T0215732

# Lecture Notes in Computer Science 9531

Commenced Publication in 1973
Founding and Former Series Editors:
Gerhard Goos, Juris Hartmanis, and Jan van Leeuwen

More information about this series at http://www.springer.com/series/7407

Guojun Wang · Albert Zomaya
Gregorio Martinez Perez · Kenli Li (Eds.)

# Algorithms and Architectures for Parallel Processing

15th International Conference, ICA3PP 2015
Zhangjiajie, China, November 18–20, 2015
Proceedings, Part IV

 Springer

*Editors*

Guojun Wang
Central South University
Changsha
China

Gregorio Martinez Perez
University of Murcia
Murcia
Spain

Albert Zomaya
The University of Sydney
Sydney, NSW
Australia

Kenli Li
Hunan University
Changsha
China

ISSN 0302-9743          ISSN 1611-3349  (electronic)
Lecture Notes in Computer Science
ISBN 978-3-319-27139-2          ISBN 978-3-319-27140-8  (eBook)
DOI 10.1007/978-3-319-27140-8

Library of Congress Control Number: 2015955380

LNCS Sublibrary: SL1 – Theoretical Computer Science and General Issues

Printed on acid-free paper

Springer International Publishing AG Switzerland is part of Springer Science+Business Media
(www.springer.com)

# Welcome Message from the ICA3PP 2015 General Chairs

Welcome to the proceedings of the 15th International Conference on Algorithms and Architectures for Parallel Processing (ICA3PP 2015), which was organized by Central South University, Hunan University, National University of Defense Technology, and Jishou University.

It was our great pleasure to organize the ICA3PP 2015 conference in Zhangjiajie, China, during November 18–20, 2015. On behalf of the Organizing Committee of the conference, we would like to express our cordial gratitude to all participants who attended the conference.

ICA3PP 2015 was the 15th event in the series of conferences started in 1995 that is devoted to algorithms and architectures for parallel processing. ICA3PP is now recognized as the main regular event in the world that covers many dimensions of parallel algorithms and architectures, encompassing fundamental theoretical approaches, practical experimental projects, and commercial components and systems. The conference provides a forum for academics and practitioners from around the world to exchange ideas for improving the efficiency, performance, reliability, security, and interoperability of computing systems and applications.

ICA3PP 2015 attracted high-quality research papers highlighting the foundational work that strives to push beyond the limits of existing technologies, including experimental efforts, innovative systems, and investigations that identify weaknesses in existing parallel processing technology.

ICA3PP 2015 consisted of the main conference and six international symposia and workshops. Many individuals contributed to the success of the conference. We would like to express our special appreciation to Prof. Yang Xiang, Prof. Andrzej Goscinski, and Prof. Yi Pan, the Steering Committee chairs, for giving us the opportunity to host this prestigious conference and for their guidance with the conference organization. Special thanks to the program chairs, Prof. Albert Zomaya, Prof. Gregorio Martinez Perez, and Prof. Kenli Li, for their outstanding work on the technical program. Thanks also to the workshop chairs, Dr. Mianxiong Dong, Dr. Ryan K.L. Ko, and Dr. Md. Zakirul Alam Bhuiya, for their excellent work in organizing attractive symposia and workshops. Thanks also to the publicity chairs, Prof. Carlos Becker Westphall, Dr. Yulei Wu, Prof. Christian Callegari, Prof. Kuan-Ching Li, and Prof. James J. (Jong Hyuk) Park, for the great job in publicizing this event. We would like to give our thanks to all the members of the Organizing Committee and Program Committee as well as the external reviewers for their efforts and support. We would also like to give our thanks to the keynote speakers, Prof. John C.S. Lui, Prof. Jiannong Cao, Prof. Wanlei Zhou, and Prof. Hai Jin, for offering insightful and enlightening talks. Last but not least, we would like to thank all the authors who submitted their papers to the conference.

November 2015
Guojun Wang
Peter Mueller
Qingping Zhou

# Welcome Message from the ICA3PP 2015 Program Chairs

On behalf of the Program Committee of the 15th International Conference on Algorithms and Architectures for Parallel Processing (ICA3PP 2015), we would like to welcome you to join the conference held in Zhangjiajie, China, during November 18–20, 2015.

The ICA3PP conference aims at bringing together researchers and practitioners from both academia and industry who are working on algorithms and architectures for parallel processing. The conference features keynote speeches, panel discussions, technical presentations, symposiums, and workshops, where the technical presentations from both the research community and industry cover various aspects including fundamental theoretical approaches, practical experimental projects, and commercial components and systems. ICA3PP 2015 was the next event in a series of highly successful international conferences on algorithms and architectures for parallel processing, previously held as ICA3PP 2014 (Dalian, China, August 2014), ICA3PP 2013 (Vietri sul Mare, Italy, December 2013), ICA3PP 2012 (Fukuoka, Japan, September 2012), ICA3PP 2011 (Melbourne, Australia, October 2011), ICA3PP 2010 (Busan, Korea, May 2010), ICA3PP 2009 (Taipei, Taiwan, June 2009), ICA3PP 2008 (Cyprus, June 2008), ICA3PP 2007 (Hangzhou, China, June 2007), ICA3PP 2005 (Melbourne, Australia, October 2005), ICA3PP 2002 (Beijing, China, October 2002), ICA3PP2000 (Hong Kong, China, December 2000), ICA3PP 1997 (Melbourne, Australia, December 1997), ICA3PP 1996 (Singapore, June 1996), and ICA3PP 1995 (Brisbane, Australia, April 1995).

The ICA3PP 2015 conference collected research papers on related research issues from all around the world. This year we received 602 submissions for the main conference. All submissions received at least three reviews during a high-quality review process. According to the review results, 219 papers were selected for oral presentation at the conference, giving an acceptance rate of 36.4 %.

We would like to offer our gratitude to Prof. Yang Xiang and Prof. Andrzej Goscinski from Deakin University, Australia, and Prof. Yi Pan from Georgia State University, USA, the Steering Committee chairs. Our thanks also go to the general chairs, Prof. Guojun Wang from Central South University, China, Dr. Peter Mueller from IBM Zurich Research, Switzerland, and Prof. Qingping Zhou from Jishou University, China, for their great support and good suggestions for a successful the final program. Special thanks to the workshop chairs, Dr. Mianxiong Dong from Muroran Institute of Technology, Japan, and Dr. Ryan K.L. Ko from the University of Waikato, New Zealand, and Dr. Md. Zakirul Alam Bhuiyan from Temple University, USA. In particular, we would like to give our thanks to all researchers and practitioners who submitted their manuscripts, and to the Program Committee and the external reviewers who contributed their valuable time and expertise to provide professional reviews working under a very tight schedule. Moreover, we are very grateful to our keynote speakers who kindly accepted our invitation to give insightful and prospective talks.

Finally, we believe that the conference provided a very good opportunity for participants to learn from each other. We hope you enjoy the conference proceedings.

Albert Zomaya
Gregorio Martinez Perez
Kenli Li

# Welcome Message from the ICA3PP 2015 Workshop Chairs

Welcome to the proceedings of the 15th International Conference on Algorithms and Architectures for Parallel Processing (ICA3PP 2015) held in Zhangjiajie, China, during November 18–20, 2015. The program this year consisted of six symposiums/workshops covering a wide range of research topics on parallel processing technology:

(1) The 6th International Workshop on Trust, Security and Privacy for Big Data (TrustData 2015)
(2) The 5th International Symposium on Trust, Security and Privacy for Emerging Applications (TSP 2015)
(3) The Third International Workshop on Network Optimization and Performance Evaluation (NOPE 2015)
(4) The Second International Symposium on Sensor-Cloud Systems (SCS 2015)
(5) The Second International Workshop on Security and Privacy Protection in Computer and Network Systems (SPPCN 2015)
(6) The First International Symposium on Dependability in Sensor, Cloud, and Big Data Systems and Applications (DependSys 2015)

The aim of these symposiums/workshops is to provide a forum to bring together practitioners and researchers from academia and industry for discussion and presentations on the current research and future directions related to parallel processing technology. The themes and topics of these symposiums/workshops are a valuable complement to the overall scope of ICA3PP 2015 providing additional values and interests. We hope that all of the selected papers will have a good impact on future research in the respective field.

The ICA3PP 2015 workshops collected research papers on the related research issues from all around the world. This year we received 205 submissions for all workshops. All submissions received at least three reviews during a high-quality review process. According to the review results, 77 papers were selected for oral presentation at the conference, giving an acceptance rate of 37.6 %.

We offer our sincere gratitude to the workshop organizers for their hard work in designing the call for papers, assembling the Program Committee, managing the peer-review process for the selection of papers, and planning the workshop program. We are grateful to the workshop Program Committees, external reviewers, session chairs, contributing authors, and attendees. Our special thanks to the Organizing Committees of ICA3PP 2015 for their strong support, and especially to the program chairs, Prof. Albert Zomaya, Prof. Gregorio Martinez Perez, and Prof. Kenli Li, for their guidance.

Finally, we hope that you will find the proceedings interesting and stimulating.

Mianxiong Dong
Ryan K.L. Ko
Md. Zakirul Alam Bhuiyan

# Welcome Message from the TrustData 2015 Program Chairs

The 6th International Workshop on Trust, Security and Privacy for Big Data (TrustData 2015) was held in Zhangjiajie, China.

TrustData aims at bringing together people from both academia and industry to present their most recent work related to trust, security, and privacy issues in big data, and to exchange ideas and thoughts in order to identify emerging research topics and define the future of big data.

TrustData 2015 was the next event in a series of highly successful international workshops, previously held as TrustData 2014 (Dalian, China, March 2012) and TrustData 2013 (Zhangjiajie, China, November, 2013).

This international workshop collected research papers on the aforementioned research issues from all around the world. Each paper was reviewed by at least three experts in the field. We feel very proud of the high participation, and although it was difficult to collect the best papers from all the submissions received, we feel we managed to have an amazing conference that was enjoyed by all participants.

We would like to offer our gratitude to the general chairs, Dr. Qin Liu and Dr. Muhammad Bashir Abdullahi, for their excellent support and invaluable suggestions for a successful final program. In particular, we would like to thank all researchers and practitioners who submitted their manuscripts, and the Program Committee members and additional reviewers for their tremendous efforts and timely reviews.

We hope you enjoy the proceedings of TrustData 2015.

Keqin Li
Avinash Srinivasan

# Welcome Message from the TSP 2015 Program Chairs

On behalf of the Program Committee of the 5th International Symposium on Trust, Security and Privacy for Emerging Applications (TSP 2015), we would like to welcome you to the proceedings of the event, which was held in Zhangjiajie, China. The symposium focuses on trust, security, and privacy issues in social networks, cloud computing, Internet of Things (IoT), wireless sensor networks, and other networking environments or system applications; it also provides a forum for presenting and discussing emerging ideas and trends in this highly challenging research area. The aim of this symposium is to provide a leading edge forum to foster interaction between researchers and developers with the trust, security, and privacy issues, and to give attendees an opportunity to network with experts in this area.

Following the success of TSP 2008 in Shanghai, China, during December 17–20, 2008, TSP 2009 in Macau SAR, China, during October 12–14, 2009, TSP 2010 in Bradford, UK, during June 29–July 1, 2010, and TSP 2013 in Zhangjiajie, China, during November 13–15, 2013, the 5th International Symposium on Trust, Security and Privacy for Emerging Applications (TSP 2015) was held in Zhangjiajie, China, during November 18–20, 2015, in conjunction with the 15th International Conference on Algorithms and Architectures for Parallel Processing (ICA3PP 2015).

The symposium collected research papers on the aforementioned research issues from all around the world. Each paper was reviewed by at least two experts in the field. We realized an amazing symposium that we hope was enjoyed by all the participants.

We would like to thank all researchers and practitioners who submitted their manuscripts, and the Program Committee members and additional reviewers for their tremendous efforts and timely reviews.

We hope you enjoy the proceedings of TSP 2015.

Imad Jawhar
Deqing Zou

# Welcome Message from the NOPE 2015 Program Chair

Welcome to the proceedings of the 2015 International Workshop on Network Optimization and Performance Evaluation (NOPE 2015) held in Zhangjiajie, China, during November 18–20, 2015.

Network optimization and performance evaluation is a topic that attracts much attention in network/Internet and distributed systems. Due to the recent advances in Internet-based applications as well as WLANs, wireless home networks, wireless sensor networks, wireless mesh networks, and cloud computing, we are witnessing a variety of new technologies. However, these systems and networks are becoming very large and complex, and consuming a great amount of energy at the same time. System optimization and performance evaluation remain to be resolved before these systems become a commodity.

On behalf of the Organizing Committee, we would like to take this opportunity to express our gratitude to all reviewers who worked hard to finish reviews on time. Thanks to the publicity chairs for their efforts and support. Thanks also to all authors for their great support and contribution to the event. We would like to give our special thanks to the Organizing Committee, colleagues, and friends who worked hard behind the scenes. Without their unfailing cooperation, hard work, and dedication, this event would not have been successfully organized.

We are grateful to everyone for participating in NOPE 2015.

Gaocai Wang

# Welcome Message from SCS 2015 Program Chairs

As the Program Chairs and on behalf of the Organizing Committee of the Second International Symposium on Sensor-Cloud Systems (SCS 2015), we would like to express our gratitude to all the participants who attended the symposium in Zhangjiajie, China, during November 18–20, 2015. This famous city is the location of China's first forest park (The Zhangjiajie National Forest Park) and a World Natural Heritage site (Wulingyuan Scenic Area).

The aim of SCS is to bring together researchers and practitioners working on sensor-cloud systems to present and discuss emerging ideas and trends in this highly challenging research field. It has attracted some high-quality research papers, which highlight the foundational work that strives to push beyond limits of existing technologies, including experimental efforts, innovative systems, and investigations that identify weaknesses in the existing technology services.

SCS 2015 was sponsored by the National Natural Science Foundation of China, Springer, the School of Information Science and Engineering at Central South University, and the School of Software at Central South University, and it was organized by Central South University, Hunan University, National University of Defense Technology, and Jishou University. SCS 2015 was held in conjunction with the 15th International Conference on Algorithms and Architectures for Parallel Processing (ICA3PP 2015), which highlights the latest research trends in various aspects of computer science and technology.

Many individuals contributed to the success of this international symposium. We would like to express our special appreciation to the general chairs of main conference, Prof. Guojun Wang, Prof. Peter Mueller, and Prof. Qingping Zhou, for giving us this opportunity to hold this symposium and for their guidance in the organization. Thanks also to the general chairs of this symposium, Prof. Jie Li and Prof. Dongqing Xie, for their excellent work in organizing the symposium. We would like to give our thanks to all the members of the Organizing Committee and Program Committee for their efforts and support.

Finally, we are grateful to the authors for submitting their fine work to SCS 2015 and all the participants for their attendance.

Xiaofei Xing
Md. Zakirul Alam Bhuiyan

# Welcome Message from the SPPCN 2015 Program Chairs

On behalf of the Program Committee of the Second International Workshop on Security and Privacy Protection in Computer and Network Systems (SPPCN 2015), we would like to welcome you to join the proceedings of the workshop, which was held in Zhangjiajie, China.

The workshop focuses on security and privacy protection in computer and network systems, such as authentication, access control, availability, integrity, privacy, confidentiality, dependability, and sustainability issues of computer and network systems. The aim of the workshop is to provide a leading-edge forum to foster interaction between researchers and developers working on security and privacy protection in computer and network systems, and to give attendees an opportunity to network with experts in this area.

SPPCN 2015 was the next event in a series of highly successful international conferences on security and privacy protection in computer and network systems, previously held as SPPCN 2014 (Dalian, China, December 2014). The workshop collected research papers on the above research issues from all around the world. Each paper was reviewed by at least two experts in the field.

We would like to offer our gratitude to the general chair, Prof. Jian Weng, for his excellent support and contribution to the success of the final program. In particular, we would like to thank all researchers and practitioners who submitted their manuscripts, and the Program Committee members and additional reviewers for their tremendous efforts and timely reviews.

We hope all of you enjoy the proceedings of SPPCN 2015.

Mianxiong Dong<br>
Hua Guo<br>
Tieming Cheng<br>
Kaimin Wei

# Welcome Message from the DependSys 2015 Program Chairs

As the program chairs and on behalf of the Organizing Committee of the First International Symposium on Dependability in Sensor, Cloud, and Big Data Systems and Applications (DependSys2015), we would like to express our gratitude to all the participants attending the international symposium in Zhangjiajie, China, during November 18–20, 2015. This famous city is the location of China's first forest park (The Zhangjiajie National Forest Park) and a World Natural Heritage site (Wulingyuan Scenic Area).

DependSys is a timely event that brings together new ideas, techniques, and solutions for dependability and its issues in sensor, cloud, and big data systems and applications. As we are deep into the Information Age, we are witnessing the explosive growth of data available on the Internet. Human beings are producing quintillion bytes of data every day, which come from sensors, individual archives, social networks, Internet of Things, enterprises, and the Internet in all scales and formats. One of the most challenging issues we face is to achieve the designed system performance to an expected level, i.e., how to effectively provide dependability in sensor, cloud, and big data systems. These systems need to typically run continuously, which often tend to become inert, brittle, and vulnerable after a while.

This international symposium collected research papers on the aforementioned research issues from all around the world. Although it was the first event of DependSys, we received a large number of submissions in response to the call for papers. Each paper was reviewed by at least three experts in the field. After detailed discussions among the program chairs and general chairs, a set of quality papers was finally accepted. We are very proud of the high number of participations, and it was difficult to collect the best papers from all the submissions.

Many individuals contributed to the success of this high-caliber international symposium. We would like to express our special appreciation to the steering chairs, Prof. Jie Wu and Prof. Guojun Wang, for giving us the opportunity to hold this symposium and for their guidance in the symposium organization. In particular, we would like to give our thanks to the symposium chairs, Prof. Mohammed Atiquzzaman, Prof. Sheikh Iqbal Ahamed, and Dr. Md Zakirul Alam Bhuiyan, for their excellent support and invaluable suggestions for a successful final program. Thanks to all the Program Committee members and the additional reviewers for their tremendous efforts and timely reviews.

We hope you enjoy the proceedings of DependSys 2015.

Latifur Khan
Joarder Kamruzzaman
Al-Sakib Khan Pathan

# Organization

## ICA3PP 2015 Organizing and Program Committees

### General Chairs

| | |
|---|---|
| Guojun Wang | Central South University, China |
| Peter Mueller | IBM Zurich Research, Switzerland |
| Qingping Zhou | Jishou University, China |

### Program Chairs

| | |
|---|---|
| Albert Zomaya | University of Sydney, Australia |
| Gregorio Martinez Perez | University of Murcia, Spain |
| Kenli Li | Hunan University, China |

### Steering Chairs

| | |
|---|---|
| Andrzej Goscinski | Deakin University, Australia |
| Yi Pan | Georgia State University, USA |
| Yang Xiang | Deakin University, Australia |

### Workshop Chairs

| | |
|---|---|
| Mianxiong Dong | Muroran Institute of Technology, Japan |
| Ryan K.L. Ko | The University of Waikato, New Zealand |
| Md. Zakirul Alam Bhuiyan | Central South University, China |

### Publicity Chairs

| | |
|---|---|
| Carlos Becker Westphall | Federal University of Santa Catarina, Brazil |
| Yulei Wu | The University of Exeter, UK |
| Christian Callegari | University of Pisa, Italy |
| Kuan-Ching Li | Providence University, Taiwan |
| James J. (Jong Hyuk) Park | SeoulTech, Korea |

### Publication Chairs

| | |
|---|---|
| Jin Zheng | Central South University, China |
| Wenjun Jiang | Hunan University, China |

# Finance Chairs

Pin Liu                     Central South University, China
Wang Yang                   Central South University, China

# Local Arrangements Chairs

Fang Qi                     Central South University, China
Qin Liu                     Hunan University, China
Hongzhi Xu                  Jishou University, China

# Program Committee

# 1. Parallel and Distributed Architectures Track

## Chairs

Stefano Giordano            Italian National Interuniversity Consortium
                              for Telecommunications, Italy
Xiaofei Liao                Huazhong University of Science and Technology,
                              China
Haikun Liu                  Nanyang Technological University, Singapore

## TPC Members

Marco Aldinucci             Universitá degli Studi di Torino, Italy
Yungang Bao                 Chinese Academy of Sciences, China
Hui Chen                    Auburn University, USA
Vladimir Getov              University of Westminster, UK
Jie Jia                     Northeastern University, China
Yusen Li                    Nanyang Technological University, Singapore
Zengxiang Li                Agency for Science, Technology and Research,
                              Singapore
Xue Liu                     Northeastern University, China
Yongchao Liu                Georgia Institute of Technology, USA
Salvatore Orlando           Universitá Ca' Foscari Venezia, Italy
Nicola Tonellotto           ISTI-CNR, Italy
Zeke Wang                   Nanyang Technological University, Singapore
Quanqing Xu                 Agency for Science, Technology and Research
                              (A*STAR), Singapore
Ramin Yahyapour             University of Göttingen, Germany
Jidong Zhai                 Tsinghua University, China
Jianlong Zhong              GraphSQL Inc., USA
Andrei Tchernykh            CICESE Research Center, Ensenada, Baja California,
                              Mexico

## 2. Software Systems and Programming Track

### Chairs

| | |
|---|---|
| Xinjun Mao | National University of Defense Technology, China |
| Sanaa Sharafeddine | Lebanese American University, Beirut, Lebanon |

### TPC Members

| | |
|---|---|
| Surendra Byna | Lawrence Berkeley National Lab, USA |
| Yue-Shan Chang | National Taipei University, Taiwan |
| Massimo Coppola | ISTI-CNR, Italy |
| Marco Danelutto | University of Pisa, Italy |
| Jose Daniel Garcia | Carlos III of Madrid University, Spain |
| Peter Kilpatrick | Queen's University Belfast, UK |
| Soo-Kyun Kim | PaiChai University, Korea |
| Rajeev Raje | Indiana University-Purdue University Indianapolis, USA |
| Salvatore Ruggieri | University of Pisa, Italy |
| Subhash Saini | NASA, USA |
| Peter Strazdins | The Australian National University, Australia |
| Domenico Talia | University of Calabria, Italy |
| Hiroyuki Tomiyama | Ritsumeikan University, Japan |
| Canqun Yang | National University of Defense Technology, China |
| Daniel Andresen | Kansas State University, USA |
| Sven-Bodo Scholz | Heriot-Watt University, UK |
| Salvatore Venticinque | Second University of Naples, Italy |

## 3. Distributed and Network-Based Computing Track

### Chairs

| | |
|---|---|
| Casimer DeCusatis | Marist College, USA |
| Qi Wang | University of the West of Scotland, UK |

### TPC Members

| | |
|---|---|
| Justin Baijian | Purdue University, USA |
| Aparicio Carranza | City University of New York, USA |
| Tzung-Shi Chen | National University of Tainan, Taiwan |
| Ciprian Dobre | University Politehnica of Bucharest, Romania |
| Longxiang Gao | Deakin University, Australia |
| Ansgar Gerlicher | Stuttgart Media University, Germany |
| Harald Gjermundrod | University of Nicosia, Cyprus |
| Christos Grecos | Independent Imaging Consultant, UK |
| Jia Hu | Liverpool Hope University, UK |
| Baback Izadi | State University of New York at New Paltz, USA |
| Morihiro Kuga | Kumamoto University, Japan |
| Mikolaj Leszczuk | AGH University of Science and Technology, Poland |

| Paul Lu | University of Alberta, Canada |
| Chunbo Luo | University of the West of Scotland, UK |
| Ioannis Papapanagiotou | Purdue University, USA |
| Michael Hobbs | Deakin University, Australia |
| Cosimo Anglano | Università del Piemonte Orientale, Italy |
| Md. ObaidurRahman | Dhaka University of Engineering and Technology, Bangladesh |
| Aniello Castiglione | University of Salerno, Italy |
| Shuhong Chen | Hunan Institute of Engineering, China |

## 4. Big Data and Its Applications Track

### Chairs

| Jose M. Alcaraz Calero | University of the West of Scotland, UK |
| Shui Yu | Deakin University, Australia |

### TPC Members

| Alba Amato | Second University of Naples, Italy |
| Tania Cerquitelli | Politecnico di Torino, Italy |
| Zizhong (Jeffrey) Chen | University of California at Riverside, USA |
| Alfredo Cuzzocrea | University of Calabria, Italy |
| Saptarshi Debroy | University of Missouri-Columbia, USA |
| Yacine Djemaiel | Communication Networks and Security, Res. Lab, Tunisia |
| Shadi Ibrahim | Inria, France |
| Hongwei Li | UESTC, China |
| William Liu | Auckland University of Technology, New Zealand |
| Xiao Liu | East China Normal University, China |
| Karampelas Panagiotis | Hellenic Air Force Academy, Greece |
| Florin Pop | University Politehnica of Bucharest, Romania |
| Genoveva Vargas Solar | CNRS-LIG-LAFMIA, France |
| Chen Wang | CSIRO ICT Centre, Australia |
| Chao-Tung Yang | Tunghai University, Taiwan |
| Peng Zhang | Stony Brook University, USA |
| Ling Zhen | Southeast University, China |
| Roger Zimmermann | National University of Singapore, Singapore |
| Francesco Palmieri | University of Salerno, Italy |
| Rajiv Ranjan | CSIRO, Canberra, Australia |
| Felix Cuadrado | Queen Mary University of London, UK |
| Nilimesh Halder | The University of Western Australia, Australia |
| Kuan-Chou Lai | National Taichung University of Education, Taiwan |
| Jaafar Gaber | UTBM, France |
| Eunok Paek | Hanyang University, Korea |
| You-Chiun Wang | National Sun Yat-sen University, Taiwan |
| Ke Gu | Changsha University of Technology, China |

# 5. Parallel and Distributed Algorithms Track

## Chairs

| | |
|---|---|
| Dimitris A. Pados | The State University of New York at Buffalo, USA |
| Baoliu Ye | Nanjing University, China |

## TPC Members

| | |
|---|---|
| George Bosilca | University of Tennessee, USA |
| Massimo Cafaro | University of Salento, Italy |
| Stefania Colonnese | Universitá degli Studi di Roma La Sapienza, Italy |
| Raphael Couturier | University of Franche Comte, France |
| Gregoire Danoy | University of Luxembourg, Luxembourg |
| Franco Frattolillo | Universitá del Sannio, Italy |
| Che-Rung Lee | National Tsing Hua University, Taiwan |
| Laurent Lefevre | Inria, ENS-Lyon, University of Lyon, France |
| Amit Majumdar | San Diego Supercomputer Center, USA |
| Susumu Matsumae | Saga University, Japan |
| George N. Karystinos | Technical University of Crete, Greece |
| Dana Petcu | West University of Timisoara, Romania |
| Francoise Sailhan | CNAM, France |
| Uwe Tangen | Ruhr-Universität Bochum, Germany |
| Wei Xue | Tsinghua University, China |
| Kalyan S. Perumalla | Oak Ridge National Laboratory, USA |
| Morris Riedel | University of Iceland, Germany |
| Gianluigi Folino | ICAR-CNR, Italy |
| Joanna Kolodziej | Cracow University of Technology, Poland |
| Luc Bougé | ENS Rennes, France |
| Hirotaka Ono | Kyushu University, Japan |
| Tansel Ozyer | TOBB Economics and Technology University, Turkey |
| Daniel Grosu | Wayne State University, USA |
| Tian Wang | Huaqiao University, China |
| Sancheng Peng | Zhaoqing University, China |
| Fang Qi | Central South University, China |
| Zhe Tang | Central South University, China |
| Jin Zheng | Central South University, China |

# 6. Applications of Parallel and Distributed Computing Track

## Chairs

| | |
|---|---|
| Yu Chen | Binghamton University, State University of New York, USA |
| Michal Wozniak | Wroclaw University of Technology, Poland |

**TPC Members**

| | |
|---|---|
| Jose Alfredo F. Costa | Universidade Federal do Rio Grande do Norte, Brazil |
| Robert Burduk | Wroclaw University of Technology, Poland |
| Boguslaw Cyganek | AGH University of Science and Technology, Poland |
| Paolo Gasti | New York Institute of Technology, USA |
| Manuel Grana | University of the Basque Country, Spain |
| Houcine Hassan | Universidad Politecnica de Valencia, Spain |
| Alvaro Herrero | Universidad de Burgos, Spain |
| Jin Kocsis | University of Akron, USA |
| Esmond Ng | Lawrence Berkeley National Lab, USA |
| Dragan Simic | University of Novi Sad, Serbia |
| Ching-Lung Su | National Yunlin University of Science and Technology, Taiwan |
| Tomoaki Tsumura | Nagoya Institute of Technology, Japan |
| Krzysztof Walkowiak | Wroclaw University of Technology, Poland |
| Zi-Ang (John) Zhang | Binghamton University-SUNY, USA |
| Yunhui Zheng | IBM Research, USA |
| Hsi-Ya Chang | National Center for High-Performance Computing, Taiwan |
| Chun-Yu Lin | HTC Corp., Taiwan |
| Nikzad Babaii Rizvandi | The University of Sydney, Australia |

# 7. Service Dependability and Security in Distributed and Parallel Systems Track

**Chairs**

| | |
|---|---|
| Antonio Ruiz Martinez | University of Murcia, Spain |
| Jun Zhang | Deakin University, Australia |

**TPC Members**

| | |
|---|---|
| Jorge Bernal Bernabe | University of Murcia, Spain |
| Roberto Di Pietro | Universitá di Roma Tre, Italy |
| Massimo Ficco | Second University of Naples (SUN), Italy |
| Yonggang Huang | Beijing Institute of Technology, China |
| Georgios Kambourakis | University of the Aegean, Greece |
| Muhammad Khurram Khan | King Saud University, Saudi Arabia |
| Liang Luo | Southwest University, China |
| Barbara Masucci | Universitá di Salerno, Italy |
| Juan M. Marin | University of Murcia, Spain |
| Sabu M. Thampi | Indian Institute of Information Technology and Management – Kerala (IIITM-K), India |
| Fernando Pereniguez-Garcia | Catholic University of Murcia, Spain |
| Yongli Ren | RMIT University, Australia |
| Yu Wang | Deakin University, Australia |
| Sheng Wen | Deakin University, Australia |

| | |
|---|---|
| Mazdak Zamani | Universiti Teknologi Malaysia, Malaysia |
| Susan K. Donohue | University of Virginia, USA |
| Oana Boncalo | University Politehnica Timisoara, Romania |
| K.P. Lam | University of Keele, UK |
| George Loukas | University of Greenwich, UK |
| Ugo Fiore | Federico II University, Italy |
| Christian Esposito | University of Salerno, Italy |
| Arcangelo Castiglione | University of Salerno, Italy |
| Edward Jung | Kennesaw State University, USA |
| Md. Zakirul Alam Bhuiyan | Central South University, China |
| Xiaofei Xing | Guangzhou University, China |
| Qin Liu | Hunan University, China |
| Wenjun Jiang | Hunan University, China |
| Gaocai Wang | Guangxi University, China |
| Kaimin Wei | Jinan University, China |

## 8. Web Services and Internet Computing Track

### Chairs

| | |
|---|---|
| Huansheng Ning | University of Science and Technology Beijing, China |
| Daqiang Zhang | Tongji University, China |

### TPC Members

| | |
|---|---|
| Jing Chen | National Cheng Kung University, Taiwan |
| Eugen Dedu | University of Franche-Comte, France |
| Sotirios G. Ziavras | NJIT, USA |
| Luis Javier Garcia Villalba | Universidad Complutense de Madrid (UCM), Spain |
| Jaime Lloret | Universidad Politecnica de Valencia, Spain |
| Wei Lu | Keene University, USA |
| Stefano Marrone | Second University of Naples, Italy |
| Alejandro Masrur | Chemnitz University of Technology, Germany |
| Seungmin (Charlie) Rho | Sungkyul University, Korea |
| Giandomenico Spezzano | ICAR-CNR, Italy |
| Jiafu Wan | South China University of Technology, China |
| Yunsheng Wang | Kettering University, USA |
| Martine Wedlake | IBM, USA |
| Chung Wei-Ho | Research Center for Information Technology Innovation in Academia Sinica, Taiwan |
| Xingquan (Hill) Zhu | Florida Atlantic University, USA |
| Nikos Dimitriou | National Center for Scientific Research Demokritos, Greece |
| Choi Jaeho | CBNU, Chonju, Korea |
| Shi-Jinn Horng | National Taiwan University of Science and Technology, Taiwan |

## 9. Performance Modeling and Evaluation Track

### Chairs

| | |
|---|---|
| Deze Zeng | China University of Geosciences, China |
| Bofeng Zhang | Shanghai University, China |

### TPC Members

| | |
|---|---|
| Ladjel Bellatreche | ENSMA, France |
| Xiaoju Dong | Shanghai Jiao Tong University, China |
| Christian Engelman | Oak Ridge National Lab, USA |
| Javier Garcia Blas | University Carlos III, Spain |
| Mauro Iacono | Second University of Naples, Italy |
| Zhiyang Li | Dalian Maritime University, China |
| Tomas Margalef | Universitat Autonoma de Barcelona, Spain |
| Francesco Moscato | Second University of Naples, Italy |
| Heng Qi | Dalian University of Technology, China |
| Bing Shi | Wuhan University of Technology, China |
| Magdalena Szmajduch | Cracow University of Technology, Poland |
| Qian Wang | Wuhan University, China |
| Zhibo Wang | Wuhan University, China |
| Weigang Wu | Sun Yat-sen University, China |
| David E. Singh | University Carlos III of Madrid, Spain |
| Edmund Lai | Massey University, New Zealand |
| Robert J. Latham | Argonne National Laboratory, USA |
| Zafeirios Papazachos | Queen's University of Belfast, UK |
| Novella Bartolini | Sapienza University of Rome, Italy |
| Takeshi Nanri | Kyushu University, Japan |
| Mais Nijim | Texas A&M University – Kingsville, USA |
| Salvador Petit | Universitat Politècnica de València, Spain |
| Daisuke Takahashi | University of Tsukuba, Japan |
| Cathryn Peoples | Ulster University, Northern Ireland, UK |
| Hamid Sarbazi-Azad | Sharif University of Technology and IPM, Iran |
| Md. Abdur Razzaque | University of Dhaka, Bangladesh |
| Angelo Brayner | University of Fortaleza, Brazil |
| Sushil Prasad | Georgia State University, USA |
| Danilo Ardagna | Politecnico di Milano, Italy |
| Sun-Yuan Hsieh | National Cheng Kung University, Taiwan |
| Li Chaoliang | Hunan University of Commerce, China |
| Yongming Xie | Hunan Normal University, China |
| Guojun Wang | Central South University, China |

# Secretariats

Zhe Tang                    Central South University, China
Feng Wang                   Central South University, China

# Webmaster

Xiangdong Lee               Central South University, China

# TrustData 2015 Organizing and Program Committees

## Steering Chairs

| | |
|---|---|
| Guojun Wang | Central South University, China |
| Peter Mueller | IBM Zurich Research Laboratory, Switzerland |

## General Chairs

| | |
|---|---|
| Qin Liu | Hunan University, China |
| Muhammad Bashir Abdullahi | Federal University of Technology, Minna, Nigeria |

## Program Chairs

| | |
|---|---|
| Keqin Li | State University of New York at New Paltz, USA |
| Avinash Srinivasan | Temple University, USA |

## Publicity Chairs

| | |
|---|---|
| Shui Yu | Deakin University, Australia |
| Weirong Liu | Central South University, China |

## Program Committee

| | |
|---|---|
| Andrei Tchernykh | CICESE Research Center, Mexico |
| Baoliu Ye | Nanjing University, China |
| Bimal Roy | Indian Statistical Institute, India |
| Chang-Ai Sun | University of Science and Technology, China |
| Chao Song | University of Electronic Science and Technology of China, China |
| Christian Callegari | The University of Pisa, Italy |
| Chunhua Su | Japan Advanced Institute of Science and Technology, Japan |
| Franco Chiaraluce | Polytechnical University of Marche (UVPM), Italy |
| Hai Jiang | Arkansas State University, USA |
| Horacio Gonzalez-Velez | National College of Ireland, Ireland |
| Imed Romdhani | Edinburgh Napier University, UK |
| Jianguo Yao | Shanghai Jiao Tong University, China |
| Joon S. Park | Syracuse University, USA |
| Kevin Chan | US Army Research Laboratory, USA |
| Lizhe Wang | Rochester Institute of Technology, USA |

# TSP 2015 Organizing and Program Committees

## Program Chairs

| | |
|---|---|
| Imad Jawhar | United Arab Emirates University, UAE |
| Deqing Zou | Huazhong University of Science of Technology |

## Program Committee Members

| | |
|---|---|
| Chao Song | University of Electronic Science and Technology, China |
| David Zheng | Frostburg State University, USA |
| Feng Li | Indiana University-Purdue University Indianapolis, USA |
| Haitao Lang | Beijing University of Chemical Technology, China |
| Huan Zhou | China Three Gorges University, China |
| Mingjun Xiao | University of Science and Technology of China, China |
| Mingwu Zhang | Hubei University of Technology, China |
| Shuhui Yang | Purdue University Calumet, USA |
| Xiaojun Hei | Huazhong University of Science and Technology, China |
| Xin Li | Nanjing University of Aeronautics and Astronautics, China |
| Xuanxia Yao | University of Science and Technology Beijing, China |
| Yaxiong Zhao | Google Inc., USA |
| Ying Dai | LinkedIn Corporation, USA |
| Yunsheng Wang | Kettering University, USA |
| Youwen Zhu | Nanjing University of Aeronautics and Astronautics, China |
| Yongming Xie | Changsha Medical University, China |

## Steering Committee

| | |
|---|---|
| Wenjun Jiang | Hunan University, China (Chair) |
| Laurence T. Yang | St. Francis Xavier University, Canada |
| Guojun Wang | Central South University, China |
| Minyi Guo | Shanghai Jiao Tong University, China |
| Jie Li | University of Tsukuba, Japan |
| Jianhua Ma | Hosei University, Japan |
| Peter Mueller | IBM Zurich Research Laboratory, Switzerland |
| Indrakshi Ray | Colorado State University, USA |

# NOPE 2015 Organizing and Program Committees

## Steering Committee Chairs

Wei Li               Texas Southern University, USA
Taoshen Li           Guangxi University, China

## Program Chair

Gaocai Wang          Guangxi University, China

## Program Committee Members

Dieter Fiems         Ghent University, Belgium
Shuqiang Huang       Jinan University, China
Juan F. Perez        Imperial College London, UK
Haoqian Wang         Tsinghua University, China
Yitian Peng          Southeast University, China
Hongbin Chen         Guilin University of Electronic Technology, China
Jin Ye               Guangxi University, China
Junbin Liang         Hong Kong Polytechnic University, Hong Kong,
                       SAR China
Xianfeng Liu         Hunan Normal University, China
Hao Zhang            Central South University, China
Chuyuan Wei          Beijing University of Civil Engineering and
                       Architecture, China
Hongyun Xu           South China University of Technology, China
Zhefu Shi            University of Missouri, USA
Songfeng Lu          Huazhong University of Science and Technology,
                       China
Yihui Deng           Jinan University, China
Lei Zhang            Beijing University of Civil Engineering and
                       Architecture, China
Xiaoheng Deng        Central South University, China
Mingxing Luo         Southwest Jiaotong University, China
Bin Sun              Beijing University of Posts and Telecommunications,
                       China
Zhiwei Wang          Nanjing University of Posts and Telecommunications,
                       China
Yousheng Zhou        Chongqing University of Posts
                       and Telecommunications, China
Daofeng Li           Guangxi University, China

# SCS 2015 Organizing and Program Committees

## Steering Chairs

Jie Li        Tsukuba University, Japan
Dongqing Xie        Guangzhou University, China

## Program Chairs

Xiaofei Xing        Guangzhou University, China
Md. Zakirul Alam Bhuiyan        Central South University, China
       and Temple University, USA

## Program Committee Members

Marco Aiello        University of Groningen, The Netherlands
David Chadwick        University of Kent, UK
Aparicio Carranza        City University of New York, USA
Mooi Choo Chuah        Lehigh University, USA
Yueming Deng        Hunan Normal University, China
Christos Grecos        Independent Imaging Consultant, UK
Dritan Kaleshi        University of Bristol, UK
Donghyun Kim        North Carolina Central University, USA
Santosh Kumar        University of Memphis, USA
Muthoni Masinde        University of Nairobi, Kenya
Satyjayant Mishra        New Mexico State University, USA
Nam Nguyen        Towson University, USA
Jean-Marc Seigneur        University of Geneva, Switzerland
Hamid Sharif        University of Nebraska, USA
Sheng Wen        Deakin University, Australia

## Publicity Chairs

Zeyu Sun        Xi'an Jiaotong University, China
Yongming Xie        Hunan Normal University, China

# SPPCN 2015 Organizing and Program Committees

## General Chair

Jian Weng — Jinan University, China

## Program Chairs

| | |
|---|---|
| Mianxiong Dong | Muroran Institute of Technology, Japan |
| Hua Guo | Beihang University, China |
| Tieming Chen | Zhejiang University of Technology, China |
| Kaimin Wei | Jinan University, China |

## Program Committee

| | |
|---|---|
| Fuchun Guo | University of Wollongong, Australia |
| Jianguang Han | Nanjing University of Finance and Economics, Nanjing, China |
| Debiao He | Wuhan University, China |
| Xinyi Huang | Fujian Normal University, China |
| Xuanya Li | Chinese Academy of Sciences, China |
| Fengyong Li | Shanghai University of Electric Power, China |
| Changlu Lin | Fujian Normal University, China |
| Chang Xu | Beijing Institute of Technology, China |
| Tao Xu | University of Jinan, China |
| Yanjiang Yang | I2R, Singapore |
| Yang Tian | Beihang University, China |
| Shengbao Wang | Hangzhou Normal University, China |
| Wei Wu | Fujian Normal University, China |
| Xiyong Zhang | Information Engineering University, China |
| Lei Zhao | Wuhan University, China |

# DependSys 2015 Organizing and Program Committees

## Steering Committee Chairs

| | |
|---|---|
| Jie Wu | Temple University, USA |
| Guojun Wang | Central South University, China |

## General Chairs

| | |
|---|---|
| Mohammed Atiquzzaman | University of Oklahoma, USA |
| Sheikh Iqbal Ahamed | Marquette University, USA |
| Md. Zakirul Alam Bhuiyan | Central South University, China and Temple University, USA |

## Program Chairs

| | |
|---|---|
| Latifur Khan | The University of Texas at Dallas, USA |
| Joarder Kamruzzaman | Federation University and Monash University, Australia |
| Al-Sakib Khan Pathan | International Islamic University Malaysia, Malaysia |

## Program Committee Members

| | |
|---|---|
| A.B.M Shawkat Ali | The University of Fiji, Fiji |
| A.B.M. Alim Al Islam | Bangladesh University of Engineering and Technology, Bangladesh |
| A. Sohel Ferdous | University of Western Australia, Australia |
| A.K.M. Najmul Islam | University of Turku, Finland |
| Abdul Azim Mohammad | Gyeongsang National University, South Korea |
| Abdur Rouf Mohammad | Dhaka University of Engineering and Technology, Bangladesh |
| Afrand Agah | West Chester University of Pennsylvania, USA |
| Andreas Pashalidis | Katholieke Universiteit Leuven – iMinds, Belgium |
| Asaduzzaman | Chittagong University of Engineering and Technology, Bangladesh |
| C. Chiu Tan | Temple University, USA |
| Changyu Dong | University of Strathclyde, UK |
| Dana Petcu | West University of Timisoara, Romania |
| Daqiang Zhang | Tongji University, China |
| Farzana Rahman | James Madison University, USA |
| Hugo Miranda | University of Lisbon, Portugal |
| Jaydip Sen | National Institute of Science and Technology, India |
| Jianfeng Yang | Wuhan University, China |
| Jinkyu Jeong | Sungkyunkwan University, South Korea |

| | |
|---|---|
| Kaoru Ota | Muroran Institute of Technology, Japan |
| Karampelas Panagiotis | Hellenic Air Force Academy, Greece |
| Lien-Wu Chen | Feng Chia University, Taiwan |
| Liu Jialin | Texas Tech University, USA |
| M.M.A. Hashem | Khulna University of Engineering and Technology, Bangladesh |
| M. Thampi Sabu | Indian Institute of Information Technology and Management, India |
| Mahbub Habib Sheikh | CASED/TU Darmstadt, Germany |
| Mahmuda Naznin | Bangladesh University of Engineering and Technology, Bangladesh |
| Mamoun Alazab | Australian National University, Australia |
| Manuel Mazzara | Innopolis University, Russia |
| Md. Abdur Razzaque | University of Dhaka, Bangladesh |
| Md. Arafatur Rahman | University Malaysia Pahang, Malaysia |
| Mohammad Asad Rehman Chaudhry | University of Toronto, Canada |
| Md. Obaidur Rahman | Dhaka University of Engineering and Technology, Bangladesh |
| Md. Rafiul Hassan | King Fahd University of Petroleum and Minerals, Saudi Arabia |
| Md. Saiful Azad | American International University, Bangladesh |
| Mehran Asadi | Lincoln University of Pennsylvania, USA |
| Mohamad Badra | Zayed University, UAE |
| Mohamed Guerroumi | University of Sciences and Technology Houari Boumediene, Algeria |
| Mohammad Asadul Hoque | East Tennessee State University, USA |
| Mohammad Mehedi Hassan | King Saud University, Saudi Arabia |
| Mohammad Shahriar Rahman | University of Asia Pacific, Bangladesh |
| Mohammed Shamsul Alam | International Islamic University Chittagong, Bangladesh |
| Morshed Chowdhury | Deakin University, Australia |
| Muhammad Mostafa Monowar | King AbdulAziz University, Saudi Arabia |
| N. Musau Felix | Kenyatta University, Kenya |
| Phan Cong | Vinh Nguyen Tat Thanh University, Vietnam |
| Qin Liu | Hunan University, China |
| Ragib Hasan | University of Alabama at Birmingham, USA |
| Raza Hasan | Middle East College, Oman |
| Reaz Ahmed | University of Waterloo, Canada |
| Risat Mahmud Pathan | Chalmers University of Technology, Sweden |
| S.M. Kamruzzaman | King Saud University, Saudi Arabia |
| Salvatore Distefano | Politecnico di Milano, Italy |
| Shan Lin | Stony Brook University, USA |
| Shao Jie Tang | University of Texas at Dallas, USA |
| Sheng Wen | Deakin University, Australia |

| | |
|---|---|
| Shigeng Zhang | Central South University, China |
| Sk. Md. Mizanur Rahman | King Saud University, Saudi Arabia |
| Subrota Mondal | Hong Kong University of Science and Technology, Hong Kong, SAR China |
| Syed Imran Ali | Middle East College, Oman |
| Tanveer Ahsan | International Islamic University Chittagong, Bangladesh |
| Tanzima Hashem | Bangladesh University of Engineering and Technology, Bangladesh |
| Tao Li | The Hong Kong Polytechnic University, Hong Kong, SAR China |
| Tarem Ahmed | BRAC University, Bangladesh |
| Tian Wang | Huaqiao University, China |
| Tzung-Shi Chen | National University of Tainan, Taiwan |
| Vaskar Raychoudhury | Indian Institute of Technology Roorkee, India |
| Wahid Khan | University of Saskatchewan, Canada |
| Weigang Li | University of Brasilia, Brazil |
| Weigang Wu | Sun Yat-sen University, China |
| William Liu | Auckland University of Technology, New Zealand |
| Xiaofei Xing | Guangzhou University, China |
| Xuefeng Liu | The Hong Kong Polytechnic University, Hong Kong, SAR China |
| Xuyun Zhang | University of Melbourne, Australia |
| Yacine Djemaiel | Communication Networks and Security, Res. Lab, Tunisia |
| Yifan Zhang | Binghamton University, USA |
| Yu Wang | Deakin University, Australia |

## Publication Chairs

| | |
|---|---|
| Jin Zheng | Central South University, China |
| Wenjun Jiang | Hunan University, China |

## Local Arrangements Chairs

| | |
|---|---|
| Fang Qi | Central South University, China |
| Qin Liu | Hunan University, China |
| Hongzhi Xu | Jishou University, China |

## Finance Chairs

| | |
|---|---|
| Pin Liu | Central South University, China |
| Wang Yang | Central South University, China |

## Web Chair

| | |
|---|---|
| Min Guo | Central South University, China |

# Contents – Part IV

## Performance Modeling and Evaluation

# Software Systems
# and Programming Models

# FT-Offload: A Scalable Fault-Tolerance Programing Model on MIC Cluster

Cheng Chen$^{(\boxtimes)}$, Yunfei Du, Zhen Xu, and Canqun Yang

School of Computer Science, National University of Defense Technology,
Changsha 410073, China
{chencheng,duyunfei,zhenx,canqun}@nudt.edu.cn

**Abstract.** Massively heterogeneous architectures are popular for modern petascale and future exascale systems. Fault-tolerance is key to the increased number of components and the complexity of these heterogeneous systems. However, standard offload programming models have traditionally been developed for supporting high performance rather than reliability. Naive fault-tolerance protocols are incapable of serving distributed MPI applications that tuned for CPU-MIC heterogeneous clusters. To address these problems, we design and implement a framework of fault tolerance programming model (FT-Offload). This enhances the reliability of heterogeneous supercomputers and retains the convenient of popular Intel Offload programming model. The effectiveness of the framework is demonstrated via numerical analysis and by porting both benchmarks and real-world applications to large-scale CPU-MIC nodes on the Tianhe-2 supercomputer. Our experimental results show that the current solution, which involves checkpoints, can efficiently strength the long running and reduce checkpointing overhead.

**Keywords:** MIC · Fault-tolerance · FT-Offload · Tianhe-2

## 1 Introduction

With the advent of many-core coprocessor architectures, which are different from CPUs in functionality, instruction set (ISA), performance, power, and energy efficiency (e.g. GPUs [1] and Intel MIC [2]), massively heterogeneous parallel systems become a hot topic in high performance computing (HPC) [3–5]. In the latest Top500 list [6], five of top the ten supercomputers are equipped with coprocessors. Packed more than 1 Tflops of double precision performance on a single chip, the first line of products based on the MIC architecture, Xeon Phi [7] has already power supercomputers on the list: Tianhe-2 [8,9] and Stampede [10].

Supercomputers may equip with a large number of coprocessors which power a relative high perk performance. Coprocessors, which lead to a significant increase in the number of system components in supercomputers installations, involve some transient and permanent failures, like any others. Because of this more complicated architecture and because of the coprocessor's unique features,

© Springer International Publishing Switzerland 2015
G. Wang et al. (Eds.): ICA3PP 2015, Part IV, LNCS 9531, pp. 3–17, 2015.
DOI: 10.1007/978-3-319-27140-8_1

large number of cores and weak fault-tolerance of coprocessor the mean time between failures (MTBF) in heterogeneous parallel systems is shorter, the mean time to repair (MTTR) is longer [11]. How to scale the heterogenous applications for these systems while keeping results reliable has become urgent. However, the standard offload programming models, such as Intel Offload [12], OpenMP4 [13] and OpenACC [14], always focus on keeping time with the coprocessor. These stress performance but not reliability for over long runtime of HPC application which typically run for several days, even several weeks or several months.

Summarizing these systems' characteristics and developing long-running high performance applications that can complete jobs pose a considerable challenge. To creators of these informatic workloads will require assistance to take advantage of state-of-the-art heterogeneous many core computers. The vast majority of current-generation HPC systems and application codes work around failures using checkpoint rollback-recovery (CR) schemes [15]: parts of the execution are lost when processes are subject to failures (either because the corresponding data is lost when the failure is a crash, or because it is corrupted due to a silent error), and the fault-tolerant protocol, when catching such errors, uses past checkpoints to restore the application in a consistent state, and re-computes the missing parts of the execution.

However, as far as we know existing application-level CR frameworks are not capable of serving distributed MPI applications that can leverage CPU-MIC heterogeneous architectures. There is no known CR implementation that supports checkpointing the massive MICs' status, even though such a CR tool may significantly enhance the dependability of MIC computing applications. In this paper, a general heterogeneous computing system checkpointing model (FT-Offload) was designed and developed. The system is as convenient as regular Offload programming but can tolerate the failures both in forward Offload and reverse-Offload applications by saving the checkpoint data under the double-in-memory principle. Then the numerical stability and real performance of this model was analyzed on Tianhe-2 supercomputer.

The rest of this paper is organized as follows. A brief introduction of the related work is drawn in Sect. 2. Section 3 illustrates the Tianhe-2 CPU-MIC heterogenous system. Section 4 describes the current checkpointing implementation on CPU-MIC system. Numerical stability is discussed in Sect. 5. Section 6 provides the details and analysis of the results of the evaluations on Tianhe-2. Conclusions and future work are presented in Sect. 7.

## 2    Related Work

When run for long periods, HPC applications need to be able to apply fault tolerance to avoid failures, which would require restarting the computation from the far beginning. There are three main methods to checkpoint HPC application: uncoordinated checkpointing, coordinated checkpointing and communication-based checkpointing. Considerable work has been done on failures tolerance of HPC applications [16,17]. Coordinated checkpointing simplifies recovering from failures because it does not suffer from rollback propagations. Checkpoint/restart has been one of the major approaches studied over the past several years. It is desirable to build systems that are able to survive partial failures with reduced overhead of systems tolerance. Kale et al. explored an in-memory checkpoint/restart scheme in a fault tolerant CHARM++ [18]. Later, they [19] presented several optimization techniques to a scalable double-in-memory checkpoint/restart scheme to improve its scalability towards exascale. CoCheck [20], Starfish [21], and AMPI [22] use coordinated checkpointing to produce fault-tolerant versions of MPI.

Heterogeneous platforms are constantly increasing their share in high performance computing. Research on fault tolerance programming is on going [23, 24]. CUDA [3] and OpenCL [25]are the most widely used programming models for CPU-GPU heterogeneous systems. CheCUDA [26] is a user-level checkpointing approach to CUDA applications running on systems with GPUs. This approach relies on the Berkeley Lab Checkpoint/Restart (BLCR) [27] tool to checkpoint the application which implements kernel level checkpointing and is widely used in applications with production quality. This tool requires that no CUDA objects exist when the check-point is taken. CheCL [25] is a user-level checkpointing tool for OpenCL applications. This tool saves only OpenCL objects and hence it works with a conventional system-level checkpointing tool, such as BLCR. One previous study [11] outlines and analyzes the intrinsic and extrinsic issues that limit the I/O performance when check-pointing parallel applications on Xeon Phi clusters.

When developing a general-purpose fault-tolerant protocol, two adversaries must be taken into account: the occurrence of failures, that hit the system at unpredictable moments, and the behavior of the application, that is designed without taking into account the risk of failure, or the fault-tolerant protocol. The advent of MIC coprocessor necessitates the development of fault tolerance programming model for CPU-MIC heterogeneous systems described herein. Such framework will run on large-scale supercomputers like Tianhe-2, and allows the developer to deal with desirable performance and reliable stabilization on the far design.

# 3 Large-Scale MICs on the Tianhe-2 Compute Nodes

Developed by the National University of Defense Technology (NUDT), Tianhe-2 supercomputer retained its position as the world's No.1 system in the latest Top500 list with a performance of 33.86 petaflop/s [6]. Tianhe-2 is a hybrid MPP(Massively Parallel Processing) system with CPUs and MICs. This section introduce the hardware configure and programming model.

## 3.1  Hardware Configure

Combining 2 Intel Xeon host processors with 3 MIC accelerators, the computing nodes in the Tianhe-2 system were installed into 500 cabinets with 32 nodes

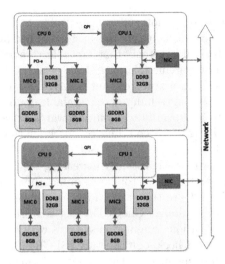

**Fig. 1.** Rough architecture of Tianhe-2 compute nodes

per cabinet, which contribute to the peak performance. The rough architecture of the heterogeneous supercomputers is shown in Fig. 1. Each node has an Intel Xeon processor with 64 GB shared memory, and three Intel MIC cards plugged in the PCIe 3.0 slot. These MIC cards consist of 57 cores, with 8 GB GDDR5 local memory each. The CPUs share the same memory space, but each MIC has its own separate memory. The three MICs can be used together or separately. Two CPUs and three MICs within a node constitute a basic heterogeneous compute unit, here called compute element. This architecture has several advantages in many aspects, such as obtaining very high performance on relatively small system scales and a much higher energy efficiency than its homogeneous counterpart.

The interconnect network topology is an opto-electronic hybrid, hierarchical fat tree. The link bandwidth is 40 Gbps with a speed of 10 Gbps per line. The network latency is 1.2 s. The network supports the communication of computation tasks, I/O access, system management, and has the characteristics of high bandwidth, low latency, and high scalability. The network supports collective communication operations.

### 3.2 MPI+X Programming on Tianhe-2

In order to use CPU and MIC cooperatively and the successful of MPI+OpenMP and MPI+CUDA in which MPI applies to inter-node and OpenMP or CUDA to intra-node programming, the MPI+X reveals potential in massively heterogeneous systems. Here X is accelerator-specific for MIC.

The MIC coprocessors from Intel support a modified x86 instruction set, thereby providing the programmability of a full-fledged multicore CPU [2]. For large MICs on Tianhe-2, Intel Offload Model is the specific X. Running a $\mu$OS, the reverse-Offload is also an alternative. Figure 2 gives a skeleton comparison of

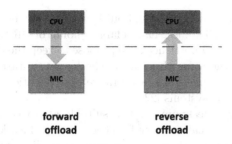

**Fig. 2.** Forward-Offload and reverse-Offload

(forward) Offload and reverse-Offload. The offload model treats the CPU cores as main processors and the MIC cores as accelerators whose role is to speed up pieces of the application. Before porting application, the programmer starts by writing code for the MIC cores. Then identifies performance-critical routines that are likely to see an improvement in performance by running on the MIC cores and correspondingly recodes those routines for the accelerators. Turning the forward Offload model upside-down, the reverse Offload treats a hybrid system as a cluster of MIC cores, each with an attached CPU core for offloading control, memory, or I/O (input/output) intensive work. Then the reverse-Offload model treats CPU as device and MIC as host and makes the program start on MIC, abundantly express the massive threads computing superiority of MIC. More details of programming and optimization on MIC system can be found in [28].

## 4    Adaptive Checkpointing on CPU-MIC Systems

In Tianhe-2 massively heterogeneous supercomputers, the memory on the MIC is completely separate from the CPU memory. Coprocessor memory is not mapped into the host's virtual memory space, so the host may not be able to read or write directly. The code and data were uploaded to coprocessor, and then the computing results is collected by Offload or reverse-Offload, which is a serials of directive provided by Intel [28]. In this section, the current FT-Offload to double in-memory checkpoint/rollback is introduced to the CPU-MIC system when the MIC is used as coprocessor or host specially for those separate memory systems. Although inspired by efficient checkpointing CPU-MIC system, it was designed as an independent software layer and can be used in any context where heterogeneous active messages might be useful.

### 4.1    Double In-Memory Checkpointing

The checkpoint is a snapshot of an application's running state that can be used to restart execution upon a failure [29], then the application do not need to restart from the far beginning. However, when checkpointing large-scale systems, tens of thousands of compute nodes write checkpoints to the parallel file system (PFS) concurrently. Then the low I/O throughput becomes a bottleneck [15]. Machines such as K computer and Tianhe-2 have a large amount of DRAM storage volume. In order to relieve the I/O bottleneck, we propose to keep the checkpoint in local storage memory. At the same time, while checkpoint/restart is a very general technique and can be applied in a wide range of application, it is still difficult to use on heterogeneous systems [23].

Double in-memory checkpointing is a suitable approach to these problems [18]. The protocol uses local memory for checkpoints, which leverages the high-speed communication network and I/O operation to alleviate bottlenecks. The basic idea is to create two checkpoints for each compute node. One checkpoint is stored in local memory, and the other is stored on a buddy node. If one fail-stop node fails, the surviving nodes restores their object data from the chosen spare node. The replacement of the failed one is done automatically from the redundancy pool. This method is capable of tolerating all single fail-stop failures and most multiple failures (if failed nodes are not buddy to each other). As single failures are the most common failure in today's HPC system, this scheme is sufficient for very large machines. In this section, the open question of applying this checkpoint principle to CPU-MIC system and retaining the compatible Offload programming is studied.

## 4.2   MIC Work as Coprocessor

The workflow of MIC-as-coprocessor is shown in Fig. 3. This model provides a flexible programming choice. First, when using the offload model, the code region is executed as a solo task, called kernels, on the accelerator. This is simple and the application can be quickly accelerated by the power of coprocessor. However, because the ever-increasing processing power of multi-core CPUs is neglected, splitting the workload between the CPU and the MIC and orchestrating the execution of multiple tasks efficiently across these devices has become fashionable for higher performance. In both case, a third component, e.g. OpenMP, MPI, is needed to handle parallelism inner-nodes and inter-nodes. In these programming models, the manner in which the program can be transferred to tolerate fault involves use the information provided by the application state which is in a state of data dependence and using the number of arrays that compose the application.

For an Offload application composed of N kernels, the data dependence is the $CPU_{task}$ input added by a snapshot taken in between two contiguous kernels $K_i$ and $K_j$ executed sequentially defined by the set of in (I) required by the kernel $K_j$ or the $CPU_{task}$ output added by the set of out (O) generated by the kernel $K_i$. In this way, data dependence between kernels is described in terms of its output and of the future inputs of CPU and MIC. The joint of output and future input in the data flow diagram will be the checkpoint location. The flowing equation presents the application state:

$$\text{Application.State} = \underbrace{\cup_c I_i + \cup_c F_i}_{Before\ CPU_{task}} + \underbrace{\cup_k I_i + \cup_k F_i}_{Before\ Kerkel} = \underbrace{\cup_c O_j + \cup_c F_i}_{After\ CPU_{task}} + \underbrace{\cup_k O_j + \cup_k F_j}_{After\ Kernel}$$

The checkpointing interval must obey the rule that the computing time between two checkpoint location added by the one time checkpointing overhead is less than MTBF. While running at the checkpoint location, the system save the checkpoint data to the memory system in case of failure. When hard error occurs, the task management system, say slurm, will stop the program and the resubmit the task. The fault tolerance view of the workflow is given in Fig. 3, on the right.

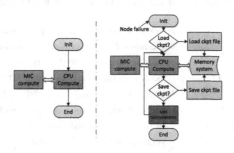

**Fig. 3.** Checkpointing protocol while MIC worke as coprocessor

### 4.3 MIC Work as Host

Running a fully user-accessible Linux OS with other operational software and services which from the Intel Many-core Platform Software Stack (MPSS), enables the MIC to work as an autonomous compute node. Specifically, it can execute programs natively, like a host. While MIC work as a host, shown in Fig. 4 on the left, the main program is initiated on MIC. The CPU only handles some of the computing task, like MPI communication and I/O operation. Similarly, dealing with the separate MIC and CPU memory becomes the main obstacle for this heterogeneous programming and checkpointing. In this section, the checkpointing protocol and implementation is described in detail. By establishing a library calls running on CPU, all the operation of MPI communication and the module of fault-tolerance is packaged as a function familiar to a computing task. This makes it easy to port existing code, and allows for accommodating the basic primitives Intel Offload pragma directives.

**Overview.** To harness the programming gap, the current FT-Offload complements the functionality of Offload with MPI communication and checkpointing API as a front-end. The API encapsulates the basic primitives **#pragma offload** directives and MPI calls. This makes it easy to port existing code. Table 1 provides an overview of the main APIs. We encapsulate the fault tolerance code with FT-Offload in a function. This function together with its arguments can then be passed to the MPI and checkpointing sub-level function. More details about the data transfer and communication will be talked in following section. The *halo_init* and the *halo_finalize* performs the remote memory allocation or free for both boundary exchange with other nodes and checking data save, returning a special remote_ptr object which ensures local and remote addresses cannot be mixed up without the compiler complaining about it. Checkpointing save and load are carried out by *checkping_save* and *checkpoint_load* functor.

**Table 1.** Overview of the main parts of the FT-Offload API

| node_t id | -address the information of coprocessor. |
|---|---|
| void exchange_wrapper() | -a packaging function of communication and fault tolerance |
| void halo_init(id) | -setup the halo boundary buffers for MPI communication |
| void mpi_communication(id, buf) | -receive/send the data updated on MIC |
| void halo_finalize(id) | -free the boundary buffers on CPU and MIC |
| void checkpoint_save(id, buf) | -save the checkpoint data on CPU and its buddy memory |
| void checkpoint_load(id, buf) | -load the checkpoint data from the buddy memory |
| volatile int s | -asynchronous transferring signal |
| int offload_signal | -asynchronous wrapper state transition signal |
| int offload_id | -asynchronous MPI communication buffer signal |
| double * send/receive_buf | -MPI communication buffer |
| double * offload_checkpoint_buf | -checkpoint data buffer |

**Checkpointing Protocol.** To deal with the relationship of CPU, MIC, data transfer, communication and checkpoint, the right part of Fig. 4 provides a simplified diagram of FT-Offload checkpointing protocol. The CPU allocates memory space, and then uploads the binary and initial data to MIC through Coprocessor Offload Infrastructure (COI). As shown in the figure. the application is initiated and does the most part of computation on MIC. Then the boundary buffer is transferred to CPU for halo exchange. This is performed by offload transfer directives. When the program reaches the checkpointing location, the checkpointing buffer is transferred to CPU memory just the same to boundary buffer, and then we perform the double in memory backup. When a hard error occurs, the task will restart by the slurm system. After restarting, the program will reach the checkpoint load location, then the workflow is the reverse of checkpoint save.

An exchange wrapper was designed to run on CPU to control these separate actions detailed in previous section. As shown in Fig. 5, there are seven tasks in the wrapper, but three tasks are active at most, and they are Receive Task (RT), Send Task (ST) and Update Task (UT). The ST is to send data to other nodes while RT is to receive. The UT is main computing task running on MIC. After MIC updating, the boundary or other data need to communicate with other node is transferred to CPU; after CPU receive the newest data to update, it transferred to MIC. The state transitions of RT, NT and UT objects is triggered by the offload signal frequently altering on MIC. The signal and data transfer

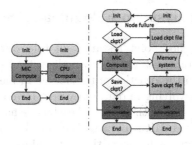

**Fig. 4.** Checkpointing protocol while MIC work as host

via an offload transfer API provided by Intel. The halo exchange setup task is to define the boundary data and all reduce data and allocate memory space both in MIC and CPU, the free work is to be done by halo exchange finalize task. As there may produce some errors while communicating, we setup a MPI error handle task to deal with.For checkpointing and recovery, a save/load memory task is used. This task deals with the checkpoint saving work, and also loads the checkpointing data once a failure occurs. The data transfer latency is hidden by asynchronous offload transfer API, provided by Intel.

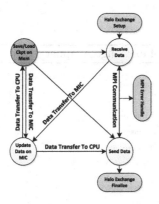

**Fig. 5.** State diagrams of exchange wrapper

**Implementation.** Algorithm 1 illustrates how the CPU listen to the signal from MIC, then organizes the execution of multiple tasks as shown in the state diagrams. The signal and wait clause is to perform the asynchronous data transfer for overlapping communication and computation. For better performance, the overlap work is done by asynchronous transfer.

# 5   Theoretical Analysis on FT-Offload's Stability

The double in memory checkpoint/restart fault tolerance presented in Sect. 4 involves restart the program with the buddy node instead from the far beginning whenever a node fails. In the practice of the double in memory fault tolerance, the numerical stability involving in data recovering have to be addressed.

Consider a parallel system with nodes and each node has four computing components, one CPU and three MICs. For a simple model similar to [18], we assume that each component failure will trigger the node failure. Each component has a failure rate of $r_1, r_2, r_3, r_4$. Then the mean time between failure (MTBF) is here set as $S_i$, the relationship between $S_i$ and r is $S_i = 1/max(r_i)$ . Without any faults, the total execution time is T. In this way, the probability to completing the long-running application without fault tolerance is $(1 - max(r_i) * T)^n$, where n is total number of nodes.

With fault tolerance, the probability may change. The total runtime set to $T'$. The checkpointing interval set in the application is $I$. Let $m$ buddy processor for a group which will give the total of $n/m$ groups of buddies. If any component of a node in a buddy group fails, then the probability of unrecoverable error running between $I$ and other value is $max(r_i) * I$. So the probability that $m$ nodes in a buddy group crash during $I$ is $max(r_i)T' * max(r_i)T$. The probability of finish the long running application with our fault tolerance model can be written as $(1 - max(r_i)T' * max(r_i)I)^{(n/m)}$.

---

**Algorithm 1.** Algorithm of exchange_wrapper

---

```
 1. while offload_sig ≠ STOP do
 2.      #pragma offload_transfer target(mic:id)out(offload_sig)signal(&s1){
 3.      #pragma offload target(mic:id)wait(&s1){
 4.      switch(offload_sig)
 5.      case INIT : //setup halo buffers
 6.          errorCode=halo_init(id)
 7.      case EXCHANGE : // MPI communication
 8.          errorCode=halo_exchange(id)
 9.      case SAVE_CKPT : // save checkpoint data
10.          errorCode=ckt_save((id))
11.      case LOAD_CKPT : // load checkpoint data
12.          errorCode=ckt_load(id))
13.      case FINALIZE : // free halo buffers
14.          errorCode=halo_finalize(id))
15.      default:
16.          return -1
17.      end switch
18.      if (errorCode ≠ 0) then
19.          handleMPIError(errorCode) // error handle
20.      end if
21.      if offload_sig ≠ STOP then
22.          offload_signal=RUN
23.          #pragma offload_transfer target(mic:id) out(offload_signal) signal(&s1){}
24.          #pragma offload target(mic:id)wait(&s1){}
25.      end if
26. end while
```

---

The numerical analysis of the probability is shown the following illustration of the equations with system parameters. At first, we set the MTBF(S) for any component of any 8192 nodes be 10 years. It may differ across different components. It was here used to simplify the system. The $r_i = 1/S = 4.8e - 5$ per hour. The application running time $R$ is 400 h. So the failure rate is about 99.999 %.

However, if the current tolerance model increase the runtime of its application to 800 h, the checkpoint interval set to 15 min, $I = 0.25$. Therefore, the probability of the unrecoverable failure is about 0.0009 %, regardless of whether the $dm$ is set to 2 or other number. That increases the likelihood that the long run application will be completed from unlikely to nearly certain. Noted that, for checkpointing is low overhead, in this analysis we do not consider the expenses of the checkpointing. The issue is addressed in experimental section.

# 6   Experimental Results

This section evaluates our FT-Offload framework. For demonstration purpose, the overhead of periodic checkpointing process and of the restarting applications after a failure was measured on Tianhe-2 supercomputer. The version of MPI library used are mpich3. The compiler used is Intel icc version 13.0.0 with optimization options "-O3". To quantify the overheads of FT-Offload, we run microbenchmarks experiments that can reveal the checkpoint overhead under different checkpoint size which is user input. Then, three real applications are used in our experiments. They are Preconditioned Conjugate Gradient (PCG) [30] algorithm, MD [31] and Euler [32].

## 6.1   Checkpointing Overhead: Benchmark Test

In this section, we use the test benchmark for the preliminary evaluation of the checkpoint design. The inputs were the checkpoint size, checkpoint save time and interval. We set the size of each node from 1 M to 1000 M. Figure 6 shows the average overhead of checkpoint-save processes. The average checkpoint time is relatively short compared to [18]. This may be attributable to the use of asynchronous transfer of MIC to CPU and taking advantage of low latency DRAM read or write, when writing the checkpoint buffer the executing pipeline needn't stop to wait for data to be saved.

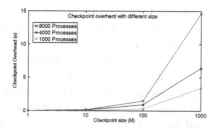

**Fig. 6.** Checkpoint overhead with different size

## 6.2    Checkpointing Overhead: Real Application

The current PCG solves the sparse linear system arising from discrediting a 3D Poisson's equation using finite-difference-method. The running time of PCG and fault-tolerance PCG (FT-PCG) is depicted on Fig. 7. The gray bar shows the running time of PCG and the black bar is for FT-PCG when no failure occurs. This demonstrates that, when no failure occurs during the computation, the overhead of our checkpointing protocol of heterogeneous system is about 6 % on 1k nodes and 8 % on 8k nodes, it's much less than 25 % labeled in [33]. Noted that, as our weak scalability scheme, the problem scale of each process is the same while running on multiple nodes. The checkpointing interval is controlled under the MTBF, so before the system corrupt the checkpoint data can be saved. And in this experiment, we can carry out the checkpoint for better analysis. To reveal the recovery of fail-stop failures, when the FT-PCG running we let down one of the working nodes through the management system manually. The main overhead for this checkpointing recovery is the time it takes to remove the failed nodes then redo the computation due to rollback, which is about 3 min. Optimistically, the recovering is automatically done by our task-submit auto script.

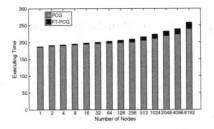

**Fig. 7.** PCG timing overheads for fault-tolerance while no failure occurs during the computation

For comparison, the current FT-Offload was used on another two application. One was frequently used in the study of nanoscale physical phenomena molecular dynamics (MD) simulation program which was poor on load balance while running on supercomputers. In this way, the size of checkpoint on one node may differ from the size of checkpoint on the others. The other is Euler, a multi uniform Goundov grid, when checkpointing the checkpoint buffer size was found to change during different running phases, but it did not show checkpoint of different sizes. Tables 2 and 3 reports the checkpoint size and overhead with different running process. Because of poor load balance, the checkpoint size of each process was different. During the parallel checkpoint buffer writing, maintaining balance took up a large amount time, it is high lined in Table 3.

To assess the recovery of fail-stop failures, when the FT-PCG running we let down one of the working nodes through the management system manually.

**Table 2.** Checkpoint overhead:Euler

| Process | Size (total) | Running time (s) | Average overhead (s) |
|---------|--------------|------------------|----------------------|
| 1000 | 7.04–32.69 G | 3858 | 1.92 |
| 4000 | 10.23–45.51 G | 2683 | 1.78 |
| 8000 | 25.12–95.34 G | 2517 | 1.96 |

**Table 3.** Checkpoint overhead:MD

| Process | Size (total) | Running time (s) | Average overhead (s) |
|---------|--------------|------------------|----------------------|
| 1000 | 1.24 G | 3848 | **5.32** |
| 4000 | 5.93 G | 3048 | **7.32** |
| 8000 | 10.88 G | 3125 | **10.56** |

The main overhead for our checkpointing recovery is the time it takes to remove the failed nodes then redo the computation due to rollback, which is about 3 min. Optimistically, the recovering is automatically done.

## 7    Conclusions

In this paper, we present FT-Offload,a fault tolerance framework for massive MIC based heterogeneous programming. It take advantage of Intel Offload and double in-memory checkpoint/recovery techniques. This FT-Offload system has several advantages over the exiting solutions, such as reliability for the long running application on massively heterogeneous systems. Existing code is rendered easily portable by providing the halo exchange wrapper and other APIs. The use of MPI and Intel Offload as communication back-end ensures its compatibility with most HPC environments.

Numerical analysis was conducted and a test benchmark and the real-word applications were ported from Offload to FT-Offload. Under the framework of halo exchange wrapper, the Offload's directives are replaced by FT-Offload. When run on large number of nodes, the checkpoint overhead can was kept is relatively low. This work demonstrates that this system can tolerate massive CPU-MIC systems and produce dependable results. This work may also serve as general guidance for heterogeneous systems.

Some observations opened up new questions that worth merit further investigation. For instance, at what point contention for the latency of transferring large checkpoint data from MIC to CPU, a new kind of checkpoint partition and latency overlap study needs further investigations. The integration of different coprocessors within a single fault tolerance programming model is also planned.

# Acknowledgments

This work is supported by the National High Technology Research and Development Program of China (863 Program)2012AA01A309, and the National Natural Science Foundation of China (NSFC) NO. 61170049, and No. 61402495.

# References

1. Luebke, D., Harris, M., Govindaraju, N., Lefohn, A., Houston, M., Owens, J., Segal, M., Papakipos, M., Buck, L.: GPGPU: general-purpose computation on graphics hardware. In: Proceedings of the 2006 ACM/IEEE Conference on Supercomputing, SC 2006. ACM, New York, USA (2006)
2. Schulz, K.W., Ulerich, R., Malaya, N., Bauman, P.T., Stogner, R., Simmons, C.: Early experiences porting scientific applications to the many integrated core (MIC) platform. In: TACC-Intel Highly Parallel Computing Symposium, Austin, Texas (2012)
3. Kirk, D.: NVIDIA CUDA software and GPU parallel computing architecture. In: Proceedings of the 6th International Symposium on Memory Management, ISMM 2007, pp. 103–104. ACM, New York, USA (2007)
4. Yang, X., Liao, X., Lu, K., Hu, Q., Song, J., Su, J.: The TianHe-1A supercomputer: Its hardware and software. J. Comput. Sci. Technol. **26**, 344–351 (2011)
5. Yang, C., Wu, Q., Tang, T., Wang, F., Xue, J.: Programming for scientific computing on peta-scale heterogeneous parallel systems. J. Cent. S. Univ. **20**, 1189–1203 (2013)
6. http://www.top500.org
7. Knights corner software developers guide, 27 April 2012
8. Liao, X., Xiao, L., Yang, C., Lu, Y.: MilkyWay-2 supercomputer: system and application. Front. Comput. Sci. **8**(3), 345–356 (2014)
9. Liao, X., Yung, C., Tang, T., Yi, H., Wang, F., Wu, Q., Xue, J.: OpenMC: towards simplifying programming for tianhe supercomputers. J. Comput. Sci. Technol. (JCST) **29**, 532–546 (2014)
10. Nasertayoob, P., Shahbazian, S.: Stampede supercomputer. http://www.top500.org/system/17793
11. Rajachandrasekar, R., Potluri, S., Venkatesh, A., Hamidouche, K., Wasi-ur Rahman, M., Panda, D.K.: MIC-Check: a distributed check pointing framework for the intel many integrated cores architecture. In: Proceedings of the 23rd International Symposium on High-Performance Parallel and Distributed Computing, pp. 121–124. ACM (2014)
12. User and reference guide for the intel c++ compiler 14.0, intel corporation (2014)
13. Intel Corporation. Openmp application program interface, version 4.0. OpenMP Architecture Review Board, July 2013
14. The openacc application programming interface, version 1.0., November 2011
15. Koo, R., Toueg, S.: Checkpointing and rollback-recovery for distributed systems. IEEE Trans. Softw. Eng. **1**, 23–31 (1987)
16. Huang, C., Lawlor, O., Kale, L.V.: Adaptive MPI. In: Rauchwerger, L. (ed.) LCPC 2003. LNCS, vol. 2958. Springer, Heidelberg (2004)
17. Xu, X., Yang, X., Xue, J., Lin, Y., Lin, Y.: PartialRC: a partial recomputing method for efficient fault recovery on gpgpus. J. Comput. Sci. Technol. (JCST) **27**, 240–255 (2012)

18. Zheng, G., Ni, X., Kalé, L.V.: A scalable double in-memory checkpoint and restart scheme towards exascale. In: 2012 IEEE/IFIP 42nd International Conference on Dependable Systems and Networks Workshops (DSN-W), pages 1–6. IEEE (2012)
19. Kale, L.V., Zheng, G.: Charm++ and ampi: adaptive runtime strategies via migratable objects. In: Advanced Computational Infrastructures for Parallel and Distributed Applications, pp. 265–282 (2009)
20. Stellner, G.: Cocheck: Checkpointing and process migration for MPI. In: Proceedings of the 10th Internationa Parallel Processing Symposium, IPPS 1996, pp. 526–531. IEEE (1996)
21. Agbaria, A.M., Friedman, R.: Starfish: fault-tolerant dynamic MPI programs on clusters of workstations. In: Proceedings. The Eighth International Symposium on High Performance Distributed Computing, pp. 167–176. IEEE (1999)
22. Bronevetsky, G., Marques, D., Pingali, K., Stodghill, P.: Automated application-level checkpointing of MPI programs. ACM Sigplan Notices 38(10), 84–94 (2003)
23. Sheaffer, J.W., Luebke, D.P., Skadron, K:. A hardware redundancy and recovery mechanism for reliable scientific computation on graphics processors. In: Graphics Hardware, vol. 2007, pp. 55–64. Citeseer (2007)
24. Karablieh, F., Bazzi, R.A.: Heterogeneous checkpointing for multithreaded applications. In: Proceedings of 21st IEEE Symposium on Reliable Distributed Systems, 2002, pp. 140–149. IEEE (2002)
25. Takizawa, H., Koyama, K., Sato, K., Komatsu, K., Kobayashi, H.: Checl: transparent checkpointing and process migration of opencl applications. In: 2011 IEEE International Parallel & Distributed Processing Symposium (IPDPS), pp. 864–876. IEEE (2011)
26. Takizawa, H., Sato, K., Komatsu, K., Kobayashi, H.: CheCUDA: a checkpoint/restart tool for cuda applications. In: 2009 International Conference on Parallel and Distributed Computing, Applications and Technologies, pp. 408–413. IEEE (2009)
27. Hargrove, P.H., Duell, J.C.: Berkeley lab checkpoint/restart (blcr) for linux clusters. J. Phys.: Conf. Ser. 46, 494 (2006)
28. Dong, X., Wen, M., Chai, J., Cai, X., Zhao, M., Zhang1, C.: Communication-hiding programming for clusters with multi-coprocessor nodes. Published online in Wiley Online Library (2015)
29. Fagg, G.E., Dongarra, J.: FT-MPI: Fault Tolerant MPI, supporting dynamic applications in a dynamic world. In: Dongarra, J., Kacsuk, P., Podhorszki, N. (eds.) PVM/MPI 2000. LNCS, vol. 1908, p. 346. Springer, Heidelberg (2000)
30. Barrett, R., Berry, M.W., Chan, T.F., Demmel, J., Donato, J., Dongarra, J., Eijkhout, V., Pozo, R., Romine, C., Van der Vorst, H.: Templates for the Solution of Linear Systems: Building Blocks for Iterative Methods, vol. 43. Siam, Philadelphia (1994)
31. Yang, C., Wang, F., Du, Y., Chen, J., Liu, J., Yi, H., Lu, K.: Adaptive optimization for petascale heterogeneous CPU/GPU computing. In: 2010 IEEE International Conference on Cluster Computing (CLUSTER), pp. 19–28. IEEE (2010)
32. Shahbazian, S.: Revisiting the foundations of quantum theory of atoms in molecules: the variational procedure and the zero-flux conditions. Int. J. Quantum Chem. 108(9), 1477–1484 (2008)
33. Chen, Z.: Algorithm-based recovery for iterative methods without checkpointing. In: Proceedings of the 20th International Symposium on High Performance Distributed Computing, pp. 73–84. ACM (2011)

# MC-RAIS: Multi-chunk Redundant Array of Independent SSDs with Improved Performance

Suzhen Wu[1], Weijian Yang[1], Bo Mao[2(✉)], and Yanping Lin[1]

[1] Computer Science Department, Xiamen University, Xiamen 361005, China
[2] Software School of Xiamen University, Xiamen 361005, China
{suzhen,maobo}@xmu.edu.cn

**Abstract.** Big Data Analytics is a big challenge for the performance of the computing and storage systems. With the rapid development of multi-core and GPU processors, the performance of HDD-based storage system becomes much more serious. The flash-based Solid State Disks (SSDs) have become an emerging alternative to HDDs and received great attentions from both academia and industry. However, a single SSD cannot satisfy the capacity, performance and reliability requirements of a modern storage system supporting increasingly demanding data-intensive computing and applications. Redundant Array of Independent SSDs (RAIS) is an effective way to build high-performance, high-reliability, and high-capacity SSD-based storage systems. In RAIS, the chunk size is an important parameter that affects the system performance. However, the existing studies are mainly focused on the efficiency of chunk size of RAID. Because of the different performance characteristics between HDDs and SSDs, the results of these studies could not be applied to the RAIS. In this paper, we first conducted extensive experiments on the efficiency of chunk size on the RAIS performance. Based on the experimental results, we proposed a Multi-Chunk RAIS (short for MC-RAIS) to improve the performance of the SSD-based storage systems. Evaluation results show that MC-RAIS outperforms the existing fix-chunk-size SSD-based disk arrays in the I/O performance measure by more than 50 %.

**Keywords:** Solid state drive · Redundant array of independent SSDs · Chunk size · Garbage collection · Performance evaluation

## 1 Introduction

Hard Disk Drives (HDDs) have become the performance wall of storage systems. Recently, the flash-based Solid State Disks (SSDs) have become an emerging alternative to HDDs and received great attentions from both academia and industry [1,6,8,19]. Different from HDDs, SSDs are based on semiconductor chips and have no mechanical parts. SSDs can provide many benefits, such as low power consumption, high robustness to vibrations and temperature, and

© Springer International Publishing Switzerland 2015
G. Wang et al. (Eds.): ICA3PP 2015, Part IV, LNCS 9531, pp. 18–32, 2015.
DOI: 10.1007/978-3-319-27140-8_2

most importantly, high small-random-read performance. Unfortunately, SSDs also have some disadvantages, such as high cost, erase-before-write problem, low small-random-write performance and limited lifetime [1].

Besides the deployment of SSDs on desktop computers, some studies also use SSDs in the high-performance computing and enterprise environments [5]. In these environments, a single SSD cannot satisfy the performance, capacity and reliability requirements. Thus, applying the RAID (Redundant Array of Independent Disks) technique [13,17] to SSDs is necessary and likely promising to build large-scale high performance and highly reliable SSD-based storage systems [2,14,20, 21]. In this paper, Redundant Array of Independent SSDs is short for *RAIS*. The different levels of RAIS are also short for *RAIS0*, *RAIS5* and so on.

By distributing user data across multiple disks in an array, RAID offers high performance, high reliability and high capacity. The chunk size is an important parameter that defines the granularity of data distribution in an array and has been traditionally determined based on characteristics of HDDs to balance throughput and response time [7]. Due to the characteristics of HDDs, the suggested chunk size by the enterprise data storage systems vendors such as IBM, HP, and EMC varies between 16 KB and 1 MB. The suggested chunk sizes can be possibly far from the optimal configuration for SSD-based disk arrays with respect to the I/O throughput and response time. Additionally, the conventional chunk size used for RAID should be revised due to the limited endurance of SSDs. To the best of our knowledge, the analysis and performance studies on the optimization of the chunk size of RAIS are missing in the previous work.

In this paper, we first conducted extensive experiments on the efficiency of the chunk size on the RAIS performance. The evaluation results show that the optimal chunk size is different for read-intensive workloads and write-intensive workloads. Based on the observations, we proposed a Multi-Chunk RAIS (short for MC-RAIS) to improve the performance of the SSD-based storage systems by exploiting the workload characteristics. To evaluate the efficiency of our proposed MC-RAIS scheme, we have implemented a prototype of MC-RAIS by integrating it into an open-source SSD simulator developed by Microsoft Research [1] and conducted extensive experiments to evaluate the performance of the MC-RAIS scheme by a wide variety of enterprise realistic workloads. The experimental results show that the MC-RAIS scheme outperforms the fix-chunk-size RAIS schemes by more than 50 %. Moreover, the MC-RAIS scheme also significantly reduces the performance variability simultaneously.

More specifically, this paper makes the following contributions:

(1) To the best of our knowledge, MC-RAIS is the first study to evaluate the impact of the chunk size on the performance of RAIS system.
(2) MC-RAIS fully exploits the parallelism characteristics of SSDs in RAIS to improve the RAIS performance and alleviate the GC impact on the performance variability.
(3) We evaluate the performance of MC-RAIS in a RAIS simulator developed by Microsoft Research [1] and Carnegie Mellon University (CMU) [4] driven by a wide spectrum of workloads. The experimental results show that the

MC-RAIS scheme outperforms the fix-chunk schemes in terms of average user response times.

The rest of this paper is organized as follows. Background and motivation are presented in Sect. 2. We describe the design detail of the MC-RAIS scheme in Sect. 3. The performance evaluation is presented in Sect. 4. The related work is presented in Sect. 5. We conclude this paper and point out the directions for the future research in Sect. 6.

## 2    Background and Motivation

In this section, we first describe the key characteristics of flash-based SSDs compared with magnetic HDDs. Then we elaborate how the configuration of the chunk size affects the RAIS performance. Based on these observations, we provide the motivation for our new multi-chunk size optimization scheme for RAIS.

### 2.1    Characteristics of Flash-based SSD

Similar to HDDs, data in SSDs is persistent when the power supply is turned off. However, unlike mechanical HDDs, flash-based SSDs are made of silicon memory chips and do not have moving parts (*i.e.*, mechanical positioning parts). SSDs can provide many benefits, such as low power consumption, high robustness to vibrations and temperature. Figure 1 illustrates a logical overview of a typical SSD with n independent channels. Each channel is shared by multiple flash chips. SSDs are inherently highly parallelized architectures, comprising different units, including page, block, plane, channel and package. The different constituent operational units can operate in parallel, thus providing the potential to achieve better performance.

Besides the advantages of high parallelism and high energy efficiency, flash-based SSDs have two main characteristics compared with HDDs, as follows.

First, the current generation of SSDs suffers from the poor performance of small random writes. The reason is that in the flash-based SSDs, each block of size 64–128 KB must be erased before any page in it can be re-written, which is known as the characteristic feature of "erase-before-write". Seriously, an erase operation typically takes several milliseconds that is one or two order of magnitude higher than the completion time of a read operation.

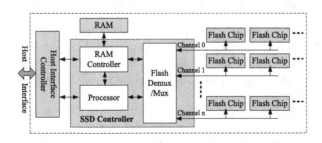

**Fig. 1.** Internal overview of a typical SSD.

Second, the flash wear-out problem caused by a large number of repeated write-erase operations affects the reliability of SSDs. Generally, the expected number of erasures per block is 100,000 for the single level cell (short for SLC) NAND flash memory while the expected number is reduced to 10,000 for the multi level cell (short for MLC) NAND flash memory.

These two above limitations of SSDs must be taken into consideration when designing SSD-based storage systems, especially SSD-based disk arrays.

## 2.2   Chunk Size

The chunk size of RAIS is an important parameter that affects the RAIS performance. To investigate the effect of different chunk sizes on the performance of SSD-based disk arrays, we conduct experiments on a RAIS5 consisting of 4 Intel DC S3700 200GB SSDs, driven by the fio benchmark.

Figure 2 shows the performance of random accesses on the RAIS5 with different chunk sizes. From Fig. 2(a), we can see that the performance is increased with the increasing chunk size of RAIS. The experimental results also shown that when the request size is 3 times of the chunk size, the read performance is the best. The reason is that the access is the full stripe read and all SSDs in the RAIS5 are involved in one request. Therefore, the access parallelism among the SSDs is fully exploited so that the RAIS performance is improved accordingly. In contrast, as shown in Fig. 2(b), when the chunk size is the smallest, the write performance is the best. The reason is that with a smaller chunk size, more write requests could be performed in all or most SSDs in the RAIS5 by exploiting the access parallelism and avoid the small-write penalty problem.

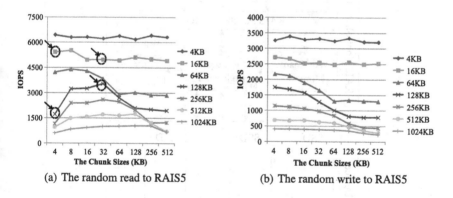

(a) The random read to RAIS5                    (b) The random write to RAIS5

**Fig. 2.** The performance of random accesses on a RAIS5 with different chunk sizes.

Based on the evaluation results, we can see that the optimal chunk sizes of SSD-based disk array in different workload conditions are diverse. To provide the best performance of RAIS, the workload characteristics must be fully exploited to guide the data layout, *i.e.*, distributing the data in different zones with different chunk sizes. These important observations motivate us to propose a multi-chunk

RAIS scheme to improve the performance of SSD-based disk arrays by exploiting the workload characteristics.

# 3    MC-RAIS

In this section, we first present the system overview of MC-RAIS, followed by a description of the request processing workflow and the data consistency in MC-RAIS.

## 3.1    System Overview of MC-RAIS

Figure 3 shows the system overview of our proposed MC-RAIS. As shown in Fig. 3, MC-RAIS interacts with the *RAIS Functional* module and can be incorporated into any existing RAIS5 schemes, including hardware and software RAIS systems. In general, MC-RAIS consists of two important functional modules added into the RAIS controller in the existing storage system: Workload Monitor and Request Redirector. The *Workload Monitor* module is responsible for identifying the user I/O requests based on the access history. The *Request Redirector* module is responsible for issuing the user I/O requests to the corresponding zones based on results of the Workload Monitor module.

In Fig. 3, the SSD-based disk array is divided into three data zones with different chunk sizes, 4 KB, 8 KB and 32 KB. The 4 KB zone is designed to store

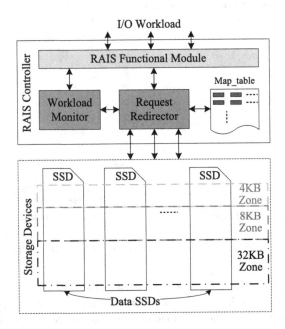

**Fig. 3.** System overview of MC-RAIS consisting of three data zones with different chunk sizes.

write-intensive data blocks (write-intensive zone), the 32 KB is designed to store the read-intensive data blocks (read-intensive zone) and the 8KB is designed for mixed data blocks. Moreover, the data blocks are classified into read-intensive, write-intensive and mixed types based on the access history. When a data block is accessed, its access frequency will be increased to track the popularity of the data block, which is a simple way to track the data popularity. However, other classic policies are also applicable in MC-RAIS to further track the data popularity to improve the efficiency of MC-RAIS.

In addition to the above two functional modules, MC-RAIS uses an important data structure, *i.e.*, Map_table, to record the mapping information of the redirected write data. As shown in Fig. 4, the *Map_table* is used to log all the write data that is stored on the different data zones. MC-RAIS uses the nonvolatile memory to store the content of the Map_table to prevent data loss in case of power failure. The Map_table is similar to the mapping information within the FTL in a single SSD. Thus, the protection schemes of mapping information within FTL are also applicable to the Map_table. Since each incoming request should be checked in the Map_Table, MC-RAIS use the bloom filter scheme to improve the query efficiency which further reduces the space overhead.

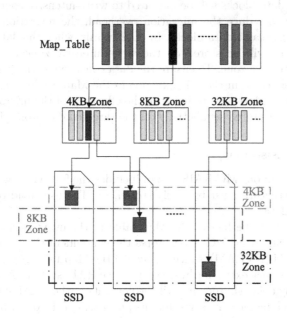

**Fig. 4.** Mapping table of MC-RAIS.

## 3.2   Request Processing Workflow

When processing the incoming requests, an important issue must be addressed for the new data blocks because no access history has been kept for the new data block. To be simple and effective, the new data blocks are first stored on the read-intensive zone. If the data blocks are read-intensive, no migration is needed. Otherwise, the data blocks will be migrated to other zones when they are updated again, thus involving on extra write operations. By doing this, the frequency of the data migration is reduced.

Upon receiving the write request, MC-RAIS first checks the Map_table to determine which data zone to service the request. If the write request hit the Map_Table, the index will be retrieved to locate the data zones to service the write request. Moreover, the corresponding $w\_count$ value in the Map_table will be increased to record the write access frequency. Otherwise, the write data will be written on the read-intensive zone and be recorded in the Map_table. For read requests, MC-RAIS also checks the Map_Table firstly to determine which data zone to service the request. If the requested data are stored on multiple data zones, the read request will be replaced by multiple read requests to the different data zones in the same RAIS. After all the these read requests have completed, the requested read data is reconstructed and returned to the upper layer. Otherwise, the read request will be serviced as usual and the corresponding $r\_value$ in the Map_table will be increased to record the read access frequency.

Once the data blocks on the read-intensive zone are identified to be write-intensive, these data blocks will be migrated to write-intensive zones in the MC-RAIS. In order to reduce the migration overhead, the migration is processed when updating the same data blocks. In other words, when the data is updated, these data blocks will be stored on the write-intensive zone rather than the original read-intensive zone. To ensure the data consistency, the log entry of the write data is deleted from the original zone in the Map_Table after the migrate process completes. Moreover, to improve the efficiency of the migration process, the data blocks are stored sequentially on the targeted data zones in MC-RAIS.

### 3.3    Data Consistency

Data consistency in our MC-RAIS design includes the following two aspects: (1) The key data structure must be safely stored, (2) The user read requests must fetch the right data.

First, to prevent the loss of the Map_table in the event of a power supply failure or a system crash, MC-RAIS stores the contents of the Map_table in the non-volatile RAM (NVRAM). Since the size of the Map_table is general small, it will not incur distinct extra hardware cost to the RAIS system. A small battery or capacitor may delay shutdown until the contents in the RAM are safely saved to an area of flash memory reserved for the purpose. On the other hand, in order to improve the write performance by using the write-back strategy, NVRAM is commonly deployed in the RAIS controller or the RAIS system. Therefore, it is easy and reasonable to use the NVRAM to store the contents of the Map_table.

Second, since the up-to-date data for a read request can be stored on different data zones, each incoming read request is first checked in the Map_table to determine whether it should be serviced by the multiple data zones. If so, the read request will be split into multiple read requests to keep the fetched data be always up-to-date. Otherwise the read request will serviced as it is.

# 4    Performance Evaluations

In this section, we first describe the experimental setup and methodology of this paper. Then we evaluate the performance of our proposed MC-RAIS scheme and the comparisons of the fix-chunk-size scheme through trace-driven simulations with realistic enterprise workloads.

## 4.1    Experimental Setup and Methodology

To evaluate the efficiency of our proposed MC-RAIS scheme, we have implemented a prototype of the MC-RAIS scheme by integrating it into an open-source SSD simulator developed by Microsoft Research (MSR) [1]. The MSR SSD simulator, an extension of DiskSim from the Parallel Data Lab of CMU [4], has been released to the public and widely used to evaluate the performance of the SSD-based storage systems in many studies [12,16,18]. In this paper, we extended the original DiskSim and the MSR SSD simulator to implement our proposed MC-RAIS scheme. The specifications of each SSD in the SSD simulator are shown in Table 1.

**Table 1.** SSD model parameters.

| SSD model | |
|---|---|
| Total Capacity | Configuable |
| Reserved Free Blocks | 15 % |
| Minimum Free Blocks | 5 % |
| Cleaning Policy | Greedy |
| Flash Chip Elements | 64 |
| Planes Per Package | 4 |
| Blocks Per Plane | 512 |
| Pages Per Block | 64 |
| Page Size | 4 KB |
| Page Read Latency | 25 us |
| Page Write Latency | 200 us |
| Block Erase Latency | 1.5 ms |

In the evaluations, we compare the performance of the MC-RAIS scheme with that of the fix-chunk-size schemes, in terms of user response time. In the fix-chunk-size configuration, we also set different chunk sizes in different experiments: 4 KB, 8 KB and 32 KB (short for 4 KB-RAIS, 8 KB-RAIS and 32 KB-RAIS). For the MC-RAIS scheme, each zone size is configured to be 60GB by default. We use three realistic enterprise-scale workloads to study the impact of our proposed MC-RAIS scheme. The three realistic enterprise-scale workloads were collected from the Microsoft Cambridge Research [3]. The main workload parameters of these traces are summarized in Table 2. Each experiment is run three times and the average results are collected.

**Table 2.** The trace characteristics.

| Traces | Read ratio | IOPS | Ave. Read Req. Size (KB) | Ave. Write Req. Size (KB) |
|--------|-----------|------|--------------------------|---------------------------|
| proj_0 | 85.5 % | 479 | 6.4 | 9.2 |
| stg_0 | 20.6 % | 354 | 9.3 | 8.6 |
| hm_0 | 68.5 % | 134 | 9.7 | 6.5 |

## 4.2    Performance Results

We first conduct experiments on an 4-disk RAIS5 system for the different schemes driven by the three workloads. Figure 5 shows the comparisons of the normalized average response times for the fix-chunk-size schemes with different chunk sizes and our MC-RAIS scheme driven by the three workloads. From Fig. 5, we can see that compared with the fix-chunk-size RAIS schemes, MC-RAIS outperforms 4 KB-RAIS, 8 KB-RAIS and 32 KB-RAIS by 40.2 %, 43.4 % and 49.8 % in terms of the average response time, respectively. The reasons are twofold. First, for the write requests, MC-RAIS reduces the overhead of the parity update, which significantly alleviates the write amplification penalty. Second, the read requests could be serviced by fully exploiting the access parallelism to improve the performance. Therefore, MC-RAIS reduces the overall response time, compared with the fix-chunk-size schemes.

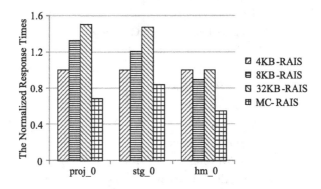

**Fig. 5.** Comparisons of the normalized average response times for the MC-RAIS scheme and three fix-chunk-size RAIS schemes driven by the three workloads.

To better understand the variance of response times for the three workloads in the experiments, Fig. 6 shows the comparisons of the standard deviation results for the MC-RAIS scheme and three fix-chunk-size RAIS schemes. From Fig. 6, we can first see that the 4 KB-RAIS scheme is capable of working with the most minimal variances. The reason is that the 4 KB chunk size is the same as the page size, which makes the performance stable in the situation. Second, we can see that the MC-RAIS scheme is capable of working with more minimal variances than 8 KB-RAIS and 32 KB-RAIS. In particular, the results show that the MC-RAIS scheme reduces the performance variance by 59.0 % and 45.8 % compared with the 8 KB-RAIS and 32 KB-RAIS schemes driven by the three workloads, respectively. In contrast, we can also see that the performance variability is a serious problem for the fix-chunk-size RAIS schemes.

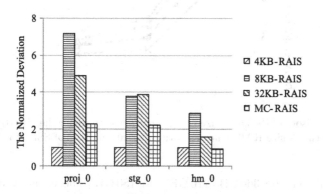

**Fig. 6.** Comparisons of the standard deviation results for the MC-RAIS scheme and three fix-chunk-size RAIS schemes driven by the three workloads.

### 4.3  Sensitivity Study

The performance of our MC-RAIS scheme is likely influenced by several important factors, including the number of SSDs in the RAIS and the zone size of the RAIS system.

*Number of SSDs.* To examine the sensitivity of MC-RAIS to the number of SSDs of the RAIS system, we conduct experiments on the RAIS5 systems consisting of different numbers of SSDs (3, 4 and 5) driven by the proj_0 workload. Figure 7 shows the comparisons of the normalized average response times for the MC-RAIS scheme and three fix-chunk-size RAIS schemes. From Fig. 7, we can see that the average response time decreases with the increasing number of SSDs in the RAIS system. The reason is that the I/O intensity on the individual SSD will decrease when increasing the number of SSDs in the RAIS system, thus reducing the service time for the user I/O requests. Moreover, a RAIS system consisting of more SSDs provides higher parallelism when processing the user I/O requests. Certainly, Fig. 7 also shows that the MC-RAIS scheme consistently outperforms the three fix-chunk-size schemes with different numbers of SSDs. We can also see that the MC-RAIS scheme is not sensitive to the number of SSDs in the RAIS system.

*Zone Size.* To examine the impact of the zone size of the RAIS system in the MC-RAIS scheme, we conduct experiments on an 4-disk RAIS5 system with zone sizes of 120 GB, 90 GB and 60 GB, respectively. Thus, the overall capacities

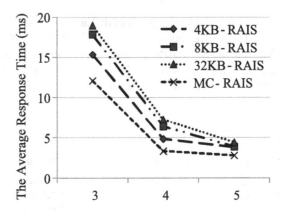

**Fig. 7.** Comparisons of the normalized average response times for the MC-RAIS scheme and three fix-chunk-size RAIS schemes with different numbers of SSDs (3, 4 and 5).

for MC-RAIS will be 360 GB, 270 GB and 180 GB. The capacity of the fix-chunk-size RAIS scheme is set to be 360 GB. Figure 8 shows the comparisons of the normalized average response times for the MC-RAIS scheme with different zone sizes and three fix-chunk-size RAIS schemes driven by the three workloads. From Fig. 8, we can see that the average response times of the user I/O requests decrease with the increasing zone size of the MC-RAIS system. The reason is that with a larger zone size, the GC operations will be fewer than that with a smaller zone size. Accordingly, the average response time is lower. Moreover, compared with the fix-chunk-size RAIS schemes, MC-RAIS reduces the average response times since it can adaptively store the data blocks with different access characteristics on the three data zones with different chunk sizes. In general, our proposed MC-RAIS scheme fully exploits the characteristics of the SSDs and the data blocks to improve the system performance.

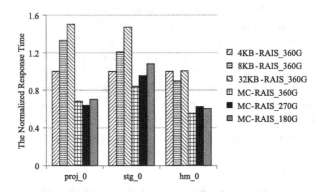

**Fig. 8.** Comparisons of the normalized average response times for the MC-RAIS scheme with different zone sizes and three fix-chunk-size RAIS schemes driven by the three workloads.

There are also some other important parameters that will affect the system performance, such as the numbers of the zone in the RAIS system and the frequency threshold. We will conduct much more experiments to evaluate their effectiveness in the future. Moreover, we will implement the MC-RAIS scheme in the real RAIS system, such as Linux MD, and evaluate it by using real applications.

# 5  Related Work

Studies conducted on SSD-based disk arrays fall into two categories, namely, pure SSD-based disk arrays that all the disks in the disk arrays are SSDs [2,9, 10,23,25] and SSD/HDD hybrid disk arrays that utilize the HDDs to assist the SSD-based disk arrays [11,14,22,24]. Our work belongs to the former.

Balakrishnan et al. [2] observed that in the pure SSD-based RAID5 disk array, the load balancing of write requests can cause correlated failures. Diff-RAID creates an age differential in an array of SSDs, distributes the parity blocks unevenly across the disk array and pre-replaces the faster degraded SSD. However, Diff-RAID does not reduce the number of parity updates on the SSDs. It only concentrates the parity updates on few SSDs to make the SSD failures be uneven in the disk array, thus increasing the reliability of the SSD-based RAID5 disk array. On the other hand, the performance of the Diff-RAID system is degraded due to the concentrated parity updates in their storage system. It essentially trades the performance for reliability for the SSD-based disk arrays.

Flash-aware RAID [10] reduces the number of internal write operations caused by the parity updates by using the delayed parity update strategy and the partial parity technique. It utilizes the cache in the upper layer to achieve this goal and then improve the performance of the RAIS system, which is orthogonal to our proposed MC-RAIS scheme. WeLe-RAID [9] introduces the Wear-leveling mechanism among the flash-based SSDs to enhance the endurance of the entire SSD-based disk arrays. It uses the age-driven parity distribution scheme to guarantee the efficiency of the wear-leveling mechanism among the flash-based SSDs and bring the performance benefit with better load balance.

On the other hand, since SSDs and HDDs have both advantages and disadvantages, none of them is the perfect choice for all applications. Some studies tried to construct hybrid disk arrays consisting of both SSDs and HDDs. Xie and Sun [22] proposed a hybrid disk array architecture, named HIT, for data-intensive applications. HIT periodically redistributes the data between SSDs and HDDs to adapt to the changing of the data access patterns. In addition, HIT balances the performance, reliability and energy efficiency to determine the appropriate data placement and migration strategy. However, HIT only considers the data placement scheme between the HDD-based disk array and the SSD-based disk array, but not in a real hybrid disk array. HPDA [14,15] is an enhanced hybrid RAID4 disk array composed of both HDDs and SSDs. It uses an HDD to service as the dedicated parity device, thus avoiding the parity updates on the SSDs. Moreover, it uses two HDDs to construct a mirroring write buffer to absorb the incoming small write requests, thus improving both the performance and reliability of the hybrid disk arrays.

However, all the above schemes have not considered the efficiency of the garbage collection operations on the RAIS performance. Kim et al. [12] found that the uncoordinated GC processes on individual SSDs amplified the performance degradation of the RAIS system and proposed a RAID-level Global Garbage Collection (GGC) mechanism to alleviate the performance variability for the RAIS system. However, GGC forces all SSDs in the RAIS system to process the GC operation at the same time, which makes the RAIS unavailable to service the applications during the GC period. Moreover, GGC requires the SSDs to be RAIS-aware and only considers RAIS0 that has lower reliability than RAIS5. Differently, our proposed MC-RAIS scheme exploits the workload characteristics to place the data blocks on multiple data zones with different chunk sizes.

## 6  Conclusion

With the rapid development and wide applications of the SSD device, the SSD-based disk arrays become one of the most effective ways to solve the performance and energy bottlenecks of HDD-based storage systems. Due to the different characteristics between HDDs and SSDs, straightforwardly applying the RAID technique to SSDs is challenging. In this paper, we first conducted extensive experiments on the efficiency of the chunk size on the RAIS performance. Based on the experimental results, we proposed a Multi-Chunk RAIS (short for MC-RAIS) to improve the performance of the SSD-based storage systems. The evaluation results show that the performance of MC-RAIS outperforms the that of existing fix-chunk-size SSD-based disk arrays by more than 50 %.

Our proposed MC-RAIS scheme is an ongoing research project and we are currently exploring several directions for the future work. First, we will implement the MC-RAIS scheme in a real RAIS system, such as Linux MD, and evaluate it by using real applications. Second, we will investigate how the system reliability is affected by the MC-RAIS scheme and evaluate its efficiency.

**Acknowledgments.** This work is supported by the National Natural Science Foundation of China under Grant No. 61100033, No. 61472336 and No. 61402385, National Key Technology R&D Program Foundation of China under Grant No. 2015BAH16F02, Fundamental Research Funds for the Central Universities (No. 20720140515).

## References

1. Agrawal, N., Prabhakaran, V., Wobber, T., Davis, J., Manasse, M., Panigrahy, R.: Design tradeoffs for SSD performance. In: Proceedings of the 2008 USENIX Annual Technical Conference (USENIX 2008), Boston, MA, June 2008
2. Balakrishnan, M., Kadav, A., Prabhakaran, V., Malkhi, D.: Differential RAID: rethinking RAID for SSD reliability. In: Proceedings of the 5th European Conference on Computer Systems (EuroSys 2010), Paris, France, April 2010

3. Block I/O Traces in SNIA. http://iotta.snia.org/tracetypes/3
4. Bucy, J., Schindler, J.S., Schlosser, S.W., Ganger, G.R.: The DiskSim Simulation Environment Version 4.0 Reference Manual, May 2008
5. Caulfield, A.M., Coburn, J., Mollov, T., De, A., Akel, A., He, J., Jagatheesan, A., Gupta, R.K., Snavely, A., Swanson, S.: Understanding the impact of emerging non-volatile memories on high-performance, io-intensive computing. In: Proceedings of the 2010 International Conference for High Performance Computing, Networking, Storage and Analysis (SC 2010), New Orleans, LA, November 2010
6. Chen, F., Koufaty, D.A., Zhang, X.: Understanding intrinsic characteristics and system implications of flash memory based solid state drives. In: Proceedings of the 11th ACM SIGMETRICS International Conference on Measurement and Modeling of Computer Systems (SIGMETRICS 2009), Seattle, WA, June 2009
7. Chen, P.M., Lee, E.K.: Striping in a RAID level 5 disk array. In: Proceedings of the 1995 ACM SIGMETRICS Conference on Measurement and Modeling of Computer Systems (SIGMETRICS 1995), Ottawa, Canada, May 1995
8. Dirik, C., Jacob, B.: The performance of PC solid-state disks as a function of bandwidth, concurrency, device architecture, and system organization. In: Proceedings of the 36th International Symposium on Computer Architecture (ISCA 2009), Austin, TX, June 2009
9. Yimo, D., Fang, L., Zhiguang, C., Xin, M.: WeLe-RAID: a SSD-Based RAID for system endurance and performance. In: Altman, E., Shi, W. (eds.) NPC 2011. LNCS, vol. 6985, pp. 248–262. Springer, Heidelberg (2011)
10. Im, S., Shin, D.: Flash-aware RAID techniques for dependable and high-performance flash memory SSD. IEEE Trans. Comput. 60(61), 80–92 (2011)
11. Kim, Y., Gupta, A., Urgaonkar, B., Berman, P., Sivasubramaniam, A.: Hybrid-Store: a cost-efficient, high-performance storage system combining SSDs and HDDs. In: Proceedings of the IEEE International Symposium on Modeling, Analysis and Simulation of Computer and Telecommunication Systems (MASCOTS 2011), Singapore, July 2011
12. Kim, Y., Oral, S., Shipman, G.M., Lee, J., Dillow, D.A., Wang, F.: Harmonia: a globally coordinated garbage collector for arrays of solid-state drives. In: Proceedings of the 27th IEEE Symposium on Mass Storage Systems and Technologies (MSST 2011), Denver, CO, May 2011
13. Mao, B., Feng, D., Wu, S., Chen, J., Zeng, L., Tian, L.: RAID10L: a high performance raid10 storage architecture based on logging technique. In: Proceedings of the 13th IEEE Asia-Pacific Computer Systems Architecture Conference (ACSAC 2008), Hsinchu, Taiwan, August 2008
14. Mao, B., Jiang, H., Feng, D., Wu, S., Chen, J., Zeng, L., Tian, L.: HPDA: a hybrid parity-based disk array for enhanced perfromance and reliability. In: Proceedings of 24th International Parallel & Distributed Processing Symposium (IPDPS 2010), Atlanta, GA, April 2010
15. Mao, B., Jiang, H., Wu, S., Tian, L., Feng, D., Chen, J., Zeng, L.: HPDA: a hybrid parity-based disk array for enhanced perfromance and reliability. ACM Trans. Storage, 8(1), 1–20 (2012). Article No. 4
16. Park, S., Seo, E., Shin, J., Maeng, S., Lee, J.: Exploiting internal parallelism of flash-based SSDs. IEEE Comput. Archit. Lett. 9(1), 9–12 (2010)
17. D.A. Patterson, G. Gibson, and R. H. Katz. A Case for Redundant Arrays of Inexpensive Disks (RAID). In Proceedings of the International Conference on Management of Data (SIGMOD 1988), Chicago IL, June 1988

18. Wu, G., He, B.: Reducing SSD read latency via NAND flash program and erase suspension. In: Proceedings of the 10th USENIX Conference on File and Storage Technologies (FAST 2012), San Jose, CA, Febuary 2012

19. Wu, S., Chen, X., Mao, B.: GC-RAIS: garbage collection aware and redundant array of independent SSDs. J. Comput. Res. Develop. **50**(1), 60–68 (2013)

20. Wu, S., Jiang, H., Feng, D., Tian, L., Mao, B.: WorkOut: I/O workload outsourcing for boosting the RAID reconstruction performance. In: Proceedings of the 7th USENIX Conference on File and Storage Technologies (FAST 2009), San Francisco, CA, Febuary 2009

21. Wu, S., Jiang, H., Mao, B.: IDO: intelligent data outsourcing with improved RAID reconstruction performance in large-scale data centers. In: Proceedings of the 26th USENIX Large Installation System Administration (LISA 2012), San Diego, CA, December 2012

22. Xie, T., Sun, Y.: Dynamic data reallocation in hybrid disk arrays. IEEE Trans. Parallel Distrib. Syst. **21**(9), 1330–1341 (2010)

23. Yi, L., Shu, J., Ou, J., Zheng, W.: CG-Resync: conversion-guided resynchronization for a SSD-based RAID array. In Proceedings of the 31st International Conference on Computer Design (ICCD 2013), Asheville, NC, October 2013

24. Zeng, L., Feng, D., Mao, B., Chen, J., Wei, Q., Liu, W.: HerpRap: A Hybrid Array Architecture Providing Any Point-in-time Data Tracking for Datacenter. In: Proceedings of the 2012 IEEE International Conference on Cluster Computing (Cluster 2012), Beijing, China, September 2012

25. Zhang, Y., Arpaci-Dusseau, A.C., Arpaci-Dusseau, R.H.: Warped mirrors for flash. In: Proceedings of the 29th IEEE Symposium on Massive Storage Systems and Technologies (MSST 2013), Long Beach, CA, May 2013

# An Energy Efficient Storage System
# for Astronomical Observation Data on Dome A

Zichao Yuan[1], Ce Yu[1](✉), Jizhou Sun[1], Jian Xiao[1],
Jianmei Wang[1], Zhaohui Shang[2,3], and Yi Hu[2]

[1] School of Computer Science and Technology, Tianjin University, Tianjin, China
{skyyuan,yuce,jzsun,xiaojian}@tju.edu.cn
[2] National Astronomical Observatories, CAS, Beijing 100000, China
[3] Astrophysics Center, Tianjin Normal University, Tianjin 300000, China

**Abstract.** In recent years, the research community has initiated different efforts to save energy consumption of the storage system in practical
application scenarios. However, restricted by Antarctic environmental
conditions, general-purpose energy-saving technologies of storage system
are not applicable for Antarctic astronomical observations. In this paper,
a new energy efficient storage system (called MCS-SSD) for astronomical
observation data on Dome A is designed, which uses multi-level caching
strategy with SSD. To boost the data disks' performance, MCS-SSD clusters correlated files and places them on the data disk via a temporal and
spatial manner. MCS-SSD further designs the prefetching and caching
techniques to create larger disk idle time intervals, then the disks that
are not in use within a certain time will be powered down. MCS-SSD
is evaluated on a trace driven simulator in TB data level and PB data
level storage systems, and the results show that compared with existing energy efficient architectures the energy consumption of MCS-SSD
is reduced about 39.34 % to 58.43 %.

**Keywords:** Energy efficient · Controllable disk array · Storage system ·
Astronomical observation

## 1 Introduction

Astronomical observations generate a large amount of data, and every telescope
has its own data format and data processing method. China is establishing a
series of telescopes for Antarctic astronomical observations. Antarctic Schmidt
Telescopes (AST3) is a trio of 50-cm optical telescope, which is being installed
on Dome A. With a surface elevation of 4093 m, Dome A is the highest place
in Antarctica with its lowest temperature reaching below −80°C in the night.
Annually, there are only around 20 days suitable for the researchers to work
there. Restricted by environmental conditions, while the power supply is strictly
limited, the data center should be energy-efficient.

The three independently and remotely controlled telescopes will be used to
study variable objects, such as supernova explosions and the afterglow of gamma-
ray bursts, and to search for extra solar planets [1,2]. Each telescope of AST3

© Springer International Publishing Switzerland 2015
G. Wang et al. (Eds.): ICA3PP 2015, Part IV, LNCS 9531, pp. 33–46, 2015.
DOI: 10.1007/978-3-319-27140-8_3

is equipped with a CCD camera of 10 K x 10K. When in operation, each of the AST3 telescopes theoretically provides 200 MB images per 2.4 min. KDUST [3] astronomical telescope project of China whose telescope is equipped with a CCD camera of 70 K x 70 K is being planned. The observation data size will be much larger and can reach petabyte level. So it is inevitable to establish a data center on Dome A to provide services for the storage of the observation data produced by the telescope and data processing services for the astronomers.

In this paper, a new energy efficient storage system (MCS-SSD) for astronomical observation data on Dome A is designed, which uses multi-level caching strategy with SSD. The disk arrays are divided into cache disks and data disks. To improve the performance of the cache disks, MCS-SSD uses the SSD as the first level cache disk which possesses high read-write speed, low power consumption and other advantages to cache the most popular data. Astronomical data are usually used according to the temporal and spatial requirements [4]. To boost the data disks' performance, MCS-SSD clusters correlated files and places them on the data disk via a temporal and spatial manner. MCS-SSD further designs the prefetching and caching techniques to create larger disk idle time intervals, then the disks that are not in use within a certain time will be powered down.

In order to meet the challenges of the PB level data, the disk arrays are divided into units, and each unit uses MCS-SSD which is composed of first-level cache disks, second-level cache disks and data disks. So the PB-level storage system is similar to a distributed architecture. This storage system based on MCS-SSD is also expected to play a significant role in the planning KDUST astronomical telescope project.

MCS-SSD is evaluated on a trace driven simulator in TB data level and PB data level storage systems, and the results show that the energy consumption of MCS-SSD is reduced about 39.34 % to 58.43 %, so MCS-SSD is more energy efficient compared with existing energy efficient architectures.

The rest of this paper is organized as follows. Section 2 presents the related works and the existing disk energy-saving strategies mainly about MAID(Massive Arrays of Idle Disks) [5] and PDC (Popular Data Concentration) [6], and the improved strategies based on them. Section 3 presents the basic architecture of MCS-SSD, and its data distribution strategy and energy consuming analysis. Section 4 presents the data access model and their corresponding energy-saving strategies. Section 5 evaluates the performance of MCS-SSD by comparing with existing approaches in TB-level and PB-level storage systems. The conclusions of the paper and the future work are presented in Sect. 6.

## 2   Related Work

The motivation of addressing the energy saving issues in the data center storage system is that a significant fraction of the operation cost of data centers is due to energy consumption of storage systems. For example, the average power consumption of top 10 super computing systems is 1.32 Mwatt, in which a large portion is contributed by storage systems [7].

The storage system is based on the disk array. For the single disk, hard disk manufacturers propose a lot of energy-saving technologies such as reducing disk rotational speed, converting disk working mode into standby mode at a certain time and so on. In addition to emerging high-performance disk drives with high power needs, several novel techniques are proposed to conserve energy in storage systems, including dynamic power management schemes [8,9], power-aware cache management strategies [10], power-aware prefetching schemes [11], software-directed power management techniques [12], redundancy techniques [13] and multi-speed settings [14–16]. The disks are not shut down in all of the technologies. But in the Antarctic, even slight energy consumption is very serious, especially in the situation of PB data level in the future. So the disk array in the Antarctic is customized through the way of powering down parts of disks for energy saving. Astronomical data are usually used or stored according to the temporal or spatial requirements, which makes heavily customizing prefer more energy saving not consideration of the generality.

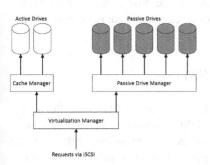

**Fig. 1.** Basic architecture of MAID

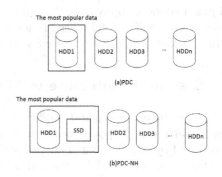

**Fig. 2.** Basic architecture of PDC and PDC-NH

Dennis Colarelli and Dirk Grunwald from University of Colorado proposed MAID [5] to save energy. Their model's architecture is shown in Fig. 1. The system is divided into zero or more "cache drives" that remain constantly spinning; the remaining "data drives" are allowed to spin-down after a varying period of inactivity. With caching, requests are checked in the cache directory at first. Requests that hit in the cache are sent to the cache drives. Reads that miss in the cache are passed on to the data drives.

Eduardo Pinheiro and Ricardo Bianchini from Rutgers University proposed PDC [6] strategies that migrates frequently accessed data to a subset of the disks. Their model's architecture is shown in Fig. 2(a). The idea behind PDC is to dynamically migrate the popular disk data (i.e., the most frequently accessed data on disk) to a subset of the disks in the array, so that the load becomes skewed towards a few of the disks and others can be sent to low-power modes.

DongKyu Lee and Kern Koh from School of Computer Science and Engineering of Seoul National University extended PDC by adding NAND flash based

Solid State Drive(SSD) [17]. They proposed PDC-NH(Popular Data Concentration on NAND Flash and Hard Disk Drive) and achieved better performance and energy savings. Their model's architecture is shown in Fig. 2(b). They developed a novel file placement policy which places popular files on either one of the flash disk or hard disk based on their size, popularity and access characteristics. Their placement policy places large and sequential read files on HDD and small and random read files on SSD. This placement takes advantage of the benefits of each medium and hides their shortcomings.

Above mentioned three researches have a similar goal of increasing the idle period of disks. MCS-SSD also aims to increase the idle period of disks. However, astronomical data are usually used or stored according to the temporal or spatial requirements, which requires the cache disks should have an efficient caching strategy for user's demands. MAID only caches the data that is hit, so it cannot afford the demand of astronomical observations. Since the meta data on data disks can't be moved, PDC and PDC-NH don't fit this situation.

MAID and PDC respectively present disk storage system energy-saving techniques' two main approaches: disk group technology and data distribution technology. MCS-SSD model takes full advantages of these two energy-saving techniques, which is shown in the next section.

## 3    System Architecture of MSC-SSD

Restricted by environmental conditions on Dome A, none of the existing storage systems can be power-aware, high availability as well as energy efficient. Motivated by strictly limited energy of the Antarctic, customized disk array of the telescopes and special usage and storage mode of astronomical observations data, a storage system designed for astronomical observations is presented in this paper. The controllable disk array of the storage system consists of two parts: industrial control computer and the disk array. The disk array consists of 40 2.5-inch mechanical hard disks which can be controlled by PDU(Power Distribution Unit) to power down or power up. The PDU can be ordered by instructions. Based on this, MCS-SSD can power down most of idle disks to reduce power consumption. The system should decide when to power down and power up the disks, what to do when the data are crashed, and how to rebuild the system. All the work should be done automatically and intelligently. The reliability strategy of AST3 is detailedly introduced in our another paper [18].

MCS-SSD model's basic architecture is shown in Fig. 3. It divides disks into data disks and cache disks. The cache disks are divided into two levels. The first-level cache disk uses solid state disk(SSD), while the second-level cache disk uses hard disk drive(HDD). Compared with HDD, SSD has a lot of advantages, such as high read-write speed, low power consumption, shockproof and anti-wrestling, wide range of operating temperature, light weight and small volume and so on. Taking into account the extremely bad weather conditions and energy conditions in Antarctica, SSD is more suitable to act as the data storage medium. However, smaller capacity and higher price of SSD make it not suitable for a wide range of applications. So after full consideration, MCS-SSD uses SSD as the first-level cache disk to store the most popular data, which will not only give full play to its advantages, but also be good to avoid its disadvantages. The second-level cache disk and data disk need to store a large amount of data, so they are composed by HDD. Data distribution strategy and energy consuming analysis of the model will be specifically described in the rest of this section.

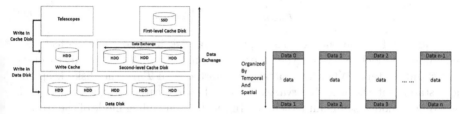

**Fig. 3.** Basic architecture of MCS-SSD          **Fig. 4.** Data distribution strategy

### 3.1  Data Distribution Strategy

As shown in Fig. 3, the data observed by telescopes directly is written into write cache disk group. When the destination disk of the observation data is active, it will write data to the corresponding data disk from the write cache disk. So writing operations of disks have a small effect on the energy saving of disks, MCS-SSD pays more attention to the reading operations.

According to the experience of long-term observations, astronomical data access is often associated with time and space. Astronomical data are usually used according to the temporal or spatial requirements, by comparing with the data observed in the same sky zone at different time, sources with changed stars or light curves will be picked out, which may help to study new extra solar planets or supernovas. So in order to achieve the greatest degree of energy saving, MCS-SSD tries to keep the data observed at different time in the same area on the same disk, the data observed in adjacent areas at the same time on the same disk. As shown in Fig. 4, in order to open less data disks when prefetching associated files, MCS-SSD puts some data copies at the edge of the adjacent disks. So when user requests the data on the edge, it only need open one disk to cache associated files.

### 3.2  Energy Consuming Analysis

The storage system saves energy by making idle disks into the standby state. But there are several challenges, one is not every idle interval of disks can be used, since the next access may arrive when the disk is shut down to standby state, which will cost more energy to spin up the disk to the idle state.

The following analysis is the energy consumption of the disk with perfect disk scheduling [8] that is when the interval time of a disk exceed a limit time

$T_{BE}$ (the limit time is a minimum interval that the disk enters standby state and will not bring additional energy consumption and it can be calculated), the disk immediately enter the standby state.

The energy consumption $E$ of the disk in time $T$ mainly consists of the active energy consumption $E_{active}$, the idle energy consumption $E_{idle}$ and the energy consumption of spinning up the disk $E_{spinup}$.

$$E = E_{active} + E_{idle} + E_{spinup} \tag{1}$$

Equation 1 is the energy consumption of a disk in time $T$. In perfect disk scheduling model [8], when the interval is longer than $T_{BE}$, the disks enter the standby state. When the interval is shorter than $T_{BE}$, the disks keep the idle state. But the next interval is hard to be predicated, so the perfect disk scheduling model is difficult to achieve. In the disk scheduling mode of the storage system based on MCS-SSD, it tries to predicate the next interval, and then decides the next state of disks. The system also uses a cache strategy to increase the interval, so the disk may have a higher probability to enter the standby state. In the storage system, it combines popular data queue and related data queue to prefetch data and it balances the load between overload disks and non-overload disks.

## 4 Operating Principles of MCS-SSD

The overall work flow of the storage system is shown as follows. When user's requests arrive, system searches data in the first level cache disk at first, requests that hit in the cache are sent to the user and the files priority is modified; requests that miss in the first level cache disk are passed on to the second level cache disk, if hit, system sends the data to users, modifies the data's priority and moves the hit data and its associated data to the cache disk; otherwise requests are passed on to the data disk. If requests are hit in data disk, system sends the data to users; if not, system sends "not found" error message to users.

All of the observed data are stored in data disks. The most popular data are stored in the first-level cache disk, and they are the copies of the observed data in data disks. The popular data are stored in the second level cache disk, and they are the copies of the observed data in data disks too.

### 4.1 Data Exchange Strategy

The data exchange strategy between layers is shown in Fig. 5. The data exchange strategy between the second-level cache disk and data disk is based on users requests. MCS-SSD will move the data which is hit(AD) and its associated data(RD) into the second-level cache disk. The data exchange strategy between the first-level cache disk and the second-level cache disk is based on a priority queue. MCS-SSD will move the data that in the most popular queue to the first-level cache disk.

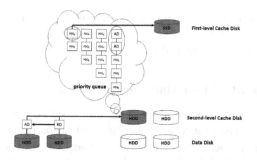

**Fig. 5.** The data exchange strategy of the storage system.

Then the placement policy of MCS-SSD is shown as follows. The most popular files should be located on either one of the first-level cache or the second-level cache, and the placement is done based on priority. MCS-SSD uses Least Recently Used (LRU) algorithm to replace files in the cache disks. To describe the priority, MCS-SSD have modeled the set of popular files as $F_C = \{f_{C1}...f_{Cn}\}$. And a file $f_{Ci}$ ($f_{Ci} \in F_C$) is modeled as a set of parameters, e.g., $f_{Ci} = (S_i, R_i, R_{total}, P_i)$, where $S_i$ is the file's size in Mbyte, $R_i$ is the request number of the file i in a fixed period of time, $R_{total}$ is the total request number of all the files in a fixed period of time, and $P_i$ is the priority to be placed in cache disk which is defined in Eq. 2. $TimeNO.$ is the request's time number of the file i in a fixed period of time. Equation 2 implies that the priority increases as request number (i.e., popularity) and the request's time number (i.e., time). The files' priority will be computed after every user's request. Based on this priority, popular files are placed on either one of the first-level cache disk or the second-level cache disk. Files will be queued based on priority from high to low. If $P_i < P_{threshold}$ file i will be discarded.

$$P_i = \frac{R_i + TimeNO.}{R_{total}} \tag{2}$$

$$P_i = \begin{cases} k_0, & if\ H_i = 1 \\ \frac{k_1}{|T_C - T_i|}, & if\ H_i = 0\ and\ SZ_C = SZ_i \\ \frac{k_2}{|SZ_C - SZ_i|}, & if\ H_i = 0\ and\ T_C = T_i \\ \frac{k_3}{|T_C - T_i| * |SZ_C - SZ_i|}, & if\ H_i = 0\ and\ T_C \neq T_i\ and\ SZ_C \neq SZ_i \end{cases} \tag{3}$$

The files on data disks are modeled as $F_D = \{f_{D1} \cdots f_{Dn}\}$. And a file $f_{Di}$ ($f_{Di} \in F_D$) is modeled as a set of parameters, e.g., $f_{Di} = (S_i, T_i, SZ_i, H_i, P_i)$, where $S_i$ is the file's size, $T_i$ is the observation time of file i, $SZ_i$ is the sky zone of the file, $H_i$ represents whether the file is hit or not, it values 0 or 1, and $P_i$ is the priority which is defined in Eq. 3. The priority increases as file association. $f_c = (S_c, T_c, SZ_c, H_c, P_c)$ is a file which is hit and in cache disk. $k_0, k_1, k_2$ and $k_3$ are configurable parameters based on the associated degree of files.

In order to reduce the computational overhead, file i's priority is calculated when the data disk is active, and only compares with the files on the same disk. If $P_i > P_{threshold}$, $f_i$ will be placed into cache disks.

## 4.2   The Access Model for the Storage System

If there are a few requests from users, it doesn't need so much cache disks, so MCS-SSD only uses the first-level cache disk and keeps the second-level cache disks closed. When requests come, system searches data in the first-level cache disk at first, requests that hit in the cache are sent to the user and the data's priority are modified; requests that miss in the first-level cache disk are passed on to the data disk, if hit, system sends data to users, modifies the data's priority and moves the hit data and its associated data to the cache disk. The Light Workload Situation is shown in Fig. 6.

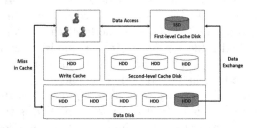

**Fig. 6.** The light workload situation.

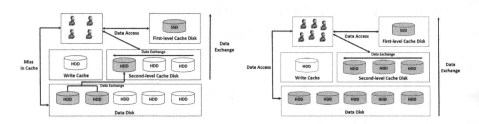

**Fig. 7.** The normal workload situation.    **Fig. 8.** The over workload situation.

If the first-level cache disk can not meet the users' requests, MCS-SSD will start part of the second-level cache disks. MCS-SSD uses Popular Data Concentration (PDC) strategies on the second-level cache disks. MCS-SSD divides the second-level cache disks into hot disks and cold disks, and puts the popular data into hot disks. So cold disks will have more opportunities to enter closed state. The Normal Workload Situation is shown in Fig. 7.

Figure 8 shows the Over Workload Situation. If the first-level cache disk and the second-level cache disks can not meet the users' requests, MCS-SSD will use all disks to support service. In the second-level cache disks, MCS-SSD also exchanges popular data to hot disks. The goal is still to make more disks enter the closed state.

# 5  Simulation Results Analysis

In this section, the performances of MCS-SSD and MAID are compared under the system with data distribution strategy, data prefetching and caching technique through simulation. Before applying to the real storage system, a lot of simulation experiments are done on the simulator. Combined with practical experience, the data access model mostly occurs to two situations such as the light workload situation and the normal situation. So a lot of simulations are running under these two situations. Furthermore, the PB-level storage system is still in the design stage.

## 5.1  Simulator Architecture

DiskSim is an efficient, accurate, highly-configurable disk system simulator [19], which is commonly used in the literature. However, the disk array in the Antarctic is customized and the number of events needed to handle a file request is highly correlated, which makes DiskSim too slow for a realistic data center simulation that involves disks. Furthermore, the disks' architecture of PB-level is complex, DiskSim can't meet the requirements.

For performance evaluation, we design and implement a special simulator to simulate the storage system based on the real one. The simulator consists of 4 parts: requests generator, trace and statistics module, resource scheduling controller and environment builder. Requests generator impersonates user requests and generates the requests' queue. Trace and statistics module will trace the process of the simulation and record the statistical data. Resource scheduling controller processes the user's requests, and controls the storage system by the given energy saving strategies. The environment builder builds the basic conditions of the simulation, and consists of data builder and disk builder.All modules of the simulator can be configured via changing parameters. The code of the simulator can be fetched at: https://github.com/yuanzichao/MCS-SSD-DiskSim.

## 5.2  The Light Workload Situation Simulation

If there are a few requests from users, it doesn't need so much cache disks, so it only uses the first-level cache disk and keeps the second-level cache disks closed. The simulator's parameters is shown in Table 1. The simulation results of MCS-SSD and MAID are shown in Figs. 9 and 10.

Comparing the results, it shows that after about 500 requests MCS-SSD's data disks open numbers begin to decline and after about 1800 requests the data disks open numbers even can reach 0. On the other hand, MAID's open disk numbers mostly range from 5 to 8. That is because MCS-SSD model prefetch

**Table 1.** The parameters of the simulator

| Parameters name | Light workload | Normal workload |
|---|---|---|
| SSD's total size | 1 TB | 1 TB |
| Second-level disks' number | 4 | 4 |
| Second-level disks' total size | 8 TB | 8 TB |
| Data disks' number | 15 | 15 |
| Data disks' total size | 30 TB | 30 TB |
| Files' number | 90,000 | 90,000 |
| Files' total size | 18 TB | 18 TB |
| Requests' number | 5,000 | 10,000 |
| Data coverage | 5.56 % | 11.1 % |

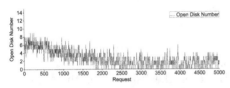

**Fig. 9.** Simulation results of MCS-SSD On light workload situation.

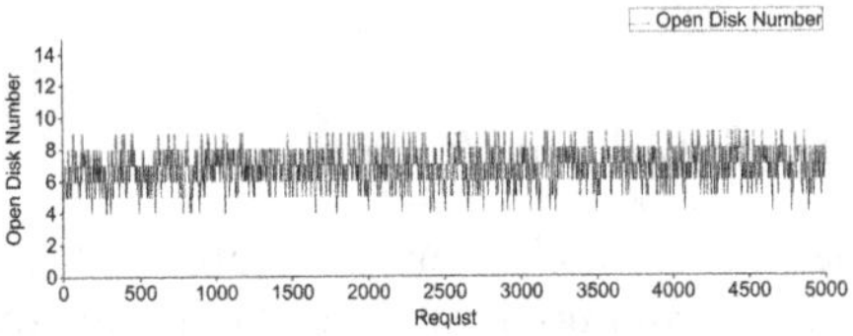

**Fig. 10.** Simulation results of MAID On light workload situation.

files that associated with the hit file to the cache disk, however MAID only prefetch the hit file to the cache disk. So after some requests, the cache disks have stored a lot of files with high priority, most data disks can change to the closed state. This will achieve a good energy saving effect.

### 5.3  The Normal Workload Situation Simulation

If the first-level cache disk can not meet the users' requests, it will start part of the second-level cache disks. The simulation results of MCS-SSD on normal workload situation are shown in Fig. 11.

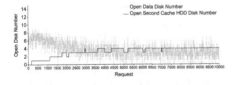

**Fig. 11.** Simulation results of MCS-SSD on normal workload.

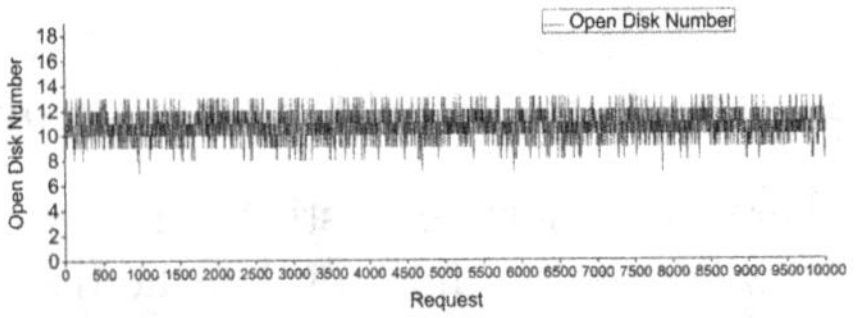

**Fig. 12.** Simulation results of MAID on normal workload.

At the beginning of the sequence of requests, MCS-SSD only opens the first level cache disk to prefetch files, but with the advent of more and more requests, the first level cache disk can't afford the users' requests, then the second level cache disks are opened. With the opening of the second level cache disks, more and more requests are responded from the second level cache disks, and the data disks have more chances to change to the closed state.

The simulation results of MAID on normal workload are shown in Fig. 12. The total open disks number of MCS-SSD is also less than MAID, furthermore the second cache disks are all in active state, so the MCS-SSD's open and close operations of data disks are far less than MAID, which need more energy than the disks in active state [20].

### 5.4   Simulation of PB-level Storage System

In the future, a larger telescope array will be installed in the Antarctic, and its data can reach PB level. So the storage system must be extended to adapt to the situation of PB-level data. In the architecture of PB-level storage system, a scheduler is responsible for handling the data produced by the telescope and the users' requests. The disk array is divided into units, and each unit uses MCS-SSD which is composed of first-level cache disk, second-level cache disks and data disks. So the PB-level storage system is similar to a distributed architecture.

**Table 2.** The parameters of the PB-level simulator

| Parameters name | Half PB-level | PB-level |
|---|---|---|
| Equipment unit's size | 30 TB | 30TB |
| Data disks' total size | 540 TB | 1,200TB |
| Files' number | 2,106,000 | 4,680,000 |
| Files' total size | 421.2TB | 936TB |
| Requests' number | 180,000 | 400,000 |
| Data coverage | 8.55 % | 8.55 % |

The simulations of PB-level storage system are also running on the simulator. The basic simulation environment is composed of many Equipment Units. The Equipment Unit in this paper consists of 15 HDD data disks, 4 second-level cache HDD disks and 1 first-level cache SSD disks, whose parameters are shown in Table 1, and the PB-level storage system's parameters are shown in Table 2.

Figure 13 shows numbers of opened data disks of all Equipment Units, as well as numbers of opened second-level cache disks of half PB-level (540 TB) storage system in normal workload situation. And the simulation results of PB-level (1200 TB) are shown in Fig. 14.

### 5.5   Conclusion of Simulation

Table 3 shows the characteristics of the hard disk used in the simulation. The disk's power consumption is mainly composed of two parts: the operating power

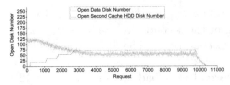
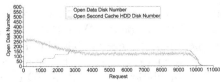

**Fig. 13.** Simulation results of half PB-level (540 TB).

**Fig. 14.** Simulation results of PB-level (1200 TB).

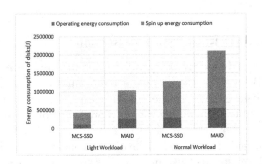

**Fig. 15.** Energy consumption in light and normal workload situation.

and the spin up power. The energy consumption of MCS-SSD and MAID in light workload situation and normal workload situation is shown in Fig. 15. According to the energy consumption, disks in MCS-SSD have more chances to change to the closed state than MAID. And the energy consumption of MCS-SSD's opened disks is about 58.43 % less than MAID in light workload situation and about 39.34 % in normal workload situations.

The PB-level storage system's architecture is similar to a distributed architecture. In PB-level storage system, every Equipment Unit with MCS-SSD performs similarly as the MCS-SSD in TB-level. So it can also achieve better energy efficiency.

**Table 3.** The characteristics of the hard disk

| Disk model | Seagate ST2000DM001 | Disk size | 2000 GB |
|---|---|---|---|
| Operating power | 8.0 Watts | Spin up power | 30 Watts |
| Spin up time | 10 s | Avg. seek time | 8.5 ms |

## 6 Conclusion and Future Work

In this paper, a storage system based on multi-level caching disk with SSD(MCS-SSD) strategy is designed for astronomical observation. Restricted by environmental conditions, while the power supply is strictly limited, the data center should be energy efficient. Since the disk array of the storage is customized, each disk can be powered down and powered up by instructions. The storage system saves energy by making idle disks into the closed state. Astronomical data are usually used according to the temporal and spatial requirements. To boost the data disks performance, MCS-SSD further clusters correlated files and places them on the data disk in a temporal and spatial manner. And several strategies including file prefetching strategy, data migration strategy and cache strategy are also applied to the system. MCS-SSD is evaluated on a trace driven simulator in TB data level and PB data level storage systems, and the results show that compared with existing energy efficient architectures the energy consumption of MCS-SSD reduces about 39.34 % to 58.43 %.

Through observations of a large amount of astronomy and astronomical research activities, what astronomers' need in astronomical research activities is a part of the file rather than the entire file. But in the existing system, it tends to directly transfer the entire file to them, and then they split the file, get the file fragment they need, and discard the remaining part of the file. This leads to a tremendous waste of resources such as the space of cache disks and the network traffic, so a more efficient way is proposed to access the astronomical data: the system only transfer the file fragment that the astronomers' need. When the user's request comes, it analyzes the detailed information of the request, get the file fragment information which the user is needed, then transfer the file fragment to users and store it and its associated data fragment to cache disks. What the cache disks stored are the files' fragment (i.e., small file) not the entire file (i.e., big file), so the cache disks can be fully used and hold more files. This model is able to meet more users requests, and at the same time it can turn more disks into closed state, so as to achieve better energy efficiency. The new model is tested in experiments in order to apply it in practical systems in the future.

**Acknowledgments.** This work was supported by The National Basic Research Program of China (973 Program 2013CB834902) and The National Natural Science Foundation of China under Grant No. 61303021 and No. 11573019.

# References

1. Zhengyang, L., Xiangyan, Y., Xiangqun, C., Daxing, W., Xuefei, G., Fujia, D. et al.: Status of the first Antarctic survey telescopes for dome A. In: Proceedings of SPIE - The International Society for Optical Engineering, vol. 8444 (2012)
2. AST3. http://aag.bao.ac.cn/ast3/
3. KDUST. http://www.kdust.org
4. Graham, M.J., Djorgovski, S.G., Mahabal, A., et al.: Data challenges of time domain astronomy. Distrib. Parallel Databases **30**(5–6), 371–384 (2012)
5. Colarelli, D., Grunwald, D.: Massive arrays of idle disks for storage archives. In: ACM/IEEE 2002 Conference on Supercomputing, November 2002
6. Pinheiro, E., Bianchini, R.: Energy conservation techniques for disk array-based servers. In: Proceedings of the International Conference on Supercomputing, pp. 68–78 (2004)

7. Power consumption of supercomputers, November 2013. http://www.top500.org/lists/2013/11/highlights
8. Douglis, F., Krishnan, P., Marsh, B.: Thwarting the power-hungry disk. In: WTEC 1994: Proceedings of the USENIX Winter 1994 Technical Conference on USENIX Winter 1994 Technical Conference, p. 23. USENIX Association, Berkeley, CA, USA (1994)
9. Li, K., Kumpf, R., Horton, P., et al.: A quantitative analysis of disk drive power management in portable computers. In: WTEC 1994: Proceedings of the USENIX Winter 1994 Technical Conference on USENIX Winter 1994 Technical Conference, p. 22. USENIX Association, Berkeley, CA, USA (1994)
10. Zhu, Q., David, F.M., Devaraj, C.F., et al.: Reducing energy consumption of disk storage using power-aware cache management. In: HPCA 2004: Proceedings of the 10th International Symposium on High Performance Computer Architecture, p. 118. IEEE Computer Society, Washington (2004)
11. Son, S.W., Kandemir, M.: Energy-aware data prefetching for multi-speed disks. In: CF 2006: Proceedings of the 3rd Conference on Computing Frontiers, pp. 105–114. ACM, New York (2006)
12. Son, S.W., Kandemir, M., Choudhary, A.: Software-directed disk power management for scientific applications. In: 19th IEEE International Proceedings on Parallel and Distributed Processing Symposium. IEEE, p. 4b (2005)
13. Pinheiro, E., Bianchini, R., Dubnicki, C.: Exploiting redundancy to conserve energy in storage systems. SIGMETRICS Perform. Eval. Rev. 34(1), 15–26 (2006)
14. Gurumurthi, S., Sivasubramaniam, A., Kandemir, M.: DRPM: dynamic speed control for power management in server class disks. In: Proceedings of 30th Annual International Symposium on Computer Architecture. IEEE, pp. 169–179 (2003)
15. Helmbold, D.P., Long, D.D.E., Sconyers, T.L., et al.: Adaptive disk spindown for mobile computers. Mob. Netw. Appl. 5(4), 285–297 (2000)
16. Krishnan, P., Long, P., Vitter, J.: Adaptive disk spindown via optimal rent-to-buy in probabilistic environments. Technical report, Durham, NC, USA (1995)
17. Lee, D.K., Koh, K.: PDC-NH: popular data concentration on NAND flash and hard disk drive. In: Proceedings of the 2009 10th IEEE/ACM International Conference on Grid Computing (GRID), pp. 196–200 (2009)
18. Li, L., Yu, C., Sun, J.: A scalable real-time photometric system for automatic astronomical observations on dome A. In: CCGrid 2014: Proceedings of the 14th IEEE/ACM International Symposium on Cluster, Cloud and Grid Computing, Chicago, Illinois, USA (2014) In Press
19. Bucy, J.S., Schindler, J., Schlosser, S.W., et al.: The disksim simulation environment version 4.0 reference manual (cmu-pdl-08-101). Parallel Data Laboratory 26 (2006)
20. Otoo, E., Rotem, D., Tsao, S.C.: Workload-adaptive management of energy-smart disk storage systems. In: Proceedings of the 2009 IEEE International Conference on Cluster Computing and Workshops. IEEE, New Orleans, pp. 1–16 (2009)

# Parallel Aware Hybrid Solid-State Storage

Dan He[1,2], Fang Wang[1(✉)], Dan Feng[1], Jingning Liu[1(✉)],
Yunxiang Wu[1], Ying He[1,2], and Yang Hu[3]

[1] Wuhan National Laboratory for Optoelectronics,
School of Computer Science and Technology,
Huazhong University of Science and Technology, Wuhan 430074, China
{hdnchu,wangfang,dfeng,jnliu,yxwu,heying}@hust.edu.cn
[2] Nanchang Hangkong University, Nanchang 330063, China
[3] China Ship Development and Design Center, Wuhan 430064, China
yanghu@foxmail.com

**Abstract.** Compared with tradition disk, NAND Flash has advantages of higher performance and shock resistance. But before write, NAND Flash must erase the old messages. That why NAND Flash based Solid State Disks (SSDs) always use the log-based schemes to improve the performance. Compared with NAND Flash, Phase Change Memory (PCM) has higher write performance, longer lifetime, and can update in-place, but its cost is high and capacity is low. So, in PCM and NAND Flash hybrid SSD, PCM is always used as log region, such as In-Page Logging-based (hybrid-IPL) SSD. The log-based SSD incurs a large number of merge operations. The cost of merge operation is very high because it involves many read, write operations, as well as an erase operation. So, how to reduce the cost of merge operations is the critical challenge to log-based hybrid (PCM and flash) SSD. In this paper, we propose a new merge scheme in PCM and NAND Flash hybrid SSD, called Parallel aware hybrid In-Page Logging-based (P-aware-IPL) SSD. This scheme can exploit the die-level and plane-level parallelism of flash. Leveraging these two levels of parallelism, the cost of full merge is significantly reduced compared with that of hybrid-IPL SSD scheme and there is no other additional overhead in our algorithm. Experiment results have shown that the proposed P-aware-IPL reduces the flash write and erase operations by up to 10 % and average response time by up to 22 % against the hybrid-IPL scheme.

**Keywords:** NAND flash · PCM · Parallelism · FTL · Hybrid SSD

## 1 Introduction

Today, NAND flash-based Solid State Disks have been widely used because of their non-volatility, fast access speed, low-power consumption, and shock resistance. However, NAND Flash has the drawback of limited write endurance [1] and "erase-before-write" requirement. That means when a block of NAND Flash is updated, it should first erase the old block before writing the new data. The procedures of erase will seriously influence the performance of the NAND Flash because erase operation needs two steps. The first step is to copy the valid pages of old block to a free block.

© Springer International Publishing Switzerland 2015
G. Wang et al. (Eds.): ICA3PP 2015, Part IV, LNCS 9531, pp. 47–60, 2015.
DOI: 10.1007/978-3-319-27140-8_4

Then system can erase the old block. In order to address this problem, NAND Flash always uses some blocks as the log area. When pages are update, the updated data is written to the log area and the old pages are signed as invalid pages. With the logs, NAND Flash can delay the merge operations. Therefore, the system performance can be improved with log area. However When the log area is full, SSD have to merge the log area with corresponding data blocks. The merge operations will serious influence the performance of SSD. During the period of merge operation, the valid pages of log block and corresponding valid pages of data block will be copied to a free block, and then the old log block and old data block will be erased. Those actions badly decrease the performance of SSD. In merge operation, copy the valid pages to a free block includes two steps. System first reads valid data from data block and log area to DRAM, then writes the data to a free NAND Flash block. Both these two steps can only be done sequentially because these data are in the same physical block (data block, log block or free block). After that, system erases the invalid NAND Flash block.

To address this problem, Guangyu Sun et al. proposed In-Page Logging with PCM hybrid Solid-State Storage (hybrid-IPL) [2]. Hybrid-IPL is a hybrid SSD, using the PCM as the log area, and NAND Flash as the data area. Compared with the NAND Flash, PCM can update in-place, and the access (read and write time) of PCM is shorter than NAND Flash. At the same time, the write endurance of PCM is also higher than the NAND Flash. With the PCM, hybrid SSDs can significantly decrease the counts of the merge operations since the PCM can update in-place.

Although hybrid-IPL can improve the performance of NAND based SSD, it still has these two shortcomings: (1) the merge operation in hybrid-IPL can only release few log areas, especially when few pages of a block (this block will be merged) are in log areas. (2) Merge operation of hybrid-IPL cannot use the parallelisms of NAND Flash, since it is only merge one block in a merge operation. So the cost of merge operation of hybrid-IPL is still high.

Therefore, in order to further improve the performance of hybrid-IPL, we believe that it is necessary to significantly reduce the cost of merge in hybrid-IPL, release more log areas in a merge operation and increase the write hit ratios of PCM.

When log area (we can see it as cache) merged (flush out from the log) with its corresponding block, the blocks which are adjacent the merge block will be merged soon, because of the spatial locality [3, 4]. Therefore flushing the merge block and its adjacent blocks simultaneously can get three advantages: (1) it can improve the hit ratio of log area because of spatial locality. (2) It can free more log area with a merge operation. (3) It can reduce the cost of merge operation because the adjacent flash blocks can operate in parallel.

Based on the above analysis, we propose a new log based hybrid solid state storage scheme, called P-hybrid-IPL. P-hybrid-IPL is designed to exploit die-level, and plane-level parallelism of NAND Flash so as to significantly reduce the cost of full merge, release more log areas in a merge operation, improve the hit ratio of PCM and it doesn't bring any other overhead. Experiment results show that Parallel awarded hybrid-IPL significantly improves the performance of hybrid-IPL, reduce the erase number and write number of flash which will improve the lifetime of hybrid SSDs.

The rest of the article is organized as follows. Background for the P-hybrid-IPL research is presented in Sect. 2. Section 3 details the design and implementation of P-hybrid-IPL, while Sect. 4 evaluates its performance. The article is concluded in Sect. 5.

# 2  Background

In this section we provide the necessary background on NAND flash, PCM, PCM based hybrid SSD, and SSD internal parallelism.

## 2.1  NAND Flash and PCM

NAND Flash architecture is shown as Fig. 1 [1]. A Flash package is composed of multiple dies, a die composed of multiple planes, a plane has a number of blocks, and a block usually consists of 64-128 pages. In NAND Flash, page is the unit for write or read operation and a block is the basic unit for the erase operation. The endurance of a block of NAND Flash memory is only 10,000 erase counts [1]. NAND Flash must obey "erase-before-write" requirement. Before writing a page, NAND-Flash memory must erase old data of the page. In a block, flash can randomly read any page, but random write is strictly prohibited. It must sequentially write a page from page 0 to page n. That means if a block writes page i, then it cannot write any pages from page 0 to page i-1, even though these pages are free.

FTL is a critical component in SSDs. It has three functions: (1) hiding the characteristics of flash– emulating the functionality of a normal block device (such as disk) with flash memory, hiding the erase-before-write characteristics. (2) address translation– translating virtual addresses from upper layers to physical addresses on the flash. (3) garbage collection– recycling invalidated physical pages and cleaning the old erase block.

FTL can be divided into three categories [5, 6]: block-level FTL [7], page-level FTL [8–10], and hybrid FTL [11, 12]. In block-level FTL, a logical block can be mapped to any physical block. In page-mapping FTL, a logical page can be mapped to any physical page. In hybrid-mapping FTL, the flash memory space is divided into the data area and log area. All the flash update are written in log area. When log area is full, SSD should merge the log with the corresponding data block. There are three types of merge operations: full merge, partial merge, and switch. Figure 2 shows the three types of merge operation. Switch only needs change the log block to data block, then erase old data block. Partial merge should copy the remaining valid pages to log block, then change log block to data block. The different between switch and partial merge is that switch updates all the pages of a block and partial merge updates partial pages of a block. In full merge, SSDs first copy the valid pages from log block and corresponding data block to a free block, and then erase the old log block and old data block.

**Parallelism in NAND Flash.** SSDs have four level parallelisms: (1) channel-level parallelism, (2) chip-level parallelism (3) die-level parallelism (4) plane-level parallelism. The priority order of the four levels parallelism in SSDs is that channel-level parallelism priority precedes die-level parallelism priority, die-level parallelism priority precedes plane-level parallelism, and plane-level parallelism priority precedes chip-level parallelism [13]. When data objects are in different channels, SSDs can use channel-level parallelism. Other levels of parallelism can be exploited by using flash advanced commands: interleave command, multiple-plane command, interleave multiple-plane command, and copy-back program command.

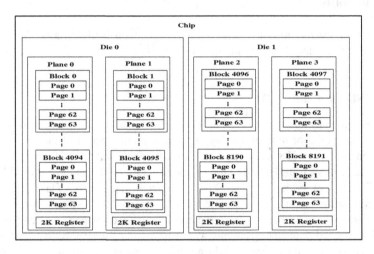

**Fig. 1.** Samsung K9K8G0U0A Flash internals.

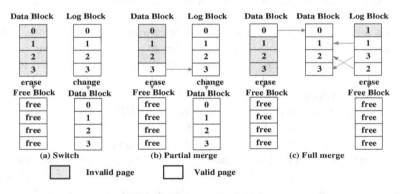

**Fig. 2.** Three types of merge

Advance command has its limitations. To use Multiple-plane command, data objects must be in different planes of the same die. For example, in Fig. 1, a two-plane read/write/erase operation into Plane 0 and Plane 2 is prohibited; whereas, a two-plane read/write/erase operation into Plane 0 and Plane 1 or into Plane 2 and Plane 3 is allowed. To use Interleave command, data objects must be in different dies of the same chip.

Multiple-plane command can exploit plane level parallelism. It is an extension of the common command. For example, the multiple-plane page write (program) command can simultaneously write (program) multiple pages. It improves the system throughput multiple compared to the common page program command. Interleave command can exploit the die level parallelism. At the same time, the interleave command can combine with the multiple-plane command to form the interleave multiple plane command, therefore, exploit the die level and plane level parallelism simultaneously.

Through precise organizing the locations of data in SSD, we can achieve maximum parallelism. Recently, many schemes have been proposed to exploit parallelism of SSD [14, 15]. But none of these algorithms can be used in merge operation. To address this problem, Dan He et al. [16] proposed Virtual Block-based Parallel FAST (VBP-FAST) to full exploit parallelism in SSD. VBP-FAST reorganizes the flash block to virtual block (Block) and physical block (PBlock). VBlock can fully exploit the channel-level, die-level, and plane-level parallelism which can significantly reduce the cost of merge. The PBlock area helps increase the number of partial merge and switch operations. Although VBP-FAST can fully exploit parallelism and reduce the cost of merge, it cannot be used in PCM based hybrid SSD. Since the PCM based hybrid SSD used PCM as the log areas. Unlike the flash, PCM can update in place.

**IPL (In-Page Logging) Method.** S. Lee et al. proposed the IPL method [17] to improve the write performance of the file system. In IPL method, a block of NAND Flash reserves some pages as the log pages. If pages of this block are updated, its update is written to the reserved pages. When the reserved pages in the block is run out, the block should merge the valid pages and log pages to a free block.

**PCM (Phase Change Random Access Memory).** Like the flash, PCM is also non-volatile memory (NVM).The origins of PCM can be traced back to the late 1960 s by S.Ovshinsky [18]. The access latency of PCM is between flash and DRAM, which means its read and write operation are faster than flash and slower than DRAM. Table 1 compares the characteristics of PCM and NAND flash memory [19].

PCM cells can sustain 1000x more writes than flash cells, currently the write times of PCM is between $10^6$—$10^8$. Like the flash, the write latency of PCM is higher than read latency. The difference between PCM and NAND flash is that PCM can update in-place. NAND flash update obeys "erase-before-write" requirement. Compared with the NAND flash, PCM has the advantage of longer lifetime, lower power consumption, random-access and in-place update. Therefore, PCM are commonly used as the log area or store the SSD's metadata [20], (such as FTL data) in PCM and NAND flash hybrid SSDs.

**Table 1.** The comparison between PCM and NAND flash

| Parameter | NAND Flash | PCM |
|---|---|---|
| Read Latency | 25 us | $200 \sim 300$ ns |
| Write Speed | 2.4 MB/s | $\sim 100$ MB/s |
| Endurance | $10^4$ | $10^6 \sim 10^8$ |

**Hybrid-IPL (In-Page Logging with PCM Hybrid Solid-State Storage).** In NAND Flash based the IPL, if system frequently updates the same block, it may cause significant performance degradation, because this procedure may quickly run out of reserved pages, and cause the merge operations. In order to address this problem, hybrid-IPL is proposed [2]. In hybrid-IPL, PCM is used as logging region and NAND Flash is used as data region. Since PCM is separated from the flash-based data region, log sectors are dynamically assigned to each erase unit to store its own updates. In order to prevent the whole system stalled for a long time waiting for merge operations to be completed, hybrid-IPL sets up a threshold of free log sectors, and the merge operations are triggered when the capacity of free log sectors is lower than it. In merge operations, updated log sectors and its corresponding valid pages in this NAND Flash erase unit are written to another free NAND Flash erase unit. After that process, log sectors are released as clean ones for future use and old NAND Flash erase unit are invalid. With the PCM, hybrid-IPL can improve system write performance; increase the NAND Flash lifetime and decrease energy consumption of the system. The hybrid-IPL has two shortcomings. Firstly, a merge operation takes place in a NAND Flash block, and all these operations (read updated log sectors, read corresponding valid pages in NAND Flash, write all the data to another free NAND Flash and erase the old NAND flash block) of merge cannot do parallelly. Secondly, a merge operation can only release few log sectors. For example, in Fig. 1, if update page 0 to page 59 of block 0, block 1,block 406,and block 4097 are all in log area (PCM). In hybrid-IPL, when log area is full and system select block 0 to merge. It need 60 times of read PCM, 4 times of read flash, 64 times of write flash and a time of erase flash block. Then system frees 60 pages of PCM. If we select block 0, block 1, block 4096, and block 4097 to merge at the same time, system can read all the valid page 60 from block 0, block 1, block 406, and block 4097 with an interleave-two-plane read command, and so on the page 61 to page 63. Then system can write all these four blocks with 64 times of interleave-two-plane write command to write the data to new adjacent blocks. At last, SSD uses an interleave-two-plane erase command to erase these four blocks. This scheme needs 240 times of PCM read, 4 times of flash read, 64 times of flash write, and one time of flash erase. Log area can free 240 pages of PCM area. The more important things is flushing these four blocks will improve the log area hit ratio, because of spatial locality. Locality of reference includes the temporal locality and spatial locality [4].Thus, in log area (like a cache), if pages of a block are flushed out, the pages adjacent to the flushed block may be flushed soon (these pages may not be references for a long time).

## 3   Parallel Aware Hybrid-IPL (P-Aware-IPL) Description

In P-aware-IPL, The PCM is used as the log areas and NAND Flash is used as data areas. Log area is dynamical assigned to all flash blocks to store the update data. The operations of parallel aware hybrid-IPL are as follows:

Read Operation. System reads the flash and PCM at the same time from different controller (data region controller and log region controller). If data is in PCM, system reads data from PCM and loads it into the buffer. Otherwise system read the data from flash into the buffer.

Write (Update) Operation. The updated page are written to PCM. If the page have already written to PCM, then we should only overwrite the sectors of PCM. If there are no existing log records for the updated page and PCM has free sectors, System allocated some sectors to store the updated page. If there are no free sectors in PCM, system will start merge operation to free some PCM sectors for the updated page.

PCM (log area) Management. In P-aware-IPL, all the updated pages of a block are linked as a list, called block list, and all the lists are linked as a LRU queue. Figure 3 shows the LRU queue of PCM.

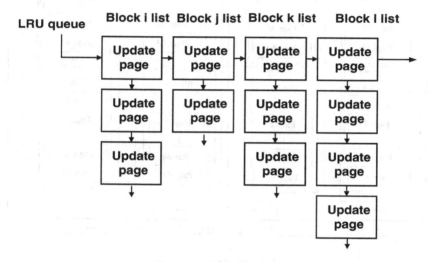

**Fig. 3.** PCM management

Merge operation. Merge operation of P-hybrid-IPL is different from that of hybrid-IPL, which uses FIFO policy. When merge operations are triggered, hybrid-IPL selects the head of the queue sectors to merge with its corresponding data block. A merge operation only deals with one flash block in hybrid-IPL. P-hybrid-IPL, uses LRU policy, and merge operation can merge one or all the adjacent blocks at the same time. The adjacent blocks is defines as follow: The adjacent blocks are the blocks which in the same package and they are in the same row. Such as in Fig. 4, the block 0, block 1, block 2 and block 3 are the adjacent blocks. In flash, adjacent blocks can use advance commands to parallel operate (read, write, and erase). For example, page 0 in block 0 and page 0 in block 1 can use two plane read/write command operate. The same operation can also be used in page 0 of block 2 and page 0 of block 3. Page 0 in block 0 and page 0 in block 2, page 0 in block 0 and page 0 in block 3, page 0 in block 1 and page 0 in block 2, and page 0 in block 1 and page 0 in block 3 can use interleave read/write to parallel operate. All page 0 in adjacent blocks can use interleave two plane read/write to parallel operate. At last, all the adjacent blocks can use interleave two plane erase to

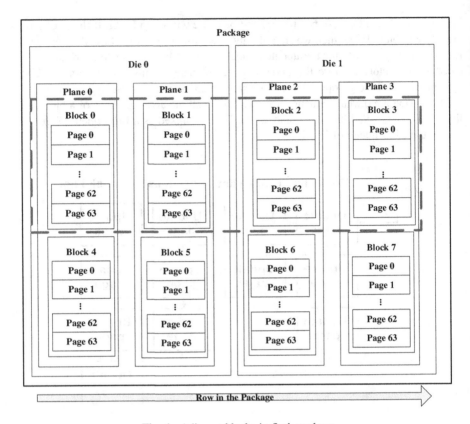

**Fig. 4.** Adjacent blocks in flash package

parallel erase. In addition, simultaneously flush a block and its adjacent block from PCM can increase the hit ratio of PCM because of the spatial locality.

Threshold value setting. The merge operation should copy all the valid pages (in PCM and valid in NAND Flash) to a clean NAND Flash block. Therefore, it is not worth merging the adjacent blocks that have only few pages in log area. In order to solve this problem, we can set up a threshold. If adjacent block have more pages than threshold in log area, we merge the adjacent blocks at the same time. Otherwise system only merge a block. The value of threshold should not set too small or too large. If threshold value is small, then merge block i and its adjacent blocks will do not release many free PCM sectors, and merge adjacent blocks will bring many flash operations (read, write, and erase). So, it is no worth merging the adjacent blocks simultaneously. In contrast, if threshold value is too large, there will be less possibility can merge block i and its adjacent blocks simultaneously. In our schemes, the value of threshold is settled two-thirds of a block's pages number.

The detailed algorithm of p-aware-IPL is described as Fig. 5. Suppose a flash package has two dies and a die has two planes:

---

Algorithm of Merge operation in P-aware-IPL

---

Program merge
1  Begin
2     Select tail of LRU queue. Its corresponding block is called block i;
3     Search adjacent blocks in the LRU queue. (Block i's adjacent blocks include these three blocks. The first block is the block
4     which is in the same die with block i, called block j. The other two blocks are the blocks which are in the same package with
5     block i but in different die with block i, called block m and block n. All the adjacent blocks are in the same row);
6     if (updated pages of block j in PCM> threshold && updated pages of block m in PCM> threshold && updated pages of block n
7     | in PCM> threshold) then
8           merge block i, j, m, and n simultaneously, these four blocks can use interleave-two-plane command to parallelly
9           operate;
10    else
11    |   if (updated pages of block j > threshold) then
12    |   |  merge block i and j simultaneously, these two blocks can use two-plane command to parallelly operate;
13    |   else
14    |   |   if (updated pages of block m > threshold) then
15    |   |   |  merge block i and m simultaneously, these two blocks can use interleave command to parallelly operate;
16    |   |   else
17    |   |   |   if (updated pages of block n > threshold) then
18    |   |   |   |  merge block i and n simultaneously, these two blocks can use interleave command to parallelly operate;
19    |   |   |   else
20    |   |   |   |  merge block i only;
21    |   |   |   end if
22    |   |   end if
23    |   end if
24    end if
25 end

**Fig. 5.** Algorithm of P-aware-IP

# 4 Evaluation

To evaluate the effectiveness of the proposed P-hybrid-IPL, we conduct a series of experiments and present the analysis results in this section. We compare P-hybrid-IPL with state-of-art scheme, hybrid-IPL by implementing them on an open-source SSD simulator called SSDSim [21]. We present the average response time, total numbers of flash write, flash erase, and PCM write comparison of P-hybrid-IPL and the baseline scheme. We do not present number of flash read and number of PCM read because flash read time and PCM read time are very shorter than their write time. At the same time, flash read, PCM read do not influence their lifetime.

Workload Traces. Four real world I/O workload traces are used in the experiments. The Financial 1 and Financial 2 trace [21] are from the Online Transaction Processing application from a large financial institution. Radius [22] was obtained from a RADIUS authentication server that is responsible for worldwide corporate remote access and wireless authentication. Display Ads Payloud [23] trace is collected over a period of 24 h for Display Ads Platform payload Server. The characteristics of the workloads are listed in Table 2.

The capacity of the flash is 2 GB, PCM capacity is 16 MB. For each given trace, the simulator counts the number of flash writes, flash erases, PCM writes, and average response time. The simulator in our experiment is configured with the key parameters listed in Table 3.

**Table 2.** Characteristics of real world I/O workloads.

| Trace | Read Request Count | Write Request Count | Read Request Average Size(512B) | Write Request Average Size(512B) |
|---|---|---|---|---|
| Fin1 | 1235596 | 4099351 | 4.5 | 7.5 |
| Fin2 | 3045784 | 653079 | 4.6 | 5.8 |
| Radius | 12760 | 109208 | 13.1 | 15.4 |
| Display | 46348 | 16060 | 57 | 21 |

**Table 3.** Configuration parameters of simulator.

| Channel | 2 |
|---|---|
| Die | Die 2/package |
| Plane | Plane 2/die |
| Block | Block 2048/plane |
| Page | Page 64/block |
| Page size | 2 KB |

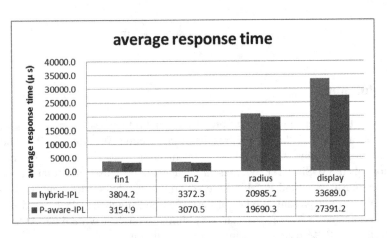

**Fig. 6.** Average response time in different workloads

Figure 6 compares the average response times of P-hybrid-IPL and hybrid-IPL under the four workloads. Among these four workloads, the average response time of P-hybrid-IPL is lower than the baseline scheme. The average response time in P-aware-IPL is about 6.6 %~22 % less than that in hybrid-IPL. The reason is that: (1) P-hybrid-IPL has less flash erase number and flash write number than that of hybrid-IPL. In flash, cost of write operation and erase operation is very high. (2) because of the locality, flushing the block and its adjacent blocks can release much more free log area and do not reduce the hit ratio of log area. This will cause more write in log area (PCM), but cost of write in PCM is less than that of in flash. Therefore, the overall response time of P-hybrid-IPL is lower than that of hybrid-IPL.

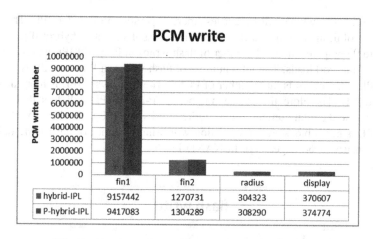

**Fig. 7.** Numbers of PCM writes in different workloads

Figure 7 compares the total number of PCM writes in P-hybrid-IPL and hybrid-IPL under the four workloads. The total number of PCM writes in P-aware-IPL is more than those of hybrid-IPL. The reason is in P-aware-IPL, a merge operation may merge a block and its adjacent blocks simultaneously. Flushing the block and its adjacent blocks can release much more free log area in a merge operation. At the same time, flushing adjacent blocks from log area (PCM) does not reduce the hit ratio of log area because of spatial locality. In other words, this procedure will increase the hit ratio of log area because pages of adjacent blocks which are in log area will not be accessed in future. Therefore, flush these pages will increase the hit ratio of log area which will increase the number of PCM writes.

In Fig. 8, the number of flash erase in P-aware-IPL are about 3 %~8 % less than that in hybrid-IPL. This is because the write number of PCM in P-aware-IPL is more than

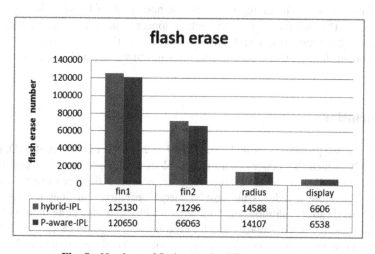

**Fig. 8.** Numbers of flash erase in different workloads

that of hybrid-IPL, which will trigger less merge operation in P-aware-IPL. Therefore, the number of flash erase in P-aware-IPL will be less than that of hybrid-IPL.

Figure 9 compares the total number of flash writes in P-hybrid-IPL and hybrid-IPL under the four workloads. The total number of flash writes in P-aware-IPL is less than hybrid-IPL. The reason is that number of PCM write in P-aware-IPL is more than that of hybrid-IPL. Therefore the merge number of P-aware-IPL will less than that of hybrid-IPL. So the total number of flash write in P-hybrid-IPL is smaller than that of in hybrid-IPL, since a block merge operation will bring 64 times of flash write (a block usually consists of 64 pages [1]). In NAND Flash.

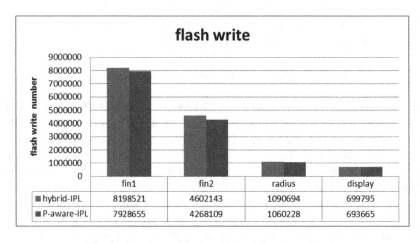

**Fig. 9.** Numbers of flash write in different workloads

In summary, P-hybrid-IPL transforms the write operation from flash to the PCM and reduces the cost of merge operation. PCM has much better endurance than the NAND flash memory. Therefore, the endurance bottleneck of hybrid SSDs is the life time of flash. The lifetime of P-hybrid-IPL is longer than that of hybrid-IPL, since P-hybrid-IPL have less write count and less erase count than that of hybrid-IPL. The most important thing is that P-hybrid-IPL does not bring any additional overhead to SSD.

## 5   Conclusion

In this article, we propose a parallel aware PCM and NAND Flash hybrid SSD, called P-hybrid-IPL, which flush pages of a updated block, and pages of its adjacent blocks from log area (PCM) at the same time. Adjacent blocks in flash can use the parallel operation. Therefore it reduces the cost of merge operation and does not bring any additional overhead. In addition, flushing adjacent blocks at the same time will bring two advantages: (1) it will improve the hit ratio because of spatial locality. (2) It will release much more free log area in a merge operation. These two points will increase the PCM write count and reduce the flash write count. Therefore, P-hybrid-IPL has higher performance, longer lifetime than hybrid-IPL.

**Acknowledgments.** This research was partially supported by the National High-tech R&D Program of China (863 Program) No. 2013AA013203, 2015AA016701, 2015AA015301, National Program on Key Basic Research Project of China (973 Program) No. 2011CB302301, NSFC No. 61402189, 61303046, 61173043, Changjiang innovative group of Education of China No. IRT0725, Key Laboratory of Information Storage System Ministry of Education. This work is also supported by Jiangxi Province Education Planning Project No. 11ZD058.

# References

1. K9XXG08XXM Flash Memory Specification. http://www.samsung.com/global/system/business/semiconductor/product/2007/6/11/NANDFlash/SLC_LargeBlock/8Gbit/K9F8G08U0M/ds_k9f8g08x0m_rev10.pdfhttp://www.samsung.com/global/system/business/semiconductor/product/2007/6/11/NANDFlash/SLC_LargeBlock/8Gbit/K9F8G08U0M/ds_k9f8g08x0m_rev10.pdf

2. Sun, G., Joo, Y., Chen, Y., Niu, D., Xie, Y., Chen, Y., Li, H.: A hybrid solid-state storage architecture for the performance, energy consumption, and lifetime improvement. In: 16th IEEE International Symposium on High-Performance Computer Architecture, pp. 51–77. IEEE Press, Bangalore (2010)

3. Jiang, S., Zhang, L., Yuan, X.H., et al.: S-FTL: An efficient address translation for flash memory by exploiting spatial locality. In: 27th International Conference on Massive Storage Systems and Technology, pp. 1–12. IEEE Press, Denver (2011)

4. Luszczek, P., Dongarra, J.J., Koester, D., Rabenseifner, R., Lucas, B., Kepner, J., McCalpin, J., Bailey, D., Takahashi, D.: Introduction to the HPC challenge benchmark suite. Technical report, UTK (2005)

5. Chung, T.-S., Park, D.-J., Park, S., Lee, D.-H., Lee, S.-W., Song, H.-J.: System software for flash memory: a survey. In: Sha, E., Han, S.-K., Xu, C.-Z., Kim, M.-H., Yang, L.T., Xiao, B. (eds.) EUC 2006. LNCS, vol. 4096, pp. 394–404. Springer, Heidelberg (2006)

6. Chung, T.-S., Park, D.-J., Park, S., Lee, D.-H., Lee, S.-W., Song, H.-J.: A survey of Flash translation layer. J. Syst. Architect. **55**, 332–343 (2009)

7. Ban, A.: Flash file system. United States Patent No. 5,404,485 (1995)

8. Hu, Y., Jiang, H., Feng, D., et al.: Achieving page-mapping FTL performance at block-mapping FTL cost by hiding address translation. In: 26th Symposium on Massive Storage Systems and Technologies, pp. 1–12. IEEE Press, Incline Village (2010)

9. Gupta, A., Kim, Y., Urgaonkar, B.: DFTL: A flash translation layer employing demand-based selective caching of page-level address mapping. In: 14th International Conference on Architectural Support for Programming Languages and Operating Systems, pp. 229–240. ACM Press, Washington (2009)

10. Ma, D., Feng, J., Li, G.: LazyFTL: A page-level flash translation layer optimized for NAND flash memory. In: SIGMOD 2011, pp. 1–12. ACM Press, Athens (2011)

11. Lee, S., Park, D., Chung, T., Lee, D., Park, S.: H. Song.: A log buffer-based flash translation layer using fully-associative sector translation. ACM Trans. Embed. Comput. Syst. **6**, 1–27 (2007)

12. Cho, H., Shin, D., Eom, Y.I.: KAST: K-associative sector translation for NAND flash memory in real-time systems. In: DATE 2009, pp. 507–512. European Design and Automation Association Press, Nice (2009)

13. Hu, Y., Jiang, H., Feng, D., et al.: Performance impact and interplay of SSD parallelism through advanced commands, allocation strategy and data granularity. In: 25th International Conference on Supercomputing, pp. 96–107. ACM Press, Tucson (2011)

14. Chen, F., Lee, R., Zhang, X.: Essential roles of exploiting internal parallelism of flash memory based solid state drives in high-speed data processing. In: 21st IEEE Symposium on High Performance Computer Architecture, pp. 266–277. IEEE Press, San Antonio (2011)

15. Jung, M., Wilson III, E.H., Kandemir, M.: Physically addressed queueing (PAQ): Improving parallelism in solid state disks. In: 39th International Symposium on Computer Architecture, pp. 404–415. IEEE Press, Washington (2012)

16. He, D., Wang, F., Jiang, H., Feng, D., Liu, J.N., Tong, W., Zhang, Z.: Improving hybrid FTL by fully exploiting internal SSD parallelism with virtual blocks. ACM Trans. Architect. Code Optim. **11**, 43 (2014)

17. Lee, S., Moon, B.: Design of flash-based DBMS: An in page logging approach. In: SIGMOD 2007, pp. 1–15. ACM Press, Beijing (2007)

18. Ovshinsky, S.R.: Reversible electrical switching phenomena in disordered structures. Phys. Rev. Lett. **21**, 1450–1453 (1968)

19. Qureshi, M.K., Srinivasan, V., Rivers, J.A.: Scalable high performance main memory system using phase-change memory technology. ACM SIGARCH Comput. Architect. News **37**, 24–33 (2009)

20. Liu, D., Wang, T., Wang, Y., Qin, Z., Shao, Z.: PCM-FTL: A write-activity-aware NAND flash memory management scheme for PCM-based embedded systems. In: 32nd IEEE Real-Time Systems Symposium, pp. 357–366. IEEE Press, Vienna (2011)

21. Huazhong University of Science and Technology SSDsim. http://storage.hust.edu.cn/SSDsim

22. UMass Trace Repository. http://traces.cs.umass.edu

23. Block I/O Traces. http://iotta.snia.org/traces/list/BlockIO

# Automatic Optimization of Software Transactional Memory Through Linear Regression and Decision Tree

Yang Xiao[1], Zhen Li[2], Ehsan Atoofian[1(✉)], and Ali Jannesari[2]

[1] Electrical Engineering Department, Lakehead University,
Thunder Bay, Canada
{yxiao4,atoofian}@lakeheadu.ca
[2] Technical University of Darmstadt, Darmstadt, Germany
{li,jannesari}@cs.tu-darmstadt.de

**Abstract.** Software Transactional Memory (STM) is a promising paradigm that facilitates programming for shared memory multiprocessors. In STM, synchronization of accesses to the shared memory locations is fully handled by STM library and does not require any intervention by programmers. While STM eases parallel programming, it results in run-time overhead which increases execution time of certain applications. In this paper, we focus on overhead of STM and propose optimization techniques to enhance speed of STM applications. In particular, we focus on size of transaction, read-set, and write-set and show that execution time of applications significantly changes by varying these parameters. Optimizing these parameters manually is a time consuming process and requires significant labor work. We exploit Linear Regression (LR) and propose an optimization technique that decides on these parameters automatically. We further enhance this technique by using decision tree. The decision tree improves accuracy of predictions by selecting appropriate LR model for a given transaction. We evaluate our optimization techniques using a set of benchmarks from NAS and DiscoPoP benchmark suites. Our experimental results reveal that LR and decision tree together are able to improve performance of STM programs up to 54.8 %.

**Keywords:** Software Transactional Memory · Linear Regression · Decision tree · Performance

## 1 Introduction

Software Transactional Memory (STM) is becoming increasingly popular as a convenient way for writing parallel programs. STM provides an atomic construct, called transaction, which is used to protect shared memory locations from concurrent accesses by threads. Reads and writes to transactional data occur at a single instance of time. Intermediate transactional values are not visible to other transactions. STM executes transactions speculatively in parallel and monitor memory locations accessed by active transactions. If executing transactions do not conflict over shared memory locations, then they safely commit. However, in the event of conflict, only one transaction can

© Springer International Publishing Switzerland 2015
G. Wang et al. (Eds.): ICA3PP 2015, Part IV, LNCS 9531, pp. 61–73, 2015.
DOI: 10.1007/978-3-319-27140-8_5

proceed and the rest should abort and restart. Transactions log operations during the execution so that they can restore state of the running program if roll-back is needed.

STM eliminates many of the problems associated with locks and enables programmers to compose scalable applications safely. In an STM program, a programmer does not need to worry about priority inversion, deadlock, or live lock. This is in contrast to lock-based programming in which a programmer needs to deal with lock placement and synchronization bugs. In an STM program, the programmer only needs to reason locally about shared memory locations and mark sections of the program that should be executed concurrently. The underlying system guarantees correctness. In addition to ease of programming, STMs are speculative in nature. The benefit of speculative approach is that transactions do not need to wait for shared memory locations; instead, they can execute concurrently and modify disjoint memory locations safely, leading to performance gains.

In the last decade, there have been several implementations of STMs [2–4]. The emergence of new STM algorithms has not been slowed down in the recent years, and the support for transactional memory in new processors [6] is likely to increase the number of TM implementations. The performance of STMs depends on several factors such as lock acquisition time, granularity of conflict detection, the mapping of memory addresses to the lock table, etc. Some researchers have explored design space of STMs and proposed changing STM parameters during the run-time. For example, Marathe et al. [5] studies lock acquisition in STMs and showed that the time at which locks are acquired has drastic impact on scalability. While eager policy (encounter-time locking) reduces overhead, lazy policy (commit-time locking) provides better throughput for some multithreaded applications. Marathe et al. [5] proposed an adaptive technique which dynamically changes lock acquisition policy in run-time. The other example is granularity of conflict detection [4]. Felber et al. [4] showed that performance of STMs varies with granularity of conflict detection and non-optimum parameterization can slow down some programs by a factor of three. While the above techniques improve performance of STMs, all of them focus on execution of STM programs during the run-time. They do not provide any guidelines for programmers to write an efficient TM program in the first place.

The first step in writing an STM program is marking regions of a sequential code as transactions. In the next step, APIs such as TM_BEGIN() and TM_END() [2] which are provided by an STM library are inserted into the program to guarantee atomicity and correctness of transactions. The size of a transaction has significant impact on performance. If the transaction is too short, then the overhead of STM APIs exceeds performance gain of parallel execution and may lead to an STM program which is slower than sequential version of the program. On the other side, if the transaction is too large, then the cost of roll-back in applications with high abort rate may reduce speed-up in STM applications.

One way to find optimal transaction size is using try and error approach. A programmer can vary transaction size and finds out the optimal transaction size by running the program multiple times. This procedure is very time consuming and requires significant programming effort. To address this challenge, we propose two optimization techniques that automatically determine near optimal transaction size: the first technique exploits Linear Regression (LR) [8] to predict transaction size. LR receives parameters of a non-optimized transaction such as transaction size, read-set size, and write-set size and predicts the optimum transaction size. While LR is simple to implement, its accuracy is low. Our second optimization technique exploits decision tree and enhances accuracy of predictions. The decision tree divides transactions into multiple groups and then uses a different LR model for each group. Using a set of benchmarks from NAS [9] and DiscoPoP [10], we show that decision tree and LR together increase accuracy of predictions significantly.

The rest of the paper is organized as follows. In Sect. 2, we explain the necessary background for our optimization techniques and discuss how LR and decision tree work. Section 3 explains the intuition behind our optimization techniques and evaluates sensitivity of STM programs to a few transactional parameters. Section 4 discusses our optimization techniques in details and reports experimental results. We review related work in Sect. 5. Finally, in Sect. 6, we offer concluding remarks.

## 2  Background

### 2.1  Linear Regression

Linear Regression (LR) is a mathematical equation which relates a response variable to a set of input parameters for a given design space [8]. LR is widely used to predict the response variable at an arbitrary point in the design space. Equation 1 shows a simple model for LR:

$$y = B_0 + \sum_{k=1}^{q} (B_k \times x_i) + \varepsilon \qquad (1)$$

where y is response variable, $x_i$ is input parameter, $B_0$ is the intercept of the fit with the y-axis, and $\varepsilon$ is the error of LR model. $B_i$ (0<i) is coefficient and represents the expected change in y per unit change in $x_i$. LR uses least square method to find the best-fitting curve to a set of test points. In this method, coefficients are calculated so that the sum of square of the errors for the test points (error of a test point is the distance of the point from the fitting curve) is minimized. While LR exploits a simple model for prediction, it shows excellent results in many applications and is able to predict the response variable with high accuracy. Examples of LR applications are prediction of stock market, oil price, and GDP [8]. Also, recently, Google used LR to predict revenue of a movie four weeks ahead of its release date [13].

Our goal in this paper is to accurately estimate transaction size so that execution time of STM applications is reduced. To do so, we explore static parameters that interact with performance. We achieve this by performing simulation-based experiments in which input parameters are varied before code compilation and the resulting transaction size is fitted as per Eq. 1. It is important to note that while parameters in Eq. 1 depend on STM library, the methodology that we use is general and can be applied to any STM implementation.

## 2.2    Decision Tree

Classification is the task of assigning objects to a set of predefined categories. Decision tree [17] is a popular approach for classification. Originally, decision tree was used in the field of statistics. However, soon it found to be effective in many other disciplines such as machine learning, image processing, etc. A decision tree classifies an input object through a set of functions organized in a hieratical manner and represented by a tree. A tree has three types of nodes: root, internal, and leaf [17]. An internal node splits the objects into two categories according to a test function. The inputs to the function are attributes of the object and the output of the function is a binary value: 0 or 1. A leaf represents a category. Objects are classified by navigating them from root down to the leaves, based on the output of the test functions along the path.

In this work, we use decision tree to classify transactions based on error of predicted transaction size. Objects in decision tree are transactions and attributes of the objects are read-set size, number of instructions between two consecutive transactions, etc. The decision tree predicts the error of transaction size to be predicted by LR. Section 4 discusses details of decision tree used in this study.

## 2.3    Benchmark Selection

To evaluate an STM system, researchers rely on a set of benchmarks. If the set of the benchmarks are selected from a specific field, then the outcome of the research is not reliable. To be able to extend the outcome of a research project to the real world applications, we need a set of comprehensive benchmarks that truly represent real world applications.

Asanovic et al. [18] proposed 13 Dwarfs as a guideline to develop benchmark suites for parallel applications. A dwarf is a high level abstraction which categorizes applications based on patterns of computation and communication. Asanovic et al. [18] showed that NAS benchmark suite [9] includes all those dwarfs and so in this work, we use NAS benchmark suite to evaluate our optimization techniques.

## 3    Motivation

In an STM program, transactions are implemented through APIs provided by an STM library. While STM does not require any changes in the architectural level, it may not result in significant speedup. This is mainly due to the overhead of STM APIs.

In this work, we use two Intel Xeon E5660 processors running at 2.8 GHz. Each processor has six cores and is capable of running up to 12 threads simultaneously. Each processor has a 12 MB shared L3 cache with 64B cache lines. Each core has a 32 KB instruction cache and a 32 KB data cache.

Figure 1a shows execution time of STM relative to sequential code for NAS benchmark suite. NAS benchmarks are originally developed using OpenMP library. We replaced critical sections in NAS with transactions. For each benchmark, the number of threads varies from two to 16. Bars more than one show speedup. On average, STM reduces performance by 43.8 %, 57.5 %, 59.1 %, and 81.7 %, when the number of threads is 2, 4, 8, and 16, respectively. From Fig. 1a, we conclude that blindly using transactions in a parallel program may result in a program that is slower than its sequential version. To boost performance of STM programs, we need to reduce the overhead of APIs. There are two main approaches to optimize STMs: static and dynamic. In static approach, the STM program is changed during the code development or compilation whereas in dynamic approach, the system is optimized during the run-time and by hacking into STM library. While many research ideas have been proposed on the latter approach, the former one did not receive enough attention from researchers. In this section, we discuss three static parameters which impact performance of STM programs: size of transaction, write-set size, and read-set size.

Figure 1b shows the impact of size of transaction on performance of NAS benchmarks. We optimized each benchmark by varying the number of instructions in transactions manually and selecting the one which minimizes execution time. It is important to note that by changing the size of a transaction, we do not violate its atomicity. Figure 2 shows an example of a large transaction. The transaction is composed of three loops. We can decompose the outer loop into several smaller loops and assign each loop to a transaction. Similarly, when we combine smaller transactions to build a large transaction, we take into account the atomicity of transactions to make sure that we do not compromise correctness of transactions.

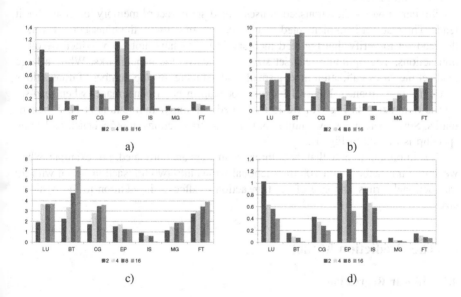

**Fig. 1.** (A) Speedup in baseline scheme. (B) Speedup when transaction size is optimized. (C) Speedup when write-set size is optimized. (D) Speedup when read-set size is optimized.

Speedup in a short transaction is limited since overhead of STM is high relative to the size of the transaction. A long transaction may increase abort rate as a large number of instructions in a transaction may increase the window during which transactions are identified as competitors. So, to boost performance of STM programs, we should merge small transactions to reduce overhead of APIs. On the other side, in a large transaction, we should split the transaction into a number of small transactions to reduce abort rate and improve performance. Figure 1b shows that transaction size, indeed, has dramatic impact on performance. In BT, performance increases up to 9.3X when we change transaction size. On average, changing transaction size improves performance by 77.7 %, 88.4 %, 89.1 %, and 89.3 % when the number of threads is 2, 4, 8, and 16, respectively.

Figure 1c shows the impact of write-set on performance. STM uses a linked-list to record transactional write operations. When a transaction writes into a shared memory location, it inserts a new node to the linked-list. In commit, the transaction traverses the linked-list to acquire locks and update memory with new transactional data. If the transaction fails to acquire a lock, then it aborts and restarts. So, a transaction with a large write-set is more likely to abort. However, if we restrict transactions to have only small write-sets, then we need to split transactions into too many short transactions. This increases overhead of STM APIs relative to the performance gains of concurrent transactions and limits speedup. The optimum write-set size depends on pattern of memory accesses by transactions and varies from one benchmark to the other. We manually optimized performance of NAS benchmarks by changing write-set size. Figure 1c shows that by changing write-set size, performance of NAS benchmarks increases up to 7.3X.

Similar to write-set, a transaction uses a read-set to record memory locations that it reads. The read-set is implemented as a linked-list. In commit, the transaction traverses the read-set to verify that the read memory locations have not been written by other transactions. The optimum read-set size varies across the benchmarks. While a large read-set increases validation time, a small read-set increases the number of transactions and hurts performance. Figure 1d shows speedup in NAS benchmarks when read-set size is optimized. In Fig. 1d, we just changed read-only transactions in NAS benchmarks. Since there are a few number of read-only transactions in NAS benchmarks, the speedup is limited in Fig. 1d.

It is important to note that these three parameters are correlated. For example, when we split a transaction with 100 transactional writes into two transactions, each with 50 transactional writes, the size of the transaction is affected in addition to the write-set size.

# 4 The Prediction Model

## 4.1 Linear Regression

Size of transaction, write-set, and read-set are three factors that affect performance of STM applications. To optimize performance of STM programs, we build a linear regression model that predicts transaction size based on these three factors. The main reason that we decided to use transaction size as the predicted value by LR is that changing STM programs based on transaction size is straightforward. Quite often, it does not require any changes in the data structure of programs. For example, Fig. 2 shows a code snippet from BT benchmark. The loop iterations are independent and so we can change transaction size by splitting the outer loop into a number of smaller loops and assigning each small loop to a transaction. On the other side, changing write-set and/or read-set of a transaction needs significant programming effort which complicates parallel programming. Hence, in all our experiments, we target transaction size for optimization. It is important to note that in some programs, it is not feasible to break down a large transaction because of dependency. For example, if the loop iterations in Fig. 2 are dependent, then we cannot break the outer loop.

While our optimization technique directly affects transaction size, it implicitly changes write-set and read-set sizes. For example in Fig. 2, if we split the k-loop into two equally sized loops, then write-set and read-set of each transaction is halved. So, by changing transaction size, we take into account the impact of all the three parameters on performance.

```
.....
TM_BEGIN();
for(k=1;...;k++)
    for(j=1;...;j++)
        rhs_t=(double)TM_SHARED_READ_F(rhs[k][j][i][0]);
        for(i=1;i<= grid_point[0]-2;i++){
            ui=rhs_t+dx1*tx1*(up1+us1-um1);
            .....
            rhs_t=ui*tx2-u[k][j][i][1];
        }
        TM_SHARED_WRITE_F(rhs[k][j][i][0],rhs_t);

    TM_END();
.....
```

**Fig. 2.** A code snippet from BT.

To train LR model, we use a set of benchmarks from NAS benchmark suite [9]. Table 1 shows the list of the benchmarks. The second column of the table shows the number of transaction per benchmark. We use 34 transactions for training of LR model. The rest are used for test. Also, we use DiscoPoP benchmark suite [10] to evaluate the impact of our optimization techniques on performance (Table 1).

We use SPSS [16] to find coefficients in our LR model. While our first LR model is simple and uses only three inputs, its accuracy is not acceptable. R_square which indicates how the data fit the regression model is only 45 %. According to this result, 55 % of data cannot be described by this model. We need to improve our LR model to reduce error rate of predicted transaction sizes.

To revise the LR model, we extend the inputs of the LR and include five more parameters: size of next transaction (SNT), number of assembly instructions between two consecutive transactions (NCT), write-set of the next transaction (WN), read-set of the next transaction (RN), and number of assembly instructions in a loop (TL). These five parameters are in addition to the original three parameters: size of transaction (ST), size of write-set (WS), and size of read-set (RS).

**Table 1.** NAS and DiscoPop benchmar suites.

| Benchmark | Number of TXs |
|-----------|---------------|
| LU | 6 |
| BT | 12 |
| CG | 4 |
| EP | 3 |
| IS | 6 |
| MG | 6 |
| FT | 9 |
| Histo_serial | 1 |
| Ann_trainig | 2 |
| Mc_light | 2 |
| mandelbort | 1 |

The first factor is called SNT. We explain why we use SNT as an input to LR model through an example. Assume that transaction A is followed by transaction B and transaction C is followed by transaction D. Transactions A, B, C, and D have 3000, 5000, 6000, and 11000 instructions, respectively, Assume that the optimum transaction size is 8000 instructions. We can combine transactions A and B and create a larger transaction with 8000 instructions. However, transactions C and D cannot be combined since the combined transaction has much more than 8000 instructions.

The second factor is called NCT. The number of instructions between two consecutive transactions affects the way we merge multiple small transactions into a large transaction. Assume that there are two transactions each with 3000 instructions. Similar to the previous example, assume that the optimum transaction size is 8000 instructions. If NCT is 2000 instructions, then the combined transaction results in optimum performance. However, if NCT is 10000, then we cannot combine the two transactions as the combined transaction is too large and hurts performance.

The third and fourth parameters are called WN and RN. Similar to SNT, write-set and read-set of the next transaction affect how we merge small transactions to build optimum transactions. So, to optimize transaction size, we need to consider WN and RN as well.

The fifth parameter is called TL. This parameter affects those transactions that are inside the body of a loop. If the total number of instructions in a loop is less than optimum transaction size, then we can move the whole loop in to a transaction. For transactions that are not inside a loop, we set this parameter to zero.

Equation 2 shows LR model using the 8 input parameters. We use SPSS [16] to calculate coefficients in Eq. 2. TS stands for transactions size.

$$TS = 5451 + 0.867 \times ST + 0.015 \times RS - 0.027 \times WS - 0.832 \times TL + 0.229 \times$$
$$NCT + 0.032 \times SNT + 0.015 \times RN - 0.026 \times WN$$

(2)

Table 2 shows accuracy of predictions by LR. The test cases in Table 2 are transactions from NAS benchmarks. While accuracy is high in some of the benchmarks, i.e. test6, in most of the benchmarks, LR predictions result in significant error. The main reason for high error is that LR tries to draw a line to cover as many points as possible. If the points are scattered, then LR is unable to fit a line that covers all the points. This reduces accuracy of predictions.

**Table 2.** Predcition accuracy in LR

| Test Cases | Original TX Size | Predicted TX Size | Optimum TX Size | Error (%) |
|---|---|---|---|---|
| test1 | 148258 | 10576.54 | 6739 | -56.9% |
| test2 | 54736 | 6985 | 2488 | -180.7% |
| test3 | 112816 | 9159 | 5128 | -78.6% |
| test4 | 636460 | 27062 | 28930 | 6.5% |
| test5 | 204192 | 5343 | 6381 | 16.3% |
| test6 | 35122 | 34385 | 35122 | 2.1% |

We need to revise the LR model to increase accuracy of predictions. Further investigation of LR model reveals that the error rate for transactions with large positive error is in the range of 6.5 %-16.3 %. On the other side, error rate of transactions with large negative error is in the range of 56 %-180.7 %. This motivates us to classify transactions into three categories: transactions with large negative error (class1), transactions with large positive error (class2), and transactions with small error (clas3). We use separate LR model for each class. This improves accuracy of predictions since the set of points within a class are well-organized and fitting a curve to the points results in less residual error. We use the same 8 input parameters for the three LR models: SNT, NCT, WN, RN, TL, ST, WS and RS. Equations 3-5 show the new LR models. TS1, TS2, and TS3 correspond to class1, class2, and class3, respectively.

$$TS_1 = 416 + 0.013 \times RS - 0.02 \times WS - 0.043 \times TL + 97.09 \times NCT + \\ 0.041SNT + 0.012 \times RN - 0.019 \times WN \tag{3}$$

$$TS_2 = 7196 + 0.824 \times ST + 0.018 \times RS - 0.033 \times WS - 0.791 \times TL - 0.015 \times \\ NCT + 0.03 \times SNT + 0.018 \times RN - 0.031 \times WN \tag{4}$$

$$TS_2 = 8142 + 0.799 \times ST + 0.024 \times RS - 0.039 \times WS - 0.765 \times TL - 0.026 \times \\ NCT + 0.03 \times SNT + 0.023 \times RN - 0.035 \times WN \tag{5}$$

## 4.2 Decision Tree

To exploit the three LR models, we need to classify transactions into three categories: class1, class2, and class3. We use decision tree [17] for classification. C4.5 [15] is a popular decision tree algorithm and is able to classify objects with continuous attributes. We train the decision tree with already classified sample transactions. Each sample $S_i$ consists of an 8-dimensional input vector (SNT, NCT, WN, RN, TL, ST, WS, and RS) as well as the class which the $S_i$ belongs to. Through the training phase, the decision tree learns how to classify transactions. For test, we feed the decision tree an 8- dimensional vector and the decision tree predicts the class of the transaction corresponding to the vector.

## 4.3 Mixed Decision Tree and Linear Regressions Model

Our last optimization technique is a mixture of decision tree and linear regression. First, decision tree determine the class of a transaction. Then, we use one of the three LR models (Eqs. 3-5) to predict optimal transaction size.

We used the same method to test the mixed model: 34 transactions from NAS are used for training and the rest are used for test.

Table 3 shows error of predictions made by our mixed model. On average, error rate drops from 59 % to 2.8 %. The error rates in most of the test cases are very low. The largest error rate is 16 % in test5. This transaction has small read- and write-sets and the decision tree categorizes it in class 3. However, this transaction has a large positive error and should be categorized in class 2. We used a small set of transactions for training. However, if we include more transactions in training phase, then this abnormality may disappear.

**Table 3.** Prediction accuracy using mixed model

| Name | Original TX Size | Predicted TX Size | Optimized TX Size | Error rate |
|------|------------------|-------------------|-------------------|------------|
| test1 | 148258 | 6739 | 6739 | 0% |
| test2 | 54736 | 2488.45 | 2488 | −0.02% |
| test3 | 112816 | 5129.87 | 5128 | −0.04% |
| test4 | 636460 | 28930 | 28930 | 0% |
| test5 | 204192 | 5359.92 | 6381 | 16% |
| test6 | 35122 | 34859.46 | 35122 | 0.75% |

To evaluate the impact of mixed model on execution time, we use benchmarks from DiscoPoP benchmark suite [10]. The last column in Table 4 shows speedup in optimized benchmarks. LR and decision tree together improve performance up to 54.8 %. On average, the performance is improved by 30.3 %.

**Table 4.** Speedup in DiscoPop [10] using mixed model

| Name | Original TX Size | Predicted TX Size | Speedup |
|---|---|---|---|
| Histo_serial | 320625 | 14186 | 47.0% |
| Mc_light | 2125000 | 77310 | 28.4% |
| Mc_light | 116250 | 11148 | 54.8% |
| Ann_trainig | 72000 | 10614.15 | 18.6% |
| Ann_trainig | 480000000 | 16328112 | 18.5% |
| mandelbort | 78208 | 9776 | 14.9% |

## 5 Related Work

Transactional memory was originally proposed by Herlihy and Moss [1]. Shavit and Touitou [7] were the first to introduce software implementation of transactional memory. Since then, many researchers offered new implementations for transactional memory or improved already existing implementations through optimizing different aspects of transactional memory.

Felber et al. [4] introduced TinySTM which is a time-based STM. The authors evaluated the impact of three parameters on performance: the number of locks, the hash function for lock table, and the size of hierarchical array in lock. The authors found that there is no one-size-fit-all value that works well across all applications. Even within an application, the optimum value of a parameter may change during the run-time. The authors proposed using hill-climbing strategy to adjust STM parameters. The dynamic optimization technique introduced in TinySTM can be combined with our static approach to improve performance of STMs further.

Wang et al. [14] proposed new techniques to optimize transactional memory in unmanaged programming languages such as C. Supporting transactions in an unmanaged language is much more challenging than managed code. For example, the lack of type safety in C forces programmers to implement validation in granularity of cache line rather than object. This makes optimization of STM overhead a challenging task. Wang et al. [14] proposed new constructs in C which allows a programmer to declare blocks that can be executed atomically. Furthermore, they exploited some compiler based optimization techniques such as inlining for fast paths, elimination of redundant barriers, and register check-pointing optimization to reduce overhead of STM. We use a different approach and focus on transaction, write-set, and read-set sizes to optimize STM applications.

DiscoPoP [10] is a tool that automatically finds parallelizable regions of a sequential code. DiscoPoP is able to identify parallelism between code regions with arbitrary granularity and does not require any predefined notion of language constructs. DiscoPoP identifies sections of the code in which data dependency does not exist. These sections are called Computational Units (CUs). Then, the tool builds a dependency graph using CUs. Nodes of the graph represent CUs and edges represent dependency between CUs. From the dependency graph, DiscoPoP determines potential parallelism available on varying levels of the code. The output of the DiscoPoP is a file that indicates which lines of the sequential code can be grouped as a task and run concurrently with other tasks. We used the set of benchmarks introduced in DiscoPoP for evaluation of our mixed model. Our mixed model can be combined with DiscoPoP to convert sequential codes into highly optimized STM codes automatically.

Castro et al. [12] used machine learning for thread mapping in STMs. In thread mapping, executing threads are assigned to processing cores dynamically so that the latency associated to the memory hierarchy is reduced. To decide on thread mapping, status of transactions and also STM platform are monitored at specific intervals. At the end of each interval, thread mapping is adjusted based on a decision tree learning method (ID3) [15]. Our work is different as we use C4.5 for classification of transactions. C4.5 is an enhanced version of ID3 which supports continuous attributes. Also, we focus on transaction, write-set, and read-set sizes for optimization. On the other side, Castro et al. [12] focus on thread mapping.

Didona et al. [11] proposed self-tuning methodologies to dynamically adjust concurrency level in STMs. One of the key factors in STM programs is concurrency level. Too many threads in a program increase contentions over shred memory locations and hurt performance. On the other side, if concurrency level is too low, then exploited parallelism by STM programs will be limited. The optimum number of executing threads depends on many parameters including but not limited to pattern of addresses generated by transactions, OS scheduler, structure of memory hierarchy, etc. So, identifying the right level of concurrency in STMs is not a trivial task. Diego et al. [11] used a hill-climbing algorithm to explore concurrency level space in shared memory STMs. This optimization technique is a dynamic approach and can be combined with our static code optimization technique to improve performance of STM applications further.

# 6 Conclusion

In this paper, we presented an optimization technique that helps programmers to write efficient STM programs. We studied the impact of three parameters on STM performance and showed that STM applications are highly sensitive to the three parameters. Then, we exploited LR to predict transaction size based on the three parameters. Our first LR model was not accurate enough and it resulted in high error rate. We revised the LR model by extending its inputs from 3 to 8 parameters. Also, to improve accuracy of LR, we classified transactions into three groups: transactions with large positive errors, transactions with large negative errors, and transaction with low errors. We used decision tree to classify transactions automatically. Our mixed model reduces error rate from 59 % to 2.8 % on average. We also evaluated the mixed model using DiscoPoP benchmark suite. The mixed model improves performance of DiscoPoP up to 54.8 %.

# References

1. Herlihy, M., Moss, J.E.B.: Transactional memory: Architectural support for lock-free data structures. In: Proceedings of the Twentieth Annual International Symposium on Computer Architecture (ISCA), pp. 289–300, May 1993

2. Dice, D., Shalev, O., Shavit, N.N.: Transactional locking II. In: Dolev, S. (ed.) DISC 2006. LNCS, vol. 4167, pp. 194–208. Springer, Heidelberg (2006)

3. Abadi, M., Harris, T., Mehrara, M.: Transactional memory with strong atomicity using off-the-shelf memory protection hardware. In: Proceedings of the 14th ACM SIGPLAN Symposium on Principles and Practice of Parallel Programming, Raleigh, NC, February 2009

4. Felber, P., Fetzer, C., Riegel, T.: Dynamic performance tuning of word-based software transactional memory. In: Proceedings of the 13th ACM SIGPLAN Symposium on Principles and Practice of Parallel Programming, Salt Lake City, UT, February 2008

5. Marathe, V.J., Scherer III, W.N., Scott, M.L.: Adaptive software transactional memory. In: Fraigniaud, P. (ed.) DISC 2005. LNCS, vol. 3724, pp. 354–368. Springer, Heidelberg (2005)

6. Dice, D., Lev, Y., Moir, M., Nussbaum, D.: Early experience with a commercial hardware transactional memory implementation. In: Proceedings of the 14th International Conference on Architectural Support for Programming Languages and Operating Systems, Washington, DC, March 2009

7. Shavit, N., Touitou, D.: Software transactional memory. In: Proceedings of the Fourteenth Annual Symposium on Principles of Distributed Computing (PODC), pp. 204–213, August 1995

8. Goldberger, S.: Best linear unbiased prediction in the generalized linear regression model. J. Am. Stat. Assoc. 57(298), 369–375 (1962)

9. Bailey, D., Barszcz, E., Barton, J., Browning, D., Carter, R., Dagum, L., Fatoohi, R., Fineberg, S., Frederickson, P., Lasinski, T., Schreiber, R., Simon, H., Venkatakrishnan, V., Weeratunga, S.: The NAS parallel Benchmarks. RNR Technical Report RNR-94-007, March 1994

10. Li, Z., Jannesari, A., Wolf, F.: Discovery of potential parallelism in sequential programs. In: Proceedings of the 42nd International Conference on Parallel Processing Workshops (ICPPW), Workshop on Parallel Software Tools and Tool Infrastructures (PSTI), Lyon, France, pp. 1004–1013, October 2013

11. Didona, D., Felber, P., Harmanci, D., Romano, P., Schenker, J.: Identifying the optimal level of parallelism in transactional memory applications. In: Gramoli, V., Guerraoui, R. (eds.) NETYS 2013. LNCS, vol. 7853, pp. 233–247. Springer, Heidelberg (2013)

12. Castro, M., Góes, L.F.W., Fernandes, L.G., Méhaut, J.-F.: Dynamic thread mapping based on machine learning for transactional memory applications. In: Kaklamanis, C., Papatheodorou, T., Spirakis, P.G. (eds.) Euro-Par 2012. LNCS, vol. 7484, pp. 465–476. Springer, Heidelberg (2012)

13. Google Inc. Quantifying Movie Magic with GoogleSearch. June 2013

14. Wang, C., Chen, W.Y., Wu, Y., et al.: Code generation and optimization for transactional memory constructs in an unmanaged language. In: The Proceedings of the International Symposium on Code Generation and Optimization, pp. 34–48. IEEE Computer Society (2007)

15. Quinlan, J.R.: C4.5: Programs for Machine Learning. Morgan Kaufmann Publishers, San Francisco (1993)

16. SPSS Inc. 2007. SPSS 16.0 Command Syntax Reference. Chicago, IL: SPSS Inc

17. Quinlan, J.R.: Induction of decision tree. Mach. Learn. 1(1), 81–106 (1986)

18. Asanovic, K., Bodik, R., Catanzaro, B.C., Gebis, J.J., Husbands, P., Keutzer, K., Yelick, K. A.: The landscape of parallel computing research: A view from berkeley. Technical Report UCB/EECS-2006-183, EECS Department, University of California, Berkeley (2006)

# A Data-Centric Tool to Improve the Performance of Multithreaded Program on NUMA

Dan Zeng, Liang Zhu, Xiaofei Liao$^{(\boxtimes)}$, and Hai Jin

Services Computing Technology and System Lab, Cluster and Grid Computing Lab,
School of Computer Science and Technology,
Huazhong University of Science and Technology, Wuhan 430074, China
{xfliao,hjin}@hust.edu.cn

**Abstract.** *Non-uniform memory access* (NUMA) is one of the main architectures of today's high-performance server. The key feature of NUMA is the non-uniformity of access latency. Access from a processor to attached memory is faster, and it also reduces the possibility of causing contention on interconnect links and memory controller. Multithreaded programs may experience high memory latency without careful placement of data and thread. Thus, it is necessary to develop a tool to identify and help ameliorate NUMA problems. In this paper, we present a data-centric tool to analyze the performance of multithreaded programs on NUMA architectures and provide advices on how to improve the performance. This paper describes the design and implementation of the tool. The tool is evaluated on Linux using three benchmark applications, and the evaluation shows how this tool helps to identify costly variables and choose optimization methods. The result shows performance improvement of up to 51.92 %.

**Keywords:** NUMA · Profiling · Thread access model · Multithread · Performance improvement

## 1 Introduction

Commercial server architecture can be divided into three categories: *symmetric multi-processing* (SMP), *massive parallel processing* (MPP) and NUMA. SMP is a system architecture where two or more identical processors connect to a single shared main memory [3], it treats processors equally and offers uniform access to memory, all processors can directly access any part of memory [21]. However, adding more microprocessors to the architecture makes the shared bus a bottleneck. All processors compete using the only bus to deliver data. MPP provides an efficient approach to expand the system [5]. It is a system combined by numerous loosely coupled processors that use their own resource. Setting up

© Springer International Publishing Switzerland 2015
G. Wang et al. (Eds.): ICA3PP 2015, Part IV, LNCS 9531, pp. 74–87, 2015.
DOI: 10.1007/978-3-319-27140-8_6

MPP is complicated because the processor is individual in the system, it requires us to determine how to partition data and assign work among the processors [2]. To improve system performance and scalability, people come up with a new architecture: NUMA. A NUMA system divides memory into parts. Each of them obtains a certain number of attached microprocessors, which access them locally. The package of memory and attached microprocessors can be called a domain. An access from a CPU to memory of other domain is called remote access. By contrast, an access from a CPU to memory of the same domain is called local access. Remote access always takes more time than local access. Domains are connected to others through interconnect links (Fig. 1).

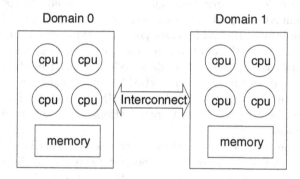

**Fig. 1.** An example of NUMA architecture

NUMA performance improvement has been a topic of fierce debate through recent years. A fundamental characteristic of NUMA hardware, non-uniform memory access, emphasizes the importance of coding properly to achieve better performance. If a thread and its relative memory are placed on the same NUMA domain, the thread will run quicker; otherwise, the thread will experience significant NUMA penalty. Significant effort has been exerted to solve this problem. Operating systems, such as Linux, Solaris and Microsoft Windows, have developed some NUMA-related features [14]. For example, Linux provides almost a whole package of tricks to help with NUMA allocation. With these tricks, users can specify how memory is allocated for a process. There are also some basic NUMA command line tools (such as *numactl* [12]) that can obtain information about NUMA characteristics of the system or bind thread on a certain domain.

Besides the support of operating systems, there are other tools that focus on NUMA problems. These tools try to make improvement mainly based on data collected during the execution of target application. Commercial tools, such as IBM Visual Performance Analyzer [4], Intel Vtune Amplifier [1] and AMD CodeAnalyst [8], have been widely used. These tools use *performance monitoring unit* (PMU) to collect NUMA-related information and identify NUMA bottleneck in the code. They point out code lines associated with NUMA problems, and this method is called code-centric method. This method is efficient in identifying which code line can be rewritten to achieve improvement. However, why it becomes a bottleneck and how the code lines can be rearranged to achieve improvement is unclear. Another method that associates NUMA problems with data used in the program is called data-centric method. The existing data-centric tools include Memphis [18] and MemProf [13], they aggregate samplings collected during the execution and analyze variables and instructions suffered from NUMA architecture.

The problem with the existing data-centric tools is that they cannot provide a clear insight into NUMA bottleneck. They cannot estimate whether an application can achieve improvement from NUMA-related adjustments, neither can they directly identify which variable accounts most of the NUMA problem. Existing tools also do not provide enough information on how to optimize codes that suffered from NUMA problem. A data-centric tool is presented in this study to provide these information and to analyze the performance of multithreaded programs. This tool has three advantages compared with existing tools. First, some metrics are computed based on data collected using hardware counters. These metrics can determine whether a NUMA problem exists. Second, the tool efficiently lists variables that suffered from NUMA problem. Third, the tool provides information to guide NUMA optimizations, including details of thread accessing variables.

The rest of the paper is organized as follows: Sect. 2 describes NUMA problems and how to identify these problems. Section 3 explains the implementation details of the tool. Section 4 presents evaluation of the tool on three benchmarks, which verify its correctness and effectiveness. Finally, Sect. 5 discusses related works, and Sect. 6 concludes the paper.

## 2 Finding and Fixing NUMA Problems

### 2.1 NUMA Problems

There are two types of problem under NUMA architecture: interconnect congestion caused by memory hot-spotting and remote access latency caused by computation-partition/data-partition mismatch [18]. Memory hot-spotting refers to a phenomenon that a variable is located on a specific domain and frequently accessed by threads on all domains, which makes a significant imbalance of accesses to domains. Memory hot-spotting causes massive accesses to one domain. Therefore accesses jam the interconnect links to the specific domain. The traffic congestion results in long latency, which slows down the program process. Memory hot-spotting is often caused by the inappropriate initialization of data. This is common under today's Linux system because it employs the default "first-touch" policy to find pages of newly allocated variables. First-touch means the operating system will always locate variables on the NUMA domain where the thread that first accesses the variable resides. In the program described by Fig. 5, thread 0 touches the whole array before any other thread is created, which means the whole array will be located on the domain where thread 0 belongs to, then every access from threads on other domains becomes remote

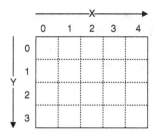

**Fig. 2.** Memory layout of a two-dimensional matrix

access. This problem can be solved by adjusting the code that first touches variable, explicitly initializing the data in the way which it is accessed throughout the rest of the application, and ensuring every thread touches its own data before other threads.

Inappropriate initialization is not only the cause of memory hot-spotting, but also the cause of massive remote accesses. Remote accesses should be avoided under the NUMA architecture because the penalty of remote accesses will harm the performance of application. Another likely cause of remote access is thread migration. Once the thread is moved to another domain for load balance by the scheduler and the data it used remains in the old domain, remote access happens. Remote access may also occur when data are accessed by loops with different data access patterns [15], we take the two-dimensional matrix in Fig. 2 as an example, when a multithreaded application attempts to access all elements in a nested loop, the data access pattern can be divided into categories based on the direction of parallel loop, in this case: $x$-wise pattern if loop is paralleled in the $x$ direction and $y$-wise pattern if the loop is paralleled in the $y$ direction. Different access patterns always result in different data distributions. Thus loops with different access pattern always come with remote accesses. This problem can be solved by matching all the access patterns of loops without violating the correctness of the application.

## 2.2   Finding and Fixing

As previously discussed, both interconnect congestion and remote accesses lead to long access latency. These problems can be detected by sampling each access activity, aggregating and analyzing the average time to obtain each variable. Thus, average access latency can be an efficient metric to detect whether an application suffers from NUMA problems.

Co-locating data and thread that frequently accesses it is the most useful optimization because it reduces the demand for interconnection delivery and decreases remote accesses at the same time. Each access of threads to a variable should be collected to get knowledge of the access model of the thread, and this information should be used to determine how multiple threads access data throughout the execution.

To help program get better performance under NUMA architecture, we need a tool to find and fix NUMA problems. This tool should pinpoint variables that suffered most from NUMA problems and then determine the access models of all threads to guide NUMA optimization.

# 3  Implementation

NumaProf is a tool that uses *precise event based sampling* (PEBS) [10] to collect access samples, analyze data, and present information helpful for NUMA optimizations. NumaProf mainly requires three steps to function properly: use PEBS to collect access samples, map virtual address from samples to corresponding variables, and process samples to obtain efficient information.

## 3.1  Sampling

Collecting useful information is an important step. During the execution of target program, NumaProf detects event and creates three event flows: malloc event flow, mmap event flow and access event flow, as we can see in Fig. 3. We get malloc event flow to mark the allocation of dynamic-allocated variable and mmap event flow to record global static variables.

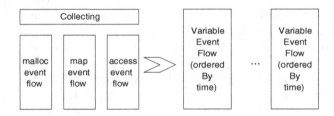

**Fig. 3.** Data flow of NumaProf

NumaProf uses PEBS on an Intel processor to track the memory accesses of each variable. PEBS is only available on Intel processors, it can be easily transformed into a similar hardware mechanism-*instruction based sampling* (IBS) on AMD processors [9]. Information provided by PEBS can be customized. Thread ID is selected in this study to identify which thread processed this access, virtual address is selected to obtain the target data, and some other useful information. With these information, we can keep track of the whole life of a variable. A variable event flow in Fig. 4 can then be created chronologically. The thread access model for each variable can be detected by searching the created flow.

The latency of each memory access should be recorded to determine variables that suffered most from NUMA, it can be provided by the load-latency facility of PEBS. It provides software a method to characterize the average load

Object was allocated from the following path:
  streamCluster(PStream*, long , long , int, long , long , char*)+0x73 [0x401cd2]  block
    main [0x40a9a9]
      __libc_start_main [0x3fe241ecdd]
        //anon [0x33b883be4a8ea]
Object is here: 2b76aa96a010-2b76b0b12010
done parseTimeline of memory access (x = load, * = write, one column per tid) - you may
need to use left/right arrows to see the function names :
      x              pgain(long , Points*, double, long *, int, parsec_barrier_t*)
        x            pgain(long , Points*, double, long *, int, parsec_barrier_t*)
      x              pgain(long , Points*, double, long *, int, parsec_barrier_t*)
          x          pgain (long , Points*, double, long *, int, parsec_barrier_t*)
  x                  pgain(long , Points*, double, long *, int, parsec_barrier_t*)
      x              pgain(long , Points*, double, long *, int, parsec_barrier_t*)
          x          pgain(long , Points*, double, long *, int, parsec_barrier_t*)

Fig. 4. Thread access stream of Streamcluster

latency to different levels of cache/memory hierarchy [10]. Latency and data source information are captured and written as part of the PEBS record.

Some load-latency information written into a PEBS record should be emphasized:

**Data Linear Address.** This information is the linear address of the target of load operation. It offers the essential information for a data-centric tool: the related data address. The linear addresses will then be translated into variable names for the convenience of users.

**Latency Value.** This information is the elapsed cycle to complete the load operation, measured in processor core clock domain. This information helps in identifying NUMA problems, as discussed in Sect. 2. Long access latency always indicates that a NUMA problem exists.

**Data Source.** This information is an encoded value that determines where the system obtained the target data. It is an additional information than can be used to identify a remote access.

Thus, samples provided by PEBS not only include the latency of every access, but also provide insight into the memory access model of a thread.

### 3.2 Mapping

So far, the data linear address of every memory access is obtained from the PEBS record. However, difficulties still exist when mapping data addresses to variables in the program. Debugging information provided by the compiler can help mapping static data addresses known at compile time, but dynamic addresses variables created on the stack or global variables created on the heap are more challenging.

Static and global data addresses can be mapped by looking into the *Executable and Linking Format* (ELF) file of mapped shared libraries and executable file of the program. When we analyze the ELF file, the symbol table is the main focus. The symbol table of an object file holds information necessary to locate and relocate the symbolic definitions and references of a program [17]. The structure symbol table entry contains two important members:

**st_name.** If it is not zero, the value represents an index in the symbol string table, which point to a string in the table, and the string table holds all the strings that represent symbol names.

**st_value.** *st_value* holds a virtual address in executable and shared object files.

*st_name* and *st_value* can help determining how to map virtual address to a symbol string. However, dynamically allocated data cannot be read from the ELF file. Thus, the code line that allocated the corresponding data can be tracked down by overloading all types of memory allocation functions. Specifically, *malloc()* is overloaded to record the allocated address range and the instruction ip that allocated it. This process is used to obtain the instruction ip for an allocated object, and the next step is to map the instruction ip to a function. It is represented as *function name + instruction offset* by NumaProf, which can be used by the user to find the correct variable in the source code.

### 3.3    Analysis

Once all the necessary information is obtained, it should be processed correctly so that useful advice can be provided to the user. The analysis is an offline work. As discussed in Sect. 2, we will present which variable is most costly and what we can do to get improvement, we mainly calculate two metrics and detect thread access model of target variable, we use aggregate latency measurements and access percentage of variable as a guide to identify whether it is necessary to consider for NUMA locality optimization, and which variable we should focus on, then we can use thread access model as a guide to understand what changes to data and/or thread mappings will be needed to improve NUMA performance.

**Average Latency.** We calculate the average latency per access for every address sampled and present to the user. Users can figure out whether a NUMA problem exists by this metric. If NUMA problems do exist, users can obtain the most costly variable based on it, and this variable is potentially the one that should be improved.

**Access Percentage.** To get performance improvement, we should improve the variable that is not only most costly but also matters the most. The variable that matters the most can be determined by calculating the access percentage of every variable. This process will prevent useless work and make the most benefit out of least work.

**Access Model.** Once the variable that requires improvement is determined, we need more detailed information about how to change the code line to make improvement. Thus, users are also provided the access model of each variable. By detecting the access model of a variable, we can get knowledge of whether the variable is accessed by multiple threads or a single thread, the accesses are all read-only accesses or both read and write accesses, we will show why this information is important to get improvement through experiment in Sect. 4. The most important meaning of these metrics is that it helps us detect which type of NUMA problem is processed, we can figure out inappropriate initial and mismatch loop access pattern as we discussed in Sect. 2.

## 4  Evaluation

This section demonstrates the effectiveness of NumaProf using three different applications: Blackscholes, Streamcluster and LU. We first analyze Blackscholes to demonstrate the metrics we offer through NumaProf is effective, and it can be used to estimate whether a NUMA problem exists and if an application can achieve improvement through some slightly adjustments of source code. As for the reserved applications, we show that the two kinds of NUMA problems we discussed in Sect. 2 can be solved and they can be improved through NumaProf. We get 23.08 % to 51.92 % performance improvement over the default Linux execution.

For all the experiments, we use a system with two 8-core Intel Xeon processors. Overall, the system has 16 cores and is divided into two NUMA domains. As for the operating system, we use Linux with kernel version 3.10. We configure all the application to run in 8 threads.

### 4.1  Blackscholes

Blackscholes is a benchmark from PARSEC benchmark suite [6]. The Blackscholes application is a benchmark, it analytically calculates the prices for European options, using the BlackScholes partial differential equation. We use the OpenMP implementation of Blackscholes and the programming language of Blackscholes is C.

The analysis result of Blackscholes is shown in Table 1, we list all variables whose average latency is over 20, and we leave out accesses to public library functions, because we cannot improve performance of accesses to these functions within dozens of source code line. We do the same thing as we represent the analysis result of the next two applications. As we can see in the table, all variables whose average weight is over 20 count less than 1 % of whole accesses, which means that we cannot get enough improvement by adjusting codes that access them and decreasing the average access latency. It is not exactly the same data for every execution, but we can draw the same conclusion from the result.

The conclusion can be verified by testing whether we can improve the performance. Ideas about proper adjustment can be obtained by searching the access model of the main concerned variables. Table 1 shows that variables allocated under the sub-range of variable *buffer* (such as *strike*, *rate* and *otime*) suffered a lot from NUMA problems, *strike* 136.73 cycles, *rate* 47.03 cycles and *otime*

**Table 1.** Data-centric analysis of Blackscholes

| Variable | Average latency | Access percentage |
|----------|-----------------|-------------------|
| strike   | 136.73          | 0.16 %            |
| rate     | 47.03           | 0.12 %            |
| otime    | 34.39           | 0.15 %            |
| sptprice | 22.10           | 0.16 %            |
| prices   | 21.25           | 0.10 %            |

34.39 cycles. Thus, the variable *buffer* is chosen. We look into its access details. Figure 5 shows the memory layout and regular access pattern of *buffer*. It is first initialized by the main thread (thread 0) on domain 0 (thread 0 runs on domain 0) because of the "first-touch" policy of Linux system, and then all threads access different parts of *buffer*. If the kernel scheduler considers load balance and distributes four threads on each domain, which is the actual situation during the execution, approximately half of these accesses become remote accesses, it will also make domain 0 become a hot spot. To eliminate these remote accesses, we parallelized the initialization using OpenMP to make sure that each thread first touches its own data. The OpenMP scheduling policy is default static policy to match with latter access loop. With this optimization, latency related to *buffer* caused by remote accesses no longer exits. The performance, however, improves less than 1 %. It verifies our tool's estimation about Blackscholes.

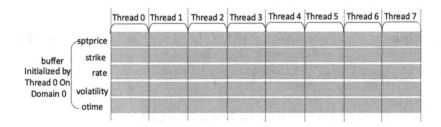

**Fig. 5.** Thread access pattern of Blackscholes

## 4.2 Streamcluster

Streamcluster is another benchmark from PARSEC benchmark suit [6], it is a common stream clustering process that deals with numerous and continuously produced data. Programming language of Streamcluster program we used in the experiment is C++.

Streamcluster performs a significant number of remote memory accesses, as is shown in Table 2. NumaProf identifies that heap-allocated variable *block*

Table 2. Data-centric analysis of Streamcluster

| Variable | Average latency | Access percentage |
|----------|-----------------|-------------------|
| is_center | 152.04 | 0.11 % |
| block | 146.35 | 92.43 % |
| center_table | 34.00 | 0.01 % |
| stack | 31.00 | 2.00 % |

accounts for 92.43 % of total access while the average latency of it is 146.35, which means we can surely get a big promotion on performance if we can adjust the thread accesses properly.

When we look into the thread access pattern of *block*, we can find out that *block* becomes a hot-spot, threads access the same variable remotely, numerous remote accesses make congestion of interconnect link, which slows the access to *block*. We find out that it is also initialized on a single domain by the main thread and then accessed by several threads. Given that it is simultaneously read and written by several threads, simply copying the variable to each domain is inappropriate. It is parallelized by pthreads, so we cannot parallelize the initial part of variable either. This problem is solved by interleaving the memory allocated for *block* to multiple domains, this process can be implemented by replacing normal *alloc()* function with *numa_alloc_interleaved()*. It cannot decrease the number of remote accesses, but it removes the memory hot spot on domain 0. Based on the result of the experiment, the average latency of the block decreases to 88.87 cycles. The performance is improved by 24 %. The experiment proves that NumaProf can be helpful in providing advice on how to adjust the source code and improving the performance of multithreaded applications.

### 4.3   LU

LU is a benchmark from the NAS parallel benchmarks [11], it is a simulated *computational fluid dynamics* (CFD) application, and it solves the equation by factorizing it into lower and upper triangular systems, which can be solved using *symmetric successive over-relaxation* (SSOR) algorithm. We use the OpenMP implementation of the benchmark and set the problem size to class C, the programming language is Fortran. Based on the output of NumaProf in Table 3, we can figure out a variable *cvar* counts for 26.80 % of total access, it is a named common block contains 6 matrices: *u*, *rsd*, *frct*, *flux*, *qs*, *rho_i*. The average latency for *cvar* is 40.81 cycles, we can focus on the access pattern of this variable to see if we can achieve improvement.

Based on the thread access model of *cvar*, a mismatch of the access model between the initial and the later parts is detected. Taking one of the four dimensional matrix *rsd* as an example, the initial loop code of *rsd* is regular, as shown in the code, the loop is parallelized with a standard OpenMP parallel for construct, and the parallelized loop iterates along the $k$ dimension of the matrix,

**Table 3.** Data-centric analysis of LU

| Variable | Average latency | Access percentage |
|----------|-----------------|-------------------|
| stack    | 62.58           | 6.27 %            |
| cvar     | 40.81           | 26.80 %           |
| buts     | 27.50           | 0.01 %            |
| cjacu    | 20.71           | 15.51 %           |

which means each thread gets $nz/8$ (we use 8 threads in the execution) of the whole computation. Then we get to one of the access loop of $rsd$, the access pattern of this loop does not match the initial loop at all, because this parallelized loop iterates along the $j$ dimension. The mismatch of loop access pattern leads to different data access pattern and therefore massive remote accesses. There are numerous access loops of $rsd$ and they are different from each other, we cannot rewrite them considering of the application's correctness. The access model mismatch also happens to other matrices inside of $cvar$. Rewriting these loops and setting the access model match will require considerable effort. So we choose the simplest way to improve the performance, we simply try to use *numactl* command to make all the threads run on the same domain. This step can solve all the problems, and an improvement of 50 % is achieved.

*Initial pattern of variable rsd*

```
!$omp do schedule(static)
    do k = 1, nz
        do j = 1, ny
            do i = 1, nx
                do m = 1, 5
                    rsd(m,i,j,k) = ce(m,1) + (ce(m,2) + ...)*zeta
                end do
            end do
        end do
    end do
!$omp end do
```

*Access pattern of variable rsd*

```
!$omp do schedule(static)
    do j = jst, jend
        do i = ist, iend
            do k = 1, nz
                flux(1,k) = rsd(4,i,j,k)
                u41 = rsd(4,i,j,k)/rsd(1,i,j,k)
                ...
```

```
              flux(2,k) = rsd(2,i,j,k) * u41
              flux(3,k) = rsd(3,i,j,k) * u41
              flux(4,k) = rsd(4,i,j,k)*u41+c2*(rsd(5,i,j,k)-q)
              flux(5,k) = ( c1 * rsd(5,i,j,k) - c2 * q ) * u41
            end do
          end do
        end do
!$omp end do
```

## 4.4 Overhead

We talk about the overhead of NumaProf in this section. Actions during the execution of program may cause overhead. First, the precise event based sampling may drag down the program. Due to the limitation of implementation, the whole number of samples we collect using NumaProf is no more than 4000. It is a relatively small number compare to the whole instructions of a program. Second, the recording of allocation and *mmap* may slower down the program. For *mmap* event, we just need to copy a file to get a list of mapped library, it is negligible. But for allocation, we overload memory allocation functions and record information during the allocation, it can be a time-consuming action. What's more, the time to store all these information can not be ignored. However, NumaProf is an offline profiling tool, so the latter processing and analysis of information will do no harm to the program performance.

## 5 Related Work

Several tools have been provided to help applications get better performance on NUMA architecture. Similar to NumaProf, some profilers collect information during the execution and provide advices on how to change source code. Most of them are based on AMD processors. Memphis [18] uses IBS to aid in identifying problematic memory accesses. NumaProf outperforms it by providing detailed thread access patterns, which further clarifies how to ameliorate NUMA problems. VTune [1] also uses PEBS to collect remote accesses and point out the virtual address, but it fails on tracking the dynamic allocated variables.

Aside from the abovementioned tools, some tools implement NUMA optimization via automatic scheduling. David Tam et al. [20] come up with a scheme to schedule threads based on sharing patterns of threads, which are detected online by PMU. Jia Rao et al. [19] proposed a NUMA-aware scheduling for virtual machine, it uses the access penalty of the uncore subsystem as a metric to predict program performance. Some tools consider other factors that cause NUMA problems. Sergey Blagodurov et al. [7] developed a contention-aware algorithm for NUMA systems, they found out that numerous remote accesses cause contention of memory controllers and interconnects, so they presented an algorithm to address this problem, and migrated threads together with its memory to solve this problem.

Other tools aim to help with NUMA improvement, Zoltan Majo et al. [16] present TBB-NUMA, a library based on *Intel Threading Building Blocks* (TBB) to provide portable and composable optimizations for NUMA systems, it allows programmer to control the computation and data placement. This kind of tools always requires programmer to use specific libraries and compilers.

## 6 Conclusion

In NUMA system, multithreaded applications suffer from two NUMA problems: interconnection congestion and memory hot-spotting. So we need a tool to find and fix NUMA problem and obtain performance improvement of multithreaded applications. In this paper, we present a tool that addresses NUMA problems and assists programmers in achieving improvement on NUMA systems. NumaProf uses PEBS to collect samples during the execution of application, these samples provides pairs of virtual address and instruction to associate variable with instructions that access it. NumaProf presents costly variables and their thread access pattern to help with NUMA improvement. We estimate the effectiveness of NumaProf by running three benchmarks, the result demonstrates the utility of NumaProf and the metrics it provides.

**Acknowledgments.** This paper is supported by National High-tech Research and Development Program of China (863 Program) under grant No. 2012AA010905, National Natural Science Foundation of China under grant No. 61322210, 61272408, 61433019, Doctoral Fund of Ministry of Education of China under grant No. 20130142110048.

## References

1. Intel VTune Amplifier 2015. https://software.intel.com/en-us/intel-vtune-amplifier-xe
2. MPP (massively parallel processing). http://whatis.techtarget.com/definition/MPP-massively-parallel-processing
3. Symmetric multiprocessing. http://en.wikipedia.org/wiki/Symmetric_multi processing
4. Visual Performance Analyzer. http://www.alphaworks.ibm.com/tech/vpa
5. Batcher, K.E.: Design of a massively parallel processor. IEEE Trans. Comput. (TOC) **100**(9), 836–840 (1980)
6. Bienia, C., Kumar, S., Singh, J.P., Li, K.: The PARSEC benchmark suite: Characterization and architectural implications. In: Proceedings of the 17th International Conference on Parallel Architectures and Compilation Techniques (PACT), pp. 72–81 (2008)
7. Blagodurov, S., Zhuravlev, S., Fedorova, A., Kamali, A.: A case for NUMA-aware contention management on multicore systems. In: Proceedings of the 19th International Conference on Parallel Architectures and Compilation Techniques(PACT), pp. 557–558 (2010)
8. Drongowski, P.J.: An introduction to analysis and optimization with AMD Code-Analyst Performance Analyzer. Advanced Micro Devices, Inc (2008)

9. Drongowski, P.J., Center, B.D.: Instruction-based sampling: A new performance analysis technique for AMD family 10h processors. Advanced Micro Devices, Inc (2007)

10. Intel: Intel 64 and IA-32 Architectures Software Developers Manual. Volume 3B: System Programming Guide (Part 2) (2013)

11. Jin, H.Q., Frumkin, M., Yan, J.: The OpenMP implementation of NAS parallel benchmarks and its performance (1999)

12. Kleen, A.: A NUMA API for Linux. Novel Inc (2005)

13. Lachaize, R., Lepers, B., Quéma, V.: MemProf: A memory profiler for NUMA multicore systems. In: Proceedings of the 2012 USENIX Conference on Annual Technical Conference (ATC), pp. 53–64 (2012)

14. Lameter, C.: NUMA(Non-Uniform Memory Access): An overview. ACM Queue 11(7), 40 (2013)

15. Majo, Z., Gross, T.R.: Matching memory access patterns and data placement for NUMA systems. In: Proceedings of the 10th International Symposium on Code Generation and Optimization (CGO), pp. 230–241 (2012)

16. Majo, Z., Gross, T.R.: A library for portable and composable data locality optimizations for NUMA systems. In: Proceedings of the 20th ACM SIGPLAN Symposium on Principles and Practice of Parallel Programming (PPoPP), pp. 227–238 (2015)

17. Matz, M., Hubicka, J., Jaeger, A., Mitchell, M.: System V Application Binary Interface. AMD64 Architecture Processor Supplement, Draft v0 99 (2005)

18. McCurdy, C., Vetter, J.: Memphis: Finding and fixing NUMA-related performance problems on multi-core platforms. In: Proceedings of IEEE International Symposium on Performance Analysis of Systems & Software (ISPASS), pp. 87–96 (2010)

19. Rao, J., Wang, K., Zhou, X., Xu, C.: Optimizing virtual machine scheduling in NUMA multicore systems. In: Proceedings of IEEE 19th International Symposium on High Performance Computer Architecture (HPCA), pp. 306–317 (2013)

20. Tam, D.K., Azimi, R., Stumm, M.: Thread clustering: sharing-aware scheduling on SMP-CMP-SMT multiprocessors. In: Proceedings of the 2007 ACM European Conference on Computer Systems (EuroSys), pp. 47–58 (2007)

21. Zheng, W., Yang, B., Lin, W., Li, Z.: Task scheduling of parallel programs to optimize communications for cluster of SMPs. Sci. China Ser. Inf. Sci. 44(3), 213–225 (2001)

# A Light-Weight Hot Data Identification Scheme via Grouping-based LRU Lists

Biaobiao Shen[1,2,3], Yongkun Li[1,2,3]([✉]), Yinlong Xu[1], and Yubiao Pan[1]

[1] School of Computer Science and Technology,
University of Science and Technology of China, Hefei 230026, China
{ykli,ylxu}@ustc.edu.cn, {ustcshen,pyb}@mail.ustc.edu.cn
[2] Guangdong Key Laboratory of Popular High Performance Computers,
Shenzhen 518060, China
[3] Shenzhen Key Laboratory of Service Computing and Applications,
Shenzhen 518060, China

**Abstract.** Real-world workloads generally exhibit high skewness in access patterns, and it is a consensus that separating hot and cold data may greatly improve storage system performance such as Solid State Drive (SSD) garbage collection(GC) performance. To achieve this, the key issue is how to accurately identify hot data, which is really challenging due to the large diversity and dynamics of workloads. In this paper, we propose a light-weight and high-accuracy identification scheme, which is developed via a group of Least Recently Used (LRU) lists and requires only a small amount of memory and CPU cycles. We further deploy our scheme on SSDs with DiskSim simulator, and results show that comparing to two state-of-the-art identification schemes, our scheme further reduces SSD GC cost by up to 59.1 % (62.1 %), and saves 44.3 % (77.5 %) of computational cost. Due to the light-weight and parameter-insensitive feature, our scheme can be easily deployed at various system levels and adaptable to different workloads.

**Keywords:** Hot data identification · LRU · Algorithm · SSD · Garbage collection

## 1 Introduction

Real-world storage workloads usually exhibit high locality and skewness, particularly, some data may be frequently updated (i.e., hot), while others are only rarely or even never updated (i.e., cold) [1–3]. Incorporating hotness awareness into storage systems design by differentiating hot data from cold ones and storing them in separate regions is considered to be an efficient way to improve the performance of storage systems [4,5]. One particular example is solid-state drives (SSDs) (see Sect. 3.1 for a detailed description on the background), without considering hotness awareness in SSD design, cold data pages may be scattered over the whole SSD due to the mixture of hot and cold data pages, thus, a large

© Springer International Publishing Switzerland 2015
G. Wang et al. (Eds.): ICA3PP 2015, Part IV, LNCS 9531, pp. 88–103, 2015.
DOI: 10.1007/978-3-319-27140-8_7

amount of cold data pages need to be moved around during the garbage collection (GC) process, and this significantly degrades both the performance and endurance of SSDs. Based on this fact, it is a consensus that separating the storage of hot and cold data should improve the SSD performance a lot [6,7].

To achieve efficient hotness-aware design of storage systems, one key issue is how to develop an adaptive algorithm to identify hot/cold data accurately and efficiently, while introduces only small system overhead. However, this is not an easy task due to the large diversity and significant dynamics of workloads. First, different workloads usually possess very different access patterns, so it is extremely hard to work out a general identification scheme to accurately capture the characteristics of various kinds of workloads. Second, even for a specific workload, the access patterns may also vary significantly due to the dynamics of workloads, and the effectiveness of an identification scheme is usually very sensitive to the algorithm parameters, so it is necessary to require the identification scheme to be less parameter-sensitive and also self-adaptive. Last but not least, hot data identification usually requires to record some history information, which introduces both memory and computational cost, so how to reduce the overhead while preserving the identification accuracy is also challenging.

Previous work on hot data identification can be classified into three categories: *time-based algorithm* [8,9], *cache replacement-based algorithm* [10], and *frequency-based algorithm* [4,11]. In particular, *time-based algorithm* usually maintains the most recent access time of all logical block addresses (LBA). Although this scheme may achieve a good hot data identification performance, it requires a significant memory consumption, which dramatically limits its application scenarios. *Cache replacement-based algorithm* was proposed in [10], and it introduces an LRU-emulated approach with a two-level LRU list (a hot list and a candidate list) to identify hot data. This scheme requires relatively fewer memory space than *time-based algorithm*, but it introduces considerable computational cost to maintain the LRU property. In contrast, *frequency-based algorithm* requires a smaller memory consumption and computational cost. Hsieh et al. [4] proposed a framework by using multiple hash functions to identify hot data, in particular, it adopts $K$ independent hash functions to hash a given request and map the results to multiple entries in a bloom filter (BF) [12] to track the write frequency. Park et al. [11] extended Hsieh's work by using multiple bloom filters to further capture the recency information of workloads. Unfortunately, these approaches may introduce false identification in the sense that a rarely updated data may be mistakenly identified as hot. Furthermore, the false identification rate heavily depends on the workload characteristics, so these approaches may not be efficient to some workloads.

Considering the above observations, we argue that an efficient hot data identification algorithm should meet the following requirements: (1) Being general in the sense that it should be applicable to various workloads, (2) Low computational cost, and (3) Small memory consumption. To meet these requirements, in this paper we develop a new hot data identification scheme based on LRU list with a grouping-based idea. Different from previous schemes, our scheme can not only achieve higher efficiency for general workloads, but also requires relatively low computational cost and small memory consumption. We make the following main contributions in this paper.

- We develop a new grouping-based hot data identification algorithm based on LRU list, which we call *GLRU*. In particular, we maintain a group of LRU lists to record the access frequency of logical data pages for hot data identification. By grouping data pages into multiple LRU lists, the runtime computational cost is reduced. Besides, we also keep the logical page number (lpn) of incoming requests in each LRU list, so false identification is avoided.
- We further exploit *spatial locality* to reduce runtime computational cost of GLRU by differentiating random and sequential requests. Simulation results show that for various workloads, our scheme can reduce the runtime computational cost up to 55.6 % compared to the state-of-the-art scheme.
- We take SSDs as a case study example, and implement our scheme in the Flash Translation Layer (FTL) of SSDs. To validate the efficiency of our proposed scheme in improving SSD performance, we conduct extensive trace-driven simulations by using the SSD simulator [13]. Evaluation results show that with our hot data identification scheme, the GC cost of SSDs which is quantified by the number of additional page writes caused by GC is reduced by up to 73.1 % under different workloads compared to the case of no identification. Even comparing to the two state-of-the-art schemes, our scheme helps further reduce the GC cost by up to 59.1 % and 62.1 %, respectively.

The remaining of this paper is organized as follows. Section 2 describes the overall architecture and design details of our proposed hot data classification scheme. Section 3 introduces the background of SSDs and illustrates on the implementation of our scheme on SSDs. Section 4 shows the DiskSim [14] simulation results and validates the efficiency of our hot data identification scheme. Finally Sect. 5 concludes the paper and discusses future work.

## 2   Design

In this section, we describe our proposed hot data identification scheme in detail. Our scheme is developed by leveraging a hash-based grouping technique with LRU list, and we call it *GLRU*. In the following, we first present the working flow of GLRU, then we illustrate on the grouping-based design in detail.

### 2.1   GLRU Working Flow

Figure 1 depicts the working flow of GLRU. Specifically, when an incoming write request arrives, we first check its accessing addresses to determine whether it is a random request or a sequential request. If it is a sequential request, i.e., the addresses being accessed are successive to the ones accessed by the last request, then we simply return the identification result of the last request instead of performing a real query. That is, if the data in the last request is identified as hot, then we also take the data in the currently processing request as hot, and vice versa. The rationale is that data pages accessed by sequential requests may have similar hotness values due to the high spatial locality of real-world workload, so we only issue a single query request to identify the hotness of multiple sequentially-accessed data pages. By doing this, we can reduce the computational cost by exploiting the spatial locality of workload.

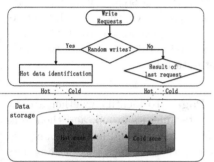

**Fig. 1.** Working flow of GLRU.

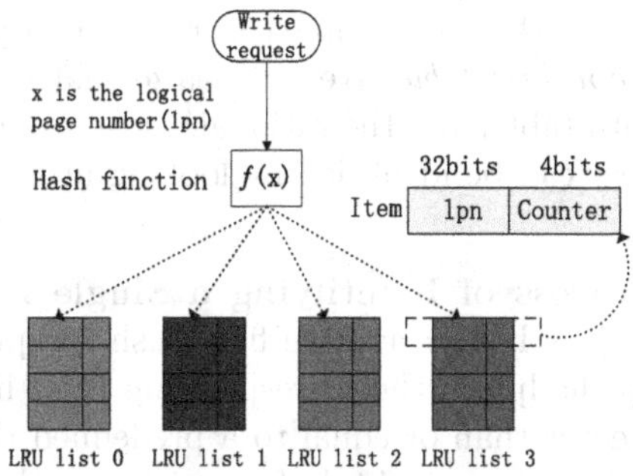

**Fig. 2.** Structure of the grouping-based LRU lists. Here, K = 4 and N = 4.

On the other hand, for a random request, we simply direct it to the hot data identification module to determine whether the accessed data is hot or not. That is, the hot data identification module accepts a data page as an input, and returns the identification result of whether the page is hot or not. To implement this functionality, we maintain a group of LRU lists, each of which keeps a fixed number of data pages with their logical page number and access frequency being both recorded. Roughly speaking, we maintain a group of LRU lists to keep potential hot data, and we then identify a requested data page as hot data if and only if it is found in a LRU list and with a large write count. After identifying whether a data page is hot or not, we update the LRU list accordingly. In particular, a data item originally residing in the LRU list may be evicted if the new data needs to be inserted into the list. We will illustrate on the detailed implementation of the grouping-based LRU lists in Sect. 2.2.

We point out that in GLRU, we only care about write requests as we implement this scheme in SSDs to evaluate its performance in this paper, while reads have no impact on SSD GC performance. However, we can easily extend the scheme by also taking read requests into account.

## 2.2 Grouping-based LRU Lists

**Data Structure of the LRU Lists.** As stated in last subsection, in GLRU, we maintain a group of LRU lists to keep tracking data pages, and each LRU list contains a fixed number of data items, each of which records the logical page number (lpn) and a write counter of a particular data page. Figure 2 depicts the structure of the LRU lists. In particular, the information of a data page may be recorded by a data item which contains a 32-bit lpn and a 4-bit write counter. The association between data pages and LRU lists are determined with a hash function, which is the division method ($f(x) = x \bmod K$, $x$ is the lpn of the requested data page, $K$ is the number of LRU lists). That is, for a data page, we compute the hash value of its lpn and take the hashing result as its group ID which is the identity of LRU list in which the lpn is stored. In particular, a data page belongs to at most one LRU list. In the whole system, we keep $K$ LRU lists with $N$ items in each. For ease of presentation, we collectively call them as a *hot data table*. We emphasize that not all data pages are recorded in the hot data table, and the rationale is that only potential hot data pages are kept, and they can be identified by looking up the hot data table.

**Process of Identifying a Single Data Page.** To identify whether a data page is hot or not, we first hash its lpn to determine its group, and then look up the lpn in the corresponding LRU list. If the lpn is found and its counter is greater than or equal to a predefined threshold, then we take this data as hot; Otherwise, as cold. Before returning the identification result, we need to update the LRU list. In particular, if the lpn already exists in the LRU, then we increase its counter by one and move this item to the head of the list so as to maintain the LRU property. We note that the write count will not be incremented if it reaches the maximum value of 15 as we use 4 bits to represent the counter. Otherwise, i.e., the lpn does not exist in the list before, then we first search the list from its tail to head to find an item with counter being equal to zero. If such an item is found, then we move all items in the list that are in front of the found item backward one position, and finally insert the new lpn in the head of the list and set its counter as one. If no item with counter being equal to zero is found, e.g., if all counters in the list are greater than or equal to one, then we evict the item in the tail with probability 0.5 and insert the new lpn into the list if the tail item is evicted. The rationale of this probabilistic evicting policy is that the data page in the list tail may not be updated for a long time and we regard it as cold.

**Aging Mechanism of Write Counters.** Considering that data becomes cold if it does not get updated for a long time, we periodically trigger a decay operation by halving the write counters like the multi-hash function scheme in [4]. In particular, if a counter is one, then we simply set it as zero. This aging mechanism is to simulate the decay behavior of data hotness. We call the time duration between two consecutive decay operations *the decay period*, and define it as a given number of incoming requests. That is, after handling a fixed number of incoming requests, we issue a decay operation to reduce all counters by half. We study the influence of *decay period* on the hot data identification performance in Sect. 4.3, and the simulation results show that our hot data identification scheme is not sensitive to the *decay period*.

**Algorithm and Discussions.** Algorithm 1 provides a pseudo-code of the above described hot data identification scheme for a single data page. We see that the time complexity of GLRU is $O(N)$ and the space complexity is $O(N*K)$, where $K$ denotes the number of LRU list and $N$ denotes the group size or number of data items in each LRU list. Since $N$ is usually set as a constant in GLRU, the time and space complexity can be regarded as $O(1)$ and $O(K)$, respectively.

We note that by explicitly recording the lpn in LRU lists, our scheme can avoid false identification. Meanwhile, by keeping the write counters for data pages, we can achieve more accurate hot data identification and make it be easily extended to realize a multi-tier classification by simply setting more than one thresholds. In particular, we implemented a multi-tier classification scheme by classifying data into three types: hot, warm and cold. We also deployed this multi-tier scheme in the FTL of SSDs, and evaluated its effectiveness of reducing the GC cost of SSDs, please refer to Sect. 4.2 for detailed results. Furthermore, we would like to emphasize that in our scheme only a proportion of data pages are recorded in the hot data table, and the total amount depends on the number of LRU list and the group size, i.e., $N*K$. Thus, our scheme usually requires a very small memory consumption, so it can be deployed at different system levels and can also be included in a large-scale storage systems.

---

**Algorithm 1. GLRU**

---

**Input:** lpn of a data page;
**Ensure:** the hotness of the data;
 1: Determine the group G associated to the data by hashing lpn;
 2: **if** lpn exists in G **then**
 3:    increase the Counter by one;
 4:    adjust the position of the items in G to maintain the LRU property;
 5:    **if** Counter $\geq$ Threshold **then**
 6:       **return** HOT;
 7:    **else**
 8:       **return** COLD;
 9:    **end if**
10: **else**
11:    search the items in G from tail to head;
12:    **if** an item whose Counter is zero exists **then**
13:       insert an item with the lpn in the head;
14:       set the Counter to one;
15:    **else if** the probability test passed **then**
16:       evict the last item in G;
17:       insert an item with the lpn in the head;
18:       set the Counter to one;
19:    **end if**
20:    **return** COLD;
21: **end if**

---

# 3   Implementation on SSDs

In this section, we take SSDs as an application example of GLRU. In particular, we deploy GLRU in the software layer inside SSDs, i.e., the flash translation layer, and then study the effectiveness of GLRU in reducing the GC cost of SSDs. In the following, we first provide the background on SSDs, then present the implementation details of GLRU on SSDs and justify the parameter settings.

## 3.1   Background on SSDs

Compared to traditional hard-disk drives (HDDs), flash-based solid-state drives (SSDs) have many technical advantages, such as higher I/O performance, better power efficiency, less noise and stronger shock resistance, etc. Although SSDs expose the same block I/O interface as HDDs, the internal architecture of SSDs is significantly different. Specifically, data on SSDs is organized into blocks, each of which contains a fixed number of pages. There are three basic operations for SSDs: *read, write and erase*. Reads and writes are performed on a page unit, while erase operates are on a block unit. At any time, a page is either in the *clean, valid* or *invalid* state. A page can be read whenever it is in the valid state, while it can only be written when it is in the clean state. Hence, when update data, SSDs use *out-of-place* updating approach which first writes data to a new clean page and then marks the previous page as *invalid*. Clearly, this approach necessitates a cleaning mechanism, named *garbage collection* (GC), to reclaim the space of invalid pages. Precisely, GC process first selects a victim block according to a certain GC algorithm, then migrates the valid pages in the block to a different clean block, and finally erases the victim block. To support the out-of-place overwrite and GC, SSDs implement a software layer in the controller, which is called *flash translation layer* (FTL). FTL also provides other functionalities like wear-leveling and bad block management, etc.

We note that GC introduces additional writes to SSDs, which are called GC cost, as it must move valid pages to other places before erasing a block. Evenworse, due to the data skewness of real-world workloads, i.e., some data is frequently updated (i.e., hot), while others are rarely or never updated (i.e., cold), the problem of GC cost is further aggregated. To view this problem, suppose that hot data and cold data are not differentiated and stored together, then we can imagine that cold data may be scattered in all flash blocks and must be moved around frequently during GC, and this finally introduces a large GC cost. It is a consensus that seperating hot and cold data should greatly improve the cleaning performance of SSDs [7,15,16]. To achieve this, an efficient online hot identification algorithm is necessary. Therefore, in this paper, we take SSDs as an application example of our hot data identification scheme by implementing it in the FTL of SSDs so as to study its effectiveness and efficiency. In the following subsection, we present the implementation details, and we show the evaluation results in Sect. 4.2.

## 3.2   Implementation Details of GLRU on SSDs

We implement GLRU in the FTL of SSDs. In our implementation, we first add a tier value into the block metadata. The tier value is denoted by an integer (e.g., 0, 1, $\cdots$) and it represents the hotness of a block. In particular, 0 means that this block is a cold block, and 1 means that it is hot (or warm in a multi-tier implementation of GLRU). We initialize the tier value of all blocks in an SSD as 0, and it implies that all blocks are considered to be cold at the beginning. Then we always maintain several active blocks with different tier values. When a page write is issued to the FTL, it will be written into an active block according to the identification results of GLRU. If the active block is full, then a clean block will be allocated from the free block pool and the tier information of the clean block will be set as the tier value of the last active block. At last, when a victim block is selected for GC, its tier value will be reset as 0 and all valid pages will be moved to an active block whose tier value is 0.

Note that as the RAM size and CPU resources is limited for SSDs, the number of LRU list and group size in GLRU can not be set as too large. We implement our GLRU with $K = 128$ and $N = 8$ in the FTL, so the memory consumption is just 5 KB. To gain better performance, we can increase the value of $K$, but the consumed memory space should be limited according to the RAM size of SSDs. Fortunately, if GLRU is implemented at the file system layer, we can set a larger $K$ and $N$, as more RAM and CPU cost are allowed.

# 4   Performance Evaluation

In this section, we conduct extensive simulations to show the effectiveness and efficiency of our proposed hot data identification scheme GLRU. We first present the evaluation setups we used in this paper, including the description of workloads, the configuration of SSDs, and the identification schemes we considered for performance comparison. We then show the identification accuracy, computational cost, and the effectiveness in reducing SSD GC cost of our scheme. At last, we study the impact of various parameter settings, including the group size, decay period and eviction probability.

## 4.1   Evaluation Setup

**Workloads.** In the evaluation, we consider the following four real-world workload traces which are all write dominant as read has no impact on SSD GC performance.

- **Financial** [17]: It is a block I/O trace collected from an On-Line Transaction Processing(OLTP) application that runs at a financial institution.
- **Webmail, Online, Webmail+Online** [18]: The first two traces depict workloads of a mail server and a course management system in a university. Webmail+Online is just the combination of Webmail and Online.

**Table 1.** Statistics of different I/O workloads.

| Trace | Total # of requests | Write ratio | # of page writes | # of unique page writes | Working set | Proportion of accessed pages |
|---|---|---|---|---|---|---|
| Financial | 4376243 | 77.8 % | 5266099 | 118745 | 4 GB | 11.3 % |
| Online | 5700499 | 73.9 % | 4211806 | 69142 | 8 GB | 3.3 % |
| Webmail | 7795815 | 81.9 % | 6381985 | 218969 | 18 GB | 4.6 % |
| Webmail+Online | 13496314 | 78.5 % | 10593791 | 249026 | 18GB | 5.3 % |

In the evaluation, we set the page size of SSDs as 4 KB, and align all the requests to be a multiple of the page size. Table 1 shows the statistics of the four traces. The size of the working set denotes the capacity of the logical address space of each trace, and it is computed by multiplying the largest logical page number with the page size. The numbers in the table are rounded to multiple gigabytes. The proportion of accessed pages is computed by dividing the working set size by the number of unique page writes, and it actually denotes the proportion of logical pages that are accessed at least once. We see that most write requests only access a very small portion of the logical space for all traces. In other words, all the traces present high *data locality*. We point out that in the Financial trace, the requests with the application-specific unit numbers ASU1, ASU3 and ASU5 are ignored as they cause a very large working set size and so require a very long time to run simulations.

**SSD Configuration.** To configure SSDs, we set the page size as 4 KB, and set the number of pages in each block as 128. We preserve 5 % of flash pages for GC. That is, the number of logical pages is only 95 % of the physical pages. We set the GC threshold as 1 %, so GC will be triggered whenever the number of clean pages drops below 1 % of total pages. For other timing parameters, we use the default setting in the simulator. We point out that although an SSD contains several flash chips, they typically operate independently with their own I/O channels and perform GC independently of other flash chips. Thus, when we evaluate the GC performance under a given workload, we set the number of chips in an SSD as one so as to preserve the workload statistics. We configure the SSD capacity according to the working set size of each trace, that is, we try to use a small-scale SSD for simulation as long as it is able to handle all write requests so as to save the simulation time.

**Identification Schemes.** In the evaluation, we consider four different hot data identification schemes and compare their performance.

- **DAMS**: It is an ideal identification scheme which assumes an infinite memory space and uses a direct address counting method. In particular, it can maintain a counter for each lpn to record the total number of writes to the lpn. A page is

**Table 2.** Parameters of GLRU & DAMS

| Parameter | GLRU | DAMS |
|---|---|---|
| # of groups | 128 | N/A |
| Group size | 8 | N/A |
| Threshold | 4 | 4 |
| Decay period | 4096 | 4096 |
| Memory space | 5 KB | N/A |

**Table 3.** Parameters of MBF & MHF

| Parameter | MBF | MHF |
|---|---|---|
| Bloom filter size | $2^{11}$ | $2^{12}$ |
| # of bloom filters | 4 | 1 |
| Decay period | $2^9$ | $2^{12}$ |
| # of hash function | 2 | 2 |
| Threshold | 4 | 4 |
| Memory space | 1 KB | 2 KB |

then identified as hot if and only if its counter is greater than or equal to a pre-defined threshold, and the counters also decay periodically by halving their values so as to simulate the workload dynamics. The parameters of threshold and decay period are shown in Table 2. Note that DAMS is an extension of the direct address method (hereafter, refer to DAM) [4] by taking a series of sequential writes as a single one, and DAM is also taken as a baseline algorithm for performance comparison in [4].

- **GLRU**: This is the scheme we proposed in this paper, and its parameter settings are stated in Table 2.
- **MHF and MBF**: These are two state-of-the-art hot data classification schemes which are developed based on hash functions and bloom filters, respectively. In particular, MHF refers to the multiple hash function scheme developed in [4], and MBF refers to the multiple bloom filter-based scheme developed in [11]. The parameters of the two schemes are shown in Table 3.

### 4.2    Evaluation Results

**Identification Accuracy.** In this paper, we take the ideal scheme DAMS as a baseline to show the identification accuracy of our scheme. In particular, we compare our scheme with the DAMS *hot ratio* which is defined as the ratio of identified hot pages over all page writes. Since DAMS assumes to know all information in advance, the hot ratio derived with this scheme can be viewed as the optimal solution. However, our scheme may drop data when the LRU list is full, so miss detection of hot data may happen. Therefore, we compare our scheme with the DAMS hot ratio to show its identification accuracy. Intuitively, the more similar results our scheme produces with DAMS, the more accurate our scheme is. Figure 3 shows the hot ratio of DAMS and GLRU under different workloads. In this evaluation, the hot ratio is measured by counting the number of pages identified as hot during a specified time duration, and precisely, the period of handling 300 K write requests. We set the X-axis as the number of write requests to display the hot ratio during different time duration. To show the impact of memory space on our scheme, we conduct the evaluations of GLRU by setting the number of groups as 128 and 256, respectively. Evaluation results

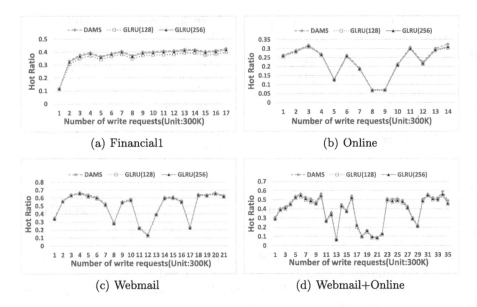

(a) Financial1

(b) Online

(c) Webmail

(d) Webmail+Online

**Fig. 3.** Comparison of hot ratio between GLRU and DAMS. Note that DAMS denotes the case of ideal identification, GLRU (128) and GLRU (256) denote the GLRU scheme with 128 and 256 groups, respectively.

show that the hot ratio of GLRU (128) is very close to that of DAMS, and the difference is at most 4.4 % in all cases. That is, our scheme achieves almost the same identification performance as the ideal scheme which assumes an infinite memory space. Besides, GLRU(256) slightly outperforms GLRU (128), especially under the Financial1 trace as shown in Fig. 3(a), mainly because it uses more LRU lists, while it also consumes more memory space.

**Computational Cost.** Note that identifying whether a data page is hot or not requires to check its metadata and examine its write count, and this lookup process inevitably introduces computational cost, and it may finally reduce the system throughput. Thus, we compare the computational cost of our scheme with two existing schemes, i.e., MHF and MBF, by using the metric called *the average CPU cycles per operation*. Precisely, we feed 100 K write requests from the Online trace to the simulator, and measure the average CPU cycles costed per identification operation. Note that each operation determines whether a page is hot or not. For comparison, we consider two variants of our scheme, GLRU_NS and GLRU without/with exploiting spatial locality. Precisely, in GLRU, we simply return the identification result of the last request when handling sequential requests (see Sect. 2.1) so that the computational cost can be reduced. We conduct this evaluation on a commodity computer attached with Intel core i3 CPU 550 (4*3.20 GHZ) and 2 GB RAM with Ubuntu 12.04 being installed. We measure the number of CPU cycles required for each identification operation by using the RDTSC instruction with limiting the process in a particular core. As shown in Fig. 4, the GLRU_NS scheme requires much fewer CPU cycles than MBF, but slightly more than MHF. However, if spatial locality is further taken into consideration, i.e., our GLRU scheme, the required CPU cycles get significantly reduced, and the reduction is up to 55.6 % even compared to MHF.

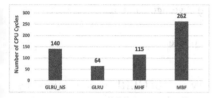

**Fig. 4.** Average computational cost per identification operation.

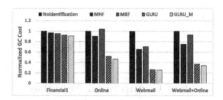

**Fig. 5.** GC cost.

**GC Cost.** In this simulation, we evaluate the efficiency of our scheme in reducing the GC cost of SSDs, which is measured as the number of pages moved in GC process. For comparison, we also deploy the other two hot data identification schemes MHF and MBF in FTL, and compare the GC cost of SSDs with/without hot data identification. In particular, we take case without hot data identification as the baseline, and normalize the GC cost in this case as one. Clearly, the smaller the GC cost is, the higher performance the SSD can achieve. To further verify the scalability of GLRU, we also deploy a multi-tier classification scheme, named GLRU_M, by setting two thresholds, i.e., 2 and 4, respectively. From Fig. 5, we can see that incorporating hot data identification into FTL indeed improves the GC performance of SSDs, as the normalized cost is always smaller than that in the case where hot data identification schemes are not deployed. Moreover, our proposed scheme GLRU outperforms MBF and MHF under all workloads. In particular, the reduction of GC cost is up to 73.1 % under **Webmail** workload. Specially, GLRU_M performs slightly better than GLRU, which suggests that we may further improve the GC performance by classifying data in a finer grain. We note that the reduction of GC cost under the Financial1 trace is very small for all schemes, including GLRU. The main reason is that Financial1 trace is random write dominated, i.e., different data pages have a similar hotness, so the benefit of separating hot/cold data is limited.

### 4.3   Impact of System Parameters

In this subsection, we study the impact of various parameter settings on the performance of GLRU, including the impact of group size, decay period, and the rate of evicting items from a LRU list.

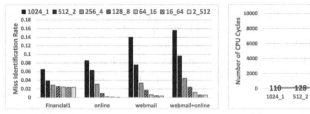
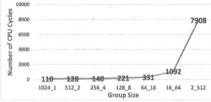

(a) Miss identification rate.    (b) Average computational cost.

**Fig. 6.** Impact of group size.

**Impact of Group Size.** Note that the memory cost of GLRU is determined by the size of the hot data table, which can be computed by multiplying the number of groups with the number of items in each group (i.e., the group size). Thus, for a given memory space, the size of the hot data table is also fixed. However, different settings of the number of groups and group size may influence both the identification accuracy and computational cost. To study their impact, we first fix the size of hot data table as 1024, and then vary the group size from 1 to 512. We characterize the identification accuracy with the difference of hot ratios between GLRU and DAMS, which is called *miss identification rate*, and quantify the computational cost with the average CPU cycles per identification operation. The evaluation results are shown in Fig. 6(a) and (b), respectively. In the figures, we use a number pair like $x\_y$ to denote a specific setting where $x$ denotes the number of groups and $y$ denotes the group size. From the figures, we can see that when the group size is small (e.g., one), GLRU may miss identifying some hot data, and the rate can be up to 16 %. As the group size increases, the miss identification rate decreases, and it can finally achieve a similar performance as the ideal identification scheme DAMS. However, the computational cost also increases as the group size increases, mainly because the lookup time increases as the LRU list contains more items. Clearly, there exists a trade-off between the identification accuracy and the computational cost. Considering that the computational cost of GLRU with the group size being equal to four or eight is very close to that of the MBF scheme, and the identification accuracy is also quite good under this setting, e.g., it is only less than 4.4 %, so we suggest to set the group size of GLRU as four or eight by default.

**Impact of Decay Period.** How to find an appropriate decay period can be regarded as a significant issue in the hot data identification scheme. For MHF and MBF, they set the decay period $D$ based on a formula, $D \leq M/(1 - R)$, where $M$ and $R$ correspond to the bloom filter size and the average ratio of hot data in a workload, respectively. However, since $R$ cannot be known in priori, it is hard to predict a good decay period for a real-world workload. In particular, if the decay period is not suitable for a workload, then the schemes of MHF and MBF will produce a high false identification rate, and in this case, incorporating these schemes in SSD cannot improve the GC performance, but may make the GC performance even worse. To study the impact of decay period on the performance of our scheme, we show the GC cost of SSDs under our scheme with the decay period varying from 2048 to 16384. Figure 7 shows the results. Note that the GC cost under the setting of 4096 is normalized as one for ease of comparison. We can see that our scheme is not sensitive to the decay period as it does not introduce flash identification. Based on this property, we can easily set a fixed decay period for different workloads, e.g., the decay period is set as 4096 in our evaluations by default.

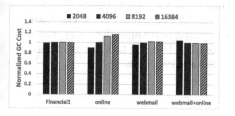    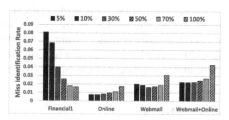

Fig. 7. Impact of decay period.          Fig. 8. Impact of eviction probability.

**Impact of Eviction Probability.** As stated in Sect. 2.2, in GLRU, when the LRU list is full and a new data item comes, we only evict an old data item with a certain probability if the write count of all items in the LRU list are greater than one. We call this probability *eviction probability*, and study its impact on the identification accuracy in this simulation. The rationale of this probabilistic eviction is that the newly arrived data may be cold as it has only received one update. Clearly, this probabilistic policy saves the computational cost, but it may miss identifying some hot data and reduce the identification accuracy. To study the impact of the eviction probability, we vary it from 0.05 to 1, and Fig. 8 shows the identification accuracy quantified by the miss identification rate. We can see that the difference is at most 0.08 under all settings, that is, GLRU only miss identifying less than 8 % of hot data. Furthermore, it is acceptable to set the eviction probability as 0.5 by default as it offers a good identification accuracy for all workloads(e.g., the miss identification rate is at most 0.025) and also saves computational cost at the same time.

# 5   Conclusion and Future Work

In this paper, we proposed a new hot data identification scheme with a group of LRU lists. Based on these LRU lists, we identify a data as hot if it exists in a LRU list with write count being greater than or equal to some pre-defined threshold. Benefit from the grouping-based data management, the size of each LRU list can be small, so our scheme enjoys a small memory space and low computational cost. To validate the effectiveness of our scheme, we further deploy it in the FTL of SSDs, and simulation results show that our scheme can help reduce the GC cost of SSDs efficiently. Comparing to two existing hot data identification schemes, MHF and MBF, our scheme can further help reduce the GC cost, and only incurs lower computational cost. Furthermore, our scheme is also insensitive to various system parameters, and can be easily deployed at different system levels.

In the future, we plan to extend our scheme to identify hot data at a finer-grained level by dividing time into multiple time slices and applying our scheme in each time slice with a self-adaptive parameter adjustment so as to address the large dynamics of workloads.

**Acknowledgments.** This work is supported in part by National Nature Science Foundation of China under Grant No. 61379038 and No. 61303048, Anhui Provincial Natural Science Foundation under Grant No. 1508085SQF214, and Guangdong Key Laboratory of Popular High Performance Computers and Shenzhen Key Laboratory of Service Computing and Applications under Grant No. SZUGDPHPCL2014.

# References

1. Gomez, M.E., Santonja, V.: Characterizing temporal locality in I/O workload. In: Proeedings of SPECTS (2002)
2. Lee, S.W., Moon, B.: Design of flash-based DBMS: an in-page logging approach. In: Proceedings of the 2007 ACM SIGMOD (2007)
3. Roselli, D.S., Lorch, J.R., Anderson, T.E., et al.: A comparison of file system workloads. In: Proceedings of USENIX ATC, General Track (2000)
4. Hsieh, J.W., Kuo, T.W., Chang, L.P.: Efficient identification of hot data for flash memory storage systems. ACM TOS **2**(1), 22–40 (2006)
5. Miranda, A., Cortes, T.: CRAID: online RAID upgrades using dynamic hot data reorganization. In: Proceedings of USENIX FAST (2014)
6. Lee, H.S., Yun, H.S., Lee, D.H.: HFTL: hybrid flash translation layer based on hot data identification for flash memory. IEEE Trans. Consum. Electron. **55**(4), 2005–2011 (2009)
7. Li, Y., Lee, P.P., Lui, J.C., Xu, Y.: Impact of data locality on garbage collection in SSDs: a general analytical study. In: Proceedings of ACM/SPEC ICPE (2015)
8. Rosenblum, M., Ousterhout, J.K.: The design and implementation of a log-structured file system. ACM TOCS **10**(1), 26–52 (1992)
9. Chiang, M.L., Lee, P.C., Chang, R.C.: Managing flash memory in personal communication devices. In: Proceedings of ISCE (1997)
10. Chang, L.P., Kuo, T.W.: An adaptive striping architecture for flash memory storage systems of embedded systems. In: Proceedings of RTAS (2002)
11. Park, D., Du, D.H.: Hot data identification for flash-based storage systems using multiple bloom filters. In: Proceedings of MSST (2011)
12. Bloom, B.H.: Space/time trade-offs in hash coding with allowable errors. Commun. ACM **13**(7), 422–426 (1970)
13. Agrawal, N., Prabhakaran, V., Wobber, T., Davis, J.D., Manasse, M.S., Panigrahy, R.: Design tradeoffs for SSD performance. In: Proceedings of USENIX ATC (2008)
14. John, B., Jiri, S., Steve, S., Greg, G.: The Disksim simulation environment (v4.0) (2008). http://www.pdl.cmu.edu/DiskSim/
15. Van Houdt, B.: Performance of garbage collection algorithms for flash-based solid state drives with hot/cold data. Perform. Eval. **70**(10), 692–703 (2013)

16. Yang, Y., Zhu, J.: Analytical modeling of garbage collection algorithms in hotness-aware flash-based solid state drives. In: Proceedings of MSST (2014)
17. Storage Performance Council (2002). http://traces.cs.umass.edu/index.php/Storage/Storage
18. Verma, A., Koller, R., Useche, L., Rangaswami, R.: SRCMap: energy proportional storage using dynamic consolidation. In: Proceedings of USENIX FAST, vol. 10, pp. 267–280 (2010)

# iPLAR: Towards Interactive Programming with Parallel Linear Algebra in R

Zhaokang Wang, Shiqing Fan, Rong Gu, Chunfeng Yuan, and Yihua Huang[(✉)]

National Key Laboratory for Novel Software Technology,
Collaborative Innovation Center of Novel Software Technology
and Industrialization, Nanjing University, Nanjing 210023, China
{wangzhaokang,fanshiqing,gurong}@smail.nju.edu.cn,
{cfyuan,yhuang}@nju.edu.cn

**Abstract.** R is a widely-used statistical programming language in the data science community. However, in the big data era, R faces the challenges from large scale data analysis tasks. It lacks the ability of distributed linear algebra computation in its local interactive shell. In this paper, we propose iPLAR, a system that runs in the interactive R environment, wraps the high performance parallel linear algebra library, and provides a group of easy-to-use interfaces. iPLAR adopts the client-server model to uncouple the interactive shell from the ScaLAPACK/MPI distributed computing backend. In addition, it provides R users with a group of parallel-detail-transparent interfaces that are similar to the native R linear algebra interfaces. We evaluate the efficiency of iPLAR with representative basic matrix operations and two widely-used machine learning algorithms. Experimental results show that iPLAR achieves the near-linear data scalability and enhances the interactive processing capability of R to large problem scales.

**Keywords:** Parallel linear algebra · R · MPI · Interactive programming · Big data analysis

## 1 Introduction

In the big data era, more and more data are generated and need to be analyzed every day. This leads to the increasing need for easy-to-use analysis tools [16]. Data analysts use matrix-based linear algebra operations [12] for rapid prototyping of analytic algorithms, including many widely-used machine learning algorithms. In addition, as the process of big data analysis is usually a trial-and-error activity, interactive programming platforms become important for the rapid prototyping. The interactive shells usually come as core components in recent big data analysis systems, such as Apache Spark [13]. We also observe that algorithms that work well on small datasets may fail on big data. Therefore, it is necessary to have the ability to carry out experiments on big data interactively.

© Springer International Publishing Switzerland 2015
G. Wang et al. (Eds.): ICA3PP 2015, Part IV, LNCS 9531, pp. 104–117, 2015.
DOI: 10.1007/978-3-319-27140-8_8

In the current data science software ecosystem, R [15] is a widely-used statistical computing language [8] with a user-friendly interactive shell UI and easy-to-use high-level linear algebra APIs. However, R is initially designed for performing the analysis on a single-node machine. It holds all data in the machine's main memory, which limits the scale of the dataset that R can handle. Moreover, native R is implemented as a single-thread program that cannot utilize the parallelism provided by multi-core CPUs. There exist some solutions to use the existing parallel processing systems in R. Those solutions enable R users to process large scale data via Hadoop (through Ricardo [4]) or Spark (through SparkR [14]). Nevertheless, these solutions lack high-level APIs to support linear algebra operations. Users have to program with complicated Jaql query language (in Ricardo) or RDD APIs (in SparkR) and rewrite existing analytical algorithms with these specific APIs in R. There is a lack of systems that enable big data processing with both interactive computing support and high-level linear algebra APIs in R language.

In this paper, we propose iPLAR (interactive Parallel Linear Algebra in R), a system that runs in the R environment and combines the easy-to-use interactive user interface with the high performance parallel linear algebra library ScaLAPACK. iPLAR adopts the client-server model to uncouple the interactive R shell from the underlying MPI distributed runtime environment. For users, iPLAR provides a group of encapsulated linear algebra APIs that are similar to the native R matrix APIs. With such a platform, users can write parallel analytic algorithms in the same API style as in the native R. This allows users to transport their single-node applications to the distributed platform without needing to know any underlying details on MPI and ScaLAPACK.

We also conducted a series of experiments on basic matrix operations and two real-world algorithms, logistic regression and back propagation neural network, to evaluate the performance of iPLAR. Experimental results show that iPLAR is efficient and achieves near-linear data scalability. Moreover, iPLAR is more scalable than the native R and the out-of-core solution when processing large scale datasets. Based on the empirical performance results, we analyze the advantages and disadvantages of the vectorization programming model which is adopted by R and Matlab, in the big data analysis scenarios.

## 2 Background

### 2.1 R and Vectorization Programming

R is a powerful widely-used scripting language and environment for statistical computing and graphics. In the survey conducted by O'Reilly [8], R language is among the most popular languages in data science community. R supports object oriented programming. iPLAR makes full use of it to override native linear algebra functions and operators of R, so that our system keeps similar APIs to the native matrix class of R.

Similar to Matlab, R suggests its users to use vectorization programming style rather than for-loop based iteration style [10]. The reason is that vectorization operators/functions predefined in R are implemented by FORTRAN or C code. They have much better performance than user-written R code. Vector and matrix are the fundamental data types in R, while scalars in R are actually considered as one-element vectors. A vectorization operator/function on two vectors/matrices is applied in an element-wise manner. For example, the R expression x+1 means adding 1 to each element of the vector/matrix x. Most of vectors/matrices' operators/functions are vectorized in R. In iPLAR, we override those operators/functions to make them work with distributed matrices.

## 2.2    Parallel Linear Algebra Library

The linear algebra computing has been studied for a long time in the high performance computing area. In the single-node environment, there are two main linear algebra libraries, namely BLAS and LAPACK. The former is for basic computing, and the latter is for advanced operations. In the distributed environment, there are corresponding extended libraries. The widely-adopted library is ScaLAPACK (Scalable LAPACK) that extends LAPACK to distributed memory machines.

The pbdR project [11] aims at wrapping those libraries in the R environment. The project consists of a group of R packages. Each package wraps a specific library in the R language. Figure 1 shows the software stack of parallel linear algebra libraries and the corresponding pbdR packages. pbdR makes ScaLAPACK much easier to use in the R environment. The server side of iPLAR is built on top of pbdR packages. In practice, the parallel linear algebra libraries and pbdR packages can only work in batch mode. iPLAR tries to address the interactive usage problem and make the parallel linear algebra computation accessible from the interactive R shell.

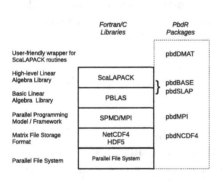

**Fig. 1.** Parallel linear algebra library software stack and corresponding pbdR packages

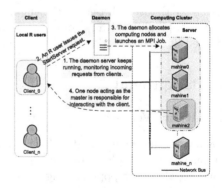

**Fig. 2.** Workflow of iPLAR

# 3   Related Work

There are mainly two approaches responding to the challenges of big data, namely the out-of-core strategy and the distributed computing method. In the out-of-core solution, most of data are stored on disk and the data are loaded into memory only when it is necessary. By this way, it can break the limit of the main memory size. In R there are two groups of out-of-core solutions. The 'ff' package group [1] enables R to process large scale vectors and data frames. However, this solution lacks APIs for the linear algebra computation. The other package group 'bigmemory' [7] provides basic linear algebra APIs for out-of-core matrices (big.matrix) and vectors but it does not support element-wise operators for vectors. In the distributed computing method, packages focus on providing R language with bindings for distributed processing systems. Rmpi [17] and pbdMPI in the pbdR project [11] wrap MPI for the R environment. Ricardo [4] enables R users to perform large scale analysis tasks via Hadoop MapReduce in the R environment. SparkR [14] provides a light-weight frontend to use Spark from R. To take advantage of those packages, users have to rewrite their existing programs in corresponding parallel programming models (SPMD for MPI, Jaql query language for Ricardo and Spark RDD for SparkR), which is a burden that cannot be ignored. Among those packages, the pbdDMAT from pbdR has friendly APIs similar to iPLAR. However, pbdDMAT package must be run in batch mode and users have to know SPMD programming model to write correct programs with pbdDMAT. In summary, the current R ecosystem still lacks packages that support the parallel linear algebra computation from the interactive R shell. iPLAR tries to fill up this vacancy.

Out of the R ecosystem, there are some efforts that try to make parallel linear algebra and interactive shells work together. Netsolve system [2] proposes the idea of making the parallel linear algebra computation as a service on the network, so that interactive clients may access the parallel linear algebra computation services via the network. PPServer [6] goes further into combining Matlab interactive analysis environment with the ScaLAPACK based parallel linear algebra computation engine. It provides near-native-style matrix APIs in Matlab for the distributed linear algebra computation. Matlab *P [3] further improves the work of PPServer. Finally, a commercial and closed source product Star-P [5] borrows ideas from Matlab *P by making the client side independent of a specific programming language and makes it accessible from Matlab, Python and R. iPLAR holds the similar goal and provides the same vectorization programming model as those work in Matlab. It also refers to the proven-to-work client-server architecture from Matlab *P to bridge the gap between the interactive R shell and the MPI runtime. However, the work in Matlab mainly focused on scientific computing. The underlying challenges in the big data analysis scenarios were not analyzed in the previous work. Considering the popularity of R in the data analysis community and the lack of support in the interactive distributed parallel matrix computation, our work is meaningful for the data science community.

# 4 System Design and Implementation

## 4.1 Overview

iPLAR adopts a client-server architecture. The server works on ScaLAPACK and serves as a computational engine. It uses the R socket to communicate with the client and is responsible for storing and operating on distributed matrices. The client on the other side is responsible for interacting with users in the R shell. There also exists a daemon module who is in charge of interacting with the cluster resource management system and launching the server MPI job.

The workflow of iPLAR is shown in Fig. 2. First, a daemon must be in the running state waiting for incoming requests. Next, an R shell user starts iPLAR computing by initializing an iPLAR client and sending a 'start server' request to the daemon. The daemon requests computing resources from the cluster resource manager and then launches an MPI job to start the server. After the server is launched, the process with MPI rank 0 will act as the master. The master on the server side will connect back to the client through the R socket. After the connection is established, the client directly communicates with the master to interactively perform calculations on distributed matrices managed on the server.

## 4.2 Modules and Features

**Server.** The server of iPLAR is actually a linear algebra computational engine for large scale matrices. It stores and conducts operations on distributed dense matrices. In addition, it supports by row, by column, and by block distribution schemes of these matrices. The server implements necessary functions, including creating/removing distributed dense matrices, performing linear algebra operations (relying on ScaLAPACK via pbdDMAT package), transforming between local R matrices on the client side and distributed matrices on the server side, and loading/saving distributed matrices from/to parallel file system/HDFS/Tachyon. Distributed matrices are managed by ddmatrix objects from pbdDMAT package [11] who provides parallel linear algebra functions. Matrix data are generated and stored on the server side in a distributed way. The client only holds a 'handle' to the data and does not store actual data. It makes the computation feasible for datasets that are too large to store for the client.

**Client.** The client module serves as a communication interface for R users to interact with the server. Adopting object oriented programming features of R, we override the matrix operators for the distributed matrices and provide near-native-matrix-style APIs to end users. The interaction with the server is transparent from users. Moreover, users are also kept transparent from ScaLAPACK/MPI programming details on the server side. They can operate on distributed matrix objects just like on ordinary R native matrix objects. All the operations on distributed matrix objects in the client will trigger corresponding operations on the server. Operations are run in a blocked and synchronous way, which means that the client will wait until the computations on the server side complete.

**Table 1.** Operation list of iddmatrix class

| Operation type | APIs |
|---|---|
| Creation & transformation | iddmatrix, as.iddmatrix, as.matrix, etc |
| Access functions | nrow, ncol, length, dim, print, show, etc |
| Logical comparisons | ==, !=, etc |
| Arithmetic reductions | sum, max, min, mean |
| Arithmetic operators | +, -(binary & unary), %*%, *, /, %/%, etc |
| Linear algebra functions | t, solve, inv, svd, lu, exp, etc |
| Data parallel | data_parallel(x,y,f,reduce_op,args) |
| Computation control | StartServer, CloseConnection |
| Other | cbind2, rep, split, apply, etc |

**iddmatrix.** The main APIs on the client side are based on a new R S4 class, namely *iddmatrix* that stands for interactive distributed dense **matrix**. This class encapsulates the *ddmatrix* class provided by pbdDMAT [11] package on the server side and the iddmatrix object serves as a handle to the remote corresponding distributed matrix. An iddmatrix object contains the size and the name information of the remote ddmatrix object. No data but only those information will be passed between the server and the client during communication, unless the user requires to pull/fetch matrices to/from the server side. In this way, iPLAR directly stores large scale matrices in the distributed environment and avoids the main memory limitation on the client side. The operations supported by iddmatrix class are listed in Table 1.

Expressing algorithms totally in distributed matrix operations may bring communication overhead and limit the overall performance of applications (see discussion in Sect. 5.4). Therefore we introduce another API (data_parallel) to support data parallel paradigm in iPLAR. Data parallel paradigm works in the MapReduce way. Algorithms adopting the data_parallel API will be executed in two stages: 1. Each process on the server side trains a local model on the local data of a distributed matrix that contains the training dataset (Map), 2. A global reduce operation is conducted over the local models to get a global model (Reduce). The global model will be returned to the client. Network communication only occurs in the global-reduce stage. Data parallel paradigm is suitable for some machine learning algorithms [9], such as SVM and neural networks, and provides better performance. We recommend users adopt this API if they have performance requirements.

The features of iPLAR are summarized below.

1. *Interactive R session support.* iPLAR supports standard interactive R session, where users can carry out calculations interactively.
2. *Easy-to-use APIs and small migration costs.* iPLAR provides users with a set of R APIs that are similar to standard R matrix APIs. A user with basic R knowledge can start to use iPLAR easily and implement a variety

of analytical algorithms for big data without mastering ScaLAPACK and MPI programming details. An example of iPLAR programs is illustrated in Fig. 3. In our implementation, only one line of code is different from the total 27 lines of native R code. Furthermore, in the BP neural network program, three lines of code are different from the total 60 lines of native R code. The code migration costs from native R to iPLAR is small.

3. *Good performance for big data.* By encapsulating parallel linear algebra library ScaLAPACK, iPLAR takes advantage of the high performance brought by parallel computing. To further improve the performance, iPLAR also provides users with the MapReduce-style `data_parallel` API to explore the parallel potential of some optimization algorithms.

```
train.lr <- function(x, y, iters, stepSize) {
  dims <- dim(x)
  m <- dims[1]
  n <- dims[2]
  intercept <- 0
  theta <- iddmatrix(0,nrow = n, ncol = 1)

  sigmoid <- function(z) {
    1.0 / (1.0 + exp(-z))
  }

  for (i in 1:iters) {
    z <- x %*% theta
    z <- z + intercept
    h <- sigmoid(z)

    #update model
    error <- h - y

    grad <- t(t(error) %*% x)
    theta <- theta - stepSize / sqrt(i) * grad
    error_sum <- sum(error)
    intercept <- intercept- stepSize /
            sqrt(i) * error_sum
  }

  theta
}
```
(a) Code in iPLAR

```
train.lr <- function(x, y, iters, stepSize) {
  dims <- dim(x)
  m <- dims[1]
  n <- dims[2]
  intercept <- 0
  theta <- matrix(0,nrow = n, ncol = 1)

  sigmoid <- function(z) {
    1.0 / (1.0 + exp(-z))
  }

  for (i in 1:iters) {
    z <- x %*% theta
    z <- z + intercept
    h <- sigmoid(z)

    #update model
    error <- h - y

    grad <- t(t(error) %*% x)
    theta <- theta - stepSize / sqrt(i) * grad
    error_sum <- sum(error)
    intercept <- intercept- stepSize /
            sqrt(i) * error_sum
  }

  theta
}
```
(b) Code in R

**Fig. 3.** Logistic Regression training algorithm implemented in iPLAR and native R

## 5    Evaluation

### 5.1    Experiment Setup

All the experiments are conducted in a cluster with 10 nodes connected by 1Gbps Ethernet. Each node has two Xeon Quad 2.4 GHz processors (altogether 8 cores) and 64 GB memory. All the nodes run on RHEL6 operating system with Ext3 file system and R environment version 3.1.1. The versions of the underlying MPI and pbdSLAP (a pbdR package, Netlib ScaLAPACK is carried with pbdSLAP) are OpenMPI 1.8.3 and 0.2-0 respectively. We adopt ATLAS 3.10.2 as the native linear algebra library for both multi-thread and single-thread versions. Moreover, in single-node native R tests we use multi-thread ATLAS to take full use of 8 cores of the node. In iPLAR tests, single-thread version ATLAS is used. In all these cases, except data parallel experiments, block cyclic distribution scheme was taken for all distributed matrices on the server side. In data parallel experiments, row cyclic distribution scheme was taken.

In this section, we mainly compare the performance of iPLAR with the native R in-memory matrix and the out-of-core matrix 'big.matrix' from 'bigmemory' [7] package. We choose them because they provide a similar linear algebra based programming model as iPLAR. Also, they both support the interactive mode of R shell. Other solutions either need re-implementation of original programs (e.g., Ricardo, SparkR, etc.), or only support the batch mode of R (e.g., pbdDMAT).

## 5.2 Performance of Basic Matrix Operations

According to the proportion of pure calculation costs to communication costs during the operations, this section takes three typical operations for scalability tests:

1. Computation intensive operation: element-wise exponential function (exp);
2. Communication intensive operation: matrix transposition (t);
3. Both intensive operation: matrix multiplication (%*%).

**Communication Overhead.** We measured the execution time of a null operation as the pure network communication overhead. The overhead is only 0.07s - 0.11s as we scale the number of MPI ranks from 16 to 80. iPLAR maintains the performance of ScaLAPACK provided by pbdR with negligible overhead.

**Data Scalability.** Data scalability experiments are carried out by scaling the size of the input matrix $A$ (rows × columns) while fixing the number of machines to 10 and the number of MPI ranks to 80. Experimental results are shown in Fig. 4 and we observe that the execution time of all three typical operations from iPLAR grows near-linearly with the increase of input matrix sizes. It indicates that iPLAR achieves good data scalability. Moreover, iPLAR outperforms the native R and big.matrix in the element-wise exponential function exp and the matrix multiplication operation when the scale of the input matrix is enlarged.

**Machine Scalability.** Machine scalability experiments are carried out by scaling the number of computing nodes while fixing the size of input matrix. Experimental results are shown in Fig. 5. It shows that for the computation intensive operation, iPLAR scales well with the increase of computing nodes. While for the computation and communication both intensive operation, the speed-up is common. The result of communication intensive operation is not ideal. Overall, iPLAR achieves the common machine scalability. If an algorithm consists of a lot of matrix transposition and multiplication operations, its machine scalability might be limited by those communication-intensive operations. For this kind of algorithm, if the data parallel paradigm applies to it, we recommend adopting the data_parallel API provided by iPLAR.

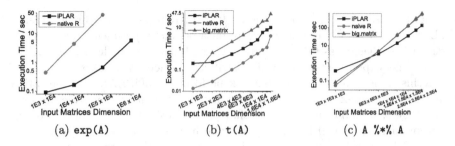

(a) exp(A)          (b) t(A)          (c) A %*% A

**Fig. 4.** Data scalability of three basic matrix operations in iPLAR. (a) computation-intensive case, (b) communication-intensive case, (c) both intensive case. 'big.matrix' does not support exp(A) operation. The vertical and horizontal axis are in log scale.

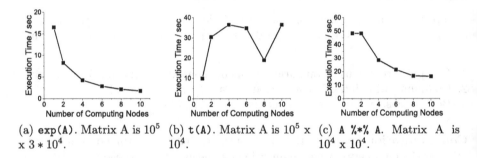

(a) exp(A). Matrix A is $10^5$ x 3 * $10^4$.    (b) t(A). Matrix A is $10^5$ x $10^4$.    (c) A %*% A. Matrix A is $10^4$ x $10^4$.

**Fig. 5.** Machine scalability of three basic matrix operations in iPLAR. (a) computation intensive case, (b) communication intensive case, (c) both intensive case. Eight MPI ranks are launched on each node.

### 5.3    Application Performance Analysis

In this section, the performance of two applications, Logistic Regression and Back Propagation Neural Network, will be evaluated. They are representatives for the linear and non-linear model machine learning algorithms respectively. In all machine scalability experiments, 8 MPI ranks are launched on each node.

**Application 1: Logistic Regression.** We present the experimental results on the gradient descent based Logistic Regression (LR) training algorithm in this subsection. The training data were randomly generated from [0, 1]. Time consumed in one iteration is measured.

From Fig. 6(a) and (b) it can be observed that iPLAR scales near-linearly as the number of training samples increases. When the sample number rises to $5 \times 10^8$, native R and big.matrix fail to return any results while iPLAR scales well. Furthermore, in Fig. 6(b) when the sample number rises to $10^7$, iPLAR achieves better performance (2.4 times faster than big.matrix and 5 times faster than native R), and the implementation with the iPLAR data_parallel API performs even better (3 times faster than iPLAR). More analyses will be presented in Sect. 5.4. As to machine scalability in Fig. 6(c) and (d), when the number of computing nodes increases, the time consumption of one iteration decreases.

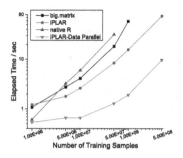

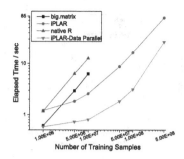

(a) LR Data Scalability. Feature number is 50. When the number of training samples $\geq 10^8$, native R is out of memory. When the number of training samples is $5 \times 10^8$, big.matrix receives the runtime exception.

(b) LR Data Scalability. Feature number is 100. When the number of training samples $> 10^7$, native R is out of memory; big.matrix receives runtime exception.

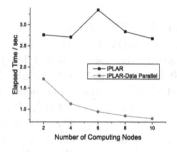

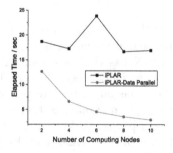

(c) LR Machine Scalability. The number of training samples is $10^7$.

(d) LR Machine Scalability. The number of training samples is $10^8$.

**Fig. 6.** Scalability of Logistic Regression. For data scalability, iPLAR (80 MPI ranks) is compared with the native R and big.matrix. The vertical and horizontal axis are both in log scale in (a)(b). The feature vector length is 100 in (c)(d).

But there is no significant performance gains on the whole. Through analysis, we find that the peaks in the iPLAR curves in Fig. 6(c) and (d) come from the improper automatic processor grid setting adopted by pbdR. Moreover, in the LR algorithm we need to conduct two large-scale matrix-vector multiplication operations who limit the machine scalability of the program. In a word, iPLAR achieves the near-linear data scalability and the common machine scalability. iPLAR can process larger dataset than native R and big.matrix. At the same time, iPLAR data_parallel API achieves both good data and machine scalability.

**Application 2: Back Propagation Neural Network.** This subsection adopts the gradient descent based Back Propagation Neural Network (BPNN) algorithm (without bias) as the benchmark and evaluates the performance of

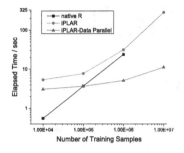

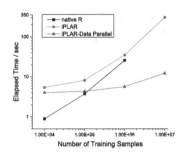

(a) The feature vector length is 50. When the number of training samples is $10^7$, native R is out of memory.

(b) The feature vector length is 100. When the number of training samples is $10^7$, native R is out of memory.

**Fig. 7.** BPNN data scalability. 80 MPI ranks were used. The vertical and horizontal axis are in log scale.

the native R and iPLAR on it. 'Big.matrix' fails in BPNN because it lacks the element-wise multiplication operator (*) for its big.matrix class. The input layer of the BPNN has the same number of neurons as the feature vector length, and the three hidden layers have 80, 100, 30 neurons respectively, while the output layer has one neuron to produce output signals. In the experiment, the time consumption of one iteration is measured. Figure 7 shows that iPLAR and iPLAR data_parallel API both achieve the near-linear data scalability. While in the Fig. 8, the performance of iPLAR has no continuous significant improvement as the number of computing nodes increases. For the BPNN application iPLAR achieves the common machine scalability while iPLAR data_parallel API scales well.

### 5.4    Analysis on Distributed Vectorization Programming

Vectorization programming is the programming model recommended by R [10] and Matlab because of its high performance. iPLAR provides the same programming model, but in an implicit parallel way. The vectorization model has its own advantages over other parallel programming models. The main attraction is its small code migration cost from serial one to parallel one, which makes it suitable for rapid prototyping.

Meanwhile, vectorization model has its inherent deficiencies, which become more severe in machine learning algorithms that take the gradient descent as their optimization methods. It has the following drawbacks:

1. *More memory footprints than for-loop based methods.* Some algorithms can be implemented in both vectorization and for-loop based methods. In the for-loop based method (such as stochastic gradient descent), the algorithm only deals with one sample at a time. The intermediate results during computation are relatively small. However, in implementations that are written

**Table 2.** Five implementations of gradient descent based logistic regression algorithm

| Implementation | Description | Characteristic |
|---|---|---|
| iPLAR | Use iPLAR matrix operation APIs | Global vectorization |
| iPLAR - Data Parallel | Use data_parallel API in iPLAR | Global data parallel, Local vectorization |
| MPI-CR | Translate iPLAR-Data Parallel into C language | Global data parallel, Local vectorization |
| Spark-MLlib | Spark-MLlib's implementation in Scala language | Global data parallel, Local for-loop based |
| MPI-CS | Translate Spark-MLlib into C language | Global data parallel, Local for-loop based |

in global vectorization paradigm, all samples are computed simultaneously. The system needs to hold all intermediate results for all samples. When the number of samples increases in big data analysis tasks, they have large memory footprints. In Fig. 8, when the number of nodes equals 2, iPLAR failed due to the out of memory error caused by the large intermediate results. In the same scenario, iPLAR data_parallel API ran smoothly.

2. *Nontrivial communication overhead.* Many machine learning algorithms can be parallelized in data parallel paradigm (such as logistic regression and BPNN). In data parallel paradigm, the communication cost in each iteration is limited by the global model size. However, in vectorization model, there will be global matrix transposition and multiplication operations as illustrated in Fig. 3. These operations involve global communications which can be avoided in data parallel paradigm. The communication overhead limits the machine scalability of iPLAR. As shown in Fig. 6(c) and (d) and Fig. 8, the machine scalability of the iPLAR data_parallel implementations is much better than global vectorization implementations.

To further verify this, we have implemented the gradient descent based LR training algorithm in 5 different ways that are described in Table 2. Those implementations can be divided into three groups: 1. Global vectorization computing (iPLAR); 2. Global data parallel, local vectorization computing (iPLAR-Data Parallel, MPI-CR); 3. Global data parallel, local for-loop based computing (Spark-MLlib, MPI-CS). iPLAR and iPLAR-Data Parallel were run in R interpreter. Spark-MLlib was run in JVM. MPI-CR and MPI-CS were compiled to native programs. They were all run in an 11-node cluster with 88 MPI ranks or Spark partitions. Two random-generated datasets were used and training sample numbers were $10^7$ and $10^8$. The feature vector length was 100 in both datasets.

All five implementations have the same amount of computation costs, but they have different communication costs and memory footprints. In Fig. 9, iPLAR gets the worst performance due to its largest memory footprints

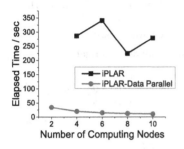

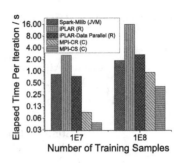

**Fig. 8.** BPNN machine scalability. The number of training samples is $10^7$. The feature vector length is 50. When the node number is 2, iPLAR is out of memory.

**Fig. 9.** Performance comparison on logistic regression model training algorithm. The vertical axis is in log scale.

and communication costs. All data parallel methods perform better than iPLAR. For iPLAR-Data Parallel and Spark-MLlib that were run in R interpreter or JVM, their performance is competitive. The implementations that have the best performance, i.e. MPI-CR and MPI-CS, are both C implementations. Between the two C implementations, for-loop based solution MPI-CS has better performance. It is about 2x faster than MPI-CR. The for-loop based implementations require less memory and are cache friendlier, therefore they have better performance. In summary, the overhead of global vectorization model is nontrivial, and for-loop based implementation is more suitable for the gradient descent algorithm. Considering the advantage of small code migration cost, iPLAR is more suitable for prototyping tests rather than for the production environment. Re-implementation of algorithms in iPLAR `data_parallel` API or in other parallel programming frameworks may be a better choice for production code.

## 6   Conclusion and Future Work

We designed and implemented a system named iPLAR, which combines the interactive R environment and parallel high performance linear algebra library together. iPLAR achieves the transparent parallel programming usability and provides end users with near-native-matrix-style APIs. iPLAR can enhance the processing capability of R to a larger problem scale. In a 10-node cluster, with the help of iPLAR, R can process 10 times more data than native R. Moreover, iPLAR achieves near-linear data scalability. iPLAR `data_parallel` API that further explores the parallel potential of many data analysis algorithms achieves near-linear data scalability and good machine scalability. In the future work, we intend to add more algorithm level APIs to iPLAR. By all, we wish to make iPLAR more usable in the production environment.

**Acknowledgments..** This work is funded in part by China NSF Grants (No. 61572250), Jiangsu Province Industry Support Program (BE2014131) and China NSF Grants (No. 61223003).

# References

1. Adler, D., Glser, C., Nenadic, O., Oehlschlgel, J., Zucchini, W.: ff: memory-efficient storage of large data on disk and fast access functions (2014). https://cran.r-project.org/web/packages/ff/
2. Casanova, H., Dongarra, J.: Netsolve: a network-enabled server for solving computational science problems. Int. J. High Perform. Comput. Appl. **11**(3), 212–223 (1997)
3. Choy, R., Edelman, A.: Parallel matlab: Doing it right. Proc. IEEE **93**(2), 331–341 (2005)
4. Das, S., Sismanis, Y., Beyer, K.S., Gemulla, R., Haas, P.J., McPherson, J.: Ricardo: Integrating R and hadoop. In: Proceedings of the 2010 ACM SIGMOD International Conference on Management of Data SIGMOD 2010, pp. 987–998. ACM, New York (2010)
5. Edelman, A.: The star-P high performance computing platform. In: 2007 IEEE International Conference on Acoustics, Speech and Signal Processing ICASSP 2007, vol. 4, pp. IV-1197–IV-1200. IEEE Press, New York (2007)
6. Husbands, P., Isbell, C.: The parallel problems server: a client-server model for interactive large scale scientific computation. In: Hernández, V., Palma, J.M.L.M., Dongarra, J. (eds.) VECPAR 1998. LNCS, vol. 1573, pp. 156–169. Springer, Heidelberg (1999)
7. Kane, M.J., Emerson, J., Weston, S.: Scalable strategies for computing with massive data. J. Stat. Softw. **55**(14), 1–19 (2013). http://www.jstatsoft.org/v55/i14/
8. King, J., Magoulas, R.: 2014 Data Science Salary Survey. O'Reilly (2014)
9. Li, H., Kadav, A., Kruus, E., Ungureanu, C.: Malt: Distributed data-parallelism for existing ml applications. In: Proceedings of the Tenth European Conference on Computer Systems EuroSys 2015, pp. 3:1–3:16. ACM, New York (2015)
10. Matloff, N.: The Art of R Programming: A Tour of Statistical Software Design. No Starch Press, San Francisco (2011)
11. Ostrouchov, G., Chen, W.C., Schmidt, D., Patel, P.: Programming with big data in R (2012). http://r-pbd.org/
12. Qian, Z., Chen, X., Kang, N., Chen, M., Yu, Y., Moscibroda, T., Zhang, Z.: Madlinq: Large-scale distributed matrix computation for the cloud. In: Proceedings of the 7th ACM European Conference on Computer Systems EuroSys 2012, pp. 197–210. ACM, New York (2012)
13. Apache Spark Project. http://spark.apache.org/
14. SparkR: R frontend for Spark. http://amplab-extras.github.io/SparkR-pkg/
15. Tippmann, S., et al.: Programming tools: Adventures with R. Nature **517**(7532), 109–110 (2015)
16. Venkataraman, S., Bodzsar, E., Roy, I., AuYoung, A., Schreiber, R.S.: Presto: Distributed machine learning and graph processing with sparse matrices. In: Proceedings of the 8th ACM European Conference on Computer Systems EuroSys 2013, pp. 197–210. ACM, New York (2013)
17. Yu, H.: Rmpi: Parallel statistical computing in R. R News **2**(2), 10–14 (2002). http://cran.r-project.org/doc/Rnews/Rnews_2002-2.pdf

# Enhancing I/O Scheduler Performance by Exploiting Internal Parallelism of SSDs

Jiayang Guo[1,2]([✉]), Yimin Hu[1]([✉]), and Bo Mao[2]([✉])

[1] School of Electrical and Computer Engineering, University of Cincinnati,
Cincinnati, USA
guojy@mail.uc.edu, huyg@ucmail.uc.edu
[2] Software School of Xiamen University, Xiamen, China
maobo@xmu.edu.cn

**Abstract.** This paper presents an SSD-based Block I/O Scheduler, short for SBIOS. SBIOS fully exploits the internal parallelism to improve the system performance. It dispatches the read requests to different blocks to make full use of SSD internal parallelism. For write requests, it tries to dispatch write requests to the same block to alleviate the block cross penalty and garbage collection overhead. Moreover, SBIOS introduces the conception of batch processing and separates read and write requests to avoid read write interference. The evaluation results show that compared with other I/O schedulers in the Linux kernel, SBIOS reduces the average response time significantly. Consequently, the performance of the SSD-based storage systems is improved.

**Keywords:** Solid state disk · I/O Scheduler · Internal parallelism · Response time

## 1 Introduction

In the last few years, with the development of Non-volatile technologies, the flash-based solid state disk becomes an essential part of the storage system. As the solid state drive becomes more and more ubiquitous, it is necessary to make full use of the potential of solid state drive to improve the performance of operating system. For instance, Flash-based solid state drives have the potential to alleviate the ever-existing I/O bottleneck problem in data-intensive computing environments, due to their advantages over conventional HDDs in aspects of performance, energy, reliability, etc. [10,14]. However, when comparing to traditional magnetic-based storage devices, the flash-based solid state drives have its own working mechanism. In order to fully dig the potential of flash-based drive in I/O performance, there are many challenges which need to be solved.

Unlike traditional magnetic-based storage devices, the flash-based solid state disk consists of semiconductor chips, which avoid considering the rotational latency in random I/O performance. So, in theory, the speed of flash-based solid state disk is one or two orders magnitude faster than mechanical disks. But,

© Springer International Publishing Switzerland 2015
G. Wang et al. (Eds.): ICA3PP 2015, Part IV, LNCS 9531, pp. 118–130, 2015.
DOI: 10.1007/978-3-319-27140-8_9

in fact, the advancements of flash-based solid state disk are not fully exploited in practice. There are two reasons. First, flash-based solid state disk has poor write performance. Such poor write performance is caused by the erase before write mechanism. In order to overwrite a previous location on SSD, the block which contains this location should be erased first, and then the new data can be written in this location. Second, mechanical disks are still the main storage devices in primary storage system. In the existing operating systems, the software I/O stack is designed for the characteristics of mechanical disks. As a consequence, the potential of flash-based solid state disk are not fully exploited. Some research studies have shown that the existing I/O software layer can cause additional overheads for flash-based solid state disks [3,4].

Due to the limitation of the erase before write mechanism, the read speed of the flash-based solid state disk is not consistent with the write speed of the flash-based solid state disk. Further aggravating the problem is that erasure granularity is much larger (64–256 KB) than the basic I/O granularity (2–8 KB) [12]. It leads to the response time of the read request is faster than the response time of the write request. Meanwhile in the upper layer application, the read operation is synchronous, so the upper layer application needs the response data of read operation to initiate the next step. While the write operation is asynchronous, it will not block the upper layer application. So if we want to fully use the characteristics of flash-based solid state disk in block layer I/O scheduler design, we need to take the read/write speed discrepancy into account.

This paper presents an SSD-based Block I/O scheduler (short for SBIOS) which combines internal device level parallelism with block characteristic of solid state disk to improve the response time. The SBIOS distinguishes the request type and rearranges the request order based on request type. In order to fully use read internal parallelism, we employ the read-preference policy and dispatch the read requests to different block in concurrent workload. For write requests, in order to avoid the block cross penalty which Marcus Dunn et al. mentioned in [6], SBIOS will try to dispatch write requests into the same block. The results of the experiment show that SBIOS improves the system performance, compared with the other I/O schedulers for SSD-based storage systems.

The rest of the paper is organized as follows. Section 2 presents the work related to SBIOS. The design and implementation is detailed in Sect. 3. The evaluation and experiment result are given in Sect. 4. Finally, we conclude the paper in Sect. 5.

## 2    Background

### 2.1    Read Write Interference

In order to design a flash-oriented IO scheduler, the first step is to analyze the characters of Flash. As we all know, the Flash write speed is significantly slower than the Flash read speed. Especially, when a reader continuously performs read requests at the presence of current writer, the reader may suffer an excessive slowdown in read performance. In order to prove this, we use fio tool to measure

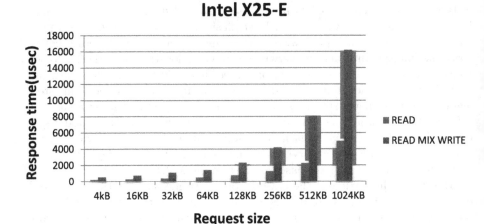

**Fig. 1.** The response time of random reads in different size with writes in concurrent execution on Intel X25-E

the read/write characteristics of flash device. The flash-based storage devices used in these experiments are Intel X25-E 64 GB and Intel 320 200 GB. To access the native characteristics of flash, we omit the memory buffer,write cache and I/O scheduler in our experiment.

Our experiment simulates two processes. One process continually sends read requests to random storage location. The other process continually sends random write requests to flash location. These two processes are concurrent. Meanwhile, Our experiment also covers the request size between 4 kB to 1 MB. Figure 1 illustrates the response time in two case- read and read mix with concurrent write. Comparing with the response time of Read mix with concurrent write, we find that the random read response time can suffer a terrible slowdown when interrupted by the concurrent write request. Especially, when the request sizes become bigger and bigger, and the slowdown effect become more and more serious. For reducing the slowdown effect brought by concurrent write, our paper introduces the conception of batch and uses the design of separating read and write requests. In this way, the problem of read write interference can be elegantly avoided.

## 2.2   Internal Parallelism

The flash-based solid state disk has a lot of internal parallelism characteristics [7,11]. Such internal parallelism characteristics can make single device to achieve close to ten thousand IO per second for Random access, as opposed to nearly two hundreds on traditional hard disk. In order to validate the importance of exploiting the internal parallelism in flash-based solid state disk, we introduce the IOPS metrics to measure the difference between hard disk and solid state disk. In our experiment, we use fio tool to show the IOPS of traditional hard disk

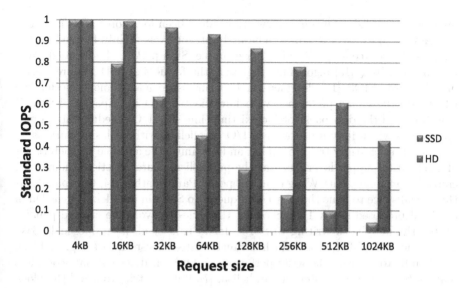

**Fig. 2.** IOPS for 4K-1M random read for Intel X25-E, the base IOPS of HD and SSD are 137 and 4492

and solid state disk. we continually issued different size requests (4 K–1 M) in random read pattern to the devices. In Fig. 2, HD represents WDC WD1600JS 500 GB, SSD represents Intel X25-E. We can see in Fig. 2. The IOPS of HD is only 137, while the IOPS of solid state disk is over than 4000. The IOPS has an over 30 folds gap between traditional hard disk and flash-based solid state disk. Why do such gaps exist? That is because of the different structures of hard ware disk and solid state disk. The traditional hard disks only have one moving head. That means one requests can be served per time. In random access pattern, the traditional hard disk wastes lots of time to rotate the platters and seek the data. That is why it only has 137 IOPS in random read pattern. But in solid state disk, the case is totally different. The solid state disk is composed of multiple channels, multiple dies, multiple packages and multiple planes. Each level internal parallelism can serve multiple requests in the same time. Especially, the random read access pattern is the most efficient pattern which can trigger the inter parallelism in flash-based solid state disk. In such a rationale, the over 30 folds gap appeared. Exploiting internal parallelism to enhance the I/O scheduler performance is very important.In our research, we dispatch the read requests to different block to trigger the internal parallelism of solid state disk.

## 3   Related Work

Since the I/O scheduler is designed for HDDs in the operating systems, the popularization of the flash-based SSDs makes the I/O scheduler for SSDs receive much more attention. There is a large body of studies on the I/O scheduler for magnetic hard disks, but only a few studies had been focus on SSDs. They can be classified into two categories. The first category was mainly focused on the fairness of resource usage of SSDs. For example, Stan park et al. proposed FIOS [12] and FlashFQ [13] algorithms that take the fairness of SSD resource usage into account. FIOS [12] designed an I/O time slice management mechanism which combines read preference with fair-oriented I/O anticipation. FlashFQ [13] discussed the drawbacks of the existing time slice I/O scheduler and a new mechanism which fully uses the flash I/O parallelism without losing fairness.

The other category tried to exploit and maximize the advance characteristics of SSDs in the upper layer, such as the parallelism characteristics among flash chips. For example, Hua Wang et al. proposed ParDispather [14] that partitions the logical space to issue the user I/O requests to SSDs in parallel. Marcus Dunn et al. [6] proposed a new I/O scheduler that tries to avoid the created penalty during the new block writing to SSDs. Jaeho Kim et al. [9] proposed IRBW-FIFO and IRBW-FIFO-RP which arrange write-requests into a logical block size bundle to improve the write performance. Our scheduler not only considers making full use of read internal parallelism [7], but also tries to avoid the block cross penalty [6].

Besides the I/O scheduler studies, there are also some researches which have revealed the advance of the flash internal organization and parallel data distribution. For example, Agrawal N et al. [1] described the internal organization of flash and some parallel data design distribution policy inside SSDs. Feng Chen et al. [5] conducted some experiments to reveal the hidden details of flash memory implementation such as unexpected performance degradation caused by the data fragmentation. Yang Hu et al. [7] divided the parallelism of the flash memory into four levels and discussed the priority and advance of these four level internal parallelisms. Based on the above observations, the SBIOS scheduler tries to exploit the internal parallelism from the aspect of I/O scheduler to boost the throughput of user applications for SSD-based storage system.

# 4    System Design and Implementation

In this section, we discuss the system design and implementation of our SBIOS scheduler.

## 4.1    System Architecture

I/O scheduling module is located between block layer and block device layer. It decides the order of the served requests by a certain sorting policy. Figure 3 shows the system overview of SBIOS and its location in the whole I/O subsystem. For the upper level, it treats the requested data entering into I/O scheduling module as inserting the request into a queue, and then the I/O scheduling module will resort the request in the queue by a certain resorting policy. For the lower layer, the request leaving from I/O scheduling module is like the operation of leaving a queue. The I/O scheduling policy in the scheduling module will decide the next

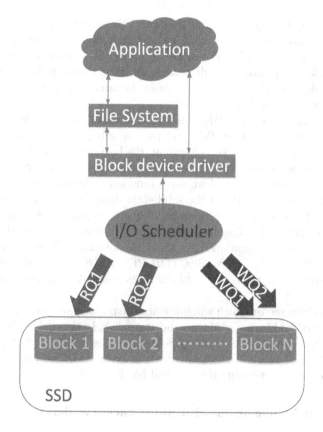

**Fig. 3.** The overview of IO scheduler

request to be served. Figure 3 details the resorting policy which we employ in SBIOS. SBIOS uses type-based queuing. We divide the requests into two types: read and write. We dispatch read requests to different blocks to make full use of the read internal parallelism [7]. For write requests, we try to dispatch them to the same block to avoid the block cross penalty. In this way, SBIOS improves the performance of solid state disk significantly.

## 4.2   Dispatching Method

Our goal of designing SBIOS is to fully use the characteristic of solid state disk, so the rich internal parallelism of solid state disk will be taken into consideration. As we all know, the read performance of solid state disk is amazing. For this reason, we sort the incoming requests based on type, and the read preference policy is employed in our scheduler. According to Yang Hu et al's paper [7], there are four levels of internal parallelism which are mentioned. In our design, we try to fully use the block level read internal parallelism, so the scheduler dispatches the read requests to different logical blocks to trigger the internal read parallelism. To exploit the full characteristic of SSD, not only we take its advantage, but also we need to avoid its drawback. Random write performance is always the bottleneck of SSD, especially for random write operations which cross the blocks [6]. To avoid this drawback, we try to dispatch the write requests to the same block. In this way, we can avoid the large response latency which is brought by crossing the blocks.

During initialization, the SBIOS uses a function to calculate the total capacity of the targeted solid state disk, and then it will find the starting sector of the solid state disk. In Linux kernel system, the basic storage unit is sector. Our design rationale is to make the logical block size which can match the physical block size of solid state disk and we use a function Calculate_Block() to achieve this. With the starting sector of the solid state disk, the Calculate_Block() can maintain the block number of incoming request. Suppose the starting sector of solid state disk is K. The beginning sector of incoming request is G. the logical block number maintained in the Calculate_Block() equals to (G-K)/SECTOR_PER_BLOCK. Here SECTOR_PER_BLOCK variable shows the number of sectors contained in a block. It is calculated at the initialization phase.

One important factor which will influence the performance of SBIOS is determining the physical block size of the solid state disk. In the real world, the block size varied from vendors to vendors. Sometimes the vendor didn't provide us the exact physical block size. However, for a given SSD, we can design some micro-tests on it to determine the physical block size [5].

### 4.3    Request Management with Interfernce Avoidence

There are two data structures which we use to track the state of the incoming requests. One is FIFO-list. We use two FIFO-lists to track the incoming requests. The other structure is red-black tree. The red-black tree is sorting by the logical address of incoming request. Because we use read-preference and small-size preference in our scheduler, this will lead to a starvation problem which some requests may be delayed for a long time. To solve this problem, SBIOS sets a time stamp which defines a time period before which the request should be dispatched into the driver. The SBIOS periodically checks the requests linked in the FIFO-lists to guarantee no request exceeds the time period assigned by time stamp.

According to Stan park et al. [12], there is a read-write interference problem when dispatching read requests and write requests concurrently. To avoid this great performance gap, the SBIOS introduces the batch processing concept into the design. Instead of dispatching one request, the SBIOS dispatches a batch of requests on each turn. Suppose we dispatch a batch of read requests in this turn, for the next turn, the SBIOS will set write as the current direction and dispatch a batch of write requests. If the last direction was set as write, the situation is just the opposite. The direction is changed when there is no pending request in this direction or the number of dispatching request in this direction is beyond the batch value.

In the experiment section, we validate that the response time of SSD is linear with the requests size. To improve the response time of SSD, the SBIOS employs the small size preference policy. When the current direction is set, the SBIOS will find two condition-satisfied requests from the red-black tree. When comparing with their size, the SBIOS will dispatch the smaller request into driver.

## 4.4    Algorithm Process

As mentioned above, in SBIOS, the entire incoming requests are placed in a red-black tree according to their logical block address. They wait in the red-black tree until the SBIOS chooses them to dispatch into the lower layer. Figure 4 shows the algorithm process of choosing a request to dispatch. As it is shown in the picture, in each next request choosing phase, the scheduler checks the request type first. If the request type is read, the scheduler goes ahead to check whether the write request is starved. We do this step because we use the read-preference policy in SBIOS. If we don't set a starved threshold to the write requests, there will be a write starvation problem in our scheduler. After checking the write starvation, the scheduler will determine the request type of the next request. Also we ensure that each request has been assigned a time stamp when it enters the I/O scheduler. If the time stamp is out of date, this request will be chosen as the next request to be served. If not, the scheduler will employ different choosing method according to the request type. If the next served request is set to read,

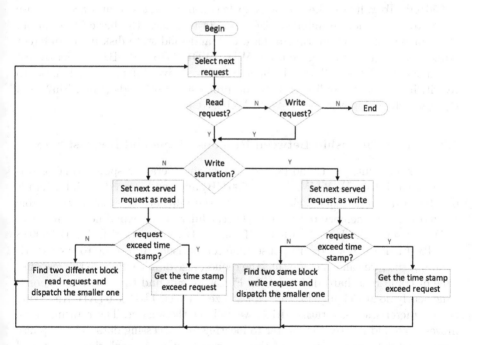

**Fig. 4.** The request processing workflow

the scheduler will find two different block requests from the read-black tree and compare their size, and then dispatch the smaller one to the lower layer. But if the next served requests are set to write, the scheduler will find the two same blocks write requests from the red-black tree and dispatches the smaller one. Finally, it continually dispatches the request pending in the red-black tree until no request pending in the tree.

# 5  Experiment Evaluation and Analysis

In this section, we set up experimental platform to analyze the performance of the SBIOS. These experiments are divided into two parts. One part is to use fio [8] tool to generate different size requests to validate that the solid state disk is linear with the request size. The other part is to run different kinds of traces to the chosen I/O scheduler to demonstrate that the SBIOS improves the response time significantly and makes full use of characteristics of SSD.

## 5.1  Experiment Setup

In this paper, the SBIOS is implemented as a kernel module in Ubuntu 14.04 with kernel 3.13.0. In our experiment, we use Intel core i3 3.00 GHZ processor and 4 GB memory in our machine. For solid state disk, we use Intel X25-E Extreme SATA Solid-State Drive 64 GB (short for Intel X25-E) and its erase block size is 256 KB. To validate the relationship between request size and SSD, we use fio [8] tool to generate different size requests to collect the basic information. We compare the response time of hard disk and solid state disk under different request size. The hard disk we use is WDC WD1600JS 500 GB. In order to test the efficiency of the SBIOS scheduler, we choose five different benchmarks to test it, including two online transaction processing workloads (Fin1, Fin2) and three search engine workloads (Web1,Web2,Web3).

## 5.2  The Relationship Between Response Time and Request Size

In our experiment, we use fio [8] tool to test the average response time of traditional hard disk (WDC WD1600JS 500 GB) and solid state disk (Intel X25-E 64 GB) in different request sizes. To avoid the influence of system, we disable the write cache, memory buffer and I/O scheduler in our experiments. In Fig. 5, SSD represents the Intel X25-E 64 GB, and HD represents WDC WD 1600JS 500 GB. Figure 5 shows the response time comparison. According to the experimental result, we can conclude that the request size didn't influence the response time of traditional hard disk a lot. In Fig. 5, we can find that the HD response time nearly no any change for the request size between 4 KB to 64 KB. Analyzing the characteristics of rotating drive, we will get the answer. The rotating drive moves head and rotates the platter to locating and accessing data. The response time of rotating drive consists of three parts. That is the seek time, rotational latency and data transfer time. When the request size is so small, the seek time

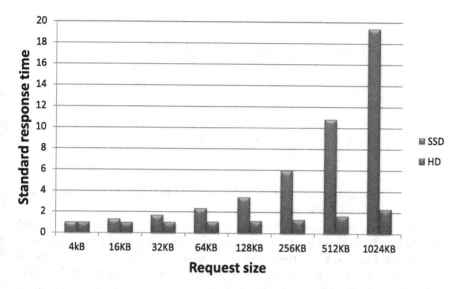

**Fig. 5.** The standard response time comparison between SSD and HD in different request size (4 KB–1 MB), the base response time of HD and SSD are 7.4 ms and 0.3412 ms.

and rotational latency occupied the main parts of the response time. When the request size becomes more and more large, the data transfer time becomes the most important part of the response time. We can see the trend in Fig. 5. When the request size is larger than 64 KB, the request size will become the main part which relates to response time of rotating drive. In Fig. 5, the standard response time of SSD and HD correspond to its base response time. We use the response time of 4 KB request as the base line for reflecting the relationship between request size and response time.

Meanwhile, we can see in Fig. 5. There is a linear relation between the request size and response time of solid state disk. When the request size becomes larger, the response time becomes slower. The reason for above observation is the different internal structure of solid state disk. Unlike rotating hard drive, the solid state disk finishes the fundamental operation (read and write) by circuit signal transmission. So we don't need to take the seek time and rotation latency into consideration. The data transfer time is the main part of the response time of solid state disk. Data transfer time is directly related to the request size. For this reason, there is a linear relationship between request size and the response time of solid state disk.

## 5.3    Performance Results and Analysis

In this section, we run different traces with different I/O schedulers (including CFQ, Deadline, Noop and SBIOS). In our experiments, we didn't compare our SBIOS to AS, because the AS scheduler has been removed from kernel 3.13.0.

**Table 1.** The workload characteristics

| Workload | Request size (byte) | Read (%) | Write (%) |
|----------|---------------------|----------|-----------|
| Fin1 | 512–17116160 | 21.6 | 78.4 |
| Fin2 | 512–262656 | 82.4 | 17.6 |
| Web1 | 512–1137664 | 99.9 | 0.01 |
| Web2 | 8192–32768 | 99.9 | 0.01 |
| Web3 | 512–23674880 | 99.9 | 0.01 |

To validate the efficiency of SBIOS, we choose five traces with different characteristics and compare their system performance.

Table 1 illustrates in detail these five traces. Fin1 and Fin2 are read mix with write workloads. In this kind of trace, read write inference problem may appear, especially for Fin1. In Fin1, read requests only account for 21.6 %. That means read requests have a big probability to be blocked by write requests. Web1, Web2 and Web3 are read-intensive workload. In this case, we need to consider write request starvation problem.

Figure 6 shows the performance results. In order to illustrate the performance clearly, we use standard response time in Y axis. In the experiment, we set the response time of Noop scheduler as the baseline (initialed to 1 in Fig. 6) to compare the efficiency of other I/O schedulers. The response time of Noop scheduler in Fin1, Fin2, Web1, Web2, Web3 are 1.20 ms, 1.45 ms, 0.59 ms, 0.92 ms and 1.07 ms. In Fig. 6, we can get two conclusions. First, except for our SBIOS,

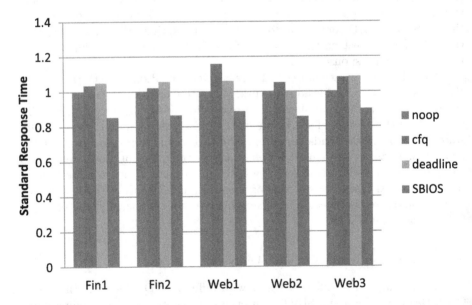

**Fig. 6.** Trace performance comparison under different IO scheduler

Noop scheduler outperforms better than the other scheduler under these five workloads. It validates that the Noop scheduler is the most suitable scheduler for SSD. Second, the SBIOS performs best among these schedulers under the five workloads. For Fin1, Fin2, Web1, Web2, Web3 trace, the SBIOS scheduler reduces the response time of best and worst of other three schedulers by 15 %–18 %, 14 %–18 %, 11 %–23 %, 14 %–18 % and 10 %–17 %. In conclusion, the SBIOS reduces the response time significantly by taking SSD characteristics into consideration.

# 6  Conclusion

In this paper, we proposed a new I/O scheduler SBIOS which makes full use of the characteristics of solid state disk. The SBIOS tries to use rich read internal parallelism provided by SSD and dispatches the read requests to different blocks to trigger the read internal parallelism. For write requests, the SBIOS dispatches them to the same block to avoid block cross penalty. Furthermore, we validate that SSD is sensitive with the request size. In SBIOS, we use the small-size preference design. The experimental results show that SBIOS reduces the response time significantly. In this way, performance of the SSD-based storage systems is improved. According to Bjrling et al. [2], IOPS of SSD will be a bottleneck for current system design. In the future work, we will introduce the IOPS as an important metric for measuring the efficiency of the I/O scheduler.

**Acknowledgments.** This work is supported by the National Natural Science Foundation of China under Grant No. 61100033, No. 61472336 and No. 61402385, National Key Technology R&D Program Foundation of China (No. 2015BAH16F02), Fundamental Research Funds for the Central Universities (No. 20720140515).

# References

1. Agrawal, N., Prabhakaran, V., Wobber, T., Davis, J.D., Manasse, M.S., Panigrahy, R.: Design tradeoffs for SSD performance. In: USENIX Annual Technical Conference, pp. 57–70 (2008)
2. Bjørling, M., Axboe, J., Nellans, D., Bonnet, P.: Linux block IO: introducing multiqueue SSD access on multi-core systems. In: Proceedings of the 6th International Systems and Storage Conference, p. 22. ACM (2013)
3. Caulfield, A.M., De, A., Coburn, J., Mollow, T.I., Gupta, R.K., Swanson, S.: Moneta: a high-performance storage array architecture for next-generation, nonvolatile memories. In: Proceedings of the 2010 43rd Annual IEEE/ACM International Symposium on Microarchitecture, pp. 385–395. IEEE Computer Society (2010)
4. Caulfield, A.M., Mollov, T.I., Eisner, L.A., De, A., Coburn, J., Swanson, S.: Providing safe, user space access to fast, solid state disks. ACM SIGPLAN Not. **47**(4), 387–400 (2012)
5. Chen, F., Koufaty, D.A., Zhang, X.: Understanding intrinsic characteristics and system implications of flash memory based solid state drives. ACM SIGMETRICS Perform. Eval. Rev. **37**, 181–192 (2009)

6. Dunn, P.M.: A new I/O scheduler for solid state devices. Ph.D. thesis, Texas A&M University (2009)
7. Hu, Y., Jiang, H., Feng, D., Tian, L., Luo, H., Zhang, S.: Performance impact and interplay of SSD parallelism through advanced commands, allocation strategy and data granularity. In: Proceedings of the International Conference on Supercomputing, pp. 96–107. ACM (2011)
8. Axboe Jens. fio-2.26 (software package) (2015)
9. Kim, J., Oh, Y., Kim, E., Choi, J., Lee, D., Noh, S.H.: Disk schedulers for solid state drivers. In: Proceedings of the Seventh ACM International Conference on Embedded Software, pp. 295–304. ACM (2009)
10. Mao, B., Jiang, H., Wu, S., Tian, L., Feng, D., Chen, J., Zeng, L.: HPDA: a hybrid parity-based disk array for enhanced perfromance and reliability. ACM Trans. Storage, vol. 8(1), Article 4, Febuary 2012
11. Mao, B., Wu, S.: Exploiting request characteristics and internal parallelism to improve ssd performance. In: Proceedings of the 33rd IEEE International Conference on Computer Design (ICCD 2015), pp. 18–21, New York City, USA, October 2015
12. Park, S., Shen, K.: FIOS: a fair, efficient flash I/O scheduler. In: FAST, p. 13 (2012)
13. Shen, K., Park, S.: FlashFQ: a fair queueing I/O scheduler for flash-based SSDS. In: USENIX Annual Technical Conference, pp. 67–78 (2013)
14. Wang, H., Huang, P., He, S., Zhou, K., Li, C., He, X.: A novel I/O scheduler for SSD with improved performance and lifetime. In: 2013 IEEE 29th Symposium on Mass Storage Systems and Technologies (MSST), pp. 1–5 (2013)

# A Performance and Scalability Analysis of the MPI Based Tools Utilized in a Large Ice Sheet Model Executing in a Multicore Environment

Phillip Dickens[✉]

School of Computing and Information Sciences,
University of Maine, Orono, ME 04426, USA
dickens@umcs.maine.edu

**Abstract.** This paper analyzes the performance and scalability characteristics of both the computational and I/O components of the Parallel Ice Sheet Model (PISM) executing in a multicore supercomputing environment. It examines the impact of multicore technologies on two state-of-the-art parallel I/O systems, both of which are based on the same underlying implementation of the MPI-IO standard, but which exhibit very different performance and scalability characteristics. It also examines these same characteristics for the MPI-based computational engine of the simulation model. One important benefit of studying these three software systems both independently and together is that it exposes a fundamental tradeoff in the ability to provide scalable I/O and scalable computational performance in a multicore environment. This paper also provides what, at least at first glance, appears to be very counter-intuitive performance results. We examine the underlying reasons for such results, and discuss the important insights gained through this examination.

**Keywords:** Parallel ice sheet model · MPI · MPI-IO · Multicore architecture · Parallel I/O · NetCDF

## 1  Introduction

The issue of global climate change is of great interest to scientists and a critical concern of society at large. One important piece of the climate puzzle is how the dynamics of large-scale ice sheets, such as those covering Greenland and Antarctica, will react in response to a changing climate. The Parallel Ice Sheet Model (PISM, [30]), is a widely used parallel simulation model designed to provide researchers with insight into the past, present, and future dynamics of such large-scale ice sheets. As with modeling in other scientific domains, the depth of knowledge that can be gained from such models is largely dependent upon the resolution at which they can be efficiently executed. The problem, however, is that even relatively small increases in the resolution of the ice sheet being modeled results in massive increases in the size of the input and output data sets and in the number of grid points that must be considered by the simulation.

© Springer International Publishing Switzerland 2015
G. Wang et al. (Eds.): ICA3PP 2015, Part IV, LNCS 9531, pp. 131–147, 2015.
DOI: 10.1007/978-3-319-27140-8_10

The tremendous challenges of scaling to higher-resolution models can be seen in Table 1, which shows the computational and I/O demands for three data sets at different resolutions. All of the data sets are for the Greenland ice sheet, and the resolution of the data sets represents the distance between grid points in the simulated ice sheet. Thus, for example, what is termed the G5 km model is a data set with 5 km between each data (or grid) point. As can be seen, moving from the 5 km resolution to the 1 km resolution increases the number of grid points by a factor of 50 (from approximately 34 million to over 1.6 billion), and the size of the output file is increased by a factor of 25 (from 1.1 GB to 28 GB). Thus for PISM to remain an important tool for scientific discovery, it must be able to scale to the data sets that are currently available, and the even higher-resolution data sets that are beginning to come online.

**Table 1.** This table shows the number of grid points in the X, Y, and Z directions for three models, and demonstrates the impact of higher resolution on the computational and I/O requirements of the PISM simulation.

| Model | X | Y | Z | Total grid points | Approximate file size |
|-------|------|------|-----|-------------------|-----------------------|
| G5 km | 301 | 561 | 201 | 33,941,061 | 1.1 GB |
| G2 km | 750 | 1400 | 401 | 421,040,000 | 7.4 GB |
| G1 km | 1501 | 2801 | 401 | 1,685,924,701 | 28 GB |

PISM derives its computational scalability from its use of the Portable Extensible Toolkit for Scientific Computation (PETSc, [1, 2, 29]), which is a widely used library of data structures and routines for scientific models that require partial differential equations for their solutions. PETSc, in turn, derives its scalability by spreading its computation across multiple processing cores and using MPI [24] for inter-process communication. The parallel I/O libraries utilized by PISM are also based on MPI (e.g., PNetCDF [17], parallel HDF5 [28], parallel NetCDF-4 [39]), and are designed to provide scalable I/O performance in much the same way that PETSc provides scalable computational performance: The file *data* is spread across multiple processes, and, in the best case, each process can write its data to *independent* regions of a shared file *concurrently*.

In this paper, we are concerned with the performance and scalability of the MPI-based computational and I/O components of the PISM model. We are approaching the problem from the point of view of high-performance computing: how such technologies are used in real applications, how they perform, how they interact with one another, and whether and/or how such performance can be improved. PISM is an excellent test-bed for this research for three reasons: First, it is a large-scale scientific model that requires high-performance computing technologies for its execution. Second, it is an important ice sheet model that is utilized in a large number of scientific studies (e.g., [4, 5, 13]). Third, it supports multiple I/O libraries via command line arguments making it reasonably simple to compare their relative performance and scalability characteristics within the same underlying MPI environment.

We examine PISM's performance using a relatively low-resolution model of the Antarctic ice sheet at the 10-kilometer resolution, and a high-resolution model of the Greenland ice sheet at the 1-kilometer resolution. This allows us to document and gain insight into those aspects of the simulation that perform well at lower resolutions but do not scale well to the higher resolution models, and to document fundamental tradeoffs between computational and I/O scalability when executing PISM in a multicore supercomputing environment.

We believe this paper makes two important contributions to the high-performance computing community. First, it documents and analyzes the performance and scalability characteristics of three state-of-the-art software systems in a very important real-world scientific model. This allows us to capture not only how such technologies behave in isolation, but also brings to light important tradeoffs between achieving scalable computational performance and scalable I/O performance that could easily be missed in isolated or benchmarking studies. Second, examining the I/O performance holistically, particularly when all are executing on top of the same MPI-IO implementation, produces some very counter-intuitive results. The diagnoses of the underlying causes of these results suggests that there may be a tradeoff between performing collective and independent I/O in multicore systems, which is contrary to the widely held belief that it is always advantageous to perform collective I/O in large-scale scientific applications.

The remainder of the paper is organized as follows. In Sect. 2, we provide background information on the study of large-scale ice sheets in general, and, in Sect. 3, we discuss the computational and parallel I/O libraries utilized by PISM in particular. In Sect. 4, we describe the experimental design and provide our results in Sect. 5. We analyze the experimental results in Sect. 6, and provide our conclusions in Sect. 7.

## 2   Ice Sheet Modeling

Ice sheet modeling is concerned with the laws that govern the ebb and flow of large glaciers on our planet, as well as on alien planets. Glaciers have been shown to have a dramatic influence on the climate of our world, and they contribute to sea-level rise when they melt [5]. The excessively slow speed at which ice sheets move presents a challenge to researchers trying to develop better insight into their behavior. Direct experimentation with ice sheets is, in general, not possible, because it is on the order of years or millennia before changes in the ice may become noticeable. For this reason, researchers are developing computer models that can efficiently simulate the evolution of ice sheets over large time scales.

The extents of a glacier can be measured with remote sensing techniques, so that we may approximate its geometry in a discrete structure. Through geological records and core samples taken from the ice itself, we are able to estimate how the physical extent of the ice has changed over time, thus providing a basis for computational models. These core samples can also provide hints about the climate conditions that accompanied changes in the ice sheet extents, thus providing one basis for explaining the complex relationship between climate and glaciers.

Ice sheet models combine physical flow laws, such as the Shallow Ice Approximation (SIA, [19]), the Shallow Shelf Approximation (SSA, [41]), and the Navier-Stokes equations [14] with observations about the current and historical state of the ice sheet. These observations include measurements of the bedrock topography, ice surface geometry, and ice thickness, all of which may be gathered with remote sensing techniques. Further information can be gathered from core samples taken from the ice itself and from geological records. The SeaRISE project (*Sea-level Response to Ice Sheet Evolution*), has aggregated many of these observations into standardized datasets for the Greenland and Antarctic ice sheets [32], two of which are used in this research.

# 3   PISM

PISM provides a highly flexible and customizable framework for the study of large-scale ice sheets. It provides a hierarchy of shallow shelf balances including the SIA and SSA models, as well as the preferred hybrid 'SSA + SIA' model [31]. It makes available a wide range of models for marine ice physics, ocean calving, and conservation of energy, and the ability to couple PISM with external ocean and atmospheric models [12].

Within PISM, the model takes place in a rectangular computational box that consists of a collection of data points in three dimensions representing the space that encloses the glacier being studied. In each of the **x** and **y** dimensions, the grid points are equally spaced, and have a relatively coarse resolution. The **z** dimension is given a relatively finer resolution than **x** or **y,** and the spacing of grid points along this dimension may vary within a given model allowing for more detail near the base of the ice where driving forces are greatest. Each **x, y** pair represents a single column of ice that is parallel with the force of gravity.

PISM takes the entire computational box and divides it into **n** rectangular sub-grids, where **n** is the number of processes being used for the simulation. It attempts to make the sub-grids as square as possible in the x and **y** dimensions because the calculation of a new value for a given grid point often only depends on the current values of variables at adjacent grid points. Therefore, the degree to which the computation of one sub-grid depends on results from another sub-grid is proportional to the perimeter of local grid, and the square has the minimum perimeter for any rectangle. However, for many computational box sizes and values of **n**, there is no way to evenly distribute the grid points to **n** non-intersecting squares. In such cases, PISM arranges the sub-grids into **r** rows and **c** columns with **n = rc**, with no row being more than one grid point wider than any other row, and no column being more than one grid point taller than any other column.

## 3.1   PISM I/O

Before discussing the I/O libraries utilized in PISM, it is important to first discuss key concepts within parallel I/O in general, and the ROMIO implementation of the MPI-IO standard in particular.

**Parallel I/O.** The I/O requirements of highly data-intensive applications such as PISM can overwhelm the capabilities of even the most sophisticated parallel I/O infrastructure, and generally present the biggest obstacle to obtaining scalable performance. In addition to the sheer *magnitude* of the data being processed, the *I/O access patterns* exhibited by PISM and other scientific applications make it exceedingly difficult to handle such datasets efficiently (e.g., [3, 9, 11, 27]). This is because individual processes in scientific applications tend to make a large number of small I/O requests, making very inefficient use of the parallel I/O subsystem. One reason for this access pattern is that parallel, scientific codes frequently operate on large, multi-dimensional arrays that are distributed across the local memories of the application processes. After a process performs some computation, it will often need to read/write its local piece of the array from/to a common file. If the process's local portion of the array is not stored on disk the same way it is stored in memory, then it will have to make a series of disjointed I/O requests to complete the operation, incurring the high costs of performing I/O across a network on each such request.

However, it has long been recognized that it is often the case that in the aggregate the entire array is being written to or read from the shared file. MPI-IO [26], the I/O component of the MPI standard [24], was developed (in part) to gather and take advantage of such global information. The *collective I/O operations* defined in MPI-IO represent one of the most important techniques through which such global information can be obtained and leveraged. In this approach, all of the processes sharing a file submit their individual requests to the underlying MPI-IO implementation, from which the aggregate I/O request is determined. Based on this global knowledge, the requests can be combined and presented to the file system in a way that makes the most efficient use of the underlying hardware and software parallel I/O infrastructure.

The MPI-IO specification defines a rich and flexible parallel I/O API, but does not specify how the API is to be implemented. It is generally agreed that ROMIO [34–36], developed and maintained at Argonne National Laboratory, is the most widely used implementation of the MPI-IO standard. ROMIO implements collective I/O operations using a technique termed *two-phase I/O* [11, 34]. In the first phase, the processes provide information about their individual I/O requests to ROMIO, which uses this information to create a picture of the aggregate I/O request. In the case of a collective write, ROMIO collects and redistributes the data from individual processes to a set of *aggregator processes*, which perform the I/O operation on behalf of all participating application processes. ROMIO uses the information about the global I/O request to redistribute the data in a way that maximizes the use of the parallel I/O subsystem. In the second phase of the algorithm, the aggregators perform the write to disk collectively.

It is important to note that the implicit assumption underlying optimizations such as two-phase I/O is that it is orders of magnitude cheaper to collect and redistribute data using inter-process communication than it is to perform a large number of disjointed requests to the file system. As will be discussed below, however, this assumption begins to break down in multi-core systems where the additional cost of *intra-node communication* must also be considered.

## 3.2    PISM I/O Libraries

PISM utilizes the software libraries, tools, and data file formats provided by the Network Common Data Form (NetCDF) [39] to handle its I/O requirements. NetCDF is actively developed and maintained by the Unidata Program, whose mission is to support high-performance scientific computing within the atmospheric and related geo-sciences [38]. It defines a set of standardized, *machine-independent* data file formats, an Application Programming Interface (API) for creating and accessing such files, and I/O libraries to provide an implementation of the API. The Unidata Program Center supports and maintains NetCDF interfaces for multiple programming languages including C, C ++, Java, and Fortran [40].

The Common Data Format (CDF) is the traditional file structure associated with NetCDF files. The first version of the Common Data Format, CDF1, also termed the *classic format*, uses 32 bits for both file and variable offsets, limiting the size of both to 4 GB. The CDF2 revision partially corrected this shortfall by using 64-bit file offsets (referred to as *large file support*), which does allow significantly larger files, but still limits the size of a single record variable, for a single record, to 4 GB.

This storage model is not well suited for high-performance computing on large, scientific data sets. The 4 GB limitation on the size of record variables is problematic for PISM, which requires 64-bit offsets for both files and record variables (systems providing 64-bit variable offsets are termed as providing *large variable support*). Another problem is the lack of support for parallel I/O (i.e., concurrent read/write access to shared files), which severely limits the size of data sets that can be processed efficiently. Until fairly recently (2012), PISM only supported the CDF {1,2} data formats, and, as a consequence of these limitations, was unable to simulate the entire Greenland ice sheet at the 1KM resolution

PISM has now added the NetCDF4 I/O library [39], which provides both large-variable and large-file support. It was developed collaboratively by Unidata and the HDF5 Group [37], with the goal of providing an enhanced NetCDF API as a front-end to the HDF5 storage technologies [28]. HDF5, in turn, is actively developed and supported by the HDF Group, and provides a data model, file format, and a set of tools to support large and complex scientific data sets. HDF5 utilizes MPI-IO as the underlying file access mechanism, from which it inherits the ability to provide scalable, *parallel I/O*. Such support is critical for PISM, enabling it to process much larger data sets, in a far more efficient manner, than in the serial I/O approach dictated by the CDF {1,2} formats. HDF5 also provides a number of options (e.g., data chunking and chunk caching [28]), through which the efficiency of parallel I/O operations can be further enhanced. It also enables data sets to be hierarchically organized, and allows multiple, unlimited dimensions. Both NetCDF and HDF5 files are *self-describing*, which means that they maintain enough meta-data to fully describe the structure and meaning of the underlying data.

PISM also supports the Parallel-NetCDF [17] I/O library (termed PNetCDF), which is actively developed and maintained at Argonne National Laboratory and Northwestern University. PNetCDF can provide excellent parallel I/O performance, but does present two challenges for PISM developers. First, it provides parallel support for CDF files only, making it incompatible with the HDF5 storage technologies. Second, it can only scale to very high-resolution data sets when utilizing the CDF5 file format [7], which extends the 64-bit file offsets available in the earlier formats with support for 64-bit variables. Unfortunately, PISM does not support the CDF5 file format because Unidata does not currently support it. This means that PNetCDF can only be used with files that can fit into the CDF{1,2} file formats. While this does provide parallel I/O support, it does not scale to the higher resolution datasets that require large variable support. As with HDF5, PNetCDF inherits its ability to perform parallel I/O though MPI-IO. It is worth noting that the data model provided by the CDF5 format is much simpler, albeit much less powerful, than that provided by HDF5. However, the I/O requirements of PISM are well served by the CDF file structure, and it does not require or make use of the additional features available through HDF5.

In the current version of PISM, the HDF5 library can be accessed directly rather than through the NetCDF4 interface, and this is the approach taken in this research. This is because for reasons that are currently unclear and under investigation, going through the NetCDF4 interface provided extremely poor performance at scale. Also, and based on our preliminary work with PNetCDF (discussed in [10]), we implemented support for the CDF5 file format in PISM so that it could be utilized with the high-resolution data sets that are too big to fit into the CDF{1,2} storage format.

## 4 Experimental Design

All of our experimental work was conducted on Stampede: a supercomputer housed at the Texas Advanced Computing Center at the University of Texas at Austin, which came on-line in February of 2013 [33]. Stampede is a Dell Linux Cluster with 6,400 Dell PowerEdge server nodes, where each node is configured with two 8-core, 64-bit Intel Xeon E5 2680 (Sandy Bridge) processors for a total of 16 cores per node. The processors operate at a rate of 2.7 GHz. Each node provides 32 GBs of memory (2 GBs per core) for a total of 32 GBs. There is also one 61-core Intel Xeon Phi Coprocessor per node, which was not utilized in this research. The operating system on a node is CentOS 6.3 with the 2.6.32 x86_64 Linux kernel. The nodes and file systems are interconnected through a FDR 56 GB Infiniband network of Mellanox switches [23].

Stampede is configured with a 14 Petabyte Lustre parallel file system, which is sub-divided into three global file systems ($WORK, $HOME, and $SCRATCH), all of which are accessible from any node. In this research, we used the $SCRATCH file system, with approximately 8.5 PB of storage and 348 OSTs. We utilized 128 OSTs and a stripe size of 1 MB in all experiments.

This research was based on PISM version 0.6, which utilizes PETSc version 3.4 as its computational engine. The parallel I/O libraries used were HDF5 version 1.8.13 and PNetCDF version 1.3.1. All of these software systems are built on top of the MVA-PICH2.1.9 implementation of the MPI standard. The collective I/O operations defined in MPI-IO were implemented via ROMIO.

## 4.1    Performance Metrics and Timing

PISM execution can be broken down into three phases: initialization, computation, and I/O. In the initialization phase, PISM reads in a configuration file and a file containing model state information. It initializes its internal data structures and distributes the model data across all of the processes participating in the simulation. In the *compute* phase, PISM models the evolution of the ice sheet over time. It carries out the computation in a series of *time steps*, where the length of a time step (i.e., the number of years or days simulated within one time step) is variable depending on current model state. In the output stage, PISM writes the final model state to disk. In this paper, we consider only the compute and output phases since these represent the primary costs of running the simulation.

As noted, we are approaching this research from the point of view of high performance computing rather than as a domain scientist. Given that we had a set allocation of time on the supercomputer, we wanted to execute only enough time steps to ensure that we captured the steady-state behavior of PISM. We determined experimentally that executing 100 time steps did provide steady-state behavior and did not burn excessive computational resources. In all experiments, we measured compute performance as the length of time required to complete 100 time steps.

All of the experimental data related to I/O performance is presented graphically, and provides the mean value, taken from a minimum of 10 experimental trials, with error bars representing the standard error.

## 4.2    Data Sets

We use two datasets based on the input data provided by the SeaRISE project. One dataset is for the Antarctic ice-sheet, at the 10-kilometer resolution, which we refer to as the A10 km model. We (loosely) categorize the A10 km model as *low-resolution* because it requires only 32 bits for both variable and file offsets. The second dataset describes the Greenland ice sheet at the one-kilometer resolution, which we refer to as the G1 km model. The state information computed by this model is on the order of 28 GB, and thus requires 64-bit offsets for both record variables and file offsets. We categorize this as a *high-resolution* model. The modeling parameters used in our test runs were derived from the first experimental control run provided in PISM's example scripts [26]. The parameters associated with each of the models are shown in Table 1.

## 5    Experimental Results

In this section, we analyze the performance and scalability of the computational and I/O components of the PISM model.

### 5.1    Computational Scalability

We first examined the scalability of the computational phase for the low- and high-resolution data sets. Our approach was to keep the number of nodes fixed, and to measure performance as the number of cores utilized per node was increased from 1 to 16 by powers of two. (Note that the number of cores used per node is referred to as the *Wayness* of the node.) We fixed the number of nodes at 64 for the A10 km, for a total count of between 64 and 1024 cores (one MPI process per core). In the case of the G1 km model, we fixed the number of nodes at 256, for a total count of 256 to 4096 MPI processes. The metric of interest was the *strong scaling efficiency,* which measures the percentage of linear speedup that is achieved as the problem size remains fixed and the number of processing elements is increased. This metric is defined in Eq. 1, where **t1** is the compute time required with one core per node, **N** is the number of cores utilized per node, and **tN** is the time required to complete the computation given **N** cores.

$$SSE = t1/(N * tN) * 100\%    \tag{1}$$

The results are shown in Table 2 below. First, consider the efficiency metric for the A10 km model. As can be seen, the computation scales reasonably well, at least up to 8 cores per node, but drops off by almost 25 % when the number of processes is increased from 8 to 16 cores per node. This suggests that the computational workload at this resolution is not sufficient to compensate for the increased communication costs at 16 processes per node.

The computational efficiency of the much larger G1 km model, however, scales extremely well with increasing process counts. In fact, when the number of processes is increased from 8 to 16 per node, the scaling efficiency only decreases by 9 % compared to the 25 % decrease observed for the lower-resolution model. Such excellent scaling results are not surprising given that each process only writes to its region of the grid, allowing the process to perform their computation independently and concurrently. And while each process must obtain data from its adjacent neighbors before each new time step, there is enough computational work to roughly offset the increased communication costs.

**Table 2.** Strong scaling efficiency based on the number of processes per node and model.

| Number of processes per node | SSE A10 km model | SSE G1 km model |
|---|---|---|
| 1 | 100 % | 100 % |
| 2 | 95 % | 96 % |
| 4 | 88 % | 88 % |
| 8 | 78 % | 87 % |
| 16 | 60 % | 79 % |

## 5.2    I/O Scalability of the Low Resolution Model

In this section, we measure the performance and scalability of the HDF5 and PNetCDF I/O libraries using the A10 km model. In these experiments, we measure the time required to write the model state to disk (approximately 1.8 GB), as a function of the I/O technique and the total number of MPI processes. In particular, we varied the number of nodes from 8 to 64, utilizing all 16 cores per node, for a total of between

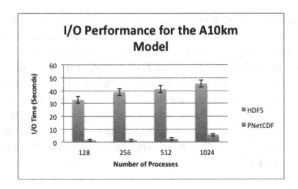

**Fig. 1.** This graph shows I/O performance as a function of the total number of processes (16 processes per node).

128 and 1024 MPI processes. The results are provided in Fig. 1, which shows the mean value of 10 experimental trials with error bars representing the standard error.

There are two very striking results that are immediately apparent. First, PNetCDF provides significantly better I/O performance, completing the write to disk on the order of 8 times faster than HDF5 at 1024 processes. Second, *neither* of the approaches scales well with increasing node/process counts. In fact, the time required to write the model state to disk *increased* in both cases when the process count increased from 128 to 1024. And while PNetCDF provided the best *overall* I/O performance, it exhibits the worst *scaling* behavior. In fact, when the node count was increased from 8 to 64, which increased the total number of processes from 128 to 1024, the time required to complete the write increased by a factor of almost *four* in the case of PnetCDF, compared to a factor of only 1.3 for HDF5.

The very different performance and scalability characteristics of the two approaches are interesting and somewhat counter-intuitive given that they both utilize the same underlying implementation of the MPI-IO standard. The poor scaling characteristics exhibited by both parallel I/O libraries is also disappointing. In the sections that follow, we attempt to identify the factors contributing to these results. We begin with a discussion of the potential impact on performance attributable to performing collective I/O operations in a multicore system such as Stampede.

**Factors Limiting I/O Scalability.** Multicore systems have been shown to present unique challenges that make the efficient implementation of MPI collective operations quite difficult. To help understand the reasons for such difficulties, reconsider the discussion of the two-phase I/O optimization implemented in ROMIO. As noted, the key assumption underlying this optimization is that the cost of data redistribution is orders of magnitude less expensive than the cost of performing multiple, disjoint I/O operations across a network. This assumption was clearly true when HPC systems typically had only one processor per node, but is becoming somewhat less true as multicore technologies begin to dominate the high-performance computing market. The following example is designed to provide an intuitive understanding of the potential scope of the problem.

When the two-phase I/O algorithm was developed, it was largely the case that each node hosted only one MPI process, and thus the cost of data redistribution involved *inter-node* process communication only. Stampede, however, supports up to 16 MPI processes per node, and the data redistribution phase requires that each process send its data to one of the aggregator processes. However, this aggregator process can now reside on the same node or on a remote node, incurring the costs of both *intra-* and *inter-node* data transfers. Further, the aggregator processes, which must now handle messages from both local and remote processes, can become communication "hot-spots", adding additional delays to the data redistribution phase. In fact, it is often the case that each process must communicate with multiple aggregator processes, in multiple iterations, in order to accomplish the desired data alignment between the aggregators. Thus data redistribution in multi-core systems can generate significant levels of simultaneous data transfer activity, placing considerable pressure on a node's underlying communication and memory subsystems. We believe it is this contention for on-node resources that is, at least in part, responsible for the relatively poor I/O performance observed above.

If this reasoning is correct, then we should observe increasing I/O costs with increasing process counts per node. To test this hypothesis, we fixed the number of nodes at 64, and measured I/O performance at 1, 8, and 16 processes per node. The idea is that at one process per node, there should be no additional delays resulting from *intra-node* messaging activity, and that such delays should be maximized at 16 processes per node.

The results are shown in Fig. 2, and, as can be seen, I/O performance is, in fact, maximized at one process per node, and increased process counts per node very clearly lead to increased I/O costs. While these results certainly lend support to our hypothesis, it is also clear that the impact on performance resulting from intra-node contention is significantly greater for PNetCDF than for HDF5. In fact, when the number of processes per node was increased from 8 to 16, the I/O costs incurred by PNetCDF increased by roughly *240 %*, while HDF5 incurred a performance penalty on the order of 20 %. We delay a more thorough analysis of these results until we compare relative performance within the context of the much higher-resolution G1 km model.

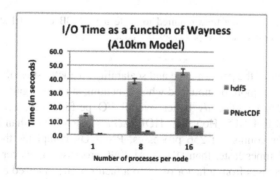

**Fig. 2.** This graph shows the increasing I/O costs with increasing process counts per node, for both I/O libraries

## 5.3    I/O Scalability of the High Resolution Model

We now turn to the investigation of I/O performance at scale. The G1 km model increases the number of grid points from 108 million to 1.6 billion, and the size of the model state from 1.8 GB to over 28 GB. In these experiments, we measured the time required to write the model state to disk as a function of the I/O technique and the total number of MPI processes. We varied the number of nodes between 64 and 256, utilizing all 16 cores per node, for a total of between 256 and 4096 MPI processes. The results of these runs are provided in Fig. 3.

The differences in the performance and scalability characteristics of the two parallel I/O libraries are even more pronounced when executing at scale. Again we observe that PNetCDF provides *significantly* better overall I/O performance, across all process counts, compared to HDF5. However, HDF5 *scales* much better than PNetCDF with increasing process counts. At 256 processes, PNetCDF completes the write to disk approximately 11 times faster than HDF5. At 4096 processes, however, this margin of improvement decreases from a factor of 11 to a factor of 3.1. Viewed another way, the I/O costs incurred by PNetCDF increased by a factor of 2.8 when the process count was increased from 1024 to 4096. In the case of HDF5, however, there was only a very minimal increase in such costs (on the order of 10 %). We investigate the reasons for these very different behaviors in the following sections.

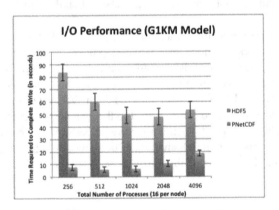

**Fig. 3.** This graph shows the time required to write the 28 GB of model state to disk as a function of total process count (16 processes per node).

The differences in the performance and scalability characteristics of the two parallel I/O libraries are even more pronounced when executing at scale. Again we observe that PNetCDF provides *significantly* better overall I/O performance, across all process counts, compared to HDF5. However, HDF5 *scales* much better than PNetCDF with increasing process counts. At 256 processes, PNetCDF completes the write to disk approximately 11 times faster than HDF5. At 4096 processes, however, this margin of improvement decreases from a factor of 11 to a factor of 3.1. Viewed another way, the I/O costs incurred by PNetCDF increased by a factor of 2.8 when the process count was increased from 1024 to 4096. In the case of HDF5, however, there was only a very minimal increase in such costs (on the order of 10 %). We investigate the reasons for these very different behaviors in the following sections.

## 6 Analysis

One significant difference between the two parallel I/O libraries is that HDF5 will, under certain circumstances, override the I/O mode requested by the application and use another I/O mode of its own choosing. In fact, it provides query functions through which the application can determine the actual I/O mode used to carry out an I/O request, and, if collective I/O was requested but not provided, the reason(s) that it was not provided. Through these mechanisms, we discovered that HDF5 was using *independent I/O* mode for what PISM refers to as diagnostic variables, and *collective I/O* for the other variables. It turned out that HDF5 was not utilizing collective I/O as requested because diagnostic variables are stored in memory as doubles but are stored in the file as floats. This requires a runtime conversion from doubles to floats, and HDF5 does not perform collective I/O when such a conversion is required. Thus the diagnostic variables were actually being written using *independent* rather than *collective I/O*, while the remaining variables, which do not require such a transformation, were written out in the requested collective I/O mode. After further investigation, it was determined that the diagnostic variables accounted for approximately *50 %* of the total 28 GB file. Thus it appears that the observed differences in performance and scalability characteristics can be attributed to the fact that PNetCDF was effectively invoking the two-phase I/O algorithm twice as often as HDF5.

This is an important result because it suggests that there may be a tradeoff between performing collective and independent I/O in multicore systems, which is contrary to the current thinking that it is always advantageous to perform collective I/O in large-scale scientific applications. And while the results presented here still support that notion, it suggests that there may be some threshold value for the number of cores per node past which it is no longer advantageous to do so. This makes it attractive to think in terms of developing simple analytic models that can help guide the choice of using collective I/O, independent I/O, or some combination of the two.

Another important result from this investigation is that there appears to be a fundamental tradeoff between the performance and scalability of the computational and I/O components of the PISM model in multicore systems. To see this tradeoff, consider Fig. 4a and b below.

Figure 4a shows the I/O and computational costs incurred by PNetCDF as a function of the number of cores per node. As can be seen, the costs of writing the 28 GB file to disk is *seven* times faster when utilizing one process per node compared to 16 processes per node. The time required to complete the 100 time steps, however, is over 12 times faster with 16 processes per node compared to one process per node. This tradeoff is certainly not (as) obvious in the case of HDF5 (shown in Fig. 4b), largely because it does not incur the costs of performing intra-node communication as often as does PNetCDF.

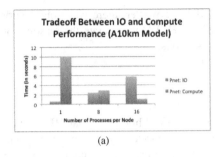
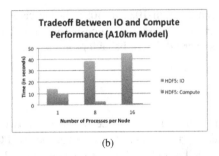

(a)                                                    (b)

**Fig. 4.** These graphs show the tradeoff between the computational and I/O components of the PISM model for both I/O libraries.

## 7    Related Work

Research related to improving the poor performance of MPI intra-node collective operations in multicore architectures is certainly of concern to PISM. For example, the MVAPICH2 installation on Stampede provides a set of lightweight communication primitives for improved intra-node communication through the LiMIC2 module [15]. KNEM provides kernel-level support to reduce the copy costs associated with intra-node data transfers, as well as awareness of the node's communication topology to reduce intra-node communication costs [6, 22, 25]. HeirKNEM [20, 21] has further enhanced this work by coordinating the activity of multiple layers of collective algorithms enabling the complete overlap of intra- and inter-node communications.

While the contention for node-level resources discussed above is related primarily to multicore systems, the overall issue of poor I/O performance in scientific applications is a well-known and widely studied problem. Many approaches have been developed to address such poor IO performance including, for example, the two-phase collective I/O optimization implemented in ROMIO [34, 35], I/O caching systems [8], data sieving [36], and adaptive file domain partitioning for collective I/O [16].

The Adaptable Input/Output System (ADIOS) [18], is a related platform that introduces a new hierarchical file format to reduce the costs of I/O is parallel applications. And while ADIOS is not currently supported in PISM, it does provide tools to translate between its format and those defined by NetCDF and HDF5. Studies comparing the performance of PNetCDF with earlier versions of the NetCDF file format are also related [17]. Finally, our preliminary work with PISM [10], where we improved the performance of PNetCDF by a factor of eight through simple modifications to the way it was being utilized in PISM, is also related.

## 8    Conclusions

In this paper, we have investigated the performance and scalability characteristics of the MPI-based tools utilized by PISM. We showed that the computational component of the PISM model scales very well with increasing process/node counts, but that the

I/O component of the model does not. We examined the very different behaviors of two state-of-the-art parallel I/O libraries, and discussed the reasons for such differences even though they are both based on the same implementation of the MPI-IO standard. Finally, we showed that there exists a fundamental tradeoff between the computational and I/O components of the PISM model in the case of PNetCDF, where I/O performance is maximized at one process per node and, as expected, computational performance is maximized at 16 processes per node.

**Acknowledgements.** This work used the Extreme Science and Engineering Discovery Environment (XSEDE), which is supported by National Science Foundation grant number ACI-1053575.

# References

1. Balay, S., et al.: PETSc Users Manual. Technical report #ANL-95/11 - Revision 3.6. Argonne National Laboratory
2. Balay, S., Gropp, W.D., McInnes, L.C., Smith, B.F.: Efficient management of parallelism in object oriented numerical software libraries. In: Arge, E., Bruaset, A.M., Langtangen, H. P. (eds.) Modern Software Tools in Scientific Computing, pp. 163–202. Birkhäuser Press, Boston (1997)
3. Baylor, S.J., Rathi, B.D.: An evaluation of the memory reference behavior of engineering/scientific applications in parallel systems. Int. J. High Speed Comput. **1**(4), 603–641 (1989)
4. de Boer, B., Dolan, A.M., Bernales, J., Gasson, E., Goelzer, H., Golledge, N.R., Sutter, J., Huybrechts, P., Lohmann, G., Rogozhina, I., Abe-Ouchi, A., Saito, F., van de Wal, R.S.W.: Simulating the Antarctic ice sheet in the late-Pliocene warm period: PLISMIP-ANT, an ice-sheet model intercomparison project. Cryosphere. **9**(3), 881–903 (2015)
5. Bueler, E., van Pelt, W.: Mass-conserving subglacial hydrology in the parallel ice sheet model version 0.6. Geosci. Mod. Dev. **8**(6), 1613–1635 (2015)
6. Buntinas, D., Goglin, B., Goodell, D., Mercier, G., Moreaud, S.: Cache-Efficient, Intranode, Large-Message MPI Communication with MPICH2-Nemesis, pp. 462–469, September 2009
7. CDF-5 Format Specifications. http://cucis.ece.northwestern.edu/projects/PnetCDF/cdf5.html. Accessed 11 September 2013
8. Coloma, K., Choudhary, A., Liao, W.: DAChe: direct access cache system for parallel I/O. In: Proceedings of the 2005 International Supercomputer Conference (2005)
9. Crandall, P., Aydt, R.A., Chien, A.A., Reed, D.A.: Input/output characteristics of scalable parallel applications. In: Proceedings of Supercomputing 1995 (1995)
10. Phillip, D., Timothy, M.: Increasing the scalability of PISM for high resolution ice sheet models. In: Workshop on Parallel and Distributed Scientific and Engineering Computing, Boston, May 2013
11. Dickens, P.M., Thakur, R.: A performance study of two-phase i/o. In: Pritchard, D., Reeve, J.S. (eds.) Euro-Par 1998. LNCS, vol. 1470, pp. 959–965. Springer, Heidelberg (1998)
12. Documentation for PISM, a parallel Ice Sheet Model. http://pism-docs.org/wiki/doku.php. Accessed 15 May 2015
13. Feldmann, J., Levermann, A.: Interaction of marine ice-sheet instabilities in two drainage basins: simple scaling of geometry and transition time. Cryosphere **9**(2), 631–645 (2015)

14. Fowler, A.C.: Mathematical Models in the Applied Sciences. Cambridge University Press, Cambridge (1997)
15. Jin, H.-W., Sur, S., Chai, L., Panda, D.K.: Lightweight kernel-level primitives for high-performance MPI intra-node communication over multi-core systems, pp. 446–451 (2007)
16. Liao, W., Choudhary, A.: Dynamically adapting file domain partitioning methods for collective i/o based on underlying parallel file system locking protocols. In: Proceedings of the ACM/IEEE Conference on Supercomputing (SC 2008), pp. 313–344 (2008)
17. Li, J., Liao, W., Choudhary, A., Ross, R., Thakur, R., Latham, R., Siegel, A., Gallagher, B., Zingale, M.: Parallel netCDF: a high-performance scientific I/O interface. In: Proceedings of Supercomputing (2003)
18. Liu, Q., et al.: Hello ADIOS: the challenges and lessons of developing leadership class I/O frameworks: HELLO ADIOS. Concurrency Comput. Pract. Experience **26**(7), 1453–1473 (2014)
19. Ma, A., Califano, F.: The shallow ice approximation for anisotropic ice- formulation and limits. J. Geophys. Res. **103**((B1)), 691–705 (1998)
20. Ma, T., Bosilca, G., Bouteiller, A., Dongarra, J.: HierKNEM: an adaptive framework for kernel-assisted and topology-aware collective communications on many-core clusters. In: 2012 IEEE 26th International Parallel & Distributed Processing Symposium (Ipdps), pp. 970–982, May 2012
21. Ma, T., Bosilca, G., Bouteiller, A., Dongarra, J.J.: Kernel-assisted and topology-aware MPI collective communications on multicore/many-core platforms. J. Parallel Distrib. Comput. **73**(7), 1000–1010 (2013)
22. Ma, T., Bosilca, G., Bouteiller, A., Goglin, B., Squyres, J.M., Dongarra, J.J.: Kernel assisted collective intra-node MPI communication among multi-core and many-core CPUs. In: 2011 International Conference on Parallel Processing (ICPP), pp. 532–541 (2011)
23. Mellanox Technologies. https://www.mellanox.com/. Accessed 21 July 2015
24. Message Passing Interface (MPI) Forum Home Page. http://www.mpi-forum.org/. Accessed 30 August 2013
25. Moreaud, S., Goglin, B., Namyst, R., Goodell, D.: Optimizing MPI communication within large multicore nodes with kernel assistance. In: IPDPS Workshops, pp. 1–7 (2010)
26. MPI-2: Extensions to the Message-Passing Interface Message Passing Interface Forum. http://mpi-forum.org/docs/mpi-20-html/mpi2-report.html. Accessed 31 August 2013
27. Nieuwejaar, N., Kotz, D., Purakayastha, A., Ellis, C.S., Best, M.: File-access characteristics of parallel scientific workloads. IEEE Trans. Parallel Distrib. Syst. **7**(10), 1075–1089 (1996)
28. Parallel HDF5. http://www.hdfgroup.org/HDF5/PHDF5/. Accessed 31 August 2013
29. PETSc Web page (2015). http://www.mcs.anl.gov/petsc
30. PISM, a Parallel Ice Sheet Model (2014). http://www.pism-docs.org
31. PISM, a Parallel Ice Sheet Model: User's Manual (2015). http://www.pism-docs.org/wiki/lib/exe/fetch.php?media=manual.pdf
32. SeaRISE Assessment - Interactive System for Ice sheet Simulation. http://websrv.cs.umt.edu/isis/index.php/SeaRISE_Assessment. Accessed 18 May 2015
33. Texas Advanced Computing Center – Stampede. http://www.tacc.utexas.edu/resources/hpc/stampede. Accessed 30 August 2013
34. Thakur, R., Gropp, W., Lusk, E.: On implementing mpi-io portably and with high performance. In: Proceedings of the 6th Workshop on I/O in Parallel and Distributed Systems, pp. 23–32 (1999)
35. Thakur, R., Lusk, E.: An abstract-device interface for implementing portable parallel-i/o interfaces. In: Proceedings of the 6th Symposium on the Frontiers of Massively Parallel Computatio, pp. 180–187 (1996)

36. Thakur, R., Lusk, E.: Data sieving and collective i/o in ROMIO. In: Proceedings of the Seventh Symposium on the Frontiers of Massively Parallel Computation, pp. 182–189 (1998)
37. The HDF Group - Information, Support, and Software. http://www.hdfgroup.org/. Accessed 11 September 2013
38. Unidata | Home. http://www.unidata.ucar.edu/. Accessed 11 September 2013
39. Unidata | NetCDF. http://www.unidata.ucar.edu/software/netcdf/. Accessed 11 September 2013
40. Unidata | Software. http://www.unidata.ucar.edu/software/. Accessed 11 September 2013
41. Weis, M., Greve, R., Hutter, K.: Theory of shallow ice shelves. Continuum Mech. Thermo-dyn. **11**(1999), 15–50 (1999)

# Performance Modeling
# and Evaluation

# An Efficient Algorithm for a Generalized LCS Problem

Daxin Zhu[1], Yingjie Wu[2]($\boxtimes$), and Xiaodong Wang[3]($\boxtimes$)

[1] Quanzhou Normal University, Quanzhou 362000, China
[2] Fuzhou University, Fuzhou 350002, China
[3] Fujian University of Technology, Fuzhou 350108, China
wangxd135@139.com

**Abstract.** In this paper, we present a simple polynomial time algorithm for a generalized longest common subsequence problem with multiple substring exclusion constraints. The problem was declared to be NP-hard, but we finally found that this is not true. A new polynomial time solution for this problem is presented in this paper. The correctness of the new algorithm is proved. The time complexity of our algorithm is analysed.

**Keywords:** Longest common subsequence problem · Dynamic programming · Substring exclusion constraints · Time complexity · Polynomial time algorithms

## 1 Introduction

In this paper, we consider a generalized longest common subsequence problem with multiple substring exclusive constraints. The longest common subsequence (LCS) problem is a well-known measurement for computing the similarity of two strings, and it is crucial in various applications. In this problem, we are interested in a longest sequence which is a subsequence of both sequences. The problem is well studied and is used in many applications, like DNA and protein analysis, text information retrieval, file comparing, music information retrieval, or spelling correction.

The most referred algorithm, proposed by Wagner and Fischer [16], solves the LCS problem by using a dynamic programming algorithm in quadratic time. Other advanced algorithms were proposed in the past decades [2,9–11].

If the number of input sequences is not fixed, the problem to find the LCS of multiple sequences has been proved to be NP-hard [12]. Some approximate and heuristic algorithms were proposed for these problems [13].

There are also a lot of generalizations of this similarity measure. One of the recent variants of the LCS problem, the constrained longest common subsequence (CLCS) which was first addressed by Tsai [14], has received much attention. It generalizes the LCS measure by introduction of a third sequence, which allows to extort that the obtained CLCS has some special properties. For two given

© Springer International Publishing Switzerland 2015
G. Wang et al. (Eds.): ICA3PP 2015, Part IV, LNCS 9531, pp. 151–160, 2015.
DOI: 10.1007/978-3-319-27140-8_11

input sequences $X$ and $Y$ of lengths $m$ and $n$, respectively, and a constrained sequence $P$ of length $r$, the CLCS problem is to find the common subsequences $Z$ of $X$ and $Y$ such that $P$ is a subsequence of $Z$ and the length of $Z$ is the maximum.

The most referred algorithms were proposed independently [3,5], which solve the CLCS problem in $O(mnr)$ time and space by using dynamic programming algorithms. Some improved algorithms have also been proposed [6].

Recently, a new variant of the CLCS problem, the restricted LCS problem, was proposed [8], which excludes the given constraint as a subsequence of the answer. The restricted LCS problem becomes NP-hard when the number of constraints is not fixed.

Some more generalized forms of the CLCS problem, the generalized constrained longest common subsequence (GC-LCS) problems, were addressed independently by Chen and Chao [4]. For the two input sequences $X$ and $Y$ of lengths $n$ and $m$, respectively, and a constraint string $P$ of length $r$, the GC-LCS problem is a set of four problems which are to find the LCS of $X$ and $Y$ including/excluding $P$ as a subsequence/substring, respectively. The four generalized constrained LCS [4] can be summarized in Table 1.

**Table 1.** The GC-LCS problems

| Problem | Input | Output |
|---------|-------|--------|
| SEQ-IC-LCS | $X, Y$, and $P$ | The longest common subsequence of $X$ and $Y$ including $P$ as a subsequence |
| STR-IC-LCS | $X, Y$, and $P$ | The longest common subsequence of $X$ and $Y$ including $P$ as a substring |
| SEQ-EC-LCS | $X, Y$, and $P$ | The longest common subsequence of $X$ and $Y$ excluding $P$ as a subsequence |
| STR-EC-LCS | $X, Y$, and $P$ | The longest common subsequence of $X$ and $Y$ excluding $P$ as a substring |

For the four problems in Table 1, $O(mnr)$ time algorithms were proposed [4]. However, their algorithm for STR-EC-LCS is not correct. In a recent paper, a correct $O(mnr)$ time dynamic programming algorithm was proposed [17].

The four GC-LCS problems can be generalized further to the cases of multiple constraints. In these generalized cases, the single constrained pattern $P$ will be generalized to a set of $d$ constraints $P = \{P_1, \cdots, P_d\}$ of total length $r$.

The problem M-SEQ-IC-LCS has been proved to be NP-hard in [7]. The problem M-SEQ-EC-LCS has also been proved to be NP-hard in [8,15]. In addition, the problems M-STR-IC-LCS and M-STR-EC-LCS were also declared to be NP-hard in [4], but without a proof. The exponential-time algorithms for solving these two problems were also presented in [4].

We will discuss the problem M-STR-EC-LCS in this paper. The failure functions in the Knuth-Morris-Pratt algorithm for solving the string matching problem have been proved very helpful for solving the STR-EC-LCS problem.

It has been found by Aho and Corasick [1] that the failure functions can be generalized to the case of keyword tree to speedup the exact string matching of multiple patterns. This idea can be very helpful in our dynamic programming algorithm. This is the main idea of our new algorithm. A polynomial time algorithm is presented for the M-STR-EC-LCS problem based on this observation and disproves that M-STR-EC-LCS problem is NP-hard.

## 2    Preliminaries

A sequence is a string of characters over an alphabet $\sum$. A subsequence of a sequence $X$ is obtained by deleting zero or more characters from $X$ (not necessarily contiguous). A substring of a sequence $X$ is a subsequence of successive characters within $X$.

For a given sequence $X = x_1 x_2 \cdots x_n$ of length $n$, the $i$th character of $X$ is denoted as $x_i \in \sum$ for any $i = 1, \cdots, n$. A substring of $X$ from position $i$ to $j$ can be denoted as $X[i : j] = x_i x_{i+1} \cdots x_j$. If $i \neq 1$ or $j \neq n$, then the substring $X[i : j] = x_i x_{i+1} \cdots x_j$ is called a proper substring of $X$. A substring $X[i : j] = x_i x_{i+1} \cdots x_j$ is called a prefix or a suffix of $X$ if $i = 1$ or $j = n$, respectively.

For the two input sequences $X = x_1 x_2 \cdots x_n$ and $Y = y_1 y_2 \cdots y_m$ of lengths $n$ and $m$, respectively, and a set of $d$ constraints $P = \{P_1, \cdots, P_d\}$ of total length $r$, the multiple STR-EC-LCS problem M-STR-EC-LCS is to find an LCS of $X$ and $Y$ excluding each of constraint $P_i \in P$ as a substring.

The most important difference between the problems STR-EC-LCS and M-STR-EC-LCS is the number of constraints. For ease of discussion, we will make the following two assumptions on the constraint set $P$.

**Assumption 1.** *There are no duplicated strings in the constraint set $P$.*

**Assumption 2.** *No string in the constraint set $P$ is a proper substring of any other string in $P$.*

Keyword tree [?], [4] is a main data structure in our dynamic programming algorithm to process the constraint set $P$ of the M-STR-EC-LCS problem.

**Definition 1.** *The Keyword tree for set $P$ is a rooted directed tree $T$ satisfying 3 conditions: 1. each edge is labeled with exactly one character; 2. any two edges out of the same node have distinct labels; and 3. every string $P_i$ in $P$ maps to some node $v$ of $T$ such that the characters on the path from the root of $T$ to $v$ exactly spell out $P_i$, and every leaf of $T$ is mapped to some string in $P$.*

For example, Fig. 1(a) shows the keyword tree $T$ for the constraint set $P = \{aab, aba, ba\}$, where $d = 3, r = 8$. Clearly, every node in the keyword tree corresponds to a prefix of one of the strings in set $P$, and every prefix of a string $P_i$ in $P$ maps to a distinct node in the keyword tree $T$. The keyword tree for set $P$ of total length $r$ of all strings can be easily constructed in $O(r)$ time for a constant alphabet size. Because no two edges out of any node of $T$ are

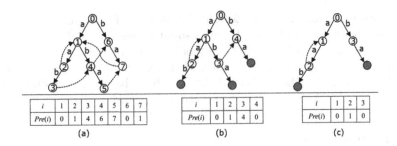

**Fig. 1.** Keyword Trees

labeled with the same character, the keyword tree $T$ can be used to search for all occurrences in a text $X$ of strings from $P$.

The failure functions in the Knuth-Morris-Pratt algorithm for solving the string matching problem can be generalized to the case of keyword tree to speedup the exact string matching of multiple patterns as follows.

In order to identify the nodes of $T$, we assign numbers $0, 1, \cdots, t-1$ to all $t$ nodes of $T$ in their preorder numbering. Then, each node will be assigned an integer $i, 0 \le i < t$, as shown in Fig. 1. For each node numbered $i$ of a keyword tree $T$, the concatenation of characters on the path from the root to the node $i$ spells out a string denoted as $L(i)$. The string $L(i)$ is also called the label of the node $i$ in the keyword tree $T$. For any node $i$ of $T$, define $lp(i)$ to be the length of the longest proper suffix of string $L(i)$ that is a prefix of some string in $T$.

It can be verified readily that for each node $i$ of $T$, if $A$ is an $lp(i)$-length suffix of string $L(i)$, then there must be a unique node $pre(i)$ in $T$ such that $L(pre(i)) = A$. If $lp(i) = 0$ then $pre(i) = 0$ is the root of $T$.

**Definition 2.** *The ordered pair $(i, pre(i))$ is called a failure link.*

The failure link is a direct generalization of the failure functions in the KMP algorithm. For example, in Fig. 1(a), failure links are shown as pointers from every node $i$ to node $pre(i)$ where $lp(i) > 0$. The other failure links point to the root and are not shown.

The failure links of $T$ define actually a failure function $pre$ for the constraint set $P$.

For example, for the nodes $i = 1, 2, 3, 4, 5, 6, 7$ in Fig. 1, the corresponding values of failure function are $pre(i) = 0, 1, 4, 6, 7, 0, 1$, as shown in Fig. 1(a).

The failure function $pre$ is used to speedup the search for all occurrences in a text $X$ of strings from $P$. As stated in [4], the failure function $pre$ can be computed in $O(r)$ time.

In the keyword tree application in our dynamic programming algorithm, a function $\sigma$ will be mentioned frequently. For a string $S$ and a given keyword tree $T$, if the label $L(i)$ of a node numbered $i$ is also a suffix of $S$, then the node $i$ is called a suffix node of $S$ in $T$.

**Definition 3.** *For any string $S$ and a given keyword tree $T$, the unique suffix node of $S$ in $T$ with maximum depth is denoted as $\sigma(S)$. That is:*

$$|L(\sigma(S))| = \max_{0 \le i < t} \{|L(i)| \, | \, L(i) \text{ is a suffix of } S\} \tag{1}$$

where $t$ is the number of nodes in $T$.

For example, if $S = aabaaabb$, then in the keyword tree $T$ of Fig. 1, the node 6 is the only suffix node of $S$ in $T$, therefore $\sigma(S) = 6$.

In our keyword tree application, we are only interested in the nonleaf nodes of the tree. So, we can renumber the nodes of the tree only for nonleaf nodes, omitting the leaf nodes of the tree, as shown in Fig. 1(b). After renumbering, the failure function of the tree will also be changed accordingly.

If a string $P_i$ in the constraint set $P$ is a proper substring of another string $P_j$ in $P$, then an LCS of $X$ and $Y$ excluding $P_i$ must also exclude $P_j$. For this reason, the constraint string $P_j$ can be removed from constraint set $P$ without changing the solution of the problem. For example, the string $ba$ is a proper substring of the string $aba$ in the keyword tree of Fig. 1(b). Therefore, the string $aba$ can be removed from the keyword tree, as shown in Fig. 1(c). We will show shortly how to remove these redundant strings from constraint set $P$ in $O(r)$ time. In the following sections, discussions are based on the Assumptions 1 and 2 on the constraint set $P$. The number of nonleaf nodes of the keyword tree for the constraint set $P$ is denoted as $s$. In the worst case $s = r - d$. The root of the keyword tree is numbered 0, and the other nonleaf nodes are numbered $1, 2, \cdots, s - 1$ in their preorder numbering. For example, in Fig. 1(c), there are $s = 4$ nonleaf nodes in $T$. The labels for the four nonleaf nodes are $L(0) = \emptyset, L(1) = a, L(2) = aa$ and $L(3) = b$ respectively.

The symbol $\oplus$ is also used to denote the string concatenation. For example, if $S_1 = aaa$ and $S_2 = bbb$, then it is readily seen that $S_1 \oplus S_2 = aaabbb$.

## 3   A Simple Dynamic Programming Algorithm

In the following discussions, we will call 'a sequence excluding each of constraint string in $P$ as a substring' a sequence excluding $P$ for short.

**Definition 4.** *Let $Z(i, j, k)$ denote the set of all LCSs of $X[i : n]$ and $Y[j : m]$ such that for each $z \in Z(i, j, k)$, $L(k) \oplus z$ excludes $P$, where $1 \le i \le n, 1 \le j \le m$, and $0 \le k < s$. The length of an LCS in $Z(i, j, k)$ is denoted as $f(i, j, k)$.*

If we can compute $f(i, j, k)$ for any $1 \le i \le n, 1 \le j \le m$, and $0 \le k < s$ efficiently, then the length of an LCS of $X$ and $Y$ excluding $P$ must be $f(1, 1, 0)$.

By using the keyword tree data structure described in the last section, we can give a recursive formula for computing $f(i, j, k)$ by the following Theorem.

**Theorem 1.** *For the two input sequences $X = x_1 x_2 \cdots x_n$ and $Y = y_1 y_2 \cdots y_m$ of lengths $n$ and $m$, respectively, and a set of $d$ constraints $P = \{P_1, \cdots, P_d\}$ of total length $r$, let $Z(i, j, k)$ and $f(i, j, k)$ be defined as in Definition 4. Suppose a* *keyword tree $T$ for the constraint set $P$ has been built, and the $s$ nonleaf nodes of $T$ are numbered in their preorder numbering. The label of the node numbered $k(0 \leq k < s)$ is denoted as $L(k)$. Then, for any $1 \leq i \leq n, 1 \leq j \leq m$, and $0 \leq k < s$, $f(i,j,k)$ can be computed by the following recursive formula (2).*

$$f(i,j,k) = \begin{cases} \max\{f(i+1,j+1,k), 1+f(i+1,j+1,q)\} & \text{if } x_i = y_j \text{ and } q < s \\ \max\{f(i+1,j,k), f(i,j+1,k)\} & \text{otherwise} \end{cases}$$

$$(2)$$

*where $q = \sigma(L(k) \oplus x_i)$, and the boundary conditions are $f(i, m+1, k) = f(n+1, j, k) = 0$ for any $1 \leq i \leq n, 1 \leq j \leq m$, and $0 \leq k \leq s$.*

**Proof.** For any $1 \leq i \leq n, 1 \leq j \leq m$, and $0 \leq k < s$, suppose $f(i,j,k) = t$ and $z = z_1 \cdots z_t \in Z(i,j,k)$.

First of all, we notice that for each pair $(i', j'), 1 \leq i' \leq n, 1 \leq j' \leq m$, such that $i' \geq i$ and $j' \geq j$, we have $f(i', j', k) \leq f(i,j,k)$, since a common subsequence $z$ of $X[i' : n]$ and $Y[j' : m]$ satisfying $L(k) \oplus z$ excluding $P$ is also a common subsequence of $X[i : n]$ and $Y[j : m]$ satisfying $L(k) \oplus z$ excluding $P$.

(1) In the case of $x_i \neq y_j$, we have $x_i \neq z_1$ or $y_j \neq z_1$.

  (1.1) If $x_i \neq z_1$, then $z = z_1 \cdots z_t$ is a common subsequence of $X[i+1 : n]$ and $Y[j : m]$ satisfying $L(k) \oplus z$ excluding $P$, and so $f(i+1, j, k) \geq t$. On the other hand, $f(i+1, j, k) \leq f(i,j,k) = t$. Therefore, in this case we have $f(i,j,k) = f(i+1,j,k)$.

  (1.2) If $y_j \neq z_1$, then we can prove similarly that in this case, $f(i,j,k) = f(i, j+1, k)$.

  Combining the two subcases we conclude that in the case of $x_i \neq y_j$, we have
  $$f(i,j,k) = \max\{f(i+1,j,k), f(i,j+1,k)\}.$$

(2) In the case of $x_i = y_j$ and $q < s$, there are also two subcases to be distinguished.

  (2.1) If $x_i = y_j \neq z_1$, then $z = z_1 \cdots z_t$ is also a common subsequence of $X[i+1 : n]$ and $Y[j+1 : m]$ satisfying $L(k) \oplus z$ excluding $P$, and so $f(i+1, j+1, k) \geq t$. On the other hand, $f(i+1, j+1, k) \leq f(i,j,k) = t$. Therefore, in this case we have $f(i,j,k) = f(i+1, j+1, k)$.

  (2.2) If $x_i = y_j = z_1$, then $f(i,j,k) = t > 0$ and $z = z_1 \cdots z_t$ is an LCS of $X[i : n]$ and $Y[j : m]$ satisfying $L(k) \oplus z$ excluding $P$, and thus $z' = z_2, \cdots, z_t$ is a common subsequence of $X[i+1 : n]$ and $Y[j+1 : m]$ satisfying $L(k) \oplus x_i \oplus z'$ excluding $P$. If $q = \sigma(L(k) \oplus x_i)$, then $L(q)$ is the longest suffix of $L(k) \oplus x_i$ that is also a label of a node of the keyword tree $T$, and therefore $z' = z_2, \cdots, z_t$ is also a common subsequence of $X[i+1 : n]$ and $Y[j+1 : m]$ satisfying $L(q) \oplus z'$ excluding $P$. In other words,
  $$f(i+1, j+1, q) \geq t - 1 = f(i,j,k) - 1. \tag{3}$$

  On the other hand, if $L(q)$ is the longest suffix of $L(k) \oplus x_i$, $f(i+1, j+1, q) = s$ and $v = v_1 \cdots v_s \in Z(i+1, j+1, q)$, then $v$ is an LCS of $X[i+1 : n]$

and $Y[j+1:m]$ satisfying $L(q) \oplus v$ excluding $P$. In this case $v' = x_i \oplus v$ is a common subsequence of $X[i:n]$ and $Y[j:m]$ satisfying $L(k) \oplus x_i \oplus v'$ excluding $P$, since $L(q)$ is the longest suffix of $L(k) \oplus x_i$ and $q < r$. Therefore,

$$f(i,j,k) \geq s+1 = f(i+1,j+,q)+1. \tag{4}$$

Combining (3) and (4) we have, in this case,

$$f(i,j,k) = 1 + f(i+1,j+,q). \tag{5}$$

Combining the two subcases in the case of $x_i = y_j$ and $q < r$, we conclude that the recursive formula (2) is correct for this case.

(3) In the case of $x_i = y_j$ and $q = s$, we must have $x_i = y_j \neq z_1$, otherwise $L(k) \oplus z$ will including the string $L(k) \oplus x_i$ corresponding to a leaf node of the keyword tree $T$. Similar to the subcase (2.1), we can conclude that in this case,

$$f(i,j,k) = f(i+1,j+1,k)$$

$$= \max\{f(i+1,j,k), f(i,j+1,k)\}.$$

The proof is complete. ∎

## 4    The Implementation of the Algorithm

According to Theorem 1, our algorithm for computing $f(i,j,k)$ is a standard 2-dimensional dynamic programming algorithm. By the recursive formula (2), the dynamic programming algorithm for computing $f(i,j,k)$ can be implemented as the following Algorithm 1.

In Algorithm 1, $s$ is the number of nonleaf nodes of the keyword tree $T$ for set $P$. The root of the keyword tree is numbered 0, and the other nonleaf nodes are numbered $1, 2, \cdots, s-1$ in their preorder numbering. $L(t)$ is the label of node numbered $t$ in the keyword tree $T$.

To implement our algorithm efficiently, the most important thing is to compute $\sigma(L(k) \oplus x_i)$ for each $0 \leq k < s$ and $x_i, 1 \leq i \leq n$, in line 9 efficiently.

It is obvious that $\sigma(L(k) \oplus x_i) = g$ if there is an edge $(k, g)$ out of the node $k$ labeled $x_i$. It will be more complex to compute $\sigma(L(k) \oplus x_i)$ if there is no edge out of the node $k$ labeled $x_i$. In this case the matched node label has to be changed to the longest proper suffix of $L(k)$ that is a prefix of some string in $T$ and the corresponding node $h$ has an out edge $(h, g)$ labeled $x_i$. Therefore, in this case, $\sigma(L(k) \oplus x_i) = g$. To speedup, we can pre-compute a table $\lambda(k, ch)$ of the function $\sigma(L(k) \oplus ch)$ for each character $ch \in \sum$ and $1 \leq k \leq s$. When we precompute the prefix function $pre$, for every edge $(k, g)$ labeled with character $ch$, the value of $\lambda(k, ch)$ can be assigned directly to $g$. The other values of the table $\lambda$ can be computed by using the prefix function $pre$. With this pre-computed table $\lambda$, the loop body of above Algorithm 1 requires only $O(1)$ time. Therefore, our

---

**Algorithm 1.** M-STR-EC-LCS

---

**Input:** Strings $X = x_1 \cdots x_n$, $Y = y_1 \cdots y_m$ of lengths $n$ and $m$, respectively, and a set of $d$ constraints $P = \{P_1, \cdots, P_d\}$ of total length $r$
**Output:** The length of an LCS of $X$ and $Y$ excluding $P$
1: Build a keyword tree $T$ for $P$
2: **for all** $i, j, k$, $1 \le i \le n, 1 \le j \le m$, and $0 \le k \le s$ **do**
3:      $f(i, m + 1, k) \leftarrow 0, f(n + 1, j, k) \leftarrow 0$ {boundary condition}
4: **end for**
5: **for** $i = n$ down to 1 **do**
6:     **for** $j = m$ down to 1 **do**
7:         **for** $k = 0$ to $s$ **do**
8:             $f(i, j, k) \leftarrow \max\{f(i + 1, j, k), f(i, j + 1, k)\}$
9:             $q \leftarrow \sigma(L(k) \oplus x_i)$
10:             **if** $x_i = y_j$ and $q < s$ **then**
11:                 $f(i, j, k) \leftarrow \max\{f(i + 1, j + 1, k), 1 + f(i + 1, j + 1, q)\}$
12:             **end if**
13:         **end for**
14:     **end for**
15: **end for**
16: **return** $f(1, 1, 0)$

---

dynamic programming algorithm for computing the length of an LCS of $X$ and $Y$ excluding $P$ requires $O(nmr)$ time and $O(r|\Sigma|)$ preprocessing time.

Until now we have assumed that our algorithm is implemented under Assumptions 1 and 2 on the constraint set $P$. We now describe how to relax the two assumptions.

If Assumption 1 is violated, then there must be some duplicated strings in the constraint set $P$. In this case, we can first sort the strings in the constraint set $P$, then duplicated strings can be removed from $P$ easily and then Assumption 1 on the constraint set $P$ is satisfied. It is clear that removed strings will not change the solution of the problem.

For Assumption 2, we first notice that a string $A$ in the constraint set $P$ is a proper substring of string $B$ in $P$, if and only if in the keyword tree $T$ of $P$, there is a directed path of failure links from a node $v$ on the path from the root to the leaf node corresponding to string $B$ to the leaf node corresponding to string $A$ [4]. For example, in Fig. 1(a), there is a directed path of failure links from node 5 to node 7 and thus we know the string $ba$ corresponding to node 7 is a proper substring of string $aba$ corresponding to node 5.

With this fact, if Assumption 2 is violated, we can remove all super-strings from the constraint set $P$ as follows. We first build a keyword tree $T$ for the constraint set $P$, then mark all nodes passed by a directed path of failure links to a leaf node in $T$ by using a depth first traversal of $T$. All the strings corresponding to the marked leaf node can then be removed from $P$. Assumption 2 is now satisfied on the new constraint set and the keyword tree $T$ for the new constraint set is then rebuilt. It is not difficult to do this preprocessing in $O(r)$ time. It is clear that the removed super-strings will not change the solution of the problem.

If we want to get the answer LCS of $X$ and $Y$ excluding $P$, but not just its length, we can also present a simple recursive back tracing algorithm for this purpose as the following Algorithm 2.

---

**Algorithm 2.** $back(i, j, k)$

---

**Comments:** A recursive back tracing algorithm to construct the answer LCS

1: **if** $i > n$ **or** $j > m$ **then**
2:     **return**
3: **end if**
4: **if** $x_i = y_j$ **and** $f(i, j, k) = 1 + f(i+1, j+1, \lambda(k, x_i))$ **then**
5:     print $x_i$
6:     $back(i+1, j+1, \lambda(k, x_i))$
7: **else if** $f(i+1, j, k) > f(i, j+1, k)$ **then**
8:     $back(i+1, j, k)$
9: **else**
10:     $back(i, j+1, k)$
11: **end if**

---

In the end of our new algorithm, a function call $back(1, 1, 0)$ will produce the answer LCS accordingly.

Since the cost of the computation $\lambda(k, x_i)$ is $O(1)$, the algorithm $back(i, j, k)$ will cost $O(\max(n, m))$ in the worst case.

Finally we summarize our results in the following Theorem.

**Theorem 2.** *The Algorithm 1 solves M-STR-EC-LCS problem correctly in* $O(nmr)$ *time and* $O(nmr)$ *space, with preprocessing time* $O(r|\Sigma|)$.

# 5 Concluding Remarks

We have suggested a new dynamic programming solution for the M-STR-EC-LCS problem. The M-STR-IC-LCS problem is another interesting generalized constrained longest common subsequence (GC-LCS) which is very similar to the M-STR-EC-LCS problem. The M-STR-IC-LCS problem is to find an LCS of two main sequences, in which a set of constraint strings must be included as its substrings. It is not clear that whether the same technique of this paper can be applied to this problem to achieve an efficient algorithm. We will investigate the problem further.

**Acknowledgments.** This work was supported by the Science and Technology Foundation of Quanzhou under Grant No.2013Z38, Fujian Provincial Key Laboratory of Data-Intensive Computing and Fujian University Laboratory of Intelligent Computing and Information Processing.

# References

1. Aho, A.V., Corasick, M.J.: Efficient string matching: an aid to bibliographic search. Commun. ACM **18**(6), 333–340 (1975)
2. Ann, H.Y., Yang, C.B., Peng, Y.H., Liaw, B.C.: Efficient algorithms for the block edit problems. Inf. Comput. **208**(3), 221–229 (2010)
3. Arslan, A.N., Egecioglu, O.: Algorithms for the constrained longest common subsequence problems. Int. J. Found. Comput. Sci. **16**(6), 1099–1109 (2005)
4. Chen, Y.C., Chao, K.M.: On the generalized constrained longest common subsequence problems. J. Comb. Optim. **21**(3), 383–392 (2011)
5. Chin, F.Y.L., Santis, A.D., Ferrara, A.L., Ho, N.L., Kim, S.K.: A simple algorithm for the constrained sequence problems. Inform. Process. Lett. **90**(4), 175–179 (2004)
6. Deorowicz, S., Obstoj, J.: Constrained longest common subsequence computing algorithms in practice. Comput. Inform. **29**(3), 427–445 (2010)
7. Gotthilf, Z., Hermelin, D., Lewenstein, M.: Constrained LCS: hardness and approximation. In: Ferragina, P., Landau, G.M. (eds.) CPM 2008. LNCS, vol. 5029, pp. 255–262. Springer, Heidelberg (2008)
8. Gotthilf, Z., Hermelin, D., Landau, G.M., Lewenstein, M.: Restricted LCS. In: Chavez, E., Lonardi, S. (eds.) SPIRE 2010. LNCS, vol. 6393, pp. 250–257. Springer, Heidelberg (2010)
9. Hirschberg, D.S.: Algorithms for the longest common subsequence problem. J. ACM **24**(4), 664–675 (1977)
10. Iliopoulos, C.S., Rahman, M.S.: A new efficient algorithm for computing the longest common subsequence. Theor. Comput. Sci. **45**(2), 355–371 (2009)
11. Iliopoulos, C.S., Rahman, M.S., Vorcek, M., Vagner, L.: Finite automata based algorithms on subsequences and supersequences of degenerate strings. J. Discret. Algorithm. **8**(2), 117–130 (2010)
12. Maier, D.: The complexity of some problems on subsequences and supersequences. J. ACM **25**, 322–336 (1978)
13. Shyu, S.J., Tsai, C.Y.: Finding the longest common subsequence for multiple biological sequences by ant colony optimization. Comput. Oper. Res. **36**(1), 73–91 (2009)
14. Tsai, Y.T.: The constrained longest common subsequence problem. Inform. Process. Lett. **88**(4), 173–176 (2003)
15. Tseng, C.T., Yang, C.B., Ann, H.Y.: Efficient algorithms for the longest common subsequence problem with sequential substring constraints. J. Complexity **29**, 44–52 (2013)
16. Wagner, R., Fischer, M.: The string-to-string correction problem. J. ACM **21**(1), 168–173 (1974)
17. Wang, L., Wang, X., Wu, Y., Zhu, D.: A dynamic programming solution to a generalized LCS problem. Inform. Process. Lett. **113**(1), 723–728 (2013)

# On Exploring a Quantum Particle Swarm Optimization Method for Urban Traffic Light Scheduling

Wenbin Hu$^{(\boxtimes)}$, Huan Wang, Liping Yan, and Bo Du

School of Computer, Wuhan University, Wuhan 430072, China
{hwb,csyan}@whu.edu.cn,
694789758@qq.com, gunspace@163.com

**Abstract.** Because of concise and efficient evolution rules, the BML model (BML) has a great potential for the two-dimension urban traffic scheduling. However, the theoretical lattice space of BML makes it difficult for the existing models based on BML to simulate the actual traffic flow. In this paper, an extended BML model (EBML) is proposed to effectively simulate the urban traffic where the quantum particle swarm optimization (QPSO) is creatively introduced to optimize traffic lights management. The main contributions include that: (1) EBML is constructed to be more consistent with the actual urban road network with different two-way multi-lane roads. Its lattice sites act as obstacles, overpasses, underground tunnels, and roads. The actual urban road network can be mapped into the lattice space of EBML. And the corresponding updating rules of each lattice site are presented; (2) A deep insight into the traffic characters is provided in EBML. And the effect of the interference among different road capacities on forming traffic congestions is elaborated. Overpasses are applied to alleviate the interferences; (3) By the scheduling simulation of EBML, QPSO optimizes the timing scheduling of traffic lights. Extensive experiments reveal that QPSO achieves excellent optimization performances in real cases.

**Keywords:** Traffic congestion · Overpasses · Roadblocks · BML · Congestion-Avoidance routing

## 1 Introduction

The dynamics of the urban traffic has attracted great attention in recent years [1, 2], which is practically important to alleviate traffic congestions and schedule the traffic flow. Many traffic models have been proposed to capture the fundamental aspects of the phase transition and congestion in cities, such as the continuous model [3], the gas kinetic model [4], the car-following model [5], the Biham, Middleton and Levine (BML) model [6]. Benefited from concise and efficient evolution rules based on the cellular automaton (CA) [7], the BML model has great advantage to model the two-dimensional urban traffic [6]. The BML model (BML) [6] describes the dynamic movement of northbound and eastbound vehicles moving on a two-dimensional square lattice with the periodic boundary conditions. At even time steps, if the next lattice site

© Springer International Publishing Switzerland 2015
G. Wang et al. (Eds.): ICA3PP 2015, Part IV, LNCS 9531, pp. 161–174, 2015.
DOI: 10.1007/978-3-319-27140-8_12

is empty, the northbound vehicle advances one lattice site. If the next lattice site is occupied, the northbound vehicle remains stationary. At odd time steps, the eastbound vehicle tries to advance one lattice site in the same way [7]. Although this model is very simple, it can describe many extremely complex behaviors very well, including jamming transition and self-organization [8].

Though the above variants based on BML have made the abundant achievements, two main weaknesses can be listed as follows: (1) In the real city, different roads have different lanes, and some roads have overpasses and underground tunnels. The existing variants based on BML only devote to integrating independent realistic feature into BML. There are still no enough traffic elements in the theoretical lattice space of BML. So the actual traffic network cannot be mapped into their lattice space; (2) The existing variants based on BML have no function to optimize urban traffic light scheduling. And the existing researches just can draw some theoretical conclusions. There are still no ways to apply the existing researches into the practical applications. In order to overcome the weaknesses above, an extended BML model (EBML) is proposed in this paper. EBML can simulate the urban traffic flow in the real urban road network, and optimize the timing scheduling of traffic lights by the quantum-behaved particle swarm optimization (QPSO). The main contributions of this paper are summarized as follows. (1) The block capacity, different unidirectional capacities and intersecting capacities are assigned to the lattice sites in EBML, which make the lattice sites act as obstacles, overpass, underground tunnels, and roads. The actual road network can be mapped into EBML. And the corresponding updating rules of vehicles are presented. (2) Compared with BML, a deep insight into the phase transition and traffic congestions is provided in EBML. And the effect of the interference among different road capacities on forming traffic congestion is elaborated. Overpasses are applied to alleviate the interference, which achieve prominent effects. (3) Based on the urban traffic simulation in EBML, the quantum-behaved particle swarm optimization (QPSO) is firstly applied to optimize the timing scheduling of traffic lights in the real city. Compared with the PSO algorithm and the random algorithm, extensive experiments show the excellent improvements of the proposed QPSO algorithm in EBML.

## 2   The IOCA-PSO Method

The framework of EBML is shown in Fig. 1. EBML includes two components: Simulation (detailed in Sect. 2.1) and Optimization (detailed in Sect. 2.2). They are introduced as follows.

(1) *Simulation*: The road network of the actual urban area is mapped into the lattice space of EBML. The dynamic movement of the vehicles at each discrete time step is controlled by updating rules. The adjustment of traffic lights at each intersection can be controlled flexibly. (2) *Optimization*: Firstly, the QPSO algorithm carries out its optimized timing scheduling in the Simulation. Secondly, making use of the simulative information in Simulation, the QPSO algorithm adjusts its timing scheduling by the QPSO algorithm. The two optimization steps will be repeated until to obtain the optimal timing scheduling of traffic lights. And the optimal timing scheduling can be implemented in the corresponding actual urban area.

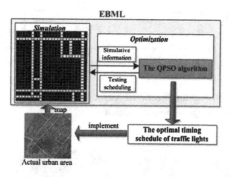

**Fig. 1.** The framework of EBML.

## 2.1   Simulation

It is unrealistic to test the timing scheduling by the tentative and repetitive applications in the real urban road network. But the timing scheduling can be tested in the simulation of EBML. EBML can model the dynamic urban traffic.

**Simulation Environment.** The finite $N \times N$ square lattice with open boundary conditions is considered in EBML, which models the actual urban road layout with different two-way multi-lane roads. The vehicles only run on the road network (including overpasses and underground tunnels) in cities, so the remaining areas can be seen as obstacles absolutely. Some lattice sites are assigned with different unidirectional capacities, which act as the roads. Some lattice sites are assigned with different intersecting capacities, which act as overpasses or underground tunnels. Except for the lattice sites with unidirectional and intersecting capacities, the remaining lattice sites are assigned with the block capacity. The lattice sites with the block capacity act as obstacles. Some lattice sites act as intersections.

Different unidirectional capacities and intersecting capacities can have different vehicle units. For example, according to the real conditions of Chinese urban roads, the number of vehicle units can be 1, 2, 3 or 4. For the northbound and eastbound vehicles, the lattice sites with unidirectional capacities can have four different structures with different vehicle units (Fig. 2). And the lattice sites with intersecting capacities can four different structures with different vehicle units (Fig. 3). The block capacity has no vehicle units. Because the roads are two-way, the southbound and westbound vehicles deal with similar structures. In the simulation of EBML, the southbound and westbound vehicles have no conflict with the northbound and eastbound vehicles. The description of capacities can be listed as follows. (1) Based on the actual urban layout, initially each lattice site should be assigned with a fixed capacity from the unidirectional capacity, the intersecting capacity and the block capacity. For a lattice site, the vehicle units of its capacity are decided by the lane number of its corresponding road or overpasses (underground tunnels). (2) A vehicle unit just can contain one vehicle in the same direction. And the number of vehicles at a lattice site should not be more than the vehicle capacity unit limitation.

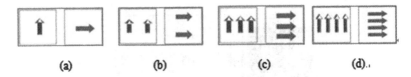

**Fig. 2.** The structures of the unidirectional capacities with different vehicle units. Right (up) arrows denote eastbound (northbound) vehicles.

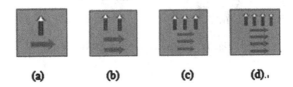

**Fig. 3.** The structures of the intersecting capacities with different vehicle units. Right (up) arrows denote eastbound (northbound) vehicles.

**Fig. 4.** The area centering Xudong in Wuhan (a) from Google maps is mapped to lattice space (b) in EBML. The white lattices denote the roads. The black lattices denote the blocks. The gray lattices denote intersections.

Most cities can be classified as grid-like cities and self-organized cities roughly, and the grid-like cities become more and more. The scheduling simulation of EBML only applies to grid-like cities. Grid-like cities are realized over a short period of time as the result of urban plans, and usually exhibiting grid structures [13]. Based on maintaining the connecting state of urban road network, the grid-like cities are easy to map in the lattice space in EBML. For example in Fig. 4, the grid-like area centering Xudong in Wuhan from Google maps is mapped to lattice space in EBML. And the configuration of traffic lights at each intersection is saved.

**Updating Rules.** In EBML, vehicles in EBML can move northward, southward, westward and eastward. The vehicles leaving EBML through the boundary lattice sites will not come back. And new vehicles are controlled to enter into the EBML through the boundary lattice sites. The number of entering vehicles is consistent with the actual traffic data.

An intersection is a junction of different roads. The movements of vehicles trying to enter an intersection are decided by traffic lights of the intersection. Under the control of traffic lights, the dynamic movement of the vehicles at each discrete time step is decided by the updating rules. Some useful parameters are introduced at first. $n$ is the number of a site in the consecutive up lattices sites, starting form 1 at the bottom. max $(n)$ denotes the maximum capacity units of a site. $M_n(n, t)$ is the amount of vehicle units occupied by northbound vehicles in the site $n$ at the time step $t$. And $M_E(n, t)$, $M_W(n, t)$, $M_S(n, t)$ are defined in the same way.

At even time steps, when the next lattice is not an intersection, the vehicle at the northbound or southbound vehicle unit tries to advance one lattice site when the next lattice has the corresponding empty vehicle unit. Otherwise, the vehicle remains stationary. At even time steps, when the next lattice is an intersection, if the movement of the vehicle is decided by the traffic lights. The updating rules of northbound vehicles at each even time step are defined as follows.

**Definition Rule₁:** When the next lattice is an intersection, if the northbound traffic light of the intersection is green, the northbound vehicle can advance. If the southbound traffic light of the intersection is green, the southbound vehicle can advance. Otherwise, the vehicle remains stationary. When the next lattice is not an intersection, $Rule_2$, $Rule_3$, $Rule_4$, and $Rule_5$ are carried out.

**Definition Rule₂:** If the site $n + 1$ owns a unidirectional capacity, and the site $n$ owns a unidirectional or intersection capacity, the $Rule_1$ can be described as follows. If $M_E(n + 1, t) > 0$, then $M_N(n, t + 1) = M_N(n, t)$, $M_N(n + 1, t + 1) = M_N(n + 1, t) = 0$. If $M_g(n + 1, t) = 0$, then $M_N(n + 1, t + 1) = M_N(n + 1, t) + temp$, $M_N(n, t + 1) = M_N(n, t) - temp$, where $temp = \min\{r, M_N(n, t)\}$, $r = \max(n + 1) - M_N(n + 1, t)$.

**Definition Rule₃:** If the site $n + 1$ owns an intersection capacity, and the site $n$ owns a unidirectional or intersection capacity, the $Rule_2$ can be described as follows. $M_N$ $(n + 1, t + 1) = M_N(n + 1, t) + temp$, $M_N(n, t + 1) = M_N(n, t) - temp$, where $temp = \min\{r, M_N(n, t)\}$, $r = \max(n + 1) - M_N(n + 1, t)$.

**Definition Rule₄:** If the site $n + 1$ owns a block capacity, no vehicles at the site $n$ can advance.

**Definition Rule₅:** When a northbound vehicle is at the site $n$ with the intersection capacity, if there are more than one sites for the northbound vehicle to advance into, the northbound vehicle will randomly select a site as the site $n + 1$, then carry out the $Rule_2$, $Rule_3$ and $Rule_4$.

The updating rules of southbound vehicles at each even time step are similar to $Rule_1$, $Rule_2$, $Rule_3$, $Rule_4$ and $Rule_5$. At odd time steps, each vehicle at the eastbound and westbound vehicle units tries to advance one lattice site when the next lattice has the corresponding empty vehicle unit. Otherwise, the vehicle remains stationary. The updating rules of the eastbound and westbound vehicles at each odd time step are in the same way with the northbound and southbound vehicle at each even time step.

## 2.2 Optimization

**Phase Encoding of Traffic Lights.** All traffic lights at a same intersection have to be necessarily synchronized for the security, and they carry out a series of common phases. A phase of an intersection includes a combination of all traffic light color states at the intersection, and the corresponding time span. The phase sequence of an inter-section and the corresponding combination of traffic light color states for each phase are determined in advance. The optimization in EBML is just for the corresponding time span of each phase, which is the timing scheduling [11].

In Fig. 5, the intersection $i+1$ has five phases, and the phases of all intersections are encoded into a one-dimensional time-span vector. A one-dimensional time-span vector provides a possible timing scheduling of the involved traffic lights. For an intersection, when a phase is terminated, they will enter into the next phase. And the first phase will follow the last phase. Based on the 1 one-dimensional time-span vector, each intersection carries out their corresponding phase circulation in a given period.

**The QPSO Algorithm.** The particle swarm optimization (PSO) is a new methodology

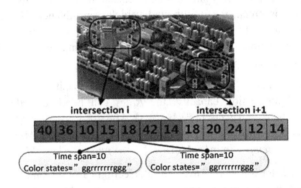

**Fig. 5.** The timing scheduling process of traffic lights by QPSO.

in the evolutionary computation, which is extremely effective in solving a wide range of engineering problems. However, the premature convergence of its most variants is very serious, which hinders its global searching ability [9]. Based on PSO by adding the quantum wave mechanics, QPSO weakens the premature convergence, and achieves a better global searching ability [10].

In EBML, the QPSO algorithm is applied to optimize the time-span values in a one-dimensional time-span vector, which determines the timing scheduling of all traffic lights. The timing scheduling by QPSO will be implemented in the simulation. The scheduling simulation provides the necessary simulative results to evaluate the opti-mization effect, which conducts the scheduling optimization by QPSO. Along with the optimization adjustment of time spans in the vectors, the timing scheduling of traffic lights is adjusted to be better. Based on the optimal timing scheduling of the final time-span vector, each intersection carries out their corresponding phase scheduling circularly in the given time period.

Some parameters are introduced firstly. $P_i$ is the state encode of the particle $i$ in the optimization of QPSO. $P_{ic}$ and $P_{is}$ are two locations occupied by a particle $P_i$, which denotes the probability amplitudes of quantum states $|0\rangle$ and $|1\rangle$. And $\tilde{P}_{ic}$ and $\tilde{P}_{is}$ denote the updating locations. The ith quantum bit of particle $P_i$ is denoted as $\left[\alpha_i^j, \beta_i^j\right]^T$, which can be transformed to the actual time spans $[X_{is}^j, X_{is}^j]^T$. $P_{ij}$ is the optimal solution that the particle $i$ has found after the current iteration. $P_g$ is the optimal solution that the whole particle swarm has found after the current iteration. $P_m$ is the mutation probability in QPSO.

As recommended in the work of Mikki and Kishk [10], the particle $P_i$ in QPSO is denoted by Eq. (2). For a particle, the probability amplitudes of quantum states $|0\rangle$ and $|1\rangle$ can be calculated by Eqs. (3) and (4), which are denoted as $P_{ic}$ and $P_{is}$. $P_{ic}$ and $P_{is}$ correspond to two one-dimensional vectors with given time-span values (Fig. 5). So a particle $P_i$ provides two one-dimensional vectors. The two locations occupied by a particle are in the unit space $I = [-1, 1]^n$, which need map to the solution space of the actual time spans. The time pan of traffic lights is among $[a_i, b_i]$. Through the solution space transformation of all quantum bits by Eqs. (5) and (6), $P_{ic}$ and $P_{is}$ can obtain their corresponding one-dimensional time-span vectors.

Assuming $P$ denotes the probability amplitude, *fitness(P)* denotes the fitness value of a one-dimensional time-span vector corresponding to $P$. The fitness value is used to evaluate the optimization result of a given time-span vector. Based on the simulative information in EBML, it is calculated by Eq. (1).

$$fitness(P) = k_0 V + k_1 H \tag{1}$$

Equation (1) is a common objective function in the traffic optimization. $V$ is the total delay of all vehicles. $H$ is the total parking number of all vehicles. $k_0$ and $k_1$ are the weighting coefficient of $V$ and $H$. $V$ and $H$ are variables that should be decreased. When the fitness value is smaller, the timing scheduling is better. QPSO is detailed in Table 1. More detail about the theoretical algorithm of QPSO can be obtained in the work of Yang et al. [9].

The final timing scheduling theoretically has the smallest fitness value. However, in the limited time of real applications, QPSO cannot always find the optimal timing scheduling in EBML. QPSO will select its existing optimal timing scheduling as its final timing scheduling. And the final scheduling is better than other state-of-the-art algorithms, which is verified in Sect. 3.4.

$$P_i = \left[ \left| \begin{matrix} \cos(\theta_{i1}) \\ \sin(\theta_{i1}) \end{matrix} \right| \begin{matrix} \cos(\theta_{i2}) \\ \sin(\theta_{i2}) \end{matrix} \left| \ldots \right| \begin{matrix} \cos(\theta_{in}) \\ \sin(\theta_{in}) \end{matrix} \right| \right] \tag{2}$$

$$P_{ic} = (\cos(\theta_{i1}), \cos(\theta_{i2}), \ldots, \cos(\theta_{in})) \tag{3}$$

$$P_{is} = (\sin(\theta_{i1}), \sin(\theta_{i2}), \ldots, \sin(\theta_{in})) \tag{4}$$

$$X_{ic}^j = \frac{1}{2} \left[ b_i(1 + \alpha_i^j) + a_i(1 - \alpha_i^j) \right] \tag{5}$$

$$X_{ic}^j = \frac{1}{2} \left[ b_i(1 + \beta_i^j) + a_i(1 - \beta_i^j) \right] \tag{6}$$

**Table 1.** The procedure of the optimization by QPSO

---

**Step 1:** Produce the initial particle swarm with a set of random values by equation (2).

**Step 2:** Carry out the conversion of the solution space by equations (3), (4), (5) and (6).

**For** $k = 1$ to the maximum iteration

    **For** $i = 1$ to the swarm size

        **If** fitness( $P_{ic}$ )<fitness( $P_{il}$ ) then $P_{il} = P_{ic}$ **End**

        **If** fitness( $P_{is}$ )<fitness( $P_{il}$ ) then $P_{il} = P_{is}$ **End**

        **If** fitness( $P_{il}$ )<fitness( $P_g$ ) then $P_g = P_{il}$ **End**

        **Step 3:** Update the state of the particle by the equations (7), (8), (9), (10) and (11).

        **Step 4:** Produce $rnd_i$ among (0,1) randomly.

        **If** $rnd_i < p_m$ , select $\left\lceil \dfrac{n}{2} \right\rceil$ quantum bit to apply the mutation operation (12).

    **End**

  **End**

**End**

**Step 5:** Carry out the conversion of the solution space of $P_g$ by equations (3), (4), (5) and (6), and output the final timing scheduling.

---

$$\Delta\theta_l = \begin{cases} 2\pi + \theta_{ilj} + \theta_{ij}(\theta_{ijl} - \theta_{ij} < -\pi) \\ \theta_{ijl} - \theta_{ij}(-\pi \le \theta_{ijl} - \theta_{ij} \le \pi) \\ \theta_{ijl} - \theta_{ij} - 2\pi(\theta_{ilj} - \theta_{ij} > \pi) \end{cases} \tag{7}$$

$$\Delta\theta_g = \begin{cases} 2\pi + \theta_{gj} + \theta_{ij}(\theta_{gj} - \theta_{ij} < -\pi) \\ \theta_{gj} - \theta_{ij}(-\pi \le \theta_{gj} - \theta_{ij} \le \pi) \\ \theta_{gj} - \theta_{ij} - 2\pi(\theta_{gj} - \theta_{ij} > \pi) \end{cases} \tag{8}$$

$$\Delta\theta_{ij}(t+1) = w\Delta\theta_{ij}(t) + c_1 r_1(\Delta\theta_l) + c_2 r_2(\Delta\theta_g) \tag{9}$$

$$\tilde{P}_{ic} = (\cos(\theta_{il}(t) + \Delta\theta_{il}(t+1)), \ldots\ldots, \cos(\theta_{in}(t) + \Delta\theta_{in}(t+1))) \qquad (10)$$

$$\tilde{P}_{ic} = (\sin(\theta_{il}(t) + \Delta\theta_{il}(t+1)), \ldots\ldots, \sin(\theta_{in}(t) + \Delta\theta_{in}(t+1))) \qquad (11)$$

$$\begin{bmatrix} 0 & 1 \\ 0 & 1 \end{bmatrix} \begin{bmatrix} \cos(\theta_{ij}) \\ \sin(\theta_{ij}) \end{bmatrix} = \begin{bmatrix} \sin(\theta_{ij}) \\ \cos(\theta_{ij}) \end{bmatrix} = \begin{bmatrix} \cos\left(\frac{\pi}{2} - \theta_{ij}\right) \\ \sin\left(\frac{\pi}{2} - \theta_{ij}\right) \end{bmatrix} \qquad (12)$$

## 3   The IOCA-PSO Method Simulations and Discussions

This section is devoted to analyzing EBML by extensive experiments. To provide a deep insight into actual urban traffic congestion, we speculate and verify the cause of traffic congestion in Sect. 3.1, which is combined with typical configurations. Furthermore, Sect. 3.2 describes the effect of the sites similar to overpass to EBML, which is practically important to alleviate the traffic congestion and improve the traffic flow. In Sect. 3.3, the timing scheduling of traffic lights in an actual urban case is optimized by EBML in extensive comparative experiments.

### 3.1   Typical Configurations and Traffic Congestions

Although 75 % of lattice sites can hold more than one vehicle in EBML, the traffic congestion happens more easily than that in BML with the same initial distribution of vehicles. In order to analysis the difference about traffic congestions in these two models, we implement numerical simulations at $\rho = 0.18$ and $\rho = 0.3$, which are the values from the first range and the second range, respectively.

As shown in Fig. 6, the velocity at the beginning in EBM is higher than that in BML at $\rho = 0.18$ and $\rho = 0.3$. Because with the same initial distribution of vehicles, most eastern or northern vehicles can still advance one lattice site in EBML, even if the next sites hold vehicles in the same direction. But only when the next site is empty can vehicles advance one site in BML. And the average velocities versus the time step have the similar changing trend in two models at $\rho = 0.18$ in Fig. 6(a). Nevertheless, the changing trends of the average velocity versus the time step are opposite obviously at $\rho = 0.3$ in Fig. 6(b). When t = 20000, the configurations in Fig. 6 can be seen as the final stable states in these two models at $\rho = 0.3$. The traffic flow in BML (Fig. 7(a)) finally self-organizes into alternating free-flow stripes (velocity = 1), but falls into global jams (velocity = 0) in EBML (Fig. 7(b)). What causes the different changing trends at $\rho = 0.18$ and $\rho = 0.3$ attracts us to discuss below.

Firstly, what uniquely differs from BML is that we add the sites with capacity 2, 3 and 4 in EBML. So it is speculated that the interference among different site capacities is the reason why the flow in EBML is jammed more easily.

Secondly, the speculation above can be verified as follows: (1) Enlarging site capacity to the same value is helpful for the flow velocity in fact. Comparing with the simulation above in BML, we implement simulations at $\rho = 0.3$ on a $150 \times 150$ lattice with the single capacity 2, 3 and 4, respectively. As shown in Fig. 8, the velocities with

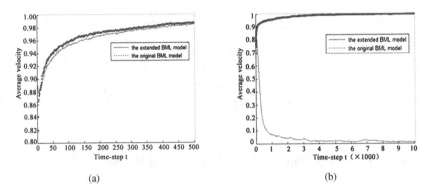

(a)                                    (b)

**Fig. 6.** (a) the average velocity of the traffic flow versus the time step in the two models at $\rho = 0.18$; (b) the average velocity of the traffic flow versus time step in the two models at $\rho = 0.3$. Red solid (blue dotted) lines are for the EBML (BML) (Color figure online).

the single capacity 2, 3 and 4 are higher than BML, which is equivalent to simulations with single capacity 1. Because there are no traffic congestions at $\rho = 0.3$, the velocities with the single capacity 2, 3 and 4 have the same outstanding performance. If the vehicle density is enlarged, the advantages of the highest single capacity 4 will increase. (2) When we implement the simulations in EBML, only the interference among different capacities can eliminate the advantage of enlarging site capacity. Let us consider two adjacent sites, the latter is filled with vehicles and the former is empty. When in EBML with single capacity, such as BML, all vehicles in the latter can advance together at the same time step. Nevertheless, when in the models with multiple capacities, assuming the latter with capacity 4 and the former with capacity 1, the vehicles in the latter need at least four corresponding time steps to evacuate. The accumulation of many similar partial phenomena results in the whole increase of the interference among different capacities, which makes the traffic flow jammed more easily in EBML.

(a)                                    (b)

**Fig. 7.** The typical configurations at $\rho = 0.3$ in $150 \times 150$ cellular space at t = 20000. (a) is in BML. (b) is in EBML.

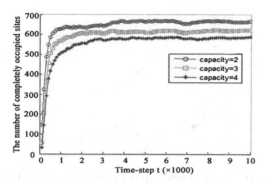

**Fig. 8.**   One kernel at $x_s$ (*dotted kernel*) or two kernels at $x_i$ and $x_j$ (*left and right*) lead to the same summed estimate at $x_s$. This shows a figure consisting of different types of lines. Elements of the figure described in the caption should be set in italics, in parentheses, as shown in this sample caption.

Furthermore, we can obtain the reason for different changing trends at $\rho = 0.18$ and at $\rho = 0.3$. Under the lower density, the interference among different capacities is non-significant in EBML, so the similar changing trends of these two models are shown in Fig. 7(a). But when the density increases, the mixed completely occupied sites with different capacities increase versus the time step. The interference among different capacities strengthens rapidly, and the changing trends of these two models become opposite in Fig. 7(b).

### 3.2   The Effect of Overpasses

After adding the mixed sites to the EBML, simulations with different $R_o$ are implemented, which are shown in Fig. 9. Because the sites ratios of four different unidirectional capacities are equivalent in EBML, we restrict that the ratios of corresponding four mixed sites are equivalent in the simulations. So we can draw conclusions as follows. (1) After we add some mixed sites, the average velocity improves at the same time step. With the ratio of overpasses increasing, the improved effect becomes increasingly evident. As the traffic congestion is mitigated, the final state always accompanies with the motion of some vehicles. As shown in Fig. 10, especially when $R_o = 0.6$ and $R_o = 0.8$, the average velocity is significantly higher than EBML. They all maintain at a steady flowing velocity finally. And more and more cars still move at last, when the ratio of overpasses increases. (2) The interference among different site capacities still exists in EBML with overpasses, which disturbs the running vehicles. At a low rate of the overpasses, the interference can be obviously reflected. As shown in Fig. 10, when at $R_o = 0.4$, the average velocity shows a small decreasing change from $t = 1000$ to $t = 4000$. It can be concluded that when the traffic congestion becomes more and more serious in EBML with overpasses, the interference among different site capacities increasingly inhibits the flowing velocity.

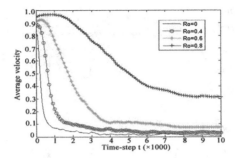

**Fig. 9.** The average velocity versus time step in EBML with the mixed sites at $\rho = 0.3$ with different $R_o$. The black solid line, the red circle line, the green star and the blue cross line denote $R_o = 0, R_o = 0.4, R_o = 0.6$ and $R_o = 0.8$, respectively (Color figure online).

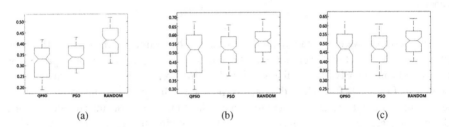

(a)                              (b)                              (c)

**Fig. 10.** Boxplots of the fitness value for three algorithms appearing in three time periods. (a) The congestion period (8:00–8:20). (b) The half free flow period (10:30–10:50). (c) The free flow period (20:30–20:50).

### 3.3    Optimization Results by QPSO

To verify the optimization by EBML, an actual urban case is selected randomly as an example in this section. As is shown in Fig. 4(a), an area centering Xudong in Wuhan is used as the objective urban area, which covers approximately 3 km$^2$ with 15 inter-sections. According to the traffic management bureau in Wuhan (http://www.whjg.gov.cn/), the traffic information in the main roads is obtained every 10 min, which is collected by sensor detections. Three typical time periods (8:00–8:20, 10:30–10:50, 20:30–20:50) in July 1, 2014 are selected, which are called as the congestion period, the half free flow period, the free flow period, respectively. The average vehicle velocities of the three time periods are 17 km/h, 34 km/h, and 51 km/h, respectively. The simulation in EBML is shown in Fig. 4(b). The swarm size in optimization is 100. The simulation time in EBML for a typical time periods are 1200 s (1200 time steps).

The PSO algorithm [12] and the RANDOM algorithm [12] are introduced as two comparison algorithms against the QPSO algorithm in EBML. The fitness function, the swarm size and the running time of two comparison algorithms are same with the QPSO algorithm, and their other parameters are set in accordance of their original settings. The boxplots of the fitness values for three algorithms in the three time periods are shown in Fig. 10. Among the three comparison algorithms, the QPSO algorithm always achieves the best performance in limited iterations. In three different time periods, the QPSO algorithm has the largest fluctuation range, and discovers the timing scheduling with the smallest fitness value. Compared with the PSO algorithm and the RANDOM algorithm, the QPSO algorithm can find a better timing scheduling in limited iterations.

# 4 Conclusion

An extended BML model (EBML) is proposed in this paper, which can model the traffic flow in the actual urban road network with different two-way multi-lane roads. Based on the scheduling simulation, the QPSO algorithm in EBML is used to improve the urban traffic flow by optimizing the timing scheduling of urban traffic lights. Several conclusions can be draw: (1) EBML exhibits a sharp phase transition from free flow to global jams. The critical density in EBML is distinctly smaller than that in BML, which means that the actual urban traffic flow can easily trap into global jams than the ideal situation in existing variants based on BML; (2) The experiments show that the interference among different site capacities in the actual urban traffic condition is the main reason why the traffic flow in EBML is jammed easily. Overpasses can alleviate the interference of EBML; (3) By on the scheduling simulation of EBML, the QPSO algorithm is improved to apply in the timing scheduling of urban traffic lights. Compared with the PSO algorithm and the RANDOM algorithm, the QPSO algorithm in EBML can find the better optimization results in the limited time.

**Acknowledgments.** This work is supported in part by the National Basic Research Program of China (973 Program) under Grant 2012CB719905, the National Natural Science Foundation of China under Grant 61572369 and 61471274, the National Natural Science Foundation of Hubei Province under Grant 2015CFB423, the Wuhan major science and technology program under Grant 2015010101010023.

# References

1. Hu, W., Wang, H., Du, B., Yan, L.: A multi-intersection model and signal timing plan algorithm for urban traffic signal control. Transport, 1–11 (2014)
2. Xing, J., Takahashi, H., Kameoka, H.: Mitigation of expressway traffic congestion through transportation demand management with toll discount. IET Intel. Transport Syst. 4(1), 50–60 (2010)
3. Finotti, C., Gaio, E.: Continuous model in dq frame of Thyristor Controlled Reactors for stability analysis of high power electrical systems. Int. J. Electr. Power Energy Syst. 63, 836–845 (2014)
4. Sazhin, S.S., Xie, J.F., Shishkova, I.N., Elwardany, A.E., Heikal, M.R.: A kinetic model of droplet heating and evaporation: Effects of inelastic collisions and a non-unity evaporation coefficient. Int. J. Heat Mass Transf. 56(1), 525–537 (2013)
5. Peng, G.H., Cheng, R.J.: A new car-following model with the consideration of anticipation optimal velocity. Physica A Stat. Mech. Appl. 392(17), 3563–3569 (2013)

6. Ding, Z.J., Jiang, R., Gao, Z.Y., Wang, B.H., Long, J.: Effect of overpasses in the Biham-Middleton-Levine traffic flow model with random and parallel update rule. Phys. Rev. E **88**(2), 022809 (2013)
7. Hu, W., Wang, H., Min, Z.: A storage allocation algorithm for outbound containers based on the outer-inner cellular automaton. Inf. Sci. **281**, 147–171 (2014)
8. Chowdhury, D., Schadschneider, A.: Self-organization of traffic jams in cities: Effects of stochastic dynamics and signal periods. Phys. Rev. E **59**(2), 1311–1314 (1999)
9. Wenbin, H., Liang, H., Peng, C., Bo, D., Qi, H.: A hybrid chaos-particle swarm optimization algorithm for the vehicle routing problem with time window. Entropy **15**(4), 1247–1270 (2013)
10. Mikki, S.M., Kishk, A.A.: Quantum particle swarm optimization for electromagnetics. IEEE Trans. Antennas Propag. **54**(10), 2764–2775 (2006)
11. Kachroudi, S., Bhouri, N. A multimodal traffic responsive strategy using particle swarm optimization. In: Control in Transportation Systems, pp. 531–537 (2009)
12. Garcia-Nieto, J., Alba, E.: Carolina olivera, a. swarm intelligence for traffic light scheduling: application to real urban areas. Eng. Appl. Artif. Intell. **25**(2), 274–283 (2012)
13. Cardillo, A., Scellato, S., Latora, V., Porta, S.: Structural properties of planar graphs of urban street patterns. Phys. Rev. E **73**(6), 95–104 (2006)

# Identifying Repeated Interleavings to Improve the Efficiency of Concurrency Bug Detection

Zhendong Wu$^{(\boxtimes)}$, Kai Lu, and Xiaoping Wang

Science and Technology on Parallel and Distributed Processing Laboratory,
College of Computer, National University of Defense Technology,
Changsha 410073, China
{wuzhendong,kailu,xiaopingwang}@nudt.edu.cn

**Abstract.** Detecting concurrency bugs is becoming increasingly important. Many pattern-based concurrency bug detectors focus on the specific types of interleavings that are correlated to concurrency bugs. To detect multiple types of concurrency bugs, general detectors focus on multiple types of interleaving patterns, including data race pattern, atomicity violation pattern, and atomic-set violation pattern. Unfortunately, they suffer from redundant analysis due to repeated interleavings, which may affect the efficiency of concurrency bug detection. Hence, we propose an approach to identify the repeated interleavings. To the best of our knowledge, this is the first approach that can prune repeated interleavings to improve the efficiency of concurrency bug detection. We apply our approach to existing general detectors (PECAN and Maple) to avoid analyzing repeated interleavings. We evaluated the general detectors with and without our approach, respectively. The experimental results show that the bug detection results are not affected. With our approach, the bug detection time of PECAN and Maple are reduced by 40.0 % and 44.4 %, respectively. Additionally, our approach does not affect the overhead of bug detection, and consumes only a little memory.

**Keywords:** Concurrency bug detection · Repeated interleaving · Pattern-based · Interleaving pattern · General detector

## 1 Introduction

Concurrent programs are prone to concurrency bugs. These bugs are difficult to be detected due to their non-deterministic characteristics. Even if a programmer manages to construct a test input that can trigger the bug, it is often difficult to expose the hidden bug. The concurrency bugs are hard to be detected during in-house testing and may cause severe damages after software deployment [1].

Recently, many detectors are proposed to detect concurrency bugs. RELAY [2], RaceMob [3], and SimRT [4] have focused on detecting data races. A data race occurs when two threads are about to access the same memory location, and at least one of the two accesses is a write, and the relative ordering of the two accesses is not enforced using synchronization primitives. These detectors can

© Springer International Publishing Switzerland 2015
G. Wang et al. (Eds.): ICA3PP 2015, Part IV, LNCS 9531, pp. 175–188, 2015.
DOI: 10.1007/978-3-319-27140-8_13

effectively detect the data races. However, atomicity violation is also one of the important types of concurrency bugs, and widely exists in concurrent programs. An atomicity violation occurs when the assumed atomicity is broken if the code region is unserializably interleaved by accesses from another thread. To detect atomicity violations, Ctrigger [5] and AssetFuzzer [6] are proposed. The above detectors are limited to detect single type of concurrency bug. Programmers need to use several existing detectors to detect all types of concurrency bugs, each of which detects a specific type of concurrency bug. However, using several detectors separately may increase detecting time significantly, and understanding different formats of results may need additional effort.

Fortunately, many general detectors are proposed to detect multiple types of concurrency bugs [7–10]. Unlike the detectors such as RELAY [2] and Ctrigger [5] which focus on specific type of interleaving pattern, general detectors are based on multiple types of interleaving patterns that can detect not only data races, but also atomicity violations and atomic-set violations. Therefore, the general detectors can detect more concurrency bugs during in-house testing. However, in those general detectors, we observe that repeated potential interleavings are analyzed since different interleaving patterns overlap, which reduces the efficiency of concurrency bug detection.

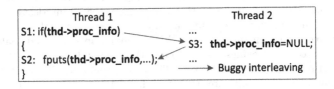

Fig. 1. A piece of code from MySQL

The general detectors always consist of multiple steps. The most important steps are predicting step and verifying step. The predicting step examines several dynamic executions to predict a set of potential interleavings based on the interleaving patterns. The verifying step actively controls thread schedule to verify the potential interleavings in many re-executions. However, the first step may produce many repeated potential interleavings, bringing many repeated re-executions in the second step, which affects the efficiency of concurrency bug detection. Figure 1 shows an example. Three potential interleavings (two data races and one atomicity violation) would be predicted in the first step. If the potential interleaving $S1$-$>S3$-$>S2$ ($S1$, $S2$, $S3$ are statements or static instructions) has been verified, it is unnecessary to verify the other two potential interleavings $S1$-$>S3$ and $S3$-$>S2$ again. Since the instance $iS1$-$>iS3$-$>iS2$ of $S1$-$>S3$-$>S2$ denotes three memory access events between two threads, and the instance $iS1$-$>iS3$ of $S1$-$>S3$ denotes two memory access events between two threads. We observe that it is unnecessary to verify the instance $iS1$-$>iS3$ as another instance $iS1$-$>iS3$-$>iS2$ has contained this instance. If the repeated potential interleavings $S1$->$S3$ and $S3$->$S2$ are not verified in re-executions, the efficiency would be improved significantly.

Based on our observation, we approximately evaluated the repeated potential interleavings in most of the general detectors. For example, in PECAN [7], 66.7 % of the potential interleavings are analyzed repeatedly in program Cache4j, and 57.1 % of the potential interleavings are analyzed repeatedly in program ArrayList. Therefore, there is a large space to improve the efficiency.

This paper proposes a new approach to identify repeated interleavings so that the general detectors can avoid verifying repeated potential interleavings. Our approach is not designed for data race detectors (e.g. RaceMob [3]) and atomicity violation detectors (e.g. Ctrigger [5]), since they focus on the specific interleaving pattern, and there are no repeated interleavings analyzed. Actually, multiple types of concurrency bugs exist in concurrent programs. General detectors that are based on general interleaving patterns suffer from verifying repeated potential interleavings.

To identify the repeated potential interleavings, we compare any two potential interleavings, checking whether one potential interleaving is repeated due to the other. We propose some metrics to determine whether a potential interleaving is repeated. If all memory access events of one potential interleaving ($P1$) are contained in another potential interleaving ($P2$), and the sequences of these memory access events in these two potential interleavings are consistent, we determine $P1$ as a repeated potential interleaving. Based on the metrics, we can compare the repeated relations between each pair of potential interleavings, and compute a set of potential interleavings which is necessary for verification. Therefore, general detectors can verify fewer potential interleavings, improving the efficiency of bug detection.

Overall, this paper makes the following contributions:

**(1) To our knowledge, this is the first approach that can identify repeated potential interleavings to improve the efficiency of concurrency bug detection.** Through analyzing potential interleavings produced by the general detectors, many repeated interleavings are identified and pruned. Therefore, the general detectors can verify fewer potential interleavings, improving the efficiency significantly.

**(2) We propose some metrics to determine whether a potential interleaving is repeated.** To avoid analyzing repeated potential interleavings in re-executions, we compare the memory access events of one potential interleaving with other potential interleavings, determining whether this interleaving is repeated.

**(3) We apply our approach to two general detectors (PECAN [7] and Maple [8]), and evaluate the enhanced general detectors on a number of real-world concurrent programs.** Results show that the bug detection results are not affected due to our approach. With our approach, the bug detection time of PECAN and Maple are reduced by 40.0 % and 44.4 %, respectively. Additionally, our approach does not affect the overhead, and consumes only a little memory.

## 2  Background

Concurrency bugs are difficult to be detected due to a combination of two conditions to manifest them. First, they require the right set of program inputs, which is exponential in number. Second, they also require the right thread interleaving, which is hidden in huge interleaving space [16]. Many previous tools assume that input design is out of the scope of concurrency bug detection, and this paper follows the same assumption.

Since different types of concurrency bugs always consist of different numbers of memory access events, some concurrency bugs reported by general detectors may be contained in other concurrency bugs. The repeated analysis may affect the efficiency of bug detection. The repeated results also need additional effort to understand. Figure 2(a) shows that the atomicity is violated due to data race. Thread 1's read-write sequence may falsely mingle with thread 2's read-write sequence to the same shared variable, leading to program's misbehavior. Since two threads read/write the same shared variable *buf->outcnt*, general detectors would report two data races and one atomicity violation in this piece of code, which may need additional effort. We observe that general detectors repeatedly analyze the interleavings that are correlated with data races. Figure 2(b) shows an atomicity violation which is data race free. In this piece of code, the three memory access events are protected by the common lock. The general detectors will report no data races. Therefore, there are no repeated interleavings analyzed.

According to the study on real world concurrency bug characteristics [20], most of the concurrency bugs involve no more than two shared variables. The study also finds that concurrency bugs can deterministically manifest, if certain orders among at most four memory accesses are enforced. These findings guide us to propose some metrics to determine whether an interleaving is repeated.

To detect the real concurrency bugs, general detectors need to verify all potential interleavings in many re-executions. During each re-execution, the general detectors actively control thread schedule to verify one potential interleaving. However, the repeated potential interleavings may cause the general detectors to repeatedly re-execute the program. We observe that there is a large space to improve the efficiency of general detectors.

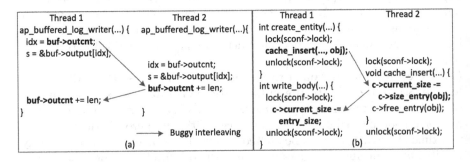

**Fig. 2.** Concurrency bugs from MySQL and Apache

# 3   Design and Implementation

## 3.1   Overview

General detectors such as PECAN [7] and Maple [8] always consist of two main phases. They use imprecise technique to predict potential interleavings. Then, for each potential interleaving, they re-execute the program by controlling thread schedule, verifying whether the potential interleaving can lead to a real concurrency bug. Unfortunately, some potential interleavings are verified repeatedly, affecting the efficiency. We propose a new approach to identify the repeated potential interleavings. Figure 3 shows the new architecture of a general detector, comprising three main components: (1) the predictor, (2) the iAnalyzer (*interleaving analyzer*), and (3) the verifier. The predictor analyzes program trace to predict potential interleavings. The verifier actively controls thread schedule to verify the potential interleavings.

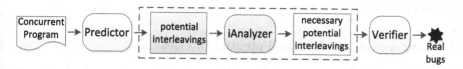

**Fig. 3.** New architecture of general detector

The iAnalyzer component is our key technique. It inputs a set of potential interleavings, and identifies the repeated ones, and outputs a set of potential interleavings which is necessary for verification. The iAnalyzer works in two phases. It first categorizes all potential interleavings into $N$ groups. The potential interleavings with the same number of memory access events are in the same group. Then, it traverses all the potential interleavings in each group, comparing each interleaving with all the potential interleavings in other groups, and determining whether it is repeated.

## 3.2   Definition

Through investigating many real-world concurrency bugs, we observe that the manifestations of most concurrency bugs involve no more than two shared variables and no more than four memory access events. According to [7,8,20], the interleaving patterns defined in general detectors are sequences of 2–4 memory access events generated by two different threads (see Fig. 4). A memory access event is a shared memory access (either a read operation or a write operation) by a thread. We use *Event(i)* to describe the interleaving patterns. For example, Pattern1 can be described as *Event1->Event2*, and Pattern2 can be described as *Event1->Event2->Event3*. An instance of Pattern1 can be described as *event1->event2*, and an instance of Pattern2 can be described as *event1->event2->event3*.

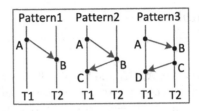

**Fig. 4.** Interleaving patterns in most general detectors

To help programmers to understand the concurrency bugs, general detectors always report concurrency bugs as sequences of statements executed by two different threads. For example, the general detectors will report $S1\text{-}>S3\text{-}>S2$ as a concurrency bug in Fig. 1. The instance of each pattern can also be described as 2–4 statements. Different from the general detectors that analyze the dynamic instances of statements to infer potential interleavings, our work is based on the inferred potential interleavings.

### 3.3   Determining Repeated Potential Interleavings

To determine whether an instance $p1$ of Pattern1 is repeated, we check whether both of the two events of $p1$ equal the two events of another instance $p2$ of Pattern2 (or another instance $p3$ of Pattern3), and the sequence of these two events are consistent in these two instances. The events are statements or static instructions that would access the same shared variables. To check whether two events are equal, we only need to compare the statements or static instructions. Therefore, two potential interleavings (data races) in Fig. 1 are both repeated since the other potential interleaving (atomicity violation) has already contained them. If the general detectors have verified $S1\text{-}>S3\text{-}>S2$, it is unnecessary to verify $S1\text{-}>S3$ and $S3\text{-}>S2$. Our strategy is checking whether the two events of $p1$ equal the first and the second events of $p2$, or equal the second and the third events of $p2$. If so, we say $p1$ is repeated due to $p2$. If we can determine $p1$ is repeated due to any instance of Pattern2, we continue to analyze the other potential interleavings. If $p1$ cannot be determined repeated due to all the instances of Pattern2, we compare $p1$ with all the instances of Pattern3. Similarly, we check whether the two events of $p1$ equal the first and the second events of $p3$, or equal the third and the fourth events of $p3$. If so, we can say $p1$ is repeated due to $p3$.

To determine whether an instance $p2$ of Pattern2 is repeated, we need to check whether all the three events of $p2$ equal the three events of another instance of Pattern3, and the sequences of these three events are consistent. Since the instances of Pattern3 contain four events, there are no other instances of other patterns which can contain all of these four events. Therefore, all the instances of Pattern3 are not repeated in our current metrics.

The definition of interleaving patterns in different general detectors may be a little different from each other, but the strategies to determine repeated potential interleavings are similar.

We have discussed how to determine whether a potential interleaving (an instance of one interleaving pattern) is repeated based on the definition of interleaving patterns. Our current metrics indicate that the potential interleavings which have 2–3 memory access events would be determined as repeated interleavings. Therefore, we need to check each pair of potential interleavings which has different number of memory access events.

Before comparing each pair of potential interleavings, we group all potential interleavings based on the number of events. The potential interleavings which have the same number of events are grouped into the same group. After grouping, we check all potential interleavings in all groups, identifying all the repeated ones. Then, before verification, we prune the repeated potential interleavings. Consequently, to detect the real concurrency bugs, the general detectors need to verify fewer potential interleavings, improving the efficiency.

## 3.4    Applying Our Approach to PECAN and Maple

We have implemented our approach as a Java tool which is called iAnalyzer. We applied iAnalyzer to two existing general detectors (PECAN [7] and Maple [8]), checking whether the efficiency of these two detectors are improved.

**PECAN.** PECAN is a persuasive bug prediction tool that can detect not only atomicity violations but also data races and atomic-set violations. It takes the bytecode of a Java program and produces two versions of this program: the record version and the replay version. The record version is executed for trace collection, and the replay version is used to create a concrete execution that exposes the predicted potential interleavings. PECAN executes the record version to collect trace. It then analyzes the collected trace, and predicts potential interleavings. To find the true concurrency bugs, it controls thread schedule to enforce a deterministic execution order of all the events, creating the potential interleaving, checking whether program failure occurs. If so, one true concurrency bug is exposed and detected. The interleaving patterns defined in PECAN are generic, which makes it can detect multiple types of concurrency bugs.

PECAN comprises four jar files that are responsible for instrumenting Java programs statically, collecting the trace of memory access events, predicting potential interleavings, and controlling thread schedule to verify the potential interleavings. These jar files can be executed separately. Therefore, it is convenient to apply iAnalyzer to PECAN. We use iAnalyzer to read the potential interleavings, identifying the repeated ones. Then, iAnalyzer deletes the schedule files which are related to the repeated interleavings. Finally, PECAN re-executes the program fewer times to verify the remaining potential interleavings.

**Maple.** Maple is a new interleaving coverage-driven testing tool that can expose untested interleavings as many as possible. It memorizes tested interleavings and actively seeks to expose untested interleavings for a given test input. To detect multiple types of concurrency bugs, Maple defines a set of interleaving patterns, including atomicity violation pattern, data race pattern, atomic-set violation pattern. Maple works in two phases. First, it uses an online imprecise technique to predict potential interleavings that can potentially be exposed for a given test input. The predicted potential interleavings are untested before. Second, the predicted potential interleavings are exposed by actively controlling thread schedule. Maple avoids testing the same interleavings across different test inputs, improving the efficiency of concurrency bug detection.

Maple is implemented as a binary instrumentation tool, and invoked by Python. To apply iAnalyzer to Maple, a little modification is needed. We modified some Python code to execute iAnalyzer between the predictor and the verifier. Before the verifier works, iAnalyzer reads potential interleavings from DB files, identifying and pruning the repeated ones, and saving the remaining potential interleavings into the same DB files. Therefore, Maple would re-execute the program fewer times to verify fewer potential interleavings.

## 4    Evaluation

The goal of our work is to identify repeated interleavings to improve the efficiency. Accordingly, our evaluation aims at two aspects:

*(1) Effectiveness-will our approach affect the bug detection results?* To answer this question, we evaluated the bug detection results of PECAN and Maple, without and with iAnalyzer, respectively. Whether the results of these two enhanced detectors are affected was to evaluate the effectiveness of iAnalyzer.

*(2) Efficiency-how efficient is our approach for general detectors?* To answer this question, we evaluated the bug detection time of PECAN and Maple. We computed how much time is reduced by iAnalyzer. We also evaluated the overhead of PECAN and Maple, checking if the overhead is affected due to iAnalyzer.

### 4.1    Benchmarks

PECAN and Maple are implemented for different programming languages. We evaluated them on different programs. Table 1 shows the benchmarks. Column 1 shows the ID of programs. Column 2, 3 show the names and lines of programs for PECAN. Column 4, 5 show the names and lines of programs for Maple.

**Programs for PECAN.** Among these programs, 4 (#1 to #4) are open libraries from JDK 1.4.2. We write test cases to test these libraries. 1 (#5) is an standard benchmark from the Java Grande Forum. 2 (#6 to #7) are from IBM ConTest. 1 (#8) is a thread-safe implementation of cache for Java objects.

**Programs for Maple.** Among these programs, 3 (#1 to #3) are kernel programs. 1 (#4) is a parallel implementation of the bzip2 block-sorting file compressor. 1 (#5) is a parallel file scanning tool. 1 (#6) is a file downloader. 2 (#7 to #8) are scientific programs from splash2 [21].

**Table 1.** Programs for PECAN and Maple

|    | PECAN | | Maple | |
| --- | --- | --- | --- | --- |
| ID | Programs | LOC | Programs | LOC |
| 1 | ArrayList | 5,866 | StringBuffer | 180 |
| 2 | HashSet | 7,086 | CircularList | 155 |
| 3 | LinkedList | 5,979 | MySQL* | 120 |
| 4 | TreeSet | 7,352 | Pbzip2 | 1,957 |
| 5 | RayTracer | 1,923 | Pfscan | 944 |
| 6 | MergeSort | 456 | Aget | 2,527 |
| 7 | BuggyProg | 385 | FFT | 901 |
| 8 | Cache4j | 3,897 | Radix | 787 |

## 4.2 Bug Detection Results

Since PECAN and Maple are designed to detect general concurrency bugs, the results reported by them always have some repeated results. For example, in Fig. 1, the detectors may report two concurrency bugs: $S1$->$S3$->$S2$ and $S3$->$S2$. However, the programmers only need to fix bug $S1$->$S3$->$S2$. Therefore, bug $S3$->$S2$ is repeatedly reported. To count the correct number of reported concurrency bugs, we group the reported bugs according to the technique in Griffin [22]. The grouping strategy is: if the memory accesses of one concurrency bug ($bug1$) are contained in another concurrency bug ($bugX$) and the sequence of these memory accesses is consistent, we determine $bug1$ as a repeated bug.

In our evaluation, the repeated results are omitted. To evaluate the effectiveness of iAnalyzer, we compared the results of general detectors with and without iAnalyzer, respectively (Table 2). Column 2, 3 show the bug detection results (the number of concurrency bugs) of PECAN, without and with iAnalyzer, respectively. As we can see, the concurrency bugs reported by PECAN and Maple with iAnalyzer are the same as without iAnalyzer, which indicates that iAnalyzer has not affected the bug detection results.

**Table 2.** Bug detection results of PECAN and Maple, without and with iAnalyzer

| PECAN | | | Maple | | |
| --- | --- | --- | --- | --- | --- |
| Programs | Original | By iAnalyzer | Programs | Original | By iAnalyzer |
| ArrayList | 2 | 2 | StringBuffer | 3 | 3 |
| HashSet | 5 | 5 | CircularList | 3 | 3 |
| LinkedList | 3 | 3 | MySQL* | 1 | 1 |
| TreeSet | 4 | 4 | Pbzip2 | 1 | 1 |
| RayTracer | 1 | 1 | Pfscan | 2 | 2 |
| MergeSort | 1 | 1 | Aget | 1 | 1 |
| BuggyProg | 1 | 1 | FFT | 2 | 2 |
| Cache4j | 2 | 2 | Radix | 8 | 8 |

### 4.3    Performance

The key contribution of our work is to improve the efficiency of concurrency bug detection. By iAnalyzer, general detectors can avoid verifying repeated interleavings, and the number of program re-executions is also reduced.

We evaluated the bug detection time of general detectors, without and with iAnalyzer, respectively, checking whether iAnalyzer can reduce the time. Table 3 shows the experimental results of PECAN and Maple. Column 2, 3 report the bug detection time of PECAN, without and with iAnalyzer, respectively. Column 6, 7 report the bug detection time of Maple, without and with iAnalyzer, respectively. The reported time numbers are the average across 10 runs. As we can see, the bug detection time of PECAN is reduced significantly, ranges from 3.9 % to 54.3 %. Therefore, iAnalyzer reduces the bug detection time of PECAN, with an average of 40.0 %. For Maple, the reduced time ranges from 10.2 % to 89.8 %, and on average is at about 44.4 %.

**Table 3.** Bug detection time of PECAN and Maple, without and with iAnalyzer

| PECAN (ms) | | | | Maple (second) | | | |
|---|---|---|---|---|---|---|---|
| Programs | Original | By iAna | Reduced | Programs | Original | By iAna | Reduced |
| ArrayList | 898 | 410 | 54.3 % | StringBuffer | 951.8 | 770.6 | 19.0 % |
| HashSet | 827 | 421 | 49.1 % | CircularList | 74.8 | 24.0 | 67.9 % |
| LinkedList | 2,105 | 1,334 | 36.6 % | MySQL* | 367.6 | 323.6 | 12.0 % |
| TreeSet | 625 | 312 | 50.1 % | Pbzip2 | 57.1 | 11.4 | 80.0 % |
| RayTracer | 470,979 | 235,936 | 49.9 % | Pfscan | 476.2 | 48.5 | 89.8 % |
| MergeSort | 8,034 | 4,789 | 40.4 % | Aget | 735.2 | 532.2 | 27.6 % |
| BuggyProg | 9,188 | 8,832 | 3.9 % | FFT | 13,329.3 | 11,967.1 | 10.2 % |
| Cache4j | 7,842 | 6,308 | 19.6 % | Radix | 86.1 | 43.9 | 49.0 % |
| Average | | | 40.0 % | Average | | | 44.4 % |

To identify the repeated potential interleavings, iAnalyzer traverses all the potential interleavings, which may affects the efficiency of general detectors. Since iAnalyzer is an off-line tool, the time spent on each program is small. For PECAN, we evaluated the time spent by iAnalyzer on each program. The average time is only 15.5 ms. Comparing with the time spent by PECAN, iAnalyzer would affect the efficiency only a littile. For Maple, the average time spent by iAnalyzer is 390 ms, which is also much smaller than the time spent by Maple.

Since general detectors dynamically control thread schedule to verify potential interleavings, runtime overhead is imposed due to instrumentation. We evaluated the overhead, without and with iAnalyzer, respectively. Table 4 shows the average overhead on each program. Column 2, 3 report the overhead of PECAN, without and with iAnalyzer, respectively. Column 5, 6 report the overhead of Maple, without and with iAnalyzer, respectively. Since general detectors execute

**Table 4.** Overhead of PECAN and Maple, without and with iAnalyzer

| PECAN | | | Maple | | |
|---|---|---|---|---|---|
| Programs | Original | By iAnalyzer | Programs | Original | By iAnalyzer |
| ArrayList | 1.4X | 1.3X | StringBuffer | 2.1X | 2.6X |
| HashSet | 1.0X | 1.1X | CircularList | 2.5X | 2.7X |
| LinkedList | 2.2X | 2.3X | MySQL* | 1.8X | 1.1X |
| TreeSet | 1.5X | 1.9X | Pbzip2 | 15.4X | 12X |
| RayTracer | 4.5X | 4.1X | Pfscan | 9.7X | 9.4X |
| MergeSort | 1.7X | 1.6X | Aget | 34.8X | 35.3X |
| BuggyProg | 2.5X | 2.8X | FFT | 14.3X | 13.9X |
| Cache4j | 0.5X | 0.7X | Radix | 13.8X | 13.3X |

the program multiple times to verify multiple potential interleavings, the overhead of each execution may be different. The reported overhead numbers are the average across all executions of each program. As we can see, the average overhead of each program is nearly not affected.

Additionally, we evaluated the memory used in each phase of PECAN. Table 5 shows the memory used by PECAN and iAnalyzer. Column 2 reports the memory used by instrumentation phase of PECAN. This phase consumes much more memory than others, because it analyzes the control flow graph of the whole program and instruments logging and replaying functions before memory access instructions. Column 3, 4 report the memory used by monitor phase and replay phase, respectively. Column 5 reports the memory used by iAnalyzer, which indicates that our approach uses only a little memory.

**Table 5.** Memory used by PECAN and iAnalyzer

| Programs | Instrumentation | Record | Replay | iAnalyzer |
|---|---|---|---|---|
| ArrayList | 1445M | 48M | 45M | 4M |
| HashSet | 1405M | 49M | 46M | 8M |
| LinkedList | 1441M | 49M | 47M | 9M |
| TreeSet | 1485M | 50M | 47M | 10M |
| RayTracer | 1312M | 48M | 42M | 7M |
| MergeSort | 1370M | 49M | 48M | 6M |
| BuggyProg | 1276M | 49M | 49M | 5M |
| Cache4j | 1381M | 229M | 163M | 13M |
| Average | 1397M | 68M | 59M | 7M |

## 5   Discussion

Since the potential interleavings are verified dynamically, general detectors may produce false negatives due to limited execution paths [13,23]. The dynamic verification can accurately identify the real bugs that are in execution paths.

To expose the real concurrency bugs quickly, what potential interleavings should be verified first is also important. The ranking strategy used in Ctrigger [5] exposes the deeply hidden atomicity violations more quickly. Our approach analyzes the potential interleavings, identifying and pruning the repeated ones. It is also easy to rank the remaining potential interleavings.

Additionally, general detectors always instrument the program to monitor execution behaviors and dynamically control thread schedule to verify potential interleavings so that runtime overhead is imposed. Our approach cannot reduce the number of instrumentation so that the overhead is not reduced. The efficiency is improved due to the pruning of repeated interleavings. We also try to design some strategies (hardware support [16]) to achieve lower overhead.

## 6   Related Work

Recently, many detectors are proposed to detect concurrency bugs. Some detectors focus on data races [2–4,11–13]. RELAY [2] is a lockset-based race detector which uses inter-procedural analysis. It flags a race whenever it sees at least two accesses to the same memory location, and at least one of the accesses is a write, and the accesses are not protected by at least one common lock. RaceFuzzer [13] is a dynamic race detector that first uses imprecise information to compute a set of data races. It then executes the program by controlling thread schedule, detecting the harmful races. RaceMob [3] is a crowdsourcing based approach for race detection. RD2 [14] is dynamic commutativity race detector which can detect the races due to concurrent interaction at the library interface.

However, atomicity violation is also common. Many detectors have been proposed [5,6,15]. AVIO [15] uses access interleaving invariants to detect atomicity violations. Ctrigger [5] focuses on unserializable interleavings that are correlated to atomicity violations. It first uses trace analysis to identify feasible unserializable interleavings. Then, it actively controls thread schedule to exercise low-probability interleavings, and exposes atomicity violations. AssetFuzzer [6] is an active randomized testing technique which can detect atomic-set serializability violations. Kivati [16] uses hardware watchpoints to efficiently detect and prevent atomicity violations. DoubleChecker [17] achieves lower overhead than previous tools, making dynamic atomicity checking more practical.

Unfortunately, both race detectors and atomicity violation detectors are easy to miss concurrency bugs due to limited interleaving patterns. For example, the race detectors cannot detect some atomicity violations in concurrent programs. To detect more types of concurrency bugs, general detectors are proposed [7–10]. PECAN [7] uses persuasive bug prediction technique, which can detect not only atomicity violations, but also data races and atomic-set violations. These detectors define general interleaving patterns, including data race pattern, atomicity violation pattern. They can detect multiple types of concurrency bugs. Since general interleaving patterns defined in these detectors overlap each other, repeated potential interleavings may be analyzed, which affects the efficiency of bug detection. Our approach can identify repeated potential interleavings.

# 7   Conclusion and Future Work

This paper proposes a new approach that can identify and prune repeated potential interleavings for concurrency bug detection. We apply our approach to two general detectors (PECAN [7] and Maple [8]). The experimental results show that our approach would not affect the results, and the efficiency is improved. To our knowledge, this is the first approach that is introduced for concurrency bug detection to improve the efficiency. Future work will concern several aspects. First, we plan to combine with other techniques [24–27] to detect more bugs. Second, we plan to apply our approach to more general detectors. Third, we plan to use deterministic techniques [18,19] to reduce interleaving space.

**Acknowledgments.** This work was partially supported by National High-tech R&D Program of China (863 Program) under Grants 2012AA01A301 and 2012AA010901, by National Science Foundation (NSF) China 61272142, 61103082, 61402492, 61170261 and 61103193, and by Innovation Fund Sponsor Project of Excellent Postgraduate Student B130608.

# References

1. SecurityFocus, Software bug contributed to blackout. http://www.securityfocus.com/news/8016
2. Voung, J.W., Jhala, R., Lerner, S.: Relay: static race detection on millions of lines of code. In: ACM Symposium on the Foundations of Software Engineering (2007)
3. Kasikci, B., Zamfir, C., Candea, G.: Racemob: crowdsourced data race detection. In: ACM Symposium on Operating Systems Principles (2013)
4. Yu, T., Srisaan, W., Rothermel, G.: Simrt: An automated framework to support regression testing for data races. In: Proceedings of the 36th International Conference on Software Engineering (2014)
5. Park, S., Lu, S., Zhou, Y.: Ctrigger: exposing atomicity violation bugs from their hiding places. In: 14th International Conference on Architectural Support for Programming Languages and Operating Systems (2009)
6. Lai, Z., Cheung, S.C., Chan, W.K.: Detecting atomic-set serializability violations in multithreaded programs through active randomized testing. In: Proceedings of the 32th International Conference on Software Engineering (2010)
7. Huang, J., Zhang, C.: Persuasive prediction of concurrency access anomalies. In: International Symposium on Software Testing and Analysis (2011)
8. Yu, J., Narayanasamy, S., Pereira, C., Pokam, G.: Maple: a coverage-driven testing tool for multithreaded programs. In: Proceedings of the ACM International Conference on Object Oriented Programming Systems Languages and Applications (2012)

9. Park, S., Vuduc, R.W., Harrold, M.J.: Falcon: fault localization in concurrent programs. In: 32th International Conference on Software Engineering (2010)
10. Park, S., Vuduc, R.W., Harrold, M.J.: A unified approach for localizing non-deadlock concurrency bugs. In: IEEE 5th International Conference on Software Testing, Verification and Validation (2012)
11. Eslamimehr, M., Palsberg, J.: Race directed scheduling of concurrent programs. In: 19th ACM Symposium on Principles and Practice of Parallel Programming (2014)
12. Zhendong, W., Kai, L., Xiaoping, W., Xu, Z.: Collaborative technique for concurrency bug detection. In: International Journal of Parallel Programming (2014)
13. Sen, K.: Race directed random testing of concurrent programs. In: ACM Conference on Programming Language Design and Implementation (2008)
14. Dimitrov, D., Raychev, V., Vechev, M., Koskinen, E.: Commutativity race detection. In: Proceedings of the 2014 ACM Conference on Programming Language Design and Implementation (2014)
15. Shan, L., Tucek, J., Qin, F., Yuanyuan, Z.: Avio: detecting atomicity violations via access interleaving invariants. In: Proceeding of the 11th International Conference on Architectural Support for Programming Languages and Operating Systems (2006)
16. Chew, L., Lie, D.: Kivati: fast detection and prevention of atomicity violations. In: Proceedings of the 5th European Conference on Computer Systems (2010)
17. Biswas, S., Huang, J., Sengupta, A., Bond, M.D.: Doublechecker: efficient sound and precise atomicity checking. In: Proceedings of the 2014 ACM Conference on Programming Language Design and Implementation (2014)
18. Xu, Z., Kai, L., Xiaoping, W., Xu, L.: Exploiting parallelism in deterministic shared memory multiprocessing. In: Journal of Parallel and Distributed Computing (2012)
19. Kai, L., Xu, Z., Bergan, T., Xiaoping, W.: Efficient deterministic multithreading without global barriers. In: Proceedings of the 19th ACM Symposium on Principles and Practice of Parallel Programming (2014)
20. Shan, L., Park, S., Seo, E., Yuanyuan, Z.: Learning from mistakes? a comprehensive study on real world concurrency bug characteristics. In: 13th International Conference on Architectural Support for Programming Languages and Operating Systems (2008)
21. Woo, S.C., Ohara, M., Torrie, E., Singh, J.P., Gupta, A.: The splash-2 programs: characterization and methodological considerations. In: Proceedings 22nd Annual International Symposium on Computer Architecture (1995)
22. Park, S., Vuduc, R.W., Harrold, M.J.: Griffin: grouping suspicious memory-access patterns to improve understanding of concurrency bugs. In: Proceedings of the 2013 International Symposium on Software Testing and Analysis (2013)
23. Shan, L., Zhou, P., Liu, W., Zhou, Y., Torrellas, J.: Pathexpander: Architectural support for increasing the path coverage of dynamic bug detection. In: IEEE/ACM International Symposium on Microarchitecture (2006)
24. Cadar, C., Sen, K.: Symbolic execution for software testing: three decades later. Commun. ACM 56(2), 82–90 (2013)
25. Xiaoguang, M., Yan, L., Ziying, D., Yuhua, Q., Chengsong, W.: Slice-based statistical fault localization. J. Syst. Softw. 89, 51–62 (2014)
26. Zhuo, Z., Xiaoguang, M., Yan, L., Peng, Z.: Enriching contextual information for fault localization. IEICE Trans. 97–D, 1652–1655 (2014)
27. Qianming, Y., Mei, W., Nan, W., Chunyuan, Z.: Accelerating thread-intensive and explicit memory management programs with dynamic partial reconfiguration. J. Supercomputing 63, 508–537 (2013)

# Global Reliability Evaluation for Cloud Storage Systems with Proactive Fault Tolerance

Jing Li[1], Mingze Li[1], Gang Wang[1]($^{(\boxtimes)}$), Xiaoguang Liu[1], Zhongwei Li[1]($^{(\boxtimes)}$), and Huijun Tang[2]

[1] Nankai-Baidu Joint Lab,
College of Computer and Control Engineering and College of Software,
Nankai University, Tianjin 300350, China
{lijing,limingze,wgzwp,liuxg,lizhongwei}@nbjl.nankai.edu.cn
[2] Qihoo 360 Technology Company, Beijing 100621, China
tanghuijun@360.cn

**Abstract.** In addition to the traditional reactive fault-tolerant technologies, such as erasure codes and replication, proactive fault tolerance can be used to improve the system's reliability significantly. To the best of our knowledge, however, there is no previous publications on the reliability of such a cloud storage system except for those on RAID systems. In this paper, several Markov-based models are respectively proposed to evaluate the reliability of the cloud storage systems with/without proactive fault tolerance from the system perspective. Since proactive measure should be coupled with some reactive measure to ensure the systems reliability, the reliability model for such a system will be very intricate. To facilitate model building, we propose the *basic state transition unit* (BSTU), to describe the general pattern of state transition in the proactive cloud storage systems. BSTU serves as the generic "brick" for building the overall reliability model for such a system. Using our models, we demonstrate the benefits that proactive fault tolerance has on a system's reliability, and also estimate the impacts of some system parameters on it.

**Keywords:** Cloud storage system · Proactive fault tolerance · Reactive fault tolerance · Global reliability model · Rack aware replication

## 1 Introduction

Replication and erasure codes are the traditional means by which cloud storage systems are made reliable. If some replicas are lost due to node failures, other survived replicas can be used to restore them to maintain the same level of reliability. This is a typical reactive fault-tolerant manner. Recently, some researchers have proposed deploying proactive fault tolerance on storage systems [1–7], which undertakes to predict failures and handle them in advance. The main advantage of proactive fault tolerance is the early head start for the rebuild while the dying drive/node is still alive.

© Springer International Publishing Switzerland 2015
G. Wang et al. (Eds.): ICA3PP 2015, Part IV, LNCS 9531, pp. 189–203, 2015.
DOI: 10.1007/978-3-319-27140-8_14

At present, the research work on the reliability for cloud storage system, has mainly been focused on a single file or an independent peer, and does not consider the rack aware placement strategy which is common in the current systems. Moreover, as said in [8], since proactive fault tolerance can not avoid failure completely, it is also necessary to be coupled with a reactive fault tolerance measure to ensure a system's reliability. Therefore the state transitions of the system are very intricate. So far, there is no relevant research on reliability for such a cloud storage system except for those on RAID-5/6 systems [7,8].

In this work we use Markov chain based methods to respectively present several global reliability evaluation models for the cloud storage systems with/without proactive fault tolerance. To construct the complex and intractable reliability models for systems with proactive fault tolerance, we propose a generic "brick" – basic state transition unit (BSTU), to describe the fundamental laws of state transitions in the model. Using our reliability models, we deduce the actual reliability gaps between systems with different replication factors, demonstrate the effects that proactive fault tolerance has on the reliability of a system given a parameterized sensitivity, and also estimate the impacts of other system parameters.

## 2   Related Work

Many studies [9,10] were on the distributed file system based on P2P networks, but their focuses were on the reliability of a single file or an independent peer, rather than on the systematic study of data reliability. Based on Markov model, Lian et al. [11] provided an analytical framework to reason and quantify the impact of replica placement policy on storage system reliability. However they did not consider the real placement strategy that replicas are random distributed across racks and nodes. And, a few studies had used probabilistic methods [12,13] to estimate the reliability of the system, however, the probability of data loss in these works took into account only the time spent by the system in failure-free state and ignored the rebuild times, which made their results not reflecting a realistic picture of the system's reliability. Moreover, KK Rao et al. [14] presented Markov models to determine the reliability of the high-end enterprise storage systems, which were realized through networked storage nodes. Our work is similar to KK Rao's, however we focus on the effect of failure prediction for rack aware replication, which is a common placement policy used in the current systems.

For storage systems with proactive fault tolerance, there are only few studies focusing on their reliability. Eckart et al. [8] first used Markov models to rigorously demonstrate the effects that failure prediction has on a system's MTTDL (mean time to data loss). They only devised models for a single hard drive, RAID-1, and RAID-5 systems. In our previous work [7], we extended this study into RAID-6 systems. However, to our best knowledge, there is no study on such cloud storage systems based on replication schemes.

# 3    Reliability Models for Reactive Cloud Storage Systems

Assuming independent exponential probability distributions for failure and repair of individual storage nodes, we build the Markov reliability evaluation models for traditional reactive cloud storage systems.

Consider cloud storage systems with $r$ racks and each rack having $n$ nodes, replicas of each data block are spread across nodes and racks. The systems are block-based storage systems, and maintain two invariants: first, no two replicas of a data block are stored on the same node; and second, replicas of a data block must be found on at least two racks. We use $c$ to denote storage capacity of each node, $\lambda$ to denote failure rate of a node, and $\mu$ to denote rebuild rate of a failure.

## 3.1    Reactive with Replication Factor Two

In a system with replication factor 2, every user data block is replicated 2 times and the 2 replicas must be stored on two separate racks. We assume that there have been enough data blocks in the system and they are fully dispersed, such that any pair of nodes from different racks share at least one data block. A system with replication factor 2 can tolerate any single node failure and a portion of $t$ node failures for $2 \leq t \leq n$. System data loss occurs if and only if node failures occur on two or more racks.

We build the reliability model for a system with replication factor 2 as shown in Fig. 1. In this model, there are $n+2$ states in total, which fall into three types: (1) $S_0$ represents a completely healthy state, during which there is no node failure at all; (2) $S_i$, where $1 \leq i \leq n$, represent the degraded states, during which $i$ nodes have already failed and all the $i$ failures are on the same rack; (3) $DL$ represents the absorbing state at which point true data loss occurs.

The system begins in the healthy state $S_0$, and will transfer to state $S_1$ with the rate of $rn\lambda$, when a storage node failure occurs. During the state $S_1$, the system initiates a rebuild process to repair the failure, then the system can transfer to any one of three states: $S_0$, with the rate of $\mu$, if the failure has been

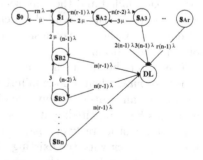

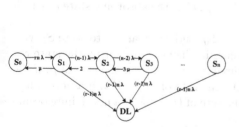

**Fig. 1.** Markov model for replication factor two without failure prediction.

**Fig. 2.** Markov model for replication factor three without failure prediction.

repaired at rate $\mu$; $S_2$, with the rate of $(n-1)\lambda$, if another failure occurs on the same rack with the existing one before the rebuild process is finished; or $DL$, with the rate of $(r-1)n\lambda$, if a new failure occurs on the other rack before the rebuild process is finished, and at this point, since there have happened some node failures on two different racks, the system goes into data loss state.

Similarly, during the state $S_i$ $(1 < i < n)$, the system can transfer to any one of three states: $S_{i-1}$, with the rate of $i\mu$, if one of the $i$ failures has been repaired; $S_{i+1}$, with the rate of $(n-i)\lambda$, if a new failure occurs on the same rack with the existing ones; or $DL$, with the rate of $(r-1)n\lambda$, if a new failure occurs on a previously healthy rack. During the state $S_n$, when all nodes on some rack have failed, the system is already in the critical condition and can transfer to either of two states: $S_{n-1}$, with the rate of $n\mu$, if one of the $n$ failures has been repaired; $DL$, with the rate of $(r-1)n\lambda$, if a new failure occurs.

## 3.2    Reactive with Replication Factor Three

In a system with replication factor 3, every user data block is replicated 3 times, and then the 3 replicas need to be stored in some 3 nodes out of which 2 nodes are on a same rack and 1 node is on another rack. We assume that there have been enough data blocks in the system and they are fully dispersed, such that any set of 3 nodes, in which 2 nodes are on a single rack and 1 node is on another rack, shares replicas of at least one data block.

The system can tolerate more than 2 failures without data loss in the following two cases: first, all the node failures happen to be on a single rack; or second, all the node failures are on different racks which means that there is up to one node failure on each rack. Therefore, the system can tolerate all the single and double node failures and a portion of $t$ node failures for $3 \le t \le max(n, r)$.

We construct the reliability model for systems with replication factor 3 as shown in Fig. 2. In this model, there are $r + n + 2$ states in total, which can be classified into five types: (1) $S_0$ represents a completely healthy state; (2) $S_1$ denotes the degraded system state, during which 1 node has already failed; (3) $S_{Ai}$, where $2 \le i \le r$, denote the degraded system states, during which $i$ nodes have already failed and they are separately on $i$ different racks; (4) $S_{Bi}$, where $2 \le i \le n$, denote the degraded system states, during which $i$ nodes have already failed and all of them are on a single rack; (5) $DL$ is the absorbing state at which point data loss occurs.

The system begins in the healthy state $S_0$, and can transfer to state $S_1$ with the rate of $rn\lambda$, when a node failure occurs in the system. During the state $S_1$, the system can transfer to any one of three states: $S_0$, with the rate of $\mu$, if the failure has been repaired; state $S_{A2}$, with the rate of $n(r-1)\lambda$, if a new failure occurs on the other rack; or $S_{B2}$, with the rate of $(n-1)\lambda$, if a new failure occurs on the same rack with the existing one.

During the state $S_{Ai}$, the system can transfer to any of three states: state $S_{A(i+1)}$, with the rate of $n(r-i)\lambda$, if a new failure occurs on a completely healthy rack; state $S_{A(i-1)}$, with the rate of $i\mu$, if one of the $i$ failures has been repaired;

or $DL$, with the rate of $i(n-1)\lambda$, if any one of the $i$ racks, which have already a node failure on them, generates a new failure.

During the state $S_{Ar}$, when each rack in the system has had one failure on it, the system is already in the critical condition and can transfer to either of two states: $S_{A(r-1)}$, with the rate of $r\mu$, if one of the $r$ failures has been repaired; or $DL$, with the rate of $r(n-1)\lambda$, if a new failure happens.

During the state $S_{Bi}$, the system can transfer to either of two states: $S_{B(i+1)}$, with the rate of $(n-i)\lambda$, if a new node failure occurs on the same rack with the existing ones; $S_{B(i-1)}$, with the rate of $i\mu$, if one of the $i$ failures has been repaired; or $DL$, with the rate of $n(r-1)\lambda$, if a new failure occurs on a previously healthy rack.

During the state $S_{Bn}$, when all nodes on some rack have failed, the system is already in the critical condition and can transfer to either of two states: $S_{B(n-1)}$, with the rate of $n\mu$, if one of the $n$ failures has been repaired; or $DL$, with the rate of $n(r-1)\lambda$, if a new failure happens.

# 4  Reliability Models for Systems with Proactive Fault Tolerance

In addition to the assumption of independent exponential probability distributions for failure and repair of individual storage nodes, we also assume independent exponential probability distributions for node warnings and their repairs, and then construct the Markov reliability models for the proactive cloud storage systems.

## 4.1  Basic State Transition Unit (BSTU)

Since no node failure predictor can guarantee 100 % accuracy, it is necessary to combine the proactive and reactive fault-tolerant measures to ensure reliability. Therefore, the state transitions in the reliability model for such a system are very intricate. One could not describe the model easily in the traditional way. Therefore, we design a generic "brick" – basic state transition unit (BSTU), by composing which we can derive the complex and intractable reliability models for cloud storage systems with proactive fault tolerance.

Using the BSTU shown in Fig. 3, we want to describe the fundamental laws of state transitions in the Markov models. The symbol $p$ represents the failure detection rate of predictors deployed in the systems, $\gamma$ represents the failure rate of a node warning, and $\mu$ represents the rebuild rate of a node failure/warning.

We use $P_{ij}$ to represent the degraded states during which $i$ nodes have actually failed and $j$ nodes are currently predicted imminent failures. The symbol $A_{ij}$ is used to represent the probability that the system can tolerate the $(i+1)$-th node failure without data loss and the new failure occurs on a previously completely healthy node. We use $B_{ij}$ to represent the probability that the system can survive from the $(i+1)$-th node failure and the new failure evolves out of a warning. And $C_{ij}$ is used to represent the probability that the $(i+1)$-th failure

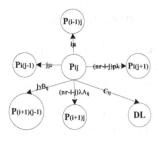

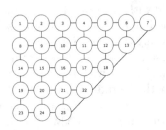

**Fig. 3.** Basic state transition unit (BSTU) for cloud storage systems with proactive fault tolerance.

**Fig. 4.** A reliability model composed by BSTUs for a proactive cloud storage system.

induces system data loss. For simplicity sake, we only draw the outgoing edges and the corresponding transition rates for state $P_{ij}$, and its incoming edges and their transition rates can be drawn similarly. We can calculate the values of $A_{ij}$, $B_{ij}$ and $C_{ij}$ for each $P_{ij}$ in some system using combinatorial analyses.

In addition to the basic internal states $P_{ij}$, there are some boundary states, the transitions of which are similar to the BSTU except for missing some incoming and outgoing edges. For cloud storage systems with proactive fault tolerance, we can construct their reliability models by combining a large number of internal and boundary BSTUs. For example, Fig. 4 is a simple diagram for a reliability model composed by 25 BSTUs for a proactive system, in which the state of data loss is omitted.

Based on Fig. 4, we want to explain some concepts used in the following. The BSTUs numbered 1–7 make up the upper boundary of the model. The ones numbered $1, 8, 14, 19, 23$ make up the left boundary. The ones numbered $7, 13, 18, 22, 25$ make up the right boundary. The ones numbered 23–25 make up the lower boundary. For the proactive systems with replication factor two, the ones numbered 9–12, 15–17, 20, 21 are the internal states. For the proactive systems with replication factor three, the ones numbered 8–13 make up the second layer of the model, and the ones numbered 15–17, 20, 21 are the internal states.

The systems with proactive fault tolerance have the same fault tolerance and characteristics as the traditional reactive systems except for having the ability of failure prediction and pre-warning treatment.

### 4.2 Proactive with Replication Factor Two

There are five types of state transition units at all, by combining which we can construct the overall reliability model for the proactive storage system with replication factor two.

The model is composed mainly of intact BSTUs, namely internal states. During an internal state $P_{ij}$ $(0 < i < n$ and $0 < j < nr - i)$, the system can transfer to any one of six states: (1) state $P_{(i-1)j}$ with the rate of $i\mu$, if one of the $i$ node failures has been repaired; (2) state $P_{i(j-1)}$ with the rate of $j\mu$, if one of the $j$ node warnings has been repaired; (3) state $P_{(i+1)j}$ with the rate of $(nr - i - j)(1 - p)A_{ij}\lambda$, if a healthy node fails, and fortunately it does not induce system data loss; (4) state $P_{i(j+1)}$ with the rate of $(nr - i - j)p\lambda$, if a healthy node is predicted to be facing an impending failure; (5) state $P_{(i+1)(j-1)}$ with the rate of $jB_{ij}\gamma$, if a warning node does not be repaired timely and actually fails at last, however it does not induce system data loss fortunately; (6) state $DL$ with the rate of $C_{ij}$, if a new failure does induce system data loss.

The value of $A_{ij}$ can be calculated by counting the proportion of healthy-to-fail transitions occurring on the faulty rack. We use $x$ to denote the number of warnings which are on the same rack with the $i$ failures. For some $x$, $(n - i - x)C^x_{n-i}C^{j-x}_{n(r-1)}$ is the number of cases for which one healthy node on the faulty rack fails. The formula $(nr - i - j)C^j_{nr-i}$ is the number of cases for which a healthy node in the system fails. So the value of $A_{ij}$ can be calculated as:

$$A_{ij} = \frac{\sum_{x=0}^{min(n-i-1,j)}(n - i - x)C^x_{n-i}C^{j-x}_{n(r-1)}}{(nr - i - j)C^j_{nr-i}}. \tag{1}$$

We calculate $B_{ij}$ by counting the proportion of warning-to-fail transitions occurring on the faulty rack. We use $x$ to denote the similar thing as in (1). For some $x$, $xC^x_{n-i}C^{j-x}_{n(r-1)}$ is the number of cases for which a previously warning node on the faulty rack fails. And, $jC^j_{nr-i}$ is the number of all cases for which a previously warning node in the system fails. So the value of $B_{ij}$ can be calculated as:

$$B_{ij} = \frac{\sum_{x=1}^{min(n-i,j)} xC^x_{n-i}C^{j-x}_{n(r-1)}}{jC^j_{nr-i}}. \tag{2}$$

The $C_{ij}$ represent the probability that the new failure is not on the faulty rack and incurs system data loss. The formula $(1 - p)\lambda(nr - i - j)(1 - A_{ij})$ denotes the probability that a failure occurring on a previously healthy node is not predicted by the predictor and induces the system data loss. So the value of $C_{ij}$ can be calculated as:

$$C_{ij} = (1 - p)\lambda(nr - i - j)(1 - A_{ij}) + j\gamma(1 - B_{ij}). \tag{3}$$

Besides the internal states, there are other four types of boundary states. They are similar to the intact BSTUs, except for missing some transitions:

(1) when $i = 0$ and $0 < j < rn$: states $P_{ij}$ make up the upper boundary of the model, during which no node failure happens and just $j$ warnings are predicted by the predictor. Since $i = 0$, there is no state $P_{(i-1)j}$ and transition $P_{ij} \rightarrow P_{(i-1)j}$; since the system can tolerate any single-failure, there is no transition $P_{ij} \rightarrow DL$.

(2) when $j = 0$ and $0 < i < n$: states $P_{ij}$ make up the left boundary of the model, during which $i$ node failures have happened and no warning is predicted. Accordingly, there is neither $P_{ij} \rightarrow P_{i(j-1)}$ nor $P_{ij} \rightarrow P_{(i+1)(j-1)}$ transition.

(3) When $i = n$ and $0 < j < (r-1)n$: states $P_{ij}$ make up the lower boundary of the model, during which all nodes on some rack have failed already and $j$ warnings are also predicted. Since the system can tolerate at most $n$ failures, there is neither $P_{ij} \rightarrow P_{(i+1)j}$ nor $P_{ij} \rightarrow P_{(i+1)(j-1)}$ transition.

(4) when $j = nr - i$ and $0 < i < n$: states $P_{ij}$ make up the right boundary of the model, during which $i$ node failures have happened and all the rest nodes in system are also predicted to be soon-to-fail. Since there is no healthy node left, neither $P_{ij} \rightarrow P_{i(j+1)}$ nor $P_{ij} \rightarrow P_{(i+1)j}$ exists.

### 4.3    Proactive with Replication Factor Three

There are six types of state transition units in the reliability model for the proactive cloud storage systems with replication factor three.

Similarly, most states are intact BSTUs, namely internal states $P_{ij}$, where $1 < i < max(n, r)$ and $0 < j < nr - i$. They are basically the same as those in the model for replication factor two, except for the values of $A_{ij}$, $B_{ij}$ and $C_{ij}$. Accordingly, we only discuss how to calculate the three probabilities here.

There are two cases for which the system survives from $i$ node failures, where $2 < i \leq min(n, r)$: first, all the $i$ node failures are on a single rack; or second, the $i$ node failures are respectively on $i$ different racks. We use $q_i$ to represent the proportion of the first case in the both, and the value of $q_i$ can be calculated as:

$$q_i = \frac{rC_n^i}{(rC_n^i + n^i C_r^i)}. \tag{4}$$

The proportion of the second case is $1 - q_i$. When $min(n, r) < i \leq max(n, r)$, the value of $q_i$ is equal to either 0 or 1.

For the case that the system tolerates the $(i+1)$-th failure which occurs on a previously healthy node, we use $N_s$ to denote the number of cases for which the new failure is on the same rack with the existing $i$ failures, and use $N_d$ to denote the number of cases for which the new failure is on a previously healthy rack. The value of $N_s$ can be calculated as:

$$N_s = \sum_{x=0}^{min(n-i-1,j)} (n - i - x) C_{n-i}^x C_{n(r-1)}^{j-x} \tag{5}$$

where $x$ denotes the number of warnings which are on the same rack with the $i$ failures.

The value of $N_d$ can be calculated as:

$$N_d = \sum_{x=0}^{min(n(r-i)-1,j)} (n(r-i) - x) C_{n(r-i)}^x C_{i(n-1)}^{j-x}) \tag{6}$$

where $x$ denotes the number of warnings which are on the healthy racks.

Then the value of $A_{ij}$ can be calculated as:

$$A_{ij} = \frac{(q_i N_s + (1 - q_i)N_d)}{(nr - i - j)C_{nr-i}^j} \tag{7}$$

Similarly, for the case that the system tolerates the (i+1)-th failure which evolves out of a warning, we use $N_s'$ to denote the number of cases for which a warning on the same rack with the existing failures fails, and use $N_d'$ to denote the number of cases for which a warning on a previously healthy rack fails. The value of $N_s'$ can be calculated as:

$$N_s' = \sum_{x=1}^{min(n-i,j)} xC_{n-i}^x C_{n(r-1)}^{j-x} \tag{8}$$

where $x$ denotes the similar thing as in (5).
The value of $N_d'$ can be calculated as:

$$N_d' = \sum_{x=1}^{min(n(r-i),j)} xC_{n(r-i)}^x C_{i(n-1)}^{j-x} \tag{9}$$

where $x$ denotes the similar thing as in (6).
Then the value of $B_{ij}$ can be calculated as:

$$B_{ij} = \frac{(q_i N_s' + (1 - q_i)N_d')}{jC_{nr-i}^j}. \tag{10}$$

And, the value of $C_{ij}$ can be calculated as:

$$C_{ij} = (1 - p)\lambda(nr - i - j)(1 - A_{ij}) + j\gamma(1 - B_{ij}). \tag{11}$$

Besides the internal states, there are other five types of boundary states. They are similar to the intact BSTUs, except for missing some transitions:

(1) when $i = 0$ and $0 < j < rn$: states $P_{ij}$ make up the upper boundary of the model, during which no node failure happens and just $j$ warnings are predicted by the predictor. Since $i = 0$, there is no state $P_{(i-1)j}$ and transition $P_{ij} \rightarrow P_{(i-1)j}$; since the system with replication factor 3 can tolerate any double-failure, there is no transition $P_{ij} \rightarrow DL$.
(2) when $i = 1$ and $0 < j < rn - 1$: states $P_{ij}$ make up the second layer of the model, during which only 1 node failure happens and $j$ warnings are predicted by the predictor. There is no transition $P_{ij} \rightarrow DL$ either.
(3) when $j = 0$ and $0 < i < max(n, r)$: states $P_{ij}$ make up the left boundary of the model, during which $i$ node failures have happened and no warning is predicted. Accordingly, there is neither $P_{ij} \rightarrow P_{i(j-1)}$ nor $P_{ij} \rightarrow P_{(i+1)(j-1)}$ transition.

(4) when $i = max(n, r)$ and $0 < j < rn - i$: states $P_{ij}$ make up the lower boundary of the model, during which the system is already in the critical condition and $j$ warnings are also predicted. Since the system can tolerate at most $max(n, r)$ failures, there is neither $P_{ij} \rightarrow P_{(i+1)j}$ nor $P_{ij} \rightarrow P_{(i+1)(j-1)}$ transition.

(5) when $j = nr - i$ and $0 < i < max(n, r)$: states $P_{ij}$ make up the right boundary of the model, during which $i$ node failures have happened and all the rest nodes in system are predicted to happen impending failure. Since there is no healthy node left, neither $P_{ij} \rightarrow P_{i(j+1)}$ nor $P_{ij} \rightarrow P_{(i+1)j}$ transition exists.

## 5   Experiment and Analyses

Table 1 shows the values of parameters used in our experiments. Typical values for practical systems are used for all parameters, except the sensitivity of node failure predictors, which have not been really used in systems. In our previous work [7], our classification tree prediction models can achieve the failure detection rate (FDR) of 95 % with the mean time in advance (TIA) of near 360 h, and can maintain a FDR above 90 % for the long-term use and for both drive families. In this paper, we have chosen a relatively conservative prediction sensitivity (the FDR of 80 % and the TIA of 360 h) for the failure predictors. Unless otherwise stated, we keep these settings unchanged in the following experiments.

Limited by the memory and computing ability, it is difficult to use Markov models to obtain the reliability values at a large data center scale, even using the best matrix algorithm. Therefore, to obtain the reliability of large scale storage systems (Sect. 5.2), we run simulations of systems using Monte Carlo methods, in which the chronological behavior of a system is simulated [15]. For each setting, we run simulation 100 times, and finally the bootstrap 95 % confidence interval for the time to data loss is computed. However, since the error margins are nearly 10 times less than the average values, to make the compared results more clearly, we only draw the average values of simulations on the figures.

We compare systems with the same effective storage space (excluding the space for redundant data). And, We transform the MTTDL to a useful measure – the

**Table 1.** The value of system parameters used in our experiments.

| Parameter | Meaning | Range |
|-----------|---------|-------|
| $c$ | storage capacity of each node | 12 TB |
| $n$ | the number of nodes on each rack | 15 |
| $1/\lambda$ | mean time to failure of storage nodes | 100000 h |
| $1/\mu$ | mean time to repair a failure/warning | 24 h |
| $p$ | failure detection rate of failure predictors | 80 % |
| $1/\gamma$ | mean time in advance of a node warning | 360 h |

expected number of data lost event per usable petabyte within one year, by which ones can better understand the reliability gaps between different cloud storage systems.

## 5.1  Sensitivity of Node Reliability

We assume that there are 40 racks in the systems with replication factor 2, and 60 racks in the systems with replication factor 3, which means that the systems can respectively store 3600 TB user data. Unless otherwise stated, we keep this assumption in the following experiments.

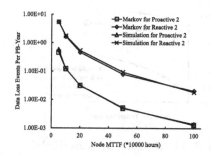 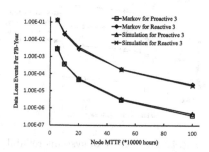

**Fig. 5.** The change of the reliability of systems with replication factor 2 according to the node reliability.

**Fig. 6.** The change of the reliability of systems with replication factor 3 according to the node reliability.

We can see from Figs. 5 and 6, with the different node MTTF, Markov-based results have a perfect match with the simulation-based values, which verifies the accuracy of our reliability models and the Monte Carlo simulations. In addition, we can learn about the following: first, all the four systems' reliability have be improved hardly with the enhanced node MTTF, which demonstrates the great value of redundancy distributed within nodes; second, the systems with replication factor 3 yield larger gains than the ones with replication factor 2 with the enhanced node MTTF. Specifically, when the node MTTF is doubled with other parameters constant, the reliability of systems with replication factor 2 will decline by three-quarters and the reliability of systems with replication factor 3 will decline by seven-eighths; and third, having the predictor with the FDR of 80 %, both the systems with replication factor 2 and 3 can reduce redundancy within their nodes to decrease the node MTTF nearly by three-quarters, while the reliability of them remain the same.

## 5.2  Sensitivity of System Size

Figure 7 shows the change of systems reliability, as the effective storage space is varied. We can adjust the storage space size by changing the number of racks in system. Three observations are evident from Fig. 7: first, for all the four systems, the reliability will be reduced by less than a half for each doubling in capacity and these decrease taper off as systems grow larger; second, having a predictor with the FDR of 80 %, the reliability of system with replication factor 2 can be improved by more than one order of magnitude and the reliability of system with replication factor 3 can be improved by nearly two orders of magnitude; and third, providing the same effective storage space, the system with replication factor 3 requires 50 % more storage nodes and achieves the reliability two orders of magnitude higher than that with replication factor 2.

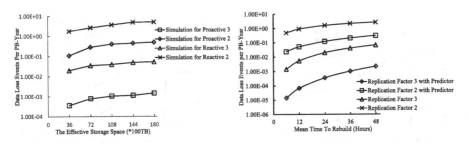

**Fig. 7.** The change of systems reliability according to the effective space size.

**Fig. 8.** The change of systems reliability according to the rebuild time.

## 5.3   Sensitivity of Rebuild Time

Figure 8 shows how the reliability of systems changes according to the rebuild time. We can also learn about that: first, the systems with replication factor 3 are more sensitivity to the rebuild time than the systems with replication factor 2. Specifically, when the rebuild time for a failure/warning is doubled with other parameters constant, the reliability of systems with replication factor 2 will decline by half and the reliability of systems with replication factor 3 will decline by three-quarters; second, having a predictor with the FDR of 80 %, both the systems can reduce the bandwidth available for rebuild process to extend the rebuild time seven times longer (by which systems can reserve more bandwidth to serve user requests), while the reliability of them remain the same.

## 5.4   Sensitivity of Failure Detection Rate (FDR)

We compare the reliability as the FDR is varied. The results are shown in Fig. 9. We can learn about the following: first, it's clear that the more accurate are the predictors the more reliable are the systems; second, for the system with replication factor 2, when the FDR of predictor is higher than 70 %, its reliability is more sensitivity to the capability of failure prediction and can be improved by 1 ~ 2 orders of magnitude with other system parameters constant; third, for the system with replication factor 3, when the FDR is higher than 60 %, its reliability is more sensitivity to the capability of failure prediction and can be improved by 1 ~ 3 orders of magnitude with other system parameters constant; and third, when the FDR achieves 97 %, the proactive system with replication factor 2 can achieve the same level of reliability as the reactive system with replication factor 3, which demonstrates the great value of the proactive fault tolerance mechanism.

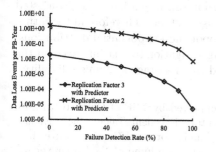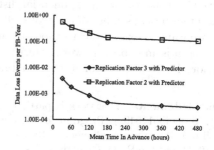

**Fig. 9.** The change of proactive systems reliability according to the failure detection rate of predictors.

**Fig. 10.** The change of proactive systems reliability according to the mean time in advance of predictors.

## 5.5  Sensitivity of Time in Advance

Figure 10 shows the effect of TIA on the reliability of proactive systems. The systems reliability is significantly improved as the increase of TIA. Beyond that, both the curves are relatively flat after the TIA of 180 h, which denotes that the TIA of 180 h is the borderline between prominent and non-prominent influence on the reliability of systems. This observation can guide designers to build a appropriate predictor for cloud storage systems. Note that, this borderline is drawn given the rebuild time of 24 h for a node warning, and a longer rebuild time may induce a higher borderline.

## 6  Conclusion

In this paper, we present several Markov-based reliability models for cloud storage systems with/without proactive fault tolerance respectively, by which one can systematically analyze the reliability of systems. To describe and compute the intricate reliability models for proactive cloud storage systems, we propose a generic "brick" – basic state transition unit (BSTU), to describe the general pattern of state transitions in the reliability models. Using our models, we evaluate the influences of some system parameters such as the sensitivity of predictor, node MTTF, rebuild time, and system size on the reliability of cloud storage systems. We wish that our models could serve as a guideline for system designers and administrators, who are not reliability experts, to decide system parameters when building cloud storage systems. For example, to ensure the system availability, users will want to take up as less bandwidth as possible for the rebuild process, which induces a long time to repair the failure or warning. However, as shown in Fig. 8, the increasing of the rebuild time will significantly decrease the reliability. Therefore, using our models, users can choose the proper rebuild bandwidth to coordinate the availability and reliability.

However, the Markov models are build by the assumptions that node failures and rebuild time follow an exponential distribution, which have been contested by recent empirical studies of real world storage systems. Therefore in the future work, we want to extend our methods to support non-exponential distributions. Moreover, it is an important work of further investigation to take into account the behavior of correlated failures to understand cloud storage system's reliability.

**Acknowledgments.** This work is partially supported by NSF of China (61373018, 11301288, 11450110409), Program for New Century Excellent Talents in University (NCET130301), the Fundamental Research Funds for the Central Universities (65141021) and the Ph.D. Candidate Research Innovation Fund of Nankai University.

# References

1. Murray, J.F., Hughes, G.F., Kreutz-Delgado, K.: Machine learning methods for predicting failures in hard drives: a multiple-instance application. J. Mach. Learn. Res. **6**, 783–816 (2005)
2. Hamerly, G., Elkan, C.: Bayesian approaches to failure prediction for disk drives. In: Proceedings of the 18th International Conference on Machine Learning, pp. 202–209 (2001)
3. Hughes, G.F., Murray, J.F., Kreutz-Delgado, K., Elkan, C.: Improved disk-drive failure warnings. IEEE Trans. Reliab. **51**(3), 350–357 (2002)
4. Murray, J.F., Hughes, G.F., Kreutz-Delgado, K.: Hard drive failure prediction using non-parametric statistical methods. In: Proceedings of the International Conference on Artificial Neural Networks (2003)
5. Zhao, Y., Liu, X., Gan, S., Zheng, W.: Predicting disk failures with HMM- and HSMM-based approaches. In: Proceedings of the 10th Industrial Conference on Advances in Data Mining: Applications and Theoretical Aspects, pp. 390–404 (2010)
6. Zhu, B., Wang, G., Liu, X., Hu, D., Lin, S., Ma, J.: Proactive drive failure prediction for large scale storage systems. In: Proceedings of 29th IEEE Conference on Massive Storage Systems and Technologies (MSST), pp. 1–5. Long Beach, CA (2013)
7. Li, J., Ji, X., Jia, Y., Zhu, B., Wang, G., Li, Z., Liu, X.: Hard drive failure prediction using classification and regression trees. In: Proceedings of 44th Annual IEEE/IFIP International Conference on Dependable Systems and Networks (DSN), pp. 383–394 (2014)
8. Eckart, B., Chen, X., He, X., Scott, S.L.: Failure prediction models for proactive fault tolerance within storage systems. In: Proceedings of IEEE International Symposium on Modeling, Analysis and Simulation of Computers and Telecommunication Systems, pp. 1–8 (2008)

9. Zhang, Z., Lian, Q.: Reperasure: replication protocol using erasure-code in peer-to-peer storage network. In: Proceedings of 21st IEEE Symposium on Reliable Distributed Systems, pp. 330–335 (2002)
10. Peric, D., Bocek, T., Hecht, F.V., Hausheer, D., Stiller, B.: The design and evaluation of a distributed reliable file system. In: Proceedings of International Conference on Parallel and Distributed Computing, Applications and Technologies, pp. 348–353 (2009)
11. Chen, M., Chen, W., Liu, L., Zhang, Z.: An analytical framework and its applications for studying brick storage reliability. In: Proceedings of the 26th IEEE International Symposium on Reliable Distributed Systems, pp. 242–252. IEEE (2007)
12. Leslie, M., Davies, J., Huffman, T.: A comparison of replication strategies for reliable decentralised storage. J. Netw. 1(6), 36–44 (2006)
13. Venkatesan, V., Iliadis, I.: A general reliability model for data storage systems. In: Proceedings of Ninth International Conference on Quantitative Evaluation of Systems Quantitative Evaluation of Systems (QEST), pp. 209–219 (2012)
14. Rao, K., Hafner, J.L., Golding, R.A.: Reliability for networked storage nodes. In: DSN 2006 International Conference on Dependable Systems and Networks, pp. 237–248 (2006)
15. Borges, C.L., Falcão, D.M., Mello, J.C.O., Melo, A.C.: Composite reliability evaluation by sequential monte carlo simulation on parallel and distributed processing environments. IEEE Trans. Power Syst. 16(2), 203–209 (2001)

# Performance Evaluation and Optimization of Wi-Fi Display on Android

Xianfeng Li[(⊠)] and Baobao Jin

School of Electronic and Computer Engineering,
Peking University, Shenzhen 518055, China
lixianfeng@pkusz.edu.cn, jinbaobao@sz.pku.edu.cn

**Abstract.** In the mobile networking environment, there is an increasing need for different devices such as computers, smartphones, and smartTVs to interact with each other. One popular type of interaction is screencast (or remote display), where the content on one device's display appears (synchronously) on another device. To facilitate this type of application, several standards have been proposed, from earlier DLNA (Digital Living Network Alliance), to Airplay by Apple, and Wi-Fi Display by Wi-Fi Alliance more recently. One distinct yet challenging requirement for screencast is synchronicity. However, despite the increasing popularity of screencast and the related standards, their performance metric has received little study. In this paper, we take Wi-Fi Display and its implementation on Android as our target, and perform an in-depth study on its performance. This evaluation identifies an important bottleneck arising from the interactions among a couple of asynchronous threads. From these findings, we propose an event-driven mechanism that shortens the latency among the relevant threads. The experimental evaluation indicates a 20 % reduction on total processing time on screencast at the Source device side, which proves the effectiveness of this new mechanism. In addition, our evaluation also identifies encoding of frame content as another major source of latency. This finding means that we either need more powerful video/image encoding hardware, or an encoding standard that takes computation requirement as a more important metric than compression ratio.

**Keywords:** Screencast · Wi-Fi display · Miracast · Latency · Performance evaluation

## 1 Introduction

With the flourishing of smartphones and smartTVs, there is a strong need for close interactions among different types of devices. One popular such interaction is screencast (or remote display), where the content on one screen is cast on the screen of another device. For example, as shown in Fig. 1, a smartphone user at home might want to share the photos on the smartphone with her family on the big screen of the smartTV, or she might want to play a game using the smartphone, but prefer to watch the scenes on the smartTV for better user experience.

The increasing popularity of screencast applications has attracted the attention of major industrial vendors and organizations, and several standards have been proposed

© Springer International Publishing Switzerland 2015
G. Wang et al. (Eds.): ICA3PP 2015, Part IV, LNCS 9531, pp. 204–215, 2015.
DOI: 10.1007/978-3-319-27140-8_15

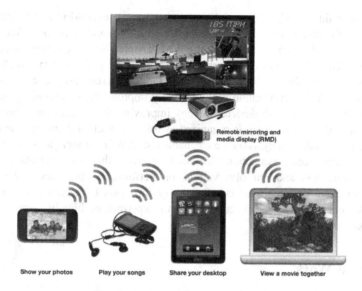

**Fig. 1.** Screencast (Remote Display)

to facilitate screencast interactions among heterogeneous devices, such as DLNA [1], Apple's Airplay [2], Wi-Fi Display [3], and Google's ChromeCast [4].

An inherent requirement for a screencast standard and its implementation is real-time performance: the content needs to be displayed synchronously on both the Source and Sink devices. This means that for each frame of content, the latency between the Source device and Sink device should be as short as possible, such that no user observable delay is experienced. Among the earlier mentioned standards, DLNA is far behind this requirement. In fact, it is primarily designed for scenarios with non-real-time content sharing. Apple's AirPlay is a proprietary standard that is designed for sceencast among Apple's devices. Wi-Fi Display is designed by WiFi Alliance, and Miracast is the authentication for devices that support Wi-Fi Display [5]. In some cases, the term Wi-Fi Display and Miracast are used interchangeably.

Despite the popularity of these standards, their performance has not received sufficient evaluation, and the reasons leading to potential screencast delays are poorly understood. In this paper, we conduct an in-depth performance evaluation on screencast, and propose optimization mechanisms from our findings. We take Wi-Fi Display and its implementation on Android (AWFD) [6] as our target, as it is an open standard (as opposed to AirPlay), and is very popular. Most importantly, the source code of the implementation is completely available.

Our performance evaluation indicates that screen content encoding is not the only source of time delay. In fact, the complex interactions among multiple Android modules and the multi-threading mechanism also introduce considerable latency. In particular, the major producer and consumer of the frame buffer along the screencast processing path work in different mechanisms, resulting in the consumption of the frame buffer being delayed sometimes, or being unnecessarily consumed multiple times in some other times. With this insight, we introduce an event-driven mechanism to facilitate timely interaction among frame buffer producers and consumers. We implement this new mechanism by modifying the Wi-Fi Display Source code of Android and run it on a Google's Nexus7 [7] tablet using a set of popular benchmarks. The experimental results show a 20 % reduction on the total screencast processing time at the Source side. This optimization will effectively improve the synchronicity between the Source devices and Sink devices, thereby improving screencast user experiences.

The remainder of this paper is organized as follows. Section 2 surveys the related work. Section 3 makes analysis on the mechanism of AWFD to serve as a guidance for subsequent performance evaluation. Section 4 describes the experimentation on performance evaluation and our observations on performance bottlenecks. Section 5 provides an event-driven framework for the optimization of a critical performance bottleneck, and evaluates its effectiveness with experiments. Finally, Sect. 6 makes conclusions on this work.

## 2  Related Work

There are many scenarios where screencast is needed, such as traditional thin client [8, 9] and remote desktops [10, 11] in the local area network consisting of personal computers, and more recently cloud computing screen sharing application [12]. Performance measurement and optimization of these screencast technologies have been done in the literature. For example, the performance of thin client has been studied, and corresponding optimization techniques have been proposed in [13–15]; the user experience of remote desktop has been studied under different network conditions in [16]; and optimization techniques for remote display of cloud applications on mobile devices have been proposed in [17].

In the context of mobile computing, many hardware- or software- based screencast technologies have emerged to facilitate the need of real-time screen sharing. Hardware-based technologies include Airplay, Chromecast, DisplayCast [18], SmartVNC [19], and CloneCloud [20], and software-based technologies include MirrorOp [21] and Splashtop [22]. Compared to those early screencast technologies mentioned above, these state-of-the-art technologies aims at achieving high visual quality for dynamic and complicated display scenes, and are mainly designed for smart devices. By far, these goals have not been well met in reality, and there is a strong need to understand the reason behind the unsatisfactory user experience, and find optimization techniques accordingly. However, the literature on this issue is very scarce. In [23], external test devices such as camera are used to detect the frame rate of screencast for some of the above mentioned technologies such as WFD, Airplay, Chromecast, MirrorOp and Splashtop. Unfortunately, the efforts stop at a very shallow understanding of the problems, and none of them conducts a deep reasoning on the mechanisms leading to these problems.

As far as we know, our work presented in this paper is the first attempt to conduct a detailed code-level analysis of AWFD, followed by an in-depth evaluation of its performance. With a detailed view on the processing procedure of the display frame and quantitative evaluation, we accurately identify a couple of bottlenecks, and propose a pure software solution for one of the bottlenecks, which are caused by inefficient multithreading and asynchronous tasking.

# 3  Analysis of AWFD Screencast Mechanism

## 3.1  Overview of AWFD

Screencast typically involves one Source device, one or multiple Sink device(s), and an underlying Wifi network connection among these devices. As illustrated in Fig. 2. A typical Source device is a smartphone or a tablet, a Sink device is a smartTV with Wifi support or a traditional TV with a Set-Top Box.

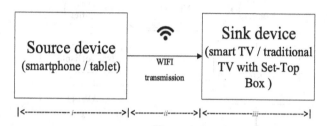

**Fig. 2.** Overview of AWFD

The Source device obtains raw graphics/video/audio data from a local frame buffer, then encodes these data with appropriate codec, e.g., h264 for video and aac for audio. The encoded frame will be disassembled into a number of packets by a packetizer, which will be sent to the Sink devices using RTP protocols over the Wifi connection. The Sink receives and reassembles the RTP packets, and decodes them to restore the original frame buffer. Note the encoding at the Source devices is usually lossy compression, and the "restoring" process cannot recover the original content. This may introduce user perceivable quality degradation for non-video content (textual content such as Word document, PowerPoint slides, etc.).

## 3.2  Source-End Display Frame Processing

From Fig. 2 processing procedure we can see total time from a display frame be produced in Source device to displayed on Sink device is mainly consisted by three parts: *i*, the time spent by the Source device to acquire, encode and packetize a display frame; *ii*, the time spent on the transmission of the frame packets from the Source device to the Sink device through Wifi network; and *iii*, the time spent on decoding and displaying the frame on the Sink device. Among them, *ii* is determined by Wifi technology, and is a relatively short time compared to *i*; similarly, *iii* is also relatively small because frame decoding is relatively simple compared to the work at the Source-end. As a result, we focus on the evaluation and optimization of the procedure at the Source device. In the subsequent part of this section, we make a reasonably detailed study on the procedure of display frame processing at the Source device.

When the AWFD service is launched at the Source device, a Remote Display BufferQueue (RDBQ) object will be created, which is responsible for maintaining buffers to be transported to the Sink device. Specifically, RDBQ is one of the output targets of the SurfaceFlinger (SF) service, which composes surfaces (layers of graphics) from applications to generate the ultimate display frame. Figure 3 highlights the procedure, and note that NDBQ and the corresponding procedure is for local display at the Source device. To support screencast, SF will fill the two BQ objects concurrently.

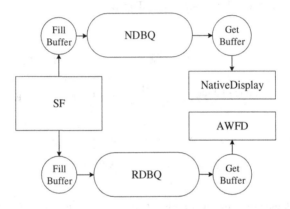

**Fig. 3.** Two BQs for SF: NDBQ for native display, and RDBQ for remote AWFD display

In more detail, the procedure of display frame processing in the Source device is presented in Fig. 4. Three related threads participate in this process: repeaterLooper (RLP), pullLooper (PLP) and wfdLooper (WLP), and they work as follows.

At first, RLP tries to obtain a buffer from RDBQ, and upon success, it will pass the data to *mBuffer*, a temporary storage object shared by RLP and PLP. Then thread PLP will obtain the display data from *mBuffer*, and will packetize it into a message object, which will be sent to thread WLP. Note that unlike RLP, PLP works periodically. If it fails to receive the data from *mBuffer* in current period, it will block itself until the next period, regardless of whether the data is fed into mBuffer between the two periods. Finally, with the message mechanism, the display data is received by a thread named WLP, which will invoke other threads. As shown in Fig. 4, when a message sent by PLP is received, WLP calls an object named Converter to conduct actual encode work. When Converter finished its work, it will send back a message to WLP, which will call an object named Packetizer to packetize the encoded display data. Eventually, WLP will call TSSender to send display data packets through Wifi network. This completes the processing of display frame at the Source-end.

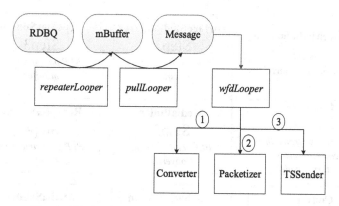

**Fig. 4.** Display frame process procedure in Source device

### 3.3 Analysis on the Disparity Between Threads

For many complex systems, multi-threading is an unavoidably technique for modular design and performance improvement. From the analysis in the previous section, we can see that there is no exception for AWFD with its reliance on multi-threading.

However, multi-threading, if misused, might be a performance detriment, and there is such a potential risk in current AWFD's multi-threading framework. Specifically, we have seen that PLP works periodically, partly due to the fixed FPS (frames-per-second) for screen update. But on the other hand, the RLP thread may feed PLP with display data right after PLP has failed to fetch the data at its beginning of current period. In this case, the time-consuming processing of the display data by PLP and WLP will be postponed to the beginning of the next period. This will eventually lead to a user perceivable delay on remote display. In essence, this problem is caused by a disparity of multi-threading between the producer (RLP) and the consumers (PLP and WLP) of the remote display frame.

To understand how serious the problem is, we perform a quantitative performance evaluation on the procedure of remote display frame processing, such that we can find the optimization technique accordingly.

## 4    Performance Evaluation on AWFD

### 4.1    Experimental Setup

With Android's support for WFD since its 4.2 release, more and more devices that run Android begin to provide hardware support for WFD. In this paper we choose Nexus7 (2013) that runs Android 4.4.2 as the Source device, whose display content needs to be transported to the Sink device, which is MiBox1S, a Set-Top Box offered by Xiaomi. MiBox1S runs Android 4.2.2, and it is attached to a TV with HDMI input.

Based on the analysis in Sect. 3.2, we further decompose the procedure of AWFD into 12 steps, and we instrument each step with logs to acquire time consumption

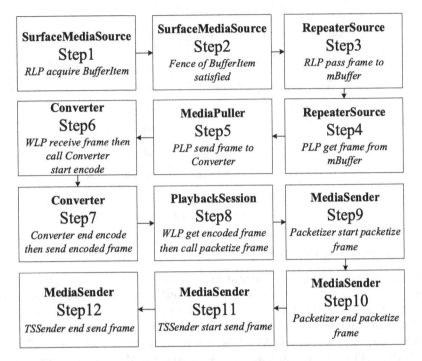

**Fig. 5.** Key points to add logs

information of the whole procedure of Source device process display frame. These corresponding 12 key points to add logs are shown in Fig. 5.

In Fig. 5, each block is depicted with three lines. The top line is the module/class name involved in that step; the middle line is the step index, and the bottom line describes the main function of this step. We calculate time of every adjacent step to evaluate time distribution of AWFD Source device process display frame.

We select six popular apps with different image complexities and refresh rates, which are: *Slide Desktop*, *Storm Player*, *Baidu Map*, *Temple Run*, *Hill Climb Racing* and *Ski Safari*.

Slide Desktop represents scenes where we slide the home screen of the smartphone. This scene has low refresh rate and simple content. Storm Player is a video player with high refresh rate and complex content. Baidu Map is a famous map application that has low refresh rate and complex content. Temple Run, Hill Climb Racing and Ski Safari are three popular games, which have high frame refresh rate and complex/dynamic content.

We install these six apps on Nexus7 (2013), which runs instrumented Android 4.4.2 to collect timing logs at different steps as listed in Fig. 5. The time distribution of the steps for each app is shown in Fig. 6, and the total processing time of each app is given in Table 1.

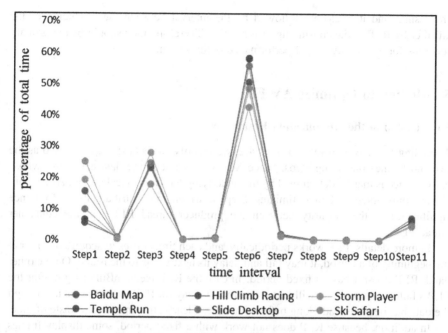

**Fig. 6.** Time distribution of every application

**Table 1.** Average value of every application's total time

| Application | Time(ms) |
|---|---|
| Slide Desktop | 36.12 |
| Storm Player | 46.93 |
| Baidu Map | 40.95 |
| Temple Run | 33.83 |
| Hill Climb Racing | 33.71 |
| Ski Safari | 42.30 |

## 4.2 Data Analysis

From Fig. 6 we can get two observations. First, although the apps that we choose to evaluate are significantly different in frame fresh rate and complexity, they have very similar time distributions among the 12 Steps. Second, from any application we can easily see that Steps 1, 3, 6, and 11 are the major part of the total processing time at the Source end. Among them, Step 6 takes more than half of the total time for most apps, with the only exceptions for Storm Player, which takes 43 % of the processing time. Second to the top is Step 3, which consumes more than 20 % processing time, except for Ski Safari (18 %).

Based on above analysis, we make the following conclusions: the time spent on encoding a display frame is the most time-consuming task for remote display frame processing; and it is closely followed by the interval between the producing of the mBuffer by RLP to the consuming of it by PLP. Therefore, they should be the primary concerns for further study and performance optimization.

# 5  Method to Optimize AWFD

## 5.1  Design of the Optimization Framework

According to analysis results in Sect. 4.2, we identify two steps: Steps 3 and 6 as the two most time-consuming steps. Since Step 6 is about frame data encoding, whose performance is mainly determined by the underlying hardware acceleration. As a result, we are only interested in optimizing Step 3, which may attribute its performance significance to the disparity between the producer thread RLP and the consumer thread PLP.

In more details, PLP works periodically, and each time it tries to acquire mBuffer at the beginning of a period, it may fail and delay its next probe to the round. On the other hand, RLP doesn't have a fixed period. In case the RLP feeds mBuffer right after the PLP's failed data probe, it will take a significant delay for PLP to get the data, although the data has become ready long before that time. Clearly, this introduces waste of time.

In addition, because RLP does not work with a fixed period, some display frames produced by RLP will not be processed by PLP, and in other cases, a display frame may be processed more than once by PLP. This phenomenon will have negative impact on the performance of AWFD because of loss of some display frames and time waste on redundant processing of display frames.

Based on above analysis, the key point is to change the interaction mechanism of thread RLP and thread PLP. For this purpose, we change the periodical work mechanism of PLP to a message driven work mechanism. In essence, PLP will no longer be driven by a fixed period; instead, it is activated each time a ready message sent by RLP is observed by PLP. Therefore, upon receiving this message, PLP will almost immediately start processing this display frame, instead of waiting a certain time as in the original periodical mechanism. The difference of the two workflows: fixed period and message-driven, is illustrated in Figs. 7 and 8.

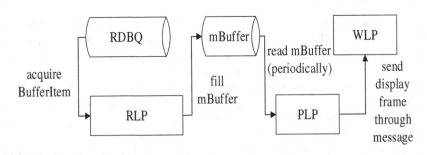

**Fig. 7.** Work flow of fixed period

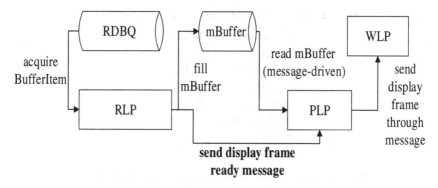

**Fig. 8.** Work flow of message driven

## 5.2    Implementation and Evaluation

We modify Android Source Code to change the work mechanism of PLP to message driven mechanism and flash the modified system to Nexus7 (2013). After that, we install and run the same set of apps mentioned in Sect. 4.1, and collect the performance data similarly as in Fig. 6. The results are presented in Fig. 9 and Table 2.

From Fig. 9, we can clearly observe that Step 3 now takes negligible time, in stark contrast to the result in the original periodic mechanism. As for the overall optimization effect, by comparing Table 2 against Table 1, we get very favorable latency reduction. As shown in Table 3, the latency reduction ranges from 18 % to 27 %, with an average of 21 % latency reduction. This optimization will reduce the chance of user perceived delays on the remote display.

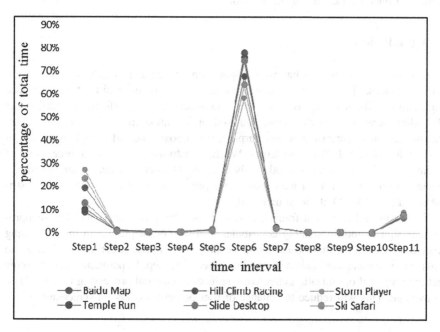

**Fig. 9.** Time distribution of every application after optimization

**Table 2.** Average value of every application's total time

| Application | Time(ms) |
|---|---|
| Slide Desktop | 29.27 |
| Storm Player | 34.15 |
| Baidu Map | 34.43 |
| Temple Run | 25.84 |
| Hill Climb Racing | 25.03 |
| Ski Safari | 34.39 |

**Table 3.** Percentage of latency reduction after optimization

| Application | Time(ms) |
|---|---|
| Slide Desktop | 19 % |
| Storm Player | 27 % |
| Baidu Map | 15 % |
| Temple Run | 23 % |
| Hill Climb Racing | 25 % |
| Ski Safari | 18 % |

Another benefit obtained from the optimization framework is the reduction of redundant work. In the new message-driven framework, because PLP is driven by RLP's output, every display frame produced by RLP will processed by PLP once and only once. So the problem that some display frames may not be processed or processed more than once by PLP is solved altogether.

## 6 Conclusions

Screencast (remote display) has wide applications in the age of heterogeneous computing devices. The major challenge of screencast is its real-time performance requirements. The main aim of this paper is to understand the performance bottlenecks of leading screencast mechanisms, and find optimization methods to improve user experiences on screencast. For this purpose, we choose Android's implementation of Wi-Fi Display (AWFD) as the target. We first instrument Android Source Code of version 4.4.2 based on an in-depth analysis of WFD work mechanism and its implementation on Android, then we choose six representative apps to collect time distribution data of AWFD at the Source end.

The result indicates that frame encoding is not the only source of delay, inappropriate design of multi-threading contributes to a significant portion in the processing procedure. Based on this observation, we propose a message-driven mechanism to replace a periodical mechanism in one key processing step. Experimental results show that the proposed optimization effectively reduces the overall processing time by 21 % on average. This will reduce the chance of user perceived delay on screencast.

**Acknowledgements.** This work is supported by the grant of Shenzhen municipal government for basic research on Information Technologies (No. JCYJ20130331144751105).

# References

1. DLNA. http://www.dlna.org/
2. Apple Airplay. https://www.apple.com/airplay/
3. Wifi-Display. http://www.wi-fi.org/discover-wi-fi/wi-fi-certified-miracast
4. Chromecast. http://www.google.com/chrome/devices/chromecast/
5. Miracast certified products. http://www.wi-fi.org/product-finder-results?capabilities=2
6. Android Wifi Display. http://developer.android.com/about/versions/android-4.2.html
7. Nexus 7 (2013). http://www.asus.com/Tablets_Mobile/Nexus_7_2013/
8. Baratto, R.A., Kim, L.N., Nieh, J.: THINC: a virtual display architecture for thin-client computing. ACM SIGOPS Operating Syst. Rev. **39**(5), 277–290 (2005)
9. Schmidt, B.K., Lam, M.S., Northcutt, J.D.: The interactive performance of SLIM: a stateless, thin-client architecture. ACM SIGOPS Operating Syst. Rev. **33**(5), 32–47 (1999)
10. RDP. https://msdn.microsoft.com/en-us/library/aa383015(VS.85).aspx
11. Richardson, T., Stafford-Fraser, Q., Wood, K.R., Hopper, A.: Virtual network computing. Internet Comput. IEEE **2**(1), 33–38 (1998)
12. Toshniwal, I.M., Kawale, P., Bhanage, L., Sonawane, S.: Virtualized Screen: A Third Element for Cloud-Mobile Convergence (2014)
13. Yang, S.J., Nieh, J., Selsky, M., Tiwari, N.: The performance of remote display mechanisms for thin-client computing. In: USENIX Annual Technical Conference, General Track, pp. 131–146, June 2002
14. Sun, Y., Tay, T.T.: Analysis and reduction of data spikes in thin client computing. J. Parallel Distrib. Comput. **68**(11), 1463–1472 (2008)
15. Tolia, N., Andersen, D.G., Satyanarayanan, M.: Quantifying interactive user experience on thin clients. Computer **39**(3), 46–52 (2006)
16. Casas, P., Seufert, M., Egger, S., Schatz, R.: Quality of experience in remote virtual desktop services. In: 2013 IFIP/IEEE International Symposium on Integrated Network Management (IM 2013), pp. 1352–1357. IEEE, May 2013
17. Simoens, P., De Turck, F., Dhoedt, B., Demeester, P.: Remote display solutions for mobile cloud computing. Computer **44**(8), 46–53 (2011)
18. Chandra, S., Boreczky, J., Rowe, L.A.: High performance many-to-many intranet screen sharing with DisplayCast. ACM Trans. Multimedia Comput. Commun. Appl. (TOMCCAP) **10**(2), 19 (2014)
19. Tsao, C.L., Kakumanu, S., Sivakumar, R.: SmartVNC: an effective remote computing solution for smartphones. In: Proceedings of the 17th Annual International Conference on Mobile Computing and Networking, pp. 13–24. ACM, September 2011
20. Chun, B.G., Ihm, S., Maniatis, P., Naik, M., Patti, A.: Clonecloud: elastic execution between mobile device and cloud. In: Proceedings of the Sixth Conference on Computer Systems, pp. 301–314. ACM, April 2011
21. MirrorOp. http://www.mirrorop.com/
22. Splashto. http://www.splashtop.com/
23. Hsu, C.F., Tsai, T.H., Huang, C.Y., Hsu, C.H., Chen, K.T.: Screencast Dissected: Performance Measurements and Design Considerations (2015)

# A Novel Scheduling Algorithm for File Fetch in Transparent Computing

Kehua Guo[1,2]([✉]), Yayuan Tang[1], and Jiacheng Gu[3]

[1] School of Information Science and Engineering,
Central South University, Changsha 410083, China
{guokehua,tangyayuan}@csu.edu.cn
[2] Key Laboratory of Intelligent Perception and Systems for High-Dimensional
Information of Ministry of Education,
Nanjing University of Science and Technology, Nanjing 210094, China
[3] Department of Computer Science and Enginnering,
Texas A&M University, College Station, TX 77840, USA
jcgu@tamu.edu

**Abstract.** A novel scheduling algorithm is proposed to optimize file fetch process in transparent computing (TC) environment. A single TC server will receive file requests for operating systems, applications or user data from multiple clients. Considering limited size of server's memory and the dependency between these file requests, the paper firstly addresses the features of valid file fetch sequence generating problem. Then explodes the methods to determine time cost for file fetch sequence. Based on the model established, we propose a heuristic and greedy (HG) algorithm at the end. According to the simulation results, we can conclude that HG algorithm can reduce overall file fetch time roughly by 50 % in the best cases compared to the time cost of traditional approaches.

**Keywords:** File dependency · File fetch · Transparent computing · Green computing

## 1 Introduction

In the past decades, the desktop terminals has gradually developed into the ubiquitous computing in the computing paradigm. Ubiquitous computing was applied to various research areas, including software adaptation [1], school learning [2] and multimedia retrieval [3], and proposed many achievements. Traditional view of computing is hardware or software-centric, now it is slowly turning into service-oriented [4]. Transparent computing (TC) [5,6] is a concrete application form of ubiquitous computing, and has become a new pervasive computing paradigm in which no OS, middle ware and any application program are installed in the clients, they are loaded from the server through network dynamically when users want to run them in a client. Users can choose any OS and application programs running on it, which has been installed in the server and can be run

© Springer International Publishing Switzerland 2015
G. Wang et al. (Eds.): ICA3PP 2015, Part IV, LNCS 9531, pp. 216–229, 2015.
DOI: 10.1007/978-3-319-27140-8_16

by the clients [7]. The goal of this computing pattern is to reduce the burden of the server and improve the system maintainability. Therefore, users simply just accomplish their tasks on their data and do not care about the machine specifics and management details [8].

One server is usually responsible for the file transmission requests from multiple clients in transparent computing environment. In the research of transparent computing, the transmission process between server and clients has a very important role. Due to the multiplicity of files requested (such as operation system(OS), application or user data), file transmission in TC has encountered a special challenge — the dependency between these files. In many cases, to successfully run applications or operating systems, files must be loaded in a specific order. All the files are fetched from the server, when multiple clients request various files, it is an important issue to generate a reasonable file fetch and transmission sequence at the server.

Solving the file dependency problem will bring critical influence upon clients concerning the Quality of Service (QoS) and also improve the efficiency of TC servers. In our model, with a file fetch sequence and a fixed size memory buffer, the best case expected is to fetch each identical file one time and send it to all clients need it. Thus, the server should provide an optimized file fetch sequence which satisfying: Each client, upon receiving any file, can directly load it without waiting for pre-required files (called "receive and load"); and (2) the server can achieve optimization in reducing overall file fetch time cost. These requirements have become new challenges in the area of file transmission in transparent computing environment.

In recent years, the research of TC has been more and more popular. Our research group is performing some important research issues. In cooperation with scholars from other universities, we are constructing an optimized algorithm to dependent file fetch in transparent computing platform. This paper proposes key definitions and features of the dependent file fetch problem, describes a heuristic and greedy approach and evaluates the performance of the proposed algorithm.

The rest of this paper is organized as follows. Sections 2 explains the related works of transparent computing and file transmission approaches, Sect. 3 describes the system model and problem description, and Sect. 4 presents the solution for the problem, including all the information related, algorithm description. Section 5 provides performance evaluation and experimental results. Section 6 concludes our work and points out the future work.

## 2   Related Works

Transparent computing is a computing pattern to provide transparent services for users [9]. In TC environment, users only need to care about the result and quality of the services they want, and do not have to pay attention to the details of the Apps in system.Therefore, users are able to freely access the services on network across heterogeneous software and hardware platforms [10].

In TC architecture, computation, storage and management are separated. The users can access the services through cross-terminal and cross-OS operations [11].

The concept of TC was proposed in 1990s, references [7] gave the concept, architecture and example to TC. In the past decade, based on the theory of TC, researchers proposed some representative architectures and developed demonstration applications. Reference [12] developed the client terminal and related systems according to their TC study and proposed a novel Meta OS approach for streaming programs named 4VP. Reference [13] proposed the performance modelling and analysis algorithm of the booting process in TC environment. In 2012, reference [14] reported the work on building a virtual machine-based network storage system for TC platform.

From 2007, a cooperated research team was established with Intel Corporation by combining a new-generation BIOS named UEFI (Unified Extensible Firmware Interface) with TC architecture [15,16], many applications were proposed based on this combination platform. Some research groups have developed TransOS clients supporting various client hardware architectures (e.g. x86, ARM and MIPS) through UEFI [6].

For the transmission protocol, Kuang et al. developed a novel network storage access protocol for TC named NSAP [17]. For the virtualization technology, references [5,9] presented a separating computation and storage strategy. In addition, references [6,18] described the relationship between TC and cloud computing.

File fetch and transmission scheme [19,20] is an indispensable part in the implementation of transparent computing. The file fetch performance is one of the most important factors in the system evaluation. The research of file fetch scheme has a close relationship to some hot research fields such as communication network, computing pattern and data optimization management, etc. The importance of file fetch is addressed in many documents, which identify it as a core area for transparent computing. The traditional file fetch schemes have three.

The first scheme is big file sharing. In this scheme, a big file (e.g. an OS image) is stored in the file system of the server. After multiple clients submitting file request lists, the server will read the blocks from the big file, then transfer the blocks from memory buffer to each clients. This method is simple and efficient in the case of clients having the same hardware platforms and requesting the same files. For example, multiple clients request Android 4.0, we only need to deploy a single OS image at the server side to be requested by clients. However, when the clients' request is various and different, this scheme will no longer be valid.

The second scheme is file packaging. When the client requests arrive, for each client, this scheme fetches the files and packages them as a single big file, and then transfers it to the corresponding client. File packaging ensures that the clients obtain the files when their requests are different. However, this approach has two disadvantages: (1) Packaging process costs much computation resources. The files, which are requested by different clients, will be repeatedly fetched and packaged. (2) The packaged file may be large, and clients have to wait for the entire package transmission is complete, and then unpack it to load the files to the memory, which costs expensive computation resources.

Another scheme is random transmission. In this scheme, we directly fetch and transfer the files according to the file request list of each client, instead of making them into one package. Some files, which are requested by multiple clients, will be fetched once from the file system of the server. This approach can save the time cost which is caused by repeated fetch. However, this scheme does not consider the file dependency in the requested list. The client may have to hold some received files and wait for some other files they rely on. This will decrease the QoS for clients.

In transparent computing environment, the hardware configuration of clients may be various, and the file request lists will be different. Meanwhile, some files may be requested by multiple clients. For example, different clients request different OS versions, but they request the same application. In this case, the above schemes are not able to possess good performance. In order to solve the problems, our group is engaged in the development of optimized file set fetch algorithm. The proposed HG algorithm is proved to possess a good performance for dependent file fetch from transparent computing server.

# 3  System Model and Problem Description

This section will present the system model on how to organize the file fetch sequence from the file system of the server. Generally, each file in the server has three parameters: (1) file path, which represents the storage location of the file in server's disk, and to each file, the file path is unique; (2) file size, which represents the space cost when it is fetched to the memory; and (3) file fetch time, which represents the time cost including searching the file on the server's disk and reading the file to the memory. After a file is fetched to the memory, it will be transferred to the corresponding client. We assume that the server has already carried out some data preprocessing to guarantee that to each file, the server stores the file size, fetch time and the file list which it must rely on.

## 3.1  System Model

Figure 1 shows the process in which the server organizes the file fetch sequence to fetch files to the memory and transfer them to the clients. This process mainly consists of 4 steps: (1) send file requests (at the clients), (2) generate file dependency graphs (at the server), (3) organize the file fetch sequence (at the server), and (4) fetch (search and read) the file from server's disk according to the sequence and then transfer it to clients (at the clients and server).

In the system, we firstly request some parameters (hardware parameters, OS requirements, application and data requirements) at the client to be obtained (Fig. 1 (1)). After the acquisition, these parameters will be packaged and sent to the server. At the server, the request package is unpackaged. The server will search the relevant file list and determine whether it is able to provide the transparent service to the client. If the server satisfies all the requirements from client, it will extract the file dependency and generate a file directed graph to store the dependency (Fig. 1(2)).

The server is able to provide services to multiple clients, and each client has its corresponding graph. Then all the graphs will be combined and a file fetch sequence will be generated (Fig. 1(3)).

Therefore, we can perform the fetch process according to the file sequence (Fig. 1(4)). In the memory, a buffer with fixed size is responsible for storing the files which will be transferred to client.

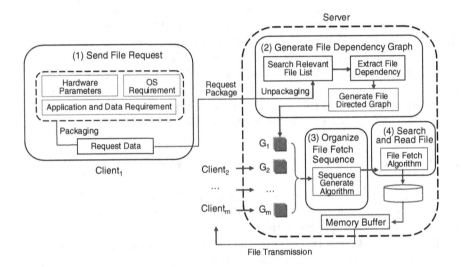

**Fig. 1.** System working process

## 3.2   Problem Description

In the system addressed above, we assume that there are $m$ clients represented as $C = \{c_1, c_2, ..., c_m\}$, and the graph set is $\Gamma = \{G_1, G_2, ..., G_m\}$, where $G_i$ is the corresponding directed graph of $c_i$ and $G_i = (V_i, E_i)$.

**Theorem 1.** $\forall G_i \in \Gamma$, $G_i$ is a directed acyclic graph.

*Proof.* Assume that we can find a cycle in $G_i$, $\forall v$ in this cycle, $v$ relies on another file. This means that we cannot find the first file which is able to be loaded at the client. So this cycle cannot exist in $G_i$.

A valid file fetch sequence can be defined as follows.

**Definition 1.** *Valid Sequence (VS): Given* $\Gamma = \{G_1, G_2, ..., G_m\}$ *, a VS is a linear sequence* $S = [s_1, s_2, ...s_N]$ *satisfying:*

1. $N = \sum_{i=1}^{m} |V_i|$, where $|V_i|$ is the number of vertices in a graph.
2. $\forall v \in V_i$, $occ(v, S){=}1$ where $occ(v, S)$ is the occurrence number of $v$ in $S$.
3. $\forall (u, v) \in E_i$, $idx(u, S) < idx(v, S)$, where $idx(v, S)$ is the index number of $v$ in $S$.

We define the process of generating a VS as Valid Sequence Generating (VSG). The VSG problem concerns that the sequence $S$ must contain all the files and keep the dependency for each client.

According to the above theorem, it can be known that if $m = 1$, VSG process is equivalent to finding a topological sort sequence of $G_i$. For $m > 1$, VSG process is equivalent to merging all the topological sort sequences of each graph.

After VSG process, the server is able to fetch the file according to the VS. The space allocation of the buffer satisfies the following criteria: (1) if the buffer has no sufficient space to accept the next file in the sequence, it will remove the file which is not used for the longest time; and (2) if the next file in the sequence has existed in the buffer, the server will directly use the existed file, instead of fetch the file from server's disk.

The problem to be solved is to organize the file sequence to minimize the total file fetch time cost under the premise of keeping the file dependency for each client. In order to compute the total time cost, $\forall s \in S$, $s.time$ should be determined according to the buffer size. We define the Time Cost Assignment (TCA) process as following.

**Definition 2.** *Time Cost Assignment (TCA): Given a buffer size $B$ and a valid sequence $S$, $\forall [s_r, ..., s_t]$, $s_r.path = s_t.path$ and $s_i.path \neq s_r.path$ $(r < i < t)$, the TCA(S,B) process assigns the file fetch time of $s_t$ as follows:*

$$s_t.time = \begin{cases} 0 & \sum_{i=r}^{t} distinct(s_i).size \leq B \\ s_t.time & others \end{cases}$$

where $\sum_{i=r}^{t} distinct(s_i).size$ represents that the $s_i.size$ is counted only once for $s_i.path$ repeatedly appears in $[s_r, ..., s_t]$. The total time cost can be represented as follows:

$$Cost(S) = \sum_{i=1}^{N} s_i.time \tag{1}$$

**Theorem 2.** *Given a buffer size $B$ and a valid sequence $S$, TCA satisfies the proper use of buffer in Algorithm 1.*

*Proof.* $\forall s_t \in S$, on the one hand, if TCA assigns $s_t.time = 0$, this means that $\exists [s_r, ..., s_t]$, where $s_r.path = s_t.path$, $s_i.path \neq s_r.path$ $(r < i < t)$ and $\sum_{i=r}^{t} distinct(s_i).size \leq B$. In other words, when the server want to read $s_t$, another file $s_r$, whose path is same as $s_t$, is still in the buffer. Assume that we change the time to $s_t.time \neq 0$, this will result in an unnecessary fetch. On the other hand, if TCA assigns $s_t.time \neq 0$, this means that $s_t.path$ is the first occurrence in $S$ or if we choose $[s_r, ..., s_t]$, where $s_r.path = s_t.path$, $s_i.path \neq s_r.path$ $(r < i < t)$, $\sum_{i=r}^{t} distinct(s_i).size$ will exceed $B$. In other words, when the server want to read $s_t$, files after $s_r$ have filled the buffer and $s_r$ has been removed. Assume that we change the time to $s_t.time = 0$, which means the file does not be fetched from disk, this will result in that the server is unable to find the file data in the buffer.

The definition of the Minimum Valid Sequence (MVS) problem is given below.

**Definition 3.** *Minimum Valid Sequence (MVS) Problem: Given* $\Gamma = \{G_1, G_2, ..., G_m\}$ *and a buffer size $B$, the MVS problem seeks $S$ in all sequences generated by VSG and satisfies Cost(TCA(S,B)) has the minimum value.*

We then consider the hardness of the MVS problem. In fact, MVS process is equivalent to find $S$ with minimum cost in all the possible topological sort merging result. The hardness can be described from two factors:(1) Given a graph $G_i$, the topological sort result may be multiple. If $G_i$ is a linear list, it only has one topological sort result; if $G_i$ has no edges, the possibility will be $|V_i|!$. (2) Given $m$ topological sort sequences, when $S$ is organized, every time we can choose the first vertex from each sequence. So the upper bound of the result space is $m^{|s|} = m^N$, the lower bound is $m!$. Therefore, the number of sequences generated by VSG may be very large. Exhaustive approach is difficult to obtain good results.

# 4    Solution for the MVS Problem

In MVS problem, because merging all the topological sort sequences into one valid sequence $S$ is infeasible, we directly generate the valid sequence $S$ from graphs and try to seek an approximate minimum case that can be solved in polynomial time. In this section, we first analyze the conditions which $S$ must satisfies and find the test algorithm. And then we propose some characters of the valid sequence $S$. Furthermore, we design a heuristic and greedy algorithm to solve the MVS problem.

## 4.1    Preliminaries

For a sequence $S$ which satisfies all the file dependency, according to the definition of VS, $\forall G_i \in \Gamma$, a topological sort sequence must exists in sequence $S$. We first propose an algorithm to test whether $S$ contains a topological sort sequence of $G_i$.

The algorithm we propose scans the sequence $S$ and finds the files which will be transferred to the corresponding client of graph $G$. If a file $s_i$ is found, we test whether it is a vertex with zero indegree in $G$. If the indegree is not zero, the algorithm will return false. Otherwise we will remove $s_i$ and all the edges starting from $s_i$ from graph $G$ and then seek the next $s_i$ in $S$. If the whole algorithm has not returned false, it means that $S$ contains a topological sort sequence of $G$.

**Theorem 3.** *The above algorithm is able to detect whether sequence $S$ contains topological sort sequence of each graph $\Gamma$.*

*Proof.* The "if statement" at line 6 guarantees that all the vertices which are checked are in graph $G$. We combine these vertices as another sub-sequence $sg$. Each file vertex in graph $G$ appears once in $sg$. On the one hand, if $sg$ is not a topological sort sequence of graph $G$, this means that there exists a directed edge $(u, v) \in E$ satisfying $idx(v) < idx(u)$. Algorithm 2 will first check vertex $v$, in this case, $v.indegree \neq 0$ because there exists an edge from $u$ to $v$, Algorithm 2 will return false. On the other hand, because every loop in Algorithm 2 will check the vertices whose indegree is zero and then remove these vertices and all the related edges. If $sg$ is a topological sort sequence of graph $G$, the algorithm will return true.

Therefore, given $\Gamma = \{G_1, G_2, ..., G_m\}$ and a sequence $S$, each graph $G_i$ can be tested by the algorithm.

### 4.2   Heuristic and Greedy (HG) Algorithm

The basic idea of HG algorithm to MVS problem is to choose the vertex which can currently save most time cost and add it to sequence $S$. The cost a vertex can save is calculated by estimated value.

**Definition 4.** *Weight Assignment (WAss) Process: Given a graph $G(V, E)$, WAss process assigns each vertex $v$ a weight $(w)$ satisfies: (1) $\forall v \in V$, if $v.indegree = 0$, then $v.w = 0$; and (2) $\forall v \in V$, if $v.indegree \neq 0$, $v.w = \sum u.size$, where $idx(u) < idx(v)$.*

We propose an algorithm to assign the weight to each vertex in graph $G$.

The algorithm first scans the graph $G$ and finds vertex $v$ whose indegree is zero and then assigns the weight as zero. Otherwise, $v.w$ will be assigned as the summation of the sizes of all the vertices whose location is before $v$.

**Definition 5.** *Choose Vertex (CV) Process: Given $\Gamma = \{G_1, G_2, ..., G_m\}$, CV process($\Gamma - v$) chooses a vertex $v$ and adds $v$ into sequence $S$, then delete $v$ and the edges starting from $v$ in corresponding graph.*

**Theorem 4.** *Given a sub-sequence $S' = [s_1, ..., s_t]$ ($t < N$), $s_{t+1}$ chosen by CV process must satisfies: $s_{t+1}.indegree = 0$.*

*Proof.* If $s_{t+1}.indegree \neq 0$, this means that $\exists (u, s_{t+1}) \in E$, and $u$ is not removed from the corresponding graph. In sequence $S$, $idx(u) > idx(s_{t+1})$ , this contradicts the definition of valid sequence $S$.

If a vertex $v$ is deleted by CV process, the weight of the rest vertices must be adjusted to satisfy the conditions in definition of WAss. The algorithm first adds $v$ into a queue. Second a vertex $u$ is popped and the vertices starting from $u$ are assigned as a new weight and added into the queue. The loop will stop when the queue is empty.

**Definition 6.** *Estimated Cost Saving (ECS): Given a sub-sequence* $S' = [s_1, ..., s_t]$ *(t < N), and* $\Gamma' = \Gamma - \sum_{i=1}^{t} s_i$ *the Estimated Cost Saving of* $s_{t+1}$ *satisfies:*

$$ECS(s_{t+1}) = \{cs(S', s_{t+1}), cs(\Gamma', s_{t+1}), ecs(\Gamma' - s_{t+1})\} \tag{2}$$

Seek $s_r$ satisfying $r < t + 1$, $s_r.path = s_{t+1}.path$ and $s_i.path \neq s_{t+1}.path$ $(r < i < t + 1)$, if $s_r$ does not exist in $S'$, $cs(S', s_{t+1})$ will be zero. Otherwise, $cs(S', s_{t+1})$ is defined as follows:

$$cs(S', s_{t+1}) = \begin{cases} s_{t+1}.time \sum_{i=r}^{t} distinct(s_i).size \leq B \\ \\ 0 \qquad others \end{cases}$$

$cs(\Gamma', s_{t+1})$ is defined as follows:

$$cs(\Gamma', s_{t+1}) = \begin{cases} s_{t+1}.time \ \exists v \in (\Gamma' - s_{t+1}) \\ \qquad where \ v.path = s_{t+1}.path \\ \qquad and \ v.indegree = 0 \\ \\ 0 \qquad others \end{cases}$$

From the formula, we can see that in $\Gamma' - s_{t+1}$, if there exists a vertex whose indegree is zero and the path is the same as $s_{t+1}.time$ the $cs(\Gamma', s_{t+1})$ will be assigned as $s_{t+1}.time$, otherwise, it will be zero.

We divide $\Gamma' - s_{t+1}$ as $\{V_1, V_2, ..., V_k\}$ satisfying: (1) for $u \in V_i$ and $v \in V_i$, $u.path = v.path$, if $idx(u) < idx(v)$, then $u.w \leq v.w$; (2) if $u \in V_i$ and $v \in V_j (i \neq j)$, $u.path \neq v.path$. It can be seen that all the files in $V_i$ have the same file path and size. $ecs(\Gamma' - s_{t+1})$ is defined as follows:

$$ecs(\Gamma' - s_{t+1}) =$$
$$\sum_{i=1}^{k} \sum_{j=1}^{|V_i|-1} exp(\frac{V_{i,j}.size - V_{i,j+1}.size}{B})V_{i,j}.size \tag{3}$$

**Definition 7.** *Heuristic and Greedy (HG) Algorithm to MVS Problem: Given* $\Gamma' = \{G_1, G_2, ..., G_m\}$, *the Heuristic and Greedy Algorithm generates a linear sequence* $S = [s_1, s_2, ..., s_N]$.

This function first scans all the vertices whose weight is zero, and then chooses a vertex $u$ with maximum positive $cs(S, u)$ value, if all the $cs(S, u)$ are zero, we chooses a vertex $u$ with maximum positive $cs(\Gamma, u)$ value, if all the $cs(\Gamma, u)$ are zero, we choose a vertex $u$ with maximum $ecs(\Gamma - u)$ value. After this step, $u$ will be added to sequence $S$ and deleted from $\Gamma$. After adjusting the weights of vertices in $\Gamma$, the function will choose the next vertex in the rest graph $\Gamma - u$. If all the vertices in $\Gamma$ are removed, this function will return $S$ and the algorithm will stop.

**Theorem 5.** *The sequence $S$ generated by HG algorithm is able to pass the sequence test in the first algorithm.*

*Proof.* If sequence $S$ generated by HG algorithm cannot pass the sequence test in Algorithm 1, this means that $\exists G_i \in \Gamma$, an edge $< u, v > \in E_i$ satisfying $idx(v) < idx(u)$. HG algorithm will first delete vertex $v$ and then delete vertex $u$. But when HG algorithm delete $v$, $v.indegree \neq 0$, $v.w$ is not zero. This contradicts the description of CV process and HG algorithm.

# 5 Simulation Experiments

## 5.1 Experiment Settings

To evaluate the performance of the proposed algorithms, we conduct a set of simulation experiments by using Java. We first investigate the performance of the three approaches to the file fetch problem, namely (1) Sequentially Merging (SM, sequentially merge the topological sort sequence of each graph); (2) Sequentially Choosing (SC, sequentially choose vertices from each graph); (3) Randomly Choosing (RC, randomly choose vertices from each graph) and HG algorithm, then study their performance in solving the MVS problem. In the experiments, we construct a database containing some files whose file sizes are randomly assigned. We will randomly generate some clients. For each client which connects to the server, we randomly generate a graph containing vertices and edges.

The primary metric concerned is the total time cost of file fetch. We consider five important parameters that may impact the total time cost of file fetch: the number of vertices ($|V_i|$), the number of edges ($|E_i|$) and vertex redundancy. The performance evaluation model is designed as follows.

**Definition 8.** *Given a sequence $S = [s_1, s_2, ..., s_N]$ , the performance of $S$ can be measured by:*

$$p(S) = \frac{cost}{lower} \tag{4}$$

*where $lower = \sum_{i=1}^{N} distinct(s_i).time$, $cost = Cost(TCA(S, B))$. Particularly, we define $p(lower) = 1$ and $p(upper) = upper/lower$, where $upper = \sum_{i=1}^{N} s_i.time$.*

From this definition we can see that when the cost is close to *lower*, $p$ will be small, which means that the sequence $S$ has good performance. The value of $p$ satisfies:

$$(p(lower) = 1) \leq p(S) \leq p(upper) \tag{5}$$

## 5.2 Performance Comparison

First of all, we testify the effectiveness of our algorithm. In the experiments, the vertices and edges are randomly generated in a database containing 100 files whose file sizes are between 10 and 20, the time cost of each file is proportional to the file size. We will randomly generate 10 clients. For each client which connects to the server, we randomly generate a graph containing 10 to 20 vertices and some edges. The buffer size is chosen as the three times of the max size of files in the database.

In order to demonstrate the performance, we record the performances of all sequences generated by each algorithm. For every algorithm, we perform 10 experiments (No. 1–10) and compute the performance of each sequence. The performances are illustrated in Fig. 2.

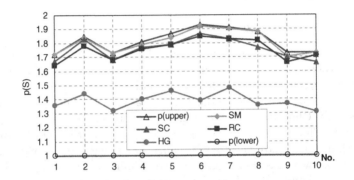

**Fig. 2.** Performance comparison of 10 experiments

Figure 2 indicates that in each experiment, the $p(S)$ of HG algorithm is about 50 % of the other three approaches, which shows that the performance of our solution is better than some traditional ones.

The second experiment will illustrate the performance comparisons between the proposed algorithm and the other three typical approaches when the number of vertices and edges changes. We define $r = |E_i|/C_{|G_i|}^2$ and choose it from 0 to 1.0. $r = 0$ means that no dependency exists in the file request list, and when $r$ increases, the dependency will be more and more. For every $r$, we perform 4 different algorithms and record the performances. The final results are listed in Fig. 3.

From Fig. 3, we can see that HG algorithm achieves good performance. Especially, when $r$ is close to zero, which means few dependencies exist in the requested file list, $p(S)$ of HG is very close to 1.0. This shows that HG algorithm is suitable for the case of not only many file dependencies, but also few file dependencies. When $r > 0.1$, the performance surpasses the other approaches.

The third experiment will illustrate the performance comparisons between the proposed algorithm and the other three typical approaches when vertex redundancy changes. We define $t = min|G_i|/fileNumber$. When $t$ is small, it means that we randomly choose a small amount of vertices from a big file database, the vertex redundancy will be small. And when $t$ increases, the choosing range will be expanded, especially when $t = 1$, the number of vertices is equal

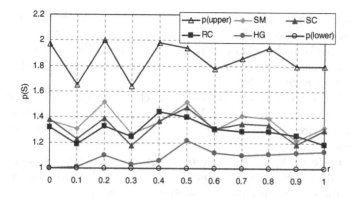

**Fig. 3.** Performance impact of the ratio of vertices and edges

to the number of files, many vertices with same path will exist in $\Gamma$. We use $t$ from 0 to 1.0. For every $t$, we perform 4 different algorithms and compute the performances. The final results are listed in Fig. 4.

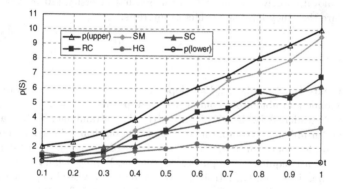

**Fig. 4.** Performance impact of the vertex redundancy

From Fig. 4, we can see that HG algorithm achieves good performance in most cases. Especially, when $t > 0.4$ and increases, clear advantages can be indicated from this experiment in comparison with the other three approaches. The performance surpasses about 50 % over the other approaches.

# 6    Conclusions and Future Work

In this paper, we propose an optimized algorithm to solve the dependent file fetch problem in transparent computing environment. We introduce the framework of file fetch problem and describe the definition of file, valid sequence, time cost assignment and minimum valid sequence problem. A heuristic and greedy algorithm has been proposed.

We have performed several experiments to evaluate the performance of HG algorithm. Comparisons in experiments demonstrate that HG algorithm obtains remarkable time saving performance.

Although this work is built on the file fetch in transparent computing, the proposed solution could be extended to be applicable to more generalized cases such as the resource generating in cloud computing and distributed computing environment.

In the future work, we will concentrate on exploring several improvements on HG, including performing the experiments in the real transparent computing environment and increasing the time saving performance.

**Acknowledgments.** This work is supported by the Major Science and Technology Research Program for Strategic Emerging Industry of Hunan (2012GK4106), International Science and Technology Cooperation Special Projects of China (2013DFB10070), Hunan Science and Technology Plan (2012RS4054), Natural Science Foundation of China (61202341), Key Laboratory of Intelligent Perception and Systems for High-Dimensional Information of Ministry of Education Innovation Fund (JYB201502), and Project of Innovation-driven Plan in Central South University (2015CXS010). The authors declare that they have no conflict of interests.

# References

1. Konstantinos, K., Paspallis, N., Papadopoulos, G.A.: A survey of software adaptation in mobile and ubiquitous computing. Enterp. Inf. Syst. **4**(4), 355–389 (2010)
2. Poole, E.S., Miller, A.D., Xu, Y., Eiriksdottir, E., Catrambone, R., Mynatt, E.D.: The place for ubiquitous computing in schools: lessons learned from a school-based intervention for youth physical activity. In: Proceedings of the 13th International Conference on Ubiquitous Computing, September, Beijing, China (2011)
3. Guo, K., Ma, J., Duan, G.: DHSR: A novel semantic retrieval approach for ubiquitous multimedia. Wireless Pers. Commun. **76**(4), 779–793 (2014)
4. Thompson, M.S., Midkiff, S.F.: Service description and dissemination for service discovery in pervasive computing environments. Int. J. Ad Hoc Ubiquitous Comput. **12**(4), 193–204 (2013)
5. Zhang, Y., Zhou, Y.: Separating computation and storage with storage virtualization. Comput. Commun. **34**(13), 1539–1548 (2011)
6. Zhang, Y., Zhou, Y.: TransOS: a transparent computing-based operating system for the cloud. Int. J. Cloud Comput. **1**(4), 287–301 (2012)
7. Zhang, Y.X.: Transparent computing: Concept, architecture and example. Acta Electronica Sinica **32**(12A), 169–173 (2004)
8. Wang, G., Bhuiyan, M., Cao, J., Wu, J.: Detecting movements of a target using face tracking in wireless sensor networks. IEEE Trans. Parallel Distrib. Syst. **25**(4), 39–949 (2013)
9. Zhang, Y., Zhou, Y.: Transparent computing: a new paradigm for pervasive computing. In: Ma, J., Jin, H., Yang, L.T., Tsai, J.J.-P. (eds.) UIC 2006. LNCS, vol. 4159, pp. 1–11. Springer, Heidelberg (2006)

10. Zhou, Y., Zhang, Y., Liu, H., Xiong, N., Vasilakos, A.: A bare-metal and asymmetric partitioning approach to client virtualization. IEEE Trans. Serv. Comput. **7**(1), 40–53 (2012)
11. Zhou, Y., Zhang, Y.: Transparent Computing: Concepts, Architecture and Implementation. Cengage Learning, Singapore (2009)
12. Zhang, Y., Zhou, Y.: 4VP: a novel Meta OS approach for streaming programs in ubiquitous computing. In: Proceedings of the IEEE 21st International Conference on Advanced Information Networking and Applications, May, Niagara Falls, Ontario, Canada (2007)
13. Guo, G., Zhang, Y., Zhou, Y., Yang, L.T., Wei, L., Tian, P.: Performance modelling and analysis of the booting process in a transparent computing environment. In: Proceedings of the 2nd International Conference on Future Generation Communication and Networking (FGCN08), December, Hainan, China (2008)
14. Gao, Y., Zhang, Y., Zhou, Y.: Building a virtual machine-based network storage system for transparent computing. In: Proceedings of 2012 International Conference on Computer Science and Service System, Nanjing, Jiangsu, China (2012)
15. Tsinghua University: Cooperation MOU on Intel platform innovation framework for EFI. 18 February 2007
16. Unified EFI Forum: Unified Extensible Firmware Interface (UEFI) (2011). http://www.uefi.org/home/. Accessed 1 November 2013
17. Kuang, W., Zhang, Y., Zhou, Y., Xu, G., Wei, L., Gao, Y.: NSAP-a network storage access protocol for transparent computing. J. Tsinghua Univ. **49**(1), 106–109 (2009)
18. Zhang, Y., Zhou, Y.: Transparent computing: Spatio-temporal extension on von Neumann architecture for cloud services. Tsinghua Sci. Technol. **18**(1), 10–21 (2013)
19. Bolosky, W.J., Douceur, J.R., Ely, D., Theimer, M.: Feasibility of a serverless distributed file system deployed on an existing set of desktop PCs. In: ACM SIGMETRICS Performance Evaluation Review, vol. 28, No. 1, pp. 34–43. ACM, June 2000
20. Nossenson, R., Attiya, H.: The distribution of file transmission duration in the web. Int. J. Commun. Syst. **17**(5), 407–419 (2004)

# Performance Evaluation of HPGMG on Tianhe-2: Early Experience

Yulong Ao[1,3], Yiqun Liu[1,3], Chao Yang[1,2]([✉]), Fangfang Liu[1],
Peng Zhang[1,3], Yutong Lu[4], and Yunfei Du[4]

[1] Institute of Software, Chinese Academy of Sciences, Beijing 100190, China
yangchao@iscas.ac.cn
[2] State Key Laboratory of Computer Science,
Chinese Academy of Sciences, Beijing 100190, China
[3] University of Chinese Academy of Sciences, Beijing 100049, China
[4] National University of Defense Technology, Changsha 410073, Hunan, China

**Abstract.** In this paper, we evaluate and analyze the performance of HPGMG on the world's largest supercomputer, Tianhe-2. We design and implement a general testing framework according to the performance-related parameters in HPGMG-FV and the architecture characteristics of Tianhe-2. This framework can automatically construct testing spaces, filter them by constrains, modify them by actual running results, and extract useful information from output files. By using this framework, we evaluate the performance of HPGMG at small-scale with different tunable parameters, and at large-scale of 8192 nodes with an overall performance of 5.511e+11 DOF/s.

**Keywords:** HPGMG-FV · Benchmark · Testing framework · Tianhe-2 · High-performance

## 1 Introduction

The High-Performance Linpack (HPL) benchmark, currently used for the TOP500 list [14], has been the most successful and broadly accepted performance metric of supercomputers for over twenty years. HPL is representative for applications with high computational intensity and uniform data access patterns. The relevance between HPL and real-world applications, however, is becoming lower, especially for problems that require high memory bandwidth and low data access latency. To better correlate computation and data access patterns found in many applications today, new benchmarks, such as the Graph500 benchmark [4,11], the High Performance Conjugate Gradient (HPCG) benchmark [7], and the High Performance Geometric Multigrid (HPGMG) benchmark [1,2], begin to draw increasingly more attention.

The Graph500 benchmark concerns data-intensive applications based on the breadth-first search in a large weighted and undirected graph. It addresses three important graph kernels, namely, concurrent search, optimization (single source

© Springer International Publishing Switzerland 2015
G. Wang et al. (Eds.): ICA3PP 2015, Part IV, LNCS 9531, pp. 230–243, 2015.
DOI: 10.1007/978-3-319-27140-8_17

shortest path), and edge-oriented (maximal independent set). Instead of using floating-point operations per second (FLOPS), Graph500 proposes a new metrics called traversed edges per second (TEPS) [11] for ranking supercomputers. The chosen data sets represent five graph-related business and scientific areas including cybersecurity, medical informatics, data enrichment, social networks, and symbolic networks.

The HPCG and HPGMG benchmarks both measure the capability of a supercomputer in solving discretized equations arising from elliptic partial differential equations on a 3D structured mesh. In HPCG, a large, sparse linear system is generated based on the 27-point finite difference scheme for the Poisson equation and is solved by using the conjugate gradient algorithm preconditioned with a geometric multigrid method. The performance metric used in HPCG is the traditional FLOP/s, but with some penalties from the overhead of generating the optimized data structures and the increased number of iterations. HPGMG, on the other hand, solves both constant- and variable-coefficient elliptic problems using the geometric multigrid algorithm, which is based on stencil computations without explicitly generating the sparse matrix. To reflect the capability of solving problems, HPGMG uses a new metric, degrees of freedom per second (DOF/s). There are two variants in HPGMG, namely the finite element version (HPGMG-FE) and the finite volume version (HPGMG-FV). All available HPGMG results, to date, are based on the HPGMG-FV version.

In this paper, we focus on the performance evaluation of HPGMG-FV on the world fastest supercomputer, the Tianhe-2. Tianhe-2 is a heterogeneous system comprised of both Intel Xeon CPUs and Intel Xeon Phi coprocessors. It is worth noting that, on most other similar hybrid systems such as Titan and Stempde [2], the current best HPGMG performances are all obtained from pure CPU configurations. This is because, for now, the support of HPGMG-FV for Xeon Phi is still premature. Therefore, in this paper we only focus on the performance evaluation on Tianhe-2 without using the Xeon Phi coprocessors.

The paper is organized as follows. We first give a detailed overview and analysis on the algorithms, data structures and implementations of HPGMG-FV in Sect. 2. Then, in Sect. 3, we setup a testing framework to help simplify the procedure of the performance evaluation of HPGMG-FV on Tianhe-2. In Sect. 4, we provide extensive experiment results, including small-scale results collected by the testing framework for helping setup parameters in larger-scale tests, and large-scale results on 8192 nodes with an aggregated performance of 5.511e+11 DOF/s. In the last two sections, we discuss some related work and give a conclusion of this paper.

# 2 Overview and Analysis of HPGMG-FV

## 2.1 Algorithm

HPGMG-FV solves both constant- and variable-coefficient elliptic problems, in a three-dimensional cubic domain, in the follow general form

$$a\alpha(\boldsymbol{x})u(\boldsymbol{x}) - b\nabla \cdot \beta(\boldsymbol{x})\nabla u(\boldsymbol{x}) = f(\boldsymbol{x}), \tag{1}$$

with homogeneous Dirichlet boundary conditions. Here the constants $a$ and $b$ control the type of the problem ($a \neq 0$ for Helmholtz and $a = 0$ for Poisson), and the variable coefficients $\alpha(\boldsymbol{x})$ and $\beta(\boldsymbol{x})$ are pre-stored variables. By default, HPGMG-FV solves the variable-coefficient Poisson equation with $a = 0$ and $b = 1$. The 7-point finite difference stencil is used to discretize the variable-coefficient Laplacian operator.

The top-level solver used in HPGMG-FV is the full geometric multigrid algorithm, which is proved, for the constant-coefficient Laplacian, to converge with an optimal computing complexity. The full multigrid (i.e. F-cycle) shown in Algorithm 1 [1,13] can be viewed as a special nested iteration method in which the smoothing step in line 6 is a V-cycle multigrid. The V-cycle multigrid, as shown in Algorithm 2, is embedded in the F-cycle multigrid to solve the fine level problem after the interpolation from the coarse to the fine level. The F-cycle multigrid is only required to sweep for one time, leading to a computing complexity of $\mathcal{O}(N)$.

---

**Algorithm 1.** F-cycle multigrid algorithm.

---

1  $h \leftarrow h_0$
2  $u^h \leftarrow A_h^{-1} f_h$                                 /* coarsest solve */
3  **while** not done **do**
4      $u^{h/2} \leftarrow \overline{I}_h^{h/2} u^h$                   /* FMG interpolation */
5      $h \leftarrow \frac{h}{2}$
6      $u^h \leftarrow$ V-cycle$(A_h, u^h, f_h)$
7      $e_h \leftarrow$ error$(u^h)$                  /* error for convergence test */
8  **end**

---

**Algorithm 2.** V-cycle multigrid algorithm.

---

1  **Function** $u^h \leftarrow V\text{-}cycle(A_h, u_0^h, f_h)$
2      **if** $h == h_0$ **then**
3          **return** $u^h \leftarrow A_h^{-1} f_h$                  /* bottom solver */
4      $u^h \leftarrow$ smooth$(A_h, u_0^h, f_h)$               /* pre-smooth */
5      $r^h \leftarrow f_h - A_h u^h$                         /* residual */
6      $r^{2h} \leftarrow I_h^{2h} r^h$                          /* restriction */
7      $u_0^{2h} \leftarrow 0$
8      $\delta^{2h} \leftarrow$ V-cycle$(A_{2h}, u_0^{2h}, r^{2h})$         /* recursive call */
9      $u^h \leftarrow u^h + I_{2h}^h \delta^{2h}$                  /* interpolation */
10     $u^h \leftarrow$ smooth$(A_h, u^h, f_h)$                 /* post-smooth */
11     **return** $u^h$
12 **end**

---

There are a number of operations [1,13] carried out in the V-cycle algorithm, which are listed as follows.

- **Smooth**: The *pre-smooth* and *post-smooth* are traditional relaxation operations. HPGMG-FV supports smoothers such as the Chebyshev polynomials, the Gauss-Seidel with red-black reordering (GSRB), the weighted and $L_1$ Jacobi, and the symmetric Gauss-Seidel (SymGS).
- **Restriction**: After reducing the error by several smooth steps, the *restriction* operation maps the residual on fine grid with grid spacing $h$ to the coarse grid with grid spacing $2h$. This progress does not stop until reaching the coarsest grid.
- **Bottom solver**: It is an iterative solver employed to solve the problem on the coarsest grid. The available *bottom solvers* in HPGMG-FV include the biconjugate gradient stabilized (BiCGSTAB) algorithm, the conjugate gradient algorithm (CG), and their corresponding communication-avoiding versions.
- **Interpolation**: The *interpolation* operation, as opposed to *restriction*, maps the coarsest correction solved by *bottom solver* back up to the finest grid level by level with *post-smooth*.

In HPGMG, the default *pre-smooth* and *post-smooth* operators are both the Chebyshev polynomials with degree 4, and the default *bottom solvers* is BiCGSTAB. These default parameters are used for the performance evaluation. The whole data flow of the full multigrid algorithm, as well as all major operations in it, are illustrated in Fig. 1.

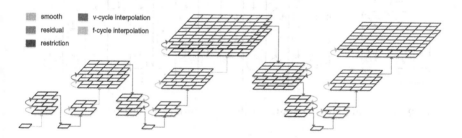

**Fig. 1.** The data flow and major operations in the full multigrid algorithm.

## 2.2 Data Structure

The global 3D domain of each level in HPGMG-FV is partitioned into subdomains called box. The resultant boxes, grouped in a list, are distributed among multiple MPI processes. The exchanging of data from different MPI processes requires allocated buffers for sending and receiving messages. Those data for boxes owned by the same MPI process are stored contiguously in the corresponding separate arrays. Further more, Memory allocation of them uses a bulk way. We can access the data in a cell by referencing the pointer plus an offset from the index calculation in a matrix-free manner.

Figure 2 shows types and layout of data for different purposes owned by one process. These data, either cell-centered or face-centered, are all double-precision. The parameter $\beta$ in Eq. (1) is face-centered coefficient and divided into three vectors $beta\_\{i, j, k\}$ which are left-right, back-front, and bottom-top, respectively. On the other hand, the parameter $\alpha$ in Eq. (1), stored in $alpha$, is cell-centered. Both the exact solution $utrue$ and the computed numerical solution $u$ are cell-centered, used for final error calculation. All the rest vectors, such as the residual $f - Av$, the original right-hand side $f$, the inverse of the diagonal $dinv$, and the L1 norm of each row $l1inv$, are cell-centered as well. There are also two special vectors $temp$ and $valid$. The former is used to keep the intermediate results from different computations and the latter is a cell-centered array to identify whether the cells are outside of boundaries of the domain and used in the stencil computation with fused boundary condition. Besides, a reserved vector will be allocated for any auxiliary bottom solver grids. All these vectors of each box also contain ghost zones which store data from their neighboring boxes.

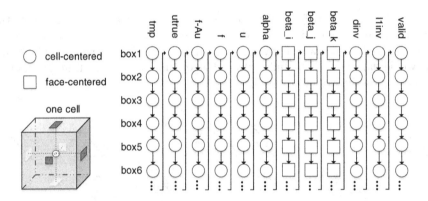

**Fig. 2.** Types and layout of data for different purpose owned by each process.

## 2.3   Implementation

HPGMG-FV is written in C based on a hybrid parallel computation model, in which MPI is used for message passing and OpenMP is used for multi-threading. The program follows a four-phase running procedure, namely: problem setup, geometry construction, solver running, and results report. At the geometry construction phase, the program firstly creates the finest level structure and then utilize it to create the rest levels progressively from the finest to the coarsest. In the process of constructing every level, the data of boxes will be flattened into smaller blocks which are the actual unit for operations. This block mechanism makes the fine-grained level parallelism control possible.

The main operations in the solver running step, as described by Algorithms 1 and 2, can be generally grouped into two classes. In the first class, there are $smooth$ and $residual$ operations. They need to exchange data with each other on the same level before computation. The second class contains operations such as *restriction* and *interpolation* which may involve communication between adjacent two levels. No matter whether the communication is intra-level or inter-level, there exist two execution paths, i.e. the remote path and the local path, both executed concurrently. On the remote path, firstly the source process packs and updates the data into the MPI send buffer and then sends to the destination process. Once the destination process receives the data in the MPI receive buffer, it will unpack them into the corresponding block. While on the local path, data exchange and update happens on the same process. This asynchronous execution mechanism will be very effective. For example, the detail procedure of these two paths in *restriction* can be seen in Fig. 3. *Interpolation* and ghost exchange in *smooth* and *residual* are similar to *restriction* except that ghost exchange just do some data moving without updating them.

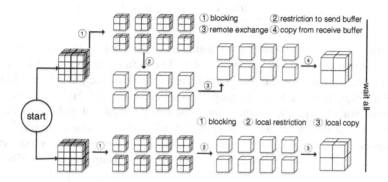

**Fig. 3.** Asynchronous execution of the remote and local restrictions.

# 3   Metric and Framework

## 3.1   Evaluated Platform and Performance Metric

We evaluate the HPGMG benchmark on the Tianhe-2 supercomputer, which ranked the first place in the latest TOP 500 list released on November 2014. It consists of 16,000 computing nodes connected with a customized network TH-Express2. The software system contains a 64-bit Kylin OS, the Intel compiler icc 14.0.2, and the MPICH2 with a customized GLEX channel. Table 1 shows the architectural characteristics of each computing node of the Tianhe-2, in which there are two Intel Xeon E5-2692 processors and three Intel Xeon Phi 31S1P coprocessors. As mentioned earlier, the Xeon Phi coprocessors are not activated in our performance evaluation.

Instead of floating point operations per second (FLOP/s) that has been widely applied as the standard performance metric for years, HPGMG-FV uses a new metric, degrees of freedom per second (DOF/s), in order to better reflect

Table 1. Architectural characteristics of Tianhe-2.

|  | Intel Xeon E5-2692 | Intel Xeon Phi 31S1P |
| --- | --- | --- |
| Frequency (GHz) | 2.2 | 1.1 |
| cores/threads | 12/24 | 57/228 |
| SIMD width (DP/SP) | 4-way/8-way | 8-way/ 16-way |
| Peak Gflop/s in D.P | 422.4 | 1003.2 |
| L1/L2/L3 cache (KB) | 32/256/30 | 32/512/- |
| Memory capacity (GB) | 64 | 8 |

the capability of problems solving. In particular, the performance is measured in HPGMG-FV as

$$perf = \frac{dim\_i \times dim\_j \times dim\_k}{avg\_time}, \qquad (2)$$

where $dim\_\{i, j, k\}$ are the respective numbers of grid points in each dimension, and $avg\_time$ is the averaged time per solve. The actual number of solves is estimated by the quotient of the minimum time the benchmark should run divided by the average time of ten warm-up solves before timing. It is obvious that the numerator of Eq. (2), which equals the total number of unknowns $dof = dim\_i \times dim\_j \times dim\_k$, is determined by three factors, including the total number of processes ($num\_procs$), the number of boxes per process ($boxes\_per\_proc$), and the dimension of each box ($2^{box\_dim}$). Their relationship can be described by

$$dof = num\_procs \times boxes\_per\_proc \times (2^{box\_dim})^3, \qquad (3)$$

where $num\_procs$ equals to the multiplication of the number of nodes ($num\_nodes$) and the number of processes per node ($procs\_per\_node$). Besides, there is another important parameter, namely the number of threads per process ($thrs\_per\_proc$), that may have a strong impact on the performance. It is worth noting that the program will automatically adjust $boxes\_per\_proc$, inputted by the user, to make the final grid size satisfy $(B \times 2^k)^3$, where $B^3$ stands for the coarsest problem size for any $1 \leq B \leq 11$.

## 3.2   The Testing Framework

Evaluating a benchmark on extreme-scale supercomputers usually requires a large number of running cases with different testing and tuning parameters. It is therefore of great importance to design a testing plan to get the maximum performance with relatively low cost. To that end, we present a basic testing framework as shown in Fig. 4. Before conducting large-scale performance evaluations, we can use this framework to do adequate experimental tests on a small number of nodes. Then we can make use of the clues we get from the small-scale tests to reduce the parameter space in a heuristic way. In the testing framework, we first construct the testing space based on the following two aspects.

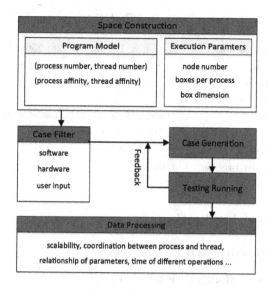

**Fig. 4.** The testing framework of HPGMG-FV.

- **Program Model.** Is the benchmark shared memory, message passing, or a combination of both? For shared memory, we need to choose the number of threads per process and set the thread affinity for them. For message passing, similar things should also be taken into consideration. For the combined situation, we should firstly decide the configuration of processes and then consider thread setting within each process.
- **Execution Parameters.** We should decide the numbers of computing nodes used in small-scale tests. Based on our experience, node numbers less than 512 can be considered as small-scale and those numbers that are the power of 2, i.e. $(1, 2, 4, 8, \cdots 512)$ , can serve as the proxy of less than 512 nodes. In HPGMG-FV, we also need to provide the number of boxes per process and box dimension. There are also some performance-related macros in HPGMG-FV, such as the blocking size and the alignment choice.

We then reduce the testing space based on the constraints from hardware, software and user input. The reduced testing space in HPGMG-FV is displayed in Table 2. Based on the reduced testing space, the framework can automatically generate all the parameters for later testing. In order to ensure the robustness, a feedback path is added for deleting unsuitable parameters based on the actual running results. At last, we can extract useful information from output files based on what purpose we want to inspect in the benchmark such as scalability, coordination between process and thread, relationship between parameters, and time of different operations etc. All the modules of the framework are implemented in script languages such as bash, awk and python.

Table 2. Testing space for HPGMG-FV on Tianhe-2.

| Number of nodes | 1, 2, 4, 8, 16, 32, 64, 128, 256, 512 |
|---|---|
| (Processes per node, Threads per process) | (1,24), (2,12), (3,8), (4,6), (6,4), (8,3), (12,2), (24,1) |
| Affinity | process: none, sockets, cache, cores thread: none, scatter, compact |
| Box dimension | 4, 5, 6, 7, 8 |
| Boxes per process | 1–64 |

## 4    Performance Evaluation

### 4.1    Effects of Box-Related Parameters

To examine how the performance is affected by the two box-related parameters, namely the box dimension, $box\_dim$, and the number of boxes per process, $boxes\_per\_proc$, we run the test on a single node of Tianhe-2 with $procs\_per\_node = 2$ and $thrs\_per\_proc = 12$. The test results are shown in Fig. 5. From the figure, we find that enlarging $box\_dim$ or $boxes\_per\_proc$ leads to an increase of the total time, and more importantly, the overall performance as well. This observation indicates that as long as the memory capacity allows, maximizing $box\_dim$ or $boxes\_per\_proc$ is an effective way to improve the performance. Similar conclusions are made when different numbers of $procs\_per\_node$ and $thrs\_per\_proc$ are set.

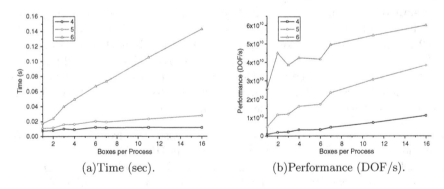

(a)Time (sec).                    (b)Performance (DOF/s).

Fig. 5. Results of tuning the box-related parameters.

### 4.2    Effects of process- and thread-related parameters

As mentioned earlier, HPGMG-FV supports both message passing and shared memory programing models. Therefore it is important to choose the number of processes per node, $procs\_per\_node$, and the number of threads per process,

$thrs\_per\_proc$, so that the performance is maximized. Since there are 24 CPU cores available in each node of Tianhe-2, we may set the parameter space to be a pair of positive integers, $(ppn, tpp) = (procs\_per\_node, thrs\_per\_proc)$, satisfying $ppn \times tpp = 24$. In the test, we fix $box\_dim = 6$ and change $boxes\_per\_proc$ to coordinate with different $(ppn, tpp)$ pairs so that the total degrees of freedom, $dof$, are fixed when number of computing nodes is fixed. For each number of computing nodes, we use the averaged performance over all $(ppn, tpp)$ pairs as the baseline, and calculate the relative performance of each $(ppn, tpp)$ configuration. The tested results are shown in Fig. 6. When measuring the performance, we try different ways for setting the thread affinity and only count the result with the highest performance. From the figure, we find that: (i) for $(1, 24)$ and $(3, 8)$ the performance is low, which is mainly because of the NUMA effect of threads from different sockets within each process; (ii) for all other cases the performance is relatively close, among which $(4, 6)$ and $(6, 4)$ seem to be the most promising. It is worth noting that in the test we fix $box\_dim = 6$ instead of other larger values, because if $box\_dim > 6$, there is not enough available memory to fully adjust $boxes\_per\_proc$ as $(ppn, tpp)$ are changed.

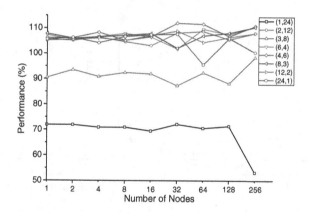

**Fig. 6.** Relative performance for different $(ppn, tpp)$ pairs with respect to the average performance.

Based on the observations made in Sects. 4.1 and 4.2, and considering the hardware restriction of Tianhe-2, we find that using a flat-MPI approach, in which we enable 24 single-threaded MPI processes in each computing node of Tianhe-2, leads to a relatively acceptable performance in all cases, especially when the memory capacity is fully exploited with an box dimension of 8. There may exist better choices of the $(ppn, tpp)$ pair, but we restrict ourself in the single-thread case to fit within the short benchmarking time-frame and simplify all tests in the sequel.

## 4.3    Scalability results

In the scalability test, we fix the number of processes per node to be $procs\_per\_node = 24$, the number of threads per process to be $thrs\_per\_proc = 1$, the number of boxes per process to be $boxes\_per\_proc = 1$, and the box dimension to be $box\_dim = 4, 5, 6, 7, 8$ to make sure the amount of work assigned to every node is a constant. Then we increase the number of computing nodes and examine the total elapsed time, which, in the ideal case, should remain constant as well. The results are shown in Fig. 7(a), from which we find that the time grows rapidly when $num\_nodes \leq 16$ and then become steady as more nodes are used. This is because when $num\_nodes$ is small, there are not enough nodes amortizing the cost of communication; and when $num\_nodes$ increases above 16, the total time approaches to a constant level. Figure 7(a) further shows the aggregate performance in the same time, from which we observe that: (i) for a same $box\_dim$, the aggregate performance increases as more nodes are used, which is straightforward due to relationship (2) and (3); and (ii) when $num\_nodes$ is fixed, a larger $box\_dim$ leads to higher performance, which is less obvious than the first observation because both the numerator and the denominator of Eq. (2) become larger.

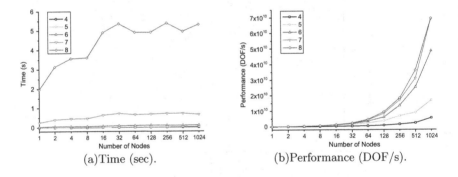

(a)Time (sec).                    (b)Performance (DOF/s).

**Fig. 7.** Results of scalability tests.

To further examine the time breakdown of different operations, we divide the total solution time of each solve into seven parts. Among them, *smooth*, *residual*, *restriction*, *interpolation*, and *ghost exchange*, are the five major operations in the multigrid algorithm, *MPI collective* stands for the time of all MPI collectives, and *other* represents other operations such as the BLAS operations and the evaluation of boundary conditions, etc. The breakdown results for the case of $box\_dim = 8$ are shown in Fig. 8. We can clearly see that the proportion of the different parts nearly keeps unchanged when increasing the number of nodes. In HPGMG-FV, Each *smooth* needs to sweep 4 times of the domain while each *residual* just requires one. So the time cost of each *smooth* is approximately 4 times of each *residual*. Each *restriction* also needs only one sweep, but the computation in it is only about 1/4 of each *residual*. So the total time spent by *residual* is about 4 times of *restriction.* Although *restriction* needs data 8 times as much as *interpolation* between adjacent two levels, they spend almost the same time. This phenomenon shows that the inter-level communication is very effective. The time spent in the two MPI-related operations, namely *ghost exchange* and *MPI collective*, is relatively small, indicating again that the communication overhead is low.

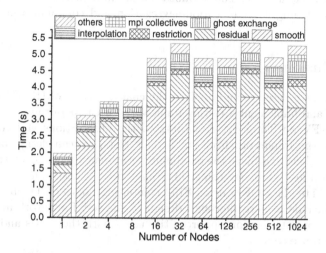

**Fig. 8.** Time breakdown for box dimension 8 given 24 processes per node and 1 thread per process

**Table 3.** The submitted HPGMG-FV performance on Tianhe-2.

| num_nodes | $(ppn, tpp)$ | boxes_per_proc | box_dim | Time (s) | Perf. (DOF/s) |
|---|---|---|---|---|---|
| 8192 | (24, 1) | 1 | 6 | 0.131047 | 3.513e+11 |
| 8192 | (24, 1) | 1 | 7 | 0.857948 | 4.293e+11 |
| 8192 | (24, 1) | 1 | 8 | 5.346149 | 5.511e+11 |

HPGMG-FV requires that the submitted results include three sets of data with increasingly larger *box_dim*. Therefore we extend the scalability test of *box_dim* = 6, 7, and 8 to the maximum available number of computing nodes, 8192, at the time of the tests. The reported performance of the three tests are shown in Table 3, in which the maximum performance is 5.511e+11 DOF/s.

# 5   Related Work

On Tianhe-2, much work is done on performance evaluation and optimization of other emerging benchmarks, such as the HPCG benchmark as in [10,17], the Graph 500 benchmark as in [4]. The main computation involved in the full multigrid algorithm is stencil computations, i.e. nearest neighbor calculations, which have low computational intensity. Lots of research has been done on the parallelism and data reuse of stencil computations, such as loop tiling [5], SIMD vectorization [9], cache oblivious [8], time skewing [3], blocking [12], and wavefront [15]. The implementation of stencil computation in HPGMG-FV uses optimizations based on [6] such as NUMA-aware allocation, multilevel blocking, and array padding etc. The optimization of full multigrid also utilizes some techniques including communication-aggregation and communication-avoiding from [16].

## 6 Conclusion

In this paper, we describe and analyze the characteristics of HPGMG-FV and then design and implement a testing framework for the performance evaluation of HPGMG-FV on Tianhe-2. According to the observations and conclusions provided by the framework from small scale tests, we can design better and fewer testing plans to achieve the maximum performance when given the limited resources with less effort. By using this framework, we reach an overall performance of 5.511e+11 DOF/s using 8192 computing nodes of Tianhe-2. Future work may include a more thorough design of the test framework and further investigation of optimization opportunities using both the CPUs and the Intel Xeon Phi coprocessors.

**Acknowledgments.** The work was supported in part by NSF China (grant# 61170075, 91530103) and 863 Program of China (grant# 2012AA010903).

## References

1. Adams, M.: HPGMG 1.0: A benchmark for ranking high performance computing systems. eScholarship, May 2014
2. Adams, M., Brown, J., Shalf, J., Straalen, B.V., Strohmaier, E., Vuduc, R., Sam, W.: HPGMG-FV Ranking of Supercomputers (2015). https://hpgmg.org/2015/02/06/updated-hpgmg-fv-ranking
3. Augustin, W., Heuveline, V., Weiss, J.-P.: Optimized stencil computation using in-place calculation on modern multicore systems. In: Sips, H., Epema, D., Lin, H.-X. (eds.) Euro-Par 2009. LNCS, vol. 5704, pp. 772–784. Springer, Heidelberg (2009)
4. Bader, D., Kogge, P., Lumsdaine, A., Murphy, R.: Top Graph 500 Supercomputer Lists (2010). http://www.graph500.org
5. Bandishti, V., Pananilath, I., Bondhugula, U.: Tiling stencil computations to maximize parallelism. In: Proceedings of the International Conference on High Performance Computing, Networking, Storage and Analysis, SC 2012, pp. 40:1–40:11. IEEE Computer Society Press, Los Alamitos (2012)
6. Datta, K., Murphy, M., Volkov, V., Williams, S., Carter, J., Oliker, L., Patterson, D., Shalf, J., Yelick, K.: Stencil computation optimization and auto-tuning on state-of-the-art multicore architectures. In: Proceedings of the 2008 ACM/IEEE Conference on Supercomputing, p. 4. IEEE Press (2008)

7. Dongarra, J., Heroux, M.: Toward a new metric for ranking high performance computing systems. Technical report SAND2013-4744, Sandia National Laboratories, Jun 2013
8. Frigo, M., Strumpen, V.: Cache oblivious stencil computations. In: Proceedings of the 19th Annual International Conference on Supercomputing, ICS 2005, pp. 361–366. ACM, New York (2005)
9. Henretty, T., Veras, R., Franchetti, F., Pouchet, L.N., Ramanujam, J., Sadayappan, P.: A stencil compiler for short-vector SIMD architectures. In: Proceedings of the 27th International ACM Conference on International Conference on Supercomputing, ICS 2013, pp. 13–24. ACM, New York (2013)
10. Liu, Y., Zhang, X., Yang, C., Liu, F., Lu, Y.: Accelerating HPCG on Tianhe-2: a hybrid CPU-MIC algorithm. In: 2014 20th IEEE International Conference on Parallel and Distributed Systems (ICPADS), pp. 542–551, December 2014
11. Murphy, R.C., Wheeler, K.B., Barrett, B.W., Ang, J.A.: Introducing the graph 500. Technical reports Sandia National Laboratories, May 2010
12. Nguyen, A., Satish, N., Chhugani, J., Kim, C., Dubey, P.: 3.5-d blocking optimization for stencil computations on modern CPUs and GPUs. In: 2010 International Conference for High Performance Computing, Networking, Storage and Analysis (SC), pp. 1–13, November 2010
13. Saad, Y.: Iterative Methods for Sparse Linear Systems, 2nd edn. Society for Industrial and Applied Mathematics, Philadelphia (2003)
14. Strohmaier, E., Dongarra, J., Simon, H., Martin, M., Meuer, H.: Top 500 Supercomputer Lists (early in 1990s). http://www.top500.org
15. Wellein, G., Hager, G., Zeiser, T., Wittmann, M., Fehske, H.: Efficient temporal blocking for stencil computations by multicore-aware wavefront parallelization. In: 33rd Annual IEEE International Computer Software and Applications Conference, COMPSAC 2009, vol. 1, pp. 579–586, July 2009
16. Williams, S., Kalamkar, D.D., Singh, A., Deshpande, A.M., Straalen, B.V., Smelyanskiy, M., Almgren, A., Dubey, P., Shalf, J., Oliker, L.: Optimization of geometric multigrid for emerging multi- and manycore processors. In: Proceedings of the International Conference on High Performance Computing, Networking, Storage and Analysis, SC 2012, pp. 96:1–96:11. IEEE Computer Society Press, Los Alamitos (2012)
17. Zhang, X., Yang, C., Liu, F., Liu, Y., Lu, Y.: Optimizing and scaling HPCG on tianhe-2: early experience. In: Sun, X., Qu, W., Stojmenovic, I., Zhou, W., Li, Z., Guo, H., Min, G., Yang, T., Wu, Y., Liu, L. (eds.) ICA3PP 2014, Part I. LNCS, vol. 8630, pp. 28–41. Springer, Heidelberg (2014)

# Joint Power and Reduced Spectral Leakage-Based Resource Allocation for D2D Communications in 5G

Mithun Mukherjee[1], Lei Shu[1(✉)], Yan Zhang[2], Zhangbing Zhou[3],
and Kun Wang[4]

[1] Guangdong Provincial Key Lab of Petrochemical Equipment Fault Diagnosis,
Guangdong University of Petrochemical Technology, Guangdong 525000, China
{m.mukherjee,lei.shu}@ieee.org
[2] Simula Research Laboratory, University of Oslo, Oslo, Norway
yanzhang@simula.no
[3] School of Information Engineering, China University of Geosciences,
Beijing 100083, China
zhangbing.zhou@gmail.com
[4] School of Internet of Things,
Nanjing University of Posts and Telecommunications, Nanjing, China
kwang@njupt.edu.cn

**Abstract.** This paper proposes a joint mode selection and resource block (RB) allocation for the direct device-to-device (D2D) communication underlying cellular network. Universal-filtered multi-carrier (UFMC) technique which is considered as a potential candidate for the future communication systems due to its robustness against inter-carrier interference (ICI), is introduced for D2D communication. In this paper, our goal is to design a network that selects the transmission mode between D2D and traditional cellular transmission mode. Unlike existing work on the mode selection which focused on network performance to improve overall throughput and providing required quality-of-service (QoS) for cellular users (CUs), we study the interference from the other D2D links operating on the edge of the neighboring cells. D2D communications provide a reliable transmission near edge of the cells but is limited by interference from CUs as well as D2D pairs belong to edge of the neighboring cells. We present an approach in UFMC-based D2D scenario to reduce the spectral leakage to nearby RBs used for same or other D2D links. Further, we develop an optimization framework that aims to maximize signal-to-interference-and-noise ratio (SINR) and improves the overall throughput.

**Keywords:** Device-to-device communication · Cellular networks · Resource management

## 1 Introduction

Researchers around the world are in pursuit of developing the technologies that enable human-centric and machine-centric networks to meet the requirements of

© Springer International Publishing Switzerland 2015
G. Wang et al. (Eds.): ICA3PP 2015, Part IV, LNCS 9531, pp. 244–258, 2015.
DOI: 10.1007/978-3-319-27140-8_18

radio systems beyond 2020 namely 5G [3]. A major focus in 5G would be on the multimedia applications such as 4K TV, high-definition (HD), and uncompressed video streaming applications with large frame sizes and uplink-downlink symmetries in case of conferencing and other applications. Due to the ever increasing demands of the proximity-based services in social networking applications, the direct device-to-device (D2D) communication [14] becomes an emerging concept in the next generation wireless networks.

Apart from the improved spectrum utilization, high data rate, and low end-to-end delay between D2D user equipment (UE), the D2D communication benefits offloading cellular traffic, that subsequently improves other non-D2D UEs. Unlike many social networking applications, where the proximity typically works in a non-autonomous manner, a self-organizing architecture design issue is actively investigated within the 3rd generation partnership project (3GPP) targeting the availability of D2D communication in long term evolution (LTE) release 12, termed as proximity service (ProSe) [11] in 3GPP.

Filter bank-based multi-carrier (FBMC) [10] has been proposed by mobile and wireless communications enablers for the twenty-twenty information society (METIS) research group with low out-of-band radiation to overcome the weakness of cyclic prefix (CP)-based OFDM that suffers from high spectrum leakage to the incumbent signals. Recently, FBMC-based scheme [17] is discussed in D2D to suppress spectrum leakage. Universal-filtered multi-carrier (UFMC) [15] based on Dolph-Chebyshev filter which is considered as an intermediate filtering technique between filtered OFDM and FBMC, uses subband-basis filtering. UFMC retains all the benefits of filtered-OFDM while uses lower the filter-length compared to FBMC. Afterward, a filter optimization technique [16] has been discussed on signal-to-in-band distortion plus out-of-band leakage ratio (SDLR). The approach shows a better performance compared to the earlier scheme [15] even in the presence of frequency offsets.

Based on the resource-block (RB) allocation, the D2D communication can be categorized into underlay- and overlay-scenario as in cognitive radio (CR). Although, the overlay-D2D UEs use RB outside of the spectrum used by cellular users (CUs), some amount of RB must be reserved for control signaling, channel state information (CSI), and synchronization to CUs via evolved node B (eNB). Most existing research have considered the underlaying [4,5,18,23] resource usage with high spectral efficiency. For the direct D2D communication underlaying cellular networks, D2D links reuse either uplink (UL) or downlink (DL) [4]. Generally, it is assumed that there will be a high-dense D2D links near the edge of the cell to offload the data of cellular links. An example of a D2D communication is illustrated in Fig. 1. It is obvious that there will be a strong interference to D2D links from the CUs in UL reused for D2D UEs due to the power control schemes used for cellular links to overcome the near-far effect [4,5]. Thus, from the D2D point of view, it can be a good choice if DL RBs are fully reused by the D2D communications. Although, it has been assumed that different sets of orthogonal RBs have been allocated to neighboring cells to minimize inter-carrier or inter-block interference, however due to high spectral

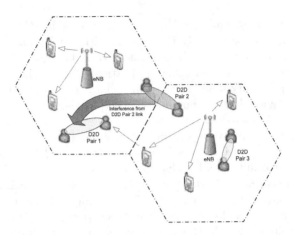

**Fig. 1.** An illustration of a interference scenario for the D2D communication under-laying cellular network that shares the downlink resource. Both the transmitter and receiver of D2D pair 1 are in the same cell, i.e., cell 1. Same follows to the D2D pair 3. However, the transmitter and the receiver of the D2D pair 2 operate on the edge of two different cells.

leakage to nearby RBs reused by D2D links, it is important to design a low spectral leakage-based RB for the D2D communication. Our contributions are summarized in the following.

- This work is concerned with the interference occurred in D2D overlaying cellular network due to the neighboring cells. We use the power efficiency as an utility function to formulate the non-linear optimization problem.
- To the best of our knowledge, we introduce UFMC-based D2D underlaying cellular network with the aim to suppress the high spectral-leakage from the edge of the neighboring cells.
- We present an efficient algorithm that jointly optimizes the number of edge subcarriers in the RB with the proposed suppressed spectrum-leakage approach and the amount of power alloted to the D2D links while protecting the target signal-to-interference-and-noise ratio (SINR) at the CU links.

The rest of the paper is organized as follows. We discuss the related work in Sect. 2. The two-cell-based system model with resource reuse of D2D links underlaying cellular network is discussed in Sect. 3. The optimization problem is formulated to jointly optimize power and number of subcarriers in RB for the D2D links in Sect. 4. In Sect. 5, an efficient algorithm is proposed to address the optimization problem. The performance results are presented in Sect. 6. Finally, conclusions and future work are discussed in Sect. 7.

## 2    Related Work

There has been a considerable research on power and resource allocation for the D2D communication to properly coordinate the interference. The authors in [19] pointed out an adaptive strategy to switch between beamforming and interference pre-processing techniques to enhance the system performance under the perfect CSI at transmitter. An interference co-ordination, termed as $\delta_D$-interference limited area control scheme [12], is discussed to limit the power of the D2D links and exclude the CUs from a $\delta_D$-interference zone. A target SINR degradation-based scheme [20] has been proposed for D2D transmitter power control to protect the required QoS for CU links.

In [24], authors studied the problem of the RB allocation to the D2D link formulated as mixed integer non-linear programming (MINLP). However, the MINLP problem is a very hard to solve within short scheduling time during UL/DL (for example, 1 ms). Thus, a greedy heuristic search algorithm was discussed for the RB allocation. An interesting scheme, called power-efficiency-based joint mode selection and power allocation scheme [9] is introduced. Although the power-efficiency-based optimization is not a concave function for transmission power, a sub-optimal solution [9] is suggested for the maximal power-efficiency among all possible modes of the UEs. Further, Gao et al. [6] developed an effective algorithm with an interesting step function of SINR with about 57 % power saving compared to the several proposed schemes. Most recently, a Stackelberg game model-based approach [4] is formulated to group the D2D links. In this approach, the D2D and the CU links are modeled as a seller and a buyer, respectively. The final price covered by both the CUs and the D2D, is equilibrium of the game-strategic model.

Aforementioned works consider mainly single-cell architecture. In addition, the mode selection-based algorithms mostly follow fixed-power allocation of CU links. Hence, it is quite promising to consider the interference effects from the nearby edge-UEs in the neighboring cells, that can be further used for the power allocation for D2D links.

# 3 System Model

Consider a hybrid two-cell network as illustrated in Fig. 1 comprised by one e-NB per cell. We consider the scenario consisting of $K^{(i)}$ pairs of the D2D links and $C^{(i)}$ orthogonal CUs with a total $N^{(i)}$ RB[1] in the $i$th cell. Both the D2D links and the base station to the mobile station (BS-MS) communication operate in the same DL frequency. We denote $RB_{c^{(i)}}$ as the number of the RB used for the $c^{(i)}$th CU in the $i$th cell. The $k^{(i)}$th D2D pair $k_{T_x^{(i)} \to R_x^{(i)}}$ in the $i$th cell consists of one D2D transmitting user $k_{T_x}^{(i)}$ and one D2D receiving user $k_{R_x}^{(i)}$. In the present scenario, there are total three D2D links in the two cells and three CUs communicating with their respective correspondent through eNB in each cell. Figure 1 represents the interference pattern in the D2D underlaying DL cellular network. Both the transmitter and the receiver of D2D pair 1 are

---

[1] As per the physical layer (PHY) standard of 3GPP LTE, each RB contains 12 subcarriers, occupies 1 slot (0.5 ms) in the time and 180 kHz in the frequency domain with a subcarrier spacing 15 kHz. The smallest unit of the RB assigned to any CU is two.

in the same cell, (i.e., in cell 1). The same follows to D2D pair 3. However, the transmitter and the receiver of the D2D pair 2 operate on the edge of two different cells (i.e., transmitter in cell 2 and receiver in cell 1).

We focus to analyze the interference due to the D2D operating on different cells and the interference due to the leakage from the other RBs used by CUs in a neighboring cells. For convenient description, we choose only to calculate the interference to receiver of D2D pair 1 due to other D2D links and CUs, further this interference calculation can be applied to other UE.

## 3.1 Data Rate and Resource Reuse Model

We assume a continuous-rate M-ary quadrature amplitude modulation (QAM) to calculate the data rate. The data rate for RB is given by $W_{RB}\log_2\left(1 + \frac{-1.5}{\ln(5\times\text{BER})}\right.$ $\left.\times\text{SINR}\right)$ b/s [7], where $W_{RB}$ is the bandwidth of each RB, SINR is the instantaneous signal-to-interference-and-noise ratio on RB, and we set the target bit-error rate (BER) equals to $1 \times 10^{-2}$. Then, the data rate for the $c^{(i)}$th CU corresponds to

$$R_{c^{(i)}} = RB_{c^{(i)}} W_{RB}\log_2\left(1 + \frac{-1.5}{\ln(5\times\text{BER})}\text{SINR}_{c^{(i)}}\right),$$  (1)

where $\text{SINR}_{c^{(i)}}$ denotes the instantaneous SINR at the $c^{(i)}$th CU. Similarly, we calculate the data rate of $k_{Tx^{(i)}\to R_x^{(i)}}$th D2D link as

$$R_{k^{(i)}} = \sum_{c^{(i)}=1}^{C^{(i)}} \zeta_{k^{(i)},c^{(i)}} W_{RB}\log_2\left(1 + \frac{-1.5}{\ln(5\times\text{BER})}\text{SINR}_{k_{R_x}^{(i)}}\right),$$  (2)

where $\text{SINR}_{k_{R_x}^{(i)}}$ is the instantaneous SINR at the $k_{R_x}^{(i)}$th receiver pair of D2D link in the $i$th cell, and $\zeta_{k^{(i)},c^{(i)}} = 1$ if the RB of the $c^{(i)}$th CU is re-used by the $k^{(i)}$th D2D link and 0 otherwise.

## 3.2 Channel Model

It is important to note that the effect of shadowing attenuation is more in D2D pair compared to eNB-CU link. Thus, we need to consider the interference from nearby UEs close to any D2D link. The distance dependent pathloss and the shadow fading pathloss model are preferred for a proximity service-based D2D service. We take the urban macro cell (UMa) model for a LTE-advanced (LTE-A) [1] for our study. The average pathloss at a distance $d$ can be measured as $PL_{\text{dB}}(d) = \alpha PL_{\text{LOS}} + (1 - \alpha)PL_{\text{NLOS}}$, where $PL_{\text{LOS}}$ and $PL_{\text{NLOS}}$ are the pathloss components in a line-of-sight (LOS) and a non-line-of-sight (NLOS) scenario, respectively, and $\alpha$ is the probability of LOS as a function of the distance $d$ (in m).

## 4   Interference Coordination and Problem Formulation

For a underlaying cellular network, we impose the target SINR to protect the quality-of-service (QoS) requirement for the $c^{(i)}$th CU in the $i$th cell as

$$\text{SINR}_{c^{(i)}} = \frac{P_{c^{(i)}} G_{c^{(i)}}}{\sum\limits_{k^{(i)}}^{K^{(i)}} \zeta_{k^{(i)},c^{(i)}} P_{k_{Tx}^{(i)}} G_{k_{Tx}^{(i)},c^{(i)}} + N_0 + \text{Leakage}} \geq \gamma_c^{(i)}, \qquad (3)$$

where $P_{c^{(i)}}$ and $P_{k_{Tx}^{(i)}}$ denote the power alloted to the $c^{(i)}$th CU at eNB and the transmitter of $k^{(i)}$th D2D pair, respectively, $G_{c^{(i)}}$ and $G_{k_{Tx}^{(i)},c^{(i)}}$ are the channel gain from BS to the $c^{(i)}$th CU and the channel gain from the $k^{(i)}$th D2D transmitter to the $c^{(i)}$th CU, respectively, and $N_0$ is the AWGN noise power density. The interference due to the spectrum leakage is discussed in next subsection. We set the target SINR as $\gamma_c^{(i)}$ to protect the QoS for the CU users in the $i$th cell. Further, $\text{SINR}_{k^{(i)}}$ can be expressed as

$$\text{SINR}_{k_{Rx}^{(i)}} = \frac{P_{k_{Tx}^{(i)}} G_{k_{Tx}^{(i)},k_{Rx}^{(i)}}}{\left( \sum\limits_{c^{(i)}}^{M^{(i)}} \zeta_{k^{(i)},c^{(i)}} P_{c^{(i)}} G_{c^{(i)},k_{Rx}^{(i)}} + \sum\limits_{j=1}^{\mathcal{M}} \sum\limits_{k'(j),k'(j)=k^{(i)}}^{M^{(i)}} \right.}$$
$$\left. \times P_{k_{Tx}'^{(j)}} G_{k_{Tx}'^{(j)},k_{Rx}^{(i)}} + N_0 + \text{Leakage} \right), \qquad (4)$$

where $G_{c^{(i)},k_{Rx}^{(i)}}$ is the channel gain from the BS to the $k^{(i)}$th D2D receiver, $G_{k_{Tx}'^{(j)},k_{Rx}^{(i)}}$ is the channel gain from $k'^{(j)}$th D2D transmitter belongs to the $j$th neighboring cell to the $k^{(i)}$th D2D receiver of the $i$th cell, $\mathcal{M}$ is the total number of first-tier interfering nearby cells. We define the leakage-effect as a error vector magnitude (EVM) concept discussed in the 3GPP specification [2]. The in-band emission is measured as the ratio of power in non-allocated RB to the allocated RB for a given UE. Finally, using (1) and (2), the total sum-rate can be expressed as

$$R_{\text{Total}} = \sum\limits_{k^{(i)}}^{K^{(i)}} R_{k^{(i)}} + \sum\limits_{c^{(i)}}^{M^{(i)}} R_{c^{(i)}} \qquad (5)$$

*Objective Function:* Generally, we consider to maximize the sum-rate to enhance the cell throughput ensuring the QoS requirement for CUs. However, it is more appealing to consider the power-efficiency [9], defined as sum-rate per total power as a maximization function. Since, the power-efficiency optimization is not a concave fuction, it is shown that this optimization function can be easily transformed to a $(log, log)$ concave function using [9, (13) and (14)]. It jointly considers the power and the sum-rate with a interference co-ordination in the D2D scenario underlaying cellular network. The power-efficiency [9] is given by

$$U = \frac{R_{\text{Total}}}{\sum\limits_{k^{(i)}}^{K^{(i)}} P_{k_{Tx}^{(i)}} + \sum\limits_{c^{(i)}}^{M^{(i)}} P_{c^{(i)}}} \tag{6}$$

Therefore, we can obtain the optimization problem as

$$\max U \tag{7}$$

$$\text{s.t. } \text{SINR}_{c^{(i)}} \geq \gamma_c^{(i)} \quad \forall i \in \{1,2\} \tag{8a}$$

$$P_{c^{(i)}} \leq P_B^{\max} \quad \forall c^{(i)} \in C^{(i)} \quad \forall i \in \{1,2\} \tag{8b}$$

$$P_{k_{Tx}^{(i)}} \leq P_{k_{Tx}^{(i)}}^{\max} \quad \forall k^{(i)} \in K^{(i)} \quad \forall i \in \{1,2\} \tag{8c}$$

$$\sum\limits_{c^{(i)}}^{C^{(i)}} \zeta_{k^{(i)},c^{(i)}} \leq 1 \quad \forall k^{(i)} \in K^{(i)} \quad \forall i \in \{1,2\} \tag{8d}$$

$$\text{Leakage} < \text{Leakage}_{\text{Th}} \tag{8e}$$

The constraint in (8a) ensures the target SINR of CUs. The upper-bound transmission power of a CU at BS $(P_B^{\max})$ and transmitter of D2D link $\left(P_{k_{Tx}^{(i)}}^{\max}\right)$ is considered as in (8b) and (8c), respectively. We also adopt the constrain in (8e) that ensures the maximum permissible leakage (Leakage$_{\text{Th}}$) to the nearby RB used by other UEs within the radius of D2D transmitter. Constrain in (8d) is to ensure that each D2D shares at most one CU's RB. During the DL RB allocation underlaying cellular network, the interference to the CUs due to D2D link need to be restricted. We note that the transmitter of the D2D pair needs to increase the power to maintain the link for a long distance between D2D pair. Accordingly, this may create more interference to the CUs. In the following, we discuss about the interference coordination for both CUs and D2D links.

## 5  Proposed Algorithm for Joint Power and Spectral Leakage-Based Resource Allocation

*Antipodal Bohman Filter-based Scheme:* It is preferred to apply the filtering or the subcarrier-weighting scheme to the edge subcarriers in the RBs with a aim to keep acceptable throughput in contrast to the transmit filtering [21] applied to the overall RBs. The filter used in the most of the out-of-band (OOB)-reduction schemes [22] is a rectangular window function that has a high-peak side-lobe power of $-13$ dB and a low side-lobe fall rate of $-6$ dB/Octave among the well-known filters. In addition, we have found that Dolph-Chebyshev filter is not the optimum filter that can be used for UFMC [15] due to its low side-lobe fall rate. A novel Bohman-window-based antipodal approach [13] was introduced that outperforms the state-of-the art on suppressed spectral leakage in overlay-CR. We observe that the Bohman filtering scheme [8] is well-suited for our purpose for the high side-lobe fall-rate of $-24$ dB/octave compared to other well-known filters. Apart from this, we also intend to combine the benefits of reduced

---

**Algorithm 1.** Joint RB and D2D power allocation scheme

---

1 **Input:** $\zeta_{k^{(i)},c^{(i)}}, N_{c^{(i)}}; P_B^{\max}, \text{SINR}_{c^{(i)}}^{\min}, P_{k_{T_x}^{(i)}}^{\max} \forall k^{(i)}, c^{(i)} \quad i \in \{1,2\}$ ;

2 $\mathbb{M}$ : Shorted list of all DL CUs with CQI in decreasing order ;

3 $\mathbb{K}$ : List of D2D connection yet to be assigned RBs and power ;

4 **Output:** $\zeta_{k^{(i)},c^{(i)}}^*, P_{k_{T_x}^{(i)}} \forall k^{(i)}, c^{(i)} \quad i \in \{1,2\}$ ;

    $\zeta_{k^{(i)},c^{(i)}} \leftarrow 0 \quad \forall k^{(i)} \in \mathbb{K}, \forall c^{(i)} \in \mathbb{M}$ ;         /* Initialize RB reuse variable */

5 **begin**

6    **while** $\mathbb{K} \neq \phi$ **do**

7       Pick RBs of the $c^{(i)}$th CU with highest CQI ;

8       Find the $c^{(i)}$th D2D pair which creates less interference to $c^{(i)}$th CU ;

9       $\text{SINR}_{c(j)} \leftarrow$ Calculate SINR according to (3) ;     /* SINR for $c^{(i)}$th CU */

10      $\text{SINR}_{k_{Rx}^{(j)}} \leftarrow$ Calculate SINR according to (4);     /* SINR for $k^{(i)}$ D2D pair */

11      **if** $\text{SINR}_{c(i)} > \text{SINR}_{c(i)}^{\min}$ **then**

12        **if** $P_{k^{(i)}} + 2\Delta P_{(i)} < P_{(i)}^{max}$ **then**

13          $P_{k^{(i)}} \leftarrow P_{k^{(i)}} + \Delta P_{(i)}$ ;     /* Increase D2D Tx power */

14          $\mathbb{K}' \leftarrow$ List of UEs in the neighboring cells within the radius of $k_{(i)}^{(i)}$;

15          use Algorithm 2 ;     /* To obtain the number of egde subcarrier of RBs where we apply antipodal Bohman-filter */

16          go to 9;

17        **else**

           /* Consider the interference to the other cell due to RB and power allocation of the current D2D pair     */

18          **if** $Rx$ of the $k^{(i)}$th D2D pair belongs to neighboring cell **then**

19            $\mathbb{K}'' \leftarrow$ List of CUs in the neighboring cells within the radius of $k_{T_x}^{(i)}$;

20            Calculate $\text{SINR}_{m(j)}$ ;    /* Calculate SINR for $j$th cell CU; $i \neq j$ */

21            $\text{SINR}_j = \left\{ \text{SINR}_{c(j)} \right\}_{c(j)=1}^{\mathbb{K}''}$;

22            **if** $\min[\text{SINR}_j] < \text{SINR}_{c(i)}^{min}$ **then**

23              $P_{k^{(i)}} \leftarrow P_{k^{(i)}} - 0.5\Delta P_{(i)}$ ;   /* Decrease the $k^{(i)}$th D2D Tx power */

24              go to 9

           **end**

         **end**

        **end**

25        $\mathbb{K} = \mathbb{K} - \{k^i\}$ ;   /* update the List of D2D connection yet to be assigned */

26        $\mathbb{C} \leftarrow \mathbb{C} + 1$ ;          /* Pick the next DL CU */

27        $\zeta_{k^{(i)},c^{(i)}}^* = 1$ ;         /* update the RB reuse variable */

28      **else**

29        Do not assign RB to the $k^{(i)}$th D2D pair ;

30        $\zeta_{k^{(i)},c^{(i)}}^* = 0$ ;         /* update the RB reuse variable */

     **end**

   **end**

 **end**

---

complexity burden and the improved flexibility with antipodal subcarrier coding scheme [22] at the edge subcarriers of the RBs. The 3-dB bandwidth of 1.71 bins of the Bohman filter, while small compared to some other filters, still creates some overlapping between subcarriers in UFMC systems with low separation between subcarriers. This can be partially solved by employing antipodal symbol pairs on adjacent Bohman-filtered edge subcarriers.

---

**Algorithm 2.** Optimize the set of edge subcarriers

---

1 **Input:** $\zeta_{k^{(i)},c^{(i)}}, RB_{c^{(i)}}; P_{c^{(i)}}, P_{k^{(i)}_{T_x}}, L^{\min}_{k^{(i)}} \forall k^{(i)}, c^{(i)} i \in \{1,2\}, \mathbb{K}';$

2 **Output:** $\zeta^*_{k^{(i)},c^{(i)}}, P_{k^{(i)}_{T_x}} \forall k^{(i)}, c^{(i)} \quad i \in \{1,2\};$

3 $\zeta_{k^{(i)},c^{(i)}} \leftarrow 0 \quad \forall k^{(i)} \in \mathbb{K}, \forall c^{(i)} \in \mathbb{M};$     /* Initialize RB reuse variable */

4 $M_{k^{(i)}} \leftarrow N_{k^{(i)}} - 2;$

5 $\mathcal{N}_{e,k^{(i)}} \leftarrow \Big\{0,1,\ldots \lceil \frac{N_{k^{(i)}} - M_{k^{(i)}}}{2} \rceil - 1, M_{k^{(i)}} + \lceil \frac{N_{k^{(i)}} - M_{k^{(i)}}}{2} \rceil - 1, M_{k^{(i)}} +$

$\lceil \frac{N_{k^{(i)}} - M_{k^{(i)}}}{2} \rceil, \ldots N_{k^{(i)}} - 1 \Big\};$     /* Edge subcarrier set */

6 $\mathcal{N}_{c,k^{(i)}} \leftarrow \mathcal{N}_{k^{(i)}} \setminus \mathcal{N}_{e,k^{(i)}};$     /* Center subcarrier set */

7 **begin**

8     Apply antipodal Bohman-filtering scheme on $\mathcal{N}_{e,k^{(i)}};$

9     Calculate $L_{k^{(i)}};$

10     **if** $L_{k^{(i)}} > L^{\max}_{k^{(i)}}$ and $M_{k^{(i)}} > \frac{N_{k^{(i)}}}{2} + 2$ **then**

11         $M_{k^{(i)}} \leftarrow M_{k^{(i)}} + 2;$     /* Increase the number of edge subcarrier */

12         Update $M_{k^{(i)}};$

13         go to 8

    **end**

**end**

---

It is important to note that, the sidelobe rolls off asymptotically as of $f^{-8}$ in the Bohman filter-based scheme [13] compared to $f^{-2}$ for the conventional OFDM and of $f^{-4}$ for the schemes in [22]. In this article, we use antipodal symbol pairs that are mapped to lower- and upper-edge subcarriers with Bohman pulse shaping. We further optimize the set of edge subcarrier indices in the proposed algorithm to control the spectrum leakage in the D2D links.

### 5.1 Power and Spectral Leakage-Based Resource Allocation

We propose an algorithm to jointly optimize power control and RB allocation for the D2D link. The basic idea of *Algorithm 1* is to consider the interference due to the neighboring UEs and adjust the number of edge subcarrier to suppress the spectrum leakage to the nearby RBs. We first take the list of D2D links yet to be assigned RBs and power. Then, we pick the D2D link that creates a low interference to the RB of CU with a highest channel quality information (CQI). In the next step, we increase the power of D2D transmitter by an amount, say $\Delta P_{(i)}$, if the allocated power of D2D link is less then the maximum permissible power $P^{\max}_{k^{(i)}_{T_x}}$ for D2D transmitter in the $i$th cell. Subsequently it increase the interference to the nearby CU links. To tackle this problem, we need to check the minimum SINR threshold at CU.

Afterwards, we take a comprehensive consideration on the leakage interference due to other nearby cells within the range of D2D transmitter. The antipodal Bohman window-based scheme is applied for the high side-lobe fall rate of RBs. We define $\mathcal{N}_{e,k^{(i)}} = \Big\{0,1,\ldots \lceil \frac{N_{k^{(i)}} - M_{k^{(i)}}}{2} \rceil - 1, M_{k^{(i)}} + \lceil \frac{N_{k^{(i)}} - M_{k^{(i)}}}{2} \rceil - 1, M_{k^{(i)}} + \lceil \frac{N_{k^{(i)}} - M_{k^{(i)}}}{2} \rceil, \ldots N_{k^{(i)}} - 1 \Big\}$ as the set of edge subcarrier indices and

**Table 1.** Simulation parameters and values

| Parameter | Values |
|---|---|
| Carrier frequency | 2 GHz |
| Bandwidth | 10 MHz |
| Cell layout | Hexagonal grid |
| Cell radius | 500 m |
| Modulation and coding scheme (MCS) | 16 QAM: 1/2 |
| Shadowing standard deviation | 4 dB |
| Shadowing decorrelation distance | $d_{corr} = 37$m |
| No of subcarrier per RB | 12 |
| Cell level user distribution | Uniform |
| RB bandwidth | 180 kHz |
| Number of available RB | 100 |
| UE noise figure | 9 dB |
| Maximum UE Transmitter power | 24 dBm |
| UE thermal noise density | $-174$ dBm/Hz |

$\mathcal{N}_{c,k^{(i)}} = \mathcal{N}_{k^{(i)}} \setminus \mathcal{N}_{e,k^{(i)}}$ as the set of center subcarrier indices, where $\mathcal{N}_{k^{(i)}}$ is the set of all available subcarriers in the RB yet to be allocated for the $k^{(i)}$th D2D link and $|\mathcal{N}_{k^{(i)}}| = N_{k^{(i)}}$.

We optimize the edge subcarrier $\mathcal{N}_{e,k^{(i)}}$ to meet the target spectrum leakage to all UEs within the radius of D2D transmitter as discussed in *Algorithm 2*. If the target SINR of all the UEs does not meet required SINR, then we roll back to the lower power by reducing $0.5\Delta P_{(i)}$ amount of power.

# 6   Numerical Results

In this section, simulation results are provided to evaluate the performance of the proposed *Algorithm 1* and *Algorithm 2* for the D2D communications underlaying cellular network. To show the advantage of *Algorithm 2*, we denote the *Algorithm 1* without *Algorithm 2* as scheme 1, and full *Algorithm 1* as scheme 2. Table 1 summarizes the list of simulation parameters and their default values.

*Normalized Aggregate Network Throughput:* In Fig. 2, we show the performance comparison in terms of the normalized aggregate network throughput. We fix the number of D2D link at 25 % of the total UEs in the cell and consider the interference due to 10 % of the total UEs from the interfering nearby cell. Generally, it is expected that the network throughput will increase with the number of active UEs. However, the capacity of a cellular link is limited by multiple access interference (MAI). From the above figure, it is observed that after a certain number of UEs, the network throughput does not increase with the number of

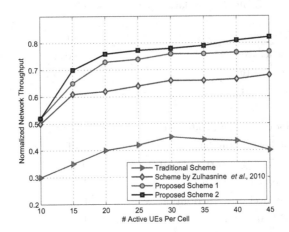

**Fig. 2.** Normalized-aggregate network throughput comparison between the proposed scheme 1, scheme 2 and the scheme by Zulhasnine *et al.*, 2010 [24]. The number of D2D link is 25 % of the cell UEs. We consider the interference due to 10 % of the total UEs from the interfering neighboring cell.

UEs. Thus, a floor is observed in all the schemes. This is because of MAI due to interference from RBs shared by both D2D and CU links, and from UEs in the neighboring cells. We term the traditional scheme that does not consider any power or resource allocation algorithm. For this reason, the traditional scheme creates higher interference on the D2D link as well as CU links. We observe that the network throughput decreases after a certain number (30 UEs/cell) of UEs in traditional scheme. An efficient resource allocation scheme [24] based on greedy heuristic search algorithm performs better than the traditional scheme. We observe that the proposed scheme 1 and scheme 2 outperform the scheme discussed in [24]. An average 16 % and 22 % improvement in throughput are achieved in scheme 1 and scheme 2, respectively, compared to the scheme [24]. The proposed scheme 2 that considers leakage interference due to nearby cells and apply antipodal Bohman filtering on the edge subcarriers, performs better compared to all schemes and achieve high normalized-network throughput capacity of about 0.9 with 45 UEs per cell.

*Total Power Consumption:* Figure. 3 illustrates the total power consumption with different values of D2D links in three scenarios. We maintain the above mentioned ratio of interfering UEs from the nearby cell. We fix the number of CU links at 16 and maintain the same ratio of interfering UEs from the nearby cell. We observe that the total power consumption monotonically increases with the number of D2D links irrespective of the schemes. It is observed from the simulation results that the power consumption increases significantly slower in both proposed schemes compared to the current state-of-the-art [6]. The proposed algorithms jointly consider the maximum permissible power for the D2D

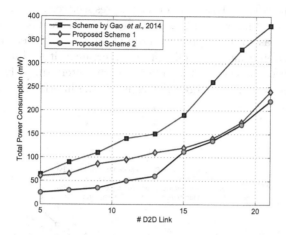

**Fig. 3.** Total power consumption comparison between proposed scheme 1, scheme 2 and the scheme by Gao et al., 2014 [6]. The number of CU links is fixed at 16. We consider the interference due to 10 % of the total UEs from the interfering neighboring cell.

link and allocate RB which minimizes the interference. The advantage of allocating D2D link that creates low interference to the RB used by CU link, benefits in total power consumption. Further, we observe that the scheme 2 performs slightly better compared to scheme 1 with lower number of D2D links. The reason is the scheme 2 adjusts the number of edge subcarriers where we apply antipodal Bohman filtering with a aim to suppress spectral leakage. However, the benefit of scheme 2 goes down with a large number of D2D links due to the limitation in the optimization technique that adjusts the number of edge subcarriers in the RBs. Nevertheless, the performance of both scheme 1 and scheme 2 significantly are better in terms of total power consumption even in a large number of D2D links. About 40 % saving in total power consumption is observed in both algorithms compared to the scheme in [6] (Fig. 4).

*Total power consumption with different number of interfering UEs from neighboring cells:* We plot the impact of number of interfering nearby UEs on the total power consumption for the proposed two algorithms. Based on the results shown in Figs. 2 and 3, we observe that the proposed scheme 2 performs better compared to the scheme 1 in terms of normalized-network throughput and total power consumption. Thus, we choose to compare scheme 2 that considers the interference due to spectrum leakage from the nearby cells with the scheme that does not consider the interference from other cells for allocating the RBs and power to the D2D links. Irrespective of both the schemes, we observe that the total power consumption increases with the number of interfering UEs from nearby cell. However, it is interesting to note that, the scheme 2 performs significantly better than the scheme without interference consideration from other cells. Total power savings of about 25 % and 22 % are observed in scheme 2 with

15 % and 20 % interfering UEs from other cell, respectively. It is intuitively clear that more number of interfering UEs from nearby cells creates more interference and leads to increase in total power consumption with a higher number of UEs under consideration from other cells. More importantly, it is observed that total power consumption in scheme 2 with 20 % nearby interfering UEs grows slowly compared to the scheme that does not consider the interference with less (i.e., 15 %) neighboring users.

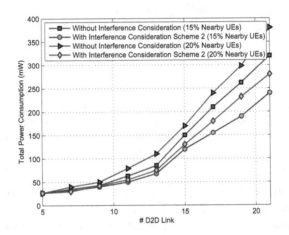

**Fig. 4.** Total power consumption comparison between proposed scheme 2 and the scheme without interference consideration. The number of CU links is fixed at 16; interference due to 15 % or 20 % of the total UEs from the interfering nearby cell.

## 7    Conclusions and Future Work

In this paper, we proposed a joint power and reduced spectral leakage-based resource allocation that considers the maximum permissible power for the D2D transmitter and the minimum threshold SINR for the CU links in UFMC systems for the D2D communication. We developed a network model that considers the interference from other UEs belong to the nearby cells. Numerical results show that the proposed algorithm achieves a higher network throughput compared to the current state-of-the art. With the increase of D2D links, the total power consumption grows slowly and about 40 % saving in power consumption is obtained in the proposed schemes compared to the recently discussed schemes. Additionally, the proposed algorithm performs better than the scheme without interference consideration even in a higher ratio of the interfering UEs from nearby cells. An analytical approach to solve the MINLP optimization would be an interesting extension.

**Acknowledgments.** This work was supported in part by the 2013 Special Fund of Guangdong Higher School Talent Recruitment, in part by the Educational Commission of Guangdong Province, China, under Project 2013KJCX0131, in part by the Guangdong High-Tech Development Fund under Grant 2013B010401035, in part by the 2013 Top Level Talents Project in Sailing Plan of Guangdong Province, in part by the National Natural Science Foundation of China under Grant 61401107, and in part by the 2014 Guangdong Province Outstanding Young Professor Project.

The work of K. Wang was supported by NSFC under Grant 61572262 and NSF of Jiangsu under Grant BK20141427.

# References

1. Guidelines for evaluation of radio interface technologies for IMT-Advanced. Techical report ITU-R M.2135-1, December 2009
2. Evolved universal terrestrial radio access (E-UTRA); user equipment (UE) Radio Transmission and Reception ( Release 10). Technical report 3GPP TS 36.101 version 10.1.1, January 2011
3. Andrews, J., Buzzi, S., Choi, W., Hanly, S., Lozano, A., Soong, A., Zhang, J.: What will 5G be? IEEE J. Select. Areas Commun. $32(6)$, 1065–1082 (2014)
4. Chen, X., Hu, R.Q., Qian, Y.: Distributed resource and power allocation for device-to-device communications underlaying cellular network. In: Proceedings of the IEEE Global Communications Conference, pp. 4947–4952, December 2014
5. Chen, X., Hu, R., Qian, Y.: Coverage study of dense device-to-device communications underlaying cellular networks. In: Proceedings of the IEEE Global Communications Conference, pp. 4353–4358, December 2014
6. Gao, C., Sheng, X., Tang, J., Zhang, W., Zou, S., Guizani, M.: Joint mode selection, channel allocation and power assignment for green device-to-device communications. In: Proceedings of the IEEE ICC, pp. 178–183, June 2014
7. Goldsmith, A., Chua, S.G.: Variable-rate variable-power MQAM for fading channels. IEEE Trans. Commun. $45(10)$, 1218–1230 (1997)
8. Harris, F.J.: On the use of windows for harmonic analysis with the discrete Fourier transform. Proc. IEEE $66(1)$, 51–83 (1978)
9. Jung, M., Hwang, K., Choi, S.: Joint mode selection and power allocation scheme for power-efficient device-to-device (D2D) communication. In: Proceedings of the IEEE VTC, pp. 1–5, May 2012
10. Lin, H., Siohan, P.: An advanced multi-carrier modulation for future radio systems. In: Proceedings of the IEEE International Conference on Acoustics, Speech and Signal Processing (ICASSP), pp. 8097–8101, May 2014
11. Lin, X., Andrews, J., Ghosh, A., Ratasuk, R.: An overview of 3GPP device-to-device proximity services. IEEE Commun. Mag. $52(4)$, 40–48 (2014)
12. Min, H., Lee, J., Park, S., Hong, D.: Capacity enhancement using an interference limited area for device-to-device uplink underlaying cellular networks. IEEE Trans. Wireless Commun. $10(12)$, 3995–4000 (2011)
13. Mukherjee, M., Chang, R.Y., Kumar, V.: OFDM-based overlay cognitive radios with improved spectral leakage suppression for future generation communications. In: Proceedings of the IEEE WCNC, March 2015
14. Tehrani, M., Uysal, M., Yanikomeroglu, H.: Device-to-device communication in 5G cellular networks: challenges, solutions, and future directions. IEEE Commun. Mag. $52(5)$, 86–92 (2014)

15. Vakilian, V., Wild, T., Schaich, F., ten Brink, S., Frigon, J.F.: Universal-filtered multi-carrier technique for wireless systems beyond LTE. In: Proceedings of the IEEE Globecom Workshops, pp. 223–228, December 2013
16. Wang, X., Wild, T., Schaich, F., Fonseca dos Santos, A.: Universal filtered multi-carrier with leakage-based filter optimization. In: Proceedings of the European Wireless Conference, pp. 1–5, May 2014
17. Xing, H., Renfors, M.: Investigation of filter bank based device-to-device communication integrated into OFDMA cellular system. In: Proceedings of the International Symposium Wireless Communication Systems (ISWCS), pp. 513–518, August 2014
18. Xu, C., Song, L., Han, Z., Zhao, Q., Wang, X., Jiao, B.: Interference-aware resource allocation for device-to-device communications as an underlay using sequential second price auction. In: Proceedings of the IEEE ICC, pp. 445–449, June 2012
19. Xu, W., Liang, L., Zhang, H., Jin, S., Li, J., Lei, M.: Performance enhanced transmission in device-to-device communications: Beamforming or interference cancellation, In: Proceedings of the IEEE Global Communications Conference, pp. 4296–4301, December 2012
20. Yu, C.H., Tirkkonen, O., Doppler, K., Ribeiro, C.: On the performance of device-to-device underlay communication with simple power control. In: Proceedings of the IEEE VTC, pp. 1–5, April 2009
21. Yu, L., Rao, B., Milstein, L., Proakis, J.: Reducing out-of-band radiation of OFDM-based cognitive radios. In: Proceedings of the IEEE SPAWC, pp. 1–5, June 2010
22. Zhou, X., Li, G., Sun, G.: Multiuser spectral precoding for OFDM-based cognitive radio systems. IEEE J. Select. Areas Commun. 31(3), 345–352 (2013)
23. Zhou, Z., Dong, M., Ota, K., Wu, J., Sato, T.: Distributed interference-aware energy-efficient resource allocation for device-to-device communications underlaying cellular networks. In: Proceedings of the IEEE Global Commununications Conference, pp. 4454–4459, December 2014
24. Zulhasnine, M., Huang, C., Srinivasan, A.: Efficient resource allocation for device-to-device communication underlaying LTE network. In: Proceedings of the IEEE WiMob, pp. 368–375, October 2010

# Performance Analysis for Job Scheduling in Hierarchical HPC Systems: A Coloured Petri Nets Method

Zhijia Li[1,2]($\boxtimes$), Li Jiao[1], and Xiang Hu[1,2]

[1] State Key Laboratory of Computer Science, Institute of Software,
Chinese Academy of Sciences, Beijing 100190, China
{lizj,ljiao,hux}@ios.ac.cn
[2] University of Chinese Academy of Sciences, Beijing 100049, China

**Abstract.** Distributed computing technology has been widely used to solve complex problems appearing in parallel processing systems. Job scheduling is very important in many distributed computing systems, like grid systems and high performance computers. Their performance is directly related to the efficiency of the distributed computing systems. Modeling them and analyzing their performance can provide quantitative performance metrics and predictions, which are helpful to guide capacity planning and scheduling optimization. In this paper, we study job scheduling systems widespread in high performance computing systems and propose a coloured Petri net method for analyzing their performance, which can be easily implemented in CPN software by potential users. We also propose an approximative modeling technique so as to reduce the model size. As a model-based performance analysis method, our method is low cost and highly flexible. Experimental results show that our method is feasible and can be applied to more complex and large-scale systems.

**Keywords:** Job scheduling · Performance analysis · Modeling · Simulation · CPNs · HPC

## 1 Introduction

Performance analysis can be used to make predictions about key performance metrics and detect possible bottlenecks, so that we can understand the as-is situations and compare them with possible to-be situations. In other words, performance analysis helps to answer questions such as "Which is the best scheduling strategy in this situation?", "How many servers we need to buy in order to handle the network traffic in the next month?", "Are the current operators enough if there are 5000 calls in this customer service center?", "How long is the average user waiting time?", "How much the average user waiting time will reduce if 10 more nodes are deployed?".

© Springer International Publishing Switzerland 2015
G. Wang et al. (Eds.): ICA3PP 2015, Part IV, LNCS 9531, pp. 259–280, 2015.
DOI: 10.1007/978-3-319-27140-8_19

As an important distributed computing technology, high performance computing (HPC) has been widely applied to various fields of science and engineering. HPC systems, like grid systems and high performance computers, integrate and coordinate resources and users with the goal of delivering various high quality services. In these distributed systems, job scheduling plays a fundamental role. Modeling them and analyzing their performance can provide quantitative performance analysis and prediction, which are very important towards the establishment of HPC infrastructure.

As a formal model, coloured Petri nets [1] inherit many merits of Petri nets. Additionally, they have more powerful modeling capabilities benefiting from colour sets, which make CPNs widely used in many fields, such as business process management, protocol verification, software engineering, and system analysis. What's more, CPNs can also be used to analyze performance based on simulation [2–7]. The method of performance analysis using CPNs is systematically proposed in [2,3], specifying how to model, simulate and analyze systems using CPNs. A new method for modeling, simulation and analysis of the network environment using CPNs is proposed in [4]. The method is different from the traditional methods on network analysis using queuing theory. It is suitable for performance analysis of many networks with different structures and workloads. A method on how to use CPNs to describe and analyze components in embedded systems is proposed in [5], which helps designers choose platforms and software with their special requirements. A CPN method to predict the performance of parallel program running on the HPC is proposed in [6]. The comparative evaluation with other simulation tools shows the method is feasible. A CPN method to analyze the performance of search engines is proposed in [7], and the most valuable contribution of this research is that tens of millions of user data can be used in its simulation, which shows that CPNs can still play a role in the era of big data. All of the above works indicate that the method of performance analysis based on CPNs is feasible and has great practical value. Besides, compared with other languages (e.g., MATLAB), CPNs are easier to program and offer a variety of other analysis techniques.

The motivation why we explore a coloured Petri nets (CPNs) method for performance analysis of job scheduling in hierarchical HPC systems, is that we have not yet found any other similar method, however we believe that CPNs are suitable for solving the problem. The second motivation is that our CPNs method helps to improve the previous work. The method proposed in [8] is not easy to be applied in large-scale systems and can't support more complex workloads. The method proposed in [9,10] also can't support complex workloads and the simulation software Flexsim is very expensive. [11] focuses on the reliability evaluation of grid services and doesn't provide modeling method of scheduling strategies. In this paper, we will propose a coloured Petri net method to improve the above problems.

This paper makes three main contributions. Firstly, we propose a new CPN method for modeling job scheduling systems in HPC and analyzing their performance. An approximative modeling technique is designed so as to reduce the model size. Secondly, we implement CPN models for many scheduling strategies using CPN Tools [12] and conduct experiments to verify that our method is feasible. We also extend the stochastic Petri net method proposed in [8] to the job scheduling system in HPC and conduct comparative experiments with it to confirm that our method is credible and can be applied to larger systems. Thirdly, we propose a kind of potential application of our method.

The rest of the paper is structured as follows. Section 2 presents an overview of CPNs and the job scheduling system. Section 3 elaborates the proposed performance analysis method for the job scheduling system in HPC using CPNs. Section 4 shows our experimental results. Section 5 introduces some related works. Section 6 provides conclusions and future implications for this work.

## 2    Preliminaries

In this section, we will give a brief introduction about CPNs and job scheduling systems. More details about them can be found in [1,13].

### 2.1    Coloured Petri Nets

**Definition 1 (Coloured Petri Nets).** A coloured Petri net (CPN) is a nine-tuple
$CPN = (P, T, F, \Sigma, V, C, G, E, I)$, where

- $P$ is a finite set of places.
- $T$ is a finite set of transitions, such that $P \cap T = \varnothing$.
- $F \subseteq P \times T \cup T \times P$ is a set of directed arcs.
- $\Sigma$ is the non-empty finite multiset of all colour sets.
- $V$ is the finite set of typed variables, so that $\forall v \in V, Type[v] \in \Sigma$.
- $C : P \to \Sigma$ is colour set function, which assigns a colour set to each place, indicating the type of tokens in this place.
- $G : T \to EXPR_v$ is a guard function, which assigns a guard, one prerequisite for transition firing, to each transition, so that $Type[G(t)] = Bool$.
- $E : F \to EXPR_v$ is an arc expression function, which assigns an expression to each arc $f$, so that $Type[E(f)] = C(P)_{MS}$, where $MS$ denotes a multiset.
- $I : P \to EXPR_v$ is an initial function which assigns a token set to each place.

A place $p \in P$ is an input place of a transition $t$ if $(p, t) \in F$; a place $p \in P$ is an output place of a transition $t$ if $(t, p) \in F$. In CPNs, a token is no longer an unidentified dot but a kind of data with special type. A transition can fire if there are enough tokens in its input places and its guard is evaluated to True. The transition is called an enabled transition if it can fire. The tokens in the input places and output places of the enabled transition will be redistributed when it fires, which also means that the state of the CPN model changes. The behaviors of the real system are modeled by the firing behaviors of the corresponding CPN model. A CPN model can be further explored in two ways, state space technology and simulation technology. State space technology explores all the possible states of the model, while simulation technology only explores one random trace in the state space. Firing behaviors make a CPN an executable model. The simulation for a model is to let the executable model run several times. We call each run a simulation and we call it a $n$-step simulation if a run contains $n$ successive firings. CPNs can be used to model complex and large-scale systems. Moreover, there are many mature CPN software tools, among which CPN Tools [1,12] is the most famous one. It is widely used for modeling, simulating and analyzing various systems.

## 2.2   Job Scheduling Systems of HPC

A job scheduling system, like the classical job scheduler LSF [13,14], is one of the most important software in HPC systems as a connector between users and machines. The cluster environment of LSF is shown in Fig. 1. The scheduling framework can be centralized or decentralized. The most common decentralized architecture is the hierarchical architecture which includes a global scheduler, various distributed local schedulers and many computing resources. In general, a classical job scheduler consists of many submission hosts and one master host. Submission hosts are used to receive the jobs submitted by the users or systems. Master host, designed as a global scheduler, is used to allocate the jobs to every node. In high performance computing systems with hierarchical architecture, distributed local schedulers exist in every node which are used to allocate the jobs to the execution hosts. The life cycle of a job consists of five main stages: submission, scheduling, dispatch, execution, and feedback. Figure 1 also describes the skeleton scheduling process of a job. Some concepts involved in this paper are described in detail as follows.

- Job: a unit of work runs in the LSF system. A job is a command submitted to LSF for execution. LSF schedules, controls, and tracks the job according to configured strategies. Jobs may be complex problems, simulation scenarios or extensive calculations, anything that needs computing power.
- Queue: a container for jobs. All jobs wait in queues until they are scheduled and dispatched to hosts. There may be many queues.
- Host: an individual computer in the cluster.
- Submission host: the host where jobs are submitted to the cluster.
- Execution host: the host where a job runs. Each execution host may have one or more CPUs. In this paper, we assume that each execution host has one CPU.
- Node: a group of computers (execution hosts) running in LSF that work together as a single unit.
- Master host: the host for scheduling and dispatching all jobs.

A job scheduling system supports a variety of scheduling strategies. For example, LSF supports the first come first served, fair share, preemption, exclusive, resource reservation and some other strategies. In addition, a job scheduling system is divided into three types: centralized scheduling, distributed scheduling and hierarchical scheduling, depending on the location of the scheduler.

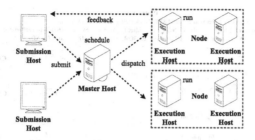

**Fig. 1.** The job scheduling process of LSF

# 3   The Performance Analysis Method Using CPNs

In this section, we will propose a performance analysis approach for job scheduling systems. Without loss of generality, we choose a two-level hierarchical job scheduling system as an example. The first level called the inter-node scheduling is responsible for scheduling a job to a node and the second level called the intra-node scheduling is responsible for scheduling a job from a node to a CPU. For model-based performance analysis methods, how to construct the model of the target system, which relates to the accuracy of the performance analysis, is the essential problem. Our modeling method can be divided into three steps. The first one is to model a job scheduling system abstractly. Then, we refine the abstract model to a more detailed model and finally propose how to analyze performance using the refined model based on simulation. The detailed steps will be listed as follows.

## 3.1   Abstractly Modeling for Job Scheduling Systems

Firstly, we construct an abstract model for a two-level hierarchical job scheduling system, in the light of the basic principles of job scheduling systems introduced in Sect. 2. The most critical parameters for modeling are the details of the system structures and workloads. More specifically, an $n \times m$ HPC contains $n$ nodes and $m$ execution hosts (CPUs) in each node. As we mentioned in Sect. 2, the workload adopted in this paper is composed of jobs which only require one computing resource. A job can be defined as $J = < Queue, ID, Time >$, where $Queue$ is the queue number of a job, $ID$ is the name of a job, and $Time$ is the arriving time of a job. The time of a job is automatically generated by different random distribution functions. CPNs support many probability distributions suitable for modeling time durations, such as the negative exponential distribution, the uniform distribution and so on [15]. Perhaps one may wonder why other important properties of jobs, like deadlines, are not considered. Actually, they are characterized in another way. We use the job arriving rate $r$ to represent that there will be $r$ jobs submitted to the HPC in each unit time (the unit time may be second, minute, hour, day or any unit of time). Similarly, we characterize each CPU with an execution speed $r_{ij}$ ($i$ denotes the sequence number of the node which

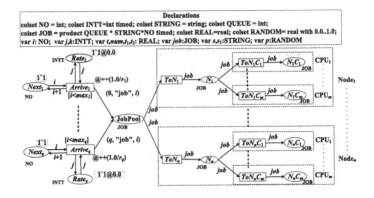

**Fig. 2.** The abstract model for a two-level hierarchical job scheduling system

the CPU belongs to and $j$ denotes the sequence number of the CPU within the node) which means how many jobs each CPU processes in each unit time. The above definitions of workload are similar with the ones in [8–10].

Besides the parameters, the behavior is another important factor that needs be considered for modeling. For a job scheduling system, scheduling each job to an execution host is the most critical behavior. Firstly, each job is scheduled to a node, after that it will be scheduled to an execution host in the node. According to the detailed information for parameters and behaviors, we construct an abstract CPN model for a two-level hierarchical job scheduling system, as shown in Fig. 2. All the declarations of colour sets and variables appeared in the CPN models in the rest of this paper are also shown in Fig. 2. The meanings of the places and transitions in Fig. 2 are described as follows, and for the symbols below, $1 \leq i \leq n$, $1 \leq j \leq m$, $1 \leq k \leq q$.

Places:

- JobPool: the place that stores all the jobs submitted from all the submission hosts. We model each submission host as a job arriving queue $Queue_k$.
- $Rate_k$: the place that controls the arriving rate of $Queue_k$.
- $Next_k$: the place that records the next arriving job of $Queue_k$.
- $N_i$: the place that stores all the jobs scheduled to the node $i$.
- $N_iC_j$: the place that stores all the jobs scheduled to the execution host CPU $j$ within node $i$.

Transitions:

- $Arrive_k$: the transition that models jobs submitted by submission host $k$. The firing rate of the transition is $r_k$ which is used to model the job arriving rate.
- $ToN_i$: the transition that models jobs scheduled to the node $N_i$ from JobPool.
- $ToN_iC_j$: the transition that models jobs scheduled to the CPU $N_iC_j$ from node $N_i$.

It should be noted that time is introduced in the models of Fig. 2 by assuming a *globalclock* representing the current *model time*. Each token in each timed

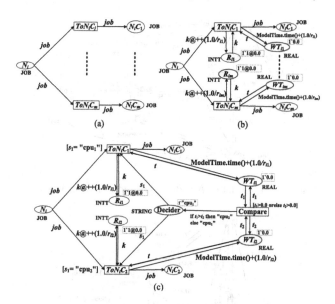

**Fig. 3.** (a): An abstract model of $N_i$; (b): The model of $N_i$ with CPU's execution speed and waiting time; (c): The basic model of $N_i$ with the MEWT scheduling strategy between two CPUs

place has a time stamp, denoted by a symbol "@", indicating when the token can be consumed. A real time delay can be expressed by a symbol "@++". More details can be found in [1].

Obviously, the model in Fig. 2 is not specific enough. Many detailed factors are not included, among which, the most important one is the scheduling strategy. Next, we will elaborate how to model the intra-node and inter-node scheduling strategy using CPNs.

### 3.2   Modeling the Intra-node Scheduling Strategy

The intra-node scheduling strategy is responsible for scheduling jobs within a node to separated CPUs. Without loss of generality, we choose the minimum expected waiting time (MEWT) scheduling strategy as an example to state our modeling method, which always schedules the next job to the CPU that has the minimum expected waiting time (specially, jobs will be scheduled evenly among CPUs if all CPUs have the same waiting time). We will build the CPN model for it step by step.

Firstly, we construct a model with implementation of the MEWT scheduling strategy between two CPUs. Figure 3(a) is the abstract model for a node $N_i$ extracted from Fig. 2. Figure 3(b) adds two places: $R_{ij}$ and $WT_{ij}$. $R_{ij}$ controls the execution speed by time delay @++$(1.0/r_{ij})$, which means the token in $R_{ij}$ can only be consumed again after $1.0/r_{ij}$ units of time. $WT_{ij}$ records the waiting time of CPU $N_iC_j$ by the expression ModelTime.time()+$(1.0/r_{ij})$, which means

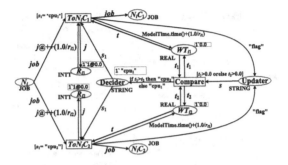

**Fig. 4.** The model of $N_i$ added an updater from Fig. 3(c)

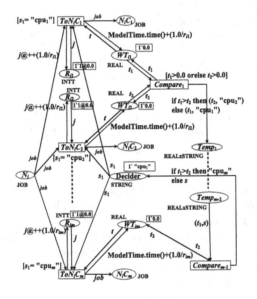

**Fig. 5.** The model of $N_i$ with the MEWT scheduling strategy among more than two CPUs

the earliest time when the CPU $N_iC_j$ becomes idle again is ModelTime.time() $+(1.0/r_{ij})$. Figure 3(c) adds one transition Compare to decide which CPU has the minimum waiting time between two CPUs, and also adds one place Decider to record the comparison results. Each time the transition $ToN_iC_j$ fires, it must satisfy that the guard of $ToN_iC_j$, $[s_1 = \text{"cpu}_j\text{"}]$, is evaluated to True which means that the only token in place Decider is "cpu$_j$", in other words, $N_iC_j$ has the minimum expected waiting time. The waiting time of CPUs will change after any $ToN_iC_j$ fires, so one place Updater is added in Fig. 4 to ensure that the minimum expected waiting time will be updated after each $ToN_iC_j$ fires. That is to say, the comparison and updating module will be triggered after each $ToN_iC_j$ fires.

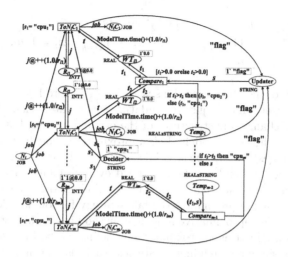

**Fig. 6.** The complete model of $N_i$ with the MEWT scheduling strategy

Next, we extend the scheduling strategy modeling method to $N_i$ with more than two CPUs in Fig. 5. Differently from the former model in Fig. 3(c), it adds $m - 1$ comparisons to decide which CPU has the minimum expected waiting time for a node with $m$ CPUs. The result of each comparison is stored in place $Temp_j$. Similar to Fig. 3(c), we add an updater and get a new model as shown in Fig. 6 which completely implements the MEWT scheduling strategy in node $N_i$.

At last, we still need to optimize the model in Fig. 6 in case that all CPUs have the same waiting time, which occurs frequently when the workloads are too low and almost all the CPUs are idle. The model shown in Fig. 6 always schedules jobs to the former CPUs when $t1 = t2$ in the if then else statement such as "if $t1 > t2$ then ($t2$, "cpu$_2$") else ($t1$, "cpu$_1$")". More improvements are required, so that every CPU has an equal opportunity to be scheduled when all their waiting time is equal. However, the CPN models will become more complex if we design an exact modeling method to meet the above requirements. Next, we will introduce an approximative modeling method so as to reduce the complexity of the exact models.

### 3.3   An Approximative Modeling Method for the Scheduling Strategy

We improve the statements by adding a random number $p$, $0 < p < 1$, in order to deal with the case that $t1$ equals to $t2$. The new improved statements are shown in Table 1.

The parameters $x_1, x_2 \cdots, x_{m-1}$ appeared in the improved statements can be solved by the following equations by guaranteeing that all CPUs have the same probability of $1/m$ to be scheduled when all their waiting time is equal.

$$
\begin{cases}
\prod_{i=1}^{m-1} x_i = (1 - x_1) \prod_{i=2}^{m-1} x_i = 1/m \\
(1 - x_k) \prod_{i=k+1}^{m-1} x_i = (1 - x_{k+1}) \prod_{i=k+2}^{m-1} x_i = 1/m, \\
1 \le k \le m - 2
\end{cases}
$$

The solution of the above equations is $x_k = \frac{k}{k+1}$, where $1 \le k \le m-1$. Thus, we can get the exact models just by updating some statements. This modeling method doesn't change any structures of the original models, but it can reduce the complexity of the exact models. This approximative modeling method almost ensures that the next job will be scheduled to the CPU which has the minimum expected waiting time and will be scheduled evenly among CPUs which have the same waiting time. In other words, the scheduling strategy modeled by the improved statements approximates the fair strategy for low workloads. We will also verify that this approximative modeling method is credible by the following experiments. Actually, this approximative modeling method is also suitable for modeling other similar scheduling strategies, such as the minimum length of queue scheduling strategy and so on.

### 3.4   Modeling the Inter-node Scheduling Strategy

The inter-node scheduling strategy is responsible for scheduling jobs to nodes from the job pool. Without loss of generality, we also choose the MEWT scheduling strategy as an example to state our modeling method. We will also construct the CPN model for it step by step.

Firstly, we construct a basic model for each node's scheduling environment as shown in Fig. 7. Place $WN_i$ is in charge of recording the number of waiting jobs in the node $N_i$. Place $WT_i$ is in charge of recording the whole waiting time

**Table 1.** Improved statements

| Statements in Fig.6 | Improved Statements |
|---|---|
| if $t1 > t2$ then $(t2,$ "cpu$_2$")<br>else $(t1,$ "cpu$_1$") | if $t1 > t2$ then $(t2,$ "cpu$_2$")<br>else if $(t1 = t2)$ then<br>  if $(p < x_1)$ then $(t1,$ "cpu$_1$")<br>  else $(t2,$ "cpu$_2$")<br>else $(t1,$ "cpu$_1$") |
| if $t1 > t2$ then "cpu$_m$"<br>else $s$ | if $t1 > t2$ then "cpu$_m$"<br>else if $(t1 = t2)$ then<br>  if $(p < x_{m-1})$ then $s$<br>  else "cpu$_m$"<br>else $s$ |

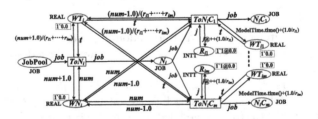

**Fig. 7.** A basic model of the scheduling environment of the node $N_i$

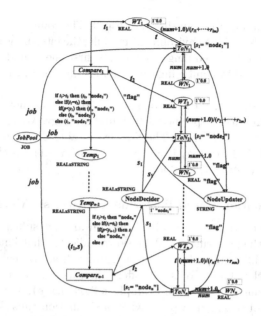

**Fig. 8.** The model with the MEWT scheduling strategy among nodes

of the node $N_i$, which is approximatively calculated by $num/(r_{i1} + \cdots + r_{im})$, where $num$ is the number of waiting jobs and $r_{ij}$ is the process speed of the CPU $N_iC_j$. Although the accurate time, when a node has an available CPU to execute the next job in a real system, may refer to the earliest time when one CPU becomes idle, we find that the model will become very large in such a situation. In addition, we find through our experiment that the errors of the approximate calculation in Fig. 7 are very small, so we still adopt this method in order to tackle large-scale systems. The number of waiting jobs will increase when a new job is scheduled to the node $N_i$ and will decrease when a job is scheduled to a CPU $N_iC_j$. At the same time, the waiting time of the node $N_i$ will increase and decrease, correspondingly. These are all implemented by arc inscriptions in the model.

Secondly, we model the scheduling strategy and get a new model with the implementation of the MEWT strategy among nodes in Fig. 8. The modeling method is similar to that stated in Subsects. 3.2 and 3.3. The parameters $y_1, y_2, \cdots, y_{n-1}$ appeared in the model can be also calculated similarly.

At last, we can get a complete model with the implementation of the MEWT scheduling strategy among nodes by combining the models in Figs. 7 and 8.

## 3.5   A Complete Model for a Job Scheduling System

In Subsects. 3.1, 3.2, and 3.4, we construct an abstract CPN model for a job scheduling system, then model the intra-node and inter-node scheduling strategies, respectively. Then we can get a complete CPN model for a job scheduling system with the MEWT scheduling strategy shown in Fig. 9. The complete model consists of three parts: the job arriving environment module, the inter-node scheduling module, and the intra-node scheduling module. The first one is modeled in Fig. 2, the second one is modeled by combining Figs. 7 and 8, and the third one is modeled in Fig. 6.

In the above section, CPN models are used to state how to model a job scheduling system with a specified scheduling strategy. We implemented their executable models in CPN tools. The final executable CPN model for an $n \times m$ HPC with the MEWT strategy is composed of $4n(m+1)+3$ places, $n(2m+1)$ transitions, and $n(16m+11)+3$ arcs.

### 3.6    The Simulation Based Performance Analysis Method

The models we construct in the above section are not sufficient enough if we want to analyze the performance. We need to indicate what kind of data should be collected for different performance metrics, such as throughput, utilization, flow time and delay. CPN Tools [12] offers the function to collect data during simulations by using monitors. For example, a **Marking size** monitor counts the average number of tokens in a place when a simulation runs. We add different monitors to our model in terms of what kind of performance metrics we need to analyze without "polluting" the model with additional places or transitions. Monitors can be directly attached to places or transitions where we need to collect data. Next, we will explain how to analyze the performance with the data collected by monitors.

The throughput of node $N_i$ can be formulated as $Th(N_i) = (D(ToN_i) - D(WN_i))/T$, where $D(ToN_i)$ is the firing number of transition $ToN_i$ during $T$ time units of simulation, and $D(WN_i)$ is the number of tokens in place $WN_i$ after the simulation stops. In other words, there are $D(ToN_i) - D(WN_i)$ jobs executed by the CPUs in the node $N_i$ during $T$ time units of simulation.

Similarly, the throughput of the CPU $N_iC_j$ can be formulated as $Th(N_iC_j) = D(ToN_iC_j)/T$, where $D(ToN_iC_j)$ is the firing number of transition $ToN_iC_j$ during $T$ time units of simulation.

The utilization of $N_i$ can be formulated as $Ut(N_i) = Th(N_i)/\sum_{j=1}^{m} r_{ij}$, where $\sum_{j=1}^{m} r_{ij}$ is the process speed of $N_i$. The utilization of $N_iC_j$ can be formulated as $Ut(N_iC_j) = D(ToN_iC_j)/(T \times r_{ij})$.

The average delay of job $DT$ comprises two parts, inter-node scheduling delay and intra-node scheduling delay. The inter-node scheduling delay can be formulated as $D(JobPool)/\sum_{i=1}^{n} Th(N_i)$, where $D(JobPool)$ is the average number of tokens in place **JobPool** indicating how many jobs are waiting in **JobPool** on average. The intra-node scheduling delay can be formulated as $\frac{\sum_{i=1}^{n}(D_{avrg}(WN_i)/Th(N_i))}{n}$, where $D_{avrg}(WN_i)$ is the average number of tokens in place $WN_i$ during one simulation. As a result, $DT$ can be formulated as

$$D(JobPool)/\sum_{i=1}^{n} Th(N_i) + \frac{\sum_{i=1}^{n}(D_{avrg}(WN_i)/Th(N_i))}{n}.$$

Many other performance metrics can also be computed by the data collected during the simulation, such as flow time of jobs, loss rate of jobs with a specified capacity of `JobPool` and so on. We will only provide the experimental results about throughput and utilization in the following section because of the paper length.

## 4  Experiment and Analysis

In this section, we will present the experimental results. At first, we verify that our method is feasible with an experiment. Then we confirm that it is credible in comparison with the stochastic Petri net method.

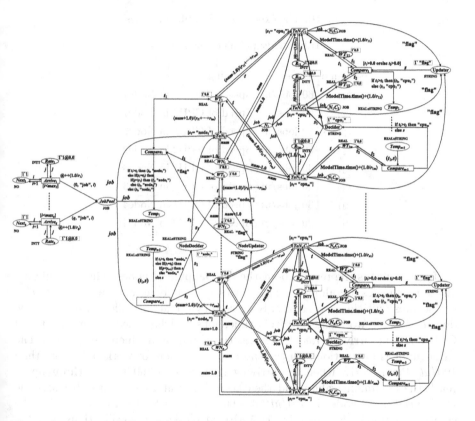

**Fig. 9.** A complete CPN model for a job scheduling system with the MEWT scheduling strategy

### 4.1  Experimental Results of Our Method

We use the software package CPN Tools [12] to implement the CPN model of a $4 \times 2$ HPC. The detailed experiment parameters are described in Table 2. We execute several 20000-step simulations for each arriving rate. The results are described as follows.

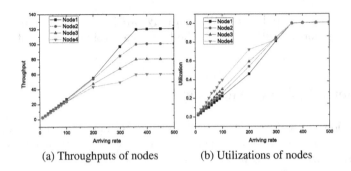

(a) Throughputs of nodes            (b) Utilizations of nodes

**Fig. 10.** The experimental results of nodes

**Table 2.** Experiment parameters

| Name | Value | Meaning |
|------|-------|---------|
| $r_{11}$ | 60 jobs/ut | Speed of CPU1 in Node1 |
| $r_{12}$ | 60 jobs/ut | Speed of CPU2 in Node1 |
| $r_{21}$ | 50 jobs/ut | Speed of CPU1 in Node2 |
| $r_{22}$ | 50 jobs/ut | Speed of CPU2 in Node2 |
| $r_{31}$ | 40 jobs/ut | Speed of CPU1 in Node3 |
| $r_{32}$ | 40 jobs/ut | Speed of CPU2 in Node3 |
| $r_{41}$ | 30 jobs/ut | Speed of CPU1 in Node4 |
| $r_{42}$ | 30 jobs/ut | Speed of CPU2 in Node4 |

Figure 10(a) is the result about the throughputs of nodes. The throughputs of the four nodes are almost the same when the arriving rate ranges from $0/ut$ ($ut$ denotes unit time) to $100/ut$, because they are almost idle during this time due to the low workloads. At this time, jobs will be scheduled evenly to all CPUs. As the arriving rate increases, the throughputs increase as well. The throughput is proportional to the speed of each node for workloads more than $100/ut$. Particularly, when the arriving rate rises to $360/ut$, the throughputs reach the maximum values and then keep stable at these values, because the total speed of all nodes is $360/ut(60 + 60 + 50 + 50 + 40 + 40 + 30 + 30)$. The similar situation is also found in Fig. 10(b), which shows the utilizations of nodes. The utilizations of all nodes achieve nearly 100 % when the arriving rate rises to $360/ut$. It is shown in Fig. 10(b) that the utilization is inversely proportional to the speed of each CPU for low workloads, which is caused by the scheduling strategy we described in Sect. 3.

Besides, the throughputs and utilizations of all CPUs are also shown in Fig. 11. The trends of CPUs' performance metrics coincide with the trends of nodes' performance metrics. It should be noted that we only observe 4 curves for 8 CPUs, since the speeds of the two CPUs in each node are the same.

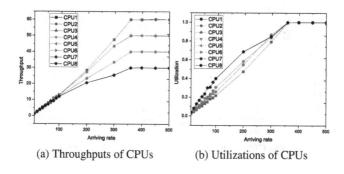

(a) Throughputs of CPUs          (b) Utilizations of CPUs

**Fig. 11.** The experimental results of CPUs

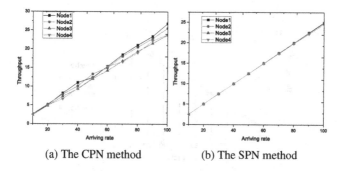

(a) The CPN method              (b) The SPN method

**Fig. 12.** The comparative experiments of throughputs

In addition, we may observe that from the experimental results of throughput, jobs are scheduled evenly to every node and CPU with low workloads (when the arriving rate ranges from $0/ut$ to $100/ut$). All about this can indicate that our approximative modeling method is feasible.

## 4.2 The Comparative Experiments with the SPN Method

We also perform comparative experiments with the method proposed in [8]. [8] proposed a SPN method for modeling and performance evaluation of a hierarchical job scheduling on the Grids. We extend it to the job scheduling system of HPC and implement the same scheduling strategy as described in Sect. 3. The configurations and parameters are exactly the same with the SPN method. The experiment results are shown in the following figures.

Figure 12 is the contrast of throughputs analyzed by the two methods, respectively. Figure 12(a) shows the curves of the throughtputs derived by our method. Figure 12(b) shows the curves of the throughputs derived by the SPN method. Obviously, the lines in Fig. 12(a) are curves, but the lines in Fig. 12(b) are straight lines. That is because our method is based on the simulation technique, whereas the SPN method is based on the state space technique. Despite a big difference between these two methods, we observe that the curves generated by our method

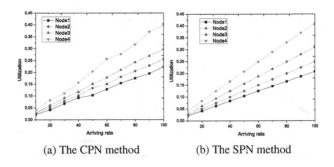

(a) The CPN method            (b) The SPN method

**Fig. 13.** The comparative experiments of utilizations

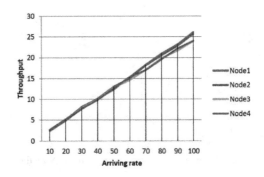

**Fig. 14.** Throughput generated by the Flexsim method

are very consistent with the curves generated by the SPN method. The slopes of curves in Fig. 12(a) are almost the same as the ones in Fig. 12(b), which indicates that the jobs are scheduled evenly to all nodes when the job arriving rates are low. We also observe that the comparison diagrams of utilizations in Fig. 13 show the similar results. The correctness of both methods is testified by each other.

Besides, we also conduct experiments with the method applied in [9], which analyzes performance using the commercial software Flexsim. The experiment result is shown in Fig. 14. We can find that the result is very similar with the above results shown in Fig. 12 generated by our method and the SPN method.

Compared with the SPN method, our method has some advantages. For example, the following case study will show that our method can be applied to HPC systems with larger scale. However, the SPN method is not easy to deal with them due to the state space explosion problem. Actually, the SPN method can't work well when the HPC system is larger than 8*2 in our another experiment. Although the SPN method can also be used for simulation, it is hard to model real workloads coming from a real HPC system since the tokens in SPN are indistinguishable. Whereas our CPN method can be easily improved to support real workloads due to CPN's modeling capacity. Figure 15 shows two kinds of

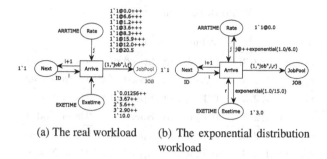

(a) The real workload    (b) The exponential distribution
                          workload

**Fig. 15.** Two kinds of workloads

workloads modeled by our method. The first one is real workload, which has more attributes, like arriving time and execution time. For example, we can use a token (1,"cal",10,0.1256)@2.3 in our models to describe a real job submitted in queue 1, named by "cal", numbered by 10, arriving at time 2.3 and whose execution time is 0.1256. The second one is exponential distribution workload which can be used to describe workload whose arriving time and execution time is exponential distribution. CPNs support more distributions, such as Erlang distribution and so on [15].

### 4.3    A Case Study

In this subsection, we will demonstrate the usefulness of our method by a case study.

Case description: A is an e-commerce company who provides online shopping services and supports online payment through the third party payment company C. B is a bank who supports quick payment service of the third party payment company C. A client of A places an online shopping order and will pay for the order by C. C sends the payment request to B. Then B fulfills the payment by transferring money from the client's bank account. In view of the payment service quality, B opens 80 servers affiliated to its branches in 20 cities to C (each branch opens 4 servers and each server process $\alpha$ payment requests every second).

We have to consider the following problems to ensure the payment service quality, such as "Are the current servers enough if there are $\beta$ payment requests every second?", "How long is the average scheduling delay?", "Which scheduling strategy is the best one to deploy on the payment system?", "How much the average user waiting time will reduce if 10 more servers are opened?".

We abstract the above payment system into a hierarchical HPC system which has 20 nodes and 4 CPUs in each node. The random first come first serve (FCFS) scheduling strategy is selected in this experiment. The detailed experiment parameters are described in Table 3. The job arriving rate is 50 jobs/ut. The experimental machine has 4 Intel Core2 CPUs, 4G memory and installs Win7 64-bit operating system. We execute a 30000-step simulation which spends about 20 s,

**Table 3.** Experiment parameters

| Name | Value | Meaning |
|------|-------|---------|
| $r_{1x}, x = 1, 2, 3, 4$ | 0.1 jobs/ut | Speed of CPUs in Node1 |
| $r_{2x}, x = 1, 2, 3, 4$ | 0.2 jobs/ut | Speed of CPUs in Node2 |
| $r_{3x}, x = 1, 2, 3, 4$ | 0.3 jobs/ut | Speed of CPUs in Node3 |
| $r_{4x}, x = 1, 2, 3, 4$ | 0.4 jobs/ut | Speed of CPUs in Node4 |
| $r_{5x}, x = 1, 2, 3, 4$ | 0.5 jobs/ut | Speed of CPUs in Node5 |
| $r_{6x}, x = 1, 2, 3, 4$ | 0.6 jobs/ut | Speed of CPUs in Node6 |
| $r_{7x}, x = 1, 2, 3, 4$ | 0.7 jobs/ut | Speed of CPUs in Node7 |
| $r_{8x}, x = 1, 2, 3, 4$ | 0.8 jobs/ut | Speed of CPUs in Node8 |
| $r_{9x}, x = 1, 2, 3, 4$ | 0.9 jobs/ut | Speed of CPUs in Node9 |
| $r_{10x}, x = 1, 2, 3, 4$ | 1.0 jobs/ut | Speed of CPUs in Node10 |
| $r_{11x}, x = 1, 2, 3, 4$ | 1.1 jobs/ut | Speed of CPUs in Node11 |
| $r_{12x}, x = 1, 2, 3, 4$ | 1.2 jobs/ut | Speed of CPUs in Node12 |
| $r_{13x}, x = 1, 2, 3, 4$ | 1.3 jobs/ut | Speed of CPUs in Node13 |
| $r_{14x}, x = 1, 2, 3, 4$ | 1.4 jobs/ut | Speed of CPUs in Node14 |
| $r_{15x}, x = 1, 2, 3, 4$ | 1.5 jobs/ut | Speed of CPUs in Node15 |
| $r_{16x}, x = 1, 2, 3, 4$ | 1.6 jobs/ut | Speed of CPUs in Node16 |
| $r_{17x}, x = 1, 2, 3, 4$ | 1.7 jobs/ut | Speed of CPUs in Node17 |
| $r_{18x}, x = 1, 2, 3, 4$ | 1.8 jobs/ut | Speed of CPUs in Node18 |
| $r_{19x}, x = 1, 2, 3, 4$ | 1.9 jobs/ut | Speed of CPUs in Node19 |
| $r_{20x}, x = 1, 2, 3, 4$ | 2.0 jobs/ut | Speed of CPUs in Node20 |

26 % of CPU and 49 M memory (actually, more simulations may be executed to improve the reliability). Some results are described as follows.

- Taking node $N_6$ as an example, it receives 512 jobs among which 497 jobs have been executed and 15 jobs are still waiting in the queue.
- Taking CPU $N_{18}C_1$ as an example, its total busy time is 77.22 ut and its utilization is 36.90 %.
- Taking node $N_{10}$ as an example, its throughput is 2.60 jobs/ut and its utilization is 65 %.
- Taking node $N_1$ as an example, its utilization is about 100 %.
- The average waiting queue length is 34.38. $N_1$ has the largest average length of waiting queue which is 236.17, and $N_{20}$ has the smallest length of waiting queue, which is only 0.0033.
- The throughput of all nodes is 43.33 jobs/ut, and the average intra-node scheduling delay is 0.79 ut.

If we compute confidence intervals based on 10 simulation runs, we can get some 90 % confidence intervals. For example, the average waiting queue length is $34.28 \pm 1.18$. That is, with 90 % confidence the average waiting queue length is between 33.10 and 35.46.

These performance results allow us to detect performance bottlenecks so that we can optimize system. For example, not all nodes' utilizations reach 100 % in current situation, but there are still some jobs waiting in the queue, which indicates that the selected scheduling strategy is not the best one. Actually, the scheduling delay decreases greatly in another experiment with the MEWT scheduling strategy. For another example, the maximum waiting queue length of $N_2$ is 327 and the average length is 166.07, however the maximum waiting queue length of $N_{16}$ is 4 and the average length is only 0.02, which indicates that the scheduling delay is different among all nodes. Besides, we can compute the quantitative curve of some performance metrics by more experiments.

## 5 Related Works

As job scheduling is very important in HPC systems and many other distributed systems, there are many works focusing on its performance analysis. [16] proposes a new method to find the optimal co-scheduling solution for a mix of serial and parallel jobs. [17] proposes a user-based grid workload model which is based on clustering users according to their behaviors in the system and their applications. [18] analyzes the performance of online scheduling in hierarchical grids using different workloads which are generated by real grid systems. [19] offers a novel abstraction framework and a heuristic, called BalancedPools, that efficiently utilizes performance properties of MapReduce jobs in a given workload for constructing an optimized job schedule. [20] proposes the use of shared resource monitoring to improve overall datacenter throughput and improve quality of service, and it also conducts detailed experiments emulating datacenter scenarios including several different kinds of workloads. [21] explores four unique approaches to achieve the scheduling goals of maximizing utilization on four distinct resources at the National Institute for Computational Sciences with a diverse job (workload) mix.

On the evaluation of solutions or on the performance analysis for the distributed computing systems (e.g. schedulers, resource management policies, throughput analysis and utilization analysis), it is desirable to analyze how the proposed solutions behave on several representative scenarios of the target system. Usually, the different scenarios are obtained by varying the workloads of the systems. All the above literatures [16–21] focus on performance analysis for HPC systems, but they use completely different workloads. In a general way, there are two kinds of workloads on the basis of different required quantity of computing resources (like CPUs, memories or others). One kind of workload is composed of jobs which require more than one computing resource, like the workload used in [18]. The other is composed of jobs which only require one computing resource [8–11]. The first one is widely used in scientific computing, such as parallel computing on supercomputers, while the second one is widely used in online systems of internet companies, such as cluster systems of search engine.

This paper focuses on modeling the job scheduling systems in hierarchical HPC systems and analyzing their performance with the second kind of workloads which is adopted in [8–11]. [8] proposes a stochastic Petri net (SPN) method for modeling and performance evaluation of hierarchical job scheduling on the grids. [9,10] analyze the performance of the scheduling strategies using a business software Flexsim, which is widely used in many fields. [11] proposes a coloured Petri nets-based method to model task scheduling and evaluate reliability of grid services. However, the method proposed in [8] is not easy to be applied in large-scale systems and can't support more complex workloads. The method proposed in [9,10] also can't support complex workloads and the simulation software Flexsim is very expensive. [11] focuses on the reliability evaluation of grid services and doesn't provide modeling method of scheduling strategies.

In this paper, we propose a new CPN method for modeling job scheduling systems in HPCs and analyzing their performance. Our method helps to improve some of the previous works. To our knowledge, we have not discovered some other methods similar with ours.

## 6    Summary and Future Work

In this paper, a modeling and performance analysis method for job scheduling systems using CPNs is proposed. A CPN modeling method and a simulation-based performance analysis method are presented. Specially, we design modeling method for some scheduling strategies, which is not considered in [11]. The experimental results show that our method is feasible and can be used to make predictions about key performance metrics. The comparative experiments with SPN method show that our method is credible and can be applied to much larger systems. What's more, our method supports real workloads which improves the SPN method [8] and the Flexsim method [9,10]. Besides, our method is low cost compared with the Flexsim method [9,10]. In the future, we still need to improve our method to support more kinds of workloads and scheduling strategies.

**Acknowledgments.** The authors would like to thank the anonymous referees for their comments and suggestions. This work is partially supported by the National Science Foundation of China (NSFC) under grant No. 91418206.

## References

1. Jensen, K., Kristensen, L.M., Wells, L.: Coloured petri nets and CPN tools for modelling and validation of concurrent systems. J. Int. J. Softw. Tools Technol. Transfer **9**(3–4), 213–254 (2007)
2. Wells, L.: Performance analysis using coloured petri nets. In: 10th International Workshop on Modeling, Analysis, and Simulation of Computer and Telecommunication Systems, pp. 217–221. IEEE Computer Society (2002)
3. Wells, L.: Performance analysis using CPN tools. In: 1st International Conference on Performance Evaluation Methodolgies and Tools, pp. 59. ACM (2006)
4. Slawomir, S., Tomasz, R.: Simulation and performance analysis of distributed internet systems using TCPNs. J. informatica (Slovenia) **33**(4), 405–415 (2009)

5. Nogueira, B., Maciel, P., Tavares, E., et al.: A formal model for performance and energy evaluation of embedded systems. J. EURASIP J. Embed. Syst. **2011**(2), 1–12 (2011). http://dx.doi.org/10.1155/2011/316510

6. Dan, M., Vintan, L.: Performance prediction for parallel applications running on HPC architectures through petri net modelling and simulation. In: 9th International Conference on Intelligent Computer Communication and Processing, pp. 267–270. IEEE (2013)

7. Gil-Costa, V., Marin, M., Inostrosa-Psijas, A., et al.: Modelling search engines performance using coloured petri nets. J. Fundam. Informaticae **131**(1), 139–166 (2014)

8. Shan, Z.G., Lin, C.: Modeling and performance evaluation of hierarchical job scheduling on the grids. In: 6th International Conference on Grid and Cooperative Computing, pp. 296–303. IEEE Computer Society (2007)

9. Styliannos, Z., Helen, D.K: Resource allocation strategies in a 2-level hierarchical grid system. In: 41st Annual Simulation Symposium, pp. 157–164. IEEE Computer Society (2008)

10. Styliannos, Z., Helen, D.K.: Performance and energy aware cluster-level scheduling of compute-intensive jobs with unknown service times. J. Simul. Model. Pract. Theory **19**, 239–250 (2011)

11. Mohammad, A.A., Reza, E.M.: Task scheduling modelling and reliability evaluation of grid services using coloured petri nets. J. Future Gener. Comput. Syst. **26**, 1141–1150 (2010)

12. CPN Tools. http://cpntools.org

13. Running Jobs with Platform LSF. http://www-03.ibm.com/systems/services/platformcomputing

14. Zhou, S.N., Zheng, X.H., Wang, J.W., Delisle, P.: UTOPIA: a load sharing facility for large, heterogeneous distributed computer systems. J. Softw. Pract. experience **23**(12), 1305–1336 (1993)

15. van der Aalst, W.M.P., Stahl, C., Westergaard, M.: Strategies for modeling complex processes using colored petri nets. In: Jensen, K., van der Aalst, W.M.P., Balbo, G., Koutny, M., Wolf, K. (eds.) Transactions on Petri Nets and Other Models of Concurrency VII. LNCS, vol. 7480, pp. 6–55. Springer, Heidelberg (2013)

16. Huanzhou, Z., Ligang, H., Stephen, A.J.: Optimizing job scheduling on multicore computers. In: 22nd International Symposium on Modelling, Analysis and Simulation of Computer and Telecommunication Systems, pp. 61–70. IEEE (2014)

17. Marcus, C., Francisco, B.: A user-based model of grid computing workloads. In: 13th ACM/IEEE International Conference on Grid Computing, pp. 40–48. IEEE Computer Society (2012)

18. Juan, M.R.A., Andrei, T., et al.: Job allocation strategies with user run time estimates for online scheduling in hierarchical grids. J. Grid Comput. **9**(1), 95–116 (2011)

19. Abhishek, V., Ludmila, C., Roy, H.C.: Two Sides of a coin: optimizing the schedule of mapreduce jobs to minimize their makespan and improve cluster performance. In: 20th IEEE International Symposium on Modeling, Analysis and Simulation of Computer and Telecommunication Systems, pp. 11–18. IEEE Computer Society (2012)

20. Jaideep, M., Ravi, L., Ramesh, L., Sadagopan, S.: Shared resource monitoring and throughput optimization in cloud-computing datacenters. In: 25th IEEE International Symposium on Parallel and Distributed Processing, pp. 1024–1033. IEEE(2011)

21. Tabitha, K.S., Troy, B., Glenn, B.R., Matt, E., Patricia, K.: Scheduling diverse high performance computing systems with the goal of maximizing utilization. In: 18th International Conference on High Performance Computing, pp. 1–6. IEEE Computer Society (2011)

# An Optimization Strategy of Energy Consumption for Data Transmission Based on Optimal Stopping Theory in Mobile Networks

Ying Peng[1], Nao Wang[2], and Gaocai Wang[2(✉)]

[1] College of Electrical Engineering,
Guangxi University, Nanning 530004, China
623833@qq.com
[2] School of Computer and Electronic Information,
Guangxi University, Nanning 530004, China
{wangzhuo,gcwang}@gxu.edu.cn

**Abstract.** With the wide deployment of mobile network, it's very important to utilize mobile networks resource efficiently and decrease energy consumption of wireless terminals for constructing green mobile computing. This paper mainly studies minimization problem of energy consumption in data transmission under the given data generation rate and transmission delay demand in wireless links. Firstly, a finite horizon optimal stopping problem with transmission data quantity constraint and energy consumption minimization is constructed, and then we prove the existence of optimal stopping rule and offer the solutions and processes. At last, we obtain the optimal transmission rate threshold of the sending terminal for each channel detection slot time, so as to form the optimization strategy of energy consumption for data transmission based on optimal stopping theory. The simulation results show that the strategy proposed by this paper has lower average energy consumption and higher average delivery success ratio than other strategies, and achieves better optimization effect in energy consumption.

**Keywords:** Mobile networks · Data transmission · Optimal stopping · Energy consumption optimization · Optimal rate

## 1 Introduction

It's necessary to reduce energy consumption of mobile terminals (MTs), which improves users' network experience and constructs green mobile computing [1]. In mobile networks environment, channel quality changes with time. The strategy which wireless networks make use of the characteristics of the time varying channel to transmit data efficiently is called opportunistic scheduling [2]. Opportunistic scheduling can be divided into centralized opportunistic scheduling and distributed opportunistic scheduling. The distributed opportunistic scheduling not only increases energy efficiency [3–6], but also improves network performance [10], such as throughput.

© Springer International Publishing Switzerland 2015
G. Wang et al. (Eds.): ICA3PP 2015, Part IV, LNCS 9531, pp. 281–292, 2015.
DOI: 10.1007/978-3-319-27140-8_20

For the minimization of average energy consumption in data transmission on the link, send terminal (ST) must detect channel quality in real time, and choose optimal time to send data according to current cumulative data quantity. Actually, this is a distributed opportunistic scheduling problem [3–6, 10]. In this distributed opportunistic scheduling, ST detects channel conditions in the link continuously, and then chooses the optimal energy efficiency time (that is the average energy consumption for data transmission is minimal) to stop observing and send data. Hence, this problem can be further turned into an optimal stopping rule strategy to be solved.

The remainder of this paper is organized as follows. Section 2 reviews the related research work. Section 3 describes the system model and the specific optimization problem. Section 4 gives the optimization strategy of energy consumption for data transmission based on optimal stopping theory. Section 5 shows simulation results and analysis. And conclude this paper and prospect the future work in Sect. 6.

## 2  Related Work

In order to decrease energy consumption in mobile networks, some researches concern how to choose the best channel quality time to deliver data [3–6], others pay attention to selecting the whole route from source to destination [7–9].

Given the access probability of multiple devices competing channel, they constructed an optimal stopping problem of infinite horizon using optimal stopping theory in [3]. They derived the optimal transmission rate threshold at each detection time in homogeneous scenario. But they didn't consider the transmission delay. Considering the maximum delay, they studied the energy consumption in the wireless link with time-varying channel in [4]. They obtained the optimal power threshold of ST at each detection time by optimal stopping theory. But they assumed an ideal situation that ST always had enough data to deliver. In real networks, when ST gets good transmission chance, the amount of data to deliver maybe more or less than the one that ST can transmit within that transmission duration. In [5], the scheduling problem that data flow is delivered from roadside unit to passing-by vehicle is studied. They obtained the optimal scheduling time using optimal stopping theory, so as to effectively save transmission cos. Furthermore, they further studied this problem in [6].

Due to rapid fluctuation of channel conditions, opportunistic route is introduced. The energy efficient cooperative communication method is proposed in [7]. They made full use of the transient characteristics of mobile network channel. Energy consumption objective functions for calculating end-to-end energy consumption are introduced into opportunistic routing in [8]. Then they designed energy-efficient routing algorithms based on Dijkstra algorithm. In [9], we proposed minimization route scheme of energy consumption in transmission with delay constraint in mobile environment, which reduced energy consumption of network efficiently.

In this paper, we study the optimization problem of energy consumption in the case of single device selecting single channel. To be different from ST always having enough data for transmission in [4], we assume that ST generates data in given rate. Moreover, the problems of the minimization of the expected energy consumption and the minimization of average energy consumption per unit time were studied in [4]. And we consider the minimization of average energy consumption per unit data transmitted, with the constraint of finishing delivering all cumulative data.

## 3 System Model and Problem Description

### 3.1 System Model

In mobile network, assume time is divided into a fixed period $T(S)$. In a wireless link composed of a wireless ST and a wireless receive terminal (RT), the channel gain g obeys certain distribution and remains constant in $T$ [3, 4, 10]. ST generates data in a given rate $c$(bit/s), and transmits data with fixed power $P$(W) to RT under delay no more than $D_m$. ST detects channel quality every $T$, and consumes energy $E_D$(J) every time. Detection duration of each time is very short and far less than T. If ST finds good channel, it'll transmit data in duration $t$. Transmission energy consumption is $P \cdot t(J)$ and its value is far more than $E_D$. Duration t satisfies $t \leq T$. The whole process is named as a round of channel detection and data transmission. It is described in Fig. 1.

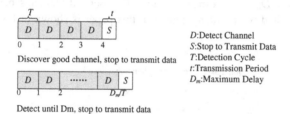

**Fig. 1.** A round of channel detection and data transmission

The total amount of data transmitted in a round is $R \cdot t$(bit), and $R$(bit/s) is the transmission rate. According to the Shannon formula:

$$R = W \log_2(1 + g \cdot P \cdot (N_0 \cdot W)^{-1}) \tag{1}$$

Transmission rate $R$ is defined by bandwidth $W$, gain $g$, transmission power $P$ and noise power spectral density $N_0$. Therefore, ST must detect the channel quality of link in real time, so as to select the optimal transmission time of best channel quality. In this paper, we obtain the optimal transmission time by the optimal stopping theory.

### 3.2 Optimal Stopping Theory

In order to maximize the expected payoff or minimize the expected cost, the decision maker observes the random variables sequentially in the optimal stopping theory, and selects a proper time to take a given action [12]. The stopping rule problem is defined:
(1) a sequence of random variables $X_1, X_2,...,$ whose joint distribution is assumed known; (2) a sequence of real-valued reward or cost functions: $y_0, y_1(x_1), y_2(x_1, x_2),...,$ $y_\infty(x_1, x_2,...)$.

The associated stopping rule may be described as: After observing $X_1 = x_1$, $X_2 = x_2$, ..., $X_n = x_n (n = 1, 2, ...)$, decision maker may stop observing and accept reward or cost function $y_n(x_1, ..., x_n)$, or continue observing $X_{n+1}$. If decision maker chooses not to take any observation, he accepts the constant value $y_0$; if he never stops observing, he accepts $y_\infty(x_1, x_2, ...)$. This rule makes the decision maker to choose the optimal time $N$ ($0 \leq N \leq \infty$) to stop, thus maximize expected reward or minimize expected cost $E[Y_N]$. Here, $Y_N = y_N(x_1, ..., x_N)$ is a random reward or cost stopping at $N$, and $E[\bullet]$ represents expected value. When $n$ doesn't exceed a maximal value $N_m$, and thus it is a problem known as an optimal stopping problem of finite horizon, which can be solved by backward induction. It is computed from $N_m$ to 0, reversely.

### 3.3 Optimal Stopping Problem About Data Transmission in Mobile Network

In this paper, we assume the ST generates data in given rate, of which the maximum delay of data transmission is $D_m(S)$. The data beyond the delay will be discarded. Therefore, this problem is an optimal stopping problem of finite horizon with maximum transmission delay $D_m$. The correspondence of associated elements between optimal stopping strategy and the problem studied in this paper is shown in Fig. 2.

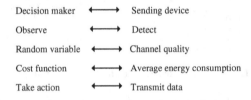

**Fig. 2.** Optimal stopping problem elements in data transmission

## 4    Optimization Strategy of Energy Consumption

### 4.1 Construction of Optimal Stopping Problem About Energy Consumption Minimization (OSPECM)

Define variable sequence $X_n = \{\Delta T_n, R_n\}$ for ST detecting channel quality at the $n$'th times. Where $\Delta T_n$ is the sequence of the total detection duration and $R_n$ is the sequence of transmission rate. ST detects channel at least once. Assume $N$ to be time index (time for short) that ST stops detecting. And assume $M$ to be the maximum time ST must stop detecting and transmit data, and $M$ is $max\{n: \Delta T_n \leq D_m\}$. Then there is $1 \leq n \leq N \leq M$. Hence, the total energy consumption of a round is:

$$E_N = NE_D + Pt \tag{2}$$

If ST repeats the stopping rule in $Y$ rounds, we get stopping time sequence $\{N_1, N_2, \ldots, N_i, \ldots, N_Y\}$ and total energy consumption sequence $\{E_{N_1}, E_{N_2}, \ldots, E_{N_i}, \ldots, E_{N_Y}\}$. $N_i$ is stopping time of the $i$'th round. It is counted from the end of the $i$-1'th round. The initial time of the first round is 0. Thus $1 \leq N_i \leq M$ holds. The total duration of the $i$'th round is $\Delta T_{N_i} + t$, and $\Delta T_{N_i}$ is $T \cdot N_i$. $E_{N_i}$ is the total energy consumption of the $i$'th round stopping at $N_i$. If ST accumulated $c(\Delta T_{N_i} + t)$ bits data waiting for transmission, and transmission rate is $R_{N_i}$, there will be $L_{N_i}$ bits data left undelivered. So,

$$L_{N_i} = (c(\Delta T_{N_i} + t) - R_{N_i}t)^+ = \begin{cases} c(\Delta T_{N_i} + t) - R_{N_i}t, & c(\Delta T_{N_i} + t) > R_{N_i}t \\ 0, & c(\Delta T_{N_i} + t) \leq R_{N_i}t \end{cases} \quad (3)$$

Define energy efficiency $\zeta$ of average consumption per bit data transmitted as:

$$\zeta = \frac{\sum_{i=1}^{Y} E_{N_i}}{\sum_{i=1}^{Y} (c(\Delta T_{N_i} + t) - L_{N_i})} \quad (4)$$

According to the law of large numbers, expression (4) converges to $E[E_N]/E[c(\Delta T_N + t) - L_N]$. Where $N$ is the time of ST's stopping detection and transmitting data. This is an optimal stopping rule, which selects stopping time $N$ to minimize $E[E_N]/E[c(\Delta T_N + t) - L_N]$. And $1 \leq N \leq M$ holds. Because we require ST to finish delivering all cumulative data in $t$, this optimal stopping problem has a constraint condition $\varphi$, and it's $R_N t \geq c(\Delta T_N + t)$. Hence, the stopping time set is defined as:

$$N^+ = \{N : 1 \leq N \leq M, E[\Delta T_N] \leq D_m, \varphi\} \quad (5)$$

And the minimization problem of energy consumption is described as:

$$\min_{N \in N^+} \frac{E[NE_D + Pt]}{E[c(\Delta T_N + t) - L_N]} \quad (6)$$
$$s.t. \quad E[R_N t] \geq E[c(\Delta T_N + t)]$$

## 4.2    Transformation of OSPECM

According to expression (4), we define the optimal energy efficiency $\zeta^*$ as:

$$\zeta^* = \inf_{N \in N^+} \frac{E[NE_D + Pt]}{E[c(\Delta T_N + t) - L_N]} \quad (7)$$

The optimal problem in expression (7) is equal to:

$$\inf_{N \in N^+} (E[NE_D + Pt] - \zeta^* E[c(\Delta T_N + t) - L_N]) = 0 \quad (8)$$

Set $Z_N = NE_D + Pt - \zeta(c(\Delta T_N + t) - L_N)$. For each $\zeta$, there is an optimal time set $N(\zeta) \in N^+$ to minimize $E[Z_N]$. To get $\zeta^*$, we must obtain optimal stopping time $N^* = N(\zeta^*)$. Then,

$$N^* = \arg \ \inf_{N \in N^+} \frac{E[NE_D + Pt]}{E[c(\Delta T_N + t) - L_N]} \tag{9}$$

Therefore, the expression (6) in Sect. 4.1 is transformed as:

$$
\begin{aligned}
&\min_{N \in N^+} \left( E[NE_D + Pt] - \zeta E[c(\Delta T_N + t) - L_N] \right) \\
&s.t. \quad E[R_N t] - E[c(\Delta T_N + t)] \geq 0
\end{aligned} \tag{10}
$$

According to the Lagrange duality theory, the above problem is turned as:

$$
\begin{aligned}
\min_{N \in N^+} E[Y_N] = \min_{N \in N^+} ( &E[NE_D + Pt] - \zeta E[c(\Delta T_N + t) - L_N] + \lambda(E[c(\Delta T_N + t)] \\
&- E[R_N t]))
\end{aligned} \tag{11}
$$

Where $\lambda$ is a Lagrange multiplier and $\lambda \geq 0$ holds.

**Remark 1.** In expression (11), there is $\begin{cases} \lambda = 0, & E[c(\Delta T_N + t)] \leq E[R_N t] \\ \lambda > 0, & E[c(\Delta T_N + t)] > E[R_N t] \end{cases}$. So,

$$\lambda(E[c(\Delta T_N + t)] - E[R_N t]) = \begin{cases} 0, & E[c(\Delta T_N + t)] \leq E[R_N t] \\ \lambda(E[c(\Delta T_N + t)] - E[R_N t]), & E[c(\Delta T_N + t)] > E[R_N t] \end{cases}$$

According to expression (3), there is $\lambda(E[c(\Delta T_N + t) - R_N t]) = \lambda E[L_N]$.
Consequently, expression (11) is expressed as follows.

$$\min_{N \in N^+} E[Y_N] = \min_{N \in N^+} \left( E[NE_D + Pt] - \zeta E[c(\Delta T_N + t) - L_N] + \lambda(E[L_N]) \right) \tag{12}$$

**Remark 2.** For $\zeta$, there is $E_D/(cT) < \zeta < Pt/(ct)$. When $L_N$ is 0 at $N$, $\zeta$ is the smallest. Its value is $(NE_D + Pt)/(cNT + ct)$. Because $t \leq T$, there is $\zeta > (NE_D + Pt)/(cNT + ct)$. According to Sect. 3.3, $Pt$ is bigger than $E_D$. So $\zeta > E_D/(cT)$. And $Pt/(ct)$ is the ratio of $Pt$ to the value of accumulative data $ct$. If $\zeta > Pt/(ct)$ holds, ST can transmit data without detecting channel to obtain less value of $\zeta$. Hence, $\zeta < Pt/(ct)$.

### 4.3   Solution to OSPECM

We first offer the following proposition 1 as follow.

**Proposition 1.** Optimal stopping rule exists in expression (12).

**Proof.** According to [12], if the problem meets the following two conditions:

A1. $E[inf_n\, Y_n] > -\infty$  A2. $\lim\, inf_{n\to\infty}\, Y_n \ge Y_\infty$ a.s.

Optimal stopping rule exists. Because $\Delta T_n$ is equal to $nT$, there is in expression (12): $Y_n = nE_D + Pt - \zeta c(nT + t) + (\lambda + \zeta)L_n$

Because $L_n \ge 0$ is satisfied, and $\zeta < Pt/ct$ holds, there is $Y_n > nE_D - \zeta cnT$.

Meanwhile, there is $\zeta > E_D/cT$. Furthermore, $nT \le D_m$ is satisfied, that is $n \le D_m/T$. Thus, $Y_n > -\infty$ holds. Consequently, condition A1 is satisfied.

When $n \to \infty$, there is $L_n \to c(nT + t)$. $nE_D \to \infty$ and $c(nT + t) \to \infty$ also hold. Hence,

$$\lim inf_{n\to\infty} Y_n = \lim\ inf_{n\to\infty}(nE_D + Pt - \zeta c(nT + t) + (\lambda + \zeta)L_n)$$
$$= \lim\ inf_{n\to\infty}(nE_D + Pt + \lambda c(nT + t)) = \infty$$

Obviously $Y_\infty = \infty$. Condition A2 is satisfied.

**End.**

For this optimal stopping problem of finite horizon, we derive the expected value from the end to the first step reversely using backward induction. According to [10], when ST stops detecting at $n$, the minimum rate of return $W_n(\lambda, \zeta)$ is as follows.

$$W_n(\lambda, \zeta) = \min(Pt + nE_D - \zeta c(nT + t) + (\lambda + \zeta)L_n, V_{M-n-1}(\lambda, \zeta)) \qquad (13)$$

Where, $n = 1, 2, \ldots, M-1$, $V_{M-n-1}(\lambda, \zeta) = E[W_{n+1}(\lambda, \zeta)|F_n]$. Here, energy consumption cost $E_D$ is considered. The rate of return at $n$ is compared with expected value $V_{M-n-1}(\lambda, \zeta)$ obtained from $n + 1$ to $M$ using optimal stopping rule. When the rate of return at $n$ is less than or equal to expected value $V_{M-n-1}(\lambda, \zeta)$, ST stops detecting. That is

$$Pt + nE_D - \zeta c(nT + t) + (\lambda + \zeta)L_n \le V_{M-n-1}(\lambda, \zeta) \qquad (14)$$

According to expression (3), if $c(nT + t) > R_n t$, expression (14) can be turned as:

$$Pt + nE_D + \lambda c(nT + t) - (\lambda + \zeta)R_n t \le V_{M-n-1}(\lambda, \zeta)$$

When $c(nT + t) \le R_n t$ is satisfied, expression (14) is transformed as:

$$Pt + nE_D - \zeta c(nT + t) \le V_{M-n-1}(\lambda, \zeta)$$

Finally, due to the delay boundary $D_m$, ST must stop detecting and transmit data if the detection time reaches $M$. So the transmission rate threshold of ST at $M$ is zero. Based on above analysis, the transmission rate threshold of ST stopping at $n$ is

$$R_{th,n}(\lambda, \zeta) = \begin{cases} \alpha, & \beta > \alpha, n = 1, 2, \ldots, M - 1 \\ \beta, & \beta < \alpha, \ and\ c1\ holds, n = 1, 2, \ldots, M - 1 \\ 0, & n = M \end{cases}$$

$$\alpha = \frac{Pt + nE_D + \lambda c(nT + t) - V_{M-n-1}(\lambda, \zeta)}{(\lambda + \zeta)t}, \qquad \beta = c(nT + t)/t$$

$$c1 : Pt + nE_D - \zeta c(nT + t) \le V_{M-n-1}(\lambda, \zeta)$$

$$\qquad\qquad (15)$$

Assume the probability density function (PDF) of transmission rate to be $f_R(r)$. The cumulative distribution function (CDF) of transmission rate at $M$ is $\int_0^{R_{max}} f_R(r)dr$, and denoted as $F\tilde{R}$. The expected value is $\int_0^{R_{max}} r f_R(r)dr$, and denoted as $\tilde{R}$. Define $R_{th} = c(MT + t)/t$. If $R_{th} < R_{max}$, the cdf of transmission rate which is less than $R_{th}$ at $M$ is $\int_0^{R_{th}} f_R(r)dr$, and denoted as $F\hat{R}_{th}$. The expected value is $\int_0^{R_{th}} r f_R(r)dr$, and denoted as $\hat{R}_{th}$. If ST stops at $M$, the expected value of the rate of return $V_0(\lambda, \zeta)$ is

$$V_0(\lambda, \zeta) = \begin{cases} (Pt + ME_D)F\tilde{R} + \lambda c(MT + t)F\hat{R}_{th} - (\lambda + \zeta)\hat{R}_{th}t \\ \quad - \zeta c(MT + t)(F\tilde{R} - F\hat{R}_{th}), & R_{th} \le R_{max} \quad (16) \\ (Pt + ME_D + \lambda c(MT + t))F\tilde{R} - (\lambda + \zeta)\tilde{R}t, & R_{th} > R_{max} \end{cases}$$

According to backward induction, combining expression (13), we obtain the expected value of the rate of return $V_{M-n}(\lambda, \zeta)$ at $n$ is as follows.

$$V_{M-n}(\lambda, \zeta) = E[\min(Pt + nE_D - \zeta c(nT + t) + (\lambda + \zeta)L_n, V_{M-n-1}(\lambda, \zeta))]$$

$$= \int_{R_{th,n}(\lambda, \zeta)}^{R_{max}} (Pt + nE_D - \zeta c(nT + t) + (\lambda + \zeta)L_n)f_R(r)dr \qquad (17)$$

$$+ \int_0^{R_{th,n}(\lambda, \zeta)} V_{M-n-1}(\lambda, \zeta)f_R(r)dr \qquad n = 1, 2, \ldots, M-1$$

Where $R_{th,n}(\lambda, \zeta)$ is given by expression (15). Consequently, we obtain the optimal stopping rule for expression (12) as follows.

$$N(\zeta^*) = \min\{M \ge n \ge 1 : R_n \ge R_{th,n}(\lambda, \zeta^*)\} \qquad (18)$$

Where $R_{th,n}(\lambda, \zeta^*)$ is given by expression (15). Next, we need to obtain the value of $\lambda$ and $\zeta^*$. The following optimal equation exists in the optimal stopping rule.

$$V^*(\lambda, \zeta^*) = E[\min(Pt + NE_D - \zeta^* c(NT + t) + (\lambda + \zeta^*)L_N, V^*(\lambda, \zeta^*))]$$

And the optimal solution is $V^*(\lambda, \zeta^*) = 0$. Consequently, we have:

$$0 = E[\min(Pt + NE_D - \zeta^* c(NT + t) + (\lambda + \zeta^*)L_N, 0)] \qquad (19)$$

Meanwhile, according to the KKT (Karush-Kuhn-Tucker) conditions, we have:

$$\lambda c E[(NT + t)] - \lambda E[R_N t] = 0 \qquad (20)$$

Next, we analyze $E[R_N]$ and $E[N]$. Assume the random variable transmission rate at $N$ to be $R_N$, and then the CDF of $R_N$ is as follows.

$$F_{R_N}(r) = \Pr[R_{N,n} \le r | stop\ at\ n] = \begin{cases} \dfrac{F_R(r) - F_R(R_{th,n}(\lambda, \zeta^*))}{1 - F_R(R_{th,n}(\lambda, \zeta^*))}, & r \ge R_{th,n}(\lambda, \zeta^*) \\ 0, & r < R_{th,n}(\lambda, \zeta^*) \end{cases} \quad (21)$$

And the probability of ST stopping at $n$ is as follows.

$$\rho_n = \left( \prod_{i=1}^{n-1} (1 - F_R(R_{th,i}(\lambda, \zeta^*))) \right) F_R(R_{th,n}(\lambda, \zeta^*)) \quad (22)$$

Hence, the expected value of $R_N$ is given as follows.

$$E[R_N] = \sum_{n=1}^{M} E[R_{N,n} | stop\ at\ n] \cdot \rho_n = \sum_{n=1}^{M} \left( \int_{R_{th,n}(\lambda, \zeta^*)}^{R_{max}} \frac{r}{1 - F_R(R_{th,n}(\lambda, \zeta^*))} dF_R(r) \right) \cdot \rho_n \quad (23)$$

The expected value of the random variable stop time $N$ is given as follows.

$$E[N] = \sum_{n=1}^{M} n\rho_n \quad (24)$$

Consequently, we have the following equations.

$$\begin{cases} 0 = \min(Pt + E[N]E_D - \zeta^* c(E[N]T + t) + (\lambda + \zeta^*)E[L_N], 0) \\ \lambda c T E[N] + \lambda c t - \lambda t E[R_N] = 0 \end{cases} \quad (25)$$

Where $E[R_N]$ and $E[N]$ are defined in expression (23) and (24), respectively. We solve expression (25) to obtain the value of $\zeta^*$ and $\lambda$. And the process is below.

--------------------------------------------------------------------------

Step 1. Start, let $k=1$, and initialize $\lambda_k$, $\lambda_{max}$ and $\lambda_\Delta$;

Step 2. If $\lambda_k \le \lambda_{max}$, initialize $\zeta_0$, carry out Step 3; else go to Step 8;

Step 3. Solve $V_0(\lambda_k, \zeta_0)$ according to expression (16), and let $n=M-1$;

Step 4. If $n \ge 1$, carry out Step 5; else go to Step 6;

Step 5. Obtain $R_{th,n}(\lambda_k, \zeta_0)$ according to expression (15), and compute $V_{M-n}(\lambda_k, \zeta_0)$ according to expression (17), and let $n=n-1$, then return Step 4;

Step 6. Obtain $E[R_N]$ and $E[N]$ according to expression (23) and (24), respectively, and solve $\zeta_{new}$ according to expression (25). If $|\zeta_{new} - \zeta_0| > \varepsilon$ (the error value predefined), let $\zeta_0 = \zeta_{new}$ and return Setp 3; else let $\zeta^*_k = \zeta_{new}$ and carry out Step 7;

Step 7. Let $k=k+1$, $\lambda_k = \lambda_{k-1} * \lambda_\Delta$, and return Step 2;

Step 8. Select the minimum value from the sequence of $\zeta^*_k$ as $\zeta^*$, and the corresponding $\lambda_k$ is saved as $\lambda$, then the process is over.

--------------------------------------------------------------------------

$R_{th,n}(\lambda, \zeta^*)$ not only offers stopping threshold of ST at each time $n$, but also gives rate threshold of the minimum average energy consumption per data transmitted. It controls the time that ST stops detecting. When ST discovers transmission rate at current time $n$ is equal to or greater than $R_{th,n}(\lambda, \zeta^*)$, it will stop detecting and start to transmit data; otherwise, it will continue detecting. If the total detection duration reaches the maximum duration $M \cdot t$, ST must send data. ST does channel detection and data transmission continuously in this policy, so as to reduce average energy consumption per unit data transmitted and increase average delivery success ratio.

## 5   Simulation Results and Analysis

In the simulation, we assume ST and RT have the same CDF of the channel conditions, and ST observe channel through periodic signal detection. According to [11], PDF of Rayleigh channel gain is $f_G(g) = g\sigma^{-2} \exp(-0.5g^2\sigma^{-2}), g \geq 0$. Where $\sigma^2$ is the correlation value of channel gain mean variance, and $g$ is channel gain. PDF of Rician channel gain is $f_G(g) = g\sigma^{-2} \exp(-0.5(g^2 + A^2)\sigma^{-2})I_0(gA\sigma^{-2}), g \geq 0$. Where $A$ is the peak value of main signal amplitude, and $I_0(\bullet)$ is the first class 0 order correction Bessel function. The parameter values in simulation are givens as follow. $W = 1[\text{MHZ}]$, $N_0 = 10^{-6}[\text{W/HZ}]$, $\sigma^2 = 1$, $g = 0 \sim 4$, $P = 100[\text{mW}]$, $A = 1$.

We compare our Energy Consumption Optimization Strategy for data transmission (ECOS) with other seven strategies in [5] using Matlab, and then analyze the results under different parameter values. Here are the seven strategies. (1) Deterministic Transmission Strategy (DTS). When ST waits until the maximum delay $D_m$, it starts to transmit data. (2) Random Transmission Strategy (RTS). During $D_m$, ST randomly selects one with the probability of $1/M$ to transmit data. (3) Probabilistic Transmission Strategy (PTS). If ST predicts the probability of a future transmission rate being greater than the current one is less than a given threshold, ST transmits data. Otherwise, it continues detecting. (4) Average Rate Transmission Strategy (ARTS). When the current transmission rate is greater than the mean value of past, ST transmits data. Otherwise, it continues detecting. (5) Optimal Transmission Strategy based on Secretary Problem (OTSSP). ST detects channel within 37 % of $D_m$ to obtain the maximum transmission rate $R_{c\text{-}max}$, then it continuously detects current transmission rate within the following 63 % of duration. It stops to transmit, if it finds a transmission rate greater than $R_{c\text{-}max}$ or detection duration reaches $D_m$. (6) Energy-Efficient Opportunistic Transmission Scheduler (E$^2$OTS): It includes E$^2$OTS-I (minimizing the expected energy consumption) and E$^2$OTS-II (minimizing the average energy consumption per unit time). When current transmission power is less than or equal to the corresponding optimal power threshold, it transmits data. Otherwise, it continues detecting.

### 5.1   Average Energy Consumption (AEC)

AEC reflects the energy consumed for each bit data transmitted, which includes $Pt$ and $E_D$. AEC comparison results are shown in Fig. 3. From Fig. 3, we can get AEC of our ECOS is the lowest. That is, the effect of energy saving is the best. ECOS obtains optimal rate threshold at each detection time through optimal stopping rule, so ST can accurately select the optimal energy-efficient time to transmit data in each round and improve energy efficiency. AEC of DTS, RTS are the largest, because they don't

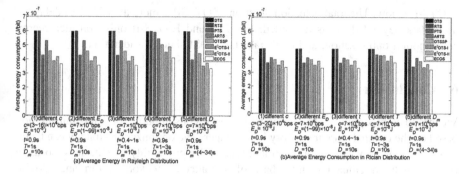

**Fig. 3.** Average Energy Consumption Comparisons

consider the energy factor. PTS, ARTS and OTSSP all select transmission time from the perspective of energy saving, so their AEC is far less than that of DTS and RTS. But they don't select the optimal energy efficiency time. Thus the effect of energy saving of those is not only far worse than that of ECOS, but also lower than that of $E^2OTS$. AEC of $E^2OTS$-I is lower than that of $E^2OTS$-II. Because $E^2OTS$-II, we consider minimize the AEC per unit time.

## 5.2    Average Delivery Success Ratio (ADSR)

ADSR is the ratio of the amount of data successfully transmitted to that generated by ST. ADSR comparison results are shown in Fig. 4. From Fig. 4, we get that ADSR of ECOS is larger. That is, the amount of data discarded is less. Because we design a constraint condition of finishing transmitting all data accumulated. The optimal transmission rate threshold of ECOS improves ADSR. However, ADSR of DTS is smallest. Because DTS selects the maximum delay time to transmit data, a considerable amount of data beyond delay is discarded. ADSR of RTS and PTS is related with the transmission rate distribution. ARTS selects transmission time through comparing the mean value of transmission rate in the past and transmission time selected is earlier. Thus the data has more opportunities to be transmitted. ADSR of OTSSP, $E^2OTS$-I and

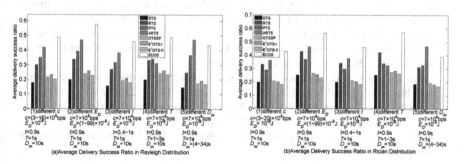

**Fig. 4.** Average Delivery Success Ratio Comparisons

$E^2$OTS-II is low. The total detection duration of OTSSP is more than 37 % of delay, so more data beyond delay is discarded. $E^2$OTS-I and $E^2$OTS-II only consider energy consumption optimization, and don't take the ADSR into consideration.

# 6 Conclusion

We propose an optimization strategy of energy consumption for data transmission based on the optimal stopping theory in this paper. The optimization strategy can better enhance the energy utilization ratio and reduce the probability of data loss, so as to optimize network efficiency on the basis of guaranteeing network performance. And it is a future research to improve energy efficiency and delivery success ratio when the data generation rate in link is variable.

**Acknowledgments.** This research is supported in part by the National Natural Science Foundation of China under Grant Nos. 61562006, 61262003, in part by the Natural Science Foundation of Guangxi Province under Grant No.2010GXNSFC013013.

# References

1. Lin, C., Tian, Y., Yao, M.: Green network and green evaluation: mechanism, modeling and evaluation. Chin. J. Comput. **34**(4), 593–612 (2011). (in Chinese)
2. Asadi, A., Mancuso, V.: A survey on opportunistic scheduling in wireless communications. IEEE Commun. Surv. Tutorials **15**(4), 1671–1688 (2013)
3. Garcia-Saavedra, A., Serrano, P., Banchs, A.: Energy-efficient optimization for distributed opportunistic scheduling. IEEE Commun. Lett. **18**(6), 1083–1086 (2014)
4. Poulakis, M.I., Panagopoulos, A.D., Constantinou, P.: Channel-aware opportunistic transmission scheduling for energy-efficient wireless links. IEEE Trans. Veh. Technol. **62**(1), 192–204 (2013)
5. Yan, Z.-J., Zhang, Z., Jiang, H., et al.: Optimal traffic scheduling in vehicular delay tolerant networks. IEEE Commun. Lett. **16**(1), 50–53 (2012)
6. Huang, L.-J., Jiang, H., Zhang, Z., et al.: Optimal traffic scheduling between roadside units in vehicular delay tolerant networks. IEEE Trans. Veh. Technol. **64**(3), 1079–1094 (2015)
7. Amin, O., Lampe, L.: Opportunistic Energy Efficient Cooperative Communication. IEEE Wirel. Commun. Lett. **1**(5), 412–415 (2012)
8. Zuo, J., Dong, C., Nguyen, H.V., et al.: Cross-layer aided energy-efficient opportunistic routing in ad hoc networks. IEEE Trans. Commun. **62**(2), 522–535 (2014)
9. Wang, G., Peng, Y., Feng, P., et al.: An energy consumption minimization routing scheme based on rate adaptation with QoS guarantee for the mobile environment. Comput. Netw. **74**, 48–57 (2014). doi:10.1016/j.comnet.2014.09.006
10. Chen, H., Baras, J.S.: Distributed opportunistic scheduling for wireless ad-hoc networks with block-fading model. IEEE J. Sel. Areas Commun. **31**(11), 2324–2337 (2013)
11. HayKin, S., Tie-Cheng, S., Ping-Ping, X., et al.: Communication System, 4. Publishing House of Electronics Industry, Beijing (2012). (in Chinese)
12. Ferguson, T.S.: Optimal Stopping and Applications, http://www.math.ucla.edu/~tom/Stopping/Contents.html. 2006

# Exploration of the Relationship Between Just-in-Time Compilation Policy and Number of Cores

Mingkai Huang[1,2], Xianhua Liu[1,2]([✉]), Tingyu Zhang[1,2], and Xu Cheng[1,2]

[1] Microprocessor Research & Development Center,
Peking University, Beijing 100871, China
[2] Engineering Research Center of Microprocessor & System, Peking University,
Ministry of Education, Beijing 100871, China
{huangmingkai,liuxianhua,zhangtingyu,chengxu}@mprc.pku.edu.cn

**Abstract.** Just-in-Time (JIT) compilation is a key technique for programs written in managed languages, such as Java and JavaScript. Traditionally, a conservative JIT compilation policy is used without impacting application threads too much on single-core machines. Nowadays, modern machines provide more and more processor cores, which are abundant computing resources. Modern virtual machines also have the ability to use an aggressive compilation policy, such as spawning multiple concurrent compiler threads, which is suitable to multicore situation. However, the suitable JIT compilation policy varies with the number of microprocessor cores. The goal of this work is to explore the relationship between the number of microprocessor cores on modern machines and the suitable JIT compilation policies that can enable existing as well as future VMs to realize better program performance.

In this work, we design novel experiments and implement new VM configurations to effectively control the compiler aggressiveness in the industry-standard Oracle HotSpot Java VM to achieve the goal. We notice that when single core is used, traditional foreground compilation with single compiler thread has better performance. As the number of cores increases, which makes more abundant computing resources available, background compilation with more compiler threads and smaller compilation threshold reaches better performance. After comparison between the foreground compilation and the background compilation, we propose a novel compilation policy, the throttling compilation, which stops interpretation when the compilation queue is too long. This policy combines the advantages of the foreground compilation and the background compilation, which gains better performance.

**Keywords:** Virtual machines · Dynamic compilation · Multicore · Java · OpenJDK

## 1 Introduction

Managed programming languages, such as Java [7] and JavaScript, are widely used in the internet era for their portability, network-mobility, and high

G. Wang et al. (Eds.): ICA3PP 2015, Part IV, LNCS 9531, pp. 293–307, 2015.
DOI: 10.1007/978-3-319-27140-8_21

software productivity. The programs written by them are distributed as platform-independent intermediate codes for a *virtual machine* (VM) architecture [19]. VMs usually employ either interpretation or Just-in-Time (JIT) to bridge the intermediate codes and the native ISA. The ability of JIT to create native code at runtime makes it a key technique to achieve high performance for VMs. JIT is a time-consuming task. However, once the native codes are generated, they can be reused many times. To reduce the JIT overheads, only those methods run enough times are selected to compile. Those are called *hot* methods. A *compilation threshold* decides which methods are hot. Considering the large JIT overheads, only conservative JIT compilation policy is used on traditional single-core machine.

Nowadays, much more opportunities appear to utilize aggressive JIT compilation policy to improve the performance of VMs [13]. That is the important trend in the microprocessor progress, i.e., more and more cores are integrated on one chip. Even a processor in a mobile phone may contain over four cores. Most of the time, there is not enough parallelism to feed so many cores, so the cores are often redundant. In order to improve the parallelism of VMs, researchers developed the strategy in which the interpretation continues after creating a compilation task. This strategy is called *background compilation*, opposite to the traditional *foreground compilation*, which stops interpretation during compilation. Later, researchers developed aggressive compilation policy spawning multiple concurrent compiler threads, which largely increases the parallelism of software running on multicore processors. At the same time, a smaller compilation threshold is employed so that more methods become *hot* sooner. However, as the number of processor cores varies, the compilation policy should be adjusted to achieve better performance.

The objective of this work is to investigate and recommend JIT compilation strategies to enable VMs to realize the best program performance on existing microprocessors. We progressively decrease the compilation threshold and increase the number of concurrent compiler threads when more numbers of microprocessor cores are used, and analyze their relationship to achieve better program performance.

This is the work to explore and evaluate these various compilation parameters and strategies as the number of utilized microprocessor cores varies. The major contributions of this research are:

- Thanks to the parallelism of JVM itself, utilizing more microprocessor cores significantly improves the performance of JVM. The configuration of threshold and thread number needs cooperation, considering the core number.
- On single-core machines, the traditional foreground compilation with a conservative compilation threshold reaches the best performance. However, the default compilation strategy is the background compilation, which lowers the performance of JVM.

- On multicore machines, background compilation is needed to supply parallelism. When there are more cores, more threads are needed to increase the parallelism of JVM to make use of these cores. When more threads are used, which increases the throughput of compilation, lower threshold is needed to supply more methods earlier.
- After comparison between the foreground compilation and the background compilation, we propose a novel compilation policy, the throttling compilation, which stops interpretation when the compilation queue is too long. This policy combines the advantages of both the foreground compilation and the background compilation, and has better performance.

The rest of the paper is organized as follows. In the next section, we present background information on existing JIT compilation policies. We describe our general experimental setup in Sect. 3. In Sect. 4, we present results that explore the most effective JIT compilation policies for different number of utilized microprocessor cores. After that, we propose the throttling compilation to combine the advantages of the foreground compilation and the background compilation in Sect. 5. In Sect. 6, we describe some related works. Finally, we present our conclusions in Sect. 7.

## 2   Background

JVM uses a platform-independent intermediate code, which is not compatible with the native ISA, so interpretation is usually adopted to run this code. The execution time distribution is illustrated in Fig. 1(a), in which the x-axis represents different methods, and the y-axis means the execution time per method. The methods are sorted by the execution time, and the total area shows the total execution time.

Interpretation is inefficient as it contains a lot of extra operations compared to native code, so Just-in-Time (JIT) compilation, which compiles the intermediate code to native code during execution, is introduced to improve the performance of JVM. The total execution cost includes the compilation cost and the native code execution cost. Though compilation is slow, it is one-run cost, which is less cost if the code runs many times. In contrast, if the code run only several times, the compilation is not afforded. Dynamic adaptive compilation (DAC) is presented to address this issue. It only compiles some hot methods, and interpret other cold methods, in which way to get a better total effect. The critical problem is how to decide the methods are hot. Theoretically speaking, if the compilation time plus the native code execution time is less than the interpretation time, it is profitable to compile this method, i.e., this method is *hot*. However, it is difficult to know the execution count before execute the method. Usually, JVM employs a simple prediction model that estimates that frequently executed current hot methods will also remain hot in the future. The method is sent for compilation if the respective method counters exceed a fixed threshold. The *ski-renting* principle is used to decide the threshold [15]. Following it, if a method

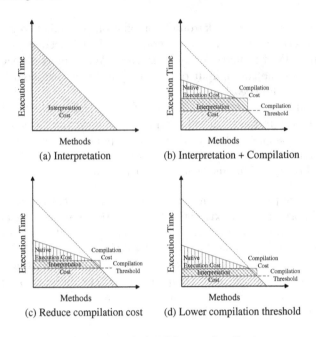

**Fig. 1.** A simplified JVM time distribution.

has already run $n$ count, it is predicted to run $n$ count later. If the successor $n$ count makes compilation profitable, the method should be compiled. Hence, the $n$ count, which makes compilation time plus the native code execution time equal to the interpretation time, is used as the threshold deciding which method is hot. This means, after $n$ count interpretation, the method is selected to compile.

When compiling a method, the interpretation can be stopped or keep going. Stopping, which is called foreground compilation, makes the method execution take more count in native mode, so this is more efficient. In contrast, keeping going, which is called background compilation, makes the interpretation and compilation concurrent. While interpretation keeps going, maybe more methods are judged to be hot, so it makes chance to concurrently compile several methods using separate compiler threads, which further increase the parallelism of JVM. Today multicore microprocessor is widely used, which need parallel software to fully utilize, so background compilation, which makes JVM running in parallel even if the application is serial, is default setting of JVM. The execution time distribution of background compilation is showed in Fig. 1(b), in which interpretation and compilation is overlapped for some time. We can see that the total execution time is reduced by DAC.

With the technique evolution, more and more cores are integrated on one microprocessor chip, so more concurrent compilation threads can be utilized to exploit these additional computing resources as the compilation of different methods is highly parallel. This situation is similar to reduce the compilation cost, which is showed in Fig. 1(c). In this figure, not only the compilation cost is reduced, but also the interpretation time is reduced by running in native mode earlier, so the total execution time is significantly reduced. While the compilation cost is reduced, the corresponding threshold $n$ also need to decrease, which is showed in Fig. 1(d). Hence, the total execution time is further reduced.

Our focus in this paper is to explore the relationship between the compilation policy and the number of available microprocessor cores, which is simply described above. The results guide better utilizing the parallelism of JVM itself to exploit the parallelism supplied by multicore for improving the performance of JVM.

## 3    Experimental Framework

Our research is performed using Oracle's OpenJDK/HotSpot Java virtual machine (64-bit, version 1.6.0_20) [16]. The HotSpot VM uses interpretation at program startup. It then employs a counter-based profiling mechanism and uses the sum of a method's *invocation* and loop *back-edge* counters to detect and promote hot methods for compilation. We call the sum of these counters the *execution count* of the method. Methods are determined to be hot if the corresponding method execution count exceeds a fixed threshold. The HotSpot VM uses separate threads to compile methods. The threads running Java application can be configured to run concurrently with the compiler threads, a.k.a. background compilation. The HotSpot VM allows the creation of an arbitrary number of compiler threads, as specified on the command line. This 64-bit Java VM makes use of a *server compiler* which applies an aggressive optimization strategy to maximize performance benefits for long running applications. Background compilation is used, unless specified otherwise. The HotSpot server VM uses a default setting of 2 compiler threads and 10 K as the compilation threshold.

Our experiments were conducted using all the benchmarks from DaCapo-9.12-bach [2] using default input. In order to limit possible sources of variation in our experiments, we set the number of application threads to 1 whenever possible (using the option -t 1).

All our experiments were performed on a machine with two 2.40 GHz Intel Xeon E5620 CPU (quad-core, 64-bit, x64) and 32 GB 1333 MHz DDR3 SDRAM, running Red Hat Enterprise Linux 6 as the operating system.

Each benchmark is run in isolation to prevent interference from other user programs. In order to account for inherent timing variations during the benchmark runs, all the performance results report the median over 5 runs (after 1 warmup run) for each benchmark.

We describe the four experimental parameters to explore the Java VM compilation policy and the way to adjust them below:

**Core Number:** Number of utilized microprocessor cores. This is adjusted by the Linux API *sched_setaffinity*, which determines the set of CPUs on which it is eligible to run.

**Background Compilation:** A thread requesting compilation is not blocked during compilation. This is controlled by the Java command line option -*XX:BackgroundCompilation*.

**Thread Number:** Number of compiler threads to run. This is controlled by the Java command line option -*XX:CICompilerCount*.

**Compilation Threshold:** Number of interpreted method invocations before (re-)compiling. This is controlled by the Java command line option -*XX: CompileThreshold*.

The remainder of this paper explores and explains the impact of different JIT compilation strategies on modern architectures using the HotSpot server VM.

## 4    Experimental Results

We change the four parameters, core number, background compilation, thread number and compilation threshold, to evaluate the relationship between the core number and the compilation policy. The settings of core number include 1, 2, 4, 8. The thread number is from 1 to 4. The compilation threshold ranges from 1 K to 20K, with step 1K. The results are presented in Fig. 2. The speedup is computed based on the compilation policy using 1 compiler thread and using 1 K as the compilation threshold while utilizing only one processor core, which we call base, and the geomean of all benchmarks' speedup is illustrated. In Fig. 2, (a) to (d) is evaluated using 1, 2, 4, 8 cores correspondingly, and (e) is formed by concatenating the lines from (a) to (d) one-by-one to compare all the compilation policies together. The default settings are denoted by red, and the best settings are denoted by green.

### 4.1    Single-Core Compilation Policy

On single-core machine, the traditional compilation strategy is foreground compilation, in which way the interpretation is stopped when a method is sent to compile. The results in Fig. 2(a) show the relative performance of foreground compilation with varied compilation threshold. Increasing the compilation threshold from 1 K to 8K improve the performance of JVM. The configuration with threshold 8 K reaches the best performance, which is 2.59 times of the baseline. The large threshold shows that only a small portion of all methods, which execute much frequently, are valuable to compile. The reason is that the compilation cost of the server compiler is expensive. The interpretation time of other methods may be less than the compilation time of them. Increasing the threshold larger than 8 K slightly lower the performance, as it delays sending valuable methods to compilation.

The background compilation is the default setting of JVM to suit the multicore era. We also evaluate whether the background compilation is suitable to the single-core machine, which is showed in Fig. 2(a). We adjust the compiler thread number and compilation threshold to get different configurations. The results show that background compilation lower the performance of JVM, so it is not suitable to the single-core machine. We think the worse performance of background compilation comes from the ineffective interpretation, i.e., the execution after the method is detected hot is more effective in native code than

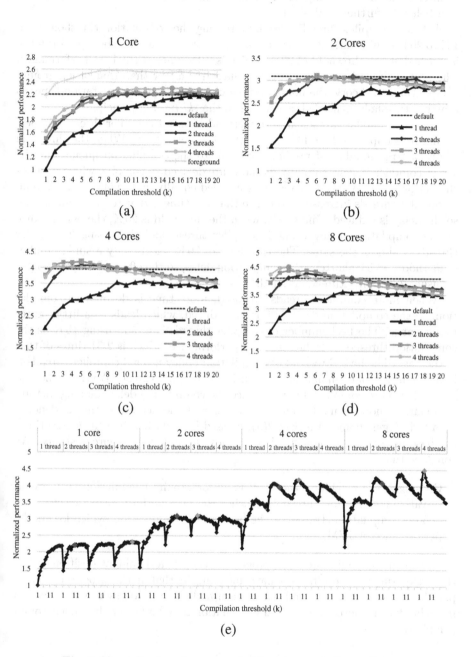

**Fig. 2.** Normalized performance of different compilation policies.

in interpretation. We compare different configurations of background compilation below to further analysis it.

When 1 compiler thread is used, increasing the compilation threshold from 1 K to 20 K significantly improve the performance of JVM. The best performance is reached at the threshold of 20 K, which is 2.18 times of the base performance. The best evaluated threshold in this situation is larger than that of foreground compilation. In theory, the non-stop policy increases the interpretation time, so a higher threshold is needed, according to the *ski-renting* principle.

When 2 compiler threads are used instead of only 1 compiler thread, the performance is improved to 1.43 times at the threshold of 1 K. When the threshold is 1 K, a large number of methods are sent to the compilation queue, but the server compiler is slow, so many methods are delayed to compile, which impacts the performance. As the threads are scheduled equally by the operating system, 2 compiler threads increase the chance that the time is devoted to compilation, so the delay is reduced. Differently, when the threshold is 20 K, the performance of the compilation policy using 1 compiler thread and that using 2 compiler threads is almost the same. The threshold of 20 K selects only a small number of methods, which shortens the compilation delay, so the effect of reducing delay by using 2 compiler threads is small.

When more compiler threads are used, more time is devoted to compilation, so the compilation delay is further reduced, which leads to a little better performance. The best number of compiler threads is 4, and using 15 K as the compilation threshold reaches the best performance, which is 2.31 times of that of the base. The best threshold of compilation policy using 4 compiler threads is lower than that of compilation policy using 1 compiler thread. We think the reason is that more compiler threads reduce the compilation delay, making method compilation more valuable. The performance of the default setting is denoted by a red bigger diamond in Fig. 2(a), crossed by a dashed line. It is 2.20 times the base performance, showing that it is less suitable to this circumstance. We conclude that:

- On single-core machines, the traditional foreground compilation with a conservative compilation threshold reaches the best performance. However, the default compilation strategy is the background compilation, which lowers the performance of JVM.

Although the multicore microprocessor occupies a dominant position today, these experimental results also have meaning in that if the program itself is parallel or there are other applications occupy the microprocessor, which leads to no redundant resource, foreground compilation may be better than background compilation.

### 4.2   Multicore Compilation Policy

The experimental results of running JVM utilizing 2, 4, and 8 cores are showed in Fig. 2(b), (c) and (d). We analysis the result of using 2 cores first. When only

1 compiler thread is used, the performance improves as the compilation threshold rising from 1 K to 17 K, at which 2.89 times performance is reached. After that, the performance slightly degrades. The best threshold 17 K is lower than the best threshold 20 K when using single-core. We think that the additional free core improves the throughput of the compiler thread and reduce the compilation delay, so as to lower the best threshold, which is similar to the comparison between the compilation policy of using 1 compiler thread and the compilation policy of using 2 compiler threads when utilizing single-core.

Similar to using single-core, more compiler threads and lower compilation threshold further improves the performance. The best 3.11 times performance is reached at using 3 compiler threads and using 6 K as the compilation threshold. This time, the best performance is reached when not using the most compiler threads. Maybe the free core significantly improve the throughput of compiler and reduce the compilation delay, so no more compiler threads are needed.

Look through Fig. 2(a), (b), (c) and (d), it is clearly that the peak value moves leftwards. When utilizing 4 cores, the configuration using 3 compiler threads and threshold 5 K reaches the best 4.19 times base performance. When utilizing 8 cores, the setting utilizing 4 compiler threads and threshold 3 K reaches the best 4.49 times base performance. As there are more cores devoted to compilation, more methods are valuable to compile. This trend is not clear for the compilation policy using only 1 compiler thread, as 1 compiler thread cannot utilize more cores. We conclude that:

– On multicore machines, background compilation is needed to supply parallelism. When there are more cores, more threads are needed to increase the parallelism of JVM to make use of these cores. When more threads are used, which increases the throughput of compilation, lower threshold is needed to supply more methods earlier.

### 4.3   Composite Results

We concatenate the lines in Fig. 2(a), (b), (c) and (d) forming (e) to show the total performance variation. Clearly, when the utilized number of microprocessor cores increases, the performance dramatically improves. This is owing to the parallel compilation ability of OpenJDK. Table 1 shows the best configurations of different core numbers and the corresponding performance improvement compared to default configuration. It is clearly that as the available core number increases, slightly more compilation threads and lower compilation threshold are needed. The default settings is somehow conservative. The performance of default setting is nearest to that of the peak setting while utilizing 2 cores, which is 3.09 times against 3.11 times, probably as the compilation thread number is equal to the core number. As more cores are available, the performance gap between the best configuration and the default configuration enlarges. The choice of such conservative setting may be owing to that the application scenario in the designer's thought is several applications running at the same time. Hence, if the load of microprocessor is low, more aggressive compilation policy can be adopted to improve the JVM's performance. We conclude that:

- Thanks to the parallelism of JVM itself, utilizing more microprocessor cores significantly improves the performance of JVM. The setting of threshold and thread number needs cooperate, considering the core number.

**Table 1.** The best configurations of different core numbers

| Core number | 2 cores | 4 cores | 8 cores |
|---|---|---|---|
| Number of compilation thread | 3 | 3 | 4 |
| Compilation threshold | 6 K | 5 K | 3 K |
| Performance improvement | 1.64 % | 23.08 % | 39.93 % |

## 5   Throttling Compilation

The comparison results in previous section show that the effectiveness of the foreground compilation is higher than that of the background compilation, i.e., the foreground compilation executes more time in native code than the background compilation, but the parallelism of the foreground compilation is lower than that of the background compilation. If combining the foreground compilation and background compilation, the effectiveness and parallelism may be both reached.

The parallelism comes from the compilation tasks which can be done by the compiler threads in parallel. The effectiveness comes from stopping the ineffective interpretation. When there are redundant cores, the parallelism is more important. When the parallelism is enough to feed the cores, effectiveness makes sense. Hence, we propose stopping interpretation when the compilation queue is too long based on background compilation, which we call throttling compilation.

As throttling compilation is based on background compilation, it can make use of parallel compiler threads to utilize the redundant cores. When the compilation queue is not long, throttling compilation acts the same as background compilation, i.e., continues to interpret to discover more compilation tasks. However, when the compilation queue becomes longer than a threshold, the parallelism is enough, so throttling compilation stops the ineffective interpretation. In this way, throttling compilation gains better performance than background compilation.

We expect the performance of the throttling compilation is about the maximum of that of the foreground compilation and the background compilation. We empirically choose the throttling threshold to be 2 × the number of compiler threads. We evaluate the three compilation policy using 2 processor cores, 2 compilation threads and 1 application thread, with the best compilation threshold in the range 1 K to 10 K, resulting Fig. 3(a). The performance is normalized to the configuration using the background compilation at compilation threshold 10 K, which is default setting, and using the same number of cores, compilation threads and application threads. Considering the performance of the throttling compilation may be about the maximum of that of the other two policies, we place it in between in the figure. The result obeys our expectation. For most of the benchmarks, the performance of the background compilation is better, and the performance of the throttling compilation is similar to the background compilation. The foreground compilation only outperforms the background compilation for *pmd*, and the performance of the throttling compilation is similar to the foreground compilation this time. Thanks to the 37.94 % performance improvement for *pmd*, the throttling compilation outperforms the background compilation 1.62 % on average.

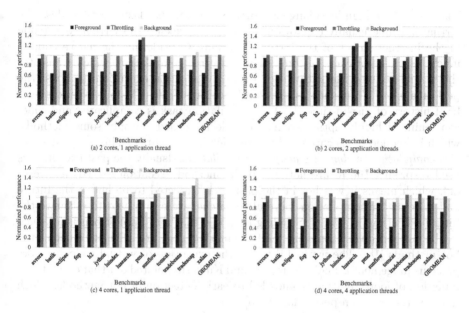

**Fig. 3.** Performance of throttling compilation.

In previous sections, we discuss that when the pressure of application is high, the performance of the foreground compilation may be better, so we increase the number of application threads to equal to the number of processor cores, which is 2, resulting Fig. 3(b). The baseline configuration is using 2 application threads too. This time, the foreground compilation outperforms the background compilation for more benchmarks, so does the throttling compilation. The throttling compilation outperforms the background compilation 4.48 % on average.

We also evaluate the three compilation policy using 4 processor cores, resulting Fig. 3(c) and (d). The results in Fig. 3(c) are evaluated using 1 application thread. The throttling compilation lower the performance by 0.64 % than the background compilation on average, as there are more free resources, which lower the need to stop interpretation. As showed in Fig. 3(d), the throttling compilation improve the performance by 3.13 % than the background compilation on average using 4 application threads, because of more application pressure.

As we run only one benchmark at a time, the redundant core left for compilation usually keeps stable. In reality, there are several applications run at
the same time, the redundant core varies. We will consider using CPU utilization information to adjust the number of compiler threads and the compilation
threshold in the future. The throttling compilation is used to adjust the balance
between the interpreter threads and the compiler threads. It can cooperate with
such adjustment, and needs no concern about the redundant core variation.

# 6    Related Work

The research on high-level language virtual machines has lasted for decades. The
virtual machine usually employs interpreters to execute the virtual code (code
in the instruction set of the virtual machine). Considering the native code is
much faster, researchers introduced just-in-time compilation, which translates
the virtual code to the native code during application execution, to boost the
performance of VMs, such as the ParcPlace SmallTalk VM [5]. Aycock gave a
brief history of just-in-time [1]. The compilation task is complicated and time-
consuming if highly optimized native code is needed, so only some methods,
which is frequently executed or *hot*, are selected to compile. This is called *selective compilation* or *dynamic adaptive compilation*. Usually the past execution is
used to predict the future hotness. If the method execution exceeds a threshold, which means it was hot in the past, it is expected to be hot in the future
and selected for compilation. Several researches were proposed to estimate the
future execution [14,15,18]. Schilling proposed that the simplest heuristics, such
as the method invocation count and the method size, are efficient to detect the
hot methods [18]. The work [14] traces the execution of virtual code, so more
precious judgement is made. Namjoshi and Kulkarni pointed out that early determination of loop iteration bounds led to early detection of hot methods, which
improve the program performance [15].

Previous works are developed considering single-core machine. As more and
more cores are integrated in a single processor chip, researchers started to pay
attention to increasing the parallelism of JIT for multicore machines, such as
background compilation [8,11,20] and parallel compilation [3,9]. Krintz et al.
investigated the impact of background compilation in a separated thread to
reduce the overhead of dynamic compilation [11]. This technique uses a single
compiler thread and employs offline profiling to determine and prioritize hot
methods to compile. While the work [11] is for Java, Ha et al. [8] introduced
background compilation to JavaScript. Unnikrishnan et al. overlap the next code
fragment compilation and the current code fragment execution [20]. Prior work
by Bohm et al. explored the issue of parallel JIT compilation with a priority
queue based dynamic work scheduling strategy in the context of their dynamic
binary translator [3]. Hong et al. uses a separate thread to optimize code, which
is concurrent with the original dynamic binary translator [9]. Existing JVMs,
such as Oracle's HotSpot server VM [16], support background compilation and
multiple compiler threads but do not present any discussions on ideal compilation
strategies for multicore machines.

As the compilation policy becomes complex, researchers investigated the adjustment of the compilation policy [6, 10, 12, 13]. Kulkarni et al. explored increasing the priority of JIT compilation thread and saw obvious performance improvement [12]. Kulkarni explored some aspects of the impact of varying the aggressiveness of dynamic compilation on modern machines for JVMs with multiple compiler threads [13]. Then Jantz and Kulkarni extended these earlier works by investigating the effects on multitiered compiler and the effects of compilation task order [10]. This paper further extends earlier works by exploring compilation policy variation when the number of utilized microprocessor cores varies on multicore machines and comparing background compilation using several concurrent compiler threads with traditional foreground compilation on single-core machines, and inspired by traditional foreground compilation, proposing throttling compilation for multicore machines. Ding et al. explored the potential of optimizing compilation task order and saw huge performance improvement potential [6].

The work [4] and [17] analyzed different mapping between JVM and asymmetric multicore processor (AMP) to exploit the asymmetric of JVM service threads, but they did not discuss the compilation policy.

# 7 Conclusion

Nowadays, there are more and more cores integrated on a single microprocessor chip. While running serial application, the JVM itself has parallelism, so the more cores can be utilized to boost the performance of JVM. In this paper, we explore the suitable compilation policy as the number of cores increases to reach better performance. We conclude that when only one core is utilized, the traditional foreground compilation is more efficient, and when more cores are utilized, a few compiler threads and smaller compilation threshold is better. We also propose a novel compilation policy, the throttling compilation, which stops interpretation when the compilation queue is too long. This policy combines the advantages of both the foreground compilation and the background compilation, and has better performance.

The availability of free resource depends not only on the number of processor cores, but also on the running workload, so it is better to adjust the compilation policy according to the processor utilization rate dynamically. We will explore this direction in the future. As there will be more and more cores in the future, we can investigate more complicated strategy to optimize the generated native code in our future work.

**Acknowledgments.** We would like to thank the anonymous reviewers for their constructive feedback. This work was supported by the National Science and Technology Major Project of China under grant 2009ZX01029-001-002 and National Science Fund of China under grant 6130004.

# References

1. Aycock, J.: A brief history of just-in-time. ACM Comput. Surv. **35**(2), 97–113 (2003)
2. Blackburn, S.M., Garner, R., Hoffmann, C., Khang, A.M., McKinley, K.S., Bentzur, R., Diwan, A., Feinberg, D., Frampton, D., Guyer, S.Z., Hirzel, M., Hosking, A., Jump, M., Lee, H., Moss, J.E.B., Phansalkar, A., Stefanovic, D., van Drunen, T., von Dincklage, D., Wiedermann, B.: The dacapo benchmarks: Java benchmarking development and analysis. In: Proceedings of the 21st Annual ACM SIGPLAN Conference on Object-Oriented Programming, Systems, Languages and Applications OOPSLA 2006, pp. 169–190. ACM, New York (2006)
3. Bohm, I., von Koch, T.J.E., Kyle, S.C., Franke, B., Topham, N.: Generalized just-in-time trace compilation using a parallel task farm in a dynamic binary translator. In: Proceedings of the 32nd ACM SIGPLAN Conference on Programming Language Design and Implementation PLDI 2011, pp. 74–85. ACM, New York (2011)
4. Cao, T., Blackburn, S.M., Gao, T., McKinley, K.S.: The yin and yang of power and performance for asymmetric hardware and managed software. In: Proceedings of the 39th Annual International Symposium on Computer Architecture ISCA 2012, pp. 225–236. ACM, New York (2012)
5. Deutsch, L.P., Schiffman, A.M.: Efficient implementation of the smalltalk-80 system. In: Proceedings of the 11th ACM SIGACT-SIGPLAN Symposium on Principles of Programming Languages POPL 1984, pp. 297–302. ACM, New York (1984)
6. Ding, Y., Zhou, M., Zhao, Z., Eisenstat, S., Shen, X.: Finding the limit: examining the potential and complexity of compilation scheduling for JIT-based runtime systems. In: Proceedings of the 19th International Conference on Architectural Support for Programming Languages and Operating Systems ASPLOS 2014, pp. 607–622. ACM, New York (2014)
7. Gosling, J., Joy, B., Steele, G., Bracha, G.: Java(TM) Language Specification. Addison-Wesley Professional, Reading (2005)
8. Ha, J., Haghighat, M.R., Cong, S., McKinley, K.S.: A concurrent trace-based just-in-time compiler for single-threaded javascript. In: Proceedings of the Workshop on Parallel Execution of Sequential Programs on Multicore Architectures PESPMA 2009 (2009)
9. Hong, D.Y., Hsu, C.C., Yew, P.C., Wu, J.J., Hsu, W.C., Liu, P., Wang, C.M., Chung, Y.C.: HQEMU: a multi-threaded and retargetable dynamic binary translator on multicores. In: Proceedings of the 10th International Symposium on Code Generation and Optimization CGO 2012, pp. 104–113. ACM, New York (2012)
10. Jantz, M.R., Kulkarni, P.A.: Exploring single and multilevel JIT compilation policy for modern machines. ACM Trans. Archit. Code Optim. **10**(4), 22:1–22:29 (2013)
11. Krintz, C., Grove, D., Sarkar, V., Calder, B.: Reducing the overhead of dynamic compilation. Softw. Pract. Experience **31**(8), 717–738 (2001)
12. Kulkarni, P., Arnold, M., Hind, M.: Dynamic compilation: the benefits of early investing. In: Proceedings of the 3rd International Conference on Virtual Execution Environments VEE 2007, pp. 94–104. ACM, New York (2007)
13. Kulkarni, P.A.: JIT compilation policy for modern machines. In: Proceedings of the 2011 ACM International Conference on Object-Oriented Programming, Systems, Languages and Applications OOPSLA 2011, pp. 773–788. ACM, New York (2011)

14. Lee, S.W., Moon, S.M., Kim, S.M.: Enhanced hot spot detection heuristics for embedded java just-in-time compilers. In: Proceedings of the 2008 ACM SIGPLAN-SIGBED Conference on Languages, Compilers, and Tools for Embedded Systems LCTES 2008, pp. 13–22. ACM, New York, NY, USA (2008)
15. Namjoshi, M.A., Kulkarni, P.A.: Novel online profiling for virtual machines. In: Proceedings of the 6th ACM SIGPLAN/SIGOPS International Conference on Virtual Execution Environments VEE 2010, pp. 133–144. ACM, New York (2010)
16. Paleczny, M., Vick, C., Click, C.: The java hotspot(TM) server compiler. In: Proceedings of the Java(TM) Virtual Machine Research and Technology Symposium JVM 2001, pp. 1–12. USENIX Association, Berkeley (2001)
17. Sartor, J.B., Eeckhout, L.: Exploring multi-threaded java application performance on multicore hardware. In: Proceedings of the ACM International Conference on Object-Oriented Programming, Systems, Languages and Applications OOPSLA 2012, pp. 281–296. ACM, New York (2012)
18. Schilling, J.L.: The simplest heuristics may be the best in java JIT compilers. SIGPLAN Not. **38**(2), 36–46 (2003)
19. Smith, J.E., Nair, R.: Virtual machines: versatile platforms for systems and processes. Morgan Kaufmann, San Francisco (2005)
20. Unnikrishnan, P., Kandemir, M., Li, F.: Reducing dynamic compilation overhead by overlapping compilation and execution. In: Proceedings of the 2006 Asia and South Pacific Design Automation Conference ASP-DAC 2006, pp. 929–934. IEEE Press, Piscataway (2006)

# CSAP: A Performance Predictor for Climate Simulation Applications on Intel CPUs

Ruizhe Li[1]([✉]), Li Liu[2], Cheng Zhang[1], and Guangwen Yang[1,2]([✉])

[1] Department of Computer Science and Technology,
Tsinghua University, Beijing 100084, China
{lrz04,zhang-cheng09}@mails.tsinghua.edu.cn, ygw@tsinghua.edu.cn
[2] Center for Earth System Science (CESS),
Tsinghua University, Beijing 100084, China
liuli-cess@mail.tsinghua.edu.cn

**Abstract.** The development of climate simulation applications highly depends on high-performance computers. A fundamental problem in constructing a high-performance computer is how to select the processors. A straightforward solution is to use a state-of-the-art processor version available from the market. However, this approach is not economical for climate simulation applications.

To pick out a suitable processor version, we propose to predict the performances of climate simulation applications on various processor versions, and design and develop a new cross-architecture performance predictor CSAP (Climate Simulation Applications performance Predictor), based on the performance characteristics of climate simulation applications. Our experimental evaluation shows that CSAP can predict the performances of climate simulation applications on various Intel CPU versions with high accuracy and low overhead.

**Keywords:** Climate simulation applications · High-performance computers · Cross-architecture performance prediction · Intel CPUs · CSAP

## 1 Introduction

Numerical simulation models play a critical role in understanding or predicting the past, present, and future climate. A number of numerical models have been developed for simulating the components of the climate system, including atmosphere models, ocean models, land surface models, sea ice models, wave models, etc. There are also coupled models, such as climate system models (CSMs) and earth system models (ESMs), each of which consists of several component models.

The numerical models has been improved substantially under the rapid development of science and technology. Many important aspects of the climate system can be successfully captured by state-of-the-art models, but uncertainties remain an important issue. These uncertainties arise in part due to limitations in the understanding of physical processes, and in part due to the relatively low

© Springer International Publishing Switzerland 2015
G. Wang et al. (Eds.): ICA3PP 2015, Part IV, LNCS 9531, pp. 308–328, 2015.
DOI: 10.1007/978-3-319-27140-8_22

**Table 1.** Information of four Intel Xeon CPU versions that are available in the market currently. The price of each CPU version was obtained from amazon.com on June 2, 2014.

| CPU version | E5-2697 v2 | E5-2650 | X5670 | E5520 |
|---|---|---|---|---|
| Peak computation performance (GFLOPs) | 518.40 | 256.00 | 140.64 | 72.64 |
| Perk memory bandwidth (GB/s) | 59.7 | 51.2 | 32.0 | 25.6 |
| Nuber of cores | 12 | 8 | 6 | 4 |
| Width of SIMD | 256 | 256 | 128 | 128 |
| Release date | Sep, 2013 | Mar, 2012 | Mar, 2010 | Mar 2009 |
| Price (USD) | 2,718 | 1,1169 | 400 | 94 |
| Peak computing performance per price (GFLOPs/USD) | 0.191 | 0.219 | 0.352 | 0.772 |
| Peak memory bandwidth per price (GB/s/USD) | 0.0220 | 0.0438 | 0.0800 | 0.2720 |

resolution of the models. The refinement of model resolutions results in rapid increase in computation amount. The peak computing performance of modern high-performance computers almost doubles every year due to the rapid development of processors, which enables models to achieve higher and higher resolutions. Now high-performance computers with a large amount of processor cores play a critical role in climate simulations. To achieve high-resolution climate simulations, scientists have to buy or hire expensive high-performance computers. On the other hand, to construct a public high-performance computer, climate simulation applications are significant benchmarks.

A fundamental question for constructing a high-performance computer is how to select the processors. To construct public high-performance computers, one popular strategy is to use the state-of-the-art processors. For example, Tianhe-2, which was announced as the fastest supercomputer in the world by TOP500 [1] from June 2013 to November 2014, contains 32,000 Intel Xeon E5-2692 12-core CPUs. This version of CPU was state-of-the-art in the middle of 2013. However, to construct a high-performance computer specifically for climate simulation applications, it is not economical to use the state-of-the-art processors due to at least three reasons. First, compared to previous processors, the state-of-the-art processors are always much more expensive without significant boost of the peak performance. For example, Table 1 lists out the information of four versions of the Intel CPU available in the market now. Peak computational performance and memory bandwidth are two important measurements of CPU. When normalizing them to per price, we can find that the older CPU versions achieve

**Table 2.** Simulation speed per price of four climate simulation applications on the four CPU versions in Table 1.

| CPU version | Simulation speed per price(SYPD/1000USD) (SYPD means simulation year per day) | | | |
| | CAM-SE ne30np4 | CAM-FV 0.9°x1.25° | GAMIL 1°x1° | CoLM 1°x1° |
| --- | --- | --- | --- | --- |
| E5-2697 v2 | 0.0632 | 0.1147 | 0.1201 | 6.6315 |
| E5-2650 | 0.0833 | 0.1361 | 0.2012 | 6.9842 |
| X5670 | 0.1968 | 0.3521 | 0.4769 | 19.8338 |
| E5520 | 0.5340 | 0.8979 | 1.2261 | 48.7234 |

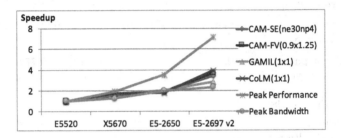

**Fig. 1.** Simulation speed of four climate model versions (CAM-FV, CAM-SE, GAMIL and CoLM) when varying the CPU versions in Table 1 from the older to the newer. The simulation speed of each model version is normalized to the Intel Xeon E5520.

higher normalized performance (the 8th and 9th column in Table 1). Second, the simulation speed of the climate models does not keep linear increase with the peak performance of processors. For example, Fig. 1 shows the simulation speed of three atmosphere model versions (CAM-FV [2], CAM-SE [3], and GAMIL [4]) and one land surface model version (CoLM [5]) on the CPU versions in Table 1. Generally, each climate model achieves a higher simulation speed on a newer CPU version. However, the increment of simulation speed is much slower than the boost of peak computing performance or peak memory bandwidth. Moreover, when normalizing the simulation speed to per price, each climate model achieves much higher normalized simulation speed on an older CPU version, as shown in Table 2. Third, different climate models have different sensitivities to the critical factors in processor architecture design, e.g., processor frequency, width of vector processing, number of cores, on-chip cache size and off-chip memory bandwidth. As shown in Fig. 1, different climate models achieve different speedups when varying the CPU version from the older to the newer. The simulation speed of CoLM is only slightly improved when upgrading the CPU version from the Intel Xeon X5670 to the Intel Xeon E5-2650.

To pick out a suitable candidate of processors for constructing a high-performance computer specifically for climate simulation applications, the application performance on each available processor version needs to be known. A straightforward solution is to directly run the applications on all processor versions available in the market. This solution is impractical because it requires users to buy or hire a lot of processors (for example, currently there are more than 100 Intel CPU versions available in the market). Moreover, accelerators such as GPGPU, Intel Xeon Phi and FPGA are also candidate processors.

A much more practical approach is to use a cross-architecture performance predictor to predict the application performance on various processor versions without buying or hiring them. In this paper, we carefully study the performance characteristics of climate simulation applications and then propose a new tool named CSAP (Climate Simulation Applications performance Predictor) for such a purpose. We take the Intel CPU versions as the first step because Intel CPUs are most widely used for climate simulations, and will extend CSAP to other kinds of processors in near future. The evaluations with real climate simulation applications and a set of CPU versions demonstrate that CSAP can achieve accurate cross-architecture performance prediction of climate simulation applications with low overheads.

The rest of this paper is organized as follows. Section 2 briefly introduces related works. Section 3 analyzes the performance characteristics of climate simulation applications. Section 4 details CSAP. Section 5 evaluates the overheads and accuracy of CSAP. We conclude this paper in Sect. 6.

## 2  Related Work

Several existing performance predictors can be used for cross-architecture performance prediction of applications.

Marin et al. [6] aim to predict the cross-architecture performance of scientific applications through profiling the reuse distances of memory accesses. Procedures for tracing the memory accesses are instrumented into the executable when running an application. After analyzing the memory reuse distances, the execution time of an application can be predicted through simulating the cache hits and misses when accessing the cache hierarchies. One dramatic drawback of this approach is that significant overheads are observed. The instrumented programs for tracing memory accesses can dramatically slow down the application execution for hundreds even thousands of times, and the size of the memory access trace can be very large (i.e., at a terabyte level). Moreover, this approach is infeasible for climate simulation applications because the computing performance of numerical models for earth science is insensitive to the cache hierarchies on modern CPUs (please refer to Sect. 3.2 for details).

Sadjadi et al. [7] and Shimizu et al. [8] aim to predict the cross-architecture performance of a specific application with a fitting function of several performance factors, i.e., processor frequency, cache size, memory size, disk I/O speed and number of processes. A number of test runs on various computer platforms with different performance factors are required for generating such a fitting function. The accuracy of the prediction highly depends on the selection of performance factors, the form of the fitting function, the diversity of the computer platforms in performance factors, and the number of the test runs. The evaluation results show that, for some applications, the prediction accuracy is less than 80%. For higher prediction accuracy, more computer platforms and test runs are required, which is inconvenient and will introduce higher overheads

Yang et al. [9] aim to predict the cross-architecture performance of a specific application according to a partial execution. To predict the computing performance on a target hardware platform A according to another hardware platform B, the first step is to run the application completely on the platform B, to draw a relationship between the partial execution and the whole execution. After obtaining the time of the partial execution on the platform A, the predicted computing performance on the platform A can be calculated according to the above relationship. Although this approach can achieve high prediction accuracy with low overheads, it requires the target hardware platform to be available for the partial execution, which is infeasible for our target in this paper.

Petit et al. [10] aim to predict the cross-architecture performance of various applications according to a database of microbenchmarks with various performance characteristics. To construct such a database, a number of microbenchmarks need to be generated and to be run on all target hardware platforms. To predict the computing performance of an application on a target hardware platform, the application will be divided into a number of small segments, each of which is mapped to a microbenchmark with similar performance characteristics in the database. This approach is infeasible for our target in this paper, because it requires the target hardware platform available for running all microbenchmarks in the database.

To achieve low-overhead and accurate cross-architecture performance prediction of climate simulation applications when target processor versions are unavailable, in this work, we develop a new tool CSAP based on the performance characteristics of climate simulation applications.

## 3    Performance Characteristics of Climate Simulation Applications

The architecture of modern CPUs becomes more and more complicated so that an increasing number of performance factors can impact the performance of applications. To develop an efficient performance prediction tool, the performance factors that are trivial to the application performance can be neglected. We therefore conduct a performance characterization of climate simulation applications to find out sensitive performance factors before designing CSAP. The sequential performance of applications is generally determined by the computing performance and memory performance. Almost all climate simulation applications are parallel applications with a number of processes, threads or the hybrid. For the parallel performance, load imbalance and communication overhead (or synchronization overhead) between multiple processes (or threads) needs to be concerned. As this work only focuses on the application performance intra a computing node, the communication overhead (or synchronization overhead) can be neglected. In the following context of this section, we use real climate simulation applications as benchmarks to characterize the memory performance, computing performance and load imbalance.

**Table 3.** Detailed setups of benchmark applications.

| Application | Version | Resolution/grid | Simulation time |
|---|---|---|---|
| CAM-FV | 5.2 | 0.9°x1.25° | 1 day |
| CAM-SE | 5.2 | ne30np4 | 1 day |
| GAMIL | 2.0 | 1°x1° | 1 day |

## 3.1 Benchmarking Applications

Several climate simulation models, which have been widely used in scientific researches, are used as benchmarking applications, including CAM5 (Community Atmosphere Model, version 5) [11] and GAMIL2 (the Grid-point Atmospheric Model of IAP (Institute of Atmospheric Physics) - LASG (State Laboratory of Numerical Modeling for Atmospheric Sciences and Geophysical Fluid Dynamics), version2) [4]. CAM5 is released as the atmospheric component of the Community Earth System Model (CESM) [12]. It has been parallelized using MPI, OpenMP and their hybrid. It contains several different dynamic cores including Eulerian Spectral, Semi-Lagrangian Spectral, Finite Volume and Spectral Element. The Finite-Volume dynamic core (CAM-FV) is often used for climate simulations. For example, CAM-FV was used for all CMIP5 (the Coupled Model Intercomparison Project, Phase 5) experiments performed by CESM. Spectral Element (CAM-SE) is the latest dynamic core of CAM5. We therefore select both CAM-FV and CAM-SE as benchmark applications.

GAMIL2 is the atmospheric component of FGOALS-g2 (the grid-point versions of the Flexible Global Ocean - Atmosphere - Land System version 2) [13], which has been widely used in model intercomparison projects and scientific researches. It also has been parallelized using MPI, OpenMP and their hybrid.

Table 3 shows the detailed setups of the benchmark application, including the version number, resolution or grid and simulation duration. All the benchmark applications are run on a computer with dual Intel Xeon E5-2650 and quad-channel 64 GB DDR3-1333 DRAM, and are compiled by Intel Composer XE 2013 SP1 at optimization level -O3.

## 3.2 Memory Performance

The memory performance of applications on modern CPUs is generally determined by the cache performance and memory bandwidth requirement. We therefore characterize them respectively.

**Cache Performance.** Different CPU versions can have different sizes of on-chip cache. Bigger size of cache can generally result in better cache performance as well as better application performance, while the sensitivity of cache performance to the variation of cache size depends on applications own characteristics. To quantify this sensitivity for climate simulation applications, we use a tool MICA

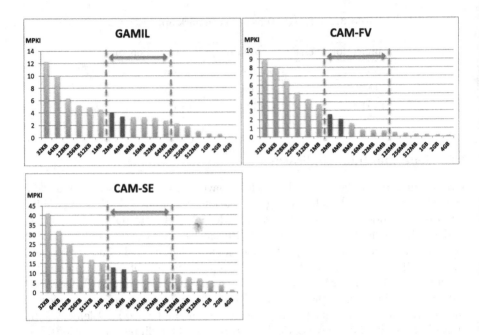

**Fig. 2.** Numbers of MPKI (misses per kilo instructions) when scaling the cache size from 32 KB to 4 GB. These results are calculated according to the memory reuse distances collected by MICA [14]. The scaling of cache sizes can be partitioned into three stages: from 32 KB to 2 MB, from 2 MB to 64 MB, and from 64 MB to 4 GB, because the sizes of L1 cache and L2 cache on modern CPUs generally range from 32 KB to 2 MB while the last level cache size generally ranges from 2 MB to 64 MB. As the last level cache is generally shared by a number of cores and the cache size per core generally ranges from 2 MB to 4 MB, we highlight the corresponding two bars in green color (Color figure online).

[14] that can calculate the number of cache misses with the variation of cache size through measuring the memory reuse distances of applications.

Figure 2 shows the numbers of MPKI (Misses Per Kilo Instructions) of the three benchmark applications when scaling the cache size from 64 KB to 4 GB, where cache prefetching is not considered. When enlarging the cache size from 64 KB to 2 MB, the MPKI is reduced rapidly. When enlarging the cache size from 2 MB to 64 MB, the MPKI gets much slower. Given a typical 3-level cache hierarchy, Fig. 3 shows the average memory access latency. When enlarging the last-level cache size from 512 KB to 4 GB, the average memory access latency is slightly decreased.

The above results without the consideration of cache prefetching indicate that the cache performance of climate simulation applications is not sensitive to the cache sizes on modern CPUs. Almost all modern CPUs provide the functionality of cache prefetching for improving the cache performance. When cache prefetching is considered, the sensitivity will be further decreased, because many

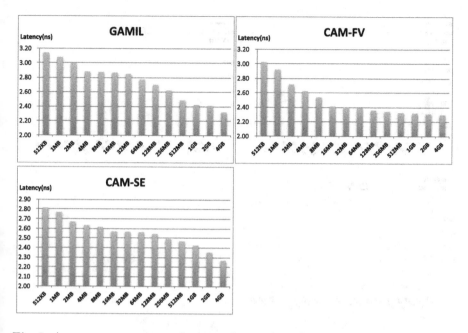

**Fig. 3.** Average memory access latency when scaling the size of the last level cache from 512 KB to 4 GB, assuming that there are three levels in the cache hierarchy, the sizes of the L1 cache and L2 cache are 32 KB and 256 KB respectively and the latencies of accessing the L1 cache, L2 cache, L3 cache (the last level cache) and main memory are 2, 6, 14 and 63 ns respectively. These results are calculated according to the MPKI in Fig. 2.

modules in climate simulation applications, such as the dynamical core, which have good spatial locality with a high proportion of sequential array accesses, can benefit from cache prefetching.

**Memory Bandwidth Requirement.** The data accesses that miss on-chip cache hierarchies will be served by the main memory. When the memory bandwidth capacity provided by the CPU cannot satisfy the main memory accesses, memory bandwidth requirement can dominate the application performance.

Figure 4 shows the average memory bandwidth requirement of the benchmark applications when scaling the cache size from 64 KB to 4 GB. Given a typical cache size between 2 MB and 64 MB, the average memory bandwidth requirement is between 0.08 GB/s and 1.53 GB/s, which can be satisfied by almost all modern CPU versions.

The above results indicate that the performance of climate simulation applications is not sensitive to the memory bandwidth capacity of modern CPUs. However, Fig. 5 shows that the memory bandwidth requirement of climate simulation applications is not constant, and can burst at some time intervals where the memory bandwidth capacity provided by most of modern CPU versions

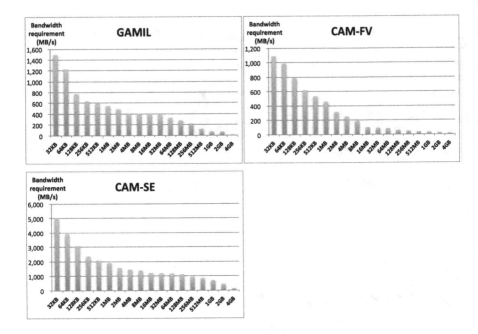

**Fig. 4.** Average memory bandwidth requirement when scaling the cache size from 32 KB to 4 GB, assuming that one third of the memory accesses are store instructions, the cycles per instruction (CPI) is 1.0, and the CPU clock rate is 2 GHz.

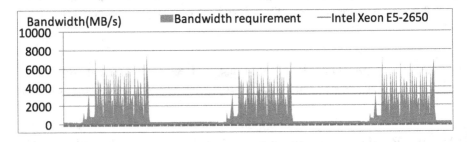

**Fig. 5.** Footprint of memory bandwidth requirement in the sequential execution of GAMIL on the Intel Xeon E5520. Instantaneous memory bandwidth requirements can be much larger the memory bandwidth capacity per core provide by the Intel Xeon E5520 (the orange line). Similar phenomenon can be observed when using the other two benchmark applications. The footprint is collected by the CSAP profiler (Sect. 4.2).

cannot fully satisfy the corresponding requirement. For example, the average memory bandwidth capacity per core of the dual Intel Xeon E5-2650 used in this paper is 3.14 GB/s (measured by STREAM [15]), which is much smaller than the peak memory bandwidth requirement of the three benchmark applications.

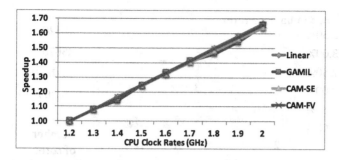

**Fig. 6.** Speedups of the benchmark applications with the scaling of the CPU clock rate when the memory bandwidth capacity provided by the CPU is sufficient. We collect these results in the sequential execution on a dual Intel Xeon E5-2650 platform that can provide enough memory bandwidth capacity to cover the memory bandwidth requirement in the sequential application execution.

### 3.3   Computing Performance

The computing performance on modern CPUs is generally determined by the CPU clock rate, SIMD (single instruction, multiple data) capability and ILP (Instruction Level Parallelism). As shown in Fig. 6, the performance of climate simulation applications can almost achieve linear speedup with the scaling of the CPU clock rate when the memory bandwidth capacity of the CPU is sufficient. As shown in Table 4, climate simulation applications can effectively benefit from the SIMD capability, and bigger performance speedup can be obtained with wider SIMD capability. Table 4 also shows the ILP (measured by the IPC (Instructions Per Clock)) achieved by the benchmark applications. Different ILP

**Table 4.** IPC (instruction per clock) and SIMD performance of benchmark applications on two Intel CPU versions (E5-2650 and X5670). These results are obtained from sequential application run, where the memory bandwidth capacity provided by the CPU versions is larger than any instantaneous memory bandwidth requirement of the applications.

| Application | version | CPU clock rate | Width of SIMD | SIMD enabled | | SIMD disabled | | SIMD speedup |
|---|---|---|---|---|---|---|---|---|
| | | | | Time(s) | IPC | Time(s) | IPC | |
| GAMIL | E5-2650 | 2.0 GHz | 256 | 6402.5 | 1.25 | 7367.8 | 1.24 | 1.151 |
| | X5670 | 2.93 GHz | 128 | 4889.4 | 1.17 | 5549.0 | 1.12 | 1.135 |
| CAM-SE | IE5-2650 | 2.0 GHz | 256 | 16590.8 | 1.51 | 18959.9 | 1.51 | 1.143 |
| | X5670 | 2.93 GHz | 128 | 13096.0 | 1.31 | 15052.9 | 1.30 | 1.149 |
| CAM-FV | E5-2650 | 2.0 GHz | 256 | 11024.8 | 1.38 | 12090.7 | 1.34 | 1.097 |
| | X5670 | 2.93 GHz | 128 | 8182.1 | 1.27 | 8813.5 | 1.25 | 1.077 |

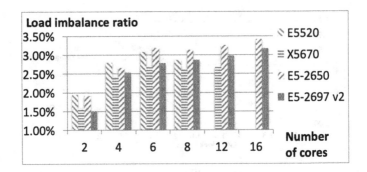

**Fig. 7.** Load imbalance ratio of CAM-SE at different core numbers on various CPU versions. Given a core number, the load imbalance ratios on different CPU versions are almost the same.

can be achieved on different microarchitectures of CPUs. Moreover, different ILP can be achieved when the SIMD capability is enabled or not.

### 3.4 Load Imbalance

To quantify the load imbalance of climate simulation applications, we use the load imbalance rate calculated by Formula 1 ($T_i$ is computation time of $i$th process/thread of the application). Figure 7 shows the load imbalance rate of the benchmark applications on different CPU microarchitectures, when increasing the number of cores from 2 to 16. It indicates that climate simulation applications also have the problem of load imbalance, and load imbalance gets more serious given a bigger number of cores.

$$L = \frac{\max T_i}{\overline{T_i}} \qquad (1)$$

## 4 Design of CSAP

Based on the performance characteristics revealed in the previous section, we designed and implemented CSAP for predicting the performance of climate simulation applications on Intel CPU versions. The overall design of CSAP will be introduced in Sect. 4.1. Guided by the overall design, we implemented a CSAP profiler (Sect. 4.2) and a CSAP predictor (Sect. 4.3).

### 4.1 Overall Design

As the average memory access latency of climate simulation applications is insensitive to the increment of cache size (Fig. 3), we neglect the factor of cache size in CSAP. We need to take consideration of other factors including memory

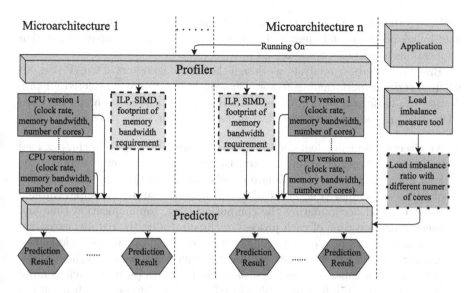

**Fig. 8.** Overall flowchart of CSAP. The squares in green, yellow and purple are the performance characteristics of climate simulation applications or the performance factors of CPU versions.

bandwidth, CPU clock rate, SIMD capability, ILP, number of cores and load imbalance because each of them affects the performance of climate simulation applications (Sect. 3).

As the footprint of memory bandwidth requirement of climate simulation applications is too uneven to predict and each application has its own memory bandwidth requirement, we implemented a profiler for sampling the footprint of memory bandwidth requirement (Sect. 4.2). The impact of CPU clock rate can be easily predicted because the performance of climate simulation applications almost keeps linear to the clock rate when the memory bandwidth capacity of the CPU is sufficient (Fig. 6).

The impact of SIMD capability and ILP is determined by the microarchitecture of the CPU when the memory bandwidth capacity of the CPU is sufficient. It is a challenge to predict the impact of SIMD capability and ILP on various microarchitectures. Although a cycle-accurate simulator can be used, it is always very complex and can significantly slow down the performance prediction. On the other hand, the microarchitectures of CPUs are not upgraded frequently. For example, there are currently more than one hundred Intel CPU versions on the market but only several different types of microarchitectures. We therefore measure the impact of SIMD capability and ILP through directly running the applications on a CPU with a certain microarchitecture.

The speedup achieved through parallelization intra a computing node generally cannot keep linear scaling with the core number, due to the overhead of load imbalance and the limit of memory bandwidth capacity provided by the

CPU. We therefore measure the impact of the parallel execution based on the load imbalance ratio and memory bandwidth requirement of climate simulation applications at certain core numbers.

Based on the above analysis, we design the overall flowchart of CSAP (Fig. 8), where a series of performance factors (squares in Fig. 8) are considered for predicting the performance of a climate simulation application on a specific Intel CPU version. These performance factors can be divided into three categories:

1. Architecture independent factors (green squares in Fig. 8), including load imbalance ratio. According to Sect. 3.4, given the same core number, the load imbalance ratios of a climate simulation application on different types of CPUs are similar (Fig. 7). Load imbalance ratio can be measured through collecting and accumulating the computing time, communication time and synchronization time of each process or thread during the parallel execution of an application at a certain number of cores. Load imbalance ratio can be measured artificially by scientists through inserting timers into the application code. A number of tools can also be used for such purpose, such as mpiP [16], Jumpshot [17], Scalasca [18] and HPCToolkit [19]. One application run is required for getting the load imbalance ratio at a core number.

2. Microarchitecture dependent factors (yellow squares in Fig. 8), including SIMD, ILP, and memory bandwidth requirement. We designed and implemented a profiler for sampling the footprint of memory bandwidth requirement on a CPU version with a specific microarchitecture. Such footprint has already taken account of the relationship between SIMD, ILP and memory bandwidth requirement. A run of the application is required for getting the footprint of memory bandwidth requirement on a specific type of microarchitecture.

3. CPU version specific factors (purple squares in Fig. 8), including clock rate, memory bandwidth capacity, and number of cores. These factors are metrics of a CPU version which can be easily obtained without an application run. The memory bandwidth capacity here is not the peak memory bandwidth of the CPU version but the maximum memory bandwidth that an application can obtain. It can be measured by STREAM on the target platform or calculated from other measured value of similar platforms.

Given a climate simulation application and a set of $N$ CPU versions of $M$ types of microarchitectures, the performance prediction can be conducted in following steps:

1. Pick out a CPU version with maximum number of cores, and then run the application with different number of cores to get the load imbalance ratios.
2. For each type of microarchitecture, select one CPU version as a reference platform and then run the application with the CSAP profiler to get the footprint of memory bandwidth requirement.
3. For each CPU version, use the CSAP predictor to get the prediction result.

Finally, the application will be run at most $K + M$ times, where K is the maximum of the core numbers, while there is almost no slowdown in each run. CSAP only requires users to run the application on one CPU version of a type of microarchitecture. Then the application performance on any other CPU version of the same type of microarchitecture can be predicted.

## 4.2  CSAP Profiler

The CSAP profiler is responsible for collecting the footprint of memory bandwidth usage of a climate simulation application. Similar to other performance profilers such as Intel VTune, the CSAP profiler also employs a sampling approach for the collection. Regarding to the Intel CPUs, a number of tools, such as Intel VTune and Intel Performance Counter Monitor (PCM), can be used to sample the memory bandwidth usage. We prefer PCM because it is an open source tool and therefore can be modified according to our specific purposes, such as the functionality of pausing and resuming the sampling (for example, I/O is not considered in the performance prediction) and various sampling frequencies, while the VTune is not open-source and cannot export the footprint for our usage. During an application run, the sampling interval is a constant physical time such as 5 ms or even shorter. The footprint of memory bandwidth usage is quantified by the total size of memory accesses (include memory read and write) and the number of clock ticks in each sampling frame.

The footprint of memory bandwidth usage can be used as the footprint of memory bandwidth requirement only when the memory bandwidth capacity of the CPU is larger than the memory bandwidth requirement at any time. Considering that the memory bandwidth requirement of an application execution increases with the increment of the core number, we propose to collect the footprint of memory bandwidth usage in a sequential execution of the application. We find that the memory bandwidth capacity of an Intel CPU for a sequential execution is generally enough for covering the memory bandwidth usage of the application.

## 4.3  CSAP Predictor

The CSAP predictor is responsible for predicting the execution time of a climate simulation application on a CPU version, taking a set of performance factors as input, including the footprint of memory bandwidth requirement, CPU clock rate, memory bandwidth capacity, number of cores and the corresponding load imbalance ratio. It iterates on all sampling frames of the footprint and predicts the execution time of each sampling frame. The execution time of a sampling frame is predicted according to Formula 2 (the definitions of the variables in Formula 2 are described in Table 5). It is determined by the maximum of computation time and memory time. The computation time is calculated according to the number of clock ticks in the sampling frame, the clock rate and the number of cores of the CPU version, because the computing performance can achieve

Table 5. Descriptions of the variables in Formulas 2 and 3.

| Variable | Definition | Unit |
|---|---|---|
| $m_i$ | Total size of memory access requirements in sampling frame $i$ | Byte |
| $k_i$ | Number of clock ticks in sampling frame $i$ | - |
| $c$ | CPU clock rate of the CPU version | Hz |
| $b$ | Memory bandwidth capacity of the CPU version | Byte/s |
| $n$ | Number of cores to use | - |
| $L$ | Corresponding load imbalance ratio of $n$ cores | - |

almost linear speedup with the scaling of the CPU clock rate and with the increment of the core number when the load imbalance is not considered. The memory time is calculated according to the total size of memory accesses in the sampling frame and memory bandwidth capacity of the CPU version.

$$t_i = \max\{\frac{k_i}{cn}, \frac{m_i}{b}\} \tag{2}$$

As shown in Formula 3, the predicted execution time of the application will be adjusted according to the corresponding load imbalance ratio.

$$t_p = (1 + L) \sum t_i \tag{3}$$

## 5  Experimental Evaluation

In this section, we will evaluate CSAP in terms of time consumption, storage consumption and accuracy, with the experimental setup described in Sect. 5.1.

### 5.1  Experimental Setup

Besides the three climate simulation applications (GAMIL, CAM-FV and CAM-SE) that have been described in Sect. 3, one more application is added for this evaluation, i.e., the land surface model CoLM (Common Land Model) [20]. CoLM is developed based on the early Common Land Model [5], which is a third-generation land surface model based on the Biosphere-Atmosphere Transfer Scheme (BATS), the Institute of Atmospheric Physics Land Surface Model (IAP94) and the Land Surface Model (LSM). CoLM has been parallelized using MPI. In our experiment, the resolution of CoLM is 1○x1○, and the simulation time is 500 hours (20.83 days).

In this evaluation, 4 real Intel CPU versions are used. They are different in microarchitecture, core number, CPU clock rate and memory bandwidth capacity, as shown in Table 6. We call them basic CPU versions. Based on a basic CPU version, a number of extended CPU versions can be generated through varying the CPU clock rate, memory bandwidth capacity or the number of cores used

**Table 6.** Information of the 4 Intel CPU versions used for the evaluation. For each CPU version, a two-way computer is used. The memory bandwidth capacity corresponding to a CPU version is measured on the corresponding two-way computer.

| CPU version | Microarchitecture | CPU clock rate | Memory configuration |
|---|---|---|---|
| Xeon E5-2650 | Sandy Bridge | 2.0 GHz | 64 GB DDR3-1333 |
| Xeon E5-2697 v2 | Ivy Bridge | 2.7 GHz | 64 GB DDR3-1333 |
| Xeon E5520 | Nehalem | 2.27 GHz | 32 GB DDR3-1067 |
| Xeon X5670 | Westmere | 2.93 GHz | 48 GB DDR3-1333 |

for running an application. The clock rate of an extended CPU version can be set in BIOS. Memory bandwidth capacity can be changed through enabling or disabling memory channels.

**Table 7.** Load imbalance ratios at different numbers of cores. These results are measured on the dual Intel Xeon E5-2697 v2.

| Cores | GAMIL | CAM-FV | CAM-SE | CoLM |
|---|---|---|---|---|
| 2 | 0.0041 | 0.0096 | 0.0151 | 0.0042 |
| 4 | 0.0188 | 0.0154 | 0.0254 | 0.0126 |
| 6 | 0.0199 | 0.0139 | 0.0278 | 0.0052 |
| 8 | 0.0242 | 0.0207 | 0.0287 | 0.0105 |
| 12 | 0.0409 | 0.0155 | 0.0298 | 0.0119 |
| 16 | 0.0667 | 0.0197 | 0.0318 | 0.0204 |
| 24 | 0.0802 | 0.0169 | 0.0342 | 0.0414 |

## 5.2   Time Consumption and Storage Consumption

For an application, we conduct the performance prediction on various CPU versions as follows:

1. For each basic CPU version, run CSAP profiler to collect the footprint of memory bandwidth usage. For different applications, the sampling interval can be different.
2. Use the dual Intel Xeon E5-2697 v2 to quantify the load imbalance ratio at different core numbers, as shown in Table 7.
3. Run CSAP predictor to predict the performance on each basic CPU version and on each extended CPU version.

Table 8 shows the time consumption and storage consumption for the performance prediction of each application, which demonstrates that CSAP is an

**Table 8.** Time consumption and storage consumption of performance prediction of the four benchmark applications in four CPUs listed on Table 6. Execution time is one process execution time on Intel Xeon E5-2650. Time consumption includes execution time for measuring load imbalance ratios, execution time for collecting memory bandwidth requirement footprint on four CPUs.

| Application | Execution time (s) | Sampling interval (ms) | Consumption | |
|---|---|---|---|---|
| | | | Time (s) | Storage |
| GAMIL | 6402.5 | 5 | 40328.8 | 324 |
| CAM-FV | 11024.8 | 10 | 57636.5 | 72 |
| CAM-SE | 16590.8 | 10 | 86622.0 | 112 |
| CoLM | 4741.2 | 10 | 24771.9 | 28 |

**Table 9.** Accuracy of performance prediction on the basic CPU versions. All CPU cores on each computer are fully used for the evaluation. The percentages between the brackets are the errors of predictions.

| Computer | Running time(s) and prediction error (%) | | | |
|---|---|---|---|---|
| | GAMIL | CAM-FV | CAM-SE | CoLM |
| E5-2650 | 497.3 ($-3.3$) | 719.2 ($-1.6$) | 1132.9 ($-1.8$) | 302.0 ($+0.6$) |
| E5-2697 v2 | 362.5 ($-2.1$) | 361.0 ($-1.6$) | 648.7 ($-0.6$) | 136.8 ($+0.3$) |
| E5520 | 1054.0 ($-2.7$) | 1340.8 ($+2.8$) | 2197.2 ($+2.3$) | 538.4 ($-0.2$) |
| X5670 | 643.6 ($-2.6$) | 791.3 ($+1.7$) | 1398.6 ($+1.7$) | 310.8 ($-0.4$) |

**Table 10.** Accuracy of performance prediction on the extended CPU versions that are generated from the dual Intel Xeon E5-2650 through varying the number of cores. The percentages between the brackets are the errors of predictions

| cores | Running time(s) and prediction error (%) | | | |
|---|---|---|---|---|
| | GAMIL | CAM-FV | CAM-SE | CoLM |
| 2 | 3223.0 ($+1.3$) | 5447.9 ($+2.2$) | 8321.3 ($+3.7$) | 2382.7 ($-0.1$) |
| 4 | 1636.4 ($+1.4$) | 2781.7 ($+0.7$) | 4264.4 ($+1.9$) | 1201.7 ($-0.1$) |
| 6 | 1115.9 ($+0.3$) | 1868.0 ($-0.2$) | 2871.0 ($+1.4$) | 789.8 ($+0.6$) |
| 8 | 860.1 ($-1.3$) | 1409.1 ($-0.1$) | 2172.2 ($+0.8$) | 596.2 ($+0.5$) |
| 12 | 621.1 ($-3.7$) | 953.6 ($-1.8$) | 1497.0 ($-2.2$) | 397.9 ($+0.7$) |
| 16 | 497.3 ($-3.3$) | 719.2 ($-1.6$) | 1132.9 ($-1.9$) | 302.0 ($+0.6$) |

efficient tool. When we increase the extended CPU versions, the time consumption will be only slightly increased because the time for the above third step can be neglected.

**Table 11.** Accuracy of performance prediction on the extended CPU versions that are generated from the dual E5-2650 through varying the CPU clock rates. All CPU cores of the dual E5-2650 are fully used for the evaluation. The percentages between the brackets are the errors of predictions.

| CPU clock rate (GHz) | Running time(s) and prediction error (%) | | | |
|---|---|---|---|---|
| | GAMIL | CAM-FV | CAM-SE | CoLM |
| 1.2 | 786.8 (−1.1) | 1188.8 (−1.3) | 1820.2 (+0.7) | 504.1 (+0.0) |
| 1.3 | 718.0 (−1.9) | 1098.5 (−1.4) | 1684.6 (+0.5) | 465.1 (+0.1) |
| 1.4 | 674.4 (−2.4) | 1019.8 (−1.3) | 1570.8 (+0.1) | 435.5 (−0.6) |
| 1.5 | 631.8 (−2.2) | 954.0 (−1.5) | 1475.4 (−0.5) | 404.1 (−0.1) |
| 1.6 | 597.9 (−2.4) | 896.5 (−1.7) | 1388.2 (−0.8) | 378.0 (+0.2) |
| 1.7 | 570.0 (−2.9) | 846.4 (−1.9) | 1312.9 (−1.2) | 356.5 (+0.1) |
| 1.8 | 544.7 (−3.4) | 800.8 (−2.0) | 1246.4 (−1.4) | 335.8 (+0.4) |
| 1.9 | 521.6 (−3.7) | 760.5 (−2.2) | 1186.4 (−1.6) | 318.4 (+0.4) |
| 2.0 | 497.3 (−3.3) | 719.2 (−1.6) | 1132.9 (−1.8) | 302.0 (+0.6) |

## 5.3   Accuracy of Performance Prediction

We first evaluate the accuracy of CSAP using the basic CPU versions when all the cores on each CPU version are used. As shown in Table 9, the errors of performance prediction range from −3.3 % to +2.8 %.

Next we generate several extended CPU versions based on the dual E5-2650 through gradually increasing the CPU clock rate from 1.2 GHz to 2.0 GHz. As shown in Table 11, the corresponding errors of performance prediction range from −3.7 % to +0.7 %.

We further generate several extended CPU versions based on the dual E5-2650 through reducing the number of memory channels from the maximum number 3 to 4. We do not consider the case of 1 or 2 memory channels because modern CPU versions generally have at least 3 memory channels. As shown in Table 12, the corresponding errors of performance prediction range from −6.6 % to +0.8 %.

Finally, we design 8 extended CPU versions based on the dual E5-2650 through combining different CPU clock rates, different memory bandwidth capacities and different numbers of cores, as shown in Table 13. The corresponding errors of performance prediction range from −4.3 % to +2.0 %.

Table 10 shows the accuracy of performance prediction on the dual E5-2650 when using different number of cores. The corresponding errors range from −3.7 % to 3.7 %.

Besides the dual E5-2650, we also use the other basic CPU versions to generate extended CPU versions for the evaluation, where small errors of performance prediction are still observed. The maximum and average absolute value of the errors are 6.9 % and 1.2 % respectively, which demonstrate that CSAP can

**Table 12.** Accuracy of performance prediction on the extended CPU versions that are generated from the dual Intel Xeon E5-2650 through varying the memory bandwidth capacity. All CPU cores of the dual Intel Xeon E5-2650 are fully used for the evaluation. The percentages between the brackets are the errors of predictions.

| Memory bandwidth capacity (MB/s) | | Running time(s) and prediction error (%) | | | |
|---|---|---|---|---|---|
| Peak | Measured | GAMIL | CAM-FV | CAM-SE | CoLM |
| 65,519 | 53,089 | 535.0 (−6.6) | 720.1 (−1.4) | 1155.5 (−2.4) | 302.4 (+0.8) |
| 87,359 | 65,457 | 497.3 (−3.3) | 719.2 (−1.6) | 1132.9 (−1.9) | 302.0 (+0.6) |

**Table 13.** Accuracy of performance prediction on 8 extended CPU versions generated from the dual Intel Xeon E5-2650 through combining different CPU clock rates, different memory bandwidth capacities and different numbers of cores. The percentages between the brackets are the errors of predictions.

| CPU clock rate | Measured memory bandwidth capacity (MB/s) | Number of cores | Running time(s) and prediction error (%) | | | |
|---|---|---|---|---|---|---|
| | | | GAMIL | CAM-FV | CAM-SE | CoLM |
| 1.8 GHz | 53,089 (triple) | 12 | 702.0 (−4.3) | 1056.1 (−1.4) | 1672.6 (−3.2) | 445.2 (+0.0) |
| 1.8 GHz | 53,089 (triple) | 8 | 979.7 (−3.0) | 1560.9 (+0.3) | 2404.8 (+0.8) | 662.8 (+0.4) |
| 1.8 GHz | 65,457 (quad) | 12 | 681.3 (−3.5) | 1055.0 (−1.5) | 1625.9 (−0.7) | 441.5 (+0.7) |
| 1.8 GHz | 65,457 (quad) | 8 | 956.5 (−1.4) | 1562.0 (+0.2) | 2398.4 (+1.0) | 658.6 (+0.4) |
| 1.4 GHz | 53,089 (triple) | 12 | 866.2 (−2.8) | 1345.6 (−0.7) | 2093.1 (−0.8) | 568.4 (+0.6) |
| 1.4 GHz | 53,089 (triple) | 8 | 1212.3 (−0.0) | 1999.7 (+0.6) | 3055.8 (+1.9) | 850.0 (+0.7) |
| 1.4 GHz | 65,457 (quad) | 12 | 851.2 (−1.9) | 1352.6 (−1.3) | 2087.0 (−0.6) | 571.7 (−0.1) |
| 1.4 GHz | 65,457 (quad) | 8 | 1199.4 (+0.9) | 1997.1 (+0.7) | 3054.7 (+2.0) | 848.7 (+0.8) |

accurately predict the performance of climate simulation applications on modern Intel CPU versions.

## 6  Conclusion and Future Works

In this paper, we propose a new tool CSAP for the performance prediction of climate simulation applications on the Intel CPU versions. Through considering the performance characteristics of climate simulation applications, CSAP can achieve high accuracy and low overhead at the same time. We believe that such an approach can help the design of specific cross-architecture performance predictors for other applications.

We take Intel CPUs as the first step of CSAP. For the future works, we will extend it to other kinds of CPUs, e.g., AMD CPUs and IBM PowerPC processors, etc. The performance characteristics of climate simulation applications need to be reanalyzed and CSAP may need to be upgraded accordingly. However, we believe that the overall flowchart of CSAP can keep the same.

**Acknowledgment.** This work is supported in part by the Natural Science Foundation of China (no. 41275098), the National Grand Fundamental Research 973 Program of China (no. 2014CB441302) and the Tsinghua University Initiative Scientific Research Program (no. 20131089356).

# References

1. TOP500.org, Top500 supercomputer sites (2014). http://www.top500.org/
2. Lin, S.-J.: A "vertically lagrangian" finite-volume dynamical core for global models. Mon. Weather Rev. **132**(10), 2293–2307 (2004)
3. Dennis, J., Edwards, J., Evans, K.J., Guba, O., Lauritzen, P.H., Mirin, A.A., St-Cyr, A., Taylor, M.A., Worley, P.H.: CAM-SE: A scalable spectral element dynamical core for the community atmosphere model. Int. J. High Perform. Comput. Appl. **26**, 74–89 (2011). doi:10.1177/1094342011428142
4. Liu, L., Li, R., Yang, G., Wang, B., Li, L., Pu, Y.: Improving parallel performance of a finite-difference agcm on modern high-performance computers. J. Atmos. Ocean. Technol. **31**, 2157–2168 (2014)
5. Dai, Y., Zeng, X., Dickinson, R.E., Baker, I., Bonan, G.B., Bosilovich, M.G., Denning, A.S., Dirmeyer, P.A., Houser, P.R., Niu, G., et al.: The common land model. Bull. Am. Meteorol. Soc. **84**(8), 1013–1023 (2003)
6. Marin, G., Mellor-Crummey, J.: Cross-architecture performance predictions for scientific applications using parameterized models. ACM SIGMETRICS Perform. Eval. Rev. **32**(1), 2–13 (2004)
7. Sadjadi, S.M., Shimizu, S., Figueroa, J., Rangaswami, R., Delgado, J., Duran, H., Collazo-Mojica, X.J.: A modeling approach for estimating execution time of long-running scientific applications. In: IEEE International Symposium on Parallel and Distributed Processing, IPDPS 2008, pp. 1–8. IEEE (2008)
8. Shimizu, S., Rangaswami, R., Duran-Limon, H.A., Corona-Perez, M.: Platform-independent modeling and prediction of application resource usage characteristics. J. Syst. Softw. **82**(12), 2117–2127 (2009)
9. Yang, L.T., Ma, X., Mueller, F.: Cross-platform performance prediction of parallel applications using partial execution. In: Proceedings of the ACM/IEEE SC 2005 Conference Supercomputing, IEEE 2005, pp. 40–40 (2005)
10. Petit, E., Herrero, P. D. O. C., Menouer, T., Krammer, B., William, J., et al.: Computing-kernels performance prediction using dataflow analysis and microbenchmarking. In: 16th Workshop on Compilers for Parallel Computing (CPC 2012) (2012)
11. Neale, R.B., Chen, C.-C., Gettelman, A., Lauritzen, P.H., Park, S., Williamson, D.L., Conley, A.J., Garcia, R., Kinnison, D., Lamarque, J.-F., et al.: Description of the ncar community atmosphere model (cam 5.0), NCAR Technical Note NCAR/TN-486+ STR (2010)
12. Hurrell, J.W., Holland, M., Gent, P., Ghan, S., Kay, J.E., Kushner, P., Lamarque, J.-F., Large, W., Lawrence, D., Lindsay, K., et al.: The community earth system model: a framework for collaborative research. Bull. Am. Meteorol. Soc. **94**(9), 1339–1360 (2013)

13. Li, L., Lin, P., Yu, Y., Wang, B., Zhou, T., Liu, L., Liu, J., Bao, Q., Xu, S., Huang, W., et al.: The flexible global ocean-atmosphere-land system model, grid-point version 2: FGOALS-g2. Adv. Atmos. Sci. **30**, 543–560 (2013)
14. Kenneth Hoste, L.E.: Mica: Microarchitecture-independent characterization of applications (2012). http://boegel.kejo.be/ELIS/mica/
15. McCalpin, J.D.: Stream: Sustainable memory bandwidth in high performance computers (1995). http://www.cs.virginia.edu/stream/
16. Vetter, J., Chambreau, C.: mpip: Lightweight, scalable mpi profiling (2005). http://www.llnl.gov/CASC/mpiP
17. Lusk, E.R., Chan, A.: Early experiments with the OpenMP/MPI hybrid programming model. In: Eigenmann, R., de Supinski, B.R. (eds.) IWOMP 2008. LNCS, vol. 5004, pp. 36–47. Springer, Heidelberg (2008)
18. Geimer, M., Wolf, F., Wylie, B.J., Ábrahám, E., Becker, D., Mohr, B.: The scalasca performance toolset architecture. Concurr. Computat.: Pract. Exp. **22**(6), 702–719 (2010)
19. Adhianto, L., Banerjee, S., Fagan, M., Krentel, M., Marin, G., Mellor-Crummey, J., Tallent, N.R.: HPCTOOLKIT: Tools for performance analysis of optimized parallel programs. Concurr. Comput.: Prac. Exp. **22**(6), 685–701 (2010)
20. Ji, D., Dai, Y.: The common land model (CoLM) technical guide (2010)

# On Routing Algorithms for the DPillar Data Centre Networks

Abbas Eslami Kiasari[1](✉), Javier Navaridas[1], and Iain A. Stewart[2]

[1] School of Computer Science, University of Manchester,
Oxford Road, Manchester M13 9PL, UK
{abbas.kiasari,javier.navaridas}@manchester.ac.uk
[2] Science Laboratories, School of Engineering and Computing Sciences,
Durham University, South Road, Durham DH1 3LE, UK
i.a.stewart@durham.ac.uk

**Abstract.** The DPillar data centre networks were introduced as an attractive topology for server-centric data centre networks and have recently received considerable attention. In this paper, we first derive analytically, and validate experimentally, the average hop count and the aggregate bottleneck throughput of the DPillar networks with a focus on single-path routing algorithms and the all-to-all traffic pattern. We use these models to explore the design space of the DPillar networks as a case study. In addition, we discuss the limitations of the original routing algorithms, showing that they do not benefit from the rich connectivity provided by the DPillar network and consequently do not tolerate link failures very well. To overcome these limitations we propose a collection of routing algorithms which keep the simplicity of the original but enable a more effective utilisation of the network. We empirically evaluate our proposed routing algorithms and we find that they outperform the original algorithms as regards network throughput ($\sim$ 2x), average hop count ($\sim 5\% - 10\%$), load balance and fault tolerance.

**Keywords:** Data centre network · Interconnection network · Routing algorithms · Performance evaluation · Analytical modelling · Design space exploration

## 1 Introduction

Computing and storage are increasingly being moved from personal computers to computing platforms resembling a warehouse full of computers that are accessed over the internet from portable computing devices [3]. The last few years have witnessed the emergence of modern data centres with tens of thousands of servers, each consisting of processors, memory, storage and a high bandwidth network interface [1]. As the number of servers in data centres and their performance continue to increase, the data centre network (DCN) plays a greater role in the overall system performance.

© Springer International Publishing Switzerland 2015
G. Wang et al. (Eds.): ICA3PP 2015, Part IV, LNCS 9531, pp. 329–343, 2015.
DOI: 10.1007/978-3-319-27140-8_23

DCNs can be roughly classified into two categories which we call switch-centric network and server-centric network [8,10]. In the former the routing intelligence is put on switches while in the latter it resides in servers and switches are used only as crossbars. In the current switch-centric design, multiple levels of switches are connected by a tree structure and servers are attached to the lowest-level switches. Fat-Tree [2] and VL2 [5] fall into this category. Tree-based architectures face difficulties in meeting the reliability and scalability requirements of DCNs; for example, a high-level switch in the tree network is a single point of failure for the sub-tree rooted from it [9,10] and the top-level switches become the cost and performance bottleneck as the number of servers grows. Conversely, server-centric DCNs use cheap low-end switches while servers are responsible for packet routing. Putting the network intelligence on servers results in a higher degree of flexibility when designing data centres. DCell [7], BCube [6], FiConn [9] and DPillar [11,12] fall into this category. Recently, the DPillar network, whose topology is inspired by the wrapped butterfly network, has attracted considerable attention [10]. It provides an interconnection topology for a large number of servers using a low number of communication channels while providing a high level of redundancy, resulting in adequate network scalability and fault tolerance [12]. The DPillar network has many desirable features including symmetry and low diameter and average inter-server hop count [12].

Routing algorithms play an essential role in the design of a DCN, in that the greatest levels of efficiency are achieved when the topological characteristics of the DCN are exploited by the routing algorithms. In order to provide maximum system performance, a routing algorithm should have high throughput and exhibit some other important features, including low-latency packet delivery, path diversity, fault-tolerance and, in general, the ability to work well under various workload conditions.

In this paper, we show the performance limitations in terms of load-balancing capability and reliability of the original routing algorithms, DPillarSP and DPillarMP from [12], which are proposed for DPillar. First, we characterize the performance of the routing algorithms DPillarSP and DPillarMP by deriving the average hop count and the aggregate throughput, and assess their accuracy by comparing them with empirical results. Furthermore, we propose a collection of routing algorithms based on the original ones, but which incorporate some simple, but effective, modifications. A detailed evaluation shows the deficiencies of the routing algorithms DPillarSP and DPillarMP and that the proposed algorithms can reduce the average hop count and increase the aggregate throughput by more than 2x, while keeping a more balanced utilisation of network resources and degrading much more gracefully with network failures.

## 2   Preliminaries

We define the DPillar topology, and then study the mathematical properties of its structure, which serve as the foundation of designing packet routing and forwarding mechanisms for DPillar.

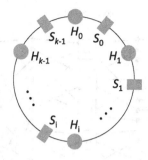

**Fig. 1.** A vertical view of DPillar with $k$ columns of servers $(H_i)$ and $k$ columns of switches $(S_i)$

## 2.1 Topology

An $(n, k)$ DPillar network is built from $k$ columns of servers $(H_i, 0 \leq i \leq k-1)$, comprising dual-port servers, and $k$ columns of $n$-port switches $(S_i, 0 \leq i \leq k-1)$ where $n$ is even and $n \geq 4$. Each server column has $(n/2)^k$ servers and each switch column has $(n/2)^{k-1}$ switches. As shown in the Fig. 1, DPillar network can be imagined as columns of servers and columns of switches, arranged alternately and vertically on the surface of a cylindrical pillar, hence the name. An $(n, k)$ DPillar network connects $k(n/2)^k$ servers via $k(n/2)^{k-1}$ switches and has bisection width of $(n/2)^k$ [11]. One server in DPillar can be uniquely addressed as $(c, v_{k-1}v_{k-2}...v_0)$ where $0 \leq c \leq k-1$ and $0 \leq v_i \leq n/2-1$. The first parameter, $c$, is the column-index and denotes the column in which the server resides, whilst the second parameter, $v_{k-1}v_{k-2}...v_0$, is the row-index and denotes the position of the server within a column. Similarly, one switch can be uniquely identified as $(c, v_{k-2}v_{k-3}...v_0)$. Note that the server row-index has $k$ coordinates $(v_{k-1}v_{k-2}...v_0)$ whereas the switch row-index has $k-1$ coordinates $(v_{k-2}v_{k-3}...v_0)$. Two servers in the server column $H_i$ are connected to the same switch in the column $S_i$ if their row-indices differ at the $i^{th}$ symbol only. Similarly, two servers in the server column $H_i$ are connected to the same switch in the column $S_{(i-1) \mod k}$ if their row-indices differ at the $((i-1) \mod k)^{th}$ symbol only. In the rest of the paper, for simplicity in the notation, we use $\oplus$ and $\ominus$ signs as modulo-$k$ addition and modulo-$k$ subtraction operations, respectively. More precisely, $i \oplus 1 = (i+1) \mod k$ and $i \ominus 1 = (i-1) \mod k$. Figure 2 shows a $(6,3)$ DPillar network in a two-dimensional view. It is worth mentioning that the servers in the rightmost and leftmost columns are identical but are shown separately to facilitate visualization.

## 2.2 Single-Path Routing (DPillarSP)

Thanks to the symmetry of the DPillar interconnection network, a straightforward packet routing was proposed whose main objective was to simplify its implementation in practical environments. In this canonical single-path routing algorithm (DPillarSP) [12], the next hop can be determined by continuously

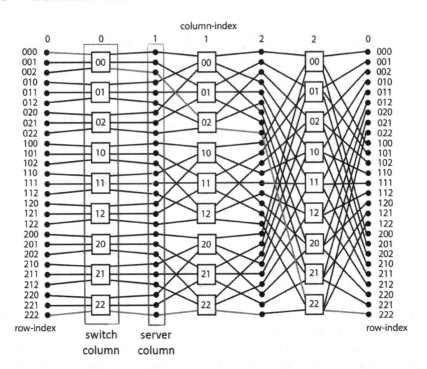

**Fig. 2.** Two-dimensional view of a (6,3) DPillar network. The red lines show the route between servers 0,000 and 2,222 computed by the routing algorithm DPillarSP in the clockwise direction. Note that the rightmost and leftmost columns are the same (color figure online).

moving clockwise (or anti-clockwise) and replacing the $i^{th}$ (accordingly $(i-1)^{th}$) coordinate in the row-index of the current server with the corresponding symbol in the row-index of the destination server.

Let $u$ and $v$ be consecutive servers on a route from source server $src$ to destination server $dst$, computed by DPillarSP. If the server $u$ in column $H_i$ forwards the packet to the server $v$ in the column $H_{i\oplus1}$ (in a clockwise direction), the $i^{th}$ symbol of the row-index of $v$ and destination are the same. Similarly, if $u$ forwards the packet from $H_i$ to $H_{i\ominus1}$ (in an anti-clockwise direction), the $(i\ominus1)^{th}$ symbol of the row-index of $v$ and the destination are the same. By continuing to do this, the packet can be forwarded to a server whose row-index is the same as the destinations row-index. After that, the packet can be sent to its destination by always forwarding to a next hop server with the same row-index. Note that in two neighbouring columns, servers with the same row-index are directly connected by a switch. Lets give an example in the (6,3) DPillar network (Fig. 2) to clarify the DPillarSP routing algorithm. The clockwise route for a packet from server (0, 000) to server (2, 222) is (0, 000), (1, 002), (2, 022), (0, 222), (1, 222), and (2, 222) and the anti-clockwise route is (0, 000), (2, 200), (1, 220), (0, 222), (2, 222). Figure 2 shows the route in the clockwise direction.

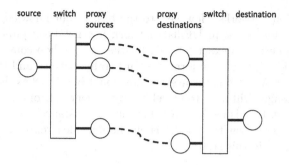

**Fig. 3.** $n/2$ disjoint paths between any source and destination

## 2.3 Multi-path Routing (DPillarMP)

In an $(n, k)$ DPillar network, each server is connected to $n/2$ servers via its clockwise neighbouring switch and $n/2$ servers via its anti-clockwise neighbouring switch. However, the routing algorithm DPillarSP uses only one of the neighbours of the source server and one of the neighbours of the destination server. In order to exploit the rich connections inside a DPillar network and to tolerate failures, the DPillar multi-path routing algorithm DPillarMP was proposed to provide $n/2$ disjoint paths between any pair of source and destination servers [12]; in [12], paths from a source server to a destination server are disjoint if they do not have any common server or switch except the switches connected to the source and destination servers. The routing algorithm DPillarMP can be summarised in three steps: (1) forward a packet from the source server to a proxy source server which is one of the $n/2$ neighbours of the source server, (2) route the packet according to the routing algorithm DPillarSP from the proxy source server to a proxy destination server which is one of the $n/2$ neighbours of the destination server, and (3) simply forward the packet from the proxy destination server to the destination server. Figure 3 shows an example of the routing algorithm DPillarMP. More details on how to pair a proxy source server with a proxy destination server can be found in [12]. It has been shown that the diameter of DPillarMP in the $(n, k)$ DPillar network is $2k + 1$ which is 2 hops more than diameter of DPillarSP [12].

## 3 Performance of DPillarSP

In this section, we continue the study of the routing algorithm DPillarSP by investigating the average hop count and throughput of DPillarSP routing algorithm.

### 3.1 Average Hop Count

As the average hop count is an indicator of expected packet latency under a moderate workload, it is widely acknowledged as an important static parameter of interconnection networks. However, to the best of our knowledge, a formula for the average hop count in DPillar network has not been published yet. In this section, we derive an exact formula for the average hop count in the DPillar network under all-to-all (uniform random) traffic pattern and the DPillarSP routing algorithm. We define the average hop count in a DCN as the mean number of hops messages will need to travel between every pair of servers, including self-sent messages. In this work we assume that the distance between any neighbouring servers (server-switch-server) is one hop. Table 1 represents parameters and notations used in this study.

**Table 1.** Parameters and notations

| | |
|---|---|
| $\oplus$ | modulo-$k$ addition |
| $\ominus$ | modulo-$k$ subtraction |
| $n$ | number of ports per switch |
| $k$ | number of columns in the DPillar network |
| $N$ | number of servers in the network |
| $F$ | number of flows in the network |
| $C$ | number of channels in the network |
| $N_i$ | number of servers which are $i$ hops away from a given server |
| $\bar{d}_c$ | average number of channels traversed per route |
| $\bar{d}$ | average hop count in the network |
| $\gamma_{max}$ | maximum channel load in the network |
| ABT | aggregate bottleneck throughput |
| DPillarSP | single-path routing algorithm [12] |
| DPillarMP | multi-path routing algorithm [12] |
| RND_SP | random direction DPillarSP |
| SHD_SP | shorter direction DPillarSP |
| RND_MP | random direction DPillarMP |
| SHD_MP | shorter direction DPillarMP |
| RND_SP+TRN | RND_SP with turn back |
| SHD_SP+TRN | RND_SP with turn back |
| RND_MP+TRN | RND_MP with turn back |
| SHD_MP+TRN | RND_MP with turn back |

**Lemma 1.** *The average hop count in the $(n, k)$ DPillar network with the routing algorithm DPillarSP is $\frac{3k-1}{2} + \frac{1-(n/2)^{-k}}{1-(n/2)}$.*

*Proof.* Consider the routing algorithm DPillarSP and let $N_i$ be the number of servers that are $i$ hops away from server $A = (c, v_{k-1}v_{k-2}...v_{c+1}v_c v_{c-1}...v_0)$.

We have $0 \leq i \leq 2k - 1$, since the maximum hop count in an $(n, k)$ DPillar when using DPillarSP is $2k - 1$ [12]. We consider first the case when $0 \leq i \leq k - 1$. It is obvious that $N_0$ represents self-sent traffic so, $N_0 = 1$. As mentioned in Sect. 2.2, the routing algorithm DPillarSP can forward a packet from server $A = (c, v_{k-1}v_{k-2}...v_{c+1}v_cv_{c-1}...v_0)$ to an adjacent server $B = (c \oplus 1, v_{k-1}v_{k-2}...v_{c+1}xv_{c-1}...v_0)$ in the clockwise direction with $0 \leq x \leq n/2 - 1$. Hence, there are $n/2$ possibilities for coordinate $c$ in the row-index of $B$. Consequently, $n/2$ servers are 1 hop away from server $A$ and all are reachable by the routing algorithm DPillarSP. Similarly, server $B$ forwards the packet to server $C = (c \oplus 2, v_{k-1}v_{k-2}...v_{c+2}yxv_{c-1}...v_0)$ with $0 \leq y \leq n/2 - 1$. It means that there are $n/2$ choices for the symbol in position $c$ and $n/2$ choices for the symbol in position $c + 1$ in the row-index of $C$. Hence, $(n/2)^2$ servers are 2 hops away from server $A$ via server $B$. Generally, we can say that $(n/2)^i$ servers are $i$ hops away from a server when $0 \leq i \leq k - 1$, i.e., during the first turn around the pillar.

Now we consider the case when $k \leq i \leq 2k - 1$. In the case of $i = k$, packets travel $k$ hops and in each hop there are $n/2$ choices from $\{0, 1, 2, ..., n/2 - 1\}$ for one of the symbols in the row-index of intermediate servers. As a result, there are $(n/2)^k$ servers which are $k$ hops away from the source node but notice that one of these servers is the source node. Hence, we can say that $N_k = (n/2)^k - N_0 = (n/2)^k - 1$.

Using the same approach, we can find $N_i$ when $k < i \leq 2k - 1$. Packets visit the destination column twice, which take place at $i^{th}$ (last) hop and $(i - k)^{th}$ hop. Hence, to calculate $N_i$, we need to exclude the possible destinations in the first round; $N_i = (n/2)^k - N_{i-k} = (n/2)^k - (n/2)^{i-k}$. To put it in nutshell

$$
N_i = \begin{cases} (n/2)^i & \text{if } 0 \leq i \leq k - 1 \\ (n/2)^k - (n/2)^{i-k} & \text{if } k \leq i \leq 2k - 1 \end{cases} \tag{1}
$$

Applying the same procedure for DPillarSP in anti-clockwise direction results in the same formula. As we calculated the distribution of the path length, it is easy to find the average hop count in the network; $\bar{d} = \sum_{i=0}^{2k-1} iN_i/N$ in which $N$ is the number of servers in the DPillar network. We compute $\sum_{i=0}^{2k-1} iN_i$ by using sum identities.

$$
\sum_{i=0}^{2k-1} iN_i = \sum_{i=0}^{k-1} i(n/2)^i + \sum_{i=k}^{2k-1} i\left((n/2)^k - (n/2)^{i-k}\right)
$$

$$
= \frac{k(3k - 1)}{2}(n/2)^k - k\frac{(n/2)^k - 1}{(n/2) - 1}
$$

Now we are able to compute $\bar{d}$.

$$
\bar{d} = \frac{\sum_{i=0}^{2k-1} iN_i}{N} = \frac{3k - 1}{2} + \frac{1 - (n/2)^{-k}}{1 - (n/2)} \tag{2}
$$

It is worth mentioning that $-1 < \frac{1-(n/2)^{-k}}{1-(n/2)} < 0$. Using this fact, we can determine lower and upper bounds for the average hop count: $\frac{3k-3}{2} < \bar{d} < \frac{3k-1}{2}$.

## 3.2 Aggregate Bottleneck Throughput

The aggregate bottleneck throughput (ABT) is a metric introduced in [6] and is well-suited to evaluate DCNs as it is based on the all-to-all traffic patterns typically found in such systems. The reasoning behind ABT is that the performance of an all-to-all operation is limited by its slowest flow, i.e., the flow with the lowest throughput. Since data centres are a form of stream processing and are therefore bandwidth limited, this is an extremely important performance metric. The ABT is defined as the total number of flows, $F$, over the maximum channel load, $\gamma_{max}$, which means $ABT = F/\gamma_{max}$. $\gamma_{max}$ is determined by the channel that carries the largest fraction of traffic and, in the case of a symmetric topology (such as DPillar), it can be calculated as $\gamma_{max} = \bar{d}_c F/C$ [4] where $\bar{d}_c$ is the average number of channels traversed per route, which equals $2\bar{d}$ because in Lemma 1, we assume that the length of a server-switch-server hop is counted as 1. $C$ is the number of channels in the network that carry traffic, and in the case of the DPillarSP routing algorithm it is equal to twice the number of servers, as each server has 2 ports. Hence, we can calculate the aggregate bottleneck throughput as $ABT = F/\gamma_{max} = C/\bar{d}_c$. Substituting $\bar{d}_c$ and $C$ with $\bar{d}$ and the number of servers results in

$$ABT = \frac{k(n/2)^k}{\bar{d}} \qquad (3)$$

# 4 Improving Routing Algorithms

The main problem of the routing algorithms DPillarSP and DPillarMP is that they route packets in a single direction around the ring (typically clockwise). Hence, half of the connection resources in the DPillar network (those going anti-clockwise) will be left unused. We propose to improve upon the routing algorithms DPillarSP and DPillarMP by utilising both the clockwise and anti-clockwise links.

## 4.1 Random Direction DPillarSP

Random direction DPillarSP (RND_SP) randomly decides a direction (either clockwise or anti-clockwise) at injection time and then applies the DPillarSP in that direction. This way, RND_SP ensures a balanced distribution of the traffic among the two directions. Because RND_SP distributes traffic over a larger number of links (exactly twice) it can sustain considerably higher throughput than DPillarSP. However, RND_SP is not able to improve upon the average hop count of DPillarSP. The rationale is that, as we showed in Lemma 1, the average hop counts in both directions are the same, so choosing randomly between them

---

**Algorithm 1.** *RND_SP(src, dst)*

1: **if** *rand*() mod 2=0 **then**                    ▷ if the random number is even
2:     *path = DPillarSP(src, dst, clockwise)*
3:     **if** *path = null* **then**                    ▷ the clockwise path is faulty
4:         *path = DPillarSP(src, dst, anti-clockwise)*
5:     **end if**
6: **else**                                             ▷ if the random number is odd
7:     *path = DPillarSP(src, dst, anti-clockwise)*
8:     **if** *path = null* **then**                    ▷ the anti-clockwise path is faulty
9:         *path = DPillarSP(src, dst, clockwise)*
10:     **end if**
11: **end if**
12: return *path*

---

leads to exactly the same value. The pseudocode of our random direction single-path routing algorithm, denoted as RND_SP, is shown in Algorithm 1. This algorithm takes the address of the source server (*src*) and the address of the destination server (*dst*) and returns the path between source and destination servers (*path*). RND_SP is based on the routing algorithm DPillarSP which takes source (*src*), destination (*dst*) and direction (*clockwise* or *anti-clockwise*) and returns the path (*path*) between source and destination servers. If the route is faulty then DPillarSP returns null. For fault tolerance purposes, if the route in the selected direction is faulty, we will try the route in the opposite direction.

## 4.2   Shorter Direction DPillarSP

Adding more intelligence to RND_SP routing algorithms, we are able to reduce the average path length in the DPillar networks. We simply estimate which direction will be shorter and try it first. Then, if due to faults in servers, switches, or links the route is not available then we will try the route in the other direction. The shorter direction is estimated on the basis of information about column-indices of source and destination servers. Although this estimation is not always accurate (in some cases it can select a longer direction) it chooses the shortest path in most of the cases and avoids a more complex computation of the shortest path. As will be shown in the next section this simple approach substantially reduces the diameter and average hop count in the DPillar data centre networks. Algorithm 2 shows the pseudocode of shorter direction single-path routing algorithm, SHD_SP.

As already discussed, DPillarMP routes a packet according to the routing algorithm DPillarSP from a proxy source server to a proxy destination server. Using RND_SP and SHD_SP instead of DPillarSP in multi-path routing, we will benefit from load balancing and fault tolerance at the same time. We name the new algorithms RND_MP and SHD_MP, respectively.

**Algorithm 2.** *SHD_SP(src, dst)*

1:  $cw\_hop = (dst.col - src.col + k) \bmod k$      ▷ estimate clockwise hop count
2:  $acw\_hop = (src.col - dst.col + k) \bmod k$    ▷ estimate anti-clockwise hop count
3:  **if** $cw\_hop < acw\_hop$ **then**                ▷ clockwise path is shorter
4:       $path = DPillarSP(src, dst, clockwise)$
5:       **if** $path = null$ **then**            ▷ the clockwise path is faulty
6:           $path = DPillarSP(src, dst, anti\text{-}clockwise)$
7:       **end if**
8:  **else if** $acw\_hop < cw\_hop$ **then**        ▷ anti-clockwise path is shorter
9:       $path = DPillarSP(src, dst, anti\text{-}clockwise)$
10:      **if** $path = null$ **then**         ▷ the anti-clockwise path is faulty
11:          $path = DPillarSP(src, dst, clockwise)$
12:      **end if**
13: **else**                             ▷ both hop counts are the same
14:      $path = RND\_SP(src, dst)$
15: **end if**
16: **return** $path$

### 4.3  Turn Back Feature

The routing algorithms DPillarSP and DPillarMP assume a server always forwards packets in one direction. However, it is possible to send packets in the reverse direction. Servers in two neighbouring columns with the same row-index are connected to the same switch. Hence, after forwarding a packet to an intermediate server whose row-index is the same as the row-index of the destination, the intermediate server estimates which direction will be shorter (similar to SHD_SP). If the route in the reverse direction is shorter, the packet forwarding direction will be changed (turn back) to bypass the longer route.

## 5  Experimental Results

We used an in-house developed software tool to carry out the experimental work. The tool provides implementations of the discussed routing algorithms and enables us to ascertain how they will compare against each other. The tool also undertakes a breadth-first search (BFS) which allows us to compute the length of the shortest path between any two servers and also to examine whether two servers become disconnected in the presence of link failures. The operation of the tool is as follows: for each flow in the workload, it computes the route using the routing algorithm and updates link utilisation accordingly. Then it reports a large number of statistics of interest about scalability (in terms of diameter, average hop count and ABT) and fault tolerance (in terms of node-to-node connectivity under link failures).

Figure 4 shows how the average hop count and ABT scale with the number of servers, for different values of $n$ and $k$ when using DPillarSP. These figures also confirm that our analytical model (Sect. 3.1) perfectly matches the experimental results.

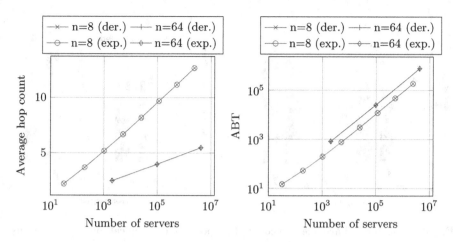

**Fig. 4.** The average hop count and the ABT for different size of DPillar DCNs when using DPillarSP, comparing experimental results with those derived in Lemma 1

Once the correctness of the analytical models has been ascertained, we proceed to discuss on how these models can be used when designing a DPillar-based data centre. Basically, they can be employed to carry out a broad exploration of the design space which would otherwise be prohibited to do based on other form of empirical or practical data. A representative example of such exploration can be seen in Fig. 5. There, we show the average hop count and ABT of a wide range of DPillar sizes and switch radices. This information, together with cost and power estimates – which are outside of the scope of this paper – can be used to decide the *best* configuration of the datacentre. Note that the *best* may have different meanings in different contexts and, indeed, may possibly lead to a Pareto front in some cases.

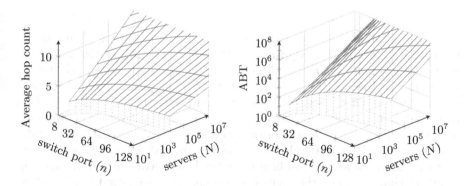

**Fig. 5.** Design space exploration of DPillar DCN based on average hop count and ABT

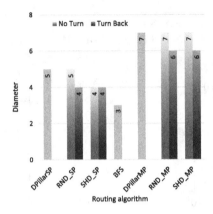
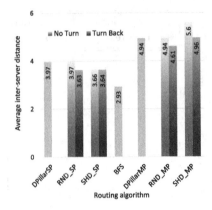

**Fig. 6.** Diameter and average hop count of proposed and canonical routing algorithms

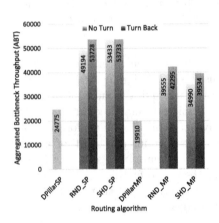
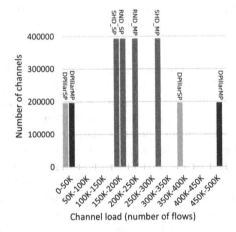

**Fig. 7.** ABT and load distribution of proposed and canonical routing algorithms

We next compare the performance of our proposed routing algorithms in the (64,3) DPillar DCN comprising 98304 servers and 3072 switches. Figure 6 shows the maximum and average hop count and compares them with the results obtained from BFS which is used to find the shortest path between any source and destination. We can see that adding randomness to the canonical algorithms (RND_SP and RND_MP) does not make any change in diameter and average hop count. However, choosing shorter direction (SHD_SP and SHD_MP) results in lower diameter and average hop count, as we expected. These figures also show that the turn back feature can help to reduce both maximum and average hop count. Having compared the average hop count with diameter in each routing algorithm, we can infer that the hop count histogram in DPillar networks follows a skewed distribution with the tail on the left-hand side.

The above figures show a clear improvement ($\sim 5\% - 10\%$) in terms of hop counts over the routing algorithms DPillarSP and DPillarMP. Figure 7 shows that when it comes to the aggregate bottleneck throughput the improvement is much more substantial ($\sim$2x). In the context of datacentres, whose performance is bandwidth limited, this can translate into a huge impact.

Our experimental results also show that in the algorithms DPillarSP and DPillarMP half of the channels are never used and the other half have exactly the same load which means that the traffic is perfectly distributed over these channels. The experimental results also reveal that in our proposed routing algorithms all channels have a very similar load that is very close to maximum load, which demonstrates very good load balancing properties.

We have seen above that the single-path routing family (DPillarSP, RND_SP, and SHD_SP with and without turn back) can sustain a better performance than multi-path routing family (DPillarMP, RND_MP, and SHD_MP with and without turn back) in terms of scalability. However, in the context of large-scale data centres, better performance may not necessarily be sufficient if it is not accompanied by a high resistance to failures. The rationale for this is that when scaling up to hundreds of thousands of servers, failures are common with the mean-time between failures being as short as hours or even minutes. In other words, failures are ubiquitous and so the DCN should be able to deal with them and remain competitively operational. Any network whose performance degrades rapidly with the number of failures is unacceptable, even if it does provide the best performance in a fault-free environment. Figure 8 shows how the (64,3) DPillar DCN is affected by link failures in the terms of connectivity. Looking at the obtained result from BFS, we can see that DPillar network offers a rich connection between servers. However, the routing algorithms DPillarSP and DPillarMP are not able to exploit this richness and in fact have a very poor resilience to failures. For a 20 % failure rate, less than 20 % of the system remains

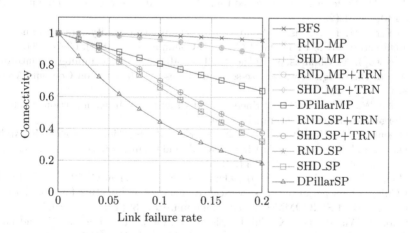

**Fig. 8.** Percentage of pairs of nodes connected by different routing algorithms

connected. This goes up to a still disappointing 64 % with DPillarMP. Our proposed MP algorithms keep a 87 % connectivity, much closer to the optimal value (96 %).

# 6 Conclusion

The DPillar DCN has attracted considerable attention as a server-centric DCN because of its nice theoretical properties (short distances, symmetry, path diversity). However, the originally proposed routing algorithms, DPillarSP and DPillarMP, have some limitations that prevent them from exploiting these properties and, hence, suffer from poor performance and resilience to failures. In this paper, we propose a collection of algorithms based on the two original ones. A detailed evaluation shows that the proposed algorithms can reduce the average hop count and increase the aggregate bottleneck throughput by more than two times, while keeping a balanced utilisation of network resources and degrading much more gracefully with network failures. Another contribution of this paper is that we derived the average hop count and ABT for DPillarSP, so it would enable a quick exploration of the design space. We provide a case study to illustrate the proposed methodology. Our next objective is to carry out timing analysis in DPillar networks and to develop an analytical model and validate it under different workload conditions.

**Acknowledgement.** This work has been funded by the Engineering and Physical Sciences Research Council (EPSRC) through grants EP/K015680/1 and EP/K015699/1.

# References

1. Abts, D., Felderman, B.: A guided tour of data-center networking. Commun. ACM **55**(6), 44–51 (2012)
2. Al-Fares, M., Loukissas, A., Vahdat, A.: A scalable, commodity data center network architecture. ACM SIGCOMM Comput. Commun. Rev. **38**(4), 63–74 (2008)
3. Barroso, L.A., Clidaras, J., Hölzle, U.: The datacenter as a computer: an introduction to the design of warehouse-scale machines. Synth. Lect. on Comput. Archit. **8**(3), 1–154 (2013)
4. Dally, W.J., Towles, B.P.: Principles and Practices of Interconnection Networks. Morgan Kaufmann, San Francisco (2004)
5. Greenberg, A., Hamilton, J.R., Jain, N., Kandula, S., Kim, C., Lahiri, P., Maltz, D.A., Patel, P., Sengupta, S.: VL2: a scalable and flexible data center network. Commun. of the ACM **54**(3), 95–104 (2011)
6. Guo, C., Lu, G., Li, D., Wu, H., Zhang, X., Shi, Y., Tian, C., Zhang, Y., Lu, S.: BCube: a high performance, server-centric network architecture for modular data centers. ACM SIGCOMM Comput. Commun. Rev. **39**(4), 63–74 (2009)
7. Guo, C., Wu, H., Tan, K., Shi, L., Zhang, Y., Lu, S.: DCell: a scalable and fault-tolerant network structure for data centers. ACM SIGCOMM Comput. Commun. Rev. **38**(4), 75–86 (2008)

8. Guo, D., Chen, T., Li, D., Li, M., Liu, Y., Chen, G.: Expandable and cost-effective network structures for data centers using dual-port servers. IEEE Trans. Comput. **62**(7), 1303–1317 (2013)
9. Li, D., Guo, C., Wu, H., Tan, K., Zhang, Y., Lu, S.: Ficonn: using backup port for server interconnection in data centers. In: INFOCOM, pp. 2276–2285. IEEE (2009)
10. Li, D., Wu, J.: On the design and analysis of data center network architectures for interconnecting dual-port servers. In: INFOCOM, pp. 1851–1859. IEEE (2014)
11. Liao, Y., Yin, D., Gao, L.: Dpillar: Scalable dual-port server interconnection for data center networks. In: 2010 Proceedings of 19th International Conference on Computer Communications and Networks (ICCCN), pp. 1–6. IEEE (2010)
12. Liao, Y., Yin, J., Yin, D., Gao, L.: Dpillar: Dual-port server interconnection network for large scale data centers. Comput. Netw. **56**(8), 2132–2147 (2012)

# MR-COF: A Genetic MapReduce Configuration Optimization Framework

Chao Liu[1,2], Deze Zeng[1(✉)], Hong Yao[1], Chengyu Hu[1],
Xuesong Yan[1], and Yuanyuan Fan[1]

[1] Hubei Key Laboratory of Intelligent Geo-Information Processing,
China University of Geosciences, Wuhan 430074, China
deze@cug.edu.cn
[2] China Services Computing Technology and System Lab and Cluster and Grid
Computing Lab, Huazhong University of Science and Technology,
Wuhan 430074, China

**Abstract.** Hadoop/MapReduce has emerged as a de facto programming framework to explore cloud-computing resources. Hadoop has many configuration parameters, some of which are crucial to the performance of MapReduce jobs. In practice, these parameters are usually set to default or inappropriate values. This severely limits system performance (e.g., execution time). Therefore, it is essential but also challenging to investigate how to automatically tune these parameters to optimize MapReduce job performance. In this paper, we propose an automatic MapReduce configuration optimization framework named as MR-COF. By monitoring and analyzing the runtime behavior, the framework adopts a cost-based performance prediction model that predicts the MapReduce job performance. In addition, we design a genetic search algorithm which iteratively tunes parameters in order to find out the best one. Testbed-based experimental results show that the average MapReduce job performance is increased by 35 % with MR-COF compared to the default configuration.

**Keywords:** Mapreduce · Massive data processing · Parameter configuration · Performance optimization · Search algorithm

## 1 Introduction

In recent years, massive data processing applications (e.g., web indexing and searching; enterprise and scientific data processing) have become increasingly more and more popular. Traditional parallel programming techniques are constrained by their development complexity, scalability, and flexibility; therefore, they cannot meet the growing requirements of large-scale data processing. To explore bulk cloud computing resources, the MapReduce programming model [1] emerges as a promising technology to deal with big data processing. Hadoop [2] is an open source implementation of MapReduce characterized by its programming simplicity, scalability, and fault tolerance. Consequently, it has been widely studied in academia and business communities. However, some recent studies show that Hadoop/MapReduce suffers some performance and cost-effectiveness problems, especially when a job occupies intensive

© Springer International Publishing Switzerland 2015
G. Wang et al. (Eds.): ICA3PP 2015, Part IV, LNCS 9531, pp. 344–357, 2015.
DOI: 10.1007/978-3-319-27140-8_24

hardware resources. For example, Pavlo et al. [3] showed that MapReduce program is 2–30 times slower than a parallel database program with the same function in the same medium-scale cluster environment.

Obviously, the values of configuration parameters in Hadoop settings have significant influence or even are crucial to job performance and system efficiency. Therefore, it is important to know how to adjust these parameters so as to improve the MapReduce job performance [4, 5]. For example, consider the configuration parameter *mapred.tasktracker.map.tasks.maximum*, which is used to control the number of map tasks within each task node. Setting the parameter to a smaller value can result in lower CPU utilization, while a larger value may lead to resource competition and job performance degradation. Hadoop administrators and users normally use default parameter settings or manually adjust the values of few parameters based on their experiences. However, there is no one-size-fits-all solution. The default settings are generally not the best for most MapReduce jobs, and manual adjustment tends to be inefficient or even error-prone. To tackle this issue, pioneering researchers and engineers have carried out some preliminary research on automatic optimization of Hadoop parameters based on different aspects. For example, Babu et al. [6] proposed a system-level code rewrite-based approach to automatically adjust Hadoop settings by adding a functional module. However, this approach has two main disadvantages. First, some parameters are subject to the application characteristics and to available resources in Hadoop; therefore, the lack of an accurate cost model makes it hard to achieve optimized results at the system level. Second, the underlying system code modification is complex, making it difficult to effectively manage and maintain.

Furthermore, parameter tuning in Hadoop is time consuming because a large number of configuration parameters (over 100) must be configured. To solve this problem, in this paper, we present a genetic MapReduce Configuration Optimization Framework (MR-COF) for massive data processing applications. MR-COF adopts a dynamic monitoring mechanism to profile the runtime behaviors of MapReduce jobs. In addition, a cost-based performance prediction model is developed and incorporated. MR-COF provides the ability to constantly adjust parameters through a heuristic search strategy to enhance MapReduce job performance in Hadoop.

The rest of this paper is organized as follows. Section 2 discusses works related to MapReduce performance optimization. The system architecture and key mechanisms of MR-COF for MapReduce parameter optimization are presented in Sect. 3. Section 4 describes the experimental environment and presents the performance evaluation. Finally, we conclude this work in Sect. 5.

## 2 Related Works

Because the basic implementation of MapReduce model has many deficiencies, researchers have conducted many optimization studies from different perspectives to improve MapReduce job performance. In this section, we summary some recent work on MapReduce optimization from three different aspects, i.e., usability optimization, process optimization and parameter configuration optimization.

**MapReduce Usability Optimization:** A number of techniques have been proposed to provide support for SQL semantics to enhance the usability of MapReduce programming [7–10]. PigLatin [7], designed by Yahoo, is a dataflow programming language on top of MapReduce and uses advanced declarative query SQL concepts to provide data manipulation primitives, such as projection and connection. Sawzall [8] is a scripting language used for Google MapReduce applications. Sawzall provides an output primitive *emit*, which transmits data to an external aggregator (e.g., Sum, Average). Hive [9, 10] is an open source data warehousing solution developed by Facebook. Hive supports a SQL subset and provides complex types (e.g., maps, lists). In addition, Hive provides HiveQL, a declarative query language. Therefore, queries written in HiveQL can be compiled into MapReduce jobs and then run in Hadoop environments.

**MapReduce Process Optimization:** The basic MapReduce framework mandatorily writes the output data of each map and reduce task to a local file. The next phase of MapReduce tasks need to read data from disk. Such process may cause performance degradation in the plurality of consecutive MapReduce jobs. The performance optimization of the MapReduce process itself has gained attention in research community [11, 12]. Yang et al. [11] proposed a Map-Reduce-Merge model, which introduces a Merge phase to MapReduce that can efficiently merge partitioned and sorted data from two different reducer outputs into one. The Map-Join-Reduce [12] system improves and extends the MapReduce runtime framework by adding a Join phase to support the implementation of complex data analyses on a large cluster and to avoid frequent checkpoints and the exchange of intermediate results.

**MapReduce Parameter Configuration Optimization:** It has been shown that MapReduce parameter configuration optimization is time consuming because the parameter space can go up to 100 [13]. Moreover, different parameters have different effects on the performance of massive data processing applications. Some of them are even interdependent. In recent years, a number of studies have concentrate on optimizing MapReduce configuration parameters.

From the perspective of Hadoop job performance predication, a variety of performance models have been proposed. For example, Shi et al. [14] proposed MRTuner, a MapReduce job overall optimization tool that uses a Production–Transmission–Consumption Model to analyze the parallel execution of MapReduce tasks. MRON-LINE [15] is an on line tuning system that provides the fine-grained control of Hadoop configuration parameters and supports different settings for different tasks. A regression-based model is proposed in [16]. This model can predict the performance of massive data processing jobs running on large-scale Hadoop clusters through data sampling and job execution within a small number of nodes. Zhang et al. [17] proposed a MapReduce job performance model based on automatic resource allocation and deduction. The model is applicable to estimate completion time using varied input data and cluster resources. Yigibasi et al. [18] studied a Support Vector Regression (SVR) model used to automatically tune Hadoop cluster configuration parameters. In [19], the time cost model of a MapReduce job is represented as the weighted linear combination of a set of non-linear functions.

In terms of the search schema to find optimal Hadoop configuration parameters, many parameter optimization search strategies in the Hadoop cloud have been studied.

Gunther [20] is a search-based automatic tuning tool using a heuristic algorithm to identify optimal Hadoop configuration parameters. Herodotou et al. [21] proposed Starfish, a cost-based self-tuning system that uses a subspace random search method to find the approximate optimal parameter configurations through enumeration.

Different methods can also be used with regard to resource usage statistics for Hadoop jobs. To achieve the goal of maximizing the MapReduce job performance while minimizing cost, a statistical signature generation model is proposed in [22], aiming to optimize MapReduce job resource provision in the cloud. The optimization method includes two components. First, a RS (Resource Set) Maximizer is responsible for calculating optimal configuration parameters to fully utilize the resources. Second, a RS Sizer is designed to determine the set of resources required to maintain the balance between costs and performance. This method improves the provision capability of Hadoop jobs by counting the resource consumption of jobs. Wang et al. [23] proposed MRPerf, a simulator to capture setup information such as node, storage capacity, network topology configuration, data layout, and the application's I/O characteristics. This information is used to predict application performance and improve the environment settings in MapReduce. Verma et al. [24] proposed SimMR, another simulation environment for MapReduce clusters that comprises three components: a trace generator, a simulator, and a scheduling policy.

# 3 Design of MR-COF

## 3.1 System Overview

The overall architecture of MR-COF is shown in Fig. 1. MR-COF is an automatic optimizer based on performance prediction to tune MapReduce configuration parameters. The design of MR-COF mainly consists of three parts: the runtime monitoring and analysis module (MAM), the performance prediction module (PPM) and the configuration parameter optimization module (POM). MAM is used to monitor and statistically analyze the running information of a MapReduce job and then write to a profile. PPM is responsible for predicting job performance based on the current configuration parameters according to the MAM output file. In accordance with the estimated job completion time, POM is then applied to adjust configuration parameters based on a genetic search algorithm.

The working process of the MR-COF system is as follows. First, the client submits a MapReduce job to the Hadoop environment through the command interface. The Hadoop Distributed File System (HDFS) is used to persistently store programs, input and output data, and configuration files. Second, MR-COF starts MAM and transmits the output information to PPM to estimate the job completion time. Third, POM iteratively searches for better configuration parameters until the termination condition is satisfied, and the result is sent back to the client, allowing the client to rerun the MapReduce job with the optimized configuration parameters.

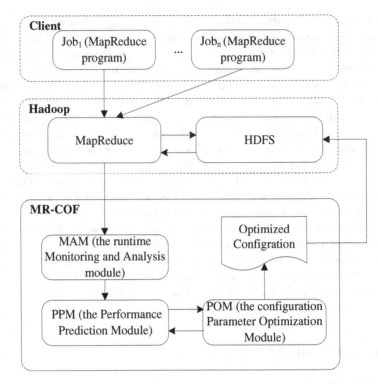

**Fig. 1.** MR-COF system architecture

## 3.2   MapReduce Monitoring and Analysis

In MR-COF, the MAM module is used to monitor and statistically analyze data flow information and the execution time of map or reduce tasks during a job running. The data flow information consists of the size of the data bytes generated by each processing phase during the execution of a MapReduce job. For example, an intermediate result created by a map task may flow to a reduce task as input data. The execution time information includes all the time cost in each phase of the map or the reduce task during the execution of a MapReduce job. The statistical operation mainly counts the aggregation or average value of the data flow or the execution time information.

The MAM module integrates Btrace [25], a dynamic monitoring tool, to support the collection of statistical information in the map or reduce tasks on each work node. At the same time, MAM allows to generate an approximate monitoring and analysis profile based on the feedback, regarding the monitoring information through the online controlling of the Btrace proxy switch on each work node and MapReduce task sampling. Afterwards, the master node can predict the MapReduce job performance and search for optimized configuration parameters. Details of the performance model and parameter configuration optimization algorithm will be described in Sects. 3.3 and 3.4.

The MAM process flow can be divided into five steps. (1) The Btrace script monitoring code is inserted into the MapReduce program in the master node.

(2) The modified MapReduce program is distributed to each work node for processing. (3) The job begins to execute map tasks. The MR-COF MAM module dynamically monitors and collects the data flow information and execution time of each phase of map tasks and then aggregates that information. (4) The job begins to execute reduce tasks, and similarly the MAM module monitors, collects, and aggregates all the information in each reduce task. (5) All the monitoring information is written to a profile and finally merged to generate MapReduce job monitoring and analysis files.

Using dynamic monitoring reduce tasks as an example, we describe how the MAM module inserts Btrace monitoring functions at the point when a job or task state changes (e.g., reduce task start time and end time). The process can be divided into four steps. (1) The map output intermediate data must be copied before performing the reduce tasks. Therefore, the *reduceTask_shuffle* monitoring point should be inserted prior to the *reduceCopier()* method. (2) The merge and sort operations are launched as soon as the full input data is fetched. Thus, the *reduceTask_merge* monitoring point should be inserted after the *copyPhase.complete()* method in the *ReduceTask* class. (3) Subsequently, the system executes the *reduce.run ()* method after completing the sort operation, so the *reduceTask_reducer* monitoring point should be inserted next to the *sortPhase.complete()* method. (4) Finally, the output results are written back to the underlying distributed file system. Therefore, the *reduceTask_writeDFS* monitoring point should be inserted before the *mapreduce.RecordWriter()* method.

### 3.3   Cost-Based Performance Prediction Model

In this section, we present the cost-based performance model used to estimate the execution time of a MapReduce job. First, we describe the basic parameters of the performance model (Table 1).

**Table 1.** Performance model parameters

| Parameter Name | Description |
| --- | --- |
| *inputBytes* | The number of bytes in the job input data |
| *mapOutputBytes* | The number of bytes in all map task output data |
| *combineOutputBytes* | The total number of bytes of all map task output data after applying the Combine function. If not applied, the number is equal to mapOutputBytes. |
| *outputBytes* | The number of bytes in the job output data |
| *numNodes* | The number of nodes in the Hadoop environment |
| *chunkBytes* | The number of bytes in a data chunk |
| *numReducers* | The number of reduce tasks actually executed |

The basic parameters can be classified into three types, i.e., input and output (I/O) parameters, cluster configuration parameters and program parameters. The I/O parameters consist of *inputBytes*, *mapOutputBytes*, *combineOutputBytes*, and *outputBytes*. The cluster configuration parameters include *numNodes* and *chunkBytes*. The program parameters contain *numReducers*.

Next, we explain the time cost of each phase of a MapReduce job and define some terms used to deduce the cost-based performance model.

**Startup Time:** The startup time is denoted as $T_{startup}$ and is related to CPU time, the disk and network I/O time for job execution, depending on the computing environment. For example, consider a user who submits a MapReduce job. First, it causes job startup cost $T_{jobStartup}$. Following the initialization of the job, the task allocation process is started and incurs task startup cost $T_{taskStartup}$. In general, the data scale of massive data-processing applications is far larger than a piece of *chunkBytes*; therefore, the startup time is usually negligible because the processing time is dominant.

**Job Processing Time:** The processing overhead of the map phase and the reduce phase constitutes the job processing time. The processing overhead of the map phase is denoted as $T_{map}$. It can be divided into five parts: $T_{readDFS}$, $T_{Mapper}$, $T_{sort}$, $T_{combiner}$, and $T_{spill}$, referring to the overhead of reading a byte from HDFS, the overhead of executing the Mapper function on the byte that was just read, the overhead of sorting a byte, the overhead of executing the Combiner function on a byte, the overhead of spilling a byte to the local file system, respectively. The processing overhead of the reduce phase is denoted as $T_{reduce}$. It consists of four parts: $T_{shuffle}$, $T_{merge}$, $T_{Reducer}$, and $T_{writeDFS}$, referring to the overhead of reading a byte that is transmitted through the network from the intermediate results generated by the Mapper function, the overhead of sorting and merging a byte from the previous step, the overhead of executing the Reducer function on a byte, the overhead of writing a byte of the resulting data to HDFS, respectively.

$$
\begin{aligned}
T = T_{jobStartup} + T_{taskStartup} * \; & \frac{\frac{inputBytes}{chunkBytes} + numReudcers}{numNodes} \\
+ \, (T_{readDFS} + T_{Mapper}) * \; & \frac{inputBytes}{numNodes} \\
(T_{sort} + T_{combiner}) * \; & \frac{mapOutputBytes}{numNodes} \\
T_{spill} * \; & \frac{combineOutputBytes}{numNodes} \\
+ \, (T_{suffle} + T_{merge} + T_{Reducer}) * \; & \frac{mapOutputBytes}{numReducers} \\
+ \, T_{writeDFS} * \; & \frac{outputBytes}{numReducers}
\end{aligned}
\tag{1}
$$

The performance prediction of a MapReduce job can be represented as the total time predicted from the job's beginning to when the job processing is complete. According to the above analysis, the execution time of a MapReduce job includes $T_{jobStartup}$, $T_{taskStartup}$, $T_{map}$, and $T_{reduce}$. Therefore, we propose a cost-based MapReduce performance prediction model, as shown in Eq. (1).

In Eq. (1), different parameters imply different costs. $T_{jobStartup}$ and $T_{taskStartup}$ involve the CPU, disk, and network costs. $T_{Mapper}$, $T_{sort}$, $T_{combiner}$, $T_{merge}$, and $T_{Reducer}$ mainly refer to the CPU cost. $T_{spill}$ and $T_{writeDFS}$ are primarily about the disk I/O cost. Finally, $T_{shuffle}$ covers the network I/O cost.

We use MRPerf [23], a lightweight Hadoop simulator, to support the establishment of a discrete-time simulating MapReduce job execution model. The structure of the performance prediction module is shown in Fig. 2. The execution flow for job performance prediction is as follows. First, a MapReduce job is given with a fixed input data size and uses the default parameter configuration. Then, the PPM actually executes the job using sampling technology to gain statistical information about the time cost of each task processing phase by monitoring and analyzing the MapReduce job. Second, the PPM can be established using the previous statistical information. Third, the virtual job profile of the same MapReduce job with a modified parameter configuration can be deduced through the combination of PPM and the MRPerf simulator. Finally, the time cost of the MapReduce job with the altered configuration is calculated.

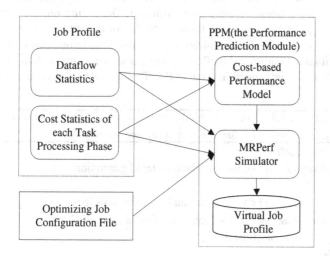

**Fig. 2.** The PPM structure

### 3.4   Automatic Parameter Configuration Optimization Algorithm

In this section, we first provide the formal definition for parameter configuration set, MapReduce job, and optimization objective. Then, we propose an automatic parameter optimization algorithm implemented in POM.

**Definition 1.** Suppose that $S$ is the parameter configuration set, which is composed of pairs of parameter names and attribute values. The value range of each attribute value can be expressed as a one-dimensional vector $\overrightarrow{S[i]}$, where the length represents the number of possible values for the $i$-th parameter.

**Definition 2.** A MapReduce job $J$ can be seen as a quad-tuple related to MapReduce program $p$, the data $d$ to be processed, the resource set $R$ in the running environment, and the specified system parameter configuration set $S$, i.e., $J = <p, d, R, S>$. In this paper, we assume that the data is sampled in fixed size and the resource in the job's running environment is unchanged. Therefore, $d$ and $R$ can both be viewed as constant.

**Definition 3.** For a certain MapReduce program $p$, we aim to find a parameter configuration set $S_i$, according to the special search schema and restriction condition so that the job execution time $T$ is approximately shortest. The optimized configuration set is expressed as $S_{opt}$, i.e.,

$$S_{opt} = \underset{s_i \in C}{\mathrm{argmin}}\ T_p$$

where $C$ is the value space of the parameter configuration set.

Our optimization objective is to find an optimized parameter configuration from the finite vector space of parameter values so that the performance of the MapReduce job is approximately optimal. Genetic algorithm (GA) is a heuristic global search algorithm that simulates the process of biological evolution. Depending on the proper fitness function, GA can effectively avoid falling into the local optimum. Therefore, GA is widely used in combinatorial optimization problems [26]. In our MR-COF system, a search algorithm to optimize MapReduce job parameter configurations is proposed based on GA and is integrated into the POM. The algorithm is shown in Fig. 3.

---

**Input:** $P(0)$, the initial population with the size of $N$ and $t$, the initial generation
**Output:** $C_{Best}$, the best individual, i.e., the optimized schema

1: $P(0) \leftarrow$ *initialize()*
2: $t \leftarrow 0$ //Assign the initial value of the number of generation
3: **do**
4:     **for** $i$ in $[0 \dots N{-}1]$ **do** //$N$ is the number of elements in the set
5:         Evaluate *fitnesss*($C_i$) //Evaluating the fitness value of $C_i$ in $P(t)$
6:         $C_{Best} = $ *maximum*(**fitness**($C_i$))
7:     **end for**
8:     $P_S(t) \leftarrow$ *select(P(t))* //execute the selection operation
9:     $P_C(t) \leftarrow$ *crossover(P(t))* // execute the crossover operation
10:    $P_M(t) \leftarrow$ *mutation(P(t))* // execute the mutation operation
11:    $P(t + 1) \leftarrow P(t)$ U $P_C(t)$ U $P_M(t)$ //generate the next generation population
12:    $t \leftarrow t + 1$
13: **while** t <= $T$ or *distance(P(t), P(t-1) )* < $\mu$ //terminate conditions

---

**Fig. 3.** Parameter configuration-optimization algorithm

The evaluation function of an individual in the population, *fitness*($C_i$), is defined as $1/JobCompletionTime_i$, and the *distance()* function is used to calculate the difference between the average fitness of the current population and the average fitness of the previous generation population. Empirically, we set $T = 20$ and $\mu = 0.05$. The algorithm is terminated until the converge condition is satisfied. Due to the quick sort method is applied to sort the $n$ individuals according to the fitness values during each *while* loop, so the time complexity of the quick sort equals to $O(N * \log N)$. As T is the number of loops, the overall time complexity of the parameter configuration optimization algorithm is $O(N * \mathrm{T}* \log N)$.

# 4 Performance Evaluation

## 4.1 Experimental Environment

The experiments are run in an in-house cloud environment comprising eight homogeneous machine nodes. One node is treated as the master node and is used to deploy NameNode and JobTracker. The other seven nodes are slavers to deploy DataNode and TaskTracker. Each node has the same software and hardware settings as follows.

**Hardware Settings:** The CPU is a 2 × Intel 2.26GHZ Xeon E5520 with four cores and an 8 MB L3 cache. The memory is 16 GB DDR 3 with a 1066 MHZ FSB frequency. The SAS disk has a 146 GB capacity. Finally, each node is equipped with 2 × 1000 M Ethernet cards.

**Software Setting:** The software installation includes RHEL 5.1 OS (kernel version 2.6.18-128.e15), Java (version 1.6.0_18), and Hadoop (version 0.20.2).

**Selected Parameters:** The selected lists of parameters tuned through the MR-COF optimizer are shown in Table 2. The other parameters are set by default.

**Table 2.** Descriptions of the 10 selected parameters

| Configuration Parameters | Default Value | Range: Step |
|---|---|---|
| *dfs.block.size* | 64 MB | [64, 512]: 64 |
| *mapred.reduce.tasks* | 1 | [5, 50]: 5 |
| *mapred.tasktracker.map.tasks.maximum* | 2 | [2, 10]: 2 |
| *mapred.tasktracker.reduce.tasks.maximum* | 2 | [2, 10]: 2 |
| *io.sort.factor* | 10 | [10, 100]: 10 |
| *io.sort.mb* | 100 | [100, 300]: 50 |
| *io.sort.record.percent* | 0.05 | [0.05,0.15]:0.02 |
| *io.sort.spill.percent* | 0.8 | [0.2, 0.8]: 0.1 |
| *mapred.job.shuffle.input.buffer.percent* | 0.7 | [0.7, 0.8]: 0.01 |
| *mapred.job.shuffle.merge.percent* | 0.66 | [0.66, 0.8]:0.01 |

## 4.2 Accuracy of Performance Prediction Model

To evaluate the prediction accuracy of MR-COF, we use the default configuration to compare the actual execution time and the MR-COF's predicted time for three different MapReduce jobs by varying the size of the input data. We run the experiments three times and record the average time. The results for Sort, WordCount, and Grep jobs with 1 GB, 5 GB, and 10 GB of input data are shown in Fig. 4. In general, the relative differences between the predicted time and the actual execution time range from 6 % to 13 %, indicating that the accuracy is within an acceptable range.

Figure 5 compares the actual and predicted execution time for the Map and Reduce breakdown phases respectively, using a WordCount MapReduce job with 1 GB of data as an example. As seen in Fig. 5(a), the predicted time is fairly close to the actual

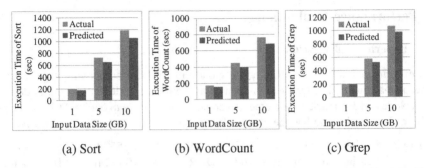

**Fig. 4.** Total execution times for three jobs from the actual run and as predicted by MR-COF

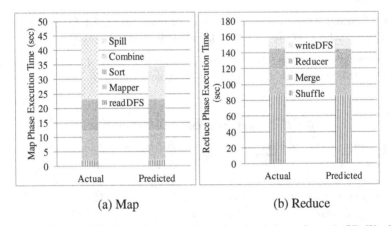

**Fig. 5.** Map phase and Reduce phase execution time breakdown for a 1 GB WordCount MapReduce job from the actual run and as predicted by MR-COF

execution time in each Map breakdown phase except for the predicted time in the Spill operation, which is significantly different from the actual time. The main reason for this is that our cost-based MapReduce performance prediction model does not consider the actual disk I/O overhead. In Fig. 5(b), we also can observe that the difference between the predicted and actual execution time for the Reduce phases is negligible.

### 4.3  Performance of Configuration Parameter Optimization

To verify MR-COF's enhanced effect on job performance, we compare the execution time of Sort, WordCount, and Grep jobs using the default configuration and the optimized configuration. For example, with 10 GB of input data, the time spent on a Sort job with the optimized configuration decreases 41 %, compared to the time spent on a job with the default configuration (Fig. 6).

Table 3 shows the optimized parameter configuration results for three different jobs with 1 GB of input data. It is noted that, the configurations are found through the proposed heuristic algorithm in Sect. 3.4. We can observe that the optimized parameter values for Grep are different from those of Sort and WordCount. The reason behind such fact is that Grep is CPU intensive, while Sort and WordCount are data intensive. For example, Sort and WordCount handle more sorting operations in memory than Grep. Therefore, Sort and WordCount set larger values for parameters related sort operation (i.e., *io.sort.mb* and *io.sort.record.percent*) compared to Grep.

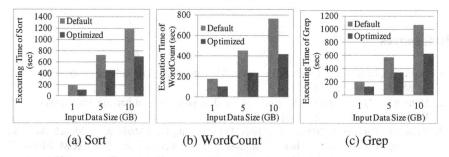

(a) Sort              (b) WordCount                (c) Grep

**Fig. 6.** Performance comparison of Sort, WordCount, and Grep jobs

**Table 3.** Optimized parameter configuration comparison of Sort, WordCount, and Grep

| Configuration Parameters | Sort | Word-Count | Grep |
|---|---|---|---|
| *dfs.block.size* | 256 | 256 | 320 |
| *mapred.reduce.tasks* | 15 | 20 | 40 |
| *mapred.tasktracker.map.tasks.maximum* | 4 | 4 | 8 |
| *mapred.tasktracker.reduce.tasks.maximum* | 4 | 4 | 6 |
| *io.sort.factor* | 80 | 90 | 30 |
| *io.sort.mb* | 200 | 250 | 150 |
| *io.sort.record.percent* | 0.15 | 0.12 | 0.06 |
| *io.sort.spill.percent* | 0.8 | 0.8 | 0.6 |
| *mapred.job.shuffle.input.buffer.percent* | 0.78 | 0.75 | 0.74 |
| *mapred.job.shuffle.merge.percent* | 0.68 | 0.68 | 0.66 |

# 5  Conclusions

In Hadoop, a large number of parameters can affect the performance of MapReduce jobs. In this paper, we present MR-COF, a genetic MapReduce parameter configuration optimization framework. The optimization framework includes three main modules: the runtime monitoring and analysis module, the performance prediction module and the configuration parameter optimization module. We propose a cost-based job performance prediction model and study a genetic parameter configuration optimization algorithm. We conduct extensive experiments using three types of massive data analysis applications: Sort, WordCount, and Grep. The experimental results show that MR-COF has good prediction accuracy. In addition, the optimized configuration substantially increases the job execution performance, compared to the default configuration.

**Acknowledgments.** This paper is supported by China National Natural Science Foundation under grant Nos. 61272470, 61305087, 61402425, 61440060, 41404076 and 61501412; the China Postdoctoral Science Foundation funded project under grant No. 2014M562086; the key projects of Hubei Provincial Natural Science Foundation under grant No. 2015CFA065; the Fundamental Research Funds for the Central Universities, China University of Geosciences, Wuhan under grant No. CUGL130233.

# References

1. Dean, J., Ghemawat, S.: Mapreduce: simplified data processing on large clusters. Commun. ACM **51**(1), 107–113 (2008)
2. Dittrich, J., Quiané-Ruiz, J.A.: Efficient big data processing in hadoop MapReduce. Proc. VLDB Endowment **5**(12), 2014–2015 (2012)
3. Pavlo, A., Paulson, E., Rasin, A., Abadi, D.J., DeWitt, D.J., Madden, S., Stonebraker, M.: A comparison of approaches to large-scale data analysis. In: The ACM SIGMOD International Conference on Management of Data, pp. 165–178. ACM Press (2009)
4. Liu, C., Jin, H., Jiang, W., Hai, L.: Research on performance optimization approach of data-intensive application with MapReduce. J. Wuhan Univ. Technol. **32**(20), 36–41 (2010)
5. Jiang, D., Ooi, B.C., Shi, L., Wu, S.: The Performance of MapReduce: An In-depth Study. Proc. VLDB Endowment **3**(1), 472–483 (2010)
6. Babu, S.: Towards Automatic Optimization of MapReduce Programs. In: 1st ACM symposium on Cloud computing, pp. 137–142. ACM Press (2010)
7. Olston, C., Reed, B., Srivastava, U., Kumar, R., Tomkins, A.: Pig Latin: a not-so-foreign language for data processing. In: The ACM SIGMOD International Conference on Management of data, pp. 1099–1110. ACM Press (2008)
8. Pike, R., Dorward, S., Griesemer, R., Quinlan, S.: Interpreting the data: parallel analysis with Sawzall. Sci. Program. **13**(4), 277–298 (2005)
9. Thusoo, A., Sarma, J.S., Jain, N., Chakka, P., Zhang, N., Antony, S., Liu, H., Murthy, R.: Hive: a warehousing solution over a map-reduce framework. Proc. VLDB Endowment **2**(2), 1626–1629 (2009)
10. Thusoo, A., Sarma, J. S., Jain, N., Chakka, P., Zhang, N., Antony, S., Liu, H., Murthy, R.: Hive-A petabyte scale data warehouse using hadoop. In: The 26th IEEE International Conference on Data Engineering, pp. 996–1005. IEEE Press (2010)
11. Yang, H., Dasdan, A., Hsiao, R.L., Parker, D.S.: Map-reduce-merge: simplified relational data processing on large clusters. In: The ACM SIGMOD International Conference on Management of Data, pp. 1029–1040. ACM Press (2008)
12. Jiang, D., Tung, A., Chen, G.: Map-Join-Reduce: toward scalable and efficient data analysis on large clusters. IEEE Trans. Knowl. Data Eng. **23**, 1299–1311 (2011)
13. White, T.: Hadoop: The Definitive Guide. O'Reilly Media, Sebastopol (2010)
14. Shi, J., Zou, J., Lu, J., Cao, Z., Li, S., Wang, C.: MRTuner: a toolkit to enable holistic optimization for MapReduce jobs. Proc. VLDB Endowment **7**(13), 1–12 (2014)
15. Li, M., Zeng, L., Meng, S., Tan, J., Zhang, L., Butt, A. R., Fuller, N.: MRONLINE: mapreduce online performance tuning. In: The 23rd International Symposium on High-Performance Parallel and Distributed Computing, pp. 165–176. ACM Press (2014)
16. Tian, F., Chen, K.: Towards Optimal Resource Provisioning for Running Mapreduce Programs in Public Clouds. In: The IEEE International Conference on Cloud Computing, pp. 155–162. IEEE Press (2011)

17. Zhang, Z., Cherkasova, L., Loo, B.T.: Parameterizable benchmarking framework for designing a mapreduce performance mode. Concurrency Comput. Pract. Experience **26**(12), 2005–2026 (2014)

18. Yigitbasi, N., Willke, T.L., Liao, G., Epema, D.: Towards machine learning-based auto-tuning of mapreduce. In: The 21st IEEE International Symposium on Modeling, Analysis & Simulation of Computer and Telecommunication Systems, pp. 11–20. IEEE Press (2013)

19. Chen, K., Powers, J., Guo, S., Tian, F.: CRESP: Towards optimal resource provisioning for mapreduce computing in public clouds. IEEE Trans. Parallel Distrib. Syst. **25**(6), 1403–1412 (2014)

20. Liao, G., Datta, K., Willke, T.L.: Gunther: search-based auto-tuning of MapReduce. In: Wolf, F., Mohr, B., an Mey, D. (eds.) Euro-Par 2013. LNCS, vol. 8097, pp. 406–419. Springer, Heidelberg (2013)

21. Herodotou, H., Lim, H., Luo, G., Borisov, N., Dong, L., Cetin, F. B., Babu, S.: Starfish: a self-tuning system for big data analytics. In: The Conference on Innovative Data Systems Research, vol. 11, pp. 261–272. ACM Press (2011)

22. Kambatla, K., Pathak, A., Pucha, H.: Towards optimizing hadoop provisioning in the cloud. In: The 1st USENIX Workshop on Hot Topics in Cloud Computing, pp. 156–172. ACM Press (2009)

23. Wang, G., Butt, A. R., Pandey, P., Gupta, K.: A Simulation Approach to Evaluating Design Decisions in MapReduce Setups. In: The IEEE International Symposium on Modeling, Analysis & Simulation of Computer and Telecommunication Systems, pp. 1–11. IEEE Press (2009)

24. Verma, A., Cherkasova, L., Campbell, R.H.: Play It Again, SimMR! In: The IEEE International Conference on Cluster Computing, pp. 253–261. IEEE Press (2011)

25. A Dynamic Instrumentation Tool for Java. http://kenai.com/projects/btrace

26. Srinivas, M., Patnaik, L.M.: Genetic algorithms: a survey. Computer **27**(6), 17–26 (1994)

# Analysis of Repair Cost in Distributed Storage Systems with Fault-Tolerant Coding Strategies

Yanbo Lu[1,2]($\boxtimes$), Jie Hao[1,2], Xin-Ji Liu[1,2], and Shu-Tao Xia[1,2]($\boxtimes$)

[1] Graduate School at Shenzhen, Tsinghua University, Shenzhen 518055, China
luyb11@mails.tsinghua.edu.cn, xiast@sz.tsinghua.edu.cn
[2] Tsinghua National Laboratory for Information Science and Technology,
Beijing 100084, China

**Abstract.** To achieve reliability in distributed storage systems, fault tolerance techniques like replication strategy are adopted. As the rapid growth of data, distributed storage systems have been transitioning replication strategy to coding strategies like Reed Solomon codes to achieve higher storage efficiency. But the repair cost of Reed Solomon codes in terms of network bandwidth is high. For repair efficiency, a new class of codes called Regenerating Codes are proposed and become more popular. However, how to quantify and evaluate the repair cost of these coding strategies at the system level remains unexplored. In this paper, we propose a metric of the repair cost at the level of whole systems, and then compare the two main classes of codes Reed Solomon codes and Regenerating codes. Our goal is to provide system designers with evaluation methods of the system level repair cost. Thus, system designers can choose optimal coding strategies according to their certain systems.

**Keywords:** Regenerating codes · Reed Solomon codes · Repair cost · Fault tolerance · Coding strategies · Distributed storage systems

## 1 Introduction

The availability and reliability of data are extremely critical to distributed storage systems. Thus, a lot of fault tolerance techniques are applied in distributed storage systems. Replication and erasure codes are used most widely. When using the same storage capacity, erasure codes are more reliable than replication. However, erasure codes require higher repair cost in terms of network bandwidth resources(data transferred through the network for repairing failed storage nodes) than replication when storage node failures occurs. To reduce the repair cost, Dimakis et al. [1] proposed a new class of codes, called Regenerating Codes, which offer significantly lower repair cost compared to erasure codes. Regenerating codes have been proven to achieve optimal repair cost at the level of repairing a single node. And then many works followed under the single node level.

To our best knowledge, Jiekak et al. [2] firstly considered the repair cost at the whole system and obtained some interesting results. However, they focused

© Springer International Publishing Switzerland 2015
G. Wang et al. (Eds.): ICA3PP 2015, Part IV, LNCS 9531, pp. 358–371, 2015.
DOI: 10.1007/978-3-319-27140-8_25

on analyzing the impact of parameters of Regenerating codes on the system repair cost and did not consider the impact of different kinds of codes on the system repair cost. So their work can not extend to compare and quantify the repair cost of coding strategies like Regenerating Codes and Reed Solomon codes from the system perspective. This motivates us to propose a general metric to evaluate and quantify the repair cost of various kinds of codes in distributed storage systems at the system level.

In this paper, we make the following contributions:

(1) We are the *first* to evaluate and quantify the repair cost at the level of whole system of various kinds of codes in distributed storage systems, to the best of our knowledge.
(2) We propose a framework of metric of the repair cost at the level of whole system under two system scenarios. We show that our metric is suitable for various kinds of codes, not just for Regenerating codes.
(3) We compare Reed Solomon codes with Regenerating codes, and we have an interesting phenomena: Regenerating codes that are optimal at the node level do not always be suitable at the system level.

## 2    Related Work

Many studies [3,4] followed [1] and focused on reducing the repair cost. However, they just considered the repair cost at the level of node not the system repair cost. [2] just models the distributed storage system repair events with Poisson process to analyze the system repair cost, and do not consider the system node failure case, and the dynamically changing process of the nodes failure and repair. Ramabhadran and Pasquale [5] developed the Markov chain model to analyze the reliability of a distributed system that using replication strategy. [6,7] used the Markov chain model to analyze the reliability of the distributed storage systems that using coding strategies. But all these studies just discussed the reliability of the distributed storage system.

## 3    Background

### 3.1    Fault Tolerant Coding Techniques in Distributed Storage Systems

Erasure codes [8] are used most widely in distributed storage systems for fault tolerance of storage nodes. As to distributed storage system with Reed Solomon codes (RS), each file is divided into $k$ blocks, which generates $n - k$ coding blocks. Then the system sends the $n$ data blocks to $n$ different storage nodes. According to Reed Solomon codes $(n, k)$, we can recover the file if there are any $k$ available blocks out of $n$ blocks. For repairing one block, the system has to recover the whole file and then encode the lost block. That is, the system has to read any $k$ blocks from $k$ nodes and transfer them in the network for repairing

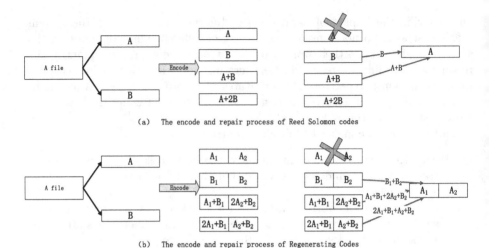

(a)     The encode and repair process of Reed Solomon codes

(b)     The encode and repair process of Regenerating Codes

**Fig. 1.** Repair methods of replication, Reed Solomon codes (RS) and Regenerating Codes (RC) and repair cost. For repairing one node size data $A$, the repair cost of Reed Solomon codes is 2 size data $A$ and $A + B$. While repairing one node (block) size data $[A_1, A_2]$, the repair cost of Regenerating Codes is $3/2$ node size data: $B_1 + B_2$ of $1/2$ size, $A_1 + B_1 + 2A_2 + B_2$ of $1/2$ size, and $2A_1 + B_1 + A_2 + B_2$ of $1/2$ size. We can see that the repair cost of RC is smaller than that of RS.

just one block, which is showed in Fig. 1(a). Note that the size of node is equal to the size of one block, so we use block and node interchangeably throughout our discussion. As to Regenerating codes, there are two kinds of repairing methods. Figure 1(b) shows the one method called *Regeneration*. And the other is the same as the repair method of Reed Solomon codes, which is showed in Fig. 1(a), and we call this method *Reconstruction*.

### 3.2    Quantification of Both Codes at the Single Node Level

Let the original file size be $\mathcal{M}$ and each block (node) size be $\alpha$, where $\mathcal{M} = k\alpha$.

*Reconstruction*: For repairing one lost block, the system has to reconstruct the whole file and then encode and store the block into a new node. In other words, the system has to read any $k$ blocks from $k$ nodes and transfer $\mathcal{M} = k\alpha$ size data in the network to repair only $\alpha$ size data. As discussed above, Reed Solomon codes apply and have to apply the repair method.

*Regeneration*: In this method, the system read data from $d$ nodes, and each node is read $\beta$, where $\beta < \alpha, k \leq d \leq n - 1$. So the repair cost for one node is $d\beta$.

Regenerating codes$(n, k, d)$: parameters $n$ and $k$ are the same as Reed Solomon codes$(n, k)$, while $d$ is the number of nodes that helps in the repair process, where $k \leq d \leq n - 1$. Each node has a mount of $\alpha$ fragments data. Let $i$ denote the number of available nodes in the system. If $i \geq d$, Regenerating codes apply *Regeneration* method for repair. If $k \leq i < d$ , Regenerating codes apply *Reconstruction* method for repair. If $i < k$, the file can not be recovered and the lost block can not be repair.

Dimakis et al. proved that the repair cost of *Regeneration* method is lower than that of *Reconstruction*, i.e., $d\beta < k\alpha$. So Regenerating codes have the lower repair cost than Reed Solomon codes at the level of a single node device. Regenerating codes proposed the tradeoff between the each node storage capacity $\alpha$ and the repair cost $\gamma$ for repairing one node. Minimum-storage regenerating codes (MSR), which correspond to the best storage cost, and minimum-bandwidth regenerating codes (MBR), which correspond to the minimum repair cost, are two extreme cases in the tradeoff. MSR has the same storage cost as Reed Solomon codes at the same parameters $(n, k)$, while MBR has higher storage cost than Reed Solomon codes. We only compare MSR with Reed Solomon codes. In this paper, we focus on analysis of Reed Solomon codes and Regenerating codes. Note that our results are also suitable to other codes, such as the locally repairable codes [9].

# 4    Definition of Metric

## 4.1    Motivation

Due to software or device failures, the storage node repairs have to be done constantly. So distributed storage systems are in a dynamical process, i.e., leaving and returning of storage nodes. That means the number of the surviving nodes changes as time grows. Thus, So it is difficult to derive the optimal repair cost of the whole system out of the optimal repair cost of the individual node device, especially under the impact of practical considerations such as network bandwidth limits and I/O performance of the system. In particular, a key question we ask is: *can optimal repair cost of single node lead to optimal repair cost of whole system, i.e. can Regenerating codes be also optimal at the system level?* Therefore, we need to propose a metric and evaluate Regenerating codes.

## 4.2    System Analysis

It is obvious that the surviving nodes are mainly determined by the repair rate and the failure rate. Different kinds of codes have different repair cost at the node level, so different kinds of codes have different failure rate under the same network bandwidth. So our work is to exactly model the dynamically changing system and define the metric for the system level repair. Note that network bandwidth represents network transfer rate, while network bandwidth resources(repair cost) represents amount of data transferred through the network.

We can see that distributed storage systems with fault tolerance are repairable systems. If we think a storage node as a repairable device, distributed storage systems with Reed Solomon codes$(n, k)$ are $k$-out-of-$n$ repairable systems. As to repairable systems, there are many schemes and models in reliability(safety) engineering [10], such as fault trees, Markov chains, stochastic Petri nets and so on. Thus, we can use them to model the systems. Here we focus on Markov chains, and then propose metric of the system level repair cost. Note that others models (e.g. fault trees) can also be suitable.

First, we discuss Markov chains for $k$-out-of-$n$ repairable systems. This is illustrated in Fig. 2. Assume that there are $n$ surviving devices in the systems at the initiate time. The symbols $\lambda$ and $\mu$ represent failure rates and repair rates respectively. Each state, represented by a circle, in the chain represents the number of devices that are surviving in the system at time $t$. There are $n - k + 2$ states in the chain, $n$ to $k - 1$, the state $n$ is the initial state and state $k - 1$ is the failed state. If system is in state $k - 1$, the system can not be repaired. As to Markov chains for distributed storage systems, we just need to consider a storage node as a repairable device. So there are also $n - k + 2$ states in the chain, and if system is in state $k - 1$, the data can not be repaired.

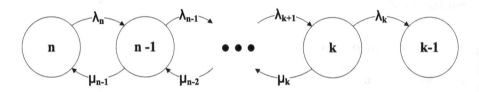

**Fig. 2.** Markov chains for $k$-out-of-$n$ repairable systems

According to Markov chains for $k$-out-of-$n$ repairable systems, we can obtain the probabilities of each state which the system be in at the time $t$, which are functions of the time $t$. And each state represents the number of surviving nodes in system. So the repair cost at each state is determinated if the coding scheme is determinated. Thus, we can take the expectation of repair cost at all repairable states(except the failed state $k - 1$) as metric for the system repair cost.

### 4.3    Formulation

Let probabilities of all repairable states be the vector $P(t)$:

$$P(t) = \begin{bmatrix} p_n(t) \\ p_{n-1}(t) \\ \vdots \\ p_k(t) \end{bmatrix} \tag{1}$$

where $p_j(t)$ is the probability of the system being in state $j$ at time $t$, $j = n, n - 1, \ldots, k$.

As discussed above, the repair cost at each state is constant, if the coding scheme is determinated. We denote $C$ repair cost in all repairable states: $C = [c_n, c_{n-1}, \cdots, c_k]$, where $c_j$ denotes repair cost in state $j$, $j = n, n - 1, \ldots, k$. And $c_n = 0$ (state $n$ is the initial state).

**Definition 1.** Define $SRC_t$ (the System Level Repair Cost at time $t$):

$$SRC_t = C \cdot P(t) \tag{2}$$

And then we give our metric for the repair cost for the system repair cost.

**Definition 2.** Define the metric as $ASRC_t$ (Average System Repair Cost in time interval $[0, t]$):

$$ASRC_t = \frac{\int_0^t C \cdot P(t)dt}{t} = \frac{\int_0^t SRC_t dt}{t} \tag{3}$$

As to the metric $ASRC_t$, the vector $P(t)$ is the key. And then we focus on obtaining $P(t)$. According to Markov model and Chapman-Kolmogorov equation [11], we need solve a system of $n - k + 2$ linear differential equations to obtain $P(t)$.

**Lemma 1.** Let $Q$ be the equations coefficient matrix.

$$\frac{dP(t)}{dt} = Q \cdot P(t) \tag{4}$$

For $Q$, different coding schemes have different $Q$. We will discuss them in the following section according to specific coding schemes.

**Lemma 2.** Let the matrix $e^Q$ be the matrix exponential. The solution of this system of Eq. 3 is

$$P(t) = e^Q \cdot P(n) \tag{5}$$

where $P(n)$ is the initial state, $P(n) = [1, 0, \ldots, 0]^T$. Now we propose the metric $ASRC_t$ for the repair cost at the level of whole system. As to $C$ in $ASRC_t$, different coding schemes have different $C$. We will discuss them in the following section according to specific coding schemes.

**Flexibility of Our Metric.** In fact, our metric is a framework. As we discussed above, many schemes and models in reliability(safety) engineering [10], such as fault trees and stochastic Petri nets are all adopted in our metric to obtain Eq. 1. Thus, it is easy for system designers to use our metric.

## 5   Analysis of $ASRC_t$

According to *Definition 2*, we can see that $C$ and $P(t)$ are key to analyze $ASRC_t$.

### 5.1   Analysis of $P(t)$

Our metric is based on Markov chains, so the key of analysis is to consider the transition paths and the transition rates of states in Markov chains.

**Transition Paths.** We consider two repair modes of Reed Solomon codes: one-node-repair mode and all-nodes-repair mode. Figure 3(a) represents one-node-repair mode and the corresponding transition rates. In one-node-repair mode, nodes are repaired one by one even facing to many multiple failed nodes. While Fig. 3(b) shows all node repair mode and the corresponding transition rates. All failed nodes are repaired at once in all-nodes-repair mode.

Regenerating codes have two kinds of repair: Regeneration and Reconstruction. Figure 3(c) shows the Markov chain for Regenerating codes. If $i \geq d$, there are enough surviving nodes for Regeneration; if $i < d$, the system has to apply Reconstruction method to repair all failed nodes. Note that Regeneration method of Regenerating codes is just one-node-repair mode, not all-nodes-repair mode. Cooperative Regenerating Codes [12] introduce all-nodes-repair mode, but we do not discuss them in this paper.

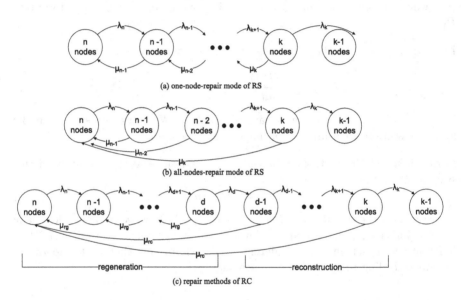

(a) one-node-repair mode of RS

(b) all-nodes-repair mode of RS

(c) repair methods of RC

**Fig. 3.** One-node-repair mode and all-nodes-repair mode of Reed Solomon codes (RS) vs. two repair methods of Regenerating codes (RC)

**Transition Rates.** Failure rates in Markov chains, i.e., transitions to lower states, are caused by hard disk crashes or system reinstalls and so on. Let $\mu$ be the node failure rate. And let the transition rate $\mu_i$ from state $i$ to state $i - 1$, where $i = k, k + 1, \ldots, n$. For the repair rate, let $\mu_i$ denote the transition rate from state $i$ to state $i + 1$, where $i = k, k + 1, \ldots, n - 1$.

While the repair rate of Regenerating codes, there are two kinds of rates. Let $\mu_{rg}$ be the repair rate of Regeneration method; $\mu_{rc}$ be the repair rate of Reconstruction method. Thus, according to Markov model and the Chapman-Kolmogorov equation, we can obtain a system of linear differential equations about $P(t)$. We just show one equation, which represents the Markov chains of ne-node-repair mode of Reed Solomon codes, which is illustrated in Eq. 6. Others are alike and are not showed here. For value of transition rates, we will discuss in Sect. 6.

$$
\begin{bmatrix} p'_n(t) \\ p'_{n-1}(t) \\ p'_{n-2}(t) \\ p'_{n-3}(t) \\ \vdots \\ p'_{k+2}(t) \\ p'_{k+1}(t) \\ p'_k(t) \end{bmatrix} = \begin{bmatrix} -\lambda_n & \mu_{n-1} & 0 & \cdots & 0 \\ \lambda_n & -\mu_{n-1}-\lambda_{n-1} & \mu_{n-2} & \cdots & 0 \\ 0 & \lambda_{n-1} & -\mu_{n-2}-\lambda_{n-2} & \cdots & 0 \\ 0 & 0 & \lambda_{n-2} & \cdots & 0 \\ \vdots & \vdots & \vdots & \ddots & \vdots \\ 0 & 0 & 0 & \cdots & \mu_{k+1} \\ 0 & 0 & 0 & \cdots -\mu_{k+1}-\lambda_k \\ 0 & 0 & 0 & \cdots & \lambda_k \end{bmatrix} \begin{bmatrix} p_n(t) \\ p_{n-1}(t) \\ p_{n-2}(t) \\ p_{n-3}(t) \\ \vdots \\ p_{k+2}(t) \\ p_{k+1}(t) \\ p_k(t) \end{bmatrix}
$$

(6)

## 5.2 Discussion of $C$

**Reed Solomon Codes.** For Reed Solomon codes, the systems apply Reconstruction method. So repair cost $c_j$ in state $j$ is $\mathcal{M}$, $c_j = \mathcal{M}$, where $j = k, k+1,, n-1$. And $c_n = 0$, the initial state of systems.

**Regenerating Codes.** For Reconstruction method, that is, $k \le i < d$, $c_i = \mathcal{M}$, where $i = d, d+1, \ldots, n-1$; $c_n = 0$.

For Regeneration method, that is, $d \le i \le n-1$, repair cost $c_i$ in state $j$, $c_i = Md/k(d-k+1)$, where $i = k, k+1,, d-1$.

# 6 Metric Under Repair Bandwidth Constraints

We introduce the key term repair bandwidth constraints in practical distributed storage systems, which are ignored in previous works about Regenerating codes [1]. For practical storage systems (e.g. cloud storage systems), the performance of reading (fetching) data for users is the most important. It has been shown that the performance of data retrieving has a large impact on user experience and service provider revenue [13]. So network bandwidth for this is account for most, with high priority; while network bandwidth for repair is with low priority. In other words, when no users ask for reading the data, i.e., the system is idle, the repair bandwidth is not constrained. When users are reading the data, the repair bandwidth is under constraint. Under this system scenario, analyze the impact of repair bandwidth constraints and give the corresponding metric. Here we consider two main factors: the system busy (reading) degree and the repair bandwidth constraint degree.

Let the system busy ratio $br$ represent the system busy (reading) degree. Let the repair bandwidth ratio $rr(0 < rr < 1)$ to reflect the repair bandwidth constraint degree. That is, when the system is idle, all nodes have $B$ repair bandwidth; when system is busy, idle nodes have $B$ repair bandwidth, and busy nodes have $rrB$ repair bandwidth. Note that not all nodes are participated in fetching data. This is showed in Fig. 4.

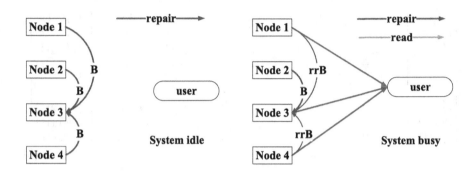

**Fig. 4.** Repair bandwidth constraints in practical storage system with Reed Solomon codes (4,3)

Now we give the definition of metric under the repair bandwidth constraints. First, we analyse two main factors the system busy ratio $br$ and the repair bandwidth ratio $rr$ in the followings, respectively.

**System Busy Ratio $br$.** We apply queueing theory to model the system to denote the system busy ratio $br$. Data retrieval (read) is provided through any $k$ nodes out of $n$ nodes. When read requests arrive, they are first enqueued. The system then determines how to allocate nodes for each request. We consider nodes allocation scheme as FCFS, that is to block subsequent read requests until the head-of-line request is processed. When users request for fetching the original data, both systems select any $i$ nodes out of $i(k \leq i \leq n)$ surviving nodes, and transfer $k$ blocks simultaneously to users. The system can serve only one request at any time. This model can be depicted as a one-server queue with arrivals of data retrieving requests and one server corresponding to any $k$ nodes. Under this setting, the systems can be modeled as $M/M/1$ queueing systems. Let read request arrivals occur at rate $\lambda'$, service times have an exponential distribution with parameter $\mu'$. Set $\rho = \lambda'/\mu'$. According to queueing theory [14], we obtain:

$$Pr[system\ idle] = 1 - \rho$$
$$Pr[system\ busy] = \rho$$

So the system busy ratio $br = \rho = \lambda'/\mu'$.

**Repair Bandwidth Ratio $rr$.** As to repair bandwidth ratio $rr$, it is determined by the situations of conditions of distributed storage systems. System designers can get the value of repair bandwidth ratio $rr$ by simulation.

## 6.1 Definition of Metric Under Repair Bandwidth Constraint

Let $ASRC_t^{idle}$ represents $ASRC_t$ if the system is idle, and the repair bandwidth is not constrained; let $ASRC_t^{busy}$ represents $ASRC_t$ if the system is busy, and the repair bandwidth is constrained. It is obvious that $ASRC_t^{idle} = ASRC_t$. And we can see that the repair bandwidth ratio $rr$ determine $ASRC_t^{busy}$. For more specific discussion of $ASRC_t^{busy}$ will be given in the following section.

**Definition 3.** Define the metric as $ASRC_t^{rbc}$ under consideration of repair bandwidth constraints:

$$ASRC_t^{rbc} = (1 - br)ASRC_t^{idle} + br\,ASRC_t^{busy} \qquad (7)$$

**Analysis of $ASRC_t^{busy}$.** In order to obtain $ASRC_t^{busy}$, we must the repair bandwidth at every state $i(k \le i \le n)$ in the Markov model of the system which is busy. The system is in state $i$, that is, there are $i$ nodes alive in system. In other words, there are $k$ busy nodes and $i - k$ idle nodes. Assume that the system selects idle nodes first for repair, if no idle nodes left, then selects busy nodes.

**Repair Bandwidth at Every State for Reed Solomon Codes**

- $k > i - k$, the repair rate at state $i$ is $rrB$ (no matter how select, busy nodes have to been chose).
- $k \le i - k$, the repair rate at state $i$ is $B$ (we assume that system selects idle nodes first for repair, there are $i - k$ idle nodes, so system can always select $k$ idle nodes for repair).

**Repair Bandwidth at Every State for Regenerating Codes**

- $i < d$ (same as Regenerating Codes, reconstruction operation)
  the repair rate at state $i$ is $rrB$, if $k > i - k$;
  the repair rate at state $i$ is $B$, if $k \le i - k$.
- $i \ge d$ (regeneration operation)
  the repair rate at state $i$ is $rrB$, if $d > i - k$;
  the repair rate at state $i$ is $B$, if $d \le i - k$.

# 7  Transition Rates

In this section, we analyse failure rates and repair rates in Marov chains.

**Failure Rates.** We make a conventional assumption that the time between failures of the node is exponentially distributed and storage nodes are independent [8]. This was shown to be valid in certain distributed storage systems (e.g. PlanetLab). So the transition rate $\lambda_i$ from state $i$ to state $i - 1$ is $i\lambda$, where $i = k, k + 1, \ldots, n$.

**Repair Rates.** For repair rates, there are two main schemes to obtain: the one is the experimental measurements and the other is simulation assumption [6,8,15]. In [6] show the repair rate mainly depends on the traffic amount and the network traffic rate. For simplicity, we adopt the scheme in [6]. This scheme showed that uploading data took almost the entire of the repair time. Let $t^u$ denote uploading time and $t^r$ denote repair time. We assume that all storage nodes have the same uploading network bandwidth. For $t_r \approx t_u$, repair rates $\mu_j$ in state $j$ is:

$$\mu_j = \frac{c_j}{t_j^r} = \frac{c_j}{t_j^u} \tag{8}$$

# 8    Evaluation

Now, we use NCCloud [6] and CORE [16] prototype to evaluate $ASRC_t$ and $ASRC_t^{rbc}$ of Reed-Solomon codes and Regenerating codes in distributed storage systems. Our evaluation consists of two parts, with $\lambda = 0.1\, pd(per day)$, network bandwidth $B = 1\, Mbps$, and $\alpha = 4\, Gb$ : (1) for $ASRC_t$, with $n = 4$ and $k = 2$; (2)for $ASRC_t^{rbc}$, with $n = 5$ and $k = 3$.

## 8.1    Evaluation of $ASRC_t$

Figure 6(a) shows in the first year $ASRC_t$ of both repair modes. Horizontal axis represents the time $t$ with a unit of per day. Vertical axis represents $ASRC_t$, and the unit is the proportion of $ASRC_t$ to the size of file $\mathcal{M}$. We can see Reed Solomon codes with all-nodes-repair mode have lower $ASRC_t$ than those with one-node-repair mode.

We compare Regenerating codes (4,2,3) with Reed Solomon codes (4,2),which is illustrated in Fig. 6(b). To be fair, we just consider Minimum Storage Regenerating codes (MSR), because MSR have the same storage efficiency as Reed Solomon codes. Figure 6(b) shows in the first year $ASRC_t$ of Reed Solomon codes with two repair modes and Regenerating codes (MSR). We can see Regenerating codes has much smaller $ASRC_t$ than all-nodes-repair mode of Regenerating codes. Under our settings of parameters, Regenerating codes just has 1/3 the system repair cost of Reed Solomon codes. It reveals that Regenerating codes have much lower repair cost than Reed Solomon codes not only at the level of a single node device but also at the level of the whole system. This result is suitable to the systems without network bandwidth constraint.

## 8.2    Evaluation of $ASRC_t^{rbc}$

For $ASRC_t^{rbc}$, two main factors: the system busy ratio $br$ and the repair bandwidth ratio $rr$, are focused on in this subsection. Here we compare Regenerating codes (5,2,3) with Reed Solomon codes (5,2) in order to analyse the impact of $br$ and $rr$ on $ASRC_t^{rbc}$.

**Discussion of** $rr$. In order to discussion $rr$, we set $br = 1$, i.e., system is always busy. And then we analyse the impact of $rr$ on $ASRC_t^{rbc}$.

In Fig. 6(a), horizontal axis represents $rr$. Note that we do not discuss the situation $0 < rr < 0.2$. Because we can not guarantee that the repair rates are much larger than the failure rates.In other words, the system goes into the failed state $k - 1$ with high probability. $ASRC_t^{rbc}$ of both codes decreases as $rr$ goes up. We can see that $rr$ has a little impact on Reed Solomon codes, while Regenerating codes are affected a lot. If $rr > 0.374$, $ASRC_t^{rbc}$ of Regenerating codes is lower than that of Reed Solomon codes. If c = 1, i.e., the repair bandwidth is not constrained, $ASRC_t^{rbc}$ of Regenerating codes is much smaller than that of Reed Solomon codes. We observe an interesting phenomena: at the opposite of the common intuition, $ASRC_t^{rbc}$ of Reed Solomon codes is lower than that of Regenerating codes, if $0.2 \leq rr < 0.374$. The explanation can be that the decrease of repair bandwidth leads to the decrease of probability of the system in the initial state and the increase of probability of the system in other states. And there is no need for repairing in the initial state.

As discussed above, Regenerating codes has much smaller $ASRC_t^{idle}$ than Reed Solomon codes. Then we consider the system busy case $ASRC_t^{busy}$. We can see that $ASRC_t^{busy}$ of Regenerating codes is smaller than that of Reed Solomon codes, if $rr > 0.374$. So $ASRC_t^{rbc}$ of Regenerating codes is always smaller than that of Reed Solomon codes, when $rr > 0.374$. We just need to discuss the impact of $br$ on $ASRC_t^{rbc}$ in the case $0.2 \leq c < 0.374$ (Fig. 5).

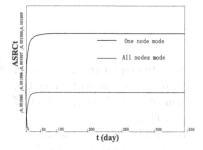 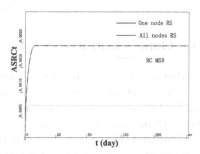

**Fig. 5.** Evaluation of $ASRC_t$ of Regenerating codes (RC) and Reed Solomon codes (RS).

**Discussion of** $br$. Here we take $c = 0.2$ and $c = 0.3$ for discussion of both codes. In Fig. 6(b), horizontal axis represents the system with busy ratio $br$, $0 < br < 1$. We can see that $ASRC_t^{rbc}$ of Reed Solomon codes keeps unchanged, as $br$ varies from 0 to 1, and is almost equal to each other for $c = 0.2, 0.3$. While $ASRC_t^{rbc}$ of Regenerating codes increases as $br$ increases. When $br$ is fixed, $ASRC_t^{rbc}$ of Regenerating codes ($c = 0.2$) is larger than that of Regenerating codes ($c = 0.3$). When $c = 0.2$ (or $c = 0.3$), if $0 < br < 0.418$, $ASRC_t^{rbc}$ of Regenerating codes is smaller than that of Reed Solomon codes. There is another phenomena of the opposite common intuition, $ASRC_t^{rbc}$ of Regenerating codes is larger than that of Reed Solomon codes, if $0.418 \leq br < 1$. We can see that the system busy ratio $br$ does influence the system repair cost, and Regenerating codes are affected more greatly. It is revealed that Regenerating codes has much smaller $ASRC_t^{rbc}$ than Reed Solomon codes in low reading load system, while in high load system Reed Solomon codes performs smaller $ASRC_t^{rbc}$, under the same repair bandwidth constraint. Repair bandwidth constrained is the basic impact factor, and system busy ratio is the extend impact factor. The latter intensify the influence of the former for $ASRC_t^{rbc}$ of both codes.

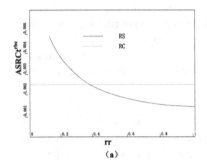
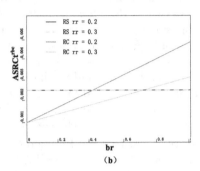

**Fig. 6.** Evaluation of $ASRC_t^{rbc}$ of Regenerating codes (RC) and Reed Solomon codes (RS).

# 9  Conclusion and Future Work

In this paper, we are the *first* to quantify and evaluate the repair cost at the level of whole system of various kinds of codes and propose a framework of metric under two system scenarios. We gave an evaluation of analysis of the effect of network bandwidth constraints on the system repair cost.

Our analysis reveals that when the repair bandwidth is not constrained, Regenerating codes have much lower repair cost than erasure codes not only at the level of a single node device but also at the level of the whole system. So Regenerating codes are more suitable for the systems in which the data stored are rarely read, such as the long-term archives storage systems. Under the condition of repair bandwidth constraint, the repair bandwidth and the system busy degree are impact factors. As for high busy (reading) load ratio system, Regenerating codes have higher average system repair cost than erasure codes. Our results can be applied to many distributed storage systems and our metric is not complex for system designers to analyze. Therefore, our work is widely applicable, practical to analyze the system repair cost for distributed storage system.

**Acknowledgments.** This research is supported in part by the Major State Basic Research Development Program of China (973 Program, 2012CB315803), the National

Natural Science Foundation of China (61371078), and the Research Fund for the Doctoral Program of Higher Education of China (20130002110051).

# References

1. Dimakis, A.G., Godfrey, P.B., Wu, Y., Wainwright, M.J., Ramchandran, K.: Network coding for distributed storage systems. IEEE Trans. Inf. Theor. **56**, 4539–4551 (2010)
2. Jiekak, S., Kermarrec, A.M., Le Scouarnec, N., Straub, G., Van Kempen, A.: Regenerating codes: A system perspective. ACM SIGOPS Operating Syst. Rev. **47**, 23–32 (2013)
3. Rashmi, K.V., Shah, N.B., Kumar, P.V.: Optimal exact-regenerating codes for distributed storage at the MSR and MBR points via a product-matrix construction. IEEE Trans. Inf. Theory **57**(8), 5227–5239 (2011)
4. Wu, Y., Dimakis, A.G.: Reducing repair traffic for erasure coding-based storage via interference alignment. In: IEEE International Symposium on Information Theory ISIT 2009 (2009)
5. Chun, B.G., Dabek, F., Haeberlen, A., Sit, E., Weatherspoon, H., Kaashoek, M.F., Kubiatowicz, J., Morris, R.: Efficient replica maintenance for distributed storage systems. In: NSDI (2006)
6. Hu, Y., Chen, H.C.H., Lee, P.P.C., Tang, Y.: NCCloud: applying network coding for the storage repair in a cloud-of-clouds. In: FAST (2012)
7. Sathiamoorthy, M., et al.: Xoring elephants: novel erasure codes for big data. In: Proceedings of the VLDB Endowment (2013)
8. Ford, D., Labelle, F., Popovici, F.I., Stokely, M., Truong, V.A., Barroso, L., Grimes, C., Quinlan, S.: Availability in globally distributed storage systems. In: OSDI, pp. 61–74 (2010)
9. Papailiopoulos, D.S., Dimakis, A.G.: Locally repairable codes. In: 2012 IEEE International Symposium on Information Theory Proceedings (ISIT) (2012)
10. Birolini, A.: Reliability Engineering, vol. 5. Springer, Heidelberg (2007)
11. Gardiner, C.W.: Stochastic Methods. Springer, Heidelberg (1985)
12. Shum, K.W.: Cooperative regenerating codes for distributed storage systems (2011). arXiv preprint arXiv:1101.5257
13. Chen, S., Sun, Y., Kozat, U.C., Huang, L., Sinha, P., Liang, G., Liu, X., Shroff, N.B.: When queueing meets coding: Optimal-latency data retrieving scheme in storage clouds. In: INFOCOM (2014)
14. Gross, D., Harris, C.: Fundamentals of Queueing Theory. Wiley Interscience, New York (1998)
15. Ramabhadran, S., Pasquale, J.: Analysis of long-running replicated systems. In: INFOCOM, pp. 1–9 (2006)
16. Li, R., Lin, J., Lee, P.P.C.: Core: Augmenting regenerating-coding-based recovery for single and concurrent failures in distributed storage systems. In: IEEE Mass Storage Systems and Technologies (MSST) (2013)

# Design Efficient In-Database Video Storage Approach by Learning from Performance Evaluation of BLOB

Hui Li[1,2(✉)], Mei Chen[1,2], Zhenyu Dai[1,2], Ming Zhu[3], and Menglin Huang[3]

[1] Department of Computer Science, Guizhou University, Guiyang 550025, China
cse.huili@gzu.edu.cn
[2] Guizhou Engineering Laboratory of ACMIS, Guiyang 550025, China
[3] CAS, National Astronomical Observatories, Beijing 100016, China

**Abstract.** Multimedia application designers often required to make the choice of whether storing multimedia objects as files in the file system, or as BLOBs (Binary Large Objects) in a database, or a combination of both. Towards small multimedia data, it often suggested to store them as BLOB data of database. However, previous study indicated that the efficiency of BLOB based video storage not always suffice. In this paper, By learning from the issues discovered from our previous performance evaluation, we proposed an efficient in-database video storage approach named *TIViS* (Temporal Interval based Video Storage). When a video object store into database by *TIViS*, it will be decomposed into temporal intervals and each interval will be sequential stored based on its temporal information. Additionally, in *TIViS* approach, a specialized buffer management mechanism is also developed to optimize the data access of multimedia objects. In our work, we implemented *TIViS* approach into the open source database system PostgreSQL 8.4. We conducted a series of experiments to verify the efficiency of *TIViS* approach, the results demonstrate that *TIViS* based video storage is significantly superior to traditional database system's built-in BLOB approach (*e.g.*, PostgreSQL's Bytea).

**Keywords:** Video data storage · Video data access · Binary large object · Database system · Performance evaluation

## 1 Introduction

### 1.1 Background

The volume of video data increased rapidly since last decade [14,26]. Video becomes popular in our everyday life for both professional and consumer applications, *e.g.*, surveillance, education and entertainment. Such needs require data management system should provide mechanism to store and access video data in an efficiency way.

© Springer International Publishing Switzerland 2015
G. Wang et al. (Eds.): ICA3PP 2015, Part IV, LNCS 9531, pp. 372–385, 2015.
DOI: 10.1007/978-3-319-27140-8_26

In video related applications, designers often have the choice of whether storing multimedia objects as files in the file system, or as BLOBs (Binary Large Objects [8,28]) in a database, or a combination of both. Generally, this decision must based on the trade-off among various application specific factors such as simplicity, manageability and performance. Although some theoretical work proves that certain storage policies will be superior to another policies in certain workloads, these analysis is either hard to adopt into real application or it often behave poorly in practice. Unfortunately, only folklore and specific experiences available to guide the decision of multimedia storage polices.

Currently, many video applications, e.g., video surveillance, video-on-demand and online video sharing system are adopting the former one, file system based video data storage. In this approach, the UNC (Universal Naming Convention) path of video files or other location description information are stored into a database-like system. While processing a video data access request, the applications should get the data file location information from database before performing the corresponding data access operation. This mechanism simplified the video data management into video data file location information management. However, there are some disadvantages in adopting the file based video storage strategy. Firstly, due to content files are outside database, it is hard to coordinate them with its location information and other metadata in consistency. Secondly, putting a large number of video thumbnails or content files in a directory of (distributed) file system will result in inefficiency for responding data request [9,12]. In fact, it has been a serious bottleneck in YouTube until it was acquired by Google and employed the distributed file system GFS [15] as the underlying infrastructure [12]. Thirdly, the development of a distributed file system based video application, is still harder than database based application. Actually, developing the GFS-like solution start from scratch, e.g., General Parallel File System (a.k.a. GPFS [24]), or deploying an application system that store and manage a large-scale video data underlying similar open source system, such as Hadoop, it's still not a easy task.

Another video storage solution is store video data in the BLOB field of the database [18–20,23]. Previous experiences have showed that, through utilizing its built-in data management functionality and the well provided development interface in DBMS, it is easy to build a large-scale application and achieve better performance [11,21,27]. Unfortunately, the folklore tells us that DBMS was only efficiently in handle small objects. But which size means "small" and where is the break-even point for accessing an object as BLOB in database will be cheaper than accessing an object as a file, is remain unanswered and need further study.

For the video related web application, e.g. YouTube, the largest video clips sharing web site, most of the uploaded clips are small and last 30 s to 2.5 min [2], the size of its temporal interval (key frame) is around 25 KB per second in standard resolution. In some others video applications, such as content based video retrieval system, video surveillance system and VoD system, the small video objects is also required. In content based video retrieval, the large video files are segmented into shots as the basic content unit for retrieval, and each shot is often less than 30 s [22]. Towards (intelligent) video surveillance system, since the video event is often to be a short video clips as in content based video retrieval system, the archived event videos also can be consider as small video objects. In VoD system, for the purpose of balancing throughput, robustness and convenient for scheduling, the video content is desired to divide into as many pieces as possible, and often take the smallest viewable unit as the basic storage unit [13,16]. For instance, recent research [16] indicate that, PPLive.com, one of the largest VoD system in China, its MPEG-1 based VoD system, using the 16 KB size as the basic viewable segment when the bandwidth is less than 1.4 Mbps. Towards above types of applications, storing the small objects into database has a high possibility to become a valid approach.

## 1.2 Motivations: The Issues We Learned from Our Previous Performance Evaluation

For both file system and database based video strategies, give a specific temporal information (timestamp), whether it is able to provide temporal interval (key frame) based video content access is important. Towards applications like video-on-demand and online video sharing, just return the required specific video clips to save the bandwidths is significant to both the customers and applications owners [7]. If a video content access approach is capable to access any part of video object directly without sequential scan and buffering, it not only decreased the respond time of the request, but also saved the bandwidth because it avoided the unnecessary data transfer and buffering.

Towards traditional relational database system, although there are some study indicate that the efficiency of BLOB based video storage not always suffice, there are still existed some folklore suggest system designer to store "small" multimedia data as BLOB data in the database. However, there still exist certain questions need to know before choose a database as multimedia storage platform: (1) Which size means "small" and where is the break-even point for accessing an object as BLOB in database will be cheaper than accessing an object as a file? This question is remain unanswered and need further study; (2) How to obtain the long-term performance impacts of a certain storage policies? Currently, most storage benchmarks focus on short-term behavior, few of people know how to evaluate the long-term performance of certain storage policies, this technical issues is important for choose a multimedia storage strategy.

Motivated by above questions, in our previous study [17], we conduct a comprehensive performance evaluation of BLOB in two popular database, one commercial database system (anonymized as *CDB* system) and one open source database system (PostgreSQL, noted it as *PG* for short). In our evaluation, we investigate the break-even point in DBMS for storing the video objects, we found that store video objects into database could be a preferred solution in some circumstance, and hence is necessary to develop more efficiently database based video content access approach. Furthermore, by evaluating long-term read/write performance, we discovered that different DBMS will vary greatly in break-even point. We also explored certain buffer parameters that usually have important effects on relational data access, however the results revealed that they have few impacts to the throughput of video objects, thus we need new buffer management approach for BLOB based data access.

By learning from the experimental study, we awared the following two problems: (1) in ceratin scenarios, store "small" multimedia objects in database can obtain optimal query performance as well as the better manageability, but its performance still need further improvement to meet the requirement of applications; (2) in current DBMS, the size of shared database buffer often have little impact in video data read/write performance, and the buffer management mechanism seems didn't work properly for BLOB data, although it often played an important role in relational data throughput.

To solve above two problems, we propose an efficient in-database video storage approach named *TIViS* (Time Interval based Video Storage) and implemented in PostgreSQL database system, which enable us to access any part of video object directly without sequential scan and buffering, thus the service response time decreased. When a video file store into database by *TIViS*, it will be decomposed into temporal intervals (*key frames*) and each interval will be sequential stored based on its temporal information (*timestamp*). Furthermore, by learning from the performance evaluation and look around the source code of PostgreSQL, we found there is no specialized buffer management mechanism for binary large objects, thus we designed and implemented a specialized buffer management strategy into PostgreSQL to optimize video data access for obtain a better performance.

## 1.3 Contributions

In this paper, our works were focused on design and implement an efficient in-database video storage approach by learning from the issues discovered in our previous extensive preformation evaluation of BLOB mechanism [17]. Our contributions were summarized as follows:

We devised a temporal interval based video content access approach for the videos stored in BLOB column of database. It provides a transparent way to wrapper the required content to the end user instead of sending the whole video file from beginning. Our experiments showed that, because the extracted temporal information enable us store video data in database in a more efficient way, and we design and implemented a specialized buffer management strategy into PostgreSQL database system to facilitate the in-database video data access.

The remainder of this paper is organized as follows: Sect. 2 present a brief description of the related work. Section 3 presents our database based in-database video content storage and access approach, the specialized buffer management mechanism also described in this section. The reports of experiments in Sect. 4. Section 5 concludes the paper.

## 2   Related Work

**Data Storage:** GFS [15] and its open source implementation HDFS is a distributed file system designed for terabyte volume archive, and GFS was the underlying infrastructure of YouTube. Benefit from its fault tolerant features and other advantages, YouTube obtained highly scalability. Tawards the modern DBMSs, all of them are adopt the EXODUS [8,28] design for efficient insertion or deletion toward a large object by a B-Tree based storage. Besides file system and BLOB [18–20,23] based storage, there is another hybrid solution named Data Links [5] which was adopted in DB2 database system. It stores BLOB data in the file system, and uses the database to coordinate the BLOB file and its metadata with a transactional semantic consistence.

**Storage Performance Evaluation:** There are little work concerned with video storage evaluation. SPC-2 [10] is a benchmark paid attentions to read-only on-demand access to video files. The performance study in [10] is measured in the view of long-run and fragmentation analysis. Similarly, the works in [25] studied the large object repository on file system and database under long-run, the fragmentation issues also were considered, furthermore, it verified the viewpoint indicated by [6] that insertions and deletions within an object can lead to fragmentation.

**Video Content Access Approach:** At present, most of the video content access approaches are developed in an application-oriented case by case way and underlying a file system based data storage. In the modern database system, some commercial DBMS products provided limited functionality to support the video content access, such as Oracle Multimedia [4], Oracle DICOM [3] and DB2 Video Extender [1]. But all of them are only capable to access some metadata of video file that is still far from enough.

## 3   TIVis: An In-Database Video Content Access Approach

### 3.1   Temporal Interval Based Video Content Access Approach

In our previous experimental study [17], our performance evaluation verified the efficiency and possibility of store small video objects into database. However, most of DBMSs only support the access to some metadata of video files, they didn't provide the capability of temporal interval based video content access or other types of raw data accessibility. This functionality can just return the required specific video clips to save the bandwidths, which is significant to both the customers and applications owners [7]. If a video content access approach is capable to access any part of video object directly without sequential scan and buffering, it not only decreased the respond time of the request, but also saved the bandwidth because it avoided the unnecessary data transfer and buffering. Therefore, we motivated to develop database based video content access approach. In our work, we implemented the functionality of access video data to three mainstream formats (AVI, MPEG-1and MPEG-4) into the open source DBMS PostgreSQL 8.4. Because the techniques issues proposed to support temporal interval based in-database AVI video content access is similar to MPEG-1, and the involved procedures are common, thus we only present the outline of how we support in-database video content access for AVI video and MPEG-4, the entire content can refer to our long version technical report [17].

Generally speaking, in order to support temporal interval based video access in database, preprocess is needed to parsing the video's format, extracting and composing the temporal-index information. Extracted temporal-index information is stored into database. When a temporal interval based video access request arrived, these extracted information were be used to locate and speed up the access.

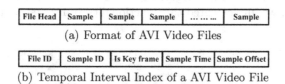

(a) Format of AVI Video Files

(b) Temporal Interval Index of a AVI Video File

**Fig. 1.** Data structures for AVI video files

The key to support temporal interval based access for AVI data is build temporal information (timestamp) index. The file format structure of AVI is presented in Fig. 1(a). Sample is the lowest granularity unit for AVI content storage. The index block is an optional component. When an AVI file is loading into database as BLOB data, we will analyze the "File header" at first, include extracting the duration time, location and length of raw video data block, then scan the "index block" to build temporal information if this component is existed, otherwise, we will scan the whole AVI file to record the position of each key sample so as to construct the temporal information index for locate the specific temporal interval.

The structure indexed the temporal information of AVI is illustrated in Fig. 1(b), it was stored in database as a table. "Sample ID" refers to the ID of video frames, "Is Key Frame" suggests whether the frame is a key frame, "Sample Time" tells the timestamp of this frame, which indicates the time of when this key frame is to be played. The "Sample Offset" expresses the offset of this frame in the video file.

When a service request is arrived and required to access certain part of AVI content, it will be handled as follows:

**Step 1:** Parse the request and get the ID of requested video file, the start time and termination time;

**Step 2:** Retrieve the temporal interval based indexing information from database based on above three data items;

**Step 3:** Locate the position in BLOB column according to the existed indexing information and read the corresponding raw video data;

**Step 4:** Rebuild the segmented content to a new file by combine file header and the wrapped raw data block based on the AVI file format standard, and then deliver the segmented clips instead of the whole file to complete this service request.

The file structure of MPEG-4 video files is shown in Fig. 2(a). There are large differences in the content organization between MPEG-4 and AVIfiles. MPEG-4 file has a complex compressed metadata structure which placed at either the front or the tail of the file. Through parsing the metadata and take a series of complex computation, the temporal interval based index information for key sample will be obtained. Due to the complexity of compressed metadata structure, split MPEG-4 video file in the style that just based on the temporal index information couldn't ensure the segmented clips is conform with the file structure standard, it will result the clip cannot decode and played correctly by video player. Therefore, in the time based MPEG-4 video content access, rebuild the new file header and metadata based on the original whole metadata that matched the raw content of segmented video are required. In our in-database based approach, we implemented this functionality transparently to users.

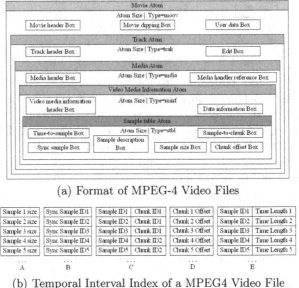

(a) Format of MPEG-4 Video Files

| Sample 1 size | Sync Sample ID1 | Sample ID1 | Chunk ID1 | Chunk 1 Offset | Sample ID1 | Time Length 1 |
| Sample 2 size | Sync Sample ID2 | Sample ID2 | Chunk ID1 | Chunk 2 Offset | Sample ID2 | Time Length 2 |
| Sample 3 size | Sync Sample ID3 | Sample ID3 | Chunk ID1 | Chunk 3 Offset | Sample ID3 | Time Length 3 |
| Sample 4 size | Sync Sample ID4 | Sample ID4 | Chunk ID2 | Chunk 4 Offset | Sample ID4 | Time Length 4 |
| Sample 5 size | Sync Sample ID5 | Sample ID5 | Chunk ID2 | Chunk 5 Offset | Sample ID5 | Time Length 5 |
| ... | ... | ... | | ... | ... | |
| A | B | C | | D | E | |

(b) Temporal Interval Index of a MPEG4 Video File

**Fig. 2.** Data structures for MPEG-4 video files

From above illustrations and file format structure showed in Fig. 2(a), we know that the preprocess procedure for loading MPEG-4 video file into database is much more complex than AVI video. Due to its complex container-style file format standard, there are many kinds of encode methods for MPEG-4 raw video content and each of them has certain distinction in file structure organization, which will course the difficulty to locate video content in a uniform way. As a result, we transform the encoded raw content into a standard organization under certain circumstance by the FFMPEG package before loading them into database.

When a temporal interval based MPEG-4 video content request arrived, it will be handled like AVI videos in the flow that has described in this section, but they are several detailed difference exist in step 2 and step 4. For example, in the step 2, we will build a 5-Array index structure with RLE (Run-Length Encoding) that given in Fig. 2(b); in the step 4, the raw content and metadata was reconstructed "chunk by chunk" rather than the way "sample by sample" or "packet by packet". It should be noted that chunk is the upper level data structure of video sample.

Figure 2(b) showed that, sample's size, ID and duration time are stored in the $A$, $B$ and $E$, respectively. Where $D$ represented the offset of each chunk, and the array $C$ mapped the relation between each sample and its upper level chunk. Due to we only want to outline the core idea of implement the in-database video content access without detail the underlying engineering techniques issue, we only introduced the core procedures, the entire approach are detailed in our technical report [17].

## 3.2 Buffer Management for In-Database BLOB Data

As we learned from our experimental study [17], traditional buffer management mechanism nearly have no impacts to the BLOB based data, such as image and video. We also taken an insight look at the source code of PostgreSQL database, there is also no buffer mechanism for BLOB based data, thus the in-database stored complex multimedia data cannot enjoy the benefit of buffer manager. This problem motivated us devise a specialized buffer management techniques for our in-database stored video data. In this section, we will describe how we implement an efficient buffer mechanism into the open source database management system PostgreSQL 8.4.

Since the data items in database buffer implicit indicates its whole data are available in main memory space across different tranactions, thus when we are implement the BLOB data buffer management strategies, we are required to insure our BLOB buffering techniques meet such characteristic. There are two technique solutions to achieve above requirement: (1) design a brand-new data structure and corresponding maintenance methods; (2) revise PostgreSQL's relational data buffer to meet the requirement of BLOB data. To simplify the implementation, we choose the latter one, revise PostgreSQL's main memory cache structure to meet the caching requirement of $TIViS$ approach.

In PostgreSQL, there are several memory data structure can be utilized as cache, such as $MemoryContext$, $TopMemoryContext$, $ExprContext$, $CacheMemoryContext$ and so on. Because above first three memory cache data structures are allocated when database system started, they cannot share the inside data across transactions, thus we have to choose revise $CacheMemoryContext$ into the needed BLOB data cache structure $BLOBCacheMemoryContex$. In PostgreSQL system, $CacheMemoryContext$ is a memory buffer data structure caching the relational data, e.g., table, schema, index and so on. In order to finish this revise, two types of work is needed: (1) revise the corresponding memory management mechanism to fit the access pattern of BLOB data. E.g., rewrite its space (page) allocation, reallocation and dispose functions, because these operations often needs refer to some metadata in catalog *pg_largeobject* (holds the data making up "large objects") to verify the validity of corresponding operations; (2) rewrite PostgreSQL's *lo_exprot* function to optimize the access of BLOB data. In PostgreSQL system, each read operation of BLOB data are resolved as certain *lo_export* operations. Since we have BLOB data buffer *CacheMemoryContext* now, the *lo_export* should be rewrite to locate needed data in *CacheMemoryContext* before take data from its original table or catalog *pg_largeobject*. The data structure of *CacheMemoryContext* is illustrated as Fig. 3.

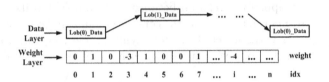

**Fig. 3.** Structure of BLOBCacheMemoryContext

*BLOBCacheMemoryContex* consist of two parts, *data layer* and *weight layer*. While the prior one is a linked list store the real BLOB data, the latter one is store the weight of corresponding BLOB data. In our work, we define the weight as the number of usage of BLOB data. When the weight is bigger than certain threshold, we will assign its values as the negative value of its absolute value, which means it has a high priority to stay in main memory. Though *BLOBCacheMemoryContex* is inherited from *CacheMemoryContex*, we still need to implement our own buffer management methods. Towards buffer replacement, we firstly handle BLOB data with positive weight by the LRU (Least Recently Used) strategy, and then replace high priority BLOB data in the same strategy if necessary. The maximum size of cached BLOB data is limited by the size of main memory, it can be setup by the parameter *BLOB_MAXIMUM_SIZE*. The evaluations of the proposed buffer management are present in the next section.

## 4    Experimental Results

In this section, we will verify the efficiency of the proposed *TIViS* approach and prove it could be used in small video related applications. Our experiments are performed on PC whose CUP is P4 2.8G, memory is 4G, and running Windows 2003 Server on a disk that is 7200 rotations per second. We compare the performance of our in-database based temporal interval based video content access approach *TIViS* with the PostgreSQL's (version 8.4) built-in BLOB approach named *Bytea*. For the simplicity, we run the experiments by simulated a client/server style application but running it in the identical machine without consider the network overheads. In the experiments, we use JDBC APIs to fulfill all the database-related operations, and the video objects are small AVI video files.

## 4.1    Effect of Temporal Interval Based Access

At first, we compare the query performance of *TIViS* and *Bytea* without enable *TIViS*'s buffer management capability, thus the evaluation will fairly demonstrate the efficiency of *TIViS*'s temporal interval based video content access. Since the performance of read 128 KB and 256 KB from *PG/Bytea* will comparative or superior than *PG/UNC*, thus we only evaluate how fast *TIViS* fetch certain part of 128 KB or 256 KB video data from a BLOB column of a given table. The procedures of how we employ *TIViS* approach to handle temporal interval based video content access has been detailed in Sect. 3.1 (Step 1 - Step 4). During the evaluation, the query service ask 128 KB from a 256 KB BLOB video data, and ask 256 KB video data from a 512 KB BLOB storage, the database buffer of PostgreSQL 8.4 are using the default settings, which means the value of parameter *shared_buffers* is 32 MB. The result of this evaluation is presented in Fig. 4.

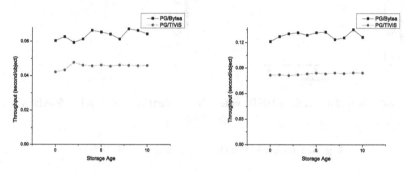

(a) Evaluation for fetch 128KB video data

(b) Evaluation for fetch 256KB video data

**Fig. 4.** Efficiency of TIViS (Disabled BLOB Buffer)

Figure 4(a) showed the performance of fetch 128 KB video data in *Bytea* and *TIViS* approach. As our other performance testing, the X-axes is storage age, and the Y-axes is throughput (second/object). From this result, we can easy to learn that *TIViS* is about 40 %–45 % faster than *Bytea* in nearly most cases. While we fetch 256 KB video data using *TIViS* approach, the experimental result in Fig. 4(b) also clearly demonstrate TIViS's efficiency, it is about 50 %–60 % faster than *Bytea*.

The overhead of our *TIViS* based video content approach is divided into two parts: one is the time consumption of calculate and locate the starting offset of segmented video content, the other is cost of fetching the designate content to the client side from the starting offset to ending offset. Since our *TIViS* approach have stored temporal interval information for the in-database video data, it is easy to get a portion of video data from the middle of a video objects. This is one of the major reason why our *TIViS* approach will faster than *Bytea* in this situation.

## 4.2    Effect of TIViS's Buffer Mechanism

The second experiment of *TIViS* is verify the efficiency our implementation of
BLOB buffer management strategy. The result is present in Fig. 5. In this evaluation, we set PostgreSQL's shared database buffer size (indicated by parameter
*shared_buffers*) to 256 MB. It should be noted that, during this performance
testing, we carefully arranged the data operations and query requests that make
the database buffer hold a constant portion (10 %) of data (about 25 MB) which
can be directly return as the result of query request.

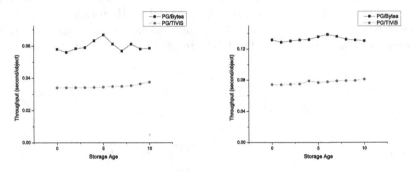

(a) Evaluation for fetch 128KB video  (b) Evaluation for fetch 256KB video
data                                    data

**Fig. 5.** Efficiency of TIViS (Enabled BLOB Buffer)

In the performance testing of fetch 128 KB video data, the result in Fig. 5(a)
showed that when storage age is less than 6, *TIViS* is about 60 %–75 % times
faster than *Bytea*. When storage age is greater than 6, *TIViS* is about 70 %
times better than *Bytea* in most scenarios. This phenomenon is in common with
folklore that the long-term performance of a storage will degrade. When we evaluate the performance of fetch 256 KB video objects, the result in Fig. 5(b) also
demonstrated *TIViS*'s superiority, it's about 60 %–80 % times faster than *Bytea*
approach. However, with the increase of storage age, its long-term performance
also showed a slightly downward trend.

## 4.3    Effect of Video Object's Size

The third experiment is to evaluate how the size of video object size impact
the performance of *TIViS* and *Bytea*. In this experiment, the database buffer
parameter *shared_buffers* is set to 256 MB and the buffer mechanism of *TIViS*
is enabled. After above settings, we evaluated the performance of fetch different
sized video objects by *TIViS* and *Bytea* approach in the condition of storage
age is 0 and 10, the results is presented in Fig. 6.

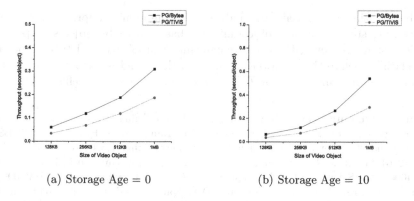

(a) Storage Age = 0               (b) Storage Age = 10

**Fig. 6.** Effects of video object size

Figure 6(a) present how video object size impact query performance of *TIViS* and *Bytea* when storage is 0. The result clearly showed *TIViS*'s superiority: *TIViS* approach is about 65 %–80 % times faster than *Bytea*. The only exception is when the video size is 512 KB, the query performance of *TIViS* is about 58 % times better than *Bytea*. When storage age is 10, the superiority of *TIViS* presented in Fig. 6(b) is similar to Fig. 6(b) as storage age is 0. Although the performance of both *TIViS* and *Bytea* are degraded, *TIViS* is still around 75 %–85 % times faster than *Bytea*. Similarly, the only exception is also occurred when video size is 256 KB. At this moment, the query performance of *TIViS* is about 63 % times better than *Bytea* approach.

## 5   Conclusions

In our previous performance evaluation [17] of video data storage revealed the break-even point of large objects storage, and verified that the small video clips related applications (*e.g.*, VoD, online video sharing, video events archive and retrieval) are have the possibility to adopt the database based storage. We also discovered that, in current DBMS, the size of shared database buffer often have little impact in video data read/write performance, although it often played an important role in relational data throughput. In order to speed up the access of small video objects which may be suitable to store into database, we devised a temporal interval based in-database video content storage approach named *TIViS*. The *TIViS* approach provides a cheap way to wrapper the required content to the end user instead of send or buffering the video file from beginning, thus we not only saved the bandwidth but also improved the response time. Additionally, a specialized buffer management mechanism is also developed to optimize the data access in the proposed *TIViS* approach. Our experiments showed that, because the *TIViS* based video storage approach enable us store video data into database in a more efficient way, and the specialized buffer further facilitate the in-database video data access, the performance was boosted.

We believe that our initial work indicated a compromise approach for video archive, $i.e.$, store small video object into database and the big objects are placed in file system. However, there are remain many problems need to be studied and clarified before this solution become practical. And we will continuous to optimize the implementation of $TIViS$ to make it become more efficiently.

**Acknowledgments.** This work was supported by the China Ministry of Science and Technology under the State Key Development Program for Basic Research (2012CB8-21800), Fund of Na-tional Natural Science Foundation of China (No. 61462012, 61562010, U1531246), Scientific Research Fund for talents recruiting of Guizhou University (No. 700246003301), Science and Technology Fund of Guizhou Province (No. J [2013]2099), High Tech. Project Fund of Guizhou Development and Reform Commission-(No. [2013]2069), Industrial Research Projects of the Science and Technology Plan of Guizhou Province (No. GY[2014]3018) and The Major Applied Basic Research Program of Guizhou Province (NO. JZ20142001, NO. JZ20142001-05).

# References

1. Db2 video extender. http://www-01.ibm.com/software/data/db2/support/aivextender_z/
2. Now starring on the web: Youtube. www.wired.com/techbiz/media/news/2006/04/70627
3. Oracle database 11g dicom medical image support. White paper, Oracle Corporation, September 2009
4. Oracle multimedia: Managing multimedia content. White paper, Oracle Corporation (2009)
5. Bhattacharya, S., Mohan, C., Brannon, K., Narang, I., Hsiao, H.I., Subramanian, M.: Coordinating backup/recovery and data consistency between database and file systems. In: SIGMOD Conference, pp. 500–511 (2002)
6. Biliris, A.: The performance of three database storage structures for managing large objects. In: SIGMOD Conference, pp. 276–285 (1992)
7. Bret, S.: The coming exaflood. Wall Street J., 20 January 2007
8. Carey, M.J., DeWitt, D.J., Richardson, J.E., Shekita, E.J.: Object and file management in the exodus extensible database system. In: VLDB, pp. 91–100 (1986)
9. Xu, C., Huang, X., Wu, N., Sun, N., Yang, G.: Performance testing and analysis to storage medium of distributed file system. J. Comput., vol.33(10), pp. 1873–1880 (2010)
10. Council, S.P.: Storage strategy of video object and performance evaluation. Official Specification (2011)
11. DeWitt, D.J., Paulson, E., Robinson, E., Naughton, J.F., Royalty, J., Shankar, S., Krioukov, A.: Clustera: an integrated computation and data management system. PVLDB 1(1), 28–41 (2008)
12. Do, C.: Youtube architecture. Google Tech Talks, March 2008 http://highscalability.com/youtube-architecture
13. Fan, B., Andersen, D.G., Kaminsky, M., Papagiannaki, K.: Balancing throughput, robustness, and in-order delivery in P2P VoD. In: CoNEXT, p. 10 (2010)
14. Gantz, J., Reinsel, D.: The digital universe in 2020: big data, bigger digital shadows, and biggest growth in the far east. In: IDC and EMC Corporation (White paper), May 2012

15. Ghemawat, S., Gobioff, H., Leung, S.T.: The google file system. In: SOSP, pp. 29–43 (2003)
16. Huang, Y., Fu, T.Z.J., Chiu, D.M., Lui, J.C.S., Huang, C.: Challenges, design and analysis of a large-scale p2p-vod system. In: SIGCOMM, pp. 375–388 (2008)
17. Li, H., Zhou, W., Zhang, X., Wang, S.: Storage strategy of video object and performance evaluation. Technical report, Renmin University of China, December 2011
18. Kunchithapadam, K., Zhang, W., Ganesh, A., Mukherjee, N.: DBFS and secure-files. Technical report, Oracle Corporation (2011)
19. Mukherjee, N., Aleti, B., Ganesh, A., Kunchithapadam, K., Lynn, S., Muthulingam, S., Shergill, K., Wang, S., Zhang, W.: Oracle securefiles system. PVLDB 1(2), 1301–1312 (2008)
20. Mukherjee, N., Ganesh, A., Djegaradjane, V., Muthulingam, S., Zhang, W., Lynn, S., Kunchithapadam, K., Aleti, B., Shergill, K., Wang, S.: Oracle securefiles: prepared for the digital deluge. PVLDB 2(2), 1501–1511 (2009)
21. Pavlo, A., Paulson, E., Rasin, A., Abadi, D.J., DeWitt, D.J., Madden, S., Stonebraker, M.: A comparison of approaches to large-scale data analysis. In: SIGMOD Conference, pp. 165–178 (2009)
22. Petkovic, M., Jonker, W.: Content-Based Video Retrieval: A Database Perspective. (Multimedia Systems and Applications). Springer, New York (2003)
23. Randal, P.S.: Filestream storage in sql server 2008. Microsoft Corporation, White paper, Ocotber 2008
24. Schmuck, F.B., Haskin, R.L.: GPFS: a shared-disk file system for large computing clusters. In: FAST, pp. 231–244 (2002)
25. Sears, R., van Ingen, C.: Fragmentation in large object repositories. In: CIDR, pp. 298–305 (2007)
26. Seltzer, M.L., Zhang, L.: The data deluge: challenges and opportunities of unlimited data in statistical signal processing. In: IEEE ICASSP, pp. 3701–3704 (2009)
27. Stonebraker, M., Abadi, D.J., DeWitt, D.J., Madden, S., Paulson, E., Pavlo, A., Rasin, A.: MapReduce and parallel DBMSs: friends or foes? Commun. ACM 53(1), 64–71 (2010)
28. Stonebraker, M., Olson, M.A.: Large object support in postgres. In: ICDE, pp. 355–362 (1993)

# Skyline Query on Anti-correlated Distributions: From the Perspective of Spatial Index

Jinchao Zhang[1,2,3], Dong Zhang[4,5], Bo Yu[1,2(✉)], Bo Li[1,2],
Weiping Wang[1,2], and Dan Meng[1,2]

[1] Institute of Information Engineering,
Chinese Academy of Sciences, Beijing 100093, China
{zhangjinchao,yubo,libo,
wangweiping,mengdan}@iie.ac.cn
[2] National Engineering Laboratory for Information Security Technologies,
Chinese Academy of Sciences, Beijing 100093, China
[3] University of Chinese Academy of Sciences, Beijing 100049, China
[4] Inspur Group Co., Ltd., Beijing 100085, China
zhangdong@inspur.com
[5] State Key Laboratory of High-End Server and Storage Technology,
Beijing 100049, China

**Abstract.** Skyline query has attracted considerable attention since its introduction in databases. Algorithms for solving skyline query are proposed consecutively, and most of them ignore data distribution or assume dimensional independence, which leads to poor performance when performing such algorithms on anti-correlated distributions. To accelerate the query process, spatial index is extensively employed, and the state-of-the-art skyline algorithm for anti-correlated distributions, SOAD, is no exception as well. However, the SOAD algorithm internally uses two index structures for the step of determination and elimination respectively, which is complex to implement and imposes extra overhead for index maintenance. In this paper, we propose an efficient algorithm RSAC for anti-correlated distributions, which solely uses one index structure to implement such two steps. Experiments reveal that RSAC achieves up to 3 times performance improvement than SOAD on various datasets.

**Keywords:** Skyline · Anti-correlation ratio · Spatial index · Kd-tree · Bound array · Tree balance maintenance

## 1 Introduction

Skyline query originates from maximal vector problem [13]. Starting with Borzsony et al. [3], database community begins to pay close attention to this issue. For an N-dimensional dataset, each item in the dataset can be described as an N-dimensional point. The skyline query finds all the points that are not dominated by any other points in the dataset. The seaside tourism problem [3] is a classic instance of skyline query.

© Springer International Publishing Switzerland 2015
G. Wang et al. (Eds.): ICA3PP 2015, Part IV, LNCS 9531, pp. 386–401, 2015.
DOI: 10.1007/978-3-319-27140-8_27

A tourist traveling to the seaside prefers to choose a hotel which has a short distance to the beach and a low price as well. Such hotels are the skyline points in the dataset of hotels, which are not dominated by any other hotels, i.e., there does not exist a hotel which is both cheaper and nearer to the beach than the tourist's choices.

Skyline query is an important operation in certain applications, such as wireless sensor networks [15, 17], and geographic based services [5, 20]. Thus, it attracts lots of attention and becomes a hotspot in database research. In the past decade, database community has made significant research efforts in this issue, and many skyline query algorithms have been proposed. However, most of these algorithms ignore data distribution or assume dimensional independence, which leads to poor performance when applying such algorithms on anti-correlated distributions.

A few previous works study skyline on anti-correlated distributions. Shang and Kitzurewaga [19] propose an algorithm termed SOAD, which is the state-of-the-art algorithm for anti-correlations. SOAD divides skyline computation into two steps, determination and elimination, and temporary skyline points are organized in spatial index. However, SOAD uses two index structures internally for the step of determination and elimination respectively, i.e., AVL tree for determination and QuadTree for elimination. Maintaining two index structures simultaneously is an expensive operation, and it increases memory consumption as well. The straightforward way for performance improvement is performing such two steps on one index structure, and this observation plays a central role in the development of our algorithm.

In this paper, we propose a novel algorithm termed RSAC for anti-correlated distributions, which promotes performance by performing the step of determination and elimination on the same index structure, and this achieves about 10 %–20 % performance improvement. In addition, we present three optimization methods for RSAC. Comparing with SOAD, a fully optimized RSAC achieves up to 3 times performance improvement.

The main contributions of this paper are summarized as follows:

- We redefine the anti-correlation ratio $c$, which is more appropriate for high-dimensional datasets.
- We propose a novel algorithm for anti-correlated distributions RSAC, which answers the skyline query by determination and elimination on one index.
- Three efficient strategies are proposed to optimize the RSAC algorithm.

The rest of the paper is structured as follows. Section 2 reviews the existing work. Section 3 describes the preliminary knowledge. Section 4 presents the algorithm and optimizations. Performance evaluation is presented in Sect. 5. Finally, we end this paper with conclusion in Sect. 6.

## 2   Related Work

Over the past decade, a large number of algorithms for skyline query have been proposed. In this section, we review the literature most relevant to this paper.

## 2.1  Skyline Algorithms Revisited

Generic skyline algorithms are extensively studied, the BNL algorithm [3] and D&C algorithm [3] are typical ones. Recent work proposes several generic algorithm as well, i.e., APSkyline [16], BSkyTree [14], and Scalagon [6]. These algorithms are simple and easy to implement, but they barely have a competitive performance. Sort-based algorithms, such as SFS [4], LESS [8] and SaLSa [1], achieve a better performance by reducing point comparisons.

Skyline algorithms with index structure avoid scanning the entire dataset, which accelerates the process of dominance check. The first index-based algorithm was proposed by Borzsony et al. [3], and refined by many following works. A variety of index structures are used in existing algorithms.

The NN algorithm is proposed by Kossmann et al. [12]. Firstly, it builds an R*-tree on candidate dataset. Next, NN finds the nearest point to the origin, denoted as p, and this point becomes the initial skyline point. Then, the data space is partitioned by the nearest neighbor to some subspaces. The spaces dominated by p are discarded. The same process is executed on other spaces recursively. Finally, results from each space will be merged. During partitioning, there may exist some overlapping points in the spaces, which will lead to duplicated computation. NN uses some methods, such as Laisser-faire, Propagate, Merge and Fine-grained Partitioning, to avoid duplicates.

The Branch and Bound Skyline (BBS) algorithm [18] is an improvement of NN. BBS collects close points as a group and finds their minimum bounding rectangles (MBR). If the minimal corner in MBR is dominated by the candidate point, all points in the same group must be dominated, so these points should be discarded directly. In addition, MBR can also be used to quickly determine if some points in the corresponding group can dominate the candidate point, because if the upper-bound vector of MBR does not dominate the candidate point, no point will.

Inspired by NN, the skyline breaker algorithm [11] exploits LSD-tree, a variant of kd-tree, to achieve nearest neighbor search. Due to the benefit from dimension-robustness of LSD-tree, parallel skyline computation is performed in skyline breaker.

## 2.2  Skyline Query Algorithms for Anti-correlated Distributions

To the best of our knowledge, there are only two lines of work that concern the issue of skyline query on anti-correlations. Köhler et al. [10] present algorithms applying to 2 or 3 dimensional dataset. Shang and Kitzurewaga [19] present a general algorithm SOAD for anti-correlations, which has no limitation in the number of dimensions. Various spatial indices can be used in SOAD, such as QuadTree [7], Octree [9], kd-tree [2], etc.

SOAD is the state-of-the-art skyline algorithm for anti-correlated distributions, which answers the skyline query in two steps: determination and elimination. In the first step, SOAD takes a candidate point and determines if it is a skyline point. If so, the point is inserted into the skyline set. Otherwise, the point has the probability of being a non-skyline point. The second step tries to eliminate the non-skyline points as many as possible. In order to execute efficiently, both steps are performed on index structures.

In SOAD, temporary skyline points are stored in index. During the steps of determination and elimination, candidate points are compared with skyline points organized in index. However, indices are conventionally employed to store candidate dataset, i.e., NN and BBS use R*-tree to store all points of the original dataset, and execute the nearest neighbor search function provided by R*-tree to compute skyline result.

# 3 Preliminaries

Symbols referred in the context are shown in Table 1.

**Table 1.** Summary of symbols

| Symbol | Meaning |
| --- | --- |
| D | The dataset for skyline query |
| S | The result of skyline |
| V[i] | The ith dimension of vector V |
| $V_c$ | Candidate vector |
| $V_t$ | Vector in skyline |
| P | A node in tree |
| Tree(P) | A tree with P as the root |
| DISC(P) | The discriminator of P in kd-tree |
| P.KEY | Data point stored in P |

Next, we give the formal definition of skyline query.

**Definition 1:** For two N-dimensional vector M, Q. M dominates Q, denoted as $M \prec Q$, iff the following conditions are satisfied, (1) $\forall i, M[i] \leq Q[i]$, $1 \leq i \leq N$ (2) $\exists j, M[j] < Q[j]$, $1 \leq j \leq N$.[1]

Based on this definition, skyline on D is defined as follows.

$$S = \{s_t | \nexists s_k, s_k \prec s_t, s_t, s_k \in D\}$$

Shang and Kitzurewaga propose the definition of anti-correlated distribution in [19], and define the anti-correlation ratio $c$ as follows.

For a set of N-dimensional points with anti-correlation ratio $c$, any points $(x_1,...,x_N)$ follow the condition of $1 \leq \sum_{i=1}^{N} x_i \leq 1 + c$, where the value of each dimension $x_i$ falls in the interval (0, 1).

However, this definition does not take the dimension $N$ into consideration, which is not appropriate for high-dimensional dataset, i.e., for a 10-dimensional dataset with a medium anti-correlated ratio (such as 0.1 which is used in [19]), the skyline cardinality

---

[1] small value is preferable in this paper.

takes up more than 99.9 % of the cardinality of the dataset. Thus, we redefine the anti-correlation ratio $c$ as follows.

**Definition 2:** For an N-dimensional dataset with the anti-correlation ratio $c$, any points $(x_1,\ldots,x_d)$ in the dataset satisfy the condition:

$$1 \leq \sum_{i=1}^{N} x_i \leq ((N-1) * c + 1)^c,$$

where the value of $x_i$ falls in the interval (0, 1).

Based on this definition, the smaller $c$ is, the more serious anti-correlation happens. As can be seen in Sect. 5, this anti-correlation ratio model avoids data skew with the growth of dimensions.

# 4   Algorithm Presentation

In this section, we present the algorithm RSAC (Reduced Skyline algorithm for Anti-Correlated distributions), and then propose three optimization strategies, which is insertion optimization, tightening bound array and maintaining a balanced tree.

## 4.1   Baseline Algorithm

To reduce the overhead induced by maintaining two index structures, we develop an algorithm termed RSAC which performs all operations on one index. The pseudocode of baseline of RSAC is shown in Algorithm 1.

---

**Algorithm 1.** baseline of RSAC($D$)
**Input**: $D$ is the N-dimensional dataset
**Output**: $S$ is the skyline of input dataset

| | |
|---|---|
| 1 | Sort $D$ by F(X) |
| 2 | $S=\emptyset$ |
| 3 | **foreach** $t$ in $D$ **do** |
| 4 |     **if** dominate($S$, $t$) is false |
| 5 |       insert($S$, $t$) |
| 6 |     **endif** |
| 7 | **endfor** |

---

At the very beginning, the algorithm sorts input dataset $D$ in the light of monotonic function F(X) (line 1). $S$ is a spatial index which holds current skyline points. Then each point $t$ in $D$ is checked whether it is dominated by any points in $S$ (line 4). If $t$ is not dominated, it is guaranteed to be a skyline point, and then will be inserted into $S$ (line 5). During the process of dominance check, determination and elimination is performed by resorting to the spatial index $S$.

RSAC employs the kd-tree [2] as the spatial index. The kd-tree is a space partitioning data structure for k-dimensional space, and it has efficient search performance for high dimensional data. Each node in kd-tree contains a bound array (BA). For a node M, all points in Tree(M) fall into the space bounded by BA of M in terms of definition. The determination step can be performed with aid of the lower-bound of BA. The proof of correctness is presented as follows.

**Theorem 1:** If a candidate point $V_c$ is not dominated by the lower-bound vector of BA of node M, then there does not exist a point in Tree(M) which dominates $V_c$.

**Proof:** Suppose there exists a point P in Tree(M) which dominates $V_c$, then the lower-bound vector of BA of M dominates $V_c$, since the value in each dimension of the lower-bound vector is less than or equal to the value in corresponding dimension of P. This leads to a contradiction, thus, such a point must not exist. The theorem holds.    □

If $V_c$ passes the determination step, then it is guaranteed to be a skyline point. Likewise, the upper-bound of BA is of great help for the step of elimination, and the correctness is proved as follows:

**Theorem 2:** If a candidate point $V_c$ is dominated by the upper-bound vector of BA of node M, then there exists a point in Tree(M) which dominates $V_c$.

**Proof:** By definition, for any point P in Tree(M), the BA of M encloses P. Thus the value in each dimension of P is less than or equal to the value in corresponding dimension of the upper-bound vector of BA. Therefore, P dominates $V_c$, the theorem holds.    □

From Theorem 2, we know that if $V_c$ is dominated by upper-bound of any node, $V_c$ is not a skyline point and should be disregarded. For a node M, if $V_c$ passes determination and elimination, and is not dominated by the point stored in M as well, then the algorithm executes the search process recursively, which is detailed in the following.

Each node in the kd-tree associates with a discriminator *DISC*, indicating which dimension is used to partition the subspace. Assume that j equals *DISC*(M), and $S_j$ be the super key, we define $S_j$ of $V_c$ as follows:

$$S_j(V_c) = V_c[j]\ V_c[j+1]\ldots V_c[N-1]\ V_c[0]\ldots V_c[j-1]$$

$S_j$ is the cyclical concatenation of all dimensions starting with j. When a candidate point $V_c$ comes, it will be compared with nodes whose data point may dominate it. This procedure starts with the root node, and descends to leaf nodes. For each node M in the search path, compare the data point stored in M with $V_c$ to determine which subtree to traverse. Let us define $V_c$ to be *j-less* than M if $S_j(V_c)$ is less than $S_j$(M.KEY), and define $V_c$ to be *j-greater* than M if $S_j(V_c)$ is greater than $S_j$(M.KEY).

If $V_c[j]$ is less than M.KEY[j], or $V_c$ is *j-less* than M, then the procedure only needs to search left subtree of M, since data points in right subtree of M cannot dominate $V_c$. If $V_c[j]$ is greater than M.KEY[j], or $V_c$ is *j-greater* than M, both subtrees have to be searched. If $S_j(V_c)$ is equal to $S_j(M)$, $V_c$ is identical to M.KEY, thus, $V_c$ will be ignored. Now we present a proof of correctness for the search process.

**Theorem 3:** Assume j equals *DISC*(M), if $V_c[j]$ is less than M.KEY[j], or $V_c$ is *j-less* than M, then there does not exist a point in the right subtree of M, which dominates $V_c$.

**Proof:** Suppose there exists a point P in the right subtree of M. If P dominates $V_c$, then $V_c[j]$ is greater than P.KEY[j], or $V_c$ is *j-greater* than P. Thus, $V_c[j]$ must be greater than M.KEY[j], or $V_c$ is *j-greater* than M. A contradiction, the theorem holds.    □

### 4.2    Algorithm Optimization

The baseline algorithm is not sufficient for salient performance promotion, therefore, we polish the algorithm in the following.

#### 4.2.1    Determine Insertion Position During Dominance Check

In RSAC, the candidate point $V_c$ is checked if it is dominated by any points in the kd-tree. If $V_c$ is not dominated, it will be inserted into the kd-tree. During this process, $V_c$ is compared with nodes in a top-down way. However, the path from the root node to the insertion position is covered by the dominance check process. Thus, the insertion operation can be combined with the process of dominance check.

For the candidate point $V_c$, the first empty node encountered by recursively traversing kd-tree in the order of root, right subtree, left subtree, is the position that $V_c$ should be inserted. For example, a kd-tree on dataset {A(25,20), B(10,70), C(5,75), D(80,15)} is shown in Fig. 1.

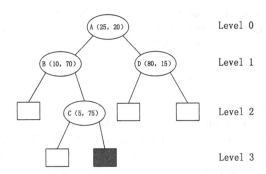

**Fig. 1.**  Determine insertion position during dominance check (Color figure online)

$V_c(8,85)$ is the current candidate point. Initially, the pointer $P_t$ points to the root node A, and the value in the first dimension of $V_c$ is less than that of $P_t$. Then traversing the left subtree of $P_t$, so $P_t$ points to B. The value in the second dimension of $V_c$ is larger than that of $P_t$, thus $P_t$ points to C. Finally, the value in the first dimension of $V_c$ is larger than that of C, and the right subtree is empty (colored in red), which is the place $V_c$ should be inserted.

Next we present a proof of correctness for this process.

**Theorem 4:** Let T be a kd-tree and $V_c$ be the candidate point. The first empty node encountered by recursively traversing T in the order of root, right subtree, left subtree, is the right position that $V_c$ be inserted in T.

**Proof:** Let $P_t$ be the current node during the traversing process, j be the discriminator of P, I be the insertion algorithm and $C_k$ be the dominance check algorithm. Initially, $P_t$ points to the root of T. If $V_c[j] < P_t.KEY[j]$, or $V_c$ is *j-less* than $P_t$, I will traverse the left subtree of $P_t$, similarly, $C_k$ will traverse the same subtree as well. If $V_c[j] > P_t.KEY[j]$, or $V_c$ is *j-greater* than $P_t$, both of the two algorithms will traverse the right subtree. Clearly, before arriving at an empty node, denoted by E, both algorithms traverse the tree along the same path. This means the node E found by I is the first empty node found by $C_k$. Therefore, $V_c$ should be inserted in E. Thus, the theorem holds.    □

Based on this theorem, we can deduce the following corollary.

**Corollary 1.** Let T be a kd-tree and $V_c$ be a vector to be inserted in T. The last empty node encountered by recursively traversing T in the order of root, left subtree, right subtree, is the right position that $V_c$ be inserted in T.

### 4.2.2  Bound Array Tightening

The native bound array in kd-tree describes the space where the node lies in, and it is determined at the time of node insertion, which simply partitions space where parent node locates, without considering nodes in subtrees. Thus, the bound array generated in such a way is too loose for the step of determination and elimination. Here, we redefine bound array.

**Definition 3:** The lower-bound vector of a point P in kd-tree is denoted as LB(P), and the upper-bound vector is denoted as UB(P). LB(P) and UB(P) are N-dimensional vectors, formalized as follows.

$$LB(P) = [\alpha_0, \alpha_1, \ldots, \alpha_{N-1}], \ \alpha_i = \min\{Q.KEY[i] | Q \in Tree(P)\}$$
$$UB(P) = [\beta_0, \beta_1, \ldots, \beta_{N-1}], \ \beta_i = \max\{Q.KEY[i] | Q \in Tree(P)\}$$

From the above definition, we can see that the value in each dimension of lower-bound(upper-bound) vector is equal to the smallest (largest) value in corresponding dimension of points in its subtree. For any node M, the initial value of LB and UB is equal to the point stored in M. When a new node P is inserted, the bound array in path from P to the root will be updated. Comparing with the native bound array which is determined by the top-down way, this bottom-up update strategy makes a much tighter bound array. Leveraging such a tight bound array, the efficiency of determination and elimination is improved.

### 4.2.3    Balanced Tree Maintenance

As we all know, unbalanced trees degrade the efficiency of insertion, query, and deletion operations in tree structure. Dynamic data insertion makes kd-tree unbalanced. In this part, we make efforts to mitigate the effect caused by such case.

It is trivial to build a balanced kd-tree on a static dataset. In each step, choosing the median of the data objects as the root, the rest of the data objects are equally divided into two subsets, which guarantees that the number of nodes in two subtrees is roughly the same. Repeat this process recursively until all the data objects are inserted. However, this method does not work in RSAC, since it is almost impossible to find the median of skyline points before all the skyline points are known. Tree rotation is a very common internal operation on self-balancing trees to maintain balance, but it does not work for kd-tree either, since rotation breaks the invariant.

The algorithm employs a strategy of periodical tree reconstruction, and uses average node depth as a measurement. For a balanced binary tree with n nodes, the depth of tree is $\lceil \log_2(n+1) \rceil$, and there are $2^i$ nodes in level $i$ (root node locates in level 0), and the average node depth of a balanced tree with n nodes can be calculated as

$$\text{DEP}_{\text{avg}}(n) = \left[ \sum\nolimits_{i=0}^{\lceil \log_2(n+1) \rceil - 2} 2^i * i + \left( n + 1 - 2^{\lceil \log_2(n+1) \rceil - 1} \right) * \left( \lceil \log_2(n+1) \rceil - 1 \right) \right] / n \tag{1}$$

When the average node depth of a kd-tree reaches a specific threshold, i.e., x times deeper than $\text{DEP}_{\text{avg}}(n)$, the reconstruction procedure is triggered to build a balanced kd-tree based on temporary skyline points.

Building a balanced kd-tree needs to find the median of data objects. However, the worst case complexity of finding the median is $O(n\log n)$, worse still, this operation will be invoked many times in a single construction process. To reduce the overhead of finding the median, we make compromise for precise median, since building a strict balanced kd-tree is not necessary. In RSAC, we use the linear-time algorithm median of medians [21] to determine an approximate median. By this way, although the newly built kd-tree is still unbalanced, the average node depth is getting lower, from which the performance benefits.

## 4.3    Algorithm Presentation

The RSAC algorithm is illustrated in Algorithm 2.

---

**Algorithm 2.** RSAC($D$)
Input: $D$ is the N-dimensional dataset
Output: $S$ is the Skyline of input dataset

| | |
|---|---|
| 1 | Sort $D$ by F(X) |
| 2 | $S=\emptyset$ |
| 3 | **foreach** $t$ in $D$ **do** |
| 4 |   pos=null |
| 5 |   **if** dominate($S.root$, $t$) is false and pos is not null |
| 6 |     insert($S$, pos, $t$) |
| 7 |     updatefilter(pos,$t$) |
| 8 |     pos=null |
| 9 |     **if** needrebuild($S$) |
| 10 |       construct ($S$) |
| 11 |     **endif** |
| 12 |   **endif** |
| 13 | **endfor** |

---

If $t$ is a skyline point, it will be inserted into $S$ with the position indicated by *pos* (line 6). Then bound array of nodes in the path from *pos* to root will be updated (line 7). If the threshold is reached (line 9), then a new tree is constructed (line 10). The function *dominate* invoked in line 5 is a key component, and it is shown in Algorithm 3.

---

**Algorithm 3.** dominate ($node$,$x$)
Input: a node in kd-tree and a candidate point
Output: true if there exists a node in TREE($node$) dominates $x$, otherwise returns false

| | | | | |
|---|---|---|---|---|
| 1 | **if** domtest($node$,$x$) | 17 |     **if** dominate ($node.right$,$x$) |
| 2 |   **return** true | 18 |       **return** true |
| 3 | **endif** | 19 |     **endif** |
| 4 | **if** equal($node$,$x$) | 20 |   **endif** |
| 5 |   **return** false | 21 | **endif** |
| 6 | **endif** | 22 | |
| 7 | **if** pos is not null and | 23 | **if** $node.left$ is null |
| |     not domtest ($node.ba$,$x$) | 24 |   **if** pos is null |
| 8 |   **return** false | 25 |     pos= $node$ |
| 9 | **endif** | 26 |   **endif** |
| 10 | cmp=veccmp($node$,$x$) | 27 | **else** |
| 11 | **if** cmp<0 | 28 |   **if** dominate ($node.left$,$x$) |
| 12 |   **if** $node.right$ is null | 29 |     **return** true |
| 13 |     **if** pos is null | 30 |   **endif** |
| 14 |       pos= $node$ | 31 | **endif** |
| 15 |     **endif** | 32 | |
| 16 |   **else** | 33 | **return** false |

---

The algorithm firstly determines if the candidate point $x$ is dominated by or equal to current node (line 1 and line 4), and then determines if $x$ is dominated by the bound array of current node (line 7). If $x$ passes all these tests, then the algorithm recursively repeats this process in the order of right subtree, left subtree of *node* (line 10–31). During this process, the algorithm determines insertion position for $x$ (line 13–15, 24–26).

# 5   Performance Evaluation

Experiments in this section are performed on a Linux server with 4 CPUs, each CPU has 8 cores with 2.2 GHz frequency. The RAM is 64 GB, and a SATA disk with 7200 RPM is attached. The RSAC algorithm is implemented in JAVA, running on JDK1.7.0. We modify the tool written by Borzsony [3] to generate anti-correlated datasets with various ratio $c$ which is defined above. We generate datasets with c = 0.1, c = 0.3 and c = 1 as strong anti-correlated datasets, medium anti-correlated datasets and week anti-correlated datasets. The size of datasets ranges from 100 k to 1 m, and dimensions from 4 to 10. To simplify statement, we use size, dimension and anti-correlation ratio to represent datasets, i.e., 1 m8d.1r for dataset with size of 1 m, dimension of 8 and anti-correlation ration ratio of 0.1. The skyline cardinality of experimental datasets is shown in Tables 2 and 3.

**Table 2.** Skyline cardinality of 100 k dataset

| Dimension \ c | 0.1 | 0.3 | 1 |
|---|---|---|---|
| 4 | 59018 | 13246 | 3095 |
| 6 | 98858 | 77904 | 4129 |
| 8 | 99997 | 87083 | 9921 |
| 10 | 100000 | 89567 | 24279 |

**Table 3.** Skyline cardinality of 1 m dataset

| Dimension \ c | 0.1 | 0.3 | 1 |
|---|---|---|---|
| 4 | 327339 | 56108 | 14141 |
| 6 | 917268 | 439807 | 14392 |
| 8 | 999739 | 609298 | 34032 |
| 10 | 999999 | 573663 | 102278 |

## 5.1   Evaluation on Impact of Anti-correlation Ratio

Section 4.2.3 describes an optimization method of maintaining a balanced tree, in which the balance threshold is a pivotal parameter that directly affects the algorithm performance. We manage to find an optimal value of the threshold through experiments. The 1 m dataset with different dimensions and anti-correlation ratio $c$ is used. The threshold ranges between 1.1 and 1.4. We use baseline algorithm solely with the optimization of maintaining a balanced tree, and the result is shown in Fig. 2.

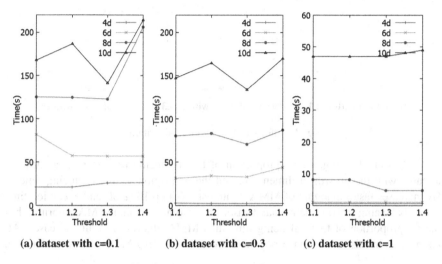

(a) dataset with c=0.1          (b) dataset with c=0.3          (c) dataset with c=1

**Fig. 2.** Effects of anti-correlation ratio

From this result, we notice that RSAC is sensitive to strong anti-correlated, high-dimensional datasets. Among all these values of threshold, 1.3 is an appropriate value for all test cases, since the algorithm with different anti-correlation ratio has a considerable performance benefits when $c$ is set to 1.3. Thus, we consider 1.3 as an optimal value of $c$, which is used in following experiments.

## 5.2    Evaluation on Balance Strategy

When maintaining the balanced kd-tree, RSAC uses the median of medians algorithm (MMA) to build an approximate balanced tree, rather than using median algorithm (MA) to build a strict balanced tree. In this section, we verify the effectiveness of this approach through experiments performing on 1 m dataset. The result is shown in Fig. 3.

From Fig. 3, we see that, comparing with MA algorithm, RSAC with MMA algorithm has an evident performance advantage on strong anti-correlated, high-dimensional dataset, i.e., RSAC with MMA is about 40 % faster than that with MA on 1m10d.1r dataset. Comparing with the linear time complexity of MA, the complexity of MMA is O(nlogn), which will efficiently degrade the performance on strong anti-correlated, high-dimensional dataset, since such dataset contains more skyline point than weak anti-correlated, low-dimensional dataset. We perform such two algorithms on 1m dataset with the anti-correlation ratio of 0.1 to investigate the proportion of tree balancing time.

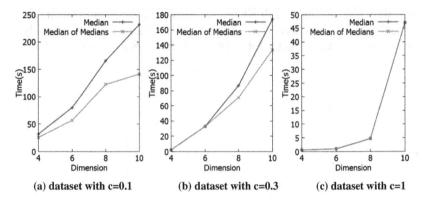

(a) dataset with c=0.1        (b) dataset with c=0.3        (c) dataset with c=1

**Fig. 3.** Effects of tree building algorithm

As illustrated in Fig. 4, the proportion of tree balancing time in both algorithms increases with the growth of dimension, and the proportion of tree balancing time of MA increases faster than that of MMA, it almost takes up 10 % of total execution time for tree balancing in 10-dimensional dataset. We also notice that the MA algorithm has a larger proportion of tree balancing time than MMA algorithm in all test cases. All experiments in this subsection verify the correctness of using MMA for tree balancing.

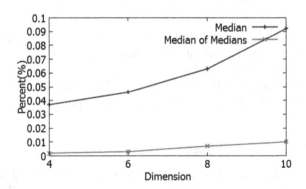

**Fig. 4.** Proportion of tree balancing time

## 5.3    Optimization Evaluation

In this section, we evaluate the performance of our algorithm RSAC, and verify the effectiveness of optimization methods, to be specific, the insertion optimization (termed as InOp), the bound array tightening optimization (termed as BTOp) and the optimization of maintaining a balanced tree (BOp), and compare all these with SOAD algorithm. Besides that, we also investigate the performance of the baseline algorithm of RSAC (termed as native RSAC). All three optimizations will be tested solely with the baseline algorithm of RSAC, i.e., RSAC InOp stands for the baseline algorithm with only optimization of insertion. The evaluation results are shown in Figs. 5 and 6.

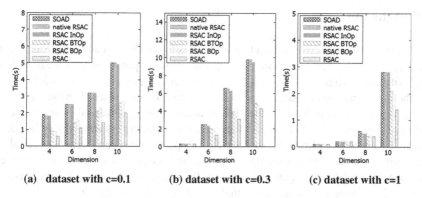

(a)  dataset with c=0.1          (b) dataset with c=0.3          (c) dataset with c=1

**Fig. 5.** Performance evaluation on 100 k dataset

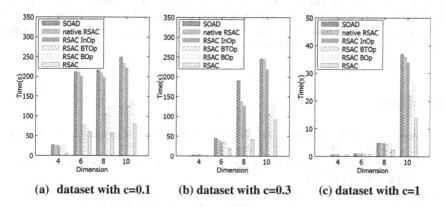

(a)  dataset with c=0.1          (b) dataset with c=0.3          (c) dataset with c=1

**Fig. 6.** Performance evaluation on 1 m dataset

Firstly, we notice that the baseline algorithm of RSAC outperforms SOAD in all test cases. The performance improvement is about 10 %–20 %, and this gap becomes prominent on dataset with large skyline cardinality (i.e., on 1m10d.1r). This phenomenon can be explained by that RSAC uses one index structure internally, which reduces the overhead of maintaining two index structures simultaneously in SOAD.

The optimizations of bound array tightening and maintaining a balanced tree do have an effect on performance promotion, and the effect of them is noticeable on strong anti-correlated, high-dimensional dataset. However, the insertion optimization has a weak effect, since the time of insertion operation takes a little proportion of the whole execution time, thus, there is not much room for improvement. Finally, comparing with SOAD, the RSAC algorithm, which is the baseline algorithm with all optimizations, has 2–3 times performance improvement.

# 6 Conclusion

The skyline cardinality on anti-correlated dataset is large, thus, a candidate point has to be compared with a large number of temporary skyline points, which leads to high complexity for skyline computation. Spatial indices are extensively utilized to accelerate the query process, especially in algorithms for anti-correlated distributions. This paper gives a new definition of the anti-correlation ratio, which takes the value of dimension into consideration. This paper also investigates skyline query on anti-correlated distributions from the perspective of spatial index, and proposes an algorithm named RSAC, which uses the kd-tree as the index structure. We improve the performance of RSAC by optimization from three aspects. Experiments demonstrate that RSAC performs 2–3 times faster than the state-of-the-art algorithm.

**Acknowledgments.** This work is supported by the National KeJiZhiCheng Project (2012B AH46B03), the National HeGaoJi Key Project (2013ZX01039-002-001-001), the National High-Tech Research and Development Plan of China (2012AA01A401), the National Natural Science Foundation of China (61402473), and "Strategic Priority Research Program" of the Chinese Academy of Sciences (XDA06030200).

# References

1. Bartolini, I., Ciaccia, P., Patella, M.: Efficient sort-based skyline evaluation. ACM Trans. Database Syst. (TODS) **33**(4), 31 (2008)
2. Bentley, J.L.: Multidimensional binary search trees used for associative searching. Commun. ACM **18**, 509–517 (1975)
3. Borzsony, S., Kossmann, D., Stocker, K.: The skyline operator. In: Proceedings of 17th International Conference on Data Engineering, pp. 421–430. IEEE (2001)
4. Chomicki, J., Godfrey, P., Gryz, J., Liang, D.: Skyline with presorting. In: ICDE, vol. 3, pp. 717–719 (2003)
5. Emrich, T., Franzke, M., Mamoulis, N., Renz, M., Züfle, A.: Geo-social skyline queries. In: Bhowmick, S.S., Dyreson, C.E., Jensen, C.S., Lee, M.L., Muliantara, A., Thalheim, B. (eds.) DASFAA 2014, Part II. LNCS, vol. 8422, pp. 77–91. Springer, Heidelberg (2014)
6. Endres, M., Roocks, P., Kießling, W.: Scalagon: an efficient skyline algorithm for all seasons. In: Renz, M., Shahabi, C., Zhou, X., Chemma, M.A. (eds.) DASFAA 2015. LNCS, vol. 9050, pp. 292–308. Springer, Heidelberg (2015)
7. Finkel, R.A., Bentley, J.L.: Quad trees a data structure for retrieval on composite keys. Acta Informatica **4**(1), 1–9 (1974)
8. Godfrey, P., Shipley, R., Gryz, J.: Maximal vector computation in large data sets. In: Proceedings of the 31st International Conference on Very Large Data Bases, pp. 229–240. VLDB Endowment (2005)
9. Jackins, C.L., Tanimoto, S.L.: Oct-trees and their use in representing three dimesional objects. Comput. Graph. Image Process. **14**(3), 249–270 (1980)
10. Kohler, H., Yang, J.: Computing large skylines over few dimensions: the curse of anti-correlation. In: Web Conference (APWEB), 2010 12th International Asia-Pacific, pp. 284–290. IEEE (2010)

11. Köppl, D.: Breaking skyline computation down to the metal: the skyline breaker algorithm. In: Proceedings of the 17th International Database Engineering & Applications Symposium, pp. 132–141. ACM (2013)

12. Kossmann, D., Ramsak, F., Rost, S.: Shooting stars in the sky: an online algorithm for skyline queries. In: Proceedings of the 28th International Conference on Very Large Data Bases, pp. 275–286. VLDB Endowment (2002)

13. Kung, H.T., Luccio, F., Preparata, F.P.: On finding the maxima of a set of vectors. J. ACM (JACM) 22(4), 469–476 (1975)

14. Lee, J., Hwang, S.W.: Scalable skyline computation using a balanced pivot selection technique. Inf. Syst. 39, 1–21 (2014)

15. Liang, W., Chen, B., Yu, J.X.: Energy-efficient skyline query processing and maintenance in sensor networks. In: Proceedings of the 17th ACM Conference on Information and Knowledge Management, pp. 1471–1472. ACM (2008)

16. Liknes, S., Vlachou, A., Doulkeridis, C., Nørvåg, K.: APSkyline: improved skyline computation for multicore architectures. In: Bhowmick, S.S., Dyreson, C.E., Jensen, C.S., Lee, M.L., Muliantara, A., Thalheim, B. (eds.) DASFAA 2014, Part I. LNCS, vol. 8421, pp. 312–326. Springer, Heidelberg (2014)

17. Pan, L.Q., Li, J.Z., Luo, J.Z.: Approximate skyline query processing algorithm in wireless sensor networks. J. Softw. 21(5), 1020–1030 (2010)

18. Papadias, D., Tao, Y., Fu, G., Seeger, B.: An optimal and progressive algorithm for skyline queries. In: Proceedings of the 2003 ACM SIGMOD International Conference on Management of Data, pp. 467–478. ACM (2003)

19. Shang, H., Kitsuregawa, M.: Skyline operator on anti-correlated distributions. Proc. VLDB Endow. 6(9), 649–660 (2013)

20. Shi, J., Lu, H., Lu, J., Liao, C.: A skylining approach to optimize influence and cost in location selection. In: Bhowmick, S.S., Dyreson, C.E., Jensen, C.S., Lee, M.L., Muliantara, A., Thalheim, B. (eds.) DASFAA 2014, Part II. LNCS, vol. 8422, pp. 61–76. Springer, Heidelberg (2014)

21. Median of medians Wiki. http://en.wikipedia.org/wiki/Median_of_medians

# PNSICC: A Novel Parallel Network Security Inspection Mechanism Based on Cloud Computing

Jin He[1]([✉]), Mianxiong Dong[2], Kaoru Ota[2], Minyu Fan[1], and Guangwei Wang[1]

[1] Department of Computer Science,
University of Electronic Science and Technology of China,
Chengdu 611731, People's Republic of China
`201111060104@std.uestc.edu.cn`, `ff98@uestc.edu.cn`,
`gwwanguestc@hotmail.com`
[2] Department of Information and Electronic Engineering,
Muroran Institute of Technology, Muroran, Japan
`{mx.dong,ota}@csse.muroran-it.ac.jp`

**Abstract.** As we all know, application firewall provides in-depth inspection to ensure application-layer security services, but brings a serious decline for network performance of application service, even more serious impact on service usability, worse, in the face of increasingly complex and diverse network application services that require an integrated network security protection, different types of application firewall collaborate together to ensure security use of integrated services, but multiple application firewalls lead to more serious performance problems than a single one. Recent efforts have provided a large number of optimization measures and algorithms, what is more, have offered a lot of new security architecture for application firewalls, unfortunately, most of them did not achieve the desired results. We have proposed a novel architecture that combines the characteristics of cloud computing, namely, parallel network security inspection Mechanism based on cloud computing (PNSICC) that is able to addresses performance problems for multiple intertwined application firewalls that protect network security of integrated service. PNSICC not only provides effective network security protections for the protected objects, but also has greatly improved security inspection efficiency. We have proved by experiments that our scheme is an effective and efficient method.

**Keywords:** Security meta-group · SW · UTM · PNSICC · Delay · Throughput · Loss rate

## 1 Introduction

Information security reports released by National Vulnerability Database [15] in February 2013 have shown that network security is a major threat to a variety of network-based application services. Although there are multiple ways to

© Springer International Publishing Switzerland 2015
G. Wang et al. (Eds.): ICA3PP 2015, Part IV, LNCS 9531, pp. 402–415, 2015.
DOI: 10.1007/978-3-319-27140-8_28

solve such security issues, today, the vast majority of ways in commercialization is that security devices (e.g., firewall, anti-virus, anti-spam) are placed at front-end of the protected objects. Once a packet or stream accesses a protected object, they must go through security devices placed at the protected objects to be inspected, thus ensuring the security of the protected object. In order to avoid direct access to these protected objects, security devices have commonly used proxy mode [5,7] to restraint data packets or stream directly access to them. Today, most commercial application firewalls (e.g., SonicWALL [22]) are based on proxy mode and dominated a large number of market. Although proxy-based application firewalls based on in-depth inspection can provide security assurance for network-based application services, they cause serious performance bottleneck [10] (e.g., latency, throughput). For example, Unified Threat Managemen (UTM) of SonicWALL [22] activates anti-virus and application firewall with much degraded system performance. Al-Aqrabi et al. [1] have presented that UTM cloud may not be a feasible approach to security protection as it may become a performance bottleneck for protecting application services when opening anti-virus, anti-spy and anti-spam application. Abdul Aziz et al. [4] have further conducted simulations on application firewalls and shows that, in the worst case, the latency seriously affected system uses.

In-depth inspection of application firewall lead to performance problems, there are a large number of related research to solve these problems, at present, these solutions can be mainly divided into two categories: single security device optimization and integrated security solutions. *For first class solutions*, Nassar et al. [12] have improved network latency by using parallel firewalls that contain SMTP in-depth inspection, however, compared to single firewall, this solution causes more decrease in link utilization. Optimization schemes of Tree-Rule Firewall and stream-based mail proxy, in some aspects of performance for anti-spam and anti-virus, have a great performance improvement, however, they cannot provides network-based application services with integrated security requirements, such as e-mail security including anti-virus, anti-spam and keyword filtering.

*For second class solutions*, Ali et al. [2] integrate multiple security middleboxes together to form UTM approach for in-depth inspection, but bring two problems: *First*, UTM causes a serious decreased performance [22]; *Second*, UTM has too large code to lead to unexpected vulnerabilities due to the large size of the trusted computing base [24]. APLOMB [21] and NetSeCC [9] present a new architecture about middlebox consolidation deployments to improve security and performance for modern enterprises' networks, but they also face the same problem: middlebox has too large code to lead to unexpected vulnerabilities. Salah et al. [19] can provide security services (e.g., anti-virus and anti-spam, and distributed denial-of-service prevention) based on virtual platform, this also faces the same performance problems as UTM, as the author finally said: future research is necessary to quantify the actual performance latency that could be associated with implementing cloud security solutions.

In short, the above approaches do not propose effective measures to resolve performance bottlenecks generated by in-depth inspection. A proposed solution is called parallel network security inspection based on cloud computing to both ensure network security and overcome the above drawbacks, and not to bring in new vulnerabilities.

The rest of the paper is organized as follows: Sect. 2 discusses issues and challenges of security devices. Section 3 provides design of PNSICC. Section 4 presents the implementation of PNSICC. Section 5 details PNSICC's performance evaluation. Finally, Sect. 6 is the conclusion.

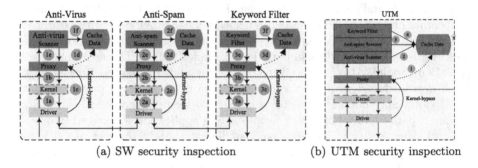

(a) SW security inspection          (b) UTM security inspection

**Fig. 1.** Working mechanism of two current popular security deployment

## 2    Issues and Challenges

In-depth inspection is based on application-layer security, different types of application services are required to go through one or more middleboxes to ensure their security. For example, e-mail service simultaneously needs anti-virus, anti-spam, keyword filtering to protect its security, where anti-virus filters e-mail with virus, anti-spam filters spam, keyword filtering filters sensitive words. Using anti-virus, anti-spam, keyword filter as an example of in-depth inspection describes how to deploy these security middleboxes to protect application-layer security. Today, there are two popular deployment: series way (SW) and UTM. A tenant chain uses SW (e.g., CoMb [20]) to go through one or more desired middleboxes, where these security middleboxes only provide a single-function protection for the protected objects, SW deployment simplify shows in Fig. 1(a). A tenant chain goes through one middlebox to ensure its security, where the middlebox is a consolidated middlebox architecture, including multiple single-function middleboxes, we simplify the model shown in Fig. 1(b). For two deployment, next, we give their working mechanism, then point out the existing problems and faces current challenges.

### 2.1    Working Mechanism

Figure 1 lists the current popular two security deployment to solve application-layer security problems. Figure 1(a) shows that SW uses multiple single-function security middleboxs to protect application service security, every middlebox uses proxy to isolate the customer and the server to prevent attackers from direct attack on the server. Using anti-virus [18] as an example describes their working mechanism [8,17].

(1) Network driver accepts network packets (1a), then forwards them to kernel or proxy. Note that some security middleboxs use zero-copy technique [11], these packets directly bypass kernel (1b and 1c) to proxy.

(2) Proxy extracts data from network packets and stores them in the data cache (1d) by a certain format. When data cache reaches a certain size or over a certain time interval, proxy informs anti-virus scanner to inspect data (1e).

(3) Anti-virus scanner inspects data to determine whether these data in the cache carry viruses (1f). If there are viruses, then terminates the forward to the next hop, otherwise proxy re-packs cache data into network packets, and forwarded them to the next hop by kernel or driver.

Anti-spam and keyword filter work the same mechanism as anti-virus. UTM shown in Fig. 1(b)has the same operating mechanism as Fig. 1(a), while the main difference of working mechanism between UTM and SW is that UTM places all scanner together sharing a proxy, while Fig. 1(a) puts to use a proxy and a scanner together.

## 2.2  Problem Analysis

*Performance.* The above mechanism shows that it takes some time for proxy to extract data from network packets to put them in the data cache, and each scanner inspects whether data in the cache have viruses, which takes some time. So both proxy and scanner cause packet latency and throughput decline. Next, The specific number is illustrated the increasing latency and throughput degradation that two employments protect network-based application services to result in.

**Definition 1 (Inspection Delay).** *A inspection delay is network delay that is due to middleboxes perform in-depth inspection traffic before reaching network-based application services. $T_{ID}$ indicates inspection delay, $T_{ID} = T_{proxy} + T_{scanner}$, where*

- $T_{proxy}$ *denotes proxy delay, including the data extraction time from network packets, the time stored in the data cache, the read data time from the cache and the time packed into network packets.*
- $T_{scanner}$ *denotes security inspection delay, including the time spent by application-layer in-depth inspection.*

**Definition 2 (Anti-Virus, Anti-Spam and Keyword-Filter Inspection Delay).** *Anti-Virus inspection delay is denoted by $T_{AV}$, $T_{AV} = T_{AVproxy} + T_{AVscanner}$; Similarly, $T_{AS}$ denotes anti-spam inspection delay, $T_{AS} = T_{ASproxy} + T_{ASscanner}$; $T_{KF}$ denotes keyword filter inspection delay, $T_{KF} = T_{KFproxy} + T_{KFscanner}$, Where*

- $T_{AVproxy}$, $T_{ASproxy}$ and $T_{KFproxy}$ denote anti-virus, anti-spam and keyword-filter proxy time, respectively.
- $T_{AVscanner}$, $T_{ASscanner}$ and $T_{KFscanner}$ denote anti-virus, anti-spam and keyword-filter inspection time, respectively.

To explain that in order to simplify the complexity of in-depth inspection, it is assumed that three types of proxy use the same mechanism and take the same time, so $T_{proxy} = T_{AVproxy} = T_{ASproxy} = T_{KFproxy}$; $T_{MAXscanner} = \mathrm{MAX}(T_{AVscanner}, T_{ASscanner}, T_{KFscanner})$.

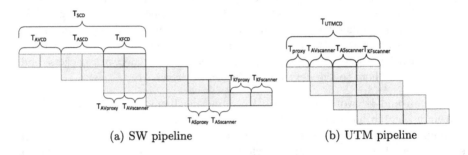

(a) SW pipeline          (b) UTM pipeline

**Fig. 2.** Pipeline of SW and UTM

**SW Inspection Delay:** $T_{SW}$ denotes the sum of SW inspection delay shown in Fig. 2(a), $T_{SW}$ is determined by $T_{AV}$, $T_{AS}$ and $T_{KF}$ by adding together.

$$
\begin{aligned}
T_{SW} &= T_{AV} + T_{AS} + T_{KF} \\
&= (T_{AVproxy} + T_{AVscanner}) + (T_{ASproxy} \\
&\quad + T_{ASscanner}) + (T_{KFproxy} + T_{KFscanner}) \\
&= 3(T_{proxy}) + T_{AVscanner} \\
&\quad + T_{ASscanner} + T_{KFscanner} \\
&= 3(T_{proxy}) + MAX(T_{AVscanner}, \\
&\quad T_{ASscanner}, T_{KFscanner}) \\
&= 3(T_{proxy}) + T_{MAXscanner}.
\end{aligned}
\tag{1}
$$

**UTM Inspection Delay:** $T_{UTM}$ denotes UTM inspection delay shown in Fig. 2(b).

$$
\begin{aligned}
T_{UTM} &= T_{proxy} + T_{AVscanner} \\
&\quad + T_{ASscanner} + T_{KFscanner} \\
&= T_{proxy} + MAX(T_{AVscanner}, \\
&\quad T_{ASscanner}, T_{KFscanner}) \\
&= T_{proxy} + T_{MAXscanner}.
\end{aligned}
\tag{2}
$$

**SW Inspection Throughput:** $TP_{SM}$ denotes SW inspection throughput, $TP_{SW} = n/T_{nSW}$ where

- n is the number of packets.
- $T_{nSW}$ is a time that n packets pass through SW to spend.

$$T_{nSW} = T_{AV} + MAX\,(T_{AV} + T_{AS})$$
$$+MAX\,(T_{AV} + T_{AS} + T_{KF})$$
$$\times (n - 2)$$
$$+MAX\,(T_{AS} + T_{KF}) + T_{KF}$$
$$\approx (n + 2)\,T_{MAXscanner}. \tag{3}$$

- $TP_{SW} \approx n/(n+2)MAXT_{scanner} \approx 1/T_{ID} = 1/(T_{proxy}+T_{scanner})$.

**UTM Inspection Throughput:** $TP_{UTM}$ denotes UTM inspection throughput, $TP_{UTM} = n/T_{nUTM}$ where $T_{nUTMCT}$ is a time that n packets pass through UTM to take.

$$T_{nUTM} = n(T_{proxy} + 3MAXT_{scanner}) \tag{4}$$
$$TP_{UTM} = n/T_{nUTM}$$
$$= n/n\,(T_{proxy} + 3T_{MAXscanner})$$
$$= 1/\,(T_{proxy} + 3T_{MAXscanner}). \tag{5}$$

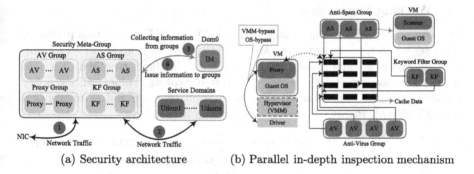

(a) Security architecture    (b) Parallel in-depth inspection mechanism

**Fig. 3.** Security architecture and working mechanism of PNSICC

In summary, it is able to get such a conclusion from the above corollaries: UTM is shorter than SW in terms of latency, while SW is higher than UTM in throughput. If network-based application services require both a short delay and a high throughput, then these two way are not suitable for this type of network-based application service. Overall, these two way are not good in terms of performance, latency and throughput are needed to be improved to ensure a safe and efficient network communication.

*Isolation.* UTM as shown in Fig. 1(b) consists of proxy, anti-virus scanner, anti-spam scanner and keyword filter, there are a lot of code in every scanner and proxy, since the greater amount of code causes the more unexpected vulnerabilities [14], so UTM may cause uncontrollable threats to seriously risk its own security. In order to reduce security threats, this is not a feasible way to cut out code in UTM, PNSICC enforces isolation of these scanners to reduce security threats being equivalent to reduce code.

### 2.3   Challenges

As shown in Fig. 1, the above existing two ways can not obtain efficient secure communications, it is needed to overcome the above two major drawbacks and to design a novel architecture that provides short delay and higher throughput for network-based application services, and also enforces isolation between scanners and between scanners and proxy.

## 3   Proposed Solution

In order to resolve the existing problems of the above popular two security deployment, existing efforts are powerless. As shown Fig. 3, we have proposed a new deployment coupled with the characteristics of virtual platform [3] (e.g., isolation, scalability, on-demand services) that is able to effectively solve the above existing disadvantages. Next, PNSICC working mechanism is first described.

### 3.1   Working Mechanism

As shown in Fig. 3(a), we have migrated AS, AV and KF into virtual platform. They, respectively, constitute AV, AS and KF group, each node in every group was deployed in a stand-alone virtual machine. To further strengthen their own security, thus avoiding too large code to lead to unexpected vulnerabilities, proxy and every scanner were isolated, thus forming proxy group and scanner group (e.g., AV group). PNSICC's working mechanism is as follows:

(1) NIC $\xrightarrow[1]{request}$ security meta-group $\xrightarrow[2]{request}$ service domains: NIC accepts request packets from client, then forwards them to security meta-group to perform parallel in-depth inspection. If these packets are valid, they are forwarded to server in service domains, otherwise drop them.

(2) Service domains $\xrightarrow[2]{response}$ security meta-group $\xrightarrow[1]{response}$ NIC: For servers' response packet, the process is similar to step 1, a valid packet is forwarded to NIC after security inspection of security meta-group, otherwise drop them.

(3) Security Meta-Group $\xrightarrow[3]{collect\ information}$ Inspection monitor (IM): Every group report their own in-depth inspection time (e.g., $T_{AVscanner}, T_{ASscanner}$) that it takes for one member (node) in every group to inspect and filter for a full cache data.

(4) IM $\xrightarrow[4]{issue\ information}$ Security Meta-Group: IM determines to create the number of proxies or scanners according to delay demand and simple indepth inspection time (§III-B).

## 3.2    Fine-Grained Scanning

Figure 3(b) shows parallel inspection mechanism of security meta-group based on virtual platform, PNSICC's parallelism reflects two aspects: not only different type of middleboxes simultaneously perform in-depth inspection in parallel, but also the same type of middleboxes cooperate together to achieve in-depth inspection in parallel. The main purpose of PNSICC design reduces network latency caused by in-depth inspection and improves network throughput, thereby providing security network with low-latency and high throughput. PNSICC is also able to dynamically adjust network latency according to delay-sensitive services (e.g., video conferencing). Given $T_{need}$ as the tolerable delay of a service, we assume $T_{proxy}$ is a constant value, so $T_{Nscanner}=T_{need}-T_{proxy}$, where $T_{Nscanner}$ denotes the inspection time it takes to complete the acceptable latency for delay-sensitive services. $\lceil T_{AVscanner}/T_{Nscanner} \rceil$ denotes the number of anti-virus required to complete synchronous parallel inspection within $T_{need}$ time. Similarly, $\lceil T_{ASscanner}/T_{Nscanner} \rceil$ denotes the number of anti-spam, $\lceil T_{KFscanner}/T_{Nscanner} \rceil$ denotes the number of keyword filter. For example, Fig. 3(b) shows that 3 anti-spam ($3*T_{Nscanner}=T_{ASscanner}$), 4 anti-virus ($4*T_{Nscanner}=T_{AVscanner}$) and 2 keyword filter ($2*T_{Nscanner}=T_{KFscanner}$) can cooperate together to achieve in-depth inspection within $T_{Nscanner}$ time. We list the efficient parallel inspection process of security meta-group.

(1) Network packets arrive proxy from driver by means of VMM-bypass and OS-bypass [11].
(2) Proxy extracts data from network packets and stores them in the data cache by means of a certain format.
(3) AS, AV and KF group simultaneously inspect data in the cache to determine whether these data have viruses, spam and sensitive keyword words. If any one of these conditions occurs, then proxy drops network packets. Otherwise, it re-packs data in the cache into network packets, and forwards them to kernel or driver.

## 3.3    Performance

Similar to Sect. 2, we can get PNSICC's packet delay and throughput.

**PNSICC Inspection Delay:** As shown in Fig. 4, $T_{PNSICC}$ denotes PNSICC inspection delay for network-based application services.

- If $T_{MAXscanner} + T_{proxy} \leq T_{need}$ then

$$T_{PNSICC} = T_{proxy} + MAX(T_{AVscanner},$$
$$T_{ASscanner}, T_{KFscanner}).$$
$$= T_{proxy} + T_{MAXscanner} \qquad (6)$$

- If $T_{MAXscanner} + T_{proxy} > T_{need}$ then

$$T_{PNSICC} = T_{need} \qquad (7)$$

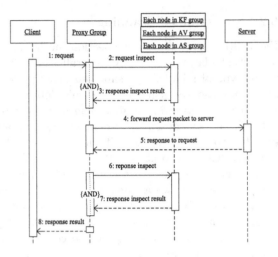

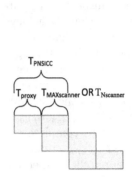

**Fig. 4.** PNSICC pipeline          **Fig. 5.** PNSICC inspection process

**PNSICC Inspection Throughput:** $TP_{PNSICC}$ denotes PNSICC Throughput, $TP_{PNSICC}=n/T_{nPNSICC}$ where $T_{nPNSICC}$ is a time that n packets pass through PNSICC to spend.

- If $T_{PNSICC} = T_{proxy}+T_{MAXscanner}$ then

$$T_{nPNSICC} = T_{proxy}$$
$$+ (n-1) MAX (T_{MAXscanner}, T_{proxy})$$
$$TP_{PNSICC} = n/T_{nPNSICC}$$
$$\approx n/ (n-1) MAX (T_{MAXscanner}, T_{proxy})$$
$$\approx 1/MAX (T_{MAXscanner}, T_{proxy}) \tag{8}$$

- If $T_{PNSICC} = T_{need}$ then

$$T_{nPNSICC} = T_{proxy}$$
$$+ (n-1) MAX (T_{Nscanner}, T_{proxy}) \tag{9}$$
$$TP_{PNSICC} = n/T_{nPNSICC}$$
$$\approx n/ (n-1) MAX (T_{Nscanner}, T_{proxy})$$
$$\approx 1/MAX (T_{Nscanner}, T_{proxy}) \tag{10}$$

Compared with SW and UTM, PNSICC is much higher than them in terms of delay and throughput. PNSICC demonstrates superior performance without affecting security protection.

### 3.4   Isolation

Compared to UTM, PNSICC not only completely isolates AS, AV and KF scanner, but also segregates proxy with every scanner, thus improving security to avoid causing the entire system failure due to a vulnerability being attacked. In the worst case, even if one scanner loses efficacy, it does not affect the normal operation of PNSICC. Compared with SW, PNSICC isolates scanner with poxy to enforce security. In short, PNSICC enforce isolation of security products or softwares to further improve virtual middleboxes' own security.

# 4   Implementation

AV, AS and KF are migrated to virtual machine, migration results are shown in Fig. 3(a). This article does not elaborate on the migration process, but implement fine-grained parallel inspection and filtering in virtual environment to improve secure communication performance. Figure 5 presents efficient parallel inspection process.

(1) Client $\xrightarrow[1]{request}$ proxy group: Client request a service through security inspection in virtual environment.

(2) Proxy group $\xrightarrow[2]{inspect\ request}$ AV, AS and KF group: Proxy group extracts data from network packets and store them in the data cache, then sends inspect requests to AV, AS and KF group that scan data in the cache in parallel.

(3) AV, AS and KF group $\xrightarrow[3]{inspect\ response}$ proxy group: Inspection results from each node of AV, AS and KF group returns to proxy group.

(4) Proxy group $\xrightarrow[4]{request}$ server: According to inspection results, proxy group determine whether to continue to forward network packets to the server or lose these packets. **Determine rules:** if any one of scanner group has intrusion problem, then throw away these data, only if all group do not detect any problems, then forward them to servers.

(5) Server $\xrightarrow[5]{request\ response}$ proxy group: Proxy group receive response packets from servers.

(6) Proxy group $\xrightarrow[6]{inspect\ response}$ AV, AS and KF group: Similar steps 2, PNSICC performs the above similar inspection for the response data.

(7) AV, AS and KF group $\xrightarrow[7]{inspect\ response}$ proxy group: Similar steps 3.

(8) Proxy group $\xrightarrow[8]{response}$ client: If there are no security risks in the response packets, proxy group forward them to client.

**Table 1.** Performance comparison between PNSICC and other scheme

| Method | Delay | Throughput |
|--------|-------|------------|
| SW | $3(T_{proxy}+T_{scanner})$ | $1/(T_{proxy}+T_{scanner})$ |
| UTM | $T_{proxy}+3T_{scanner}$ | $1/(T_{proxy}+3T_{scanner})$ |
| PNSICC | $T_{proxy}+T_{scanner}$ | $1/\mathrm{MAX}(T_{proxy},T_{scanner})$ |

# 5    Performance Evaluation

## 5.1    Theoretical Analysis

Next, we present performance evaluation of PNSICC. According to Sects. 2 and 3, Table 1 has theoretically shown that PNSICC has rendered more excellent than SW and UTM in term of latency and throughput. By the actual environment, it is needed to further prove whether the above theoretical result is right.

**Table 2.** The list of open source security software

| Middlebox name | Open source software |
|---|---|
| Anti-virus | ClamAV [6] |
| Anti-spam | SpamAssassin [23] |
| Keyword filter | Amavisd-new [13] |

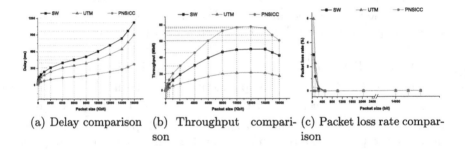

(a) Delay comparison    (b) Throughput comparison    (c) Packet loss rate comparison

**Fig. 6.** Performance comparison about three kinds of security architecture

## 5.2    Actual Simulation

*Experimental environment.* Virtual platform was conducted on a Dell Server with 4 core, 3.42 GHz Intel CPU, 16GB memory. IXIA [16] is considered as a performance test instrument. Open source security software shown in Table 2. Three experimental simulation scenarios is as follows:

(1) *SW simulation environment*: Open source security middleboxs in Table 2 were installed in a independent VM, respectively. According to virtual isolation technology, each VM in virtual platform is equivalent to a separate security middleboxes, these softwares in VMs constitute SW employment (AV-AS-KF) as shown in Fig. 1(a).

(2) *UTM simulation environment*: Open source security middleboxs are moved to the same VM, thus forming UTM as shown in Fig. 1(b).

(3) *PNSICC environment*: This article has achieved PNSICC system as shown in Fig. 3.

To evaluate PNSICC system performance, we focus on latency, throughput and packet loss rate that are important indicator of system performance, Fig. 6 shows performance comparison results. According to three sets of comparative test, we can observe PNSICC's advantage performance comparing with SW and UTM.

*Latency*: Figure 6(a) has presented three characteristics: First, network latency of three kinds of security employment is larger as the packet size increases, specifically, UTM and SW increase rapidly, mainly because there are multiple proxies in SW whose latency increases with the packet size, while UTM has three serial scanner, every scanner's latency increases as the packet size increases; Second, UTM is lower than SW in term of latency, this was mainly due to SW has several proxies than UTM to lead to delay increase. Finally, PNSICC has lower delay than UTM and SW, mainly because PNSICC provides parallel inspection, and decreases the number of proxies. Figure 6(a) indicates that PNSICC not only meets the same network security as UTM and SW, but also provides better network service, especially low-latency network requirements, such as video conference, video surveillance, etc.

*Throughput*: Figure 6(b) has shown throughput of three kinds of security employment, it is easy to see that their throughput increases with the packet size increase, PNSICC' growth rate is more rapid than UTM and SW with the packet size from 1Kbit to 10000Kbit, and PNSICC has higher throughput than UTM and SW in the same packet size. In a good case, PNSICC's throughput sometimes is even twice as UTM.

*Packet Loss Rate*: Experimental environment of packet loss rate is not the same as latency and throughput, all open source security middleboxs are used the default configuration (such as cache memory, the number of threads), and we always keep 50Mbit/s throughput regardless of packet size from 64bit to 16000bit. In the stress test, Fig. 6(c) has shown packet loss rate of three kinds of security architecture, PNSICC had no packet loss, while packet loss of SW and UTM occurred, this was mainly due to SW and UTM having high delay and low throughput to cause packet loss.

In summary, PNSICC is a high-performance security architecture whose delay, throughput and packet loss rate are far superior to existing framework, at the same time, PNSICC also enhances their own security of security softwares or products, and is easily applied to cloud platform.

# 6 Conclusion

It can be seen from the above design, implementation and experiments that PNSICC based on cloud platform provides parallel network security inspection with a novel efficient architecture. It not only overcomes the shortcomings of the current popular two security deployment, but also improves the security inspection performance of the system. In the future research, we will provide a better load balancing algorithm in security meta-group to further improve

PNSICC inspection efficiency, in the face of such a efficient parallel inspection architecture, we have reason to believe that PNSICC is able to obtain a wide range of applications in the actual business.

**Acknowledgments.** This work is partially supported by JSPS KAKENHI Grant Number 26730056, 15K15976, JSPS A3 Foresight Program.

# References

1. Al-Aqrabi, H., Liu, L., Xu, J., Hill, R., Antonopoulos, N., Zhan, Y.: Investigation of it security and compliance challenges in security-as-a-service for cloud computing. In: 2012 15th IEEE International Symposium on Object/Component/Service-Oriented Real-Time Distributed Computing Workshops (ISORCW), pp. 124–129. IEEE (2012)
2. Ali, S., Lawati, M.H.A., Naqvi, S.J.: Unified threat management system approach for securing SME's network infrastructure. In: 2012 IEEE Ninth International Conference on e-Business Engineering (ICEBE), pp. 170–176. IEEE (2012)
3. Armbrust, M., Fox, A., Griffith, R., Joseph, A.D., Katz, R., Konwinski, A., Lee, G., Patterson, D., Rabkin, A., Stoica, I., et al.: A view of cloud computing. Commun. ACM **53**(4), 50–58 (2010)
4. Aziz, A., Zafran, M., Ibrahim, M.Y., Omar, A.M., Ab Rahman, R., Zan, M., Mahfudz, M., Yusof, M.I.: Performance analysis of application layer firewall. In: 2012 IEEE Symposium on Wireless Technology and Applications (ISWTA), pp. 182–186. IEEE (2012)
5. Chao, Y., Bingyao, C., Jiaying, D., Wei, G.: The research and implementation of UTM. In: IET International Communication Conference on Wireless Mobile and Computing (CCWMC 2009), pp. 389–392. IET (2009)
6. ClamAV. www.clamav.net
7. Dong, M., Li, H., Ota, K., Yang, L.T., Zhu, H.: Multicloud-based evacuation services for emergency management. IEEE Cloud Comput. **1**(4), 50–59 (2014). http://dx.doi.org/10.1109/MCC.2014.85
8. Dong, M., Li, H., Ota, K., Zhu, H.: HVSTO: efficient privacy preserving hybrid storage in cloud data center. In: 2014 Proceedings IEEE INFOCOM Workshops, Toronto, ON, Canada, 27 April - 2 May 2014, pp. 529–534 (2014). http://dx.doi.org/10.1109/INFOCOMW.2014.6849287
9. He, J., Dong, M., Ota, K., Fan, M., Wang, G.: NetSecCC: A scalable and fault-tolerant architecture for cloud computing security. Peer-to-Peer Netw. Appl., pp. 1–15 (2014)
10. He, J., Dong, M., Ota, K., Fan, M., Wang, G.: NSCC: Self-service network security architecture for cloud computing. In: 2014 IEEE 17th International Conference on Computational Science and Engineering (CSE), pp. 444–449. IEEE (2014)
11. Mauch, V., Kunze, M., Hillenbrand, M.: High performance cloud computing. Future Gener. Comput. Syst. **29**, 1408–1416 (2012)
12. Nassar, S., El-Sayed, A., Aiad, N.: Improve the network performance by using parallel firewalls. In: 2010 6th International Conference on Networked Computing (INC), pp. 1–5. IEEE (2010)
13. amavisd new. http://www.amavis.org/

14. Nguyen, A., Raj, H., Rayanchu, S., Saroiu, S., Wolman, A.: Delusional boot: securing hypervisors without massive re-engineering. In: Proceedings of the 7th ACM European Conference on Computer Systems, EuroSys 2012, pp. 141–154. ACM, New York (2012). http://doi.acm.org/10.1145/2168836.2168851
15. NVD. http://nvd.nist.gov/
16. I. http://www.ixiacom.com/
17. Proxy, H.A.V. http://www.server-side.de/download.htm
18. for Proxy Server, K.A.V.:http://www.kaspersky.com/anti-virus_proxy_server
19. Salah, K., Calero, A.J., Zeadally, S., Almulla, S., ZAaabi, M.: Using cloud computing to implement a security overlay network. IEEE Secur. Priv. **11**, 44–53 (2012)
20. Sekar, V., Egi, N., Ratnasamy, S., Reiter, M.K., Shi, G.: Design and implementation of a consolidated middlebox architecture. In: Proceedings of NSDI (2012)
21. Sherry, J., Hasan, S., Scott, C., Krishnamurthy, A., Ratnasamy, S., Sekar, V.: Making middleboxes someone else's problem: network processing as a cloud service. ACM SIGCOMM Comput. Commun. Rev. **42**(4), 13–24 (2012)
22. SonicWALL. http://www.sonicwall.com/
23. SpamAssassin. http://spamassassin.apache.org/
24. Szefer, J., Lee, R.B.: Architectural support for hypervisor-secure virtualization. SIGARCH Comput. Archit. News **40**(1), 437–450 (2012). http://doi.acm.org/10.1145/2189750.2151022

# Simulation Platform for X-Ray Computed Tomography Based on Low-Power Systems

Estefania Serrano$^{(\boxtimes)}$, Javier Garcia Blas, Alberto Verza,
and Jesus Carretero

Computer Architecture and Technology Area,
Universidad Carlos III, 28911 Madrid, Spain
esserran@inf.uc3m.es

**Abstract.** Reconstruction of Computed Tomography (CT) images is a computationally and memory demanding tool. The creation of new algorithms for the reduction of the X-Ray dose and the increasing resolution of the detectors have complicated the obtaining of a good performance. Accelerators have become essential for the processing of the algorithm in a reasonable time. Nowadays, with the emergence of new mobile architectures that are not only powerful but also energy efficient and the possibility of easily porting the already existing code thanks to different programming models they could become an alternative to desktop and high performance accelerators. We evaluate four different platforms for our simulation framework for CT images. The evaluation results demonstrate that although in terms of performance, low-power platforms are still far from GPGPUs, the reduction of the energy consumption to almost a half in the case of the Jetson TK1 is an evident incentive that can lead to the creation of smaller and mobile medical image scanners.

**Keywords:** Computed Tomography (CT) · Iterative reconstruction · Simulation

## 1 Introduction

The medical image field, and more concretely the field of image reconstruction in Computed Tomography (CT), is a multidisciplinary topic that draws on knowledge from medicine, physics, and computer science. The CT scanner allows us to obtain images from the interior of the body through the application of X-Rays. These rays are directed from different angles to create the scanner images, which means increasing the dose received by the patient. This may be harmful for patients undergoing CT and it may have secondary effects and ulterior consequences, as X-Rays are considered harmful and carcinogenic in high and repeated doses.

One of the research lines in this field is related to the reduction of the dose applied to the patient without affecting the diagnosis capacity. New algorithms have been created, which are able to reconstruct images obtained using scanners

© Springer International Publishing Switzerland 2015
G. Wang et al. (Eds.): ICA3PP 2015, Part IV, LNCS 9531, pp. 416–426, 2015.
DOI: 10.1007/978-3-319-27140-8_29

with less number of angles or with lower voltage, at the cost of more computational resources. Those algorithms, called iterative reconstruction algorithms, are based on applying the reconstruction process several times until obtaining accurate results. For each iteration the projections obtained from the scanner are processed to obtain a final 3D image of the body. Error correction is made on each iteration, so that the final results may be even better than, for example, those of the Feldkamp, Davis and Kress (FDK) algorithm.

Due to the increasing size and resolution of the scanners, the computational cost of the reconstruction has also augmented. Considering that the iterative algorithms represent a high computational overhead over the basic algorithms, it has become unfeasible to execute these algorithms in multicore machines. To cope with those needs, new paradigms and architectures, such as GPGPUs, have been adopted. The usage of heterogeneous computing allows the user to obtain results in a reasonable time and, because of the existence of a standardized programming model available (OpenCL), the solutions implemented can be executed in many architectures. One of them are ARM devices, that have become very popular nowadays because of their usage in mobile devices. Moreover, they have also been integrated in mini-computers with very-low power consumption, which is a major advantage for embedded devices. OpenCL programming model is available for both previously mentioned architectures, apart from CPU or many-core solutions. Opposite to CUDA, which is an NVidia proprietary model, OpenCL allows us to execute the same code in several different devices without major changes.

In this work we present the implementation and the evaluation of a modular Scan CT 3D image simulator, which includes an iterative reconstructor with two main stages: backprojection and projection. This simulator has been implemented using both CUDA and OpenCL and ported for evaluation to three different hardware platforms: NVidia GPUs, AMD GPUs, and ARM architectures. Apart from the performance, power consumption and installation constraints are also studied in the paper, as the small size in the case of ARM architecture can lead to a future generation of mobile and miniaturized scanner computer units.

In two previous works [11,12], we presented an evaluation of the reconstruction algorithm over different high performance devices, such as modern GPGPU, cloud computing platforms, and Intel Xeon Phi. In this paper, we describe our advances in image processing, showing an integrated simulation tool that contains the backprojector mechanism discussed previously and a novel projector implementation. Additionally, we evaluate a new implementation based on OpenCL.

The remainder of the paper is structured as follows. Section 2 presents some related work. Main operation and implementation of the iterative simulator are shown in Sect. 3. Evaluation results from the different platforms are shown in Sect. 4. Finally, conclusions are presented in Sect. 5.

## 2    Related Work

Due to the nature of reconstruction algorithms, researchers have sought ways to accelerate execution by using high-performance techniques [7], being nowadays very popular using many-core accelerators based on GPGPUs [1]. To ensure full usage of heterogeneous architectures, it is essential to use well-established programming models, such as OpenMP 4.0, CUDA, or OpenCL. CUDA and OpenCL programming models have already been used in previous works for the reconstruction of 3D medical imaging. Examples are the works presented in [8] and [13]. In the last one, Siegl et al. studied the usage of OpenCL for high-performance medical image reconstruction by using RabbitCT [10] as a benchmarking platform for CT reconstruction algorithms implemented in OpenCL. They proved that the use of the standard programming model available for different platforms does not penalize the performance excessively, being able to run on different architectures with a loss of around 10%.

Leeser et al. [6] presented a more complete example, comparing programming models for heterogeneous computing systems (OpenMP, CUDA, and OpenCL) in 3D image processing. In this work, phase and rear projections were parallelized, and implementations for both AMD and NVIDIA cards were evaluated. Their results show that OpenCL performs better on AMD that on NVIDIA and, unlike in our case, the implementation in CUDA got the worst outcomes. The usage of filtering libraries and optimizations in our work may be related to this difference in results. The authors also performed a comparison of the obtained results, showing that image errors are not noticeable between both implementations. Finally, Park et al. [9] presented an implementation of the overhead projector based on OpenCL, showing high performance in GPGPUs. They also performed a quality comparison, showing that using GPUs in the reconstruction process does not affect the final image accuracy.

As for the projection module, studies focus on making forward projection access. As an example, Zhou et al. [15] face the usage of OpenCL to accelerate the projection phase, obtaining a speedup of 543 compared to sequential CPU implementation. In [5], the authors propose to optimize iterative image reconstruction by accelerating forward-projection through a water-filling buffer to remove pipeline stalls, and out-of-order processing to reduce the off-chip memory access by up to three orders of magnitude. In both cases, the proposals try to enhance parallelism by overlapping computing and input/output, as much as possible.

With respect to the usage of mobile platforms for the execution of scientific applications, there are some recent studies that use, i.e. NVidia Jetson TK1 boards. In [2] the authors evaluate an audio processing application with a GPU-based implementation on these boards, demonstrating that Jetson TK1 is capable of executing the application in real time and that even if it is a low power device it can provide with a real good performance. Another example is [14] where they also study the energy efficiency of video encoding applications on mobile platforms maintaining the minimum performance requirements.

As we will see in Sect. 4, in general, previous studies are consistent with our results. However, our work provides new contributions by comparing 3D images generated using different programming models to asses quality, by including both modules (reconstruction and projection) in performance evaluation, and by the inclusion of energy as a parameter to consider for a mobile CT Scan computing platform.

# 3    ScanCT Iterative Simulation Tool

Based on our previous reconstruction algorithms [11,12], an Iterative Simulation Tool (IST) has been developed. IST includes different algorithms and modules to, not only reconstruct, but also simulate the functionality of the scanner.

The iterative reconstruction functionality relies on both backprojector and projector operators. The iterative process starts with a dummy volume composed by constant values. This volume will be refined on each iteration. Following Fig. 1, first the backprojector is applied to the volume to get the new projections. Those projections are compared with the original projections obtained from the scanner. If the difference is bigger than a threshold, the projections are passed to the backprojector in order to generate a new volume. This volume is combined with the former one to get the entry volume for the new iteration. If the error is lower than a threshold the algorithm stops.

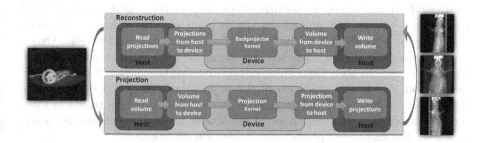

**Fig. 1.** Workflow of the IST when executing an iterative reconstruction.

In this work we are focused on the two main modules used for iterative reconstruction: projection and reconstructor. Both of them have been implemented in the two main programming models for accelerators: CUDA and OpenCL. A generic modular software API has been designed and implemented to transparently offer the functionality of the different programming models to the upper levels of the application.

## 3.1    Reconstruction and Projection Modules

The reconstruction module transforms 2D projections into a 3D volume through the use of an optional filter and a backprojector kernel. The backprojection kernel is based on the FDK algorithm for cone-beam geometry in flat panel detectors [3]. The filter used in this solution is a *rampfilter*, implemented through a discrete Fourier transform in both programming models (CUDA and OpenCL). In the case of CUDA, we rely on the native library cuFFT[1]. In OpenCL, an open source library called clFFT[2] is used.

---

[1]  https://developer.nvidia.com/cuFFT.
[2]  http://clmathlibraries.github.io/clFFT.

The other main module, the projection one, transforms a 3D volume into a configurable number of 2D projections, in a similar way that the scanner process to obtain projections. The projector module is considered as the inverse of the backprojection operation. In this case, no filter is applied during the process and execution model is computationally easier.

## 3.2   Generic Application Programming Interface

This API is a wrapper that includes the necessary functions for the execution of the algorithm. It transparently provides the functionality for the different programming models to the application. The functions have been grouped in four fundamental blocks described below: Memory allocation functions; Memory transfer functions; Kernel calls; and Platform management.

The memory allocation functions consist of the methods necessary to allocate memory in the accelerator and the host, including utilities for the entire volume (or the corresponding volume partition depending on the available memory) and projections. Volume and projections act as input or output data respectively, depending on the module executed, projection and backprojection respectively.

Regarding the memory transfer functions, they allow the data movement from accelerator to host. Data are maintained inside the accelerator, until their destruction, during the execution of the application. These functions include: host to accelerator transfer of projections and accelerator to host transfer of volume (reconstruction module), host to accelerator transfer of volume and accelerator to host transfer of projections (projection module).

**Listing 1.1.** Example of the API functions used by the projection.

```
int create_textures_gpu(int numDevices, short roi_coronal, short roi_sagittal
    , short roi_axial);
int send_projection_gpu(int thread, float * volume, short roi_coronal, short
    roi_sagittal, short roi_axial );
int execute_projection_gpu(int thread, long position, const size_t roi_s,
    size_t roi_z, float rad_angle, struct propar param);
int receive_projection_gpu(int thread, float * st, long position, size_t
    count);
int allocate_memory_projections_gpu(int countDevices, long size);
int free_memory_projections_gpu(int countDevices);
int memset_projections_gpu(int thread, long size);
```

The Kernel calls are used to invoke the execution of the different kernels for both programming models. For the execution of the iterative reconstructor method, there are currently three kernels available: rampfilter, backprojection (part of the reconstruction module); and projection (projection module). These kernels can be customized through the parameters that can specify the geometry and characteristics of the scanner.

Finally, the platform management functions provide information, setup, and destruction utilities for the platform and software configuration. It contains generic functions for obtaining information needed for the correct operation of the application, such as devices that will run the application or, the adaptation of the volume size to the memory available. In addition, if OpenCL is used, an additional context initialization of the device must be performed. This initialization is included within this set of functions.

We have used this API to construct the two main modules of the iterative simulation tool: reconstructor and projection. It could be used to generate new functionality by the user, abstracting its design from the programming model in which they can be implemented. An example of the functions used by the projection modules is shown in Listing 1.1.

## 4    Experimental Evaluation

In order to evaluate the proposed solution, we have implemented the IST using both CUDA and OpenCL programming paradigms. The goal of the evaluation is to study and compare the performance of that implementation in terms of performance and energy consumption to assess the feasibility of each platform. We have evaluated the solution under four different platforms: ARM ODROID XU3-lite (low-power profile), NVidia Jetson (low-power profile), NVidia GTX 760 (desktop profile), and AMD Radeon R9 290 (HPC profile).

The ODROID XU3-lite device includes a Samsung Exynos 5 Octa (5422) processor with a quad core Cortex-A15 2.0 GHz and another CPU with 4 Cortex-A7 cores (ARM architecture big.LITTLE). The NVidia Jetson system comprises a quad-core ARM Cortex A15 processor and an NVIDIA "Kepler" GPU with 192 CUDA cores. We also evaluated two regular GPUs, a GTX 760 and an AMD Radeon R9 290 with, 1152 and 2560 cores respectively.

The operating system chosen for the evaluation is Linux Ubuntu 14.04 LTS. The compiler used was GCC 4.8. A SSD drive was connected to the USB port 3.0 in the devices to store the experimental data. Total energy consumed by the board during application execution was measured using an external device. The energy measurements include the overall computer components, such as PSU, memory, etc. The results plotted in the figures correspond with an average of five consecutive executions.

The original projection images were taken from a PET/CT scanner with resolution of $512^2$ pixels. The scanned object was a crocodile scapula. For the evaluation of lower resolution studies, the original projections were partitioned. The complete original size study was only used in the case of the GPGPU platforms due to the memory limitations of the ARM platforms.

### 4.1    Platform Evaluation

Due to the requirements of the application, an evaluation of the support provided by the different platforms was done. This evaluation has as objective the selection of the most suitable architecture considering performance and energy comparisons. Since CUDA is clearly a non standard programming model (only valid for NVidia devices), OpenCL is the option that, theoretically, will be supported in most cases. The main problem with OpenCL support is the existence of several types of profiles, which shorten the compatibility of the application with the different platforms. Those profiles provide different features, such as types of memory objects, floating point calculations, etc. that can affect to the execution of our algorithms. Table 1 shows the features offered by each computing platform evaluated plus Intel Xeon Phi. These platforms were selected taking into account their theoretical compatibility with the two programming models chosen. The features presented, along with the support for one or both of the programming models represent the minimum requirements for the correct execution of the application in the different platforms.

Table 1. Features offered by each computing platform.

| Platform | NVidia GPU | AMD GPU | Odroid XU3 Lite | Wandboard Quad | Jetson TK1 | Intel Xeon Phi |
|---|---|---|---|---|---|---|
| Architecture | Kepler | GCN | ARM | ARM | ARM+Kepler | x86 |
| Peak Perf. (GFlops) | 2985 | 2000 | 60 | ? | 200 | 2000 |
| CUDA version | 7.0 | ✗ | ✗ | ✗ | 6.5 | ✗ |
| OpenCL version | 1.2 | 2.0 | 1.2 | 1.2 | ✗ | 1.1 |
| 3D memory objects | ✓ | ✓ | ✓ | ✗ | ✓ | ✗ |
| 2D memory objects | ✓ | ✓ | ✓ | ✓ | ✓ | ✗ |
| FFT library | ✓ | ✓ | ✓ | ✓ | ✓ | ✓ |

At the end, and despite of the OpenCL standardization, we could only evaluate the following platforms: NVidia, AMD, Odroid XU 3 Lite, and Jetson TK1. The OpenCL modules were executed in the AMD, Odroid and NVidia GTX 760 platform meanwhile CUDA was only executed on Jetson TK1 that lacks of OpenCL support.

## 4.2   Performance Evaluation

To evaluate performance on the different platforms, we have compared the GFLOPS provided by the different modules of the iterative simulation tool. Figure 2 shows the computing performance results over the four different architectures proposed using OpenCL and CUDA. As may bee seen, the ODROID platform provides a poor performance as compared to the platforms using high-performance GPUs, but Jetson TK1, which also uses ARM architecture, provides better results in terms of performance than AMD for low resolution studies. This demonstrates that, for projections and volumes of lower sizes, architectures designed for mobile platforms can be a serious alternative to GPUs and other parallel architectures.

In general, the results obtained for accelerators (both OpenCL and CUDA) are good comparing with other implementation in the literature (for example

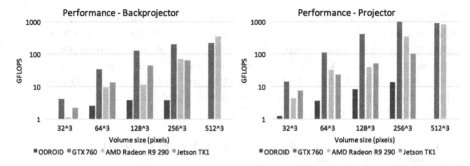

**Fig. 2.** Computing performance of the simulator modules on the different architectures evaluated for different image sizes: Backprojector (left) and Projector (rigth).

the one in [9] or [4]). However, the results are far from the ones obtained by [7], in which the authors complete the reconstruction in less than one second for floating point precision and $1024^3$ voxels. Taking into account that our kernel is generalized for the support of several geometries and execution modes, the optimizations that can be done must be less specific and therefore not as efficient as the ones presented in that work.

### 4.3   Energy Consumption

Another point to take into account is the energy consumption depending of the size of the problem, which is directly proportional to the computational load. The metric used in this section is Joules (J), by showing the energy consumed during the execution of the different kernels for the same problem. Figure 3 shows the results of this evaluation. In all cases, Jetson TK1 obtains the best results, consuming approximately half of the energy with respect to the AMD card. In the case of the ODROID, its advantages disappear when the problem size increases, consuming the same as the NVidia card for the $256^3$ study.

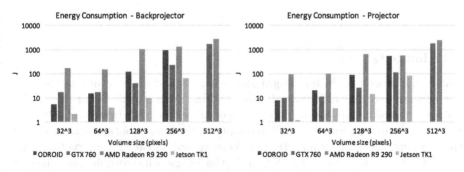

**Fig. 3.** Energy consumption of the simulator modules on the different architectures evaluated for different image sizes: Backprojector (left) and Projector (right).

We also show the results for the performance per unit of energy of each kernel in each of the devices in Tables 2 and 3. The results are coherent with respect the previous data shown in this study. The best performance per unit of energy is given by the NVidia GTX 760 when using CUDA although the Jetson TK1 is near. Odroid and AMD are far, the first because of the evident lack of performance and the second because of the higher consumption and lower performance compared to the NVidia GTX 760.

**Table 2.** Performance per unit of energy of the backprojection kernel for the different devices and programming models.

| Device | Programming model | Performance/Unit of energy (GFlops/J) | | | | |
|---|---|---|---|---|---|---|
| | | 32 | 64 | 128 | 256 | 512 |
| AMD R9 | OpenCL | 0.006 | 0.064 | 0.011 | 0.053 | 0.126 |
| NVidia GTX 760 | CUDA | 0.427 | 4.062 | 5.037 | 1.342 | 0.179 |
| | OpenCL | 0.250 | 2.024 | 3.268 | 0.863 | 0.130 |
| NVidia Jetson TK1 | CUDA | 0.916 | 3.342 | 4.185 | 1.005 | - |
| Odroid XU3 | OpenCL | 0.161 | 0.168 | 0.032 | 0.004 | - |

**Table 3.** Performance per unit of energy of the projection kernel for the different devices and programming models.

| Device | Programming model | P erformance/Unit of energy (GFlops/J) | | | | |
|---|---|---|---|---|---|---|
| | | 32 | 64 | 128 | 256 | 512 |
| AMD R9 | OpenCL | 0.047 | 0.326 | 0.062 | 0.620 | 0.328 |
| NVidia GTX 760 | CUDA | 1.263 | 10.401 | 14.601 | 8.934 | 0.841 |
| | OpenCL | 1.731 | 10.401 | 17.376 | 9.160 | 0.302 |
| NVidia Jetson TK1 | CUDA | 5.999 | 6.582 | 3.800 | 1.189 | - |
| Odroid XU3 | OpenCL | 0.166 | 0.173 | 0.095 | 0.026 | - |

## 4.4    Image Quality

Due to the differences in the programming models and architectures supported, one concern was that differences in the resulting images could occur due to the different precision and optimizations supported both by hardware and software. For this reason, an evaluation of the quality of the images obtained is necessary to asses that obtaining of a better performance and a faster reconstruction time does not imply a severe degradation of the image which would not make it suitable for diagnosis.

In our case, the difference between images reconstructed using different programming paradigms and devices are, in the worst case, lower or equal to

$0.1x10^{-7}$. When talking about projections, the difference is even lower, in the order of $0.1x10^{-9}$. Between the images obtained with CUDA in Jetson TK1 and the GTX 760 there were no differences, which means that there are not precision looses due to the low-power architecture.

## 5 Conclusions

In this work we have shown the main components of the ScanCT Iterative Simulation Tool, projection and backprojection, and the algorithms used in them. Those components have been implemented for heterogeneous platforms using two well known programming models: CUDA and OpenCL. OpenCL compatibility has allowed us to execute the IST on four heterogeneous platforms. We have executed the IST on the different platforms using OpenCL and CUDA and measured results in terms of computational performance and energy efficiency.

The results obtained for computational performance are similar for the GPUs, independently of the programming model used. Performance is smaller in the ARM platforms, but energy efficiency is much better, which makes them an alternative for processing small volumes and for embedded systems. But not all ARM chips consume the same amount of energy. In our evaluation, while the Jetson TK1 platform saved almost half of the energy comparing it with a GPGPU, the Odroid board consumed quantities similar to the NVidia card and even slightly more in very large volume cases. Whatever, the main problem found with the mobile platforms was memory size, which, in a memory bound application, such as the IST, leads to results in performance that can be far away from the maximum of the platform. This probably will be solved due to the current trends of increasing the memory available in mobile platforms and the arrival of 64 bit ARM architectures.

**Acknowledgments.** This work has been partially supported by the grant TIN2013-41350-P, *Scalable Data Management Techniques for High-End Computing Systems* from the Spanish Ministry of Economy and Competitiveness, and by the EU under the COST Programme Action IC1305, *Network for Sustainable Ultrascale Computing (NESUS)*. We gratefully acknowledge the support of NVidia Corporation with the donation of the Tesla K40 GPU used for these projects.

## References

1. Archirapatkave, V., Sumilo, H., See, S.C.W., Achalakul, T.: GPGPU acceleration algorithm for medical image reconstruction. In: 2014 IEEE International Symposium on Parallel and Distributed Processing with Applications, pp. 41–46 (2011)
2. Belloch, J.A., Gonzalez, A., Mayo, R., Vidal, A.M., Quintana-Orti, E.S.: Evaluating the potential of low power systems for headphone-based spatial audio applications. Procedia Comput. Sci. **51**, 191–200 (2015)
3. Feldkamp, L., Davis, L., Kress, J.: Practical cone-beam algorithm. JOSA A **1**(6), 612–619 (1984)

4. Jian-Lin, C., Lei, L., Lin-Yuan, W., Ai-Long, C., Xiao-Qi, X., Han-Ming, Z., Jian-Xin, L., Bin, Y.: Fast parallel algorithm for three-dimensional distance-driven model in iterative computed tomography reconstruction. Chin. Phys. B **24**(2), 028703 (2015)

5. Kim, J.K., Fessler, J.A., Zhang, Z.: Forward-projection architecture for fast iterative image reconstruction in X-ray CT. IEEE Trans. Signal Process. **60**(10), 5508–5518 (2012)

6. Leeser, M., Mukherjee, S., Brock, J.: Fast reconstruction of 3D volumes from 2D CT projection data with GPUs. BMC Res. Notes **7**(1), 582 (2014)

7. Mendl, C.B., Eliuk, S., Noga, M., Boulanger, P.: Comprehensive analysis of high-performance computing methods for filtered back-projection (2013)

8. Mukherjee, S., Moore, N., Brock, J., Leeser, M.: CUDA and OpenCL implementations of 3D CT reconstruction for biomedical imaging. In: 2012 IEEE Conference on High Performance Extreme Computing (HPEC), pp. 1–6. IEEE (2012)

9. Park, H.G., Shin, Y.G., Lee, H.: A fully GPU-based ray-driven backprojector via a ray-culling scheme with voxel-level parallelization for cone-beam CT reconstruction. Technol. Cancer Res. Treat. tcrt-2012 (2014)

10. Rohkohl, C., Keck, B., Hofmann, H., Hornegger, J.: Technical note: RabbitCT - an open platform for benchmarking 3D cone-beam reconstruction algorithms. Med. Phys. **36**(9), 3940–3944 (2009)

11. Serrano, E., Bermejo, G., Blas, J.G., Carretero, J.: High-performance X-ray tomography reconstruction algorithm based on heterogeneous accelerated computing systems. In: 2014 IEEE International Conference on Cluster Computing (CLUSTER), pp. 331–338. IEEE (2014)

12. Serrano, E., Bermejo, G., Garcia Blas, J., Carretero, J.: Evaluation of the feasibility of making large-scale X-ray tomography reconstructions on clouds. In: 2014 14th IEEE/ACM International Symposium on Cluster, Cloud and Grid Computing (CCGrid), pp. 748–754. IEEE (2014)

13. Siegl, C., Hofmann, H., Keck, B., Prümmer, M., Hornegger, J.: OpenCL: a viable solution for high-performance medical image reconstruction? In: SPIE Medical Imaging, p. 79612Q. International Society for Optics and Photonics (2011)

14. Stokke, K.R., Stensland, H.K., Griwodz, C., Halvorsen, P.: Energy efficient video encoding using the tegra K1 mobile processor. In: Proceedings of the 6th ACM Multimedia Systems Conference, pp. 81–84. ACM (2015)

15. Zhou, L., Chao, K.C., Chang, J.: Fast polyenergetic forward projection for image formation using OpenCL on a heterogeneous parallel computing platform. Med. Phys. **39**(11), 6745–6756 (2012)

# STRUCTURE: A Strategyproof Double Auction for Heterogeneous Secondary Spectrum Markets

Yu-E Sun[1], He Huang[2]([✉]), Miaomiao Tian[3], Zehao Sun[3], Wei Yang[3],
Hansong Guo[3], and Liusheng Huang[3]

[1] School of Urban Rail Transportation, Soochow University, Suzhou 215131, China
[2] School of Computer Science and Technology, Soochow University,
Suzhou 215006, China
huangh@suda.edu.cn
[3] School of Computer Science and Technology,
University of Science and Technology of China, Hefei 230027, China

**Abstract.** Auction has been regarded as one of the promising methods
for the scarce resources allocation due to its fairness. Thus, spectrum auction is an efficient way to allocate licensed spectrum to new demanders
for mitigating the spectrum scarcity. Most of the existing studies assume
that the spectrum resources are homogeneous. However, spectrums with
different frequencies are intrinsically heterogeneous due to their different
licensed areas and interference ranges. In this paper, we concentrate on
the heterogeneity of spectrum resources and propose a strategyproof double auction mechanism STRUCTURE. The STRUCTURE assumes that
all the buyers are selfish and rational, and they will submit their bids
for each interested spectrum. To achieve the strategyproofness, many
existing double spectrum auction mechanisms adopt the bid-independent
methods to construct buyer groups, which may cause unfairness for the
buyers with high bid values. To tackle this, we turn to choose a bid-
related buyer group construction algorithm, which is more suitable for
the laws of market and can further avoid the collusion between buyers. After that, we propose a collusion-free allocation mechanism and
a bid-independent payment mechanism to ensure the strategyproofness
for both buyers and sellers. Simulation results show that the proposed
mechanism significantly improves the spectrum utilization with low running time. Furthermore, we also find that the buyers with higher bid
values have a higher winning ratio than the buyers with low bids in the
STRUCTURE.

**Keywords:** Spectrum allocation · Double auction · Heterogeneous ·
Strategyproof · Spectrum utilization

## 1 Introduction

In recent years, with the increasing popularity of various mobile devices and
applications [7], the demand for available radio spectrum resources are increasing

© Springer International Publishing Switzerland 2015
G. Wang et al. (Eds.): ICA3PP 2015, Part IV, LNCS 9531, pp. 427–441, 2015.
DOI: 10.1007/978-3-319-27140-8_30

rapidly. Unfortunately, many new spectrum demanders cannot access the limited spectrum licensees in time while a large pool of spectrum resources are extremely underutilized. Spectrum auction is regarded as one of the most promising methods and natural ways to solve the spectrum scarcity due to its fairness and allocation efficiency. Through the auction, spectrum owners (*a.k.a* sellers) could gain utilities by leasing the idle resources while new demanders (*a.k.a* buyers) could gain access to the spectrum.

The design of a spectrum auction mechanism mainly faces three major challenges. First, spectrum can be reused by multiple users without interference in spatial or temporal domains. Second, the spectrum channels are heterogeneous, which have different frequencies, coverage areas and so on. Third, strategyproofness (*a.k.a* truthfully, we will use these two words interchangeably in the following paragraph) is one of the most critical properties of auction mechanisms, which ensures that the dominant strategy of each buyer or seller is to bid the true valuation of channels. However, it is not a trivial job to design a strategyproof auction mechanism for heterogeneous spectrum channels when the channels can be reused in spatial or temporal domains.

Spectrum auction has been well studied in recent years. These studies can be mainly categorized into two types: single-sided auction and double auction. One strategyproof spectrum auction mechanism design often includes two procedures: channel allocation mechanism design and payment calculation. Since spectrum channels are reusable, the auctioneer will choose a set of conflict-free buyers to share one channel. Clearly, how to choose the conflict-free buyers and allocate them in channels will affect the utility of buyers. Most of the existing single-sided spectrum auctions are aiming to maximize the social efficiency or the profit of sellers, which means their channel allocation mechanisms are bid-dependent. In these bid-dependent channel allocation mechanisms, if one given buyer wins by bidding a bid value $b_i$, it will always win by any bid values higher than $b_i$ to ensure the strategyproofness of buyers. Thus, buyers with higher bid values will have more chances to win the auction than the buyers with low bid values. By considering the reusability and heterogeneity of spectrum channels, many effective single-sided spectrum auctions have been proposed [1,8,10,12,14,23–26,30]. However, there is only one seller in this single-sided spectrum auctions, which may restrict the auction model to falling within a very limited scenario. To support multiple sellers in one spectrum auction, many double spectrum auction mechanisms were proposed. In a strategyproof double auction mechanism, both the buyers and sellers should submit their true valuations of channels to the auctioneer. Thus, it is more challenging to design a strategyproof double spectrum auction mechanism than the single-sided one. To tackle this challenge, the existing studies mainly use a bid-independent buyer set constructing method to construct a set of conflict-free buyer sets. Then, they view each buyer set as a super buyer and adopt the traditional double auction mechanism to decide which super buyer will win the auction [31]. Unfortunately, the higher bid values of buyers will not guarantee higher winning probabilities in the auctions with bid-independent allocation mechanism, which is against the laws of market and unfair to the buyers with high bid values. To avoid being involved in a buyer group with lower bid value by the auctioneer, buyers with higher bid values may prefer to collude with each other.

In this paper, we design STRUCTURE, A STRategyproof DoUble AuCtion mechanism for HeTerogeneoUs SecondaRy SpEctrum markets, which includes a bid-monotone channel allocation mechanism and a bid-independent payment calculation mechanism. We say a channel allocation mechanism is bid-monotone if a buyer/seller wins by bidding a bid value $b_i$, then it will always win by any bid values larger/smaller than $b_i$. And we say a payment calculation mechanism is bid-independent if there is no relationship between the payment and bid value of each winner $i$. In our bid-monotone channel allocation mechanism, we first propose a bid-dependent buyer group formation algorithm, which can maximize the winning probability of buyers and can further avoid the case that the buyers with high bid values collude with each other. We allocate heterogeneous channels to the buyers iteratively in STRUCTURE. In each iteration, we first find the buyer group with the highest bid value for each channel. Then, we allocate channels to the buyers in the buyer groups with highest bid values. We assume that each buyer only wants to buy one channel. However, one buyer may be involved into multiple buyer groups in each iteration. If different buyer groups with no less than one same buyer, we say they conflict with each other. In this case, only the buyer group with the largest number of buyers will win the auction in this iteration. The losing channels and buyers will participate in the next iteration of the auction until there is no buyer wins in the auction. In our bid-independent payment calculation mechanism, we prove that the payments or charges of winners will not be decided by the bid values of their own. To the best of our knowledge, we are the first to design strategyproof double spectrum auction for heterogeneous spectrum channels with bid-dependent buyer group constructing algorithm, which can avoid the collusion between buyers.

The major contributions of the proposed STRUCTURE can be identified as follows:

- We propose a bid-dependent buyer group construction algorithm for heterogeneous spectrum channels, which can maximize the winning probability of buyers and can further avoid the case that the buyers with high bid values collude with each other.
- We design a strategyproof double spectrum auction mechanism for heterogeneous spectrum channels, which allocates channels to buyers iteratively and can significantly improve the utilization of spectrums.

## 2  Preliminaries

### 2.1  Wireless Network Model

Consider a wireless network consisting of $M$ spectrum owners (a.k.a sellers) $\mathcal{Q} = \{q_1, q_2, ..., q_M\}$, a set of new users (a.k.a buyers) $\mathcal{V} = \{1, 2, ..., N\}$ and a third-party auctioneer who hosts the auction. Spectrum owner $q_i$ holds some heterogeneous spectrum channels. We use $\mathcal{S} = \{s_1, s_2, ..., s_K\}$ to denote channels contributed by all the primary users. Each spectrum channel is denoted as $s_j = \{b_j, r_j, D_j\}$, where $b_j$ is the bid of spectrum owner for the channel, $r_j$ is the interference range of the channel and $D_j$ is the description of the channel. The description of channels may include their frequency, bandwidth, coverage area and so on. The channels supplied by the spectrum owners may have different frequencies and coverage areas, and these channels can accommodate to different cellular networks. Thus, each buyer will only be interested in a part of them. After reading the description of channels, the buyers will submit their profiles to the auctioneer. The profile of each buyer $i$ can be defined as $i = \{\{b_{i,k}\}_{s_k \in \mathcal{S}_i}, L_i\}$, where $\mathcal{S}_i$ is the interested channel set of buyer $i$, $b_{i,k}$ is the bid value of buyer $i$ for channel $s_k$ and $L_i$ is the location where buyer $i$ wants to access in the channel. We stress that if buyer $i$ wins the auction, it only wants to buy one of the channels in set $\mathcal{S}_i$. Thus, the auction result of different channels will influence with each other. We also use $v_{i,k}$ to denote the true valuation of secondary user $i$ for channel $s_k$. Note that buyers may submit bid values which are not equal to their true valuations. Thus, we need to design mechanism to make sure that the dominate strategy of buyers are bidding their true valuations. We also assume that $b_{i,k}$ may not be equal to $b_{i,p}$ if $k \neq p$ in our work, which is very different with the previous homogeneous spectrum auctions and makes our work more challenging.

We say two secondary users $i$ and $l$ are conflicted with each other if the distance between $L_i$ and $L_l$ is smaller than twice of the interference radius of the channel they used. Since the heterogeneous channels may have different interference radii, the conflict relationships may be different for the same buyers when they use different channels. Thus, we use a matrix $C = (c_{i,j,l})_{N*N*M}$ to represent the conflict relationships of buyers, where $c_{i,j,l} = 1$ if buyers $i$ and $l$ conflict with each other in channel $j$, or $c_{i,j,l} = 0$ otherwise. Since each buyer is only interested in a part of the channels, we need a matrix $Y = (y_{i,j})_{N*M}$ to represent whether $s_j$ is in set $\mathcal{S}_i$, where $y_{i,j} = 1$ if $s_j \in \mathcal{S}_i$, or $y_{i,j} = 0$ otherwise. Thus two buyers $i$ and $l$ can share channel $s_j$ if and only if $c_{i,j,l} = 0$ and $y_{i,j} = 1$, $y_{l,j} = 1$.

## 2.2   Problem Formulation

The target of our work is to design a strategyproof double auction mechanism for heterogeneous channels. The spectrum auction studied in this work is the sealed-bid auction, which will be executed periodically. In each round, the buyers and sellers first send their concealed profiles to the auctioneer, then the auctioneer decides the winners as well as their payments.

We say a double auction mechanism is strategyproof if buyers or sellers bid their true valuations then they will maximize their profits regardless of the bids of others. If the auctioneer allocates channel $s_j$ to some buyers in the allocation phase, we say channel $s_j$ wins the auction. A winning channel $s_j$ is getting paid $p_j^s$ by the auctioneer. Then, the utility of the channel $s_j$ is $u_j^s = p_j^s - b_j$. The utility (payment) of a seller is the total utility (payment) of winning channels that it supplied. If the auctioneer allocates a buyer $i$ in one channel in the allocation phase, then we say buyer $i$ wins the auction. Each winning buyer $i$ is charged $p_i^u$ by the auctioneer. Suppose $x_{i,j}$ denotes whether the auctioneer allocates channel $s_j$ to buyer $i$ or not. Then, we let $x_{i,j} = 1$ when the auctioneer allocates $s_j$ to $i$, and $x_{i,j} = 0$ otherwise. The payment of buyer $i$ is $p_i^u = \sum_{s_j \in \mathcal{S}_i} p_{i,j}^u x_{i,j}$, where $p_{i,j}^u$ is the value of the auctioneer charged buyer $i$ for channel $s_j$. Thus, the utility of buyer $i$ is $u_i^u = \sum_{s_j \in \mathcal{S}_i} (b_{i,j} - p_{i,j}^u) x_{i,j}$. The payments, charges, and corresponding utilities are all equal to zero for all losing buyers and channels. The utility of the auctioneer is $u^A = \sum_{i \in \mathcal{V}} p_i^u - \sum_{s_j \in \mathcal{S}} p_j^s$.

### 2.3   Economic Requirements

Since some economic properties are essential in the double auction mechanism design, we will briefly introduce these properties in this subsection.

(1) *Individual Rationality*: The auctioneer cannot charge $p_{i,j}^u \geq b_{i,j}$ for each buyer $i$ who wins channel $s_j$, then the utility of each buyer will no less than zero. At the same time, the auctioneer cannot pay $p_j^s \leq b_j$ for each winning channel, then the utility of each seller will no less than zero.

(2) *Ex-post Budget Balance*: The gain of the auctioneer should be no less than zero, i.e., the overall payment of all buyers who win in the auction should be no less than the auctioneer's total payment to the sellers.

(3) *Strategy-Proofness (Truthfulness)*: Both buyers and sellers who participate in the auction can achieve the maximum utilities only if they submit their bids truthfully.

## 3   STRUCTURE: Mechanism Design

Given a set of heterogeneous spectrum channels $\mathcal{S}$ that is supplied by multiple sellers and a set of buyers $\mathcal{V}$, the STRUCTURE mechanism allocates channels to buyers iteratively. In each iteration, STRUCTURE performs the auction in three steps. We first forms a buyer group with highest bid value for each unallocated heterogenous spectrum channel. Then, it decides which buyer groups and channels win the auction in this iteration. Finally, the proposed mechanism computes a bid-independent payment or charge for each winner.

### 3.1   Buyer Group Construction

Since the spectrum channels can be reused by some non-conflicting buyers, we organize the buyers that are assigned to the same channel into one buyer group. Moreover, all the channels are heterogenous and have different interference radii. Thus, the conflict relationships of buyers are different for different channels. To tackle this issue, the STRUCTURE first constructs the conflict graph $\mathcal{G}_j$ for each channel $s_j$, where one vertex in conflict graph $\mathcal{G}_j$ denotes the buyer who is interested in $s_j$ and there exists an edge between two buyers if they are conflict

---

**Algorithm 1.** Bid-dependent buyer group constructing mechanism

---

**Require:** The set of channels $\mathcal{S}$, and the set of buyers $\mathcal{V}$ ;
**Ensure:** The buyer group sets with the highest bid values $G^f = \{g_1^f, ..., g_K^f\}$, and the
   buyer group sets with the second highest bid values $G^s = \{g_1^s, ..., g_K^s\}$;
 1: **for** $j = 1$ to $K$ **do**
 2:    $g_j^f$=Max_weight_g_f($\Phi$, $\mathcal{G}_j$);
 3:    $g_j^s$=Max_weight_g_s($\Phi$, $\mathcal{G}_j$);
 4: **return** $G^f$ and $G^s$;

---

with each other. Then, the STRUCTURE forms one buyer group for each channel
$s_j$ based on $\mathcal{G}_j$ since each channel can only be allocated to one buyer group finally.

   In the existing studies, most of the buyer group formation algorithms are bid-independent. For instance, [31] forms buyer groups through a random algorithm
and [21] views the buyer group formation problem as a *unweighted maximum
K-colorable subgraph problem*. In fact, a bid-independent buyer group forma-tion method can greatly make the problem of designing strategyproof auction
mechanism becoming easier to solve. However, in order to ensure the proper-ties of strategyproofness, almost all the winner determination mechanisms are
bid-dependent. We use $B_{g_k}$ to denote the bid value of buyer group $g_k$, $b_{g_k}^{min}$ to
denote the minimum bid value of buyers in $g_k$ and $|g_k|$ to denote the number of
buyers in $g_k$. Then, $B_{g_k} = b_{g_k}^{min} * |g_k|$. It means that the bid value of each buyer
group is decided by the buyer with the lowest bid value in this group, which
in turn decides whether the buyer group can win the auction or not. Therefore,
unsuitable buyer group formation method may cause the buyers with high bid
values are willing to collude with each other to avoid being formed into one
buyer group with low bid value. To tackle this problem, we judiciously design a
*bid-dependent* buyer group constructing mechanism, as shown in Algorithm 1.

---

**Algorithm 2.** $Max\_weight\_g\_f$(IS, $\mathcal{G}$)

---

 1: **if** $\mathcal{G} = \Phi$ **then**
 2:    **return** IS;
 3: **else**
 4:    randomly choose one buyer $i$ in $\mathcal{G}$;
 5:    delete $i$ from $\mathcal{G}$;
 6:    $Temp\_\mathcal{G} = \mathcal{G}$;
 7:    delete all the buyers which are conflicted with $i$ from $Temp\_\mathcal{G}$;
 8:    $Temp\_IS1$=Max_weight_g_f($IS$, $\mathcal{G}$);
 9:    $Temp\_IS2$=Max_weight_g_f($IS \cup \{i\}$, $Temp\_\mathcal{G}$);
10:    **if** $B_{Temp\_IS1} > B_{Temp\_IS2}$ **then**
11:       **return** $Temp\_IS1$;
12:    **else**
13:       **return** $Temp\_IS2$;

---

In Algorithm 1, the function of Max_weight_g_f($\Phi$, $\mathcal{G}_j$) will return the buyer group $g_j^f$ which has the highest bid value for each channel $s_j$. Then, the STRUC-TURE constructs $K$ buyer groups with top bid values for $K$ channels, and prepares to allocate channels to these buyer groups. To ensure the strategyproofness of buyers, the payments of winning buyers should be independent of their own bids. Assume that $g_j^s$ is the buyer group constructed based on $\mathcal{G}_j$, which has the highest bid value and $b_{g_j^s}^{min}$ does not come from a member of $g_j^f$. The STRUC-TURE finds the buyer group $g_j^s$ for each channel $s_j$ by running the function of Max_weight_g_s($\Phi$, $\mathcal{G}_j$). The payment of $g_j^f$ is $B_{g_j^s}$ if it wins in the auction. The details of Max_weight_g_f(IS, $\mathcal{G}$) and Max_weight_g_s(IS, $\mathcal{G}_j$) are shown in Algorithms 2 and 3.

---

**Algorithm 3.** $Max\_weight\_g\_s$(IS, $\mathcal{G}_j$)

1: **if** $\mathcal{G} = \Phi$ **then**
2:     **return** IS;
3: **else**
4:     randomly choose one buyer $i$ in $\mathcal{G}_j$;
5:     delete $i$ from $\mathcal{G}_j$;
6:     $Temp\_\mathcal{G} = \mathcal{G}_j$;
7:     delete all the buyers that are conflicted with $i$ from $Temp\_\mathcal{G}$;
8:     $Temp\_IS1$=Max_weight_g_s($IS$, $\mathcal{G}_j$);
9:     $Temp\_IS2$=Max_weight_g_s($IS \cup \{i\}$, $Temp\_\mathcal{G}$);
10:    **if** $B_{Temp\_IS1} > B_{Temp\_IS2}$ **then**
11:        **return** $Temp\_IS1$;
12:    **else if** $i \in g_j^f \& b_{i,j} = b_{Temp\_IS2}^{min}$ **then**
13:        **return** $Temp\_IS1$;
14:    **else**
15:        **return** $Temp\_IS2$;

---

We assume that all the buyers are rational and selfish, and each of them view the process of buyer group construction as a game among buyers. In this game, it is obvious that all the buyers want to improve their winning probabilities. Since one buyer group with higher bid value also has a higher winning probability in the auction, each buyer always wants to join into a group with higher bid. Thus, we construct the buyer group with highest bid value for each channel in the STRUCTURE, and the sellers are willing to sell channels to the buyers in these buyer groups. The utility of buyers which are constructed in the buyer groups with highest bid values are maximized by the STRUCTURE. Therefore, these buyers have no incentive to collude with other buyers. Moreover, the collusion between the buyers which are not in the buyer groups with highest bid values will not affect our auction results. Thus, we can get that:

**Theorem 1.** *STRUCTURE can avoid the collusion among buyers.*

## 3.2    Winner Determination and Payment Calculation

Let $G^f = \{g_1^f, ..., g_K^f\}$ be the buyer groups constructed by the STRUCTURE. We say two buyer groups $g_j^f$ and $g_k^f$ are conflicting with each other if they have same buyers. The STRUCTURE may construct one buyer into multiple buyer groups if this buyer is interested in multiple heterogeneous channels. However, one buyer only wants to pay for one channel if it wins the auction based on our assumption. To improve the utilization of channels, the STRUCTURE always chooses the buyer group with the largest number of buyers as winner if there exists conflicting relationship. The details of the winner determination and payment calculation algorithm in each iteration is shown in Algorithm 4.

---

**Algorithm 4.** The winner determination and payment calculation algorithm

1: Sort the buyer groups in $G^f$ in the descending order according to $|g_j^f|$;
2: **for** $j = 1$ **to** the remaining buyer groups in $G^f$ **do**
3:    **if** $B_{g_j^s} \geq b_j$ **then**
4:       allocate $s_j$ to $g_j^f$;
5:       **for** each buyer $i \in g_j^f$ **do**
6:          set $p_i^u = B_{g_j^s}/|g_j^f|$;
7:       set $p_j^s = B_{g_j^s}$;
8:       delete all the buyer groups that conflict with $g_j^f$ from $G^f$;

---

Let $|g_j^f|$ be the number of buyers in $g_j^f$. In Algorithm 4, the proposed STRUCTURE first sorts the buyer groups in descending order according to $|g_j^f|$, then scans all the buyer groups one by one. When the buyer group $g_j^f$ is being scanned, we first compare the bid of $g_j^s$ and the bid of channel $s_j$. Then, STRUCTURE allocates channel $s_j$ to the buyers in $g_j^f$ if $B_{g_j^s} \geq b_j$. To ensure the strategyproofness of buyers and sellers, the payment of each winning buyer $i$ is $p_i^u = B_{g_j^s}/|g_j^f|$ if $g_j^f$ wins the auction, and the payment of channel $s_j$ is $B_{g_j^s}$, if it wins the auction. After that, STRUCTURE deletes all the buyer groups which conflict with $g_j^f$ from $G^f$, and scans the next buyer group in $G^f$ until all the buyer groups in $G^f$ have been scanned.

# 4    Analysis of the STRUCTURE

In this section, we will demonstrate all the essential economic properties of the STRUCTURE mechanism.

**Theorem 2.** *STRUCTURE is ex-post budget balanced and individual rational.*

*Proof.* Due to page limits, the proof is referred to [18].

In order to prove the strategyproofness of the STRUCTURE, we need to show that for any buyer or seller, it cannot improve its own utility by bidding any other bid values than its true valuation. For this, we first show that the STRUCTURE is strategyproof for buyers.

**Lemma 1.** *STRUCTURE is strategyproof for buyers.*

*Proof.* There are only two cases that each buyer $i$ may benefit from its untruthful bidding. We now examine the two cases one by one.

*Case 1:* Buyer $i$ loses the auction when it bids its true valuation and wins when it bids untruthfully. That means buyer $i$ fails to be constructed in the buyer group with highest bid value of any its interested channel, or the buyer groups which include $i$ lose in the auction. If $i$ wants to win the auction, it needs to increase its bid value. Suppose $i$ is allocated in $s_j$ when it increases its bid value to $b'_{i,j}$. Let $g^f_j$ be the buyer group constructed by Algorithm 1 when $i$ bids truthfully. Let $g^{f'}_j$ and $g^{s'}_j$ be the buyer groups constructed by Algorithm 1 when $i$ bids untruthfully. Then, we can get that $b'_{i,j} * |g^{f'}_j| > B_{g^f_j} > v_{i,j} * |g^f_j|$. Moreover, the probability of $B_{g^{s'}_j} > v_{i,j} * |g^{f'}_j|$ is much larger than that of the opposite. In the other words, $p^u_i$ is larger than $v_{i,j}$ in most of time. Thus, the expected utility of buyer $i$ will decrease when $i$ bids $b'_{i,j} > v_{i,j}$ in this case, while a rational buyer will not do that.

*Case 2:* Buyer $i$ wins either it bids truthfully or untruthfully. In the situation of STRUCTURE allocates the same channel $s_j$ to $i$ when $i$ bids truthfully and untruthfully, $B_{g^s_j}$ is also the same in this two situations. The payment of $i$ is decided by $B_{g^s_j}$ and $|g^f_j|$. If $i$ wants to decrease its payment, it needs to decrease its bid lower than $b^{min}_j$. However, $i$ has more opportunity to lose the auction but not decrease its payment. Thus the expected utility of buyer $i$ will not increase if $i$ decreases its bid lower than $b^{min}_j$. The other possible situation is STRUCTURE allocates different channels $i$ when $i$ bids truthfully and untruthfully. Since $i$ has no way to get the bids and conflict relationship of buyers in our sealed-bid auction, $i$ has no idea about how to improve its utility even by telling untruthful bid values.

In conclusion, buyers cannot improve their utilities by bidding untruthful bids. Thus, the STRUCTURE is strategyproof for buyers.     □

**Lemma 2.** *STRUCTURE is strategyproof for sellers.*

*Proof.* We first show that each seller cannot obtain a higher utility from one channel by bidding an untruthful bid value. According to Algorithm 4, STRUCTURE scans the buyer groups according to their $|g^f_j|$. In other words, changing the bid of a channel will not change the order it been scanned in each or which iteration. This is only decided by the conflict relationships and the bids of buyers, but not the bids of channels. When channel $s_j$ has been scanned, it will win as long as $b_j \leq B_{g^s_j}$ and the payment is always equal to $B_{g^s_j}$. Thus, each seller cannot obtain a higher utility from one channel by bidding an untruthful bid value.

Since each seller has multiple spectrum channels, sellers may improve their utility by misreporting the bid values of parts of their channels. According to the STRUCTURE, the auction between different channels will interfere with each other only when there are common buyers in their buyer groups with highest bid value and only one of them can win the auction. Assume that $s_j$ wins the auction and $s_k$ loses and their owners bid their true valuations. We further assume that $s_j$ and $s_k$ belong to the same seller and there are common buyers in $g_j^f$ and $g_k^f$. Note that we study the sealed-bid auction in this work. Thus, sellers have no idea of the relationships or the bids of buyers. The expectation utility of the seller that owns $s_j$ and $s_k$ will decrease if it changes its bid value to make $s_k$ wins the auction and $s_j$ loses. This finishes our proof.    □

We have proved that the STRUCTURE is strategyproof for both buyers and sellers, then we can get that:

**Theorem 3.** *The proposed STRUCTURE mechanism is strategyproof.*

# 5    Simulation Results

In this section, we conduct extensive simulations to evaluate the performance of the proposed STRUCTURE. In order to show the improvement of the STRUCTURE, we compare it with the existing double auction mechanism TAMES [2].

## 5.1    Simulation Setup

We first introduce three major metrics to evaluate the performance of spectrum auction mechanism, which are the buyer's satisfaction ratio, spectrum transaction ratio, and spectrum utilization. We define the buyer's satisfaction ratio as the ratio between the number of buyers who take part in the auction and the number of buyers who win the auction. We define the spectrum transaction ratio as the ratio between the total number of spectrum channels that supplied by sellers and the number of spectrum channels that win the auction. The spectrum utilization is the ratio between the number of winning buyers and the number of winning spectrum channels.

In our simulation, we assume that all the buyers are randomly distributed in a fixed area of $100 \times 100$ square units, the bid values of buyers are randomly distributed in $[70, 130]$, and the bid values of sellers for each spectrum channel are randomly distributed in $[100, 110]$. The total number of spectrum channels that supplied by sellers is 10, and the interference range of these spectrum channels are randomly distributed in $[20, 30]$. In each set of evaluations, we vary the number of buyers, and fix the other settings. All the results are averaged over 1000 rounds.

## 5.2   Simulation Results

Figure 1 shows that the buyer's satisfaction ratios achieved by TAMES and STRUCTURE. We notice that the satisfaction ratios of the two auctions increase as the number of buyers increases at first. This is because that more buyers may lead to higher buyer group bid values, and more buyers and spectrum channels will win the auction in the case of that there are plenty of spectrum channels. Then, the satisfaction ratios will decrease as the number of buyers increases after the number of buyers larger than 10. This is because there are only 10 spectrum channels in our setting, and the increasing number of buyers means more competition among them. Many buyers will lose the auction due to the confliction. Thus, the increasing speed of the number of winning buyers will slower than the increasing speed of number of losing buyers when there are plenty of buyers.

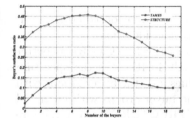
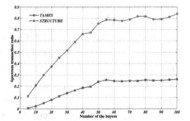

**Fig. 1.** The comparison of the buyer's satisfaction ratio with the increasing number of buyers between STRUCTURE and TAMES.

**Fig. 2.** The comparison of the spectrum transaction ratio with the increasing number of buyers between STRUCTURE and TAMES.

Further, the STRUCTURE adopts a bid-dependent buyer group constructing mechanism, which can ensure that the buyer group constructed for each spectrum channel is the buyer group with highest bid values. However, the auction mechanisms with bid-independent buyer group construction mechanisms, such as TAMES, may construct a set of buyer groups with small bid values, whose bid values are smaller than the sellers' bids. Thus, the buyer groups in STRUCTURE have more chances to win the auction than the buyer groups in TAMES. As shown in Fig. 1, the buyer's satisfaction ratio of STRUCTURE is obviously higher than that of the TAMES, which indicates that our evaluation results corroborate our theoretical analysis.

Figure 2 shows the relationship between the spectrum transaction ratio and the number of buyers. Since the bid values of buyer groups increases as the number of buyers increases, the number of winning spectrum channels increases. Moreover, the number of spectrum channels that supplied by the seller is unchanged in our setting, thus spectrum transaction ratio increases as the number of buyers increases. We can also get that the STRUCTURE performs better than TAMES, because STRUCTURE maximizes the bid value of each buyer

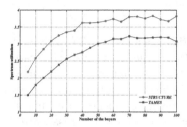     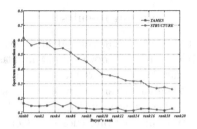

**Fig. 3.** The comparison of the spectrum utilization with the increasing number of buyers between STRUCTURE and TAMES.

**Fig. 4.** The relationship between the buyer's satisfaction ratio and buyer's rank.

group, but the TAMES only uses a greedy-like buyer group constructing mechanism without taking the bid values of buyers into consideration.

As shown in Fig. 3, the spectrum utilization of the STRUCTURE is better than that of the TAMES. This is because STRUCTURE sells the spectrum channels to the buyer groups with highest bid values, and the buyer groups with higher bid value often have more buyers than the buyer groups with lower bid values. Thus, the winning buyer groups of the STRUCTURE often have more buyers than the winning buyer groups of the TAMES, which further enlarges spectrum utilization.

In the STRUCTURE, the buyers with high bid values have more chances to win the auction, as shown in Fig. 4. From Fig. 4, we also find that the bid values of buyers in the TAMES have no direct relationship with their winning probabilities. It means that buyers with high bid values in the TAMES are willing to collude with others to improve their winning probabilities. However, buyers cannot improve their winning probabilities by colluding with others in the STRUCTURE. Thus, Fig. 4 shows why the STRUCTURE performs better in avoiding the collusion of buyers.

# 6   Literature Review

Auction theory, regarded as an important subfield of economics and game theory, serves as an efficient and fair way to redistribute various scarce resources among competing participators. In recent years, auction theory has been successfully applied in the wireless communication and networking fields [13,22,27–29].

Due to the demand for available spectrum resource is experiencing a rapid growth, auction has also been widely studied in the scope of spectrum allocation. Many traditional state-of-art spectrum allocation studies failed to address the truthful properties in mechanism design. To encourage participation, the spectrum auction should be economically robust. Truthfulness (Strategyproofness) is considered as one of the most critical economic factors in the auction design [4, 9, 17, 19]. However, most of the classical strategyproof auction cannot be directly applied in spectrum auction without changes due to some constraints, such as spatial and temporal reuse.

The spectrum auction studies can be categorized into two major groups: single-sided spectrum auction (one-seller and multi-buyer) [1, 8, 10, 12, 14, 16, 23, 25, 26, 30] and double spectrum auction (multi-seller and multi-buyer) [2, 3, 5, 6, 11, 15, 20, 21, 31]. In the study of single-sided auction, most of the literatures concentrate on maximizing social efficiency or revenue with consideration of spatial and temporal reuse. Strategyproofness is first addressed in [30] for single-sided spectrum auction, where only spatial reuse is considered. [1] and [14] mainly focus on the revenue maximization for auctioneer. [8] studied the trade-off between social efficiency maximization and fairness while designing strategyproof auction mechanism. Huang et al. first proposed a series of near-optimal strategyproof spectrum auction mechanisms with performance guarantee, which jointly considered spatial and temporal reuse [12]. Compared to the single-sided auction, double auction framework is more suitable for spectrum redistribution due to its fairness and efficiency. TRUST [31] first took the extended McAfee double auction model [17] into spectrum redistribution to achieve the essential economic properties. Wang et al. proposed an economically robust double auction with consideration of spectrum locality property [21]. Huang et al. first considered multi-unit double spectrum auction mechanism design [11]. Feng et al. [6] first took the spectrum heterogeneity factor into consideration in the double auction mechanism design. TAMES also focused on heterogeneous double spectrum auction design, and it can be extended to comply with the multi-unit spectrum trading [2]. However, all the above mentioned double auction mechanisms choose to adopt the bid-independent buyer group formation method to achieve the strategyproofness, which may greatly simplify the economic properties demonstration. In comparison, this paper proposes a bid-dependent buyer group constructing algorithm for heterogeneous spectrum channels, which can maximize the winning probability of buyers and can further avoid the buyers with high bid value colluding with each other.

# 7  Conclusion

We propose a strategyproof double auction mechanism, STRUCTURE, for heterogeneous spectrum channels. To avoid the collusion between buyers with high bid values, we first design a bid-dependent buyer group constructing mechanism. Then, we design a channel allocation mechanism, which can allocate spectrum channels to the buyer groups iteratively and tackle the competition between spectrum channels. At last, we use a second-price payment calculation mechanism to ensure the strategyproofness of both buyers and sellers. Our evaluation results demonstrate that the proposed STRUCTURE not only achieves good buyer's satisfaction, spectrum transaction ratio and utilization, but also can avoid the collusion of buyers.

**Acknowledgements.** This work is partially supported by National Natural Science Foundation of China under Grant No. U1301256, No. 61303206, No. 61202028, No. 61572342, Natural Science Foundation of Jiangsu Province under Grant No. BK20151240, Priority Academic Program Development of Jiangsu Higher Education Institutions, and Jiangsu Collaborative Innovation Center on Atmospheric Environment and Equipment Technology. Any opinions, findings, conclusions, or recommendations expressed in this paper are those of author(s) and do not necessarily reflect the views of the funding agencies (NSFC).

# References

1. Al-Ayyoub, M., Gupta, H.: Truthful spectrum auctions with approximate revenue. IEEE INFOCOM **2011**, 2813–2821 (2011)
2. Chen, Y., Zhang, J., Wu, K., Zhang, Q.: TAMES: A truthful double auction for multi-demand heterogeneous spectrums. IEEE Trans. Parallel Distrib. Syst. **25**(11), 3012–3024 (2014)
3. Chen, Z., Huang, H., Sun, Y., Huang, L.: True-MCSA: A framework for truthful double multi-channel spectrum auctions. IEEE Trans. Wirel. Commun. **12**(8), 3838–3850 (2013)
4. Clarke, E.H.: Multipart pricing of public goods. Public choice **11**(1), 17–33 (1971)
5. Dong, W., Rallapalli, S., Qiu, L., Ramakrishnan, K., Zhang, Y.: Double auctions for dynamic spectrum allocation. IEEE INFOCOM **2014**, 709–717 (2014)
6. Feng, X., Chen, Y., Zhang, J., Zhang, Q., Li, B.: TAHES: Truthful double auction for heterogeneous spectrums. IEEE INFOCOM **2012**, 3076–3080 (2012)
7. Fu, Z., Sun, X., Liu, Q., Zhou, L., Shu, J.: Achieving efficient cloud search services: multi-keyword ranked search over encrypted cloud data supporting parallel computing. IEICE Trans. Commun. **98**(1), 190–200 (2015)
8. Gopinathan, A., Li, Z., Wu, C.: Strategyproof auctions for balancing social welfare and fairness in secondary spectrum markets. IEEE INFOCOM **2012**, 2813–2821 (2011)
9. Groves, T.: Incentives in teams. Econometrica: J. Econometric Soc. **41**, 617–631 (1973)
10. Huang, H., Sun, Y., Li, X.-Y., Chen, S., Xiao, M., Huang, L.: Truthful auction mechanisms with performance guarantee in secondary spectrum markets. IEEE Trans. Mob. Comput. **14**(6), 1315–1329 (2015)
11. Huang, H., Sun, Y., Xing, K., Xu, H., Xu, X., Huang, L.: Truthful multi-unit double auction for spectrum allocation in wireless communications. In: Wang, X., Zheng, R., Jing, T., Xing, K. (eds.) WASA 2012. LNCS, vol. 7405, pp. 248–257. Springer, Heidelberg (2012)
12. Huang, H., Sun, Y.E., Li, X.-Y., Chen, Z., Yang, W., Xu, H.: Near-optimal truthful spectrum auction mechanisms with spatial and temporal reuse in wireless networks. MobiHoc **2013**, 237–240 (2013)
13. Huang, J., Han, Z., Chiang, M., Poor, H.V.: Auction-based resource allocation for cooperative communications. IEEE J. Sel. Areas Commun. **26**(7), 1226–1237 (2008)
14. Jia, J., Zhang, Q., Zhang, Q., Liu, M.: Revenue generation for truthful spectrum auction in dynamic spectrum access. ACM Mobihoc **2009**, 3–12 (2009)
15. Jing, T., Zhao, C., Xing, X., Huo, Y., Li, W., Cheng, X.: A multi-unit truthful double auction framework for secondary market. IEEE ICC **2013**, 2817–2822 (2013)

16. Li, W., Cheng, X., Bie, R., Zhao, F.: An extensible and flexible truthful auction framework for heterogeneous spectrum markets. ACM MobiHoc **2014**, 175–184 (2014)

17. McAfee, R.P.: A dominant strategy double auction. J. Econ. Theor. **56**(2), 434–450 (1992)

18. Sun, Y.E., Huang, H., Tian, M., Sun, Z., Yang, W., Guo, H., Huang, L.: STRUC-TURE: A strategyproof double auction for heterogeneous secondary spectrum markets. Technical report, Soochow University, September 2015. http://home.ustc.edu.cn/~huang83/huang-ica3pp.pdf

19. Vickrey, W.: Counterspeculation, auctions, and competitive sealed tenders. J. Financ. **16**(1), 8–37 (1961)

20. Wang, S.G., Xu, P., Xu, X.H., Tang, S.J., Li, X.-Y., Liu, X.: TODA: truthful online double auction for spectrum allocation in wireless networks. IEEE Dyspan **2010**, 1–10 (2010)

21. Wang, W., Li, B., Liang, B.: District: Embracing local markets in truthful spectrum double auctions. IEEE SECON **2011**, 521–529 (2011)

22. Wang, X., Huang, L., Xu, H., Huang, H.: Truthful auction for resource allocation in cooperative cognitive radio networks. In: IEEE ICCCN 2015 (2015)

23. Wu, F., Vaidya, N.: SMALL: A strategy-proof mechanism for radio spectrum allocation. IEEE INFOCOM **2011**, 3020–3028 (2012)

24. Xu, H., Jin, J., Li, B.: A secondary market for spectrum. IEEE INFOCOM **2010**, 1–5 (2010)

25. Xu, P., Li, X.-Y.: Online market driven spectrum scheduling and auction. In: Proceedings of the CoRoNet workshop of ACM MobiCom 2009, pp. 49–54 (2009)

26. Xu, P., Wang, S.G., Li, X.Y.: SALSA: Strategyproof online spectrum admissions for wireless networks. IEEE Trans. Comput. **59**(12), 1691–1702 (2010)

27. Yang, D., Fang, X., Xue, G.: Truthful auction for cooperative communications. In: ACM MobiHoc 2011, p. 9 (2011)

28. Yang, D., Xue, G., Fang, X., Tang, J.: Crowdsourcing to smartphones: incentive mechanism design for mobile phone sensing. In: ACM Mobicom 2012, pp. 173–184 (2012)

29. Zhang, L., Li, X.-Y., Liu, Y., Huang, Q., Tang, S.: Mechanism design for finding experts using locally constructed social referral web. IEEE INFOCOM **2012**, 2896–2900 (2012)

30. Zhou, X., Gandhi, S., Suri, S., Zheng, H.: ebay in the sky: strategy-proof wireless spectrum auctions. ACM Mobicom **2008**, 2–13 (2008)

31. Zhou, X., Zheng, H.: TRUST: A general framework for truthful double spectrum auctions. IEEE INFOCOM **2009**, 999–1007 (2009)

# Reality Mining with Mobile Data: Understanding the Impact of Network Structure on Propagation Dynamics

Yuanfang Chen[1,2]([✉]), Noel Crespi[1,2], Lei Shu[3], and Gyu Myoung Lee[4]

[1] Institut Mines-Télécom, Télécom SudParis, 91000 Evry, France
yuanfang_chen@ieee.org, noel.crespi@mines-telecom.fr
[2] Department of Computer Science,
Université Pierre et Marie CURIE, 75005 Paris, France
[3] Guangdong University of Petrochemical Technology, Maoming 525000, China
lei.shu@ieee.org
[4] Liverpool John Moores University, Liverpool L3 3AF, UK
g.m.lee@ljmu.ac.uk

**Abstract.** Recent studies have increasingly turned to graph theory to model Realistic Contact Networks (RCNs) for characterizing propagation dynamics. Several of these studies have demonstrated that RCNs are best described as having exponential degree distributions. In this article, based on the mobile data gathered from in-vehicle wireless devices, we show that RCNs do not always have exponential degree distributions, especially in dynamic environments. On this basis, a model is designed to recognize the structure of networks. Based on the model, we investigate the impacts of network structure on disease dynamics that is an important empirical study to the propagation dynamics. The time-varying infected number $R$ is the important parameter that is used to quantify the disease dynamics. In this study, the prediction accuracy for $R$ is improved by utilizing realistic structural knowledge mined by our recognition model.

**Keywords:** Reality mining · Mobile data · Structural knowledge · Propagation dynamics

## 1 Introduction

In recent years, there have been increasing efforts to uncover, model, and understand propagation processes arising over a wide variety of networks, e.g., propagation of infectious diseases [3,4], propagation of information [9,10,15,23], and even propagation of computer viruses [5,8]. Observing a propagation process, and quantifying and predicting the dynamics of the propagation, are important for: (i) reducing the transmission rate of an infectious disease, (ii) decreasing the number of infected individuals during an epidemic, (iii) allocating public health resources and responding to public health events, (iv) acquiring timely

© Springer International Publishing Switzerland 2015
G. Wang et al. (Eds.): ICA3PP 2015, Part IV, LNCS 9531, pp. 442–461, 2015.
DOI: 10.1007/978-3-319-27140-8_31

and accurate information, (v) capturing a new behavior or a new development tendency from the propagation of information/knowledge, and (vi) controlling the number of infected nodes with the propagation of computer viruses. And these propagation processes arise over a wide variety of networks. It is necessary to figure out the impacts of network structure on the propagation dynamics, and automatically recognize the network structure based on a recognition model.

As an important aspect of propagation dynamics [25], the quantification and prediction of disease dynamics during epidemics [30,31] are very important in allocating public health resources and in responding to public health events. Underestimating the impact of a disease can lead to an inadequate public health response, while overestimating can lead to the misallocation of limited public health resources. The time-varying infected number $R^1$ can be used to quantify the disease dynamics during an epidemic, and a wide range of methods have been proposed to estimate or predict the parameter $R$ [1,11,21,27,28] with time-based or network-based models. However, the existing methods are based on Exponential Networks (ENs)[2]. Compared with the ENs, Realistic Contact Networks (RCNs) [2] contain realistic structural knowledge that is helpful to improve the prediction accuracy for disease dynamics during an epidemic.

In this article, based on the mobile data gathered from in-vehicle and handheld wireless devices, we show that RCNs do not always have exponential degree distributions. On this basis, a model is designed to recognize the structure of networks, for mining the knowledge of network structure. With the model, we investigate the impacts of network structure on propagation dynamics. As the important empirical study for the propagation dynamics, we investigate the impacts of network structure on disease dynamics, and the key parameter $R$ is used to quantify the disease dynamics.

The scientific contributions of this article are shown as follows:

- We compare RCNs with ENs, and measure the differences between them in their network structures with precise measurements.
- A model is designed to recognize the structure of networks.
- Real surveillance data is used to evaluate the prediction performance for $R$. And realistic structural knowledge is used into the prediction, which is mined and acquired by our recognition model.

The achieved main results of this article are: (i) RCNs do not always have exponential degree distributions, (ii) the structural knowledge from RCNs is helpful to improve the prediction accuracy for propagation dynamics, and (iii) as the basic and important structural knowledge for networks, degree distribution, is effective to reflect the structure of a network, and to improve the accuracy of predicting for the infected number $R$.

---

[1] $R$ is defined as the number of infected cases during an epidemic over time.

[2] In this study, the network with exponential degree distribution is named as "Exponential Network".

The remainder of this article is organized as follows. Section 2 introduces the preparatory work and methods of carrying out our study. In Sect. 3, fitting results are shown and discussed in detail, and these results are about fitting the network structure of RCNs into exponential, normal, poisson and power-law distributions. Based on these results, in Sect. 4, a model is designed to recognize the structure of networks. In Sect. 5, we investigate the impacts of network structure on propagation dynamics. With the structural knowledge of respective networks, the prediction accuracy for $R$ on the RCNs and ENs is measured respectively, and the prediction results for $R$ are compared with real surveillance data. As the background of this study, Sect. 6 provides related work. This article is concluded in Sect. 7.

# 2    Methods

Two types of networks and the real surveillance data of a disease outbreak are used in our study. For evaluating the impacts of the structural knowledge about networks on propagation dynamics, extensive experiments for a knowledge-based Susceptible-Infected-Recovered (SIR) model [29] are run on these networks.

## 2.1    Networks

Two types of networks are used: (i) Exponential Networks, and (ii) Realistic Contact Networks from the real physical world.

**Exponential Networks.** It has recently been demonstrated that empirical contact networks are best described as having exponential degree distributions [2].

Through analyzing empirical contact networks [2] and based on the analysis and proof of literature [1], a Bansal Network (BN) is implemented and used as the EN. In the BN, each pair is generated using an algorithm of Bansal et al. [2] (Greedy Rewiring Algorithm (Algorithm 1)).

The probability mass function (pmf) of BN's degree distribution meets Eq. (1).

$$f(x; \lambda) = \begin{cases} \lambda e^{-\lambda x}, & x \geq 0, \\ 0, & x < 0, \end{cases} \tag{1}$$

where $x \in [0, \infty)$ is the degree of a node, and $\lambda > 0$ is the key parameter of an exponential distribution, which is called "rate parameter". This can be described as: $X \sim Exp(\lambda)$, which means the random variable $X$ has an exponential distribution.

The nodes of BN are labeled $(1, ..., N)$, and an edge between two nodes indicates the presence of a transmission probability for a disease from one node to another. For example, there is a pair of nodes, $i$ and $j$, $i \neq j$, the edge between them is $e_{\{i,j\}}$, and the transmission probability on the edge between $i$ and $j$ is given by $p_{\{i,j\}}$.

The input of Greedy Rewiring Algorithm is a connected and undirected network $G$, and the algorithm rewires edges until the degree distribution of the network becomes approximately exponential. In particular, the algorithm runs until the coefficient of variation ($\frac{standard\ deviation(sd)}{mathematical\ expectation(E[fx])}$) of the degree distribution is less than 1 (this ensures an exponential distribution of network). The algorithm is described below and illustrated in Fig. 1.

---

**Algorithm 1.** Greedy rewiring algorithm

**Input:** A fully connected, undirected network $G$
1: select a random node $i$ from the network $G$.
2: select a random edge $e_{\{i,j\}}$ from the network $G$ such that the degree of node $j$ is greater than one.
3: select a random edge $e_{\{j,m\}}$ from the network $G$, where the selected node $m$ has the maximum probability of $k_m / \sum k_m$, and $k_m$ means the degree of node $m$. Meanwhile $m \neq i$ and the node $m$ is not the neighbor of node $i$.
4: If we find the appropriate node $j$ and $m$, we remove the edge $e_{\{i,j\}}$ and add the edge $e_{\{i,m\}}$ to the network $G$.
5: The termination condition for re-building the network $G$ is: $sd/E[fx] < 1$
    – $sd$ is the standard deviation of the degree distribution
    – The degree distribution of network $G$ is fitted into an exponential distribution $fx$
    – $E[fx]$ is the mathematical expectation of $fx$
**Output:** A network with exponential degree distribution

---

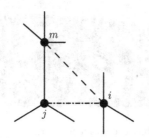

**Fig. 1.** Greedy rewiring process: node $i$ is chosen at random, the edge $e_{\{i,j\}}$ is selected at random from the edges of node $i$, and the edge $e_{\{j,m\}}$ is selected at random from the edges of node $j$ with probability proportion to the degree of node $m$. The edge $e_{\{i,j\}}$ (shown with a dotted line) is removed and the edge $e_{\{i,m\}}$ (shown with a dashed line) is added.

**Realistic Contact Networks.** Two RCNs from the real physical world are studied in this article.

Vehicle-based contact network (Fig. 2). There are 2483 nodes in this network with spatio-temporal GPS traces of vehicles, and the traces come from in-vehicle and GPS-enabled wireless devices. The network can be modelled as a dynamic graph $G_t$ with the time-varying velocities of different traffic segments, and the velocities can be estimated using a combination of sources, including Automatic Number Plate Recognition (ANPR) cameras, in-vehicle and GPS-enabled wireless devices and inductive loops built into road surfaces (a scenario is illustrated in Fig. 3).

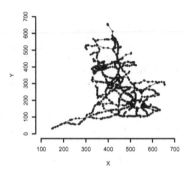

**Fig. 2.** Vehicle-based contact network. Using the coordinates of junctions of each traffic segment, the network can be built, where the black nodes are junctions, and the lines between these junctions are traffic segments that are with different traffic velocities.

**Fig. 3.** A scenario of vehicle-based contact network. This network includes Automatic Number Plate Recognition (ANPR) cameras, in-vehicle and GPS-enabled wireless devices and inductive loops built into road surfaces. With this network, massive mobile data of different traffic segments can be gathered based on various sensor nodes and wireless devices. The mobile sensing data is gathered by the Highways Agency, in England.

The dynamic graph $G_t$ can be described as follows. An undirected weighted graph $G_t = (V_t, E_t, W_t)$, where $V_t$ is a set of $n_t$ vertices with an online sequence of updates: (i) Delete($e_{\{i,j\}}$): delete the edge $e_{\{i,j\}}$ from $E_t$ and corresponding vertices $i$ and $j$ from $V_t$; (ii) Insert($e_{\{i,j\}}$): insert the edge $e_{\{i,j\}}$ into $E_t$ and corresponding vertices $i$ and $j$ into $V_t$; (iii) Update($w_{\{i,j\}}$): update the weight

$w_{\{i,j\}}$ related to the edge $e_{\{i,j\}}$ to $W_t$, and the weight $w_{\{i,j\}}$ is the velocity on the corresponding edge $e_{\{i,j\}}$. On the above (i), (ii) and (iii) basis, the graph $G_t$ is updated, from $G_t = (V_t, E_t, W_t)$ to $G_{t+1} = (V_{t+1}, E_{t+1}, W_{t+1})$. It means that at different time points, with different velocities on different traffic segments, the transmission rates on these traffic segments are different. This vehicle-based contact network is time-varying.

Moreover, the data for this network is gathered from all motorways and 'A' roads managed by the Highways Agency, in England. The data provides average velocities and traffic flow information for 15-minute periods since April 2009 on these motorways and roads. The data includes these variables: (i) Segment ID. A unique alphanumeric segment id represents a segment from one junction (intersection) to another junction; (ii) Date. There is a date for each record; (iii) Time Period. There are 96 time periods, 0-95, with 15-minute intervals, in a day (1440 minutes); (iv) Average Velocity. The average velocity (km/h) of vehicles on a traffic segment within a given 15-minute time period; (v) Segment Length. The length of a traffic segment (km).

Human-based contact network. There are 942 nodes in this network. With the wireless communication devices held by volunteers of epidemic areas, the volunteers report new cases (confirmed and suspected cases), corresponding locations, and relationships between these cases, and then, these reported cases with corresponding locations can be used to build the human-based contact network (an example is shown in Fig. 4). During an epidemic, the network is time-varying along with the propagation of an infectious disease, with the order of time stamps of reports. As the vehicle-based contact network, the human-based contact network can be modelled as a dynamic graph $G_t$. However, the weight $w_{\{i,j\}}$ is the transmission probability ($p_{\{i,j\}}$) of a disease from vertex $i$ to vertex $j$ (on the corresponding edge $e_{\{i,j\}}$). For this network, there are four variables: (i) Case ID. A unique number indicates a case; (ii) Source ID. A source id indicates the source of infection for a case; (iii) Date. It is the date that a case is reported; (iv) Location. It indicates the coordinates (longitude and latitude) of a reported case.

## 2.2 Outbreak Data

The outbreak data of Ebola in West Africa from March 2014, is used as real surveillance data to evaluate the prediction performance for $R$ on RCNs and ENs.

As a latest outbreak of disease, until February 15, 2015, Ebola Virus Disease (EVD. It is commonly known as "Ebola") has killed 9380 people, and the total cases have reached 23253. Researchers generally believe that from a 2-year-old boy of Guinea to his mother, sister and grandmother (a human-based contact network), Ebola rapidly spreads in West Africa, from March 2014.

The reported Ebola cases with time series and location information are gathered by the World Health Organization (WHO), as well as the ministries of health of epidemic countries. And in this study, we select part of data from three typical outbreak countries, Guinea, Nigeria and Liberia. Guinea is the source of this outbreak and is with relatively high quantity of confirmed cases (2727, as of

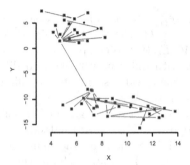

**Fig. 4.** An example of our human-based contact network. This example displays 50 cases and their relationships (contact), from three typical countries and seven regions of the Ebola outbreak in 2014. Three countries are: Guinea, Nigeria and Liberia. Seven regions are: Gueckedou, Macenta, Kissidougou, Conakry, Monrovia, Lagos and Port Harcourt. The black nodes of this network are cases (suspected and confirmed) and if there is an edge between two nodes, it means that there is contact between the individuals of the two cases.

February 15, 2015), and Nigeria is far away from the source of the outbreak, and is with relatively low quantity of confirmed cases (19, as of February 15, 2015), and Liberia is close to the source of the outbreak, and is with high quantity of confirmed cases (3149, as of February 15, 2015). And seven regions of these three countries are: Gueckedou of Guinea, Macenta of Guinea, Kissidougou of Guinea, Conakry of Guinea, Monrovia of Liberia, Lagos of Nigeria, and Port Harcourt of Nigeria. And these variables are included in the outbreak data: (i) Case ID. A unique number indicates a case; (ii) Source ID. A source id indicates the source of infection for a case; (iii) Date. It is the date that a case is reported; (iv) Location. It indicates the coordinates (longitude and latitude) of a reported case.

## 2.3   Methods

A knowledge-based SIR model is used to evaluate the impacts of network structure on disease dynamics. As the results of this evaluation, the number of infected cases (infected number $R$) is calculated for each time period (different time periods have different network structures along with the propagation of a disease during an epidemic).

The SIR model is a model from epidemiology [13]. This model is developed to describe the propagation of an epidemic that occurs during a period of time. The individuals of a contact network might be in three states: Susceptible (S), Infected (I) and Recovered (R). Susceptible individuals become infected at a given rate through contact with infected individuals. Infected individuals recover with a given rate and become recovered. The model is capable of showing the important parameter $R$ which is measured to quantify the disease dynamics during an epidemic. The parameter $R$ is the number of infected cases over time. In this study, we consider a knowledge-based SIR model with the knowledge of network structure.

Moreover, we consider different time periods $(t)$, for our RCNs. For the vehicle-based contact network, the unit of time period is "15 minutes", and for the human-based contact network, the unit of time period is "day". And for comparing the impacts of different networks, the ratio $R_{A/B}$ is used to measure the different impacts of the network $A$ and the network $B$. And for a network, the degree distribution is used to characterize and reflect the structure of the network.

# 3  Results and Analysis

To evaluate the impacts of network structure on disease dynamics, the basic and important structural knowledge of networks, degree distribution, is measured and compared for each network that is studied in this article.

In a network, the degree of a node is its most basic structural knowledge, and it indicates the number of adjacent edges of the node. The degree distribution is the probability distribution of these degrees over the network. It gives the overall structural information of the network. For a real-world network, the relationships between nodes are complex. The degree distribution is helpful to characterize and model a real-world network. On this basis, the structural knowledge of a complex network can be acquired and formulated. The formulated knowledge is effective for analyzing and solving network-related problems.

In this study, we analyze the degree distributions of RCNs in detail, by conducting maximum-likelihood fitting to fit the degree distributions of these networks into exponential, normal, poisson and power-law distributions [2], and calculating and comparing the estimated standard deviations and the estimated variance-covariance matrices of these fittings.

**Vehicle-based Contact Network.** Figure 5 illustrates the degree distribution of vehicle-based contact network.

From Fig. 5, we can observe that the degrees of nodes are not exponential distribution, in this real-world contact network. For figuring out the differences between them, the degree distribution of vehicle-based contact network and exponential, normal, poisson and power-law distributions, maximum-likelihood fitting is conducted to fit the degree distribution of vehicle-based contact network into exponential, normal, poisson and power-law distributions (Fig. 6), and then the estimated standard deviations and the estimated variance-covariance matrices of these fittings are measured to quantify "how many differences between two different degree distributions".

With these fittings that are shown in Fig. 6, corresponding parameter estimates can be calculated, for example, using maximum-likelihood fitting, the most likely value of parameter $\lambda$ (rate parameter) is 0.4966, for the fitting with the exponential distribution. Corresponding estimated standard deviations and estimated variance-covariance matrices are measured, and these deviations and

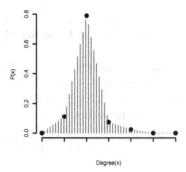

**Fig. 5.** Degree distribution of our vehicle-based contact network. There are 2483 nodes and 2500 edges in this network. The black spots are the probability distribution of nodes' degrees.

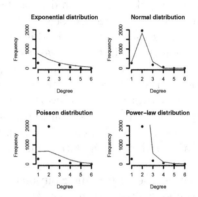

**Fig. 6.** Maximum-likelihood fitting of degree distributions. The degree distribution of vehicle-based contact network is fitted into exponential, normal, poisson and power-law distributions with maximum-likelihood fitting. The black spots display the probability distribution of nodes' degrees to the vehicle-based contact network, and the red lines are the corresponding fittings for exponential, normal, poisson and power-law distributions.

matrices are calculated by comparing with standard distributions that are with corresponding parameter estimates, for example, the exponential distribution with $\lambda = 0.4966$ is used as the standard distribution for the fitting with the exponential distribution. These deviations and matrices show how many differences between two distributions. Moreover, the parameter estimates for different distributions from maximum-likelihood fitting, are listed as follows: (i) the rate parameter $\lambda$ of exponential distribution is 0.4966, (ii) $\mu = 2.013693113$ and $\sigma = 0.539810394$ for the normal distribution, (iii) $\lambda = 2.013693$ for the poisson distribution, (iv) $xmin = 2$ and $\alpha = 5.785002$ for the power-law distribution.

Table 1 shows the estimated standard deviations and the estimated variance-covariance matrices of these fittings.

**Table 1.** Estimated standard deviations and estimated variance-covariance matrices for different fittings

| Distribution | Standard deviation | Variance-covariance matrix | | |
|---|---|---|---|---|
| Exponential | $\lambda$ (rate parameter): 0.009965942 | | *rate parameter* | |
| | | *rate parameter* | $9.932e - 05$ | |
| Normal | $\mu$ (mean): 0.010833103, $\sigma$ (standard deviation (sd)): 0.007660161 | | *mean* | *sd* |
| | | *mean* | 0.0001173561 | 0.0000000000 |
| | | *sd* | 0.0000000000 | $5.867806e - 05$ |
| Poisson | $\lambda$ (lambda): 0.02847792 | | *lambda* | |
| | | *lambda* | 0.000810992 | |
| Power-law | $xmin + \alpha$: 0.006375843 | NULL | | |

From the fitting results displayed in Fig. 6 and Table 1, the degree distribution of nodes for the vehicle-based contact network, is approximate to the power-law distribution with $xmin = 2$ and $\alpha = 5.785002$ and with the standard deviation 0.006375843.

**Human-based Contact Network.** Fig. 7a illustrates the degree distribution of human-based contact network. On Fig. 7a basis, for figuring out the degree distribution of human-based contact network, maximum-likelihood fitting is conducted to fit the degree distribution of human-based contact network into exponential, normal, poisson and power-law distributions, and then the estimated standard deviations and the estimated variance-covariance matrices of these fittings are measured to quantify "how many differences between two different distributions". The results of fittings are illustrated in Fig. 7b.

In Fig. 7, the results show that the degree distribution of human-based contact network is approximate to the exponential distribution with $\lambda = 0.50159915$.

The parameter estimates for different distributions from maximum-likelihood fitting are: (i) the rate parameter $\lambda = 0.50159915$ for the exponential distribution, (ii) $\mu = 1.99362380$ and $\sigma = 2.77914691$ for the normal distribution, (iii) $\lambda = 1.9936238$ for the poisson distribution, and (iv) $xmin = 2$ and $\alpha = 2.803973$ for the power-law distribution.

Table 2 shows the estimated standard deviations and the estimated variance-covariance matrices of these fittings.

Comparing the estimated standard deviations and estimated variance-covariance matrices listed in Table 2, the minimum standard deviation for these fittings is 0.01635166. This minimum standard deviation is corresponding to the exponential distribution with the rate parameter $\lambda = 0.50159915$.

However, based on the descriptions for the networks that are studied in this article, the human-based contact network is time-varying along with the propagation of an infectious disease. As an example, the analysis results of the subnetwork that is with 96 time periods of August 26th, 2014[3], are shown in Fig. 8 and Table 3.

---

[3] This subnetwork is obtained by a time-based sample. It is the contact network of this day, August 26th, 2014.

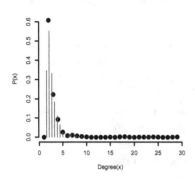

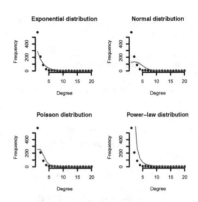

(a) Degree distribution of our human-based contact network. There are 942 nodes and 938 edges in this network. The black spots are the probability distribution of nodes' degrees.

(b) Maximum-likelihood fitting of degree distributions. The degree distribution of human-based contact network is fitted into exponential, normal, poisson and power-law distributions with maximum-likelihood fitting. The black spots display the probability distribution of nodes' degrees to the human-based contact network, and the red lines are the corresponding fittings for exponential, normal, poisson and power-law distributions.

**Fig. 7.** Degree distribution and maximum-likelihood fitting for our human-based contact network.

**Table 2.** Estimated standard deviations and estimated variance-covariance matrices for different fittings

| Distribution | Standard deviation | Variance-covariance matrix | | |
|---|---|---|---|---|
| Exponential | $\lambda$ (rate parameter): 0.01635166 | | | *rate parameter* |
| | | *rate parameter* | | $2.673769e - 04$ |
| Normal | $\mu$ (mean): 0.09059760, $\sigma$ (standard deviation (sd)): 0.06406218 | | *mean* | *sd* |
| | | *mean* | 0.008207925 | 0.000000000 |
| | | *sd* | 0.000000000 | 0.004103963 |
| Poisson | $\lambda$ (lambda): 0.0460285 | | *lambda* | |
| | | *lambda* | 0.002118623 | |
| Power-law | $xmin + \alpha$: 0.03831463 | NULL | | |

With the fittings for the subnetwork of human-based contact network, the parameter estimates for different distributions are: (i) the rate parameter $\lambda = 0.74796748$ for the exponential distribution, (ii) $\mu = 1.33695652$ and $\sigma = 1.00841216$ for the normal distribution, (iii) $\lambda = 1.33695652$ for the poisson distribution, and (iv) $xmin = 1$ and $\alpha = 3.041947$ for the power-law distribution.

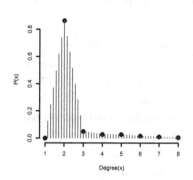

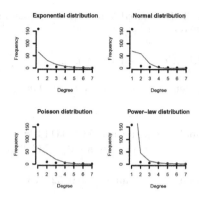

(a) Degree distribution for the subnetwork of human-based contact network. There are 96 time periods of August 26th, 2014 in this network. The black spots are the probability distribution of nodes' degrees.

(b) Maximum-likelihood fitting of degree distributions. The degree distribution for the subnetwork of human-based contact network is fitted into exponential, normal, poisson and power-law distributions with maximum-likelihood fitting. The black spots display the probability distribution of nodes' degrees to the subnetwork, and the red lines are the corresponding fittings for exponential, normal, poisson and power-law distributions.

**Fig. 8.** Degree distribution and maximum-likelihood fitting for the subnetwork of human-based contact network.

Table 3 shows the estimated standard deviations and the estimated variance-covariance matrices of the fittings for the subnetwork.

From the fitting results for the subnetwork of August 26th, 2014, which are listed in Table 3, the degree distribution of the subnetwork is approximate to the power-law distribution with $xmin = 1$ and $\alpha = 3.041947$.

With the above detailed analyses on the structure of networks, this fact can be observed: network structure is different to different networks, and is time-varying to dynamic networks.

## 4    Recognition Model of Network Structure

Because network structure is different to different networks, and the network structure is time-varying to dynamic networks, it is necessary to recognize the structure of a network, for analyzing the propagation dynamics on the network.

Our recognition model consists of: fitting, selection and parameter adjustment, and it can be formulated and described as follows:

**Table 3.** Estimated standard deviations and estimated variance-covariance matrices for different fittings

| Distribution | Standard deviation | Variance-covariance matrix | | |
|---|---|---|---|---|
| Exponential | $\lambda$ (rate parameter): 0.05514089 | | | *rate parameter* |
| | | | *rate parameter* | 0.003040518 |
| Normal | $\mu$ (mean): 0.07434113, $\sigma$ (standard deviation (sd)): 0.05256712 | | *mean* | *sd* |
| | | *mean* | 0.005526604 | 0.000000000 |
| | | *sd* | 0.000000000 | 0.002763302 |
| Poisson | $\lambda$ (lambda): 0.08524123 | | *lambda* | |
| | | *lambda* | 0.007266068 | |
| Power-law | $xmin + \alpha$: 0.02865438 | NULL | | |

- As the first step of model, the fitting is to fit the structure of a network into exponential, normal, poisson and power-law distributions with maximum-likelihood fitting, and the fitting calculates the parameter estimates and standard deviations to corresponding distributions. The parameter estimates and standard deviations to corresponding distributions, can be denoted as: (i) $pe_{exp}$ and $sd_{exp}$ for the exponential distribution, (ii) $pe_{norm}$, $sd_{\mu,norm}$ and $sd_{\sigma,norm}$ for the normal distribution, (iii) $pe_{pois}$ and $sd_{pois}$ for the poisson distribution, and (iv) $pe_{pl}$ and $sd_{pl}$ for the power-law distribution.
- And then, the selection is to select an approximate distribution by comparing the calculated standard deviations of four distributions. This step is denoted as:
$\min\{sd_{exp}, sd_{norm} = \frac{sd_{\mu,norm}+sd_{\sigma,norm}}{2}, sd_{pois}, sd_{pl}\}$.
- Finally, our model uses the standard deviation of the selected approximate distribution to adjust the degree distribution function of the selected approximate distribution, and the selected approximate distribution is with the corresponding parameter estimate calculated by the fitting of first step.

Degree distribution functions and the detailed process of adjustment are introduced as follows:

(i) The degree distribution functions of exponential, normal, poisson and power-law distributions:

- The degree distribution function of exponential distribution is: $f(x; \lambda) = \lambda e^{-\lambda x}(x \geq 0)$.
- The degree distribution function of normal distribution is: $f(x; \mu, \sigma) = \frac{1}{\sigma\sqrt{2\pi}}e^{-\frac{(x-\mu)^2}{2\sigma^2}}$.
- The degree distribution function of poisson distribution is: $f(x; \lambda) = \frac{\lambda^x e^{-\lambda}}{x!}$.
- The degree distribution function of power-law distribution is: $f(x; xmin, \alpha) = \frac{\alpha-1}{xmin}\left(\frac{x}{xmin}\right)^{-\alpha}$.

(ii) The detailed process of adjustment:

Based on (i) above degree distribution functions, and (ii) the parameter estimates and standard deviations to corresponding distributions, the adjusted degree distribution functions can be obtained and these adjusted degree distribution functions reflect the structure of real networks. The adjusted degree distribution functions to corresponding distributions are listed in Eq. (2).

$$f(x; (\lambda \pm sd_{exp})) = (\lambda \pm sd_{exp})e^{-(\lambda \pm sd_{exp})x}(x \geq 0),$$

$$f(x; (\mu \pm sd_{\mu,norm}, (\sigma \pm sd_{\sigma,norm})$$

$$= \frac{1}{(\sigma \pm sd_{\sigma,norm})\sqrt{2\pi}}e^{-\frac{(x-(\mu \pm sd_{\mu,norm}))^2}{2(\sigma \pm sd_{\sigma,norm})^2}},$$

$$f(x; (\lambda \pm sd_{pois})) = \frac{(\lambda \pm sd_{pois})^x e^{-(\lambda \pm sd_{pois})}}{x!}, \tag{2}$$

$$f(x; (xmin \pm sd_{pl}), (\alpha \pm sd_{pl}))$$

$$= \frac{(\alpha \pm sd_{pl}) - 1}{(xmin \pm sd_{pl})}(\frac{x}{(xmin \pm sd_{pl})})^{-(\alpha \pm sd_{pl})}.$$

An example is provided to explain the adjustment. The human-based contact network is approximate to the exponential distribution with $\lambda = 0.50159915$, and the standard deviation from the rate parameter $\lambda$ of this exponential distribution is $0.01635166$, so the degree distribution function of this human-based contact network can be denoted as: $f(x; 0.50159915 \pm 0.01635166) = (0.50159915 \pm 0.01635166)e^{-(0.50159915 \pm 0.01635166)x}(x \geq 0)$. And the degree distribution function can be used to reflect the network structure of this human-based contact network.

## 5   Evaluation

We investigate the impacts of network structure on propagation dynamics. With the structural knowledge of respective networks, the prediction accuracy for $R$ on the RCNs and ENs is measured respectively, and the prediction results for $R$ are compared with real surveillance data.

**Knowledge-based SIR Model.** For a SIR model, the following differential equations represent this model:

$$\frac{dS}{dt} = \delta R - \beta SI,$$

$$\frac{dI}{dt} = \beta SI - \gamma I, \tag{3}$$

$$\frac{dR}{dt} = \gamma I - \delta R,$$

where $\beta$ is the rate at which susceptible individuals contract the disease when exposed to infection, $\gamma$ is the rate at which infected individuals recover from the disease and $\delta$ is the rate at which recovered individuals lose immunity and become susceptible again.

The important parameter $I$ in Eq. (3) indicates an individual is infected, and is used to calculate the infected number $R$. In this study, our SIR model is based on the knowledge of network structure. For our knowledge-based SIR model, the important parameter $I$ is formulated in Eq. (4).

$$I = \beta_0 + \beta_1 f(x), \tag{4}$$

where $f(x)$ is the degree distribution function of a network, and it can be acquired by our recognition model.

**Parameter Configuration of Experiments.** Based on the description of BN, a BN is an exponential network. For the comparability with RNs, the values of rate parameter $\lambda$ for BNs are set to: (i) 0.4966 corresponding to our vehicle-based contact network, and (ii) 0.50159915 corresponding to our human-based contact network. And the number of nodes: (i) the BN with $\lambda = 0.4966$, is 2483, and (ii) the BN with $\lambda = 0.50159915$, is 942.

We repeat the process 100000 times for each network in our experiments with different randomly selected individuals. We use the average number of infected cases across all 100000 realizations as the value of $R$ for each network.

**Prediction Accuracy for R.** Based on our knowledge-based SIR model, extensive experiments are run on different networks, and on these experiments basis, the infected number $R$ can be predicted, and the parameter $R$ is time-varying to reflect the propagation dynamics of a disease. And the prediction results for $R$ from different networks are compared with real surveillance data, to show network structure impacts the propagation dynamics on the network. And utilizing realistic structural knowledge can help to improve the prediction accuracy for $R$ that is used to reflect the propagation dynamics on a network. Figure 9 illustrates: (i) the prediction results, and (ii) the comparison of the prediction results and real surveillance data.

From Fig. 9, we acquire: with realistic structural knowledge of networks, the prediction accuracy for $R$ is improved, and network structure impacts propagation dynamics. For comparing the impacts of different networks, the ratio $R_{A/B} = \frac{R_A}{R_B}$ is calculated, at different time points, respectively, to measure the different impacts of the network A and the network B. First, we use A to denote real surveillance data, B to denote our vehicle-based contact network, C to denote our human-based contact network, D to denote the BN with $\lambda = 0.4966$ and 2483 nodes, and E to denote the BN with $\lambda = 0.50159915$ and 942 nodes. And then, $R_{A/B}^t$ denotes the ratio for network A and network B, at the $t^{th}$ time point. Finally, $R_{B/A}^t$, $R_{C/A}^t$, $R_{D/A}^t$ and $R_{E/A}^t$ ($t = 1, 2, 3, 4, 5, 6, 7, 8, 9, 10, 11, 12$ (12 months)) are calculated and listed in Table 4.

The ratios listed in Table 4, are all different, so the impacts of these networks on propagation dynamics are different.

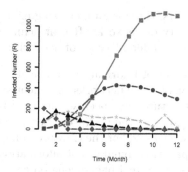

**Fig. 9.** Comparison of prediction results and real surveillance data. (i) The black line with triangular spots displays the acquired result by mining real surveillance data. (ii) The green line with star spots is the prediction result on our vehicle-based contact network. (iii) The red line with diamond-shaped spots is the prediction result on our human-based contact network. (iv) The pink line with square spots is the prediction result on the BN with $\lambda = 0.4966$ and 2483 nodes. (v) The blue line with circular spots is the prediction result on the BN with $\lambda = 0.50159915$ and 942 nodes (Color figure online).

**Table 4.** Ratios of $R$ to measure the different impacts of two different networks on propagation dynamics

|        | $R^t_{B/A}$ | $R^t_{C/A}$ | $R^t_{D/A}$ | $R^t_{E/A}$ |
|--------|-------------|-------------|-------------|-------------|
| t=1    | 0.91        | 2.6         | 0.039       | 0.052       |
| t=2    | 0.82        | 0.58        | 0.11        | 0.16        |
| t=3    | 1.3         | 0           | 0.43        | 0.75        |
| t=4    | 1.8         | 0           | 1.7         | 2.5         |
| t=5    | 2.2         | 0           | 5.5         | 5.8         |
| t=6    | 3.1         | 0           | 14          | 11          |
| t=7    | 5.2         | 0           | 31          | 19          |
| t=8    | 6.7         | 0           | 60          | 28          |
| t=9    | 8           | 0           | 105.7       | 40.9        |
| t=10   | 5           | 0           | 186.5       | 63.5        |
| t=11   | 35          | 0           | 281.5       | 84          |
| t=12   | 10          | 0           | 550         | 148.5       |

# 6    Related Work

## 6.1    Propagation Dynamics

Understanding the propagation processes arising over a wide variety of network structures is very important to mine useful knowledge about how a behavior on a network to impact the nodes of the network, and even is helpful to model the behavior. In recent years, there is an increasing effort to study propagation dynamics based on a variety of networks. Recent achievements can be divided into two categories based on different types of networks:

- The propagation dynamics of information on social networks [14,17]. In the information propagation of social networks, exponential and power-law models that reflect network structure have been widely used to model the dynamics of propagation [9,26]. Not only the network structure but also the prior probabilities of activation of edges [22] or the transmission rates of networks [7] are used to study the propagation dynamics of information on social networks.
- The propagation dynamics of real phenomena on contact networks. The contact networks describe the real relationships between individuals/systems of the physical world. Based on the real relationships from the physical world, the propagation dynamics on these networks is different from the propagation dynamics on social networks. With the development of the IoT (Internet of Things) and the help of various sensors and wireless devices, some researchers have paid their attention to this propagation dynamics, and have obtained some achievements: (i) for the propagation of infectious diseases [6,12,18,24], and (ii) for the propagation of contaminants [16]. Analyzing and studying the dynamics of propagation between individuals/systems can help us to understand and control the propagation dynamics on these real networks.

Some previous achievements assume networks to be static so that information propagates over these networks that their structures remain constant over time, and these achievements consider that different networks possess similar network structures and the structures of different networks can be modelled into unified models, e.g., exponential models and power-law models.

### 6.2  Disease Dynamics

As an important aspect of propagation dynamics, the disease dynamics on contact networks has been widely studied.

The quantification and prediction of disease dynamics during epidemics [20,30,31] are very important to public health [19] in allocating public health resources and in responding to public health events.

The infected number $R$ can be used to quantify the disease dynamics during epidemics. For studying the quantized disease dynamics, a wide range of methods have been proposed to estimate or predict $R$ [1,11,21,27,28] based on the assumptions of network structure, e.g., the contact networks for the spread of disease are best described as having exponential degree distributions [2].

However, realistic contact networks are not always and absolutely with the assumptions of network structure (e.g., exponential degree distributions). For improving the accuracy of estimating and predicting for $R$ during an epidemic on a network, the realistic structure of the network needs to be mined.

# 7   Conclusion

In this article, we have mined the impacts of network structure on propagation dynamics through studying the disease dynamics that is an important aspect of propagation dynamics. Our study is based on the mobile data gathered from the real physical world, and with the mobile data, two RCNs are built, and as a comparison, we have implemented exponential networks using the greedy rewiring algorithm that is proposed by Bansal et al. Exponential networks are widely used into RCN-based studies, and it has been demonstrated that the RCNs are best described as having exponential degree distributions. As a key result of this study, we have observed that RCNs do not always have exponential degree distributions, especially in dynamic environments. On this result basis, we have designed a model to recognize the structure of a network. Based on the model, we have investigated the impacts of network structure on propagation dynamics with evaluating and comparing the accuracy of prediction for the time-varying infected number $R$. In this comparing, the prediction results for $R$ from different networks are compared with real surveillance data. From this investigation, we have obtained another key result of this study, the structure of a network impacts the propagation dynamics related on this network, and the prediction accuracy for $R$ can be improved by utilizing realistic structural knowledge mined by our recognition model.

**Acknowledgments.** This work is supported by Guangdong University of Petrochemical Technology's Internal Project No. 2012RC106, Educational Commission of Guangdong Province, China Project No. 2013KJCX0131, Guangdong High-Tech Development Fund No. 2013B010401035, 2013 Special Fund of Guangdong Higher School Talent Recruitment, National Natural Science Foundation of China under Grant 61401107, 2013 Top Level Talents Project in "Sailing Plan of Guangdong Province", and 2014 Guangdong Province Outstanding Young Professor Project.

# References

1. Ames, G.M., George, D.B., Hampson, C.P., Kanarek, A.R., McBee, C.D., Lockwood, D.R., Achter, J.D., Webb, C.T.: Using network properties to predict disease dynamics on human contact networks. In: Proceedings of the Royal Society B: Biological Sciences, pp. 1–7 (2011)
2. Bansal, S., Grenfell, B.T., Meyers, L.A.: When individual behaviour matters: homogeneous and network models in epidemiology. J. Roy. Soc. Interface 4(16), 879–891 (2007)
3. Belik, V., Geisel, T., Brockmann, D.: Natural human mobility patterns and spatial spread of infectious diseases. Phys. Rev. X 1(1), 011001 (2011)
4. Charaudeau, S., Pakdaman, K., Boëlle, P.Y.: Commuter mobility and the spread of infectious diseases: application to influenza in france. PloS one 9(1), e83002 (2014)
5. Chen, Z., Gao, L., Kwiaty, K.: Modeling the spread of active worms. In: INFO-COM 2003. Twenty-Second Annual Joint Conference of the IEEE Computer and Communications. IEEE Societies. vol. 3, pp. 1890–1900. IEEE (2003)

6. Colizza, V., Barrat, A., Barthelemy, M., Valleron, A.J., Vespignani, A.: Modeling the worldwide spread of pandemic influenza: baseline case and containment interventions. PLoS Med. **4**(1), e13 (2007)

7. Du, N., Song, L., Yuan, M., Smola, A.J.: Learning networks of heterogeneous influence. Adv. Neural Inf. Proc. Syst, 2780–2788 (2012)

8. Garetto, M., Gong, W., Towsley, D.: Modeling malware spreading dynamics. In: INFOCOM 2003. Twenty-Second Annual Joint Conference of the IEEE Computer and Communications. IEEE Societies. vol. 3, pp. 1869–1879. IEEE (2003)

9. Gomez Rodriguez, M., Leskovec, J., Krause, A.: Inferring networks of diffusion and influence. In: Proceedings of the 16th ACM SIGKDD International Conference on Knowledge Discovery and Data Mining, pp. 1019–1028. ACM (2010)

10. Gomez-Rodriguez, M., Leskovec, J., Krause, A.: Inferring networks of diffusion and influence. ACM Trans. Knowl. Discov. Data (TKDD) **5**(4), 21 (2012)

11. Groendyke, C., Welch, D., Hunter, D.R.: A network-based analysis of the 1861 hagelloch measles data. Biometrics **68**(3), 755–765 (2012)

12. Hufnagel, L., Brockmann, D., Geisel, T.: Forecast and control of epidemics in a globalized world. Proc. National Acad. Sci. U.S.A. **101**(42), 15124–15129 (2004)

13. Keeling, M.J., Rohani, P.: Modeling infectious diseases in humans and animals. Princeton University Press, Princeton (2008)

14. Lappas, T., Terzi, E., Gunopulos, D., Mannila, H.: Finding effectors in social networks. In: Proceedings of the 16th ACM SIGKDD International Conference on Knowledge Discovery and Data Mining, pp. 1059–1068. ACM (2010)

15. Leskovec, J., Backstrom, L., Kleinberg, J.: Meme-tracking and the dynamics of the news cycle. In: Proceedings of the 15th ACM SIGKDD International Conference on Knowledge Discovery and Data Mining, pp. 497–506. ACM (2009)

16. Leskovec, J., Krause, A., Guestrin, C., Faloutsos, C., VanBriesen, J., Glance, N.: Cost-effective outbreak detection in networks. In: Proceedings of the 13th ACM SIGKDD International Conference on Knowledge Discovery and Data Mining, pp. 420–429. ACM (2007)

17. Leskovec, J., Lang, K.J., Dasgupta, A., Mahoney, M.W.: Statistical properties of community structure in large social and information networks. In: Proceedings of the 17th International Conference on World Wide Web, pp. 695–704. ACM (2008)

18. Lipsitch, M., Cohen, T., Cooper, B., Robins, J.M., Ma, S., James, L., Gopalakrishna, G., Chew, S.K., Tan, C.C., Samore, M.H., et al.: Transmission dynamics and control of severe acute respiratory syndrome. Science **300**(5627), 1966–1970 (2003)

19. Luke, D.A., Stamatakis, K.A.: Systems science methods in public health: dynamics, networks, and agents. Annu. Rev. Publ. Health **33**, 357–376 (2012)

20. Martín, G., Marinescu, M.C., Singh, D.E., Carretero, J.: Leveraging social networks for understanding the evolution of epidemics. BMC Syst. Biol. **5**(Suppl 3), S14 (2011)

21. Mukandavire, Z., Liao, S., Wang, J., Gaff, H., Smith, D.L., Morris, J.G.: Estimating the reproductive numbers for the 2008–2009 cholera outbreaks in zimbabwe. Proc. National Acad. Sci. **108**(21), 8767–8772 (2011)

22. Myers, S., Leskovec, J.: On the convexity of latent social network inference. In: Advances in Neural Information Processing Systems, pp. 1741–1749 (2010)

23. Myers, S.A., Zhu, C., Leskovec, J.: Information diffusion and external influence in networks. In: Proceedings of the 18th ACM SIGKDD International Conference on Knowledge Discovery and Data Mining, pp. 33–41. ACM (2012)

24. Riley, S., Fraser, C., Donnelly, C.A., Ghani, A.C., Abu-Raddad, L.J., Hedley, A.J., Leung, G.M., Ho, L.M., Lam, T.H., Thach, T.Q., et al.: Transmission dynamics of the etiological agent of sars in hong kong: impact of public health interventions. Science 300(5627), 1961–1966 (2003)

25. Rodrigue, M.G., Leskovec, J., Balduzzi, D., Schölkopf, B.: Uncovering the structure and temporal dynamics of information propagation. Netw. Sci. 2(01), 26–65 (2014)

26. Rodriguez, M.G., Schölkopf, B.: Submodular inference of diffusion networks from multiple trees (2012). arXiv preprint arXiv:1205.1671

27. Stadler, T., Kouyos, R., von Wyl, V., Yerly, S., Böni, J., Bürgisser, P., Klimkait, T., Joos, B., Rieder, P., Xie, D., et al.: Estimating the basic reproductive number from viral sequence data. Mol. Biol. Evol. 29(1), 347–357 (2012)

28. Team, W.E.R.: Ebola virus disease in west africathe first 9 months of the epidemic and forward projections. N Engl. J. Med. 371(16), 1481–1495 (2014)

29. Tomé, T., Ziff, R.M.: Critical behavior of the susceptible-infected-recovered model on a square lattice. Phys. Rev. E 82(5), 051921 (2010)

30. Vazquez-Prokopec, G.M., Bisanzio, D., Stoddard, S.T., Paz-Soldan, V., Morrison, A.C., Elder, J.P., Ramirez-Paredes, J., Halsey, E.S., Kochel, T.J., Scott, T.W., et al.: Using gps technology to quantify human mobility, dynamic contacts and infectious disease dynamics in a resource-poor urban environment. PloS one 8(4), e58802 (2013)

31. Woolhouse, M.: How to make predictions about future infectious disease risks. Philos. Trans. Royal Soci. B: Biol. Sci. 366(1573), 2045–2054 (2011)

# Reducing Journaling Overhead with Hybrid Buffer Cache

Zhiyong Zhang$^{(\boxtimes)}$, Lei Ju, and Zhiping Jia

School of Computer Science and Technology, Shandong University,
Jinan 250101, China
zhangzhiyongschool@163.com, {julei,jzp}@sdu.edu.cn

**Abstract.** Journaling technique is widely used in modern file systems for high reliability and fast recovery from system failures. However, journaling mechanism accounts for extra journal traffic flushed from the buffer cache to storage, greatly impeding the performance of file systems. Emerging non-volatile memory (NVM) technologies bring a new perspective of resolving this issue. But replacing DRAM with NVM as the whole buffer cache encounters the challenge of limited lifetime of NVM. As such, in this paper, we exploit a hybrid NVM-DRAM buffer cache architecture to optimize the journaling overhead using the non-volatility of NVM and the unlimited write endurance of DRAM. We propose a novel page management policy to direct page placement and migration while ensuring DRAM absorb most writes. Besides, a write-burst predictor is presented to further reduce write activities on NVM to prolong the lifespan of the hybrid buffer cache. Furthermore, we present a hybrid-commit journaling scheme to support the in-place commit of NVM and the in-memory commit of DRAM. We implement the proposed techniques on Linux 2.6.38 and measure the performance with various file I/O benchmarks. The experimental results show that our scheme significantly improves the I/O performance compared with the existing Linux buffer cache with ext4 and prolongs the lifetime compared with the NVM based buffer cache.

**Keywords:** Reliability · Journaling · Non-volatile memory · Performance

## 1   Introduction

Reliability is an important issue in computer systems. But in traditional systems, an unexpected event, such as a system crash or a power failure, may result in an inconsistent and/or out-of-date file system. In order to relieve this problem, modern file systems exploit the journaling technique, which keeps track of the changes that will be made in a journal space before committing them to the main file system, to improve the reliability and robustness. Though the journaling is designed for high reliability and fast recovery from system failures, it is a serious impediment to high I/O performance since the journal space is usually a

© Springer International Publishing Switzerland 2015
G. Wang et al. (Eds.): ICA3PP 2015, Part IV, LNCS 9531, pp. 462–475, 2015.
DOI: 10.1007/978-3-319-27140-8_32

dedicated area in storage, which causes extra write traffic and frequent storage accesses. For example, one source [1] reports that the write traffic with journaling is about 2.7 times more than that without journaling on average. Besides, in cloud storage systems, even though there is consensus that journaling is necessary, it is not deployed due to the high cost of network accesses involved in journaling [2]. Thus, high journaling overhead hinders the reliability benefit of the journaling technique.

Fortunately, emerging non-volatile memory (NVM) technologies bring a new perspective of resolving this issue. Non-volatile memories, such as PCM (Phase-change memory), STT-RAM (Spin-Transfer Torque RAM) and RRAM (Resistive RAM), have recently been extensively studied as promising alternative of DRAM, which has been widely used as main memory for decades. Compared with DRAM, NVM shows its advantages of non-volatility, higher density, better scalability and energy efficiency. However, the drawbacks of asymmetric read/write operations and limited write endurance make NVM unfit for completed replacement of DRAM. As such, hybrid NVM-DRAM main memory, as an ideal architecture, is proposed to utilize the respective strengths of NVM and DRAM [3–7].

The hybrid NVM-DRAM architecture brings a non-volatile main memory which maintains data even after a power failure. Therefore, compared with traditional file systems, introducing NVM to buffer cache can effectively remove the journal traffic since the data in buffer cache can act its own journal without committing to permanent storage, e.g. flash or disk. However, directly replacing DRAM with NVM as the buffer cache encounters the challenge of limited lifetime of NVM since in most caces, the buffer cache is accessed when reading from or writing to storage. Hence, in order to avoid NVM being worn out within a short period of time, in this paper, we adopt a hybrid NVM-DRAM based buffer cache, utilizing the non-volatility of NVM and the unlimited write endurance of DRAM, to relieve the performance degradation caused by journaling and improve the lifespan of the hybrid main memory.

However, the hybrid buffer cache architecture complicates the page management policy of traditional file systems. Writing to NVM removes the journal traffic from buffer cache to storage since NVM is non-volatile, but a bulk of writes affects the lifetime of the hybrid memory. Writing to DRAM has no impacts on the lifetime of NVM, but it causes extra in-memory migrations between DRAM and NVM since the updates to file system have to be copied from DRAM to NVM as journal. Though the in-memory copy is much faster than that from main memory to storage, it still impedes the performance of file system.

Our goal is to improve the performance of journaling file system without any loss of reliability. Meanwhile, we utmostly prolong the lifetime of the hybrid buffer cache by reducing write accesses to NVM. The main contributions of this paper can be summarized as follows:

(1) We propose a novel page management policy for the hybrid NVM-DRAM based buffer cache. The policy directs page placement and migration between NVM and DRAM, taking both high performance and less writes to NVM into account.

(2) We put forward a hybrid-commit journaling mechanism for the hybrid buffer cache. The mechanism comprises the in-place commit of NVM and the in-memory commit of DRAM, removing all the I/O traffic caused by journaling.

(3) We implement our page management policy and the hybrid-commit journaling scheme on Linux 2.6.38. The experimental results show the hybrid buffer cache with proposed techniques significantly improve the I/O performance compared to the existing Linux buffer cache with ext4 and prolong the lifetime compared to the NVM based buffer cache.

The remainder of this paper is organized as follows. Section 2 reports the background of NVM and DRAM, journaling technique and the hybrid buffer cache architecture employed in our work. Section 3 presents our page management policy. Section 4 describes the hybrid-commit journaling scheme for the hybrid buffer cache. Experimental results and correlation analysis are presented in Sect. 5. Section 6 describes the previous work and finally, this paper is concluded in Sect. 7.

## 2    Background and Problem Analysis

### 2.1    Non-volatile Memory

Recently, non-volatile memory technologies have received intensive attention. Compared with DRAM, NVM shows the advantages in many aspects, such as non-volatility, better scalability and low power. It is worth mentioning that the access time of NVM is in the nanosecond range. For example, one source reports a read latency of 50 ns and a write latency of 60-120 ns for PCM, and less than 20 ns read and write latency for STT-RAM [8]. In addition, NVM has higher density than DRAM. For example, PCM holds about four times more data than DRAM cells in the same area [7]. As such, all these benefits make NVM become a promising substitute main memory of DRAM, especially for embedded devices and energy hungry computer systems, providing disk-like data persistence at DRAM-like latency.

However, NVM has limited number of writes which significantly limits its lifetime. For example, state-of-the-art process technology has demonstrated that the maximum writes number of PCM is only around $10^8$ to $10^9$. Therefore, hybrid main memory architecture, as an ideal architecture, has been proposed to utilize the respective strengths of DRAM and NVM.

### 2.2    Journaling Technique

Journaling technique employs transaction based recovery protocols to provide the ACID (Atomicity, Consistency, Isolation, Durability) properties for file systems. Journaling file system reserves a journal space in addition to the real file system image in permanent storage. The file system periodically creates transactions to log the updates to file system and commits the updates to journal space.

Unfortunately, journaling technique greatly impedes the system performance. As mentioned above, the write traffic from the buffer cache to storage with journaling is about 2.7 times more than that without journaling on average [1]. The emergence of NVM relieves this problem. Since NVM is non-volatile, the update in NVM can act as its own journal without committing to the journal space in permanent storage. However, frequent writes to NVM affect the lifetime of the hybrid main memory. Therefore, how to improve the performance of journaling file systems and prolong the lifetime of the hybrid buffer cache without any loss of reliability is the problem to be addressed in this study.

### 2.3 Hybrid Buffer Cache Architecture

The hybrid buffer cache employed in this paper is composed of DRAM and NVM. We aim to exploit the hybrid buffer cache to remove the I/O traffic caused by journaling, while ensuring minimal writes to NVM to prolong the lifetime of the hybrid main memory. To this end, firstly, an intelligent page management policy is required for the hybrid buffer cache. The page management policy should be designed for two requirements. First, the DRAM portion should absorb as many write requests as possible, thus prolonging the lifetime of NVM. Secondly, the pages with less writes should be placed in NVM to remove the bursty synchronous in-memory copy since NVM has the characteristics of non-volatility and higher density.

Moreover, a hybrid-commit journaling scheme is demanded for the hybrid buffer cache architecture. Since NVM is non-volatile, when a journal commit occurs, the updates in NVM are committed in-place. But the updates in DRAM have to be copied to NVM as journal. Thus, the journaling scheme for the hybrid buffer cache need to be carefully designed to coordinate the different journaling patterns of NVM and DRAM.

## 3    Page Management Policy for the Hybrid Buffer Cache

### 3.1    Policy Design

Figure 1 shows the flow chart of our proposed page management policy upon receiving a write request. As shown in this figure, when a new page enters into the buffer cache, since we don't know its access pattern, we place it to DRAM to prevent excessive writes on NVM. The pages in DRAM are managed by our proposed *WA-CLOCK* (Write-aware CLOCK) algorithm. The WA-CLOCK algorithm distinguishes the write pattern, write-hot or write-cold, from the perspective of write recency. When a new page need to be entered into buffer cache and there is no free space in DRAM buffer, WA-CLOCK chooses a write-cold victim page and migrates it to NVM to make space for it.

Since we unite the buffer cache and journaling layers in our hybrid buffer cache, both data blocks and journal blocks reside in the buffer cache. We set the state of journal blocks to *frozen* to distinguish from the normal data blocks.

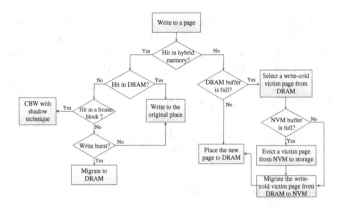

**Fig. 1.** Flow chart of the proposed page management policy

As the journal blocks record the previous changes, they are important to ensure consistency of the file system. As such, the frozen blocks are write protected. If a write request hits in a frozen block, we have to copy it to a new location and write the updated data to the copy, i.e. copy before writing (CBW). Here, we propose a shadow mechanism to aid CBW to be performed in a more reasonable way to further reduce writes to NVM, which will be detailed in Sect. 4. Moreover, if a normal data block in NVM is written frequently within a short period of time, we migrate it to DRAM with consideration of the lifetime of the hybrid buffer cache. To this end, a write-burst predictor is integrated into our page management policy. If a write hit in NVM is predicted to be a write burst access, the data block will be migrated to DRAM.

In our proposed page management policy, when a new page is loaded into the buffer cache from the storage, it is placed in DRAM. If it needs to be evicted from the buffer cache, it is evicted from NVM. The write-hot pages reside in DRAM, while the write-cold pages and journal pages are maintained in NVM. The effective migration policy ensures high performance of the file system and less writes to NVM.

## 3.2   WA-CLOCK Policy for the DRAM Buffer Cache

In our design, we divide the data pages into two categories: write-hot pages and write-cold pages. The write-hot pages are placed to DRAM, while the write-cold pages are maintained in NVM. We manage the pages in NVM and DRAM separately so as to fully exploit the characteristics of each memory media. For DRAM buffer cache, we use a variant of CLOCK algorithm. CLOCK algorithm is a well-known page replacement algorithm, which is widely used in virtual memory environments.

CLOCK algorithm was introduced as a one-bit approximation to LRU. Different from LRU, which keeps pages in the order of access time, CLOCK only monitors whether a page has recently been accessed or not. To do this, a *reference bit* is associated to each page. When a page is referenced (read/write), the corresponding reference bit is set to 1. CLOCK keeps a circular list with the *hand pointer* to the last referenced page in the list. When a replacement occurs, the reference bit is inspected at the hand pointer location. If it is 0, the page is replaced out, otherwise, the reference bit is cleared to 0 and the hand pointer is increased to check the next page in the circle. The process is repeated until a page is replaced out. The schematic diagram of CLOCK is shown in Fig. 2.

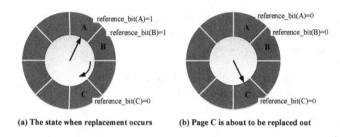

(a) The state when replacement occurs        (b) Page C is about to be replaced out

**Fig. 2.** Schematic diagram of the CLOCK algorithm

Unlike traditional DRAM based buffer cache, the proposed hybrid buffer cache is write-sensitive since NVM has limited write endurance. Thus, in our design, we evaluate the access pattern of a page only exploiting the write history since the write temporal locality based on write history alone and that based on both read/write histories show similar results [9]. Since the CLOCK algorithm does not have the ability to distinguish the write-cold and write-hot pages, several extra fields, *write_bit*, *rotation_count* and *write_count*, are associated to each page in our proposed WA-CLOCK algorithm. Where, the *write_bit* replaces the reference bit to record the write recency, and the *write_count* is used to record the write frequency. Our goal is to allocate the write-hot pages in DRAM and the write-cold pages in NVM. As such, if a page is write-hot, WA-CLOCK does not evict it but the *rotation_count* is increased by one. The *rotation_count* records how many times the page was overlooked even though the *write_bit* is 0. The detailed rules of the WA-CLOCK policy are listed as follows.

**Rule 1:** When a page enters into DRAM and the DRAM buffer cache is not full, we put it into the DRAM buffer cache and initialize the *write_bit*, *write_count* and *rotation_count* to 0.

**Rule 2:** When a write request hits in DRAM, WA-CLOCK sets the corresponding *write_bit* to 1 and increases the *write_count* by one.

**Rule 3:** When a page enters into DRAM but the DRAM buffer cache is full, page replacement occurs. WA-CLOCK traverses the circular list to find a victim page with *write_bit* is 0. However, if a page's *write_bit* is 0 but it is a write-hot page, WA-CLOCK does not evict it but the *rotation_count* is increased by one. Only when the *rotation_count* reaches to the preset threshold value, which means the page has not been written for a long time and it is no longer write-hot, it is evicted from DRAM to NVM. The algorithm of the replacement is shown in Algorithm 1.

---

**Algorithm 1.** Replacement Rule of the WA-CLOCK Policy

```
1: while (1) do
2:      p= the page pointed by the hand pointer;
3:      hand pointer points to next page;
4:      if (write_bit(p)==1) then
5:          write_bit(p)=0;
6:          rotation_count(p)=0;
7:      else
8:          if (write_count(p)⩾hot_page_threshold &&
9:              rotation_count(p)<expiration_threshold) then
10:             rotation_count(p)++;
11:         else
12:             evict the page p from DRAM to NVM;
13:             the new page enters into DRAM;
14:             return;
15:         end if
16:     end if
17: end while
```

---

### 3.3  Pre-CLOCK Policy for the NVM Buffer Cache

WA-CLOCK algorithm allocates most of the write-hot pages in DRAM while moves the write-cold pages to NVM. In order to further reduce write accesses to NVM and correct *the unreasonable judgments* of the write-cold pages, a write-burst predictor is designed to monitor the pages in NVM and migrate the write-burst pages to DRAM in real time. When a write request hits in NVM, the predictor is accessed to predict whether it is a write-burst request. Similarly, the write-burst predictor is designed based on the information of write frequency and write recency. If a page in NVM is written frequently within a short period of time, we migrate it to DRAM to increase the lifespan of the hybrid buffer cache. Here, we design another variant of CLOCK algorithm, called Pre-CLOCK (Clock with Prediction), to manage the NVM buffer cache. The Pre-CLOCK policy integrates the write-burst predictor, whose rules are detailed as follows.

**Rule 1:** When a write request hits in NVM, Pre-CLOCK sets the corresponding *write_bit* to 1 and increases the *write_count* by one. The write-burst predictor examines whether the *write_count* exceeds the preset *write-burst threshold*. If so, this is a write-burst request and the page is migrated to DRAM. It is worth noting that, if the page is frozen, it is copied to a new location and the updates are written to the copy. Here, we introduce a shadow scheme which will be detailed in Sect. 4.

**Rule 2:** When a write-cold page of DRAM is moved to NVM and the NVM buffer cache is not full, we put it into the NVM buffer cache and initialize the *write_bit*, *write_count* and *rotation_count* to 0. Otherwise, page replacement occurs. Different from CLOCK algorithm, Pre-CLOCK does not evict the potential write-burst pages (the *write_count* is not less than a preset ratio, e.g. 50 %

of the write-burst threshold) but with the *rotation_counts* increased by one, even their *write_bits* are 0. However, If the *rotation_count* reaches the *expiration_threshold*, which means this page has not been written for a long time, it is evicted from NVM to storage.

### 3.4  Page Management Policy for the Hybrid Buffer Cache

Now we are ready to present our page management policy for the hybrid buffer cache, which is depicted in Algorithm 2. In our policy, we use WA-CLOCK and Pre-CLOCK algorithm to manage the DRAM buffer cache and the NVM buffer cache, respectively. The WA-CLOCK allocates the write-hot pages to DRAM and the write-cold pages to NVM, while the Pre-CLOCK integrates a write-burst predictor to migrate the write-burst pages from NVM to DRAM.

---

**Algorithm 2.** Page Management Policy (page $p$, operation $op$)

---

1: **if** ($p \in$ DRAM) **then**
2:     **if** ($op$==write) **then**
3:         execute Rule 2 of WA-CLOCK;
4:     **end if**
5: **else if** ($p \in$ NVM) **then**
6:     **if** ($op$==write) **then**
7:         execute Rule 1 of Pre-CLOCK algorithm;
8:         If $p$ is a write-burst page, Rule 3 of WA-CLOCK
9:             and Rule 2 of Pre-CLOCK are executed;
10:     **end if**
11: **else**   /*page fault*/
12:     If there is free page in DRAM, Rule 1 of WA-CLOCK
13:         algorithm is executed;
14:     If there is no free page in DRAM, Rule 3 of WA-
15:         CLOCK and Rule2 of Pre-CLOCK are executed;
16: **end if**

---

## 4   Hybrid-Commit Journaling Scheme

The journaling scheme in the hybrid buffer cache comprises the in-place commit of NVM and the in-memory commit of DRAM. We reference the idea of *frozen blocks* proposed in [1], which changes the state of updated cache blocks to frozen right at where they are currently located when a commit operation is issued. But for the updated blocks in DRAM, they are copied to NVM and then are changed to frozen as journal, while the original data blocks in DRAM are free and can be reclaimed by other processes. When a read request hits in a frozen block, if the frozen block is up-to-date, it can still be used as a cache block. As mentioned above, the frozen blocks are write protected, that is, writing to a frozen block leads to a copy be made to a new location and then the updated data is written to the copy. Accordingly, the copy becomes up-to-date, while the original frozen block becomes out-of-date. This guarantees the journal remain unchanged before the corresponding data is written to the real file system.

When writing to a frozen block, the block can be copied to a new location, NVM or DRAM. If the block will only be written one time before next commit, it should be copied to NVM which results in one block written to NVM. Otherwise, if it is copied to DRAM, it leads to one block written to DRAM, one block in-memory copy from DRAM to NVM and one block written to NVM. However, if the block will be written two or more times, it should be copied to DRAM to reduce writes to NVM since in these kinds of cases, only one journal block is written to NVM. To do this, we propose a *shadow* mechanism for the distinction. We introduce two extra lists: list L1 records the dirty pages which have been modified only once since last commit, and list L2 records the dirty pages modified two or more times. The design is on the assumption that if a page was written frequently, it is likely to be written frequently again in the future. Hence, if a block is in list L1 before being committed, the write copy will be performed in NVM, or if it is in list L2, it will be copied to DRAM.

In the NVM buffer cache, we maintain a shadow table to keep track of the committed blocks in L2 list. The shadow table maintains the entries instead of the whole pages. This can be implemented very easily in modern file systems. When a write operation occurs on a frozen block, if it is in the shadow table, it is copied to DRAM, otherwise, it is copied to NVM.

## 5    Experiments

### 5.1    Experiment Setup

We implemented our page management policy and the hybrid-commit journaling mechanism on Linux 2.6.38. We compared our scheme with ext4 file system and the Union of Buffer cache and Journaling (UBJ) scheme proposed in [1]. As mentioned above, UBJ adopts NVM as the entire buffer cache while our scheme employs the hybrid buffer cache. As such, UBJ represents the performance upper bound of our scheme since there are no overheads of migrations and in-memory copies. We set the journaling option of ext4 to journal-mode, which logs both data and metadata, to provides the same consistency semantics as UBJ and our scheme.

Since our proposed techniques provide the same reliability with traditional journaling schemes, we focus on the performance improvement and writes reduction on NVM. Furthermore, since NVM is not commercially available now, we use a small portion of DRAM as NVM, with the assumption that NVM provides disk-like data persistence at DRAM-like latency according to the recent research reports.

### 5.2    Experimental Results

Filebench is a file system and storage benchmark which uses loadable work-load personalities to allow easy emulation of complex applications. Here, we use four applications, varmail, webproxy, fileserver and webserver, to measure the throughput of the three different journaling schemes. The characteristics of the four workloads is shown in Table 1. Respectively, we run the four workloads 30 min under different schemes. The results are shown in Fig. 3.

**Table 1.** Characteristics of different workloads

| workload | avg. file size | # of files | avg. op. size | r:w ratio |
|----------|----------------|------------|---------------|-----------|
| *Varmail* | 16K | 1000 | 4K | 1:1 |
| *Webproxy* | 16K | 10000 | 4K | 5:1 |
| *Fileserver* | 128K | 10000 | 72K | 1:2 |
| *Webserver* | 16K | 1000 | 16K | 10:1 |

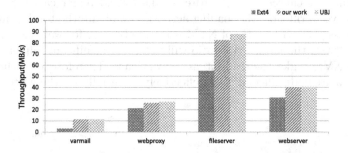

**Fig. 3.** Throughput of Filebench workloads

As shown in Fig. 3, the throughput of our journaling scheme is better than ext4 by 89.6 %, while with only 4.75 % performance gap compared to UBJ, on average. Specifically, the performance improvement of varmail is the largest among the four workloads. This is because that varmail generates a large number of writes, incurring frequent commit operations. However, since the small memory footprint, the varmail workload does not cause frequent checkpointing. Hence, the introduce of NVM significantly improves the performance in this situation. As for the fileserver workload, the situation is different. The large writes trigger frequent checkpointing. Therefore, the performance gains of NVM is relatively small compared to varmail.

It is worth noting that, frequent commits affect the performance benefits of our scheme since the DRAM portion of the hybrid buffer cache has to commit the updates to NVM as journal. Since the memory footprint is small in varmail workload, compared with UBJ, the in-memory commit does not lead a significant performance drop. But for the fileserver workload, the large writes cause large in-memory copy, which leads to largest performance gap, about 10 %, compared with UBJ.

Additionally, even for read-intensive workloads like webproxy and webserver, our scheme and UBJ scheme improve I/O performance due to the reduction of journal traffic relieves the contention to hardware resources like memory bus and DMAs.

Figure 4 shows the write distribution on NVM with the baseline of the writes under UBJ. We observe that, varmail issues frequent writes to small files. In addition, our scheme ensures that write-hot data is located in DRAM and write-burst data is migrated out of NVM. As such, for varmail workload, the large memory portion, i.e. NVM, absorbs only 35 % of the total write size compared to UBJ. But for fileserver, the write size of NVM is relatively large, 58.4 %, since the large memory footprint leads to considerable in-memory copy on NVM. Therefore, for write-intensive workloads, varmail and fileserver, our scheme improve the lifetime of NVM by 185 % and 71 %, compared to UBJ, respectively. It is worth noting that, for the read-intensive workloads, DRAM absorbs almost all the writes. However, in our statistics, when a data block is loaded into DRAM/NVM for the first time, it causes a block write on the hybrid buffer cache. So, for the read-intensive workloads, the loading activities dominate the total write traffic. As we can see, the write ratio of NVM is relatively large for webproxy and webserver. However, the large write ratio will not cause significant influence on the lifetime of NVM under the read-intensive workloads. Therefore, our scheme alleviates the write endurance of NVM effectively, especially for the write-intensive workloads.

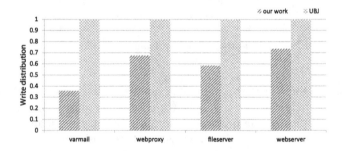

**Fig. 4.** The normalized write size on NVM with different workloads

# 6   Related Work

Traditional DRAM based main memory is volatile, the unexpected system crashes may result in an inconsistent file system. To relieve this problem, journaling file systems exploit the journaling technique to log the updates to non-volatile storage. However, journaling mechanism is transaction based [10–14] and leads to a large number of journal traffic, greatly impeding system performance. The introduction of NVM brings a new perspective of resolving this issue. Youyou

Lu et al. designed a new embedded transaction mechanism for SSDs with non-volatile disk cache to improve performance of data consistency [12]. In order to reduce overhead caused by strict ordering of writes, a loose-ordering consistency mechanism was proposed for persistent memory [15]. Previous work [16,17] attempted to reduce journaling overhead using NVM for database and file system. However, these techniques either were not integrated into file system or kept NVM separately from the buffer cache. A UBJ scheme uniting the buffer cache and journaling layers with NVM was proposed in [1]. But this study employed NVM as the whole main memory without considering the write endurance of NVM. Therefore, in this paper, we employ a hybrid NVM-DRAM buffer cache. However, the hybrid buffer cache complicates the traditional DRAM based or NVM based journaling mechanism, but the problem has not been studied extensively yet.

Emerging non-volatile memory technologies, such as PCM and RRAM, have been intensively studied as a promising candidate main memory. Compared with DRAM, NVM shows the advantages of non-volatility, low power, better scalability and high density [18,19]. However, considering the disadvantage of NVM in terms of write operation, architectures integrating NVM and DRAM into the main memory have been proposed in [3–5,20,21].

In modern computer systems, a large amount of main memory is used as a page cache. Traditional page management algorithms, such as LRU, LIRS [22], ARC [23], and CLOCK-Pro [24], were designed for DRAM based main memory and did not consider the different characteristics of NVM and DRAM. H-ARC, an extended ARC algorithm, was proposed in [25] to improve NVM based cache performance. Focusing on caching and endurance problem, the migration policy between NVM and DRAM is presented in [26,27]. In order to predict future write references of pages, a CLOCK-DWF algorithm is presented in [9]. However, all these studies were only dedicated to reducing write operations on NVM and did not take the journaling mechanism into account to reduce the in-memory journal traffic between DRAM and NVM.

Therefore, in this paper, we focus on reducing the storage accesses caused by journaling using NVM. We study the page management policy and the hybrid-commit journaling scheme for the hybrid buffer cache architecture. The proposed techniques aim to enormously improve the performance of file system without any loss of reliability while reducing write accesses to NVM.

# 7    Concluding Remarks

In this paper, we aim to optimize the performance overhead caused by journaling for modern file systems. We solve the problem using emerging NVM technologies. Considering the non-volatility of NVM and the unlimited write endurance of DRAM, we exploit a hybrid NVM-DRAM buffer cache architecture. We propose a page management policy to direct page placement and migration between NVM and DRAM. The policy distinguishes the write-hot and write-cold data to ensure DRAM absorb most writes. Meanwhile, a predictor is integrated to avoid the write-burst activity on NVM. Furthermore, we present a hybrid-commit journaling scheme to support the in-place commit of NVM and the in-memory commit of DRAM. We implement the page management policy and the hybrid-commit journaling scheme on Linux 2.6.38 and the experimental results show the proposed techniques significantly improve the performance of file system and prolong the lifetime of the hybrid buffer cache.

**Acknowledgments.** This research is sponsored by the Natural Science Foundation of China (NSFC) under Grant No. 61070022 and 61202015, Shandong Provincial Natural Science Foundation under Grant No. ZR2011FQ036, ZR2013FM028 and 2015ZRE27478, the Fundamental Research Funds of Shandong University under No. 2015JC030, and Guangdong Key Laboratory of Popular High Performance Computers, Shenzhen Key Laboratory of Service Computing and Applications (SZU-GDPHPCL2014).

# References

1. Lee, E., Bahn, H., Noh, S.H.: Unioning of the buffer cache and journaling layers with non-volatile memory. In: FAST, pp. 73–80 (2013)
2. Rubin, M.: File systems in the Cloud. Linux Foundation Collaboration Summit (2011)
3. Mogul, J.C., Argollo, E., Shah, M.A., Faraboschi, P.: Operating system support for nvm+ dram hybrid main memory. In: HotOS (2009)
4. Qureshi, M.K., Srinivasan, V., Rivers, J.A.: Scalable high performance main memory system using phase-change memory technology. ACM SIGARCH Comput. Architect. News **37**(3), 24–33 (2009)
5. Dhiman, G., Ayoub, R., Rosing, T.: Pdram: a hybrid pram and dram main memory system. In: Design Automation Conference, DAC 2009. 46th ACM/IEEE, pp. 664–669. IEEE (2009)
6. Li, Y., Chen, Y., Jones, A.K.: A software approach for combating asymmetries of non-volatile memories. In: Proceedings of the 2012 ACM/IEEE International Symposium on Low Power Electronics and Design, pp. 191–196. ACM (2012)
7. Ramos, L.E., Gorbatov, E., Bianchini, R.: Page placement in hybrid memory systems. In: Proceedings of the International Conference on Supercomputing, pp. 85–95. ACM (2011)
8. Zhirong, S., Wei, X., Jiwu, S.: Research on new non-volatile storage. J. Comput. Res. Dev. **51**(2), 445–453 (2014)
9. Lee, S., Bahn, H., Noh, S.: Clock-dwf: A write-history-aware page replacement algorithm for hybrid pcm and dram memory architectures (2013)
10. Tweedie, S.C.: Journaling the linux ext2fs filesystem. In: The Fourth Annual Linux Expo (1998)
11. Lu, Y., Shu, J., Wang, W.: Reconfs: a reconstructable file system on flash storage. In: FAST, pp. 75–88 (2014)
12. Lu, Y., Shu, J., Guo, J., Li, S., Mutlu, O.: Lighttx: A lightweight transactional design in flash-based ssds to support flexible transactions. In: 2013 IEEE 31st International Conference on Computer Design (ICCD), pp. 115–122. IEEE (2013)
13. Lu, Y., Shu, J., Zheng, W., et al.: Extending the lifetime of flash-based storage through reducing write amplification from file systems. In: FAST, pp. 257–270 (2013)

14. Coburn, J., Bunker, T., Schwarz, M., Gupta, R., Swanson, S.: From aries to mars: Transaction support for next-generation, solid-state drives. In: Proceedings of the Twenty-Fourth ACM Symposium on Operating Systems Principles, pp. 197–212. ACM (2013)

15. Lu, Y., Shu, J., Sun, L., Mutlu, O.: Loose-ordering consistency for persistent memory. In: 2014 32nd IEEE International Conference on Computer Design (ICCD), pp. 216–223. IEEE (2014)

16. Fang, R., Hsiao, H.-I., He, B., Mohan, C., Wang, Y.: High performance database logging using storage class memory. In: 2011 IEEE 27th International Conference on Data Engineering (ICDE), pp. 1221–1231. IEEE (2011)

17. Phillips, D.: Zumastor linux storage server. In: Proceedings of the Linux Symposium, pp. 135–143. Citeseer (2007)

18. Lee, B.C., Ipek, E., Mutlu, O., Burger, D.: Phase change memory architecture and the quest for scalability. Commun. ACM **53**(7), 99–106 (2010)

19. Mutlu, O.: Memory scaling: A systems architecture perspective. In: 2013 5th IEEE International Memory Workshop (IMW), pp. 21–25. IEEE (2013)

20. Zhang, W., Li, T.: Exploring phase change memory and 3d die-stacking for power/thermal friendly, fast and durable memory architectures. In: 18th International Conference on Parallel Architectures and Compilation Techniques, 2009 PACT 2009, pp. 101–112. IEEE (2009)

21. Condit, J., Nightingale, E.B., Frost, C., Ipek, E., Lee, B., Burger, D., Coetzee, D.: Better i/o through byte-addressable, persistent memory. In: Proceedings of the ACM SIGOPS 22nd Symposium on Operating Systems Principles, pp. 133–146. ACM (2009)

22. Jiang, S., Zhang, X.: Lirs: an efficient low inter-reference recency set replacement policy to improve buffer cache performance. ACM SIGMETRICS Perform. Eval. Rev. **30**(1), 31–42 (2002)

23. Megiddo, N., Modha, D.S.: Arc: A self-tuning, low overhead replacement cache. In: FAST, vol. 3, pp. 115–130 (2003)

24. Jiang, S., Chen, F., Zhang, X.: Clock-pro: An effective improvement of the clock replacement. In: USENIX Annual Technical Conference, General Track, pp. 323–336 (2005)

25. Fan, Z., Du, D.H.C., Voigt, D.: H-arc: A non-volatile memory based cache policy for solid state drives. In: 2014 30th Symposium on Mass Storage Systems and Technologies (MSST), pp. 1–11. IEEE (2014)

26. Seok, H., Park, Y., Park, K.H.: Migration based page caching algorithm for a hybrid main memory of dram and pram. In: Proceedings of the 2011 ACM Symposium on Applied Computing, pp. 595–599. ACM (2011)

27. Seok, H., Park, Y., Park, K.-W., Park, K.H.: Efficient page caching algorithm with prediction and migration for a hybrid main memory. ACM SIGAPP Appl. Comput. Rev. **11**(4), 38–48 (2011)

# A Green Scheduler for Cloud Data Centers Using Renewable Energy

Chonglin Gu[1], Chunyan Liu[1], Chen Shi[1], Zhixiang He[1],
Hejiao Huang[1,2(✉)], and Xiaohua Jia[1]

[1] Harbin Institute of Technology Shenzhen Graduate School, Shenzhen 518055, China
hjhuang@hitsz.edu.cn
[2] Shenzhen Key Laboratory of Internet Information Collaboration,
Shenzhen 518055, China

**Abstract.** In recent years, a large number of cloud data centers have been built around the world to provide all kinds of service. The high power consumption of the servers in those data centers deteriorates the already serious global warming. Many Internet operators have devoted much effort in power-aware scheduling using renewable resources. However, the intermittent nature of renewable resources proposes new challenges for us: how to distribute the incoming requests to the data centers that are powered by renewable energy, while minimizing the carbon emissions under a certain budget. In this paper, we model the problem as a constraint optimization problem. The goal is to minimize total carbon emissions of those geographically distributed data centers, while satisfying the constraints: (1) The electricity budget in each time slot; (2) The intermittent supply of renewable energy; (3) The number of each type of heterogeneous servers in each data center; (4) QoS constraint in request processing time. We ingeniously transformed this problem into a mixed integer linear programming problem, and solved it using Cplex. Our simulation is based on traces from real world, and we can get optimum solution when problem scale like Wiki workload is not so large. Experiments show that our scheduler can minimize carbon emissions while satisfying the above mentioned constraints.

**Keywords:** Cloud computing · Data center · Renewable resource · Green scheduling · Carbon emissions

## 1 Introduction

Cloud computing is developing so fast that a large number of data centers have been built in recent years. It is the servers running in those data centers that cause high power consumption as well as high electricity cost. According to a recent report, the power consumption of Google is over 1,120 GWh with 67 million dollars per year, and Microsoft consumes 600 GWh with 36 million dollars [1] annually. The power consumption of data centers accounts for 1.3 % currently, and it is estimated to reach 8 % in 2020. Thus, cloud data centers

© Springer International Publishing Switzerland 2015
G. Wang et al. (Eds.): ICA3PP 2015, Part IV, LNCS 9531, pp. 476–491, 2015.
DOI: 10.1007/978-3-319-27140-8_33

contribute greatly to global warming, since 2/3 of the electricity of the world is generated by burning fossil fuels [2]. Some Internet service providers have already taken steps to promote the usage of renewable energy for data centers. For example, Facebook has built solar-powered data center in Oregon, and Green House Data built its wind-powered data center in Wyoming [3]. Besides, Google and Yahoo have already powered their own data centers using clean energy, which account for 39.4 and 56.4, respectively. Therefore, it is significant for cloud data centers to make green scheduling using renewable energy.

Existing work on scheduling for cloud data centers mainly focus on energy saving policy designs, minimizing total electricity, or maximally using renewable energy, as to be discussed in Sect. 2. Different from the work in literature, our focus is to design a green scheduler for requests dispatching, so that the carbon emissions can be minimized. In this paper, we first model our problem as a constraint optimization problem with the goal of minimizing total carbon emissions of geographically distributed data centers. The constraints are: (1) the electricity budget in each time slot; (2) the intermittent supply of renewable energy; (3) the number of each type of heterogeneous servers in each data center; (4) QoS constraint in request processing time. It should be noted that the supply of renewable energy and the electricity price in different locations are fluctuating with time. We ingeniously transform our problem into mixed integer programming problem, and solved it using Cplex. Our simulation is based on traces from real world. Some data are collected in a coarse granularity such as one hour. However, our scheduling granularity is 5 min, so there is need to divide each value of the original traces into several ones in a finer granularity. We propose to use quadratic function discretization to generate the traces in a finer granularity while maintaining the trend of data in time series. To evaluate our method, we give four baselines: Minimum Cost Scheduling, Maximum Cost Scheduling, Minimum Carbon Emission Scheduling, and Minimum Transmission Time Scheduling. Experiments show that our method can minimize carbon emissions while satisfying the constraints. And our method can get optimum solution when the problem scale is not large enough like Wiki workload in simulation.

The rest of this paper is organized as follows. Section 2 reviews related work. Section 3 demonstrates the architecture of green scheduler. In Sect. 4, details of the modeling for our problem is discussed and solution is given. In Sect. 5, we will show how the simulation is made using traces from real world, and evaluate the performance of our model. Finally, Sect. 6 concludes this paper.

## 2    Related Work

Scheduling for cloud data centers has been a hot topic in recent years. In general, it can be classified into three categories: energy saving, managing electricity cost, and utilizing renewable energy.

**In Energy Saving.** Chen et al. in [4] and Chase in [5] propose a request response service model to reduce power consumption from long-lived TCP connections. Elnozahy et al. in [6] combine DVFS and power on/off techniques to reduce power consumption of data centers. But none of these work take varying electricity price into consideration, and they did not consider that data centers may be powered by renewable energy besides brown energy.

**In Cost Management.** Qureshi et al. in [7] propose to reduce total cost of the data centers in geographically distributed locations with varying electricity prices. Rao et al. in [8] consider the multi-electricity market to reduce electricity cost. Zhang et al. in [9] propose an electricity capping algorithm to minimize electricity cost under certain budgets. Lin te al. in [10] propose a dynamic right sizing method to minimize energy cost with delay cost. But none of these work consider the supply of renewable resource to power data centers.

**In Utilizing Renewable Energy.** Le et al. in [11,12] propose a capping method for brown energy while satisfying SLA constraint. Liu et al. in [13] exploit how to lower brown energy price using renewable resources in a specific market. Brown et al. in [14] propose an infrastructure called Rerack to simulate data center with renewable energy simulation. Stewart in [15] propose to maximize renewable resources for data centers. Li et al. in [16] try to characterize the renewable resource pattern. They also give a scheme for power management by tuning workload with renewable resources. Authors in [17] built a demo system with scheduler designed to maximize the usage of solar energy. Green Hadoop [18] and Green Slot [19] are the two schedulers based on this system. The two schdulers try to use as much solar energy as possible while satisfying the finishing deadlines of all incoming tasks. The authors in [20] try to use renewable energy as much as possible while maintaining load balancing between data centers.

Similar to our work, Zhang et al. in [21] propose GreenWare, a scheduler that maximally uses renewable resources under a certain budget. The shortage of GreenWare is that it can not quantify how green the scheduler is. And maximizing the usage of renewable resource does not mean minimizing carbon emissions, because some cheap renewable resource may emit more carbon compared with expensive ones. Another work in [22] simulates requests dispatching for data center powered by renewable resource. But they only build a simple model that assume the data centers are composed of homogeneous servers. In their simulation, the granularity is one hour, which is too large to reflect the intermittency of renewable resources very well. In our work, we assume all the data centers are composed of different types of servers. Furthermore, our scheduling frequency is 5 min, a fine scheduling granularity. As far as we know, we are the first to propose green scheduling for heterogeneous data centers using renewable energy with fine grained scheduling time slot. The following section will give the architecture of our green scheduler.

## 3    Architecture of Green Scheduler

Internet service operators like Google always build their data centers in geographically distributed locations for special purposes. In this paper, we mainly focus on minimizing carbon emissions of each data center. We assume the data centers are built near the locations abundant in renewable resources such that the losses of electricity during transmission can be neglected. Wind and solar energy are the dominant renewable resources, which account for 62 percent and 13 percent non-hydro renewable resources, respectively [23]. In this paper, we assume that all the data centers are powered by solar energy, wind energy, as well as traditional brown energy. The architecture of our scheduling system is shown in Fig. 1.

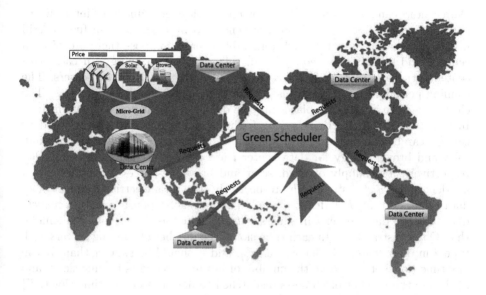

**Fig. 1.** Architecture of green scheduler [22]

As can be seen in Fig. 1, the green scheduler is responsible for dispatching the incoming requests to each data center. The scheduler itself is a high performance server or a cluster of servers. It should be noted that the servers in the same data center are heterogeneous. The request transmission delays from scheduler to each data center are different. Each data center is powered by wind, solar and brown energy, and the supply of each type of energy can be switched seamless using micro-grid technology. Thus, the applications running in the data center will not be affected when there are switchings between different energy supply. The input for each scheduling includes: (1) predicted climate condition (including temperature, solar illumination and wind speed), which are used for calculating the power supply of wind and solar in this time slot; (2) the budget for this time slot; (3) QoS, the maximum response time of the requests. (4) electricity price in this time slot. (5) the number of each type of servers in the data center. Different from existing architectures, the task of our scheduler is to dispatch requests to the data centers, with the goal of minimizing total carbon emissions. It should satisfy the constraints like: response time, number of different types of servers in each data center, renewable power supply, and budget per hour.

Since the servers in each data center are heterogenous, the task for dispatching the incoming requests to different types of servers are also considered in this system. Servers with no requests dispatched should be in sleeping state with little power consumed. In the following section, modeling for this problem will be given in detail.

# 4    Problem Modeling and Solution

Data centers can not be powered only by renewable energy due to its intermittent nature. And traditional brown energy generated by burning fossil fuels is still needed when there is not enough renewable energy. Suppose there are $N$ data centers, and each is powered by wind, solar and brown energy. In each data center $i$, there are $M_i$ types of servers, and each type has $M_{ij}$ servers. The running period of our scheduler is $T$ time slots, and for each slot $t$, $t \in T$. The electricity price in different places may be different, and it fluctuates with time. In time slot $t$, the electricity price of wind, solar and brown energy for data center $i$ can be denoted as $Pw_i^t$, $Ps_i^t$ and $Pb_i^t$, respectively. The demand of wind, solar and brown energy for data center $i$ are denoted as $Dw_i^t$, $Ds_i^t$, and $Db_i^t$, respectively. The supply of wind, solar and brown resources for data center $i$ are denoted as $Sw_i^t$, $Ss_i^t$, and $Sb_i^t$, respectively. The total electricity budget of all data centers during $T$ is denoted as $C$. The average response time of a request dispatched to data center $i$ in time slot $t$ is denoted as $r_i^t$, it should be smaller than QoS constraint $R_i$. In each time slot $t$, the number of running servers with type $j$ in data center $i$ is denoted as $x_{ij}^t$, and it should be smaller than $M_{ij}$ in any time slot. Let $\lambda^t$ denote the number of incoming requests in time slot $t$, and $\lambda_i^t$ denote the number of requests dispatched to data center $i$ in time slot t. $E_i^t$ denotes the carbon emissions of data center $i$ in time slot $t$.

In our scheduler, the response time of a request in data center $i$ is denoted as $r_i$. It is composed of three parts: waiting time, processing time, and the transmission delay from scheduler to each data center. Each data center has heterogeneous servers. When requests are dispatched to each data center, the scheduler will determine how many requests are dispatched to each type of servers. Let $\lambda_{ij}^t$ denote the number of requests dispatched to servers with type $j$ in data center $i$ during time slot $t$. We have:

$$\lambda_i^t = \sum_{j=1}^{M_i} \lambda_{ij}^t$$

Suppose all the requests need waiting in queue for homogeneous servers of a certain type. Thus, M/M/n model can be used to simulate waiting time and processing time of each request. Let the service rate of a server with type $j$ in data center $i$ be denoted as $\mu_{ij}$, then the waiting time and processing time are denoted as $1/(\mu_{ij} \cdot x_{ij}^t - \lambda_{ij}^t)$, and $1/\mu_{ij}$, respectively. The transmission delay from scheduler to data center $i$ is $d_i$. So we have:

$$r_i = \frac{1}{\mu_{ij} \cdot x_{ij}^t - \lambda_{ij}^t} + \frac{1}{\mu_{ij}} + d_i, \quad \mu_{ij} \cdot x_{ij}^t > \lambda_{ij}^t$$

When QoS constraint of $R_i$ is given, the minimum number of running servers with type $j$ in data center $i$ during time slot $t$ can be deduced like this:

$$x_{ij}^t = \frac{\mu_{ij} + \lambda_{ij}^t \cdot R_i \cdot \mu_{ij} - \lambda_{ij}^t \cdot d_i \cdot \mu_{ij} - \lambda_{ij}^t}{\mu_{ij}(R_i \cdot \mu_{ij} - d_i \cdot \mu_{ij} - 1)} = f(\lambda_{ij}^t)$$

Obviously, $x_{ij}^t$ is in linear relationship with $\lambda_{ij}^t$. In fact, $\lambda_{ij}^t$ can further be decomposed into the number of requests dispatched to servers with type $j$ in datacenter $i$ using wind, solar and brown energy in time slot $t$, denoted as $\lambda w_{ij}^t$, $\lambda s_{ij}^t$, and $\lambda b_{ij}^t$, respectively.

$$\lambda_{ij}^t = \lambda w_{ij}^t + \lambda s_{ij}^t + \lambda b_{ij}^t$$

It should be noted that $\lambda w_{ij}^t$, $\lambda s_{ij}^t$, and $\lambda b_{ij}^t$ may not be integers, but the sum $\lambda_{ij}^t$, and $\lambda_i^t$ are integers.

Suppose $P_{ij}$ is the peak power of a server with type $j$ in data center $i$, and its real power is in proportion to load. Thus, the amount of wind, solar, and brown energy in each time slot $t$ can be denoted as follows:

$$Dw_i^t = \sum_{j=1}^{M_i} \left( \frac{\mu_{ij} + \lambda w_{ij}^t \cdot R_i \cdot \mu_{ij} - \lambda w_{ij}^t \cdot d_i \cdot \mu_{ij} - \lambda w_{ij}^t}{\mu_{ij}(R_i \cdot \mu_{ij} - d_i \cdot \mu_{ij} - 1)} \cdot P_{ij} \right)$$

$$Ds_i^t = \sum_{j=1}^{M_i} \left( \frac{\mu_{ij} + \lambda s_{ij}^t \cdot R_i \cdot \mu_{ij} - \lambda s_{ij}^t \cdot d_i \cdot \mu_{ij} - \lambda s_{ij}^t}{\mu_{ij}(R_i \cdot \mu_{ij} - d_i \cdot \mu_{ij} - 1)} \cdot P_{ij} \right)$$

$$Db_i^t = \sum_{j=1}^{M_i} \left( \frac{\mu_{ij} + \lambda b_{ij}^t \cdot R_i \cdot \mu_{ij} - \lambda b_{ij}^t \cdot d_i \cdot \mu_{ij} - \lambda b_{ij}^t}{\mu_{ij}(R_i \cdot \mu_{ij} - d_i \cdot \mu_{ij} - 1)} \cdot P_{ij} \right)$$

To calculate carbon emissions, we can use CER (carbon emission rate) for calculation. CER represents the amount of carbon emissions in unit energy (kWh), as can be seen in Table 1.

**Table 1.** CER of the energy sources [2]

| Energy Source | Coal | Wind | Solar |
|---|---|---|---|
| Carbon Emission Rate(g$CO_2$e/kWh) | 968 | 22.5 | 53 |

In many power plant around the world, coal is still the most widely used brown energy, so we use coal as our brown energy in this paper. The CER of brown, wind and solar energy are denoted as $Eb$, $Ew$, and $Es$, respectively. We have:

$$E_i^t = Eb \cdot Db_i^t + Ew \cdot Dw_i^t + Es \cdot Ds_i^t$$

Thus, our problem can be formulated as follows:

$$Minimize: E = \sum_{i=1}^{N} \sum_{t=1}^{T} E_i^t \tag{1}$$

$$0 \le x_{ij}^t \le M_{ij} \tag{2}$$

$$Dw_i^t \le Sw_i^t \tag{3}$$

$$Ds_i^t \le Ss_i^t \tag{4}$$

$$\sum_{i=1}^{N} \sum_{t=1}^{T} (Dw_i^t \cdot Pw_i^t + Ds_i^t \cdot Ps_i^t + Db_i^t \cdot Pb_i^t) \le C \tag{5}$$

$$\lambda^t = \sum_{i=1}^{N} \sum_{j=1}^{M_i} (\lambda w_{ij}^t + \lambda s_{ij}^t + \lambda b_{ij}^t) \tag{6}$$

$$\lambda w_{ij}^t, \ \lambda s_{ij}^t, \ \lambda b_{ij}^t \in \mathbb{R}^+ \quad (\mathbb{R}^+ \ denotes \ set \ of \ positive \ real \ number) \tag{7}$$

$$\sum_{j=1}^{M_i} \lambda w_{ij}^t + \lambda s_{ij}^t + \lambda b_{ij}^t \in \mathbb{N} \quad (\mathbb{N} \ denotes \ set \ of \ natural \ number) \tag{8}$$

In this optimization problem, there are $N$ data centers, each is powered by 3 types of energy. Suppose each data center has $M$ types of servers. Thus, this optimization problem has $N \times M \times 3$ decision variables in total during each time slot $t$. They are $\lambda w_{ij}^t$, $\lambda s_{ij}^t$, and $\lambda b_{ij}^t$ in our formulation, where $i \in N$ and $j \in M$. It is not a classical programming problem, especially for constraint (8). To solve this problem, auxiliary variables are needed. We consider $\lambda_{ij}^t$ as integer variables added to the formulation, and then we replace constraints (6)–(8) by (6-1)–(9-1) as follows:

$$\lambda^t = \sum_{i=1}^{N} \sum_{j=1}^{M_i} \lambda_{ij}^t \tag{6-1}$$

$$\lambda_{ij}^t = \sum_{j=1}^{M} \lambda w_{ij}^t + \lambda s_{ij}^t + \lambda b_{ij}^t, \tag{7-1}$$

$$\lambda_{ij}^t \in \mathbb{N} \tag{8-1}$$

$$\lambda w_{ij}^t, \ \lambda s_{ij}^t, \ \lambda b_{ij}^t \in \mathbb{R}^+ \tag{9-1}$$

Thus, our problem is transformed into a mixed integer linear programming problem with $N \times M \times 4$ variables in both real and integer type. They are $\lambda w_{ij}^t$, $\lambda s_{ij}^t$, and $\lambda b_{ij}^t$, and $\lambda_{ij}^t$.

Since each time slot is a separate scheduling unit, there is no close relationship between decision variables between two consecutive time slots. Thus, the whole problem can be divided into $T$ sub-problems, each is a separate mixed integer linear programming problem. In this paper, our scheduler is implemented using mixed integer linear programming solver in Cplex. Though mixed integer linear programming problem is an NP-hard problem, the optimum solution can be calculated quickly when the problem scale is not large enough. In simulation using data from Wiki, our scheduler can obtain optimum solution.

# 5    Performance Evaluation

## 5.1    Simulation Setup

To verify the effectiveness of our green scheduler in reducing carbon emissions for data centers, our simulation data are based on traces from real world, including climate data, server capacity, statistical request traces, prices in different locations with time.

For servers in each data center, we use the same parameters in [24]. There are four types of servers in each data center. The power consumption of each type of server are 88.88, 34.10, 149.19, and 141.28 watts, respectively. The service rates are 50, 30, 75, and 65 requests per second, respectively. Each data center has 200 servers, in which there are 50 servers for each type in each data center.

For the availability of renewable resources, we use models of solar panel and wind turbines based on climate data from MIDC of National Renewable Energy Laboratory [25]. The climate traces contain irradiation, wind speed and temperature information from June 1st to June 30st in 2014. It includes four stations: Loyola Marymount University, University of Arizona, Solar Technology Acceleration Center, and National Energy Laboratory Hawaii Autoraty. We use 10000 BP-MSX-120 solar panels to power each data center. Based on P-V model [26], the maximal power generated by a solar panel can be calculated using Lamberts function with optimization technique proposed in [27]. We also use 200 NE-3000 wind turbines to power each data center. The power generated by wind can be calculated using the model proposed in [28].

For workload traces, Wiki dump data is used [29]. We also choose traces from June 1st to June 30st in 2014. It should be noted that the workload pattern of Wiki in each month are similar, so that the traces can be used as prediction in real scheduler.

For prices in different locations, we use traces from New York Independent System Operator (NYISO). To make the prices consistent with the workload in time, we also choose history prices from June 1st to June 30st in 2014. The NYISO only provides brown energy prices. The simulation is based on the assumption that given the price of brown energy $Pb_i$, wind energy charges $Pb_i + 1.5$ cents, and solar energy charges $Pb_i + 18$ cents per KWh [21].

For requests transmission from scheduler to each data center $i$, the delays are $d_1 = 0.2$, $d_2 = 0.25$, $d_3 = 0.15$, $d_4 = 0.1$, respectively.

In simulation, some traces from real world may be collected in a coarse granularity. We need to divide the data in a much finer granularity so that the scheduler can be designed in a proper granularity. The dividing must reflect the trend of data changes with time slots. We propose a method using quadratic function discretization processing like this. Suppose there are three points $(x_1, y_1)$, $(x_2, y_2)$, $(x_3, y_3)$ consecutive in time series. For each point $(x, y)$, $x$ denotes the sequential number of time slot, and $y$ denotes the value in this time slot (eg. the number of requests). We first built a quadratic function using these three points. Suppose the original scheduling granularity of each time slot will be further divided into $n$ smaller time slots. We insert $n$ points between $x_1$ and $x_3$, and $x$ values of those points are $x_1 + i * (x_3 - x_1)/n, i \in [1, n]$. Take these values into the calculated quadratic function, we can obtain y value for each inserted point. The $y$ value of each point will be multiplied by a proportion ratio, such that the sum of those values is equal to $y_2$. Thus, we successfully simulate the traces in time slot $x_2$ in a much finer granularity while reflecting the real trend of the data using values in time series like $y_1$ and $y_3$.

## 5.2   Model Evaluations

### A. Baselines

To evaluate our method, we give four baselines: (1) Minimum Cost Scheduling; (2) Maximum Cost Scheduling; (3) Minimum Carbon Emission Scheduling; (4) Minimum Transmission Time Scheduling. Thus, we can estimate the upper bound and lower bound of our budget.

(1) **Minimum Cost Scheduling:** This scheduling dispatches incoming requests to data centers with low electricity price as many as possible. It is used to estimate the lower bound of the total cost.

(2) **Maximum Cost Scheduling:** This scheduling dispatches incoming requests to data centers with high electricity price as many as possible. It is mainly used to estimate the upper bound of total cost.

(3) **Minimum Carbon Emission Scheduling:** This scheduling dispatches incoming requests to data centers using as much renewable energy as possible. It is used to estimate the lowest carbon emission we can achieve without considering the cost.

(4) **Minimum Transmission Time Scheduling:** This scheduling dispatches incoming requests to the nearest data centers so that the total request transmission time can be minimized. It is mainly used to show the cost and carbon emission as a tradeoff for best QoS.

For baselines, we propose to use simple greedy algorithm to solve each problem. For baseline (1) and (2), we first calculate the price per request using formula like this: $P_{ij} * Pb_i^t / \mu_{ij}$ for each server with type $j$ in data center $i$. Then we sort different types of servers in ascending or descending order, and dispatch our requests to different types of servers in each data center until finish dispatching all requests. For baseline (3), we dispatch requests to data centers powered by the cheapest renewable energy with low carbon emission. For baseline (4), we dispatch as many requests as possible to the nearest data centers. In simulation, our scheduling granularity is 5 min.

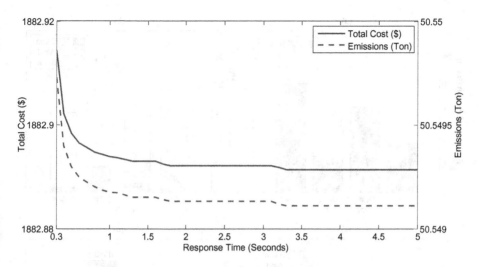

**Fig. 2.** The trend of cost and carbon emissions with response time

Before scheduling, we will first exploit how the changes of response time $R_i$ affect total cost and emission, as can be seen in Fig. 2. From this Figure, it can be easily found that the total cost and carbon emissions of all data centers are decreasing with the increase of response time for baseline (1), which is representative for all baselines. It can be explained using the Queue Theory we used in the model. When the response time becomes larger, more requests will be waiting in a queue, so that fewer servers are needed to process the heading requests in the queue. Thus, the power consumption in this time slot can be reduced. The saved money can also be used for purchasing green energy, so that the total carbon emission is reduced. As is mentioned in Sect. 3, $\mu_{ij}x_{ij}^t > \lambda_{ij}^t$, so we have:

$$R_i > \frac{1}{\mu_{ij}} + d_{ij}$$

So we set response time range from 0.3 s to 5 s.

Figure 3 is a verification for the four baselines, here we set $Ri = 1$ s for all data centers. From this Figure, interesting discussions will be made as follows: In (a), the goal is to use the cheapest energy as much as possible. Renewable energy is usually much more expensive than brown energy, so brown energy is consumed most in all of the four data centers. The usage of renewable energy such as wind and solar is not so obvious in this Figure, because their usage is so little compared with brown energy. The disadvantage of this scheduling is that it will produce a lot of carbon emissions. In fact, the price of the most expensive renewable energy in one place may even be lower than the cheapest brown energy in other places, so that this scheduling is not so dirty because it uses cheap renewable energy sometimes. In (b), the goal is to spend as much money as possible. Solar energy is usually the most expensive energy, so that it is consumed most in this case, as is shown in Figure (b). In fact, more money

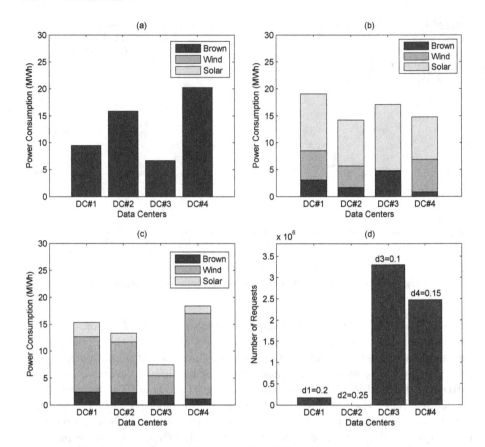

**Fig. 3.** Verifications for the four baselines. (a) Different types of energy consumed in each data center using Minimum Cost Scheduling. (b) Different types of energy consumed in each data center using Maximum Cost Scheduling. (c) Different types of energy consumed in each data center using Minimum Carbon Emission Scheduling. (d) The average requests per slot dispatched to each data center using Minimum Transmission Scheduling.

does not mean much greener, because some cheap renewable energy can be much greener with low carbon emissions. In (c), the goal is to use the energy with least carbon emission. From this Figure, we found that wind is the greenest renewable energy, it has merits of both low price and low carbon emission. In (d), requests will be dispatched to the nearest data centers. In this Figure, the transmission time of $d3 = 0.1$ s is the smallest, so that most of the requests will be dispatched to data center3 with high priority, and then to data centers with transmission time to be $d4 = 0.15$ s, $d1 = 0.2$ s, and $d2 = 0.25$ s, respectively. For data center 2, the number of requests dispatched to it is almost 0, because all requests are dispatched to the other 3 data centers and they indeed have enough capacity to process all the requests, so that no requests are left for this data center.

**Table 2.** Upper bound and lower bound of cost and emissions

|  | Electricity cost ($) | Carbon emission (Ton) |
|---|---|---|
| MinCost | 1882.89 | 50.55 |
| MaxCost | 7316072.40 | 12.36 |
| MinEmission | 1977012.70 | 8.70 |
| MinTrans | 63001.72 | 54.27 |

Table 2 gives upper bound and lower bound of cost and carbon emissions based on the baselines mentioned above. We found that maximum cost does not incur lowest carbon emission, because it uses only the most expensive energy instead of cheapest renewable energy. It is better to make budgeting based on Minimum Carbon Emissions Scheduling, because extra investment will not reduce carbon emissions any more after reaching minimum carbon emission.

## B. Comparisons for Our Scheduler

Renewable energy is usually much more expensive than brown energy. The four baselines did not consider budget constraints in using renewable energy. In reality, the energy generated in the next time slot can not be predicted very well, and the electricity price also changes with time. So our budgeting is designed like this. Let the total budget for the whole month of 30 days be denoted as $B$, then we divide the total budget into each time slot. Our scheduling granularity is 5 min, so there are $30 * 24 * 12 = 8640$ time slots during this month, and the initial budget for each time slot is $B/8640$. If the budget of the previous time slot is not used up, the remained unused money can be added to current time slot. So we have: $b_t = B/8640 + Remainer_{t-1}$, where $b_t$ denotes the real budget in time slot $t$, and $Remainder_{t-1}$ denotes the remained unused budget from previous time slot $t-1$. Our budget is set to be 150$ per time slot. The following are the analysis of experiment results based on our scheduler.

In our experiment, we define **server slots** as the number of servers accumulated with time slots, such that we can quantify the usage of heterogenous servers in each data center over the whole period of time. Figure 4 show the server slots for each type of servers in the data centers. For each data center, it can be found that servers of Type2 is the used most, then Type1, Type3 and Type4. Type3 and Type4 are the most powerful servers among the four types, but used less compared with Type1 and Type2. The reason behind this is that Type3 and Type4 consumes high power. We define the Power Consumption per Request (PCR) as $P_{ij}/\mu_{ij}$, which is used to weigh how green the server is. We found that the higher PCR is, the greener this server is. In our simulation, Type2 and Type1 are the servers with high PCR. Although the service rates are low, these two types of servers consume lower power. Thus, it is still a good choice to dispatch requests to these two types of servers considering PCR.

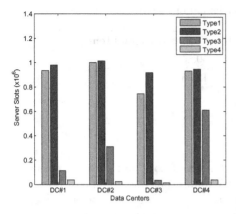

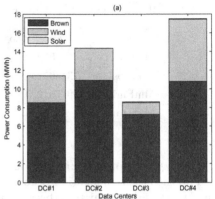

**Fig. 4.** Server slots of each type of servers in the data centers

**Fig. 5.** Different types of energy consumed in each data center using our scheduler

Figure 5 shows different types of energy consumed in each data center using our scheduler. Due to budget constraint, it can be seen that brown energy still accounts for a large part in all data centers due to its low price. And then the wind energy is used as much as possible, since it is cheap compared with solar energy. We find that solar energy is used little due to its highest price among the three types of energy. It is used only when budget of current time slot is sufficient and wind energy has been used up.

Figure 6 gives a comprehensive comparison of our method with the four baselines in brown energy used, carbon emission, and total cost. Let the values of brown energy, carbon emission and total cost of our scheduler be base with value 1. The values of other baselines are the ratios to our scheduler in brown energy used, carbon emission, and total cost. It can be seen that the ratios between the two groups of brown energy and carbon emissions are so similar. The reason lies in that carbon emission is mainly generated by brown energy, while renewable energy such as wind and solar emit little compared with brown energy. So, the carbon emission seems in proportion to brown energy used in this Figure. As can be seen, MinEmission Scheduling uses least brown energy so that it produces least carbon emissions, costing more money, about 8.2 times of base cost. MaxCost Scheduling uses as much expensive energy as possible, so that solar energy is used most, with 30.4 times of base cost. And its emission is very low. However, highest cost does not mean lowest carbon emissions, because there are some cheap renewable energy with lower carbon emissions like wind energy that should be considered with higher priority. For the MinCost Scheduling, energy with low price is considered first, so that brown energy is used most, and its carbon emission is very high. We are surprised to find that MinTransmission Scheduling has even higher carbon emissions than MinCost, but with higher cost. It is because MinTransmission Scheduling are more concerned with QoS, with the goal of minimizing transmission time, but at the expense of high

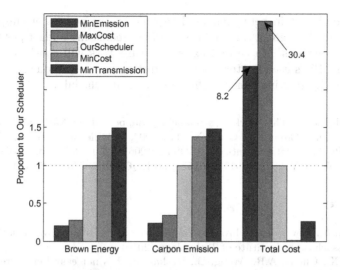

**Fig. 6.** Comparisons of five scheduling policies in brown energy, carbon emissions, and total cost with baselines

cost and emissions. This is not always true for MinTransmission Scheduling, because in this simulation, most of requests are dispatched to the data centers whose transmission time is smallest, but have very high electricity prices and less renewable energy provided. This is a special case, and the condition may differ when simulation parameters change.

From our experiments, we find that wind is currently the most ideal renewable energy with low emission as well as low price. The response time and budget also affect the final emission. In general, more budget means more renewable energy can be used for green scheduling. However, extra budget (like that of MaxCost) is not necessary when budget of the whole period is equal to the total cost of MinEmission. Experiments proved that our scheduler can minimize carbon emissions in consideration of budget for data centers with heterogenous servers. Therefore, it can be a good guide for real cloud data centers.

## 6    Conclusion

Cloud data centers are always consuming a large amount of power. Therefore, it is significant to make green scheduling using renewable energy. In this paper, we first build a green scheduling model for geographically distributed data centers with heterogenous servers. It must satisfy constrains such as budget per time slot, QoS, number of each type of servers in different data centers, the supply of intermittent renewable energy. We formulate the problem into a constraint optimization problem. The whole problem can be divided into separate sub-problems of the same type. We ingeniously transform each sub-problem into a mixed integer problem, and solved it using Cplex tools in Matlab. Experiments show our scheduler can minimize carbon emissions under a certain budget.

We also found that in heterogenous data centers, the power consumption per request reflects how green the server is. Besides, increasing budget per time slot can reduce emissions in a certain extend. Future work will consider electricity losses when UPS is used to store energy to further reduce carbon emissions, and tasks with strict starting time and finishing time in scheduling.

**Acknowledgment.** This work was financially supported by National Natural Science Foundation of China with Grant No. 11371004, and Shenzhen Strategic Emerging Industries Program with Grants No. ZDSY20120613125016389, No. JCYJ20120613 1512014-51, No. JCYJ20130329153215152, and KQCX20150326141251370.

# References

1. Qureshi, A.: Power-demand routing in massive geo-distributed systems. Ph.D. thesis, Massachusetts Institute of Technology (2010)
2. Gao, P.X., Curtis, A.R., Wong, B., Keshav, S.: It's not easy being green. ACM SIGCOMM Comput. Commun. Rev. **42**(4), 211–222 (2012)
3. Deng, W., Liu, F., Jin, H., Li, B., Li, D.: Harnessing renewable energy in cloud datacenters: opportunities and challenges. IEEE Netw. **28**(1), 48–55 (2014)
4. Chen, G., He, W., Liu, J., Nath, S., Rigas, L., Xiao, L., Zhao, F.: Energy-aware server provisioning and load dispatching for connection-intensive internet services. NSDI. **8**, 337–350 (2008)
5. Chase, J.S., Anderson, D.C., Thakar, P.N., Vahdat, A.M., Doyle, R.P.: Managing energy and server resources in hosting centers. ACM SIGOPS Oper. Syst. Rev. **35**, 103–116 (2001)
6. Elnozahy, E.N.M., Kistler, J.J., Rajamony, R.: Energy-efficient server clusters. In: Falsafi, B., VijayKumar, T.N. (eds.) PACS 2002. LNCS, vol. 2325, pp. 179–197. Springer, Heidelberg (2003)
7. Qureshi, A., Weber, R., Balakrishnan, H., Guttag, J., Maggs, B.: Cutting the electric bill for internet-scale systems. ACM SIGCOMM Comput. Commun. Rev. **39**(4), 123–134 (2009)
8. Rao, L., Liu, X., Xie, L., Liu, W.: Minimizing electricity cost: optimization of distributed internet data centers in a multi-electricity-market environment. In: INFOCOM, 2010 Proceedings IEEE, IEEE (2010) 1–9
9. Zhang, Y., Wang, Y., Wang, X.: Capping the electricity cost of cloud-scale data centers with impacts on power markets. In: Proceedings of the 20th International Symposium on High Performance Distributed Computing, pp. 271–272. ACM (2011)
10. Lin, M., Wierman, A., Andrew, L.L., Thereska, E.: Dynamic right-sizing for power-proportional data centers. IEEE/ACM Trans. Netw. (TON) **21**(5), 1378–1391 (2013)
11. Le, K., Bianchini, R., Martonosi, M.: Nguyen, T.D.: Cost-and energy-aware load distribution across data centers. In: Proceedings of HotPower, pp. 1–5 (2009)
12. Le, K., Bilgir, O., Bianchini, R., Martonosi, M., Nguyen, T.D.: Managing the cost, energy consumption, and carbon footprint of internet services. ACM SIGMETRICS Perform. Eval. Rev. **38**, 357–358 (2010)
13. Liu, Z., Lin, M., Wierman, A., Low, S.H., Andrew, L.L.: Greening geographical load balancing. In: Proceedings of the ACM SIGMETRICS Joint International Conference on Measurement and Modeling of Computer Systems, pp. 233–244. ACM (2011)

14. Brown, M., Renau, J.: Rerack: Power simulation for data centers with renewable energy generation. ACM SIGMETRICS Perform. Eval. Rev. **39**(3), 77–81 (2011)
15. Stewart, C., Shen, K.: Some joules are more precious than others: managing renewable energy in the datacenter. In: Proceedings of the Workshop on Power Aware Computing and Systems (2009)
16. Li, C., Qouneh, A., Li, T.: Characterizing and analyzing renewable energy driven data centers. ACM SIGMETRICS Perform. Eval. Rev. **39**(1), 323–324 (2011)
17. Bianchini, R.: Leveraging renewable energy in data centers: present and future. In: Proceedings of the 21st International Symposium on High-Performance Parallel and Distributed Computing, pp. 135–136. ACM (2012)
18. Goiri, Í., Le, K., Nguyen, T.D., Guitart, J., Torres, J., Bianchini, R.: Greenhadoop: leveraging green energy in data-processing frameworks. In: Proceedings of the 7th ACM European Conference on Computer Systems, pp. 57–70. ACM (2012)
19. Goiri, Í., Beauchea, R., Le, K., Nguyen, T.D., Haque, M.E., Guitart, J., Torres, J., Bianchini, R.: Greenslot: scheduling energy consumption in green datacenters. In: Proceedings of 2011 International Conference for High Performance Computing, Networking, Storage and Analysis, vol. 20. ACM (2011)
20. Liu, Z., Lin, M., Wierman, A., Low, S.H., Andrew, L.L.: Geographical load balancing with renewables. ACM SIGMETRICS Perform. Eval. Rev. **39**, 62–66 (2011)
21. Zhang, Y., Wang, Y., Wang, X.: GreenWare: greening cloud-scale data centers to maximize the use of renewable energy. In: Kon, F., Kermarrec, A.-M. (eds.) Middleware 2011. LNCS, vol. 7049, pp. 143–164. Springer, Heidelberg (2011)
22. Chonglin, G., Chunyan, L., Jiangtao, Z., Hejiao, H., Jia, X.: Green scheduling for cloud data centers using renewable resources. In: IEEE INFOCOM 2015 Workshop on Mobile Cloud and Virtualization (MCV 2015), pp. 132–137. IEEE (2015)
23. Ren, C., Wang, D., Urgaonkar, B., Sivasubramaniam, A.: Carbon-aware energy capacity planning for datacenters. In: 2012 IEEE 20th International Symposium on Modeling, Analysis & Simulation of Computer and Telecommunication Systems (MASCOTS), pp. 391–400. IEEE (2012)
24. Li, J., Li, Z., Ren, K., Liu, X.: Towards optimal electric demand management for internet data centers. IEEE Trans. Smart Grid **3**(1), 183–192 (2012)
25. Measurement and Instrumentation data center. http://www.nrel.gov/midc. Accessed 2015
26. Sera, D., Teodorescu, R., Rodriguez, P.: Pv panel model based on datasheet values. In: IEEE International Symposium on Industrial Electronics, ISIE 2007, pp. 2392–2396. IEEE (2007)
27. Ding, J., Radhakrishnan, R.: A new method to determine the optimum load of a real solar cell using the lambertw-function. Solar Eng. Mater. Solar Cells **92**(12), 1566–1569 (2008)
28. WindPower Program. http://www.wind-power-program.com/index.htm. Accessed 2015
29. Wiki Dump Data. http://dumps.wikimedia.org/other/pagecounts-raw/. Accessed 2015

# Fine-Grained Fault-Tolerant Adaptive Routing for Networks-on-Chip

Junxiu Liu[1(✉)], Jim Harkin[1], Liam Maguire[1], Yuhua Li[2], Lei Wan[3], and Yuling Luo[3]

[1] School of Computing and Intelligent Systems,
University of Ulster, Derry BT48 7JL, UK
{liu-j4,jg.harkin,lp.maguire}@ulster.ac.uk
[2] School of Computing Science and Engineering,
University of Salford, Manchester M5 4WT, UK
y.li@salford.ac.uk
[3] Guangxi Key Lab of Multi-Source Information Mining & Security,
Faculty of Electronic Engineering, Guangxi Normal University,
Guilin 541004, China
vanley_lei@139.com, yuling0616@mailbox.gxnu.edu.cn

**Abstract.** Due to the increase of physical defects in advanced manufacturing processes, Networks-on-Chip (NoC) system reliability is a critical challenge as faults often occur post manufacturing. Therefore it is important to add fault tolerance to the NoC system. In this paper, a novel routing algorithm for 2D mesh NoCs is proposed which aims to enhance the fault-tolerant capabilities via a look-ahead function. A traffic status informing mechanism is developed to provide information to local NoC routers on the interconnect conditions in far distant routers. In addition, a weighted path mechanism is used to forward the packets. The routing algorithm is implemented and verified on FPGA hardware. Real-time throughput and traffic information were collected by a monitoring unit on the FPGA. Results show that the proposed routing algorithm can maintain the system function under low fault rates and only has a marginal (∼5 %) throughput degradation under high fault rate of 20 %. The router area is also relatively low which demonstrated its scalability.

**Keywords:** NoC · Fault-tolerant · Adaptive routing · FPGA · Look-ahead

## 1 Introduction

NoC is an efficient interconnection strategy for various applications such as brain-inspired computing [1, 2], multicore systems [3]. Research undertaken in [4] showed that fault tolerance is especially crucial for NoC. Adaptive routing algorithms are widely investigated in order to enhance the fault-tolerant capabilities of NoC systems [5]. Several key challenges and capabilities need to be investigated and achieved as follows: (a) To tolerate faults and to proceed in retaining system functionality in the event of a physical impairment; (b) To make routing decisions under complex traffic conditions. The traffic condition of an entire NoC system, a region, or even just a node, cannot be classed as a single and simple condition, it's more complex

© Springer International Publishing Switzerland 2015
G. Wang et al. (Eds.): ICA3PP 2015, Part IV, LNCS 9531, pp. 492–505, 2015.
DOI: 10.1007/978-3-319-27140-8_34

as the condition depends on a combination of different traffic statuses across many paths. An adaptive routing algorithm should consider all the different types of traffic statuses and make routing decisions based on these conditions in order to balance the traffic workloads effectively across the entire NoC; and (c) To obtain sufficient knowledge of the traffic information in the neighbouring regions and to make the optimal routing decisions under various fault rates, avoid traffic starvation or overhead and balance traffic loads across the NoC. The interconnect fault distribution problem was summarized in [6]. In most of these fault patterns, the faulty interconnect are clustered which requires the routing algorithm to have the capability to gauge the interconnect condition in advance by looking ahead in each channel path and make routing decisions in advance of packets arriving so as to avoid entering a faulty region. Therefore, in this paper, a novel adaptive fault tolerant routing algorithm with fine-grained look-ahead function, namely FG routing algorithm, is proposed. It addresses the aforementioned challenges and investigates routing strategies that can select the fault-free and minimal congested paths to route packets, reduce the overall latency of packets and maintain the throughput performance of the NoC systems when faults occur.

## 2    Previous Works

A fault-tolerant routing algorithm was proposed in [7] where detected faulty routers are deactivated, and the routing algorithm is modified according to the change of topology. It is only tolerant of faulty routers (node). The Gradient routing scheme [8] models the NoC across eight different zones. Routing directions are then established according to the zone where the destination node is located. EDXY routing algorithm [9] used two dedicated wires per channel of the router to indicate the congestion status in the same row or column as the current router. Its weakness is the potential for traffic starvation and loss of traffic balance, as the congested flag does not provide positional information regarding the congested node. FADyAD routing algorithm [10] combines the advantages of both deterministic and adaptive routing schemes, but it only tolerates immediate connected link faults. Most of the aforementioned routing algorithms make routing decisions based solely on the immediate channel traffic conditions, i.e. they are routing algorithms with only local-awareness. They do not have global knowledge of the link status in the distant regions of the NoC; therefore the routing decisions are non-optimal which may cause traffic starvation and traffic overload for other regions of the NoC system. A fault-on-neighbour aware deflection routing algorithm makes routing decisions to avoid faulty links and routers based on the link conditions within a 2-hop range or region [6]. FTDR used a routing table to store the distance for every direction between the current and destination nodes [11]. The routing table is updated if the link status changes. The current node can choose a fault-free path to forward the packets. The main limitation of [6, 11] is that a faulty link has to be shut down in both directions. Similar to [11], routing algorithms in [12–14] also used a routing table to make routing decisions where the table was updated when a node or link was faulty. The routing table prohibits these approaches in facilitating large NoC implementations, i.e. scalability. In [15], a fault-tolerant routing algorithm was proposed where it uses a hierarchical model to route the packets. If the links or nodes are faulty, an echo model is activated which can choose a valid path for routing. It employs a node stamping mechanism which adds the router IDs to the packets while transmitting through them. It increases the packet size linearly and can cause NoC traffic overload, especially for long distance communications. LAFT routing algorithm receives the fault status from the immediate neighbouring nodes and selects the routing path based on this information [16]. If there are several candidates, the path with minimum distance and large diversity will be chosen. However, the node with a large path diversity is probably busy or faulty and not suitable for forwarding the packets. Current adaptive routing algorithms do not meet the required characteristics to provide an efficient routing strategy for modern NoC. In this paper, the FG routing algorithm is proposed which aims to enhance the fault-tolerant capabilities via fine-grained look-ahead capability with a relatively low area overhead.

## 3    Fine-Grained Routing Algorithm

In this section, the traffic status and link condition informing mechanism of FG routing algorithm are presented firstly; then the FG routing algorithm is discussed in detail. In addition, the deadlock and livelock avoidance techniques are also given.

### 3.1    Traffic Status and Link Condition Informing Mechanism

In the FG router, a traffic status and link condition informing mechanism is proposed to provide regional traffic data. The data includes the immediate connected link traffic statuses and the link conditions several hops away in each coordinate direction.

(1)  *Traffic Statuses of Immediate Connected Link.* The number of free slots ($F_s$) in the input FIFO of the receiver (RX) side reflects the channel traffic status. When the input FIFO is empty or less than half-full, the channel is termed as *Idle*. If the FIFO is half-full, or more than half-full and less than full, the channel is *Busy*. If the FIFO is full, it is defined as *Congested*. Two dedicated traffic status signals of *Busy* and *Congested* are connected from the RX side to the transmitter side [17]. These traffic statuses aid the NoC router in making effective routing decisions that improves throughput during busy traffic periods in the network.

(2)  *Link Conditions of Neighbouring Nodes.* Besides the traffic signals of *Idle/Busy/Congested*, another dedicated '*Faulty*' signal is provided by the monitor module in our previous work [17]. If it is high, the channel under test is classed as faulty. In this paper, this fault flag signal is encoded to provide a 'fault flag code'. The fault flag coding and decoding modules aim to enhance the router with the capability of sensing the traffic information of the links beyond a nearest neighbour, i.e. several hops away. All the signals connected to the fault flag encoding and decoding modules are labelled with a fault flag code presented in the Fig. 1(a). In total there are 12 different fault flag codes which are named according to the directions shown by Fig. 1(b). Figure 1(c) is a 9 × 9 2D-mesh NoC. There are 36 links labelled numerally from link #0 (L0) up to link #35 (L35) where the

condition of several links are represented by a fault flag code. The corresponding links of a fault flag code are ranked by the priority. The link which is closest to the current node is defined as #1 link and the furthest link is defined as #3, e.g. in Fig. 1(c), corresponding links (#1-#3) of URL for current node (5,5) are L8, L7, L6. Similar to the *Busy/Congested* signals, the fault flag code is also represented by dedicated signals, which are connected to the decoding module of each router.

Fault flag code is a 2-bit data. The coding process is given as follows. If all the links are fault-free, the fault flag code is '00'. If #1 link is faulty, the fault flag code is '01'. In this scenario, the conditions of #2 and #3 links are not important as #1 link is the closest link to the current node which has the highest priority. Similarly, the fault flag code is '10' if the #1 link is fault-free, #2 link is faulty and the condition of #3 is not important. If the links of #1, #2 are fault-free and #3 link is faulty, the fault flag code is '11'. Decoding is the reverse of the coding process. After the current node receives a fault flag code, the conditions for corresponding #1 – #3 links are decoded. Therefore, after receiving the 12 fault flag codes, the current node has knowledge of all the link conditions of L0–L35 (green links in Fig. 1(c)) which provides key visibility of the fault-status in the region and aids in making routing decisions.

The connecting combinations of L0–L35 are defined as a *Regional Communication Path* (RCP). Figure 1(c) shows all the RCPs in the solid red or dash blue colours, e.g. ranging from *rcp*[0] to *rcp* [19], within a bounding region. RCPs are combined by the links along the path, e.g. *rcp[0]* includes L13, L9, L10, L11; the same rules are applied to other RCPs. This bounding region is a sliding window as the flit is transmitted from node to node on its destination journey. The RCPs include *rcp[0-9]* on the x-axis and *rcp [10-19]* on the y-axis. They are divided into two categories according to the RCP length; namely, *Side RCP* which has one or two turns (e.g. rcp[0], rcp [1]) and *Middle RCP* which is straight (e.g. rcp[4]).

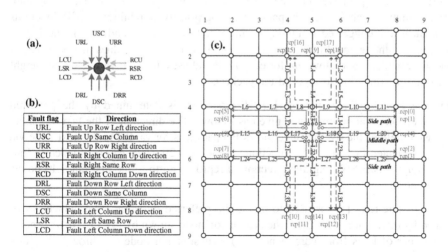

**Fig. 1.** Fault flag coding mechanism

When the router receives a packet, it needs to know the length of *RCP[i]*, i.e. *rcp_len[i]*. The *rcp_len[i]* is determined by the relative position of the destination node, where $1 \leq rcp\_len[i] \leq 4$. However, *rcp_len* varies according to the positions of current and destination nodes. The *rcp_len* are initialized to 4 for side RCPs and 3 for middle RCPs. For the *rcp[0-4]*, if the current node is on the right border, *rcp_len[0-4]* are equal to 1; if the current node is one hop away to the right border or the destination node, *rcp_len[0-3]* are equal to 2 and *rcp_len[4]* is equal to 1; if the current node is two hops away to the right border or the destination node, *rcp_len[0-3]* are equal to 3 and *rcp_len[4]* is equal to 2. For all other scenarios, i.e. the current node is three or more hops away to the border or the destination node, *rcp_len[0-3]* are equal to an initial value 4 and *rcp_len[4]* is equal to an initial value of 3. A similar path length calculation process is applied to the *rcp[5-19]*.

The *rcp_len* provides the information of the number of links contained in a specific path when a current node attempts to transmit packets to a destination node. The RCP is different from the Complete Communication Path (CCP), where CCP specifies the complete path between source and destination nodes. The length of an RCP, *rcp_len*, is defined by the number of hops. It can be smaller, equal or greater than the length of CCP, *ccp_len*. If $rcp\_len \geq ccp\_len$, the destination node is inside or on the edge of the cross-shape region; if $rcp\_len < ccp\_len$, the destination node is outside of the cross-shape region. When $rcp\_len \geq ccp\_len$, the FG algorithm can always find the optimal direction to forward the packets. When $rcp\_len < ccp\_len$, the packets are forwarded through an optimal path toward the destination; however, the status-known region is a sliding window and the destination node will be in this region eventually.

## 3.2   Fine-Grained Routing Algorithm

After the FG router receives the regional traffic information, it gets an idea about the environment, and based on this traffic status it makes routing decisions. The FG algorithm uses a path weight function to measure the quality of the path. The path weight function includes several parameters: the priority weighting of RCP directions ($w_p$), Busy and congested weighting of immediate link ($w_{lk1b}$ and $w_{lk1c}$), and Faulty weighting of the regional links ($w_f$). Based on these parameter values, the path weight function calculates a total weight for each RCP and uses the RCP with a lowest weight as an optimal direction to forward the packets.

(1) *The Priority Weighting of RCP directions.* It is determined by the preferred direction definition which is given as follows: The direction of the first link in an RCP defines the overall direction as the packet is forwarded to the next node via the selected first link. The directions of the total 20 RCPs can be divided to four groups – N/E/S/W, e.g. the direction of rcp[0] is north as the first link L13 points to north.

A Q-value term [11] is used to define the preferred direction level, which is calculated by the number of hops to the destination node shown by (1). $Q_{dir}^c(d, n)$ denotes the number of hops from current node (c) to destination node (d) through direction (dir) and neighbouring node (n). It is a deterministic value which is equal to one hop plus the minimum number of hops from node $n$ to $d$ over all directions ($minQ^n(d,o)$). Note that among all the directions of node $n$, the direction has the minimum number of hops from $n$ to $d$ as defined as $o$.

$$Q_{dir}^C(d,n) = 1 + minQ^n(d,o) \tag{1}$$

When a router forwards packets, the destination node can be one of 8 directions denoted by D1–D8 (from east to south east) shown in the top half of Fig. 2. In the case where the coordinates of the destination node is equal to the current node, this indicates that the packet has arrived at its destination and should be forwarded to the local port. When the destination node is located in D1-D8, it can be classed as type (1) diagonal position (i.e. in D2, D4, D6, D8 directions) or (2) direct position (i.e. in D1, D3, D5, D7). For each type, one example is provided to illustrate the concept of the preferred direction definition. The preferred direction is defined as the direction which the current node should choose preferably to forward a packet to its destination. The bottom left of Fig. 2 presents the examples where the destination node is (4, 9) in the *diagonal position* relative to the current node (2,7). Based on (1), the following can be calculated: $Q_{East}^{(2,7)}((4,9),(3,7)) = 4$, $Q_{South}^{(2,7)}((4,9),(2,8)) = 4$, $Q_{West}^{(2,7)}((4,9),(1,7)) = 6$ and $Q_{North}^{(2,7)}((4,9),(2,6)) = 6$. Therefore, the east is defined as Preferred Direction 1 (PD1), south as Preferred Direction 2 (PD2) and west and north directions are both defined as Preferred Direction 3 (PD3). The levels are set in this ranking as the Q-values of the E and S directions are smaller than W/N. The east port is defined as a higher level than the south port as the FG algorithm gives the x-dimension priority to forward the packets. The bottom right of Fig. 2 illustrates the Q-levels when the destination node is in the *direct position*. Note, in this example N and S are assigned the same level (PD2) as both have the same Q-value (i.e. 5) to the destination node.

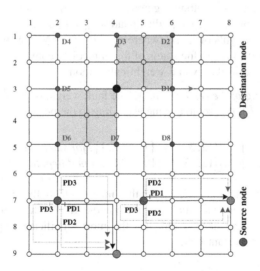

**Fig. 2.** Relative directions between source node and destination node (top half) and different preferred port definition (bottom half)

The symbol $w_p[rcp\_dir[i]]$ denotes the direction priority weighting of $rcp[i]$, where the $rcp\_dir[i]$ is the direction of first link in the $rcp[i]$. It is determined by the preferred direction level. If the direction of $rcp[i]$ is a PD1 direction, the $w_p$ is equal to 1; if it is a PD2 direction, $w_p = 2$; if it is a PD3 direction, $w_p = 3$. For example, in Fig. 1(c) the current and destination nodes are (5,5) and (8,5); then the destination node is in the D1 direction (according to the top half of Fig. 2) and $w_p[N] = \{2\}, w_p[E] = \{1\}, w_p[S] = w_p[W] = \{3\}$. The priority weight of rcp[5] is equal to $w_p[N]$, i.e. 2. It is a second preferred path to transmit packets as the east direction is the first choice. Therefore, ideally a lower priority weight value is sought and the direction with the lowest value is selected as the preferred direction to route the packets from the current node.

(2) *Busy and Congested Weighting of Immediate Link.* Every node has the knowledge of the traffic statuses of the first links (neighbours) via dedicated *Busy/Congested* input signals which are generated based on the FIFO occupancy of neighbouring nodes. The notation of $s_b$ and $s_c$ is used to denote the *Busy* and *Congested* status of the first link. If the status of the link is busy then $s_b = 1$ and if the link is congested $s_c = 1$. If the link is not busy or congested then $s_b = s_c = 0$. The busy and congested statuses determine two corresponding weights, $w_{lk1b}$ and $w_{lk1c}$. The weight values of $w_{lk1b}$ and $w_{lk1c}$ can be calculated using (2). It can be seen that the weight $w_{lk1c}$ is given precedence (i.e. $w_{lk1c} > w_{lk1b}$ when $s_b = 1, s_c = 1$) as the channel status of *Congested* has the more significant performance impact on a channel over *Busy*.

$$w_{lk1b} = \begin{cases} 0, s_b = 0 \\ 2, s_b = 1 \end{cases}, w_{lk1c} = \begin{cases} 0, s_c = 0 \\ 3, s_c = 1 \end{cases} \tag{2}$$

Each node connects to neighbouring nodes via four immediate links at the N/E/S/W directions. The notations of $w_{lk1b}[rcp\_dir[i]]$ and $w_{lk1c}[rcp\_dir[i]]$ are used to denote the busy and congested weights of $rcp[i]$, where $rcp\_dir[i] \in \{N, E, S, W\}$. The weighting of $w_{lk1b}$ and $w_{lk1c}$ reflect the traffic status of the immediate connected links of a current node and will be used in the overall weight calculation.

(3) *Faulty weighting of the regional links.* The fault weight of the $j^{th}$ link in the rcp[i] is defined as $w_f[j]$. It is set to a value according to the position as expressed by (3),

$$\begin{cases} w_f[1, 2, 3, 4] = \{10, 2, 2, 1\}, \textit{for sidepath} \\ w_f[1, 2, 3] = \{10, 4, 1\}, \textit{for middlepath} \end{cases} \tag{3}$$

where $w_f[j]$ is set to be $\{10, 2, 2, 1\}$ for the links sequentially in the side RCP, and $\{10, 4, 1\}$ for the links sequentially in the middle RCP. The weights are set in a decreased manner as the nearest link has the most significant impact for the path selection over a more distant link.

(4) *Total weight of the direction.* Equation (4) illustrates the weight of *rcp[i]* calculation process for the FG routing algorithm,

$$W[i] = w_p[\text{rcp\_dir}[i]] + w_{lk1b}[\text{rcp\_dir}[i]] + w_{lk1c}[\text{rcp\_dir}[i]] + \sum_{j=1}^{rcp\_len[i]} w_f[j] \quad (4)$$

where $0 \le i < 20$, $W[i]$ is the total weight for *rcp[i]*, *rcp_dir[i]* is the direction of the first link in the *rcp[i]*, $w_p[\text{rcp\_dir}[i]]$ is the direction priority of the *rcp[i]*, $w_{lk1b}[\text{rcp\_dir}[i]]$ and $w_{lk1c}[\text{rcp\_dir}[i]]$ are the busy and congested weights of *rcp[i]*, and $w_f[j]$ is the fault weight of the $j^{th}$ link in the *rcp[i]* which is accumulated from 1 to the RCP length.

The FG routing algorithm weights each of the links in a RCP to differentiate between faulty and non-faulty links. It calculates the weights for all 20 RCPs and selects the RCP with the lowest weight as the output path to forward the packets. For complex fault patterns, it has the analysis capability to look ahead in more detail (finer levels within a path) to make better routing decisions. This ultimately can reduce communication latency of packets and improve system performance.

### 3.3   Deadlock and Livelock Avoidance

The FG router architecture is similar to a 5-stage NoC router architecture where the technique of VC is employed to avoid deadlock. The VCs are used to temporarily store the packets which cannot be forwarded on time; the packets that requesting the same output port from different inputs can share the output physical channel based on the time multiplexing division; and the adaptive arbitration policy (AAP) module in our previous work [2] is employed to decide the arbitrations of VCs requesting the same physical channel. Using this mechanism, all the packet can arrive at the destinations eventually without deadlock occurring.

For the livelock avoidance, the FG algorithm imposes the restriction that data packets from any given direction cannot return on the same direction. The FG algorithm is livelock free when the path is fault-free and not congested. If congestion occurs, for most cases, the path delay is a little longer but it does not introduce livelock. For extreme scenarios, e.g. the congested links build up a circle, due to the AAP module [2] that combines the fairness policy of a round-robin arbiter and a first-come first-served priority scheme, the access to the busy channel can be granted regularly; therefore the livelock is avoided. If the NoC system has faulty channels, the livelock avoidance is restricted for some fault patterns, e.g. for convex faulty regions and the concave faulty regions within a depth of 3 router hops, the packets can avoid livelock. To avoid livelock with other concave faulty regions (e.g. larger than 3 hops depth) or serious scenarios, a re-routing constraint mechanism [18] can be employed. It is an efficient solution by adding a *state* component to the router. After adding a *state* component, the router has two parts of traffic information – one is the traffic information of the observed region from the sensor and the other is the additional knowledge of the unobserved region which is deduced by the *state* component. If the re-routing number of a packet is beyond the threshold number, the *state* component can deduce that this packet has fallen into a region with a complex fault pattern where the sensor cannot completely observe the traffic conditions, and a livelock probably occurs; then this packet is discarded. Therefore, the re-routing constraint mechanism based on *state* component can be used to avoid livelock for the serious scenarios.

## 4    Hardware Verification and Evaluation

### 4.1    Hardware Verification of FG

The FG routing algorithm is validated on the FPGA hardware platform in real-time. The open-source monitor tool in our previous work [19] is employed to evaluate the performances under different fault rates. The NoC system is implemented in the FPGA device and the traffic data is acquired in real time and uploaded to the monitor software; the monitor software quantitatively analyses the NoC system's fault-tolerant capability by calculating throughput, the number of lost/corrupted packets calculation and the generation of traffic heat maps for visualisation.

An $8 \times 8$ 2D-mesh NoC system is implemented. The NoC system implements the matrix multiplication application which is one of the most common numerical operations used in many applications, e.g. engineering and image processing. The detail about matrix multiplication can be found in [20]. It calculates the multiplication product of two matrices, A and B, resulting in a matrix C. Average throughput, the number of lost packets and throughput degradation are used as the performance analysis metrics. Each NoC router has four ports to connect neighbouring nodes and a local port to connect the local processing element. For a given window time of $N$ clock cycles, the router throughput, $T$, can be calculated by (5), where $\sum R = R_N + R_E + R_s + R_w + R_L$, i.e. the number of received packets through North/East/South/West/Local ports.

$$T = \frac{\sum R}{N} \tag{5}$$

Average throughput is defined by (6), where the $T_{avg}$ is the average throughput, $T(i,j)$ is the throughput of router $(i,j)$, $DIM_x$ and $DIM_y$ are the size of NoC system in x and y dimension.

$$T_{avg} = \sum_{i=1}^{DIM_x} \sum_{j=1}^{DIM_y} T(i,j)/(DIM_x * DIM_y) \tag{6}$$

The throughput degradation, $T_d$, is defines by (7) where $T_h$ is the throughput when all the channels are healthy, and $T_f$ is the throughput when channels are faulty. The number of lost packets is equal to the number of received packets while no fault occurs, minus the number of received packets when faults occur.

$$T_d = (T_h - T_f)/T_h \tag{7}$$

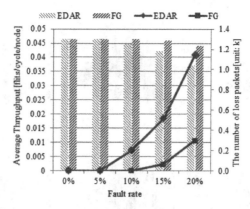

**Fig. 3.** Average throughput (bars) and the number of lost packets (lines) of the EDAR and FG router under various fault rates

Figure 3 gives the experimental results of average throughput and the number of lost packets under variable fault rates. The EDAR router with local fault-tolerant capability in our previous work [21] is chosen as the benchmark. When the fault rate is low (e.g. 5 %), both the EDAR and FG routers maintain the system performance and don't have throughput degradation. When the fault rate increases, they loss packets but with different rates – the FG router loses fewer. When the fault rate is high at 20 %, the EDAR and FG routers have 20 % and 5 % throughput degradation, respectively. In Fig. 3, it can be seen the FG router achieves better throughput performance than the EDAR router with increased fault rates.

Using the monitor tool, we can also plot the throughput of the NoC systems as a distribution across the 2D NoC, e.g. 3D-columns. Figure 4 depicts the distribution with fault rates of 5 %, 15 % and 20 %. When the fault rate is 5 %, the EDAR and FG routers have very similar throughput distributions. Because of the matrix multiplication traffic pattern and great path diversity in the middle region, the traffic load in the middle is heavier, i.e. the throughput in the middle region is higher than the edges. However, when the fault rate is 15 % or 20 %, their throughput distributions are different. In contrast, when the fault rate is 15 % as shown in Fig. 4(c and d), the throughput distributions change. For example, as the fault rate increases and the number of fault-free channels decreases, these fault-free channels undertake more traffic; therefore the number of channels with heavy traffic is increased. Overall, the maximum throughput of the FG router is much higher than the EDAR router, as it has the capability to use the limited healthy channels to transmit more packets which permits the system performance to be more attainable. Figure 4(e) and (f) shows these channels to have a higher throughput, e.g. the coloured rows of orange and green in (f) shows a more even distribution than the EDAR in (e). When the fault rate is 20 %, due to the fine grained look-ahead function, the FG algorithm has more distributed channels which are used than the EDAR router; therefore it has a lower throughput degradation as more packets are transmitted across the larger number of visible paths.

In this subsection, we evaluated the throughput performance and traffic load balance of the EDAR and FG routing algorithms based on a real application. The throughput

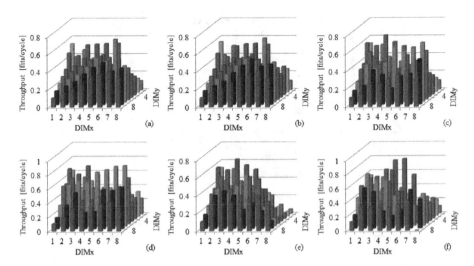

**Fig. 4.** Throughputs of EDAR/FG routers under fault rates of 5 % (a/b), 15 % (c/d) and 20 % (e/f). Colour code represents each row of the 8 × 8 NoC.

display in 3D-column demonstrated that the FG achieves a better fault-tolerant capability than the EDAR router due to the look-ahead functions, i.e. it has a lower throughput degradation and a better traffic load balance capability under high fault rates. In the next subsection, we will continue to evaluate the EDAR and FG routing algorithms by considering the area overhead and power consumption. The relationship between the performance and cost will be further explored.

## 4.2    Hardware Evaluation

The hardware evaluation process followed an FPGA design flow based on the Stratix IV EP4SGX530KH40C2 using Quartus II software. Altera's PowerPlay Power Analysis tool was used to analyse power dissipation. The NoC systems with EDAR and FG routing algorithms were designed; the toggle rate of data was derived sufficiently from the Value Change Dump (.vcd) file which represents the system operation at gate level; this aids estimating the power analysis in high level confidence.

Table 1 gives the resource utilization and power consumption of one router with the EDAR and FG routing algorithms. Resource utilization includes combinational ALUTS, dedicated logic registers and number of input/output signals; power consumption includes static power dissipation. For the combinational ALUTs, the FG router requires more than the EDAR router due to the additional look-ahead capability however for dedicated logic registers, the FG is a less than the EDAR. The number of input and output signals is the number of required signals of the router for the connection and communication with processing element and other routers, where these signals include clock, reset, router address, channels and traffic status flag (e.g. B/C/F of EDAR router, fault flag of FG router etc.). The number of input/output signals is 366 for the EDAR router, 406 for FG routers. The FG router requires additional 10 fault

**Table 1.** Resource utilization and power consumption of one router with EDAR [21] and FG routing algorithm

| Resource utilization and Power consumption | EDAR | FG |
|---|---|---|
| Combinational ALUTs | 2,696 | 3,932 |
| Dedicated Logic Registers | 4,190 | 4,142 |
| Number of Input/Output signals | 366 | 406 |
| Dynamic Power Dissipation (mW) | 47.05 | 72.31 |

**Table 2.** Area overhead comparison of adaptive routing scheme

| The approach | Fault detection | Router capability | | | Area overhead ($\mu m^2$) | |
|---|---|---|---|---|---|---|
| | | Congestion aware | Fault tolerant | Router | Router | Device technology |
| [22] | ✗ | ✓ | ✗ | | 56,000 | 90 nm CMOS |
| [17] | ✓ | ✓ | ✗ | | 182,076 | SAED 90 nm |
| EDAR [21] | ✓ | ✓ | ✓ | | 241,132 | SAED 90 nm |
| FG | ✓ | ✓ | ✓ | | 342,172 | SAED 90 nm |

flag signals per direction; therefore in total an additional 40 signals are required. For the power consumption, the dynamic power dissipation of the FG router is 72.31 mW, whereas the EDAR router is 47.05 mW. It can be seen that the EDAR and FG routers vary in values on the metrics of combinational ALUTs, number of input/output signals and dynamic power dissipation. These metrics mainly reflect the hardware overhead and power consumption of the router. The FG router has a larger resource utilization than the EDAR; however, FG has a significant fault-tolerant capability over the EDAR as demonstrated in the previous sections.

The implementation approach also followed the standard ASIC cell design flow, synthesis and verification based on a SAED 90 nm CMOS technology. Table 2 provides a comparison of the FG algorithm against existing benchmark adaptive routing schemes and illustrates the routing capabilities and router area. The approach in [22] provides congestion-aware adaptive routing however it does not provide a fault-tolerant capability, therefore the router area is relative low (56,000 $\mu m^2$). Based on [22], the router in [17] was extended with the monitor module to provide a level of fault detection capability which increased the area overhead (182,076 $\mu m^2$). However the routing algorithms in [22] and [17] are not fault-tolerant. The EDAR router [21] is able to detect interconnect faults and make routing decisions based on traffic status of the link with a router area of 241,132 $\mu m^2$. Although that the area overhead of the EDAR router is smaller, the FG router has an improved fault-tolerant capability, e.g. $\sim 15$ % throughput improvement at 20 % fault rate. In consideration of the added fault tolerance capability and improved throughput performance of the FG, the additional area overhead can be traded-off for higher reliability.

# 5 Conclusion

In this paper, a fault-tolerant routing algorithm with fine-grained look-ahead function was presented which improves the NoC throughput performance under high fault rates. It employs the fault status encoding/decoding mechanisms to transmit the channel conditions; then selects the fault-free direction or regional path with minimal congestion/faults to forward the packets. Hardware verification and validation procedures were given and a performance monitoring and analysing mechanism was employed to evaluate real-time performance of the proposed FG algorithm in hardware under a real application with various fault rates. The results demonstrated that the FG algorithm achieves a significant improvement in throughput, especially when high fault rates are present. The hardware overhead was presented and demonstrated scalability as a low area constraint was met for the algorithm.

**Acknowledgements.** This research was partially supported by the Guangxi Natural Science Foundation under Grant 2015GXNSFBA139256 and 2014GXNSFBA118271, the Research Project of Guangxi University of China under Grant ZD2014022, Guangxi Key Lab of Multi-source Information Mining & Security under Grant MIMS14-04, Guangxi Key Lab of Wireless Wideband Communication & Signal Processing under Grant GXKL0614205, the Education Development Foundation and the Doctoral Research Foundation of Guangxi Normal University, the State Scholarship Fund of China Scholarship Council under Grant [2014]3012.

# References

1. Furber, S.B., Lester, D.R., Plana, L.A., Garside, J.D., Painkras, E., Temple, S., Brown, A.D.: Overview of the SpiNNaker system architecture. IEEE Trans. Comput. **62**, 2454–2467 (2013)
2. Carrillo, S., Harkin, J., McDaid, L.J., Morgan, F., Pande, S., Cawley, S., McGinley, B.: Scalable hierarchical network-on-chip architecture for spiking neural network hardware implementations. IEEE Trans. Parallel Distrib. Syst. **24**, 2451–2461 (2013)
3. Abdelfattah, M.S., Betz, V.: The power of communication: energy-efficient NoCs for FPGAs. In: 23rd International Conference on Field Programmable Logic and Applications (FPL), pp. 1–8 (2013)
4. Agarwal, A., Raton, B., Iskander, C., Multisystems, H., Shankar, R.: Survey of network on chip (NoC) architectures & contributions. J. Eng. Comput. Architect. **3**, 1–15 (2009)
5. Duong, T.D., Kaneko, K.: Fault-tolerant routing based on approximate directed routable probabilities for hypercubes. In: Xiang, Y., Cuzzocrea, A., Hobbs, M., Zhou, W. (eds.) ICA3PP 2011, Part I. LNCS, vol. 7016, pp. 106–116. Springer, Heidelberg (2011)
6. Feng, C., Lu, Z., Jantsch, A., Jinwen, L., Zhang, M.: FON: Fault-on-neighbor aware routing algorithm for networks-on-chip. In: 23rd IEEE International SoC Conference, pp. 441–446 (2010)
7. Zhang, Z., Greiner, A., Taktak, S.: A reconfigurable routing algorithm for a fault-tolerant 2D-mesh network-on-chip. In: 45th IEEE/ACE Design Automation Conference, pp. 441–446 (2008)

8. Pratomo, I., Pillement, S.: Gradient - An adaptive fault-tolerant routing algorithm for 2D mesh Network-on-Chips. In: Design and Architectures for Signal and Image Processing (DASIP), pp. 1–8 (2012)
9. Lotfi-Kamran, P., Rahmani, A.M., Daneshtalab, M., Afzali-Kusha, A., Navabi, Z.: EDXY - A low cost congestion-aware routing algorithm for network-on-chips. J. Syst. Architect. **56**, 256–264 (2010)
10. Mehranzadeh, A., Khademzadeh, A., Mehran, A.: FADyAD- fault and congestion aware routing algorithm based on DyAD algorithm. In: 5th International Symposium on Telecommunications, pp. 274–279 (2010)
11. Feng, C., Lu, Z., Jantsch, A., Zhang, M., Xing, Z.: Addressing transient and permanent faults in NoC with efficient fault-tolerant deflection router. IEEE Trans. Very Large Scale Integr. VLSI Syst. **21**, 1053–1066 (2013)
12. Ali, M., Welzl, M., Hessler, S., Hellebrand, S.: A fault tolerant mechanism for handling permanent and transient failures in a network on chip. In: 4th International Conference on Information Technology, pp. 1027–1032 (2007)
13. Aisopos, K., DeOrio, A., Peh, L.-S., Bertacco, V.: ARIADNE: agnostic reconfiguration in a disconnected network environment. In: International Conference on Parallel Architectures and Compilation Techniques, pp. 298–309. IEEE (2011)
14. Parikh, R., Bertacco, V.: uDIREC: unified diagnosis and reconfiguration for frugal bypass of NoC faults. In: 46th Annual IEEE/ACM International Symposium on Microarchitecture, pp. 148–159 (2013)
15. Chaix, F., Avresky, D., Zergainoh, N.-E., Nicolaidis, M.: A fault-tolerant deadlock-free adaptive routing for on chip interconnects. In: Design, Automation & Test in Europe Conference & Exhibition (DATE), pp. 1–4 (2011)
16. Ahmed, A.B., Abdallah, A.B.: Graceful deadlock-free fault-tolerant routing algorithm for 3D network-on-chip architectures. J. Parallel Distrib. Comput. **74**, 2229–2240 (2014)
17. Liu, J., Harkin, J., Li, Y., Maguire, L.: Online traffic-aware fault detection for networks-on-chip. J. Parallel Distrib. Comput. **74**, 1984–1993 (2014)
18. Alhussien, A., Wang, C., Bagherzadeh, N.: Design and evaluation of a high throughput robust router for network-on-chip. IET Comput. Digit. Tech. **6**, 173–179 (2012)
19. Liu, J., Harkin, J., Li, Y., Maguire, L., Barranco, A.L.: Low overhead monitor mechanism for fault-tolerant analysis of NoC. In: IEEE 8th International Symposium on Embedded Multicore/Many-core Systems-on-Chip, pp. 189–196, Aizu-Wakamatsu, Japan (2014)
20. Chen, P., Dai, K., Wu, D., Rao, J., Zou, X.: The parallel algorithm implementation of matrix multiplication based on ESCA. In: 2010 IEEE Asia Pacific Conference on Circuits and Systems, pp. 1091–1094 (2010)
21. Liu, J., Harkin, J., Li, Y., Maguire, L.: Low cost fault-tolerant routing algorithm for networks-on-chip. Microprocess. Microsyst. **39**, 358–372 (2015)
22. Carrillo, S., Harkin, J., McDaid, L., Pande, S., Cawley, S., McGinley, B., Morgan, F.: Advancing interconnect density for spiking neural network hardware implementations using traffic-aware adaptive network-on-chip routers. Neural Netw. **33**, 42–57 (2012)

# On the Optimal Provider Selection for Repair in Distributed Storage System with Network Coding

Chengjin Jia[1], Jin Wang[1]([⊠]), Yanqin Zhu[1],
Xin Wang[2], Kejie Lu[3,4], Xiumin Wang[5], and Zhengqing Wen[1]

[1] Department of Computer Science and Technology,
Soochow University, Suzhou 215006, China
wjin1985@suda.edu.cn
[2] School of Computer Science, Fudan University, Shanghai 200433, China
[3] College of Computer Science and Technology,
Shanghai University of Electronic Power, Shanghai 200444, China
[4] Department of Electrical and Computer Engineering,
University of Puerto Rico at Mayagüez, Mayagüez 00681-9000, USA
[5] School of Computer and Information, Hefei University of Technology,
Hefei 230000, China

**Abstract.** In large-scale distributed storage systems (DSS), reliability is provided by redundancy spread over storage servers across the Internet. *Network coding* (NC) has been widely studied in DSS because it can improve the reliability with low repair time. To maintain reliability, an unavailable storage server should be firstly replaced by a new server, named *new comer*. Then, multiple storage servers, called *providers*, should be selected from surviving servers and send their coded data through the Internet to the new comer for regenerating the lost data. Therefore, in a large-scale DSS, provider selection and data routing during the regeneration phase have great impact on the performance of regeneration time. In this paper, we investigate a problem of optimal provider selection and data routing for minimizing the regeneration time in the DSS with NC. Specifically, we first define the problem in the DSS with NC. For the case that the providers are given, we model the problem as a mathematical programming. Based on the mathematical programming, we then formulate the optimal provider selection and data routing problem as an integer linear programming problem and develop an efficient near-optimal algorithm based on linear programming relaxation (BLP). Finally, extensive simulation experiments have been conducted, and the results show the effectiveness of the proposed algorithm.

**Keywords:** Network coding · Distributed storage system · Provider selection · Routing · Linear programming · LP relaxation

## 1 Introduction

With the rapid development of big data, the information explosion results in the rapid development of data storage. There are about 5 Exabytes independent

© Springer International Publishing Switzerland 2015
G. Wang et al. (Eds.): ICA3PP 2015, Part IV, LNCS 9531, pp. 506–520, 2015.
DOI: 10.1007/978-3-319-27140-8_35

information created in 2015 and 8.6 Zettabytes of data center traffic by 2018 [1]. Therefore, many large-scale DSSs, e.g., Google File System [2], Azure [3], are widely used for achieving high reliability by storing the data redundantly over multiple unreliable storage servers.

Reliability is one of the basic requirements for these DSSs that users can get data anywhere anytime. The traditional methods for providing reliability in DSSs include replication and Reed-Solomon codes [4]. In 2000, NC was proposed to increase the throughput of the network, balance network load and so on [5]. It has been proved distributed storage applications can achieve good benefits with NC [6]. When using NC, it keeps the MDS property of erasure code that the original file is divided into $k$ packets, then encoded into $n$ coded packets [7]. Users can recover the original file by any set of $k$ coded packets among $n$ coded packets. Therefore, more and more researchers pay attention on NC in DSS.

Although NC can improve storage reliability, the data of distributed storage systems is prone to be damaged, such as an outage of the server, invasion by the hackers, disk damaged. To keep the same level of reliability, when a server fails or leaves the system, a new server has to join the system and accesses existing servers to regenerate the lost data, which leads to repair bandwidth consumption and regeneration time. Based on the ideas of NC, the functional minimum storage regeneration (FMSR) codes have been proposed to minimize the repair bandwidth or regeneration time in DSS [8,9].

Although FMSR code can significantly minimize repair bandwidth, it cannot ensure that the regeneration time is minimized. In order to reduce the regeneration time, Li *et al.* proposed a tree-structured data regeneration in the heterogeneous network [10,11]. Most of current studies focus on obtaining data from multiple surviving servers to regenerate the lost data under the condition that the bandwidth of the path between each servers and the new comer is given. However, each link in physical network may be shared by multiple paths, which means the bandwidth of each link should be shared between different paths. Therefore, in practice, the bandwidth of the routing path from each selected server, i.e., provider, to the new comer may not be achieved.

Next, we introduce an example that shows the effect for regenerating the lost data by selecting a given number of servers as the providers and routing paths from the providers to the new comer. Figure 1(a) gives the original network topology and includes routers denoted as $R_j$ and storage servers denoted as $F_i$. In this example, each server $F_i$ stores different coded packets of the same file. When $F_4$ is unavailable, to keep the same level of reliability, a new server should be installed to replace $F_4$ and acquire data packets from multiple available storage servers to regenerate the lost data. Therefore, in this example, we also denote the new comer as $F_4$. We assume the number of providers is 3, which is denoted as $d$ in the rest of the paper and the size of the file is $M = 300\,Mb$. With the minimum-storage regenerating code [12,13], each server storages $\alpha = M/k = 150\,Mb$ data and $F_4$ needs to download $\beta = \alpha/(d - k + 1) = 75\,Mb$ data from each provider. The bandwidths of the links range from $30\,Mbps$ to $100\,Mbps$. As shown in Fig. 1(a), the maximum transmission rate from each storage server to

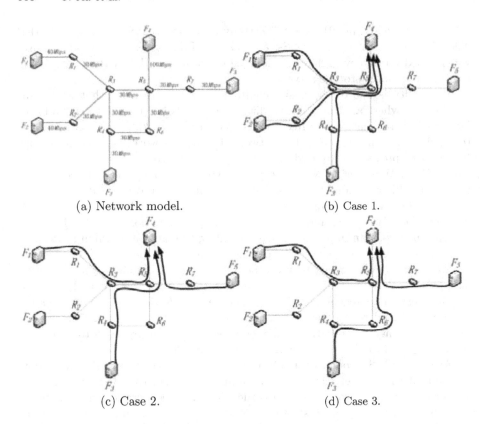

(a) Network model.    (b) Case 1.

(c) Case 2.    (d) Case 3.

**Fig. 1.** Examples for providers and routing paths selection.

$F_4$ is 30 *Mbps*. Figure 1(b), (c) and (d) respectively show different selections of the providers and routing paths. Next, we show different regeneration time of these three kinds of selections as follows:

In Fig. 1(b), $F_1$, $F_2$ and $F_3$ are selected as providers. Since all the routing paths pass through the link between $R_3$ and $R_5$. The bandwidth is only 30 *Mbps*. Therefore, the transmission rate can be achieved per provider is 10 *Mbps* and the regeneration time is $75/10 = 7.5$ s.

In Fig. 1(c), $F_1$, $F_3$ and $F_5$ are selected as providers. As shown in the figure, two routing paths pass through the link between $R_3$ and $R_5$. The transmission rates for $F_1$ and $F_3$ can be achieved are 15 *Mbps*. Although the maximum transmission rate of $F_5$ can be 30 *Mbps*, the regeneration time depends on the transmission time of $F_1$ and $F_3$ (15 *Mbps*). Therefore, the regeneration time is $75/15 = 5$ s.

In Fig. 1(d), $F_1$, $F_3$ and $F_5$ are also selected as providers. In this figure, different routing paths are selected. The transmission rates for $F_1$, $F_3$ and $F_5$ can be achieved are 30 *Mbps*, respectively. Therefore, the regeneration time is $75/30 = 2.5$ s.

The example above has well demonstrated that not only the selection of providers but also routing paths can significantly affect the regeneration time, which motivates the work of this paper. In this paper, we focus on selecting a given number of providers and deciding the routing paths from them to the new comer to minimize the regeneration time. The main contributions of this paper are summarized as follows.

- We define the providers and routing paths selection (PRPS) problem in the DSS with NC and model the problem as a mathematical programming.
- For the case that the providers are given, we model the PRPS problem as a linear programming. Based on the linear programming, we then formulate the optimal provider selection and data routing problem as an integer linear programming.
- We develop an efficient near-optimal algorithm based on linear programming relaxation (BLP).
- We conduct extensive simulation experiments and the results show the effectiveness of the proposed algorithm.

The rest of the paper is organized as follows: in Sect. 2, we introduce the related works. In Sect. 3, we show network model and notations. We propose a linear programming(LP) in Sect. 4 to calculate the optimal regeneration time when the selection of the providers is fixed. In Sect. 5, we formulate the optimal provider selection problem as a mixed integer linear programming (MILP) problem and develop an efficient near-optimal algorithm based on LP-relaxation (BLP). We conduct extensive simulation experiments in Sect. 6. Finally, we conclude the paper in Sect. 7.

## 2    Related Works

Hu *et al.* considered functional minimum storage regenerating (FMSR) codes, which achieved the minimum repair bandwidth [13]. However, in the practical network, minimizing the repair bandwidth does not mean to minimize the regeneration time. Based the heterogeneous network, Sun *et al.* proposed a tree-structure regeneration model to reduce the regeneration time, which can reduce significantly the regeneration time [14]. To further reduce the regeneration time, Wang *et al.* reconsidered how to solve the problem in the heterogeneous network [15].

In [19,20], Gong *et al.* studied the provider selection problem of DSS in overlay networks, which are represented as a complete graph, to minimize the regeneration time. Comparing with previous works shown in [19,20], the main differences of our paper is summarized as follows: Firstly, routing paths from each server to the new comer are not given and the general physical network topology is studied in this paper. Secondly, multiple routing paths can be utilized from each selected server, i.e., provider, which makes the transmission topology from the providers to the new comer may not be a tree. Thirdly, each link in the network can be used simultaneously by different flows from different providers and the bandwidth of the link can be shared between them. Moreover, the total bandwidth of each link is assigned to different flows based on the algorithm proposed in Sect. 5 instead of assigning the bandwidth equally to different flows. Finally, by considering the general physical network with heterogeneous bandwidth on each links, we jointly study the provider selection from survival servers, the routing path decision in physical network and the bandwidth assignment of each link together to optimize the regeneration time.

# 3    Problem Formulation

In this section, we mainly give the definitions of the problem studied in this work. Specifically, we firstly introduce the network model. We then introduce important parameters and variables to be used in the rest of this paper.

## 3.1    The Network Model

The network consists of routers and storage servers. We assume that each server is connected with a router[1]. Different links in the network may have different bandwidths or transmission rates. In the DSS, the servers distribute in different geographical area of the world [2,3]. In repair phase, the lost data are regenerated by minimum-storage regenerating code with functional repair [7–10]. Moreover, we assume each provider sends the same amount of data packets to new comer (such transmission model has been investigated [13,14]). We also assume the providers for regenerating the data in the network can be controlled to minimize the regeneration time.

We model the network as a directed graph $G = (N, E)$, where $N$ consists of the routers. Since each storage server is connected with a router, we use the router to represent the connect server. We denote the set of routers, each of which connects to a available storage server, as $M_p$, and $M_p \subseteq N$. Moreover, we use $g$ to represent the new comer or the connected router, $g \in N$. We assume the router connected to each server represents it to transmit and receive data. Therefore, in this paper, the problem is equivalent to selecting $d$ routers as providers from the subset of routers $M_p$. Specifically, we want to select $d$ routers to regenerate the lost data, denoted $M_d$, $M_d \subseteq M_p$. Therefore, we also call the subset of routers $M_p$ as servers in the rest of this paper.

## 3.2    Notations

In order to facilitate the discussion, we define the parameters and variables as follows.

Parameters used in the rest of the paper are shown as follows:

- $M_p$: The subset of routers, each of which connects a surviving server which can be selected as providers, $M_p = \{n_1, n_2, ..., n_{|M_p|}\}$.

---

[1] If a server is connected with multiple routers, we can add a virtual router and this virtual router is connected with multiple routers.

- $g$: The router which connects the new comer.
- $M_n$: The set of the routers in the network, not including $M_p$ and $g$.
- $N$: The set of the routers in the network, $N = M_p \cup M_n \cup \{g\}$.
- $E$: The set of links between routers in the network $G$.
- $N(u)$: The set of downstream neighbor nodes of the router $u$. There exists a link from node $u$ to each node in $N(u)$.
- $N'(u)$: The set of upstream neighbor nodes of the router $u$. There exists a link from each node in $N'(u)$ to node $u$.
- $B_{uv}$: The bandwidth of link $e_{uv}$ from $u$ to $v$ in the network, $e_{uv} \in E$.
- $\beta$: The number of transmission data each provider need to send.
- $d$: The number of the providers.

Decision variables of the problem are shown as follows:

- $\lambda$: The regeneration time.
- $f_{uv}^i$: The traffic load of traffic flow $i$ on link $e_{uv}$. We note that each flow denotes the data transmission from a available server to the new comer $g$.
- $r_i$: The transmission rate routed to $g$ for traffic flow $i$.
- $w_l$: 0–1 variable, which indicates whether a server is selected as a provider.

### 3.3 Problem Definition

In the DSS, server failures are unavoidable. Therefore, it is desirable to regenerate the lost data in order to maintain the system reliability. In this paper, we consider selecting optimal servers as the providers for regenerating the lost data to minimize the regeneration time, which contains the selection of $d$ providers and routing paths from them to new comer, named *providers and routing paths selection (PRPS)* problem.

## 4 Problem Formulation

In this section, we firstly assume $d$ providers have been fixed, and give the mathematical formulation to minimize the regeneration time. Specifically, to solve the PRPS problem, we then develop a mixed integer linear programming (MILP) to select $d$ optimal servers as providers.

### 4.1 The PRPS Problem Formulation with Fixed Providers

When given parameter: $M_d$, which denotes the set of fixed providers, $M_d = \{s_1, s_2, ..., s_d\}$, $M_d \subseteq M_p$. Let $Q = \{1, 2, ...d\}$. We assume there are $d$ flows, each of which from one provider to new comer. $s_i$ is equivalent to the source node of traffic flow $i$, $i \in Q$. The non-linear programming formulation for the case of fixed providers is shown as follows:

$$Minimize: \lambda \tag{1}$$

Subject to:

$$\lambda \geq \beta/r_i, \forall i \in Q \tag{2}$$

$$\sum_{v \in N(u)} f_{uv}^i - \sum_{v \in N'(u)} f_{vu}^i = r_i, \forall i \in Q, u = s_i \tag{3}$$

$$\sum_{v \in N(u)} f_{uv}^i = \sum_{v \in N'(u)} f_{vu}^i, \forall i \in Q, \forall u \in N - \{s_i, g\} \tag{4}$$

$$\sum_{v \in N'(u)} f_{vu}^i - \sum_{v \in N(u)} f_{uv}^i = r_i, \forall i \in Q, u = g \tag{5}$$

$$0 \leq \sum_{i \in Q} f_{uv}^i \leq B_{uv}, \forall e_{uv} \in E \tag{6}$$

$$0 \leq f_{uv}^i, \forall i \in Q, \forall e_{uv} \in E \tag{7}$$

The objective (1) is to route the data stored in providers to the new comer through the network such that the regeneration time is minimized. Constraint (2) gives the regeneration time no less than transmission time from each provider to new comer $g$. $r_i$ denotes the transmission rate routed to $g$ for traffic flow $i$. Constraints (3)– (5) put network flow constraints between each provider and new comer. Constraint (6) gives the bandwidth constraint for different flows through the same link in the network. Constraint (7) gives value range of variables.

Although we have given the constraints of the problem, the constraint (2) is a non-linear constraint. Next, we try to convert the non-linear constraint to a linear constraint. The objective can be equally converted by the three steps:

- First, the optimal value of the objective is equivalent to minimize the value of $\max_{i \in Q}(\beta/r_i)$;
- Second, the value $\max_{i \in Q}(\beta/r_i)$ can be simplified to the value $\beta \max_{i \in Q}(1/r_i)$, and is equivalent to $\beta/\min_{i \in Q}(r_i)$;
- Finally, the objective can be converted to minimize the value of $\beta/\min_{i \in Q}(r_i)$, which is equivalent to maximize the value of $\min_{i \in Q}(r_i)$. Suppose the maximum value of $\min_{i \in Q}(r_i)$ is $r$, $\lambda$ can be obtained by $\beta/r$.

### 4.2   The PRPS Problem

In this section, we assume $d$ providers are not fixed but should be selected from the set of available servers $M_p$. We assume there are $|M_p|$ flows, each of which from one server $n_i$ to the new comer $g$, $n_i \in M_p$. Let $Q = \{1, 2, \ldots |M_p|\}$. We then formulate PRPS problem as a mixed integer linear programming (MILP):

$$Maximize: \quad r \tag{8}$$

Subject to:

$$r \le o_i, \forall i \in Q \tag{9}$$

$$o_i = r_i + (1 - w_l)\theta, \forall i \in Q, l = n_i \tag{10}$$

$$\sum_{v \in N(l)} f^i_{lv} - \sum_{v \in N'(l)} f^i_{vl} = r_i, \forall i \in Q, l = n_i \tag{11}$$

$$\sum_{v \in N(u)} f^i_{uv} = \sum_{v \in N'(u)} f^i_{vu}, \forall i \in Q, \forall u \in N - \{n_i, g\} \tag{12}$$

$$\sum_{v \in N'(u)} f^i_{vu} - \sum_{v \in N(u)} f^i_{uv} = r_i, \forall i \in Q, u = g \tag{13}$$

$$0 \le \sum_{i \in Q} f^i_{uv} \le B_{uv}, \forall e_{u,v} \in E \tag{14}$$

$$0 \le f^i_{lv} \le w_l B_{lv}, \forall i \in Q, l = n_i, v \in N(n_i) \tag{15}$$

$$\sum_{l \in M_p} w_l = d \tag{16}$$

$$0 \le f^i_{uv}, \forall i \in Q, \forall e_{uv} \in E \tag{17}$$

$$w_l \in \{0, 1\}, \forall l \in M_p \tag{18}$$

In above MILP, we use the 0–1 variable $w_l$ denotes whether server $n_l \in M_p$ is selected as a provider. Constraint (16) shows that only $d$ servers can be selected as providers. Constraints (11)–(13) and Constraint (15) give that there has a non-zero transmission rate $r_i$ from server $n_i$ to the new comer $g$ if only if server $n_l \in M_p$ is selected as a provider. Constraint (10) is equivalents to

$$o_i = \begin{cases} r_i, & \text{if } r_i > 0; \\ \theta, & \text{if } r_i = 0. \end{cases}$$

Let $\theta$ be a sufficiently large number. Consider the objective and Constraint (9), $r = \min_{i \in Q} o_i$. Since $\theta$ is set to be a sufficiently large constant value, $i.e.$, $\theta > \max_{i \in Q} r_i$, we have $r = \min_{i \in Q \text{ and } r_i > 0} r_i$, which means the objective $r$ is to maximize the minimum transmission rate of the providers. Finally, we can get the minimum regeneration time, which is equivalent to $\beta/r$.

## 5  An Efficient Algorithm for Optimal Providers and Routing Paths Selection

According to the MILP proposed in above section, we can obtain the minimum regeneration time. The PRPS problem can be optimally solved by the proposed MILP formulation when the size of the problem is small. However, when the problem size is large, the computational complexity of MILP is considerably large, which has been proved as NP-hard problem [16]. Therefore, when the problem size is large, we need to develop a novel efficient algorithm to select $d$ providers and corresponding routing paths.

Next, we propose a novel efficient algorithm based on the LP-relaxation of the proposed MILP, which contains three steps is shown as follows:

---

**Algorithm 1.** The Effective Algorithm Based on LP Relaxation (BLP)

---

**Step 1**: Solve the LP-relaxation with the objective (8), constrains (9)– (17), (19) to obtain an optimal solution $\{w_l^M\}$.

**Step 2**: For each $l \in M_p$.

set $w_l^* = 1$ for the $d$ largest $w_l^M$ in $\{w_l^M | l \in M_p\}$.

**Step 3**: Set other $w_l^* = 0$.

**Step 4**: Fix the $d$ selected providers with $w_l^* = 1$, solve the LP with the objective (8), constrains (3)–(7), $r <= r_i$ and obtain the value of $f_{uv}^i$, which denotes the data transmission rate on link $e_{uv}$ for each provider $i$.

**Step 5**: Return the sub-optimal solution: $\{w_l^* | l \in M_p\}$ and $\{f_{uv}^i | e_{uv} \in E, i \in Q\}$.

---

(1) We replace the constraint (18) by:

$$0 \leq w_l \leq 1, \forall l \in M_p \tag{19}$$

We obtain the LP-relaxation of the proposed MILP.

(2) We solve the obtained LP-relaxation and use $w_l^M$ to represent the optimal solution, where some values of $w_l^M$ may not be integers.

(3) We select $d$ servers as providers based on the values of $w_l^M$. Specifically, Algorithm 1 gives the BLP algorithm. For each variable $w_l^M, l \in M_p$, the first $d$ servers, which have first $d$ highest value, will be selected as the providers, and the corresponding variable $w_l^M$ is set to 1. Otherwise, it is set to 0.

It is known that LP can be efficient solved. The time complexity will take $O(M_p \log M_p)$ for sorting the elements in $w_l^M$. Therefore, the time complexity of our algorithm is dominated by solving the LP relaxation.

## 6    Performance Evaluation

In this section, we will give simulation results to compare with the proposed BLP algorithm, a random selection (RS) scheme and the maximum-flow (MF)scheme.

The RS scheme randomly selects $d$ available servers as the providers. On the other hand, in the MF scheme, we calculate maximum-flow $H_u$ from each available server $u$ to $g$ individually without considering that different flows may pass through the same link, $u \in M_p$. Specifically, for each value $H_u$, the first $d$ servers, which have first $d$ highest value, will be selected as the providers.

Moreover, let $\lambda_r$ denote the regeneration time achieved by the RS scheme, $\lambda_m$ denote the regeneration time by MF scheme, and $\lambda_b$ denote the regeneration time achieved by the BLP algorithm. Compared with the RS scheme, the improvement ratio of the BLP algorithm is defined as $I_{RS} = (\lambda_r - \lambda_b)/\lambda_r$. On the other hand, the improvement ratio of the BLP algorithm is defined as $I_{MF} = (\lambda_m - \lambda_b)/\lambda_m$ compared with the MF scheme.

### 6.1    Simulation Setup

In this simulation, we assume the nodes in the network are randomly generated in the $10 \times 10$ $m^2$ square region, where the nodes denote servers, the routers and the new comer. As we know, the encoding time from each provider and decoding time on the new server are ignored with the reason these operations can be performed with the data transmission at the same time [10].

Moreover, the random network graph $G$ is generated by the widely used Waxman algorithm [17]. The nodes in $G$ are a Poisson process mainly with three kinds of variables, denoted as $a$, $b$ and $c$. $a$ denotes the intensity of the Poisson process. Two nodes are connected by a link with probability $P(u,v) = be^{-\overline{d}(u,v)/(c*L)}$, $\overline{d}(u,v)$ is Euclidean distance and $L$ is the maximum distance between any two nodes. In the simulation, we firstly let the set of nodes with serial number in $\{1,\cdots,D\}$ as $M_p$, $i.e.$, the set of available servers, and let the node has largest serial number as the new comer, denoted as $g$. Other nodes in $G$ are routers.

In this section, the file is coded with the redundancy of an $(n = 10, k = 2)$-MDS code. The size of the file is $M = 1024\,Mb$ and each server stores $\alpha = M/k = 512\,Mb$. Moreover, with the minimum-storage regenerating (MSR) codes [8], each provider needs to send $\beta$ data to the new comer for regenerating the lost data and $\beta$ can be calculated as the formula $\beta = \alpha/(d - k + 1)$, where $d$ represents the number of providers. We set $\theta$ as a sufficiently large number when solve the LP relaxation of the MILP. Moreover, we use CPLEX [18] to solve the linear programming in the simulation.

## 6.2   Simulation Results

In this section, we change different combinations of parameters to compare the RS method, MF method and the proposed BLP algorithm.

In Fig. 2, we set $b$=0.4, $c$=0.4, $D$=7, $d$=4 and $U$=[10, 40]. Figure 2(a) shows the regeneration time of all algorithms decreases with the increase of $a$. With the increase of $a$, there are more nodes and links in the network, which leads to multiple paths can be selected to routing the data and higher transmission rate can be achieved. Therefore, the regeneration times of the three algorithms decrease. Figure 2(a) shows our algorithm can achieve lower regeneration time compared with other two schemes. In Fig. 2(b), the improvement ratios of BLP

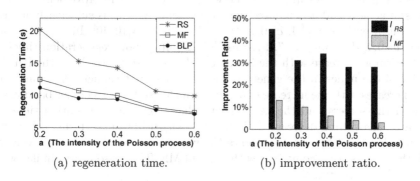

(a) regeneration time.                    (b) improvement ratio.

**Fig. 2.** Different values of $a$ with $b$=0.4, $c$=0.4, $d$=4, $U = [40, 90]$ and $D$=7.

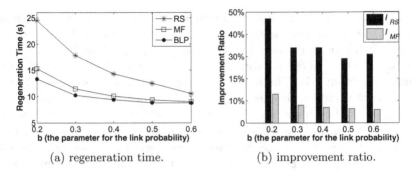

(a) regeneration time.                    (b) improvement ratio.

**Fig. 3.** Different values of $b$ with $a=0.4$, $c=0.4$, $d=4$, $U = [40, 90]$ and $D=7$.

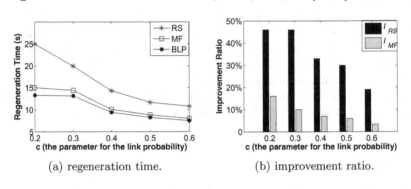

(a) regeneration time.                    (b) improvement ratio.

**Fig. 4.** Different values of $c$ with $a=0.4$, $b=0.4$, $d=4$, $U = [40, 90]$ and $D=7$.

decrease with the increase of $a$ compared with RS and MF. The reasons include that (1) the number of $D$ is fixed, the optimization space is limited; and (2) when multiple paths can be selected to routing the data and higher transmission rate can be achieved with the increase of $a$, the selection of providers has lower impact on the regeneration time. Our algorithm can achieve lower regeneration time compared with MF because that MF does not consider the link sharing between different flows and using network coding. The improvement ratio of BLP still achieves 30 % compared with RS scheme when $a$ is sufficiently large.

In Fig. 3, we set $a=0.4$, $c=0.4$, $D=7$, $d=4$ and $U=[10, 40]$. In Fig. 4, we set $a=0.4$, $b=0.4$, $d=4$ and $D=7$. Figures 3(a) and 4(a) show regeneration times of all algorithms decrease with the increase of $b$ and $c$, respectively. Although the density of the nodes in the generated network does not change, the number of links increases with the increase of $b$ and $c$, which also leads to higher bandwidth between the servers and the new comer. Therefore, the regeneration times of the three algorithms decrease and the BLP algorithm outperforms other two schemes. Figures 3(b) and 4(b) shows the improvement ratios of BLP decrease with the increase of $a$ compared with RS and MF. The reasons are similar with the case shown in Fig. 2.

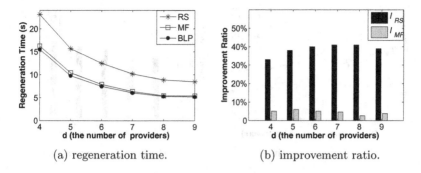

(a) regeneration time.          (b) improvement ratio.

**Fig. 5.** Different values of $d$ with $a$=0.4, $b$=0.4, $c$=0.4, $U = [40, 90]$ and $D$=10.

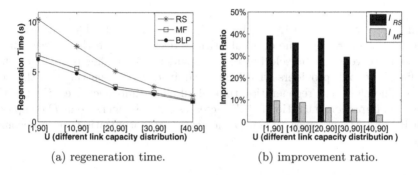

(a) regeneration time.          (b) improvement ratio.

**Fig. 6.** Different values of $U$ with $a$=0.4, $b$=0.4, $c$=0.4, $d = 4$ and $D$=7.

In Fig. 5, we set $a$=0.4, $b$=0.4, $c$=0.4, $D$=10 and $U$=[10, 40]. Figure 5(a) shows the regeneration time of all algorithms decreases with the increase of $d$. The more servers can be selected as providers the less data that each provider needs to transmit to the new comer, which leads to the decrease of regeneration time. In Fig. 5(b), the improvement ratio of BLP is low in the cases that $d$ is small and large. On the other hand, the improvement ratio of BLP achieves the highest value when $d$ is median. The reason is that considering $D$ is fixed, when $d$ is too small or too large, the optimization space of the BLP algorithm is small comparing with the case that $d$ is median.

In Fig. 6, we set $a$=0.4, $b$=0.4, $c$=0.4, $D$=7 and $d$=4. Figure 6(a) shows that the regeneration time of all algorithms decreases because the range of link bandwidth increases. Figure 6(b) shows the improvement ratio of BLP decreases. The reason is that the optimization space of the BLP algorithm is small when the range of the link bandwidth decreases. The simulation results also show that the proposed BLP algorithm is suitable in heterogenous network. Note that the proposed BLP algorithm can reduce about 40 % and 10 % regeneration time comparing with RS scheme and MF scheme, respectively, when the range of the link bandwidth is sufficiently large.

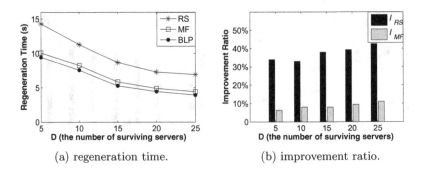

Fig. 7. Different values of $D$ with $a$=0.4, $b$=0.4, $c$=0.4, $d$=4 and $U = [40, 90]$.

In Fig. 7, we set $a$=0.4, $b$=0.4, $c$=0.4, $d$=4 and $U$=[10, 40]. The Fig. 7(a) shows the regeneration time of all algorithms decreases with the increase of $D$. The more servers can be selected to be providers, the higher probability that can find $d$ "good" providers with higher bandwidth between them to the new comer. Therefore, the regeneration time of all algorithms decreases. Figure 7(b) shows the improvement ratio of BLP increases with the increase of $D$ compared with RS and MF schemes. When $D$ increases, the optimization space becomes larger.

## 7   Conclusion

In this paper, we investigate a problem of optimal provider selection to minimize the regeneration time. Specifically, we first give the definitions of the PRPS problem in the DSSs with NC. For the special case that the providers are given, we model the PRPS problem as a mathematical programming. On the basis of the special case, we then formulate the optimal provider selection problem as a mixed integer linear programming problem and develop an efficient algorithm based on LP-relaxation (BLP) to solve the PRPS problem. Finally, extensive simulation experiments have been conducted, and the effectiveness of the proposed algorithm are shown from the results. Specifically, when the range of link bandwidth is large, the proposed BLP algorithm can reduce about 40 % and 10 % regeneration time comparing with RS scheme and MF scheme, respectively.

In the future, we will conduct more experiments by using setups and traces from a real-world scenario. Moreover, we will also take more characteristics of the network into consideration.

**Acknowledgments.** This work was supported in part by Natural Science Foundation of China No. 61202378, 61373164, China Postdoctoral Science Foundation No. 2013M531402, 2014T70544, Research Project of Jiangsu Province No. BY2013030-06 and Application Foundation Research of Suzhou No. SYG201401.

# References

1. Cisco prediction. http://www.ctiforum.com/news/guonei/438872.html
2. Ghemawat, S., Gobioff, H., Leung, S.-T.: The google file system. ACM SIGOPS Oper. Syst. Rev. **37**(5), 29–43 (2003)
3. Calder, B.: Windows azure storage: a highly available cloud storage service with strong consistency. In: Proceedings of the 23rd ACM Sympossium on Operating Systems Principles (2011)
4. Reed, I., Solomon, G.: Polynomial codes over certain finite fields. J. Soc. Ind. Appl. Math. **8**(2), 300–304 (1960)
5. Ahlswede, R., Cai, N., Li, S.-Y.R., Yeung, R.W.: Network information flowem. In: Proceedings of the 8th International Workshop on Quality of Service (IWQOS), vol. 46(4), pp. 1204–1216 (2000)
6. Hu, Y., Chen, H., Lee, P., Tang, Y.: NCCloud: applying network coding for the storage repair in a cloud-of-clouds. In: Proceedings of the 10th USENIX Annual Technical Conference (2012)
7. Rashmi, K.V., Shah, N.B., Kumar, P.V.: Optimal exact-regenerating codes for distributed storage at the MSR and MBR points via a productmatrix construction. In: Proceedings of 19th International Workshop on Quality of Service (IWQOS), vol. 57(8), pp. 5227–5239 (2011)
8. Cadambe, V.R., Jafar, S.A., Maleki, H.: Distributed data storage with minimum storage regenerating codes - exact and functional repair are asymptotically equally efficient. arXiv: 1004.4299 [cs.IT] (2010)
9. Wu, Y., Dimakis, A.G., Ramchandran, K.: Deterministic regenerating codes for distributed storage. In: Proceedings of 45th Annual Allerton Conference on Communication, Control, and Computing (2007)
10. Li, J., Yang, S., Wang, X., Li, B.: Tree-structured data regeneration in distributed storage systems with regenerating codes. In: Proceedings of the 29th Internationnal Conference on Computer Communications (2010)
11. Li, J., Yang, S., Wang, X., Xue, X., Li, B.: Tree-structured data regeneration with network coding in distributed storage systems. In: Proceedings of 17th International Workshop on Quality of Service(IWQoS) (2009)
12. Cullina, D., Dimakis, A.G., Ho, T.: Searching for minimum storage regenerating codes. In: Proceedings of 47th Annual Allerton Conference on Communication, Control, and Computing (2009)
13. Hu, Y., Lee, Patrick P.C., Shum, Kenneth W.: Analysis and construction of functionalregenerating codes with uncoded repair for distributed storage systems. In: Proceedings of the 32nd IEEE International Conference on Computer Communications, vol. 63(01), pp. 31–44 (2013)
14. Sun, W., Wang, Y., Pei, X.: Tree-structured parallel regeneration for multiple data losses in distributed storage systems based on erasure codes. Proc. Commun. **10**(4), 113–125 (2013)
15. Wang, Y., Wei, D., Yin, X., Wang, X.: Heterogeneity-aware data regeneration in distributed storage systems. In: Proceedings of the 33rd IEEE International Conference on Computer Communications (2014)
16. Al-khedhairi, A.S.: Simulated annealing metaheuristic for solving p-median problem. Int. J. Contemp. Math. Sci. **3**(28), 1357–1365 (2008)
17. Waxman, B.M.: Routing of multipoint connections. Int. J. Sel. Areas Commun. **6**(9), 1617–1622 (1988)
18. IBM ILOG CPLEX. http://www-03.ibm.com/software/products/zh/ibmilogcple

19. Gong, Q., Wang, J., Wei, D., Wang, J., Wang, X.: Optimal node selection for data regeneration in heterogeneous distributed storage systems. In: Proceedings of the 44th International Conference on Parallel Processing (ICPP) (2015)
20. Gong, Q., Wang, J., Wang, Y., Wei, D., Wang, J., Wang, X.: Topology-aware node selection for data regeneration in heterogeneous distributed storage systems. preprint arXiv: 1506.05579 (2015)

# Local State Reusing for Efficient Model Checking of Multithreaded Programs

Junrui Zhou[✉], Hong An, Yunyun Wang, and Junshi Chen

School of Computer Science and Technology,
University of Science and Technology of China, Hefei 230027, China
{junrui09,wyy183,cjuns}@mail.ustc.edu.cn,
han@ustc.edu.cn

**Abstract.** Applying model checking to detect concurrency errors in larger-scale multithreaded programs is limited by state explosion problem stemming from nondeterminism. We propose a novel approach established on the insight into the relationship between thread interference and nondeterminism to break the limitation. The approach works for particular parallel region that can be divided into disjoint groups among which there is no thread interference. We demonstrate that the set of reachable states of the parallel region is the Cartesian product of reachable states of each disjoint group. Local states of disjoint groups explored in previous runs can be reused to avoid redundant state transitions such that the time consumed by successive runs is decreased. The empirical results indicate that the efficiency of model checking can be improved by orders of magnitude through local state reusing.

**Keywords:** Software model checking · State explosion · Thread interference · Concurrent control flow · Local state reusing

## 1 Introduction

In the area of concurrency testing, stateless model checking [8,13] based on state transition system occupies a unique seat. However, state explosion problem incurred by intrinsic nondeterminism of multithreaded programs limits its application to large-scale multithreaded programs. Partial-order reduction techniques [5,15,17] have been proposed to strike the problem through pruning equivalent states. The mechanism of detecting dependence relations between transition determines the optimization effect.

We propose a novel local state reusing technique to accelerate stateless model checking. Aided by concurrent control flow graph [19,20] which depicts the control flow, parallel flow, synchronization dependence and thread interference between basic blocks in a multithreaded program, some parallel regions can be divided into disjoint groups among which there is no thread interference. The set of reachable states of such parallel region is equivalent to the Cartesian product of the set of reachable states of each disjoint group. It means that a large

© Springer International Publishing Switzerland 2015
G. Wang et al. (Eds.): ICA3PP 2015, Part IV, LNCS 9531, pp. 521–538, 2015.
DOI: 10.1007/978-3-319-27140-8_36

number of end states reached by each disjoint group may be repeatedly explored in simulated runs during state exploration. This fact motivates our local state reusing technique.

Normalized state exploration, executing disjoint groups in order, is proposed to simplify local state reusing. In normalized state exploration, it is feasible to detect when exploration of disjoint groups is accomplished. The end states of disjoint groups recorded in previous runs are reused to generate successive states. Therefore the cost of computing persistent sets and performing state transitions can be reduced. According to empirical results, the efficiency of stateless model checking by SPIN can be improved in orders of magnitude. Our contributions consist of mathematically analyzing the relation between reachable states of disjoint groups and corresponding parallel region, the insight into the redundant exploration of states reached by disjoint groups, and the implementation of SR-SPIN model checker equipped with local state reusing technique.

This paper is organized as follows. Section 2 briefly introduces model checker SPIN and concurrent control flow graph, a powerful method for statically analyzing multithreaded programs. Preliminaries including notations, definitions and theorems are given in Sect. 3. The implementation of state reusing is depicted in Sect. 4. Experimental results are shown in Sect. 5. Sections 6 and 7 give related work and conclusion and future work respectively.

## 2    Background

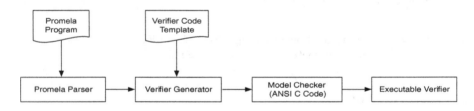

**Fig. 1.** The structure of SPIN verification (Source: [21])

### 2.1    SPIN Model Checker

SPIN is a static model checker developed at Bell Labs [16,21]. Figure 1 illustrates its framework. The input is a Promela language program used to model concurrent system. The output is a test harness (verifier) consisted of state transition system which takes charge of model checking using state exploration. The semantics supported by Promela language is limited. The only way to express parallelism is creating child thread using fork directive. Except for atomic, none explicit synchronizations is supported. Condition statement involved in global variable can be used as synchronizer between threads [22]. Dynamic memory allocation, call-by-reference and pointer are illegal. Static analysis of Promela program is relatively simple.

## 2.2 Concurrent Control Flow Graph

CCFG, an intermediate representation of parallel programs, is a counterpart of CFG (control flow graph) of sequential programs. It is a common method to make static analysis of parallel programs [19,23], such as computing slices. We utilize the edges in CCFG to visualize the disjointness relations between parallel threads in Sect. 3.

Each node in CCFG corresponds to a statement. There are four classes of edges in CCFG-control flow, parallel flow, conflict dependence and synchronization dependence. Two nodes are linked by the parallel flow edge in two cases: they represent creation of a thread and the entry of created thread respectively; two nodes represent the exit of a thread and thread join operation respectively. The bidirectional conflict edge links two concurrent basic blocks that can be executed in parallel and reference the same shared variable (with one of the references being a write) [14,19]. The synchronization edge connects synchronization operations, such as barrier, post, wait, lock, and unlock.

# 3   Preliminaries

This section builds theory foundation for our local state reusing technique based on Mazurkiewicz trace theory [27] and traditional formal representation of transition system [10].

## 3.1   Disjoint Groups

**Definition 1 (Disjointness Relation).** *Let $\alpha$ and $\beta$ denote two code snippets from parallel threads $\sigma$ and $\omega$. The disjointness relation between $\alpha$ and $\beta$ hold iff the following properties are satisfied.*

*Property 1. There is no conflict dependence or synchronization dependence between $\alpha$ and $\beta$.*

*Property 2. There is no parallel flow between $\alpha$ and $\beta$. If $\Omega$ is the set of enclosing threads [19] of $\beta$ $(\alpha)$, then $\alpha$ $(\beta)$ doesn't contain the statement where a thread $t \in \Omega$ is forked.*

**Definition 2 (Disjoint Groups).** *Assume a parallel region $R$ can be split into disjoint groups $g_1,\ldots,g_n$ $(n \geq 2)$. Each disjoint group $g_i$ $(1 \leq i \leq n)$ consists of code snippets of which each code snippet is a code block extracted from a thread in $R$. If $\alpha \in g_i$ and $\beta \notin g_i$ $(1 \leq i \leq n)$ $(\beta$ belongs to $R)$, the disjointness relation between $\alpha$ and $\beta$ holds. It implies that if $\alpha \in g_i$ and $\beta \in g_j$ $(i \neq j)$, then disjointness relation between $\alpha$ and $\beta$ holds.*

Here we only discuss multithreaded shared-memory programs. To simplify the illustration, we map the Promela language to generic parallel programming language Pthreads. The "run" is mapped to "fork". The term "disjoint groups" is explained with the CCFG of a multithreaded program shown in Fig. 2.

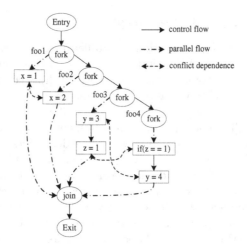

**Fig. 2.** A case of concurrent control flow graph

The main thread "init" [11] creates four child threads foo1, foo2, foo3 and foo4 successively. The edge between main thread and each child thread is parallel flow edge. In total, there are three bidirectional conflict edges between the four child threads. Let group g0 consist of foo1 and foo2 and group g1 consist of foo3 and foo4. g0 and g1 are two disjoint groups.

In the following two subsections, we introduce the notion of normalized state exploration and reason the concurrent behavior of parallel region which can be split into disjoint groups as Cartesian product. Take a parallel region $R$ that can be split into a bunch of disjoint groups $g_1, g_2, \ldots, g_n$ ($n \geq 2$) as an example. Let $S$ represent the set of reachable states of $R$. Let $s \in S$ ($s$ is an element of $S$). The projection of the state $s$ on group $g_i$ is represented by $s[g_i]$ which consists of program counter and local variables of each thread $t$ ($t \in g_i$) and global variables shared among the threads owned by $g_i$. Let $S[g_i]$ represents the set of reachable states of group $g_i$.

### 3.2 Normalized State Exploration

**Definition 3 (Normalized Transition Sequence).** *Let $s_0$ be the initial state of the parallel region $R$ mentioned above. Let $T_{norm}$ and $T$ be two sequences of transitions of $R$. Sequence $T_{norm}$ is considered as the normalization of $T$ iff the following properties hold.*

*Property 1. There is a unique state $s$ such that $s_0 \xRightarrow{T_{norm}} s$ and $s_0 \xRightarrow{T} s$, i.e., $T_{norm} \equiv T$ (Mazurkiewicz equivalence trace [27]).*

*Property 2. Let $t_1$ and $t_2$ are the first transition and the last transition of $g_i$ in $T_{norm}$ respectively. If $t$ lies between $t_1$ and $t_2$ in $T_{norm}$, then $t \in g_i$. In other words, the transitions of each disjoint group are consecutively executed in explored transition sequences.*

*Property 3. All disjoint groups are sequentially executed. If $t_1$ is the last transition of $g_i$, and $t_2$ is the first transition of $g_{i+1}$ in $T_{norm}$, then $t_2$ is next to $t_1$.*

The first property of normalized transition sequence implies that if $t_1$ and $t_2$ are a pair of transitions in $T_{norm}$ such that $t_1 \prec t_2$ ($\prec$ is a happens-before relation [10]), then $t_1 \prec t_2$ must hold in the sequence $T$, i.e., the relative position of each pair of dependent transitions in $T_{norm}$ is the same as $T$. The second and the last property formalize the transitions sequences explored in normalized state exploration where disjoint groups are sequentially executed in each trace path. Given the independence relation between disjoint groups (Definition 2) and the properties of transition sequences in normalized state exploration (Definition 3), it is feasible to yield a normalized state exploration of R such that there is at least one equivalent transition sequence for unnormalized transition sequence associated with R.

**Theorem 1** *(Feasibility of Normalized State Exploration). Assume the parallel region R mentioned above is deadlock-free. For each sequence of transitions $T$ associated with R, there is a sequence $T_{norm}$ such that $T_{norm} \in [T]_\equiv$.*

*Proof* Denote the set of transitions of group $g_i$ as $T[g_i]$. For each group $g_i$, there is no race relation and deadlock between $T[g_i]$ and the other transitions in $T$. For each pair of transitions $t \in T[g_i]$ and $t' \notin T[g_i]$, independence relation [10] holds (Definitions 1 and 2). Hence, according to trace theory [27], $T_{norm}$ resulted from repeatedly exchanging the locations of adjacent transitions which are from different disjoint groups in $T$ satisfies the relation $T_{norm} \in [T]_\equiv$.

### 3.3  Cartesian Product

We consider two cases of state exploration of $R$. One case is searching all partial orders of the entire $R$. The other case is only searching partial orders of group $g_i$. Denote the set of reachable states of $R$ and $g_i$ as $S$ and $S'$ respectively. Use $s[g_i]$ to denote the projection of the state $s$ on $g_i$ under the first case and $s'[g_i]$ to denote the state under the second case. The persistent set of a state $s$ is denoted as $PSet(s)$. The concatenation of a state and a transition (sequence) is denoted as $s.t$ ($s.T$).

Let $S[g_i]$ denote the set of the projection of reachable states on group $g_i$ under the first case. Let $S'[g_i]$ denote the set of reachable states under the second case. The sets of local state of any group $g_i$ resulted from state exploration under the two cases are the same, $S[g_i] = S'[g_i]$ (Theorem 2).

**Theorem 2** *(Local State Equivalence). $S[g_i] = S'[g_i]$ holds ($1 \leq i \leq n$).*

*Proof* If $s_0$ and $s_0'[g_i]$ are the initial states at the entry of $R$ in the two cases respectively, then $s_0[g_i] = s_0'[g_i]$. Let $S_{inter} = S[g_i] \cap S'[g_i]$. Since $s_0[g_i] \in S[g_i]$ and $s_0'[g_i] \in S'[g_i]$, $S_{inter} \neq \emptyset$. If $S[g_i] = S'[g_i]$ doesn't holds, then there exists at least one pair of states $s$ and $s'$ and a transition $t \in g_i$ such that $s[g_i] = s'[g_i]$ and $s.t \neq s'[g_i].t$. We prove this situation won't happen below by induction on the consistency of successive states of $s[g_i]$ and $s'[g_i]$ with respect to $g_i$ ($1 \leq i \leq n$).

Due to absence of dependence between any pair of transitions from different disjoint groups, a subset of transitions from $g_i$ can be used as the persistent set of each state $s \in S$ under the first case.

**Basic Case.** Denote the successive states of state $s$ as $Succ(s)$. As mentioned above $s_0[g_i] = s_0'[g_i]$. There are two situations for the persistent sets of $s_0$ and $s_0'[g_i]$ with respect to $g_i$. If $PSet(s_0) \subseteq g_i$, $PSet(s_0) = PSet(s_0'[g_i])$. Else, given the independence relation between disjoint groups (Definition 2), $PSet(s) \cap g_i = \emptyset$. In the second situation, for each successive state $s_{succ}$ of $s_0$, $s_{succ}[g_i] = s_0'[g_i]$ still holds. For each $s_{succ}$ and $s_0'[g_i]$, the second situation may repeat until $enabled(s_{succ}) \subseteq g_i$ and $PSet(s_{succ}) = PSet(s_0'[g_i])$. Eventually $s_0[g_i]$ and $s_0'[g_i]$ will be transformed to the same set of successive states. Consequently, the consistency of successive states of $s_0[g_i]$ and $s_0'[g_i]$ with respect to $g_i$ ($1 \leq i \leq n$) is satisfied. $Succ(s_0[g_i]) = Succ(s_0'[g_i])$ with respective to $g_i$ holds.

**Inductive Step.** Consider any pair of states $s[g_i]$ and $s'[g_i]$ such that $s[g_i] = s'[g_i]$. The situation of consistency of successive states of $s[g_i]$ and $s'[g_i]$ with respect to $g_i$ is the same as that of $s_0$ and $s_0'[g_i]$. Consequently, the procedures of state transformation related to $g_i$ under the two cases of state exploration are identical, $Succ(s[g_i]) = Succ(s'[g_i])$. In conclusion, $S[g_i] = S'[g_i]$ ($1 \leq i \leq n$) holds.

Assume that the parallel region $R$ mentioned above is deadlock-free. The concurrent behavior of $R$ can be reasoned as the Cartesian product of each disjoint group, $S = \prod_{i=1}^{n} S'[g_i]$ (Theorem 3).

**Theorem 3 (Cartesian Product).** *The set $S$ of reachable states of $R$ is the Cartesian product of the set of reachable states of each disjoint group,*

$$S = \prod_{i=1}^{n} S'[g_i].$$

*Proof* Let $S[g_i]$ denote the projection of the set of reachable states $S$ of $R$ on $g_i$ ($1 \leq i \leq n$). State $s \in S$ and $s[g_i]$ is the projection of state $s$ on $g_i$. $S[g_i] = \{s[g_i] \mid s \in S\}$. According to the definition of normalized state exploration of $R$, $s = (s[g_1], s[g_2], \ldots, s[g_n])$ ($n \geq 2$) ($s$ is an ordered set of reachable states of each group). Hence, $S = \prod_{i=1}^{n} S[g_i]$. In addition, $S'[g_i] = S[g_i]$ (Theorem 2). It can be inferred that $S = \prod_{i=1}^{n} S'[g_i]$.

## 4    Implementation

Our technique is implemented in SR-SPIN framework, an variant of SPIN [16,21]. Particular extensions are made to each module of the SPIN framework in SR-SPIN. Grammatical rules associated with disjoint groups are added to Promela parser. The source code used to perform state reusing is integrated into the template code of verifier. Rules of translating the entry and exit of disjoint group into pseudo transitions are incorporated into verifier generator. The verifier generated by SR-SPIN is equipped with local state reusing.

## 4.1    Normalized State Exploration

After static analysis of thread interferences aided by CCFG, a parallel region $R$ may be split into $n$ disjoint groups. Each group identity $i \in [1, n]$ is assigned to one randomly selected group. In the normalized state exploration (Definition 3), disjoint groups are sequentially executed: $g_{i+1}$ is executed after $g_i$ ($i \in [1, n-1]$). Algorithm 1 gives the procedure of normalized state exploration and local state reusing. The depth-first search algorithm is augmented with well-controlled manipulations to runtime scheduler. The manipulations consist of interferences to exploration status. When a transition is executed from state $s$, new exploration status is computed according to the status at state $s$ and the type of transition. Runtime scheduler makes decisions on how to compute successive states according to exploration status.

**Exploration Status Maintenance.** The exploration status consists of the exploration stage, the identity of group being explored and the execution state of threads. The exploration status relative to each explored state of transition system is recorded in stack $Status$. An element $status_0$ which represents the initial exploration status is pushed onto $Status$ (in initialization of Algorithm 1). Once a new state $s'$ is generated, exploration status is refreshed and newly generated status relative to $s'$ is pushed onto $Status$ (line 10 and line 17). When depth-first search backtracks to state $s$ from successive state $s'$, the exploration status relative to $s'$ is pulled from $Status$ (line 27). Therefore, when state search procedure backtracks to a history state $s$, the top element on stack $Status$ is the exploration status relative to $s$.

The relative location of program counter and the entry (and exit) of disjoint group splits each simulated run performed by verifier into three stages: $before\_group$, $in\_group$, and $after\_group$. The shift among the three stages happens when searching successive states or backtracking to history states. The $before\_group$ stage in each simulated run starts from the initial state $s_0$. Runtime supervises the relative position of program counter and the disjoint group entry for each thread. Once a thread reaches the entry, it will be blocked until all the other threads in the same parallel region reach the entry. As soon as all active threads reach the entry of disjoint group, the stage is transformed to $in\_group$ from $before\_group$. Meanwhile, the active group is set to the first group $g_0$ and all the threads associated with $g_0$ are waked up.

During $in\_group$ stage in each simulated run, runtime monitors the relative position of program counter of each related thread and the disjoint group exit for each active group. As soon as all the threads of active disjoint group $g_i$ reach the disjoint group exit, these threads are blocked and the active group is set to the next disjoint group $g_{i+1}$ (this is performed when refreshing the exploration status). The way in which each disjoint group is set as the active group ensures the normalized state exploration. Exploration stage is switched to $after\_group$ from $in\_group$ when all active threads from current parallel region reach the disjoint group exit. At the end of this stage, all the blocked threads related to disjoint groups are waked up.

**Algorithm 1.** Depth-First State Searching Equipped with Local State Reusing

**Initialization:**     $S = \phi$; $H = \phi$; $Status = status_0$; $Tran = \phi$; $stage = 0$; $s = s_0$;
1: **function** Search($s$)
2:     **if** $s \notin H$ **then**
3:         $S$.push($s$);
4:         $H$.insert($s$);
5:         $status = Status$.top();
6:         $g_i = status.active\_group$;
7:         **if** $i \in [1, n]$ and $g_i.finished = true$ **then**
8:             **for** each end state $es[g_i]$ in $ES[g_i]$ **do**
9:                 Generate successive state $s'$ through replacing $s[g_i]$ with $es[g_i]$;
10:                Refresh the exploration status;
11:                Search($s'$);
12:            **end for**
13:        **else**
14:            **for** each transition $t \in$PersistentSet($s$)\$s.sleepset$ **do**
15:                $Tran$.push($t$);
16:                $s' = s \cdot t$;
17:                Refresh the exploration status;
18:                **if** the group exit of $g_i$ is reached **then**
19:                    $ES[g_i]$.insert($s[g_i]$);
20:                **end if**
21:                $s'.sleepset = \{t' | t \in s.sleepet(s)$ and $t'$ is independent with $t\}$;
22:                Search($s'$);
23:                $s.sleepset$.insert($t$);
24:            **end for**
25:        **end if**
26:        $S$.pop();
27:        $Status$.pop();
28:        **if** $s$ is generated via state transition **then**
29:            $tran = Tran$.top();
30:            $Tran$.top();
31:            **if** $tran$ is the finish indicator of the group $g_j$ **then**
32:                $g_j.finished = true$;
33:            **end if**
34:        **end if**
35:    **end if**
36: **end function**

**Persistent Set Computation.** The procedure of computing the persistent set of transitions at each explored state is shown in Algorithm 2. To ensure sequential execution of disjoint groups, candidate transitions performed from each state is limited to unblocked threads owned by the active disjoint group (line 3). When exploring the active disjoint group, the persistent set is the subset of enabled transitions in the active group. Except this, there is no difference between our persistent set computation and original persistent set computation in SPIN.

The computation of persistent set for each state is a greedy procedure that continually checks whether there are dependence relations between the remaining transitions in the set of candidate transitions and the transitions in the persistent set (line 7–19). Consequently, all possible partial orders of transitions can be searched. This procedure halts only if no dependence relation is left or a transition related to the dependence n doesn't belong to the candidate transitions of current state.

---

**Algorithm 2.** Computing Persistent Set

---

**Initialization:**    $Pset(s) = \phi$;
**Output:**    $PSet(s)$;
 1: **function** PersistentSet()
 2:     $status = Status.top()$;
 3:     $T=\{t \mid$ thread $t$ is not blocked in $status\}$;
 4:     $Trans = \{tran \mid tran \in enabled(s)$ and $active(t) \cap T \neq \phi\}$;
 5:     $tran$ is a transition arbitrarily selected from $Trans$;
 6:     $Pset = Pset \cup \{$corresponding thread for $tran\}$;
 7:     **for** each transition $tran_i \in Trans$ **do**
 8:         set $t_i$ to corresponding thread for transition $tran_i$;
 9:         **for** each transition $tran_j$ such that $s(t_i) = pre(tran_j)$ **do**
10:             **for** each active corresponding thread $t_j$ for $tran_j$ **do**
11:                 $Pset = Pset \cup \{t_j\}$;
12:             **end for**
13:         **end for**
14:         **for** each transition $tran_j$ **do**
15:             **if** $tran_i$ and $tran_j$ are not commutative **then**
16:                 $Pset = Pset \cup \{$corresponding thread for $tran_j\}$;
17:             **end if**
18:         **end for**
19:     **end for**
20: **end function**

---

## 4.2 Local State Reusing

Directly performing local state reusing during original state exploration procedure is intractable. We address this problem through normalizing the state exploration procedure and only reusing the end states of each disjoint group. Local end state $es[g_i]$ is the state where the program counter of each thread $t$ associated with $g_i$ ($t \in g_i$) points to the disjoint group exit. $ES[g_i]$ denotes the set of end states reached by $g_i$. Each local end state $es[g_i] \in ES[g_i]$ consists of program counter and local variables of each thread $t$ ($t \in g_i$) and global variables shared among the threads owned by $g_i$.

Consider a parallel region $R$ that consists of four threads $t_1$, $t_2$, $t_3$, and $t_4$. There is a write-write dependence on shared variable x between $t_1$ and $t_2$, while there is a write-write dependence on shared variable y between $t_3$ and $t_4$.

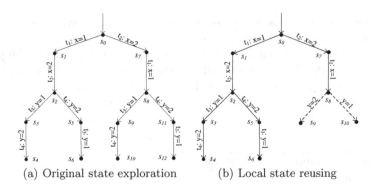

(a) Original state exploration          (b) Local state reusing

**Fig. 3.** The simulated trace paths resulted from state exploration without and with local state reusing

According to Definition 2, $R$ can be split into two disjoint groups: $g_1$ consisting of $t_1$ and $t_2$ and $g_2$ consisting of $t_3$ and $t_4$. Figure 3 visually makes a comparison between the state exploration of $R$ with (Fig. 3(b)) and without (Fig. 3(a)) local end state reusing.

In Fig. 3, the nodes represent the states which the state exploration procedure goes through. The subscripts of state nodes increase progressively with the order in which the states are explored. The directed edges represent the state transitions during model checking. The source state at the beginning of each solid arrowed line is transferred to the destination state through executing a single transition or an atomic region. Instead, each dotted arrowed line denotes local end state reusing. Correspondingly, the label with thread identity attached to each solid arrowed edge denotes the transition executed from the source state node, such as t1: x=1 executed from $s_0$ in Fig. 3(a) and (b), while the label attached to each dotted arrowed edge without thread identity denotes the reusing of a local end state, such as y=2 executed from $s_8$ in Fig. 3(b).

In the normalized state exploration (Definition 3), $n$ disjoint groups are sequentially executed: $g_{i+1}$ is executed after $g_i$, $i \in [1, n-1]$. Each local end state $es[g_i] \in ES[g_i]$ represents a partial order related to $g_i$. We call the ordered end states $(es[g_0], \ldots, es[g_{i-1}])$ the partial order prefix of $g_i$ $(1 \le i \le n)$. In each simulated run resulted from normalized state exploration, the first transition (not pseudo transition corresponding to the entry of $g_i$) of $g_i$ is performed from the state $s$ where $s[g_j] \in ES[g_j]$ $(1 \le j \le i-1)$ and $s[g_i]$ is the initial state of $g_i$.

With optimal partial order reduction [5], only the representatives of all possible states of $R$ are explored, as shown in Fig. 3(a). We use $ES[R]$ to denote the end states of $R$ where all the threads in $R$ reach the disjoint group exits. Each element $ES[R]$ is an ordered set of the end states of each disjoint group in $R$. The end states of $g_1$, $g_2$ and $R$ are given in Eqs. (1), (2) and (3). The "exit" denotes that the threads in a disjoint group reach the exit of the disjoint group section.

In normalized state exploration, $g_1$ is executed before $g_2$ in each simulated trace. The partial order prefix of $g_2$ is the end state of $g_1$. Under different partial order prefix of $g_2$, the set of end states of $g_2$ are equal. For example, $s_4[g_2] = s_{10}[g_2]$ and $s_6[g_2] = s_{12}[g_2]$. Such local state equivalence motivates our local state reusing technique.

$$ES[g_1] = \{(x = 2, exit), (x = 1, exit)\} \tag{1}$$

$$ES[g_2] = \{(y = 2, exit), (y = 1, exit)\} \tag{2}$$

$$ES[R] = \{((x = 2, exit), (y = 2, exit)), ((x = 2, exit), (y = 1, exit)), \\ ((x = 1, exit), (y = 2, exit)), ((x = 1, exit), (y = 1, exit))\} \tag{3}$$

The local state equivalence with respect to a disjoint group under different partial order prefixes allows local state reusing. According to Theorem 4, the sets of end states of each disjoint group explored from different partial order prefixes are identical. Hence, the feasibility of local state reusing technique gets proved.

**Theorem 4 (Feasibility of Reusing Local End States).** *Consider any two partial order prefixes $\gamma_1$ and $\gamma_2$ of $g_i$ consisting of transitions of all the disjoint groups executed in ahead of $g_i$. Let $s_{\gamma_1}$ and $s_{\gamma_2}$ represent two states such that $s_0 \overset{\gamma_1}{\Rightarrow} s_{\gamma_1}$ and $s_0 \overset{\gamma_2}{\Rightarrow} s_{\gamma_2}$ where $s_0$ is the initial state at the entry of R. Let $ES_{\gamma_1}[g_i]$ and $ES_{\gamma_2}[g_i]$ represent the set of end states of $g_i$ explored from $s_{\gamma_1}$ and $s_{\gamma_2}$ respectively, then $ES_{\gamma_1}[g_i] = ES_{\gamma_2}[g_i]$.*

*Proof.* We prove the equality between the end states of $g_i$ explored from $\gamma_1$ and $\gamma_2$ via induction on the equality between successive states of $s_{r_1}$ and $s_{r_2}$. Since there is no thread interferences between $g_i$ and $g_j$ $(j \neq i)$, $s_{r_1}[g_i] = s_{r_2}[g_i]$.

**Basic Case.** At the beginning of executing $g_i$, the persistent set for $s_{\gamma_1}$ and $s_{\gamma_2}$ are identical, i.e., $PSet(s_{r_1}) = PSet(s_{r_2})$. Therefore, $s_{\gamma_1}$ and $s_{\gamma_2}$ should have identical successive states. For each pair of successive states $s'_{r_1}$ and $s'_{r_2}$, $s'_{r_1}[g_i] = s'_{r_2}[g_i](1 \leq i \leq n)$.

**Inductive Step.** Due to $s'_{r_1}[g_i] = s'_{r_2}[g_i]$ ($g_i$ is the active group), $PSet(s'_{r_1}) = PSet(s'_{r_2})$. Hence, the equality of successive states of $s'_1$ and $s'_2$ still holds.

In conclusion, the equality between the end states of $g_i$ explored from $\gamma_1$ and $\gamma_2$ holds, i.e., $ES_{\gamma_1}[g_i] = ES_{\gamma_2}[g_i]$.

Once possible partial orders related to $g_i$ are fully searched, $ES[g_i]$ contains all the end states that can be reached by $g_i$. In order to ensure the completeness of state exploration equipped with local state reusing, reusing states of $g_i$ is forbidden until all possible interleavings related to $g_i$ have been explored (line 7, Algorithm 1). If successive states can't be generated through reusing end states, the procedure to compute the persistent set of enabled transitions at each reached is called.

And the set of transitions explored from current state is the set difference of the persistent set and the sleep set of current state $s$ (line 14, Algorithm 1).

During *in_group* stage in state exploration, runtime maintains the exploration status of $g_i$ according to the backtracking of the accomplishment indicator of $g_i$. The accomplishment indicator of exploring $g_i$ is set to the predecessor transition of the firstly executed non-pseudo transition of $g_i$. When runtime detects that backtracking happens to the indicator of $g_i$, the accomplishment flag of exploration related to $g_i$ is set to true (line 32, Algorithm 1). In the subsequent simulated runs where the exploration relative to $g_i$ is accomplished, the end states recorded in $ES[g_i]$ are reused. The reusing is generating each successive state $s'$ of state $s$ where groups $g_1, g_2, \ldots, g_{i-1}$ reach their ends through replacing local state $s[g_i]$ with each end state $es[g_i]$ stored in $ES[g_i]$ (line 9, Algorithm 1).

Take the state exploration in Fig. 3(b) as an example. After all possible end states of $g_2$ are explored under the prefix order (x=2,exit), the end states of $g_2$ are recorded in $ES[g_2]$. Instead of performing transitions in $g_2$ under the prefix order (x=1,exit), the value of variable $y$ and program counters (exit) related to end states of $g_2$ are copied to $s_8$ to generate the successive states $s_9$ and $s_{10}$. The average trace path resulted from exploration with reusing local states is shorter than without reusing local states. Model checking time could be saved with such reduction of exploration.

## 5    Experimental Results

Our experiments are performed on a machine with i5 CPU (2.30 GHZ), 6 GB of RAM running Linux operating system. We elaborately design a suit of Promela programs to help us measure the effectiveness of state reusing. The Promela programs in the suit of benchmarks are divided into two categories: 2 disjoint groups and 3 disjoint groups. For each benchmark $\alpha$ with 3 groups, there is a benchmark $\beta$ with 2 groups such that the entire code of $\beta$ is a part of $\alpha$.

We use the verifier generated by SPIN which doesn't support local state reusing as the baseline to evaluate the local state reusing technique implemented in SR-SPIN. We measure the effectiveness and the runtime overhead of state reusing in certain metrics. The counts of state resulted from state exploration without and with state reusing are represented by #*State* and #*SRState* respectively. State reusing ratio, denoted by $\epsilon$, is used to directly characterize the effectiveness of state reusing. The state reusing ratio is

$$\epsilon = \frac{\#State}{\#SRState}. \tag{4}$$

The state exploration time consumed by test harnesses generated by SPIN and SR-SPIN are denoted as Time and SRTime respectively. The speedup on model checking time provided by state reusing is denoted by $\theta$,

$$\theta = \frac{Time}{SRTime}. \tag{5}$$

The ratio between the state reusing ratio $\epsilon$ and the time speedup $\theta$ is used to measure the additional time overhead arising from state reusing, denoted $\varphi$,

$$\varphi = \frac{\epsilon}{\theta}. \tag{6}$$

Table 1 shows the performance results for the benchmarks with 2 and with 3 disjoint groups: state count, reusing ratio $\epsilon$, state exploration time, time speedup $\theta$ and runtime overhead of local state reusing $\varphi$. The columns with the prefix "SR" provide the results associated with local state reusing. The states explored with local state reusing can be classified into two categories: the normal states which are generated by performing transitions and the states which are generated by reusing local states. #SRState is the count of normal states. The time result for each benchmark is the average of the total time spent on executing each benchmark 50 times.

**Table 1.** Performance results for the benchmarks

| Benchmarks | #State | #SRState | $\epsilon$ | Time(ms) | SRTime(ms) | $\theta$ | $\varphi$ |
|---|---|---|---|---|---|---|---|
| 2 disjoint groups | | | | | | | |
| Kmeans | 427958 | 1246 | 343.47 | 5438 | 27 | 201.41 | 1.71 |
| Boundary_50 | 244084 | 3181 | 76.73 | 933 | 24 | 38.88 | 1.97 |
| Boundary_100 | 449345 | 5296 | 84.85 | 1649 | 25 | 65.96 | 1.29 |
| Boundary_150 | 579808 | 7292 | 79.51 | 2289 | 27 | 84.78 | 0.94 |
| Boundary_200 | 730515 | 9414 | 77.60 | 2568 | 28 | 91.71 | 0.85 |
| Boundary_250 | 884275 | 11525 | 76.73 | 2495 | 29 | 86.03 | 0.89 |
| Boundary_300 | 942138 | 13521 | 69.68 | 2749 | 29 | 94.79 | 0.74 |
| 3 disjoint groups | | | | | | | |
| Kmeans | 1521771 | 14312 | 106.33 | 25009 | 213 | 117.41 | 0.91 |
| Boundary_50 | 2016932 | 1972 | 1022.78 | 9177 | 30 | 305.9 | 3.34 |
| Boundary_100 | 2113079 | 2268 | 931.69 | 10215 | 32 | 319.22 | 2.92 |
| Boundary_150 | 2222419 | 2552 | 870.85 | 11126 | 32 | 347.69 | 2.50 |
| Boundary_200 | 2247212 | 2855 | 787.11 | 11491 | 35 | 328.31 | 2.40 |
| Boundary_250 | 2259605 | 3147 | 718.02 | 11694 | 36 | 324.83 | 2.21 |
| Boundary_300 | 2269089 | 3431 | 661.35 | 11477 | 37 | 310.19 | 2.13 |

Kmeans with 2 or 3 disjoint groups aims to partition 24 objects into 2 or 3 clusters iteratively until a threshold is reached. The cyclic boundary condition should be reached in Kmeans after partition is performed once, because SR-SPIN is unable to dynamically split the concurrent region corresponding to subsequent partition iterations into disjoint groups. The numbers after "Boundary_" is the cyclic boundary in each benchmark which has a positive correlation with the size of interleaving space of each benchmark. The state count grows with the increase of cyclic boundary.

The benchmarks listed in the first column in the table have 2 or 3 disjoint groups. We call the firstly executed group in each explored trace during state exploration the root group. Each code snippet owned by the root group is a loop body iteratively operating on a shared variable. The condition of the loop compares the global variable with the cyclic boundary ranging from 50 to 300.

To measure the scalability of the effectiveness of our technique, comparison analyses are made in two dimensions: the number of disjoint groups and the cyclic boundary. The trend of each curve in the following coordinate graphs exposes whether our technique performs well when the benchmarks scales up. Each number on the horizontal axis is the cyclic boundary used by each benchmark.

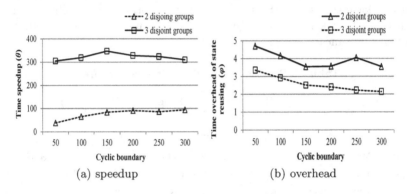

(a) speedup    (b) overhead

**Fig. 4.** Performance improvement and additional overhead resulted from local state reusing

Figure 4(a) shows the time speedup across the benchmarks except for Kmeans. We use $\theta_2$ and $\theta_3$ to denote the time speedup for 2 groups and 3 groups respectively. $\theta_2 \in [38, 94]$, and $\theta_3 \in [305, 347]$. The significant margin between speedup for the benchmarks with 2 and with 3 disjoint groups suggests the good scalability of our technique. Figure 4(b) exposes the additional time overhead of state reusing by the value of $\varphi$. Under the same cyclic boundary, the runtime overhead for 3 disjoint groups is much less than overhead for 2 disjoint groups. This is another proof for the good scalability. The overhead decreases with the increase of cyclic boundary overall. Figures 4(a) and (b) expose the potential of applying local state reusing to large-scale multithreaded programs.

Due to the reduction of redundant local state exploration, memory space used to store states is reduced dramatically. Figure 5 depicts the ratio between memory space consumed without and with state reusing. For the benchmarks with 2 disjoint groups, the ratio ranges from 10 to 30. And for benchmarks with 3 groups, the ratio ranges from 70 to 90. According to the amount of simulated runs explored per micro second shown in Fig. 6, the average time spent on each simulated run (trace) is cut down, which is the consequence of local state reusing. Reusing previously explored states is more time-efficient than computing the outgoing transitions at each state (persistent set).

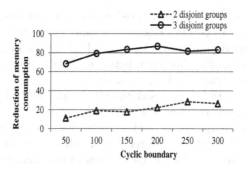

**Fig. 5.** Reduction of memory consumption

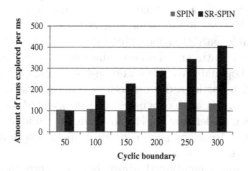

**Fig. 6.** The speed of exploration

# 6 Related Work

In spite of the state explosion problem arising from nondeterminism of concurrent programs, stateless model checking based on thoroughly searching states is still attractive in that it can prove the absence of concurrency error. A rich body of partial order reduction techniques have been proposed to strike state explosion problem such as persistent sets [25], stubborn sets [26], and ample sets [24]. Such techniques are established on the Mazurkiewicz trace theory [27] which provides the criterion for pruning redundant states. Each pair of interleavings leading to the same state can be obtained from each other through repeatedly exchanging adjacent independent transitions. According to the way to compute the outgoing transitions at each explored state, such techniques are classified into two categories: static and dynamic partial order reduction.

Classical static partial order reduction (SPOR) techniques [12, 24–26] heavily rely on static analysis to make state reduction. Model checking incorporated with SPOR is usually protected from missing any state related to safe properties through conservatively approximating inter-thread interferences. Due to the limitation of static analysis, these techniques are helpless to prune state space when working with the concurrent programs using dynamic memory. Dynamic partial order reduction (DPOR) techniques accurately detect dependences on the fly with the aid of instrumentation on shared memory operations, leading to a better state reduction than SPOR. Besides, in most cases, the runtime overhead brought by detecting dependences can be paid off by the improvement of time and memory efficiency. The difference between DPOR techniques [5,7,9,15,17] lies in the way to construct the backtracked set.

The rules of state reduction used by SPOR and DPOR are all heuristic. Consequently, a part of redundant states may escape from being eliminated. Sleep sets [25] and wakeup tree [5] are integrated with persistent sets and source sets respectively to strengthen state reduction. All the SPOR and DPOR techniques mentioned above exploit the independence relations between transitions to prune redundant exploration. State reduction employed in Zing [17] leverages the independence relations between atomic code blocks. The exploited fact is that concurrent program is a sequence of transactions in essence.

Static partial order reduction alone suffers from inaccuracy of dependence relations and dynamic partial order reduction alone suffers runtime overhead. The synergy between static and dynamic analysis of thread-locality completes each other in an orthogonal way. Static and on-the-fly escape analysis techniques are incorporated with partial order reduction techniques to deal with the challenges arised when working with concurrent object-oriented programs which may use dynamic memory or deferencing [4]. Heap shape model is leveraged to analyze state equivalence to adapt partial order reduction techniques to dynamic memory operations [18].

The POR techniques mentioned above only concern the nondeterminism stemming from thread scheduling. Recently, [1,2,6] adapt dynamic partial order reduction technique to work with the nondeterminism resulted from store buffering in concurrent programs under relax memory model. Nidhugg [1] introduces chronological traces to characterize the equivalence between traces to support state space reduction under TSO and PSO memory model. CDSchecker [6] combines schedule-driven partial order reduction with relaxed model-checking technique to overtake substantial state search space of the multithreaded programs written in C11/C++11. The similarity among partial order reduction techniques for multithreaded programs under sequential consistency and relax memory model lies in that redundant states should be eliminated according to state equivalence.

## 7  Conclusion

We implement SR-SPIN framework aimed to further address state explosion problem through local state reusing. Under the assumption that there exist certain parallel regions in multithreaded programs that can be partitioned into disjoint groups, we achieve the insight that the concurrent behavior of concurrent systems can be reasoned as the Cartesian product of concurrent behavior of each disjoint group. Based on this insight, our local state reusing technique for efficient model checking is established.

According to the experimental results, the potential of applying state reusing to large-scale multithread programs is confirmed from the perspective of its good scalability. SR-SPIN only can statically split parallel region into disjoint groups, because the mechanism of dynamically analyzing thread interferences is still absent. Dynamically splitting parallel region into disjoint groups will be incorporated into SR-SPIN in the near future.

**Acknowledgments.** We thank the anonymous reviewers for their valuable comments. This work is supported financially by the National Hi-tech Research and Development Program of China under contracts 2012AA010902.

# References

1. Abdulla, P.A., Aronis, S., Atig, M.F., Jonsson, B., Leonardsson, C., Sagonas, K.: Stateless model checking for TSO and PSO. In: Baier, C., Tinelli, C. (eds.) TACAS 2015. LNCS, vol. 9035, pp. 353–367. Springer, Heidelberg (2015)
2. Zhang, N., Kusano, M., Wang, C.: Dynamic partial order reduction for relaxed memory models. In: ACM SIGPLAN Conference on Programming Language Design and Implementation (2015)
3. Thomson, P., Donaldson, A.F.: The lazy happens-before relation: better partial order reduction for systematic concurrency testing. In: Proceedings of the 20th ACM SIGPLAN Symposium on Principles and Practice of Parallel Programming, pp. 259–260. ACM (2015)
4. Kusano, M., Wang, C.: Assertion guided abstraction: a cooperative optimization for dynamic partial order reduction. In: Proceedings of the 29th ACM/IEEE International Conference on Automated Software Engineering, pp. 175–186. ACM (2014)
5. Abdulla, P.A., Aronis, S., Jonsson, B., Sagonas, K.: Optimal dynamic partial order reduction. ACM SIGPLAN Not. **49**(1), 373–384 (2014)
6. Brian, N., Brian, D.: CDSchecker: checking concurrent data structures written with C/C++ atomics. ACM SIGPLAN Not. **48**(10), 131–150 (2013)
7. Lauterburg, S., Karmani, R.K., Marinov, D., Agha, G.: Evaluating ordering heuristics for dynamic partial-order reduction techniques. In: Rosenblum, D.S., Taentzer, G. (eds.) FASE 2010. LNCS, vol. 6013, pp. 308–322. Springer, Heidelberg (2010)
8. Jhala, R., Majumdar, R.: Software model checking. ACM Comput. Surv. (CSUR) **41**(4), 21 (2009)
9. Kastenberg, H., Rensink, A.: Dynamic partial order reduction using probe sets. In: van Breugel, F., Chechik, M. (eds.) CONCUR 2008. LNCS, vol. 5201, pp. 233–247. Springer, Heidelberg (2008)
10. Sen, K., Agha, G.: A race-detection and flipping algorithm for automated testing of multi-threaded programs. In: Bin, E., Ziv, A., Ur, S. (eds.) HVC 2006. LNCS, vol. 4383, pp. 166–182. Springer, Heidelberg (2007)
11. http://spinroot.com/spin/Man/init.html
12. Gueta, G., Flanagan, C., Yahav, E., Sagiv, M.: Cartesian partial-order reduction. In: Bošnački, D., Edelkamp, S. (eds.) SPIN 2007. LNCS, vol. 4595, pp. 95–112. Springer, Heidelberg (2007)
13. Strunk, E.A., Aiello, M.A., Knight, J.C.: A Survey of Tools for Model Checking and Model Based Development. University of Virginia (2006)
14. Nanda, M.G., Ramesh, S.: Interprocedural slicing of multithreaded programs with applications to java. ACM Trans. Program. Lang. Syst. (TOPLAS) **28**(6), 1088–1144 (2006)

15. Flanagan, C., Godefroid, P.: Dynamic partial order reduction for model checking software. ACM Sigplan Not. **40**, 110–121 (2005)
16. Holzmann, G.J.: The SPIN Model Checker: Primer and Reference Manual. Addison-Wesley, Reading (2004)
17. Andrews, T., Qadeer, S., Rajamani, S.K., Rehof, J., Xie, Y.: Zing: exploiting program structure for model checking concurrent software. In: Gardner, P., Yoshida, N. (eds.) CONCUR 2004. LNCS, vol. 3170, pp. 1–15. Springer, Heidelberg (2004)
18. Dwyer, M.B., Hatcliff, J., Iosif, R.: Space reduction strategies for model checking dynamic software. In: Proceedings of the 2nd Workshop on Software Model Chekcing (2003)
19. Hisley, D., Bridges, M.J., Pollock, L.L.: Static interprocedural slicing of shared memory parallel programs. PDPTA **2**, 658–664 (2002)
20. Lee, J.J.: Compilation Techniques for Explicitly Parallel Programs (1999)
21. Holzmann, G.J.: The model checker SPIN. IEEE Trans. Softw. Eng. **23**(5), 279–295 (1997)
22. http://spinroot.com/spin/Man/condition.html
23. Krinke, J.: Static slicing of threaded programs. ACM Sigplan Not. **33**, 35–42 (1998)
24. Peled, D.: All from one, one for all: on model checking using representatives. In: Courcoubetis, C. (ed.) CAV 1993. LNCS, vol. 697. Springer, Heidelberg (1993)
25. Godefroid, P., Wolper, P.: Using partial orders for the efficient verification of deadlock freedom and safety properties. In: Larsen, K.G., Skou, A. (eds.) CAV 1991. LNCS, vol. 575. Springer, Heidelberg (1992)
26. Valmari, A.: Stubborn sets for reduced state space generation. In: Rozenberg, G. (ed.) Advances in Petri Nets 1990. Lecture Notes in Computer Science, pp. 491–515. Springer, Heidelberg (1991)
27. Mazurkiewicz, A.: Trace theory. In: Brauer, W., Reisig, W., Rozenberg, G. (eds.) Petri Nets: Applications and Relationships to Other Models of Concurrency. Lecture Notes in Computer Science, vol. 255, pp. 278–324. Springer, Heidelberg (1987)

# Intelligent Road Congestion Prediction Employing Queueing Based Model

Lianghao Gao[1], Chengfang Ma[1], Lei Liu[1(✉)], and Xinjing Wei[2]

[1] School of Computer Science and Technology,
Shandong University, Jinan 250101, China
l.liu@sdu.edu.cn
[2] Division 2, Audit Bureau Jinan Branch,
Agriculture Bank of China, Jinan 250002, China

**Abstract.** Road traffic has long been recognized to represent a country's prosperity. Unfortunately, traffic congestion coming with it is considered as one of the most significant challenge in modern cities. Thus, a promising paradigm, namely, Intelligent Transportation System (ITS) has become a research focus which lies on its feasibility and efficiency of solving transportation issues. In the open literature, researchers have proposed theories and developed corresponding models to alleviate traffic congestion. However, many solutions are static, which means they serve to analyze and evaluate the traffic systems rather than schedule the road traffic dynamically. To this end, this paper develops a road traffic congestion prediction model to forecast the congestion level. The congestion performance metrics are obtained by developing a queueing system subject to self-similar traffic. This is because Hurst parameter evaluation, subject to road traffic flow at rush hour, presents strong self-similar characteristic. The developed model is validated by comparing results derived from model with that of simulations on real road traffic data provided by government authorities.

**Keywords:** Queueing system · ITS · Traffic prediction · Queueing analysis · Traffic engineering

## 1 Introduction

In modern society, road traffic system is an indispensable part of human life. According to the authorities, an average of 40 % of the urban dwellers spend at least an hour on road each day. Congestion poses a lot of problems such as fuel consumption, air pollution and time waste [1]. Moreover, accident risks increase with the expansion of traffic systems, particularly in several developing countries. Some reports published by the U.S. Federal Highway Administration indicated traffic accidents that happened in cities account for about 50 %–60 % of all congestion delays [2]. Last but not least, the competitiveness of a country, its economic strength, and productivity heavily depends on the performance of its traffic systems [3]. Thus, due to such urgent situations, Intelligent Transportation Systems (ITS) are brought to deal with congestion.

There are researchers who try to provide a solution for congestion by adopting the vehicles desired speed [4]. The research above yields interesting result yet it fails to

© Springer International Publishing Switzerland 2015
G. Wang et al. (Eds.): ICA3PP 2015, Part IV, LNCS 9531, pp. 539–548, 2015.
DOI: 10.1007/978-3-319-27140-8_37

look at the problem in a dynamic way as well as fails to focus on prediction other than static analysis. In this paper, we develop an analytical model to make prediction of the congestion dynamically by employing a queueing based model.

In open literature, there exists various strategies to modulate network traffic, and in the worst case, we can just restart the network to avoid a system's breaking down. Yet, in real life, it is impossible to restart traffic systems when congestion happens. To fill this gap, this paper proposes a solution to predict traffic congestion based on current traffic status. By analyzing the data collected from a large amount of auxiliary instruments in Jinan, we can derive the self-similar characteristics of the traffic system. This paper applies service rate subject to exponential distribution to corresponding traffic system because of the randomness characteristic traffic system has. This paper presents numerical validation on real traffic data presented by government authorities with different utilization.

The remainder of the paper is organized as follows. In Sect. 2, some preliminaries are presented. In Sect. 3, a queueing based prediction model has been introduced in detail. Section 4 validates the correctness as well as accuracy of the developed model. Finally, the paper is concluded in Sect. 5.

## 2 Self-similarity Evaluation of Road Traffic

### 2.1 Measurement of Traffic Self-similarity

Self-similarity is an important and widespread phenomenon in nature. The self-similarity of traffic can be examined by the following process [5]. $\{X_t : t \in N\}$ is an arbitrary time-series. Its autocorrelation function is denoted by $R(k)$.

$$R(k) \sim Mk^{-\beta_1} \tag{1}$$

where, $M > 0$ and $\beta_1 \in (0, 1)$. Hurst parameter which presents the degree of self-similarity can be obtained by

$$H = 1 - \frac{\beta_1}{2} \tag{2}$$

The evaluation of Hurst parameter is critical. Rescaled Range (R/S) estimator and Variance Time estimator are employed in this work [14].

**Rescaled Range Estimator.** R/S estimator is to provide means of evaluating variability changes with the length of time-ranged being concerned of a series [6].

$$\log(E[r(n)/S(n)]) \sim \log M_H + H \log n \tag{3}$$

where $r(n)$ is the range of the rescaled series, n is the block length and S stands for the standard deviation of the rescaled series. And $M_H$ is a positive finite constant independent of $n$. H, the Hurst parameter, is the slope of the line Eq. (3).

**Variance Time Estimator.** Variance Time (VT) estimator, also known as aggregated variance, which will be introduced in this section has low computational complexity [7].

$$\log \operatorname{var}(X^{(m)}) \sim -\beta_3 \log m + \log M_v \qquad (4)$$

By selecting different block size $m$, we can get a number of points by plotting $\log \operatorname{var} X^{(m)}$ against $\log m$ where $M_v$ is a finite positive value which is independent of block size $m$. $\beta_3$ is connected with Hurst parameter by equation $H = 1 - \beta_3/2$. These points are converged on a line which is presented by Eq. (4) with a slope $-\beta_3$.

## 2.2 Measurement of Road Traffic

The data collected by the cameras depicts the number of vehicles that pass through an intersection. 20 days' data starting from May 6th, 2013 is employed.

In Table 1, passing time refers to the time that the car passes the camera placed at the crossing and the time unit is millisecond. In our model, we ignore license number as well as license type. Each crossing number represents a crossing in Jinan and speed is calculated by cameras placed at the crossing. There are different types of crossings so the number of directions may vary.

**Table 1.** The sample of the real traffic data

| Passing time | License number | Vehicle type | Crossing number | Direction | Speed |
|---|---|---|---|---|---|
| 1367769600000 | XX14090 | 99 | 9 | 4 | 0 |
| 1367769600060 | XXL556S | 2 | 384 | 3 | 3 |

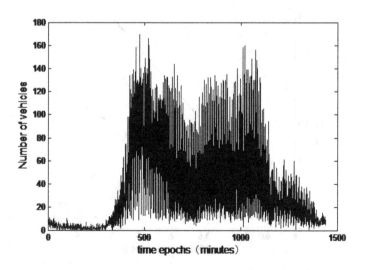

**Fig. 1.** Traffic dataset collected on May 6, 2013

Figure 1 plots the number of vehicles against the time epoch in minute, standing for the number of vehicles on May 6, 2013. Estimating the rush hours from the time information of all day, we select the period from 14:01:00 to 18:41:00. Figure 2 is plotted to demonstrate the number of vehicles at rush hours on May 6, 2013.

By referring to the figures above, the road traffic flow conforms to self-similar characteristics.

As aforementioned, the lines in Figs. 3 and 4 are mentioned in measurement of traffic self-similarity, and the slopes of these lines are the parameters, respectively. In Table 2,

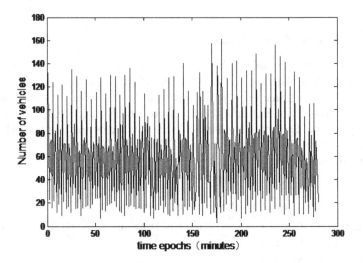

**Fig. 2.** Traffic dataset collected on May 6, 2013 (at rush hours)

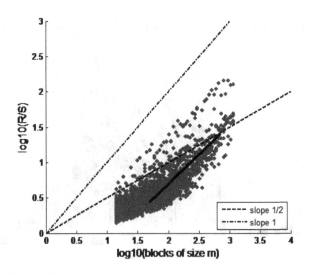

**Fig. 3.** Hurst parameter approximations by using R/S method

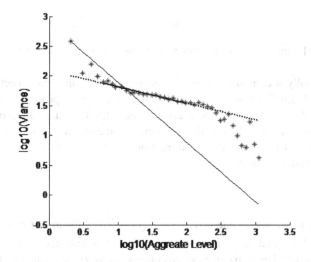

**Fig. 4.** Hurst parameter approximations by using VT method

**Table 2.** Hurst estimation of road data

| RS | 0.83534 |
|----|---------|
| VT | 0.86246 |

we present the Hurst parameter approximations according to the aforementioned estimators.

It is clear that all two estimators can measure the desired value well. The result shows that the road traffic flow conforms to a strong self-similar characteristic.

## 3   Analytical Model of Traffic Prediction

### 3.1   Modelling Self-Similar Road Traffic

This paper manages to develop an analytical model subject to self-similar traffic flow. In queueing theory study, exponential distribution is often used to depict service rate of real traffic system whose traffic flow possesses randomness, so we apply exponential distribution to determine how many cars pass an intersection during a green light period.

In this section, we consider our real world traffic system as a single server queueing system. This paper emulates the traffic light as a server since the traffic light operates periodically. So, the performance of the traffic system can be obtained by examining this queueing system.

Let $\{X = X_t\}, t \in N$ be a covariance stationary stochastic process with variance $\sigma^2$ and autocorrelation function $r(k), k \geq 0$. Process $X$ is said to be LRD [8], if

$$r(k) \sim \rho(k)k^{-\alpha}, k \to \infty \tag{5}$$

where $\alpha \in (0,1)$ and $\rho(k)$ is a slowly varying function. For $\forall x > 0, p(tx) \sim p(t)$ as $t \to \infty$.

It is essentially a continuous time Gaussian process with zero expectation at any time. In general, a traffic flow can be modelled as a stochastic process in a cumulative arrival form as $A = \{A(t)\}, t \in N$ where $A(t)$ is the cumulative amount of traffic arrived up to time t. Then $A(s,t) : A(t) - A(s)$ can denote the amount of traffic arrived in time interval $(s, t]$. For a fractional Brownian motion (fBm) traffic flow, the corresponding $A_f(t)$ can be expressed as [9]

$$A_f(t) = \lambda_f(t) + Z_f(t) \tag{6}$$

where $\lambda_f$ is the mean arrival rate and $Z_f(t) = \sqrt{a_f \lambda_f} \overline{Z_f}(t)$. Parameter $a_f$ is the variance coefficient of $A_f(t)$ and $\overline{Z_f}(t)$ is a standard fBm with variance $\overline{v_f}(t) = t^{2H_f}$, where $H_f \in [0.5, 1]$ is the Hurst parameter. According to $\overline{v_f}(t)$, we can get the variance function of $A_f(t)$ as follows [9]:

$$v_f(t) = a_f \lambda_f \overline{v_f}(t) = a_f \lambda_f^{2H_f} \tag{7}$$

## 3.2    Performance Metrics

In this section, the expression is derived to calculate the queue length distribution of the self-similar exponential queueing system by adopting an LDP-based method [10] to handle the real time traffic flows. An LDP characterizes the behavior of self-similar traffic based on a non-negative rate function especially examining the exponential decay of the probability measures of extreme or tail events. LDP has been successfully applied in information theory and risk management. This paper is built on the LDP specialized for Gaussian processes where the reproducing kernel Hilbert space is used to deal with the Gaussian case. This method requires that the variance $v_k(t)$ of Gaussian traffic flow $A_k$ fed into the queuing system satisfies $\exists \alpha < 2$, such that $\lim_t \to \infty, v_k(t)/t^\alpha = 0$.

It has been successfully used to study the queue length distribution of self-similar exponential queueing system subject to Gaussian traffic flows [10]. The Gaussian characteristic of real network traffic has been demonstrated by measurement studies (e.g., [11, 12]).

Now let us consider the self-similar exponential system. Let $A = \{A(t)\}, t \in N$ be the traffic flow fed into the queuing system and $A(s,t)$ be the amount of this traffic flow arrived during time interval $(s, t]$. Consequently, the total queue length, $Q(t)$, of the system at time t can be denoted as [10]

$$Q(t) = \sup_{s \le t} \{A(s,t) - C(t-s)\} \tag{8}$$

where C represents the service capacity of the self-similar exponential system. Note that theoretically, as long as the sum of the mean arrival rates of the traffic flow is less than the service capacity, the self-similar exponential system is able to converge to a steady state.

Based on the LDP method [10], we can derive the upper and lower bounds of the total queue length distribution, $P(Q > x)$, of the self-similar exponential queueing system as follows:

$$\frac{\exp(-\frac{1}{2}\theta(t_x))}{\sqrt{2\pi(1+\sqrt{\theta(t_x)})^2}} \leq P(Q > x) \leq \exp(-\frac{1}{2}\theta(t_x)) \tag{9}$$

where $\theta(t)$ is referred to as the determinative function of the queue length distribution and is given by

$$\theta(t) = \frac{(-x+(C-\lambda)t)^2}{v(t)} \tag{10}$$

Parameter $t_x(<0)$ minimizes $\theta(t)$, i.e. $t_x = \arg\min_t \theta(t)$ Function and $v(t)$ by Eq. (7).

Observing Eq. (9), we can find that the difference between the upper and lower bounds of the queue length distribution is the coefficient of $\exp(-0.5 \times \theta(t_x))$. This fact motivates us to take a certain mean (e.g., arithmetic mean, geometric mean) of the upper and lower bounds to approximate the queue length distribution. In this paper, we adopt the geometric mean that has been proven effective [13]. As a result, the total queue length distribution can be given by

$$P(Q > x) \approx \frac{\exp(-\frac{1}{2}\theta(t_x))}{\sqrt[4]{2\pi(1+\sqrt{\theta(t_x)})^2}} \tag{11}$$

From the above, it is easy to see that the queue length distribution is simply decided by the minimum value of the determinative function of $\theta(t)$. Upon solving the equation, $\theta'(t) = 0$, and substituting the root, denoted as $t_x(<0)$, into the equation, we obtain the minimum value of $\theta(t)$ as $\min_t \theta(t) = \theta(t_x)$.

Additionally, based on the queue length distribution of the self-similar exponential queueing system, we can easily get the waiting time distribution of the vehicles waiting in the queue. The result can be derived by Eq. (12),

$$P_w(q < t) = 1 - \pi^{-t/w} \tag{12}$$

where $P_w(q < t)$ is the probability of a random vehicle's waiting time less than time period t and w is average waiting time which can be calculated by the following equation,

$$W = \frac{p}{\mu(1-p)} \tag{13}$$

where p is arrival rate(lambda)/service rate(C).

## 4  Numerical Validation

### 4.1  Standardization of the Dataset

According to the raw dataset, we can get some valuable information of Jinan's traffic system. Then, some preprocessings are done to each dataset to help to pick out the data types that this paper needs.

Step1. Removal of irrelevant information and retaining useful information like passing time, intersection number and driving direction.

Step2. By referring to dataset, the crossing that has the largest traffic flow is found. The reason this paper uses the dataset with largest traffic flow is that our goal is to evaluate and model the traffic flow at rush hours and high throughput is likely to have self-similar feature. After doing the same work with crossing number 409 for a four successive day in May, we derive the final dataset.

Step3. Further filtration is done to pick out the time period with the most vehicles crossing the intersection. As a result, we get the busiest time period from 14:01:00 to 18:41:00, lasting for 20 days.

Step4. Converting the time unit of the raw dataset. We convert the time unit from millisecond to minute as the data cumulates. We add a twenty days' data during the rush hour with same time gap, deriving the final dataset. By expanding the dataset, we can get a more accurate result both from simulation and analytical model.

Step5. This paper takes the dataset derived from step 4 as input of simulation and the dataset we use to calculate Hurst parameter is the number of vehicles.

By the way, we can draw the variance coefficient by

$$S^2 = \frac{(x_1 - A)^2 + (x_2 - A)^2 + \ldots + (x_n - A)^2}{n} \tag{14}$$

where n is the data set number, A is the mean, $x_1, x_2, \ldots, x_n$ is the number of vehicles every minute according to the time sequence.

### 4.2  Analytical Model Versus Simulation

According to Figs. 5 and 6, we can prove that the analytical model is able to be applied to real traffic system.

Those two figures above illustrate the results of our model against the results derived by simulation on the real traffic data. From the pictures, we can see the queue length distribution, which is an essential parameter we should consider in network traffic researches and real world traffic studies. The results are perfectly matched thus strongly indicate the correctness as well as the accuracy of our model. Moreover, we are convinced that our analytical model is capable to be applied to evaluate traffic flows at rush hours.

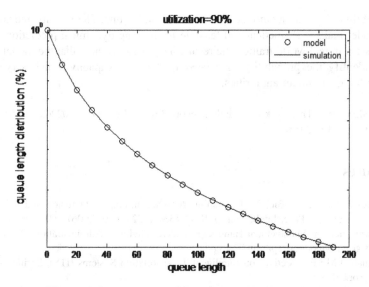

**Fig. 5.** Queue length distribution with utilization = 90 %

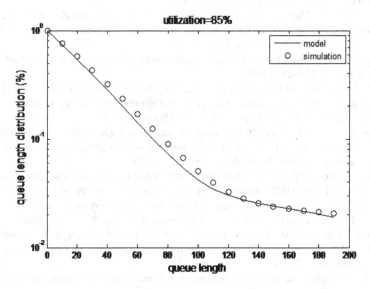

**Fig. 6.** Queue length distribution with utilization = 85 %

# 5 Conclusion

Road traffic prediction plays an important role in mitigating traffic congestion. This paper has developed an analytical model for a single server queueing system in the presence of self-similar road traffic system. We have obtained the performance metrics of queue length distribution of the traffic system. Queue length distribution suggested the probability of a certain number of cars waiting in the line. The validity and accuracy of the model make it a practical and feasible for making dynamical predictions of the traffic system in real world traffic. The results have demonstrated that the model can be used to identify the probability of exceeding the road capacity which serves as a guidance for government authorities.

**Acknowledgments.** This work is partially supported by NSFC NO. 61402262 and 61572295, SDSF NO. ZR2013FQ013.

# References

1. Shawe-Taylor, J., De Bie, T., Cristianini, N.: Data mining, data fusion and information management. IEE Proc. Intell. Transp. Syst. **153**(3), 221–229 (2006). IET Digital Library
2. Freeway Incident Management Handbook, Federal Highway Administration (2000). http://ntl.bts.gov/lib/jpodocs/rept_mis/7243.pdf
3. Sussman, J.M.: Perspectives on Intelligent Transportation Systems (ITS). Springer-Verlag, New York (2005)
4. AlGhamdi, A.S., Eren, H., Salem, A.: FLS modeling and using ITS to adopt traffic congestion. In: 2013 4th International Conference on Intelligent Systems Modelling & Simulation (ISMS). IEEE, pp. 112–115 (2013)
5. Daszczuk, W.B., Choromański, W., Mieścicki, J., et al.: Empty vehicles management as a method for reducing passenger waiting time in personal rapid transit networks. IET Intell. Transp. Syst. **9**(3), 231–239 (2014)
6. Mandelbrot, B.B., Wallis, J.R.: Computer experiments with fractional gaussian noise. Water Resour. Res. **5**, 228–267 (1969)
7. Beran, J.: Statistics for Long-Memory Processes. Chapman and Hall, New York (1994)
8. Beran, J., Sherman, R., Taqqu, M.S., et al.: Long-range dependence in variable-bit-rate video traffic. IEEE Trans. Commun. **43**(2–4), 1566–1579 (1995)
9. Norros, I.: A storage model with self-similar input. Queueing Syst. **16**(3–4), 387–396 (1994)
10. Mannersalo, P., Norros, I.: A most probable path approach to queueing systems with general Gaussian input. Comput. Netw. **40**(3), 399–412 (2002)
11. Kilpi, J., Norros, I.: Testing the Gaussian approximation of aggregate traffic. In: Proceedings of 2002 ACM SIGCOMM Workshop Internet Measurment, pp. 49–61 (2002)
12. van de Meent, R., Mandjes, M., Pras, A.: Gaussian traffic everywhere? In: Proceedings of 2006 IEEE International Conference on Communications, pp. 573–578 (2006)
13. Quan, Z., Chung, J.-M.: Priority queueing analysis for self-similar traffic in high-speed networks. In: Proceedings of 2003 IEEE International Conference on Communications, vol. 3, pp. 1606–1610 (2003)
14. Liu, L.: Analytical modelling of scheduling schemes under self-similar network traffic. Traffic Modelling and Performance Analysis of Centralized and Distributed Scheduling Schemes. University of Bradford (2011)

# Evaluation and Analysis of Three Typical Resource Allocation Algorithms in Virtual Router Platform

Xianming Gao[(⊠)], Baosheng Wang, Xiaozhe Zhang, and Shicong Ma

School of Computer Science,
National University of Defense Technology, Changsha 410073, China
nudt_gxm9000@163.com

**Abstract.** Virtual router is regarded as one of key platforms for the deployment and application of network virtualization technology, which can run multiple router instances in parallel and in independent. However, due to the frequent creation and deletion of router instances, there may be lots of resource fragmentations that can prevent this platform from establishing new router instances in it. In order to analyze influences of above problem, this paper firstly establishes resource evaluation model for virtual router platform. And we evaluate three typical resource allocation algorithms including first-fit algorithm, best-fit algorithm, and worst-fit algorithm in terms of failure magnitude of creation of router instances, magnitude of resource fragmentations, ratio of resource fragmentation, and execution time. At last, we further analyze advantages and disadvantages of three algorithms through our designed simulator, namely SoRAA. Our experimental results show that best-fit algorithm is the best among three typical algorithms in the processing of resource allocation.

**Keywords:** Network virtualization · Virtual router · Resource fragmentation · First-fit · Best-fit · Worst-fit

## 1 Introduction

Network virtualization technology [1–3] has been regarded as a gradual solution to innovation of Internet architecture, which attracts lots of attentions from research communities and equipment venders. This technology can run several virtual networks synchronously, and these virtual networks may be isomorphic or isomerous network architecture. Moreover, it has the ability to provide differential service, which can establish a test-bed for evaluation of new protocols, or can provide different network-resources for lessees in cloud environment [4, 5]. Virtual router is regarded as one of key equipment for the deployment and implement of virtual networks, whose role is the same as the traditional routers in the Internet [6, 7]. Virtual router platform can run multiple router instances in parallel and in independent, and each router instance plays an important role on packet forwarding in one virtual network. Thus, service providers can rent network resources to lessees by creating virtual networks and establishing router instances. Meanwhile, they can release network resources occupied by virtual network after the lifecycle of virtual router comes to end.

© Springer International Publishing Switzerland 2015
G. Wang et al. (Eds.): ICA3PP 2015, Part IV, LNCS 9531, pp. 549–568, 2015.
DOI: 10.1007/978-3-319-27140-8_38

During service providers continually creating and deleting of router instances in one virtual route platform, there will be lots of resource fragmentations whose resource space is too small to meet requirements of new incoming requests of creation of router instances. And these resource fragmentations are non-sequential spaces, which cannot be combined to establish router instances. The meaning of resource fragmentation is similar to "memory fragmentation" in general computers. In special, as the amount of resource fragmentation increases, virtual router platform will have less available resources. At last, it cannot normally dispose incoming requests any more, even though it has enough resources including lots of resource fragmentations for new router instances. For instance, one platform has two network interfaces with 10Gbps: NIC-A and NIC-B, and service providers has partitioned one virtual interface with 4Gbps off from NIC-A and another virtual interface with 4Gbps off from NIC-B. At the moment, this platform has two resource fragmentations: one resource block with 6Gbps in NIC-A and another resource block with 6Gbps in NIC-B. When one new request of the creation of router instance including one interface with 8Gbps comes, this platform cannot use the remainder of two network interfaces to create one virtual interface with 8Gbps, even though it has interface resources of 12Gbps. Thus, the resource fragmentations generated by the creation and deletion of router instances hinder virtual router platform from continually establishing new router instances. In fact, "resource fragmentation" problem in virtual router platform is a severe problem. Unluckily, researchers don't pay any attention on this problem, while they had put lots of efforts to ensure the independence of router instances [8, 9] and made many attempts to advance the overall performance of virtual router platform [10–12]. If we want virtual routers to provide supports for network virtualization, we should change our research way and start to attach importance to "resource fragmentation" problem.

In order to analyze influences of "resource fragmentation" problem on virtual router problem, this paper firstly establishes resource evaluation model, and we can evaluate resource allocation algorithms in terms of failure magnitude of creation of router instances, magnitude of resource fragmentation, ratio of resource fragmentation, and execution time. At present, virtual router platform usually adopts three typical resource allocation algorithms to calculate the mapping relationship between router instances and physical infrastructure, and these three algorithms include first-fit algorithm, best-fit algorithm, and worst-fit algorithm. We design a simulator that is called as SoRAA to analyze advantages and disadvantages of three algorithms. The simulator can save appointed magnitude of physical resources (such as line-card number, link-bandwidth, CPU number, and memory size), randomly create or delete router instances, and set resource size of each router instance. Our experimental results that best-fit algorithm is better than the other algorithms in terms of failure magnitude of creation of router instances, magnitude of resource fragmentation, and ratio of resource fragmentation. Although execution time of best-fit algorithm is longer than the others', best-fit algorithm is fit for resource allocation in virtual router platform. We hope that our results can provide supports for the deployment of virtual routers.

The remainder of this paper is organized as follow. Section 2 discusses and illustrates the features and limitations of related works about resource allocation in virtual router platform. Section 3 presents a general model for virtual router, and establishes evaluation model for our platform. Section 4 mainly exhibits three algorithms in static allocation: first-fit algorithm, best-fit algorithm, and worst-fit algorithm. Section 5 presents our experimental results about three algorithms, and analyzes advantages and disadvantages of three algorithms. Section 6 concludes this paper with a summary of our studies and discusses next works in the future.

## 2  Related Works

Many major router vendors and research communities have begun to follow suit in building support for router virtualization [6, 7, 10–12], and explore how the virtual routers can support for multiple router instances running on the same underlying physical device where the behavior of router instance is identical to the behavior of physical router. It is a key device for bridging the gap between the new network architectures and physical platforms. Thus, many focus on the virtual routers that can support for polymorphic network architectures rather than monolithic network architectures and accommodate simultaneous coexistence of several router instances including the traditional router in the current Internet.

However, how to control and manage virtual router platform to create (or delete) router instance is cold topic relative to the above research topics. At the same time, a real platform supporting virtual router doesn't come down to earth. Dynamic migration of router instances may provide a solution to "resource fragmentation" problem, as shown in Fig. 1 [13]. The logical control plane of router instance RC2 is migrated from one control blade to another control blade, the logical forwarding plane of router instance Rf2 is migrated in the same way, and the two virtual network interfaces of router instance are also migrated. At last, we can clearly see that these two router instances are deployed in the same blades, which can efficiently reduce the amount of resource fragmentation.

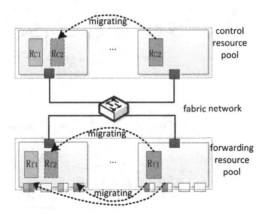

**Fig. 1.** Dynamic re-configuration processing

However, dynamic migration of router instance must take time to move router instances from one blade to another blade, which may results in cutoff of migrated router instances. The best way to solve the "resource fragmentation" problem is static allocation that must try to decrease the amount of resource fragmentations in the processing of calculation of mapping relationship between router instances and physical infrastructure.

# 3   System Overview

In this section, we mainly present a general framework of virtual router platform. We further establish resource evaluation model based on this framework and point out which criterions can be used to evaluate resource allocation algorithms.

## 3.1   Platform Framework

We put forward three-layer model supporting the deployment of router instances. It includes: resource management plane, control plane, and data plane, as shown in Fig. 2. This model can provide a good interactive interface for service providers to manage their platforms. Moreover, physical infrastructure adopts "pool" idea, which includes a cluster of resource blades to provide high performance and high expansibility.

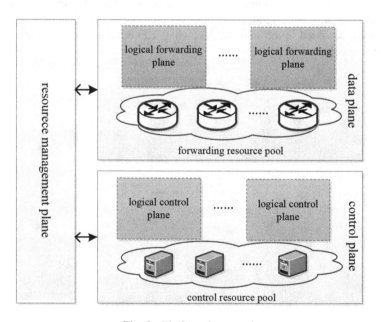

**Fig. 2.** Platform framework

From the description of our proposed platform framework, it mainly includes three key planes as follows:

Resource management plane: it is responsible for management tasks of overall platform, such as providing an interactive interface for operators, managing physical platform, translating high-level language into executable content, calculating the mapping relationship between router instances and physical infrastructure, deploying the router instances, and releasing the occupied resources. Resource Management plane usually run in a single server, which interconnect with any equipment in control and forwarding resource pool via Ethernet or other ways. So three typical resource allocation algorithms included in this paper are deployed in this plane.

Control plane: it is used to run multiple logical control planes in parallel by using system virtualization technology, such VMware [14], XEN [15], LXC [16], and KVM [17] etc. These logical control planes share the same physical resources in control-resource pool. And each logical control plane can either run routing demos, such as Quagga [18] and XORP [19], or customized protocols to support new network architecture. When any equipment of control-resource pool joins, it must notify its resource information to resource management plane as soon as possible. So that the latter can create logical control plane of router instance onto it.

Data plane: it is used to run multiple logical forwarding planes in parallel. It doesn't use system virtualization technology to virtualize data plane, due to the low performance of the latter. Data plane can provide fixed of physical resources (such as interface number, link-bandwidth, CPU number, and memory size) for each logical forwarding plane. And each logical forwarding plane can adopt function-based router (such as click [20]) or flow-based router (such as OpenFlow Switch [21]). Each logical forwarding plane must have a corresponding logical control plane in control plane. When any equipment of forwarding-resource pool joins, it must notify its resource information to resource management plane as soon as possible. So that the latter can create logical forwarding plane of router instance onto it.

When managers want to create one new router instance, resource management plane firstly calculates the mapping relationship between router instance and physical infrastructure based on installed resource allocation algorithm. It then sends configuration rules to control and forwarding plane to create one logical control plane and one logical forwarding plane of a single router instance. When the lifecycle of a router instance is over, resource management plane should callback the resources occupied by router instance. And, this platform will generate lots of resources fragmentations in the processing of creation and deletion of router instances. The magnitude of resource fragmentations is determined by resource allocation algorithms. Thus, it's necessary to evaluate these typical resource allocation algorithms in virtual router platform.

## 3.2    Resource Evaluation Model

Virtual router platform mainly includes two physical resources: control resource pool and forwarding resource pool. These two types of physical resources are responsible for different functional planes. In order to judge whether or not physical resources meet the requirements of router instances and calculate the amount of resource fragmentations, we firstly establish an evaluation model for virtual router platform, which includes three types of resource models as follows:

Physical control resource model: it is used to describe physical resources in control resource pool, which determines whether available resources meet requirements of logical control plane. Cx refers to physical control blade that can run logical control planes. Each Cx includes three parts of resources: (1) CPU, which is responsible for calculation function of logical control plane; (2) link-bandwidth, which is mainly used to communicate with the corresponding logical forwarding plane in data plane; and (3) memory, which can save state information, such as routing tables, as shown in Formula (1).

$$Cx = \sum \left( C_{cpu} + C_{link} + C_{mem} \right) \tag{1}$$

And C refers to the total physical resources of control resource pool, which is calculated as shown in Formula (2).

$$C = \sum_{i=1}^{N} Ci \ (i \in control - blade) \tag{2}$$

Physical forwarding resource model: it is used to describe forwarding resources in forwarding resource pool. Fx refers to physical forwarding blade that running logical forwarding planes. Each Fx also includes three parts of resources: (1) CPU, which is responsible for calculation function of logical forwarding plane; (2) link-bandwidth, which is used to communicate with the corresponding logical control plane in control plane and interconnect with other nodes in underlying network; (3) memory, which can save forwarding rules, such as forwarding tables or flow tables, as shown in Formula (3).

$$Fx = \sum \left( F_{cpu} + F_{link} + F_{mem} \right) \tag{3}$$

And F refers to the total physical resources of forwarding resource pool, which is calculated as shown in Formula (4).

$$F = \sum_{i=1}^{N} Fi \ (i \in forwarding - blade) \tag{4}$$

Router instance resource model: it is used to describe resources occupied by route instances in virtual router platform. Rx refers to physical resources occupied by router instance, which include two parts: $R^x_{C(m)}$, which stands for resources (onto control blade m) occupied by logical control of router instance x, and $R^x_{F(n)}$, which stands for resources (onto forwarding blade n) occupied by logical forwarding of router instance x, as shown in Formula (5).

$$Rx = R^x_{C(m)} + R^x_{F(n)} (m \in control - blade; n \in forwarding - blade) \qquad (5)$$

And R refers to the total physical resources occupied by router instances, which is calculated as shown in Formula (6).

$$R = \sum_{i=1}^{N} Ri(i \in router - ins\tan ce) \qquad (6)$$

We can use three types of resource models to calculate resource utilization that is an important criterion. The resource utilization refers to the ratio of resource occupied by router instances to overall resources including overall control-resources and overall forwarding-resources, as shown in Formula (7):

$$R_{utilization} = \frac{R}{C+F} \qquad (7)$$

### 3.3 Evaluation Criterion

In order to evaluate resource allocation algorithms in virtual router platform, we put forwarding four evaluation criterions: (1) failure magnitude of creation of router instances, (2) magnitude of resource fragmentations, (3) ratio of resource fragmentation, and (4) execution time based on above resource evaluation model. The details of four evaluation criterions are as follows.

1. Failure magnitude of creation of router instances

This evaluation criterion is used to record failure times in the processing of creation of router instances. If requirements of logical forwarding plane or requirements of logical control plane exceeds maximum of remainder in a single blade, resource management plane cannot allocate any resource for them, as shown in Formula (8).

$$sum(failure) = \begin{cases} sum(failure) + 1 & \begin{array}{l} if(R^x_{C(m)} > MAX\{\text{Remainder}(Cx)\}) \\ if(R^x_{F(n)} > MAX\{\text{Remainder}(Fx)\}) \end{array} \\ sum(failure) & other \end{cases} \qquad (8)$$

- *MAX{Remainder (Cx)}*: it refers to the maximum of resource block in control-resource pool;
- *MAX{Remainder (Fx)}*: it refers to the maximum of resource block in forwarding-resource pool;

We can use this above formula to know failure magnitude of creation of router instances. If this evaluation criterion is too big, resource allocation algorithms has worse ability to meet needs of creation of router instances. Otherwise, operators can establish router instances with a lower possibility of failure of creation of router instances.

## 2. Magnitude of resource fragmentations

This evaluation criterion can refer to how many resource fragmentations are located in our platform. We can calculate the sum of resource fragmentations in each blade, as shown in Formula (9).

$$sum(frag) = \sum_{i}^{M} \sum_{p} P_{C(m)}^{p} + \sum_{j}^{N} \sum_{q} P_{F(n)}^{q} \, (m \in control - blade;$$

$$n \in forwarding - blade) \tag{9}$$

- $P_{C(m)}^{p}$: it refers to a resource fragmentation p in control blade m;
- $P_{F(n)}^{q}$: it refers to a resource fragmentation q in forwarding blade n;
- $\sum_{i}^{M} \sum_{p} P_{C(m)}^{p}$: it refers to magnitude of resource fragmentations in control-resource pool;
- $\sum_{j}^{N} \sum_{q} P_{F(n)}^{q}$: it refers to magnitude of resource fragmentations in forwarding-resource pool.

The value of this evaluation criterion is continually changing in the processing of creation and deletion of router instances. If platform has low magnitude of resource fragmentations, resource allocation algorithms have higher chance to allocate resources for incoming requests of creation of router instances; otherwise, it may fails to establish new router instances.

## 3. Ratio of resource fragmentation

In order to further analyzing "resource fragmentation" problem, we use an evaluation criterion, namely ratio of resource fragmentation. It refers to the ratio of the largest resource block to all resource space. The calculation of this evaluation criterion is as shown in Formula (10):

$$f_R = \begin{cases} f_C \text{ if } (f_C \geq f_F) \\ f_F \text{ if } (f_F > f_C) \end{cases} \tag{10}$$

- $f_C$: it refers to ratio of resource fragmentation in control-resource pool, as shown in Formula (10);
- $f_F$: it refers to ratio of resource fragmentation in forwarding-resource pool.

When the ratio of resource fragmentation in control plane is no smaller than the ratio of resource fragmentation in forwarding plane, the ratio of resource fragmentation in our platform is determined by the ratio of resource fragmentation in control plane.

And when the ratio of resource fragmentation in control plane is smaller than the ratio of resource fragmentation in forwarding plane, the ratio of resource fragmentation in our platform is determined by the ratio of resource fragmentation in forwarding plane. $f_R$ is lower than 1; only when this platform only includes one control blade and one forwarding blade, and doesn't establish any router instance, $f_R$ is equal to 1. For example, our platform has two control blades and four forwarding blades without deploying any router instance, so $f_C$ is 0.5, $f_F$ is 0.75, and $f_R$ is 0.75. The smaller this evaluation criterion is, the better resource allocation algorithm is.

Formula (11) is used to calculate the ratio of resource fragmentation in control plane, numerator refers to the largest resource block in control plane, and denominator refers to the total resources of control plane.

$$f_F = 1 - \frac{MAX(size(P^q_{F(n)}))}{F} \tag{11}$$

Formula (12) is used to calculate the ratio of resource fragmentation in forwarding plane, numerator refers to the largest resource block in forwarding plane, and denominator refers to the total resources of forwarding plane.

$$f_C = 1 - \frac{MAX(size(P^q_{C(n)}))}{C} \tag{12}$$

4. Execution time

Execution time refers to how long resource allocation algorithm calculates the mapping relationship between router instances and physical infrastructure. In this paper, we mainly make an experiment on execution time of three typical algorithms including first-fit, best-fit, and worst-fit based on our simulator.

The shorter the execution time of resource allocation algorithm is, the better it is. If an algorithm has a short execution time, it can calculate the wanted results as soon as possible. And operators usually hope that resource allocation algorithm can calculate mapping relationship in millisecond, which can provide quality of experience.

## 4 Description of Three Typical Algorithms

Static allocation arms to calculate mapping relationship between router instances and underlying infrastructure before router instances are established by resource management plane. The way of static allocation tries to solve "resource fragmentation" problem by adopting the best configuration of creation of router instances. It makes efforts to avoid occurrence of resource fragmentation during the creation of router instance. However, the way may also increase the amount of resource fragmentations in the processing of the creation and deletion of router instances. At last, our platform may have lots of resource fragmentations, and cannot provide service for new requests until it has enough physical resources.

Though the way of static allocation cannot fundamentally solve "resource fragmentation" problem, it's a useful way to slow the processing of increasing of resource fragmentations. In this part, we introduce three typical algorithms into our platform: first-fit algorithm [22], best-fit algorithm [23], and worst-fit algorithm [23]. And these typical algorithms are usually used to solve "memory fragmentation" in traditional computer architecture. So we hope that these three algorithms also have the ability to solve "resource fragmentation" in virtual router platform.

## 4.1    First-Fit Algorithm

First-fit algorithm generally searches the first resource block that including enough remained resources to establish new router instances. Only when both resource block in control-resource pool and resource block in forwarding-resource pool meet needs of new router instances, resource management plane will establish new router instances.

In first-fit algorithm, it includes four types of linked lists: C-idle list using to manage idle resource blocks in control resource pool; C-allocated list using to manage control resources occupied by router instances; F-idle list using to manage idle resource blocks in forwarding resource pool; and F-allocated list using to manage forwarding resources occupied by router instances, as shown in Figs. 3a and b.

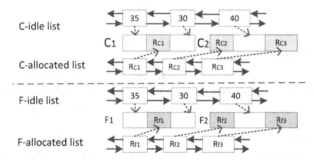

a. Resource lists before allocating resources for incoming requests

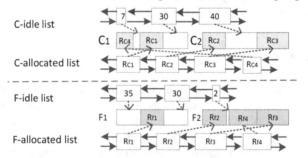

b. Resource lists after allocating resources for incoming requests

**Fig. 3.**  First-fit algorithm

When resource management plane establishes one router instance, it allocates two types of physical resources for the latter. Firstly, first-fit algorithm searches C-idle list from head to tail, and finds the first resource block that meets the requirement of logic control plane. And then this algorithm searches F-idle list to find the first resource block that meet the requirement of logical forwarding plane. At last, if it finds selected resource blocks both in C-idle list and in F-idle-allocated list, resource management plane can allocate resources for this request; otherwise, resource management plane cannot establish any router instance. For example, when a request of creation of router instance including control resources with 28-unit and forwarding resources with 38-unit comes, resource management plane will establish logical control plane on resource block with 35-unit of C-idle list and logical forwarding plane on resource block with 40-unit of F-idle list based on the theory of first-fit algorithm, as shown in Fig. 3b. From the above description, this algorithm generated two resource fragmentations: one resource block with 7-unit in C-idle list and another resource block with 2-unit in F-idle list after this request is executed.

After one router instance is released, resource management plane should search C-allocated list to find resource block occupied by this router instance, and search C-idle list to judge whether or not the searched resource block can be consolidated with resource blocks in C-idle list. At the same time, it also has to search F-allocated list to find resource block occupied, and search F-idle list to judge whether or not the searched resource block can be consolidated with resource blocks in F-idle list. Thus, overhead of first-fit algorithm when it calculates mapping relationship between router instance and physical resources is lower than overhead when it releases the resources occupied by router instances.

## 4.2 Best-Fit Algorithm

Best-fit algorithm searches the best resource blade to establish new router instance. And the best resource block isn't smaller than resources required by router instance, and is the smallest among idle resource blocks. So best-fit algorithm must ensure that the best resource block in forwarding-resource pool is allocated for logical forwarding plane and the best resource block in control-resource pool is allocated for logical control plane. If platform doesn't have the best resource block for logical forwarding plane or logical control plane, it will give up this request.

In best-fit algorithm, it also includes four linked lists: C-idle list using to manage idle resources in control resource pool; C-allocated list using to manage control resources occupied by router instances; F-idle list using to manage idle resource in forwarding resource pool; and F-allocated list using to manage the forwarding resources occupied by router instances, as shown in Fig. 4a and b. Compared with first-fit algorithm, both C-idle list and F-idle list in best-fit algorithm sort from smallest to largest.

When resource management plane establishes one router instance, it allocates two types of physical resources for the latter. Firstly, best-fit algorithm searches C-idle list from head to tail, and find the first resource block that meets the requirement of logic control plane. And then this algorithm searches F-idle list to find the first resource

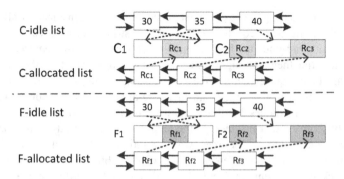

C-idle list

C-allocated list

F-idle list

F-allocated list

a. Resource lists before allocating resources for incoming requests

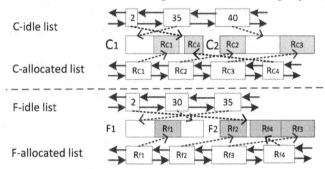

C-idle list

C-allocated list

F-idle list

F-allocated list

b. Resource lists after allocating resources for incoming requests

**Fig. 4.** Best-fit algorithm

block that meet the requirement of logical forwarding plane. At last, if it finds its selected resource blocks both in C-idle list and in F-idle-allocated list, resource management plane can allocate resources for this request; otherwise, resource management plane cannot establish this router instance. For example, when a request of creation of router instance including control resources with 28-unit and forwarding resources with 38-unit comes, resource management plane will establish logical control plane on resource block with 30-unit of C-idle list and logical forwarding plane on resource block with 40-unit of F-idle list based on the theory of best-fit algorithm. And, it also sorts C-idle list and F-idle list from smallest to largest, as shown in Fig. 4b. From the above description, this algorithm generated two resource fragmentations: one resource block with 2-unit in C-idle list and another resource block with 2-unit in F-idle list after this request is executed.

After one router instance is released, resource management plane should search C-allocated list to find resource block occupied by this router instance, and search C-idle list to judge whether or not the searched resource block can be consolidated with resource blocks in C-idle list. At the same time, it also has to search F-allocated list to find resource block occupied, and search F-idle list to judge whether or not the searched resource block can be consolidated with resource blocks in F-idle list. Besides the above tasks, it also sorts C-idle list and F-idle list from smallest to largest.

Thus, the overhead of best-fit algorithm when it calculates the mapping relationship between router instance and physical resources is lower that the overhead when it releases the resources occupied by router instances.

### 4.3 Worst-Fit Algorithm

Worst-fit algorithm usually searches the worst resource blade to establish new router instance. And the worst resource block isn't smaller than resources required by router instance, and is the largest among idle resource blocks. So worst-fit algorithm must ensure that the worst resource block in forwarding-resource pool is allocated for logical forwarding plane and the worst resource block in control-resource pool is allocated for logical control plane. If platform doesn't have the worst resource block for logical forwarding plane or logical control plane, it will give up this request.

In worst-fit algorithm, it also includes four linked lists: C-idle list using to manage the idle resources in control resource pool; C-allocated list using to manage the control resources occupied by router instances; F-idle list using to manage the idle resource in forwarding resource pool; and F-allocated list using to manage the forwarding resources occupied by router instances, as shown in Fig. 5a and b. Compared with best-fit algorithm, both C-idle list and F-idle list in worst-fit algorithm sort from largest to smallest. So worst-fit can quickly find the wanted result in the shortest time.

When resource management plane establishes one router instance, it allocates two types of physical resources for the latter. Firstly, worst-fit algorithm searches C-idle list from head to tail, and find the first resource block that meets the requirement of logic control plane. And then this algorithm searches F-idle list to find the first resource block that meet the requirement of logical forwarding plane. At last, if it finds its selected resource blocks both in C-idle list and in F-idle-allocated list, resource management plane can allocate resources for this request; otherwise, resource management plane cannot establish this router instance. For example, when a request of creation of router instance including control resources with 28-unit and forwarding resources with 38-unit comes, resource management plane will establish logical control plane on resource block with 40-unit of C-idle list and logical forwarding plane on resource block with 40-unit of F-idle list based on the theory of worst-fit algorithm. And, it also sorts C-idle list and F-idle list from largest to smallest, as shown in Fig. 5b. From the above description, this algorithm generated two resource fragmentations: one resource block with 12-unit in C-idle list and another resource block with 2-unit in F-idle list after this request is executed.

After one router instance is released, resource management plane should search C-allocated list to find resource block occupied by this router instance, and search C-idle list to judge whether or not the searched resource block can be consolidated with resource blocks in C-idle list. At the same time, it also has to search F-allocated list to find resource block occupied, and search F-idle list to judge whether or not the searched resource block can be consolidated with resource blocks in F-idle list. Besides the above tasks, it also sorts C-idle list and F-idle list from largest to smallest.

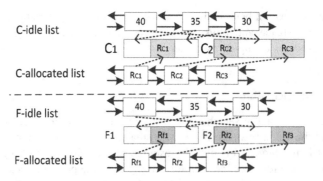

a. Resource lists before allocating resources for incoming requests

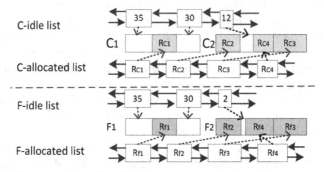

b. Resource lists after allocating resources for incoming requests

**Fig. 5.** Worst-fit algorithm

Thus, the overhead of worst-fit algorithm when it calculates the mapping relationship between router instance and physical resources is also lower that the overhead when it releases the resources occupied by router instances.

## 5    Experimental Results and Analysis

In order to analyze the advantages and disadvantages of static allocation, we firstly design a simulator which can calculate four evaluation criterions including failure magnitude of creation of router instances, magnitude of resource fragmentations, ratio of resource fragmentation, and execution time. At last, we contrast three typical resource allocation algorithms based our experimental results.

### 5.1    Description of Simulator

We design a simulator to achieve goals of evaluation of three typical resource allocation algorithms including first-fit, best-fit, and worst-fit. The simulator is called as

SoRAA[1] (Simulator of Resource Allocation Algorithm). The inputs and outputs of SoRAA are as follows.

1. Inputs of SoRAA

   - Quantity of control blades including CPU, link-bandwidth, and memory;
   - Quantity of forwarding blades including CPU, link-bandwidth, and memory;
   - Range of resources occupied by router instances;
   - Appointed resource utilization;
   - Times of resource allocation once runtime;
   - Selection of resource allocation algorithm;

2. Outputs of SoRAA

   - Failure magnitude of creation of router instances;
   - Magnitude of resource fragmentations;
   - Ratio of resource fragmentation;
   - Execution time;

We mainly make an experiment on four evaluation criterions based on different values of resource utilization. After operators set value of resource utilization, SoRAA will randomly create router instances and delete the existing router instances. During this processing, SoRAA will calculate these four evaluation criterions and record experimental results into appointed files.

## 5.2    Failure Magnitude of Creation of Router Instances

We firstly measure failure magnitude of creation of router instances based on different values of resource utilization, as shown in Fig. 6. This evaluation criterion is used to reflect failure frequency whiling operators creating new router instances.

It shows failure magnitude of creation of router instances increases as value of resource utilization continually increases. Besides, failure magnitude increases severely, when value of resource utilization is larger than 70 %, because there are only less than 30 % available resources and magnitude of resource fragmentations increases. At the same time, worst-fit algorithm appears the first failure of creation of router instances when the value of resource utilization is about 60 %; while the other two algorithms cannot meet needs of router instances, when value of resource utilization is no lower than 80 %. Besides, failure magnitude introduced by worst-fit algorithm is larger than the other two algorithms, and best-fit algorithm is the best among them in terms of failure magnitude of creation of router instances. However, three algorithms have a high failure magnitude of creation of router instances.

---

[1] SoRAA is developed by using "soft-thread" mechanism based on library functions provided by Quagga. We can easily append other resource allocation algorithms to SoRAA. Both best-fit and worst-fit use Quicksort to sort idle-lists. If you are interest in it, you can contact with us via e-mail.

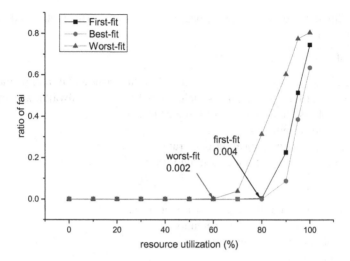

**Fig. 6.** Failure magnitude of creation of router instances

## 5.3 Magnitude of Resource Fragmentations

In order to further reflect the influences introduced by resource fragmentations on failure magnitude, we measures magnitude of resource fragmentations based on different values of resource utilization, as shown in Fig. 7. This value can reflect how many resource fragmentations are located in current platform.

It shows that when value of resource utilization ranges from 0 % to 90 %, magnitude of resource fragmentations increases continually as value of resource utilization

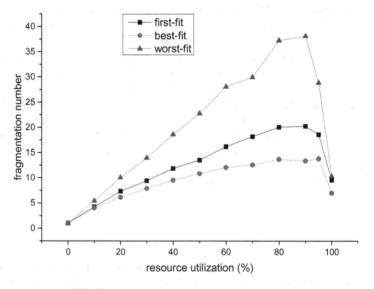

**Fig. 7.** Magnitude of resource fragmentations

increases; while magnitude of resource fragmentations appears a declining trend when value of resource fragmentations is larger than 90 %. Because there are less than 10 % available resources, many resource fragmentations may be allocated for new router instances. Besides, magnitude of resource fragmentations introduced by worst-fit algorithm is larger than other two algorithms, and best-fit algorithm is better than other two algorithms in terms of magnitude of resource fragmentation. And the amount of resource fragmentations is about 12 in the processing of creation and deletion of router instances.

## 5.4   Ratio of Resource Fragmentation

We put forward a formula to reflect status of resource fragmentations. Thus, we measure the maximum of size of source fragmentations and calculate ratio of resource fragmentation when value of resource utilization is 50 %, as shown in Fig. 8.

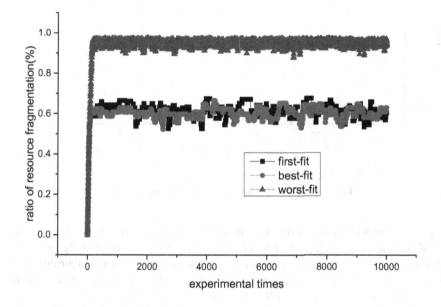

**Fig. 8.** Ratio of resource fragmentation

It shows that ratio of resource fragmentation increases severely with a start, and stays a fixed position. The fixed value in worst-fit algorithm is approximately 92 %, and the fixed value of first-fit algorithm is 60 %, which is equal to the fixed value in best-fit algorithm. The reason is that worst-fit algorithm always allocates maximal size of resource fragmentations for router instances; while first-fit algorithm randomly selects resource block to establish router instances and best-fit algorithm selects the best resource block. From the point of ratio of resource fragmentation, first-fit algorithm and best-fit algorithm are better than worst-fit algorithm. It means that best-fit and first-fit always have large size of resource blocks, which are fit for requests of creation of router instances including large resource needs.

## 5.5    Execution Time of Three Algorithms

We use execution time to reflect efficiency of each algorithm. And we measure execution time of each algorithm based on different values of resource utilization, as shown in Fig. 9.

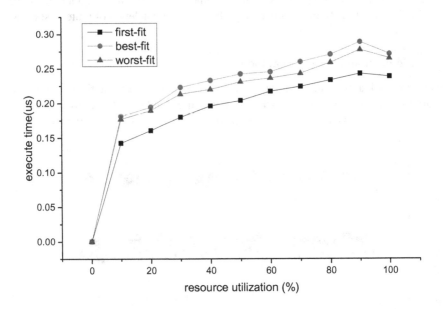

**Fig. 9.** Execution time of three typical algorithms

It shows that when value of resource utilization ranges from 0 % to 90 %, execution time of each algorithm increases as value of resource utilization continually increases. The reason is that the amount of resource fragmentations increases and algorithms will take more time to select fitted resource block from idle lists. However, once value of resource utilization is larger than 90 %, execution time appears a declining trend, because the amount of resource fragmentation decreases, which is resulted in by the failure of creation of router instances. Besides, execution time of first-fit algorithm is lower than other two algorithms, because it doesn't sort resource fragmentations when one router instance is created or deleted. And worst-fit algorithm is better than best-fit algorithm in terms of execution time, because worst-fit can quickly select fitted resource block, while best-fit should search idle-lists until it finds the best resource block.

## 5.6    Summary and Contrast

We summarize the above experimental results to enumerate advantages and disadvantages of three algorithms, as shown in Table 1.

**Table 1.** Summary of advantages and disadvantages of three algorithms

| Algorithm name | Evaluation Criterion | | | |
|---|---|---|---|---|
| | Failure magnitude of creation of router instances | Magnitude of resource fragmentation | Ratio of resource fragmentation | Execution time |
| First-fit | □□ | □□ | □□□ | □□□ |
| Best-fit | □□□ | □□□ | □□□ | □ |
| Worst-fit | □ | □ | □ | □□ |

Although execution time of best-fit is worse than the other algorithms, best-fit is no worse than the other algorithms in terms of other evaluation criterions. Thus, best-fit algorithm is fit for resource allocation in virtual router platform.

## 6 Conclusion and Future Works

In this paper, we firstly put forward "resource fragmentation" problem in virtual router platform, and further propose static allocation including three typical algorithms: first-fit, best-fit, and worst-fit. Static allocation just can avoid the occurrence of resource fragmentations. Our experimental results show that best-fit algorithm is the best selection for static allocation in virtual router platform.

However, when value of resource utilization is higher, best-fit algorithm also has higher failure magnitude of creation of router instances. Thus, we should find a better solution to "resource fragmentation" problem based on our analysis of this paper.

## 7 Acknowledge

This work is supported by Program for National Basic Research Program of China (973 Program) 'Reconfigurable Network Emulation Testbed for Basic Network Communication', and research on XXX access authentication and authorization protocol standards.

## References

1. Chowdhury, N.M.M.K., Boutaba, R.: A survey of network virtualization. Comput. Netw. **54**(5), 862–876 (2010)
2. Chowdhury, N.M.M.K., Boutaba, R.: Network virtualization: state of the art and research challenges. Commun. Mag. IEEE **47**(7), 20–26 (2009)
3. Guo, C.: Secondnet: a data center network virtualization architecture with bandwidth guarantees. ACM Conext **24**, 620–622 (2010)

4. Hao, F., Lakshman, T.V., Mukherjee, S., et al.: Enhancing dynamic cloud-based services using network virtualization. ACM Sigcomm Comput. Commun. Rev. **40**(1), 67–74 (2010)
5. Zaheer, F., et al.: Multi-provider service negotiation and contracting in network virtualization. In: IEEE/IFIP Noms, pp. 471–478 (2010)
6. Bozakov, Z.: An open router virtualization framework using a programmable forwarding plane. ACM Sigcomm Comput. Commun. Rev. **40**(4), 439–440 (2010)
7. Xie, G., He, P., Guan, H., et al.: PEARL: a programmable virtual router platform. IEEE Commun. Mag. **49**(7), 71–77 (2011)
8. Yang, M., Liu, Z., Yong, L.I., et al.: Control plane of a programmable hardware-based virtual router. J. Tsinghua Univ. **52**(5), 586–591 (2012)
9. Gao, X., Zhang, X., Lu, Z., et al.: A general model for the virtual router. In: 2013 15th IEEE International Conference on Communication Technology (ICCT), pp. 334–339. IEEE (2013)
10. Primet, P., Anhalt, F.: Analysis and evaluation of a XEN based virtual router. Netw. Internet Archit. (2008)
11. Mattos, D.M.F., Ferraz, L.H.G., Costa, L.H.M.K., et al.: evaluating virtual router performance for a pluralist future internet. Proc. Int. Conf. Inform. Commun. Syst. **7198** (5), 699–703 (2012)
12. Egi, N., Greenhalgh, A., Handley, M., et al.: Evaluating Xen for router virtualization. In: Proceedings of 16th International Conference on Computer Communications and Networks, ICCCN 2007, pp. 1256–1261. IEEE (2007)
13. Chen, X., Phillips, C.: Virtual router migration and infrastructure sleeping for energy management of IP over WDM networks. In: 2012 International Conference on Telecommunications and Multimedia (TEMU), pp. 31–36. IEEE (2012)
14. VMware. http://www.vmware.com/
15. XEN. http://www.citrix.com/products/xenserver/overview.html
16. LXC. http://zh.wikipedia.org/wiki/LXC
17. KVM. http://www.linux-kvm.org/
18. Quagga. http://www.nongnu.org/quagga/
19. XORP. http://www.xorp.org/
20. Morris, R., et al.: The Click modular router. Symp. Operating Syst. Principles Kiawah Island Sc **18**(3), 263–297 (1999)
21. Naous, J., Erickson, D., Covington, G.A., et al.: Implementing an OpenFlow switch on the NetFPGA platform. In: ACM ANCS, pp. 1–9 (2008)
22. Sun, X., Li, Y., Lambadaris, I., et al.: Performance analysis of first-fit wavelength assignment algorithm in optical networks. In: Proceedings of the 7th International Conference on Telecommunications, 2003. ConTEL 2003, pp. 403–409. IEEE (2003)
23. Bays, C.: A comparison of next-fit, first-fit, and best-fit. Commun. ACM **20**, 191–192 (1977)
24. Cheocherngngarn, T., Jin, H., Andrian, J., et al.: Depth-First Worst-Fit Search based multipath routing for data center networks. In: Global Communications Conference (GLOBECOM), 2012 IEEE, pp. 2821–2826. IEEE (2012)

# Beyond Data Parallelism: Identifying Parallel Tasks in Sequential Programs

Zhen Li[1]([✉]), Bo Zhao[2], Ali Jannesari[1], and Felix Wolf[1]

[1] Technische Universität Darmstadt, 64289 Darmstadt, Germany
{li,jannesari,wolf}@cs.tu-darmstadt.de
[2] Xi'an Jiaotong University, Xi'an 710049, China
zhaobo36@stu.xjtu.edu.cn

**Abstract.** Today, millions of legacy programs are awaiting their parallelization. For this reason, the automatic discovery of parallelism in sequential programs is now receiving considerable attention. However, past efforts mainly concentrated on data parallelism hidden inside loops. As programming models begin to support more irregular types of parallelism, centered around the notion of tasks in various forms, methods are needed to identify code sections that could potentially represent parallel tasks. In this paper, we present a novel approach to automatically finding parallel tasks in sequential programs. We first created a dynamic dependence graph, then isolated tasks, and finally produced a task graph according to the dependences we find. With the help of a source-to-source code translator, parallel code is automatically generated. We conducted a range of experiments to cover both tasks executing the same code and tasks executing different code. Results showed that our method achieved reasonable speedups on the test cases.

**Keywords:** Parallelism discovery · Task parallelism · Computational unit · Data dependence · Parallel programming

## 1 Introduction

While writing parallel programs from scratch has always been considered a difficult task, parallelizing legacy programs written by someone else, today a common scenario in many organizations, is even harder [8]. For this reason, many methods have been proposed to assist programmers in parallelizing sequential programs. The most attractive idea is to build a compiler that automatically translates a sequential into a parallel program. Such compilers support a set of directives that the programmer has to insert into the source code to mark sections that can run in parallel. Although this approach requires only minor changes to the source code, it leaves an important but time-consuming job to the programmer: finding parallelism in the sequential program.

To support programmers also in this initial stage of the process, methods have been proposed to discover potential parallelism automatically. So far, their main target has been data parallelism in loops, which can be exploited by distributing

© Springer International Publishing Switzerland 2015
G. Wang et al. (Eds.): ICA3PP 2015, Part IV, LNCS 9531, pp. 569–582, 2015.
DOI: 10.1007/978-3-319-27140-8_39

iterations of a loop among multiple threads. However, as more programming models such as OpenMP and Intel TBB [18] aim at task-based parallelism, this original focus of parallelism discovery becomes too narrow. In contrast to loop-based data parallelism, task parallelism does not require that every thread to execute the same code. Tasking can exploit parallelism between arbitrary code sections, including parallelism within individual iterations of a loop or between different loops.

In this paper, we present an approach to the detection of parallel tasks in sequential programs. As the first step, we run our data-dependence profiler [14] to extract the dynamic data-dependence graph. This graph is then transformed into another graph, whose edges represent only true data dependences and whose nodes are small pieces of computation without any noteworthy internal parallelism. We call these nodes *computational units* (CUs) and we call the graph *CU graph*. Then we search the graph for *strongly connected components* (SCCs) and *chains*, we merge the CUs they contain, and label them as potential tasks. Finally, we feed the generated task graph to a code transformation component that can transform serial C/C++ code into Intel TBB [18] parallel code. The code transformation component then translates the sequential source code into equivalent parallel code using TBB flow graph template.

The remainder of the paper is structured as follows. In the next section, we review related work and highlight the differences to our own. In Sect. 3, we explain our approach in more detail. Evaluation results and case studies are presented in Sect. 4. Finally, Sect. 5 summarizes our paper and discusses possible improvements.

## 2    Related Work

Methods for assisting parallelization mainly fall into one of two not necessarily disjoint categories. Methods in the first category focus primarily on data dependence analysis to find parallelism, whereas methods in the second category put more emphasis on the runtime system as their primary vehicle of parallelization.

***Dynamic Dependence Analysis.*** After purely static approaches including auto-parallelizing compilers had turned out to be too conservative for the parallelization of general-purpose programs, a range of predominantly dynamic approaches emerged. As a common characteristic, all of them capture dynamic dependence to asses the degree of potential parallelism. Using dependence information, Kremlin [6] determines the length of the critical path in a given code region. Based on this knowledge, it calculates a metric called self-parallelism, which quantifies the parallelism of a code region. Finally, Kremlin reports self-parallelism for each region, in the same way as an ordinary performance profiler such as gprof would report the time. Alchemist [20] is centered around the notion of futures, treating predefined constructs as candidates for asynchronous execution. It profiles the dependence distance (the number of instructions between the source and sink of a dependence) to estimate the effectiveness of parallelizing a certain construct. AutoFutures [15] adopts a similar idea, but goes one step further in that it automatically transforms the code. However, it seems to be still at a preliminary stage with negative speedup results reported for some of the test programs. Previous work [5] identified task parallelism in C applications for multiprocessor System-on-Chip (MPSoC) platforms based on the notion of a coupled block, which is a group of statements tightly coupled by dependences. A coupled block is treated as a task.

All of the approaches mentioned above discover parallelism from massive raw data dependences without respecting computation patterns. They overlook the truth that the computation of a task usually does not contain any noteworthy parallelism inside, and the set of variables used for communication among tasks usually does not overlap with the set of variables used for computations.

Other approaches primarily concentrate on the efficiency of profiling dependences. Parwiz [10] is an optimized data-dependence profiler that attaches the dependences it finds to the nodes of an execution tree (i.e., a generalized call tree that also includes basic blocks) that it maintains. Based on this execution tree, it can identify DOALL [9] loops in sequential programs. Prospector [11] is a parallelism-discovery tool based on the memory-efficient data dependence profiler SD3 [12]. It tells whether a loop can be parallelized and provides a detailed dependence analysis of the loop body.

**Scheduling.** Runtime scheduling frameworks are another way of adding parallelism to sequential programs. DSWP [16] and DOMORE [2] target DOACROSS [9] loops, scheduling their iterations in a pipeline style according to previously identified (static) dependences. Anantpur and Govindarajan [7] profile cross-iteration dependences for DOACROSS loops and try to accelerate their execution using GPUs. Ye and Chen [19] profile data dependences on the superblock level. Using a meta-reorder buffer to measure and exploit the available parallelism, superblocks are dynamically analyzed, reordered, and dispatched, respecting data dependences.

Generally, scheduling techniques incur a non-negligible fixed overhead, which changes very little if the number of data dependences in the program varies. Moreover, most scheduling approaches focus solely on DOACROSS loops, missing the potential parallelism outside such loops. While scheduling approaches do not require any effort on the part of the programmer, the above limitations often render the speedup they can achieve inferior to manual parallelization.

## 3   Approach

Our approach consists of the following steps. First, we profile the target program to extract the dynamic data-dependence graph. This graph then undergoes two transformations aimed at isolating tasks and dependences between them. During both transformations, nodes are merged to simplify the graph structure. At the end, some nodes may emerge as independent or dependent tasks. Finally, we submit the generated task graph to a code transformation component that transforms serial C/C++ code into Intel TBB parallel code.

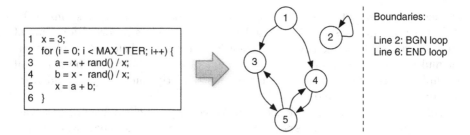

**Fig. 1.** Data-dependence graph and control-structure boundaries produced by DiscoPoP. Vertices are source lines and edges are data dependences.

## 3.1 Extracting Data Dependences

To generate the data-dependence graph, we use an efficient dynamic dependence profiler [14]. The nodes of the graph are source-code lines and the edges are data dependences between them. Figure 1 shows the profiler's output for a sample code section. The output also includes control-structure boundaries and the names of variables involved in dependences. Of course, relying on dynamic dependences makes our approach input-sensitive. However, the effects of the input sensitivity can be ameliorated by (i) running the target program with a range of inputs and merge the outputs (ii) letting the user specify a representative input that covers the typical execution flow.

## 3.2 Identifying Computational Units

The first transformation of the dependence graph isolates small pieces of code without any noteworthy internal parallelism, which we call *computational units* (CUs). A CU is built for a collection of instructions following the *read-compute-write* pattern: a set of variables is read by a collection of instructions and used to perform computation, then the result is written back to another set of variables. We call the two sets *read set* and *write set*, respectively. The two sets do not have to be disjoint. The load instructions reading variables in the read set form *read phase* of the CU, and the store instructions writing variables in the write set form *write phase* of the CU.

We define a CU by read-compute-write pattern because in practice, tasks communicate with one another by reading and writing values to variables that are global to them. Thus, we require the variables in a CU's read set and write set to be global to the CU, and the variables used in a CU's computation should be local. To distinguish variables that are global to a code section, we analyze variable scope information, which is available in any ordinary compiler. Note that the global variables in read set and write set do not have to be global to the whole program. They can be variables that are local to an encapsulating code section, but global to the target code section.

---

**Algorithm 1.** Algorithm of building CUs (pseudocode).

---

```
 1  for each region R in the program do
 2      globalVars = variables that are global to R
 3      isCautious = true
 4      for each variable v in globalVars do
 5          if v is read then
 6              readSet += v
 7              for each instruction Irv reads v do
 8                  | readPhase += Irv
 9              end
10          end
11          if v is written then
12              writeSet += v
13              for each instruction Iwv writes v do
14                  | writePhase += Iwv
15              end
16          end
17      end
18      for each instruction Ir in readPhase do
19          for each instruction Iw in writePhase do
20              if Ir happens after Iw then
21                  isCautious = false
22                  break
23              end
24          end
25      end
26      if isCautious then
27          cu = new computational unit
28          cu.scope = R
29          cu.readSet = readSet
30          cu.writeSet = writeSet
31          cu.readPhase = readPhase
32          cu.writePhase = writePhase
33          cu.computationPhase =
34          (instructions in R) - (readPhase + writePhase)
35      end
36  end
```

---

We further require that the load and store instructions in read phase and write phase are *cautious* [17]. Cautious property is previously defined for operators in unordered algorithms. By adapting it to CU, we say a CU is cautious if it reads all the variables in its read set before it writes any variables in its write set. Cautious property guarantees the read-compute-write pattern. It does not only give a clear way of separating read phase and write phase, but also allows multiple CUs to be executed speculatively without buffering updates or

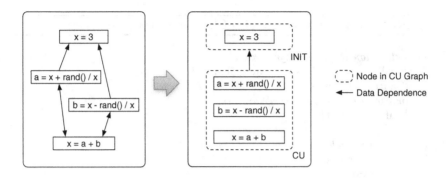

**Fig. 2.** Building a CU.

making backup copies of modified data because all conflicts are detected during
the read phase. Consequently, tasks extracted based on CUs do not have any
special requirement on runtime frameworks.

CUs are built for every *region*. A region is a single-entry-single-exit code
block. The difference between a region and a basic block is that not every instruction inside a region is guaranteed to be executed, meaning a region could be a
group of basic blocks with branches inside. A region can be a function, a loop,
an if-else structure, or a basic block. In practice, a basic block rarely contains
noteworthy parallelism because it usually contains a small number of instructions. Code in different branches of an if-else structure are semantically exclusive,
thus rarely run in parallel. Hence, we mainly focus on regions like functions and
loops, which usually contain important computations that can potentially run
in parallel. In our approach, regions of a program are traversed by implementing
the algorithm of building CUs shown in Algorithm 1 using the *region pass* in
LLVM [13].

Figure 2 shows a CU built from the code section shown in Fig. 1. Each loop
iteration calculates a new value of x with the help of local variables a and b.
For a single iteration, the loop region is cautious since all the read to x happen
before the write to x. Following the read-compute-write pattern, lines 3–5 are in
one CU, and the CU depends on the initialization of x, as shown in Fig. 2. Note
that CUs never cross control-region boundaries. Otherwise a CU could grow
too large, possibly swallowing all the iterations of a loop and many other code
sections, and hiding important parallelisms that we actually want to expose.

Identifying CUs simplifies the dependence graph by not only merging vertices
into CUs, but also hiding dependences that are local to the computations of CUs.
After identifying CUs, edges in the dependence graph are all inter-CU dependences, which are always among instructions in read phases and write phases.
Giving the truth that the number of global variables to a code section is usually
far less than the number of local variables, identifying CUs delivers a significant
simplification for the dependence graph. We call the simplified dependence graph
*CU graph*.

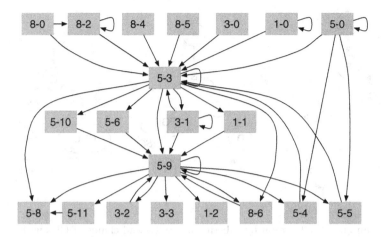

**Fig. 3.** Part of the CU graph of *rot-cc*.

Figure 3 shows a part of the CU graph of *rot-cc*, a benchmark from Starbench parallel benchmark suite [1]. According to the figure, although it is quite clear that some CUs can run in parallel (e.g. 8–4 and 8–5), it still requires effort to tell whether other CUs can run in parallel. Thus, we simplify CU graph further into a directed acyclic graph (DAG), which we call *task graph*.

### 3.3  Forming Tasks

The second transformation of the dependence graph helps identify either independent or dependent tasks, the latter in a potential pipeline arrangement. Whenever possible, we merge CUs contained in *strongly connected components* (SCCs) or in *chains*. The idea of merging CUs in SCC comes from previous work [16]. In graph theory, an SCC is a subgraph in which every vertex is reachable from every other vertex. Thus, every CU in an SCC of the CU graph depends on every other CU either directly or indirectly, forming a complex knot of dependences that is likely to defy internal parallelization. Identifying SCCs is important for two reasons:

1. Algorithm design. Complex dependences are usually the result of highly optimized sequential algorithm design oblivious of potential parallelization. In this case, breaking such dependence requires a parallel algorithm, which is beyond the scope of our method.
2. Coding effort. Even if such complex dependences are not created by design, breaking them is usually time-consuming, error-prone, and may cause significant synchronization overhead that may outweigh the benefit of parallelization.

Hence, we hide complex dependences inside SSCs, exposing parallelization opportunities outside, where only a few dependences need to be considered. Figure 4 shows the graph simplification process by substituting SCCs and chains

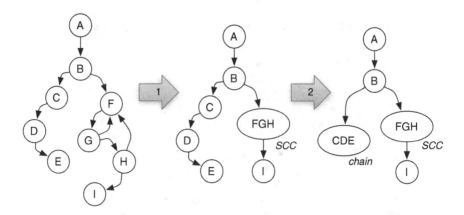

**Fig. 4.** Simplifying CU graph by substituting SCCs and chains of CUs with vertices.

of CUs with vertices. In step 1, CU $F$, $G$ and $H$ are grouped into $SCC_{FGH}$. After contracting each SCC to a single vertex, the graph becomes a directed acyclic graph. Moreover, we group CUs that are connected in a row without a branching or joining point in between into a *chain* of CU since a chain of CU does not contain significant parallelism inside, and merging them can lower the communication overhead among tasks. In step 2, CU $C$, $D$ and $E$ are grouped into $chain_{CDE}$. We call the simplified graph *task graph*.

Finally, we declare each vertex in the task graph a potential task. If the task graph has more than one entries, a virtual task ($task_0$) is added to be the predecessor of all the entry nodes. The virtual task ensures that a task graph has only one entry node, which simplifies the code transformation algorithm mentioned below.

### 3.4    Automatic Code Transformation

In the end, we submit the generated task graph to a code transformation component that transforms serial C/C++ code into Intel TBB [18] parallel code. Transformation is performed at AST level using Clang libraries. The transformation module traverses the Clang AST of the source code in order to locate the code sections targeted by the task graph. Afterwards, a source code rewriting module rewrites the targeted source code strings in the Clang AST context using TBB flow graph templates. The transformation component also supports DOALL loops. A DOALL loop is transformed into a TBB `parallel_for` template with its loop body filled as a lambda expression.

The flow graph transformation algorithm is divided into three steps:

Step 1: **Identifying Code Sections Corresponding to Each Task.** For each task in the task graph, the transformation module gets all its source code lines via the AST context and save them to *CU.codeBody* in the corresponding task. Note that the virtual task does not correspond to any code section.

Step 2: **Generating Source Code of the Flow Graph Node.** The source code rewriting module generates the flow graph node based on the following three cases:

- The current task has a single or none incoming edge and multiple outgoing edges. If all its successors receive the same data, we insert a TBB `broadcast_node`. Otherwise, a TBB `split_node` is inserted. When there is no input data for `broadcast_node` or `split_node`, the node template uses type `continue_msg` defined in TBB. Otherwise the corresponding data types must be obtained via AST and be passed to the template.
- The current task has a single incoming edge and single or none outgoing edge. In this case, the source code rewriting module directly transforms it to a flow graph `function_node` using a lambda function.
- The current task has multiple incoming edges and single out going edge, which means at least two variables need synchronization before they are passed to the current task. Hence, we must first add a `join_node` to synchronize the operations on these variables and then insert the `function_node`. A `join_node` has multiple input ports and generates a single output tuple that contains a value received from each port.

Step 3: **Generating Source Code of Flow Graph Edges.** After all of the flow graph nodes have been defined in the source code, the corresponding code for edges must be added according to the task graph.

It's worth mentioning that `join_node` supports three different buffering policies: `queueing`, `reserving`, and `tag matching`. Currently the buffering policy need to be determined by users, because it is usually semantic related and can not be solved by our tool. When all the nodes and edges have been defined, the transformation terminates and the parallel code is complete.

## 4    Evaluation

As we mentioned in Sect. 1, task parallelism does not require that every thread to execute the same code. Like loop-based data parallelism, tasking can certainly exploits parallelism among iterations of a loop (each task executes the same code). However, tasking also exploits parallelism between different loops and functions (each task executes different code). In this section, we show that our method can handle both kinds of task parallelism.

We have mentioned that the buffering policy of TBB `join_node` needs to be determined by users. Another thing that has to be determined by users is the data chunk size when data decomposition is needed. They are the only two things our method requires. Determining data chunk size automatically requires an auto-tuning technique, which is beyond the scope of this paper.

We conducted a range of experiments to evaluate our method. All experiments ran on a server with $2 \times 8$-core Intel Xeon E5-2650 2 GHz processors with 32 GB memory, running Ubuntu 12.04 (64-bit server edition). Time and speedup numbers represent an average of five independent executions.

## 4.1   Tasks Executing the Same Code

When tasks execute the same code, it means the parallelism comes from data decomposition. In sequential code, such parallelism usually resides in loops, where each iteration perform computation on a piece of input data. To determine whether a loop in sequential code can be parallelized, we only need to check if the partial CU graph of the loop has no circle, including edges that come from a CU and point to itself. Otherwise, an iteration of the loop reads data produced in the previous iteration, and the loop cannot be parallelized.

Programs containing loops where each iteration can be emitted as a task are easy to find. In our experiments, we chose three benchmarks (*BT*, *SP*, and *CG*) from NAS parallel benchmark suite [3], *blackscholes* from PARSEC benchmark suite [4], and two applications (*mandelbrot*, *ann training*) that are commonly used in parallel programming courses.

Instead of transforming each iteration into a tbb::task, we use tbb::parallel_for for loops because it utilize the thread pool in TBB for better efficiency. On the other hand, tbb::task always creates a new thread for a task.

Table 1. Summary of parallelization results for tasks executing the same code.

| Program | # parallel loops | | # of threads | Speedup(auto) | Speedup(manual) |
|---|---|---|---|---|---|
| | auto | manual | | | |
| BT | 22 | 30 | 16 | 2.17 | 6.78 |
| SP | 26 | 34 | 16 | 2.03 | 5.07 |
| CG | 5 | 16 | 16 | 2.15 | 8.36 |
| blackscholes | 3 | 1 | 16 | 3.19 | 7.12 |
| mandelbrot | 2 | 2 | 4 | 2.02 | 3.96 |
| ann training | 4 | 2 | 4 | 1.91 | 3.07 |

Table 1 shows the results on parallelizing tasks residing in loops. In general, our method exploits fewer parallelism than experienced programmers and results in lower speedups, which is common to all of the automatic parallelization approaches. In *blackscholes* and *ann training*, our method parallelized more loops than the manually parallelized versions. However, all the additional loops that are automatically parallelized are small loops doing initialization. Parallelizing such loops does not bring any speedup, but rather incurs additional overhead in creating and destroying threads.

An interesting case is *mandelbrot*, where our method parallelized exactly the same places as the programmer did. However, the automatic parallelized version still has a lower speedup due to imbalanced workload. In *mandelbrot*, whether the matrix is divided row-wise or column-wise gives a different workload to each worker thread. Unfortunately, there is no way to get such information before running a parallel version of the program. This case shows that although automatic parallelization method can bring some speedup for free, user's knowledge is still critical for a higher speedup.

## 4.2    Tasks Executing Different Code

In our experiments, we found that applications containing task parallelism that different tasks run different code are mainly from multimedia processing area. Thus, we chose Intel CnC sample program FaceDetection, and Ogg Vorbis codec libVorbis as representative cases.

**FaceDetection.** FaceDetection is an abstraction of a cascade face detector used in the computer vision community. The face detector consists of three different filters. As shown in Fig. 5(a), each filter rejects non-face images and lets face images pass to the next layer of cascade. An image will be considered a face if and only if all layers of the cascade classify it as a face. The corresponding TBB flow graph is shown in Fig. 5(b). A join node is inserted to buffer all the boolean values. In order to decide whether an image is a face, every boolean value corresponding to that specific image is needed. Thus we configure the transformation tool to use `tag_matching` buffering policy in the join node. `tag_matching` policy creates an output tuple only when it has received messages at all the ports that have matching keys.

The three filters take 99.9 % of sequential execution time. We use 20,000 images as input. The speedup of our transformed flow graph parallel version is $9.92\times$ using 32 threads. To evaluate the scalability of the automatically transformed code, we compare the speedups achieved by official Intel CnC (short for "Concurrent Collections") parallel version and our transformed TBB flow graph version using different number of threads. The result is shown in Fig. 6. The performance is comparable using two and four threads. When more than eight threads are used, the official CnC parallel version outperforms ours. The reason is that the official CnC parallel code is heavily optimized and restructured. For example, some data structures are altered from `vector` to CnC `item_collection`. As shown in Fig. 6, when using just one thread, the speedup of official CnC parallel version is already $2\times$ because of the optimization (Fig. 6).

**LibVorbis.** We also tested the encoder of LibVorbis, a reference implementation of the Ogg Vorbis codec. In contrast to previous test cases, it contains a pipeline pattern, which is a special case of task flow graph. Four `function_nodes` are constructed for the four-stage pipeline, and our automatic version achieved a speedup of 2.41 with four threads. We got a lower speedup mainly because the code transformation tool uses task flow graph to mimic pipeline, which is less efficient than the specialized `tbb::pipeline` class. This test case enlightened us to improve our code transformation component to support pipeline pattern. We consider this task as a future work (Table 2).

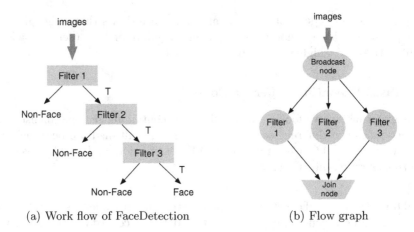

(a) Work flow of FaceDetection          (b) Flow graph

**Fig. 5.** Work flow of FaceDetection and the corresponding flow graph

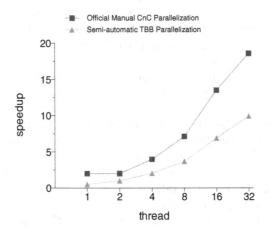

**Fig. 6.** FaceDetection speedups with different threads

**Table 2.** Summary of parallelization results for tasks executing different code.

| Program | Function | % of time | # of threads | Speedup(auto) | Speedup(manual) |
|---------|----------|-----------|--------------|---------------|-----------------|
| FaceDetection | facedetector | 99.9 | 32 | 9.92 | 18.60 |
| LibVorbis | main (encoder) | 100.0 | 4 | 2.41 | 3.62 |

## 5    Conclusion and Outlook

Many efforts have been made to find potential parallelism in sequential programs. However, most of them focused on loop-based data parallelism. In this paper, we propose a novel method that can identify parallel tasks—another promising source of parallelism but harder to find because more irregular. We extract the dependence graph dynamically from the program and subject it to several (simplifying) transformations at the end of which the tasks emerge. The main idea of this paper is the identification of computational units (CUs) and the localization of strongly connected components (SCC) and chains as representations of potential tasks. While CUs hide dependences that are local to computations, SCCs encapsulate complex dependences inside a task. The generated task graph is further submitted to a code transformation component that translate the sequential code into parallel TBB code. Experiment results showed that for both tasks executing the same code and different code, reasonable speedup is secured. The bottom line is that, we believe this work closes a gap in parallelism discovery technology, which is especially important for the systematic parallelization of larger general-purpose application portfolios, a challenge many organizations are facing today.

In the future, we want to support further types of task parallelism including, for example, TBB pipeline. Furthermore, we want to develop heuristics to validate the automatically generated code before submitting them to the programmer, providing more accurate and reliable results.

# References

1. Andersch, M., Juurlink, B., Chi, C.C.: A benchmark suite for evaluating parallel programming models. In: Proceedings 24th Workshop on Parallel Systems and Algorithms, PARS 2011, pp. 7–17 (2011)
2. August, D.I., Huang, J., Beard, S.R., Johnson, N.P., Jablin, T.B.: Automatically exploiting cross-invocation parallelism using runtime information. In: Proceedings of the 2013 IEEE/ACM International Symposium on Code Generation and Optimization, CGO 2013, pp. 1–11. IEEE Computer Society (2013)
3. Bailey, D.H., Barszcz, E., Barton, J.T., Browning, D.S., Carter, R.L., Fatoohi, R.A., Frederickson, P.O., Lasinski, T.A., Simon, H.D., Venkatakrishnan, V., Weeratunga, S.K.: The NAS parallel benchmarks. Int. J. Supercomput. Appl. 5(3), 63–73 (1991)
4. Bienia, C.: Benchmarking Modern Multiprocessors. Ph.D. thesis, Princeton University, January 2011
5. Ceng, J., Castrillon, J., Sheng, W., Scharwächter, H., Leupers, R., Ascheid, G., Meyr, H., Isshiki, T., Kunieda, H.: Maps: an integrated framework for mpsoc application parallelization. In: Proceedings of the 45th Annual Design Automation Conference, DAC 2008, pp. 754–759. ACM (2008)
6. Garcia, S., Jeon, D., Louie, C.M., Taylor, M.B.: Kremlin: Rethinking and rebooting gprof for the multicore age. In: Proceedings of the 32nd ACM SIGPLAN Conference on Programming Language Design and Implementation, PLDI 2011, pp. 458–469. ACM (2011)
7. Govindarajan, R., Anantpur, J.: Runtime dependence computation and execution of loops on heterogeneous systems. In: Proceedings of the 2013 IEEE/ACM International Symposium on Code Generation and Optimization, CGO 2013, pp. 1–10. IEEE Computer Society (2013)
8. Johnson, R.E.: Software development is program transformation. In: Proceedings of the FSE/SDP Workshop on Future of Software Engineering Research, FoSER 2010, pp. 177–180. ACM (2010)

9. Kennedy, K., Allen, J.R.: Optimizing Compilers for Modern Architectures: A Dependence-based Approach. Morgan Kaufmann Publishers Inc., San Francisco (2002)
10. Ketterlin, A., Clauss, P.: Profiling data-dependence to assist parallelization: framework, scope, and optimization. In: Proceedings of the 45th Annual IEEE/ACM International Symposium on Microarchitecture, MICRO 45, pp. 437–448. IEEE Computer Society (2012)
11. Kim, M., Kim, H., Luk, C.K.: Prospector: discovering parallelism via dynamic data-dependence profiling. In: Proceedings of the 2nd USENIX Workshop on Hot Topics in Parallelism, HOTPAR 2010 (2010)
12. Kim, M., Kim, H., Luk, C.K.: SD3: A scalable approach to dynamic data-dependence profiling. In: Proceedings of the 43rd Annual IEEE/ACM International Symposium on Microarchitecture, MICRO 43, pp. 535–546. IEEE Computer Society (2010)
13. Lattner, C., Adve, V.: LLVM: A compilation framework for lifelong program analysis & transformation. In: Proceedings of the 2nd International Symposium on Code Generation and Optimization: Feedback-Directed and Runtime Optimization, CGO 2004, pp. 75–86. IEEE Computer Society, Washington(2004)
14. Li, Z., Jannesari, A., Wolf, F.: An efficient data-dependence profiler for sequential and parallel programs. In: Proceedings of the 29th IEEE International Parallel & Distributed Processing Symposium, IPDPS 2015, pp. 484–493 (2015)
15. Molitorisz, K., Schimmel, J., Otto, F.: Automatic parallelization using autofutures. In: Pankratius, V., Philippsen, M. (eds.) MSEPT 2012. LNCS, vol. 7303, pp. 78–81. Springer, Heidelberg (2012)
16. Ottoni, G., Rangan, R., Stoler, A., August, D.I.: Automatic thread extraction with decoupled software pipelining. In: Proceedings of the 38th Annual IEEE/ACM International Symposium on Microarchitecture, MICRO 38, pp. 105–118. IEEE Computer Society (2005)
17. Pingali, K., Nguyen, D., Kulkarni, M., Burtscher, M., Hassaan, M.A., Kaleem, R., Lee, T.H., Lenharth, A., Manevich, R., Méndez-Lojo, M., Prountzos, D., Sui, X.: The tao of parallelism in algorithms. SIGPLAN Not. 46(6), 12–25 (2011)
18. Reinders, J.: Intel Threading Building Blocks. O'Reilly Media, Sebastopol (2007)
19. Ye, J.M., Chen, T.: Exploring potential parallelism of sequential programs with superblock reordering. In: Proceedings of the 2012 IEEE 14th International Conference on High Performance Computing and Communication & 2012 IEEE 9th International Conference on Embedded Software and Systems, HPCC 2012, pp. 9–16. IEEE Computer Society (2012)
20. Zhang, X., Navabi, A., Jagannathan, S.: Alchemist: A transparent dependence distance profiling infrastructure. In: Proceedings of the 7th Annual IEEE/ACM International Symposium on Code Generation and Optimization, CGO 2009, pp. 47–58. IEEE Computer Society (2009)

# Fast Data-Dependence Profiling by Skipping Repeatedly Executed Memory Operations

Zhen Li$^{1(\boxtimes)}$, Michael Beaumont$^2$, Ali Jannesari$^1$, and Felix Wolf$^1$

$^1$ Technische Universität Darmstadt, 64289 Darmstadt, Germany
{li,jannesari,wolf}@cs.tu-darmstadt.de
$^2$ RWTH Aachen University, 52062 Aachen, Germany
michael.beaumont@rwth-aachen.de

**Abstract.** Nowadays, more and more program analysis tools adopt profiling approaches in order to obtain data dependences because of their ability of tracking dynamically allocated memory, pointers, and array indices. However, dependence profiling suffers from high time overhead. To lower the overhead, former dependence profiling techniques either exploit features of the specific program analyses they are designed for, or let the profiling process run in parallel. Although they successfully lowered the time overhead of dependence profiling by a certain amount, none of them have tried to solve the fundamental problem that causes the high time overhead: the memory operations that are repeatedly executed in loops. In most of the time, these memory operations lead to exactly the same data dependences. However, a profiling method has to profile all these memory operations over and over again in order to not miss a single dependence that may occur just once. In this paper, we present a method that allow a dependence profiling technique to skip memory operations that are repeatedly executed in loops without missing any single data dependence. Our method works with all types of loops and does not require any prepossessing like source annotation of the input code. Experiment results show that our method can lower the time overhead of data-dependence profiling by up to 52 %.

**Keywords:** Data-dependence · Profiling · Optimization · Program analysis · Parallel programming

## 1 Introduction

Extracting data dependences from programs serves as the foundation of many program analysis and transformation methods. Especially, since data dependence is one of the main factors that preventing parallelism, data-dependence analysis is the base of nearly all the tools that discover parallelism in parallel programming area. Tools for discovering parallelism [6,10,11,15,18,24] identify the most promising parallelization opportunities. Runtime scheduling frameworks [4,7,17,22] add more parallelism to programs by dispatching code sections in a more effective way. Automatic parallelization tools [1,8,13,25] transform

© Springer International Publishing Switzerland 2015
G. Wang et al. (Eds.): ICA3PP 2015, Part IV, LNCS 9531, pp. 583–596, 2015.
DOI: 10.1007/978-3-319-27140-8_40

sequential into parallel code automatically. Method that suggests parallel patterns [9] helps programmer to choose the most promising pattern for parallelizing code. All the tools and methods mentioned above have in common the fact that they rely on data-dependence information to achieve their goals.

Data dependences can be obtained in two main ways: static and dynamic analysis. Static approaches determine data dependences without executing the program. Although they are fast and even allow fully automatic parallelization in some cases [1,8], they lack the ability to track dynamically allocated memory, pointers, and dynamically calculated array indices. This usually makes their assessment conservative, limiting their practical applicability. In contrast, dynamic dependence profiling captures only those dependences that actually occur at runtime. Although dependence profiling is inherently input sensitive, the results are still useful in many situations, which is why such profiling forms the basis of many program analysis tools [3,6,10,11,15]. Moreover, input sensitivity can be addressed by running the target program with changing inputs and computing the union of all collected dependences.

However, a serious limitation of data-dependence profiling is high time overhead. It may significantly prolong the analysis, sometimes requiring an entire night [19]. This is because dependence profiling requires all memory operations to be instrumented and records of all accessed memory locations to be kept. Many solutions have been proposed to lower the overhead. The first solution is to limit the scope to the subset of the dependence information needed for the analysis they have been created for, sacrificing generality and, hence, discouraging reuse. The second solution is sampling, also tries to analyze a subset of all the memory operations but without losing generality. Based on sampled memory operations combined with a probabilistic model, the second solution profiles data dependence with a sacrifice of accuracy. The last solution is to let the data-dependence profiling process run in parallel. This is possible because some data dependences related to one memory address do not affect other dependences related to another memory address. It does not lose generality or accuracy, but it surely needs much more effort to implement.

An observation is that many memory operations in loops are repeatedly executed. In most of the time they lead to always the same data dependences, but still need to be analyzed over and over again just because of some special data dependences that rarely occur. None of the solutions mentioned above tried to deal with this problem. In this paper, we present a method that allow a dependence profiling technique to skip memory operations that are repeatedly executed in loops without missing any data dependence. Our method works with all types of loops, and allows nesting. Furthermore, our method can be applied in combination with the existing overhead-reducing techniques mentioned above. Experiments results on applications from NAS Parallel Benchmarks 3.3.1 [5] and Starbench parallel benchmark suite [2] show that our method can lower the time overhead of data-dependence profiling by up to 52 %.

The remainder of the paper is organized as follows. First, we summarize related work in Sect. 2. Then, we introduce the work flow of data-dependence profiling in Sect. 3, providing a background of our method. In Sect. 4, we describe the details of skipping memory operations in loops. Evaluation of our method and a discussion on the characteristics of skipped memory operations are presented in Sect. 5. Finally, we conclude the paper and outline future prospects in Sect. 6.

## 2 Related Work

In previous dynamic data-dependence profiling techniques, their overhead was reduced through three major ways: tailoring the profiling technique to a specific analysis, sampling memory operations, or parallelizing the profiling process.

Using dependence profiling, Kremlin [6] determines the length of the critical path in a given code region. Based on this knowledge, it calculates a metric called self-parallelism, which quantifies the parallelism of the region. Instead of pair-wise dependences, Kemlin records only the length of the critical path. Alchemist [24], a tool that estimates the effectiveness of parallelizing program regions by asynchronously executing certain language constructs, profiles dependence distance instead of detailed dependences. Although these approaches profile data dependences with low overhead, the underlying profiling technique has been tailored to the specific analysis, and has difficulty in supporting other program analyses.

Another solution to decrease the profiling overhead is to use approximate representation rather than instrument every memory operation. Previous work [20] tried to ignore memory operations in a code section when it had been executed more than $2^{32-k}$ times. However, when setting $k = 10$, only 33.7% of the memory operations are covered, which can lead to significant inconsistency in profiled data dependences. Vanka and Tuck [21] profiled data dependencies based on signature and also compared the accuracy under different sampling rates. In this work, sampling was done in function level. A sampling rate of $M$ means the next $M - 1$ invocations of a function will be skipped. When decreasing the sampling rate from 1 to 100, an obvious drain of accuracy was observed.

There are also approaches that reduce the time overhead of dependence profiling through parallelization. For example, SD3 [12] exploits pipeline and data parallelism to extract data dependences from loops. DiscoPoP [16] distributes all the memory operations of a program among a number of worker threads based on the accessed address, and a redistribution table is used to ensure balanced workload. Multi-slicing [23] leverages compiler support for parallelization. Before execution, the compiler divides the profiling job into multiple profiling tasks through a series of static analyses. All these approaches successfully reduced the time overhead of data-dependence profiling without losing generality or accuracy. However, they still analyze all memory operations. At a certain time, the parallelism exist among different memory addresses cannot be exploited further by increasing the number of worker threads, and the huge number of memory operations that need to be processed sequentially dominates the profiling overhead.

Like Kremlin, Alchemist, and former work [20,21], our method also profiles only a subset of all the memory operations of a program. Unlike these methods,

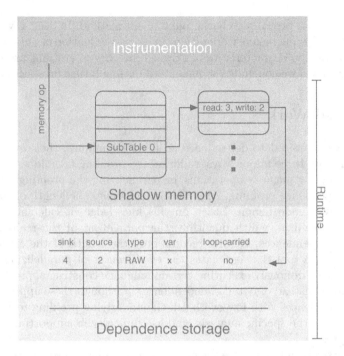

**Fig. 1.** Work flow of data-dependence profiling.

our approach does not lose generality or accuracy. The skipped memory operations are those repeatedly executed and lead to identical data dependences. Theoretically, our approach can work with any code sections that are executed more than once.

## 3    Background

A profiling techniques usually contains two parts: an instrumentation component that inserts analysis functions into the target code following specific rules, and a runtime library that implements the analysis functions and data structures. In data-dependence profiling, the instrumentation component inserts analysis functions for every memory operation. Instrumented code will be linked against the runtime library and executed. The runtime library is further divided into two components. The first component is called *shadow memory*. During runtime, the analysis functions keep tracking each memory locations accessed in the target application, and maintain access status of each memory location in a separate memory space. The second component is data-dependence storage, where data dependences are built and stored when the statuses in shadow memory are changed.

Figure 1 shows the work flow of data-dependence profiling. Among the three phases, instrumentation can be done statically, and time overhead of instrumentation is usually negligible. The main time overhead are caused by the remaining two phases: updating shadow memory and building dependence. Both shadow memory and dependence storage are typically implemented based on table-like data structures where each memory address or data dependence has an entry. Given the truth that the number of memory operations and data dependences are usually very large, the overhead is mainly incurred by searching, updating, and inserting elements to the data structures. As a result, data-dependence profiling typically slows the program down by a factor ranging from 100 to 150. [10]

However, not every memory operation has to be processed through all the three phases. Let us take the loop shown in Fig. 2 as an example. After profiling two iterations of the loop, data dependences are complete. Table 1 shows the dependences. *Source* and *sink* are the source code locations of the former and the latter memory operations, respectively. *Type* is the dependence type, including read after write (RAW), write after read (WAR), and write after write (WAW). *Variable* is the variable that causing a dependence. When source and sink of a dependence belong to different iterations of a loop, we call the dependence a *loop-carried* dependence.

```
1   while (k > 0) {
2       sum += k * 2;
3       k--;
4   }
```

**Fig. 2.** A simple loop where data dependences will not change over iterations.

**Table 1.** Data dependences of the loop shown in Fig. 2.

| ID | Sink | Source | Type | Variable | Loop-carried |
|----|------|--------|------|----------|--------------|
| 1 | 2 | 2 | write after read (WAR) | sum | no |
| 2 | 3 | 1 | write after read (WAR) | k | no |
| 3 | 3 | 2 | write after read (WAR) | k | no |
| 4 | 3 | 3 | write after read (WAR) | k | no |
| 5 | 1 | 3 | read after write (RAW) | k | yes |
| 6 | 2 | 2 | read after write (RAW) | sum | yes |
| 7 | 2 | 3 | read after write (RAW) | k | yes |
| 8 | 3 | 3 | read after write (RAW) | k | yes |

Among the dependences shown in Table 1, dependence 1–4 can be obtained within the first iteration, and dependence 5–8 will be added once the second iteration is done. After that, no more data dependence will be built, no matter how many iterations the loop has. In this case, profiling these memory operations over and over again is just a waste of time. It may be necessary to keep updating statuses in shadow memory for correctness, but we definitely do not want to touch dependence storage after data dependences for a code section are complete. In the next section, we show how we skip these memory operations after the dependences are fully obtained to accelerate the profiling process.

# 4    Approach

An abstract analysis function for a memory operation looks like this:

$$\text{mem\_op}(\text{accessType, accessInfo, addr}).$$

For a memory operation, accessType can be either read or write. It does not change over time. In practice, two analysis functions will be created for read and write operations, respectively. Necessary information needed to update shadow memory are stored in accessInfo, and passed into the analysis function. Usually, accessInfo is the identifier of the associate memory operation. For example, the address of the instruction, the source line location, the variable name, or a combination of such information. Depending on concrete implementation, accessInfo may or may not be unique to each memory operation. However, for one memory operation, its accessInfo does not change. addr is the memory address accessed by the memory operation. It can change if the address is referred by pointers.

## 4.1    Condition on **addr**

If a memory operation can be safely skipped, the memory address it accesses must not change over time. For simplicity, we create a variable called lastAddr for each memory operation storing the memory address accessed by the memory operation last time. And we require

$$\text{addr} == \text{lastAddr}$$

to be a necessary condition if a memory operation can be safely skipped. last Addr should be initialized with an address which is rarely accessed, like $0 \times 0$.

When the condition on addr holds, it only means that the current memory operation has been profiled before. It does not mean all data dependences that are related to the current memory operation have been obtained. Again, let us take the loop shown in Fig. 2 as an example. After applying the condition on addr, all the memory operations in the first iteration will be profiled, and dependence 1–4 in Table 1 are obtained. However, from the second iteration, memory operations are skipped because the addresses they access do not change. Thus, we name the condition on addr a necessary condition, and we still need other conditions to decide if a memory operation can be skipped.

## 4.2    Condition on **accessInfo**

The key to cover all data dependences is to decide when to resume profiling once the profiling has been paused. Our solution is to have a mechanism that allows a memory operation be notified if the access status of its memory address has changed, so that the memory operation must be profiled again.

In order to track the access status of a memory address, the shadow memory stores accessInfo of the last read operation and the last write operation to the address. We call them statusRead and statusWrite, respectively. We then create two variables lastStatusRead and lastStatusWrite for each memory operation, storing the accessInfo of the last read operation and the last write operation to the memory address when the memory operation was profiled *last* time, respectively. Then we require

```
statusRead == lastStatusRead &&
statusWrite == lastStatusWrite
```

to be another necessary condition if a memory operation can be safely skipped. Both lastStatusRead and lastStatusWrite should be initialized with impossible values for accessInfo.

When the condition on accessInfo holds, it means that the access status of the memory address has been seen before. We say "has been seen before" because the address may change, and the access status of the current memory address may just coincidentally be the same as the access status of another address. This is very likely to happen when accessInfo is not unique to each memory operation. However, combing the two conditions on addr and accessInfo will give the sufficient condition if a memory operation can be safely skipped: a memory operation has been profiled before, and the access status of its memory address has not changed since it was profiled last time.

When the conditions do not hold anymore, it means either the memory operation accesses a different memory address, or the access status of the memory address has changes. No matter which situation it is, the memory operation must be profiled again in order to cover new data dependences.

### 4.3    Example

In this section, we show how our method works on a simple example, and a special case where a memory operation can be skipped even without updating its status in shadow memory.

```
1   loop:
2        op1:   write  x
3        op2:   read   x
4        op3:   read   x
5        op4:   write  x
6   end
```

**Fig. 3.** A loop containing for memory operations on the same memory address.

Figure 3 shows a loop with four memory operations (op1–op4). All the memory operations access the same memory address x. We show memory operations instead of source code so that the profiling process can be clearly illustrated. Data dependences of the loop shown in Fig. 3 are listed in Table 2.

**Table 2.** Data dependences of the loop shown in Fig. 3.

| ID | Sink | Source | Type | Variable | Loop-carried |
|----|------|--------|------|----------|--------------|
| 1 | op2 | op1 | read after write (RAW) | x | no |
| 2 | op3 | op1 | read after write (RAW) | x | no |
| 3 | op4 | op3 | write after read (WAR) | x | no |
| 4 | op1 | op4 | write after write (WAW) | x | yes |

**Table 3.** Changing process of values of `lastStatusRead` and `lastStatusWrite` in the profiling process on the loop shown in Fig. 3.

| Op | lastStatusRead | | | | lastStatusWrite | | | |
|----|------|-----|-----|-----|------|-----|-----|-----|
|    | init | 1st | 2nd | 3rd | init | 1st | 2nd | 3rd |
| write x | — | 0 | 3 | S | — | 0 | 4 | S |
| read x | — | 0 | 3 | S | — | 1 | 1 | S |
| read x | — | 2 | S | S | — | 1 | S | S |
| write x | — | 3 | S | S | — | 1 | S | S |

**Table 4.** Changing process of the statuses in shadow memory in the profiling process on the loop shown in Fig. 3.

|  | init | op1 | op2 | op3 | op4 | op1 | op2 | op3 | op4 |
|--|------|-----|-----|-----|-----|-----|-----|-----|-----|
| statusRead | 0 | 0 | 2 | 3 | 3 | 3 | 2 | 3 | 3 |
| statusWrite | 0 | 1 | 1 | 1 | 4 | 1 | 1 | 1 | 4 |

The changing process of values stored in `lastStatusRead` and `last StatusWrite` for each memory operation is shown in Table 3. "1st", "2nd"", and "3rd" refer to the first, the second, and the third iteration of the loop, respectively. An "S" means the memory operation is skipped, otherwise the memory operation is processed and the value of `lastStatusRead` and `lastStatusWrite` are updated.

The changing process of the accessing status of x in shadow memory is shown in Table 4. We adopt the most common design, where for each memory address the last read operation and the last write operation to the address are stored. In both Tables 3 and 4, we use "1" for op1, "2" for op2, and so fort.

Let us examine the profiling process step by step. In the beginning, `last StatusRead` and `lastStatusWrite` are initialized to "–", `statusRead` and `statusWrite` are 0, and `lastAddr` is 0 × 0. Now comes op1. Since addr is not equal to `lastAddr`, op1 is processed. Statuses in shadow memory are loaded into `lastStatusRead` and `lastStatusWrite`, which are both 0 in case of op1. Then op1 updates shadow memory. `statusWrite` of x is now 1.

The same process happens to op2. The difference is that when op2 is executed, `statusRead` and `statusWrite` of x has been changed to 0 and 1, respectively. With `statusWrite` is no longer zero, a read-after-write (RAW) dependence from op2 to op1 is built, which is the first dependence shown in Fig. 2. The profiling process continues, and dependence 2, 3 are built when op3 and op4 are profiled.

Now the profiling process enters the second iteration, and op1 comes again. Although the condition on addr holds this time, the condition on AccessInfo fails. The last time op1 was profiled, the last read operation (stored in last StatusRead) and the last write operation (in lastStatusWrite) to x were 0. After the first iteration is completed, they are 3 and 4. op1 must be profiled again in order to cover new dependences. Thus, the last data dependence in Table 2 is built. The same situation also happens to op2, but it only leads to a read-after-read (RAR) dependence, which is ignored in most of the data-dependence profilers.

Both condition holds when op3 is executed again, and it is skipped. No dependence instance is built, and no query to the dependence storage. Note that shadow memory is still updated for correctness. From then on, all further memory accesses to x in the same loop are skipped, and no dependence is missed. The dependence storage is touched only four times, exactly as the number of dependences the loop contains.

**Special Case.** When the loop contains only op1, op2, and op3, statusWrite to x will be always 1. This is a special case where the following condition holds:

    currentWrite == statusWrite == lastStatusWrite.

In this case, a write operation can be skipped without updating shadow memory. The same applies for read operation as well.

## 5    Evaluation

We implemented our method in the data-dependence profiler [16] of DiscoPoP [14,15]. The profiler contains several different implementations of shadow memory. In this paper, we choose an implementation where statusRead and statusWrite of a memory address are stored in two separate sets called *readSet* and *writeSet*, respectively. Both of the two sets are non-approximate representation, meaning no false positives or false negatives will be built.

We conducted a range of experiments to evaluate the effectiveness of our method. Test cases are the NAS Parallel Benchmarks 3.3.1 [5] (NAS), a suite of programs derived from real-world computational fluid-dynamics applications, and a few applications from the Starbench parallel benchmark suite [2], which covers programs from diverse domains, including image processing, information security, machine learning and so on.

### 5.1    Time Overhead

Figure 4 shows the slowdowns of the data-dependence profiler on NAS benchmarks and *kmeans* from Starbench before (dp) and after (dp+opt) applying the

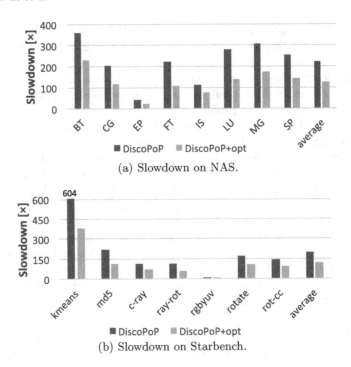

(a) Slowdown on NAS.

(b) Slowdown on Starbench.

**Fig. 4.** Slowdowns of the data-dependence profiler of DiscoPoP on NAS and Starbench benchmarks with (DiscoPoP+opt) and without (DiscoPoP) skipping repeatedly executed memory operations.

mechanism of skipping memory operations that are repeatedly executed in loops. As it shown, our method reduces the slowdown of data-dependence profiling on all of the test cases. The highest slowdown reduction shows in *FT* (52.0 %), and the lowest shows in *rot-cc* (31.1 %). On average, our method reduces the time overhead of data-dependence profiling by 41.3 %. The outputs after applying our method were compared to the original ones using *diff* tool, and no difference is observed.

Whether our method reduces the time overhead of data-dependence profiling on an application depends on the computation pattern of the application. Theoretically, the more work done in loops (or other repetitive manner), the more effective our method will be. If a program does not have any code sections that are executed more than once, which is obviously very uncommon for a real-world application, our method should actually bring a minor time overhead due to condition checking. In test cases *FT*, *LU*, and *CG*, the biggest hot spots are all loops. Applying our method on these test cases give reductions on slowdown of 52 %, 51 %, and 44 %, respectively.

Memory access pattern is another factor that can affect the effectiveness of our method. In the worst case, accessed memory addresses change in every iteration, which means the profiling process cannot be paused. This usually

**Table 5.** Statistics of memory operations that lead to data dependence but skipped on NAS benchmarks and *kmeans* from Starbench.

| Benchmark | read | | write | | read+write | |
|---|---|---|---|---|---|---|
| | total | skipped [%] | total | skipped [%] | total | skipped [%] |
| BT | 743 969 748 | 71.94 | 104 153 401 | 22.66 | 848 123 149 | 65.89 |
| CG | 562 665 608 | 79.20 | 82 428 819 | 92.32 | 645 094 427 | 80.88 |
| EP | 1 268 263 496 | 96.75 | 528 633 275 | 89.00 | 1 796 896 771 | 94.47 |
| FT | 1 034 144 426 | 99.68 | 274 436 113 | 99.53 | 1 308 580 539 | 99.65 |
| IS | 26 061 226 | 82.69 | 10 596 042 | 73.53 | 36 657 268 | 80.04 |
| LU | 368 187 710 | 87.09 | 36 303 260 | 41.92 | 404 490 970 | 83.04 |
| MG | 66 160 096 | 82.60 | 5 876 449 | 53.88 | 72 036 545 | 80.26 |
| SP | 450 997 264 | 83.54 | 51 853 149 | 44.31 | 502 850 413 | 79.50 |
| kmeans | 1 124 603 733 | 65.27 | 225 500 303 | 87.97 | 1 350 104 036 | 69.06 |
| md5 | 3 908 055 | 91.05 | 1 368 725 | 97.99 | 5 276 780 | 92.85 |
| c-ray | 1 251 777 658 | 64.77 | 264 217 429 | 48.35 | 1 515 995 087 | 61.91 |
| ray-rot | 500 462 138 | 56.48 | 133 222 408 | 47.65 | 633 684 546 | 54.62 |
| rgbyuv | 25 639 777 | 89.28 | 15 977 310 | 85.32 | 41 617 087 | 87.76 |
| rotate | 328 610 773 | 89.17 | 53 662 659 | 56.59 | 382 273 432 | 84.60 |
| rot-cc | 427 139 027 | 91.67 | 76 733 411 | 57.34 | 503 872 438 | 86.44 |
| average | — | 82.08 | — | 66.56 | — | 80.06 |

happens when computation is based on array or matrix. Results on test cases *BT*, *IS*, *rotate*, and *rot-cc* are affected due to this problem.

## 5.2 Skipped Memory Operations

In the second experiment, we get statistics of the memory operations that lead to data dependence but skipped in each test case. As most of the data-dependence profilers do, read-after-read (RAR) dependences are not profiled in our experiment.

Table 5 shows the statistics. In each column group, "percent" gives the percent of memory operations skipped of the type specified for the group. As it is shown, on average 80.06 % of the memory operations that lead to data dependences are skipped. It is surprising that the full data dependence set of an application can be obtained by profiling only 20 % of its memory operations (or even less because those do not lead to dependences are skipped already). The results give us an insight of how much time were wasted in a classic data-dependence profiler that profiles identical data dependences over and over again.

Although on average about 80 % of the memory operations that lead to data dependence are skipped, the slowdown reductions shown in Fig. 4 never achieve 60 %. There are two reasons for this. Firstly, in most cases, skipping a memory operation means skipping the data dependence building phase. Overhead is still incurred by updating shadow memory. The second reason is that profiling a write operation is more complex than profiling a read, and the percentage of skipped write operations (66.56 %) is less than the percentage of read (82.08 %). Profiling a write operation needs to check both WAW and WAR dependences, while profiling read operation only needs to check RAW.

## 5.3  Memory Overhead

Our method introduces a minor overhead on memory consumption of data-dependence profiling because of the variables created for condition check. However, compared to the memory overhead of shadow memory, the memory overhead of our method can be ignored. In our experiments, one 64-bit integer (lastAddr) and two 32-bit integers (lastStatusRead and lastStatusWrite) are created for each *distinct* memory operation. However, the number of distinct memory operations is usually small comparing to the number of total memory operations due to loops and other code blocks that are repeatedly executed. For example, *kmeans* has $10^9$ memory operations in total and iterates 300 times. Thus, the number of distinct memory operations in *kmeans* is roughly $3 \times 10^6$. With 16 Bytes memory overhead each, our method results in about 50 MB memory consumption. The memory overhead of shadow memory, however, is almost ten times of that. Memory consumption of the state-of-the-art data-dependence profilers [12, 16] ranges from several hundred mega bytes to several giga bytes. Using 10 % memory more to reduce the time overhead by 30–50 % is definitely a bargain.

## 6  Conclusion

Data-dependence profiling has a huge time overhead because it applies heavy analysis to every memory operation of the target program. Existing solutions to reduce the number of memory operations needed to be analyzed includes static analysis and sampling. However, the number of data dependences that can be determined statically is usually limited. Sampling, on the other side, skips memory operations according to certain pre-defined rules with no respect to the memory access pattern of the target program.

In this paper, we proposed a fast data-dependence profiling method that can skip memory operations repeatedly executed in loops. By storing a short profiling history for each memory operation, our method recognizes memory operations that have been recently profiled and skips them, and, which is more important, resumes profiling when the access pattern changes. According to the experiment results, our method reduces the time overhead of data-dependence profiling by 42.5 % on average. Furthermore, in contrast to sampling approaches, our method ensures consistent state in shadow memory, lowering the time overhead without losing accuracy. Finally, our method can cooperate with existing overhead-lowering techniques for data-dependence profiling like static analysis and parallelization.

We plan to develop a fast data-dependence profiler with the help of both former techniques of reducing overhead like parallelization and the method presented in this paper. We are also interested in applying our method to profilers that built on top of virtual machines, where the original code without instrumentation can be scheduled into execution when all its memory operations are marked as skipped.

## References

1. Amini, M., Goubier, O., Guelton, S., Mcmahon, J.O., Pasquier, F.X., Pan, G., Villalon, P.: Par4All: From convex array regions to heterogeneous computing. In: Proceedings of the 2nd International Workshop on Polyhedral Compilation Techniques, IMPACT 2012 (2012)
2. Andersch, M., Juurlink, B., Chi, C.C.: A benchmark suite for evaluating parallel programming models. In: Proceedings 24th Workshop on Parallel Systems and Algorithms, PARS 2011, pp. 7–17 (2011)
3. Atre, R., Jannesari, A., Wolf, F.: The basic building blocks of parallel tasks. In: Proceedings of the 2015 International Workshop on Code Optimisation for Multi and Many Cores, COSMIC 2015, pp. 3:1–3:11. ACM, New York (2015)
4. August, D.I., Huang, J., Beard, S.R., Johnson, N.P., Jablin, T.B.: Automatically exploiting cross-invocation parallelism using runtime information. In: Proceedings of the 2013 IEEE/ACM International Symposium on Code Generation and Optimization, CGO 2013, pp. 1–11. IEEE Computer Society (2013)
5. Bailey, D.H., Barszcz, E., Barton, J.T., Browning, D.S., Carter, R.L., Fatoohi, R.A., Frederickson, P.O., Lasinski, T.A., Simon, H.D., Venkatakrishnan, V., Weeratunga, S.K.: The NAS parallel benchmarks. Int. J. Supercomput. Appl. $5$(3), 63–73 (1991)
6. Garcia, S., Jeon, D., Louie, C.M., Taylor, M.B.: Kremlin: rethinking and rebooting gprof for the multicore age. In: Proceedings of the 32nd ACM SIGPLAN Conference on Programming Language Design and Implementation, PLDI 2011, pp. 458–469. ACM (2011)
7. Govindarajan, R., Anantpur, J.: Runtime dependence computation and execution of loops on heterogeneous systems. In: Proceedings of the 2013 IEEE/ACM International Symposium on Code Generation and Optimization, CGO 2013, pp. 1–10. IEEE Computer Society (2013)
8. Grosser, T., Groesslinger, A., Lengauer, C.: Polly - performing polyhedral optimizations on a low-level intermediate representation. Parallel Process. Lett. $22$(04), 1250010 (2012)
9. Huda, Z.U., Jannesari, A., Wolf, F.: Using template matching to infer parallel design patterns. ACM Trans. Archit. Code Optim. $11$(4), 64:1–64:21 (2015)
10. Ketterlin, A., Clauss, P.: Profiling data-dependence to assist parallelization: Framework, scope, and optimization. In: Proceedings of the 45th Annual IEEE/ACM International Symposium on Microarchitecture, MICRO 45, pp. 437–448. IEEE Computer Society (2012)
11. Kim, M., Kim, H., Luk, C.K.: Prospector: discovering parallelism via dynamic data-dependence profiling. In: Proceedings of the 2nd USENIX Workshop on Hot Topics in Parallelism, HOTPAR 2010 (2010)
12. Kim, M., Kim, H., Luk, C.K.: SD3: A scalable approach to dynamic data-dependence profiling. In: Proceedings of the 43rd Annual IEEE/ACM International Symposium on Microarchitecture, MICRO 43, pp. 535–546. IEEE Computer Society (2010)

13. Lee, S.I., Johnson, T., Eigenmann, R.: Cetus - an extensible compiler infrastructure for source-to-source transformation. In: Rauchwerger, L. (ed.) Languages and Compilers for Parallel Computing. Lecture Notes in Computer Science, vol. 2958, pp. 539–553. Springer, Heidelberg (2004)

14. Li, Z., Atre, R., Ul-Huda, Z., Jannesari, A., Wolf, F.: DiscoPoP: A profiling tool to identify parallelization opportunities. In: Niethammer, C., Gracia, J., Knüpfer, A., Resch, M.M., Nagel, W.E. (eds.) Tools for High Performance Computing 2014, 1st edn, pp. 1–10. Springer International Publishing, Switzerland (2015)

15. Li, Z., Jannesari, A., Wolf, F.: Discovery of potential parallelism in sequential programs. In: Proceedings of the 42nd International Conference on Parallel Processing, PSTI 2013, pp. 1004–1013, vol. 13. IEEE Computer Society (2013)

16. Li, Z., Jannesari, A., Wolf, F.: An efficient data-dependence profiler for sequential and parallel programs. In: Proceedings of the 29th IEEE International Parallel & Distributed Processing Symposium, IPDPS 2015, pp. 484–493 (2015)

17. Ottoni, G., Rangan, R., Stoler, A., August, D.I.: Automatic thread extraction with decoupled software pipelining. In: Proceedings of the 38th Annual IEEE/ACM International Symposium on Microarchitecture, MICRO 38, pp. 105–118. IEEE Computer Society (2005)

18. Rul, S., Vandierendonck, H., De Bosschere, K.: Function level parallelism driven by data dependencies. SIGARCH Comput. Archit. News **35**(1), 55–62 (2007)

19. Rul, S., Vandierendonck, H., De Bosschere, K.: A profile-based tool for finding pipeline parallelism in sequential programs. Parallel Comput. **36**(9), 531–551 (2010)

20. Serebryany, K., Potapenko, A., Iskhodzhanov, T., Vyukov, D.: Dynamic race detection with LLVM compiler. In: Khurshid, S., Sen, K. (eds.) RV 2011. LNCS, vol. 7186, pp. 110–114. Springer, Heidelberg (2012)

21. Vanka, R., Tuck, J.: Efficient and accurate data dependence profiling using software signatures. In: Proceedings of the 10th International Symposium on Code Generation and Optimization, CGO 2012, pp. 186–195. ACM, New York (2012)

22. Ye, J.M., Chen, T.: Exploring potential parallelism of sequential programs with superblock reordering. In: Proceedings of the 2012 IEEE 14th International Conference on High Performance Computing and Communication & 2012 IEEE 9th International Conference on Embedded Software and Systems, HPCC 2012, pp. 9–16. IEEE Computer Society (2012)

23. Yu, H., Li, Z.: Multi-slicing: a compiler-supported parallel approach to data dependence profiling. In: Proceedings of the 2012 International Symposium on Software Testing and Analysis, ISSTA 2012, pp. 23–33. ACM (2012)

24. Zhang, X., Navabi, A., Jagannathan, S.: Alchemist: a transparent dependence distance profiling infrastructure. In: Proceedings of the 7th Annual IEEE/ACM International Symposium on Code Generation and Optimization, CGO 2009, pp. 47–58. IEEE Computer Society (2009)

25. Zhao, B., Li, Z., Jannesari, A., Wolf, F., Wu, W.: Dependence-based code transformation for coarse-grained parallelism. In: Proceedings of the 2015 International Workshop on Code Optimisation for Multi and Many Cores, COSMIC 2015, pp. 1–10. ACM, New York (2015)

# P-index: An Efficient Searchable Metadata Indexing Scheme Based on Data Provenance in Cold Storage

Jinjun Liu, Dan Feng$^{(\boxtimes)}$, Yu Hua, Bin Peng, Pengfei Zuo, and Yuanyuan Sun

Wuhan National Laboratory for Optoelectronics,
School of Computer Science and Technology,
Huazhong University of Science and Technology, Wuhan 430074, China
{liujinjun,dfeng,csyhua,pengbin,pfzuo,sunyuanyuan}@hust.edu.cn

**Abstract.** Cold data are infrequently accessed in data centers. Cloud storage service providers commonly store cold data and their metadata in low-cost commodity hardware for cost-effective storage. While, there are several kinds of storage services which need to ensure the high-performance access and retrieval to cold data. Since some of cold data have not been accessed for a long time, traditional metadata are not useful for searching them. In order to solve these problems, we propose an efficient and effective searchable metadata indexing based on data provenance, called P-index. P-index partitions correlative files into logical groups via provenance relationships of files. This method quickly cuts off the subtrees which do not contain the query results to improve the efficiency of metadata search. Moreover, P-index adds the metadata extracted from data provenance into index structure to improve the effectiveness of metadata search. We evaluate the performance of P-index via two complex queries, range and k-nearest-neighbor(KNN) queries. Compared with state-of-the-art metadata index methods, P-index improves the efficiency and effectiveness of metadata search.

**Keywords:** Provenance relationship · Cold storage · Searchable metadata · Index structure · Metadata query

## 1 Introduction

In order to ensure data reliability or to share digital artifacts, current personal users and enterprisers upload the enormous number of data to cloud storage systems via various devices. At the same time, modern storage systems also store a lot of plain copies for reliably storing large amount of data in datacenters. While, most of the data are rarely accessed. This kind of data is regarded as cold data.

There are at least two reasons which make us focus on the index of cold data. First, since cold data are infrequently accessed and can not be lost, cloud storage service providers commonly move cold data and their metadata into low-cost commodity hardware for cost-effective data storage. While, there are several

© Springer International Publishing Switzerland 2015
G. Wang et al. (Eds.): ICA3PP 2015, Part IV, LNCS 9531, pp. 597–611, 2015.
DOI: 10.1007/978-3-319-27140-8_41

kinds of storage services which need to ensure the high-performance accessing and searching even if the data have become *cold*. For example, when users request to access or search the photos which have not been accessed for several years in a social media platform, the platform needs to finish the requests and returns the results within three seconds [1]. Current storage systems commonly use the metadata search to provide data retrieval service. Hence, cold storage systems need an efficient metadata index structure.

Second, since the data are cold and are not accessed for a long time, cold storage systems need to collect as much information as possible to help users to find the data which they need. Usual method is to index the metadata information of the data in storage systems. While, a recent study [2] reveals that traditional metadata could be unhelpful to search data, and most of data are uploaded with few metadata. Hence, it is a challenge for cold storage systems to build an effective metadata index structure.

Cold storage systems of several enterprises [3,4] use database management systems (DBMS) to store and index the metadata of files. Since DBMS must check each B+-tree index for each attribute during searching metadata and lack the support for scalability, existing DBMS do not fully satisfy the requirements of metadata retrieval in the large-scale cold storage systems. There are several kinds of index trees which are used to organize and index metadata for metadata search. While these index trees only use the current attributes or features within a short time to index metadata.

In order to improve the performance of metadata search in cold storage, we propose an efficient and effective searchable metadata indexing scheme based on data provenance, called **P-index**. P-index leverages two kinds of semantic information which are extracted from provenance to improve the performance of metadata index. The first one is the provenance relationship. Since the provenance relationship is a kind of compact relationship, P-index partitions correlative files into logical groups via the relationship, and then uses a tree to index the centroids of each group. By building metadata index in this way, P-index quickly cuts off the subtrees which do not contain the query results to improve the efficiency of metadata search. The second one is the metadata information which is extracted from data provenance. These metadata are added into index structure for enhancing the accuracy of searching metadata. Hence, P-index improves the effectiveness of metadata search.

Compared with state-of-the-art metadata index methods, P-index demonstrates its efficiency and efficacy in terms of response latency and query accuracy. The average speed of the metadata query in P-index can be up to one order of magnitude faster than traditional index tree structure and to two orders of magnitude faster than DBMS.

The contributions of this paper are summarized as two aspects.

- **Efficient and Effective Metadata Index Structure.** We propose a novel searchable metadata indexing scheme based on data provenance, called P-index, which takes advantage of both the relationship and the metadata coming from data provenance to speed up metadata search and improve the accuracy in cold storage.

- **Evaluation on Real-Word Trace.** We achieve the prototype of P-index. We evaluate the performance via using two complex queries, range and KNN queries. The test results show that P-index improves metadata searching performance by 1 - 2 orders of magnitude.

The rest of the paper is organized as follows. Section 2 shows research backgrounds and our motivations. We give the overview of the P-index in Sect. 3. Section 4 presents the system design and implementation. We give extensive experimental results in Sect. 5. Section 6 describes the related work, and Sect. 7 concludes the paper.

## 2 Background and Motivations

In this section, we first show the research backgrounds about the cold storage systems. We then present our motivations.

### 2.1 Cold Storage Systems

A cold storage system stores cold data with low storage costs and correspondingly accepted performance levels [1], such as Amazon Glacier [5], Microsoft Pelican [4] and Facebook Cold Data Storage [3]. Cold data are the data which can not be lost in a long term, and rarely accessed.

According to the concerned requirements except low cost, cold storage systems are classified into two categories. The first kind of cold storage systems pursue expected storage life, such as, archive systems and disaster recovery systems. The design of these systems mainly focuses on the reliability of systems and data. The second kind of cold storage systems are more concerned with access speed. For example, online social media systems and several backup systems. These systems need to provide real-time services (the response time is less than three seconds) [1].

With the development of cloud applications, the amount of cold data become larger and larger. There are over 100 hours of videos being uploaded every minute on YouTube, and 2 billions of photos each day shared across Facebook sites [3]. Since most of the data are accessed infrequently, several cheap and lower-performance equipments are used for cost-effective storage. Hence, ensuring the system performance becomes a great challenge in the second kind of cold storage systems mentioned above.

### 2.2 Motivations

When the data that users need are "cold", metadata search is used to find the data. There are two methods which are used to speed up metadata search. The first method is improving the efficiency of index structure, such as spyglass [6], smartstore [7], vsfs [8] and so on. By using the methods, the systems quickly cut off the branches which do not contain the query results. The second method is collecting and storing more information of files. Once users remember a little information about the files they need, they can find the files easily.

**Fig. 1.** Provenance information

In order to improve the performance of metadata search, we use not only the present information of files, but also their historical information. Provenance data of a file record its historical information. We extract data correlations from provenance data, as shown in Fig. 1. The data correlation is the provenance relationship. Since provenance relationship is a more compact relation, we use it to group files. The files within a group have the similar properties and access features. Adopting this method, we build an efficient index structure to speed up the metadata search. On the other hand, we obtain more semantic attributes from provenance. When we use the attributes to add the metadata of index structure, we build an effective index structure and improve the query accuracy.

## 3    System Overview

In current storage systems, users search files via searching file metadata in metadata server cluster. Figure 2 shows the logical diagram of P-index. P-index includes three parts: client-side, the metadata server cluster and the data server cluster.

The first part mainly collects application-level provenance data. When the applications are moved from the client-side to cloud, the provenance collector is moved to the cloud together with applications. In order to reduce the network overhead of transferring provenance data, the raw provenance need to be preprocessed. For example, the identical records are deduplicated, and the provenance data of system files are filtered.

The second part which includes three function domains provides two kinds of metadata query services, and metadata management and storage. The first function domain includes provenance manager module and provenance storage module. After receiving the provenance from provenance collector, provenance manager extracts provenance relationships of files for logic grouping, and several searchable metadata from provenance data. The provenance manager then sends

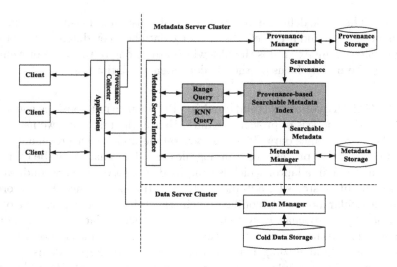

**Fig. 2.** The architecture of P-index.

the selected provenance data to the provenance storage module to store them. The second function domain includes two metadata search modules and the provenance-based searchable metadata indexing module. Our work focuses on this domain. Two query modules achieve the whole processes of searching metadata, such as receiving the requests of range query, extracting query conditions, searching the index structure and returning search results. The last function domain is responsible for metadata management and storage. The metadata manager chooses searchable metadata for all file metadata to build the searchable metadata index structure.

The third part provides cold data management and storage. The data manager is mainly responsible for accessing and migrating cold data.

# 4    Design and Implementation

In this section, we first present the new insights of provenance relationship and searchable metadata. We then present our design of the efficient and effective index structure and metadata search in cold storage.

## 4.1    Provenance Relationship

**The Definition.** Through the analysis of provenance data, we get the provenance relationships, also known as ancestry relationships, dependency correlations, lineage relationships or causal relationships [9]. For example, an application software reads data from file $A$ and then writes them to file $B$. We consider that $B$ is a child of $A$. There is the provenance relationship between $A$ and $B$.

The Open Provenance Model defines three kinds of nodes, including artifact, process and agent, and five types of causal dependency relationships among them [10]. The mode defines a directed graph of causal relationships to represent provenance graph, and it is useful to exchange data between different provenance systems. Since P-index groups the files which are belong to the same provenance subgraph. We mainly focus on the file dependency relationship.

**How to Get Provenance Relationship.** Provenance relationships commonly come from the analysis of provenance data. Hence, the first thing we need to do is to collect provenance data. There are several methods to get provenance data. First, we can derive provenance from log files [11]. Provenance can be extracted from log files via an adaptor which is composed of a set of rules. Second, we can design or modify systems for automatically collecting provenance [12]. According to the particular points of modification in the software stack, we can obtain application-level provenance, system-level provenance or dataflow provenance.

In addition to these methods, we can obtain the provenance relationships via metadata or data analyzing. For example, in online backup systems or online storage systems, a user uploads several files in a day and uploads other files at the next day. If many of them are similar in pathnames or have the same filename, like */backup/jun07/paper/main.tex* and */backup/jun08/paper/main.tex*, we easily deduce that the latter is the child of the former.

In P-index, we get provenance relationship via the analysis of application-level provenance. There are two main benefits from this method. First, collecting and storing application-level provenance have less overhead. We do not concern the information about operation system and file system. Second, since users are more likely to remember the application-level information, application-level provenance is much helpful for searching cold data. P-index collects and indexes the metadata coming from application-level provenance to speed up file queries.

**How to Use Provenance Relationship.** In the present study, provenance relationship is commonly used in intrusion detection, reliability analysis and data rebuilding. These approaches only focus on the places where objects come from and the applications which are using or used objects. P-index takes the advantage of the provenance correlation to achieve logical grouping of files. The files within same provenance subgraph are partitioned into one group. Since the provenance relationships of files reflect more compact correlations between files than the relationships that only come from file attributes, P-index exploits this kind of relationships to speed up file queries. Hence P-index provides efficient metadata search.

In order to reduce the overhead of index updates, P-index uses a buffer to temporarily store the provenance relationships. Whenever the buffer becomes full, P-index updates the index structure and removes the records about provenance relationships. Hence, P-index does not maintain and store a provenance graph in the cold storage system.

### 4.2   Searchable Metadata

**The Definition of Searchable Metadata.** There are two concepts which are relevant to searchable metadata. *File metadata*, such as size, owner, retention policy and timestamps, are the attributes of files. In large-scale file systems, *Metadata search* is helpful to address the file management and locating [6]. Searchable metadata are a kind of metadata which can help users or administrators to accomplish complex, ad hoc metadata search about the files which are stored in storage systems or digital libraries [13]. P-index extracts searchable metadata from two sources, traditional file metadata and file provenance.

**Extracting Searchable Metadata from Common Metadata.** Not every attributes of files really contributes to help users to find their files. A recent study [2] reveals that concerning the time of last usage of a document, the common search criteria, only 4.8 % of the recalls are correct and 47.6 % of the recalls are utterly incorrect.

There are several common attributes of files which are firmly remembered by people, such as file type, keywords and visual elements [2]. These metadata are searchable metadata. Each file has dozens of metadata attributes. If all of attributes are used to build index structure, the space and time overheads of storing and retrieving the index are unacceptable. P-index selects several searchable metadata as a part of the searchable multidimensional index metadata. We call these metadata as CSM below.

**Extracting Searchable Metadata from Provenance Data.** Besides extracting searchable metadata from common metadata, P-index extracts several searchable metadata from application-level provenance, PSM for short. There are two reasons which prompt us to do this. First, since many files uploaded by users have no or very poor metadata, it is not enough to perform precision query and recommendation [14]. For example, most of programmers like to name the installation program as "setup.exe". Second, application-level information is easier to be remembered, such as receiving a PDF file from the email coming from Tom, using Storm Codec (a popular media player software in China) to play a video last month. Adding the attributes of PSM into the index structure improves the accuracy ratio of inquires. Hence P-index provides effective metadata search.

**Table 1.** Definition of provenance semantics

| Provenance element | Attribute | Definition | Examples |
| --- | --- | --- | --- |
| When | Time | Time of the event | February 24, 2013, morning, 5 PM |
| Where | Space | Location of the event where the data came from | Dropbox, YouTube |
| Which | Instrument | Softwares or tools in the event | Email, MS Powerpoint, |
| Who | Agent | Individuals involved in the event | Mr. Huang, Tom, home.jpg |
| How | Action | Actions that lead to the event | download, creation, publication |

Towards a provenance event, P-index adopts a W5 mode, like W7 [15], to extract the PSM. We define that a provenance record include *when*, *where*, *which*, *who* and *how* associated with each provenance event. Table 1 shows these 5 Ws and the corresponding attributes. For example, Towards a event "I downloaded a file named presentation.ppt from the email of SOHU coming from Tom at 8 AM, June 1, 2015", *when* is 8 AM, June 1, 2015, *where* is SOHU, *which* is email, *who* is Tom, and *how* is download. We provide a string as a unique identifier of a provenance record. Hence, P-index uses key/value pairs to store the PSM.

### 4.3   P-Index Structure

After collecting the provenance relationships of files, P-index first uses k-proto types algorithm [16] to compute the features of each provenance group-(subgraph). The features represent each group and are treated as first-level index nodes. The features include two parts, PSM and CSM. P-index then imports the first-level index nodes into a KD-tree and builds the searchable metadata index structure, as shown in Fig. 3.

In our design, the KD-tree is stored on a server cluster with distributed shared memory. The speed of accessing data from the memory of neighboring nodes is quicker than local disks. There are two reasons that we use the KD-tree in P-index. First, a main memory index structure can ensure the performance of searching metadata. It is necessary to ensure the high-performance accessing and searching in several kinds of storage services, even if the data have become cold [1]. Second, the distributed index structure improves the system reliability. P-index can address the single-point-failure problem.

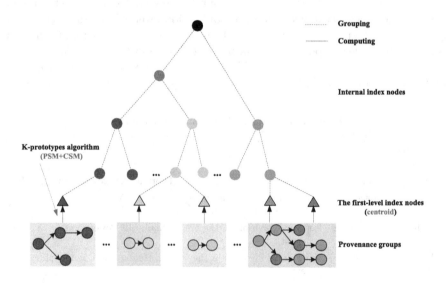

**Fig. 3.** The index structure of P-index

**Computing the Features of Provenance Group.** K-prototypes algorithm integrates the k-means and k-modes algorithms. K-means algorithm partitions $n$ objects with numeric attributes into $k$ clusters so as to minimize the within-cluster sum of squares (WCSS). K-modes algorithm addresses the objects with categorical values. Since PSM and CSM include numbers and characters respectively, P-index uses k-prototypes algorithm to partition a provenance group (provenance subgraph) into $k$ subgroups and obtain the centroid of each subgroup. The attributes of the centroid can be considered as the features of each cluster.

The usage of k-prototypes algorithm in P-index offers three advantages. First, this method computes the features of each provenance group. Second, this method improves the accuracy of the features of each provenance group. When a provenance group is too large, it is inaccurate to use a mean as the feature. Third, this method increases the balance of index tree. P-index partitions a huge group into several small groups with relatively average number of nodes.

**Building Basic Index.** By using k-prototypes algorithm, P-index gets the first-level index nodes, and then uses KD-tree to index them. Since KD-tree is not suitable for high-dimensional data, P-index adopts the median of medians algorithm to improve the efficiency of searching metadata.

When P-index receives a new provenance relationship among files $A_1$, $A_2$,..., $A_n$ ($n > 1$), P-index can address the changes of provenance groups.

- When all files do not belong to any provenance group, P-index adds a new group which includes the files $A_i$ ($1 < i \leq n$).
- When a part of the files belong to provenance group $G_j$ ($1 \leq j < n$) and others do not belong to any group, P-index merges the groups $G_j$ ($1 \leq j < n$) into a new group and adds other files into the new group.
- When $A_i$ ($1 < i \leq n$) do belong to group $G_j$ ($1 < j \leq n$), P-index merges the groups $G_j$ ($1 < j \leq n$) into one new group.

In order to ensure the index robustness, P-index uses a common KD-tree to index CMS of the files without provenance relationship. When obtaining the provenance relationship of a file, P-index moves its CMS and PMS to the provenance-based searchable metadata index structure.

**Storing and Maintaining P-Index.** To ensure metadata search efficiency, P-index stores the index nodes in memory. Since P-index only uses PSM and CSM, the other file metadata and provenance information (if these information need to be stored) are stored at data server cluster. After a file is migrated to the cold storage system, its changes of PSM and CSM are few.

When a provenance group have excessive amounts of files, The time overheads of metadata searching and metadata update in this group far exceeds other groups. Therefore, a huge provenance group affects the balance of index tree. We define a threshold $S$ to limit the size of each group. If the number of files which belong to same group is more than $S$, we divide the group into several

---

**Range_Query_Algorithm(Root,R)**

S = Root
if  S is the first-level index node **then**
   **while** ( S ≠ NULL) **do**
      w = Get_Node(S)
      w is the result if it lies in R
   **end while**
**else**
   **if** Region(Left_Subtree(S))is fully contained in R **then**
      S = Left_Subtree(S)
      Range_Query_(S,R)
   **end if**
   **if** Region(Right_Subtree(S))is fully contained in R **then**
      S = Right_Subtree(S)
      Range_Query_(S,R)
   **end if**
**end if**

---

**Fig. 4.** Algorithm for Executing Range Query in P-index.

subgroups in which the number of files is less than $S$. When the number of nodes within a provenance group is $n$, P-index sets $k$ (the number of clusters) to $\lceil n/S \rceil$.

When P-index removes a file, the metadata of the file will be deleted. Once all files of a group are removed, the first-level index node corresponding to the group will be removed. Similarly, P-index adopts a lazy adjusting index strategy, like LA-tree [17]. P-index uses several cascaded buffers to cache the nodes that need to be updated. When the buffers become full, P-index starts to adjust the index structure.

### 4.4   Metadata Search Based on P-Index

We present on-line approaches to satisfy two kinds of complex query requests which are range and KNN query in this subsection.

**The Range Query.** The range query is to find files which contain within the query domain. When receiving a range query request, P-index finds the first-level index nodes which satisfying range constraints. The first-level index nodes correspond to several provenance groups. And then P-index finds the final results via comparing the attributes of files which belonging to the groups with the given query domain. The pseudo-code for the range query algorithm is shown in Fig. 4.

**The K-nearest-neighbor Query.** The KNN query gets the files which attributes are closest to the given query condition. The time overhead of KNN query is $O(k*\log n)$, n is the number of index nodes. Since n is less than the number of files due to logical grouping based provenance relationship, the overhead is low than $O(k*\log n)$ and is $O(k*\log(n/v))$, $v$ is the average number of a logical group.

# 5   Performance Evaluation

In this section, we evaluate the performance of P-index by implementing a meta-data index and search prototype. The evaluation metrics include the time over-head of building P-index and the performance of two kinds of common metadata queries, range and KNN query.

## 5.1   Experiment Setup

Since there are not authoritative datasets which record both provenance data and file attributes of a storage system, we demonstrate our design via a trace which comes from two resources. First, we analyze the HP trace [18] to obtain metadata information and provenance relationships of files. For example, when a process reads and writes several files in a short period of time, we consider that the files have provenance relationships between them. Second, we collect a trace recording our history of uploading our files into Baidu cloud storage which is a cloud backup system for several months. In order to reduce the overhead of collecting provenance, we only track the usage and uploading of several special files, such as Word, Excel, PowerPoint and PDF. We collect the provenance and attributes of more than 6 millions.

We compare our design with three kinds of metadata index structure. The identifiers *R-tree* and *KD-tree* means only use KD-tree or R-tree to index the traditional metadata of files. We also compare the performance of searching file with DBMS.

## 5.2   Result and Analysis

**Building Latency.** The overhead of building index tree can not be ignored by searchable file system designers. For example, when we use DBMS to index the metadata, we first import the metadata into DB. As shown in Fig. 5a, we find that P-index needs less time to build index structure than DBMS. We also find that, with the increase of files, the time cost of building P-index is less than KD-tree and R-tree, as shown in Fig. 5b. When the dataset is smaller, the k-prototypes algorithm occupies most time overhead due to the iteration com-puting centroids. We can reduce the time cost of building P-index via computing the centroids of each provenance group in parallel. From Fig. 5b, we can also find that the time overhead of computing K-prototype algorithm decreases with the increase of dataset.

**Query Latency.** In the P-index prototype system, we mainly exploit the numeric metadata and provenance data to achieve range query. Figure 6a shows that the average time consumption of each range query in our P-index. We exam-ine the latency as a function of the number of files from 1000 k to 6000 k with the increase of 1000 k in dataset. The latency of P-index is one order of magni-tude better than R-tree and KD-tree, and is two order of magnitude better than

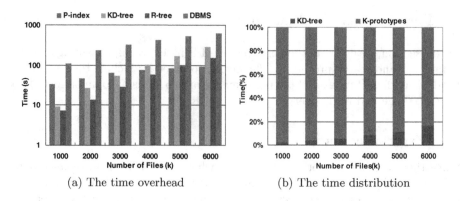

(a) The time overhead                    (b) The time distribution

**Fig. 5.** The overhead of constructing P-index

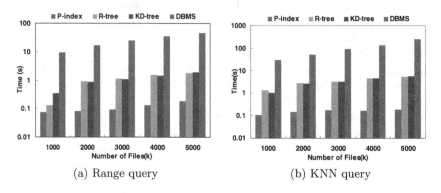

(a) Range query                          (b) KNN query

**Fig. 6.** The average latency of each metadata query

DBMS. Due to logical grouping based on provenance relationships, P-index can quickly prune out the branches which do not contain the query results.

We compare the time efficiency of searching files of different metadata index methods. Figure 6b shows the average time cost of each KNN query when k = 8. We discover that P-index spends 10 × - 30 × less time than KD-tree and R-tree to finish a KNN(k = 8) query. We also discover that P-index costs 282 × -1370 × less time than DBMS to finish a KNN(k = 8) query due to DBMS needing to check each B+-tree index for each attribute in searching metadata.

**Query Accuracy.** P-index adds the large quantities of metadata extracted from data provenance into the index structure. When users remember one or more keywords about the history of the files which they need, the keywords will filter many irrelevant query results and make P-index provide a relatively high accuracy. Figure 7a shows that over 90 % range query requests are served accurately by P-index. Since DBMS, KD-tree and R-tree lack the metadata coming from data provenance. Their accuracy is lower than P-index. The same conclusions about KNN query are observed in Fig. 7b

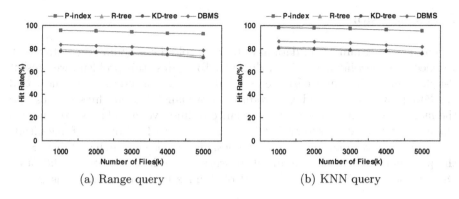

(a) Range query                    (b) KNN query

**Fig. 7.** The average hit rate of each metadata query

# 6 Related Work

In recent years, a lot of researches have focused on the application of provenance in storage systems. In the personal filesystem, provenance have been used
to improve file searching performance. Shah et al. [19] used a context-enhanced
architecture to improve the precision rate of file retrieval. The architecture was
built via the analysis of file correlations coming from provenance data. Liu
et al. [20] used a provenance graph to speed up the file search in storage systems. Their system can get the final results and do not need to access the disk
except that the result metadata are stored on the disk. These two methods store
and search the provenance graph for enhancing the accuracy ratio of inquiries.
P-index is different with them. P-index only exploits the provenance relationships
for logical grouping and exacts several searchable metadata. Hence P-index does
not need to store and search the provenance graph and reduce a lot of overhead.

There are some studies which use the keywords extracted from the provenance
data to help users to retrieve file and enhance the function of file retrieval.
Feldspar [21] allows users to easily construct, edit and visualize the connections
among entities which can obtain from provenance and to help users to retrieve
information. Keiko Yamamoto et al. [22] proposed a retrieval method based
on provenance which came from monitoring six kinds of file operations, such as,
copy, move, rename, edit, download and receive. These methods only capture the
provenance of specific applications. P-index can collect provenance of different
kinds of applications and extract searchable metadata from it.

Towards the metadata index in cold storage system, several enterprises use
database to store and index the metadata of files [3]. Pelican uses catalog, a off-
rack metadata service to store and maintain the metadata of files [4]. A metadata
catalog service commonly uses MySQL relational database as backend to store
and index metadata. While, DBMS limits efficiencies of scalability and require
lots of system resources. P-index uses key/value pairs to store the metadata and
uses KD-tree to index searchable metadata.

# 7  Conclusion

As an increasing number of data have become cold data, finding the data which you need has become increasingly difficult. To address this problem, we present P-index, an efficient and effective searchable metadata indexing scheme based on data provenance. P-index introduces provenance relationships of files and the metadata coming from data provenance to improve metadata search performance. Our evaluation shows that P-index has up to 1 - 2 orders of magnitude faster search performance than existing designs and also has high accuracy. Since the provenance is immutable, in future work, we seek to use SSD (Solid State Disk) to persist the unchangeable part of P-index for lowers memory usage.

**Acknowledgments.** The work reported in this paper is supported by National Basic Research 973 Program of China under Grant 2011CB302301 and National Natural Science Foundation of China (NSFC) under Grant 61025008, 61173043, 61232004 and 61402189.

# References

1. Mendoza, K.: Cold storage in the cloud: Trends, challenges, and solutions (2013). http://www.intel.com/content/dam/www/public/us/en/documents/white-papers/cold-storage-atom-xeon-paper.pdf
2. Blanc-Brude, T., Scapin, D.L.: What do people recall about their documents?: implications for desktop search tools. In: Proceedings of the 12th International Conference on Intelligent User Interfaces, pp. 102–111. ACM, Honolulu (2007)
3. Patiejunas, K.: Freezing exabytes of data at facebook's cold storage (2014). http://www.digitalpreservation.gov/meetings/documents/storage14/Kestutis_Pat-iejunas_Facebook_FreezingExabytesOfDataFacebooksColdStorage.pdf
4. Balakrishnan, S., Black, R., Donnelly, A., England, P., Glass, A., Harper, D., Legtchenko, S., Ogus, A., Peterson, E., Rowstron, A.: Pelican: A building block for exascale cold data storage. In: Proceedings of the 11th USENIX Conference on Operating Systems Design and Implementation, pp. 351–365. USENIX Association, Broomfield (2014)
5. Baron, J., Kotecha, S.: Storage options in the AWS cloud. Technical report, Amazon Web Services (2013)
6. Leung, A.W., Shao, M., Bisson, T., Pasupathy, S., Miller, E.L.: Spyglass: fast, scalable metadata search for large-scale storage systems. In: Proceedings of the 7th USENIX Conference on File and Storage Technologies, pp. 153–166. USENIX, Berkeley (2009)
7. Hua, Y., Jiang, H., Zhu, Y., Feng, D., Tian, L.: Smartstore: a new metadata organization paradigm with semantic-awareness for next-generation file systems. In: Proceedings of the Conference on High Performance Computing Networking, Storage and Analysis, pp. 1–12. IEEE, Portland (2009)
8. Xu, L., Huang, Z., Jiang, H., Tian, L., Swanson, D.: VSFS: A versatile searchable file system for HPC analytics. Technical report, University of Nebraska-Lincoln (2013)

9. Muniswamy-Reddy, K.K., Macko, P., Seltzer, M.I.: Provenance for the cloud. In: Proceedings of the 8th USENIX conference on File and storage technologies, pp. 197–210. USENIX, San Jose (2010)
10. Moreau, L., Clifford, B., Freire, J., Futrelle, J., Gil, Y., Groth, P., Kwasnikowska, N., Miles, S., Missier, P., Myers, J., et al.: The open provenance model core specification (v1. 1). Future Gener. Comput. Syst. **27**(6), 743–756 (2011)
11. Ghoshal, D., Plale, B.: Provenance from log files: a bigdata problem. In: Proceedings of the Joint EDBT/ICDT 2013 Workshops, pp. 290–297. ACM, New York (2013)
12. Braun, U., Garfinkel, S.L., Holland, D.A., Muniswamy-Reddy, K.-K., Seltzer, M.I.: Issues in automatic provenance collection. In: Moreau, L., Foster, I. (eds.) IPAW 2006. LNCS, vol. 4145, pp. 171–183. Springer, Heidelberg (2006)
13. Leung, A., Adams, I., Miller, E.L.: Magellan: A searchable metadata architecture for large-scale file systems. Technical Report UCSC-SSRC-09-07, University of California, Santa Cruz (2009)
14. Davidson, J., Liebald, B., Liu, J., Nandy, P., Van Vleet, T., Gargi, U., Gupta, S., He, Y., Lambert, M., Livingston, B., et al.: The youtube video recommendation system. In: Proceedings of the Fourth ACM Conference on Recommender Systems, pp. 293–296. ACM, Barcelona (2010)
15. Ram, S., Liu, J.: A semantic foundation for provenance management. J. Data Semant. **1**(1), 11–17 (2012)
16. Huang, Z.: Extensions to the K-means algorithm for clustering large data sets with categorical values. Data Min. Knowl. Disc. **2**(3), 283–304 (1998)
17. Agrawal, D., Ganesan, D., Sitaraman, R., Diao, Y., Singh, S.: Lazy-adaptive tree: An optimized index structure for flash devices. Proc. VLDB Endowment **2**(1), 361–372 (2009)
18. Riedel, E., Kallahalla, M., Swaminathan, R.: A framework for evaluating storage system security. In: Proceedings of the 1st USENIX Conference on File and Storage Technologies, pp. 15–30. USENIX, Monterey (2002)
19. Shah, S., Soules, C.A., Ganger, G.R., Noble, B.D.: Using provenance to aid in personal file search. In: USENIX Annual Technical Conference, pp. 1–14. USENIX, Santa Clara (2007)
20. Liu, J., Feng, D., Hua, Y., Peng, B., Nie, Z.: Using provenance to efficiently improve metadata searching performance in storage systems. Future Gener. Comput. Syst. **50**, 99–110 (2014)
21. Chau, D.H., Myers, B., Faulring, A.: What to do when search fails: finding information by association. In: Proceedings of the SIGCHI Conference on Human Factors in Computing Systems, pp. 999–1008. ACM, Montreal (2008)
22. Yamamoto, K., Kuriyama, T., Shigemori, H., Kuramoto, I., Tsujino, Y., Minakuchi, M.: Provenance based retrieval: File retrieval system using history of moving and editing in user experience. In: Proceedings of the IEEE 35th Annual Conference on Computer Software and Applications, pp. 618–625. IEEE, Munich (2011)

# Performance Optimization and Evaluation of Space Management in Cloud Storage Systems

Guangping Xu[1,2(✉)], Huan Li[1,2], Qunfang Mao[1,2],
Sheng Lin[1,2], and Hua Zhang[1,2]

[1] Tianjin Key Laboratory of Intelligence Computing
and New Software Technology, Tianjin 300384, China
xugp2008@aliyun.com
[2] Computer and Communication Engineering School,
Tianjin University of Technology, Tianjin 300384, China

**Abstract.** Cloud service providers and enterprises usually deploy high performance storage to manage the unrelenting growth of data. In this paper, we focus on performance optimization and evaluation by using optimal regeneration codes in such cloud storage systems. We present an efficient data maintenance management framework to reduce network repair traffic with the minimum data movement while keeping the desired fault-tolerance in storage systems. In the management framework, it has two phases including the traditional erasure coding process and the optimal placement process. We formally represent the optimal placement as a variant of the bin packing problem by bipartite graphs. Then, we model the placement transform by the interchange graph and propose an efficient heuristic algorithm to find the optimal solution. All feasible solutions are linked together by interchange operation and thus the search space can be taken as an interchange graph. Finally, we evaluate the performance of the optimal placement during data maintenance with different practical settings in our experiments. The experimental results show that the amount of network repair traffic can be reduced by about $10\%$ than the initial placement and by about $2X$ than traditional erasure coding placement.

**Keywords:** Cloud storage systems · Data maintenance · Optimal placement · Bin packing · Performance evaluation

## 1 Introduction

It is reported that the global total data amount is growing $40\%$ per year into the next decade and will reach 44 zettabytes by 2020 [1]. The demand for large-scale storage systems is ever-increasing to keep up with the ever-growing data amount. Today cloud object storage is becoming popular which is ideal for cost effective, scalable storage requirements, like Amazon $S3$ [2], OpenStack Storage [3], etc.

© Springer International Publishing Switzerland 2015
G. Wang et al. (Eds.): ICA3PP 2015, Part IV, LNCS 9531, pp. 612–625, 2015.
DOI: 10.1007/978-3-319-27140-8_42

In such cloud storage systems, storage nodes are typically built using a large number of inexpensive commodity machines that may fail frequently. Data maintenance is one of the most important aspects in cloud storage systems. To maintenance the massive amount of data storage, it desires to have the least network traffic to repair the lost data in case of failures. We present an efficient data maintenance management framework to reduce network repair traffic with the minimum data movement while keeping the desired fault-tolerance in storage systems. Since it has the potential to improve the system performance, data reliability and load balance, it is a very active research topic in large-scale storage systems.

## 1.1 Motivation

Redundancy based on erasure coding techniques has been paid much attentions in these systems, especially, Maximum Distance Separable (MDS) codes. MDS codes achieve the optimal tradeoff between storage redundancy and fault-tolerance and existing most erasure codes allow to minimize the storage overhead.

Consider that network bandwidth is more concerned than storage overhead in distributed networks. The optimization design of the fault-tolerance in cloud storage networks need tradeoff such constraints between storage redundancy and network bandwidth. Even though MDS codes achieve the optimal storage overhead, these codes may become the barrier due to the large amount of bandwidth overhead. In fact, the majority of network bandwidth overhead is caused by *the whole file recovery* and *the storage node repair* in cloud storage systems. The upper-level access of the stored file needs to recover the whole file in case of the node failure, called the whole file recovery. Their recovery only needs the minimum amount of data which is the size of $\mathcal{F}$. When a single node failure occurs, it needs to replenish the lost packets on the failed nodes to a new storage node, which is called the storage node repair. For a file $\mathcal{F}$ with an MDS code, the bandwidth cost of the repair process needs is the same as the whole file recovery, i.e., the whole size of $\mathcal{F}$. As mentioned above, the failure of storage nodes may occur more frequently and hence the repair of failures will take up much more amount of network bandwidth for the MDS storage model.

From the philosophy above, Dimakis et al. proposed a new family of erasure codes, called regenerating codes, which allow for efficient single node repairs by minimizing repair bandwidth. Moreover, they discussed two extreme points on the trade-off, minimum storage regenerating (MSR) and minimum bandwidth regenerating (MBR) codes [8,9]. Thereafter the proposed constructions in [6,7] achieve MBR for the efficient storage node repair. For example, Rouayheb and Ramchandran called such a new family of codes, called Fraction Repetition (FR) codes [7]. In these hybrid codes of replication and MDS codes, the optimal placement is taken as the open problem. In this paper we study the optimal data placement under a unified framework and evaluate its performance with various practical experimental settings.

## 1.2  Contributions

Our contributions of this paper have the following three-fold: *First*, we model the optimal placement management by the interchange graph. All feasible solutions are linked together by interchange operation and thus the search space can be taken as an interchange graph. *Second*, we propose an efficient heuristic algorithm to find the optimal placement and speedup its process. *Third*, the performance of the optimal placement is evaluated during data maintenance with different practical settings.

## 1.3  Paper Organization

The rest of the paper is organized as follows. In Sect. 2 we present a two-phase framework of the data placement management. In Sects. 3 and 4, we model the optimal problem and propose our novel heuristic algorithms, respectively. Then in Sect. 5 we analyze the algorithm. In Sect. 6 we evaluate the proposed algorithm and the storage performance of the optimal placement. In the final section we conclude this paper.

## 2  Related Work

In cloud like distributed storage systems, much more attentions have been paid on data management such as scalability, load balance, reliability and etc. Among them, fault-tolerance is much more concerned. It can be provided either by replicating data or using various MDS erasure codes [4,5]. However, neither of them can provide the perfect solution to storage data in networks in terms of storage redundancy, network bandwidth and coding complexity. The appropriate storage design involves the tradeoff among these metrics which were studied deeply. In particular, bandwidth may be the dominant constrained resource in distributed networks.

In [8], Dimakis et al. studied their termed regenerating codes which allow for efficient single node repairs by minimizing repair bandwidth. And they presented the extremal points on the tradeoff between storage capacity and repair bandwidth, namely Minimum Storage Regenerating (MSR) codes and Minimum Bandwidth Regenerating (MBR) codes. Subsequent research works paid attention to the construction of both classes of regenerating codes. Here we merely concern about the related literature on MBR codes.

In [6] Rashmi et al. presented a construction for MBR codes which is based on a concatenation of an MDS code with a repetition code based on a complete graph. Rouayheb and Ramchandran [7] generalized the construction of [6] and defined a new family of codes belong to MBR codes, called fraction repetition codes. The node repair of an FR code can be performed not only at the minimum bandwidth cost but also without complex coding process. At the same time, several different design schemes were studied.

Different with the node repair of MBR codes that any fixed sized node set is involved, the node repair of an FR code instead uses certain of fixed sized node set specified by an table (i.e., table-based repair). As the gain of the table-based repair, the capacity of an FR code may exceed the storage capacity of MBR codes and such FR codes are universally good. The upper bound of FR codes with given parameters are presented in [6]. Several constructions have been proposed by some combinatorial objects such as regular graphs [7], resolvable designs [11] and cage graphs [10]. In [17,18] some algorithms to generate the matrix of FR codes were presented. Based on these works, the constructions of optimal FR codes are based on combinatorial designs and on different families of regular graphs and transversal designs which attain the capacity bounds were presented.

As stated in the recent literatures [12,13], the optimal construction is an important problem that is still open in general. This paper makes a contribution towards solving this problem by proposing a optimal solution that achieve the optimal tradeoff between storage and bandwidth in cloud storage systems. To our best knowledge, this is the first time to evaluate the storage performance by the practical experiments.

## 3   Framework

In the section, we briefly present a two-phase management framework in the data management and then formally describe the optimal problem.

For a file $\mathcal{F}$, it first is encoded into $\theta$ packets by an MDS code; then these packets are replicated $\rho$ times and stored on $n$ storage nodes uniformly (say $d$ packets on each node) such that $\mathcal{F}$ can tolerate any $n - k$ node failures.

The data placement management framework consists of two phases: the traditional erasure coding phase and the replicating placement phase. During the traditional erasure coding phase, it often employ Reed-Solomon like codes to encode a file. Then we replicate the encoded packets into a set of storage nodes during the replicating placement phase. This framework ensures the node repair can be done in an efficient way without decoding and the storage nodes involved in a storage node repair just transfer certain of packets which will be directly stored on the new storage node.

In this paper, we focus on optimization of the placement phase and evaluating the storage performance. The formal definition of the storage framework can be presented into the following colored bin packing model: Here balls correspond to coded packets and bins correspond to storage nodes. We are given a set of balls with different $n$ colors and each color has the same amount balls, say $\rho$; then we place these balls into $m$ bins so that each bin has an equal number of balls, say $\theta$. Clearly, it can be observed that the relation of these parameters holds: $nd = \theta\rho$. It can prove that FR codes exist in a wide range of parameters constrained with the relation.

The placement of balls-in-bins ensures remained balls have certain of colors after *any* $n - k$ bins are removed. So consider the following optimal goal: What is the minimum ball amount of distinct colors with such constraints? How can we construct explicitly such the feasible placement?

To formally represent the optimal goal, we define the storage capacity as follows.

**Definition 1.** *Given parameters $n, \theta, d, \rho$, the storage capacity of a placement $C$, denoted by $R_c(k)$ is*

$$R_c(k) := \min_{\substack{I \in [n] \\ |I| = k}} \left| \bigcup_{i \in I} V_i \right|$$

*where $[n]$ denotes the integer set $\{1, 2, \cdots, n\}$ and $V_i$ is a subset of $[\theta]$ such that $|V_i| = d$.*

From this definition, the storage capacity $R_c(k)$ is the minimum number of distinct packets stored in any $k$ storage nodes. Given the same parameters $n, \theta, d, \rho$, the storage capacity $R_c(k)$ may be different for different placements $C$. So a feasible algorithm is needed to find the optimal storage capacity and determine the corresponding placement. Therefore, we formally describe the following optimal problem: *For fixed parameters $n, \theta, d, \rho$ and $k$, it is to determine a placement with the maximum $R_c(k)$.*

In the following two sections, we present the graph model and propose our search algorithm.

## 4    Model

### 4.1    Representation of Optimal Placement

We use a bipartite graph $G(X \cup Y, E)$ and the corresponding adjacency matrix $A$ to represent a placement. Recall that a *bipartite graph* $G(X \cup Y, E)$ is a graph with two classes $X$ and $Y$ of vertices such that edges are only connected between vertices in $X$ and $Y$. Let vertices in $X$ be storage nodes and vertices in $Y$ be distinct packets; and then an edge $e_{ij} \in E$ represents storage node $i \in X$ stores one packet $j \in Y$. Thus $|X| = n$, $|Y| = \theta$ and the degree of each vertex in $X$ is $d$ and the degree of each vertex in $Y$ is $\rho$. Such the bipartite graph calls the bipartite biregular graph.

A bipartite graph $G(X \cup Y, E)$ can be represented by an *adjacency matrix*, which is a Boolean matrix with $n$ rows indicating vertices of $X$ and $\theta$ columns indicating vertices of $Y$, denoted by $A = (a_{ij})_{n \times \theta}$, where

$$a_{ij} = \begin{cases} 1 & \text{node } i \text{ stores packet } j, \\ 0 & \text{otherwise.} \end{cases}$$

for $i \in [n]$ and $j \in [\theta]$.

Thus a Boolean matrix $A$ has constant row weight $d$ and constant column weight $\rho$, respectively. From the bipartite biregular graph and the correspond Boolean matrix, it is obvious that $nd = \theta\rho$. Figure 1 shows two examples with the same parameters.

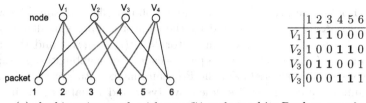

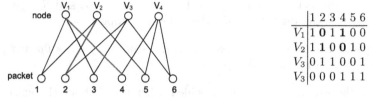

(b) the bipartite graph without $C4$ cycles and its Boolean matrix

**Fig. 1.** Two examples of packet placement with the same parameters: $n = 4, \theta = 6, d = 3, \rho = 2$.

We take the Boolean matrix $A$ as *a feasible solution*. All such Boolean matrices with appropriate parameters form a solution space, denoted by $\mathcal{A} = \{A\}$. So our goal is to find an optimal placement with the maximum storage capacity, $R_c(k)$.

**Definition 2.** *A $C4$-cycle represents a complete subgraph $K_{2,2}$ in its bipartite graph $G$, i.e., a cycle of length 4.*

That is, from the view of the corresponding Boolean matrix, a $C4$-cycle corresponds to a $2 \times 2$ sub-matrix in a Boolean matrix $A$ whose all elements are 1s.

As shown in Fig. 1, both examples have different cycle structures: the former in Fig. 1(a) has two $C4$ cycles which has $R_c(2) = 4$ while the latter in Fig. 1(b) has no $C4$ cycle (i.e., it is $C4$-free) which has $R_c(2) = 5$. So we get the following observation.

**Proposition 1.** *The different cycle structures of the placements in $\mathcal{A}$ with the same coding parameters (i.e., the $(0, 1)$ patterns in the Boolean matrices) may result in different storage capacities $R_c(k)$.*

In the following sections, we first ensure the existence of placements with given parameters, and then propose an efficient search algorithm to find an optimal placement in $\mathcal{A}$ by so called interchange operation to transform one solution to another.

## 4.2 Existence of a Placement

For the given parameters $n, \theta, d, \rho$, we first determine whether a placement exists. It should point out a connection of the Boolean matrix of a placement with the class of the Boolean matrix which has prescribed row and column sum vectors.

For a Boolean matrix of $m$ rows and $n$ columns, let the sum of row $i$ be denoted by $r_i$ for $i = 1, \cdots, m$ and let the sum of column $i$ be denoted by $s_i$ for $i = 1, \cdots, n$. Thus the row sum vector $R = (r_1, \cdots, r_m)$ and the column sum vector $S = (s_1, \cdots, s_m)$. In the past decades, the combinatorial properties and the construction algorithm of the Boolean matrix with prescribed row and column sum vectors were well studied by Ryser and Brualdi et al. in [14,15] Here the Boolean matrix of a feasible placement is special that row sum vector and column sum vector are constant vectors, $R = (d, \cdots, d)$ and $S = (\rho, \cdots, \rho)$, respectively. We can directly obtain the following proposition.

**Proposition 2.** *Let positive integers* $n, \theta, d, \rho$ *stratifying* $nd = \theta\rho$ *and* $\rho \leq n$; *then placement* $\mathcal{C}(n, \theta, d, \rho)$ *always exists.*

Note that the literature [17] also provided other proof about the existence of feasible placements. We next will detail an efficient search algorithm in $IG(\mathcal{A})$.

## 5   Algorithm and Analysis

In this section we first present the framework of the whole search algorithm and then detail its implementation.

### 5.1   Search Algorithm

With the given parameters $n, d, \theta, \rho$ and $k$, our aim is to output a Boolean matrix whose storage capacity $R_c(k)$ is maximum. Our proposed search algorithm follows the hill climbing methodology, which belongs to the family of local search.

It is an iterative algorithm which can be described as follows: we first generate an initial solution with the given parameters as current feasible solution; then for current feasible solution, its neighborhood can be determined by the interchange operation; we evaluate the storage capacity of the neighborhood solutions and take one solution which has better storage capacity as current feasible solution. Repeat the iterative search until the optimal solution is found.

The algorithm of the search process is shown as the pseudocode in Algorithm 1. After checking the feasibility of the given parameters (line 1), the algorithm generates an initial solution (line 2), set it as current optimal solution $OPT$ and add it into the candidate list (line 3-5). Then taking a solution $A$ from $\mathcal{L}$, we evaluate each neighbor $N$ of $A$. If $N$ is close to $OPT$, then we add it to $\mathcal{L}$ and set it as $OPT$ if it is better than $OPT$ (line 8-3). Note that if $L$ is full, some elements is allowed to expire in the order they are added (line 14). In the following subsections, we will detail its implementation.

### 5.2   Initial Solution

When performing the search process, we consider the question of how to generate the initial solution arises. As shown in Fig. 1, the storage capacity of a feasible

**Algorithm 1.** The heuristic algorithm for finding an optimal placement.

**Input:**
    the parameters: $n, \theta, d, \rho$;
    the number of storage nodes involved in a repair, $k$;
**Output:**
    an optimal solution $OPT$.
1: **if** existence of a placement$(n, \theta, d, \rho)$ **then**
2:    $A \leftarrow$ generate an initial solution;
3:    $\mathcal{L} \leftarrow$ initialize a candidate list;
4:    $\mathcal{L} = \mathcal{L} \cup \{A\}$;
5:    $OPT \leftarrow A$;
6:    **while** $\mathcal{L}$ is not empty **do**
7:        $A \leftarrow$ take a solution in $\mathcal{L}$;
8:        **for** each neighbor $N$ of $A$ and $N \notin \mathcal{L}$ **do**
9:            **if** evaluate the structure of $N$ close to $OPT$ **then**
10:                $\mathcal{L} = \mathcal{L} \cup \{N\}$;
11:                **if** $N$ is better than $OPT$ **then**
12:                    $OPT = N$;
13:                **end if**
14:                **if** $\mathcal{L}$ is full **then**
15:                    remove the first solution in $\mathcal{L}$;
16:                **end if**
17:            **end if**
18:        **end for**
19:    **end while**
20: **end if**
21: **return** $OPT$;

solution closely depends on its cycle structure. Here we define a heuristic rule by the number of $C4$-cycles in a solution. So it is better to generate the initial solution with few $C4$-cycles to improve the search performance. Although Ryser gives a matrix structure in the proof of Proposition 1, the matrix is obviously very far away from the optimal solution. There are some other methods to generate the initial solution. In [17,18], they presented how to construct such a placement directly. However, these constructed placements are not optimal in the storage capacity, which we will detail them in the following experiment results.

### 5.3 Solution Space

In order to search the optimal solution, we need to link all solutions in $\mathcal{A}$ together by a specific operation, termed the interchange operation. We are concerned with the following $2 \times 2$ sub-matrices of $A$ of the types

$$T_1 = \begin{bmatrix} 1 & 0 \\ 0 & 1 \end{bmatrix} \text{ and } T_2 = \begin{bmatrix} 0 & 1 \\ 1 & 0 \end{bmatrix}.$$

**Definition 3.** *An interchange is a transformation of the elements of A that changes a specified submatrix of type $T_1$ into type $T_2$, or vice versa, and keep all other elements of A unchanged.*

It can be observe that the interchange operation does not change the weights of any row or column of the matrix. By the terms in graph theory, let that $A_1$ and $A_2$ in $\mathcal{A}$ be vertices and then join them by an edge if they differ by an interchange. The resulted graph is called the interchange graph $IG(\mathcal{A})$. For example, the matrix in Fig. 1(a) can be transformed into the matrix Fig. 1(b) by an interchange. Thus an edge in $IG(\mathcal{A})$ connect them directly. Followed the result in [15], we get the following proposition.

**Proposition 3.** *The interchange graph $IG(\mathcal{A})$ is connected.*

This proposition makes it possible to design a search algorithm to find the optimal FR code in $\mathcal{A}$. After applied an interchange to a matrix in $\mathcal{A}$, then it is transformed to another matrix. Since the connectivity of $IG(\mathcal{A})$, the vertices corresponded to the optimal solutions can be reached by a series of interchanges.

### 5.4 Heuristic Criterion

The proposed algorithm uses the following method as a heuristic criterion to speedup the computation of $R_c(k)$. As known, the fault tolerance of a placement is the girth of its bipartite graph from coding theory. The bipartite graph having the least number of 4-cycles tend to have the larger girth [16]. So we try to reduce the number of 4-cycles in a Boolean matrix during the search process. We take the number of $C4$ cycles in matrix of solution as the criterion of our algorithm. If the number of $C4$ cycles in matrix $X$ is less than the number in matrix $Y$, we believe that $X$ is batter than $Y$. We count C4 cycles of current solution based on its previous solution with the time complexity of $O(n^2)$ during the search. The number of $C4$ cycles of current solution is gradually decreased and tends to a constant value in the search process.

## 6    Experimental Results

In the following section, we present the experimental results. We first focus on analyzing our proposed algorithms and then evaluate the performance of the optimal placement in our prototype storage system.

### 6.1    Algorithmic Evaluation

**Initial Placement.** As discussed in Sect. 5.2, initial placements can be generated by different algorithms. Here we first implement both algorithms and evaluate their initial placements. The experimental results are shown in Fig. 2 in which the initial placement 1 is generated by [17] and the initial placement 2 is generated by [18], respectively.

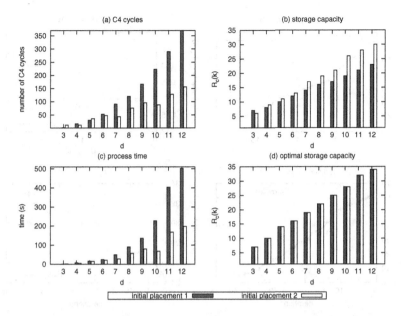

**Fig. 2.** The comparison between two initial placements during the optimization process with the following parameters: $n = 12, \rho = 3$ and $d = 3 \ldots 12$.

It can be observed that the number of $C4$ cycles in the initial placement 1 is much larger than in the initial placement 2 (Fig. 2(a)) and therefore the storage capacity of the initial placement 1 is worse than the initial placement 2 (Fig. 2(b)). To reduce so many $C4$ cycles in the initial placement 1, it takes much more time than to the initial placement 2 (Fig. 2(c)) by our algorithm. After the optimization for both initial placements, both resulted optimal placements reach the same storage capacity as shown in Fig. 2(d). The results show that the proposed method in [18] can generate better initial placement for storage systems; They also show that our proposed algorithm is robust to optimize the placement. So the following experiments use it to generate the initial placement.

**$C4$ Cycles Reduction.** As we know from Subsect. 5.4, the reduction of $C4$ cycles helps to speedup the search process. Here consider the relation between the storage capacity and $C4$ cycles during the optimization process. In both cases shown in Fig. 3, we evaluate and record the number of $C4$ cycles and the storage capacities $R_c(4)$ during the whole process. Along with the reduction of $C4$ cycles in the process, the corresponding storage capacities increase steadily. From such the trend, it validates that the reduction of $C4$ cycles indeed results to increase the storage capacity.

## 6.2 Storage Performance

In this subsection we evaluate the performance of the optimal placement in our prototype system. The prototype system is implemented based Openstack Swift

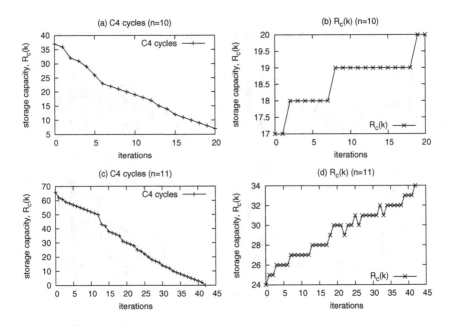

**Fig. 3.** The storage capacity $R_c(k)$ and $C4$ cycles during the optimization process ($k = 4$). In subfigure (a) and (b), $n = 10, d = 7, \theta = 35, \rho = 2$ while in subfigure (c) and (d), $n = 11, d = 10, \theta = 55, \rho = 2$.

in C++ and deployed on our cluster system consisting of 6 storage nodes. We can create arbitrary containers to emulate distributed storage nodes which are distributed into physical storage nodes.

**Experimental Settings.** Consider that $\theta = 16$ distinct packets are generated by an MDS code, replicated $\rho = 3$ times and then placed into $n = 12$ storage nodes uniformly, i.e., $\theta = 4$. There are the following alternative placements represented by the adjacency matrices $A_{G_1}(12, 16)$ and $A_{G_2}(12, 16)$. Here $A_{G_1}(12, 16)$ is the optimal placement found by our algorithm from the initial placement $A_{G_2}(12, 16)$ which is generated by [18]. To tolerate at most any $n - k$ failures, we can obtain $R_c(k)$ for both cases.

In our experiments, in both placements to tolerate 4 failures, $R_{c1}(8) = 15, R_{c2}(8) = 14$, respectively. Similarly, to tolerate 5 failures, $R_{c1}(7) = 14, R_{c2}(7) = 12$, respectively. That is, it can download the stored file by accessing at least $R_c(k)$ packets from any $k$ nodes. Thus we placed packets on 12 nodes in accordance with $A_{G_1}$ and $A_{G_2}$ for files with different sizes, 10 MB, 50 MB and 200 MB, respectively. As a comparison, we also stored these files by using the traditional Reed-Solomon codes. As shown in Fig. 4, it plots the storage performance of the initial placement, the optimal placement and Reed-Solomon coding placement.

$$
A_{G_1}(12,16) = \begin{pmatrix}
1\,1\,1\,1 & & & \\
& 1\,1\,1\,1 & & \\
& & 1\,1\,1\,1 & \\
& & & 1\,1\,1\,1 \\
1 & 1 & 1 & 1 \\
1 & 1 & 1 & 1 \\
& 1 & 1 & 1 & 1 \\
1 & 1 & 1 & 1 \\
1 & 1 & 1 & 1 \\
& 1 & 1 & 1 \\
1 & 1 & 1 & 1 \\
1 & 1 & 1 & 1
\end{pmatrix}
\tag{1}
$$

$$
A_{G_2}(12,16) = \begin{pmatrix}
1\,1\,1\,1 & & & \\
1 & 1\,1\,1 & & \\
1 & & 1\,1\,1 & \\
1 & & & 1\,1\,1 \\
1 & & & 1\,1\,1 \\
1 & 1 & 1\,1 & 1 & 1 \\
1 & & & \\
& 1 & 1\,1 & 1\,1\,1 \\
& 1\,1\,1 & & \\
& & 1\,1\,1\,1 & 1 \\
& & 1\,1\,1\,1
\end{pmatrix}
\tag{2}
$$

**Performance Results.** We concern about the file operations including storing files, retrieving files and repairing failed nodes.

We first evaluate the time cost to store files into the prototype storage system. The experimental results are shown in Fig. 4 (a) and (b). It can observe that the initial placement $A_{G_2}(12,16)$ takes the most time overhead to store files while the traditional Reed-Solomon placement is the most efficient. As expected, we observe that the optimal placement $A_{G_1}(12,16)$ is much more efficient than the initial placement $A_{G_2}(12,16)$ by about 5 %, 8 % and 12 % for three different kinds of files, respectively in both cases. Since $A_{G_1}(12,16)$ is better than $A_{G_2}(12,16)$ in the redundancy overhead, the size of each packet in $A_{G_2}(12,16)$ is smaller than the size of each packet in $A_{G_1}(12,16)$. It is easy to understand the efficiency of storing files by Reed-Solomon codes since it has the optimal storage cost to achieve the required tolerant failures.

We also evaluate the performance of retrieving files. In either of these three cases, it needs to download the whole size of each file. So it takes nearly the same time overhead to retrieve files. Due to the space limitation of the paper, the results are not plotted.

At last, we measure the performance of the repair of single node failure. During the repair of a failed node, it needs to transfer some packets from other available nodes and upload these packets to a new node. If there is more than one failure, then we repair each failed node one by one. From Fig. 4(c) and (d), we observe that the optimal placement $A_{G_1}(12,16)$ has the best performance. Its performance is improved by at least 10 % than the initial placement $A_{G_2}(12,16)$ and by up to 2X than Reed-Solomon coding placement. Of course, such savings in network overheads is at the cost of much more redundancy compared to Reed-Solomon codes. As discussed in Subsect. 1.1, it significantly reduces much more network traffic after the optimization of data placement.

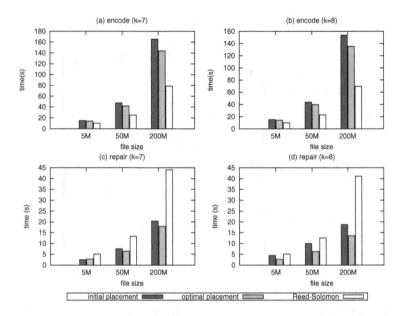

**Fig. 4.** The performance evaluation for the file operations including storing files with different sizes and repairing failed nodes. Files are stored into 12 storage nodes according with $A_{G_1}(12,16)$, $A_{G_2}(12,16)$ and Reed-Solomon codes, respectively.

# 7   Conclusion

We presented a data placement management framework for cloud storage systems in this paper. It is formulated into a variant of bin packing problem and propose an efficient heuristic algorithm to place encoded packets of files to store on storage nodes. The optimization ensures to obtain the maximum storage capacity by the optimal placement. The experimental results showed that the amount of network repair traffic can be reduced significantly. So it can effectively reduce the maintenance overhead for the large-scale storage system.

**Acknowledgments.** This work was supported in part the National Science Foundation of China Projects under Grant 61201234, 61202381, 61202168, 61572357 and 61170301, and also Tianjin Science Foundation Project under Grant 13JCQNJC00400.

# References

1. IDC. The Digital Universe of Opportunities: Rich Data and the Increasing Value of the Internet of Things. http://www.emc.com/leadership/digital-universe/2014iview/executive-summary.htm
2. Amazon S3. http://aws.amazon.com/s3/
3. OpenStack Storage. http://www.openstack.org/software/openstack-storage/

4. Khan, O., Burns, R., Plank, J., et al.: Rethinking erasure codes for cloud file systems: miniminzing I/O for recovery and degraded reads. In: Proceedings of the FAST, February 2012
5. Huang, C., Simitci, H., Xu, Y., Ogus, A., Calder, B., Gopalan, P., Li, J., Yekhanin, S.: Erasure coding in windows azure storage. In: Proceedings of the 2012 USENIX Conference on Annual Technical Conference, USENIX ATC12, Berkeley, CA, USA (2012)
6. Rashmi, K., Shah, N.B., Kumar, P.V., Ramchandran, K.: Explicit construction of optimal exact regenerating codes for distributed storage. In: Proceedings of the 47th Annual Allerton Conference on Communication, Control, and Computing (Allerton), pp. 1243–1249 (2009)
7. El Rouayheb, S., Ramchandran, K.: Fractional repetition codes for repair in distributed storage systems. In: Proceedings of the 48th Annual Allerton Conference on Communication, Control, and Computing (Allerton), pp. 1510–1517 (2010)
8. Dimakis, A.G., Godfrey, P., Wainwright, M., Ramachandran, K.: Network coding for distributed storage system. IEEE Trans. Inform. Theory **56**(9), 4539–4551 (2010)
9. Dimakis, A.G., Ramchandran, K., Wu, Y., Suh, C.: A survey on network codes for distributed storage. In: Proceedings of the IEEE, pp. 476–489 (2011)
10. Koo, J.C., Gill III, J.T.: Scalable constructions of fractional repetition codes in distributed storage systems. In: Proceedings of the 49th Annual Allerton Conference on Communication, Control, and Computing (Allerton), pp. 1366–1373 (2011)
11. Olmez, O., Ramamoorthy, A.: Repairable replication-based storage systems using resolvable designs. In: Proceedings of the 50th Annual Allerton Conference on Communication, Control, and Computing (Allerton), pp. 1174–1181 (2012)
12. Silberstein, N., Etzion, T.: Optimal Fractional Repetition Codes, January 2014. arXiv:1401.4734
13. Goparaju, S., El Rouayheb, S., Calderbank, R.: New Codes and Inner Bounds for Exact Repair in Distributed Storage Systems, February 2014. arXiv:1402.2343
14. Ryser, H.J.: Combinatorial properties of matrices of zeros and ones. Canad. J. Math. **9**, 371–377 (1957)
15. Brualdi, R.A.: Matrices of zeros and ones with fixed row and column sum vectors. Linear Algebra Appl. **33**, 159–231 (1980)
16. Chen, R., Huang, H., Xiao, G.: Relation between parity-check matrixes and cycles of associated tanner graphs. IEEE Commun. Lett. **11**(8), 674–676 (2007)
17. Anil, S., Gupta, M.K., Gulliver, T.A.: Enumerating some fractional repetition codes, March 2013. arXiv:1303.6801
18. Toni, E.: The Existence of Fractional Repetition Codes (2012). arXiv: 1201.3547

# Performance Prediction for Concurrent Workloads in Distributed Database Systems

Hui Li[1,2(✉)], Xiaohuan Hou[1,2], Mei Chen[1,2], Zhenyu Dai[1,2],
Ming Zhu[3], and Menglin Huang[3]

[1] Department of Computer Science, Guizhou University, Guiyang, China
{cse.HuiLi,gychm,cse.zydai}@gzu.edu.cn
[2] Guizhou Engineering Laboratory of ACMIS, Guiyang 550025, China
[3] National Astronomical Observatories,
Chinese Academy of Sciences, Beijing, China
{mz,huangmenglin}@nao.cas.cn

**Abstract.** In order to store and process data at large-scale, distributed databases are built to partition data and process it in parallel on distributed nodes in a cluster. When the database concurrently execute heterogeneous query workloads, performance prediction is needed. However, running queries in a distributed database heavily touches upon the network overhead as the data transmission between cluster nodes. Hence, in this work, we take network latency into account when predict concurrent query performance. We propose a linear regression model to estimate the interaction when execute concurrent query for analytical workloads in distributed database system. Since network latency and overheads of local processing are the two most significant factors for query execution, we analyze the query behavior with multivariate regression on both of them at different degree of concurrency. In addition, we use sampling techniques to obtain various query mixes as concurrency level increasing. The experiments for evaluation the performance of our prediction model are conducted over a PostgreSQL database cluster with a representative analytical workloads of TPC-H, the experimental results demonstrates that the query latency predictions of our model can minimize the relative error within 14 % on average.

**Keywords:** Performance prediction · Concurrent workloads · Distributed database · Distributed processing · Performance modeling

## 1 Introduction

As the data rapidly increased in many domains of industry and everyday life, distributed database system is needed to be able to store and manage massive data with parallelism and highly scalability. In a distributed database system, data is partitioned and stored at multiple, distributed nodes in a cluster, and the cluster often can be easily scaled out by adding new nodes. A query issued to a distributed database can be transformed into several sub-queries and then processed by many database nodes concurrently, the partial results in each nodes will be returned and combined as final output. In general, distributed database system is designed to support concurrent query

© Springer International Publishing Switzerland 2015
G. Wang et al. (Eds.): ICA3PP 2015, Part IV, LNCS 9531, pp. 626–639, 2015.
DOI: 10.1007/978-3-319-27140-8_43

execution to decrease the response time of execute analytical workloads. However, concurrent execution brings numerous challenges as well as benefits for resources competition, e.g., it's become hard to estimating the interaction of multiple queries in a distributed database cluster. For instance, there may be a positive interaction when two queries share a table scan. In this lucky case, both of the two queries can enjoy an appropriate speedup for the pre-fetched data. In contrary, if both two queries are incur high bandwidth network transmission, they will be slow down by each other as the heavy network traffic.

While build distributed database system on the cloud to provide data analytics as a service, e.g., Aliyun's DRDS (Distribute Relational Database Service) [27], it is significant for service providers to offer effective resource allocation and user experience. Thus the service provider should confer with users in term of service level agreements (SLAs). Generally, SLAs often expressed in Quality-of-Service (QoS) as query latency. SLAs/QoS violation often means lost revenue and reputation. Therefore, in the QoS prediction, workload latency often choose as the critical indicator rather than throughput or resource utilization.

In this work, we proposed a composite, multivariate regression models based on logical I/O latency and network latency to characterize the interaction of queries in distributed database system under concurrent environment. For the purpose of efficient estimate the performance in heavy concurrent workloads, we revise this model by introduce sampling technique. Our major contributions can be summarized as follows:

- We develop multivariate regression models to estimate the interaction of query mixes and predict the query latency when query is executed in distributed database system. During the model design and performance estimation, both logical I/O latency and network latency are considered.
- We conduct experiments in a PostgreSQL database cluster with TPC-H workload and comprehensively analyzed the results, we demonstrates that the effectiveness of our predictive models minimized the relative error within 14 % on average.

The rest of this paper is organized as follows. Related work is presented in Sect. 2. Section 3 introduces some critical performance indicators of distributed database system with preliminary analysis. Our performance prediction model is detailed in Sect. 4. The experimental evaluation of our models are described in Sect. 5. Finally we conclude and discuss our future work in Sect. 6.

## 2  Related Work

There has been many significant studies for predict performance for database workloads. In this section, we briefly review the major difference between our work and prior representative researches.

Literature [1] presented performance prediction models for database cloud to predict performance and resource utilization, which introduced multiple challenges about deploy databases applications in the cloud. They propose primary prediction models for the essential class of OLTP/Web workloads, while our models target OLAP workloads and are more suitable for database cloud. A similar study for portable database workload performance prediction in the cloud can be found in [2], which focus on lightweight workloads. As contrast to our work, we concentrate exclusively on medium-weight analytical workloads.

In literature [3–6], the researchers predict the performance metrics for both short and long-running queries by machine learning method, the involved metrics include elapsed time, disk I/O, message count, message bytes etc. Similarly, our approach primarily employ I/O block reads and data transfer volume to predict query latency, which is our critical QoS metric. There are two major difference between literature [3–6] and our work. Firstly, they do not address concurrent workloads issues, which is a typical application scenarios of database applications. Secondly, prior research focus on make use of the performance predication to obtain precise indicator of query progress, while our work just ignored this issue and only focus on concurrent workload modeling.

In literature [7, 8], the researchers built models of query interactions to predict the end-to-end latency of analytical queries. Query performance prediction for concurrent analytical workloads was also explored in [9–14]. They primarily work on propose regression models based on sampled query mixes to predict performance of single node database system. In the contrary, our focus in predicting query interactions in distributed database system with take network latency into account.

## 3 Performance Prediction

Our target is to predict the concurrent query latency in distributed database system which is mainly affected by resource contention as the share in fundamental resources such as RAM, CPU, disk I/O, network bandwidth, and so on [15–17]. In this section, we discuss the effective indicators which can be used for the query latency prediction under concurrent workloads of distributed database scenarios. And a simple motivated evaluation is also presented.

### 3.1 Indicators in Distributed Database System

We emphasize predicting query latency of concurrent queries for distributed analytical workloads. These workloads mainly involve network latency and local processing in a distributed database system.

Local processing is to retrieve and process the data needed for a query at the node from which it is accessed. The local processing time is an average time when a request for retrieving data at the node is submitted and when the required block is returned. For logical I/O requests, the local processing needs more than thousands of interactions of disk retrieve, a series of sequential reads and a few writes, or many cache and buffer pool hits. Generally, most of the local processing time is used to perform I/O operations and read operations are more than writes. In this paper, we use the average I/O block reads as one of our query latency indicators in term of local processing according to informed research [18–21].

As the data in distributed database system is processed in a scatter/gather pattern, network communication is required to run a query. Data is partitioned and stored at multiple, distributed nodes in a cluster. Transmission could be partial results from local node, or final results need to be sent back to the original node that issues the query [22, 23]. The impact of query latency in distributed database system is data transfer volume. So we use this metric as the indicator on the dimension of network response.

## 3.2 A Simple Motivated Evaluation

In this paper, we target medium-weight analytical workloads. We choose 10 medium-weight queries from TPC-H to form our queries mixes. The queries mixes in our workloads focus on concurrent performance in distributed database systems. We study the variance of the 10 queries in observed latencies (in seconds) on a four-nodes PostgreSQL cluster, the dataset is generated from TPC-H benchmark and the scale factor of dataset is set as 10 for different multiprogramming levels (MPLs). The results of this simple evaluation is list in Table 1, and we can see that not all the query latency increase linearly with the multiprogramming levels.

**Table 1.** Variance of 10 TPC-H queries

| Query | MPL1 | MPL2 | MPL3 | MPL4 |
|-------|-------|-------|-------|-------|
| Q3 | 0.07 | 0.13 | 0.12 | 0.10 |
| Q4 | 5.23 | 5.48 | 5.32 | 5.61 |
| Q5 | 8.92 | 9.62 | 9.70 | 10.46 |
| Q6 | 2.63 | 3.14 | 2.76 | 2.80 |
| Q7 | 27.80 | 29.48 | 31.03 | 32.06 |
| Q8 | 26.95 | 28.24 | 31.85 | 28.12 |
| Q10 | 3.13 | 3.68 | 3.61 | 3.71 |
| Q14 | 3.50 | 4.10 | 3.84 | 4.11 |
| Q18 | 83.14 | 93.47 | 87.93 | 86.03 |
| Q19 | 4.83 | 5.90 | 5.92 | 6.19 |

## 4   Modeling Interactions

As we discuss in the previous section, when we predict performance with different query mixes as well as various concurrency levels, we use block I/O and data transfer volume as the indicators of local processing and network response. We propose two multivariate regression models to study the interaction when the query mix is executed under concurrency in this section. Then we present a linear regression model to predict the query execution latency by block I/O and network latency. After that, we train our prediction models by sampling.

### 4.1   Prediction Query Interactions

In order to predict the impact of a query under concurrent workloads, we first examine how their block I/O and data transfer volume are affected when they are run in pairs and generally increase the multiprogramming level. Specifically, we build our multivariate regression model by analyzing how they affect each other in pairs. To make our model intelligible, we classify queries into primary and complement queries. The primary query is the query that we want to predict its performance while the concurrent query is the complement one. To better understand our model, we introduce following four variables that used in our models, and their values would be calculated from training data.

- Isolated: We present the variable as indicator values when the primary query is run in isolation which is taken as a baseline to estimate the concurrent values. For *query* i, we denote the block I/O as $B_i$ and data transfer volume as $N_i$.
- Complement: Likewise, the value of this variable is the accumulation of other concurrent queries' isolated $B_i$ or $N_i$ for *query* i.
- Direct: We adopt this variable to represent the impact of complement queries on the primary query, it is an aggregation of the change of indicator values. For example, as for data transfer volume of query i with concurrent *query* j, we take $N_{i/j}$ as the direct interaction and the change is $\Delta N_{i/j} = N_{i/j} - N_i$.
- Indirect: We present the indirect variable to reflect the interaction between the complement queries, its value is the accumulation of the direct variable among concurrent queries.

Therefore, we predict average concurrent block I/O and data transfer volume for *query* q with concurrent queries $p_1, ..., p_n$ as following, then we apply the ordinary least square method to estimate the coefficients $\beta_1$, $\beta_2$, $\beta_3$, $\beta_4$ for all of the query over training set.

$$B = \beta_1 B_q + \beta_2 \sum_{i=1}^{n} B_{p_i} + \beta_3 \sum_{i=1}^{n} \Delta B_{q/p_i} + \beta_4 \sum_{i=1}^{n} \sum_{j=1}^{n,j!=i} \Delta B_{p_i/q_j} \tag{1}$$

$$N = \beta_1 N_q + \beta_2 \sum_{i=1}^{n} N_{p_i} + \beta_3 \sum_{i=1}^{n} \Delta N_{q/p_i} + \beta_4 \sum_{i=1}^{n} \sum_{j=1}^{n,j!=i} \Delta N_{p_i/q_j} \tag{2}$$

## 4.2    Query Latency

In this work, we build a binary linear regression model to predict the execution latency of query by utilize both I/O block reads and data transfer volume. In general, query latency of distributed database system is mainly consisted of network latency and local processing overheads. While local processing overheads mainly includes overhead of CPU time and the average time of waiting for a logical I/O. Therefore, the latency of a query q L can be given by the equation:

$$L = C_q + \beta_1 \times B_q + \beta_2 \times N_q \tag{3}$$

In above equation, $C_q$ is the CPU overhead of *query q*, $B_q$ is the average block I/O while $N_q$ is the average data transfer volume of multiple nodes in the distributed database system. The coefficient $\beta_1$, $\beta_2$ are obtained by ordinary least squares method based on our experimental generated samples.

Let's give a specific example to illustrate our model. If we want to predict the query latency of *query a* with complement *query b* and *c* in a distributed database system, we first need the following values:

- The average of isolated block I/O and data transfer volume of $a$, $b$, $c$: $B_a$, $B_b$, $B_c$ and $N_a$, $N_b$, $N_c$.
- The direct variable of $a$ with concurrent queries $b$ and $c$: $\Delta B_{a/b}$, $\Delta N_{a/b}$, $\Delta B_{a/c}$, $\Delta N_{a/c}$.
- The indirect variable: $\Delta B_{c/b}$, $\Delta N_{c/b}$, $\Delta B_{b/c}$, $\Delta N_{b/c}$.

We can respectively obtain the indicator values using the following equations.

$$B_a = \beta_1 B_a + \beta_2 (B_b + B_c) + \beta_3 (\Delta B_{a/b} + \Delta B_{a/c}) + \beta_4 (\Delta B_{b/c} + \Delta B_{c/b}) \qquad (4)$$

$$N_a = \beta_1 N_a + \beta_2 (N_b + N_c) + \beta_3 (\Delta N_{a/b} + \Delta N_{a/c}) + \beta_4 (\Delta N_{b/c} + \Delta N_{c/b}) \qquad (5)$$

Then we predict the query latency of *query a* using Eq. 3:

$$L_a = C_a + \beta_1 \times B_a + \beta_2 \times N_a \qquad (6)$$

In order to illustrate how to get the specific models for each query, especially for how to obtain the coefficients of our models, we present following detailed example. If we desire to get the model to predict network latency for *query a* when MPL is 3, we need to conduct experiments to obtain following three sample sets:

$$N_s = \begin{bmatrix} 13 & 21 & -10 & 4 \\ 13 & 22 & -12 & 1 \\ 13 & 23 & -6 & -10 \\ 13 & 22 & -13 & -3 \\ 13 & 28 & 2 & -10 \\ 13 & 23 & -18 & -4 \\ 13 & 24 & -9 & -6 \\ 13 & 28 & -5 & -3 \end{bmatrix} \quad N_p = \begin{bmatrix} 13 \\ 13 \\ 14 \\ 6 \\ 14 \\ 13 \\ 9 \\ 10 \end{bmatrix} \quad \beta = \begin{bmatrix} 4.3182 \\ -1.5097 \\ 1.0895 \\ 0.1702 \end{bmatrix}$$

$N_s$ is the sample matrixes and $N_p$ is the samples of observed network latency. Then we can obtain the coefficients $\beta = regress(N_p, N_s)$. To be noted that, the *regress* function realizes multiple linear regression using ordinary least squares. Consequently, the model is as following:

$$N_a = 4.3128 N_3 - 1.5097 (N_b + N_c) + 1.0895 \left( \Delta N_{\frac{a}{b}} + \Delta N_{\frac{a}{c}} \right) 0.1702 \left( \Delta N_{\frac{b}{c}} + \Delta N_{\frac{c}{b}} \right)$$

When we predict network latency for *query a* with concurrent *query b* and *c* in different MPL contexts, the method used to obtain the coefficients of block I/O and execution latency are identical.

### 4.3   Training Our Models Based on Sampling

In order to obtain the query latency through Eq. 3, we need to train our prediction models. Our experimental context is identical to Sect. 3.2. Firstly, we figure out the features of the 10 representative TPC-H analytical queries when they are run in isolation, which is also the baseline to analyze the variance with various query mixes under different MPLs. Then we run queries in pairs, it means 55 pairwise queries are repeatedly executed in our experiments so as to get the specific characteristics of how they impact each other.

Towards the queries run on multiple nodes of cluster, we use Latin Hypercube Sampling (LHS) to generate the query mix from our workload. LHS is a stratified sampling method which can easily produce any number of samples [24]. In Fig. 1, we give an example of LHS at MPL 2. In this example, we can see that LHS generates five unique pairwise queries for five queries. In our experiments, we record block I/O and data transfer volume for each query mix to constitute the samples, which are used for estimating the coefficients of our models. For each query, we generate many query mixes to form the samples. For example, Q3 is the mix query (Q3, Q4, Q5), while Q3 is the primary query, and Q4, Q5 are complement queries.

| Query | 1 | 2 | 3 | 4 | 5 |
|-------|---|---|---|---|---|
| 1     |   | X |   |   |   |
| 2     |   |   |   |   | X |
| 3     | X |   |   |   |   |
| 4     |   |   | X |   |   |
| 5     |   |   |   | X |   |

**Fig. 1.**   Example of 2-DLHS

In our work, we generate query mixes $x$ to form the samples by employ $X = 1+10*LHS(10, 3)$, while *LHS* is a Latin Hypercube Sampling implementation, and the parameter *3* represents the MPL is set as *3*, the parameter *10* denotes there are *10* queries will be executed concurrently in different MPL scenarios. If we repeat above query mixes generation in three times, then we can obtain a query mixes matrix $x$.

We rounds each element of $x$ to the nearest integer less than or equal to that element, then we get matrix $y$, which denote the query id of query mixes. Based on the mapping showed in Table 2, we can obtain the final query mixes as matrix $z$. During our model training, query mixes as (Q14, Q8, Q8) will be discarded for the existed same concurrent running queries. In the matrix $z$, the query mixes such as (Q3, Q19,

Q4) indicate Q3 is the primary query while Q19 and Q4 are complement queries, we consider the mix query belongs to Q3. Similarly, the query mix (Q3, Q19, Q4) can also be consider as one of query mixes of Q19 or Q4 when it became the primary query. Therefore, we can get enough samples to train our models using the method mentioned in the previous section.

**Table 2.** Mapping of the query id which used in matrix

| Query ID in query mixes | 1 | 2 | 3 | 4 | 5 | 6 | 7 | 8 | 9 | 10 |
|---|---|---|---|---|---|---|---|---|---|---|
| TPC-H Query ID | 3 | 4 | 5 | 6 | 7 | 8 | 10 | 14 | 18 | 19 |

$$
x = \begin{bmatrix} 5.0803 & 10.2730 & 2.4644 \\ 2.1591 & 8.5054 & 10.8071 \\ 4.8186 & 5.5875 & 8.5465 \\ 10.9145 & 3.7100 & 5.3774 \\ 7.4941 & 4.7706 & 3.3528 \\ 1.2875 & 1.1593 & 4.6290 \\ 3.4101 & 2.7732 & 9.4096 \\ 6.6834 & 9.5371 & 7.4935 \\ 9.2353 & 7.0790 & 1.1291 \\ 8.4832 & 6.3443 & 6.8173 \end{bmatrix} \Rightarrow y = \begin{bmatrix} 5 & 10 & 2 \\ 2 & 8 & 10 \\ 4 & 5 & 8 \\ 10 & 3 & 5 \\ 7 & 4 & 3 \\ 1 & 1 & 4 \\ 3 & 2 & 9 \\ 6 & 9 & 7 \\ 9 & 7 & 1 \\ 8 & 6 & 6 \end{bmatrix} \Rightarrow z = \begin{bmatrix} 3 & 19 & 4 \\ 4 & 14 & 19 \\ 6 & 7 & 14 \\ 19 & 5 & 7 \\ 10 & 6 & 5 \\ 3 & 3 & 6 \\ 5 & 4 & 18 \\ 4 & 18 & 10 \\ 18 & 10 & 3 \\ 14 & 8 & 8 \end{bmatrix}
$$

## 5 Evaluation

In this section, we would like to evaluate the accuracy and effectiveness of our modules. We start with briefly reviewing our experimental setups. Then we present the observed result of query execution latency, network latency and block I/O, meanwhile, mean relative errors of each queries in different MPL scenarios are presented and discussed with the corresponding predicted values.

### 5.1 Experimental Setup

To estimate the accuracy of our models, we run the benchmark TPC-H 2.14 over a TPC-H data set generated by QGEN at scale 10 [25]. As we target OLAP workloads, we choose the queries with id 3, 4, 5, 6, 7, 8, 10, 14, 18, 19, namely 10 of 22 queries in the benchmark to make up our query mixes. Those queries are relative complex queries and often need long time to return the result, thus it can give us more time to collect block I/O and data transfer volume when they are running. Our distributed database system is a four nodes PostgreSQL cluster. We implement the distributed system by Postgres-XL, which is an open source PostgreSQL database cluster with horizontal scalability and enough flexibility to handle various database workloads [26]. The cluster is deployed on a machine with four-core Intel(R) Xeon(R) CPU E5-2620 2.0 GHz processor and 8 GB of RAM. Each node run on Centos 6.4 with kernel of Linux 2.6.32.

During the experiments, we repeatedly issues the chosen 10 queries against the PostgreSQL cluster to obtain the performance metrics. Specifically, we use the Linux utility SystemTap to write scripts to dynamically track and collect performance metrics such as block I/O and data transfer volume during query execution. Furthermore, we moderately adjust the value of PostgreSQL's parameter *shared_buffer* to ensure we can obtain more accurate performance metrics. Part of the collected performance data will be utilized as training sets to train our linear regression model, and the rest of them will be used as test data to predict block I/O and network latency when the queries is running concurrently.

## 5.2 Results Discussion

The fitted curve of predicted and observed query execution latency (in seconds) is depicted in Fig. 2. We use determination coefficient (R2), one of the measures that estimate the regression model, to evaluate whether predicted and observed values fit well. The range of R2 is from 0 to 1. When R2 is closer to 1, it indicates that the predicted value is closer to the corresponding observed value, and it means our model is better. Figures 2, 3 and 4 show the fitting situation of predicted and observed query execution latency, network latency, I/O block reads at context of MPL 3 and MPL 4. The value of R2 are 0.94, 0.58 and 0.84. We examine our ability to predict query latency by composing network latency with block I/O. In our experiment, we pick up the network transmission packets between each node as the source data to evaluate data

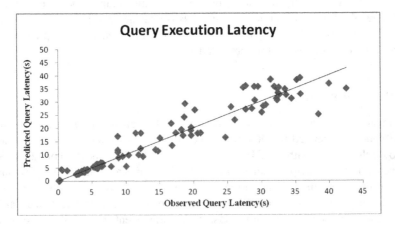

**Fig. 2.** Query latency at MPL 3 and MPL 4

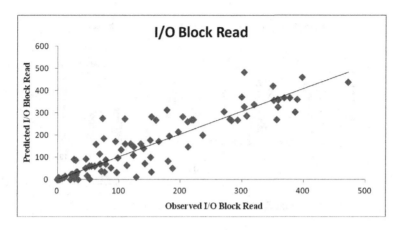

**Fig. 3.** Block I/O (×1000) at MPL 3 and MPL 4

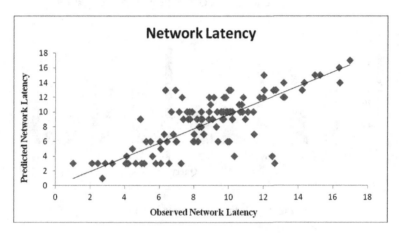

**Fig. 4.** Network latency at MPL 3 and MPL 4

transfer volume during query execution. In Fig. 4, we can found there are exist some underestimated and overestimated network latency prediction, based on our performance profiling and analysis, it is mainly raised for the reason that there are some network stability issues occurred and it then lead to the packets loss during performance metrics collecting.

As stated earlier, we apply Ordinary Least Squares (OLS) approach to estimate the coefficients of our models. According to our experience of using OLS, we need at least 30 samples to obtain acceptable results. In most cases of our experiments, we use 120 samples. Similarly, when we predict network latency and block I/O, there are need at least 30 samples by experiences. Actually, we use 140 samples in most cases of our evaluation. We also tried to use more samples in model training and prediction, however, the overall trend of results are similar, and it just makes the points denser.

Furthermore, in order to make our experimental scenarios are close to real application environments, we don't clear the cache during our experiments, which is one of

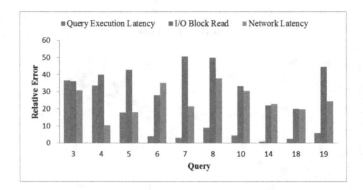

**Fig. 5.** Mean relative error at MPL 3.

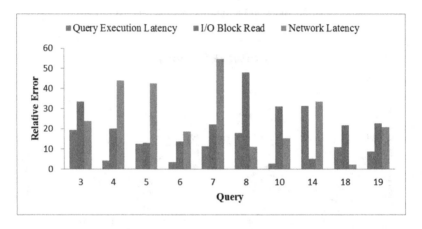

**Fig. 6.** Mean relative error at MPL 4.

**Table 3.** R2 and mean relative error for execution latency, block I/O and network latency

| Indicators | $R^2$ | Relative error |
|---|---|---|
| Query execution latency | 0.94 | 14 % |
| Block I/O | 0.58 | 30 % |
| Network Latency | 0.84 | 37 % |

the reasons why our estimates become slightly less accurate as we increase the value of MPL. We can find this issue when we compare the mean relative error of block I/O predication in Figs. 5 and 6.

Figures 5 and 6 depicted the mean relative error at the context of MPL 3 and MPL 4, which is calculated as |*(observed-predicted)/observed*|. We found that the mean relative error of *Q3* at MPL 3 and MPL 4 are relatively high. It's mainly because the execution time needed for *Q3* is too short to accurately capture enough performance metrics data to generate the samples needed by model training, thus the quality of samples are reduced. The total mean relative error of query latency, network latency and block I/O are showed in Table 3, they are 14 %, 30 % and 37 %, respectively. Our experimental results showed that our approach is promising to accurately predict the performance of concurrent workloads in distributed database system.

## 6  Conclusions

In this work, we propose multivariate regression models to predict concurrent query latency for analytical workloads in distributed database system. As far as we know it is the first work focus on predict performance for analytical workloads of distributed database. We first figure out the indicators in distributed database system and establish a binary linear regression model which involve block I/O and network latency. Then we propose two multivariate regression models to extrapolate the block I/O and network latency. Our experimental results showed that our predictions approach can minimize the relative error within 14 % on average.

**Acknowledgments.** This work was supported by the China Ministry of Science and Technology under the State Key Development Program for Basic Research (2012CB821800), Fund of National Natural Science Foundation of China (No. 61462012, 61562010, U1531246), Scientific Research Fund for talents recruiting of Guizhou University (No. 700246003301), Science and Technology Fund of Guizhou Province (No. J [2013]2099), High Tech. Project Fund of Guizhou Development and Reform Commission (No. [2013]2069), Industrial Research Projects of the Science and Technology Plan of Guizhou Province (No. GY[2014]3018) and The Major Applied Basic Research Program of Guizhou Province (NO. JZ20142001, NO. JZ20142001-05).

## References

1. Barzan, M., Carlo, C., Samuel, M.: Resource and performance prediction for building a next generation database cloud. In: Proceedings of the Conference on Innovative Data Systems Research (CIDR), Asilomar, California, USA (2013)
2. Jennie, D., Yun, C., Hakan, H., Shenghou, Z., Ugur, C.: Packing light: portable workload performance prediction for the cloud. IEEE Computer Society (2013)
3. Ganapathi, A., Kuno, H., Dayal, U., Wiener, J.L., Fox, A., Jordan, M., Patterson, D.: Predicting multiple metrics for queries: better decisions enabled by machine learning. In: Proceedings of the 29th International Conference on Data Engineering, ICDE 2009, pp. 592–603, Shanghai, China, 29 March – 2 April 2009
4. Chaudhuri, S., Narasayya, V., Ramamurthy, R.: Estimating progress of execution for sql queries. In: Proceedings of ACM SIGMOD/PODS 2004 Conference, pp. 803–814, Maison de la Chimie, Paris, France, 13–18 June 2004
5. Luo, G., Naughton, J.F., Yu, P.S.: Multi-query SQL progress indicators. In: Ioannidis, Y., Scholl, M.H., Schmidt, J.W., Matthes, F., Hatzopoulos, M., Böhm, K., Kemper, A., Grust, T., Böhm, C. (eds.) EDBT 2006. LNCS, vol. 3896, pp. 921–941. Springer, Heidelberg (2006)
6. Luo, G., Nanughton, J.F., Ellmann, C.J., Watzke, M.W.: Toward a progress indicator for database queries. In: Proceedings of ACM SIGMOD/PODS 2004 Conference, pp. 791–802, Maison de la Chimie, Paris, France, 13–18 June 2004

7. Ahmad, M., Aboulnaga, A., Babu, S., Munagala, K.: Modeling and exploiting query interactions in database systems. In: Proceedings of ACM 17th Conference on Information and Knowledge Management, CIKM 2008, Napa Valley, California, USA, 26–30 October 2008

8. Ahmad, M., Aboulnaga, A., Babu, S., Munagala, K.: Interaction aware scheduling of report-generation workloads. VLDB J. **20**(4), 589–615 (2011)

9. Ahmad, M., Aboulnaga, A., Babu, S.: Query interactions in database workloads. In: Proceedings of 2nd International Workshop on Testing Database Systems, DBTest 2009, Providence, Rhode Island, USA, 29 June 2009

10. Akdere, M., Cetintemel, U., Riondato, E., Upfal, E., Zdonik, S.: Learning-based query performance modeling and prediction. In: Proceedings of the 2012 IEEE 28th International Conference on Data Engineering, pp. 390–401, Washington, DC, USA, 1–5 April 2012

11. Elnaffar, S., Martin, P., Horman, R.: Automatically classifying database workloads. In: Proceedings of 11th International Conference on Information and Knowledge Management, CIKM 2002, pp. 622–624. ACM, New York (2002)

12. Ahmad, M., Bowman, I.T.: Predicting system performance for multitenant database workloads. In: Proceedings of 4th International Workshop on Testing Database Systems, DBTest 2011, Athens, Greece, Article no. 6, 13 June 2011

13. Mozafari, B., Curino, C., Madden, S.: Performance and resource modeling in highly-concurrent OLTP workloads. In: Proceedings of the 2013 International Conference on Management of Data, SIGMOD 2013, pp. 301–312, New York, USA, 22–27 June 2013

14. Jennie, D., Uger, C., Olga, P., Eli, U.: Performance prediction for concurrent database workloads. In: Proceedings of the ACM SIGMOD International Conference on Management of Data, SIGMOD 2011, pp. 337–348, Athens, Greece, 12–16 June 2011

15. Mehta, A., Gupta, C., Dayal, U.: BI batch manager: a system for managing batch workloads on enterprise data-warehouses. In: Proceedings of the 11th International Conference on Extending Database Technology: Advances in Database Technology, EDBT 2008, pp. 640–651, New York, NY, USA (2008)

16. Lo, J.L., Barroso, L.A.: Eggers, S.J., Gharachorloo, K., Levy, H.M., Parekh, S.S.: An analysis of database workload performance on simultaneous multithreaded processors. In: Proceedings of the 25th Annual International Symposium on Computer Architecture, vol. 26(3), pp. 39–50. ACM, New York, June 1998

17. Chaudhuri, S., Kaushik, R., Ramamurthy, R.: When can we trust progress estimators for SQL queries? In: Proceedings of the 2005 ACM SIGMOD International Conference on Management of Data, SIGMOD 2005, pp. 575–586, Baltimore, Maryland, USA, 14–16 June 2005

18. Wu, W., Chi, Y., Zhu, S., Tatemura, J., Hacıg, H., Naughton, J.F.: Predicting query execution time: are optimizer cost models really unusable? In: Proceedings of the 2013 IEEE International Conference on Data Engineering, ICDE 2013, pp. 1081–1092. IEEE Computer Society, Washington, DC, USA, 8–11 April 2013

19. Curino, C., Jones, E.P.C., Popa, R.A., Malviya, N., Wu, E., Madden, S., Balakrishnan, H., Zeldovich, N.: Relational cloud: a database service for the cloud. In: Proceedings of 5th Biennial Conference on Innovative Data Systems Research, CIDR 2011, pp. 235–240, Asilomar, CA, January 2011

20. Hacıg, H., Tatemura, J., Hsiung, W.P., Moon, H.J., Po, O., Sawires, A., Chi, Y., Jafarpour, H.: CloudDB: One size fits all revived. In: Proceedings of 6th World Congress on Services, SERVICES 2010, pp. 148–149, Miami, Florida, USA, 5–10 July 2010

21. Xiong, P., Chi, Y., Zhu, S., Moon, H.J.; Pu, C., Hacig, H.: Intelligent management of virtualized resources for database systems in cloud environment. In: Proceedings of 2011 IEEE 27th International Conference on Data Engineering, ICDE 2011, pp. 87–98, Hannover, Germany, 11–16 April 2011
22. Marin, G., Mellor-Crummey, J.: Cross-architecture performance predictions for scientific applications using parameterized models. In: Proceedings of the International Conference on Measurement and Modeling of Computer Systems, SIGMETRICS 2004, pp. 2–13. ACM, New York, 12–16 June 2004
23. Jesper, M.: On the impact of network latency on distributed systems design. Inf. Technol. Manage. **1**, 183–194 (2000)
24. Latin hypercube sampling. http://en.wikipedia.org/wiki/Latin_hypercube_sampling (Accessed: 25 November 2014)
25. Postgres-XL. http://www.postgres-xl.org/ (Accessed: 25 November 2014)
26. TPC-H. http://www.tpc.org/tpch/ (Accessed: 25 November 2014)
27. Aliyun's DRDS (Distribute Relational Database Service). http://www.aliyun.com/product/drds/ (Accessed: 25 November 2014)

# An Energy-Aware File Relocation Strategy
# Based on File-Access Frequency
# and Correlations

Cheng Hu[1] and Yuhui Deng[1,2(✉)]

[1] Department of Computer Science, Jinan University, Guangzhou 510632, China
hucheng_public@163.com, tyhdeng@jnu.edu.cn
[2] State Key Laboratory of Computer Architecture, Institute of Computing,
Chinese Academy of Sciences, Beijing 100190, China

**Abstract.** Energy consumption has become a big challenge of the traditional storage systems due to the explosive growth of data. A lot of research efforts have been invested in reducing the energy consumption of those systems. Traditionally, the frequently accessed data are concentrated into a small part of hot storage nodes, and other cold storage nodes are switched to a low-power state, thus saving energy. However, due to the energy penalty and time penalty, it takes extra energy and generates additional delay to switch a cold storage node from a low-power state to an active state. In contrast to the existing work, this paper proposes a Skew File Relocate (SFR) strategy which aggregates the correlated cold files to the same cold storage node in addition to concentrating the frequently accessed files to the hot nodes. Because the correlated files are normally accessed together, SFR can significantly reduce the number of power state transitions and lengthen the idle periods that the cold storage nodes are experienced, thus saving more energy and improving the system response time. Furthermore, other three relocation strategies are designed to explore the performance behavior of SFR. Experimental results demonstrate that SFR can significantly reduce the energy consumption while maintaining the system performance at an acceptable level.

**Keywords:** Energy aware · File relocation strategy · File-access frequency · File-access correlations · Clustered storage system

## 1 Introduction

Commercially component-based clustered storage systems with the advantage of high scalability become the architecture of next generation storage systems. However, with the explosive growth of data, this system will become more and more complex, and then it will consume enormous energy and require a mass of storage resources. Deng [1] indicated that energy efficiency has become one of the most important challenges in designing disk drive storage systems. EPA

© Springer International Publishing Switzerland 2015
G. Wang et al. (Eds.): ICA3PP 2015, Part IV, LNCS 9531, pp. 640–653, 2015.
DOI: 10.1007/978-3-319-27140-8_44

(U.S. Environmental Protection Agency) [2] estimated that about 61 billion kilowatt-hours (kWh) are consumed by data centers in 2006 (1.5 percent of total U.S. electricity consumption) with a total electricity cost of about $4.5 billion, and the energy efficiency trends reveal that the power consumption keeps a growth rate of 18 % per year.

To reduce the energy consumed by storage system, many approaches dynamically transfer the power state of storage nodes [3–5]. 80/20 rule [6] indicates that roughly 80 % of the effects come from 20 % of the causes. Cherkasova and Ciardo [7] found that in web workloads, 90 % of the requests go to 10 % of files. Because the storage nodes which store cold files are occasionally accessed, these nodes can be transferred to a low-power state. Due to the extended idle length of those storage nodes, energy conservation can be achieved.

However, those approaches did not consider the impact of file-access correlations on system performance and energy consumption. In most cases, correlated files are accessed together. And if correlated files are put into the same node in the standby state, the number of wake-ups will be reduced, which leads to a further reduction of energy consumption. Besides, based on 80/20 rule we can maintain a minimal number of active storage nodes. As a result, the energy consumption of a specific clustered storage system can be significantly reduced.

Many empirical studies [8,9] have shown that it's viable to identify the file-access frequency and correlations. In this paper, we design a Skew File Relocation (SFR) strategy which is energy-aware. And we present a novel method to mine the file-access frequency and correlations, which is crucial to realize SFR strategy. In order to explore the system behavior of the proposed strategy, we design other three strategies for comparison. Furthermore, we simulate a clustered storage system to evaluate these file relocation strategies. Experimental results demonstrate that our strategy can significantly reduce the energy consumption, while maintaining the system performance at an acceptable level. Our main contributions are as follows:

1. We propose an energy-aware file relocation strategy—SFR which leverages both file-access frequency and correlations.
2. Frequency and Correlations Mining (FCM) method is presented to mine file-access frequency and correlations.
3. To evaluate SFR, we design other three strategies for comparison, and perform a simulation to measure the energy consumption and response time of a specific clustered storage system.

The rest of this thesis is organized as follows. Section 2 discusses related work. Next, Sect. 3 introduces a clustered storage system, SFR, and the FCM method. Then, in Sect. 4 we construct a simulator, in which other three file relocation strategies designed for comparison are evaluated along with SFR. Finally, a summary is given in Sect. 5.

# 2    Related Work

## 2.1    Energy Saving of Clustered Storage Systems

Many efforts have been made to reduce the energy consumption of clustered storage systems. To improve the energy efficiency of server clusters, Chase et al. [4] designed an architecture for resource management in a hosting center. They put unused clusters into a sleep state. Pinheiro et al. [3] developed a system that dynamically turns cluster nodes on/off to handle the load imposed on the system. Power management techniques were implemented by Verma et al. [10] to reduce the power consumption of high performance applications on modern power-efficient servers with virtualization support. And Bostoen et al. [11] listed and classified a variety of energy saving techniques.

Recent work by Krioukov et al. [12] designed a power-proportional cluster which consists of a power-aware cluster manager and a set of heterogeneous machines. Thereska et al. [13] presented Sierra, a power-proportional distributed storage subsystem for data centers. This subsystem powers down servers during troughs. About 23 % of power was saved in their experiment. Zhang et al. [5] presented a power-aware data replication strategy by leveraging data access activities. Deng et al. [14] designed a power-aware web cluster scheduler which divides cluster nodes into an active group and a low-power group. Many researches also reduced energy consumption through task scheduling [15–17]. Power-saving storage systems based on dynamic voltage scaling (DVS) of processors have been also proposed [17,19]. The intuition behind the power savings is that the energy consumption of CPU is proportional to the square of the voltage [18].

Besides, reducing the energy consumption of hard disk drives is also a widely used way for reducing the energy consumption of a storage system. RAID [20] is a well-known technology to resolve this issue. EERAID [21], PARAID [22] and GRAID [23] are all based on RAID. There are also several approaches for reducing energy consumption of hard disk drives grounded on the skewed distribution of file-access frequency [24]. Iritani and Yokota [25] further propose Placement of files for Latency and Energy Consumption Optimization (PLECO), a novel method achieves the goal of energy conservation by placing correlated files into the same hard disk drive.

Different from ignoring file-access correlations or aiming to reduce the energy consumption of CPUs or hard disk drives, in this paper, we propose a novel method to mine the correlations among the accessed files. With this method we design an energy-aware file relocation strategy which can significantly reduces the energy consumption of clustered storage systems.

## 2.2    Mining File-Access Frequency and Correlations

In order to optimize I/O performance and mitigate the problem that the speed of cache, memory and hard disk is dramatically unmatched, many early researchers put forward several approaches to derive relationships between files rooted in access sequences. Tait et al. [26] investigated a client-side cache management technique for detecting file access patterns, and then they exploit them to prefetch files from servers. Lei and Duchamp [27] extended this approach and introduced the last successor predictor. Kroeger and Long [28] used traces of file system activity to compare four different models: last-successor prediction model, Finite Multi-Order Context modeling (FMOC), graph based modeling and an improved FMOC model called Partitioned Context Model (PCM). In order to prefetch more file (not only would be accessed next time but also some times later) and further reduce I/O latencies, Kroeger and Long [29] modified PCM and thus create a technique called Extended Partition Context Modeling. All these works told us, accurate prediction of future access pattern can be made by studying the past access pattern. Ishii et al. [30] inserted a memory access map into a prefetcher. This map is a data structure like bitmap for holding past memory accesses whose access patterns can be detected in turn. He et al. [31] advocated to accumulate I/O information, and then by exploring these information they reveal data usage patterns. Jiang et al. [32] presented a disk-level prefetching scheme, which leverages data layout and access history on disk drives to find out access pattern.

To derive the file-access correlations, there are also several approaches. Among them, FARMER [8] is an approach to mine file-access correlations leveraging file access sequence and semantic distance among files. And SUGOI (Search by Utilizing Groups Of Interrelated files in a task), a file search system, was introduced by Wu et al. [9]. SUGOI contains a task mining component, which extracts tasks and then discovers the interrelation between them from file-access logs.

In contrast to the existing work, this paper proposes a novel method for mining file-access frequency and correlations. The method is then employed to design an energy-aware file relocation strategy. In order to explore the system behavior of the proposed strategy, we design other three strategies for comparison. Furthermore, we simulate a clustered storage system to evaluate these file relocation strategies.

## 3    System Design

### 3.1    System Overview

**System Architecture.** A clustered storage system is designed in this paper. In terms of 80/20 rule, hot files are a small part of file set. So, in our design, storage nodes are divided into hot ones and cold ones. Hot files are relocated into the hot nodes. And cold files are relocated into the cold nodes with other cold files correlated to them. We only consider the file-access correlations of cold files and place correlated cold files together. That's because the hot nodes never go into a standby state, whether correlated hot files are in the same storage node has no impact on system performance and energy consumption. The hot nodes are kept in the active state (or the idle state when there's no request) all the time, owing to the accesses to hot files would be more than 80 % of the total requests. However, the cold nodes are in the standby state unless a request is received.

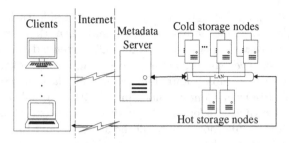

**Fig. 1.** System architecture.

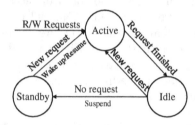

**Fig. 2.** Power state migration of a storage node.

And after all the requests are finished and there are no subsequent requests for a predetermined period of time, they are transferred to the standby state again.

As depicted in Fig. 1, the system contains one metadata server and several storage nodes. Hot nodes and cold nodes are divided from those storage nodes. The metadata server is the manager of the system. For the purpose of adapting to those relocation strategies, every storage node contains a file relocation buffer memory. Only when the file relocation buffer is full, can the files be relocated to the hard disk drive of this storage node. The intuition behind is that SFR relocates related cold files to the same storage node, so the files in a relocate buffer memory are related, thus they can be flushed to the hard disk drive and stored sequentially, and when these files are accessed in the future, this management will dramatically reduce the latency. We detail the process of file relocation in Sect. 3.2.

**Power State Transition of Nodes.** In general, the storage nodes of a clustered storage system have three power states: active state, idle state and standby state. The power state migration of a storage node is presented in Fig. 2. When the data in a storage node need to be accessed, the storage node will be switched to the active state to serve the read/write requests. After the requests are completed and there are no subsequent requests waiting, the storage node is then transferred to the idle state. The power of the idle state is slightly lower than the active state. The node will be transferred back to the active state when a new request is received.

To conserve energy, the node can be further suspended to the standby state, in which the CPU, RAM and hard disk drives of the node are all switched to the standby state. The power of a storage node in the standby state is much lower than that in the active state or the idle state. To perform requests after entering the standby state, the storage node must be woken up and then resumed to the active state. Suspending a storage node to the standby state only takes a little time and energy. However, resuming a storage node from the standby state to the active state takes extra energy and time due to the energy penalty and time penalty.

### 3.2   Mining File-Access Frequency and Correlations

FCM method is proposed to mine the file-access frequency and correlations. The file-access frequency. is easy to identify. FCM sorts all the files by the number of accesses, then in terms of 80/20 rule, the top 20 % files are hot files and the remaining files are cold ones. However, mining the file-access correlations is not a simple work. Wu et al. [9] presented a method for the frequent itemset task mining in order to search files in file systems. But here we improve it to mine the file-access correlations.

The basic idea of the frequent itemset task mining is that files accessed within the same period of time are related to each other. FCM applies this ideal and improves it to mine the file-access correlations. First, FCM divides the file-access logs into several transactions. A transaction is a series of file-accesses in a certain duration. We use 15 min as a duration (transaction duration). Figure 3 illustrates a instance of three successive transactions. As shown, in the first transaction (8:00–8:15), file a, b and c are accessed. To mine file-access correlations from transactions, a data-mining algorithm—Apriori [33] is adopted in this paper. Apriori is a best-known basic algorithm for mining frequent item sets in a set of transactions. Of course, it is feasible to use other data-mining algorithms.

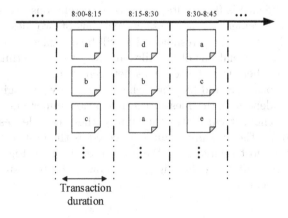

**Fig. 3.** Files accessed in transactions.

The Apriori algorithm uses two measurements (support and confidence) to discover the rules. In this paper, we also use these two measurements, but to discover the correlation degree of two files. We take file $F_A$ and $F_B$ as an illustration. Support is the probability that the two files appear in a transaction. Confidence is the probability that the file $F_B$ appears in a transaction when the file $F_A$ appears.

We calculate support and confidence by adding a weighted factor $\alpha$, for the sake that FCM could adapt to the latest file-access cases. $\alpha$ is a weighted factor related to the order of a transaction. E.g., as in Fig. 3, if we take the time duration 8:00–8:15 as the first transaction and there are 3 transactions in total, the $\alpha$ of the transaction (8:00–8:15) is $1 + 1/3$. We calculate the $\alpha$ of the $ith$ transaction by

$$\alpha_i = 1 + i/n. \tag{1}$$

In where, $i$ represents the order of the transaction and $n$ represents the total number of transactions. Support of two files is calculated by

$$Support = (\alpha_i + \alpha_j + ... + \alpha_k)/(\alpha_1 + \alpha_2 + ... + \alpha_n). \tag{2}$$

Confidence (short for "conf" due to the length) of two files is calculated by

$$Conf = (\alpha_i + \alpha_j + ... + \alpha_k)/(\alpha_i + \alpha_j + ... + \alpha_k + ... + \alpha_l). \tag{3}$$

In (2), the subscripts $i$, $j...k$ represent the order of transactions in which the two files appear, and the divisor represents the sum of $\alpha$ of all transactions. In (3), the subscripts $i$, $j...k$ represent the order of transactions in which the two files appear, and the divisor represents the sum of $\alpha$ of all transactions in which the first file appears. In this paper, the file-access correlations of two file is represented by the form $< abc \rightarrow xyz >$.

The maximum value of support is 1. This happens when the two files appear in every transaction. And the maximum value of confidence is 1 as well. This happens when the two files appear together all the time. The minimum value of support and confidence is 0. To filter file-access correlations, we set thresholds for these two measurements. File-access correlations of two files whose support or confidence is less than the threshold value will be considered to be 0. In other words, if file-access correlations of two files are very weak, we think that is just a coincidence, and there is no correlations between them.

When SFR relocates a cold file, for each cold node, by leveraging FCM, SFR first get the confidences of the files in the relocation buffer and the file needs to be relocated. Then, it calculates the sum of these confidences. Finally, the cold node which has the maximum sum is selected as the best one, because this node contains the most related files. We give an example in Fig. 4, the data in the table is figured out based on Fig. 3. As shown, the best storage node for relocation is the node B.

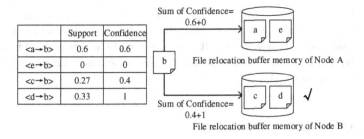

**Fig. 4.** File relocation of SFR.

# 4   Simulation Setup

We take a simulation experiment to evaluate all those strategies. The experiment models a clustered storage system which contains 16 storage nodes and one metadata server. Among those storage nodes, two nodes are used as hot nodes, and the other 14 nodes are cold nodes. To reduce the number of wake-ups of cold nodes and provide a good performance, when cold nodes perform requests, every of the them will keep in a active state (or a idle state when there is no request to perform) for 30 s.

In fact, data-mining process is executed when the metadata server receives a file-access request. This process can be inserted into the process of file information retrieval. Therefore, the effect of the data-mining process on system performance would be negligible. In the experiment, we do not include the execution time and energy overheads of the data-mining process. In addition, relocating files into a cold node happens when the cold node finished all the requests and have not be suspended into the standby state. Similarly, only when a hot node is idle, files can be relocated into the hot node. So, executing relocations almost have no impact on system performance. We also neglect the overheads of relocations in the experiment. We plan to do more accurate experiments in future work.

In order to explore the system behavior of our proposed strategy—SFR, we also implement other three file relocation strategies.

- High-Performance (HP) strategy is used as the baseline. HP does not divide the storage nodes into hot ones and cold ones. So it does not suspend any storage node to a standby state. And all the files in the storage system will not be relocated.
- File Relocate Once (FRO) relocates files into storage nodes only once. At first, FCM identifies the hot files and cold files after a learning stage. Then, FRO executes the relocation only once after this learning stage. Storage nodes are divided into hot ones and cold ones in this strategy. Hot files are relocated into hot nodes and cold files are relocated into cold nodes. FRO does not leverage the file-access correlations to relocate cold files.

– Equal File Relocate (EFR) relocates files when a mismatching situation
  appears, namely, hot file(s) in cold node or cold file(s) in hot node. If a hot file
  is in a cold node, EFR relocates it into a hot node in a round robin method.
  Similarly, if a cold file is in a hot node, EFR relocates it into a cold node in
  a round robin method.

## 4.1    Platform Environment

We use a PC as the experimental platform, the detailed specs are showed in
Table 1. And the parameters of storage nodes used in our experiment are given
in Table 2. The transmission rate of a hard disk drive is set according to a
performance evaluation in [34]. And the RAM transmission rate is the theoretical
value of a DDR-III RAM with the frequency of 1.33 GHz. The other parameters
of the storage nodes are set based on the measured value in [5].

Real network file system traces are used in this paper. Network file system
traces trace files' access behaviors and record those behaviors in a specific format.
In order to investigate the real situations and insure our research is universal,
we use three different traces: lair62b, home02 and deasna02. The characteristics
of these traces are given in Table 3. R/W represents the read/write request.

**Table 1.** Simulation platform specs

|  | Specification |
| --- | --- |
| OS: | Windows 7 professional x64 |
| RAM: | 4 GB DDR III |
| CPU: | Intel i3-3240 |
| Hard drive: | 500 GB/5400rpm |

**Table 2.** Characteristics of simulated storage node

| Parameter | Qualification | Value |
| --- | --- | --- |
| Power(Watt) | Active | 60 |
|  | Idle | 40.2 |
|  | Standby | 4 |
| Energy(Joule) | Suspend | 4 |
|  | Wake up | 519 |
| Delay(Second) | Suspend | 1 |
|  | Wake up | 10 |
| Hard disk drive transmission rate(MB/s) | Read | 60 |
|  | Write | 50 |
| RAM transmission rate(GB/S) | Read/write | 10 |

**Table 3.** Characteristics of the Network file system traces

| Trace name | Size | Time length | R/W per hour |
|---|---|---|---|
| lair62b | 11 GB | 984hours | 63k/h |
| home02 | 48 GB | 2160hours | 260k/h |
| deasna02 | 32 GB | 960hours | 840k/h |

As shown, deasna02 has the heaviest workloads. Lake of space we do not give the detailed information of these traces here, and it can be obtained in the web page: http://www.eecs.harvard.edu/sos/traces.html.

## 4.2 Evaluation

We take the 8:00–18:00 traces of a weekday respectively from those network file system traces. The traces of 8:00–10:00 is used as the learning sample which is provided to FCM. So, these two hours is the learning stage of FCM. After the learning stage, FCM keeps on updating file-access frequency and correlations by tracing the file-access behaviors. All mentioned file relocation strategies are adopted. Then, we test the average response time and energy consumption of the storage nodes with remainder 8 h traces respectively. We set 0.1 as the threshold of support and 0.4 as the threshold of confidence. We believe that the values of thresholds will affect the result of experiment. But we do not discuss them here, because we just want to show the availability of SFR.

**Energy Consumption.** Energy consumptions of the storage nodes with the four file relocation strategies are compared in Fig. 5.

As shown, in every traces SFR consumes the least energy. This is because that waking cold nodes up from the standby state will spend a large amount of energy. If correlated files are scattered across different cold nodes, all these cold nodes which have already been suspended to the standby state should be woke up. SFR relocates correlated cold files to the same cold node, this will reduce the number of wake-ups, thus the energy consumption could also be reduced. HP consumes the most energy because all storage nodes work as hot nodes, and it does not suspend any storage node to the standby state. FRO relocates files based on file-access frequency, and it executes the relocation only once after the learning stage. Although file-access behaviors will change as time goes by, FRO still saved more than 11 % energy compared with HP. It reveals the locality of file-access. In other words, file-access pattern would be kept on for a long time. Compared with SFR, EFR does not select the optimal cold node for cold file relocation, it relocates files in a round robin. EFR could not prevent correlated files scattered across different cold nodes, so it consumes higher energy compared with SFR.

Experimental result demonstrates that the file relocation strategy we proposed is effective. SFR which leverages the file-access frequency and correlations

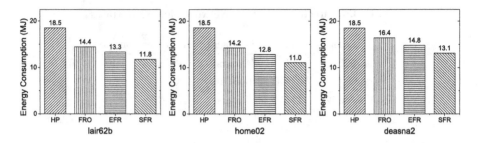

**Fig. 5.** Energy consumption comparison with four file relocation strategies.

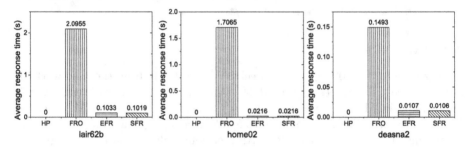

**Fig. 6.** Average response time comparison with four file relocation strategies.

saved the most energy compared with other strategies. And compared with the baseline—HP, SFR reduces the energy consumption of storage nodes by more than 29 %.

**Response Time.** Figures 6 and 7 show the average response time and the variance of response time of the four different file relocation strategies with the three traces.

HP does not suspend any storage node to the standby state, so it have the best performance. Please note that the experiment value of HP is too small, that it is rounded to 0 by statistical software. FRO could not adapt to the latest file-access behaviors, because it executes the relocation only once after the learning stage. And the performance of FRO is the worst. EFR have a good performance owe to leverage the file-access frequency. Furthermore, by relocating correlated cold files into the same cold node, SFR could reduce the wake-ups to perform requests for accessing cold files. And because waking up cold nodes will spend a much long time relative to data transmission rate, SFR gains a lower average response time. The variance of response time shows the same trend: HP is the most steady strategy, the next is SFR, then EFR is tinier poor than SFR, and the worst is FRO.

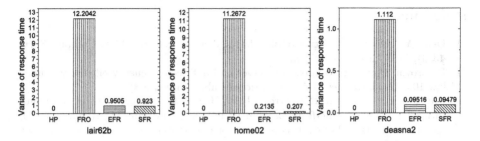

**Fig. 7.** Variance of response time comparison with four file relocation strategies.

## 5   Conclusion

In this paper we proposed an energy-aware file relocation strategy—SFR. By leveraging the file-access frequency and correlations, SFR relocates files when mismatching situation appears. In this strategy, storage nodes are divided into a hot node set and a cold node set. By reason that more than 80 % of total requests go to those hot files, the hot nodes are always kept in an active state (or an idle state when there's no request) to satisfy the system performance. While, the cold nodes are maintained in the standby state unless requests are received. And the cold nodes go back to the standby state only if file-access requests are accomplished, and there are no subsequent requests for a predetermined period of time. Furthermore, FCM method is proposed to mine file-access frequency and correlations.

To explore the system behavior of SFR, we implement four file relocation strategies in a simulation experiment, including SFR. Compared with the baseline, SFR reduced the energy consumption of storage nodes by more than 29 %. It is demonstrated that SFR which relocates files by leveraging the file-access frequency and correlations can significantly reduce the energy consumption while maintaining the system performance at an acceptable level.

For future work, we would like to assign the number of hot nodes according to the workload (increase in a heavy workload and decrease in a light one). Obviously, we could obtain a further reduction of energy consumption and provide better service. Then due to the changes of hot/cold nodes, it is necessary to relocate files among nodes, and it deserves careful study. Finally, it's so appealing to evaluate our strategy by real implementation instead of simulation.

**Acknowledgments.** This work is supported by the National Natural Science Foundation (NSF) of China under Grant (No. 61572232, and No. 61272073), the key program of Natural Science Foundation of Guangdong Province (No.S2013020012865), the Open Research Fund of Key Laboratory of Computer System and Architecture, Institute of Computing Technology, Chinese Academy of Sciences (CARCH201401), and the Fundamental Research Funds for the Central Universities, and the Science and Technology Planning Project of Guangdong Province (No. 2013B090200021). And the corresponding author is Yuhui Deng from Jinan University.

# References

1. Deng, Y.: What is the future of disk drives, death or rebirth? ACM Comput. Surv. **43**(3), 1–27 (2011). Article 23
2. R. Brown: Report to congress on server and data center energy efficiency: Public law 109–431. Lawrence Berkeley National Laboratory (2008)
3. Pinheiro, E., Bianchini, R., Carrera, E.V., Heath, T.: Dynamic cluster reconfiguration for power and performance. In: Benini, L., Kandemir, M., Ramanujam, J. (eds.) Compilers and Operating Systems for Low Power, pp. 75–93. Springer, New York (2003)
4. Chase, J.S., Anderson, D.C., Thakar, P.N., Vahdat, A.M., Doyle, R.P.: Managing energy and server resources in hosting centers. ACM SIGOPS Operating Syst. Rev. **35**(5), 103–116 (2001). ACM
5. Zhang, L., Deng, Y., Zhu, W., Peng, J., Wang, F.: Skewly replicating hot data to construct a power-efficient storage cluster. J. Netw. Comput. Appl. **50**, 168–179 (2015). Elsevier Science
6. Pareto Principle. http://en.wikipedia.org/wiki/Pareto_principle
7. Cherkasova, L., Ciardo, G.: Characterizing temporal locality and its impact on web server performance. Technical Report HPL-2000-82, Hewlett Packard Laboratories (2000)
8. Xia, P., Feng, D., Jiang, H., Tian, L., Wang, F.: FARMER: a novel approach to file access correlations mining and evaluation reference model for optimizing peta-scale file system performance. In: Proceedings of the 17th International Symposium on High Performance Distributed Computing. ACM (2008)
9. Wu, Yi, Otagiri, Kenichi, Watanabe, Yousuke, Yokota, Haruo: A file search method based on intertask relationships derived from access frequency and RMC operations on files. In: Hameurlain, Abdelkader, Liddle, Stephen W., Schewe, Klaus-Dieter, Zhou, Xiaofang (eds.) DEXA 2011, Part I. LNCS, vol. 6860, pp. 364–378. Springer, Heidelberg (2011)
10. Verma, A., Ahuja, P., Neogi, A.: Power-aware dynamic placement of HPC applications. In: Proceedings of the 22nd Annual International Conference on Supercomputing. ACM (2008)
11. Bostoen, T., Mullender, S., Berbers, Y.: Power-reduction techniques for data-center storage systems. ACM Comput. Surv. (CSUR) **45**(3) (2013). Article No. 33
12. Krioukov, A., et al.: NapSac: design and implementation of a power-proportional web cluster. ACM SIGCOMM Comput. Commun. Rev. **41**(1), 102–108 (2011)
13. Thereska, E., Donnelly, A., Narayanan, D.: Sierra: practical power-proportionality for data center storage. In: Proceedings of the Sixth Conference on Computer Systems. ACM (2011)
14. Deng, Y., Hu, Y., Meng, X., Zhu, Y., Zhang, Z., Han, J.: Predictively booting nodes to minimize performance degradation of a power-aware web cluster. Cluster Comput. **17**(4), 1309–1322 (2014). Springer, New York
15. Mashayekhy, L., Nejad, M., Grosu, D., Zhang, Q., Shi, W.: Energy-aware scheduling of mapreduce jobs for big data applications. IEEE Trans. Parallel Distrib. Syst. **PP**(99), 1 (2014)
16. Ebrahimirad, V., Goudarzi, M., Rajabi, A.: Energy-aware scheduling for precedence-constrained parallel virtual machines in virtualized data centers. J. Grid Comput. **13**(2), 233–253 (2015)
17. Tang, Z., Qi, L., Cheng, Z., Li, K., Khan, S.U., Li, K.: An energy-efficient task scheduling algorithm in DVFS-enabled cloud environment. J. Grid Comput., 1–20 (2015)

18. Weiser, M., Welch, B., Demers, A., Shenker, S.: Scheduling for reduced CPU energy. In: Imielinski, T., Korth, H.F. (eds.) Mobile Computing, pp. 449–471. Springer, New York (1996)

19. Zikos, S., Karatza, H.D.: Performance and energy aware cluster-level scheduling of compute-intensive jobs with unknown service times. Simul. Model. Pract. Theory 19(1), 239–250 (2011)

20. Patterson, D.A., Gibson, G., Katz, R.H.: A case for redundant arrays of inexpensive disks(RAID). In: Proceedings of the 1988 ACM SIGMOD International Conference on Management of Data, SIGMOD 1988, pp. 109–116. ACM, New York (1988)

21. Li, D., Wang, J.: EERAID: energy efficient redundant and inexpensive disk array. In: Proceedings of the 11th Workshop on ACM SIGOPS European Workshop, EW 11. ACM, New York (2004)

22. Weddle, C., et al.: PARAID: A gear-shifting power-aware RAID. ACM Trans. Storage (TOS) 3(3), 13 (2007)

23. Mao, B., et al.: GRAID: A green RAID storage architecture with improved energy efficiency and reliability. In: 2008 IEEE International Symposium on Modeling, Analysis and Simulation of Computers and Telecommunication Systems, MAS-COTS 2008. IEEE (2008)

24. Colarelli, D., Grunwald, D.: Massive arrays of idle disks for storage archives. In: Proceedings of the 2002 ACM/IEEE Conference on Supercomputing. IEEE Computer Society Press (2002)

25. Iritani, M., Yokota, H.: Effects on performance and energy reduction by file relocation based on file-access correlations. In: Proceedings of the 2012 Joint EDBT/ICDT Workshops. ACM (2012)

26. Tait, C.D., Duchamp, D.: Detection and exploitation of file working sets. In: 11th International Conference on Distributed Computing Systems. IEEE (1991)

27. Lei, H., Duchamp, D.: An analytical approach to file prefetching. In: USENIX Annual Technical Conference (1997)

28. Kroeger, T.M., Long, D.D.E.: The case for efficient file access pattern modeling. In: Proceedings of the Seventh Workshop on Hot Topics in Operating Systems. IEEE (1999)

29. Kroeger, T.M., Long, D.D.E.: Design and implementation of a predictive file prefetching algorithm. In: USENIX Annual Technical Conference, General Track (2001)

30. Ishii, Y., Inaba, M., Hiraki, K.: Access map pattern matching for high performance data cache prefetch. J. Instr. Level Parallelism 13, 1–24 (2011)

31. He, J., Sun, X.H., Thakur, R.: Knowac: I/O prefetch via accumulated knowledge. In: 2012 IEEE International Conference on Cluster Computing (CLUSTER). IEEE (2012)

32. Jiang, S., Ding, X., Xu, Y., Davis, K.: A prefetching scheme exploiting both data layout and access history on disk. ACM Trans. Storage (TOS) 9(3), 10 (2013)

33. Agrawal, R., Imieliski, T., Swami, A.: Mining association rules between sets of items in large databases. ACM SIGMOD Rec. 22(2), 207–216 (1993). ACM

34. Deng, Y.: Deconstructing network attached storage systems. J. Netw. Comput. Appl. 32(5), 1064–1072 (2009)

# Projective Synchronization for Complex Dynamical Networks of Non-delayed and Delayed Coupling with Different Scale Factors via Impulsive Control

Yuxiu Li[(⊠)] and Guoliang Cai

School of Mechanical Engineering,
Jiangsu University, Zhenjiang 212013, China
1000002122@ujs.edu.cn

**Abstract.** Based on Lyapunov stability theory and impulsive control method, this paper investigates the projective synchronization problem of complex dynamical networks with non-delayed and delayed coupling. Some projective synchronization rules in complex dynamical networks of non-delayed and delayed coupling with different scale factors were proposed and testified by two different methods, respectively. Moreover, numerical examples are presented to verify the feasibility and effectiveness of the synchronization scheme.

**Keywords:** Complex dynamical networks · Impulsive control · Projective synchronization · Non-delayed and delayed coupling · Different scale factors

## 1 Introduction

Complex dynamical networks have been shown to exist in many different fields in the real world and have been intensively studied in the last few years. Common examples of complex networks include the Internet, the World Wide Web (WWW), food webs, scientific citation webs, as well as many other systems made up of a large number of intricately connected parts. Indeed, complex networks are the important part of our daily lives. Generally speaking, complex networks are made up of interconnected nodes and are used to describe various systems of real world. Synchronization of all dynamical nodes is an interesting phenomenon and has been intensively studied in the recent years since Pecora and Carroll [1] introduced a method for synchronization two identical chaotic systems with different initial conditions. Especially in recent decades, as the Internet and the WWW are continuously expanding over our world, all things in our world are connected much more closely than before. As a result, some new types of synchronization have appeared in the literatures, such as global synchronization [2, 3], linear generalized synchronization [4], cluster synchronization [5], projective synchronization (PS) [6, 7], adaptive function projective synchronization [8], mixed synchronization [9], impulsive synchronization [10], and so on.

The PS characterized by a scaling factor (a constant $\lambda$) such that two systems synchronies proportionally, are a generalized method of synchronization. It can be used

© Springer International Publishing Switzerland 2015
G. Wang et al. (Eds.): ICA3PP 2015, Part IV, LNCS 9531, pp. 654–666, 2015.
DOI: 10.1007/978-3-319-27140-8_45

to the digital communications of the secure communications. Mainieri and Rehacek investigated the PS first. Furthermore, J. D. Cao testified to the PS for a class of delayed chaotic systems by impulsive control and some sufficient conditions are derived by the stability analysis of the impulsive functional differential equations [11]. Recently, S.Q. Jiang studied on the Adaptive cluster general projective synchronization of complex dynamic networks in finite time by time-varying adaptive control gains and nonlinear feedback controllers [12].

In this paper, the projective synchronization problem with non-delayed and delayed coupling between complex dynamical networks was investigated. The nodes did not need to be partially linear. Based on Lyapunov stability theory and impulsive control method, some projective synchronization rules in complex dynamical networks of non-delayed and delayed coupling with different scale factors were proposed, respectively.

The layout of this paper is as follows. Section 2 describes the networks model and some necessary mathematical preliminaries. The projective synchronization problem with non-delayed and delayed coupling between complex dynamical networks was investigated in Sect. 3. Section 4 gives some numerical simulation examples to demonstrate the feasibility and effectiveness of the proposed approach. Finally some concluding remarks are given in Sect. 5.

## 2 Networks Model and Preliminaries

In this section, a complex dynamical networks with non-delayed and delayed coupling consisting of $N$ identical nodes with linear coupling is considered, which is characterized by

$$
\begin{cases}
\dot{x}_i(t) = Ax_i(t) + f(x_i(t), x_i(t-\tau)) + \sum_{j=1}^{N} b_{ij}\Gamma x_j(t) + \sum_{j=1}^{N} c_{ij}\Gamma x_j(t-\tau(t)), \\
x(t) = x_0, t \in [-\tau, 0].
\end{cases} \quad i = 1, 2, \cdots N.
$$

(1)

where $x_i(t) = (x_{i1}(t), x_{i2}(t), \cdots, x_{in}(t))^T \in R^n$ is the state vector of the $i$th node, $A \in R^{n \times n}$ is a constant matrix, $f: R \times R^n \to R^n$ is a smooth nonlinear function, $\tau(t) \geq 0$ is the coupling delay. $\Gamma \in R^{n \times n}$ is inner-coupling matrix and $B = (b_{ij})_{N \times N} \in R^{N \times N}$, $C = (c_{ij})_{N \times N} \in R^{N \times N}$ are the weight configuration matrices. If there is a connection from node $i$ to node $j$ $(j \neq i)$, then the coupling $b_{ij} \neq 0$, $c_{ij} \neq 0$; otherwise, $b_{ij} = c_{ij} = 0(j \neq i)$, and the diagonal elements of matrices $B$, $C$ are defined as

$$
b_{ii} = -\sum_{j=1, j \neq i}^{N} b_{ij}, \quad c_{ii} = -\sum_{j=1, j \neq i}^{N} c_{ij}, \quad i = 1, 2, \cdots N.
$$

The response system of networks (1) can be written as

$$\begin{cases} \dot{y}_i(t) = Ay_i(t) + \alpha_i f(\dfrac{y_i(t)}{\alpha_i}, \dfrac{y_i(t-\tau)}{\alpha_i}) + \displaystyle\sum_{j=1}^{N} b_{ij}\Gamma y_j(t) + \sum_{j=1}^{N} c_{ij}\Gamma y_j(t-\tau(t)), & t \neq t_k, \\ \Delta y_i(t_k) = y_i(t_k^+) - y_i(t_k^-) = B_{ik}[y_i(t_k^-) - \alpha_i x(t_k)], & t = t_k, k \in Z^+, \\ y_i(t) = y_{i0}, & t \in [-\tau, 0], \end{cases} \qquad i = 1, 2, \cdots N.$$

$$(2)$$

where $y_i(t) = (y_{i1}(t), y_{i2}(t), \cdots \in, y_{in}(t))^T \in R^n, i = 1, 2, \cdots, N$ is the response state vector of the $i$th node, $y_i(t_k^+) = \lim\limits_{t \to t_k^+} y_i(t), y_i(t_k^-) = \lim\limits_{t \to t_k^-} y_i(t), \alpha_i \neq 0 (i = 1, 2, \cdots N)$ is different scale factors. Moreover, any solution of (2) is left continuous at each $t_k$, i.e. $y_i(t_k^-) = y_i(t_k)$.

Define the synchronization errors $e_i(t) = y_i(t) - \alpha_i x_i(t)$, $(i = 1, 2, \ldots, N)$, the following errors dynamics system is obtained:

$$\begin{cases} \dot{e}_i(t) = Ae_i(t) + \alpha_i F_i(e_i(t), e_i(t-\tau) + \displaystyle\sum_{j=1}^{N} b_{ij}\Gamma e_j(t) + \sum_{j=1}^{N} c_{ij}\Gamma e_j(t-\tau(t)), & t \neq t_k, \\ \Delta e_i(t_k) = e_i(t_k^+) - e_i(t_k^-) = B_{ik}e_i(t_k^-), & t = t_k, k \in Z^+, \\ e_i(t) = e_{i0}, & t \in [-\tau, 0], \end{cases} \qquad i = 1, 2, \cdots N.$$

$$(3)$$

where $F_i(e_i(t), e_i(t-\tau)) = f(\frac{y_i(t)}{\alpha_i}, \frac{y_i(t-\tau)}{\alpha_i}) - f(x_i(t) - x_i(t-\tau))$,

$$e_i(t_k^+) = e_i(t_k), \quad e_i(t_k^-) = \lim_{t \to t_k^-} e_i(t),$$

$$e_{i0}(t) = y_{i0}(t) - \alpha_i x_{i0}(t),$$

$$\text{Let } e(t) = (e_1^T(t), e_2^T(t), \cdots, e_N^T(t))^T,$$

$$e_0(t) = (e_{10}^T(t), e_{20}^T(t), \cdots, e_{N0}^T(t))^T,$$

$$A_\alpha = diag(\alpha_1, \alpha_2, \cdots \alpha_N),$$

$$e_0(t) = (e_{10}^T(t), e_{20}^T(t), \cdots, e_{N0}^T(t))^T,$$

$$A_\alpha = diag(\alpha_1, \alpha_2, \cdots \alpha_N),$$

$$B_k = diag(B_{1k}, B_{2k}, \cdots B_{Nk}),$$

$$F(e(t), e(t-\tau)) = (F_1^T(e_1(t), e_1(t-\tau)), \cdots, F_N^T(e_N(t), e_N(t-\tau))^T.$$

Equation (3) can be written as

$$\begin{cases} \dot{e}(t) = (I_N \otimes A)e(t) + (A_\alpha \otimes I_n)F(e(t), e(t-\tau)) + (B \otimes \Gamma)e(t) + (C \otimes \Gamma)e(t-\tau), & t \neq t_k \\ e(t_k) = e(t_k^+) - e(t_k^-) = B_k e(t_k^-), & t = t_k, k \in Z^+, \\ e(t) = e_0, & t \in [-\tau, 0]. \end{cases}$$

Throughout this paper, the following basic and useful definitions and lemmas are required for achieving projective synchronization.

**Definition 1.** The complex delayed dynamical systems (1) and (2) are said to be projective synchronized with different scale factors $\alpha = (\alpha_1, \alpha_2, \cdots, \alpha_N)^T$, if

$$\lim_{t \to \infty} \|e_i(t)\| = \lim_{t \to \infty} \|y_i(t) - \alpha_i x_i(t)\| = 0, \quad i = 1, 2, \ldots, N.$$

**Definition 2.** The complex delayed dynamical systems (1) and (2) are said to be globally exponentially synchronized if there exist constant $\eta > 0$ and continuous function $V(t)$ such that

$$V(t) \le \left( \sup_{-\tau \le s \le 0} V(s) \right) \exp\{-\eta t\}, \quad t \ge 0$$

**Lemma 1.** [11] For a $r \times r$ real symmetric matrix $\Omega$, $\Omega$ is positive definite if and only if all its eigenvalues are positive. Moreover, the inequality holds:

$$\lambda_{\min}(\Omega) x^T x \le x^T \Omega x \le \lambda_{\max}(\Omega) x^T x. \forall x \in R^n$$

**Lemma 2.** $P = \text{diag}(p_1, p_2, \cdots, p_n)$ is positive matrix, there exist symmetric matrix $D_i$, $i = 1, 2$, such that

$$(x-y)^T P[f(x,u) - f(y,v)] \le (x-y)^T PD_1(x-y) + (u-v)^T PD_2(u-v), \quad \forall x, y, u, v \in P^n.$$

**Lemma 3.** [10] For any vectors $x, y \in R^n$ and positive-definite matrix $Q \in R^{n \times n}$, the following matrix inequality holds:

$$2x^T y \le x^T Q x + y^T Q^{-1} y.$$

# 3  Projective Synchronization of Complex Dynamical Networks

In this section, we will present our main results about how to employ both synchronizing and desynchronizing impulses to realize globally exponential synchronization in mean square.

**Theorem 1.** System (1) is projective synchronization with system (2) about different scale factors $\alpha = (\alpha_1, \alpha_2, \cdots, \alpha_N)^T$, if the following conditions are satisfied:

(1)   $(I_n + B_{ik})P(I_n + B_{ik}) - dP \leq 0, \quad k \in Z^+, i = 1, 2, \cdots, N;$

(2)   $\sup(t_k - t_{k-1}) < -\dfrac{\ln d}{\lambda_{\max}(\Omega)},$

where

$$\Omega = A + P^{-1}A^T P + 2D_1 + 2\lambda_{\max}(B)\Gamma + \lambda_{\max}(CC^T)\Gamma^2 + \frac{I_n}{d}(2\lambda_{\max}(D_2) + 1)$$

$$\lambda_{\max}(\Omega) > 0.$$

**Proof.** Choose the following Lyapunov function:

$$V(t, e(t)) = e^T(t)(I_N \otimes P)e(t) = \sum_{i=1}^{N} e_i^T(t)Pe_i(t) = \sum_{j=1}^{n} p_j \tilde{e}_j^T(t)\tilde{e}_j(t),$$

where $e_i(t) = (e_{i1}(t), e_{i2}(t), \cdots, e_{iN}(t))^T$, $\tilde{e}_j(t) = (e_{1j}(t), e_{2j}(t), \cdots, e_{Nj}(t))^T$.
Under Lemma 1, we gain:

$$\lambda_{\min}(p) \sum_{i=1}^{N} e_i^T(t)e_i(t) \leq V(t, e(t)) \leq \lambda_{\max}(p) \sum_{i=1}^{N} e_i^T(t)e_i(t).$$

It is easy to obtain that

$$V(t_k, e(t_k)) = \sum_{i=1}^{N} e_i^T(t_k^-)[(I_n + B_{ik})P(I_n + B_{ik}) - dP]e_i(t_k^-)$$

$$+ dV(t_k^-, e(t_k^-)) \leq dV(t_k^-, e(t_k^-)), \quad k = 1, 2 \cdots.$$

Let $\varphi(s) = ds, V(t, e(t))$ be defined for $\forall s \in [-\tau, 0)$ which satisfies:

$$V(t + s, e(t + s)) \leq \varphi^{-1}(V(t, e(t))),$$

then

$$e^T(t + s)(I_N \otimes P)e(t + s) \leq \frac{1}{d}e^T(t)(I_N \otimes P)e(t).$$

$$D^+V(t,e(t)) = \sum_{i=1}^{N} e_i^T(t)(PA + A^TP)e_i(t) + \sum_{i=1}^{N} 2\alpha_i e_i^T(t)PF_i(e_i(t), e_i(t-\tau))$$
$$+ 2\sum_{j=1}^{n} p_j\gamma_j\tilde{e}_j^T(t) \times B\tilde{e}_j(t) + 2\sum_{j=1}^{n} p_j\gamma_j\tilde{e}_j^T(t)C\tilde{e}_j(t-\tau)$$

In terms of Lemma 2, we have:

$$D^+V(t,e(t)) \leq \sum_{i=1}^{N} e_i^T(t)(PA + A^TP)e_i(t)$$
$$+ 2\sum_{i=1}^{N} [e_i^T(t)PD_1e_i(t) + e_i^T(t-\tau)PD_2e_i(t-\tau)]$$
$$+ 2\sum_{j=1}^{n} p_j\gamma_j\tilde{e}_j^T(t)B\tilde{e}_j(t)$$
$$+ \sum_{j=1}^{n} p_j\gamma_j^2\tilde{e}_j^T(t)CC^T\tilde{e}_j(t) + \sum_{j=1}^{n} p_j\tilde{e}_j^T(t-\tau)\tilde{e}_j(t-\tau)$$
$$\leq \sum_{i=1}^{N} e_i^T(t)(PA + A^TP + 2PD_1 + 2\lambda_{\max}(B)\Gamma P + \lambda_{\max}(CC^T)\Gamma^2 P)e_i(t)$$
$$+ (2\lambda_{\max}(D_2) + 1)\sum_{i=1}^{N} e_i^T(t-\tau)Pe_i(t-\tau)$$
$$\leq \sum_{i=1}^{N} e_i^T(t)P\Omega e_i(t)$$
$$\leq \lambda_{\max}(\Omega)V(t,e(t)).$$

Let $g(s) \equiv 1, h(s) = s\lambda_{\max}(\Omega)$, we obtain:

$$\int_{\varphi(\mu)}^{\mu} \frac{ds}{h(s)} - \int_{t_{k-1}}^{t_k} g(s)ds = \frac{-\ln d}{\lambda_{\max}(\Omega)} - (t_k - t_{k-1}) >$$
$$> \frac{-\ln d}{\lambda_{\max}(\Omega)} - \sup\{t_k - t_{k-1}\} > 0 \, as \, \mu > 0$$

Therefore, the error system (3) is globally asymptotically stable about zero. Therefore, system (1) is projective synchronization with system (2). The proof is completed.

**Theorem 2.** Let $\lambda_1, \lambda_2, \lambda_3$ and $\beta_k$ be the largest eigenvalue of $(I_1 \otimes A) + (I_1 \otimes A)^T$, $(B \otimes \Gamma) + (B \otimes \Gamma)^T, (C \otimes \Gamma) + (C \otimes \Gamma)^T$ and $(I_2 + B_{ik})^T(I_2 + B_{ik})(1,2,\cdots)$, respectively. $d^*$ is the minimum value of the initial feedback strength $d_{i0}(d_{i0} \leq d_i, 1 \leq i \leq N)$ and $0 < \tau \leq \inf_k\{t_{k+1} - t_k\}$. If there exists a constant $\xi > 1$ such that

$$(\lambda_1 + \lambda_2 + \lambda_3 + 2\lambda_{\max}(D_1) + M - 2d^*)(t_{k+1} - t_k) + \ln(\xi\beta_k) \leq 0.$$

where $I_1 \in R^{N \times N}, I_2 \in R^{n \times n}$ denote the identity matrices. Then the drive dynamical networks (1) and the response dynamical networks (2) can achieve synchronization.

**Proof.** We construct the Lyapunov function as follows:

$$V(t, e(t)) = \sum_{i=1}^{N} e_i^T(t)Pe_i(t) + M \int_{t-\tau}^{t} \sum_{i=1}^{N} e_i^T(\theta)e_i(\theta)d\theta, \quad M \geq \lambda_{\max}(D_2),$$

$M$ is a constant. Since $0 < \tau \leq \inf_k\{t_{k+1} - t_k\}$, we gain:

$$V(t, e(t)) \leq \sum_{i=1}^{N} e_i^T(t)e_i(t) + \tau M \sum_{i=1}^{N} \|e_i\|^2,$$

where $\|e_i\| = \sup_{t-\tau \leq \theta \leq t} \|e_i(\theta)\|$.

Under the condition, we need linear controllers $u_i$ and updating laws are designed as follows:

$$u_i = -d_i e_i(t), \; \dot{d}_i = k_i e_i^T(t)e_i(t) = k_i\|e_i(t)\|^2, \; i = 1, 2, 3, \ldots, N,$$

where $d_i$ is the feedback strength and $k_i > 0$ is arbitrary constant. And we choose the linear impulsive controller $B_{ik}$ which is a $n \times n$ constant matrix. Then, the objective of this Letter is to design adaptive feedback controller $u_i$, an impulsive controller $B_{ik}$ and the impulsive distances $\Delta k + 1 = t_{k+1} - t_k < \infty$ ($k = 1, 2, \ldots$) such that the state of drive dynamical networks (1) synchronize with the state of response dynamical networks (2). That is $\lim_{t \to \infty} \|e_i(t)\| = 0$.

For $t \neq t_k$, by Lemmas 2 and 3, the derivative of $V(t, e(t))$ along the trajectories of (3) is

$$\dot{V}(t, e(t)) = \sum_{i=1}^{N} e_i^T(t)[Ae_i(t) + \alpha_i F_i(e_i(t), e_i(t - \tau))$$

$$+ \sum_{j=1}^{N} b_{ij}\Gamma e_j(t) + \sum_{j=1}^{N} c_{ij}\Gamma e_j(t - \tau(t)) - d_i e_i(t)]$$

$$+ \sum_{i=1}^{N} [Ae_i(t) + \alpha_i F_i(e_i(t), e_i(t - \tau))$$

$$+ \sum_{j=1}^{N} b_{ij}\Gamma e_j(t) + \sum_{j=1}^{N} c_{ij}\Gamma e_j(t - \tau(t))e_i(t) - d_i e_i(t)]^T e_i(t)$$

$$+ M \sum_{i=1}^{N} e_i^T(t)e_i(t) - M \sum_{i=1}^{N} e_i^T(t - \tau)e_i(t - \tau)$$

$$
\begin{aligned}
&= e^T[(I_1 \otimes A) + (I_1 \otimes A)^T]e + e^T[(B \otimes \Gamma) + (B \otimes \Gamma)^T]e \\
&\quad + e^T[(C \otimes \Gamma) + (C \otimes \Gamma)^T]e(t-\tau) + 2\sum_{i=1}^{N} \alpha_i e_i^T(t) I_2 F_i(e_i(t), e_i(t-\tau)) \\
&\quad - 2\sum_{i=1}^{N} d_i e_i^T(t) e_i(t) + M \sum_{i=1}^{N} e_i^T(t) e_i(t) - M \sum_{i=1}^{N} e_i^T(t-\tau) e_i(t-\tau) \\
&\leq e^T[(I_1 \otimes A) + (I_1 \otimes A)^T]e + e^T[(B \otimes \Gamma) + (B \otimes \Gamma)^T]e \\
&\quad + 2\left(\frac{1}{2} e^T (C \otimes \Gamma)(C \otimes \Gamma)^T e + \frac{1}{2} e^T(t-\tau)(C \otimes \Gamma)(C \otimes \Gamma)^T e(t-\tau)\right) \\
&\quad + 2\sum_{i=1}^{N} [e_i^T(t) D_1 e_i(t) + e_i^T(t-\tau) D_2 e_i(t-\tau)] \\
&\quad - 2\sum_{i=1}^{N} d_i e_i^T(t) e_i(t) + M \sum_{i=1}^{N} e_i^T(t) e_i(t) - M \sum_{i=1}^{N} e_i^T(t-\tau) e_i(t-\tau) \\
&\leq e^T[(I_1 \otimes A) + (I_1 \otimes A)^T]e + e^T[(B \otimes \Gamma) + (B \otimes \Gamma)^T]e + e^T(C \otimes \Gamma)(C \otimes \Gamma)^T e \\
&\quad + e^T(t-\tau)(C \otimes \Gamma)(C \otimes \Gamma)^T e(t-\tau) + 2\lambda_{\max}(D_1) \sum_{i=1}^{N} e_i^T(t) e_i(t) \\
&\quad + 2\lambda_{\max}(D_2) \sum_{i=1}^{N} e_i^T(t-\tau) e_i(t-\tau) - 2\sum_{i=1}^{N} d_i e_i^T(t) e_i(t) \\
&\quad + M \sum_{i=1}^{N} e_i^T(t) e_i(t) - M \sum_{i=1}^{N} e_i^T(t-\tau) e_i(t-\tau) \\
&\leq (\lambda_1 + \lambda_2 + \lambda_3 + 2\lambda_{\max}(D_1) + M - 2d_{i0}) \sum_{i=1}^{N} e_i^T(t) e_i(t) \\
&\leq (\lambda_1 + \lambda_2 + \lambda_3 + 2\lambda_{\max}(D_1) + M - 2d^*) \sum_{i=1}^{N} e_i^T(t) e_i(t) \\
&\leq (\lambda_1 + \lambda_2 + \lambda_3 + 2\lambda_{\max}(D_1) + M - 2d^*)\left(\sum_{i=1}^{N} e_i^T(t) e_i(t)\right. \\
&\quad \left. + M \int_{t-\tau}^{t} \sum_{i=1}^{N} e_i^T(\theta) e_i(\theta) d\theta\right) \\
&= (\lambda_1 + \lambda_2 + \lambda_3 + 2\lambda_{\max}(D_1) + M - 2d^*) V(t, e(t)).
\end{aligned}
$$

which implies that

$$
V(t, e(t)) \leq V(t_{k-1}^+, e(t_{k-1}^+)) e^{(\lambda_1 + \lambda_2 + \lambda_3 + 2\lambda_{\max}(D_1) + M - 2d^*)(t-t_{k-1})}, \quad t \in [t_{k-1}, t_k]
$$

When $t = t_k$, we have:

$$V(t_k^+, e(t_k^+)) = \sum_{i=1}^{N} e_i^T(t)(I_2 + B_{ik})^T(I_2 + B_{ik})e_i(t)$$

$$+ M \int_{t-\tau}^{t} \sum_{i=1}^{N} e_i^T(\theta)(I_2 + B_{ik})^T(I_2 + B_{ik})e_i(\theta)d\theta$$

$$\leq \lambda_{\max}[(I_2 + B_{ik})^T(I_2 + B_{ik})](\sum_{i=1}^{N} e_i^T(t)e_i(t) + M \int_{t-\tau}^{t} \sum_{i=1}^{N} e_i^T(\theta)e_i(\theta)d\theta)$$

$$\leq \beta_k V(t_k), \quad k = 1, 2 \cdots.$$

When $k = 1$ in inequality, then for any $t \in (t_0, t_1)$

$$V(t_1, e(t_1)) \leq V(t_0^+, e(t_0^+))e^{(\lambda_1 + \lambda_2 + \lambda_3 + 2\lambda_{\max}(D_1) + M - 2d^*)(t_1 - t_0)}.$$

Also we have

$$V(t_1^+, e(t_1^+)) \leq \beta_1 V(t_0^+, e(t_0^+))e^{(\lambda_1 + \lambda_2 + \lambda_3 + 2\lambda_{\max}(D_1) + M - 2d^*)(t_1 - t_0)}.$$

In the same way for any $t \in (t_k, t_{k+1}]$, we obtain:

$$V(t, e(t)) \leq \beta_1 \beta_2 \cdots \beta_k V(t_0^+, e(t_0^+))e^{(\lambda_1 + \lambda_2 + \lambda_3 + 2\lambda_{\max}(D_1) + M - 2d^*)(t - t_0)}.$$

From the assumption given in the theorem, we have

$$\xi \beta_k e^{(\lambda_1 + \lambda_2 + \lambda_3 + 2\lambda_{\max}(D_1) + M - 2d^*)(t_{k+1} - t_k)} \leq 1.$$

Therefore, one finds that

$$V(t, e(t) \leq V(t_0^+, e(t_0^+))[\beta_1 e^{(\lambda_1 + \lambda_2 + \lambda_3 + 2\lambda_{\max}(D_1) + M - 2d^*)\Delta_1}] \times \cdots$$

$$\times [\beta_k e^{(\lambda_1 + \lambda_2 + \lambda_3 + 2\lambda_{\max}(D_1) + M - 2d^*)(t - t_0)\Delta_k}] \times e^{(\lambda_1 + \lambda_2 + \lambda_3 + 2\lambda_{\max}(D_1) + M - 2d^*)(t - t_k)}$$

$$\leq V(t_0^+, e(t_0^+))\frac{1}{\xi k} e^{(\lambda_1 + \lambda_2 + \lambda_3 + 2\lambda_{\max}(D_1) + M - 2d^*)(t - t_k)}.$$

This implies that the error system (3) is globally asymptotically stable about zero. Therefore, synchronization of the dynamical networks (1) and the dynamical networks (2) is achieved. The proof is completed, too.

## 4    Numerical Simulation Examples

In this section, the numerical simulation examples are performed to verify the effectiveness of the proposed synchronization scheme in the previous section.

**Example 1.** We consider a time delayed complex networks to verify the correctness of theorem 1.

$$x(t) = (x_1(t), x_2(t))^T,$$

$$f(x(t), x(t - \tau)) = Bg(x(t)) + Dg(x(t - \tau)), g(x(t)) = (\tan h(x_1(t)), \tan h(x_2(t)))^T,$$

$$A = \begin{pmatrix} -1 & 0 \\ 0 & -1 \end{pmatrix}, B = \begin{pmatrix} 2.1 & -0.1 \\ -5.0 & 3.0 \end{pmatrix}, D = \begin{pmatrix} -1.5 & -0.1 \\ -0.2 & -2.5 \end{pmatrix}, N = 5,$$

and $y(t) = (y_1(t), y_2(t))^T$, $\Gamma = I_2$, $\sum_{i=1}^{N} b_{ij}\Gamma = 0$, the asymmetric coupling matrix is

$$C = \begin{pmatrix} -3 & 3 & 1 & -1 & 0 \\ 3 & -3 & -1 & 1 & 0 \\ 1 & -1 & -3 & 1 & 2 \\ -1 & 1 & 1 & -1 & 0 \\ 0 & 0 & 2 & 0 & -2 \end{pmatrix}.$$

Let $B_{ik} = -0.5I_2, d = 0.26, \tau = 0.01, t_k - t_{k-1} = 0.02, \alpha = (-5, -1, 7, 1, 6).$

Based on theorem 1, the complex dynamical networks we have discussed can achieve projective synchronization. The numerical simulation results are shown in Fig. 1.

**Example 2.** We consider another complex networks with non-time-delay and time delayed coupling consisting of the Chua's circuit system 5 nodes to verify the correctness of Theorem 2. The Chua's circuit chaotic system is described by $\dot{x} = Ax + f(x)$, where $x = (x_1, x_2, x_3)^T$, matrix $A$ and the function $f$ satisfy:

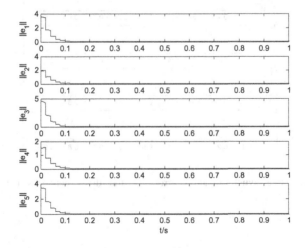

**Fig. 1.** The projective synchronization errors of system (1) and system (2)

$$A = \begin{pmatrix} -a & a & 0 \\ 1 & -1 & 1 \\ 0 & \gamma & 0 \end{pmatrix}, \quad f(x) = \begin{pmatrix} -af(x_1) \\ 0 \\ 0 \end{pmatrix},$$

where $f(x_1) = nx_1 + 0.5(m-n)(|x_1+1| - |x_1-1|)$ the parameters $(a, \gamma, m, n)$ are chosen to be $(9, \frac{7}{100}, -\frac{8}{7}, -\frac{5}{7})$. The asymmetric coupling configuration matrix $B$ is

$$B = \begin{pmatrix} -3 & 2 & 0 & 0 & 1 \\ 1 & -4 & 1 & 1 & 1 \\ 0 & 1 & -2 & 1 & 0 \\ 0 & 1 & 1 & -3 & 1 \\ 1 & 1 & 0 & 1 & -3 \end{pmatrix}, C = 0.$$

$\Gamma = I, B_{ik} = \mathrm{diag}(-1.5, -1.5, -1.5), k_i = 1, d_{i0} = 1, \alpha = (1, 1, 1, 1, 1)^T, \xi = 2,$ $\delta = -1.5, \lambda_{\max}(D_1) = 10.2857, \lambda_{\max}(D_2) = 3.3375, M = 3.49.$ After calculations, we getting $\lambda_1 = 13.8669, \lambda_2 = 0.0438, \lambda_3 = 30.00860$ and $\beta = 0.25$. The impulsive interval $\Delta$ can be estimated as follows:

$$0 < \Delta < -\frac{\ln \xi + \ln(1+\delta)^2}{\lambda_1 + \lambda_2 + \lambda_3 + 2\lambda_{\max}(D_1) + M - 2d^*} = 0.1285.$$ Let the impulsive interval $\Delta = 0.1$ and the time delay $\tau = 0.09$.

Based on Theorem 2, the projective synchronization of the dynamical networks (1) and the dynamical networks (2) is achieved. The numerical simulation results are shown in Fig. 2.

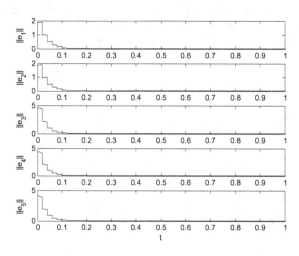

**Fig. 2.** The projective synchronization errors of the drive networks (1) and response networks (2)

# 5 Conclusions

In this paper, the problem of the projective synchronization between two complex networks of non-delayed and delayed coupling with different scale factors via impulsive control is discussed, which has been used two different methods. Based on the comparison theorem for the stability of impulsive control system, projective synchronization criterions are obtained, respectively. Moreover, the weight configuration matrix is not assumed to be symmetric or irreducible, and the inner coupling matrix need not be symmetric. Numerical simulations are presented to verify the effectiveness of the proposed synchronization criteria finally.

**Acknowledgments.** This work was supported by the National Nature Science foundation of China (Grants 51276081, 11402100), the Society Science Foundation from Ministry of Education of China (Grants 12YJAZH002, 15YJAZH002), the Project Funded by The Priority Academic Program Development of Jiangsu Higher Education Institutions (Grant1033000001), and the Society Science Foundation of Jiangsu University (Grant JDR2008B04).

# References

1. Pecora, L.M., Carroll, T.L.: Synchronization in chaotic systems. Phys. Rev. Lett. **64**, 821–824 (2012)
2. Cai, G.L., Yao, Q., Shao, H.J.: Global synchronization of weighted cellular neural networks with time-varying coupling delays. Commun. Nonlinear Sci. Numer. Simu. **17**, 3843–3847 (2012)
3. Cai, G.L., Shao, H.J., Yao, Q.: A Linear Matrix Inequality approach to global synchronization of multi-delay Hopfield Neural Networks with parameter perturbations. Chin. J. Phys. **50**, 86–99 (2012)
4. Yao, Q., Cai, G.L., Fan, X.H., et al.: Linear generalized synchronization between two complex networks. Advan. Intell. Soft Comp. **128**, 447–452 (2011)
5. Cai, G.L., Jiang, S.Q., Cai, S.M., et al.: Cluster synchronization of overlapping uncertain complex networks with time-varying impulse disturbances. Nonlinear Dyn. **80**, 503–513 (2015)
6. Cai, G.L., Yao, Q., Fan, X.H., et al.: Adaptive projective synchronization in an array of asymmetric neural networks. J. Comp. **7**, 2024–2030 (2012)
7. Cai, G., Ma, H., Li, Y.: Adaptive projective synchronization and function projective synchronization of chaotic neural networks with delayed and non-delayed coupling. In: Wang, J., Yen, G.G., Polycarpou, M.M. (eds.) ISNN 2012, Part I. LNCS, vol. 7367, pp. 293–301. Springer, Heidelberg (2012)
8. Cai, G., Ma, H., Gao, X., Wu, X.: Generalized function projective lag synchronization between two different neural networks. In: Guo, C., Hou, Z.-G., Zeng, Z. (eds.) ISNN 2013, Part I. LNCS, vol. 7951, pp. 125–132. Springer, Heidelberg (2013)
9. Wang, J.W., Ma, Q.H., Zeng, L., et al.: Mixed outer synchronization of coupled complex networks with time-varying coupling delay. Chaos **21**, 013121 (2011)
10. Zheng, S.: Adaptive-impulsive projective synchronization of drive-response delayed complex dynamical networks with time-varying coupling. Nonlinear Dyn. **67**, 2621–2630 (2012)

11. Cao, J.D., Ho, W.C., Yang, Y.Q.: Projective synchronization of a class of delayed chaotic systems via impulsive control. Phys. Lett. A **373**, 3128–3133 (2009)
12. Jiang, S.Q., Cai, G.L., Cai, S.M., et al.: Adaptive cluster general projective synchronization of complex dynamic networks in finite time. Commun. Nonlinear Sci. Numer. Simu. **28**, 194–200 (2015)

# Elastic Database Replication in the Cloud

Xianxia Zou[1]($\boxtimes$), Jiuhui Pan[1], Wei Du[2], and Shuhong Chen[3]

[1] Department of Computer Science, Jinan University, Guangzhou 510632, China
{zouxianxia,jh_pan}@163.com
[2] Department of Computer Science, Gong Dong Police College,
Guangzhou 510232, China
weiduzxx@163.com
[3] College of Computer and Communication, Hunan Institute of Engineering,
Xiangtan 411101, China

**Abstract.** Cloud computing is a prevailing paradigm of service oriented computing and has revolutionized the computing infrastructure in terms of abstraction and usage. But its model requires significant changes in data management systems due to the requirements on scalability, availability, performance and quality of service. Many researchers proposed database replication techniques to address these challenges. However, only a few existing solutions to database replication in the cloud are attacking the issues with elasticity and quality of service. In this paper, we concern about the problem of relational database replication in the cloud. We present Scalable Relational Database Cloud ($SRDC$), an approach that adopts database replication in the cloud with elasticity. Experiments with the popular benchmarks demonstrate that our approach is viable and has achieved scalability with strong consistency.

**Keywords:** Cloud computing · Database replication · Generalized snapshot isolation ($GSI$) · Scalability

## 1 Introduction

The success and popularity of cloud infrastructures are majorly contributed by its Scalability, elasticity, pay-as-you-go and economies of scale. Many web service providers, like Google's Bigtable [1], Apache Cassandra [2], and Amazon's Dynamo [3], adopt Key-Value stores that provide more scalability and availability than traditional Relational Database Management System ($RDBMS$).

However, the Key-Value stores' simplified data model is lack of transactional support and attributed based accesses, which can result in considerable overhead in re-architecting legacy applications that are predominantly based on RDBMS technology. For those applications that rely on traditional relational databases, features, such as elasticity, flexible deployment, or reduced capital expenses through the use of cloud services, are severely limited. Recent studies show that RDBMS such as Microsoft'S SQL Azure [4], and Amazon's RDS [5] have obtained good results in different cloud application scenarios. Relational

© Springer International Publishing Switzerland 2015
G. Wang et al. (Eds.): ICA3PP 2015, Part IV, LNCS 9531, pp. 667–681, 2015.
DOI: 10.1007/978-3-319-27140-8_46

Cloud, a scalable relational database-as-a-service for cloud computing environment, is introduced in [8,9]. It focuses on efficient multi-tenancy, elastic scalability and database privacy and also uses workload-aware partitioning strategy. But Relational Cloud does not have efficient strategy for replication. In this paper, we will address the problem of relational database replication in the cloud.

Database replication techniques have been used to improve availability, performance and scalability in different environments. Conventional solutions of database replication focused on these aspects of the system using a static setting of replicas. Aspects related to dynamic provisioning of capacity, such as adding replicas on-the-fly, have received little attention. This issue is critical and needs cost-efficient approach to handle changes of workload when initializing new replicas of database [23]. We propose an architecture named SRDC (Scalable Relational Database Cloud) which uses data partition techniques on a cluster. With data partition, each node of the cluster is responsible for a few partitions and every partition runs as independent instance of RDBMS server.

The consistency model describes how different replicas are kept in sync. Strong consistency guarantees that all replicas appear identical to applications. Although strong consistency is clearly a desirable property for building applications, it is impossible to achieve without sacrificing either availability or tolerance to network partitions. The CAP Theorem [7] states that among Consistency, Availability, and Partition tolerance, only two out of three are possible. For example master-slave replication is not an ideal solution at cloud scale [6]. Systems like Dynamo [3] use eventual consistency to provide high availability and partition tolerance for cross-datacenter replication. With eventual consistency, failures, network partitions, or conflicting writes can cause replicas to diverge, and applications may see multiple versions of the same data item. As a result, applications must be prepared to do conflict detection and resolution themselves. The familiar isolation guarantees of ACID transactions are not supported. While a small class of applications with availability requirements may be able to tolerate the nuances of eventual consistency.

This work presents a study of the replication techniques for partition database applied in a cloud scheme to achieve transactional support combining the high availability and scalability that characterizes cloud system. More concretely, we make the following contributions:

☐ We present a prototype of scalable relational database cloud and show the details of implementation of partition database replication in the cloud.
☐ We propose a solution to extract the writeset of update transactions that prevents from distributed transaction rollback.
☐ We experimentally evaluate the performance of the prototype with the popular benchmark, proving the viability and elasticity.

The paper is structured as follows. Section 2 introduces the background of this paper. Section 3 presents the related work on database replication. Section 4 presents an overview of SRDC's architecture, and the implement of SRDC is described in Sects. 5 and 6.

## 2    Related Work

Replicated database provide high scalability and availability for storage systems. Replication presents the problem of keeping all data stored in all replicas consistent. A categorization of traditional replication techniques to minimize this consistency problem can be done by three design criteria [15]: the first criteria determines where updates take place which can be distinguished between primary copy [21] and update everywhere [12,15,17]; the second criteria determines when replicas coordinate which can be distinguished between eager replication [11,22] and lazy replication [20]; the third criteria determines whether an approach is based on changes to the database kernel [13] or by middleware that uses unmodified single node DBMS engines for the replicas [14,18].

Traditional database replication protocols do not scale well for a cloud environment. It is known that few cloud storage systems provide full transactional support and strong consistency in order to achieve scalability and elasticity. ElasTras [19] is an elastic transactional relational database with the characteristics of scalability and elasticity and transactional access. ElasTras is based on the philosophy of key-value stores and partition the data at a schema. ElasTras has a restricted transaction semantics that is executed in one data partition.

EcStore [16] provides Snapshot Isolation applying a protocol where all transactions at the commit time are validated. Each transaction at commit time is validated against other transactions successfully committed, except for the read-only transactions which are executed in a consistent snapshot of the database and they do not need the validation phase. To avoid the bottleneck in the primary copy the read-only transaction access the replicas, but the update transactions access to the primary copy to ensure that the updates are well-behaved.

Azure SQL implements the primary copy protocol with strong consistency [4]. Each database hosted in the SQL Azure has three replicas: one primary replica and two secondary replicas. All reads and writes go through the primary replica, and any changes are replicated to the secondary replicas asynchronously.

In [23] Dolly is proposed, a database provisioning system based on a virtual machine cloning technique to spawn database replicas in the cloud. In Dolly, each database replica runs in a separate virtual machine and Dolly clones the entire virtual machine. [24] presents a study about data replication in a virtualized environment, focusing on provisioning when the master database server is heavily loaded or when it fails. This work implements primary copy protocol but does not address other aspects of database replication in the cloud. Amazon Relational Database Service (RDS) [5] implements the primary copy protocol and works similar to traditional databases.

The MIT based database-as-a-service propose the Relational Cloud [8,9], a scalable relational for cloud computing environment. Relational Cloud focuses on efficient multi-tenancy, elastic scalability and database privacy. This work uses a workload-aware partition strategy. Relational Cloud does not detail the strategy of replication.

## 3   Architecture

The architecture (shown in Fig. 1) consists of four main components: (1) Public
Interfaces, (2) Coordinator, (3) Virtual Machine (VM), and (4) Certifier which
are replicated mainly for higher availability. Data is divided into different partition. Every partition is managed by standalone DBMS instance in a virtual
machine. A partition is replicated into other VM. If the scope of transaction
is limited to a single partition, the transaction is directly committed after the
partition is certified, otherwise the transaction will be committed only when all
partitions are certified. The goal here is to provide just enough background to
understand replication protocol, which is the main focus of this paper.

Public Interfaces receives requests from client applications using a standard
connectivity layer such as JDBC and relays responses from partition replica to
client.

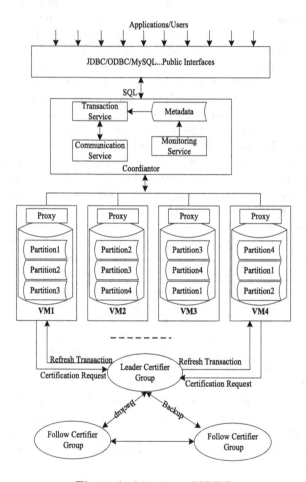

**Fig. 1.** Architecture of SRDC

Coordinator consists of a set of services that address the management of replicas. Metadata stores the information of partition, the number of transaction in every partition, the information of VM, and cohort set of which every cohort is consisted of all replicas of a partition. Monitoring Service is responsible for managing the information about the state of the VMs and the DBMS collected by the proxy. Transaction Service receives SQL statements from clients, analyzes each SQL statement, uses its metadata to determine the execution nodes and plan, and decides the submission of update transaction by executing in partition replica. Communication Service distributes sub-transaction based on partition, receives the message of proxy.

VM contains DBMS employing snapshot isolation and proxies. Every instance of DBMS manages a partition. Each proxy is thread-safe. Every partition in a VM has a proxy that intercepts partition requests. The proxy tracks the partition version, maintains a small amount of state for each active transaction, invokes certification, and applies the remote writesets. Each proxy has a write-ahead log which helps the proxy recovers from a crash.

Certifier performs the following tasks: (a) detects and prevents system-wide conflicts, and assigns a total order to update transactions that commit, (b) ensures the durability of its decisions and committed transactions, and (c) forwards the writeset of every committed update transaction or cycle affairs to replicas of the partition in form of refresh transactions. Certifier is replicated for availability across a small set of nodes using Paxos. The replication algorithm uses a leader elected from the set of Certifier. The leader is responsible for receiving all certification request of a partition replication group. Every cohort has absolute certifier group.

# 4 Proxy

Each replica node of the partition maintains its own version number $v_i$ which indicates the version number of its current version, and which may be different from the current version at the certifier or other replicas. For each p-transaction T that is active at a replica node, the replica node maintains the version number of its starting p-snapshot tx_start_version. To pre-commit an update p-transaction, the node sends a certification request containing tx_start_version, the p-transaction readset and writeset. The leader certifier ensures that there is neither committed nor pre-committed update p-transaction which is read-impacting and write-impacting.

## 4.1 Proxy Task

In the first phase of transaction processing, a proxy in front of each partition database intercepts incoming partition database requests. The proxy tracks the database version, maintains a small amount of state for each active transaction, invokes certification, and applies the remote writesets. In the second phase of transaction processing, a proxy receives the command of the Coordinator, commit or abort the partition transaction on the partition database. The pseudo code for actions at the proxy is shown in Algorithm 1.

## 4.2   Extracting Writeset

Writeset is used for certification and for update propagation. We assume that each tuple in database is identified by its primary key value. Tuples in the writeset can be introduced by UPDATE, INSERT or DELETE SQL statements in a transaction. A writeset is a list of tuples, including the old and new values for each attribute in the tuple. If certification is successful, the certifier adds the writeset to its database, and sends the writeset to replicas for update propagation.

**Algorithm 1.** THE PSEUDO CODE OF THE PROXY

1. On proxy intercepting partition transaction T from the Coordinator:
    1.1 *T receives a snapshot of the database;*
    1.2 *T.tx_start_version ← replica_version*
        *of partition database;*
    1.3 *extracting writeset;*
        *IF T.writeset is empty(i.e., T is read − only)*
        *THEN send T commits to the Coordinator;*
        *ELSE*
        *{confirm the readset;*
        *invoke certification request(T.tx_start_version, T.writeset, T.readset);*
        *Empty the temp table; }*
2. Receiving the reply from the Coordinator
    2.1 *If commit*
    *{Apply writetset;*
        *Vi ← T.tx_commit_version;*
        *Empty the temp table;*
        *Send < T, commit > to the Certifier; }*
    2.2 *if abort*
        *{Clear the temp table;*
        *Send < T, abort > to the Certifier}*
3. Receive the answer <decision,writesets,T.tx_commit_version> from certification:
    3.1 *if decision = "abort"*
        *{Apply < writeset >;*
        *Vi ← T.tx_commit_version;*
        *Send < T, abort > to the Coordinator; }*
    3.2 *if decision = pre − commit*
        *Send < T, commit > to the Coordinator;*
    3.3 *if decision = "refresh"*
        *{Apply writeset;*
        *Vi ← T.tx_commit_version; }*
4. cycle ending:
    4.1 *T.tx_start_version ← replica_version*
        *of partition database;*
    4.2 *invoke certification request(T.tx_start_version, null, null);*

There are several approaches to extract writeset, including triggers, log sniffing or direct support from the database engine (e.g., in Oracle). Although the methods are usually preferred all methods have limitations and disadvantages. For example the system performance will be degraded as the inserted and deleted tables are created dynamically and the records are inserted in these tables in triggers. It is difficult to access and to parse database log file for most database vendor because of database security. More importantly, all methods obtain the writeset through executing the transaction on the database, but the transaction must rollback regardless of being certified in order to keep the total order of distributed transaction. In our prototype the writeset is extracted by converting the update statements to two steps. Firstly the update statements are transformed the select queries, the results of the select queries are inserted into a temp table. And then the update statements are executed on temp table, these transaction need not rollback.

We observe that the UPDATE, INSERT or DELETE SQL statements involve only one relation, it is easy to create corresponding temp table. In order to perform the query transformation and extract the writeset, the proxy separates the UPDATE, INSERT or DELETE SQL statements from the transaction. TEMP-I-R and TEMP-D-R respectively stores the new value and the old value of tuples which the UPDATE, INSERT or DELETE SQL statements involve.

(1) INSERT statement:

The basic form of insertion statement is not modified, only corresponding temp table instead of the original relation:

INSERT INTO TEMP-I-Ri (A1, A2,, An) VALUES (v1,v2,,vn) or

INSERT INTO TEMP-I-Ri (A1, A2, , An) SELECT expr_list FROM Rj,Rk WHERE pred;

(2) DELETE statement:

The basic form of deletion statement is:

DELETE FROM Rd WHERE predd; where predd denotes a predication.

The DELETE statement will be executed the following INSERT statement on corresponding temp table.

INSERT INTO TEMP-D-Rd (A1, A2, , An) SELECT * FROM Rd WHERE pred.

(3) UPDATE statement:

The basic form of deletion statement is:

UPDATE Ru SET attrj=valuej where pred; or

UPDATE Ru SET attrj=case pred1 then value1j

case pred2 then value2j

......

case predn then valuenj;

The UPDATE statement will be divided into the following INSERT statement UPDATE statement:

INSERT INTO TEMP-I-Ru (A1, A2, , An) SELECT * FROM Ru WHERE predd; or

INSERT INTO TEMP-I-Ru (A1, A2, , An) SELECT * FROM Ru WHERE

pred1 and pred2 and ⋯ and predn;
INSERT INTO TEMP-D-Ru (A1, A2, , An) SELECT * FROM Ru WHERE predd; or
INSERT INTO TEMP-D-Ru (A1, A2, , An) SELECT * FROM Ru WHERE pred1 and pred2 and ⋯ and predn;
UPDATE TEMP-I-Ru SET attrj=valuej where pred; or
UPDATE TEMP-I-Ru SET attrj=case pred1 then value1j
　　　　　　　　case pred2 then value2j
　　　　　　　　......
　　　　　　　　case predn then valuenj;

TEMP-I-Ru stores the new value of UPDATE statement and TEMP-D-Ru stores the old value of UPDATE statement. The writeset of p-transaction is consisted of a set of TEMP-I-R and TEMP-D-R.

Readset of p-transaction is consisted of SELETE statement, values of INSERT statement, predicate of DELETE and UPDATE statement in the transaction.

## 5   Certifier

### 5.1   Certification Algorithm

We present the SRDC certification algorithm for the partition replication model. Read-only transactions do not need certification. We certify the readset and writeset of the update transaction in order to ensure that the updated transaction executes on the latest version; that is, no concurrent update transaction committed writes into the readset and writeset. In order to detect and prevent conflicts, the certifier manages the writesets produced by the committed and pre-committed transactions together with the commit order. The certifier maintains two databases: the persistent database in the disk and the memory database. The two databases have a schema similar to that of the partition augmented with a version attributed in each relation. Every schema of the two databases has two tables named as C-I-Ri and C-D-Ri which respectively store the new value and the old value of tuples which the UPDATE, INSERT and DELETE SQL statement of the p-transaction.

After a successful pre-commit of which the writeset of an update p-transaction has no read-write and write-write conflict with the persistent database and the memory database, each tuple in the p-transactions writeset is extended with a new version number assigned by the certifier forming the global commit order of the partition and inserted in the corresponding relation of C-I-Ri and C-D-Ri. Once when the transaction is committed, the corresponding memory tables of the p-transation are bulked into the persistent database. The data with versions older than the minimum for all partition replicas in the persistent database will be truncated.

**Algorithm 2.** CERITFICATION ALGORITHM

**INPUT:** a certification request having <T.tx_start_version, T.writeset, T.readset > or a
certification command having <T, command>;

**OUTPUT:** < decision, writesets, T.tx_commit_version>

1. IF T.writeset is not empty

   1.1 *IF it is true that the input T.writeset and T.readset are tested for conflict
detection against entries of the persistent database whose tx_commit_version is greater
than T.tx_start_version*

   *THEN*

     {*decision* ← "abort";

     *writesets* ← *null*;

     *T.tx_commit_version remains unchanged;*

     *go to step 5;* }

   1.2 *ELSE IF it is true that the input T.writeset and T.readset are tested for
conflict detection against entries of the memory database*

     *Then suspend the transaction;*

   1.3 *ELSE*

     {*decision* ← "pre-commit";

     *writeset* ← *union writeset of the persistent database from T.tx_start_version
to system.version;*

     *increment System_version;*

     *writeset* ← *writeset unionT.writeset;*

     *T.tx_commit_version* ← *System_version;*

     *Write < T.writeset, System.version > into the
memory database;*

     *Go to step 5;* }

2. IF T.writeset is empty

   *then*{*decision* ← "refresh";

   *writeset* ← *union writeset of the persistent database from T.tx_start_version
to system.version;*

   *T.tx_commit_version* ← *System_version;*

   *Go to step 5;* }

3. if <T,commit>

   {*Flush the memory table into the persistent table;*

   *abort all conflicting suspend transactions;*

   *decision* ← "abort";

   *writesets* ← *null*;

   *T.tx_commit_version remains unchanged;*

   *go to step 5;* }

4. if <T,abort>

   {*delete tuples of T from the memory table;*

   *select the oldest transaction of the conflicting suspendtransactions;*

   *decision* ← "pre-commit";

   *writeset* ← *union writeset of the persistent databasefromT.tx_start_version
to system.version;*

   *writeset* ← *writeset union T.writeset;*

   *increment System_version;*

   *T.tx_commit_version* ← *System_version;*

   *Write < T.writeset, System.version > into the memory database;*

   *Go to step 5*}

5. The output of the procedure contains:

   *Output (writesets, decision, T.tx_commit_version);*

   }

As presented in Algorithm 2, the certifier receives a certification request
containing the writeset, the readset and the version number of a replica
node. Given a certification request from replica $node_j$ for a transaction with
$p\text{-}snaphot(T)$=tx_start_version, firstly the certifier accesses all committed writesets with a version greater than in the persistent database, because writesets with

version number smaller than $p$-$snaphot(T)$ belong to transactions that committed before the snapshot of T was taken and transaction T sees their effects. For each accessed writeset item X of the persistent log, the certifier checks if $X \in writeset(T)$ and $X \in readset(T)$, in which case T is aborted since its commit would introduce an impacted transaction in the history and an abort message is send to the replica node. Otherwise the certifier again access the memory database, for each accessed writeset item $X'$ of the memory database, the certifier checks if $X' \in writeset(T)$ and $X' \in readset(T)$, in which case T is suspended until the conflicting pre-committed transaction is committed or aborted.

To avoid the long delay led by no transaction at replica node, we set a counter in node and periodically pull data from the certifier. Once a new sub-transaction is executed at the node, the counter is cleared. If the counter reaches a predetermined value, the node sends a certification request only with $p$-$snapshot(T)$ to the lead certifier. The leader certifier accesses all committed writesets with a version greater than $p$-$snapshot$ of the persistent log and send sets of writesets to the node.

If the certifier receives the reply of commit from the proxy of the pre-committed transaction, the memory table of pre-committer is bulked into the persistent table, and all conflicting suspend transaction is aborted meanwhile the proxy aborts the transaction. If the certifier receives the reply of abort from the proxy of the pre-committed transaction, the oldest suspend transaction is pre-committed.

## 5.2  Conflict Detection

If only checking write-write conflicts without detecting read-write conflicts, phantoms might be introduced, causing the anomalies under SI. But in contrast to writesets, identifying readsets using the tuples is a poor choice, because the readset of a transaction is typically much larger than the writeset, and it is expensive to send the set of rows read in a transaction from the replica to the certifier. [22] introduced novel techniques to provide a stronger global isolation level, namely readset extraction and enhanced verification that prevents read-write and write-write conflicts in a replicated setting [22] The readset is extracted by applying an automatic query transformation to each SQL statement inside an update transaction. The transformation creates the certification queries which are evaluated during the certification process. We make use of the idea based on our data model and architecture.

(1) SELECT Queries The readset of a SELECT statement includes any tuple that matches the predicate $pred(Query)$ on the certifier. The certification query uses the original SQL statement by combining the version predicate [22]. The certification query can be rewritten as:

$Certification\ Queries: SELECT\ Query$

$select * from\ C\text{-}I\text{-}R_i,\ C\text{-}D\text{-}R_i$

$where\ pred(Query)$

$and\ system\text{-}version > p\text{-}snapshot(T);$

FROM clause includes all the corresponding tables with the original SQL statement. The certification query will be performed on the persistent database and the memory database respectively.

(2) Update Statements In [22] proved that certifying the readset of update statement also detects write-write cnflicts and it is, therefore, not necessary to certify the writeset.

The readset of an UPDATE SQL statement includes any tuple matches the predicate on the target table. Similarly, the readset of a DELETE statement contains any tuple that matches the deletion predicate. The readset of an INSERT statement is identified the primary key of the new inserted tuples, based on the fact that the database checks the uniqueness of the primary key. These conditions are captured by the following certification queries:

*Certification Queries : Update Queries*

(1) *select \**
    *from $C$-$I$-$R_i$, $C$-$D$-$R_i$, $Temp$-$I$-$R_i$*
    *where $TEMP$-$I$-$R_i.key = C$-$I$-$R_i.key$*
    *and $TEMP$-$I$-$R_i.key = C$-$D$-$R_i.key$*
    *and $system$-$version > p$-$snapshot(T)$;*

(2) *select \* from $C$-$D$-$R_i$*
    *where $pred(R_i)$*
    *and $system$-$version > p$-$snapshot(T)$;*

(3) *select \* from $C$-$I$-$R_i$, $C$-$D$-$R_i$*
    *where $pred(R_i)$ and $system$-$version > p$-$snapshot(T)$*

The certification query will be performed on the persistent database and the memory database respectively.

# 6  Performance Evaluation

Our main objective is to show the proposed approaches of SRDC are practical replication algorithms with competitive performance. We investigate its overhead and scalability. We use the TPC-W benchmark to assess performance as it is widely used to evaluate replicated database system.

## 6.1  Experimental Setup

We use a cluster of virtual machines to deploy the replicated database system. The master and clone VMs used in our evaluation are running MySQL 5.0 with 1 GB of RAM, one virtual CPU, and a 10 GB disk. Each is hosted on a SunFire X4450 with 4 intel xeon DPes, 128 G RAM, and 8 SCSI RAID. Xeon processors are running on Fedore core 12 with version 2.6.31 of Linux Kernel and dual gigabit Ethernet NICS.

We experiment with the TPC-W benchmark. TPC-W is designed to evaluate e-commerce systems and it implements an on-line bookstore. It consists of three workload mixed that differ in the relative frequency of the transaction types. The browsing in the relative frequency of the transactions, the shopping mix has 20 % update transactions, and the ordering mix has 50 % update transaction. The shopping mix is the most representative mix, while the ordering mix is update-intensive and therefore is the most challenging mix for replicated databases. TPC-W is widely used to evaluate replicated database system. We use one machine running the application server and another hosting a remote terminal emulator. The application server (TOMCAT 6.0) executes the requested JSP pages that access the database. The remote terminal emulator is a multi-threaded eclipse program in which each thread represents one client issuing requests in a closed loop.

We adopt the following metrics: system throughput, which is the number of completed transactions per second (TPS), and response time, denoting the time taken from receiving the transaction at the Coordinator until knowing the commit or abort time at the Coordinator (in ms). The proposed approaches of SRDC shortened the response time. It will increase the throughput under a certain condition.

## 6.2   Performance Evaluation

**Response Time:** we report response time results for the shopping and ordering mix in Fig. 2. The X-axis gives the number of replicas that varies between one and eight, while the curves represent the performance of each partition when the load is fixed. The Y-axis shows response time in million second (ms).

The results of the TPC-W shopping mix (20 % update transactions) and ordering mix (50 % update transactions) are shown in Fig. 2.

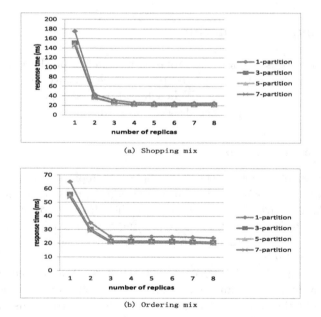

(a) Shopping mix

(b) Ordering mix

**Fig. 2.** Response time

When the load is fixed, response time gradually decrease and stabilizes when using five or more replicas. When the number of replicas increases, the number of partition has less effect on response time. The number of partition decreases the time of every sub-transaction, but the time of the message transport increases, so the delay time of the global certifier increases.

**Throughput:** We report throughput for the shopping mix under different number of partition and different number of replicas, the result is shown in Fig. 3. The shopping mix has 20 % update transaction and 80 % read-only transaction. Our manual partitioner attempted to minimize the number of distributed transaction.

From Fig. 3, the partitioning system has higher throughput than no partitioning system. But the throughput is not improved with the number of partition. That is because the number of distributed transaction increases with the number of partition. The number of distributed transaction will reduce the throughput.

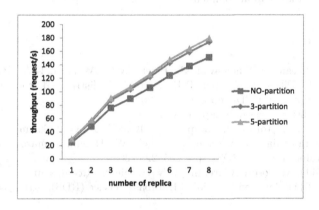

**Fig. 3.** Throughput for TPC-W shopping mix

Figure 3 showed that the throughput for the shopping mix almost rises linearly as the number of replicas increase. But it is not difficult to find by analysis that the conflict probability of update transactions will increase when the number of update transaction increases, because the time of certification to commit transaction will delay. So the benefits of replication depend on the ratio of update.

The result of experiment and analysis shows that SRDC is applied the database with the lower ratio of update transaction and needs an algorithm of database partitioning for transactional workloads.

## 7    Conclusion

This research investigates providing a serializable snapshot isolation in the cloud stronger than eventual consistency. We introduce a concurrency control technique that ensures one-copy serializability in partition replicated database system (SRDC) in which each replica is snapshot isolated. We employ novel techniques to extract transaction readsets and writeset, and perform enhanced certification. We build a prototype SRDC and implement algorithms of extract data set and certification, and evaluate its performance. The performance results under the TPC-W workload mixes show that the response time gradually decrease using the appropriate number of replicas and the appropriate number of partitions, and that the prototype SRDC has higher throughput with the lower ratio of update transaction.

**Acknowledgements.** This work was supported in part by Natural Science Foundation of GuangDong Province Grant No. 2015A030310208, Technology Research Project of the Ministry of Public Security Grant No. 2014JSYJB048, and National Natural Science Foundation of China Grant No. 61502163. Jiuhui Pan is the corresponding author of the paper. The authors are grateful to the anonymous referee for a careful checking of the details and for helpful comments that improved this paper.

# References

1. Chang, F., Dean, J., Ghemawat, S., Hsieh, W.C., Wallach, D.A., Burrows, M., Chandra, T., Fikes, A., Gruber, R.E.: Bigtable: a distributed storage system for structured data. In: OSDI, pp. 205–218 (2006)
2. Cassandra. http://cassandra.apache.org
3. DeCandia, G., Hastorun, D., Jampani, M., Kakulapati, G., Lakshman, A., Pilchin, A., Sivasubramanian, S., Vosshall, P., Vogels, W.: Dynamo: amazons highly available key-value store. In: SOSP, pp. 205–220 (2007)
4. Azure (2011). Microsoft Azure. http://www.microsoft.com/azure/
5. Amazon (2011). Amazon Relational Database Service (RDS). http://aws.amazon.com/rds/
6. Rao, J., Shekita, E.J., Tata, S.: Using paxos to build a scalable, consistent, and highly available datastore. Proc. VLDB Endow. **4**(4), 243–254 (2011)
7. Brewer, E.A.: Towards robust distributed systems. In: PODC, p. 7 (2000)
8. Curino, C., Jones, E.P.C., et al.: Schism: a workload-driven approach to database replication and partitioning. VLDB **3**, 48–57 (2010)
9. Curino, C., Jones, E.P.C., Popa, R.A., et al.: Relational cloud: a database service for the cloud. In: CIDR, pp. 235–240 (2011)
10. Gray, J., Helland, P., O'Neil, P., Shasha, D.: The dangers of replication and a solution. In: SIGMOD, pp. 173–182 (1996)
11. Kemme, B., Alonso, G.: A new approach to developing and implementing eager database replication protocols. ACM TODS **25**(3), 333–379 (2000)
12. Kemme, B., Alonso, G.: Don't be lazy, be consistent: Postgres-R, a new way to implement database replication. In: Proceedings of VLDB 2000, pp. 134–143 (2000)
13. Wu, S., Kemme, B.: Postgres-R(SI): combining replica control with concurrency control based on snapshot isolation. In: Proceedings of ICDE 2005, pp. 422–433 (2005)
14. Kemme, B., Alonso, G.: Database replication: a tale of research across communities. PVLDB **3**(1), 5–12 (2010)
15. Martnez, M.P., Peris, R.J., Kemme, B., Alonso, G.: MIDDLER: consistent database replication at the middleware level. ACM TOCS **23**(4), 375–423 (2005)

16. Vo, H.T., Chen, C., Ooi, B.C.: Towards elastic transactional cloud storage with range query support. PVLDB **3**(1), 506–517 (2010)
17. Elnikety, S., Zwaenepoel, W., Pedone, F.: Database replication using generalized snapshot isolation. In: Proceedings of SRDS 2005, pp. 73–84 (2005)
18. Elnikety, S., Dropsho, S., Pedone, F.: Tashkent: uniting durability with transaction ordering for high-performance scalable database replication. In: EuroSys, pp. 117–130 (2006)
19. Das, S., Agarwal, S., Agrawal, D., et al.: ElasTras: an elastic, scalable, and self managing transactional database for the cloud. Technical report UCSB-CS-2010-04, University of California, Sabtaba Barbara (2010)
20. Daudjee, K., Salem, K.: Lazy database replication with snapshot isolation. In: Proceedings of VLDB 2006, pp. 715–726 (2006)
21. Plattner, C., Alonso, G., Ozsu, M.T.: Extending DBMSs with satellite databases. VLDB J. **17**(4), 657–682 (2008)
22. Bornea, M.A., Hodson, O., Elnikety, S., Fekete, A.: One-copy serializability with snapshot isolation under the hood. In: Proceedings of ICDE 2011, pp. 625–636 (2011)
23. Cecchet, E., Singh, R., Sharma, U., and Shenoy, P.: Dolly: virtualization-driven database provisioning for the cloud. In: ACM VEE, pp. 51–62 (2011)
24. Savinov, S., Daudjee, K.: Dynamic database replica provisioning through virtualization. In: CloudDB, pp. 41–46 (2010)

# A Predetermined Deployment Technique for Lifetime Optimization in Clustered WSNs

Subir Halder$^{(\boxtimes)}$ and Amrita Ghosal

Department of CSE, Dr. B.C. Roy Engineering College, Durgapur 713206, India
sub.halder@gmail.com, ghosal_amrita@yahoo.com

**Abstract.** In wireless sensor networks, preserving energy requires utmost attention due to their high resource constraint feature. Clustering is commonly considered as one of the most efficient energy conservation technique. Firstly, considering Rician channel model for inter-cluster communication and a shortest path routing protocol, we analyze the optimization of network lifetime by balancing the energy consumption among different cluster heads (CHs). It is found that cluster radius of each level has significant role in maximization of network lifetime. To meet the requirement of optimization of network lifetime, we devise a routing aware clustering strategy. We also identify Archimedes' spiral, based on which a deployment function is proposed for distributing member node (MN) and CH. Simulation results demonstrate that the proposed technique significantly outperforms two competing schemes in terms of energy balance, network lifetime and throughput.

**Keywords:** Clustering · Energy balance · Network lifetime · Node deployment · Wireless sensor network

## 1 Introduction

Due to the impetuous advancement of technologies in recent years, wireless sensor networks (WSNs) have become a reliable and mature technology, widely used in several applications ranging from industry to military and home [1]. Almost for all the available platforms of WSNs, sensor nodes are designed to run on batteries, which have very limited energy. Due to the limited on-board energy supply of sensor nodes, the design objective of these systems is normally to conserve as much energy as possible to achieve prolonged network lifetime.

Node deployment is a fundamental issue in WSNs that affects many facets of network operation, including energy management, routing, security. Based on the means of deployment, there are broadly two types of deployment: (i) random deployment, and (ii) predetermined deployment [2]. Random deployment is typically used for inhospitable environments e.g., battlefields surveillance, environmental monitoring [2]. On the contrary, many applications of WSNs serve in controlled setups where predetermined deployment of node is feasible and desirable [2]. Examples of these applications include habitat monitoring, safety assessment of factory floor. The controlled nature of the application allows pre-planning and careful selection for node placement.

© Springer International Publishing Switzerland 2015
G. Wang et al. (Eds.): ICA3PP 2015, Part IV, LNCS 9531, pp. 682–696, 2015.
DOI: 10.1007/978-3-319-27140-8_47

To improve scalability and energy efficiency, sensors in WSNs are often organized into clusters [3] that reduce channel contention and packet collisions, resulting in better network throughput under high load [3]. The role of CHs in the clustering paradigm increases the burden on the CHs, forcing them to drain out their energy much faster. Even if the CH is equipped with a more durable battery than the MNs, the large difference in energy consumption between the two can lead to its shorter lifetime. Once the CH dies, no communication can take place between the MNs in that cluster and the rest of the network. The clusters with comparable area coverage and node density have roughly the same volume of intra-cluster data traffic. Nevertheless, the traffic from far away CHs needs to be relayed via CHs closer to the sink. Thus, CHs closer to the sink drain their energy reservoir faster than the other CHs, resulting in energy hole problem [1, 2] that may effect the whole network leading to premature decrease in network lifetime. To avoid this, care should be taken during deployment such that energy dissipation in all nodes takes place uniformly ensuring load balancing throughout the network.

Many works [4] - [8] reported so far deal with the issue of balancing the energy consumption in WSNs, by dividing the network into clusters. Nevertheless, except [4], none of the existing works consider optimization of cluster radius of each level while devising clustering structure. Further, to the best of our knowledge, no attempt has been made yet to identify a mathematical model and design a deployment scheme based on which MNs and CHs are deployed at some predetermined locations. The main contributions of this paper are as follows: Initially, different from [4] - [8], we analyze the energy balancing approach for optimization of network lifetime by jointly considering Rician fading channel and a shortest path routing protocol. Based on the analysis, principle of optimal clustering structure is derived and that in turn computes the optimal cluster radius of each level using a linear program. Similar to [8], we propose a deployment strategy based on Archimedes' spiral using which both CH and MN are deployed at some predetermined locations. Finally, performance of the optimal clustering strategy is evaluated through quantitative analysis under both ideal and realistic scenarios.

The rest of this paper is organized as follows: In Sect. 2, literature review is provided. The system model considered for the present work is described in Sect. 3. Section 4 theoretically analyzes the network lifetime optimization problem and obtains the clustering strategy. The proposed clustering structure including a deployment strategy based on Archimedes' spiral is described in Sect. 5. In Sect. 6, simulation results under ideal and more realistic scenarios are provided. Finally, concluding remarks are given in Sect. 7.

## 2   Literature Review

The state-of-the-art works that deal with the issue of balancing the load throughout the network, by dividing the network into clusters are elaborated in this section.

Shu et al. [4] provided energy balanced alternatives that try to maximize network lifetime directly by accounting for the interaction between clustering and routing. To obtain balanced power consumption, two mechanisms are proposed, viz. routing-aware optimal cluster planning and the clustering-aware optimal random relay. Unlike [4],

Lai et al. presented a cluster based routing protocol, ACT (arranging cluster sizes and transmission ranges for wireless sensor networks) [5]. The protocol aims in reducing the size of the clusters with closer proximity to the sink as they take the burden of relaying more data than the clusters farther away from the sink. This is achieved by keeping cluster radii near the sink smaller while the clusters located farther away from the sink have larger radii. In another work to conserve energy, Darabkh et al. [6] proposed three clustering algorithms namely adaptive head, static head, and selective static head for mobile target tracking in WSN. Among these algorithms, the static and selective static heads algorithms follow static clustering while the other one follows dynamic clustering. Recently, in order to maximize the lifetime of deployed nodes, Li et al. [7] investigated the problem of constructing optimal clustering architectures in homogeneous WSNs. Most recently, in [8], authors proposed an optimal clustering technique to maximize the lifetime of WSNs. Initially, the authors analyzed the energy balancing approach. Based on the analysis, they derived the principle for optimal clustering structure which, in turn, decides the number of clusters in each layer and the number of MNs associated with each cluster.

Similar to [4, 5, 8] we derived clustering structure by computing the optimal cluster radius. Unlike [4, 5, 8], we analyzed the energy balancing approach for optimization of network lifetime by jointly considering Rician fading channel and a shortest path routing protocol. Further, similar to [8], we propose a deployment strategy based on Archimedes' spiral using which both CH and MN are deployed at some predetermined locations.

## 3 System Models

### 3.1 Network Model

We virtually cover the network area $\chi$ of radius $R$ by a disk sector of angle $\varphi$ (Fig. 1). The disk sector is divided into $i$ number of ring sectors or slices, where $i = 1,...,N$. In this network model, the sink is considered to be located at the vertex, as shown in Fig. 1 and responsible for collecting data from sensors. Sensors are uniformly deployed across $\chi$ with

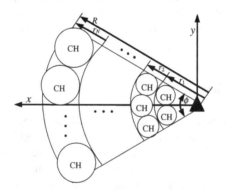

**Fig. 1.** Network area division into slices.

density $\rho$. Although, we assume a slice based network area, we argue this slice shape is general enough to approximate many other shapes e.g., triangle, square, rectangle etc.

In this work, we assume deployment of static heterogeneous node where nodes are organized into clusters. The nodes are heterogeneous in terms of both functionality and battery capability. By functional heterogeneity, we mean a cluster consisting of two types of nodes: MNs and CHs. Similar to [6], we assume a WSN where nodes are divided proactively into many clusters at the time of node deployment. Each MN senses the environment, generates data, and periodically transmits the data to its CH. On the contrary, the CH fuses and forwards the data received from both its MNs and neighbouring CHs which are farther away from the sink. In this way data from a MN reaches the sink through intermediate CHs. We consider that MNs have limited battery capability, whereas CHs are equipped with more durable battery. Without loss of generality, we assume that each CH is located at the centre of its cluster [4]. Because of the symmetric nature of area $\chi$ and uniform deployment, the formation of clusters in a slice is also symmetric i.e., any two clusters with the same distance from the sink to their centres cover the same area. We divide the area $\chi$ into $N$ number of slices; therefore, $N$ types of clusters exist in the network. Here, the clusters located closest to the sink are placed in 1st slice (1st type) and farthest from the sink are placed in $N$th slice ($N$th type). Finally, we assume that in $i$th slice, there are $j$ $(j > 1)$ number of clusters.

## 3.2 Network Operation

We assume that each MN generates data at a rate $n$ bits/sec. Further, we assume that a CH transmits data to the sink via the shortest path. Precisely, a CH in the $i$th slice forwards the data packet (formed by fusing the data received from its MNs and CH of ($i$ +1)th slice) to the closest CH in the ($i$-1)th slice. Next, the CH in the ($i$-1)th slice employs the same procedure to choose the next forwardee CH for sending its data packet. This process repeats till the data packet arrives at the sink. From the network operation, it is clear that the CH bears more data pressure than the MN and hence, the CH depletes its energy at a much faster rate than the MN. As a strategic point of view, the role of a CH is more critical in maintaining network connectivity than the MNs. Therefore, in this work, we focus our attention on energy depletion at the CHs.

## 3.3 Energy Model

We consider the first order radio model [7, 8] as the energy model, where energy consumption of a node is dominated by its wireless transmissions and receptions; so the other energy consumption factors such as for sensing is ignored. In addition to transmission and reception, a CH also consumes energy for data fusion. According to this radio model, energy consumed by a node for transmission and reception is as follows: Energy consumption for transmitting a $n$ bits packet over a transmission range $R_c$ is $e_{tr}(n, R_c) = \left(e_{elec} + e_{amp} R_c^2\right)n = e_t n$, where $e_t = e_{elec} + e_{amp} R_c^2$ and $e_t$ is the energy required to transmit one bit of data. Whereas, the energy consumption for receiving a $n$ bits packet is $e_{re}(n) = e_{elec} \, n = e_r \, n$, where $e_r = e_{elec}$ and $e_r$ is the energy required for receiving one bit of data. Finally, energy consumption for fusing $n$ bits packet is $e_{da}(n) = e_a \, n$, where $e_a$ is the energy required for fusing one bit of data.

### 3.4   Channel Model

Motivated by [9], we use a Rician fading channel model to describe the channel between two CHs and also between the CH and the sink. In this channel model, the probability density function of the received signal amplitude is given by:

$$f_R(\xi) = \frac{\xi}{\sigma^2} e^{-\left(\xi^2 + s^2/2\sigma^2\right)} I_0\left(\frac{\xi \sqrt{2R_f}}{\sigma}\right)$$

where $\xi$ is a normalized random variable that represents the fluctuation in the fading process, $\sigma^2$ is the variance of the multipath components, $s$ is the amplitude of the Line-of-Sight component, $I_0(\cdot)$ is the zero-order Bessel function of the first kind and $R_f$ is the Rician factor, given by: $R_f = s^2/2\sigma^2$. In this channel model, for a transmitter-receiver separation distance $l$, channel gain is given as:

$$h(l) = \frac{G_t G_r \omega^2}{(4\pi l_0)^2} \left(\frac{l}{l_0}\right)^{-\eta} \xi = L(l_0)\left(\frac{l}{l_0}\right)^{-\eta} \xi \tag{1}$$

where $L(l_0) = \frac{G_t G_r \omega^2}{(4\pi l_0)^2}$ is the path loss of the close-in distance $l_0$, $G_t$ and $G_r$ are the corresponding gains of the transmitting and receiving antennas, $\omega$ is the wavelength of the carrier signal, $\eta$ is the path loss exponent ($2 \leq n \leq 6$). Since $\xi$ is random, correct reception of a signal can be guaranteed only when it is represented on a probabilistic basis. Accordingly, in our work, reliable reception of a signal is represented as $\Pr\{e_{rx} \geq \tau\} \geq \delta_r$, where $e_{rx}$ is the energy of the received signal, $\tau$ is a predefined energy threshold and $\delta_r$ is the required link reliability.

## 4   Analysis of Network Lifetime Optimization

We consider the definition of network lifetime as follows:

**Definition (Network Lifetime):** The network lifetime is defined as the time until the first CH dies [4]. A CH is considered as dead when the residual energy is less than a predetermined threshold. The threshold value for a CH is considered as when it is neither able to transmit nor able to receive any data.

The average intra-cluster and inter-cluster traffic load carried by the CHs in the $i$th ($i = 1, \ldots, N - 1$) slice is given by $\pi\left(r_i^2 - r_{i-1}^2\right)\rho \, n \, \varphi/2\pi$ and $\pi\left(R^2 - r_i^2\right)\rho \, n \, \varphi/2\pi$, respectively. On the contrary, the average intra-cluster traffic carried by the CHs in the $N$th slice is given by $\pi\left(R^2 - r_{N-1}^2\right)\rho \, n \, \varphi/2\pi$. Let $C_i$ be the number of CHs in the $i$th slice. Therefore, $C_i$ is approximately given by $\frac{2r_i}{r_i - r_{i-1}}\frac{\varphi}{2\pi}$. Let $E_{ij}$ be the expected energy consumed by $j$th CH in the $i$th slice for transmitting all of its traffic to the nearest CH in the $(i-1)$th slice and $l_i$ be the physical distance between these two CHs. Therefore, the expected energy consumed by $j$th CH in the $i$th $(i = 1, \ldots, N - 1)$ slice is given by:

$$E_{ij} = \pi(R^2 - r_{i-1}^2)\rho n \frac{\varphi}{2\pi} \frac{(r_i - r_{i-1})}{2r_i} \frac{2\pi}{\varphi}(e_r + e_t + e_a)$$

$$E_{ij} = \frac{(R^2 - r_{i-1}^2)(r_i - r_{i-1})}{2r_i}\rho n(e_r + e_t + e_a) \tag{2}$$

where $e_t = e_{elec} + e_{amp}l_i^2$. The expected energy consumed by $j$th CH in the $N$th slice can be calculated applying (2) and using the standard convention that a sum of terms is zero if its lower index is greater than its upper bound.

Let $e_{ti}$ be the over-the-air RF energy consumed when transmitting one bit from $j$th CH in the $i$th slice to $j$th CH in the $(i-1)$th slice. So, the above (2) can be rewritten as:

$$E_{ij} = \frac{(R^2 - r_{i-1}^2)(r_i - r_{i-1})}{2r_i}\rho n(e_r + e_t + e_a + e_{ti}). \tag{3}$$

According to the network model, the distance between two CHs in the $i$th slice and the $(i-1)$th slice is given by:

$$l_i = \begin{cases} \frac{r_i}{2} & \text{for } i = 1, 2 \\ \frac{r_i - r_{i-2}}{2} & \text{for } i = 3, 4, \ldots, N \end{cases}$$

Now, for given $l_i$ and channel model (1), the over-the-air RF energy consumed for receiving one bit, $e_{ri}$, is given as:

$$e_{ri} = e_{ti} L(l_0)\left(\frac{l_i}{l_0}\right)^{-\eta}\xi.$$

For a Rician fading channel, the link reliability requirement can be expressed as:

$$\delta_r = \Pr\{e_{ri} \geq \tau\}$$

$$= \Pr\left\{\xi \geq \frac{\tau}{e_{ti} L(l_0)}\left(\frac{l_i}{l_0}\right)^{\eta}\right\}$$

$$= e^{\frac{-\tau}{e_{ti} L(l_0)}\left(\frac{l_i}{l_0}\right)^{\eta}}$$

From the above expression, we can express $e_{ti}$ as:

$$e_{ti} = \frac{-\tau}{L(l_0) \, \log \delta_r} \left(\frac{l_i}{l_0}\right)^\eta$$

Under shortest path routing, the maximum number of links of an end-to-end path is $N$ (i.e., maximum number of slices). Therefore, to generate the constraint on path reliability, $\delta_p$, the minimum link reliability must be:

$$\delta_r = \delta_p^{\frac{1}{N}}$$

Therefore,

$$e_{ti} = \frac{-N\tau}{L(l_0) \, \log \delta_p} \left(\frac{l_i}{l_0}\right)^\eta = \beta \, l_i^\eta$$

where $\beta = \frac{-N\tau}{L(l_0) \, l_0^\eta \, \log \delta_p}$ and it is a constant. Consequently, the energy consumed by $j$th CH in the $i$th slice, given in (3), can be rewritten as:

$$E_{ij} = \frac{\left(R^2 - r_{i-1}^2\right)(r_i - r_{i-1})}{2r_i} \, \rho \, n(e_r + e_t + e_a + \beta \, l_i^\eta) \tag{4}$$

From (4), the expected energy consumption of a CH in a slice can be approximately represented as a function of cluster radius. Our objective is to determine the optimal radius of a cluster in slices that minimizes the expected energy consumption among all CHs. This optimization problem can be formulated as follows:

$$\begin{cases} \min\limits_{r_1, r_2, \ldots, r_N} \quad \{E_{1j}, E_{2j}, \cdots, E_{Nj}\} \\ \text{such that} \quad r_1 < r_2 < \cdots < r_N = R \end{cases} \tag{5}$$

*subject to*

$$\left[\pi\left(\left(r_i^2 - r_{i-1}^2\right) + \sum\nolimits_{h=i}^N \left(r_{h+1}^2 - r_h^2\right)\right)\rho \, n \frac{\varphi}{2\pi}\right] \\ - \pi \sum\nolimits_{h=i-1}^N \left(r_{h+1}^2 - r_h^2\right)\rho \, n \frac{\varphi}{2\pi} = 0 \; \forall \, 1 \leq i \leq N \tag{6}$$

$$n \sum\nolimits_{i=1}^N \pi(r_i^2 - r_{i-1}^2)\rho \frac{\varphi}{2\pi} = n \, \pi R^2 \rho \frac{\varphi}{2\pi} \quad \forall \, 1 \leq i \leq N \tag{7}$$

The constraint (6) guarantees inter-cluster flow preservation i.e. all data packets generated at or forwarded to a slice are pushed out of it. The constraint (7) specifies that the sum of all data packets generated at a given time duration in the network is constant. If we examine both the function to be optimized and the constraints given above, we see that its objective function is monomial and the constraints are signomials. Hence, its optimal solution can be found using generalized geometric programming (GGP) as introduced in [10]. Once the radius profile of clusters is obtained by solving the above optimization problem, we can ensure that all CHs deployed in the sensor field deplete their energy at minimum rate and hence, optimal network lifetime is achieved.

It has been observed in the recent past state-of-the-work [11] that, except mitigating energy hole problem, predetermined node deployment shows significant improvement in end-to-end delay, throughput, etc. Motivated by [8, 12], we proposed a predetermined deployment strategy based on Archimedes' spiral. We have examined different standard geometric models e.g., Gaussian distribution and found Archimedes' spiral to be one that can be modeled as slice based network architecture because the successive circular turns of Archimedes' spiral have a constant separation distance. This feature primarily motivates us to consider Archimedes' spiral as a node distribution function. The detailed features of the said spiral is given in the next section where we have shown how Archimedes' spiral based node deployment can be mapped or used for ring sector based network architecture.

## 5  The Clustering Technique

The proposed energy balanced clustering strategy consists of evaluation of optimal cluster radius, MNs/CHs deployment, cluster setup and routing path formation phases. The evaluation of optimal cluster radius and routing path formation are already discussed in Sect. 4 and Sect. 3.2, respectively. In this section, we describe MNs/CHs deployment and cluster setup phases.

### 5.1  Deployment Phase

In this section, a deployment function based on Archimedes' spiral is proposed.

#### 5.1.1  Archimedes' Spiral
A spiral is defined as a curve, which emanates from a central point, getting progressively farther away as it revolves around the point. An Archimedes' spiral is a continuous spiral [8, 12] with polar equation $R_d = \theta B$ where $R_d$ is the radial distance, $\theta$ is the polar angle and $B$ is a real number whose value is constant. The distance between two successive circular turns can be calculated using the value of $B$. One of the features of the Archimedes' spiral is that its successive circular turns have a constant separation distance equal to $2\pi B$ (Fig. 2)

#### 5.1.2  Deployment with Discrete Archimedes' Spiral
As the Archimedes' spiral is a continuous curve, to use it as a deployment function, it should be transformed into discrete form so that MNs/CHs may be deployed at those discrete locations. We propose the discrete spiral, as in (8) and (9), to be used as the node deployment function.

$$f(\theta_k) = \theta_k B \tag{8}$$

where $\theta_k \in [2(k-1)\pi, \, 2k\pi]$ for $k = 1, \ldots, K$.

Now, within the designated range of locations in each circular turn, discrete points need to be identified for deployment. We propose to decompose $\theta_k$ for each $k$ into $m$ discrete locations and at each discrete location nodes are deployed. The decomposition of $\theta_k$ is given as follows:

$$\theta_k(m) = [2(k-1)\pi + m\,\varphi_k] \tag{9}$$

for $k = 1, \ldots, K$ and for each $k$, $m = 1, \ldots, \frac{2\pi}{\varphi_k}$. In (9), $\varphi_k$ represents the angular gap between two adjacent nodes in $k$th circular turn as shown in Fig. 2. While deploying the nodes at $m$ discrete locations in each circular turn, we assume that deployment starts at location $m = \frac{2\pi}{\varphi_k}$ and ends at $m = 1$.

Our objective is to model Archimedes' spiral as a node deployment function in such a way that it approximately represents the ring sector based network area (Fig. 1). In order to achieve our goal, we propose to decompose the $i$th slice into multiple regions of size $w_i \times w_i$, where $w_i = r_i - r_{i-1}$. Each of the regions would hold an Archimedes' spiral. We consider this spiral as a cluster, where point of origin of this spiral is CH. MNs are deployed uniformly at discrete locations in each circular turn.

- The radius $(r_k')$ of circular turn (Fig. 2) of proposed Archimedes' spiral is considered approximately as:

$$\frac{1}{2}[2\pi k B + 2\pi(k+1)B] = \pi(2k+1)B$$

$$r_k' = \pi(2k+1)B.$$

Therefore, the separation distance between two successive circular turns of Archimedes' spiral is $r_k' - r_{k-1}' = 2\pi B$.
- The relationship between the width of two successive circular turns in the proposed Archimedes' spiral and $R_s$ is $\pi B \leq R_s$ (Fig. 2).
- For the proposed node deployment function, the number of MNs and CHs deployed in clusters of $i$th type is $(r_i^2 - r_{i-1}^2)\varphi\rho/2$ and $r_i\,\varphi/(r_i - r_{i-1})$, respectively. Further, the number of MNs in any cluster is deployed uniformly at discrete locations using a point as the centre where CH is located by controlling the values of $\theta_k$ and $\varphi_k$, respectively.

Once the optimal cluster radius of each slice is obtained by solving (5)-(7), it is required to know $K$ and $\varphi_k$ to implement the deployment scheme. The following lemmas derived $K$ and $\varphi_k$ for a given region while maintaining coverage and connectivity.

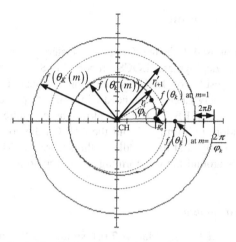

**Fig. 2.** Node distribution function based on Archimedes' spiral.

**Lemma 1:** For a given region $w_i \times w_i$, the required number of circular turns $(K)$ should stand in relation with $w_i$ as $K \leq \lceil w_i / 2\sqrt{2}\,\pi B \rceil$, where $B \leq R_s/\pi$.

**Lemma 2:** In a given $K$ circular region, for Archimedes' spiral based node deployment function, the angular gap $\varphi_k$ between two adjacent MNs in $k$th circular turn stands in relation with $R_s$ as follows:

$$\varphi_k = 2\,\cos^{-1}\left(\frac{(f(\theta_k))^2 + (r'_k)^2 - R_s^2}{2\,f(\theta_k)\,r'_k}\right).$$

Due to page limitation, the proofs of Lemma 1 and 2 could not be incorporated.

## 5.2    Cluster Setup Phase

Since the number of clusters in a slice, number of MNs under any cluster and deployment locations are known a priori, no separate algorithm is designed for the CH selection. Once the CH and MNs are deployed in a circular region based on the proposed deployment function, a cluster is formed. In each such region, nodes (i.e., both MN and CH) are deployed using (8) and (9). The CHs are deployed at the origin of each circular region. We claim that the proposed deployment is feasible. As reported in [13], air-dropped deployment in a controllable manner is feasible even in an inaccessible terrain. We propose to compute the optimal cluster radius of each slice and number of nodes in each circular region of the network off-line prior to the actual deployment. At last, the pre-computed nodes are to be dropped (e.g. from helicopter) using a point (i.e., CH) as the centre following the proposed deployment function. Real life applications e.g., precision agriculture [11] implement node deployment using such methods.

# 6  Performance Evaluation

Performance of the proposed Lifetime Oriented Clustering Structure using Archimedes' spiral based node deployment (LOCS), reported in Sect. 5 is measured through simulation. Simulation results of LOCS scheme are compared with two existing clustering approaches namely Energy Balanced Clustering Approach (EBCA) [4] and ATC [5]. During simulation of EBCA, CH is deployed at the centre of each cluster and MNs are deployed random uniformly around the CH. On the contrary, during simulation of ATC, CH is deployed at the middle of the square and MNs are deployed at predetermined locations around the CH forming a grid topology.

## 6.1  Simulation Environment

The evaluation is performed using Matlab 7.0.1 simulator. We model all the three schemes, under both ideal and realistic scenarios. Here, by ideal scenario we mean the scenario considered during theoretical analysis in Sect. 4. On the contrary, in realistic scenario, in addition to ideal scenario we consider a medium access control (MAC) protocol which includes idle/sleep schedule of the nodes. Moreover, in realistic scenario, energy consumption is considered for idle, sleeping and sensing in addition to transmission, reception and fusion. The MAC protocol is implemented by IEEE 802.11 carrier sense multiple access with collision avoidance (CSMA/CA) [14]. This MAC protocol defines two medium access mechanisms viz. distributed coordination function (DCF) and point coordination function. Considering the decentralized nature of WSN, DCF is the considered mechanism while simulating all the schemes. Further, we considered a network area consisting of 6 slices. To bring all the schemes in the same platform, during simulation, we have deployed same number of MNs and clusters in a slice. Extensive simulation is performed with a confidence level of 95 % and average of 200 independent runs is taken while plotting the simulation graphs.

## 6.2  Simulation Metrics

To evaluate the performance of all the three schemes, energy balance, network lifetime and throughput are considered as performance metrics. In our experiment, energy balance is measured by the parameter energy consumption rate per CH in a slice as given in (4). We define throughput as the amount of data (in terms of bits) received at the sink per unit time and it is measured over a period of 1 s. We conducted three sets of experiments where first set measures energy balancing in the network, second set verifies the enhancement of network lifetime and third set measures the throughput. During simulation, we consider initial energy of a CH and a MN as 50 J and 5 J, respectively. Further, similar to [4], radio and channel models parameters are considered as $e_t = 60\,nJ$, $e_r = e_a = 50\,nJ$, $l_0 = 10\,m$, $G_t = G_r = 1$, $\eta = 4$, $\tau = 10^{-17}$ J, $\delta_r = 0.99$, $\omega = 0.125\,m$ and $R_f = 20$ [9]. Finally, similar to [2], we assume $R_s = 10\,m$ and $n = 400$ bits. Unless, specified otherwise, we use the same parameters with same values of the DCF mechanism as described in [14] during implementation of MAC protocol e.g., queuing delay, saturation point. In plots, scheme names with '(R)' signify performance under realistic scenario and without it under ideal scenario.

### 6.3   Energy Balance

Figure 3 shows ECR per CH for network consisting of 6 slices. We observe from the plot that the nature of the graph for the LOCS is fairly straight. Further, it is observed that in LOCS, for both ideal and realistic scenarios, the plot is almost constant for all slices. For example, in ideal scenario, ECR per CH is 35.70 μJ/sec whereas in realistic scenario, it is 62.48 μJ/sec. On the contrary, in both EBCA and ATC, it is observed that ECR per CH varies abruptly in different slices. Also, in both the competing schemes, it is observed that CHs in the 1st slice have maximum ECR per CH and CHs in the 6th (farthest) slice have the lowest ECR per CH. This justifies that LOCS is relatively more energy balanced compared to the competing schemes viz. EBCA and ATC. Now, for all the schemes if we compare the results of both scenarios, it is observed that ECR per CH (realistic) in all the cases is higher compared to ECR per CH (ideal). The additional energy usage for realistic scenario is due to the implementation of MAC protocol.

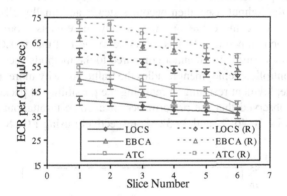

**Fig. 3.** Energy consumption rate per CH under ideal and realistic scenarios.

### 6.4   Network Lifetime

The graphs illustrated in Fig. 4 represent the network lifetime. For ideal scenario, it is observed that the network lifetime of LOCS is 11.57 % and 23.67 % more than that of EBCA and ATC, respectively. On the contrary, for realistic scenario, it is 10.82 % and 19.74 % more than that of EBCA and ATC, respectively. Moreover, in LOCS the flat nature of the plot ensures that in all the slices, network lifetime terminates in more or less the same time as compared to EBCA and ATC. This ensures that energy in LOCS is balanced to a greater extent than both the competent schemes. Now, if we compare the simulation results of network lifetime both for ideal and realistic scenarios, network lifetime is reduced in realistic scenario, as there is additional energy consumption due to the implementation of MAC protocol.

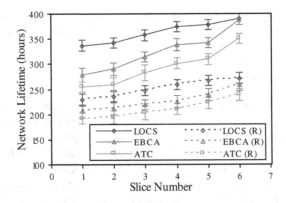

**Fig. 4.** Network lifetime under ideal and realistic scenarios.

## 6.5   Throughput

Figure 5 shows data throughput of LOCS, EBCA and ATC as measured at the sink under the multi-hop benchmark. It is observed from Fig. 5 that for each of the competing schemes' throughput rises, then becomes steady and finally falls. Nevertheless, in case of LOCS, once the curve becomes steady, it remains more or less steady compared to all the competing schemes. It is due to the fact that in LOCS, nodes are deployed in a more controllable manner compared to the methods used in both EBCA and ATC. The controlled deployment handles the traffic intensity more judiciously than other means of deployment resulting in reducing the possibility of packet collision and congestion. We observed that the performance of average throughput improves over EBCA and ATC by 10.46 %, and 39.32 %, respectively using LOCS.

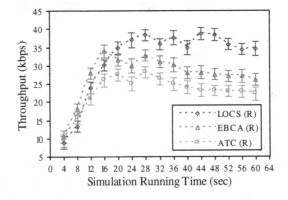

**Fig. 5.** Throughput comparison over simulation running time.

# 7  Conclusion and Future Work

In this work, we analyzed the problem of network lifetime optimization by balancing energy consumption at different CHs in a clustered WSN. Analysis revealed the cluster radius of each level have significant role in optimization of network lifetime by avoiding energy hole [2]. Considering the results of this analysis, we developed a joint deployment and routing aware optimal clustering strategy. Our proposed optimal clustering strategy considered the deployment of both CH and MN at some predetermined locations. To deploy both CH and MN at some predetermined locations, we identified Archimedes' spiral, based on which a deployment function is proposed for distributing MN and CH. Simulation results clearly demonstrate our strategy's dominance over the existing two competing clustering strategies [4, 5] in terms of all the three performance metrics viz. energy balance, network lifetime and throughput. In future, the proposed clustering strategy may be made more realistic by considering 3-D environment.

# References

1. Rault, T., Bouabdallah, A., Challal, Y.: Energy efficiency in wireless sensor networks: a top-down survey. Comput. Netw. **67**, 104–122 (2014)
2. Halder, S., Ghosal, A.: A Location-wise predetermined deployment for optimizing lifetime in visual sensor networks. IEEE Trans. Circ. Syst. Video Technol. (2015). doi: 10.1109/TCSVT.2015.2441391
3. Younis, O., Krunz, M., Ramasubramanian, S.: Node clustering in wireless sensor networks: recent developments and deployment challenges. IEEE Netw. **20**(3), 20–25 (2006)
4. Shu, T., Krunz, M.: Coverage-time optimization for clustered wireless sensor networks: a power-balancing approach. IEEE/ACM Trans. Netw. **18**(1), 202–215 (2010)
5. Lai, W.K., Fan, C.S., Lin, L.Y.: Arranging cluster sizes and transmission ranges for wireless sensor networks. Inf. Sci. **183**(1), 117–131 (2012)
6. Darabkh, K.A., Ismail, S.S., Shurman, M.A., Jafar, I.F., Alkhader, E., Mistarihi, M.F.A.: Performance evaluation of selective and adaptive heads clustering algorithms over wireless sensor networks. J. Netw. Comput. Appl. **35**(6), 2068–2080 (2012)
7. Li, H., Liu, Y., Chen, W., Jia, W., Li, B., Xiong, J.: COCA: constructing optimal clustering architecture to maximize sensor network lifetime. Comput. Commun. **36**(3), 256–268 (2013)
8. Ghosal, A., Halder, S.: Lifetime optimizing clustering structure using archimedes' spiral based deployment in WSNs. IEEE Syst. J. (2015). doi:10.1109/JSYST.2015.2434498
9. Wyne, S., Singh, A.P., Tufvesson, F., Molisch, A.F.: A statistical model for indoor office wireless sensor channels. IEEE Trans. Wirel. Commun. **8**(8), 4154–4164 (2009)
10. Boyd, S., Kim, S.J., Vandenberghe, L., Hassibi, A.: A tutorial on geometric programming. Optim. Eng. **8**(1), 67–127 (2007)
11. Sanchez, A.J.G., Sanchez, F.G., Haro, J.G.: Wireless sensor network deployment for integrating video-surveillance and data-monitoring in precision agriculture over distributed crops. Comput. Electron. Agric. **75**(2), 288–303 (2011)
12. Halder, S., Ghosal, A.: Lifetime optimizing clustering structure using archimedes spiral based deployment in WSNs. In: Proceedings of 14th IFIP/IEEE Symposium on Integrated Network and Service Management (IM), pp. 592–598 (2015)

13. Bernard, M., Kondak, K., Maza, I., Ollero, A.: Autonomous transportation and deployment with aerial robots for search and rescue missions. J. Field Robot. **28**(6), 914–931 (2011)
14. Li, X., Yan, S., Xu, C., Nayak, A., Stojmenovic, I.: Localized delay-bounded and energy-efficient data aggregation in wireless sensor and actor networks. Wirel. Commun. Mob. Comput. **11**(12), 1603–1617 (2011)

# Traffic Replay in Virtual Network Based on IP-Mapping

Lun Li, Zhiyu Hao[✉], Yongzheng Zhang,
Zhenquan Ding, and Haiqiang Fei

Institute of Information Engineering,
Chinese Academy of Science, Beijing 100093, China
{lilun,haozhiyu}@iie.ac.cn

**Abstract.** Building a controllable, reproducible, and flexible network environment is essential for network behavior research. One key is to generate real traffic data in a virtual network; this helps a virtual network perform as physical network, and further facilitates analysis of the traffic characteristics. However, due to the divergence between physical and virtual network topologies, the traffic generated in virtual network are far from practice. In this paper, we propose a traffic generating approach called IP-Mapping Traffic Replay. We attempt to find an optimal IP mapping from physical network to virtual network by computing the similarity. Once the mapping is known, we replay the traffic data collected from a physical network on associated nodes in the virtual network, so that the generated traffic in the virtual network reflects the trace in physical. We implement IP-Mapping Traffic Replay in a simulated virtual network using NS-3, and conduct a set of experiments to show its effectiveness. The results demonstrate that our approach can replay the traffic data effectively and efficiently in a virtual network that is mapped from physical network.

**Keywords:** Virtual network · Traffic generating · Traffic Replay · IP-Mapping · Network simulator

## 1 Introduction

The explosive growth of information contains valuable information, but at the same time, a huge amount of information would generate harmful traffic which poses a great threat to cyber security. Recording the traffic data and then replaying them when necessary is an important tool for analyzing the traffic characteristics. Mathematical model, historical traffic [1, 2], Tcpreplay [3] and Tcpopera [4] provide approaches to generate traffic data and replay the data in a network. Unfortunately, these existing approaches cannot always capture the changing behavior of network attacks. First, most proposed approaches such as network security tools testing, network attack scenario building is extremely difficult to be fully implemented in a complex physical network. Second, the historical traffic data are still not fully utilized due to the difficulty of data replaying in a physical network. Finally, these works focus on the unit of traffic upon replaying, and ignore the network environment impact on data replaying. As a result, they cannot reflect the practical communication scenarios.

© Springer International Publishing Switzerland 2015
G. Wang et al. (Eds.): ICA3PP 2015, Part IV, LNCS 9531, pp. 697–713, 2015.
DOI: 10.1007/978-3-319-27140-8_48

One well known approach in cyberspace research nowadays is to build a controllable, reproducible, and flexible network environment using virtualization technology and then conduct research in the virtual network. These virtualization tools include Xen [5], KVM [6], etc., network simulators NS-3 [7], Omnet++ [8], etc. Although a virtual network provides several features such as easy deployment, isolation, scalability and flexibility, it is still difficult to satisfy the practical requirement of researchers on replaying the network traffic collected from physical network, mainly due to the divergence between virtual and physical network topologies.

In this paper, we focus on how to generate real traffic data in a virtual network. We collect the trace data from a physical network, and use the trace as the traffic to be generated. Then we build two models from physical and virtual network topologies respectively, and formulate an interface similarity to describe the similarity between the two. We then present the algorithm to solve the problem for acquiring the mapping from physical network into virtual network. The mapping with the largest interface similarity promotes the generated traffic data in virtual to approximate the real data in physical. Lastly, we replay the data on the nodes in the virtual network for retransmitting the traffic.

The main contributions of the paper are two-fold:

First, we formulate an interface similarity problem to match the physical and virtual network topologies, and propose IP-Mapping Traffic Replay approach to generate traffic data in virtual network.

Second, we implement the approach in **NS-3** simulator, and conduct a set of experiments to justify its effectiveness.

The rest of this part is organized as follows. The next section introduces the background and existing works related to traffic data generation. Section 3 presents the design of IP-Mapping Traffic Replay approach, and Sect. 4 reports the experimental results. Finally, we conclude our work in Sect. 5.

## 2  Related Work

Tcpreplay is currently the most widely used traffic replay tool. It sequentially replays traffic in a specific format at the link layer; the upper layer protocol does not need to know the details. Similar to Tcpreplay, NBTRL [9] reads the packet file in pcap format using Libpcap [10] to a certain replay point, then uses Libnet to send packets on the replay point previously chosen.

Tomahawk [11] extracts client and server packets respectively from the original traffic data, and sends the packets at the server node and client node. Tools such as Monkey [12] send HTTP traffic to evaluate the performance of web service. WireReplay [13] extends Tcpreplay to replay traffic at the transport layer rather than the link layer. Tcpopera and improved Tcpopera [14] extract the TCP netflow from the raw traffic file for building a sequence of status messages, they then replay the traffic upon status change of client and server in the netflow unit. [15] designs and implements ProxyReplay system to replay application layer traffic to test application proxy network device.

The essential difference of these traffic replay systems lays in the replay units. For example, Tcpreplay and other similar tools replay traffic in the packet unit on the link layer to create a complete reproduction of the original packet, but they cannot reflect the interaction in the data transmission. Other tools that replay data at transport layer focus on replaying TCP/UDP protocol sessions, but they ignore other protocols. Other than the packet unit upon replaying, environmental effects also play an important role upon traffic replay. Unfortunately, the existing replay systems always neglect the environment elements; they simply replay the traffic using two roles: one server part and several client parts. Figure 1 is a common example of a traffic replay system.

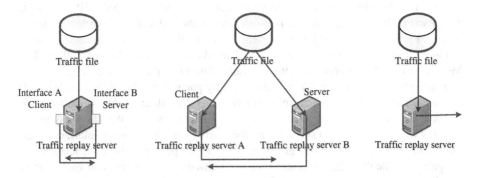

**Fig. 1.** Common design of traffic replay systems

The importance of the authenticity of traffic is emphasized on [16] and the authors design the LegoTG system, but without the environmental support, we still need to feature extraction from the traffic trace. Mahimahi [17] records and replays HTTP traffic and using multi Unix network namespaces to simulate clients and servers, but the network topologies is limited. Van et al. [18] propose an approach based on IP aggregation to improve the throughput, but, due to lack of environmental considerations, the replay results do not reflect the details of network behavior which should be signified by the raw data. For example, replaying the data that contain a DDoS attack with the characteristics of a group attack behavior can only be used to test the functionality of security devices, but they cannot reflect the characteristics of the attack itself. Therefore, their approach cannot replay real traffic data well. The approach proposed in [19] takes both replay control and environment emulation into account, it models the WLAN environment and involves complex state transitions, but it is not a common replay method to be straightly used in the virtual network platform.

## 3 IP-Mapping Traffic Replay

In this section, we will first present the overview of IP-Mapping Traffic Replay approach, and then we introduce how to build the physical network model and virtual network model. With the two models, we formulate the network mapping as interface similarity problem and describe an effective solution. Finally, we describe the implementation details on data replaying and prove the complexity.

### 3.1  Design Overview

We capture the real traffic data from a particular router interface named as traffic capture point. The traced data contain multiple endpoints and communication details which can be distinguished by the IP addresses. It is worth noting that we cannot acquire the whole physical network topology, since we just get the data from one interface of the router. In contrast to the physical network, the virtual network is built on demand by the administrator, so the topology is known.

Motivated by this, upon replaying the real traffic in a virtual network, we can map the physical network endpoints into virtual network endpoints; replace the physical endpoint IP addresses extracted from traffic data with virtual endpoint IP addresses. Then, each endpoint in the virtual network fetches the traffic data collected from the associated physical node, and replays them following the physical traffic sequence.

Figure 2 shows the overall framework of IP-Mapping Traffic Replay method. The physical router takes charge of capturing traffic data from the interface, after the data are acquired; a physical network model is built by parsing the data that records the IP addresses. Then, the network is split into two sets according to the communication direction, i.e., R_IPA and R_IPB. For the virtual network, because the topology is known, it can be divided into several candidate pairs by different virtual interfaces, e.g., $v\_interface_i$ and $v\_interface_j$ will generate two different pairs of sets. To determine the best pair, we calculate the interface similarity between physical sets and each pair of virtual sets, and denote the one that is the largest similarity. This will generate a mapping between physical nodes and virtual nodes. Finally, we replay the physical traffic data in the virtual node, thereby helps the virtual network performs as real.

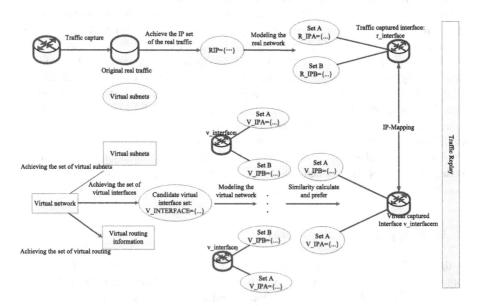

**Fig. 2.** Framework of IP-Mapping Traffic Replay

The challenges of this method mainly consist of three parts: (i) how to map the traffic capture physical point to a virtual interface (called virtual capture interface), (ii) how to assign real IP addresses to virtual nodes, and (iii) how to replay the packets in physical traffic order. We will describe our solution in the following sections.

### 3.2 Practical Network Modeling

We employ network capture tools like Libpcap to analyze the traffic in an offline manner; we record the source IP address, destination IP address, as well as the timestamp of each packet. After removing the duplicated IP addresses, we can acquire the set defined as below:

$$R\_IP = \{R\_IP_1, R\_IP_2, \ldots R\_IP_n | n > = 2\} \tag{1}$$

We define the traffic capture interface as *r_interface*, therefore, $R\_IP_1, R\_IP_2, \ldots,$ $R\_IP_n$ are the IP addresses in the traffic data captured over *r_interface*.

Take the *R_IP* as vertices, considering that each req packets is always associated with an ack packet, we view each packet as an undirected edge, i.e., $e=(R\_IP_i, R\_IP_j)$. Then, we get the edge set $E= \{e=(R\_IP_i, R\_IP_j) | R\_IP_i, R\_IP_j \in R\_IP\}$. Finally, we can construct an undirected graph $R\_Graph=(R\_IP, E)$ from the real traffic data.

**Proposition 1:** *R_Graph* is a bipartite graph, i.e. *R_IP* can be partitioned into two disjoint subsets *R_IPA* and *R_IPB* which satisfy: $R\_IPA \cap R\_IPB = \phi$, $R\_IP = R\_IPA \cup R\_IPB$. That is, each edge $(R\_IP_i, R\_IP_j)$ in *R_Graph* is associated with two vertices, $R\_IP_i$ and $R\_IP_j$ which belong to two different sets for $R\_IP_i \in R\_IPA$, $R\_IP_j \in R\_IPB$.

**Proof:** To prove Proposition 1, we should firstly prove that *R_Graph* has least two vertices, and its length of all circuits is even [20].

**Sufficiency:** Without doubt, $|R\_IP| >= 2$, C is a circuit in *R_Graph*, so that $C=(R\_IP_0, R\_IP_1, R\_IP_2, \ldots, R\_IP_{n-1}, R\_IP_n, R\_IP_0)$. Consider that *R_Graph* is a bipartite graph, the element in *R_IPA* (or *R_IPB*) does not communicate with IP addresses in the same set. $R\_IP_i$ (i = 0, 1,..., n) must occur alternately in R_IPA and R_IPB. We can provide $\{R\_IP_0, R\_IP_2, R\_IP_4, \ldots R\_IP_n\} \in R\_IPA$, $\{R\_IP_1, R\_IP_3, R\_IP_5, \ldots, R\_IP_{n-1}\} \in R\_IPB$, suggesting that *n* is even; therefore, the number of edges in *C* is even.

**Necessity:** Apparently, $|R\_IP| >= 2$. If the graph R_*Graph* is not completely connected, then all the branches of *R_Graph* follow the discussion below.

We suppose that $R\_IP_x, R\_IP_y, R\_IP_z \in R\_IP$. If $R\_IP_x$ communicates with $R\_IP_y$ and $R\_IP_y$ communicates with $R\_IP_z$, then $R\_IP_z$ cannot communicate with $R\_IP_x$ over the interface of physical router, so that the circuit number will be 0 which is even. As a result, $R\_IP_x$ and $R\_IP_z$ can be put into *R_IPA*, while $R\_IP_y$ can be put into *R_IPB*. Otherwise, if $R\_IP_z$ communicates with $R\_IP_x$, the circuit length is odd, the edge connecting vertices $R\_IP_x$ and $R\_IP_y$ indicates that there exists a communication packet in the traffic data, as well as $R\_IP_y$ and $R\_IP_z$,. If $R\_IP_x$ communicates with $R\_IP_z$ through *r_interface* and $R\_IP_y$ communicates with $R\_IP_z$ through *r_interface* as well, according to the routing definition, $R\_IP_x$ and $R\_IP_y$ should be placed in the same side of the r_interface and they should not communicate across the *r_interface*. Therefore, the communication data between $R\_IP_x$ and $R\_IP_y$ should not exist in the real traffic. This contradicts the assumption, so that the necessity is established. Finally, Proposition 1 is proved.

```
Input: R_Graph
Output: R_IPA and R_IPB
procedure PartitionGraph(R_Graph)
    for each r_ip in R_Graph.R_IP:
        node[r_ip].color = GRAY
        node[r_ip].visited = false
    end for
    for each r_ip in R_Graph.R_IP:
        if node[r_ip].visited == false   then
            node[r_ip].color = BLACK
            DFS(r_ip);
        end if
    end for
    for each r_ip in R_Graph.R_IP:
        if node[r_ip].color == BLACK then
            add r_ip to R_Graph.R_IPA
        else if node[r_ip].color == WHITE then
            add r_ip to R_Graph.R_IPB
        end if
    end for
end procedure
procedure DFS(r_ips)
    node[r_ips].visited = true;
    color = OppositeColor(node[r_ips].color)
    for each node r_ipd linked to r_ips
        if node[r_ipd].visited == false then
            node[r_ipd].color = color
            DFS(r_ipd)
        else if node[r_ipd].color != color then
            report error
        end if
    end for

end procedure
```

**Algorithm 1.** Partition Algorithm

The algorithm described in Algorithm 1 partitions the bipartite graph *R_Graph* into two disjoint sets *R_IPA*, *R_IPB*. First, all the nodes are not marked and regarded as not being visited. Then the algorithm traverses all nodes. If it finds that a node has not been accessed, it sets the node's color BLACK, and then employs the depth first search algorithm (DFS). In the DFS procedure, the root node and its children nodes will be marked with an opposite color. Note that if the node and its children nodes cannot be marked with the opposite color in the procedure, which means the pcap file is mixed with muti interfaces captured traffic, this occasion cannot be handled in this paper. Finally, all nodes will be traversed. The nodes labeled as **BLACK** will be put into R_IPA and nodes labeled as **WHITE** are placed into R_IPB.

## 3.3   Virtual Network Modeling

As mentioned before, the virtual network topology is known upon deployment. Similar to the physical network model, there exist two disjoint IP address sets associated with a virtual network interface. The virtual router's interface set is determined by:

$$V\_INTERFACE = \{v\_intreface_1, v\_intreface_2 \ldots V\_intreface_n | n > 2\}$$

The problem is that there exist several cuts to divide the virtual network. For example, as shown in Fig. 3.

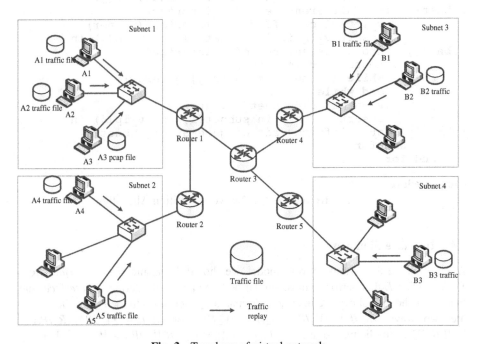

**Fig. 3.** Topology of virtual network

For any virtual router's interface $v\_interface_i$, virtual nodes communicating through $v\_interface$ can be partitioned into two disjoint sets: V_IPA and V_IPB. We calculate the virtual network model under the assumption that the global routing information is known. The algorithm described in Algorithm 2 traverses each routing path between the virtual network subnets. The main idea behind is that each skip will encounter one interface; so that we can insert nodes of different virtual subnets into *V_IPA* and *V_IPB* of the encountered *v_interface$_i$*. After a two-for-loop, the algorithm calculates the *V_IPA* and *V_IPB* for all interfaces in *V_INTERFACE*.

```
Input: VirtualNetwork
Output: V_IPA_i and V_IPB_i of each v_interface
procedure Partition (VirtualNetwork)
    for i=0 to VirtualNetWork.subnet.size()
        for j=i+1 to VirtualNetWork.subnet.size()
            insert v_ip(i) in subnet[i] and v_ip(j) in
subnet[j] into different set of gateway of subnet[i]
            router = subnet[i].gateway
            do
                if(routing path reachs gateway of
subnet[j])
                    break
            end if
            router = subnet[i].gateway
            v_interface = find_src_interface(router)
            insert v_ip(i) in subnet[i] and v_ip(j) in
subnet[j] into different set of v_interface
            v_interface = find_dst_interface(router)
            insert v_ip(i) in subnet[i] and v_ip(j) in
subnet[j] into different set of v_interface
            router = v_interface
            while (router!= subnets[j].gateway)
            end while
            v_interface=subnet[j].gateway
            insert v_ip(i) in subnet[i] and v_ip(j) in
subnet[j] into different set of gateway of subnet[j]
        end for
    end for

end procedure
```

**Algorithm 2.** Virtual Network Partition Algorithm

## 3.4   Interface Similarity

After obtaining the virtual network model, we should determine one *v_interface* from *V_INTERFACE* that performs most similar with the physical interface *r_interface*, and treats it as the virtual capture interface. To map a v_interface into the *r_interface*, there are two ways: (*R_IPA→V_IPA*, *R_IPB→V_IPB*) or (*R_IPB→V_IPA*, *R_IPA→ V_IPB*). For simplicity, we assume that$|V_IPA|>=|V_IPB|,|R_IPA|>=|R_IPB|$. For any *v_interface$_i$* in *V_INTERFACE* we will encounter three conditions:

1. $|V\_IPA_i| >= |R\_IPA|, |V\_IPB_i| >= |R\_IPB|$
2. $|V\_IPA_i| <= |R\_IPA|, |V\_IPB_i| <= |R\_IPB|$
3. $|V\_IPA_i| >= |R\_IPA|, |V\_IPB_i| <= |R\_IPB|$ or $|V\_IPA_i| <= |R\_IPA|, |V\_IPB_i| >= |R\_IPB|$

We need to define a measurement metric to calculate the comprehensive similarity of the two sets, for acquiring the best-fit mapping. In this paper, the similarity is defined by *a_factor*, which is the absolute similarity of mapping ($R\_IPA \rightarrow V\_IPA$, $R\_IPB \rightarrow V\_IPB$). To avoid the absolute similarity deviation of condition 3, we introduce $x$ as a smoothing factor, and define *s_factor* as a smooth similarity. If $|V\_IPA| >= |R\_IPA|$, $|V\_IPA|/|R\_IPA| = x$. In the case of fewer gaps between a virtual network model and a real network model, generally select $x = 1$. Then, *a_factor* and *s_factor* are determined by:

$$a\_factor = (|V\_IPA|/|R\_IPA|) * (|V\_IPB|/|R\_IPB|)$$

$$s\_factor = (|V\_IPA|/|R\_IPA| > 1?x : (|V\_IPA|/|R\_IPA) * /(|V\_IPB|/|R\_IPB|)$$

The similarity comparison is conducted as follows. We compare the smooth similarity *s_factor* first. If *s_factor* is different to the previous value, the $v\_interface_i$ with a larger *s_factor* suggests that it is more similar with *r_interface*. If the $s\_factor_i$ is the same with $s\_factor_j$, we need to further compare *a_factor*. Similarly, if the value of *a_factor* is larger than the previous one, the *v_interface* would be more similar with the r_interface. We sort the v_interfaces in *V_INTERFACE* set according to the steps above and finally choose the best *v_interface* whose *s_factor* and *a_factor* are the largest among all interfaces. This interface will be regarded as the mapping point for the physical capture point.

Let the virtual capture point be $v\_interface_m$, the corresponding map is ($R\_IPA \rightarrow V\_IPA_m$, $R\_IPB \rightarrow V\_IPB_m$). We can map elements of $R\_IPA$ and $V\_IPA_m$ one-to-one, so as to $R\_IPB$ and $V\_IPB_m$. If either condition 2 or condition 3 occurs, implying that multiple IP addresses in $R\_IPA$ (or $R\_IPB$) will be mapped into the same virtual IP address, we can continue to scratch the elements of $V\_IPA_m$ or $V\_IPB_m$ from the beginning of the set.

## 3.5    Traffic Replay

We replay the traffic data in IP layer and only replay non-broadcasting IP packets. Once the mapping from physical nodes to virtual nodes is known, the real traffic will be retraversed for data replay. The source and destination IP addresses in the real traffic will be re-placed with the corresponding virtual IP addresses, meanwhile, the traffic data will be split by the virtual source nodes. The traffic data after being split will be transmitted by the virtual nodes using socket APIs, which are provided by the virtualization tools.

To guarantee that the replayed traffic in the virtual network can arrive at the virtual capture point following the order in real traffic, the recorded timestamps should be recalculated. For each packet $pkt_i$, $t_i$ is referred to as the original timestamp of packet, and $pkt_i$ will be send by $v\_node_j$. According to global virtual network routing information, we can calculate the link delay $delay_j$ from $v\_node_j$ to interface $v\_interface_m$, so the new timestamp of $pkt_i$ in the virtual network should be $t_i$-$delay_j$. In order to avoid negative relative, let $t\_off$ be a global non-negative time offset. Consequentially, $pkt_i$

will be transmitted in the virtual network at the timestamp $T_i$, where $Ti=t_i\text{-}delay_j+t\_off$. Finally, the virtual network system will unify the sequential order and control the transmission speed when replaying the packets.

## 3.6 Complexity

The IP-Mapping Traffic Replay approach mainly consists of the IP-Mapping phase and the Traffic Replay phase. The Traffic Replay phase just takes charge of sending packets and is easy to implement. Therefore, we mainly discuss the complexity of IP-Mapping phase.

Let **n** be the total number of the packets in the original traffic from the physical network, **m** is the number of IP addresses (i.e., $|R\_IP|$), and k is the number of the subnets in virtual network topology. As mentioned before, the IP-Mapping phase can be divided into four phases, and the time complexity of each phase is discussed as follows:

**Phase 3.1:** Real traffic handle. The time of this phase should be the sum of the time to traverse real traffic and the time to remove the duplicated IP addresses. The complexity of data traversing is $O(n)$. The IP address is an unsigned long integer. The time complexity of IP addresses removal using a sorting algorithm will be $O(nlog_2n)$; thus, the complexity of phase 3.1 is $O(n)+O(nlog_2n)$;

**Phase 3.2:** Calculate $R\_IPA$ and $R\_IPB$. The time of this phase is directly related to the complexity of $R\_Graph$. In our implementation, we leverage the adjacency table to store the graph. Therefore, the complexity is $O(m+e)$, where e is the number of edges;

**Phase 3.3:** Calculate $V\_IPA$ and $V\_IPB$ of each $v\_interface$. Phase 3.3 compromises two level loops for $k$, to the overhead of these loops is $O(k^2)$. The inside loop traverses the routing information to implement set division ($O(k^2*log_2k)$). Let x be the average length of routings, the total time complexity will be $O(k^2*log_2k)$;

**Phase 3.4:** IP-Mapping. Time for mapping the real IP to the virtual IP will be $O(m)$.

Consequentially, the time complexity of IP-Mapping is $O(n) + O(nlog_2n) + O(m+e) + O(m) = O(nlog_2n) + O(m+e) + O(k^2*log_2k)$.

The above analysis demonstrate that the IP-Mapping processing time is mainly affected by the number of packets in the real traffic, the number of IP addresses, and the complexity of the virtual network. Since the number of packets (i.e., n) is far larger than the other parameters, the overall complexity is considered to be $O(nlog_2n)$.

## 4    Evaluation

### 4.1    Experimental Setup

We use the widely used LLS_DDOS_1.0 attack scenario data set from MIT Lincoln Laboratory [21], and adopt their method to process the LLS_DDOS_1.0 attack. The five phases of the attack scenario are:

**(1) IP Sweeping**: Sending ICMP Requests to multi-type IP addresses and determining the active hosts through the ICMP replies; **(2) Probing**: Probing the live IP addresses to search the Sadmind daemon that are running on these hosts; **(3) Breakin**: Breaking in the hosts via the Sadmind vulnerability; **(4) Installation**: Installing Mstream DDoS [22] attack software into three hosts selected from phase 3); **(5) Attack**: Starting attack.

Our case chooses the internal network scanning data LLS_DDOS_1.0-inside.-dump. We use this data because it contains an integrated attacking scenario, which will help to clearly present how to replay traffic in a virtual network. Our experiments aim to demonstrate the attack behavior through traffic replaying in one case of virtual network topology, as shown in Fig. 4.

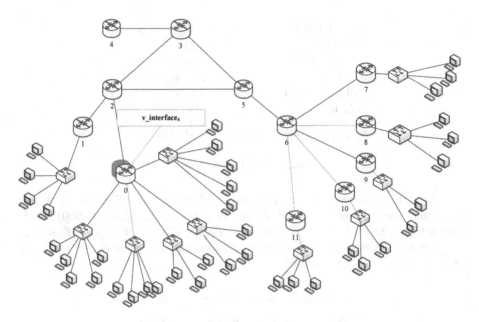

**Fig. 4.** Virtual network topology

To construct the virtual network, we employ NS-3 simulator which provides sufficient APIs for simply scheduling a specific event at a specific time. In addition, it also provides a tracing mechanism for acquiring traffic file in *pcap* format from any expected interface.

## 4.2   Experimental Results

First, LLS_DDOS_1.0-inside.dump was processed, and the error in Algorithm 1 is occurred. This error indicates that LLS_DDOS_1.0-inside.dump is mixed with traffic from multi-interfaces. According to the information provided from [21], the data should mix the communication traffic between inside and outside hosts and the mirror traffic of the inside switch. We filter the packets that don't satisfy the prerequisite. The LLS_DDOS_1.0-inside.dump described below is referred to as the filtered data.

In the original file, there exist 30744 IP addresses to be mapped. The number after bipartite graph partition is 34055 for R_IPA and 319 for R_IPB. The partition result illustrated in Fig. 5 indicate that the set of IP addresses of this traffic is very large, implying that it is in full compliance with the characteristics of the attack.

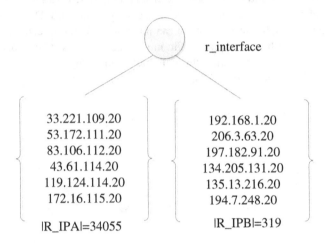

**Fig. 5.** Model of real traffic

Finally, the interface $v\_interface_4$ which is marked shadow in Fig. 4 is selected as the virtual capture interface. $|V\_IPA|=50$, $|V\_IPB|=27$, real factor=0.000124265, smooth factor=0.000124265. As a result, $|V\_IPA|<|R\_IPA|$, $|V\_IPB|<|R\_IPB|$, so that multi real IP addresses would be mapped to a single virtual IP address. Some cases of the mapping are illustrated in Table 1.

**Table 1.** Part of the mapping results

| R_IPA | V_IPA | R_IPB | V_IPB |
|---|---|---|---|
| 172.16.115.20 | 11.0.0.38 | 216.40.24.2 | 14.0.1.12 |
| 99.32.44.0 | | 206.3.63.20 | |
| ... | | ... | |
| 172.16.116.20 | 11.0.0.35 | 192.254.26.2 | 14.0.1.8 |
| 15.107.45.0 | | 197.182.91.20 | |
| ... | | ... | |

There are 77 virtual nodes for transmitting the traffic, so the original traffic file will be split into 77 smaller files. The source IP and destination IP address would be replaced with the corresponding virtual IP address. We use NS-3 APIs to capture the traffic flow over each router interface, with the aim to analyze the results upon data replaying.

**IP Sweeping Phase:** We observe the ICMP Request packets in Virtual_LLS_DDOS. pcap, and then we pay particular attention to packets whose ping destination is multiple IP addresses. Finally we find that the source IP of these packets is 14.0.5.7, as shown in Fig. 6. We identify that 14.0.5.7 is the attacker who is in charge of the whole attacking process. Figure 7 shows several replies of Ping command that are recorded in the traffic attacker.pcap captured at this node.

| Source | Destination | Protocol | Length | Info |
|---|---|---|---|---|
| 14.0.5.7 | 11.0.0.29 | ICMP | | 64 Echo (ping) request |
| 14.0.5.7 | 11.0.0.38 | ICMP | | 64 Echo (ping) request |
| 14.0.5.7 | 14.0.7.4 | ICMP | | 64 Echo (ping) request |
| 14.0.5.7 | 14.0.7.6 | ICMP | | 64 Echo (ping) request |
| 14.0.5.7 | 11.0.0.27 | ICMP | | 64 Echo (ping) request |
| 14.0.5.7 | 11.0.0.38 | ICMP | | 64 Echo (ping) request |
| 14.0.5.7 | 14.0.7.5 | ICMP | | 64 Echo (ping) request |
| 14.0.5.7 | 11.0.0.12 | ICMP | | 64 Echo (ping) request |
| 14.0.5.7 | 14.0.7.5 | ICMP | | 64 Echo (ping) request |
| 14.0.5.7 | 14.0.7.4 | ICMP | | 64 Echo (ping) request |
| 14.0.5.7 | 11.0.0.20 | ICMP | | 64 Echo (ping) request |

**Fig. 6.** IP Sweeping generated by 14.0.5.7

| Source | Destination | Protocol |
|---|---|---|
| 14.0.6.4 | 14.0.5.7 | ICMP |
| 11.0.0.29 | 14.0.5.7 | ICMP |
| 11.0.0.38 | 14.0.5.7 | ICMP |
| 11.0.0.38 | 14.0.5.7 | ICMP |
| 14.0.7.4 | 14.0.5.7 | ICMP |
| 14.0.7.4 | 14.0.5.7 | ICMP |
| 14.0.6.4 | 14.0.5.7 | ICMP |

**Fig. 7.** Ping replies to 14.0.5.7

**Probing Phase:** We search for the Sadmind and Portmap packets in attacker.pcap to find out which node has the Sadmind vulnerabilities. As we can see from the results illustrated in Fig. 8, the attacker has probed 11.0.0.38, 14.0.7.4, 11.0.0.27, 14.0.7.5, 11.0.0.12, 14.0.6.8, 11.0.0.29, 11.0.0.21, 14.0.7.6, 14.0.6.4 respectively, and gets responses from 11.0.0.38, 14.0.6.8, 11.0.0.29, 14.0.6.8, 11.0.0.12 etc.

| Source | Destination | Protocol |
|---|---|---|
| 14.0.5.7 | 11.0.0.12 | Portmap |
| 14.0.5.7 | 11.0.0.12 | Portmap |
| 14.0.5.7 | 14.0.6.8 | Portmap |
| 14.0.6.8 | 14.0.5.7 | Portmap |
| 14.0.5.7 | 14.0.6.8 | SADMIND |
| 14.0.6.8 | 14.0.5.7 | SADMIND |

**Fig. 8.** Probing phase

**Breakin Phase:** Attackers choose the victims according to the list of hosts that exhibit Sadmind vulnerability, so we filter the packets associated with the Telnet protocol. Figure 9 shows a fraction of the communication data. As we can see, the attacker chose 11.0.0.38, 11.0.0.29 and 14.0.6.8 and begins to take charge of these three hosts.

| Source | Destination | Protocol |
|---|---|---|
| 14.0.5.7 | 11.0.0.38 | TCP |
| 11.0.0.38 | 14.0.5.7 | TELNET |
| 14.0.5.7 | 11.0.0.38 | TCP |
| 11.0.0.38 | 14.0.5.7 | TELNET |
| 14.0.5.7 | 11.0.0.38 | TCP |
| 14.0.5.7 | 11.0.0.38 | TCP |
| 11.0.0.38 | 14.0.5.7 | TCP |

**Fig. 9.** Breakin Phase

**Installation Phase:** Fig. 10 shows that the attacker selects 14.0.6.8, 11.0.0.38, 11.0.0.29 as victims to install MStream DDoS attacking program. We mark 14.0.6.8, 11.0.0.38, and 11.0.0.29 as victim1, victim2 and victim3, respectively. Figure 10 illustrates a part of the RSH communication process. As we can see, WireShark tells that the application layer information is a Server->Client Data of hacker2.

| Source | Destination | Protocol | Length | Info |
|---|---|---|---|---|
| 14.0.5.7 | 11.0.0.38 | RSH | 75 | Session Establishment |
| 14.0.5.7 | 11.0.0.38 | RSH | 103 | Session Establishment |
| 11.0.0.38 | 14.0.5.7 | RSH | 71 | Server username:hacker2 Server -> Client Data |
| 11.0.0.38 | 14.0.5.7 | RSH | 103 | Server username:hacker2 Server -> Client Data |
| 14.0.5.7 | 11.0.0.38 | RSH | 75 | Session Establishment |
| 14.0.5.7 | 11.0.0.38 | RSH | 122 | Session Establishment |
| 11.0.0.38 | 14.0.5.7 | RSH | 71 | Server username:hacker2 Server -> Client Data |
| 11.0.0.38 | 14.0.5.7 | RSH | 128 | Server username:hacker2 Server -> Client Data |
| 14.0.6.8 | 14.0.5.7 | RSH | 64 | Session Establishment |
| 14.0.6.8 | 14.0.5.7 | RSH | 143 | Session Establishment |
| 14.0.5.7 | 14.0.6.8 | RSH | 64 | Server username:root Server -> Client Data |
| 14.0.5.7 | 14.0.6.8 | RSH | 109 | Server username:root Server -> Client Data |
| 14.0.6.8 | 14.0.5.7 | RSH | 64 | Session Establishment |
| 14.0.6.8 | 14.0.5.7 | RSH | 129 | Session Establishment |

**Fig. 10.** Installation Phase

**Mstream DDOS Attack Phase**: Before sending a large amount of sequential TCP packets, we search for packets that satisfy: (i) the source is one of 11.0.0.38, 11.0.0.29, 14.0.6.8 and (ii) the destination is the other two IP addresses respectively. From the filtered result we can observe that the Master program is installed in the host with IP 11.0.0.38, i.e., victim2. From the results of attack process shown in Fig. 11, we are confirmed that 14.0.3.10 was attacked. The attacked port is not fixed, and the source IP addresses in the attacking traffic are not limited to the three victims. All these information obtained from the replayed traffic in the virtual network conform to the signatures of MStream DDoS attack.

| Source | Destination | Protocol | Length | Info |
|---|---|---|---|---|
| 14.0.6.7 | 14.0.3.10 | TCP | 64 | 33369 > 31586 [ACK] Seq=1 |
| 14.0.6.4 | 14.0.3.10 | TCP | 64 | 33025 > 29879 [ACK] Seq=1 |
| 14.0.6.3 | 14.0.3.10 | TCP | 64 | 38852 > 22121 [ACK] Seq=1 |
| 11.0.0.37 | 14.0.3.10 | TCP | 64 | 32955 > 23587 [ACK] Seq=1 |
| 14.0.7.3 | 14.0.3.10 | TCP | 64 | 23988 > 29451 [ACK] Seq=1 |
| 11.0.0.35 | 14.0.3.10 | TCP | 64 | 33533 > 21395 [ACK] Seq=1 |
| 14.0.6.5 | 14.0.3.10 | TCP | 64 | 33162 > bfd-control [ACK] |
| 11.0.0.28 | 14.0.3.10 | TCP | 64 | 32804 > 22945 [ACK] Seq=1 |
| 14.0.7.3 | 14.0.3.10 | TCP | 64 | 33295 > 8255 [ACK] Seq=1 |
| 14.0.6.3 | 14.0.3.10 | TCP | 64 | 38987 > ibprotocol [ACK] |
| 14.0.6.5 | 14.0.3.10 | TCP | 64 | 24079 > 26026 [ACK] Seq=1 |
| 14.0.6.8 | 14.0.3.10 | TCP | 64 | 32766 > 9973 [ACK] Seq=1 |
| 14.0.6.4 | 14.0.3.10 | TCP | 64 | 23975 > 17608 [ACK] Seq=1 |
| 14.0.6.3 | 14.0.3.10 | TCP | 64 | 32473 > cnrp [ACK] Seq=1 |
| 14.0.6.5 | 14.0.3.10 | TCP | 64 | 33275 > bpmd [ACK] Seq=1 |

**Fig. 11.** Mstream DDOS Attack Phase

According to data obtained from the virtual network we can infer the following conclusions. (1) The IP address of the attacker is 14.0.5.7. (2) The IP addresses which are controlled by the attacker are 11.0.0.38, 11.0.0.29, 14.0.6.8. (3) The MStream DDoS Attack master node's IP is 11.0.0.38. (4) The node who is being attacked is 14.0.3.10. The IP-Mapping Traffic Replay approach maps the real traffic completely to the virtual network so that users could get data from any expected interface and then handle these data on demand. This mapping between IP addresses mentioned above and the real IP addresses is shown in Table 2.

**Table 2.** Mapping relation

| Mapped IP | Real IP |
| --- | --- |
| 14.0.5.7 | 207.46.179.15 |
| 11.0.0.38 | 172.16.115.20 |
| 14.0.6.8 | 172.16.112.10 |
| 11.0.0.29 | 172.16.112.50 |
| 14.0.3.10 | 131.84.1.31 |

The labeled data set provided in [21] also indicate the results in practical scenario: (1) The IP address of the attacker is 207.46.179.15. (2) The inside network nodes controlled by the attacker are 172.15.115.20, 172.16.112.10, 172.16.112.50. (3) The node that is attacked is 131.84.1.31. It is different from the fact that the source IP addresses of the attack packet are spoofed in LLS_DDOS_1.0-inside.dump, however, in the virtual network, these spoofed IP addresses are mapped into the corresponding virtual IP addresses, and the attack traffic is send by all these mapped nodes, but these do not influence the replay process and result.

It is worth noting that we only present one case to show how to replay real traffic in a virtual network. In practical scenarios, users can change the virtual network topology and modify the properties of virtual network elements such as adding an ACL function for a virtual router or changing the routing protocols so that the traffic information is free to access and process. This suggests that our approach will provide great convenience to users with the high controllability and flexibility which are introduced by the virtual network.

## 5  Conclusions and Future Work

In this paper, we analyze the traffic replay problem in a virtual network, and propose an IP-Mapping Traffic Replay approach to generate real traffic in the virtual network based on IP-Mapping which maps the physical nodes into virtual nodes. We implement a prototype system and evaluate it on an NS-3 built virtual network. The results show that our approach greatly improves the reality of the network emulation or simulation by replaying the traffic collected from the physical net-work. We believe that this approach help researchers to build a more authentic virtual network for further exploring the potential value of real traffic.

In the future, we plan to collect real traffic from multiple physical interfaces, and replay them over multiple interfaces in a virtual network. In addition, we plan to implement distributed traffic replay system in a virtual network to improve the capability and scalability of IP-Mapping Traffic Replay.

**Acknowledgments.** This work is supported by National Key Technology Support Program of China (Grant No. 2012BAH46B02).

# References

1. Park, K., Kim, G., Crovella, M.: On the relationship between file sizes, transport protocols, and self-similar network traffic. In: 1996 International Conference on Network Protocols, 1996. Proceedings, pp. 171–180. IEEE (1996)
2. Abry, P., Baraniuk, R., Flandrin, P., Riedi, R., Veitch, D.: Multiscale nature of network traffic. Signal Proc. Mag. IEEE **19**, 28–46 (2002)
3. Tcpreplay. http://tcpreplay.synfin.net/
4. Hong, S.-S., Wu, S.: On interactive internet traffic replay. In: Valdes, A., Zamboni, D. (eds.) RAID 2005. LNCS, vol. 3858, pp. 247–264. Springer, Heidelberg (2006)
5. Xen. http://www.xenproject.org/
6. KVM. http://www.linux-kvm.org/
7. NS-3. http://www.nsnam.org/
8. Omnet++. http://www.omnetpp.org/
9. Kuo, Z., Kuo, T., Jianfeng, C., Liang, H.: NBTRL: A software platform for network background traffic replay based on log. In: Control Conference, 2007. CCC 2007. Chinese, pp. 607–611. IEEE (2007)
10. Libpcap. http://www.tcpdump.org/pcap3_man.html
11. Tomahawk. http://sourceforge.net/projects/tomahawk/
12. Cheng, Y.-C., Hölzle, U., Cardwell, N., Savage, S., Voelker, G.M.: Monkey see, monkey do: A tool for TCP tracing and replaying. In: Proceedings of the 2004 USENIX Annual Technical Conference (2004)
13. Wireplay. http://code.google.com/p/wireplay/
14. Weibo, C., Zhongmin, C., Xiaohong, G., Mingxu, C.: A new method for interactive TCP traffic replay based on balance-checking between transmitted and received packets. Chin. J. Comput. **32**, 835–846 (2009). Chinese
15. Huang, C.-Y., et al.: Stateful traffic replay for web application proxies. Secur. Commun. Netw. **8**(6), 970–981 (2015)
16. Mirkovic, J., Genevieve, B.: Techreport ISI-TR-699 LegoTG: Composable Traffic Generation with a Custom Blueprint (2015)
17. Netravali, R., et al.: Mahimahi: Accurate Record-and-Replay for HTTP. In: 2015 USENIX Annual Technical Conference (USENIX ATC 15). USENIX Association (2015)
18. Van, D.P., Zhanikeev, M., Tanaka, Y.: Effective high speed traffic replay based on IP space. In: 11th International Conference on Advanced Communication Technology, 2009. ICACT 2009, pp. 151–156. IEEE (2009)
19. Ku, C.-Y., Lin, Y.-D., Lai, Y.-C., Li, P.-H., Lin, K.-J.: Real traffic replay over WLAN with environment emulation. In: Wireless Communications and Networking Conference (WCNC), 2012 IEEE, pp. 2406–2411. IEEE (2012)

20. Bipartite graph. http://en.wikipedia.org/wiki/Bipartite_graph
21. Lincoln Laboratory Scenario (DDoS) 1.0. http://www.ll.mit.edu/mission/communications/cyber/CSTcorpora/ideval/data/2000/LLS_DDOS_1.0.html
22. MStream DDoS. http://staff.washington.edu/dittrich/misc/mstream.analysis.txt

# Optimizing the Overheads for Uncoordinated Proactive Checkpointing

Lei Zhu$^{(\boxtimes)}$, Jianhua Gu, and Zhennao Cai

School of Computer, Northwestern Polytechnical University,
Xi'an 710072, China
zeiier@126.com,
{gujh, caizn}@nwpu.edu.cn

**Abstract.** Fault tolerance is one of the crucial challenges for HPCs to achieve exascale. In this paper, we consider the impact of the predictions that fail to precisely identify the fault-occurrence time on uncoordinated proactive checkpointing/restart (C/R). We extended Aupy's model in the presence of the uncoordinated proactive C/R and distorted predictions. We then propose optimal strategies for deciding when to accept the predictions, and provide algorithms for the optimal storage interval for the periodic C/R. The results show that the proposed method can significantly improve the performance of the system. Furthermore, our case study indicates that the recall of the predictor is more important than precision for our system.

**Keywords:** Proactive fault tolerance · Uncoordinated checkpointing · Prediction · High performance computer (HPC)

## 1 Introduction

Fault tolerance is a crucial technique for high performance computer (HPC) to achieve exascale. The overall mean time between failure (MTBF) of HPCs decreases with the system size since the reliability of modern processors is not perfect [1, 2]. This issue will threaten the productivity of extreme-scale systems [3]. The most widely used fault tolerance approach is coordinated periodic checkpointing/restart (C/R) which will be prohibitively expensive for extreme-scale systems [5]. Thus, the multi-level checkpointing technical [6–8] was proposed to alleviate this issue. Although this technique can reduce the system-downtime caused by C/R, it remains a reactive technique: these methods cannot handle the failure until system has been suspended by the failure [12]. Thus, the rework overheads are huge if the failure occurs at the later part of the computing fragment. In cooperation with failure prediction methods, proactive fault tolerance techniques handle failures by performing proactive actions before the failure occurs. Even though remarkable failure prediction methods have been introduced over the past few years [9–11], none of them can perfectly predict all failures. Therefore, proactive fault tolerance and failure prediction methods have to be used in conjunction with reactive fault tolerance (e.g. periodic C/R). This paper focuses on the system with both proactive and reactive fault tolerance.

© Springer International Publishing Switzerland 2015
G. Wang et al. (Eds.): ICA3PP 2015, Part IV, LNCS 9531, pp. 714–728, 2015.
DOI: 10.1007/978-3-319-27140-8_49

The coordinated proactive C/R [12] is a popular technique for reducing the rework time by writing a checkpoint right before the failure occurs. Although this technique is reliable, it is also costly. One ideal mechanism is the uncoordinated proactive C/R. However, the system needs to deal with the domino effect [16]. In this paper, we consider only the case of fault tolerant protocols that provide a consistent recovery (by using message logging techniques), immune to the domino effect [14].

This paper aims at providing a better understanding of the uncoordinated proactive C/R method with prediction. The key contributions of this paper are as follows.

- We extend Aupy's model [13] to characterize the proactive fault tolerance system using the uncoordinated proactive C/R.
- Based on our model, we design the optimal periodic C/R and proactive action policies.
- We propose policies that determine whether the prediction should be accepted.
- We propose a method for determining the optimal length of the computing fragment. When we choose the optimal length of the computing fragment the fault tolerance overheads will be minimized.
- We evaluate our method under different system settings using a discrete event simulator.
- Our case study shows that the recall of the predictor is more important than the precision in the context.

The main notation of this paper is presented in Table 1.

**Table 1.** Description of symbols

| Symbol | Decription |
|---|---|
| $r, p$ | Recall(precision) of the predictor |
| $q$ | Probability to take prediction into account |
| $\tau$ | Time inverval of periodic checkpoint |
| $T_s$ | The effective operating time |
| $T_{nf}$ | The fault-free execution time of the application with periodic C/R |
| $T_{lost}$ | The average extra overhead induced by one failure |
| $D$ | The average prediction distortion |
| $\Delta l$ | The overhead factor of message loading during recovery |
| $\varnothing$ | Uncoordinated recovery factor |
| $m$ | MTBF of the platform |
| $m'$ | MTBF of single component |
| $m_{lost}$ | Mean time between unpredicted failures |
| $m_{hit}$ | Mean time between predicted failures |
| $C$ | The overhead of writing a periodic checkpoint |
| $R$ | The restart time |
| $C_p$ | The overhead of writing a uncoordinated proactive checkpoint |
| $t$ | fault-occurrence time |
| $T_{total}$ | The expected execution time |

## 2    Related Work

There are two key techniques of proactive fault tolerance: the failure prediction and the proactive action. Considerable researches in the field of failure predicting method have been proposed in the past few years. In order to analyzing the system logs, a dynamic meta-learning approach was introduced by Gu [17]. Depending on different rules, the predicting engine can switch between different methods. Nakka [18] investigated the logs of a productive system and proposed an approach which is able to extract the past and future failure distributions for each failure event. Based on these methods, they use different decision tree classifiers to predict the failures. However, these two methods are difficult to implement in practice since they require the precise overview of the system architecture. Based on signal analysis concepts, Gainaru [9] proposed Event Log Signal Analyzer (ELSA). ELSA is a toolkit which can get a more realistic overview of the entire system. The experimental results showed that this approach improve the effectiveness of proactive fault tolerance. By using data mining techniques, the ELSA has been improved in [19].

The most widely used techniques of proactive action are the C/R and migration. Remarkable optimization strategies had been developed for reducing the overheads of C/R techniques [6–8]. There are also many studies focus on modeling uncoordinated reactive C/R [15].

Few studies focused on the impact of prediction and proactive action on the periodic C/R. Gainaru [10] studied the influence of prediction on the periodic C/R. However, they only replace the MTBF by the mean time between unpredicted faults of an existing model. Mohamed [12] studied the combination of failure prediction, coordinated proactive C/R and coordinated periodic C/R. A model that reflects the expected computing efficiency of fault tolerance has been proposed by them. They also optimized the periodic checkpointing interval by the model. Aupy [13] further extended the classical first-order model by providing the optimal strategy to decide whether and when to accept the prediction. They also derived the optimal length of the computing fragment in this context. Compared to a fault tolerant method without prediction, their approach is capable of improving system productivity significantly. All of these studies considered the coordinated proactive C/R method as the proactive action. These methods can be further improved, because it is prohibitively expensive for extreme-scale systems [5].

The uncoordinated C/R has been less frequently modeled. Zheng [4] proposed a local C/R technique and prove it has a positive impact on the proactive C/R overheads. However, the midplanes of the system they considered are independent. Thus, the model doesn't consider the overheads of message logging. Bosilca [15] introduced a unified model to characterize both coordinated C/R and uncoordinated C/R (with message logging). The results of their analytical comparison proved the validity of the model. However, all these studies only consider reactive C/R methods.

Unlike all the previously mentioned studies, we focused on improving the uncoodinated proactive C/R approaches with message logging. To the best of our knowledge, this paper is the first to consider the mathematics of the combination of failure prediction, uncoordinated proactive C/R with message logging and coordinated periodic C/R. We have also provided a model and a detailed analysis of the extra overheads caused by the fault tolerance approach and failures.

# 3 Framework Design

This paper aims at a combinative fault tolerant method including fault prediction, uncoordinated proactive C/R and coordinate periodic C/R. Our objective is to minimize the expected execution time ($T_{total}$) of the application. For simplification, we wish to minimize the waste ratio. The waste ratio is the time that the platform is not executing effective applications divided by $T_{total}$ of the execution.

## 3.1    The Strategy of Checkpointing

Like [13], this study considers a HPC system subject to a fault tolerance and failure events, and ignores the specific architecture of the system. A failure event is defined as an event that immediately interrupts the system. We consider a system with $N$ processors that work concurrently, and use coordinated periodic C/R for back up fault tolerance. The periodic checkpoints are written to stable storage at fixed intervals of length $\tau$. The average overhead of taking a periodic checkpoint is denoted as $C$. We enforce that $\tau > C$ in this study. Periodic C/R is responsible for the failures that fail to be forecasted by the predictor. When a failure interrupts the platform, the application must recover from the last checkpoint.

## 3.2    Prediction and Proactive Action

Different from most related works, this paper dose not assumes that the predictor can precisely predict the failure-occurrence time. The average prediction distortion is denoted as $D$. In fact, if the predictor can precisely predict the fault-occurrence time, the system states are always consistent because we can write a checkpoint just before the fault occurs. Thus, there is no *orphan* process in the system. In this case, the system can be characterized by Aupy's model [13], and one only needs to reset the cost of proactive C/R. Thus, we only model the system with imperfect predictor. As shown in Fig. 1, if process $P_2$ rolls back, $P_1$ and $P_3$ become *orphan* process because their state depends on the messages ($m_4$ and $m_5$) that are seen as not sent yet. In this paper, we consider the system use an improved pessimistic message logging technique to deal with this issue. Instead of logging all messages of the application, the system only log the messages that sent and received by the suspected processes after an accepted prediction.

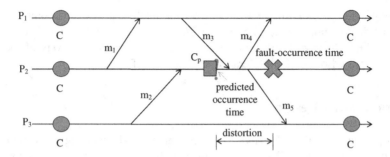

**Fig. 1.** Uncoordinated proactive C/R with imperfect prediction

The duration of writing a uncoordinated proactive checkpoint is $C_p$. The recall and precision of the predictor are defined as $\frac{T_p}{T_p+F_n}$ and $\frac{T_p}{T_p+F_p}$, respectively. $T_p$ is true positive events. $F_p$ is false positive events. $F_n$ is false negative events. The reliability of the platform is characterized by the system MTBF. The system MTBF is denoted as $m$. Consider a platform with $N$ processors whose individual MTBF is $m'$, then $m = m'/N$ [13]. To characterize the impact of the failure prediction and proactive actions, we consider two quantities: $m_{lost}$ (mean time between missed failures) and $m_{hit}$ (mean time between predicted failures). Thus, the rate of missed failures is $\frac{1}{m_{lost}} = \frac{1-r}{m}$, and the rate of identified failures is $\frac{1}{m_{hit}} = \frac{r}{m \times p}$.

## 4    Model

### 4.1    The Model Without Failure Prediction and Proactive Fault Tolerance

In this section, we revisit Aupy's approach. If the waste ratio is defined as $O$, and $O = \frac{T_{total} - T_s}{T_{total}}$. Their work [13] proposed that

$$O = \frac{C}{\tau} + \left(1 - \frac{C}{\tau}\right)\frac{1}{m}\left(\frac{\tau}{2} + R\right). \tag{1}$$

The $\tau_{opt}$ that minimizes $O$ is approximated as $\tau_{opt} = \sqrt{2(m-R)C}$.

### 4.2    The Complete Model

In this section, we propose a mathematical model that characterizes the platform with failure prediction, uncoordinated proactive C/R, and coordinated periodic C/R.

We consider the following policies.

- The length of computing fragment is denoted as $\tau$.
- If there is enough time to finish the proactive operation, the system may still ignore the prediction. This happens with a probability $1 - q$. Thus, the system accepts the prediction with probability $q$.
- The average prediction distortion is denoted as $D$. $D = t - t'$ where $t$ denots the actual fault-occurrence time and $t'$ denotes the fault-occurrence time predicted by the predictor.
- Remain that we consider only the case of fault tolerant protocols that provide a consistent recovery (by using message logging techniques), immune to the domino effect. The overhead of message logging is characterized by an overhead factor $\Delta l$. Thus, the overhead of message logging can be denoted as $D \times \Delta l$.
- The recovery overheads of the uncoordinated C/R is $\varnothing R$. $\varnothing \in [0, 1]$ is the unco-ordinated recovery factor.

Our objective is to derive an expression for the waste ratio. Obviously, the fault-free overheads are unchanged: $O_{nf} = \frac{C}{\tau}$. We only need to refine $O_f$. There are three scenarios of $O_f$:

(1) Unpredicted failures: Obviously, the waste due to false negative events is $\frac{1}{m_{lost}} \left( \frac{\tau}{2} + R \right)$.

(2) Reject the prediction: This extra overhead occurs because the system rejects the prediction, it happens in two different scenarios. First, if there isn't enough time to perform the proactive action (which is the uncoordinated proactive checkpointing in this paper), the system surfer an overhead if the prediction is a true positive event. All the work done between the fault-occurrence time $t$ and the completion of the last periodic checkpoint will be lost. The expected time lost is

$$L_1 = \frac{1}{\tau} \int_0^{c_p} [p(t+R)]dt. \tag{2}$$

Second, if the system can implement the proactive action, the platform will also suffer an extra overhead if the prediction is correct. Recall that the probability of accepting the prediction is $q$. Then, the expected time lost can be defined as follows.

$$L_2 = \frac{1}{\tau}(1 - q) \int_{c_p}^{\tau} [p(t+R)]dt. \tag{3}$$

(3) Accept the prediction: These extra overheads happen when the system accepts the prediction. If the prediction is a false alarm, the time lost will be the overhead of the proactive action. On the contrary, if the prediction is valid, the system loses time because of performing the proactive action and recovery. Thus, the expected time lost can be defined as follows.

$$L_3 = \frac{1}{\tau} q \int_{C_p}^{\tau} \left[ p(C_p + D + D \times \Delta l + \emptyset R) + (1-p)C_p \right] dt \qquad (4)$$

Using the law of total probability, the waste ratio of fault ($O_f$) can be derived from the disjunction of all possible cases. The final value of $O_f$ is

$$O_f = \frac{1}{m_{lost}} \left( \frac{\tau}{2} + R \right) + \frac{1}{m_{hit}} (L_1 + L_2 + L_3) \qquad (5)$$

### 4.3   Identify the Probability of Accepting the Prediction

In practice, the system cannot always accept the prediction even though it is true positive event. The recovery overheads may be less than the avoiding overheads if the failure occurs at the beginning of a computing fragment. On the contrary, the prediction may be a false alarm. This means we will lose time by performing an extra proactive action. If the system chooses to accept the prediction, the waste is

$$O_p = p[C_p + D + D \times \Delta l + \emptyset R] + (1-p)C_p. \qquad (6)$$

If the proactive action is not performed, the waste is $O_{np} = p(t + R)$.

Obviously, the platform can only benefit from the proactive action if $O_p < O_{np}$. By solving this inequality, we get

$$\frac{C_p}{p} + (1 + \Delta l)D + \emptyset R - R < t. \qquad (7)$$

Let $(1 + \Delta l)D + \emptyset R - R = \delta$ and $\varepsilon = C_p/p + \delta$. Thus, the probability that the system accepts the prediction within a computing period is defined as

$$q = \begin{cases} 0 & t \le \varepsilon \\ 1 & t > \varepsilon \end{cases}. \qquad (8)$$

Let us refine the former model with this Eq. (8). If the inequality $\tau \le \varepsilon$ holds, the system always rejects the prediction. In this case, it seems that the platform adopted no proactive action, and the waste ratio is given by Eq. (1). If $\tau > \varepsilon$, the system rejects all prediction in the interval $[0, \varepsilon]$ and accepts all predictions in the interval $(\varepsilon, \tau]$. Thus, the waste due to failures is

$$O_f = \frac{1}{m_{lost}} \left( \frac{\tau}{2} + R \right) + \frac{1}{m_{hit}\tau}$$
$$+ \left\{ \int_0^{\varepsilon} p(t+R)dt + \int_{\varepsilon}^{\tau} \left[ p(C_p + D + D \times \Delta l + \emptyset R) + (1-p)C_p \right] dt \right\}.$$

For simplicity, we only consider the case that $\varepsilon > C_p$. In fact, this assumption is reasonable except the most extreme cases. The proactive checkpoint cannot be taken if the time interval between the fault-occurrence time ($t$) and the beginning of the computing fragment is less than $C_p$. Plugging all these values into Eq. (1), we obtain the refined expression for the invalid-overhead ratio:

$$
\begin{cases}
O_1(\tau) = \frac{C}{\tau}\left(1 - \frac{R}{m}\right) + \frac{R - C/2}{m} + \frac{\tau}{2m} & \text{if } \tau \leq \varepsilon \\[2mm]
O_2(\tau) = \frac{rC\varepsilon\left(2C_p + 2p\delta - p\varepsilon\right)}{2p} \times \frac{1}{m\tau^2} + \frac{2C(m - \delta r - R) + \varepsilon r(\varepsilon - 2\delta)}{2m\tau} \\[2mm]
\quad + \frac{1-r}{2m}\tau + \frac{\delta r + R - (1-r)\frac{C_{pd}}{2}}{m} + \frac{rC_p}{pm}\left(1 - \frac{C+\varepsilon}{t}\right) & \text{if } \tau > \varepsilon
\end{cases}
\tag{9}
$$

Obviously, $O_2(\tau)$ equal $O_1(\tau)$ if the recall of the predictor is zero. If we set $\emptyset = 1$ and $D = \Delta l = 0$, Eq. (9) become Aupy's approach.

## 5  Optimization Algorithm

In this section, we propose an optimization algorithm that minimizes the waste ratio. As before, we assume that $\tau > C$ holds.

We first consider the case when $C > \varepsilon$. Obviously, $\tau > \varepsilon$. The optimal solution can be found by differentiating $O_2$ with respect to $\tau$. In this paper, we only consider the case where $O_2''(\tau) > 0(O_2'' = \partial O_2(\tau)/\partial \tau)$, because this is typical for realistic parameter settings (we will discuss the case when $y$ is negative later). Actually, we do have $O_2''(\tau) > 0$ for the whole range of simulations. When $O_2''(\tau) > 0, O_2(\tau)$ must be a convex function on the corresponding interval, and we can obtain a unique minimum $\tau_{opt\_o2}$ using Cardano's method [13]. Furthermore, we must add the constraint $\tau > \varepsilon$. Then, the optimal computing period is $\max(\tau_{opt\_o2}, \varepsilon)$. Recall that we assumed that $\tau > C$ and $C > \varepsilon$, in this case. Thus, the optimal computing period for $C_{pd} > \varepsilon$ is

$$
\hat{\tau}_{p\_2} = \max\left(\tau_{opt\_o2}, C\right). \tag{10}
$$

When $C \leq \varepsilon$, we divide it into interval $\tau \in [C, \varepsilon]$ and $\tau > \varepsilon$. For the case $\tau \in [\varepsilon, +\infty]$, we only need to replace $C$ by $\varepsilon$ because the constraint $C > \varepsilon$ no longer holds. For the case $\tau \in [C, \varepsilon]$, the optimal value can be determined using classical algorithms, because the system rejects all predictions.

Combining all these terms, the optimization algorithm can be expressed as follows.

$$
\begin{cases}
\hat{\tau}_{p\_2} = \max\left(\tau_{opt\_o2}, C\right) & \text{if } C > \varepsilon \\[2mm]
\hat{\tau}_{p\_2} = \max\left(\tau_{opt\_o2}, \varepsilon\right) & \text{if } C \leq \varepsilon < \tau \\[2mm]
\hat{\tau}_{np} = \max\left(C, \min\left(\tau_{opt}, \varepsilon\right)\right) & \text{if } C \leq \tau \leq \varepsilon.
\end{cases}
\tag{11}
$$

We only need to replace $m$ by $m_{lost}$ when $m$ is very large. In fact, the system works well without the predictor and proactive fault tolerance if $m$ is very large.

If we cannot ensure $O_2''(\tau) > 0$, we only need to compute all the non-negative real roots of the corresponding polynomial [13]. The optimal value of $\tau$ is either a root or a sub-interval bound (the roots divide the admissible interval into several sub-intervals).

# 6  Evaluations

Our experiments were based on a simulation framework used by previous works [4, 13]. Section 6.1 describes the simulation framework and our parameter settings, the experimental results are reported in Sect. 6.2, and our observations are discussed in Sect. 6.3.

## 6.1  Simulation Framework

- The simulator: The simulator is a discrete-event simulator which is driven by various events (e.g. failure events, fault tolerance events etc.). First, we input a random trace of faults in the simulator. Then the application will be executed by the simulator. When a failure event occurs, the simulator suspends the application and calculates the corresponding overheads. Then the system will resume the task and add the time delay into the task completion time. A random trace of failure predictions according to the failure trace (we assumed the prediction arriving time follows a uniform distribution [4, 13] ) is generated by the simulator. The accuracy of the predictor is characterized by the recall and precision. A proactive action event is driven by a prediction which is accepted.
- Synthetic failure traces: We used random fault traces with Exponential distribution. The MTBF of the single processor was set as 120 years. In this simulation, the number of processing units of the platform varied from 65,536 (64 k) to 2,097,152 (2M). Thus the system MTBF $m$ varied from 481 min to 30 min.
- Checkpoint and recovery: we took $C = 10$ min and $R = 5$ min. We considered two scenarios for proactive action: $C_p = 0.2C$ or $C_p = 0.6C$. We only considered $D = 3$ min and $\Delta l = 0.8$ in the tests. In fact, this is sufficient for the proof of validity of our model.
- Failure prediction: we used two predictors: one 'ideal' predictor with very high accuracy $(r = 0.85$ and $p = 0.80)$, another 'practical' predictor with $r = 0.60$ and $p = 0.35$ [4].
- In the simulations, we mainly considered two proactive strategies. UPC is the proactive strategy of our work. The SPA is the refined algorithm of Aupy's work [13]. The proactive action of CPC was proactive checkpointing.

- To assess the quality of our model, we compared the 'OPTIMAL' results with its 'BEST' counterparts (defined as the same strategy but using the best possible period $\tau$). The former was computed via our algorithm which is described in Sect. 4. The latter was computed via a numerical search for the optimal period.

## 6.2   Simulation Results of Synthetic Traces

To evaluate our work, we compared the results using the proposed method with the fixed proactive action method. Figures 2 and 3 show the average results for the two proactive policies as a function of the number of processors ($N$). We used MatLab to compute and plot the optimal value of the waste for different $N$. The left plots show the results calculated by using our model. The right plots show the simulation results for the exponential distribution via the discrete-event simulator.

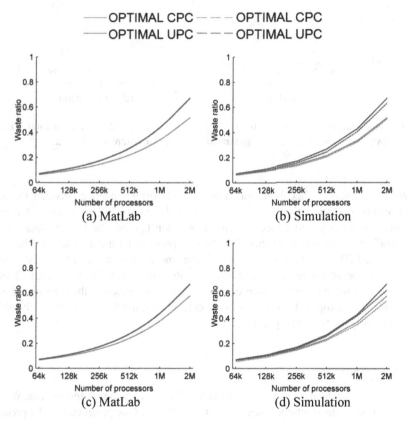

**Fig. 2.** Simulation results with $r = 0.85$, $p = 0.80$, $C_p = 0.2C$, $\varnothing = 0.2$ (first row), $\varnothing = 0.8$ (second row) and with a failure trace generated via different failure distribution.

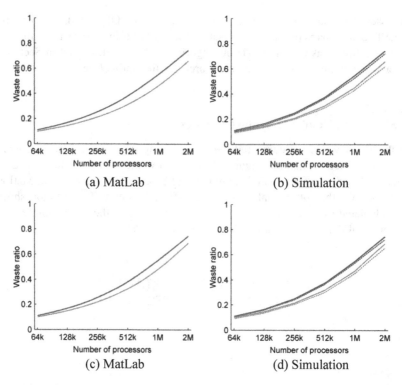

**Fig. 3.** Simulation results with $r = 0.60$, $p = 0.35$, $C_p = 0.2\ C$, $\emptyset = 0.2$ (first row), $\emptyset = 0.8$ (second row) and with a failure trace generated via different failure distribution.

We first observed that there was a very good correspondence between the theoretical results and simulation results. This proves the validity of our model. Due to the conceptual similarity and space limitation, we don't show the results obtained via $C_p = 0.6C$. We also observed that 'OPTIMAL' produced similar results to the corresponding 'BEST' counterparts, even in the most extreme cases. These results demonstrate the accuracy of our optimization algorithm. What's more, Figs. 2 and 3 also show that the uncoordinated proactive C/R is more efficient than the coordinated proactive C/R. Compared with Aupy's model, our approach can dramatically reduce the waste ratio for the large platform.

## 6.3  Case Study

In this section, we assess the impact of the recall and precision on the system. We first ran simulations with synthetic traces for both predictors. One parameter of the predictor was fixed while the other varied. We chose a small platform with 256 k processors

($m$ = 240.6 min) and a large platform with 2M processors ($m$ = 30.075 min). In both cases, we studied the impact of the recall and precision assuming an exponential fault distribution, under scenarios $C_p = 0.2C$ and $C_p = 0.6C$. We first fixed the precision and let the recall vary from 0.2 to 0.99, as shown in Fig. 4. In these four plots, we can see that the recall significantly affected the performance.

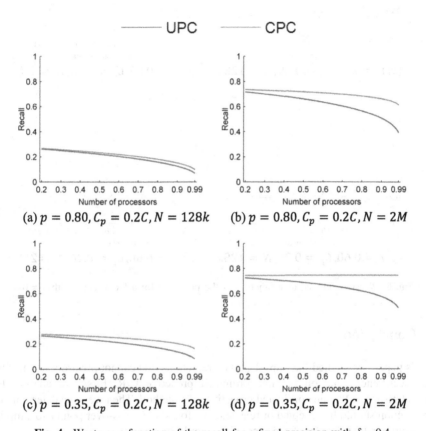

**Fig. 4.** Waste as a function of the recall for a fixed precision with $\delta = 0.4$

Figure 5 shows the results when we fixed the recall and let the precision vary from 0.2 to 0.99. We observed that, like most studies [12, 13], the precision had a minor effect on the performance for the platform.

We conclude that it is more important to focus on improving the recall rather than the precision for the uncoordinated proactive C/R method.

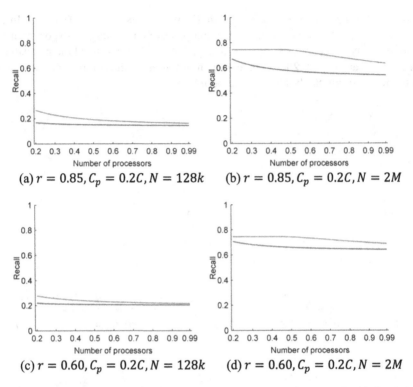

(a) $r = 0.85, C_p = 0.2C, N = 128k$    (b) $r = 0.85, C_p = 0.2C, N = 2M$

(c) $r = 0.60, C_p = 0.2C, N = 128k$    (d) $r = 0.60, C_p = 0.2C, N = 2M$

**Fig. 5.** Waste-overhead as a function of the precision for a fixed recall with $\delta = 0.4$

## 7   Conclusion

In this paper, we studied the impact of the predictions that cannot precisely identify the fault-occurrence time on the uncoordinated proactive C/R. First, we analyze the characteristics of the uncoordinated proactive C/R method. Then we have determined if a prediction should be accepted or rejected. We found the cross-over point $\varepsilon$ to simplify the arbitrator that decides if the prediction should be accepted.

We ran simulations involving synthetic failure traces following exponential distribution. These experiments proved that our model is valid. The evaluation results also indicate that our approach can effectively reduce the waste caused by failures and fault tolerance operations. In our case study, we showed that the recall of the predictor is more important than the precision.

In the further, we will expand this work to hierarchical C/R protocols.

# References

1. Robert, F.: What it'll take to go exascale. Science **27**, 394–396 (2012)
2. Sato, K., Moody, A., Mohror, K., Gamblin, T., et al: Design and modeling of a non-blocking checkpointing system. In: The 2012 International Conference for High Performance Computing, Networking, Storage and Analysis (SC 2012), Article No. 19 (2012)
3. Cappello, F.: fault tolerance in petascale/exascale systems: current knowledge, challenges and research opportunities. Int. J. High Perform. Comput. Appl. **23**, 212–226 (2009)
4. Zheng, Z., Lan, Z., Gupta, R., Coghlan, S., Beckman, P.: A practical failure prediction with location and lead time for blue gene/p. In: Dependable Systems and Networks Workshops (DSN-W 2010), pp. 15–22 (2010)
5. Varela, M.R., Ferreira, K.B., Riesen, R.: Fault-tolerance for exascale systems. In: 2010 IEEE International Conference on Cluster Computing Workshops and Posters (CLUSTER WORKSHOPS), pp. 1–4 (2010)
6. Leonardo, B.G., Seiji, T., Komatitsch, D., Cappello, F., Maruyama, N., et al.: FTI: high performance fault tolerance interface for hybrid systems. In: Proceedings of 2011 International Conference for High Performance Computing, Networking, Storage and Analysis, pp. 1–32 (2011)
7. Moody, A., Bronevetsky, G., Mohror, K., Bronis, R., et al.: Design, modeling, and evaluation of a scalable multi-level checkpointing system. In: Proceedings of the 2010 ACM/IEEE International Conference for High Performance Computing, Networking, Storage and Analysis (SC 2010), pp. 1–11 (2010)
8. Jangjaimon, I., Tzeng, N.F.: Adaptive incremental checkpointing via delta compression for networked multicore systems. In: The 27th IEEE International Symposium on Parallel & Distributed Processing (IPDPS 2013), pp. 7–18 (2013)
9. Gainaru, A., Cappello, F., Kramer, W.: Taming of the shrew: modeling the normal and faulty behavior of large-scale HPC systems. In: IEEE 26th International Parallel & Distributed Processing Symposium (IPDPS), pp. 1168–1179 (2012)
10. Gainaru, A., Cappello, F., Kramer, W., Snir, M.: Fault prediction under the microscope—a closer look into hpc systems. In: The 2012 International Conference for High Performance Computing, Networking, Storage and Analysis(SC 2012), Article No. 77 (2012)
11. Yu, L., Zheng, Z., Lan, Z., Coghlan, S.: Practical online failure prediction for bluegene/p: period-based vs event-driven. In: Dependable Systems and Networks Workshops (DSN-W), pp. 259–264
12. Mohamed, S.B., Gainaru, A., Leonardo, B.G., Franck, C., et al.: Improving the computing efficiency of HPC systems using a combination of proactive and preventive checkpointing. In: The 27th IEEE International Symposium on Parallel & Distributed Processing (IPDPS 2013), pp. 501–512 (2013)
13. Aupy, G., Robert, Y., Vivien, F., Zaidouni, D.: Checkpointing algorithms and fault prediction. J. Parallel Distrib. Comput. **74**(2), 2048–2064 (2014)
14. Elnozahy, E.N.M., Alvisi, L., Wang, Y.M., Johnson, D.B.: A survey of rollback-recovery protocols in message-passing systems. ACM Comput. Surv. **34**, 375–408 (2002)
15. Bosilca, G., Bouteiller, A., Brunet, E., Cappello, F., et al.: Unified model for assessing checkpointing protocols at extreme-scale. Concurrency Computat **26**, 2772–2791 (2014)
16. Ifeanyi, P., Egwutuoha, D.L., Bran, S., Shiping, C.: A survey of fault tolerance mechanisms and checkpoint/restart implementations or high performance computing systems. J. Supercomputing **65**(3), 1302–1326 (2013)

17. Lan, Z., Gu, J.X., Zheng, Z.M., Thakur, R., et al.: Dynamic meta-learning for failure prediction in large-scale systems: A case study. In: Proceedings OfInternational Conference on Parallel Processing, pp. 157–164 (2008)
18. Nakka, N., Agrawal, A., Coudhary, A.: Predicting node failure in high performance computing systems from failure and usage logs. In: IEEE Workshop on Dependable Parallel, Distributed and Network-Centric Systems, pp. 1557–1566 (2011)
19. Gainaru, A., Cappello, F., Snir, M., Kramer, W.: Fault prediction under the microscope: a closer look into HPC systems. In: proceedings of the International Conference on High Performance Computing (SC 2012), Article No. 77 (2012)

# Tunneling-based Multi-path Routing Mechanism in Packet-Switched Non-Geostationary Satellite Networks

Guyu Hu[1], Zhaofeng Wu[1(✉)], Fenglin Jin[1],
Bowei Yang[2], Yu Song[1], and Yinjin Fu[1]

[1] PLA University of Science and Technology,
Nanjing 210007, People's Republic of China
qqk20080915@163.com
[2] School of Aeronautics and Astronautics, Zhejiang University,
Hangzhou 310027, People's Republic of China

**Abstract.** A new tunneling-based multi-path routing mechanism tailored for the packet-switched non-geostationary (NGEO) satellite networks is proposed and evaluated. The proposed routing mechanism exploits both the predictable topology and inherent multi-path property of the NGEO satellite networks to construct the tunnels between satellites. The ingress satellite distributes the traffic along the tunnels to the egress satellite while the egress satellite sends the feedback packets periodically along the tunnels. The maximum link utilization along each tunnel is retrieved via the feedback packet, thus the ingress satellite could form a partial global view of the network congestion status and adaptively move the traffic from the over-utilized tunnels to the under-utilized tunnels. The simulation results corroborate the improved performance of the proposed mechanism compared with the existing in the literature, and also verify the proved convergence property corresponding to the Wardrop equilibria.

**Keywords:** NGEO Satellite Networks · Dynamic routing · Load balancing · Tunneling · Multi-path routing · Traffic engineering · Wardrop equilibria

## 1 Introduction

The packet-switched NGEO satellite networks with inter-satellite links (ISLs) are of particular interest among researchers for its advantages, such as the comparable end-to-end delay with the terrestrial networks and the relaxed power requirement for the hand-held devices. Notwithstanding all its merits, the drawbacks induced by the dynamics of the NGEO satellite networks, e.g. the variance of the ISL length and the discontinuous operation of the ISLs, make the routing a daunting challenge. Several routing mechanisms of the early works were proposed to shield the dynamics of the constellations [1]. Yet due to the non-homogeneous distribution of the users around the globe, the satellites covering

© Springer International Publishing Switzerland 2015
G. Wang et al. (Eds.): ICA3PP 2015, Part IV, LNCS 9531, pp. 729–742, 2015.
DOI: 10.1007/978-3-319-27140-8_50

the dense population areas may easily get congested while others are under-utilized at the same time [3], it is also pivotal for the routing algorithm to be able to achieve a balanced traffic distribution in the NGEO satellite networks. This paper proposes the tunneling-based multi-path routing (TMPR) mechanism in the NGEO satellite networks. TMPR makes use of both the predictable topology and multi-path property of the NGEO satellite networks to construct the tunnels between satellites. The ingress satellite distributes the traffic along the tunnels according to the splitting ratio associated with each tunnel and adjusts the splitting ratios periodically based on the feedback packets initiated from the egress satellites. Compared with the existing researches, TMPR shows the following advantages: (1) adaptability, each satellite could form a partial global view of the network congestion status and adapt proactively to the unbalanced traffic distribution across the satellite network; (2) convergence, the NGEO satellite networks employing the TMPR mechanism could converge to the Wardrop equilibria [14,25]; (3) the signaling overhead in TMPR is also carefully managed. The simulation results corroborate the improved gains of the proposed mechanism.

This paper is organized as follows. Section 2 presents the related works along with the motivation of the proposed mechanism. Section 3 describes the network model briefly while the detailed TMPR mechanism is delineated in Sect. 4. Section 5 gives the simulation results and discussion. Finally, concluding remarks are drawn in Sect. 6.

## 2   Related Works

Routing in NGEO satellite networks has been the subject of considerable study since 1990s [1]. The routing mechanisms originally proposed were connection-oriented [27]. As the IP traffic gradually dominates the Internet, the connection-less routing becomes the hot topic. The former studies mainly focused on the mechanism to shield the dynamics of the NGEO satellite networks and found a feasible path to reduce the end-to-end delay, e.g. the datagram routing algorithm based on the virtual node routing strategy [8] and the Dijkstra's shortest path (DSP) routing based on the virtual topology routing strategy [6,17]. This type of routing algorithm assumes the light traffic load on the NGEO satellite networks and the propagation delay between neighboring satellites is the main factor that contributes to the whole end-to-end delay. As the earth is mostly covered by sea and the majority of the hot spots are located in the northern hemisphere, the routing with load-balancing capability is of great importance to avoid congestion, thus improves the efficiency the NGEO satellite networks.

As has been pointed out in [11] that the first consideration of the routing in the satellite network is the dissemination of the network state information. From this point of view, Franck et al. [12] firstly provided the criterion for the classification of the routing algorithm, that is the static routing vs. the adaptive routing which can be further classified into the isolated routing vs. the non-isolated routing. Then, they evaluated a number of routing strategies and pointed out that the adaptive and non-isolated routing is superior provided that the signaling overhead of the distribution of the network status is properly managed.

Motivated by the traffic concentration at the higher latitudes, Mohorčič et al. [18] proposed the alternate link routing (ALR) strategy. ALR tries to distribute the traffic via alternate links and reduces the traffic peak effectively. However, the ability of ALR to achieve a better traffic distribution across the network is limited. Then Mohorčič et al. [16] proposed the traffic dependent routing (TCD) which classifies the traffic as different classes. TCD tries to optimize the routes for each traffic class with specified QoS requirement, e.g. routing the throughput-intensive traffic via the path with the maximum available bandwidth. The simulation model in [16] assumes that the network state is updated before the routing tables are calculated. Yet the signaling overhead induced by the network status distribution, as pointed out in [12], could also harm the routing performance significantly.

Bai et al. [3] proposed the compact explicit multi-path routing (CEMR) algorithm for the LEO satellite networks. CEMR assigns an orbit speaker for each orbit to periodically collect and exchange the link status of its representative orbit. Based on the network status from the orbit speaker, CEMR calculates two disjoint paths to the destination satellite and evenly distributes the traffic along these two paths, which takes limited advantage of the multi-path properties of the satellite networks. Aiming at reducing the routing overhead, Papapetrou et al. [19] presented the location-assisted on-demand routing (LAOR). On receiving the user's communication request with specific QoS requirement, the satellite searches for the path to the destination satellite proactively. The satellite set reached by the request packets is limited to the area formed by the request area formation process, thus reducing the signaling overhead compared with that incurred by the periodic distribution of the network status. Yet for a large number of users with frequent requests, the routing overhead could still be staggeringly high. Rao et al. [20] proposed the agent-based load balancing routing (ALBR). ALBR employs two kinds of agents, i.e. the mobile agent to explore the available paths and the stationary agent to calculate the routes based on the information from the mobile agents. The mobile agent explores the random-chosen destination, thus could cause unnecessary routing overhead if there is no traffic to the corresponding destination. Besides, although LAOR and ALBR actively probe the satellite network status, yet considering the relative long propagation delay of the satellite network and the highly variable traffic pattern, both mechanisms could fail to obtain the actual network status.

Taleb et al. [24] proposed the explicit load balancing (ELB) scheme which capitalizes on the congestion information exchanged between neighboring satellites to avoid the packet dropping due to the already congested neighboring satellite. Once receiving the congestion notification from the neighboring satellite, a proper portion of packets whose next hop is the congested satellite are diverted to another path that excludes the already congested neighboring satellite. Guanghua et al. [23] extends the idea of ELB and brought forward the traffic light based routing (TLR) mechanism. Moreover, TLR introduces the public waiting queue to exploit the fact that often one or two links of the satellite are highly utilized while the rest are used lightly or even idle. Both ELB and TLR effectively reduce the routing overhead due to the information exchanged between the neighboring satellites, but the diverted traffic could possibly incur cascaded congestion on other satellites.

Yet for the already proposed routing mechanisms, either the multi-path property of the NGEO satellite networks is not effectively utilized or just local congestion information is used lacking even the partial congestion status of the satellite network. In this paper, we propose the tunneling-based multi-path routing mechanism for the packet-switched NGEO satellite networks. The simulation results show that the proposed mechanism not only achieves a balanced traffic distribution across the satellite network, but could also converge to the Wardrop equilibria which denotes a stable network state [4].

## 3   Network Model

The topology of the NGEO satellite network is dynamic due to the motion of the NGEO satellites, and the virtual topology strategy [27] is adopted to shield the dynamics of the NGEO satellite constellation in this paper. The dynamic topology of the NGEO satellite network can be regarded as a series of snapshots each of which corresponds to a static yet temporary topology of the satellite network. In each snapshot, the satellite network can be denoted as a directed graph $G = (V, E)$ where $V$ is the set of the satellites and $E$ denotes the set of the inter-satellite links in the network. Each directed link $e, e \in E$ is with a positive, continuous and non-decreasing cost function $c_e : \mathbb{R}_+ \to \mathbb{R}_+$. We define the commodity $i \in I = \{1, \ldots, n\}$ as the traffic demand from the source node $s_i$ to the destination node $d_i$, thus each commodity $i$ can be represented by the ordered source-destination pair $\langle s_i, d_i \rangle \in V \times V$. For each commodity $i \in I$, $D_i > 0$ denotes the demand from $s_i$ to $d_i$. Let tunnel $t$ be defined as an acyclic directed path from node $s_i$ to node $d_i$, and there exists multiple tunnels to deliver the demand $D_i$ in the network $G$. All the tunnels from node $s_i$ to $d_i$ form a set which is denoted by $T_i$. Figure 1 depicts just a pair of source and destination satellites sending data and feedback packets respectively. Note that there could exist a number of source-destination pairs simultaneously in the network and the inter-satellite links are highly coupled. Let $f_t, t \in T_i$ represent the flow on the tunnel $t$ connecting the node $s_i$ to node $d_i$ and $T = \cup_{i \in I} T_i$ denotes the available tunnels in the network. Then the load on the directed link $e \in E$ can be represented by $f_e = \sum_{t \in T, e \in t} f_t$. For the tunnel $t$, the cost function, which is also known as the payoff function, corresponding to the tunnel thus can be the combination of the link cost along the tunnel, i.e. $c_t(f) = com\{c_e(f_e), e \in t\}$ where $com\{\cdot\}$ can be the summation of the delay over the links, e.g. in the transportation system, or any other metric imposed on the tunnel, e.g. the maximum link utilization along the tunnel. Then the weighted average cost of commodity $i \in I$ is given by:

$$C_i(f) = \sum_{t \in T_i} \frac{f_t}{D_i} c_t(f) \tag{1}$$

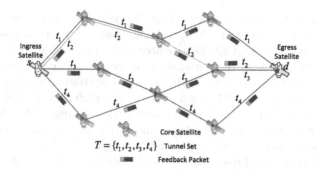

**Fig. 1.** The TMPR mechanism.

A non-negative flow vector $(f_t), t \in T$ is feasible if it satisfies the flow demands, i.e.,

$$\sum_{t \in T_i} f_t = D_i \quad \forall i \in I \tag{2}$$

$$f_t \geq 0 \quad \forall t \in T$$

In the evolutionary game model [26], the flow vector $(f_t), t \in T$ is interpreted as a population vector. Specifically, we assume infinite number of agents each of which wants to send an infinitesimal amount of data through the network, and $f_t$ is the fraction of agents sending their load over the tunnel $t$. Agents aim at minimizing their own cost without considering the effect on the global congestion. One could fairly assume that the agents would come to a flow allocation where no agent could improve its own gains by deviating from its current tunnel. This is exactly what the Wardrop equilibrium trying to convey. Formally, we have:

**Definition 1 (Wardrop Equilibrium [25]).** *A feasible flow vector $(f_t), t \in T$ is at Wardrop eqilibrium if for every commodity $i \in I$ and tunnels $t_1, t_2 \in T_i$ with $f_{t_1} > 0$ it holds that $c_{t_1}(f) \leq c_{t_2}(f)$.*

In the NGEO satellite networks, each satellite acts as a router connected with one or more terminals on the ground while each terminal could send data up to the satellite which we call the ingress satellite. In spite of the dynamic topology of the satellite networks, TMPR takes advantage of the predictable topology of the NGEO satellite networks to construct the tunnels, i.e. the control center on the ground could in advance use proper methods, e.g. the top $K$-shortest path algorithm, to compute the $K$ tunnels that connect any two satellites in each snapshot. With proper technique, e.g. the multi-protocol label-switching routing mechanism [7] or the source routing [23], the ingress satellite thus could determine the tunnel where the packets take to reach the egress satellite from which the packet are sent down to the destination terminals.

As has been previously noted that the routing mechanism with load balancing capability is of great importance in the NGEO satellite networks, and TMPR is designed for the satellite router to be able to adapt to the variable nature of the traffic due to both the dynamics of satellite network and the inhomogeneous distribution of the population. As the satellite network spans across the globe, the routing coordination of all the satellites under the central control paradigm is obviously insensitive to the outburst of the traffic that is especially common in the NGEO satellite networks. TMPR is thus a distributed routing mechanism employed on each satellite. Although each satellite under the TMPR mechanism acts on its own behalf to minimize the cost $C_i(f_t)$ on any of its tunnels, there still exists a flow vector $(f_t), t \in T$ that converges relatively fast to the Wardrop equilibria under the collective cooperation among the satellites.

There has been lots of researches on the Wardrop equilibria under the replicator dynamics [2,4,10,15,21,22] all of which adopt the additive path cost, i.e. the cost of the path is the sum of the link cost along the path. As we focus on the load balancing of the NGEO satellite networks, the tunnel cost in the proposed mechanism is the maximum link cost along the tunnel, i.e. $c_t(f) = \max\{c_e(f_e), e \in t\}$, which can also be denoted as bottleneck game [5,9,13]. However, the relation between the bottleneck game and the replicator dynamics hasn't been well investigated, e.g. although the work in [9] considers the maximum link utilization, the backing theory is still the Wardrop equilibria with the additive path cost. In this paper, we point out explicitly that the bottleneck game with the link cost as the simple link utilization conforms to the non-atomic potential game whose equilibrium state, i.e. Wardrop equlibria, can be reached by the replicator dynamics. The convergence property of the TMPR mechanism is also verified by the simulations.

## 4    Proposed TMPR Mechanism

There are three schemes, i.e. cost information gathering (CIG), splitting ratio adjustment (SRA) and satellite status monitoring (SSM) in the TMPR mechanism. The CIG scheme is responsible for the dissemination of the network status information while the SRA scheme is used for the route computation. The SSM scheme reduces the signaling overhead effectively.

### 4.1    Cost Information Gathering

In the CIG phase, the ingress satellite delivers the traffic along the tunnels according to the splitting ratio associated with each tunnel once the data arrives at the ingress satellite. For the satellite acting as an egress point, the satellite maintains a feedback timer which fires at regular interval denoted by $I_{cig}$. When the timer times out, the egress satellite sends the feedback packets along all the tunnels to the ingress satellite. The feedback packet gathers the maximum link utilization along the tunnel where the intermediate satellite checks if its output link utilization along the tunnel is greater than the link utilization in the packet in which case it overwrites the utilization with its own. Once the feedback packet reaches the ingress satellite, the latest tunnel utilization denoted by $u_{t,k}$

is recorded as the $k$th value corresponding to the tunnel $t$. Then the utilization of the tunnel $t$ represented by $u_t$ can be updated using the iterative exponential averaging:

$$u_t = (1 - \lambda)u_t + \lambda u_{t,k}, \forall k \in \mathbb{N} \tag{3}$$

where $0 < \lambda < 1$.

## 4.2  Splitting Ratio Adjustment

The SRA phase involves only the ingress satellite which maintains the splitting ratio adjustment timer that fires at regular interval $I_{sra}$. When the timer fires, the ingress satellite updates the splitting ratio corresponding to each tunnel based on the maximum link utilization along the tunnels. The updating procedure is similar to that in [4,13]. Specifically, suppose there is the stable traffic demand $D_i > 0$ between the ingress satellite $s_i$ and egress satellite $d_i$ during a short period. $\forall i \in N, t \in T_i, p_t$ represents the traffic splitting ratio associated with the tunnel $t$ such that $\sum_{t \in T_i} p_t = 1$. Then $C_i(f)$ becomes the weighted average maximum link utilization of the tunnels between the ingress satellite $s_i$ and egress satellite $d_i$ and can be reformulated as follows:

$$C_i(f) = \frac{\sum_{t \in T_i} f_t \cdot u_t}{D_i} \tag{4}$$

Then the ingress satellite updates the temporary splitting ratio $\tilde{p}_t$ corresponding to the tunnel $t$ as follows:

$$\tilde{p}_t = \max\{0, p_t + \Delta p_t + \xi\} \tag{5}$$

where $0 < \xi \ll 1$ is a random variable enabling the ingress satellite to explore the alternate tunnels and $\Delta p_t$ can be calculated as follows:

$$\Delta p_t = \frac{f_t}{D_i}(C_i(f) - u_t) \tag{6}$$

Finally, the ingress satellite normalizes the new splitting ratio $p_t^{new}$ corresponding to the tunnel $t$:

$$p_t^{new} = \frac{\tilde{p}_t}{\sum_{t' \in T_i} \tilde{p}_{t'}} \tag{7}$$

It is emphasized that the feedback packet is treated as normal data packets and could be dropped due to the link congestion. When the splitting ratio adjustment timer fires, there could be no feedback packet corresponding to the tunnel $t$ during the last $I_{sra}$ interval, in which case the value $u_t$ is simply set to 1.0 indicating that the tunnel is congested.

### 4.3   Satellite Status Monitoring

The SSM module monitors the status of the ingress satellite $s$ that whether the satellite $s$ is actively sending the traffic destined to itself. Each satellite maintains the satellite status monitoring timer and the timestamp vector $\overrightarrow{TS}$ with length $|V| - 1$. The element $ts_s \in \overrightarrow{TS}$ represents the most recent time that the satellite has received data destined to itself from the satellite $s$. When the satellite received a packet from the satellite $s$, the value $ts_s$ is updated as the current time. When the timer that fires at regular interval $I_{ssm}$ times out, the satellite checks each value $ts_s \in \overrightarrow{TS}$ and sees if the current time is larger than the value $ts_s$ beyond $I_{ssm}$ in which case the satellite stop sending the feedback packets to the satellite $s$. It is in this way that the SSM scheme avoids the unnecessary exploration of the tunnels and reduces the signaling overhead.

### 4.4   Convergence of the TMPR Mechanism

Let $C_e$, $C_{max}$ and $C_{min}$ denote the capacity of the link $e \in E$, the maximum and minimum link capacity of the whole network respectively. As has been noted in Sect. 3 that the payoff function of the tunnel $t \in T$ for any mixed strategy profile $f$ is:

$$c_t(f) = \max\{c_e(f_e), e \in t\} \tag{8}$$

where $c_e(f_e) = \frac{f_e}{C_e}, e \in E$. It is clear that the payoff function $c_t(f)$ is a Lipschitz-continuous, convex and non-decreasing scalar function. Although not everywhere differentiable, the value of the sub-differential of $c_t(f)$ is bounded between $\frac{1}{C_{max}}$ and $\frac{1}{C_{min}}$. The typical capacity of link in the production network is Mbps or even Gbps, so the value of $c_t'(f)$ can be approximated as zero. Thus for any two commodities $i, j \in I$, we have:

$$\frac{\partial c_t(f)}{\partial \hat{t}} \approx \frac{\partial c_{\hat{t}}(f)}{\partial t}, t \in T_i, \hat{t} \in T_j \tag{9}$$

So the game considered in this paper can be regarded as the potential game [22].

If we ignore the boundary condition $max\{\cdot\}$ and the random variable $\xi$, the Eq. (5) then translates into the following equation:

$$\tilde{p}_t - p_t = \Delta p_t = \frac{f_t}{D_i}(C_i(f) - u_t) \quad t \in T_i, i \in I \tag{10}$$

The splitting ratio $p_t$ corresponding to the tunnel $t$ is proportional to the flow $f_t$, thus if the $I_{sra}$ interval is small enough, then the left side of the Eq. (10) becomes the differential of the splitting ratio $p_t$ corresponding to the tunnel $t$. We thus have:

$$p_t' = p_t(C_i(f) - u_t) \quad t \in T_i, i \in I \tag{11}$$

where $p_t(0) = p_{t,0}$ is the initial traffic splitting ratio corresponding to tunnel $t, t \in T_i, i \in N$. Equation (11), i.e. the replicator dynamics, is a set of differential equations representing the dynamics of the whole network.

As has been proved in [10] that the Eq. (11) can converge to the Wardrop equilibria provided that the initial traffic splitting ratio satisfies $p_{t,0} > 0$. Moreover, the variable $\xi$ can be regarded as the dynamic perturbation mentioned in [15] which states that the time-average of the traffic flows of sufficiently patient agents is still concentrated in a neighborhood of evolutionary stable equilibria. Thus TMPR has the provable convergence property.

### 4.5  Considerations Regarding the TMPR Mechanism

The TMPR mechanism is similar to some parts of the TeXCP [13] proposed for the terrestrial networks. Yet there are three crucial aspects in the TMPR mechanism different from the load balancing mechanism of the TeXCP. First and foremost, TeXCP employed sophisticated measures to stabilize the link utilization of the network while TMPR mechanism is in fact a discrete version of the replicator dynamics which has been proved to be able to converge to the Wardrop equilibria in the potential game. Secondly, instead of the probing packets initiated by the ingress router in the TeXCP, TMPR adopts the feedback packets originating from the egress satellites to obtain the maximum link utilization along the tunnels. The underlying reason lies in the relatively large end-to-end delay of the satellite networks compared with that in the terrestrial networks such that the probing packets could probably get a stale link utilization of the network when reaching the ingress satellites. Finally, as the buffer in the satellite is limited, $I_{sra}$ is set to a value slightly larger than the value of $I_{cig}$, thus enabling the ingress satellites to react timely to the congestion of the satellite network before its dropping packets. All in all, TMPR is a self-sustaining routing mechanism suitable for the NGEO satellite networks and can adapt to the variable traffic in a simple and efficient way.

## 5    Performance Evaluation

### 5.1  Simulation Setup

To evaluate the proposed TMPR mechanism, we use the NS2 as the simulation tool to conduct the simulations in an Iridium-like NGEO satellite network. The polar constellation contains 6 orbits each with 11 satellites. Each satellite typically maintains 4 ISLs to its neighbors. The capacity of ISLs and the link capacity between satellite and terminal are set to 25Mbps. The average packet size is set to 1000Bytes and the queue length is set 100 packets. We adopt the virtual topology mechanism [27] to shield the dynamics of the satellite network and therefore the topology of the satellite network is represented by a series of snapshots each of which corresponds to a static yet temporary topology of the satellite network. In each snapshot, we exploit the top $K$-shortest path algorithm to construct the tunnels between any two satellites. At the end of each snapshot, the tunnels in the next snapshot is loaded and used for routing. Besides, the source routing technique is employed in the TMPR mechanism to simplify the actual implementation of the tunnel in the NS2.

We utilize 1200 ON-OFF flows and the ON/OFF period of each flow follows a Pareto distribution with the shape of 1.5. The average burst and idle time are both set to 200 ms. The source terminals send data with varying rates from 0.3 Mbps to 0.75 Mbps. The $\xi$ is a random variable uniformly chosen from $(0, 0.1)$. The tunnel number $K$ between any two satellites is set to 4 while the values of $I_{cig}$, $I_{sra}$ and $I_{ssm}$ are set to 200 ms, 210 ms and 4 s respectively. The value of $\lambda$ is set to 0.9 and the reason is to comply with the latest network congestion status as accurate as possible. The initial traffic splitting ratio $p_{t,0}$ corresponding to the tunnel $t \in T_i, \forall i \in I$ is simply set to $1/K$. The user distribution model is the same as that in [23, 24].

We also evaluate the TLR mechanism and the DSP routing algorithm under the same scenario for the comparison. The performance metrics considered in this paper are the packet drop rate, ideal packet drop rate, throughput, average delay and traffic distribution index. The ideal packet drop rate is the total number of the dropped packets without the dropped packets between the satellites and the terminals divided by the total packets sent out by the source terminals. The average delay denotes the mean of the end-to-end delay between all the sending and receiving terminals on the ground. The traffic distribution index is used to indicate how well the traffic is distributed across the network and has been defined in [24]. The higher the traffic distribution index is, the better the traffic distributes across the network. We finally analyze the stability of the TMPR mechanism. The simulation duration is 20.51 s the same as that in [23] and the simulation for each of the three routing mechanisms under different sending rates were conducted 10 times.

## 5.2   General Performance Metrics

Figures 2, 3, 4, 5 and 6 show the packet drop rate, ideal packet drop rate, throughput, average delay and traffic distribution index for both the three routing mechanisms. From Figs. 2, 3, 4, 5 and 6 we could in general conclude that both TLR

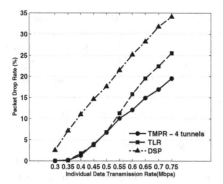

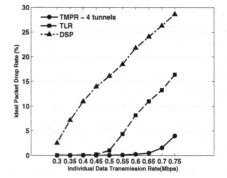

**Fig. 2.** The packet drop rate for different sending rates.

**Fig. 3.** The ideal packet drop rate for different sending rates.

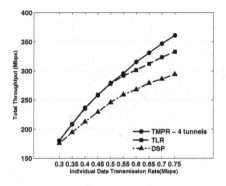

**Fig. 4.** The total throughput for different sending rates.

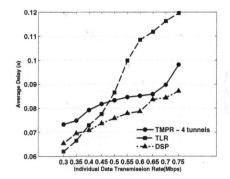

**Fig. 5.** The average delay for different sending rates.

and TMPR mechanisms are more effective compared with that of the DSP algorithm excluding the average delay. In terms of the packet drop rate and the ideal packet drop rate, both TLR and TMPR are more or less the same under the light network load, yet as the network load increases, the packet drop rate, especially the ideal packet drop rate, under the TMPR mechanism grows more slowly compared with that of the TLR mechanism. It is because the TMPR could form a partial global view of the network to react to the congestion of not only the neighboring satellites, but also the core satellites along the tunnels. Moreover, the ideal packet drop rate curve shows that a large portion of the packets under TMPR mechanism has reached the egress satellites, yet has been dropped due to the limited downlink rate and the buffer size between the egress satellites and the ground terminals. The asymmetric nature of the uplink and downlink rates exist in both the GEO satellites as well as the wireline networks on the ground. The future NGEO satellite networks could, to a large extent, be as asymmetric as current networks, thus the TMPR mechanism could be more suitable for the future NGEO satellite networks. The reduced packet drop rate results in the increased throughput, as shown in Fig. 4. However, as both the TMPR and the TLR mechanisms try to send the packets to its destinations via alternate tunnels and links, the average delay is large compared with the DSP algorithm, as shown in Fig. 5. Since the TMPR mechanism attempts to send the traffic on all its tunnels, the average delay is large compared with the TLR mechanism even at the light traffic load. As the number of the hops that the packets take under the TMPR mechanism are bounded by the tunnels, the average delay thus is bounded resulting in the reduced average delay compared with the TLR mechanism under higher traffic load. The traffic distribution index for the three mechanisms is shown in Fig. 6. Because the DSP algorithm only tries the shortest path, the traffic is thus distributed across a limited set of the links in the network, so the traffic distribution index is low compared with the TMPR and TLR mechanisms. As the users' sending rate increases, the former under-utilized links gradually become over-utilized while the former over-utilized links remain

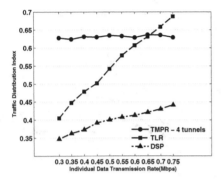
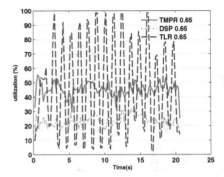

**Fig. 6.** The traffic distribution index for different sending rates.

**Fig. 7.** The link utilization between two specified satellites.

unchanged, so the traffic distribution index of DSP increases. The TLR could avoid congestion of neighboring satellites dynamically and it is also confirmed by the traffic distribution index of TLR which increases in accordance with the users' sending rates. For TMPR, the ingress satellite tries to balance the traffic all the time, so the traffic distribution index is high under light traffic load. As the tunnels in TMPR are fixed, the increased traffic could only distribute across the same limited links, so the traffic distribution index is almost constant. All in all, the TMPR mechanism shows the overall improved performance compared with the that of the TLR and DSP routing mechanisms.

### 5.3  Convergence Property of the TMPR Mechanism

We pick the inter-satellite link between two neighboring satellites randomly and measure its link utilization during the simulation period. The corresponding link utilization under the data transmission rate 0.65 Mbps is shown in Fig. 7. It is clear that the link utilization under both the TMPR and DSP mechanisms are relatively stable while the link utilization under TLR mechanism shows drastic oscillation. The traffic between any two satellites under the DSP routing algorithm follow the same paths due to the static routes generated by DSP, so the link utilization under the DSP routing algorithm shows less variance. However, as TLR reacts to the congestion provided the queue length of the link is beyond a certain threshold which signifies a certain congestion on the corresponding satellite, and the simultaneous congestion avoidance measures taken by the neighboring satellites of the congested satellite can easily cause the oscillation on the congested link and the cascaded congestion on other satellites, as can be seen from the link utilization curve of TLR in Fig. 7. The TMPR mechanism, on the other hand, tries to balance the traffic on all the available tunnels, thus the link utilization curve shows less variance compared with the TLR mechanism. The perturbation of the link utilization under TMPR and DSP mechanisms are mainly from the variable nature of the ON/OFF traffic pattern. The utilization of the rest of the links in the network show similar results and are omitted here for brevity. The simulation results also verify that the TMPR mechanism could converge relatively fast to the Wardrop equilibria, thus stabilize the network under the dynamic traffic pattern.

# 6    Conclusion

This paper proposes and evaluates the TMPR mechanism proposed for the packet-switched NGEO satellite networks. The core idea, i.e. tunnels, behind the proposed mechanism relies on the exploitation of the predictable topology and the inherent multi-path property of the NGEO satellite networks. The tunnels acting as the manageable resource not only collaboratively support the traffic but could also limit the routing overhead. Ample simulation experiments provide corroboration of the enhanced performance along with the convergent property corresponding to the Wardrop equilibria for the proposed mechanism.

**Acknowledgment.** This work was supported by the grants from the National High Technology Research and Development Program of China (863 Program) under No. 2012AA01A510 and NO. 2012AA01A509 and was also partially supported by the National Science Foundation of China (NSFC) under grant NO. 61402518. The authors also would like to thank Prof. Jennifer Rexford for the valuable advice.

# References

1. Alagöz, F., Korçak, Ö., Jamalipour, A.: Exploring the routing strategy in next-generation satellite networks. IEEE Wirel. Commun. **7**(4), 79–88 (2007)
2. Altman, E., Boulogne, T., El-Azouzi, R., Jiménez, T., Wynter, L.: A survey on networking games in telecommunications. Comput. Oper. Res. **33**(2), 286–311 (2006)
3. Bai, J., Li, X., Li, Z., Peng, W.: Compact explicit multi-path routing for leo satellite networks. In: Proceedings 2005 High Performance Switching Routing Workshop, pp. 386–390 (2005)
4. Borkar, V.S., Kumar, P.R.: Dynamic cesaro-wardrop equilibration in networks. IEEE Trans. Autom. Control **48**(3), 382–396 (2003)
5. Cole, R., Dodis, Y., Roughgarden, T.: Bottleneck links, variable demand, and the tragedy of the commons. In: Proceedings of the 17th Annual ACM-SIAM Symposium on Discrete Algorithms, SODA 2006, pp. 668–677. Miami, FL, USA, January 2006
6. Dijkstra, E.W.: A note on two problems in connexion with graphs. Numer. Math. **1**(1), 269–271 (1959)
7. Donner, A., Berioli, M., Werner, M.: Mpls-based satellite constellation networks. IEEE J. Sel. Areas Commun. **22**(3), 438–448 (2004)
8. Ekici, E., Akyildiz, I.F., Bender, M.D.: A distributed routing algorithm for datagram traffic in leo satellite networks. IEEE/ACM Trans. Netw. **9**(2), 137–147 (2001)
9. Fischer, S., Kammenhuber, N., Feldmann, A.: Replex-dynamic traffic engineering based on wardrop routing policies. In: Proceedings 2nd Conference on Future Networking Technologies, CoNext 2006, pp. 6–17. Lisboa, Portugal, December 2006

10. Fischer, S., Vöcking, B.: On the evolution of selfish routing. In: Albers, S., Radzik, T. (eds.) ESA 2004. LNCS, vol. 3221, pp. 323–334. Springer, Heidelberg (2004)
11. Franck, L., Maral, G.: Routing in networks of intersatellite links. IEEE Trans. Aerosp. Electron. Syst. **38**(3), 902–917 (2002)
12. Franck, L., Maral, G.: Static and adaptive routing in ISL networks from a constellation perspective. Int. J. Satell. Commun. **20**, 455–475 (2002)
13. Kandula, S., Katabi, D., Davie, B., Charny, A.: Walking the tightrope: responsive yet stable traffic engineering. In: Proceedings ACM SIGCOMM (2005)
14. Matthias, E., Thomas, F., Lars, O.: Sensitivity of wardrop equilibria. Theor. Comput. Syst. **47**(1), 3–14 (2010). http://dx.doi.org/10.1007/s00224-009-9196-4
15. Mertikopoulos, P., Moustakas, A.L.: Selfish routing revisited: degeneracy, evolution and stochastic fluctuations. In: Lasaulce, S., Fiems, D., Harrison, P.G., Vandendorpe, L. (eds.) 5th International ICST Conference on Performance Evaluation Methodologies and Tools Communications, VALUETOOLS 2011, Paris, France, 16–20 May 2011, pp. 217–226. ICST/ACM (2011). http://dx.doi.org/10. 4108/icst.valuetools.2011.245732
16. Mohorčič, M., Švigelj, A., Kandus, G.: Traffic class dependent routing in isl networks. IEEE Trans. Aerosp. Electron. Syst. **40**(4), 1160–1172 (2004)
17. Mohorčič, M., Švigelj, A., Kandus, G., Werner, M.: Performance evaluation of adaptive routing algorithms in packet-switched intersatellite link networks. Int. J. Satell. Commun. **20**, 97–120 (2002)
18. Mohorčič, M., Werner, M., Švigelj, A., Kandus, G.: Alternate link routing for traffic engineering in packet-oriented ISL networks. Int. J. Satell. Commun. **19**, 463–480 (2001)
19. Papapetrou, E., Karapantazis, S., Pavlidou, F.N.: Distributed on-demand routing for leo satellite systems. Comp. Netw. **51**(15), 4356–4376 (2007)
20. Rao, Y., Wang, R.: Agent-based load balancing routing for leo satellite networks. Comp. Netw. **54**(17), 3137–3195 (2010)
21. Roughgarden, T., Tardos, É.: How bad is selfish routing? J. ACM **49**(2), 236–259 (2002)
22. Sandholm, W.H.: Potential games with continuous player sets. J. Econ.Theor. **97**, 81–108 (2001)
23. Song, G., Chao, M., Yang, B., Zheng, Y.: TLR: A traffic-light-based intelligent routing strategy for NGEO satellite IP networks. IEEE Trans. Wirel. Commun. **13**(6), 3380–3393 (2014)
24. Taleb, T., Mashimo, D., Jamalipour, A., Kato, N., Nemoto, Y.: Explicit load balancing technique for NGEO satellite IP networks with on-board processing capabilities. IEEE/ACM Trans. Netw. **17**(1), 281–293 (2009)
25. Wardrop, J.G.: Some theoretical aspects of road traffic research. Proc. Inst. Civil Eng, Part 2 **1**, 325–378 (1952)
26. Weibull, J.W.: Evolutionary Game Theory. MIT press, Cambridge (1995)
27. Werner, M., Delucchi, C., Vögel, H.J., Maral, G., Ridder, J.J.D.: ATM-based routing in LEO/MEO satellite networks with intersatellite links. IEEE J. Sel. Areas Commun. **15**(1), 69–82 (1997)

# Cost-Effective Scheduling Analysis Through Discrete Event Simulation for Distributed Systems

Siti Fajar Jalal[✉], Masnida Hussin, Abdullah Muhammed, and Rohaya Latip

Department of Communication Technology and Networks,
Faculty of Computer Science and Information Technology,
University Putra Malaysia (UPM) Serdang, 43400 Seri Kembangan,
Selangor, Malaysia
fajarupm@gmail.com,
{masnida,abdullah,rohayalt}@upm.edu.my

**Abstract.** Large computing systems where globally distributed can be best characterized by their dynamic nature particularly in terms of resource provisioning and scheduling. Users of the systems normally aim to maximize their own interest when consuming the shared resources. Apart from that, the processing requirements that submitted by the systems' users are diverse in their properties (e.g., size, priority). This condition makes the resources in distributed system overwhelmed by heterogeneity of task to be processed; that leads to fluctuation in resource availability. There are researchers' proposed scheduling algorithms and evaluated through simulation system in order to improve resource availability. It is because the simulation system is able to save cost rather than real test bed experimental. In response to this, we proposed priority-based scheduling algorithm for improving resource availability that developed using discrete-event simulation approach. We defined several events in the simulation to represent various execution statuses that used to monitor resource state in the distributed systems. Our simulation system successfully gives better performance in terms of waiting time compared than other works that also used simulation as their experimental platform.

**Keywords:** Discrete event simulation · Task scheduling · Cost-Effective computing · Distributed systems · Heterogeneous resources

## 1 Introduction

Along with rapid growth of modern distributed system (e.g., Grid, Cloud), IT community is also facing an operational cost problem in order to provide comprehensive computing support. In response to the issue, some organizations have introduced an ideology of computational-effective resource allocation [1, 2]. One of its aims is to provide comprehensive processing activity without excessive operational cost. Basically, in the distributed systems there are massive computations that happen mostly 24/7 to process large number of users' tasks. Therefore, it is a huge challenge to sustain

© Springer International Publishing Switzerland 2015
G. Wang et al. (Eds.): ICA3PP 2015, Part IV, LNCS 9531, pp. 743–755, 2015.
DOI: 10.1007/978-3-319-27140-8_51

better performance and fulfil all processing requirements in distributed systems especially in dynamic computing environment. The computing resources are also needed to be regularly maintained to sustain their processing power. Therefore, in order to stabilize computing expenses, we needed effectively to consider heterogeneity in both resources and users' tasks in resource management.

Task scheduling algorithm is one of the important factors that influence the system optimal performance [3–5]. A task scheduler is important in managing distribution of users' tasks to available resources that according to scheduling policy. In scheduling algorithm for heterogeneous environment, basically, the schedulers consider several criteria of the tasks and resources in order to find the best suitable match between them. It aims for providing an efficient resource management while improving the resource utilization. The efficiency of resource management can be achieved through effective scheduling and allocation decision strategies. In order to satisfy the systems' users, both strategies are typically used several performance metrics, such as response time, speedup, or throughput. Meanwhile, better performance in execution becomes an indicator for the resource providers to show their reliability in processing. It mainly involved many evaluation processes for analyzing processing satisfaction for users and providers in resource management.

In order to analyse the effectiveness in processing activities in distributed system, many researchers are used simulation approach for their experimental system. The fundamental advantage of the simulators is their independence to the execution platform while constructing large and complex network model. It has been used extensively as a way to evaluate and compare scheduling strategies as simulation experiments are configurable, repeatable and generally fast. The authors in [6] has listed three advantages of implementing simulation as follows:

- Experimental cost of time is compressed:
  It takes lengthy of time to implement dynamic task scheduling in real distributed systems but through simulation, the duration of operation or execution is shorten and can be controlled and save cost.
- Reduced analytic requirements:
  Researchers from wider background of expertise have an opportunity to perform analysis systems without to study complex systems in prior.
- Models can be easily demonstrated:
  Researchers are capable to understand the simulation system that they developed for analysing experiment results. The interpretation of the results also can be made easily and reduced time.

One of popular simulation approach that used for investigating task scheduling problem is Discrete Event Simulation (DES) [7–9]. Basically, DES approach drives toward an analytical study with an overall understanding of the behaviour of a system. Through DES, a visualization of a scheduling algorithm can be obtained and responsive solution can be planned and assigned to any understandable problem. DES improves the flexibility of the system that make it easier to use. We can manipulate scheduling and execution parameters (e.g., response time, waiting time, and throughput) with respect to investigational purposes for producing different results of study.

In this work, we addressed cost-effective scheduling through prioritization of queue in resource site. Our task scheduling approach has been modelled through Discrete Event Simulator (DES) that develops by using C++ programming language. We defined the scheduling events in the simulation that aims to control task-resource matching process while monitoring system performance. Next, we embedded the queuing policy as part of our scheduling approach to identify the effect of the queue size towards waiting time. Results from our simulator demonstrate that the task waiting time is subjected to the number of available resources in the system. The scheduling events of our simulator are capable to deal with heterogeneous computing environment while achieving better waiting time.

The remainder of this paper is organized as follows. Section 2 describes related work on energy management using scheduling approach. Section 3 details the models used in the paper. Our design of event-based simulator is presented in Sect. 4. Experimental settings and results are presented in Sect. 5. Finally, Sect. 6 concludes the paper.

## 2   Related Works

Many researchers exercised simulation as part of their methodology in distributed systems. One of the factors promoting this approach is because there are several of good simulation tools that use to model the distributed computing environment. The authors in [10] introduced SimJava simulation toolkit for heterogeneous resource modelling and scheduling simulation that uses a basic discrete event simulation infrastructure. The Simgrid version 2 gives a higher level abstraction to build a complex simulation with the ability to support large number of resources and applications. The GridSim toolkit [8] has also been widely used in distributed computing system that means to study issues in Grid. Particularly, they provide scalable and extensible simulation engine to make them possible for simulating the arbitrary network topologies, dynamic compute and network resource availabilities, as well as resource failure. Expectedly, the simulation tools are difficult to use by others contexts than the ones for which they were intended. Moreover, only few of them are sufficiently documented and maintained over time that hinder the comparison of published results. In response to that, we developed our own scheduling simulator using discrete event approach.

There are studies on dynamic task scheduling that developed using their own simulation systems. Zikos and Helen [11] performed their experimental results by using a simulation model to evaluate the performance and energy behaviours in three different scheduling policies. Their scheduling policies are applied on Local Scheduler (LS) for distributing tasks to resources with assumption that LSs have all the information of resources in the system. Our work also applied the same assumption for studying our scheduling strategy. Authors in [12] evaluated the scheduling performance using DES for heterogeneous environment. The simulation events in their simulation system are identified through arrival and departure events. Their work initialized computing environment that runs the arrival of tasks through class Cluster. Each of the tasks that arrive into the system is denoted by class Transaction where the information of task is kept. Each of processors is represented by class Processor.

There are two arrays that assigned for class Processor are service rate and power consumption. Unlike from their work, we do not dedicate any class for our system component in order to simplify our simulation system.

# 3   The Models

## 3.1   System Model

Our system model consists of users that submitted their tasks to the available resources. The tasks initially submitted to global scheduler (GS) that is connected to other resource sites. In order to handle the tasks distribution successfully, the system model is designed based on hierarchical structure. There is local scheduler (LS) at each resource site that connected directly to GS. The LS in the site is responsible to assign tasks to its processors for execution. Figure 1 shows the hierarchical structure of our system model.

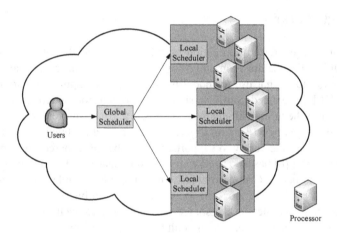

**Fig. 1.** System model

With the intention to address the heterogeneity of distributed systems, the resource sites contain a set of processors and each processor composes with different number of cores. The speed of all cores in a particular processor is homogeneous but may different with core speed in another processor. Hence, there is heterogeneity issue in task scheduling that required to handle for effective resource allocation decisions.

In response to two schedulers; GS and LS, there is various queue sizes that needs to take into account in making the allocation decisions. Both schedulers have their own task queues; global-queue (gq) that resides in GS while local-queue (lq) occupying for LS. For each LS in the systems, there is other three local queues, lq (i.e., low -pq, med-pq and high-pq) for handling the tasks that have different priorities. Note that, the tasks are been prioritizing only in local-queue, lq. Hence, LS is responsible to generate task's priority when the task arrived at the resource site. The tasks prioritization technique is based on our previous work [9] that used both requested time (rt) and actual runtime (art) of each task. Specifically, if art of a task is at least 70 % of rt, it is determined as high priority; meanwhile if its art is at most 20 %, the task is determined as low priority. Otherwise, the task is considered as medium priority. We use Eq. (1) to identify the priority of tasks in lq.

$$task\,priority = artrx100\%$$ (1)

## 3.2 Dynamic Scheduling Model

In response to improve system performance while managing cost-effective processing in the system, we designed dynamic scheduling model in our simulation system. Due to there are different priorities among tasks, we designed an adaptive queuing policy in both queues (i.e., gq and lq). For each incoming task in the system, the GS will be provided a sign based on its arrival time. The sign of a task si is used to monitor the current status of the task in the system. For example, GS can checked either the task is still in the local-queue or already been processing. Basically, there are three stages of task completion; (i) arriving, (ii) waiting and (iii) executing. The task will be monitored according to those completion stages. We assumed that each task completion stage represents as a fraction 1/3; ratio 1:3. The value of sign $s_i$ will be reduced according to fraction of reduction as given in Table 1. Hence, for each task, the value of $s_i$ denotes arrival time subtracted fraction of reduction for the stage.

Table 1. Fraction of reduction in completion stage

| Stage of completion | Fraction of reduction |
|---------------------|----------------------|
| Arriving | 0 |
| Waiting | 1/3 |
| Executing | 2/3 |

Meanwhile, the queuing policy in local-queue, lq is based on first-come-first-serve (FCFS) queuing policy. It is because the tasks in lq are already in their particular queue that depends on their priority. For the resource allocation, we implemented several policies as follows:

Policy 1:  Every task is assigned based on the processing capacity of available processor. The fitness value is created to identify the suitability between processor capacity and task priority. This policy is concerned on tasks with high priority from *high-pq*. It will be assigned to the processor that gives the highest fitness value.

Policy 2:  In this policy, the tasks are randomly assigned into available processors. It improves the resource allocation by minimizing task waiting time and maximizing resource utilization. This policy is meant for low priority task that queued in *low-pq*.

The LS uses the first policy to schedule the tasks in med-pq. However, if it is detected that the waiting time keeps increasing, it will switch into the second policy for scheduling the task. In response to cost-effective processing, we used a power-threshold [8] to define processing power limit for every processor. It aims to prevent the processors from overwhelmed from the executing process. The processing power limit is defined based on the system's load; either light-loaded or weight-loaded. The lightly loaded in the system is identified when the difference of average task waiting time and minimum waiting time is at least 80 % of average waiting time; else, the system is in heavy loaded. To ensure the effectiveness of our priority-based task scheduling, every processor's power limit is monitored. If a processor reaches its power limit, the newly incoming task will be then assigned to other available processor.

## 4  Event-Based Scheduling Simulator

### 4.1  Simulation Model

We designed our simulation structure by identifying key events. There are several events in our DES that identified to fulfil task queuing and task-resource matching processes. We used a main function called scheduler() for controlling alternation between the queuing and matching processes. The scheduler() mainly checked the all event schedule that provides the information of arrival time, waiting time, requested processing time, execution time and finish time. If the actual execution time is smaller than the requested time, the scheduler() will then updated the number of tasks, otherwise the task is considered as null value. It aims to calculate the number of successful task that meets their processing requirements. To ensure that the right event occurs at the right time, the scheduler() function spots the closest event time and calls the appropriate events according to the time order. Through the simulation, the scheduler() checks the event time regularly and the nearest or the smallest event time will be called by returning the type of event to be called back to the system. Initially, the simulation defines all the variables including random number and simulation clock. The arrival time of every task is set to be in random manner and independent from each other's. It allows then to be in sequential and processed separately.

Specifically, the main events in our simulation model are arrival() and departure() events. The arrival() event denotes the submission time of task into the system and the departure() event refers to time when the task leaves the system. The arrival() event is focusing on obtaining the task information from the workload trace, then scheduled them into the respective queue (i.e., gq and lq). We introduced two sub-events are GS() and LS() that represent procedures for Global Scheduler and Local Scheduler, respectively. The system used *GS()* event for obtaining task parameters (e.g., requested time (rt) and actual runtime (art)) from the workload trace. The event also capable to schedule the tasks into *gq* according to FCFS policy. In response to monitoring the stage of completion status, we designed a function called *sign()* function inside *GS()* event in order to calculate and trace all tasks in the systems. The information of the current completion status of each task will be kept in a table at *GS()* event. Note that, the *sign()* function merely activated when the task departed from *gq* for matching process at LS. The table is frequently updated in order to gain up-to-date information of tasks that are still in operating in the system. In the *GS()* event, there is *power()* function to identify light-loaded and weight-loaded of the system workload. Hence, the tasks from *gq* will be assigned to the resource site that gives light-loaded state. It aims to avoid the tasks been dropped by the LS; due to full occupied queue in *lq*. The calculation of light-loaded and weight-loaded is same as discussed in Sect. 3 (Fig. 2).

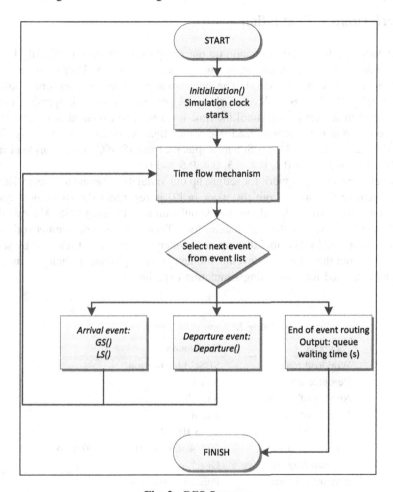

**Fig. 2.** DES Structure

The tasks are then assigned to the resource site where the LS() event started to operate. The LS() event calculated the priority of the incoming tasks and scheduled into respective lq that according to the level of task's priority (i.e., (i.e., low-pq, med-pq and high-pq). We assumed that the LS have the information about its processors. It allows LS() event to perform resource-task matching process to find the most suitable processor for the task. When the processor is allocated for the task and started the execution process, the LS() event will the blocked the processor by changing the processor's flag to 1 (occupied). When the execution process is completed, the main function, scheduler() calls the departure() event to send back the task to user. Once the departure() event is activated, the LS() event will set the processor's flag to 0 (free). Hence, the LS() event can assigned another task into the processor to fulfil the user's demand. The process continues until all the tasks have been executed.

## 5    Performance Evaluation

We conduct a performance evaluation on our developed simulator to identify its level of performance. The performance metric used to analyse our simulator is queue waiting time that measured in second (s). The queue waiting time, or sometime known as queuing delay [9, 13], is defined as the total period of time task spends from the beginning of its arrival into gq until the time it starts to be executed in processor. We used two different existing workload traces the High Performance Computing Center North (HPC2N) and San Diego Supercomputer Center (SDSC) Blue workload traces with the workload factor 0.1, 0.2, 0.3, 0.4, 0.5 and 0.6.

We refer our previous work for setting up our simulation parameters, as in Table 2. The different in this work from the work in [9] is regarding the simulation system, where in this work we designed our own simulation system using DES. Meanwhile, in [9] they used GridSim as their evaluation tool. There are open source network simulators or commercial simulators that are now widely available, that released by several developers. Note that, the well-develop simulation tools provide a library of functions that can be utilized for conducting simulation experiment.

**Table 2.**  Simulation parameters

| Parameter | Description |
|---|---|
| Workload trace | SDSC blue horizon |
| Resource sites | 4 to 8 |
| Number of processors | 8 to 20 |
| Number of cores | 2 to 8 |
| Core speed of a processor | 50 to 100 MIPS |
| Number of tasks | 200, 400, 600, 800 and 1000 tasks |
| Programming language | C++ |
| Inter arrival time | Poisson distribution |

## 6    Result and Discussion

In this section, we discuss the result of the performance evaluation from the simulation system. We analysed the effectiveness of our scheduling approach that investigated through our simulator (CEDES) compared to simulator that developed using Grid simulation toolkit (GridSim). Next, we study the impact of number of resource sites that involved in the system towards queuing time.

### 6.1    Result 1: Priority-Based Scheduling in Two Different Simulation Designs

Figures 3 and 4 show the queue waiting time between CEDES and simulation tool, Ref. Tool that used in [9]. Both studied on the HPC2N and SDSC Blue workload traces with load factor of 0.1, 0.2, 0.3, 0.4, 0.5 and 0.6. It shows that the queue waiting times for both simulations are increased when the load factor increases. Interestingly, the queue waiting time of CEDES generates same pattern of the results of Ref.Tool for both workload traces. However, the queuing time shows better result when it is been investigated using simulation tool. It is due to the different specification of machine that used to run the simulation. Furthermore, programming library from the simulation toolkits helps the queuing policy to approximately emulate real task scheduling. Meanwhile, our simulation system is designed with effective functions and procedures using C++ programming language. We conclude that discrete event simulation approach is capable to use for analysing scheduling problem in heterogeneous environment.

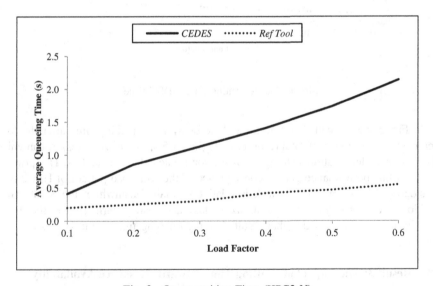

**Fig. 3.** Queue waiting Time (HPC2 N)

### 6.2    Result 2: The Impact of Waiting Time Towards System Size

In this experiment, we investigate on how waiting time is influenced by the size of resource sites that setin CEDES. Results from the Figs. 5 and 6 shows that both workload traces give comparable output. From the figures, it clearly demonstrates the minimizing of queuing time when there is many resource sites in the systems; it assumed that many resources are available to perform task execution. This also can be happened when the scheduling decisions are able to comparatively allocate the task into its suitable resource that reduces task waiting time in the queue. It indicates that the waiting time is explicitly effected by the system sizes. We claimed that our simulator closely represent the real scheduling scenario.

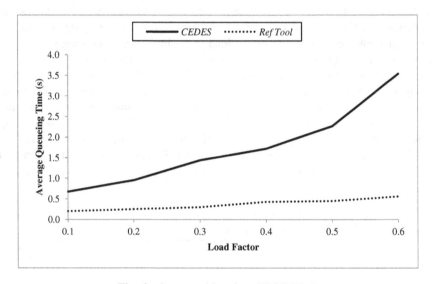

**Fig. 4.** Queue waiting time (SDSC Blue)

In Fig. 5 we noticed that there is a slope of average queuing time after the load factor 0.5 in both range of total resource sites (i.e., 4-5 sites and 7-8 sites). Meanwhile, Fig. 6 shown degradation pattern when the load reached to factor 0.6. The primary source of this performance gain is consequence of the workload pattern of HPC2 N— considering the overall size of task is relatively small. Meanwhile, the SDSC Blue workload exhibits huge variation in size of task and load pattern. Hence, the queue capacity becomes overloaded that results lengthy queuing time in the systems.

### 6.3    Result 3: The Impact of Waiting Time Towards Resource Availability

Table 3 shows result of the processing ratio of resources in both HPC2N and SDSC Blue workload traces. In this experiment we set the number of sites into two different mode; static (i.e., 4 sites) and dynamic (i.e., 4-6 and 4–8). As expected, the processing ratio is increased when we have fixed number of resource sites in the systems. With the dynamic resource site setting, it indicates that our simulator works well with the fluctuation of resource availability with minimal task waiting time. The also demonstrates the waiting time of SDSC workload is slightly higher than HPC2N workload which gives the same performance pattern in the previous experiment (Result 2). Hence, we claimed that our simulation system that designed through DES provides cost-effective processing without needed complex and comprehensive functions and procedures for queuing policy while effectively improving the system performance.

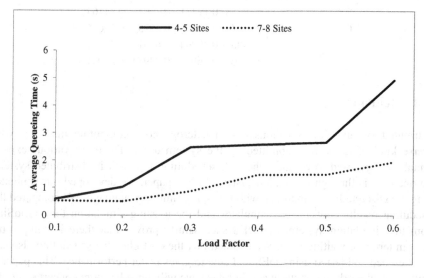

**Fig. 5.** Queue waiting time (HPC2N)

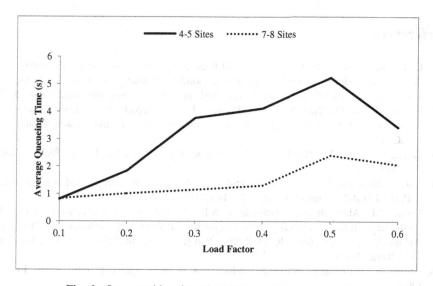

**Fig. 6.** Queue waiting time (SDSC Blue) (Color figure online)

**Table 3.** Processing ratio of resource sites

| Workload Traces | HPC2N | | SDSC Blue | |
|---|---|---|---|---|
| Load Factor | 4 sites | 4-8 sites | 4 sites | 4-8 sites |
| 0.1 | 0.13309 | 0.06634 | 0.15474 | 0.10189 |
| 0.2 | 0.33166 | 0.16412 | 0.27531 | 0.16969 |
| 0.3 | 0.38218 | 0.19471 | 0.4094 | 0.24769 |
| 0.4 | 0.63378 | 0.23508 | 0.5525 | 0.29665 |
| 0.5 | 0.79067 | 0.29994 | 0.6951 | 0.41991 |
| 0.6 | 0.92503 | 0.36956 | 0.98974 | 0.59051 |

## 7 Conclusion

Distributed systems consists thousands of heterogeneous computing machines with diverse kind of tasks that submitted by the system users. There are various experimental strategy used to evaluate the task scheduling approach in distributed system, and one of it is through simulation system. In this paper, we developed our simulator using the Discrete Event approach with C++ programming language. We compared the scheduling results between our simulator and the existing simulation tool, GridSim. From the simulation system, our DES successfully proves that there is comparable result in terms of waiting time. We claimed that the cost-effective scheduling also can be developed and tested using DES and able to gives better performance. This paper is only an initial work of our study and in future, we will consider more concerns into the study to map the dynamic heterogeneous attribute of a more complex and large system.

## References

1. Calheiros, R.N., Buyya, R.: Cost-Effective provisioning and scheduling of deadline-constrained applications in hybrid clouds. In: Wang, X., Cruz, I., Delis, A., Huang, G. (eds.) WISE 2012. LNCS, vol. 7651, pp. 171–184. Springer, Heidelberg (2012)
2. Zhu, M.M., Wu, Q., Zhao, Y.: A cost-effective scheduling algorithm for scientific workflows in clouds. In: IEEE 31st Int'l Performance Computing and Communications Conference (IPCCC) (2012)
3. Gupta, K., Singh, M.: Heuristic based task scheduling in grid. Int. J. Eng. Technol. **4**(4), 254–260 (2012)
4. Liu, C., Baskiyar, S.: A general distributed scalable grid scheduler for independent tasks. J. Parallel Distrib. Comput. **69**(3), 307–314 (2009)
5. Hussin, M., Abdullah, A., Subramaniam, S.K.: Adaptive resource allocation for reliable performance in heterogeneous distributed systems. In: Aversa, R., Kołodziej, J., Zhang, J., Amato, F., Fortino, G. (eds.) ICA3PP 2013, Part II. LNCS, vol. 8286, pp. 51–58. Springer, Heidelberg (2013)
6. Chung, C.: Simulation modeling handbook: A practical approach. CRC Press, Florida (2004)
7. Moschakis, I.A., Karatza, H.D.: Evaluation of gang scheduling performance and cost in a cloud computing system. J. Supercomput. **56**(2), 975–992 (2012)

8. Buyya, R., Murshed, M.: GridSim: A Toolkit for the modelling and simulation of distributed resource management and scheduling for Grid computing. Concurrency Comput. Pract. Experience **14**(13), 1175–1220 (2002)

9. Hussin, M., Lee, Y.C., Zomaya, A.Y.: Priority-based scheduling for large-scale distribute systems with energy awareness. In: Proceedings of the 2011 IEEE Ninth International Conference on Dependable, Autonomic and Secure Computing. Sydney, Australia: IEEE Computer Society (2011)

10. Casanova, H., Legrand, A., Quinson, M.: SimGrid: a generic framework for large-scale distributed experiments. In: 10th Int'l Conference on Computer Modelling and Simulation, p. 126–131. IEEE Computer Society (2008)

11. Zikos, S., Karatza, H.D.: Performance and energy aware cluster-level scheduling of compute-intensive jobs with unknown service times. Simul. Model. Pract. Theor. **19**(1), 239–250 (2011)

12. Terzopoulos, G., Karatza, H.: Energy-efficient real-time heterogeneous cluster scheduling with node replacement due to failures. J. Supercomput. **68**(2), 867–889 (2014)

13. Eryilmaz, A., Srikant, R.: Fair resource allocation in wireless network using queue-length-based scheduling & congestion control. IEEE/ACM Trans. Netw. **15**(6), 1333–1344 (2007)

# Energy Consumption Prediction Based on Time-Series Models for CPU-Intensive Activities in the Cloud

Juan Li[1], Xiao Liu[2], Zhou Zhao[2], and Jin Liu[1(✉)]

[1] State Key Laboratory of Software Engineering,
Wuhan University, Wuhan 430072, China
ljwuse2012@whu.edu.cn, mailjinliu@yahoo.com
[2] Shanghai Key Laboratory of Trustworthy Computing,
East China Normal University, Shanghai 200241, China
xliu@sei.ecnu.edu.cn

**Abstract.** Due to the increasing energy consumption in cloud data centers, energy saving has become a vital objective in designing the underlying cloud infrastructures. A precise energy consumption model is the foundation of many energy-saving strategies. This paper focuses on exploring the energy consumption of virtual machines running various CPU-intensive activities in the cloud server using two types of models: traditional time-series models, such as ARMA and ES, and time-series segmentation models, such as sliding windows model and bottom-up model. We have built a cloud environment using OpenStack, and conducted extensive experiments to analyze and compare the prediction accuracy of these strategies. The results indicate that the performance of ES model is better than the ARMA model in predicting the energy consumption of known activities. When predicting the energy consumption of unknown activities, sliding windows segmentation model and bottom-up segmentation model can all have satisfactory performance but the former is slightly better than the later.

**Keywords:** Cloud computing · Energy consumption prediction · Time-series model · Time-series segmentation

## 1 Introduction

Cloud computing is a new and popular platform used in industry and academia which refers to a business model for delivering resources (e.g. computing, storage, network and software services) in the form of utility over the Internet [1]. Cloud computing adopts a pay-as-you-go model, which provides available, convenient, on-demand network access to the sharing resource pool. This model makes the interaction among the data center, network, service providers and users more rapidly and implements the self-management of computing systems. Users can obtain and release their computing and storage resources in a more flexible and economical fashion. However, with the promising application of cloud computing and the growing demands for big data processing, the amount of energy consumed of cloud infrastructure is rising at a fast speed [2]. According to a study in China Net (http://www.china.com.cn/), the electricity consumed by China Unicom data center is 9.9 billion KWH each year. Globally,

© Springer International Publishing Switzerland 2015
G. Wang et al. (Eds.): ICA3PP 2015, Part IV, LNCS 9531, pp. 756–769, 2015.
DOI: 10.1007/978-3-319-27140-8_52

the total power consumed by information and communication technology accounts for roughly 8 % of the world's total power consumption. Clearly, there will be a surprising result if we consider all the power consumption of the cloud computing systems in the world together. Therefore, improving the energy efficiency and reducing the power usage is a critical challenge and concern for cloud computing.

Currently, many efforts have been made to improve the energy efficiency in cloud systems [3–5, 7, 8]. It is well known that the more the number of active servers, the higher the energy consumption is in the cloud. Based on this, the virtualization technology used to manage the cloud resource try to reduce the number of active servers to save energy [3]. Besides, using Dynamic Voltage/Frequency Scaling (DVFS) to adjust the voltage dynamically according to the requirement of processing speed is another feasible solution to reduce the processor energy consumption but it has limited range of application [4]. Some technology reduces the energy consumption from the perspective of resources utilization, such as live migration, task consolidation, resource consolidation. Live migration refers to a process of moving a running virtual machine or workload between different servers [5, 7, 8]. The under-utilized resources can merge into a new one by live migration, which has reduced the resource waste and improved the energy efficiency. Combining task consolidation or resource consolidation can get better resource utilization. And furthermore, it can reduce the energy consumption by turning off the servers or put them into sleeping mode. However, all these technologies did not consider the relationship between system energy consumption and the characteristics of the system configurations and the application workloads.

In addition, the quality of service (QoS) is an important requirement in designing the system. Guaranteeing the targeted QoS is a condition before reducing the energy consumption. Some research has devoted to exploring the relationship between system performance and energy consumption. Swinburne University has designed an automatic performance and energy consumption analysis tool for cloud applications, named StressCloud. It can model the cloud application workloads, and generate the load tests automatically, and finally profile the system performance and energy consumption [6]. Besides, many attempts have been made to model the energy consumption of cloud system. The most commonly used method is modeling the energy consumption with the multiple linear regressions [9, 10]. However, there are many uncertainty factors affecting the energy consumption of the system, some of which is difficult to monitor.

In this paper, we focus on the energy consumption of the cloud system for running CPU-intensive activities. As a fact that the power series can be gotten directly, we use the time-series models to address this problem. Overall, we analyze and model the energy consumption from two aspects. First, for a known CPU-intensive activity, we can use its historical power data to model its energy consumption and further make a prediction by using traditional time-series models such as ARMA(Autoregressive-Moving-Average) and ES (Exponential Smoothing). Second, for a new-coming CPU-intensive activity, we can find its similar statistical time-series pattern from the historical time-series patterns obtained by the time-series segmentation model such as sliding windows and bottom-up. Afterwards, we can make a prediction about the power consumption of the new activity. Finally, we demonstrate and compare the prediction results with different models which are essential for the relationship analysis between different workloads, different system configuration and system energy consumption.

To the best of our knowledge, this paper is the first to apply time-series segmentation models to predict the energy consumption of CPU-intensive activities in the cloud.

The rest of the paper is organized as follows: Sect. 2 presents some related work of the energy research in cloud. Section 3 describes the background and the overview of energy consumption prediction strategy. The process of predicting the energy consumption based on time-series model is shown in Sect. 4 in detail. Section 5 shows the experiment environment and the performance evaluation results. Finally Sect. 6 offers the conclusion of the paper and a discussion of the future work.

## 2  Related Work

Energy consumption in cloud systems is a hot research topic for the past several years. Many policies and technologies have been taken to save the energy consumption of cloud system. Virtualization [11, 12] is a mature technology which is a key feature of cloud systems that can improve the system efficiency and save the computing resource. Different with the other environment, the virtualization technologies in the cloud contains the computing resource virtualization, the network resource virtualization and the storage resource virtualization and so on [13, 15]. Virtualization is considered as the preconditions to resource or power management in cloud data center. The work in [9] designs an energy saving approach which combines task consolidation into virtualization, considering that the energy consumption of under-utilized resources in the cloud is wasted and abundant. But it does not consider the characteristics of the tasks and the resource configuration. The work in [14] explores the energy cost of the virtual machine and proposes an energy-efficient framework concerned with cloud architectures which can save 25 % of the computing nodes' electrical consumption. Dynamic voltage and frequency scaling (DVFS) is a feasible solution to reduce the processor energy consumption in the cloud server side. Depending on the circumstances, it can not only decrease or increase the voltage used in a CPU dynamically, but also change the clock frequency. During some idle time, energy consumption can be reduced by lowering the clock frequency and decreasing the voltage [17]. Live migration between different virtual machines greatly improves the efficiency of resource management and reduces the waste of cloud resources. First-Fit Decreasing (FFD), Best-Fit and Worst-fit are frequently used algorithms [16]. These technologies are able to reduce the system energy consumption and improve the resource utilization to a large extent. However, no specific energy consumption models have been proposed so far.

Some existing study has made efforts on analyzing the relationship between the system performance and the energy consumption in the cloud. The work in [21] explores the performance and energy consumption data with different system configurations and three types of tasks: computation-intensive, data-intensive and communication-intensive in the cloud system. Furthermore, it proposes an analysis tool StressCloud for cloud system to profile and visualize the relationship between system performance and energy consumption with different tasks and system configurations. The results of these studies can be used for designing energy monitors and guiding the system configurations. But these research works did not analyze the energy data further and propose an efficient energy consumption model.

Extensive studies have been dedicated to predicting the energy consumption of cloud system. The work in [18] proposed a system-wide energy consumption model for servers by combing the server energy consumption with its thermal envelope. Most existing predicting approaches represent the power consumption as a linear model that correlates with CPU utilization, memory access count, hard disk I/O rate and network I/O rate and so on. Study has proved that 60 % of the power can be used when the CPU is at full speed [20]. Based on this phenomenon, many researches establish the energy consumption model related with the peak power and the idle power [19]. These studies have proposed an energy consumption prediction model based on a linear model or polynomial models. However, time-series models and the type of the tasks have been ignored. In this paper, we analyze the energy consumption data in cloud for CPU-intensive activities and predict the energy consumption with time-series models. Furthermore, we investigate the energy model from two aspects: traditional time-series models (AMRA, ES) [22, 23] for known activities and the time-series segmentation models for unknown activities respectively. The experimental results show that the performance of ES model is better than AMRA model for predicting the energy consumption when there are historical power data available. Meanwhile, the performance of sliding window segmentation model is a slightly better than the bottom-up segmentation model in the prediction of unknown activities.

## 3   Strategy Overview

There are various types of activities running in different quantities in the cloud. To reduce energy consumption, when we are planning to run a specific CPU-intensive activity in the cloud, we need to predict its energy consumption before we reserve the resource and schedule the task. If the activity has been run before and its historic energy consumption has been recorded, its energy consumption can be calculated and predicted by the traditional time-series models, such as the ARMA $(p, q)$ and ES, which are depicted as $T$ (short for traditional as in this paper). As for a new activity, traditional time-series models are not practical since there is no historic trace for their energy usage. However, by a test run for a small period of time, we can obtain its similar statistical time-series pattern from the historical time-series patterns using the time-series segmentation model, which is depicted as $S$ (short for segmentation in this paper). In the meantime, we notice that some systems record the power for running an activity on some discrete time points while some other may record the energy consumption in a continuous fashion. Since the energy consumption can be simply calculated with the power and the duration of the activity, we focus on the power prediction of CPU-intensive activities in this paper without losing generality.

The prediction process is described as follows. Our prediction strategy is consisted of four phases: power series building, power series segmentation, power pattern recognition & matching and power predicting, just as shown in Fig. 1. The inner ring represents the main factors which influence the energy consumption of system. It contains three basic aspects: the characteristics of workload activities (like the number of the requests, the problem size etc.), the performance of the various resources (including metrics such as CPU use, disk reads and writes, storage resource etc.), and the

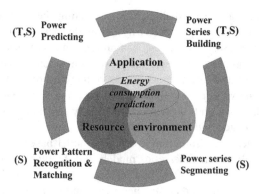

**Fig. 1.** Strategy overview

feature information of the environment (e.g. the network traffic and the bandwidth). As depicted in Fig. 1, the traditional time-series model does not contain phase 2 and 3, while the time-series segmentation model contains all the four phases.

Phase 1: *Power series building.* For each kind of time-series models, designing a time-series according to the historical data is necessary. In this paper, the power series of a specific activity is built by repeatedly running the activity and colleting the relevant historical power data at equal observation unit. Adopting this periodical sampling plan, we can obtain a representative power series by the sample mean of each unit.

Phase 2: *Power series segmentation.* This phase is only applied to time-series pattern segmentation model (*S*), which is the key and basis step. The representative power series will be segmented into several segmentations using sliding window model and bottom-up model respectively.

Phase 3: *Power pattern recognition and matching.* This phase contains two steps: one is power pattern recognition which is to discover the power-series pattern and the other is power matching to find out the closest pattern for a new power series sequence. This phase is only applied to the time-series segmentation model (*S*), but not to the traditional time-series model (*T*).

Phase 4: *Power predicting.* Power predicting is applied to both the traditional time-series model and the time-series pattern segmentation model. The main task of this phase is to predict the descendant power sequence of the limited power series for a new-coming activity using the models.

## 4  Energy Consumption Prediction Based on Time-Series Models

As demonstrated in Sect. 3, the energy consumption prediction based on traditional time-series models contains two phases: power-series building and power predicting And the energy consumption prediction based on time-series segmentation models contains four phases: power-series building, power series segmentation, power pattern recognition and matching and power predicting. This section will introduce the predicting process in detail.

## 4.1  Power-Series Building

For both traditional time-series models and time-series pattern segmentation models, the first step is designing a power-series according to the historical data. The power-series is built by recording the power data in the cloud server center at equal observation unit and this process is repeated numerous times. Then the representative power-series can be built with the sample mean of each observation unit. There is a little difference in this phase from the traditional models and segmentation models. For traditional time-series models, the power data is recorded when the cloud system is running a specific CPU-intensive activity. But for the time-series pattern segmentation models, the power data is recorded when the cloud system is randomly running several CPU-intensive activities.

## 4.2  Power-Series Segmentation

For a new-coming activity, its historical power data doesn't exist and using the traditional time series models is not ideal. And we need to find out the similar time-series segment with the similar features by the aid of time-series segmentation model. In this section, we introduce the time-series segmentation models for these activities in detail.

Time-series segmentation refers to these types of models, whose input is a time series and output is several segmented sub time-series or a piecewise linear representation (PLR). Its main idea is that time series T can be divided into several segments and get the best representation after using some models. First of all, how to describe the features of these time-series segments? In statistics, the factors, such as sample mean, standard deviation, and median value etc., can be used to characterize the behavior of each time-series sample. Based on this, we use statistical features to describe the segments and chose two basic statistical features (sample mean and standard deviation) to represent each segment. Next, we will introduce the two segmentation models used in this paper.

**Sliding Windows.** For a time-series T, the sliding window model is anchoring the left of its first window at the first data of T. And try to find the right of the window by increasing the length of segments according to a given threshold. The series from the anchor to the point i is transmitted as a segment until the standard deviation of the possible segment larger than the given threshold.

**Bottom-Up.** For a time-series T, the first step is to connect the adjacent points in the time-series and get the finest segmentation method. Then calculate the fitting error of all the segments, and merge the two adjacent segments with the minimum fitting error into one segment until all the fitting error larger than a given threshold. The fitting error in this paper is the residual value of the time-series.

### 4.3 Power Series Pattern Recognition and Matching

After segmenting the time-series into several segments, the next phase is to recognize the power pattern and to do a match. Power pattern recognition aims to ensure that the segmented patterns are valid. The Algorithm 1 describes this process.

```
Algorithm 1: power pattern validation
Input: Segmented power series Seg={seg₁,seg₂,…,segₘ},
       Const Min_pattern_length
Output: Real power pattern[]
For (i=1, i≤Seg.length, i++)
    Real_pattern(i)=segᵢ;    // Initialized the real power pattern
    Real_pattern(i).mean= segᵢ.mean;
    Real_pattern(i).std= segᵢ.std;
    If segᵢ.length<Min_pattern_length
    //compare the length of segᵢ with Min_pattern_length
        Real_pattern(i).valid=false;
    else
        Real_pattern(i).valid=true;
    end
end
```

Power matching is built to find out the most similar power-series pattern from the whole segmented patterns for the current activity. First of all, the new power-series is built for the current activity. Then the new power-series matches with the validation segmented patterns. Finally, the most similar series sequence is identified based on the mean and standard deviation. The detail is presented in Algorithm 2.

```
Algorithm 2: power pattern matching
Input: Latest power series DS, Power pattern[],
       Const Max_std_error
Output: Matched pattern MP
 If DS.std≥ Max_std_error
     While DS.std≥ Max_std_error
     //remove the turning point for the latest power series
         If length(latest_time_series)≠1
             DS=DS-DS.firstvalue;
         End
         Break
     End
     m=compare(DS,pattern);
     //compare DS with pattern[], return the most similar pat-
tern with the closest mean.
   else
       m=compare(DS,pattern);
   end
   MP=pattern(m);    //return matched pattern MP
```

## 4.4 Power Predicting

After the above phases, the last step is predicting the power consumption for the current activity. As presented in Sect. 3, phase 3 is applied to both traditional time-series models and time-series pattern segmentation models. For an activity which has historical power data, the power is predictable to a certain degree from the past recording data using the traditional time-series models. But for an activity which a new-coming, we can obtain its limited power sequence and find out the most similar power-series pattern to predict the descendant power sequence using time-series pattern segmentation models (as described in Sect. 4.2). The whole predicting process is described as follows:

*Power Predicting Process for an Activity which has Historical Power Data.* The AMRA model and the ES model can be trained by the historical power sequence data of the activity. According to the smoothing coefficient, the ES models can be divided into simple exponential smoothing (SES), double exponential smoothing model (DES) further. Thus, we use AMRA, SES and DES models to analysis the power sequence. In this process, we obtain the parameters of the models using the tool: Eviews. In the end, the power sequence in the future can be predicted by the models.

*Power Predicting Process for an Activity which is a New Coming.* After phase 2, we can obtain the most similar power-series pattern for this new-coming activity. Then the descendant power sequence is built. Thus the whole power-series pattern is seen as the new-coming activity's power-series.

## 5 Evaluation

In order to evaluate the proposed energy consumption prediction strategy, we design a simulation testbed where we deploy and run some benchmarks. At the same time, we record the power consumption by a physical power meter. In this section, we introduce the experimental environment firstly, and demonstrate the prediction results in detail.

### 5.1 Experimental Environment

Our experiments were designed on OpenStack (https://www.openstack.org/), which is a free and open-source cloud computing software platform. In the private cloud established by OpenStack, we created three virtual machines. We assign 2 virtual cores for each of the VMs. The amount of RAM is 4 GB and the amount of hard disk is 40 GB assigned for each VM. Recording the power consumed in cloud system requires an external physical power meter. In our work, we use the HP-8713 power meter connected with the server by USB interface. We use Linux operating system in the experiment.

Our paper focuses on the energy consumption of CPU-intensive activities running in the cloud. The major cloud resources consumed by CPU-intensive activities are CPU cores and RAM. In order to obtain valid samples, we use Prime 95 (http://www.mersenne.org/) as the benchmark running in the system. Prime 95 is dedicated to test the stability of the CPU by loading the test procedure incrementally and the test environment of Prime 95 is very cruel. Thus Prime 95 can be used as different kinds of CPU-intensive activities loading on the server one by one.

## 5.2     Results Using Traditional Time-Series Models

We run Prime 95 test standard procedure in the VM. The experiment process and results are as follows:

*Power Series Building.* The step one is to build the power series. In the experiment, the collecting time unit is 1 s for Prime 95 and we collect the power value for 2 min. Finally, we obtain the representative power series of the training data by the mean of the 7 times observations.

*Power Predicting.* In this section, the regression results of the traditional models, including ARMA, SES and DES, will be depicted and analyzed. The power series of Prime 95 is nonstationary sequence, based on the correlation test and unit root test. The results of autocorrelation partial autocorrelation test shows that AR(3) model can used to fit the power series of Prime 95. The predicting result is as shown in Fig. 2.

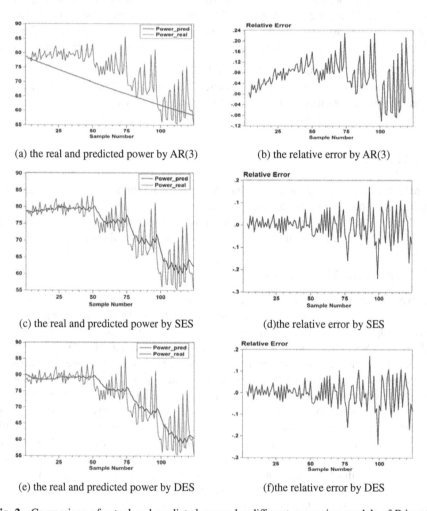

(a) the real and predicted power by AR(3)          (b) the relative error by AR(3)

(c) the real and predicted power by SES          (d) the relative error by SES

(e) the real and predicted power by DES          (f) the relative error by DES

**Fig. 2.** Comparison of actual and predicted power by different regression models of Prime 95

The relative error of the training data shows that the fitting efficiency of the model and the smaller the relative error is, the better the fitting efficiency of the model is. Figure 2 shows the fitting results by different regression models, such as AR(3), SES (Simple exponential smoothing model) and DES(Double exponential smoothing model), for the power series of Prime 95. Figure 2(a), (c) and (e) depict that the fitting results of SES and DES are better than AR(3). And the fitting result of SES is pretty close to DES. In addition, the linear regression AR(3) model is not ideal for fitting the power series of Prime 95. From the Fig. 2(b), (d) and (f), the relative error has a great fluctuation. The relative error of AR(3) changes from -12 % to 20 %. There are no big differences between the relative error of both SES and DES, which ranges from -10 % to 10 %. Overall, the performance of ES is better than ARMA.

### 5.3   Results Using Time-Series Segmentation Models

The test standard procedure, Prime 95, is deployed on the VMs. The process is repeatedly 7 times at the same running pattern. And the collected power data is used for training the time-series segmentation pattern model.

*Power Series Building.* As depicted in Sect. 5, the first step is to build the power series. We collected 7 groups of power data in the same observation time unit. The power data sampling frequency is 10 s. In the observation time unit, the VMs in the cloud system is in turn started and Prime 95 is running on the VMs in order. Obviously, the power series is consisted of several segmentations, which is a basis of the time-series segmentation pattern model. The representative power series is obtained by composing the mean of samples in each observation unit sequentially, which will be analyzed in the future.

*Power Series Segmentation.* In this phase, we conduct two segmentation models: sliding window model and bottom-up model to find out the potential pattern sequence set for the representative power series.

Table 1 shows the segmentation results of sliding window model. First of all, we assign the value for the parameter: max_error = 1.000, that means the standard deviation of the sub-segment is no more than 1.000 in the final results. As depicted in Table 2, the representative power series has been segmented into 10 segments. Each mean of segments is 67.2455, 84.1934, 78.1096, 84.6891, 78.5088, 84.7123, 80.0286, 9.1854, 116.5964 and 124.9851. And the standard deviation of the segments is 0.3080, 0.3166, 0.2404, 0.3737, 0.2268, 0.2993, 3.1171, 0.5677, 0.2632 and 0.4340 respectively.

Table 2 shows the segmentation results of bottom-up model. First of all, we need assign the value for the parameter: the number of the segments. The number of the segments is a decisive parameter of the model. In the experiment, we estimate the number of segments from the scatter of the representative power series and set the value for the parameter: num_of_segments = 12. As depicted in Table 2, the representative power series has been segmented into 12 segments. Each mean of segments is 67.2679, 75.3765, 84.2099, 78.1096, 84.4829, 78.5092, 84.7123, 79.4077, 98.7849, 108.3705, 117.2054 and 125.0000. The standard deviation of the segments is 0.3150, 11.8165, 0.3095, 0.2404, 1.1876, 0.2369, 0.2993, 0.2885, 1.1844, 11.0797, 2.1791 and 0.4426.

*Power Pattern Recognition and Matching.* After segmentation the representative power series, we verify the correction of these patterns firstly. In the experiment, the minimum length of each pattern in Algorithm 1 is set as 3. The results of pattern validation are shown in the right of Tables 1 and 2. As present in Table 1, all the 10 patterns segmentation with sliding windows are valid. But Table 2 shows that 10 valid patterns are identified from 12 segments with bottom-up model. The step two of this phase is pattern matching. The latest power series is built by randomly running the Prime 95 in one of the VMs and recording the power sequence in 2 min. The recording frequency is 10 s. We select the first five data to match the patterns and the last 7 data value is used as the target to be predicted.

The matching result shows that segment 9 of Table 1 is the most similar pattern with the latest power series and the segment 11of Table 2 is the most similar pattern with the latest power series. Finally, we use the average value of these two segments to predict the last 7 data value and the relative error of the prediction is shows as Fig. 3. The maximum relative error is 1.5 % for sliding window and the maximum one for bottom-up is around 2 %. The relative error of sliding window is less than that of bottom-up and thus the performance of sliding window is better.

**Table 1.** The segmentation results of sliding window model

| Representative power series | Mean= 89.3189, Standard Deviation= 15.7208, Length=193 | | | |
|---|---|---|---|---|
| Segmentation model | sliding window model, where max_error=1.000 | | | |
| segments description | mean | Standard Deviation | Length | validation |
| Segment 1 | 67.2455 | 0.3080 | 11 | true |
| Segment 2 | 84.1934 | 0.3166 | 29 | true |
| Segment 3 | 78.1096 | 0.2404 | 12 | true |
| Segment 4 | 84.6891 | 0.3737 | 29 | true |
| Segment 5 | 78.5088 | 0.2268 | 13 | true |
| Segment 6 | 84.7123 | 0.2993 | 28 | true |
| Segment 7 | 80.0286 | 3.1171 | 25 | true |
| Segment 8 | 99.1854 | 0.5677 | 14 | true |
| Segment 9 | 116.5964 | 0.2632 | 14 | true |
| Segment 10 | 124.9851 | 0.4340 | 18 | true |

**Table 2.**  The segmentation results of bottom-up model

| Representative power series | Mean= 89.3189, Standard Deviation= 15.7208, Length=193 | | | |
|---|---|---|---|---|
| Segmentation model | bottom-up model, where number of segments is 12 | | | |
| segments description | mean | Standard Deviation | Length | validation |
| Segment 1 | 67.2679 | 0.3150 | 10 | true |
| Segment 2 | 75.3765 | 11.8165 | 2 | false |
| Segment 3 | 84.2099 | 0.3095 | 28 | true |
| Segment 4 | 78.1096 | 0.2404 | 12 | true |
| Segment 5 | 84.4829 | 1.1876 | 30 | true |
| Segment 6 | 78.5092 | 0.2369 | 12 | true |
| Segment 7 | 84.7123 | 0.2993 | 28 | true |
| Segment 8 | 79.4077 | 0.2885 | 24 | true |
| Segment 9 | 98.7849 | 1.1844 | 14 | true |
| Segment 10 | 108.3705 | 11.0797 | 2 | false |
| Segment 11 | 117.2054 | 2.1791 | 14 | true |
| Segment 12 | 125.0000 | 0.4426 | 17 | true |

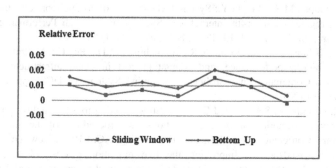

**Fig. 3.**  Relative error of the prediction by different segmentation models

# 6   Conclusion and Future Work

Energy saving in cloud computing is an important goal for scheduling the cloud resources and designing the cloud applications. This paper explored the energy consumption of CPU-intensive activities in the cloud from two aspects: one is traditional time-series models and the other is time-series segmentation models. The traditional time-series model, such as ARMA and ES, is used for predicting the energy consumption of these activities which have historical power data. The experimental results show that the performance of ES model, including SES and DES models, is better than the ARMA model. Meanwhile, the time-series segmentation models, such as sliding windows and bottom-up, are used for forecasting the energy consumption of new-coming activity in the system. The experimental results show that the relative error of the prediction is small and the performance of sliding windows is slightly better than bottom-up. These results can provide some fundamental guidelines for scheduling the cloud resources and improving the energy efficiency.

While this paper focused on the CPU-intensive activities, in the future we will study the energy consumption of I/O-intensive or Memory-intensive activities in the cloud. In addition, we will compare the results and further explore the energy consumption of an entire business process instead of a single activity in the cloud.

**Acknowledgments.** This work was partially supported by the grants of the National Natural Science Foundation of China (61572374, 61070013, U1135005) and the Fundamental Research Funds for the Central Universities (No. 2042014kf0272, No. 2014211020201).

# References

1. Armbrust, M., Fox, A.: A view of cloud computing. Commun. ACM **53**, 50–58 (2010)
2. Koomey, J.G.: Estimating total power consumption by servers in the U.S. and the world. In: Lawrence Berkeley National Laboratory, Stanford University (2007)
3. Graziano, C.D.: A performance analysis of Xen and KVM hypervisors for hosting the Xen worlds Project. In: Digital Repository (2011)
4. Kim, W., Gupta, M.S., Wei, G.Y.: System level analysis of fast, per-core dvfs using on-chip switching regulators. In: 14th International Symposium on High Performance Computer Architecture, pp. 123–134. IEEE Press, Salt Lake City, UT (2008)
5. Jung, G., Hiltunen, M.A., Joshi, K.R., Schlichting, R.D., Pu, C.: Mistral: dynamically managing power, performance, and adaptation cost in cloud infrastructures. In: 30th International Conference on Distributed Computing Systems (ICDCS), pp. 62–73. IEEE Press, Genova (2010)
6. Chen, F., Grundy, J., Schneider, J.G., et al.: StressCloud: a tool for analysing performance and energy consumption of cloud applications. In: Proceedings of the 5th ACM/SPEC International Conference on Performance Engineering. ACM Press, New York (2014)
7. Hacking, S., Hudzia, B.: Improving the live migration process of large enterprise applications. In: Proceedings of the 3rd International Workshop on Virtualization Technologies in Distributed Computing, pp. 51–58. ACM Press, New York (2009)
8. Lee, Y.C., Zomaya, A.Y.: Energy efficient utilization of resources in cloud computing systems. J. Supercomput. **60**(2), 268–280 (2012)
9. Bartalos, P., Blake, M.B.: Green web services: modeling and estimating power consumption of web services. In: 19th International Conference on Web Services (ICWS), pp. 178–185. IEEE Press, Honolulu, HI (2012)

10. Bartalos, P., Blake, M.B., Remy, S.: Green web services: models for energy-aware web services and applications. In: International Conference on Service-Oriented Computing and Applications (SOCA), pp. 1–8. IEEE Press, Irvine, CA (2011)
11. Bellino, J., Hans, C.: Virtual machine or virtual operating system. In: Proceedings of the ACM Workshop on Virtual Computer Systems, pp. 20–29. ACM Press, New York (1973)
12. Goldberg, R.P.: Survey of virtual machine research. Computer 7(6), 34–45 (1974)
13. Nurmi, D., et al.: The eucalyptus open-source cloud-computing system. In: 9th IEEE/ACM International Symposium on Cluster Computing and the Grid, pp. 124–131. IEEE Press, Shanghai (2008)
14. Lefèvre, L., Orgerie, A.C.: Designing and evaluating an energy efficient cloud. J. Supercomput. 51(3), 352–373 (2010)
15. Alshaer, H.: An overview of network virtualization and cloud network as a service. Int. J. Netw. Manag. 25(1), 1–30 (2015)
16. Xu, J., Fortes, J., A.B.: Multi-objective virtual machine placement in virtualized data center environments. In: Conference on Green Computing and Communications (GreenCom), and Conference on Cyber, Physical and Social Computing (CPSCom), pp. 179–188. IEEE Press, Hangzhou (2010)
17. Wang, L., Von, L.G., Dayal, J.: Towards energy aware scheduling for precedence constrained parallel tasks in a cluster with DVFS. In: 10th IEEE/ACM International Conference on Cluster, Cloud and Grid Computing (CCGrid), pp. 368–377. IEEE Press, Melbourne, VIC (2010)
18. Lewis, A.W., Ghosh, S., Tzeng, N.F.: Run-time energy consumption estimation based on workload in server systems. HotPower 8, 17–21 (2008)
19. Guo, Y., Gong, Y., Fang, Y.: Energy and network aware workload management for sustainable data centers with thermal storage. Parallel Distrib. Syst. IEEE Trans. 25(8), 2030–2042 (2014)
20. Chase, J.S., Anderson, D.C., Thakar, P.N., Vahdat, A.M.: Managing energy and server resources in hosting centers. Proc. ACM Symp. Operating Syst. Principles 35(5), 103–116 (2001)
21. Chen, F., Grundy, J., Schneider, J.G.: Automated analysis of performance and energy consumption for cloud applications. In: 5th ACM/SPEC International Conference on Performance Engineering, pp. 39–50. ACM Press, New York (2014)
22. Dinda, P.A., OHallaron, D.R.: Host load prediction using linear models. Cluster Comput. 3(4), 265–280 (2000)
23. Commander, E.S.G.: Exponential smoothing: the state of the art. J. Forecast. 4(1), 1–28 (1985)

# HYPAD: Hyper-Graph-Driven Approach for Parallel Data Warehouse Design

Ahcene Boukorca[1], Ladjel Bellatreche[1], and Soumia Benkrid[2]($\boxtimes$)

[1] LIAS/ISAE-ENSMA - Poitiers University, Futuroscope, Poitiers, France
{ahcene.boukorca,ladjel.bellatreche}@ensma.fr
[2] Ecole Nationale Suprieure d'Informatique (ESI), Algiers, Algeria
s_benkrid@esi.dz

**Abstract.** Small, medium and large companies all face three well-identified problems, precisely: **(i)** the data deluge, **(ii)** the large number of interacted exploratory queries and **(iii)** the economic crisis. Hence, it becomes a real necessity to consider those problems and develop low-cost database deployment solutions. Data parallel architectures are one of the relevant deployment platforms that may manage efficiently this deluge of data. The process of designing such architecture has to integrate the interaction that may exist between queries. Although, the state-of-art on parallel data warehouses is quite rich, to the best of our knowledge, the query interaction is not highlighted. Amazingly, the queries are in the core of the parallel design. Ignoring their interaction may impact the quality of the final design. In this paper, we propose a new scalable hyper-graph approach, called *HYPAD*, for designing cluster warehouses by considering concurrent analytical highly interacted queries. Our approach is validated through a data warehouse cluster simulator. The obtained results show the effectiveness and efficiency of our proposal.

**Keywords:** Parallel data warehouse design · Fragmentation · Allocation · Big queries management · Query processing

## 1 Introduction

With rising of *Big Data* era, we are facing a *data deluge*. Multiple data providers are contributing to this deluge. We can cite three main factors: **(i)** the massive use of sensors (e.g. *10 Terabyte of data* are generated by planes *every 30 min*), **(ii)** the massive use of social networks (e.g., 340 million tweets per day), and **(iii)** transactions (*2.5 Petabytes* in the Wal-Mart databases per minute). The decision makers need fast response times to their *very large number of queries* in order to predict in real time the behaviour of users, so they can offer them services via analysing large volumes of data. This situation generates *Big Queries phenomenon*. These queries are highly interacted, since they may share several sub-expressions (joins, selections). The causes of this interaction are multiple: (i) the OLAP queries defined on relational data warehouses ($\mathcal{RDW}$) modelled by a star schema or its variants pass through the fact table, (ii) the interactive $\mathcal{DW}$ exploration generates more personalized and recommended queries [9].

© Springer International Publishing Switzerland 2015
G. Wang et al. (Eds.): ICA3PP 2015, Part IV, LNCS 9531, pp. 770–783, 2015.
DOI: 10.1007/978-3-319-27140-8_53

The query interaction is one of the important field in databases. It has been widely studied in all generations of databases (traditional databases [19], Object oriented databases [14], semantic databases [10], and data warehouses [22], etc.).

Considering three above cited dimensions: data deluge, big queries phenomenon and the economic crisis, deploying $\mathcal{RDW}$ on conventional platforms (e.g. centralized) becomes obsolete, even with the spectacular progress in terms of advanced optimization structures (e.g., materialized views, indexes, storage layouts, etc.). Despite this, the sole use of these structures is not sufficient to gain efficiency during the evaluation of complex OLAP queries over relational $\mathcal{DW}$. As a consequence, distributed and parallel platforms are one of the relevant robust and scalable solutions to store, process and analyse data, with the layers of modern analytic infrastructures [8]. Editors of DBMS already propose a large choice of solutions to companies to adopt these solutions (e.g., *Teradata*) or to go to the Cloud (e.g. Amazon Redshift). Note that these solutions may become rapidly expensive when data size grows. For instance, the cost of storing 1 Terabyte of data per year in *Amazon Redshift* is about 5 500 USD. Several efforts have been deployed to ensure a balance between low cost and high performance solutions to manage this deluge of data. Even large companies like *Alibaba* work towards this direction. In their recent works published in VLDB 2014 [7], they propose a MySQL driven solutions to deal with the data deluge over the Cloud.

In this study, we follow this direction by designing parallel data warehouses over clusters and considering the two dimensions: *Big* and *Interacted* Queries. The query interaction has been incorporated in selecting optimization structures in the context of relational $\mathcal{DW}$ (e.g. the work of [23] for selecting materialized views), query scheduling [22], query caching in the context of distributed data stream [20], etc. To deal with Big queries phenomenon, we recently proposed a scalable hyper-graph data structure to manage both dimensions [6]. This structure contributes in selecting materialized views by considering many interacted queries.

In this paper, we propose and experimentally assess an innovative methodology guided by the *big query interaction* for designing Parallel $\mathcal{RDW}$ ($\mathcal{PRDW}$) on shared nothing database cluster architecture. To explore the large number of queries, we use the hyper-graph structure that helps us in visualizing our workload and partitions it, if necessary, into several components to reduce the complexity of the design. Our main contributions are: (i) establishment of strong coupling between *Multiple Query optimization* ($\mathcal{MQO}$) problem and $\mathcal{PRDW}$ design, (ii) the use of hyper-graph data structure to handle the large search space of all possible Unified Query plans (UQP) and (iii) the elaboration of a modular joint design including the data partitioning and the fragment allocation.

The rest of the paper is organized as follows. Section 2 provides an overview of related work. Section 3 depicts a motivating example. Section 4 contains the details of the $\mathcal{PRDW}$ design methodology *HYPAD*, which represents the main contribution of our research. Section 5 provides our experimental results obtained from testing the performance of HYPAD using dataset of the Star Schema Benchmark (SSB). Finally, Sect. 6 concludes the paper and discusses some open issues.

## 2    Related Work

In this section, we review the most important state-of-art studies on $\mathcal{PRDW}$ design and $\mathcal{MQO}$. At the end of discuss the projection of $\mathcal{MQO}$ on this design.

$\mathcal{PRDW}$ **Design**. It consists first in fragmenting the warehouse schema using any partitioning algorithm [16] and allocating the so-generated fragments over the processing nodes using a particular algorithm such that the allocation scheme generated must optimize the workload performance [13]. Then, the designer duplicates the generated fragments on processing nodes to ensure high availability of data and the high performance of the system [24]. Once the fragmentation and allocation schemes are generated, a load balancing policy is applied to optimize the workload and achieve a high performance of the system [1,17].

Note that the different phases of the parallel design life-cycle (fragmentation, allocation, replication and load balancing) have the merit to be largely studied, in an isolation way, over all database generations [13,18]. Afterwards, iterative $\mathcal{PRDW}$ design approaches were proposed [21]. Recently, some research efforts recommended combining some phases of the life-cycle in order to get benefit from the interaction between these phases [3]. In our previous studies, we proposed a methodology for designing $\mathcal{PRDW}$ that considers the dependency issue between fragmentation and allocation phases of the parallel design life-cycle. This methodology has been implemented on Teradata machine – a shared nothing DBMS with proven scalability and robustness in real life user environments [2]. The obtained results outperform the iterative design.

**Multi-Query Optimization.** The $\mathcal{MQO}$ has been widely studied by in the literature. At first, it has been dealt as a problem of reusing intermediate results of some queries to optimize other queries [19]. Researchers used this philosophy to recommend materializing intermediate results [23], proposing query scheduling strategies based on the intermediate results that may exist in the buffer [17,22].

**The Projection of the $\mathcal{MQO}$ on the $\mathcal{PRDW}$ design.** When this projection is done, we figure out that it shows its impact in phases in isolated way. In the work of [4], the authors show the contribution of $\mathcal{MQO}$ in selecting the best horizontal partitioning schemes of a $\mathcal{DW}$. Mehta et al. [12] tackle the problem of scheduling queries in a parallel database by considering batches of queries. The authors propose to divide the batch of queries into sub-batches, so that the memory requirement of the queries in each sub-batch adds up to available memory.

To the best of our knowledge, even there exists some works that consider interaction when designing $\mathcal{PRDW}$, none of them considers the *Big Interacted Queries Phenomenon*. In this paper, we propose to study the impact of this phenomenon in designing of $\mathcal{PRDW}$; especially for data partitioning and fragment allocation. To deal efficiently with the big queries, we propose the use of hyper-graph structure that contributes in splitting the workload into disjoint components *collaborating* to partition and allocate data over the nodes of the cluster. To illustrate this approach, we consider a motivating example in the next section.

## 3 Motivating Example

We assume the following configuration of our parallel warehouse:

- A star schema composed of one fact table: *Lineorder* and four dimension tables : *Supplier, Dates, Customer,* and *Part.*
- On the top of this schema, 10 star queries $\{Q_1, .., Q_{10}\}$. The unified plan is described in Fig. 1-a. Three types of nodes of this plan are distinguished: a selection operation (with the form *Attribute* $\theta$ *value*, where *Attribute* $\in$ *Table*, $\theta \in \{=, <, >, ...\}$ and *Value* $\in$ *Domain(Attribute)*), denoted by $S_i$, a join operation, denoted by $J_i$ and a projection operation denoted by $\pi$. We note that seven (7) selections and joins are identified.
- The candidate attributes with their respective domains to perform the partitioning are given in Fig. 1-c.
- A cluster with four nodes $N = \{N_1, .., N_4\}$.

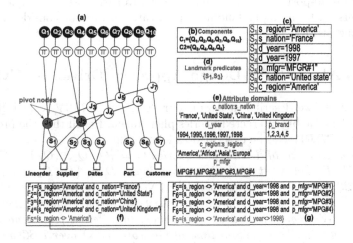

**Fig. 1.** UQP representation example

By examining the UQP, we figure out that the queries can be regrouped into two main groups called *components* (Fig. 1-b): $C_1 = \{Q_1, Q_2, Q_5, Q_7, Q_8, Q_{10}\}$ and $C_2 = \{Q_3, Q_4, Q_6, Q_9\}$. Each component contains a set of queries that share at least one join operation. The first shared join node is called the *pivot node* of the component and the set of selection predicates of its branches called *set of landmark predicates*. In our case, we have two pivot nodes ($J_1$ for the component $C_1$ and $J_2$ for the component $C_2$) with their sets of landmark predicates are $\{s\_region =$ "America"$\}$ and $\{d\_year = 1998\}$, respectively.

Note that the *pivot node* notion is quite important, since it guides the partitioning process of a component by the means of its *set of landmark predicates*. A landmark predicate partitions its corresponding table (a leaf node of the plan) into two partitions, one with all instances satisfying the predicate (e.g., $s\_region$ = "America") and another representing the *ELSE* partition ($s\_region \neq$ "America"). Note that the partitioning of dimension tables will be *propagated* to partition the fact table. This partitioning is called *derived partitioning* [3]. This initial partitioning schema of a component will be refined by considering other predicates of the set of landmark predicates and other predicates do not belonging to pivot node (e.g., $S_4$). In the case, where the obtained fragments of each component are allocated over these nodes in *round robin fashion*, the maximum number of algebraic operations will be executed over all the cluster nodes. Therefore, queries of a given partitioned component (e.g., $C_1$) will get benefit from this process.

The remaining fragment of the initial component ($F_5$ in our example) will be concerned by the partitioning process of the component $C_2$. The above partitioning and allocation reasoning applied to $C_2$ (Fig. 1-g). Note that the queries of the component $C_2$ need fragments of the component $C_1$.

A partitioning order has to be defined among components. In our proposal, we give more importance to component that involves most costly queries. The components with an empty landmark predicate set are not considered for the partitioning process.

# 4   HYPAD: PRDW Design Approach Driven by UQP

In this section, we describe in details our design of $\mathcal{PRDW}$ (called *HYPAD*) that considers the big interacted queries phenomena. Recall that the problem of designing a $\mathcal{PRDW}$ can be described as follows [3]:

*Given a workload of L star join queries $Q = \{Q_1, Q_2, .., Q_L\}$, a $\mathcal{DW}$ with a fact table F and a set of d dimensions tables $D = \{D_1, D_2, .., D_d\}$ and a cluster $\mathcal{DBC}$ with M processing node $N = \{N_1, N_2, .., N_M\}$, where each node $N_i$ has its storage capacity. Our problem consists in fragmenting the fact table F of $\mathcal{DWS}$ in W fragments and assigning them to different processing nodes in order to minimize the execution time of the workload Q over $\mathcal{DBC}$ and satisfy all constraints related to storage and maintenance.*

Our proposed approach aims at ensuring an equitable node processing by generating effective data placement schema (data partitioning and fragments allocation schemes) using query interaction. *HYPAD* is based on the clustering of the workload in several small components to ensure the scalability of the design. The partitioning process is guided by sharing operations, so their tables (determined by the means of the predicate landmarks) are partitioned and distributed over cluster-nodes.

The sharing operations are described using the UQP, where they are divided in several components. Thus, the partitioning is driven by one operation shared by one or more components (called *component area*). Each component area becomes the subject of a module of sub-partition and sub-allocation. So, the $\mathcal{PRDW}$ designing consists on the following tasks: (1) capturing the interaction between queries, (2) data partitioning and allocation using disjoint modules of sub-partition and sub-allocation. The flowchart for our proposed $\mathcal{PRDW}$ design methodology is sketched in Fig. 2.

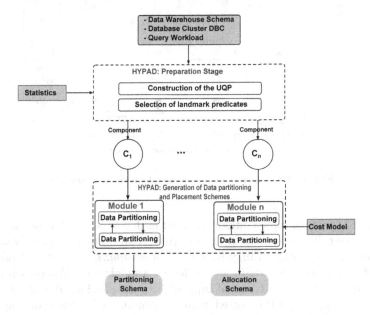

**Fig. 2.** Flowchart for our proposed $\mathcal{PRDW}$ design methodology

### 4.1 Construction of the Unified Query Plan (UQP)

To generate the UQP, we have used our previous work [6]. We use *hypergraph data structure* issued from *VLSI* layout design [11]. Both queries and theirs operations are represented by a hypergraph (see Fig. 3-*a*). To ensure the scalability of our algorithm when dealing with big queries, we regroup the queries in many connected components, such that queries belonging in the same component shall have a high interaction and minimal interaction with others components. This problem is known in *VLSI* domain as *k-way hypergraph partitioning with minimum cut problem*. We have used *HMETIS*[1] [11] that can partition efficiently hypergraph of millions nodes using recursive multi-level partitioning. The result of the partitioning is several disjoint sub-sets (sub-hypergraphs), called *connected components* (Fig. 3-b). Each component can be processed independently to generate a local UQP by ordering the nodes using a cost model [6]. At the end, the global UQP is generated by merging the sub-hypergraphs (Fig. 3-c).

### 4.2 Annotation of UQP

Note that a potential fragment of a component, generated by a landmark predicate, can be shared by many components. This is because landmark predicate *lp*

---

[1] http://glaros.dtc.umn.edu/gkhome/metis/hmetis/overview.

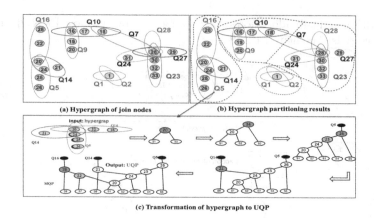

(a) Hypergraph of join nodes          (b) Hypergraph partitioning results

(c) Transformation of hypergraph to UQP

**Fig. 3.** An overview of capturing of interaction method

is associated to one or more components, but each component has one landmark predicate. We call *Components Area* of lp ($CA_{lp}$) all components involved by lp. Note that a given workload may have a set of *landmark predicates*, denoted by $LP$. Each *landmark predicate* lp, is labelled by a weight ($w(l_p)$) representing the sum of processing cost, in terms of Inputs/Outputs, of all queries of its component area ($CA_{lp}$). The $LP$ is sorted in the descending order based on the weight of its landmark predicates.

A candidate fragment of a component (generated by a landmark predicate) can be shared by many components. To maximize its benefit, it will be interesting if it affects the components with higher query processing cost.

## 4.3   Generation of Partial Data Partitioning Schema

Each component of our hyper-graph is concerned by the partitioning process. For each component, a fragmentation preparation is needed. It consists in decomposing the fact table based on landmark predicates into two fragments: one defined by the clause of landmark predicates (noted $Candidate_{Frag}$) and the second containing the rest of the data (ELSE Clause), (noted by $NoCandidate_{Frag}$). The partitioning process will use this fragment by considering other predicates. This partitioning passes through two main steps: preparation and iterative splitting.

– **Preparation of Attributes Partitioning.** We identify all possible attributes, which have more than one value in their sub-domains in the definition of the fragment object to the partial partition. These attributes are divided into two categories: the first one, called *first candidates* ($FC$), contains attributes that are not used by the queries in the *component area*. The second one contains the remaining attributes (called *second candidates* ($SC$)). The partition starts using first attributes ($FC$) to split the fragment such that each query can be processed by the maximum of cluster nodes. When none attribute exists in $FC$, the partition process uses $SC$ to select the attributes used in the partitioning process.

- **Iterative Fragment Splitting.** The partial partitioning is a sequence of splitting operations, where each split is applied on one fragment to produce two fragments. So, the partial partition schema starts with a fragment and it increases by one in each splitting. Each split is applied on the most voluminous fragment. The volume is defined by the selectivity factor calculated as the multiplication of selectivity factors of all attributes participating on the definition of the fragment. The selectivity of a given attribute is the *sum of the selectivity of their sub-domain* [3].

  The splitting attribute corresponds to the attribute that has the minimum values in its sub-domain. The splitting operation divides the sub-domain of $n$ values into two sub-domains, each one has $n/2$ values if $n$ is pair else one sub-domain has $(n + 1)/2$ values and the other has $(n - 1)/2$ values. The splitting process continues till $M$ fragments ($M$ is number of cluster nodes) are produced.

- The previous steps are repeated for all *components*.

### 4.4   Generation of the Partial Fragment Allocation Schema

The fragments of a Partial Data Partitioning Schema is allocated in *round robin fashion* over the cluster nodes. Once allocated, the maintenance constraint (represented by the number of fragments $W$ that the designer wants to have) is verified. If this constraint is violated ($W > M$), the merging operations of small fragments are necessary.

### 4.5   Evaluation of the Partial Fragment Placement Schema

An analytical cost model measures the quality of the selected placement schema by estimating the number of inputs/outputs required for executing the workload. More precisely, this model receives as input a horizontal fragmentation schema $SF$, an allocation schema $AS$ and a set of queries $W$, it returns the execution cost of the workload $W$. The processing cost of all queries equal to the maximum execution time of the processing nodes.

   Indeed, the coordinator nodes of the Shared nothing database cluster ensure the execution of the queries. For each query $Q_i$ of $W$, an optimal execution plan is generated by:

- identifying the appropriate facts fragments;
- identifying the necessary joins;
- defining the join execution order and specifying the data access methods. The so-generated sub-queries are allocated to the processing nodes. Since the allocation is not redundant, the so-generated sub-queries are allocated to only one processing nodes.
- Finally, all intermediate results are submitted to a suitable coordinator node that merges them and accomplishes the needed aggregations.

## 5  Experimentation

This section reports the results of an experimental evaluation of our proposed approach. Our simulation conducted on a computer with 3.4 GHz Intel(R) Core(TM) i7-3770 equipped with 8 GB RAM. Algorithms were carried out in Java programming language. For the hardware architecture, we simulate a homogeneous Database Cluster of 8 to 128 nodes. We use the dataset of the Star Schema Benchmark (SSB) [15] with different sizes (from 100 GB to 2 TB). Several workloads randomly generated are used with a size varying from 32 to 10,000 queries. Our star join queries are generated from the 13 queries proposed by the star schema benchmark (SSB). Specifically, we convert each reference query to a template, by replacing each range predicate with a parameter. Thereby, to obtain a workload query, we just replace the parameter in the query template with a random value.

In all experiments, we use the same cost model, estimating the number of inputs/outputs (I/O) when executing a given workload, developed in [3]. Our tests have two objectives: (i) compare the performance of HYPAD approach with a recent design approach called ($\mathcal{F\&A}$) that shows its efficiency in *Teradata* machine [2] and (ii) check the quality and scalability of HYPAD, where workload and the size of dataset changes.

### 5.1  Comparing HYPAD Against $\mathcal{F\&A}$

As a first experiment, we study the performance of our proposed methodology HYPAD, compared against $\mathcal{F\&A}$ approach [3], where allocation phase is done at partitioning phase. In this approach, the fragmentation phase uses a Genetic Algorithm and the allocation phase is based in innovative matrix-based formalism and a related fuzzy k-means clustering. For each $\mathcal{PRDW}$ design methodology, we set the fragmentation threshold $W$ to 500 and we measured the query execution time versus the variation of the number of database cluster nodes $M$ over the interval [8:32]. Figure 4 shows the obtained results. We can see that HYPAD approach performs 18 %–39 % better than $\mathcal{F\&A}$.

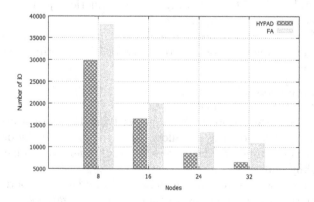

**Fig. 4.** Computational overhead performance of HYPAD against $\mathcal{F\&A}$ Design

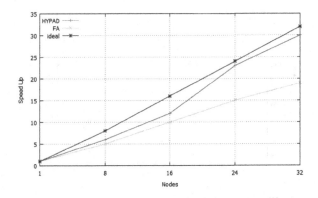

**Fig. 5.** Performance of HYPAD against $\mathcal{F}\&\mathcal{A}$ design approach

To check the quality of the placement schema generated by HYPAD when changing the number of cluster, we conduct the same experiment and we calculate the speed up factor for each approach. Figure 5 shows that this factor is not linear, since HYPAD does not perform the load balancing processing. To determine the cause of this imbalance processing and to see how data is distributed, we run a second experiment. We fix the number of nodes to M=8 and we check the amount of data stored in each node. As sketched in the Fig. 6, both approaches ($\mathcal{F}\&\mathcal{A}$, HYPAD) suffers by data placement skew with 43% and 48% respectively. This is due to the selectivity skew. Indeed, both approaches are based on the multi-level partitioning that is based on the splitting of the attribute's domain. This type of splitting depends on the nature of the distribution of the attribute's domain. As shown in [5], the solution of this problem requires removing from the list of partitioning attribute candidates the attributes that suffer from selectivity skew problem.

In the third experiment, we study the effect of the size of the workload on the performance of HYPAD comparing with the $\mathcal{F}\&\mathcal{A}$ approach. Here, we fix the number of nodes to $M = 16$ and we range the workload size over the interval [30:60] in order to study how the HYPAD query performance varies accordingly. Figure 7 gives more details for executing a workload with 30 queries. For HYPAD, all queries get benefit from the partitioning schema, whereas in $\mathcal{F}\&\mathcal{A}$, only queries involving fragmentation attributes get benefit. This result shows the efficiency of our approach.

## 5.2 Influence of the Workload Query Pattern in Query Performance

To evaluate the HYPAD scalability, we have to vary several parameters: the number of queries, the number of nodes, and the size of datasets. We perform these experiments on HYPAD and not in the $\mathcal{F}\&\mathcal{A}$; *since it does scale when the number of queries is high.*

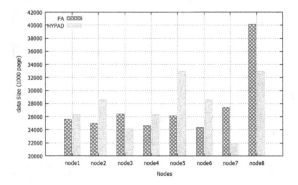

**Fig. 6.** HYPAD data placement distribution

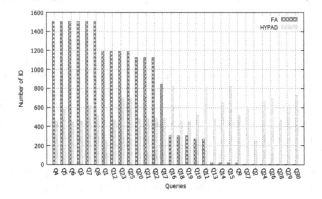

**Fig. 7.** Queries makspen

The first experiment aims to evaluate the impact of the workload size on the quality of data distribution. We consider the following configuration: a cluster with 32 nodes, a 2 TB dataset and two workloads with 100 and 1000 queries, respectively. The obtained results are given in Fig. 8. The main lesson of these experiments is that the data placement skew of HYPAD may be improved when more queries are involved.

The second experiment aims to check the scalability of HYPAD. Intensive tests were applied using different configurations by varying the number of cluster nodes ([8:128]), number of queries (from 100 to 10 000 queries) and the size of dataset (100 GB, 1 TB and 2 TB). In each configuration, the simulator estimates the total cost of query processing. To check the scalability of HYPAD when database size increases, we fix the number of query on 1 000 queries. Figure 10, shows that HYPAD scales-up when the data size increases.

To check the scalability of HYPAD when the workload size increases, we fix the size of dataset to 2 TB. The obtained results in Fig. 9 confirm that an increase of the workload size results in raising the speed-up and making it more linear.

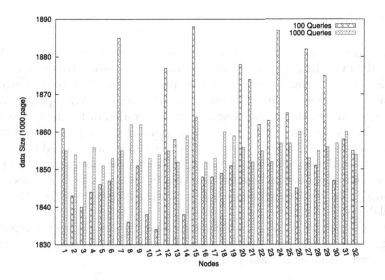

**Fig. 8.** The impact of workload size on data distribution quality.

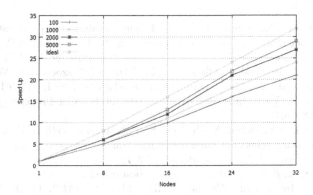

**Fig. 9.** Scale-up of HYPAD when the workload size increases

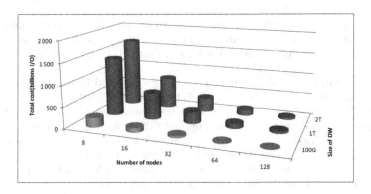

**Fig. 10.** Scale-up of HYPAD when database size increases

# 6    Conclusion

In this paper, we motivate the consideration of query interaction in designing parallel data warehouses under concurrent analytical queries. We proposed a new scalable $\mathcal{PRDW}$ designing approach that can generate effective data partition and data placement schemes. The main steps of our HYPAD approach are: (i) capturing of interaction among queries. (ii) Generation of landmark predicates that performed by using connected components that compose the UQP. (iii) Elaboration of modular data partition and data allocation, guided by the components of UQP. Our approach is compared against the most important state of art works and the obtained results show the efficiency and effectiveness of our approach. It has been tested under big size workload (10000 queries), that shows its scalability.

Currently, we are working into two directions: (i) introducing the replication of fragment to ensure the availability and the (ii) applying query interaction to on-line load balancing in parallel database.

# References

1. Akal, F., Böhm, K., Schek, H.-J.: OLAP query evaluation in a database cluster: a performance study on intra-query parallelism. In: Manolopoulos, Y., Návrat, P. (eds.) ADBIS 2002. LNCS, vol. 2435, pp. 218–231. Springer, Heidelberg (2002)
2. Bellatreche, L., Benkrid, S., Ghazal, A., Crolotte, A., Cuzzocrea, A.: Verification of partitioning and allocation techniques on teradata DBMS. In: 11th International Conference on Algorithms and Architectures for Parallel Processing (ICA3PP), pp. 158–169 (2011)
3. Bellatreche, L., Cuzzocrea, A., Benkrid, S.: Effectively and efficiently designing and querying parallel relational data warehouses on heterogeneous database clusters: the f&a approach. J. Database Manage. **23**(4), 17–51 (2012)
4. Bellatreche, L., Kerkad, A.: Query interaction based approach for horizontal data partitioning. Int. J. Data Warehouse. Min. (IJDWM) **11**(2), 44–61 (2015)
5. Benkrid, S., Bellatreche, L., Cuzzocrea, A.: A global paradigm for designing parallel relational data warehouses in distributed environments. T. Large Scale Data Knowl. Cent. Syst. **15**, 64–101 (2014)
6. Boukorca, A., Bellatreche, L., Senouci, S.-A.B., Faget, Z.: SONIC: scalable multi-query optimization through integrated circuits. In: Decker, H., Lhotská, L., Link, S., Basl, J., Tjoa, A.M. (eds.) DEXA 2013, Part I. LNCS, vol. 8055, pp. 278–292. Springer, Heidelberg (2013)
7. Cao, W., Yu, F., Xie, J.: Realization of the low cost and high performance mysql cloud database. Proc. VLDB Endow. **7**(13), 1742–1747 (2014)
8. Eavis, T.: Parallel and distributed data warehouses. In: Liu, L., Ozsu, T. (eds.) Encyclopedia of Database Systems, pp. 2012–2018. Springer, US (2009)
9. Eirinaki, M., Abraham, S., Polyzotis, N., Shaikh, N.: Querie: collaborative database exploration. IEEE Trans. Knowl. Data Eng. **26**(7), 1778–1790 (2014)
10. Goasdoué, F., Karanasos, K., Leblay, J., Manolescu, I.: View selection in semantic web databases. Proc. VLDB Endow. **5**(2), 97–108 (2011)
11. Karypis, G., Kumar, V.: Multilevel k-way hypergraph partitioning. In: ACM/IEEE Design Automation Conference (DAC), pp. 343–348. ACM (1999)

12. Mehta, M., Soloviev, V., DeWitt, D.J.: Batch scheduling in parallel database systems. In: Proceedings of the Ninth International Conference on Data Engineering, 19–23 April 1993, Vienna, Austria, pp. 400–410 (1993)
13. Menon, S.: Allocating fragments in distributed databases. IEEE Trans. Parallel Distrib. Syst. **16**(7), 577–585 (2005)
14. Mitchell, G.: Extensible query processing in an object-oriented database. Ph.D. thesis. Citeseer (1993)
15. O'Neil, P., O'Neil, B., Chen, X.: Star schema benchmark (2009)
16. Pavlo, A., Curino, C., Zdonik, S.: Skew-aware automatic database partitioning in shared-nothing, parallel oltp systems. In: Proceedings of the 2012 ACM SIGMOD International Conference on Management of Data, pp. 61–72 (2012)
17. Phan, T., Li, W.-S.: Load distribution of analytical query workloads for database cluster architectures. In: 11th International Conference on Extending Database Technology (EDBT), pp. 169–180 (2008)
18. Saccà, D., Wiederhold, G.: Database partitioning in a cluster of processors. In: VLDB, pp. 242–247 (1983)
19. Sellis, T.K.: Multiple-query optimization. ACM Trans. Database Syst. **13**(1), 23–52 (1988)
20. Seshadri, S., Kumar, V., Cooper, B.F.: Optimizing multiple queries in distributed data stream systems. In: Proceedings International Conference on Data Engineering Workshops, p. 25. IEEE (2006)
21. Stöhr, T., Märtens, H., Rahm, E.: Multi-dimensional database allocation for parallel data warehouses. In: VLDB, pp. 273–284 (2000)
22. Thomas, D., Diwan, A.A., Sudarshan, S.: Scheduling and caching in multiquery optimization. In: Proceedings of the 13th International Conference on Management of Data (COMAD), pp. 150–153 (2006)
23. Yang, J., Karlapalem, K., Li, Q.: Algorithms for materialized view design in data warehousing environment. In: VLDB, pp. 136–145 (1997)
24. Zhu, H., Gu, P., Wang, J.: Shifted declustering: a placement-ideal layout scheme for multi-way replication storage architecture. In: Proceedings of the 22nd Annual International Conference on Supercomputing, ICS 2008, pp. 134–144 (2008)

# Efficient Space Management and Wear Leveling for PCM-Based Storage Systems

Zhangling Wu[1], Peiquan Jin[1,2(✉)], and Lihua Yue[1,2]

[1] School of Computer Science and Technology,
University of Science and Technology of China, Hefei 230027, China
jpq@ustc.edu.cn
[2] Key Laboratory of Electromagnetic Space Information,
Chinese Academy of Sciences, Hefei 230027, China

**Abstract.** Phase change memory (PCM) has emerged as a promising candidate for next-generation storage media, owing to its low power consumption, non-volatility, and high scalability. However, PCM has limited write endurance, or more particularly, it can only undergo a limited number of write operations. This problem is much critical to the lifetime of PCM. Aiming to solve this problem, in this paper we propose an efficient space management scheme for PCM-based storage systems, which is able to level the write operations to PCM and lengthen the lifetime of PCM. In particular, we propose a new structure (called *dual dynamic bucket lists*) to manage the spaces of PCM, and further devise an efficient page management policy for page allocation, migration, and swaps. With these mechanisms, write operations are distributed to PCM chips in a balanced manner and the write amplification ratio of PCM incurred by page swaps is decreased, yielding less write operations to PCM and longer lifetime of PCM. Our experimental results on a simulated PCM-based device show that our proposal is effective in lengthening the lifetime of PCM, and thus offers a more practical solution for the space management on PCM-based storage systems.

**Keywords:** Phase change memory · Space management · Wear leveling

## 1 Introduction

Phase change memory (PCM) is a new kind of storage media that has received much attention from both academia and industries in recent years [1]. PCM is non-volatile and has fast read/write speeds than other storage media such as flash memory and magnetic disks. As I/O latency is always a performance bottleneck in computer systems, PCM is expected to be incorporated into future storage systems, which we call PCM-based storage systems, to offer much higher I/O performance than the existing storage media.

However, PCM has some special properties compared to existing storage media like flash memory and magnetic disks, such as byte-addressable and limited write endurance [2]. Specially, PCM can only undergo a limited number of write operations. This is much critical to the lifetime of PCM, as well as to its practicability.

© Springer International Publishing Switzerland 2015
G. Wang et al. (Eds.): ICA3PP 2015, Part IV, LNCS 9531, pp. 784–798, 2015.
DOI: 10.1007/978-3-319-27140-8_54

Although flash memory is also regarded to have limited write endurance, we cannot simply use existing flash-memory-optimized techniques such as hot-DL [3] for PCM-based storage systems. For example, flash memory offers page-level read/write operations and block-level erase operations but has to use the erase-before-write policy when updating data, which is called out-of-place updating [4]. However, PCM supports in-place updating because of its byte-addressable feature.

In this paper, aiming at leveling write operations to PCM and therefore lengthening the lifetime of PCM, we propose an efficient approach for the space management on PCM-based storage systems. In brief, we make the following contributions in this paper:

1. The spaces of PCM are organized by a unit of page and we propose a new structure (called *dual dynamic bucket lists*) to manage these pages. With this design, all the pages of PCM are organized into a free dynamic bucket list for maintaining free pages and an allocated dynamic bucket list for allocated pages. (Section 3.1)
2. Based on the dynamic bucket lists, we propose a page management algorithm for page allocation, page migration, and page swaps. With this mechanism, write operations are distributed to PCM chips in a balanced manner and the write amplification ratio of PCM incurred by page swaps is decreased, yielding less write operations to PCM. (Section 3.2)
3. We conduct experiments on a simulated PCM-based storage system to compare our proposal with several existing approaches including PTL [5], the bucket-based WL algorithm [6], and the random swapping algorithm [7]. The results show the efficiency of our approach. (Section 4)

## 2 Background and Related Work

As a kind of non-volatile memories, PCM is a promising candidate for storage and main memory because of its non-volatility, high density and so on. A PCM cell uses phase change material that can switch the state between amorphous and crystalline with electrical pulses to store a bit information. Write a PCM cell includes two operations called SET and RESET. SET operation requires wild pulse and low current to crystallize the phase change material. RESET operation is controlled by high-power pulse to make the material amorphous. While reading a PCM cell is done with very low power by sensing the resistivity of phase change material. Basically, the great advantages of PCM are non-volatile, low idle power, high scalability, bit addressable and low read latency. However, the long SET operation increases the write latency, and the PCM cell can only sustain a limited number of writes which is known about $10^6$-$10^8$ in general [8]. Therefore, frequently writing to PCM will impact the performance and lifetime.

Some researchers believe that PCM will not completely replace DRAM and design new memory architecture either using a small amount of DRAM in front of PCM to cache PCM data [9, 10] or use PCM as an alternative main memory [11, 12]. In the hybrid memory systems, DRAM is used to store frequently accessed or write intensive data by effective memory management that consists of data partition methods, page replacement and migration policies. There are a large number of buffer managing policies based on different storage media and different kinds of architecture. For example, the classical LRU policy [13] is widely used in modern systems. Lazy-write organization [9] and CLOCK-DWF [12] are proposed for PCM-based hybrid memory. These buffer managing policies aim to the assumption that there is a big read/write latency gap between buffer and secondary storage, so that every request must be cached in the buffer. Finally, request for a cold page may evict a frequently accessed page because of the behavior of mandatory buffering.

As PCM has limited write endurance, many researchers proposed approaches to overcome the PCM write-endurance problem. These approaches can be roughly divided into two categories: *write count reduction* and *wear leveling*. The combination of DRAM and PCM described above is one way to reduce write count. But this cannot prolong the life-span of PCM if the writes to PCM are seriously localized. Thus wear leveling is necessary. In the past years, many policies such as DAC [14], PWL [15], and Hot-DL [3] have been proposed for flash memory, which are based on dynamic or static wear leveling. However, wear leveling researches on PCM are not like flash-based wear leveling methods because PCM is different from flash in some features like byte-addressable and in-place updating.

One kind of PCM-based wear leveling methods is the deterministic algorithm based on the age of pages. The age of a PCM page can be estimated by recording the write count information of the page. If one page whose life exceeds a given threshold, then we swap it with another page on which few write operations occur [16]. Park et al. [10] proposed an adaptive multiple data swapping and shifting scheme for PCM. They monitor the write pattern of PCM to determine whether swapping and shifting should be performed or not, and then perform page-level swaps and line-level shifting operations. This scheme implements wear leveling in multiple granularity and performs well, but it brings heavy storage overhead for maintaining the write counts of PCM. Zhou et al. [16] proposed two methods, row shifting and segment swapping, to achieve wear leveling of PCM. Comparing to literature [10], the two methods spend less storage to maintain metadata. However, they will introduce high search costs for the segments to be swapped if the PCM capacity becomes large, and swapping pages at a fix swap interval might not prevent wearing out the PCM pages from the attacks of malicious processes. Space overhead is the main drawback of age-based wear leveling schemes if they use a fine-granularity. To solve the space overhead, wear leveling policies that utilize random algorithms to swap data to another randomly selected place [7] are proposed. In these techniques, the accurate determination of a random algorithm and a swapping interval is important because they highly impact time performance and the effect of wear leveling.

Unfortunately, both age-based swapping and random-based swapping algorithms will incur the write amplification problem. Choi et al. [5] proposed PRAM translation layer (PTL) that dynamically translates logical addresses to physical addresses. Although PTL avoids write amplification, the age difference between read-only pages and frequently updated pages will become bigger if there is no update.

## 3  Space Management for PCM-Based Devices

Figure 1 shows the overall architecture of a PCM-based device. Though the PCM-based device can support multi-grained accesses, such as line-level or page-level access, we manage all spaces of PCM using a page granularity. If a request needs to access $x$-bytes data, we first check which pages the $x$-bytes data belong to. If these pages have been cached in the DRAM buffer, we just need to read or update the requested $x$-bytes data in the buffer. If the pages are not in the buffer, we read the pages from PCM to DRAM and then operate the $x$-bytes data in the buffer.

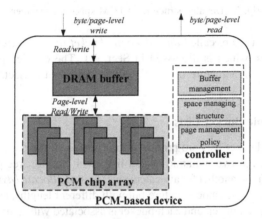

**Fig. 1.** Overall architecture of a PCM-based device

Figure 2 shows the detailed structure of our space management scheme. The spaces of PCM are divided into two parts: a data area and a metadata area. The data area is the actual physical space available for data storage. The metadata area maintains two kinds of metadata about the pages in the data area. The first kind of metadata is the age information of the pages in the data area. The age of a page is determined by its write count. Every time when a page is updated, its corresponding write count is increased. The second kind of metadata is a reversed mapping table that maps physical page numbers (PPN) to logical page numbers (LPN). This mapping table is dynamically reconstructed when the device is initialized. The reason for storing PPN-LPN reverse mapping table instead of LPN-PPN mapping table is explained as follows. If we store mapping table and the mapping relationships of LPN to PPN change frequently, the wear counts of the cells which are used to store the LPN-PPN mapping information are uncontrollable and mapping table area may be worn out if no finer granular wear leveling method is performed. On the contrary, storing PPN to LPN reverse mapping table will not incur such wearing problem because the write count of PCM cells storing the reverse mapping information is always less than the wear count of the corresponding data area page.

In addition, the pages in the data area are grouped into three categories: young group, middle-age group, and old group, according to the write count of the pages.

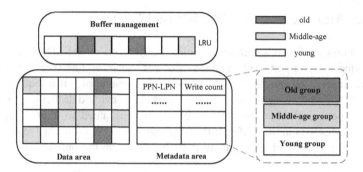

**Fig. 2.** Detailed structure of PCM space management

We design a new structure called *dual dynamic bucket lists* to classify the pages into the three categories, which is discussed in Sect. 3.1. The detailed page management algorithm based on the structure of Fig. 2 will be described in Sect. 3.2.

## 3.1   Dual Dynamic Bucket Lists

The dual dynamic bucket lists are proposed to organize all the pages in the data area. Particularly, we design two dynamic bucket lists, with one for free pages (called *free dynamic bucket list*) and another for allocated pages (called *allocated dynamic bucket list*).

The two lists have the same structure but with different lengths, as shown in Fig. 3. Each node in a list is a bucket, and each bucket is associated with a number denoting the age information of the pages in the bucket. We set $w$ as the basic value of the age of a page. Once a page is updated $n$ times $((i - 1) * w \leq n < i * w)$, its age is updated to $i * w$. Then, we put the pages whose write counts are within a certain range into the same bucket. For example, if the write count of a page is between $n*w$ and $(n + 1)*w$, we put the page into the bucket whose associated number is $(n + 1)*w$ (its age is $(n + 1)*w$). With the increasing of the write count of a page, we may need to move the page to a new bucket. Note that in the structure shown in Fig. 3, the pages among different buckets are ordered, while the pages in the same bucket are disordered. At the beginning, there is

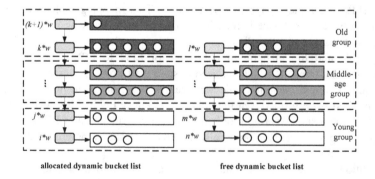

**Fig. 3.** Dual dynamic bucket lists

only one bucket node in the free dynamic bucket list containing all available pages in PCM. The allocated dynamic bucket list is initially empty because there is no real data stored in PCM.

The purpose of wear leveling is to prevent old pages from being worn out, thus we need to identify the oldness of the pages in the data area. For this purpose, we divide the pages in the lists into three groups: young group, middle-age group, and old group. Each group contains a set of pages and is denoted by the dotted boxes in Fig. 4. The partitioning of the three groups is based on average write count of pages. As we have maintained the write count of each page within the data area in the dynamic bucket lists, we can calculate the average write count of all the pages in PCM by (3.1).

$$averagewritecount = \frac{totalwritecount}{totalpages} \tag{3.1}$$

Then, given the average write count $AW$, we say a page is within the middle-age group if the absolute difference between the write count of the page and the average write count $AW$ is less than a threshold $TH$. Similarly, a page whose write count is over $(AW + TH)$ is identified as an old page and is put in the old group, and pages with write counts less than $(AW + TH)$ are put in the young group. The group to which the pages belong may change as $AW$ will increase after several writes.

Thus, for ensuring wear leveling, we can simply select the pages from the youngest bucket in the free dynamic bucket list if a request of page allocation arrives. However, the challenging problem is that this policy will lead to poor effectiveness if the free dynamic bucket list only contains old pages (pages in the old group). This is because allocating old pages may bring more writes to these pages and worsen the write endurance of PCM. Therefore, we propose a new effective approach for page management, which is described in Sect. 3.2.

## 3.2    Page Management for Wear Leveling

In this section, we introduce a novel PCM page management based on the dual dynamic bucket lists.

Previous PCM-based wear leveling policies, such as segment swapping [16], random swapping [7], and adaptive multiple data swapping and shifting scheme [10], relied on the parameters of operation timing and the number of swapping pages which have a high impact on the performance of wear leveling. Differing from previous approaches, our proposal does not need such parameters and the swapping or migration operations are controlled by page allocations. In addition, we perform in-place updates on young pages and out-of-place updates on old pages, which can improve the performance of wear leveling.

We use an LRU list to maintain the request information about each data page. Thus, for each write to PCM, we can easily identify the exact group to which the updated page belongs based on the write count information of pages in the LRU list. Generally, in order to improve the performance of wear leveling, we aim to make the write counts of each page close to the average write count. Therefore, young pages should absorb more write requests than old pages. For this purpose, we let young pages be updated by the in-place updating policy, but old pages have to be updated in the manner of out-of-place updating, because we need to reduce writes to old pages. For example, in Fig. 4, a dirty page C which belongs to the old group is evicted from the buffer, and an out-of-place writing operation to C is performed. Figure 4 shows the procedure of writing back an old page from the buffer to PCM. The parts marked by (1) show the initial state when C is evicted from the buffer. The parts marked by (2) are the states after page C has been written back to PCM. We can see that page C was stored in physical page PPN10 which belongs to the old group before performing the update operation. We allocate a new empty young page PPN7 for the required out-of-place write and update the mapping table. Then, we write page C to PPN7. Finally, PPN10 is reclaimed to be a free page. With this mechanism, the write count of PPN10 does not increase, yielding better performance of wear leveling for PCM.

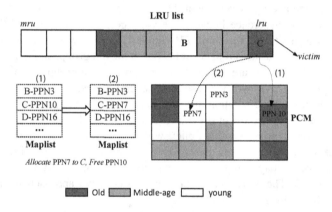

**Fig. 4.** The procedure of out-of-place updating

| **Algorithm 1:** *Page Allocation* |
| --- |
| 1:      $p$=the page from the youngest bucket of the free dynamic bucket list; |
| 2:      **if** ($p.write\_count - AW < TH$) **then** |
| 3:           allocate $p$ and **return** $p$; /* $p$ is in the young or middle-age group*/ |
| 4:      **else** /*page $p$ belongs to old group*/ |
| 5:           $q$= the youngest bucket of the allocated dynamic bucket list; |
|              /*$q$ is in the young or middle-age group*/ |
| 6:           update the mapping information from $q$ to $p$ and copy the data of $q$ to $p$; |
| 7:           release $q$ and add $q$ into the free dynamic bucket list; |
| 8:           allocate $q$ and **return** $q$; |

Generally, a page allocation command originates from either an updating of an old page or a new logical page mapping, both of which may introduce write operations. Thus, the allocated new page is first regarded as a hot page due to the temporal locality of page requests. If the newly allocated page belongs to the old group, possible write operations will worsen the performance of wear leveling. Therefore, we suggest that only the pages in the young or middle-age groups can be allocated as new pages. If a page allocation request arrives but the free dynamic bucket list only contains old pages, a young page in the allocated dynamic bucket list needs to be released. Since the page to be released is relatively young, meaning that it will not be written frequently in the near future, we move the page to a free old page, so that the young page can be released and reallocated. As a consequence, a page allocation request will introduce additional page migration and page swapping operations.

**Algorithm 1** shows the detailed process of page allocation. When a free page is needed, a page $p$ in the youngest bucket of free dynamic bucket list is selected. If $p$ belongs to young or the middle-age group, it is allocated directly (Line 1-3). Otherwise, if $p$ belongs to the old group, another page $q$ in the youngest bucket of the allocated dynamic bucket list is selected as victim. In order to allocate $q$ to response the page allocation request, $p$ should be allocated to store the data of $q$, and the LPN of $q$ is updated to link to $p$ (Line 4-6). Finally, $q$ is released and reallocated (Line 7-8).

Figure 5 shows an example of data migration caused by a page allocation. In Fig. 5, each cycle represents a physical page number, and the letter in the cycle denotes the associated logical page number of the physical page. For instance, the physical page PPN4 is mapped to the logical page $A$. Figure 5(a) shows the initial state of the dual dynamic bucket lists before executing the data migration, PPN4 is a young page, and all the free pages in the free dynamic bucket list belong to the old group. When a page migration is performed, the page PPN4 in the allocated dynamic bucket list is selected as the victim. The mapping information of its logical page $A$ is changed to a new page,

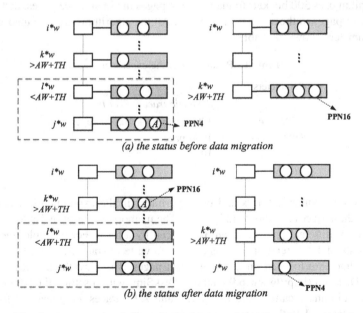

(a) the status before data migration

(b) the status after data migration

**Fig. 5.** An example of data migration incurred by allocating command

namely PPN16, which is selected from the free dynamic bucket list. The data in PPN4 is then copied to PPN16 and PPN4 is reclaimed and put into the free dynamic bucket list, as shown in Fig. 5(b). After that, the free dynamic bucket list has a free young page that is used to response the page allocation request.

We summarize the storage overhead for managing 4 GB PCM. The information stored in metadata area includes age information of all pages and the reverse mapping table from PPN to LPN (To reduce space overhead, we set the basic managing unit as a page). Since our system allows byte-level reading or writing, if the system updates several bytes, we increase the wear count of the pages which these updated bytes belong to. For a 4 GB PCM storage, the page size is set to 4 KB, so there are $2^{20}$ pages. We use 4B to store the age information per page since the write limitation is $10^6$-$10^8$, the space used to store age information is 4 MB. Meanwhile, 4 B is also enough to maintain the reverse mapping information per a page, so another 4 MB is needed. So the total space overhead to store metadata for a 4 GB PCM storage is 8 MB.

## 4 Performance Evaluation

### 4.1 Experimental Settings

We implemented a PCM simulator according to the architecture of Fig. 1. The page size of the DRAM buffer as well as PCM is set to 4 KB. The DRAM buffer is managed by the LRU policy. We compare our proposal with several existing algorithms including the random swapping algorithm [7], PTL [5], and the bucket-based WL algorithm [6]. The random swapping algorithm swaps the page to be written with a randomly selected page after every 512 write operations to PCM. The bucket-based WL algorithm uses 500 buckets to maintain the pages in use and free pages, and the age difference of pages in the same buckets is 10. All the algorithms are executed with the same parameters shown in Table 1.

**Table 1.** Parameters in the experiments

| Parameters | Value | |
|---|---|---|
| | Synthetic traces | Real traces |
| PCM size | 12000 pages | 52000 pages |
| DRAM buffer size | 1000 pages | |
| w | 10 | |
| TH | 30 | |

We use two synthetic traces and two real traces in the experiments. The characteristics of these traces are shown in Table 2. The memory footprint in Table 2 refers to the number of different pages that are referenced by a trace. For example, the T1982 trace consists of 10 % read operations and 90 % write operations, and 80 % requests within the trace are focused on 20 % different pages. These synthetic traces are generated by DiskSim (http://www.pdl.cmu.edu/DiskSim) within setting the parameters of read/write ratio and locality. And the OLTP and ZIPF traces are generated from real database systems when the systems access to disk data.

**Table 2.** Synthetic and real traces used in the experiments

| Trace | Memory Footprint | Read/Write Ratio | Locality | Total Requests |
|-------|------------------|------------------|----------|----------------|
| T1982 | 10,000 | 10 % / 90 % | 80 % / 20 % | 300,000 |
| T1955 | 10,000 | 10 % / 90 % | 50 % / 50 % | 300,000 |
| OLTP | 51,880 | 77 % / 23 % | ~ | 607,390 |
| ZIPF | 47,023 | 51 % / 49 % | ~ | 500,000 |

## 4.2  Experimental Results

### 4.2.1  Impact of the Parameter TH and W

We first conduct an experiment to see the impact of the parameter TH and w. In this experiment, we run our algorithm on the four traces with various values of TH and w. We focus on measuring the maximum write count on one PCM page after the execution of a trace. This metric is an important factor that affects the lifetime of PCM. Figure 6 shows the results of maximum write count by varying TH from 10 to 80 and varying w from 10 to 20. We can see that the maximum write count increases with w and TH in most cases, especially when TH is over 30. This is because the numerical age range of pages that belong to the middle-age group becomes larger as TH and w increases, and the pages can tolerate more writes before they belong to the old group, making the maximum write count larger. This also causes a degradation of the total migration count. In the following experiments, we set TH to 30 and w to 10.

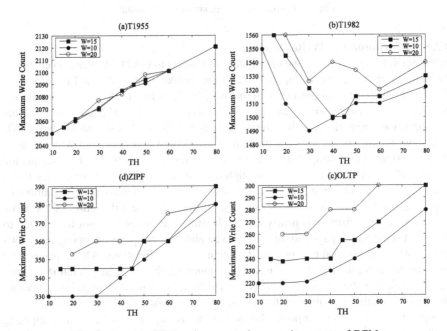

**Fig. 6.** Impact of TH and w on maximum write counts of PCM

### 4.2.2     Maximum Write Count on PCM

Figure 7 shows the maximum write counts on PCM for various traces. We can see that
the maximum write count of our proposal is much less than that of competitor algorithms, indicating that our algorithm brings less writes to each PCM page, which is
helpful to lengthen the lifetime of PCM. The random swap algorithm gets the worst
result because in this algorithm, the page to be accessed may not be the oldest pages
when a page swapping is triggered. Note that when T1955 is used, our proposal has
similar result with PTL. This is because of the special feature of T1955, in which the
trace all the requests are evenly distributed.

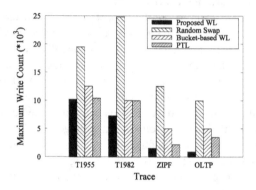

**Fig. 7.**   Comparison of maximum write count

### 4.2.3     Distribution of Write Requests

In this section, we will show the distribution of write count in PCM after implementing
the same number of requests. Figure 8 shows the comparative results on T1982, and the
results on other traces are similar with that on T1982. In Fig. 8, the $y$-axis refers to the
number of writes on each page and the $x$-axis refers to the physical page numbers. Note
that the value range of $y$-axis is different in each sub-figure. For the bucket-based WL
algorithm, the difference between maximum write count and minimum write count is
about 5000 and the writing distribution is about from 4700 to 10000. PTL adopts the
strategy of out-of-place updating, although most of the pages are worn evenly (from
7700 to 8200), there are still a few pages that have been tolerated a large number of
write operations. The random swap method shows the largest deviation of the write
count than others (from 0 to nearly 25000) because old pages may not be selected to
swap and some empty pages are not likely to be allocated for page swapping. As shown
in Fig. 8(a), our proposal narrows the deviation of write operations. All the pages have
been written at least 7190 times, but the maximum number of write operations is only
7284. A red line shown in Fig. 8(a) is formed by a large number of points gathering
together. Actually, this line is the boundary of the old group and the middle-age
group. The result of our proposal shows that the average age is 7247 after applying
T1982, and the pages whose write count is over $ave + TH$ (that is, $7247 + 30 = 7277$)
belong to the old group, indicating that our proposal can guarantee most of the pages
are below the line.

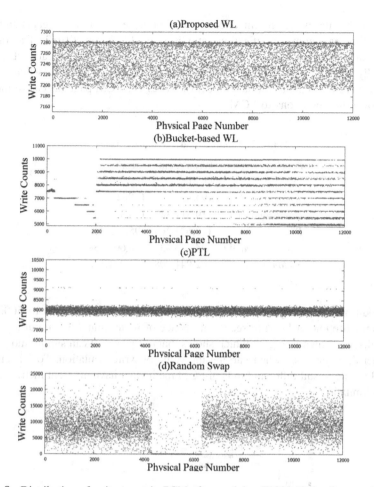

**Fig. 8.** Distribution of write count in PCM after applying T1982 (Color figure online)

### 4.2.4 Lifetime of PCM

The life time of PCM is evaluated based on the first failure time, that is, the first time that a PCM page is worn out. Previous literature has reported that a PCM cell can tolerate about $10^6 \sim 10^8$ writes in general [5]. In this experiment, the write limitation of a PCM page is set to $10^4$. Since some write requests are cached in the buffer before being written back to PCM, we do not use the overall number of write requests but use the actual writes to PCM. If a page management scheme can undergo more writes than others, it is considered to be a better policy. The number of pages in PCM is set to 12000, thus the total number of write operations that PCM can tolerate in the ideal case is *pages × limitation* (12000 × 10000). Table 3 shows the comparative results. Our approach can tolerate more write operations before a PCM page is worn out than other three methods, and achieve about 99.5 % and 96.9 % of the ideal lifetime when T1955 and T1982 are executed. By contrast, PTL, the bucket-based WL, and the random swap algorithm only achieve 89 %, 75.5 %, and 37 % of the ideal lifetime. The experiments also shows that the write amplification ratio of proposed method is very small. Particularly, the maximum amplification ratio is only 2.7 % on T1982. The random swapping algorithm incurs more extra writes than others on T1955 because it invokes periodically page swaps. On the contrary, in our proposed method, whether wear leveling is invoked depends on the number of writes to a PCM page instead of the total number of write operations to PCM.

**Table 3.** Lifetime under synthetic traces

| Policies | Write count of wearing out PCM | |
|---|---|---|
| | 1955 | T1982 |
| *Our Proposal* | 119,511,349 | 116,328,780 |
| *PTL* | 117,628,266 | 95,740,849 |
| *Bucket-based WL* | 94,416,434 | 86,691,668 |
| *Radom swap* | 62,941,008 | 26,001,132 |

In addition, we change the write limitation of a page from 10000 to 50000 and measure the lifetime of PCM to see the influence of write limitation on our algorithm. The results are shown in Fig. 9, which shows that our proposal can supply more writes than other three methods when varying the value of write limitation. To this end, our proposal is able to suit different kinds of PCM media that have different metrics in term of write limitation.

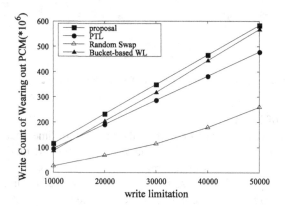

**Fig. 9.** Life time of PCM when varying write limitation

## 5   Conclusion

In this paper, we propose a PCM-based device and present an efficient approach for the page management of PCM-based device. Specially, we propose a new structure (called dynamic bucket list) to manage the pages of PCM. With this design, all the pages of PCM are organized into a free dynamic bucket list for maintaining free pages and an allocated dynamic bucket list for allocated pages. Based on the dynamic bucket lists, we propose a page management scheme for page allocation, page migration, and page swaps. With this mechanism, write operations are distributed to PCM chips in a balanced manner and the write amplification ratio of PCM incurred by page swaps is reduced. We conduct experiments on a simulated PCM-based storage system to compare our proposal with several existing approaches including PTL, the bucket-based WL algorithm, and the random swapping algorithm. The results show the efficiency of our approach.

**Acknowledgements.** This work is partially supported by the National Science Foundation of China under the grant (61379037 and 61472376) and the Fundamental Research Funds for the Central Universities.

# References

1. Wu, Z., Jin, P., Yang, C., Yue, L.: APP-LRU: A new page replacement method for PCM/DRAM-based hybrid memory systems. In: Hsu, C.-H., Shi, X., Salapura, V. (eds.) NPC 2014. LNCS, vol. 8707, pp. 84–95. Springer, Heidelberg (2014)
2. Chen, K., Jin, P., Yue, L.: A novel page replacement algorithm for the hybrid memory architecture involving PCM and DRAM. In: Hsu, C.-H., Shi, X., Salapura, V. (eds.) NPC 2014. LNCS, vol. 8707, pp. 108–119. Springer, Heidelberg (2014)
3. Kwon, S.J., Chung, T.S.: Hot-LSNs: Distributing Wear-Leveling Algorithm for Flash Memory. ACM Transactions on Embedded Computing Systems, 12(1 s), no. 62 (2013)
4. Lu, K., Jin, P., Yang, P., Wan, S., Yue, L.: Adaptive in-page logging for flash-memory storage systems. Front. Comput. Sci. 8(1), 131–144 (2014)
5. Choi, G.S., On, B.W., Choi, K., Yi, S.: PTL: PRAM translation layer. Microprocess. Microsyst. 37(1), 24–32 (2013)
6. Chen, C.H., Hsiu, P.C., Kuo, T.W., Yang, C.-L., Wang, C.-Y.:. Age-based PCM wear leveling with nearly zero search cost. In: 49th Design Automation Conference, pp. 453–458. ACM, New York (2012)
7. Ferreira, A.P., Zhou, M., Bock, S., Childers, B., Melhem, R., Mosséet, D.: Increasing PCM main memory lifetime. In: 13th International Conference on Design, Automation, and Test in Europe, pp. 914–919. IEEE Press, New York (2010)
8. Chang, H.S., Chang, Y.H., Hsiu, P.C., Kuo, T.W., Li, H.P.: Marching-based wear-leveling for PCM-based storage systems. ACM Trans. Des. Autom. Electron. Syst. 20(2), 25 (2015)
9. Qureshi, M., Srinivasan, V., Rivers, J.: Scalable high performance main memory system using phase-change memory technology. In: 36th International Symposium on Computer Architecture, pp. 24–33. ACM, New York (2009)
10. Park, S.K., Maeng, M.K., Park, K.W., Park, K.H.: Adaptive wear-leveling algorithm for PRAM main memory with a DRAM buffer. ACM Trans. Embedded Comput. Syst. 13(4), 88 (2014)
11. Shin, D.J., Park, S.K., Kim, S.M., Park, K.H.: Adaptive page grouping for energy efficiency in hybrid PRAM-DRAM main memory. In: 2012 ACM Research in Applied Computation Symposium, pp. 395–402. ACM, New York (2012)

12. Lee, S., Bahn, H., Noh, S.H.: Characterizing memory write references for efficient management of hybrid PCM and DRAM memory. In: 19th Annual IEEE/ACM International Symposium on Modeling, Analysis and Simulation of Computer and Telecommunication Systems, pp. 168–175. IEEE Press, New York (2011)
13. Coffman, E.G., Denning, P.J.: Operating Systems Theory. Prentice-Hall, New Jersey (1973)
14. Chiang, M.L., Chang, R.C.: Cleaning policies in mobile computers using flash memory. J. Syst. Softw. **48**(3), 213–231 (1999)
15. Chen, F.H., Yang, M.C., Chang, Y.H., Kuo, T.W.: PWL: A progressive wear leveling to minimize data migration overheads for NAND flash devices. In: 18th International Conference on Design, Automation, and Test in Europe, pp. 1209–1212 (2015)
16. Zhou, P., Zhao, B., Yang, J., Zhang, Y.: A durable and energy efficient main memory using phase change memory technology. ACM SIGARCH Comput. Architect. News **37**(3), 14–23 (2009)

# An Investigation of the Impact of Double Bit-Flip Error Variants on Program Execution

Fatimah Adamu-Fika$^{(\boxtimes)}$ and Arshad Jhumka

Department of Computer Science, University of Warwick Coventry,
Coventry CV4 7AL, UK
{fatimah,arshad}@dcs.warwick.ac.uk

**Abstract.** The objective of this paper is to investigate two existing variants of the double bit-flip error models and their impact on program execution. The two variants are (i) flipping two bits in a given word or register and (ii) flipping one bit in two different words or registers. The goal of the study is to determine whether there is relevance for consideration for both variants during program validation. Specifically, we seek to determine if the profile failures induced on software by the variants are different. This then motivates that both are needed for validation. We conduct a large-scale experiment on five different software systems from two target systems. Our results show that each variant induces a different failure profile in software. Hence, we conclude that both variants are important during validation.

**Keywords:** Multiple bit-flip errors · Fault injection · Failure profile · Evaluation

## 1 Introduction

The rate of hardware transient faults is increasing with reducing hardware sizes and with issues such as temperature hotspots [3,15,20]. These transients faults cause errors to exist in running programs [9] by subverting bits in CPU registers or memory words [5,8]. To emulate these errors, system execution is artificially perturbed by injecting bit-flip errors into program state during a process called fault injection [6]. Traditionally, a single bit is flipped in a single run of the program. This typically involves selecting a location and inverting a bit at that location at some given time. However, the occurrence of multiple transient faults limits the usefulness of single bit-flip errors in uncovering vulnerabilities and, in turn, necessitates the injection of multiple bit-flip errors in a single run. To evaluate the ability of software to tolerate these faults, fault injection is widely used for the validation of dependable systems. Its recommendation as a highly valuable assessment method in the recently published ISO 26262 standard [7] for functional safety of road vehicles supports the recognition of its increasing importance.

There is some evidence that shows several bit upsets occurring within a single memory word and single bit upsets occurring across several memory words, while

© Springer International Publishing Switzerland 2015
G. Wang et al. (Eds.): ICA3PP 2015, Part IV, LNCS 9531, pp. 799–813, 2015.
DOI: 10.1007/978-3-319-27140-8_55

also there has been observations that errors may occur chip-wide [11,17]. On the other hand, there is lack of field data on the manifestation of multiple faults in registers. Several works have started investigating double bit-flip errors fault models, in anticipation of hardware being susceptible to multiple faults [1,2,19]. The works in [2,19] focused on the variant of double bit-flip errors occurring at a given location (i.e., memory word or register), where *two bits* are selected and are subsequently flipped. We call this variant the *double bit-flip* model (DBF). A novel variant of the double bit-flip error model called the *Double Single Bit-flip* (DSB) fault model was considered in [1], where *two locations are selected and a single bit-flip error is injected at each location*. Hence, we need to investigate whether the DBF and DSB give rise to different failure profiles and in turn determine whether *both variants need to be considered during validation*.

The utility of a fault model lies in its ability to discover weaknesses in a system during validation. In particular, it is common that the *error sensitivity* of a software system is evaluated with respect to the errors being introduced according to the assumed fault model. Error sensitivity is often defined as the likelihood that a software component, as a result of a hardware error, will produce an error that may go undetected by the system. This type of error is called a silent data corruption (SDC).

It has also been observed that different fault models will induce different failure profiles in software, thereby motivating the need to consider various fault models for coverage [13]. Thus by injecting double faults variants the coverage of double bit-flips is expected to increase thereby decreasing inaccuracy. Hence, we have conducted an extensive fault injection campaign, in excess of one and a half million fault injection experiments on five different software modules from two different target systems, each with different software structures, to test our hypothesis.

The objective of our study is to determine whether the failure profile induced by DSB differs from DBF. As such, our main contributions are (i) we provide a categorisation based on injection location, (ii) we conduct a large scale fault injection experiments for DSB and DBF errors, and (iii) we conduct traditional SBF fault injections as a baseline comparison. The main result shows that DSB induces a failure profile different from the one induced by DBF.

The remainder of this paper is structured as follows: We describe our system and fault models in Sect. 2. In Sect. 4, we describe the fault injection conducted, including target programs used and input set processed during fault injections and the experimental setup used. We present the results of our experiments in Sect. 5. Section 6 discusses the limitations of our study and overarching issues. In Sect. 7, we conclude the paper, and provide some areas of future research.

## 2   Models

We now present the system and fault models we assume in the rest of the paper.

## 2.1   System Model

We consider modular software systems, i.e., software that consists of a number of components which offer discrete software functions. Each component may consist of one or more sub-components. These components interact with each other to deliver the requisite functionality. We consider a component to be *white-box*, i.e., the codebase is available, having possibly multiple inputs and outputs. We do not assume knowledge of the implementation details though. The codebase is only needed to enable the software to be instrumented to enable artificial bit-flip errors to be injected.

Components communicate with each other in some specified way using different forms of signalling, e.g., shared memory, parameter passing etc. A component performs computations using the inputs received on its input channels to generate the outputs, which are then placed on the requisite output channels. At the lowest abstraction level, a component may be a procedure or a function and a process at the highest level. Such type of software is commonplace nowadays and can be seen in many different applications areas, such as embedded systems.

## 2.2   Fault Model

In this paper, we consider transient hardware faults originating at the transistor level, that ultimately impact on the software modules. These faults are usually caused by issues such as temperature hotspots and cosmic ray or alpha particle strikes. Also, the faults impact on the program state by altering the content of memory and registers, and through the process of error propagation results in *errors* [9] existing in the software modules. These errors are usually mimicked by injecting bit-flip errors in memory and registers. We consider faults that occur in the data, sdata, bss, sbss and stack segments of the Static Random Access Memory (SRAM), which, hereon, we refer to as words. In addition, we consider faults that occur in general purpose registers, stack pointer registers and Arithmetic Logic Unit (ALU) input and output registers. The general assumption is any number of bit-flip errors may occur in any number of locations. In this paper, we only consider two bit-flip errors occurring. We implemented this as either *double single bit-flips (DSB)*, where we flip one bit in two different target words or registers or *DBF*, where we flip two bits within one target word or register.

## 3   Problem Statement

In this paper, we investigate the differences in impact on software of two variant implementations of the double bit-flip errors fault models (the double single bit-flip (DSB) proposed in [1] and double bit-flip fault (DBF) model variant used in [2,19]), injected in the same injection locations (an injection location being either one main memory word or register, or two main memory words or registers). The overall objective of the study is to determine whether there is need for considering the two variants during software validation. Specifically, if the variants induce different failure profiles on the target software, then we conclude that there is a need for both variants.

To achieve this objective, we consider the following goals:

– We study the impact of the injection location with respect to the failure mode of the program.
– We study the failure profiles induced by both DSB and DBF on programs and, subsequently, compare the induced failure profiles. However, the comparison does not extend to decide which of the models is better.
– As a baseline comparison, we study the failure profile induced by SBF errors.

## 4    Fault-Injection Experiments

In this section, we provide details about the fault injection experiments conducted, including details about target modules and the input set that are processed by the modules during fault injection, and experimental setup and procedure.

### 4.1    Target Programs

We conducted fault injections for five different modules selected from two different software systems[1].

**SUSAN (Smallest Univalue Segment Assimilating Nucleus).** The first system is an image recognition package[2], developed for noise filtering and for recognising corners and edges in Magnetic Resonance Image (MRI) of the brain [16]. In SUSAN, we targeted three different modules for corners detection, edges detection and noise filtering, for simplicity we refer to them as corners, edges and smoothing respectively in this paper.[3]

**Flight Control.** The second system we instrumented is a flight longitudinal motion control system of an aircraft. First order linear approximations of the aircraft and actuator behaviour are connected to an analog flight control design that uses the pilot's stick pitch command as the set point for the aircraft's pitch attitude and uses aircraft pitch angle and pitch rate to determine commands. To perturb the system, a simplified Dryden wind gust model is incorporated [12].

---

[1] One is a soft computing application, SUSAN [16] and the second a safety-critical system, Mathwork's implementation of a flight control system for the longitudinal motion of an aircraft [12].

[2] SUSAN is available as self-contained C program from [16]. SUSAN is also available as a program in the automative package of the MiBench suite [4].

[3] Each module is ran with input files of varying sizes, small, medium and large. The medium file comes with the SUSAN package from [16], while the small and large files comes with the SUSAN package in the MiBench suite [4].

Within the flight control system, we used two modules for instrumentation, one for updating derivatives for the root system and the other for updating the model step, we refer to the two modules as derivatives and step respectively in the rest of the paper.[4]

Description of the input set used in the fault injection experiments is provided in Table 1.

**Table 1.** Sizes of target modules and description of their input set

| Target Module | Size (bytes) | Input description | Output |
|---|---|---|---|
| Corners | 7975 | File format: PGM | |
| Edges | 6053 | Input set: A simple four-sided geometric shape (7292 bytes) | PGM file |
| Smoothing | 3488 | Multiple geometric shapes of various shapes and sizes (65551 bytes) An image (111666 bytes) | |
| Derivatives | 2915 | Input format: Pilot Frequency in rads/secs | |
| Step | 10249 | Input set: Variable of type unsigned long long between 0.030000000000000000 to 0.1199999999999999 | MAT logging file |

## 4.2 Experimental Setup

In this section, we provide details about the experimental setup and the fault injection experiments that we conducted.

**System Specification.** The experiments were executed on a Darwin (Kernel version 14.1.0) machine having a 22 nm Haswell 3.0 GHz Intel Core i7 processor, with dual independent processor cores on a single silicon chip, with 16 GB of 1600 MHz DDR3L SDRAM and 500 GB solid state drive.

**Fault Injection Tool.** Faults were injected using LLVM Fault Injection Tool (LLFI)[5] [18]. LLFI is a LLVM-based fault injection tool that works at the LLVM [10] compiler's intermediate representation (IR) level[6].

---

[4] Each module is ran with three different pilot frequencies, small, medium and large.

[5] An extended version of LLFI (*extended FR-LLFI*) as reported in [1] was used for the experiments.

[6] The IR is a low-level programming language similar to assembly. The IR is a strongly types RISC instruction set which abstracts away details of the target platform.

**Instrumentation.** To perform fault injection, we first compiled the source files of the software system into a single IR file. The IR file along with a fault injection configuration script[7] are passed through to the *instrumentor* of the extended FR-LLFI to produce an instrumented IR files and executable C/C++ object files. The profiling executable C/C++ object file generated by the instrumentor is fed to the *profiler* of the extended FR-LLFI to generate setup files to be used for the injection phase and to execute the *golden run*, i.e. a fault-free execution of the program. Finally, the setup files generated in the profiling phase together with IR file and fault-injection executable C/C++ object files produced in the instrumentation phase and the initial configuration script are passed to the fault-injector of the extended FR-LLFI to execute the fault-injection experiments. The output of the fault-injector is the fault injection experiments, including program output, log and stat files[8]. Figure 1 depicts the workflow of the *extended FR-LLFI* [1].

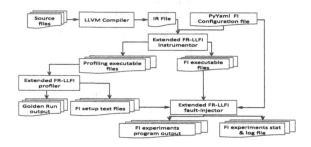

**Fig. 1.** Extended FR-LLFI fault-injection workflow

**Experimental Procedure.** To achieve the goals we stated in Sect. 3, we executed a number of fault injection experiments into a number of different variables (or combination of variables) in five different modules. We executed each target module on three inputs to cover all parts of the module's source code.

Before commencing these experiments, we choose six variables at random, since we do not have any implementation knowledge. We define a *target location* as a particular word in memory or a particular register. Alternatively, it also means a variable at a particular location in the program. An *injection location* is the target location(s) selected to inject faults into, according to the assumed fault model. When a DBF error is injected, a single target location is selected, whereas two target locations are selected when injecting a DSB error. A fault injection *experiment* is the injection of an error at the selected location(s), according to

---

[7] Written in PyYaml format [14].

[8] The log files captures execution information including program exceptions and system crashes etc., while the stat files stores execution information such as injected fault type, injection location etc.

the assumed fault model. A fault injection *campaign* is a set of fault injection experiments on a given input set using the same fault model. Errors are only injected in target location(s) immediately before the target location is read to avoid unnecessary overwrites.

For each of the chosen variable, two injection locations are selected, the word in memory it corresponds to and a register it correlates with. For each injection location, we exhaustively inject double bit-flip errors to cover all possible combination. For the DBF fault model, we conducted $\binom{n}{r}$ experiments in each injection location, $n$ being the size of (number of bits in) the word or register and $r = 2$ (the number of bits to flip). We injected a total of *278,208* DBF errors across the five different modules. For the DSB fault model, for each injection location we ran $n \times m$ experiments, $m, n$ being the size of its target locations. In total, we injected *1,332,686* DSB errors over all the target modules. We injected a total of *9,984* SBF errors across the different modules.

*Injection Location Data Categorisation.* We categorised an injection location as follows:

- *Control.* If it holds a control data in at least one of its target locations and neither target locations is a pointer. Control data items are usually loop termination condition and branching condition.
- *Pointer.* If it holds a pointer data in any of its target locations and neither target locations is control. Pointer data include pointer, array and struct data items.
- *Control and Pointer.* If it holds control data in one of its target locations and pointer data in the other. DBF errors do not get categorised as such since they only have a single target location in their injection location.
- *Neither.* If it holds neither control nor pointer data in any of its target locations. The data under this category are usually normal data such as signed and unsigned integer numbers etc.

*Target Register Categorisation.* We partitioned injection location having register target locations into:

- *General Purpose.* If at least one of its target locations is a general purpose register. This target location stores either data or address.
- *Stack Pointer.* If it has a stack pointer register as one of its a target location. This target location stores addresses.
- *ALU Input.* If either of its target locations holds the input operand for the ALU.
- *ALU Output.* If at least one of its target location holds the result of an ALU operation, including address computation.

*Fault Injection Outcome Categorisation.* We classified the outcome of each fault injection experiment as follows:

- *Safe Run.* If the program execution terminates normally, and the output produced is identical to that of the golden run's.

- *Data failure.* If the program execution terminates normally, but fails to produce an output or produces an output that differs from that of the golden run's.
- *Time Out failure.* If the program execution hangs, i.e. fails to terminate within predefined time. We set this time to be approximately 15 times larger than the execution time of the golden run.
- *Crash failure.* If the program execution is terminated due to an exception either by the program or by the OS.

**Table 2.** Average number of fault injections according to injection locations

(a) For data categories across target modules

| Data Category | Fault Injections |
|---|---|
| Control & Pointer | 174080 |
| Control | 199632 |
| Pointer | 1164125 |
| Neither | 83808 |

(b) For register categories across target modules

| Register Category | Fault Injections |
|---|---|
| General purpose | 272384 |
| Stack pointer | 379946 |
| ALU intput | 202666 |
| ALU output | 541085 |

## 5    Experimental Results

In this section, we analyse the results of the various fault injection experiments, as presented in Tables 3, 4 and Figs. 2, 3 and 4. Specifically, we wish to analyse the results in light of the goals defined in Sect. 3.

### 5.1    Failure Profile of DSB Errors Vs. DBF Errors.

The first goal of the paper was to evaluate the impact of DSB errors on programs compared to that of DBF errors in the same variables. The results for all the modules are summarised in Table 3, while an overall summary is presented in Fig. 2.

Figure 2a shows the failure profile across all campaigns for DSB, and Fig. 2b shows that of DBF. As observed in these figures, there is no noticeable overall difference between the failure profile induced by DSB errors compared to that by DBF errors. The Safe Run category has the most observed difference of only 1.6 %.

However, at the module-level, the failure profile induced by the two variants differs considerably, specifically in the Crash failure outcome. Table 3 shows fault injection outcomes between DSB errors and DBF errors per different target location across the modules.

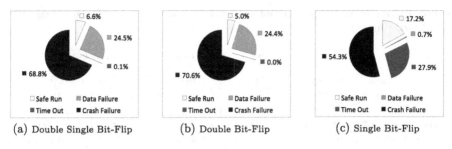

(a) Double Single Bit-Flip        (b) Double Bit-Flip        (c) Single Bit-Flip

**Fig. 2.** Average fault injection outcome distributions over all target modules

**Flight Control Modules.** In the modules from the flight control, we observe that the proportion of Crash failures is ≈ 7% higher for the DSB errors than for DBF errors. On the other hand, the Data failure outcome is ≈ 7% higher for the DBF errors than for DSB errors. Also, we observe no difference between the two fault models for the Time Out and Safe Run outcomes.

**SUSAN's Modules.** We observe in the edges and corners modules from SUSAN that the Crash failure outcome is ≈ 8% higher for DBF errors. On the other hand, the Crash failure outcome is only 1.5% higher for DSB errors in the smoothing module. We observe no considerable difference between the two types of errors in the other fault outcome categories. However, in the corners module the Safe Run outcome is ≈ 9% lower for the DBF error. Further, we observe in the edges module the Data failure outcome is ≈ 9% higher for the DSB error.

**Baseline Comparison.** Figure 2c shows the failure profile across all campaigns for SBF. We observed that there is marked difference between the failure profile induced by both DSB and DBF errors to that of SBF errors. Further, the proportion of Safe Run under SBF is more than double compared to that observed under DSB errors and almost three times more compared to the proportion of safe run under DBF (see Fig. 2). Whereas, the proportion of Crash failure is considerably higher (≈ 18%) under DSB errors and (≈ 20%) under DBF errors than under SBF errors. On the other hand, we observe a reduction in the occurrence Data failure (≈ 9%) under DSB and DBF errors. We conjecture that this is due to the fact DSB and DBF errors induce more Crash failure, which cause the program to prematurely exit and hence such executions cannot display Data failures. We reckon that similar with the Data failures because DSB and DBF errors mostly causes the program to prematurely exit, little and no executions tend to hang. We conclude that DSB and DBF errors induce a failure profile different to that induced by SBF errors. As such, we conclude that both DSB and DBF errors uncover new vulnerabilities in the system, and hence, need to be considered when validating dependable software systems.

**Table 3.** Average fault injection outcome distribution between DSB, DBF and SBF for all target modules

| Target Module | Safe Run | | | Data Failure | | | Time Out | | | Crash Failure | | |
|---|---|---|---|---|---|---|---|---|---|---|---|---|
| | DSB | DBF | SBF | DSB | DBF | SBF | DSB | DBF | SBF | DSB | DBF | SBF |
| Corners | 19.2% | 10.3% | 33.1% | 3.9% | 5.2% | 2.9% | 0.1% | 0.0% | 0.6% | 76.7% | 84.6% | 63.4% |
| Edges | 11.5% | 12.3% | 28.6% | 15.6% | 6.9% | 11.5% | 0.0% | 0.0% | 1.1% | 72.9% | 80.8% | 58.8% |
| Smoothing | 2.2% | 2.2% | 11.5% | 19.6% | 18.3% | 39.0% | 0.3% | 0.2% | 2.5% | 77.9% | 79.4% | 47.0% |
| Derivatives | 0.0% | 0.0% | 0.0% | 20.9% | 28.0% | 37.1% | 0.0% | 0.0% | 1.8% | 79.1% | 72.0% | 61.2% |
| Step | 0.0% | 0.0% | 0.0% | 62.7% | 63.5% | 76.3% | 0.0% | 0.0% | 0.2% | 37.3% | 36.5% | 23.4% |

## 5.2    Impact of Injection Location on Failure Profile

Here, we evaluate the effect of injection location on fault outcome as shown in Figs. 3, 4 and 5 and Table 4.

**Impact of Data Category on Fault Outcome.** Figure 3 shows the average results for each fault model across modules for different failure categories, while Table 2a shows the average number of injections across campaigns per different data categories.

Data categorisation for the two fault models differs in the sense that both bits for DBF errors are flipped from the same data item while, for DSB errors, the two bits are either flipped within the same data item or in a combination of two data items having different data types.

As can be observed in Fig. 3, the failure outcome distribution for the different data categories follows the following trend:

*Control.* For DSB errors, errors in control data leads to a high proportion of Time Out-related failures. We notice errors in control data also leads to a high proportion of Safe Run outcome, however it is lower to that observed for Time Out outcomes. We also observe that errors in control data lead to failures in the other two fault categories in similar proportion.

For DBF errors, we notice that errors in control data leads to high proportion of Safe Run outcome. Similar to DSB errors, we notice that the errors in control data induce similar proportion of Crash and Data failures. However, we notice that unlike for DSB errors, errors in control data do not induce Time Out failures.

*Pointer.* We observe pointer errors lead to a high proportion of Crash or Data failures but only a small proportion of Time Out failures under the DSB error model. We observe a very similar pattern for the DBF model.

*Control and Pointer.* We observe that a combination of errors in control and pointer data is only possible under the DSB model. We observe that this causes a relatively high proportion of Crash failures and a non-negligible proportion of Data failures.

*Neither.* We observe that when errors are injected in locations that are neither control nor pointer items under the DBF, the proportion of Time Out failures is very high, around 97 %.

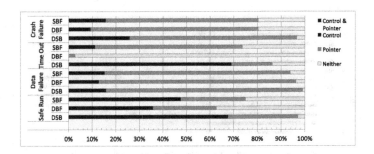

**Fig. 3.** Average fault injection outcome distributions between DSB, DBF and SBF experiments per different data categories for all target modules

**Impact of Register Category on Fault Outcome.** Figure 4 shows the average results for each fault model across modules for different fault outcomes, while Table 2b shows the average number of injections across campaigns per different register categories.

The difference between register categorisation for DBF errors and DSB errors is for DBF errors both bits are flipped within the same target register, while for DSB errors, the two bits are flipped in a combination of two target registers, either of the same type or of different types.

From Fig. 4, we make the following observations:

*General Purpose.* We observe that errors injected in general purpose registers are often harmless under the DBF model. We observe also, they cause Data failures only under the DSB model. However, under both the DSB and DBF models they induce a similar proportion of Crash and Time Out failures.

*Stack Pointer.* We observe that most Time Out failures are caused by errors in the stack pointer under the DBF model. Errors in the stack pointer under the DSB model induce a higher proportion of Crash failures than under the DBF model. We also observe that errors in the stack pointer under the DSB model give rise to a high proportion of Safe Runs.

*ALU Input.* We observe that errors in ALU input registers do not cause any Time Out failures under the DBF model while, under the DSB model, it induces a higher proportion of Crash failures than under the DBF model. Errors in the ALU input registers cause a higher proportion of Data failures under DBF model than under the DSB model.

*ALU Output.* We observe that errors in ALU output registers do not cause any Time Out failures under the DBF model, while under the DSB model, it induces about 15 % of Time Out failures. Otherwise, errors in ALU registers under either model shows similar failure profile.

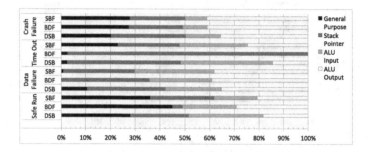

**Fig. 4.** Average fault injection outcome distributions between DSB and DBF experiments per different register categories for all target modules

**Word Vs. Register Target Locations.** Figure 5 and Table 4 summarises the results per target location for different failure categories.

Figure 5a shows the failure profile across all fault models for injections in word locations, Fig. 5b shows that for register locations and Table 4 shows fault injection outcomes between errors in word and register target locations per fault model across all campaigns. We observe that the Data failure outcome rate is more than halved when errors are injected into registers, irrespective of fault model. Further, we observe Safe Run outcome is significantly lower for errors injected into registers. However, we observe up to $\approx 33 \%$ higher rate of Crash failures for errors injected in registers.

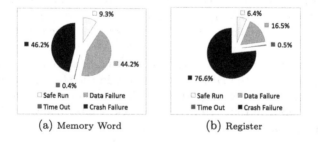

(a) Memory Word                    (b) Register

**Fig. 5.** Average outcome distributions per injection location across all modules

From both Fig. 5 and Table 4, we observe no considerable difference between the two locations for the Time Out fault outcome.

**Table 4.** Average fault injection outcome distribution between memory word and registers for all target modules

| Fault Model | Safe Run | | Data Failure | | Time Out | | Crash Failure | |
|---|---|---|---|---|---|---|---|---|
| | Word | Register | Word | Register | Word | Register | Word | Register |
| DSB | 7.2% | 4.1% | 43.0% | 13.1% | 0.0% | 0.1% | 49.8% | 82.7% |
| DBF | 6.0% | 2.9% | 40.6% | 14.0% | 0.0% | 0.0% | 53.3% | 83.1% |
| SBF | 14.6% | 12.0% | 48.9% | 22.5% | 1.0% | 1.4% | 35.4% | 64.1% |

### 5.3 Related Work

Single and/or multiple bit-flip errors were injected in main memory and registers of software programs and their impact on the programs execution were investigated [1,2]. These studies have shown that multiple fault injections can be very effective in detecting software vulnerabilities. However, both studies did not investigate the impact of variations of multiple bit-flip errors on program execution, which is our goal.

## 6 Discussion and Limitations

We first discuss some observations about the results and then provide some limitations of the work.

### 6.1 Discussion

We make several important observations:

1. The failure profile induced by the DSB model is very different to that induced by the DBF model. For example, errors injected in control under the DSB model tends to cause a high proportion of Time Out failures.
2. The failure profile induced by the DSB model cause software to fail in some unique ways. For example, errors injected in general purpose registers under the DSB model cause a significant proportion of data failures. On the other hand, errors injected in the same general purpose registers under the DBF model do not cause any data failure.
3. Errors injected in ALU registers under the DBF model do not cause any Time Out failures, in contrast to errors injected in the same registers under the DSB model, which causes around 50% of Time Out failures.
4. Errors injected in both control and pointer locations induced data and crash failures under the DSB model. This is a unique failure profile.
5. Overall, errors injected under the DSB model lead to a wider range of failures.

Although we have observed differences between the failure profiles induced by DSB and DBF, we did not look for uniqueness.

## 6.2  Limitations

A first limitation of the work is the range of applications used to evaluate the two fault models. A wider range of software from different target systems is needed to confirm the observations made in this paper. Nevertheless, the modules used for this assessment are very varied and shared very little overlap in terms of data structures. However, we believe that the results are statistically significant, especially after conducting over 1.5 million fault injection experiments.

A second limitation in the results presented here is that, to the best of our knowledge, there is scarcity of field data that shows how multiple bit upsets will manifest themselves. There is however increasing evidence that the rate of hardware errors is increasing. We only consider the two variants of double bit-flip errors in this paper. The relevance of the results presented here is only as far as the field data matches the pattern of error injection used.

# 7  Conclusion and Future Work

We consider the two variants of double bit-flip errors that have appeared in dependability evaluation recently. The objective, in this paper, is to determine whether there is relevance in using both variants during validation. Our answer is positive: yes, we need both variants as they induce very different failure profiles in software and, in some cases, the failures are unique to a given variant. We considered errors being injected in a range of memory words or register locations and we considered the impact of the type of locations on failures.

# References

1. Adamu-Fika, F., Jhumka, A.: An investigation of the impact of double single bit-flip errors on program executions. DEPEND 2015. In: The Eight International Conference on Dependability, pp. 15–22. IARIA, Venice, Italy August 2015
2. Ayatolahi, F., Sangchoolie, B., Johansson, R., Karlsson, J.: A study of the impact of single bit-flip and double bit-flip errors on program execution. In: Bitsch, F., Guiochet, J., Kaâniche, M. (eds.) SAFECOMP. LNCS, vol. 8153, pp. 265–276. Springer, Heidelberg (2013)
3. Georgakos, G., Huber, P., Ostermayr, M., Amirante, E., Ruckerbauer, F.: Investigation of increased multi-bit failure rate due to neutron induced SEU in advanced embedded SRAMs. In: IEEE Symposium on VLSI Circuits, pp. 80–81 (2007)
4. Guthaus, M.R., Ringenberg, J.S., Ernst, D., Austin, T.M., Mudge, T., Brown, R.B.: MiBench: A free, commercially representative embedded benchmark suite. In: Proceedings of the Workload Characterization, 2001. WWC-4. 2001 IEEE International Workshop, pp. 3–14. WWC 2001, IEEE Computer Society, Washington, DC, USA (2001)
5. Hiller, M., Jhumka, A., Suri, N.: An approach for analysing the propagation of data errors in software. In: Proceedings of the 31st IEEE/IFIP International Conference on Dependable Systems and Networks, pp. 161–172, July 2001
6. Hsueh, M., Tsai, T.K., Iyer, R.K.: Fault injection techniques and tools. IEEE Comput. 30(4), 75–82 (1997)

7. ISO 26262–1:2011, road vehicles - functional safety - part 1: Vocabulary. ISO, Geneva, Switzerland (2011)

8. Kanawati, G.A., Kanawati, N.A., Abraham, J.A.: FERRARI: A flexible software-based fault and error injection system. IEEE Trans. Comput. **44**(2), 248–260 (1995)

9. Laprie, J.C.: Dependability: Basic Concepts and Terminology. Springer, Heidelberg (1992)

10. Lattner, C., Adve, V.: LLVM: A compilation framework for lifelong program analysis & transformation. In: Proceedings of the International Symposium on Code Generation and Optimization: Feedback-directed and Runtime Optimization, p. 75. CGO 2004, IEEE Computer Society, Washington, DC, USA (2004)

11. Li, X., Huang, M.C., Shen, K., Chu, L.: A realistic evaluation of memory hardware errors and software system susceptibility. In: Proceedings of the 2010 USENIX Conference on USENIX Annual Technical Conference, p. 6. USENIXATC 2010, USENIX Association, Berkeley, CA, USA (2010)

12. MATLAB: version 8.3 (R2014a). The MathWorks Inc., Natick, Massachusetts (2014). http://www.mathworks.co.uk/products/matlab/

13. Powell, D.: Failure model assumptions and assumption coverage. In: Proceedings of the 22nd International Symposium on Fault-Tolerant Computing, pp. 386–395 (July 1992)

14. PyYaml: PyYaml (2011). http://pyyaml.org/wiki/PyYAMLDocumentation. Accessed 19 November 2014

15. Reed, R., et al.: Heavy ion and proton-induced single event multiple upset. IEEE Trans. Nucl. Sci. **44**(6), 2224–2229 (1997)

16. Smith, S.: SUSAN version 2l (1999). http://users.fmrib.ox.ac.uk/steve/susan/susan2l.c. Accessed 19 November 2014

17. Sridharan, V., Liberty, D.: A study of DRAM failures in the field. In: 2012 International Conference for High Performance Computing, Networking, Storage and Analysis (SC), pp. 1–11, November 2012

18. Thomas, A., Pattabiraman, K.: LLFI: An intermediate code level fault injector for soft computing applications. In: Proceedings of IEEE Workshop on Silicon Errors in Logic, System Effects (SELSE) (2013)

19. Winter, S., Tretter, M., Sattler, B., Suri, N.: simFI: From single to simultaneous software fault injections. In: Proceedings of Dependable Systems and Networks (DSN) (2013)

20. Yang, C., Orailoglu, A.: Processor reliability enhancement through compiler-directed register file peak temperature reductionprocessor reliability enhancement through compiler-directed register file peak temperature reduction. In: Proceedings Dependable Systems and Networks, pp. 468–477 (2009)

# An Efficient Dynamic Programming Algorithm for SEQ-IC-SEQ-EC-LCS Problem

Daxin Zhu[1], Lei Wang[2], Yingjie Wu[3], and Xiaodong Wang[4][✉]

[1] Quanzhou Normal University, Quanzhou 362000, China
[2] Facebook, 1 Hacker Way, Menlo Park, CA 94052, USA
[3] Fuzhou University, Fuzhou 350002, China
[4] Fujian University of Technology, Fuzhou 350108, China
wangxd135@139.com

**Abstract.** In this paper, we consider a generalized longest common subsequence problem, in which a constraining sequence of length $s$ must be included as a subsequence and the other constraining sequence of length $t$ must be excluded as a subsequence of two main sequences and the length of the result must be maximal. For the two input sequences $X$ and $Y$ of lengths $n$ and $m$, and the given two constraining sequences of length $s$ and $t$, we present an $O(nmst)$ time dynamic programming algorithm for solving the new generalized longest common subsequence problem. The correctness of the new algorithm is demonstrated.

**Keywords:** Longest common subsequence problem · Dynamic programming · Similarity · Constraining sequences · Time complexity

## 1 Introduction

The longest common subsequence (LCS) problem is a well-known measurement for computing the similarity of two strings. It can be broadly applied in diverse areas, such as file comparison, pattern matching and computational biology [3,4,8,9].

Given two sequences $X$ and $Y$, the longest common subsequence (LCS) problem is to find a subsequence of $X$ and $Y$ whose length is the longest among all common subsequences of the two given sequences.

For some biological applications some constraints must be applied to the LCS problem. These kinds of variant of the LCS problem are called the constrained LCS (CLCS) problem. Recently, Chen and Chao [1] proposed the more generalized forms of the CLCS problem, the generalized constrained longest common subsequence (GC-LCS) problem. For the two input sequences $X$ and $Y$ of lengths $n$ and $m$,respectively, and a constraint string $P$ of length $r$, the GC-LCS problem is a set of four problems which are to find the LCS of $X$ and $Y$ including/excluding $P$ as a subsequence/substring, respectively.

© Springer International Publishing Switzerland 2015
G. Wang et al. (Eds.): ICA3PP 2015, Part IV, LNCS 9531, pp. 814–821, 2015.
DOI: 10.1007/978-3-319-27140-8_56

In this paper, we consider a more general constrained longest common subsequence problem called SEQ-IC-SEQ-EC-LCS, in which a constraining sequence of length $s$ must be included as a subsequence and the other constraining sequence of length $t$ must be excluded as a subsequence of two main sequences and the length of the result must be maximal. We will present the first efficient dynamic programming algorithm for solving this problem.

The organization of the paper is as follows.

In the following 3 sections, we describe our presented dynamic programming algorithm for the SEQ-IC-SEQ-EC-LCS problem.

In Sect. 2 the preliminary knowledge for presenting our algorithm for the SEQ-IC-SEQ-EC-LCS problem is under discussion. In Sect. 3 we give a new dynamic programming solution for the SEQ-IC-SEQ-EC-LCS problem with time complexity $O(nmst)$, where $n$ and $m$ are the lengths of the two given input strings, and $s$ and $t$ the lengths of the two constraining sequences. Some concluding remarks are located in Sect. 4.

## 2    Characterization of the Generalized LCS Problem

A sequence is a string of characters over an alphabet $\sum$. A subsequence of a sequence $X$ is obtained by deleting zero or more characters from $X$ (not necessarily contiguous). A substring of a sequence $X$ is a subsequence of successive characters within $X$.

For a given sequence $X = x_1 x_2 \cdots x_n$ of length $n$, the $i$th character of $X$ is denoted as $x_i \in \sum$ for any $i = 1, \cdots, n$. A substring of $X$ from position $i$ to $j$ can be denoted as $X[i : j] = x_i x_{i+1} \cdots x_j$. If $i \neq 1$ or $j \neq n$, then the substring $X[i : j] = x_i x_{i+1} \cdots x_j$ is called a proper substring of $X$. A substring $X[i : j] = x_i x_{i+1} \cdots x_j$ is called a prefix or a suffix of $X$ if $i = 1$ or $j = n$, respectively.

An appearance of sequence $X = x_1 x_2 \cdots x_n$ in sequence $Y = y_1 y_2 \cdots y_m$, for any $X$ and $Y$, starting at position $j$ is a sequence of strictly increasing indexes $i_1, i_2, \cdots, i_n$ such that $i_1 = j$, and $X = y_{i_1}, y_{i_2}, \cdots, y_{i_n}$. A compact appearance of $X$ in $Y$ starting at position $j$ is the appearance of the smallest last index $i_n$. A match for sequences $X$ and $Y$ is a pair $(i, j)$ such that $x_i = y_j$. The total number of matches for $X$ and $Y$ is denoted by $\delta$. It is obvious that $\delta \leq nm$.

For the two input sequences $X = x_1 x_2 \cdots x_n$ and $Y = y_1 y_2 \cdots y_m$ of lengths $n$ and $m$, respectively, and two constrained sequences $P = p_1 p_2 \cdots p_s$ and $Q = q_1 q_2 \cdots q_t$ of lengths $s$ and $t$, the SEQ-IC-SEQ-EC-LCS problem is to find a constrained LCS of $X$ and $Y$ including $P$ as a subsequence and excluding $Q$ as a substring.

**Definition 1.** *Let $S(i, j, k, r)$ denote the set of all LCSs of $X[1 : i]$ and $Y[1 : j]$ such that for each $z \in S(i, j, k, r)$, $z$ includes $P[1 : k]$ as a subsequence, and excludes $Q[1 : r]$ as a subsequence, where $1 \leq i \leq n, 1 \leq j \leq m, 0 \leq k \leq s$, and $0 \leq r \leq t$. The length of an LCS in $S(i, j, k, r)$ is denoted as $f(i, j, k, r)$.*

The following theorem characterizes the structure of an optimal solution based on optimal solutions to subproblems, for computing the LCSs in $S(i, j, k, r)$, for any $1 \leq i \leq n, 1 \leq j \leq m, 0 \leq k \leq s$, and $0 \leq r \leq t$.

**Theorem 1.** *If* $Z[1 : l] = z_1, z_2, \cdots, z_l \in S(i, j, k, r)$, *then the following conditions hold:*

1. *If* $r = 1$ *and* $x_i = y_j = q_r$, *then* $z_l \neq x_i$ *and* $Z[1 : l] \in S(i - 1, j - 1, k, r)$.
2. *If* $r > 1$ *and* $x_i = y_j = q_r$,
   *(1)* $x_i = p_k$, $z_l \neq x_i$ *implies* $Z[1 : l] \in S(i - 1, j - 1, k, r)$.
   *(2)* $x_i = p_k$, $z_l = x_i$ *implies* $Z[1 : l - 1] \in S(i - 1, j - 1, k - 1, r - 1)$.
   *(3)* $k = 0$ *or* $k > 0, x_i \neq p_k$, $z_l \neq x_i$ *implies* $Z[1 : l] \in S(i - 1, j - 1, k, r)$.
   *(4)* $k = 0$ *or* $k > 0, x_i \neq p_k$, $z_l = x_i$ *implies* $Z[1 : l-1] \in S(i-1, j-1, k, r-1)$.
3. *If* $k > 0$, $x_i = y_j = p_k$ *and* $r = 0$ *or* $r > 0, x_i \neq q_r$, *then* $z_l = x_i$ *and* $Z[1 : l - 1] \in S(i - 1, j - 1, k - 1, r)$.
4. *If* $x_i = y_j$ *and* $k = 0$ *or* $x_i \neq p_k$ *and* $r = 0$ *or* $x_i \neq q_r$, *then* $z_l = x_i$ *and* $Z[1 : l - 1] \in S(i - 1, j - 1, k, r)$.
5. *If* $x_i \neq y_j$, *then* $z_l \neq x_i$ *implies* $Z[1 : l] \in S(i - 1, j, k, r)$.
6. *If* $x_i \neq y_j$, *then* $z_l \neq y_j$ *implies* $Z[1 : l] \in S(i, j - 1, k, r)$.

**Proof.**

1. In this case, if $x_i = z_l$, then $Z[1 : l]$ includes $Q[1 : r]$, a contradiction. Therefore, we have $x_i \neq z_l$, and $Z[1 : l]$ must be an LCS of $X[1 : i - 1]$ and $Y[1 : j - 1]$ including $P[1 : k]$ as a subsequence and excluding $Q[1 : r]$ as a subsequence, i.e. $Z[1 : l] \in S(i - 1, j - 1, k, r)$.

2. In this case, we have $x_i = y_j = q_r$.

(1) We have $x_i = p_k$ furthermore, if $z_l \neq x_i$, then $Z[1 : l]$ must be a common subsequence of $X[1 : i - 1]$ and $Y[1 : j - 1]$ including $P[1 : k]$ as a subsequence and excluding $Q[1 : r]$ as a subsequence. It is obvious that $Z[1 : l]$ must also be an LCS of $X[1 : i - 1]$ and $Y[1 : j - 1]$ including $P[1 : k]$ as a subsequence and excluding $Q[1 : r]$ as a subsequence, i.e. $Z[1 : l] \in S(i - 1, j - 1, k, r)$.

(2) We have $x_i = p_k$ furthermore, if $z_l = x_i$, then $Z[1 : l - 1]$ must be a common subsequence of $X[1 : i - 1]$ and $Y[1 : j - 1]$ including $P[1 : k - 1]$ as a subsequence and excluding $Q[1 : r - 1]$ as a subsequence. It is readily seen that $Z[1 : l - 1]$ must also be an LCS of $X[1 : i - 1]$ and $Y[1 : j - 1]$ including $P[1 : k - 1]$ as a subsequence and excluding $Q[1 : r - 1]$ as a subsequence, i.e. $Z[1 : l - 1] \in S(i - 1, j - 1, k - 1, r - 1)$.

(3) We have $k = 0$ or $x_i \neq p_k$ furthermore, if $z_l \neq x_i$, then $Z[1 : l]$ must be a common subsequence of $X[1 : i - 1]$ and $Y[1 : j - 1]$ including $P[1 : k]$ as a subsequence and excluding $Q[1 : r]$ as a subsequence. It is obvious that $Z[1 : l]$ must also be an LCS of $X[1 : i - 1]$ and $Y[1 : j - 1]$ including $P[1 : k]$ as a subsequence and excluding $Q[1 : r]$ as a subsequence, i.e. $Z[1 : l] \in S(i - 1, j - 1, k, r)$.

(4) We have $k = 0$ or $x_i \neq p_k$ furthermore, if $z_l = x_i$, then $Z[1 : l - 1]$ must be a common subsequence of $X[1 : i - 1]$ and $Y[1 : j - 1]$ including $P[1 : k]$ as a subsequence and excluding $Q[1 : r - 1]$ as a subsequence. It is readily seen that $Z[1 : l - 1]$ must also be an LCS of $X[1 : i - 1]$ and $Y[1 : j - 1]$ including $P[1 : k]$ as a subsequence and excluding $Q[1 : r - 1]$ as a subsequence, i.e. $Z[1 : l - 1] \in S(i - 1, j - 1, k, r - 1)$.

3. Since $x_i = y_j = p_k$, and and $r = 0$ or $r > 0, x_i \neq q_r$, we have $x_i = z_l$ and $Z[1 : l - 1]$ is a common subsequence of $X[1 : i - 1]$ and $Y[1 : j - 1]$ including $P[1 : k - 1]$ as a subsequence and excluding $Q[1 : r]$ as a subsequence. We can show that $Z[1 : l - 1]$ is an LCS of $X[1 : i - 1]$ and $Y[1 : j - 1]$ including $P[1 : k - 1]$ as a subsequence and excluding $Q[1 : r]$ as a subsequence. Assume by contradiction that there exists a common subsequence $a$ of $X[1 : i - 1]$ and $Y[1 : j - 1]$ including $P[1 : k - 1]$ as a subsequence and excluding $Q[1 : r]$ as a subsequence, whose length is greater than $l - 1$. Then the concatenation of $a$ and $z_l$ will result in a common subsequence of $X[1 : i]$ and $Y[1 : j]$ including $P[1 : k]$ as a subsequence and excluding $Q[1 : r]$ as a subsequence, whose length is greater than $l$. This is a contradiction.

4. In this case we have no constraints on adding $x_i$ to $Z[1 : l - 1]$, and thus $Z[1 : l - 1]$ is a common subsequence of $X[1 : i - 1]$ and $Y[1 : j - 1]$ including $P[1 : k]$ as a subsequence and excluding $Q[1 : r]$ as a subsequence. We can show that $Z[1 : l - 1]$ is an LCS of $X[1 : i - 1]$ and $Y[1 : j - 1]$ including $P[1 : k]$ as a subsequence and including $Q[1 : r]$ as a subsequence. Assume by contradiction that there exists a common subsequence $a$ of $X[1 : i - 1]$ and $Y[1 : j - 1]$ including $P[1 : k]$ as a subsequence and including $Q[1 : r]$ as a subsequence, whose length is greater than $l - 1$. Then the concatenation of $a$ and $z_l$ will result in a common subsequence of $X[1 : i]$ and $Y[1 : j]$ including $P[1 : k]$ as a subsequence and including $Q[1 : r]$ as a subsequence, whose length is greater than $l$. This is a contradiction.

5. Since $x_i \neq y_j$ and $z_l \neq x_i$, $Z[1 : l]$ must be a common subsequence of $X[1 : i - 1]$ and $Y[1 : j]$ including $P[1 : k]$ as a subsequence and excluding $Q[1 : r]$ as a subsequence. It is obvious that $Z[1 : l]$ is also an LCS of $X[1 : i - 1]$ and $Y[1 : j]$ including $P[1 : k]$ as a subsequence and excluding $Q[1 : r]$ as a subsequence.

6. Since $x_i \neq y_j$ and $z_l \neq y_j$, $Z[1 : l]$ must be a common subsequence of $X[1 : i]$ and $Y[1 : j - 1]$ including $P[1 : k]$ as a subsequence and excluding $Q[1 : r]$ as a subsequence. It is obvious that $Z[1 : l]$ is also an LCS of $X[1 : i]$ and $Y[1 : j - 1]$ including $P[1 : k]$ as a subsequence and excluding $Q[1 : r]$ as a subsequence.

The proof is completed. $\qquad\square$

## 3   A Simple Dynamic Programming Algorithm

Let $f(i,j,k,r)$ denote the length of an LCS in $S(i,j,k,r)$. By the optimal substructure properties of the SEQ-IC-SEQ-EC-LCS problem shown in Theorem 1, we can build the following recursive formula for computing $f(i,j,k,r)$.

**Theorem 2.** *For any* $1 \leq i \leq n, 1 \leq j \leq m, 0 \leq k \leq s$, *and* $0 \leq r \leq t$, *the values of* $f(i,j,k,r)$ *can be computed by the following recursive formula (1).*

$$f(i,j,k,r) =$$

$$
\begin{cases}
\max\left\{f(i-1,j,k,r), f(i,j-1,k,r)\right\} \\
\qquad \text{if } x_i \neq y_j \\
f(i-1,j-1,k,r) \\
\qquad \text{if } r = 1 \wedge x_i = y_j = q_r \\
\max\left\{1 + f(i-1,j-1,k,r-1), f(i-1,j-1,k,r)\right\} \\
\qquad \text{if } r > 1 \wedge (k = 0 \vee x_i \neq p_k) \\
\max\left\{1 + f(i-1,j-1,k-1,r-1), f(i-1,j-1,k,r)\right\} \\
\qquad \text{if } r > 1 \wedge k > 0 \wedge x_i = p_k) \\
1 + f(i-1,j-1,k-1,r) \\
\qquad \text{if } k > 0 \wedge x_i = y_j = p_k \wedge (r = 0 \vee x_i \neq q_r) \\
1 + f(i-1,j-1,k,r) \\
\qquad \text{if } x_i = y_j \wedge (k = 0 \vee x_i \neq p_k) \wedge (r = 0 \vee x_i \neq q_r)
\end{cases}
\tag{1}
$$

*The boundary conditions of this recursive formula are*
$f(i,0,0,0) = f(0,j,0,0) = 0$ *and* $f(i,0,k,r) = f(0,j,k,r) = -\infty$
*for any* $0 \leq i \leq n, 0 \leq j \leq m, 0 \leq k \leq s$, *and* $0 \leq r \leq t$.

**Proof.**
    The formula (1) is a summation of the all cases proved in Theorem 1 with a recursive formula, which is more convenient for us to implement it as the following Algorithm 1.
    The proof is completed.                                                     □

Based on this formula, our algorithm for computing $f(i,j,k,r)$ is a standard dynamic programming algorithm. By the recursive formula (1), the dynamic programming algorithm for computing $f(i,j,k,r)$ can be implemented as the following Algorithm 1.
    It is obvious that the algorithm requires $O(nmst)$ time and space. For each value of $f(i,j,k,r)$ computed by algorithm $Suffix$, the corresponding LCS of $X[1:i]$ and $Y[1:j]$ including $P[1:k]$ as a subsequence, and excluding $Q[1:r]$ as a subsequence, can be constructed by backtracking through the computation paths from $(i,j,k,r)$ to $(0,0,0,0)$. The following algorithm $back(i,j,k,r)$ is the backtracking algorithm to obtain the LCS, not only its length. The time complexity of the algorithm $back(i,j,k,r)$ is obviously $O(n+m)$.

---

**Algorithm 1.** SEQ-IC-SEQ-EC-LCS

---

**Input:** Strings $X = x_1 \cdots x_n$, $Y = y_1 \cdots y_m$ of lengths $n$ and $m$, respectively, and two constrained sequences $P = p_1 p_2 \cdots p_s$ and $Q = q_1 q_2 \cdots q_t$ of lengths $s$ and $t$

**Output:** $f(i, j, k, r)$, the length of an LCS of $X[1:i]$ and $Y[1:j]$ including $P[1:k]$ as a subsequence, and excluding $Q[1:r]$ as a subsequence, for all $1 \leq i \leq n, 1 \leq j \leq m, 0 \leq k \leq s$, and $0 \leq r \leq t$.

1: **for all** $i, j, k, r$ , $0 \leq i \leq n, 0 \leq j \leq m, 0 \leq k \leq s$ and $0 \leq r \leq t$ **do**
2:     $f(i, 0, k, r), f(0, j, k, r) \leftarrow -\infty, f(i, 0, 0, 0), f(0, j, 0, 0) \leftarrow 0$ {boundary condition}
3: **end for**
4: **for all** $i, j, k, r$ , $1 \leq i \leq n, 1 \leq j \leq m, 0 \leq k \leq s$ and $0 \leq r \leq t$ **do**
5:     **if** $x_i \neq y_j$ **then**
6:         $f(i, j, k, r) \leftarrow \max\{f(i-1, j, k, r), f(i, j-1, k, r)\}$
7:     **else if** $r > 0$ and $x_i = q_r$ **then**
8:         **if** $r = 1$ **then**
9:             $f(i, j, k, r) \leftarrow f(i-1, j-1, k, r)$
10:         **else if** $k > 0$ and $x_i = p_k$ **then**
11:             $f(i, j, k, r) \leftarrow \max\{1 + f(i-1, j-1, k-1, r-1), f(i-1, j-1, k, r)\}$
12:         **else**
13:             $f(i, j, k, r) \leftarrow \max\{1 + f(i-1, j-1, k, r-1), f(i-1, j-1, k, r)\}$
14:         **end if**
15:     **else if** $k > 0$ and $x_i = p_k$ and $(r = 0$ or $x_i \neq q_r)$ **then**
16:         $f(i, j, k, r) \leftarrow 1 + f(i-1, j-1, k-1, r)$
17:     **else**
18:         $f(i, j, k, r) \leftarrow 1 + f(i-1, j-1, k, r)$
19:     **end if**
20: **end for**

---

# 4 Concluding Remarks

We have suggested a new dynamic programming solution for the new generalized constrained longest common subsequence problem SEQ-IC-SEQ-EC-LCS. The new dynamic programming algorithm requires $O(nmst)$ in the worst case, where $n, m, s, t$ are the lengths of the four input sequences respectively. It is not difficult to show that this problem can also be solved in $O(\min(n, m)st)$ space based on Hirschbergs Algorithm [5].

Numerous other generalized constrained longest common subsequence (GC-LCS) problems have similar structures. It is not clear that whether the same technique of this paper can be applied to these problems to achieve efficient algorithms. We will explore these problems further.

---

**Algorithm 2.** $back(i, j, k, r)$

---

**Input:** Integers $i, j, k, r$
**Output:** The LCS of $X[1 : i]$ and $Y[1 : j]$ including $P[1 : k]$ as a subsequence and $Q[1 : r]$ as a suffix

```
 1: if i < 1 or j < 1 then
 2:     return
 3: end if
 4: if x_i ≠ y_j then
 5:     if f(i − 1, j, k, r) > f(i, j − 1, k, r) then
 6:         back(i − 1, j, k, r)
 7:     else
 8:         back(i, j − 1, k, r)
 9:     end if
10: else if r > 0 and x_i = q_r then
11:     if r = 1 then
12:         back(i − 1, j − 1, k, r)
13:     else if k > 0 and x_i = p_k then
14:         if 1 + f(i − 1, j − 1, k − 1, r − 1) > f(i, j − 1, k, r) then
15:             back(i − 1, j − 1, k − 1, r − 1)
16:             print x_i
17:         else
18:             back(i − 1, j − 1, k, r)
19:         end if
20:     else
21:         if 1 + f(i − 1, j − 1, k, r − 1) > f(i, j − 1, k, r) then
22:             back(i − 1, j − 1, k, r − 1)
23:             print x_i
24:         else
25:             back(i − 1, j − 1, k, r)
26:         end if
27:     else if k > 0 and x_i = p_k and (r = 0 or x_i ≠ q_r) then
28:         back(i − 1, j − 1, k − 1, r)
29:         print x_i
30:     else
31:         back(i − 1, j − 1, k, r)
32:         print x_i
33:     end if
34: end if
```

---

**Acknowledgments.** This work was supported by the Science and Technology Foundation of Quanzhou under Grant No. 2013Z38, Fujian Provincial Key Laboratory of Data-Intensive Computing and Fujian University Laboratory of Intelligent Computing and Information Processing.

# References

1. Chen, Y.C., Chao, K.M.: On the generalized constrained longest common subsequence problems. J. Comb. Optim. **21**(3), 383–392 (2011)
2. Crochemore, M., Hancart, C., Lecroq, T.: Algorithms on Strings. Cambridge University Press, Cambridge (2007)
3. Deorowicz, S.: Quadratic-time algorithm for a string constrained LCS problem. Inform. Process. Lett. **112**(11), 423–426 (2012)
4. Deorowicz, S., Obstoj, J.: Constrained longest common subsequence computing algorithms in practice. Comput. Inform. **29**(3), 427–445 (2010)
5. Hirschberg, D.S.: Algorithms for the longest common subsequence problem. J. ACM **24**, 664–675 (1977)
6. Gotthilf, Z., Hermelin, D., Lewenstein, M.: Constrained LCS: hardness and approximation. In: Ferragina, P., Landau, G.M. (eds.) CPM 2008. LNCS, vol. 5029, pp. 255–262. Springer, Heidelberg (2008)
7. Gotthilf, Z., Hermelin, D., Landau, G.M., Lewenstein, M.: Restricted LCS. In: Chavez, E., Lonardi, S. (eds.) SPIRE 2010. LNCS, vol. 6393, pp. 250–257. Springer, Heidelberg (2010)
8. Gusfield, D.: Algorithms on Strings, Trees, and Sequences: Computer Science and Computational Biology. Cambridge University Press, Cambridge (1997)
9. Peng, Y.H., Yang, C.B., Huang, K.S., Tseng, K.T.: An algorithm and applications to sequence alignment with weighted constraints. Int. J. Found. Comput. Sci. **21**(1), 51–59 (2010)
10. Tang, C.Y., Lu, C.L.: Constrained multiple sequence alignment tool development and its application to RNase family alignment. J. Bioinform. Comput. Biol. **1**, 267–287 (2003)
11. Tseng, C.T., Yang, C.B., Ann, H.Y.: Efficient algorithms for the longest common subsequence problem with sequential subsequence constraints. J. Complexity **29**, 44–52 (2013)

# A Hybrid QoS Evaluation Tool Based on the Cloud Computing Platform

Yanjun Shu[✉], Yan Zhao, Hongwei Liu, Decheng Zuo,
and Xiaozong Yang

School of Computer Science and Technology,
Harbin Institute of Technology, Harbin 150001, China
{yjshu,yanzhao,liuhw,zuodc,xzyang}@hit.edu.cn

**Abstract.** Centralized and distributed evaluation approaches have been proposed for Quality of Services (QoS) measurement. The centralized evaluation approach cannot reflect the user-side QoS and the distributed evaluation approach depend on users to provide evaluation records. In this paper, a hybrid evaluation tool comprising two approaches is proposed. In particular, the centralized evaluation is deployed on a cloud computing platform which is the Amazon web services (AWS). Therefore, the hybrid tool can make evaluation from several AWS regions even if there are no test volunteers. Both the collaborative filtering model and the multiple regression model are implemented in the hybrid evaluation tool for predicting the unknown QoS value. To illustrate the advantages of the hybrid QoS evaluation tool, the scene of a traveler who wants to evaluate and select a best web service in the real world is presented. The results show that the hybrid tool is effective and convenient for users to evaluate the QoS of web services.

**Keywords:** Qos evaluation · Qos prediction · Hybrid evaluation · Web services · Cloud computing

## 1 Introduction

The web service is a software system designed to support interoperation between machines over network [1]. Nowadays the web service gains more popularity, it has been used widely in various areas. The need for Quality of Services (QoS) has become a significant factor for building a dependable service application. Providers must evaluate web services before and after release it. On the other side, users also want to know the QoS measurements when they are using the web services. Therefore, the evaluation tools are required for both the convenience of users and providers.

The QoS evaluation research attracts little attention contrast to the prosperity of service selection [2], composition [3] or ranking [4], though the QoS measurements are the basis consideration in these service application researches. Generally, the existing evaluation approaches of web services are two kinds, the centralized approach and the distributed approach. The centralized approach evaluates the web services from a single place. It is proposed earlier and easy to implement [5]. However, the centralized

© Springer International Publishing Switzerland 2015
G. Wang et al. (Eds.): ICA3PP 2015, Part IV, LNCS 9531, pp. 822–835, 2015.
DOI: 10.1007/978-3-319-27140-8_57

evaluation cannot acquire the real user-side quality of web service as the internet environment is quite different in various regions. For example, a user from China may find the real experience is different to the evaluation result by using a centralized evaluation tool implemented in USA, for the internet environment of USA and China is quite different.

Then, the distributed evaluation approach was proposed. It can establish a user-side evaluation when there are lots of the web services testing records from all over the world. Zheng, Z. et al. first presented a distributed evaluation framework [6]. Noor, T. et al. also proposed a distributed trust management method to manage the experience of users on web service [7]. Though the distributed evaluation can reflect the different internet environment in the different regions, when there is not enough distributed testing records, the evaluation cannot work out. To solve this problem, Zheng, Z. et al. employed the PlanetLab to achieve the distributed experiments [8]. The PlanetLab is a useful platform to perform distributed experiments for it has many computing nodes distributed around the world. But it is unsteady for every host server may crash at any time. Moreover, there are many constraints on PlanetLab, such as bandwidth and resource limitations.

Since evaluating all web services from all the places is impossible, there are many cases that users want to know the QoS of web services in some places but they were not been evaluated at there. For the distributed evaluation approach, predicting the unknown QoS measurements is another important issue. By assuming similar users had similar evaluations, the collaborative filtering model has been used widely to make the QoS prediction [6, 9]. The collaborative filtering model has been widely used in recommendation system. The Pearson correlation coefficient is often used to characterize the similarity. However, it is difficult to use a simple correlation coefficient to reflect the complex relation between different services and users [10]. Shi, Y. et al. considered applying the linear regression algorithm for the QoS prediction based on location and network condition [11]. But they did not demonstrating the effectiveness of the proposed algorithm.

To improve the efficiency of centralized and distributed approach, this paper proposes a hybrid evaluation tool which integrates the two approaches. In particular, the centralized evaluation is deployed on a famous cloud computing platform, Amazon Web Services (AWS). Thus, the centralized evaluation can test web services and collect data from different AWS regions. Moreover, both the multiple regression and the collaborative filtering are implemented to make the QoS prediction. For the conveniences of users, the hybrid evaluation tool is implemented on the internet and users can access it on the web page for evaluating the web services easily.

The rest of this paper is organized as follows: Sect. 2 presents the architecture of hybrid tool. Section 3 describes the evaluation and prediction of QoS. Section 4 illustrates the experiments in real world. Section 5 contains the conclusions and some ideas for further work.

## 2   The Hybrid QoS Evaluation Tool

Users can access the hybrid QoS evaluation tool through the web page[1] which is presented on Fig. 1. The tool is deployed on a famous cloud computing platform, AWS, which is one of the most prevailing cloud computing platforms provided by Amazon.com. AWS provides the cloud computing services in 9 regions, and China will be the 10th region. Other cloud computing platforms, for example, Microsoft Azure and IBM Bluemix can also be used to deploy the tool. The centralized evaluation can be used directly on the web page. The distributed evaluation should be downloaded from the web page before use, which is at the bottom of the web page. The User Interface (UI) is very user-friendly. Follow the instruction on the web page, users can evaluate the QoS of the web services from different AWS regions conveniently.

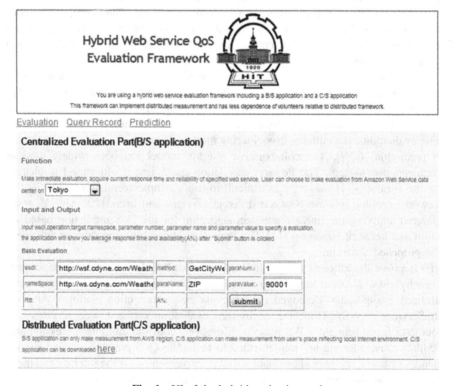

**Fig. 1.**   UI of the hybrid evaluation tool

### 2.1   Architecture of the Tool

The hybrid tool is composed of the centralized evaluation and the distributed evaluation. The centralized evaluation is implemented in the Browser/Server (B/S) mode and it is called the B/S application in the paper. The B/S application is deployed on the

---

[1] http://54.65.143.60/BSSpecificWS/evaluation.jsp.

Elastic Computer Cloud (EC2) which is provided by AWS in 9 regions over the world. Thus, users can achieve the evaluation of a web service from these 9 regions through the browser. Moreover, with the help of the great computation ability of AWS, the centralized evaluation can be achieved not only rapidly but also continuously for weeks or months to find the varying trend of web services' QoS. The distributed evaluation is implemented in the Client/Server (C/S) mode and it is called the C/S application. The user who wants to get the evaluation of web services at his place should download the distributed evaluation program from the web page and runs it on the local computer. Through the C/S application, the web service can be evaluated from wherever there is a user. Furthermore, with the locating ability of the distributed evaluation program, neighboring users can share test records and evaluate the web service in a collaborative way.

As Fig. 2 shows, the two kinds of applications provide the same evaluating functions and share a common database. The Amazon RDS (Relational Database Service) is used to establish the unified database. Since the hybrid evaluation tool deployed on the cloud computing platform, the dataset can be managed. When the new record inserts, the QoS measurements are calculated automatically. Thus, users can obtain the QoS analysis in real time.

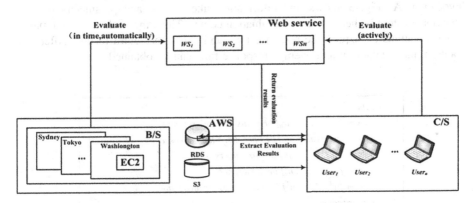

**Fig. 2.** Architecture of the hybrid evaluation tool

## 2.2   Measurement of QoS

The Quality of Service is usually used for describing nonfunctional characteristics of web services [9]. Among the QoS properties of web services, some properties are user-independent which are identical for different users (e.g., price, popularity, reliability, etc.). These user-independent properties are usually offered by the service providers or the third-party registers. On the other hand, some QoS properties are user-dependent and have different values for different users (e.g., response time, availability, etc.). The evaluation of these user-dependent QoS properties needs the client-side invocation of services. The hybrid evaluation tool aims to measure these user-dependent QoS attributes. Thus, the availability and response time are chosen to represent it.

Availability ($A\%$) is calculated by the successful invocation counts ($C_s$) divided by the total invocation counts ($C_t$) as Eq. (1) shows.

$$A\% = C_s/C_t \tag{1}$$

The response time ($Rtt$) means the time taken to receive a response after making a request, which composes of the internet latency and execution time. We use average response time to represent the response time of a web service which is calculated by total response time of all successful invokes divided by successful invocation counts as Eq. (2) shows.

$$T_{avg} = \sum_{i=1}^{C_s} T_i/C_s \tag{2}$$

The response time of unsuccessful invokes is not considered in the computation of average response time to avoid the influence of extreme large response time caused by unsuccessful invokes.

To make the evaluation result reflecting the experience of users, the real invocations are brought out to measure the metrics of QoS. Axis2 is employed to make the invocation. As Fig. 3 shows, the information like WSDL and parameters of web services are stored when request of evaluation comes. Then, the evaluation tool makes real invocations to acquire the response time and check the return results. After calculation, the availability and average response time can be obtained.

```
Begin
    Let  w = {w₁, w₂,......, wₙ} be wsdls of n web services
        o = {o₁, o₂,......, oₙ} be operations to be invoked
        p = {p₁, p₂,......, pₙ} be parameters
        n = {n₁, n₂,......, nₙ} be namespace
        U = {wᵀ, oᵀ, pᵀ, nᵀ} be n use cases for invocation
    wait for request.
    Set  total_num to be Loop_Num
        client to be the Axis invocation client.
    For i = 0;i < num; i ++
        For j = 0; j < n; j ++
            cⱼ make the invocation according to Uᵢ
            get and store invocation results
            if (invoke successfully)
                store response time and the number
    End
```

**Fig. 3.** Measurement process

## 2.3  Functions of the Tool

The hybrid evaluation tool includes three functions: evaluation, query record and prediction. Figure 4 shows the workflow of the tool.

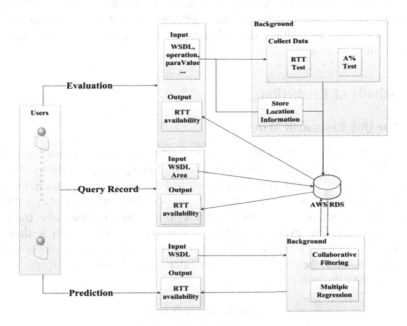

**Fig. 4.** Workflow of the tool

## 2.4  Functions of the Tool

The hybrid evaluation tool includes three functions: evaluation, query record and prediction. Figure 4 shows the workflow of the tool.

**The Evaluation Function.** Both of the centralized and distributed approaches are implemented with the same evaluating functions. As Fig. 1 shows, user need to input the WSDL (Web Services Description Language) url, parameters information, name space and other information of web services in the evaluation interface and click the submit button. Then, the evaluation tool measures attributes of QoS like response time, availability, location information of the user and web service. The evaluation information will be shown to the user. Meanwhile, the invocation parameters, the evaluation results and the geographical information of the user and web service are stored in the database.

**The Query Function.** The query function includes two parts, 1. Query record of the AWS regions and 2. Query record of the users' places. Both these two parts of query need users to input the WSDL information of web service. Part 1 will return users the evaluation records from all AWS regions and Part 2 will return users the evaluation records according to the users' location. Compare to other existing QoS evaluation tool, the hybrid tool offers the query record function, which is very convenient for users to find the evaluation history record.

**The Predict Function.** If users can't find the evaluation record of a web service from a specific region, they can choose this part to make the prediction. Users need to input WSDL url and a region, then the hybrid evaluation tool will apply both the collaborative fileting and the multiple regression model to make the prediction based on history evaluation data.

# 3    Methods of Prediction

## 3.1    The QoS Evaluation Matrix

Some symbols and inventions are introduced first to discuss the prediction method clearly. The web services set is represented by $W=\{w_1,w_2,...,w_l\}$. As the hybrid evaluation tool comprises the distributed approach and the centralized approach, the users set includes the real world users and the AWS severs of different regions. Let $u_i$ denotes a real evaluation user, and $a_i$ denotes an AWS region's server. The user set is $U=\{u_1,u_2, ...u_m, a_1,a_2,...,a_n\}$. The evaluation record is an $(m+n)\times l$ matrix which is shown as Table 1, and $q_{i,j}$ is the evaluation of QoS. If user $i$ didn't evaluate web service $j$, then $q_{i,j}$ is *null*. For example, the element $q_{m,l}$ in the Table 1 is *null*, which means the user $u_m$ did not evaluate the web service $w_l$.

**Table 1.**  Matrix of QoS

|  | $w_1$ | $w_2$ | $w_3$ | $w_4$ | ... | $w_l$ |
|---|---|---|---|---|---|---|
| $u_1$ | $q_{1,1}$ | *null* | $q_{1,3}$ | $q_{1,4}$ | ... | *null* |
| $u_2$ | $q_{2,1}$ | $q_{2,2}$ | $q_{2,3}$ | *null* | ... | $q_{2,l}$ |
| ... | ... | ... | ... | ... | ... | ... |
| $u_m$ | *null* | $q_{m,2}$ | $q_{m,3}$ | $q_{m,4}$ | ... | *null* |
| $a_1$ | $q_{m+1,1}$ | $q_{m+1,2}$ | $q_{m+1,3}$ | $q_{m+1,4}$ | ... | $q_{m+1,l}$ |
| $a_2$ | $q_{m+2,1}$ | $q_{m+2,2}$ | $q_{m+2,3}$ | $q_{m+2,4}$ | ... | $q_{m+2,l}$ |
| ... | ... | ... | ... | ... | ... | ... |
| $a_n$ | $q_{m+n,1}$ | $q_{m+n,2}$ | $q_{m+n,3}$ | $q_{m+n,4}$ | | $q_{m+n,l}$ |

In the QoS matrix, the upper $m$ rows are the distributed evaluation records and the lower $n$ rows are the centralized evaluation records. Compare to the upper $m$ rows, there is no *null* value in the lower $n$ rows since the AWS severs will evaluate all web services automatically. Thus, the submatrix of lower $n$ rows is an effective supplement to the evaluation records.

## 3.2    Prediction of QoS

To predict the *null* value in the QoS matrix, the collaborative filtering model has been widely used [2, 6, 8–10]. The basic of the collaborative filtering model is the similar users have a similar evaluation. The prediction of the collaborative filtering needs three steps: normalization, similarity mining and QoS prediction. It is very complex and when there are too many *null* values, it cannot work.

Shi, Y. et al employed the linear regression for predicting the unknown QoS [11]. However, they did not give any example to demonstrate it. The multiple regression model is an classical statistics prediction method by the regression analysis to determine the interdependence of the quantitative relationship between two or more variables. It is applied here to prediction the unknown QoS value. Assuming the different users' evaluation of the specific web services are linear correlation. The calculate formula of the multiple regression model is represented as Eq. (3).

$$Y = b_0 + b_1 X_1 + b_2 X_2 + \ldots + b_K X_K \tag{3}$$

$Y$ is the unknown QoS value to predict and $X$ is the different users' QoS evaluation. First, select $K$ users from user set $U$ that they both evluate $h$ web services. Then, an $K \times h$ QoS matrix is fitted for estimating the coefficient $b_i$. Finally, the unknown $Y$ can be calculated with $X$ and the estimated $b_i$.

The key of applying the multiple regression model is establishing an $K \times h$ QoS matrix which is all $K$ users have evaluated the same $h$ web services. It is stricter than applying the collaborative filtering model. This condition is difficult to be fulfilled when the evaluation is carried out by the distributed users. But, for the hybrid tool, all the web services can be evaluated from 9 AWS regions automatically. Thus, $K$ is equal or great than the number of AWS regions and the enough data will be acquired for the multiple regression model fitting.

## 3.3    Prediction Effect Analysis

Mean Absolute Error (MAE) and Root Mean Square Error (RMSE) are the metrics to evaluate the prediction effect. The value of MAE and RMSE is less means the prediction is better. As Eqs. (4) and (5) show, $q_{i,j}$ and $\overline{q_{i,j}}$ in equations represent the real value and predicted value, $h$ represents the amount of values.

$$MAE = \frac{\sum\limits_{j=0}^{h-1} |q_{i,j} - \overline{q_{i,j}}|}{h} \tag{4}$$

$$RMSE = \sqrt{\frac{\sum\limits_{j=0}^{h-1} (q_{i,j} - \overline{q_{i,j}})^2}{h}} \tag{5}$$

## 4   Implement and Experiments

To show the effectiveness of the hybrid evaluation tool, some experiments in the real world are carried out. Assuming Mr. Li is a Chinese businessman. While he takes the business travels, he always uses the web services to acquire some information. Recently, his friend introduced him the hybrid evaluation tool of the web services which can get the QoS measurements online easily. As Mr. Li often travels around world, he wants to use the tool to evaluate the QoS of web services which he often uses and find some better ones. Moreover, Mr. Li planned to travel from Beijing to Paris in the near future. Thus, he also wants to know if the web services are available and efficient there.

In order to solve these problems, Mr. Li invited his friends around the world to evaluate the web services by using the C/S applications of the hybrid evaluation tool. He also offered 12 web services which he often used to his friends for evaluation. In particular, the web services 6, 7, 10 and 12 are weather forecasting services, Mr. Li wanted to know which had the best QoS in Paris. His friends' IP and geographic information and the AWS regions' IP and geographic information are shown in Table 2.

**Table 2.** Users and AWS IP and Geographic Information

|      | IP              | Country & Region          |
|------|-----------------|---------------------------|
| User | 111.204.219.197 | China (Beijing)           |
|      | 111.78.228.213  | China (Jiangxi)           |
|      | 117.71.239.148  | China (Anhui)             |
|      | 202.118.239.144 | China (Heilongjiang)      |
|      | 58.53.20.186    | China (Liaoning)          |
|      | 14.136.173.241  | China (HongKong)          |
|      | 137.132.200.160 | Singapore                 |
|      | 83.204.131.232  | France (Clermont)         |
| AWS  | 54.67.9.85      | United States (California)|
|      | 54.68.210.18    | United States (Oregon)    |
|      | 52.0.93.162     | United States (Delaware)  |
|      | 54.169.89.99    | Singapore                 |
|      | 54.65.143.60    | Japan                     |
|      | 54.171.241.57   | Ireland                   |
|      | 54.93.98.189    | Germany                   |
|      | 54.94.231.75    | Brazil                    |
|      | 54.79.4.10      | Australia                 |

### 4.1   Evaluation of QoS

The experiment had been carried out from 2014.08.07 to 2015.02.14 and collected 1,011,234 records. Among the total records, the B/S applications on AWS contributed 864,579 records. The B/S application is deployed on AWS by using EC2.

The AWS RDS is used to establish the unified database. As described in Sect. 2.2, the hybrid evaluation tool aims to measure these user-dependent QoS attributes. Here, the QoS attributes include the availability and response time. The evaluation results evaluated by the hybrid tool are shown in Table 3.

**Table 3.** Evaluation Results of 12 Web Services

| | | $w_1$ (CN) | $w_2$ (CN) | $w_3$ (CN) | $w_4$ (CN) | $w_5$ (CN) | $w_6$ (CN) | $w_7$ (US) | $w_8$ (US) | $w_9$ (US) | $w_{10}$ (US) | $w_{11}$ (AU) | $w_{12}$ (IS) |
|---|---|---|---|---|---|---|---|---|---|---|---|---|---|
| $u_1$ | Rtt | 324.4 | 290.3 | 509.8 | 537.8 | 639.0 | 205.3 | 3509 | 878.8 | 762.6 | 1557 | 1165.7 | NaN |
| | A% | 1.000 | 1.000 | 1.000 | 1.000 | 1.000 | 1.000 | 0.924 | 0.992 | 1.000 | 1.000 | 1.0000 | 0.000 |
| $u_2$ | Rtt | 692.2 | 578.3 | 517.9 | 703.7 | 542.1 | 544.5 | 902.7 | 1075 | 793.1 | 1622 | 974.3 | NaN |
| | A% | 0.999 | 0.999 | 0.999 | 0.998 | 0.999 | 0.999 | 1.000 | 0.997 | 0.999 | 0.790 | 0.9894 | 0.000 |
| $u_3$ | Rtt | 236.5 | 162.8 | 296.8 | 336.0 | 366.0 | 192.3 | 1582 | 1730 | 1014 | 2230 | 1534.4 | NaN |
| | A% | 0.996 | 0.996 | 0.996 | 0.996 | 0.996 | 0.996 | 0.920 | 0.902 | 0.972 | 0.586 | 0.9375 | 0.000 |
| $u_4$ | Rtt | 560.9 | 407.1 | 587.7 | 804.4 | 1419 | 518.5 | 1312 | 1456. | 832.0 | 1002 | 806.5 | NaN |
| | A% | 1.000 | 1.000 | 1.000 | 1.000 | 1.000 | 1.000 | 0.930 | 0.991 | 1.000 | 1.000 | 0.9492 | 0.000 |
| $u_5$ | Rtt | 519.7 | 746.7 | 713.5 | 493.0 | 2010 | 645.0 | 2025 | 1036 | 709.8 | 1269 | 1188.0 | NaN |
| | A% | 1.000 | 1.000 | 1.000 | 1.000 | 0.985 | 1.000 | 1.000 | 1.000 | 1.000 | 0.985 | 1.0000 | 0.000 |
| $u_6$ | Rtt | 1245 | 747.0 | 835.2 | 1221 | 1116 | 1069 | 738.7 | 651.0 | 670.1 | 1520 | 709.7 | NaN |
| | A% | 0.984 | 0.988 | 0.988 | 0.988 | 0.991 | 0.916 | 0.904 | 1.000 | 0.998 | 0.995 | 1.0000 | 0.000 |
| $u_7$ | Rtt | 543.5 | 421.1 | 417.5 | 606.5 | 504.7 | 421.3 | 539.6 | 627.8 | 545.1 | 1004 | 742.4 | NaN |
| | A% | 0.999 | 0.999 | 0.999 | 0.999 | 0.999 | 0.999 | 0.999 | 0.999 | 1.000 | 0.999 | 0.9997 | 0.000 |
| $u_8$ | Rtt | 3495 | 1736 | 1632 | 2534 | 2052 | 1710 | 330.6 | 444.1 | 536.6 | 953.4 | 164.7 | 595.8 |
| | A% | 0.992 | 0.990 | 0.993 | 0.991 | 0.992 | 0.991 | 1.000 | 1.000 | 1.000 | 1.000 | 1.0000 | 1.000 |
| $a_1$ | Rtt | 3708 | 2300 | 2415 | 2606. | 2109 | 2217 | 200.0 | 163.0 | 197.6 | 506.9 | 470.3 | 598.2 |
| | A% | 0.993 | 0.993 | 0.994 | 0.995 | 0.993 | 0.995 | 1.000 | 0.997 | 1.000 | 1.000 | 1.0000 | 0.465 |
| $a_2$ | Rtt | 1439 | 685.9 | 698.2 | 1009. | 669.2 | 674.3 | 173.2 | 179.8 | 237.1 | 426.2 | 489.0 | 621.5 |
| | A% | 1.000 | 0.999 | 0.999 | 1.000 | 1.000 | 0.999 | 1.000 | 0.999 | 1.000 | 1.000 | 1.0000 | 0.298 |
| $a_3$ | Rtt | 2863 | 1406 | 1396 | 2058 | 1435 | 1419 | 25.1 | 80.2 | 202.0 | 475.1 | 302.6 | 466.6 |
| | A% | 0.999 | 1.000 | 0.999 | 0.999 | 0.999 | 0.999 | 1.000 | 0.999 | 1.000 | 1.000 | 1.0000 | 0.400 |
| $a_4$ | Rtt | 979.4 | 518.1 | 511.3 | 752.4 | 523.8 | 522.8 | 523.5 | 535.7 | 512.6 | 716.0 | 769.0 | 1007 |
| | A% | 0.999 | 0.999 | 0.999 | 0.999 | 0.999 | 0.999 | 1.000 | 0.999 | 1.000 | 0.999 | 1.0000 | 0.425 |
| $a_5$ | Rtt | 665.6 | 221.2 | 217.5 | 446.2 | 226.5 | 240.3 | 399.1 | 405.4 | 373.4 | 456.9 | 633.6 | 781.9 |
| | A% | 1.000 | 0.999 | 0.999 | 1.000 | 0.999 | 0.999 | 1.000 | 0.999 | 0.999 | 1.000 | 1.0000 | 0.429 |
| $a_6$ | Rtt | 4146 | 2888 | 3639 | 3785 | 3411 | 3740 | 252.5 | 234.3 | 408.8 | 791.6 | 153.4 | 322.4 |
| | A% | 0.979 | 0.980 | 0.992 | 0.988 | 0.979 | 0.984 | 1.000 | 0.998 | 1.000 | 1.000 | 1.0000 | 0.603 |
| $a_7$ | Rtt | 3706 | 1757 | 1719 | 2664 | 1821. | 1779 | 214.1 | 261.3 | 1288 | 1726. | 104.5 | 280.1 |
| | A% | 1.000 | 0.968 | 0.998 | 1.000 | 0.967 | 0.999 | 1.000 | 0.998 | 0.990 | 0.992 | 1.0000 | 0.543 |
| $a_8$ | Rtt | 2460 | 1251 | 1289 | 1841 | 1287 | 1271 | 454.4 | 360.5 | 773.1 | 1056 | 540.7 | 719.0 |
| | A% | 1.000 | 1.000 | 1.000 | 1.000 | 0.999 | 0.999 | 1.000 | 1.000 | 0.997 | 0.999 | 1.0000 | 0.437 |
| $a_9$ | Rtt | 1442 | 704.3 | 693.5 | 1042 | 714.8 | 701.9 | 585.8 | 553.1 | 567.5 | 736.7 | 811.0 | 962.4 |
| | A% | 1.000 | 1.000 | 1.000 | 1.000 | 1.000 | 0.999 | 1.000 | 0.999 | 1.000 | 1.000 | 1.0000 | 0.260 |

As the 1,011,234 experiments records are brought out by the users and AWS servers for 12 web services. In Table 3, the first column is the users $u_1$-$u_8$ and AWS servers $a_1$-$a_9$ which are listed in Table 2, and the first row is the web services $w_1$-$w_{12}$. Underlined $w_6$, $w_7$, $w_{10}$, $w_{12}$ are weather forecasting services and underlined $u_8$ is the country France where Mr. Li plans to travel.

Every QoS value $q_{i,j}$ includes two attributes, the availability ($A\%$) and response time ($Rtt$). The availability is the success accessing ratio. The response time is the time duration between the request and the response. Here, the unit of the $Rtt$ is the millisecond which is abbreviated to "$ms$". To avoid the influence of large response time introduced by fail access cases, the response time only considers the successful invocation cases. Therefore, when there is no successful invocation, like $u_3$-$w_{12}$, the $A\%$ is 0.0 and the $Rtt$ is represented as $NaN$. Moreover, there is not the $NaN$ value in Table 3 as all the web services have been evaluated by the users.

In Table 3, most $A\%$ values are more than 0.99 and most $Rtt$ values are less than 2000 $ms$, which means the majority web services work well in all regions. However, some web services show quite different $Rtt$ and $A\%$ value in different regions. For example, the last column is the QoS values of $w_{12}$. $w_{12}$ is a weather forecasting web service in Israel. The $A\%$ values of the users $u_1$-$u_6$ for the $w_{12}$ are 0.0 which means $w_{12}$ cannot be accessed in China. But $w_{12}$ is usable in France and United States. Therefore, the distributed evaluation approach is essential for user-sides QoS evaluation.

In addition to the QoS of web service is different in different regions, the QoS of web service shows better to the local users from Table 3. There are two boxes in Table 3. The upper box is the QoS values for the web services $w_1$-$w_6$ and users $u_1$-$u_5$. Both these web services and users are in Mainland China. The QoS values in this box show the better $Rtt$ and $A\%$ value than other regions. Moreover, the lower box is the QoS values for the web services $w_7$-$w_{10}$ and users $a_1$-$a_3$. Both these web services and users are in United States and they show the better $Rtt$ and $A\%$ value than other regions. The circumstance of these two box shows that the web services and users in the same region have a stable network environment which is a main factor influenced the QoS.

As mentioned in the beginning of this Section, Mr. Li wanted to know whether the 12 web services are available and efficient in Paris. In particular, Mr. Li wanted to find which has the best QoS of web services $w_6$, $w_7$, $w_{10}$ and $w_{12}$ in Paris. Mr. Li can obtain the QoS of web services in different place by the hybrid evaluation tool. From Table 3, the $A\%$ and $Rtt$ of $w_7$ in France are 1.0000 and 330.6 $ms$, which is the highest availability and lowest response time. Thus, Mr. Li should choose $w_7$ to acquire the weather information at there.

The lower 9 rows of Table 3 are the QoS value of 12 web services from AWS regions. The hybrid tool can also provide the evaluation results even there are no users, like Japan or Brazil. Assuming Mr. Li will go to Columbia next time but he does not have a friend in there can test the web services. Moreover, there are no test records from Columbia in the hybrid tool. As the neighboring region in users is Brazil, the QoS evaluation results by Brazil AWS can be used as the QoS value in Columbia.

Hence, for the places which exit users share the test records, like Hong Kong or Harbin, the C/S application of the hybrid tool can provide the evaluation results straightly. On the other side, if there are not users, but in AWS regions like Brazil, the B/S application of the tool can evaluate web services from there. The AWS platforms are distributed in all over the world, the neighboring AWS region can be used to make out the unknown QoS value for the places there are no users. Hence, the hybrid QoS evaluation tool can help to evaluate in more regions and less dependence of users when making analysis.

## 4.2  Prediction of QoS

In this section, the QoS prediction effectiveness by the collaborative filtering and the multiple regression will be analyzed. Assuming Mr. Li's friend in France did not evaluate the w1, and Mr. Li will use $w_1$ to check the stock price at there. So he wants to predict the availability and response time ranges of $w_1$.

As introduced in Sect. 3.2, there are two kinds of the prediction methods, the collaborative filtering and the multiple regression. Mr. Li first compares these two methods by using the available data in Table 3, and then decides which method is used to predict the QoS of $w_1$ in France. By applying the hybrid evaluation tool on AWS, Mr. Li can acquire the QoS prediction of $w_2$-$w_{12}$ in France with the two methods respectively. The prediction results of the availability and response time are listed in Table 4.

**Table 4.** The QoS Prediction and Effectiveness of $w_2$-$w_{12}$ in France

| Prediction Methods | QoS | Prediction Effectiveness | |
|---|---|---|---|
| | | MAE | RMSE |
| Multiple Regression | Rtt | 499.13 | 604.52 |
| | A% | 0.0015 | 0.0038 |
| Collaborative Filtering | Rtt | 798.81 | 1360.39 |
| | A% | 0.0048 | 0.0050 |

Then, Mean Absolute Error (MAE) and Root Mean Square Error (RMSE) are used for evaluating the prediction effectiveness. The MAE and RMSE have described in Sect. 3.3. The last two columns of Table 4 list the MAE and RMSE results of the two prediction methods. The MAE and RMSE values of *Rtt* by the multiple regression method are 499.13 and 604.52. On the other side, the MAE and RMSE values of *Rtt* by the collaborative filtering method are 479.81 and 1360.39. Although the *A%* values in Table 4 are very close to 1.0, the multiple regression also shows less the MAE and RMSE values. Therefore, in case of France, the QoS prediction of $w_1$ by the multiple regression is more reliable.

Table 5 shows the two methods prediction QoS results of $W_1$ in France, Mr. Li will take the response time of $w_1$ as 2691.0 *ms* and the availability of $w_1$ as 0.9914. After a few days, Mr. Li arrives Paris and uses $w_1$. He finds the real the response time of $w_1$ is 3495.7 *ms* and the availability is 0.9928. These real QoS results are more close to the prediction by the multiple regression. Therefore, compare to the real QoS, the multiple regression shows better predict ability than the collaborative filtering.

The collaborative filtering method uses the similar users' QoS to predict the unknown value. In this case, the number of web services and users is small. It is difficult

**Table 5.** Prediction Results of $w_l$ in France

| QoS | Prediction methods | Prediction | Real |
|-----|-------------------|------------|------|
| *Rtt* | Multiple Regression | 2691.0 | 3495.7 |
| | Collaborative Filtering | 970.62 | |
| *A%* | Multiple Regression | 0.9914 | 0.9928 |
| | Collaborative Filtering | 0.9969 | |

to find the exactly similar users to predict. On the other hand, the multiple regression can determine the interdependence of the quantitative relationship between two or more users. Compare to the collaborative filtering, applying the multiple regression needs more complicate calculations. Therefore, when there are few web services and users, the multiple regression may be more suitable than the collaborative filtering for prediction.

## 5  Conclusions

This paper proposes a hybrid evaluation tool to improve the centralized and distributed approaches on their limitations. The cloud computing platform, AWS is employed to measure QoS of web services to make sure the evaluation can be brought out from different places around the world even when lack of volunteers. Furthermore, the hybrid QoS evaluation tool is the first tool which provides the evaluation, query and prediction functions on the web page. Users can access it and apply it easily. With the hybrid evaluation data by the tool, a similarity QoS evaluation result can be made out straightly even there are no test volunteers. Both the collaborative filtering model and the multiply regression model are implemented in the tool for predicting the unknown QoS. The experiments of the scene of Mr. Li show that the hybrid evaluation tool can be used conveniently and effectively. Compare to the common-used collaborative filtering, the multiple regression has better prediction ability in the case of France.

In future, more metrics will be considered in the hybrid tool, such as the process time and throughput. For making a more accurate prediction, the predicting methods will be improvement by location and clustering the cloud regions in the different users' places.

**Acknowledgments.** This work was supported by the National Natural Science Foundation of China (Grant No. 61202091) and the Fundamental Research Funds for Central Universities (Grant No. NSRIF.2016050).

## References

1. Booth, D., Haas, H., McCabe, F., Newcomer, E., Champion, M., Ferris, C., Orchard, D.: Web services architecture. W3C Group (2004)
2. Saleem, M., Ding, C., Liu, X., Chi, C.H.: Personalized decision making for QoS-based service selection. In: Proceedings of the 15th IEEE International Conference on Web Services, pp. 17–24 (2014)

3. Feng, Y., Ngan, L.D., Kanagasabai, R.: Dynamic service composition with service-dependent QoS attributes. In Proceedings of the 14th IEEE International Conference on Web Services, pp. 10–17 (2013)
4. Almulla, M., Almatori, K., Yahyaoui, H.: A qos-based fuzzy model for ranking real world web services. In: Proceedings of the 12th IEEE International Conference on Web Services, pp. 203–210 (2011)
5. Al-Masri, E, Mahmoud, Q.: Quality of web services dataset. http://www.uoguelph.ca/~qmahmoud/qws/index.html
6. Zheng, Z., Zhang, Y., Lyu, M.R.: Distributed qos evaluation for real-world web services. In: Proceedings of the 11th IEEE International Conference on Web Services, pp. 83–90 (2010)
7. Noor, T., Sheng, Q., Zeadally, S., Yu, J.: Trust management of services in cloud environments: Obstacles and solutions. ACM Comput. Surv. (CSUR) 46(1), 12–25 (2013)
8. Zheng, Z., Ma, H., Lyu, M.R., King, I.: Collaborative web service QoS prediction via neighborhood integrated matrix factorization. Serv. Comput. IEEE Trans. 6(3), 289–299 (2013)
9. Sillic, M., Delac, G., Krka, I., Srblijc, S.: Scalable and accurate prediction of availability of atomic web services. IEEE Trans. Serv. Comput. 7(2), 252–264 (2014)
10. Shao, L., Zhou, L., Zhao, J., Xie, B., Mei, H.: Web Service QoS predication approach. J. Softw. 20(8), 2062–2073 (2009)
11. Shi, Y., Zhang, K., Liu, B., Cui, L.: A new QoS prediction approach based on user clustering and regression algorithms. In: Proceedings of the 11th IEEE International Conference on Web Services, pp. 726–727 (2011)

# Author Index

Printed in the United States
By Bookmasters